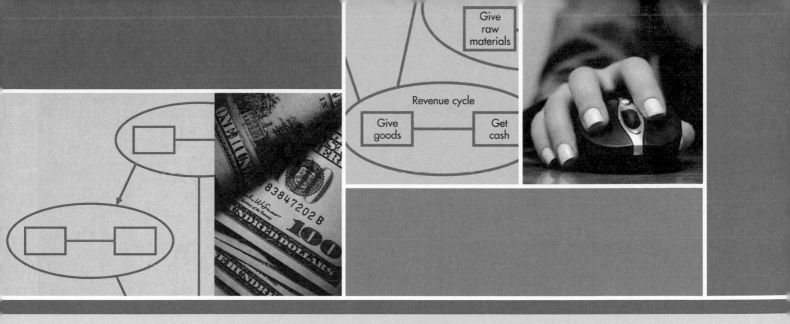

ACCOUNTING INFORMATION SYSTEMS

TWELFTH EDITION

Marshall B. Romney
Brigham Young University

Paul J. Steinbart
Arizona State University

Prentice Hall

Boston Columbus Indianapolis New York San Francisco Upper Saddle River
Amsterdam Cape Town Dubai London Madrid Milan Munich Paris Montreal Toronto
Delhi Mexico City Sao Paulo Sydney Hong Kong Seoul Singapore Taipei Tokyo

Editorial Director: Sally Yagan
Editor in Chief: Donna Battista
Executive Editor: Stephanie Wall
Product Development Manager: Ashley Santora
Editorial Project Manager: Christina Rumbaugh
Editorial Assistant: Brian Reilly
Director of Marketing: Patrice Jones
Sr. Marketing Assistant: Kimberly Lovato
Sr. Managing Editor: Cynthia Zonneveld
Sr. Production Project Manager: Rhonda Aversa
Sr. Operations Specialist: Natacha Moore
Sr. Art Director: Jonathan Boylan
Text and Cover Designer: Jonathan Boylan
Cover Art: © Shutterstock, Inc.
Media Editor: Allison Longley
Media Project Manager: John Cassar
Full-Service Project Management: PreMediaGlobal, Inc.
Composition: PreMedia Global, Inc.
Printer/Binder: Edwards Brothers
Cover Printer: Lehigh-Phoenix Color/Hagerstown
Text Font: 10/12 Times

Credits and acknowledgments borrowed from other sources and reproduced, with permission, in this textbook appear on appropriate page within text.

Microsoft® and Windows® are registered trademarks of the Microsoft Corporation in the U.S.A. and other countries. Screen shots and icons reprinted with permission from the Microsoft Corporation. This book is not sponsored or endorsed by or affiliated with the Microsoft Corporation.

Romney, Marshall B.
Accounting information systems / Marshall B. Romney, Paul John Steinbart. — 12th ed. p. cm.
Includes index.
ISBN 978-0-13-255262-2
1. Accounting—Data processing. 2. Information storage and retrieval systems—Accounting. I. Steinbart, Paul John. II. Title.
HF5679.A34 2012
657.0285—dc22

                                                                                            2010032521

10 9 8 7 6 5 4 3 2

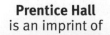

Prentice Hall
is an imprint of

www.pearsonhighered.com

ISBN 10:   0-13-255262-0
ISBN 13: 978-0-13-255262-2

Brief Contents

Contents

Preface

To the Student

The twelfth edition of *Accounting Information Systems* is designed to prepare you for a successful accounting career in public practice, industry, or government. All of you will be users of accounting information systems (AIS). As such, you should participate in the design of those systems. Doing so effectively, however, requires that you have a sound understanding of how they work. In addition to being users, some of you will become managers. Others will become internal and external auditors, and some of you will become consultants. All of these roles require you to understand how accounting information systems work so that you can measure their cost-effectiveness, assess their reliability and the reliability of the information produced, or lead the redesign and implementation of new and better systems. Mastering the material presented in this text will give you the foundational knowledge you need in order to excel at all those tasks.

This text discusses important new information technology (IT) developments, such as virtualization, cloud computing, the use of RFID tags to track inventory, and the adoption of XBRL for financial reporting, because such developments affect business processes and often cause organizations to redesign their accounting systems to take advantage of new capabilities. The focus, however, is not on IT for the sake of IT, but on how IT affects business processes and controls. Indeed, new IT developments not only bring new capabilities, but also often create new threats and affect the overall level of risk. This text will help you understand these issues so that you can properly determine how to modify accounting systems controls to effectively address those new threats and accurately assess the adequacy of controls in those redesigned systems. We also discuss the effect of recent regulatory developments, most notably the Sarbanes–Oxley Act and the upcoming switch from GAAP to IFRS, on the design and operation of accounting systems.

In addition to technology- and regulatory-driven changes, companies are responding to the increasingly competitive business environment by reexamining every internal activity in an effort to reap the most value at the least cost. As a result, accountants are being asked to do more than simply report the results of past activities. They must take a more proactive role in both providing and interpreting financial and nonfinancial information about the organization's activities. Therefore, throughout this text we discuss how accountants can improve the design and functioning of the accounting information system (AIS) so that it truly adds value to the organization.

Key Learning Objectives

When you finish reading this text, you should understand the following key concepts:

- The basic activities performed in the major business cycles
- What data need to be collected to enable managers to plan, evaluate, and control the business activities in which an organization engages
- How IT developments can improve the efficiency and effectiveness of business processes
- How to design an AIS to provide the information needed to make key decisions in each business cycle

- The risk of fraud and the motives and techniques used to perpetrate fraud
- The COSO and COSO-ERM models for internal control and risk management, as well as the specific controls used to achieve those objectives
- The Control Objectives for Information and Related Technology (COBIT) framework for the effective governance and control of information systems and how IT affects the implementation of internal controls
- The AICPA's Trust Services framework for ensuring systems reliability by developing procedures to protect the confidentiality of proprietary information, maintain the privacy of personal information collected from customers, assure the availability of information resources, and provide for information processing integrity
- Fundamentals of computer information security
- Goals, objectives, and methods for auditing information systems
- Fundamental concepts of database technology and data modeling and their effect on an AIS
- The tools for documenting AIS work, such as REA diagrams, data flow diagrams, and flowcharting
- The basic steps in the system development process to design and improve an AIS

Features to Facilitate Learning

To help you understand these concepts, the text includes the following features:

1. **Each chapter begins with an integrated case that introduces that chapter's key concepts and topics and identifies several key issues or problems that you should be able to solve after mastering the material presented in that chapter.** The case is referenced throughout the chapter, and the chapter summary presents solutions to the problems and issues raised in the case.
2. **Focus boxes and real-world examples** help you understand how companies are using the latest IT developments to improve their AIS.
3. **Hands-on Excel exercises in many chapters** help you hone your computer skills. Many of these exercises are based on "how-to" tutorials that appeared in recent issues of the *Journal of Accountancy*.
4. **Numerous problems in every chapter** provide additional opportunities for you to demonstrate your mastery of key concepts. Many problems were developed from reports in current periodicals. Other problems were selected from the various professional examinations, including the CPA, CMA, CIA, and SMAC exams.
5. **Cases in each chapter** require more extensive exploration of specific topics.
6. **Chapter quizzes** at the end of each chapter enable you to self-assess your understanding of the material. We also provide detailed explanations about the correct answer to each quiz question.
7. **Extensive use of graphics** enhance your understanding. The text contains hundreds of figures, diagrams, flowcharts, and tables that illustrate the concepts taught in the chapters.
8. **A comprehensive glossary** located at the back of the book makes it easy to look up the definition of the various technical terms used in the text.
9. **Extensive online support** is available at Prentice Hall's content-rich, text-supported Web site, at www.prenhall.com/romney.

Content and Organization

This text is divided into five parts, each focused on a major theme.

Part I: Conceptual Foundations of Accounting Information Systems

Part I consists of four chapters that present the underlying concepts fundamental to an understanding of AIS. Chapter 1 introduces basic terminology and discusses how an AIS can add value to an organization. Chapter 2 provides an overview of basic business processes. It introduces transaction processing in automated systems, presenting basic information processing and data storage concepts. You will see the wide range of data that must be collected by the AIS. This information helps you to understand what an AIS does; as you read the remainder of the book, you will see how advances in IT affect the manner in which those functions are performed. Chapter 3 covers two of the most important tools and techniques used to understand, evaluate, design, and document information systems: data flow diagrams and flowcharts. Chapter 4 introduces the topic of databases, with a particular emphasis on the relational data model and creating queries in Microsoft Access.

Part II: Control and Audit of Accounting Information Systems

The seven chapters in Part II focus on threats to the reliability of AIS and applicable controls for addressing and mitigating the risks associated with those threats. Chapter 5 discusses fraud and explains how and why it occurs. Chapter 6 continues the discussion of fraud, focusing specifically on computer fraud. Chapter 7 uses the COSO framework, including the expanded enterprise risk management (COSO-ERM) model, to discuss the basic concepts of internal control. Chapters 8–10 use both COBIT and the AICPA's Trust Services frameworks to discuss effective governance and control of information systems. Chapter 8 introduces the fundamental concepts of defense-in-depth and the time-based approach to security. The chapter provides a broad survey of a variety of security topics, including access controls, firewalls, encryption, and incident detection and response. Chapter 9 discusses the many specific computer controls used in business organizations to achieve the objectives of ensuring privacy and confidentiality, and it includes a detailed explanation of encryption. Chapter 10 addresses the controls necessary to achieve the objectives of accurate processing of information and ensuring that information is available to managers whenever and wherever they need it. Chapter 11 describes principles and techniques for the audit and evaluation of internal control in a computer-based AIS and introduces the topic of computer-assisted auditing.

Part III: Accounting Information Systems Applications

Part III focuses on how a company's AIS provides critical support for its fundamental business processes. Most large and many medium-sized organizations use enterprise resource planning (ERP) systems to collect, process, and store data about their business processes, as well as to provide information reports designed to enable managers and external parties to assess the organization's efficiency and effectiveness. To make it easier to understand how an ERP system functions, Part III consists of five chapters, each focusing on a particular business process. Chapter 12 covers the revenue cycle, describing all the activities involved in taking customer orders, fulfilling those orders, and collecting cash. Chapter 13 covers the expenditure cycle, describing all the activities involved in ordering, receiving, and paying for merchandise, supplies, and services. Chapter 14 covers the production cycle, with a special focus on the implications of recent cost accounting developments, such as activity-based costing, for the design of the production cycle information system. Chapter 15 covers the human resources management/payroll cycle, focusing primarily on the activities involved in processing payroll. Chapter 16 covers the general ledger and reporting activities in an organization, discussing topics such as XBRL, the balanced scorecard, the switch from GAAP to IFRS, and the proper design of graphs to support managerial decision making. Each of these five chapters explains the three basic functions performed by the AIS: efficient transaction processing, provision of adequate internal controls to safeguard assets (including data), and preparation of information useful for effective decision making.

Part IV: The REA Data Model

Part IV consists of three chapters that focus on the REA data model, which provides a conceptual tool for designing and understanding the database underlying an AIS. Chapter 17 introduces the REA data model and explains how it can be used to design an AIS database. The chapter focuses on modeling the revenue and expenditure cycles. It also demonstrates how the REA model can be used to develop an AIS that not only can generate traditional financial statements and reports but also can more fully meet the information needs of management. Chapter 18 explains how to implement an REA data model in a relational database system and shows how to query a relational database in order to produce various financial statements and management reports. Chapter 19 explains how to develop REA data models of the production, HR/payroll, and financing cycles. It also discusses a number of advanced modeling issues, such as the acquisition and sale of intangible products and services and rental transactions.

Part V: The Systems Development Process

Part V consists of three chapters that cover various aspects of the systems development process. Chapter 20 introduces the systems development life cycle and discusses the introductory steps of this process (systems analysis, feasibility, and planning). Particular emphasis is placed on the behavioral ramifications of change. Chapter 21 discusses an organization's many options for acquiring or developing an AIS (e.g., purchasing software, writing software, end-user–developed software, and outsourcing) and for speeding up or improving the development process (business process reengineering, prototyping, and computer-assisted software engineering). Chapter 22 covers the remaining stages of the systems development life cycle (conceptual design, physical design, implementation, and operation and maintenance) and emphasizes the interrelationships among the phases.

To the Instructor

This book is intended for use in a one-semester course in accounting information systems at the undergraduate or graduate level. Introductory financial and managerial accounting courses are suggested prerequisites, and an introductory information systems course that covers a computer language or software package is helpful. The book can also be used as the main text in graduate or advanced undergraduate management information systems courses. Indeed, the topics covered in this text provide information systems students with a solid understanding of transaction processing systems that they can then build on as they pursue more in-depth study of specific topics such as databases, data warehouses and data mining, networks, systems analysis and design, computer security, and information system controls.

Enhancements to the Twelfth Edition

The twelfth edition has been extensively revised and rewritten to incorporate recent developments while retaining the features that have made prior editions easy to use. Every chapter has been updated to include current examples of important concepts. Specific changes include the following:

1. More extensive coverage of both fraud and computer fraud, replacing the one chapter in the eleventh edition that covered both topics with two chapters in this new edition.
2. More detailed discussion of internal control frameworks: COSO, COSO-ERM, and COBIT.
3. Updated discussion of information security countermeasures, including the security and control implications associated with virtualization and cloud computing.
4. Additional Excel exercises, based on *Journal of Accountancy* articles, to help students develop the skills used by practitioners.
5. Many new end-of-chapter discussion questions and problems.

Supplemental Resources

As with prior editions, our objective in preparing this twelfth edition has been to simplify the teaching of AIS by enabling you to concentrate on classroom presentation and discussion, rather than on locating, assembling, and distributing teaching materials. To assist you in this process, the following supplementary materials are available to adopters of the text:

- *Solutions Manual* prepared by Marshall Romney at Brigham Young University and Paul John Steinbart at Arizona State University.
- *Instructors Manual/PowerPoint Presentations* prepared by Steven Hornik at the University of Central Florida.
- *PowerPoint Presentations* prepared by Steven Hornik at the University of Central Florida. The twelfth edition includes an entirely new set of PowerPoint slides that makes extensive use of high-quality graphics to illustrate key concepts. The slides do not merely consist of

bullet points taken verbatim from the text, but instead are designed to help students notice and understand important relationships among concepts. The large number of slides provides instructors a great deal of flexibility in choosing which topics they wish to emphasize in class.

- *Test Item File* prepared by Debra Cosgrove at the University of Nebraska–Lincoln.
- *TestGen testing software,* a computerized test item file.

In addition, you can access these supplements from the protected instructor area of www.pearsonhighered.com. Free online course support is also available on Blackboard and CourseCompass platforms. CourseCompass is Prentice Hall's nationally hosted solution.

We recognize that you may also wish to use specific software packages when teaching the AIS course. Contact your local rep to learn about bundling options with software packages such as Peachtree or other texts such as *Comprehensive Assurance & Systems Tool: Assurance Practice Set*, 2nd ed.; *Comprehensive Assurance & Systems Tool: Manual AIS Practice Set*, 2nd ed.; *Comprehensive Assurance & Systems Tool: Computerized AIS Practice Set*, 2nd ed., all written by Laura R. Ingraham of San Jose State University and J. Gregory Jenkins, at Virginia Polytechnic Institute and State University.

Acknowledgments

We wish to express our appreciation to all supplements authors for preparing the various supplements that accompany this edition. We thank Martha M. Eining of the University of Utah and Carol F. Venable of San Diego State University for preparing the comprehensive cases included on our Web site. Perhaps most important, we are indebted to the numerous faculty members throughout the world who have adopted the earlier editions of this book and who have been generous with their suggestions for improvement. We are especially grateful to the following faculty who participated in reviewing the twelfth edition throughout various stages of the revision process:

Bill Brewer, *Sam Houston State University*

Lawrence Chui, *University of Northern Texas*

Sandra Devona, *Northern Illinois University*

Rong Huang, *CUNY–Baruch College*

Vankataraman Iyer, *UNC–Greensboro*

Diane Janvrin, *Iowa State University*

Teresa Phinney, *Texas A&M–College Station*

Leslie Porter, *University of Southern California*

Laura Rickett, *Kent State University*

Jesse Robertson, *University of Northern Texas*

Winston Shearon, *Texas A&M–College Station*

James Stinson, *University of Houston*

Wendy Tietz, *Kent State University*

Barbara Uliss, *Metropolitan State College*

Louie Walker, *Metropolitan State College*

We are grateful for permission received from four professional accounting organizations to use problems and unofficial solutions from their past professional examinations in this book. Thanks are extended to the American Institute of Certified Public Accountants for use of the CPA Examination materials, to the Institute of Certified Management Accountants for use of CMA Examination materials, to the Institute of Internal Auditors for use of CIA Examination materials, and to the Society of Management Accountants of Canada for use of SMAC Examination materials.

Of course, any errors in this book remain our responsibility. We welcome your comments and suggestions for further improvement.

Finally, we want to thank our wives and families for their love, support, and encouragement. We also want to thank God for giving us the ability to start and complete this book.

—Marshall B. Romney
Provo, Utah

—Paul John Steinbart
Tempe, Arizona

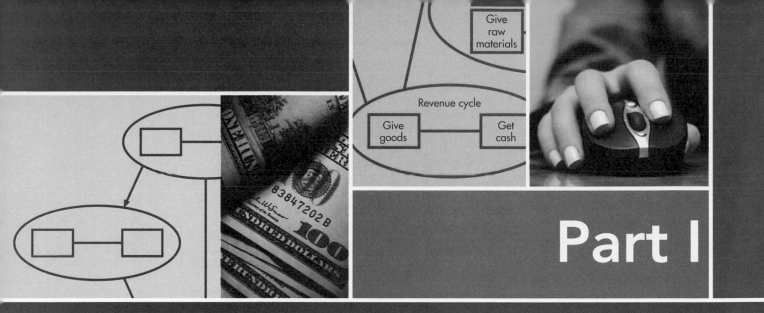

Part I

Conceptual Foundations of Accounting Information Systems

Chapter 1

Accounting Information Systems: An Overview

Learning Objectives

After studying this chapter, you should be able to:

1. Distinguish data from information, discuss the characteristics of useful information, and explain how to determine the value of information.

2. Explain the decisions an organization makes and the information needed to make them.

3. Identify the information that passes between internal and external parties and an AIS.

4. Describe the major business processes present in most companies.

5. Explain what an accounting information system (AIS) is and describe its basic functions.

6. Discuss how an AIS can add value to an organization.

7. Explain how an AIS and corporate strategy affect each other.

8. Explain the role an AIS plays in a company's value chain.

INTEGRATIVE CASE S&S

After working for years as a regional manager for a retail organization, Scott Parry opened his own business with Susan Gonzalez, one of his district managers, as his partner. They formed S&S to sell appliances and consumer electronics. Scott and Susan pursued a "clicks and bricks" strategy by renting a building in a busy part of town and adding an electronic storefront.

Scott and Susan invested enough money to see them through the first six months. They will hire 15 employees within the next two weeks—three to stock the shelves, four sales representatives, six checkout clerks, and two to develop and maintain the electronic storefront.

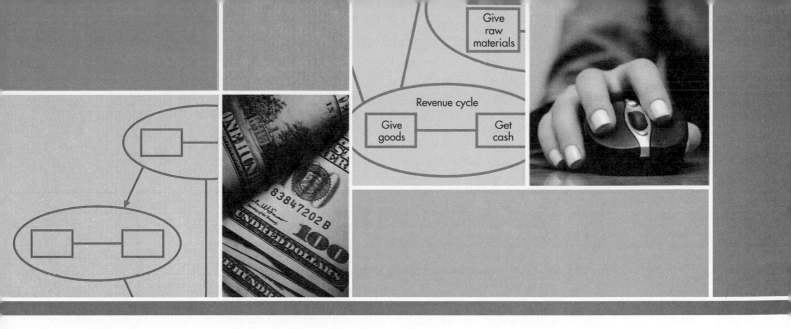

Scott and Susan will host S&S's grand opening in five weeks. To meet that deadline, they have to address the following important issues:

1. What decisions do they need to make to be successful and profitable? For example:
   a. How should they price products to be competitive yet earn a profit?
   b. Should they extend credit, and, if so, on what terms? How can they accurately track what customers owe and pay?
   c. How should they hire, train, and supervise employees? What compensation and benefits package should they offer? How should they process payroll?
   d. How can they track cash inflows and outflows to avoid a cash squeeze?
   e. What is the appropriate product mix? What inventory quantities should they carry, given their limited showroom space?
2. What information do Scott and Susan need to make those decisions?
   a. What information do the external entities they interact with need?
   b. What information do management and other employees need?
   c. How can they gather, store, and disseminate that information?
3. What business processes are needed, and how should they be carried out?
4. What functionality should be provided on the Web site?

Although Scott and Susan could use an educated guess or "gut feeling" to make these decisions, they know they can make better decisions if they obtain additional information. A well-designed *accounting information system (AIS)* can solve these issues and provide the information they need to make any remaining decisions.

Introduction

We begin this chapter by explaining important terms and discussing the kinds of information that organizations need and the business processes used to produce that information. We continue with an exploration of what an accounting information system (AIS) is, how an AIS adds value to an organization, how an AIS and corporate strategy affect each other, and the role of the AIS in the value chain.

A *system* is a set of two or more interrelated components that interact to achieve a goal. Most systems are composed of smaller subsystems that support the larger system. For example, a college of business is a system composed of various departments, each of which is a subsystem. Moreover, the college itself is a subsystem of the university.

Each subsystem is designed to achieve one or more organizational goals. Changes in subsystems cannot be made without considering the effect on other subsystems and on the system as a whole. *Goal conflict* occurs when a subsystem is inconsistent with the goals of another subsystem or with the system as a whole. *Goal congruence* occurs when a subsystem achieves its goals while contributing to the organization's overall goal. The larger the organization and the more complicated the system, the more difficult it is to achieve goal congruence.

Data are facts that are collected, recorded, stored, and processed by an information system. Businesses need to collect several kinds of data, such as the activities that take place, the resources affected by the activities, and the people who participate in the activity. For example, the business needs to collect data about a sale (date, total amount), the resource sold (good or service, quantity sold, unit price), and the people who participated (customer, salesperson).

Information is data that have been organized and processed to provide meaning and improve the decision-making process. As a rule, users make better decisions as the quantity and quality of information increase.

However, there are limits to the amount of information the human mind can absorb and process. *Information overload* occurs when those limits are passed, resulting in a decline in decision-making quality and an increase in the cost of providing that information. Information system designers use *information technology (IT)* to help decision makers more effectively filter and condense information. For example, Walmart has over 500 terabytes (trillions of bytes) of data in its data warehouse. That is equivalent to 2,000 miles of bookshelves, or about 100 million digital photos. Walmart has invested heavily in IT so it can effectively collect, store, analyze, and manage data to provide useful information.

The *value of information* is the benefit produced by the information minus the cost of producing it. Benefits of information are reduced uncertainty, improved decisions, and improved ability to plan and schedule activities. The costs are the time and resources spent to produce and distribute the information. Information costs and benefits can be difficult to quantify, and it is difficult to determine the value of information before it has been produced and utilized. Nevertheless, the expected value of information should be calculated as effectively as possible so that the costs of producing the information do not exceed its benefits.

To illustrate the value of information, consider the case of 7-Eleven. In 1973, a Japanese company licensed the very successful 7-Eleven name from Southland Corporation. As it opened its stores, 7-Eleven Japan invested heavily in IT, but the U.S. stores did not. Each 7-Eleven store in Japan was given a computer that:

- Keeps track of the 3,000 items sold in each store and determines what products are moving, at what time of day, and under what weather conditions.
- Keeps track of what and when customers buy to make sure it has in stock the products most frequently purchased.
- Orders sandwiches and rice dishes from suppliers automatically. Orders are placed and filled three times a day so that stores always have fresh food. In addition, 7-Eleven allows its suppliers to access sales data in their computers so that they can forecast demand.
- Coordinates deliveries with suppliers. This reduces deliveries from 34 to 12 a day, resulting in less clerical receiving time.
- Prepares a color graphic display that indicates which store areas contribute the most to sales and profits.

Average daily sales of 7-Eleven Japan were 30% higher and its operating margins almost double those of its closest competitor. What happened to Southland and its 7-Eleven stores in the United States? Profits declined, and Southland eventually had to file for bankruptcy. Who came to the company's rescue? Along with its parent company, 7-Eleven Japan purchased 64% of Southland.

Table 1-1 presents seven characteristics that make information useful and meaningful.

TABLE 1-1 Characteristics of Useful Information

Relevant	Reduces uncertainty, improves decision making, or confirms or corrects prior expectations.
Reliable	Free from error or bias; accurately represents organization events or activities.
Complete	Does not omit important aspects of the events or activities it measures.
Timely	Provided in time for decision makers to make decisions.
Understandable	Presented in a useful and intelligible format.
Verifiable	Two independent, knowledgeable people produce the same information.
Accessible	Available to users when they need it and in a format they can use.

Information Needs and Business Processes

All organizations need information in order to make effective decisions. In addition, all organizations have certain business processes that they are continuously engaged in. A *business process* is a set of related, coordinated, and structured activities and tasks that are performed by a person or by a computer or a machine, and that help accomplish a specific organizational goal.

To make effective decisions, organizations must decide what decisions they need to make, what information they need to make the decisions, and how to gather and process the data needed to produce the information. This data gathering and processing is often tied to the basic business processes in an organization. To illustrate the process of identifying information needs and business processes, let's return to our case study of S&S.

Information Needs

Scott and Susan decide they must understand how S&S functions before they can identify the information they need to manage S&S effectively. Then they can determine the types of data and procedures they will need to collect and produce that information. They created Table 1-2 to summarize part of their analysis. It lists S&S's basic business processes, some key decisions that need to be made for each process, and information they need to make the decisions.

Scott and Susan realize that the list is not exhaustive, but they are satisfied that it provides a good overview of S&S. They also recognize that not all the information needs listed in the right-hand column will be produced internally by S&S. Information about payment terms for merchandise purchases, for example, will be provided by vendors. Thus, S&S must effectively integrate external data with internally generated data so that Scott and Susan can use both types of information to run S&S.

S&S will interact with many external parties, such as customers, vendors, and governmental agencies, as well as with internal parties such as management and employees. To get a better handle on the more important interactions with these parties, they prepared Figure 1-1.

Business Processes

Scott decides to reorganize the business processes listed in Table 1-2 into groups of related transactions. A *transaction* is an agreement between two entities to exchange goods or services or any other event that can be measured in economic terms by an organization. Examples include selling goods to customers, buying inventory from suppliers, and paying employees. The process that begins with capturing transaction data and ends with informational output, such as the financial statements, is called *transaction processing*. Transaction processing is covered in more depth in Chapter 2.

Many business activities are pairs of events involved in a *give-get exchange*. Most organizations engage in a small number of give-get exchanges, but each type of exchange happens many times. For example, S&S will have thousands of sales to customers every year in exchange for cash. Likewise, S&S will continuously buy inventory from suppliers in exchange for cash.

TABLE 1-2 Overview of S&S's Business Processes, Key Decisions, and Information Needs

Business Processes	Key Decisions	Information Needs
Acquire capital	How much Find investors or borrow funds If borrowing, obtaining best terms	Cash flow projections Pro forma financial statements Loan amortization schedule
Acquire building and equipment	Size of building Amount of equipment Rent or buy Location How to depreciate	Capacity needs Building and equipment prices Market study Tax tables and depreciation regulations
Hire and train employees	Experience requirements How to assess integrity and competence of applicants How to train employees	Job descriptions Applicant job history and skills
Acquire inventory	What models to carry How much to purchase How to manage inventory (store, control, etc.) Which vendors	Market analyses Inventory status reports Vendor performance
Advertising and marketing	Which media Content	Cost analyses Market coverage
Sell merchandise	Markup percentage Offer in-house credit Which credit cards to accept	Pro forma income statement Credit card costs Customer credit status
Collect payments from customers	If offering credit, what terms How to handle cash receipts	Customer account status Accounts receivable aging report Accounts receivable records
Pay employees	Amount to pay Deductions and withholdings Process payroll in-house or use outside service	Sales (for commissions) Time worked (hourly employees) W-4 forms Costs of external payroll service
Pay taxes	Payroll tax requirements Sales tax requirements	Government regulations Total wage expense Total sales
Pay vendors	Whom to pay When to pay How much to pay	Vendor invoices Accounts payable records Payment terms

FIGURE 1-1

Interactions Between S&S and External and Internal Parties

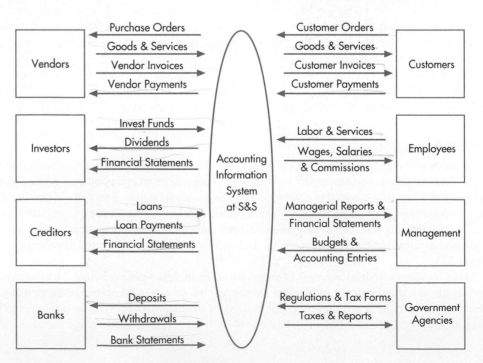

These exchanges can be grouped into five major *business processes or transaction cycles*:

- The *revenue cycle*, where goods and services are sold for cash or a future promise to receive cash. This cycle is discussed in Chapter 12.
- The *expenditure cycle*, where companies purchase inventory for resale or raw materials to use in producing products in exchange for cash or a future promise to pay cash. This cycle is discussed in Chapter 13.
- The *production* or *conversion cycle*, where raw materials are transformed into finished goods. This cycle is discussed in Chapter 14.
- The *human resources/payroll cycle*, where employees are hired, trained, compensated, evaluated, promoted, and terminated. This cycle is discussed in Chapter 15.
- The *financing cycle*, where companies sell shares in the company to investors and borrow money and where investors are paid dividends and interest is paid on loans.

These cycles process a few related transactions repeatedly. For example, most revenue cycle transactions are either selling goods or services to customers or collecting cash for those sales. Figure 1-2 shows the main transaction cycles and the give-get exchange inherent in each cycle.

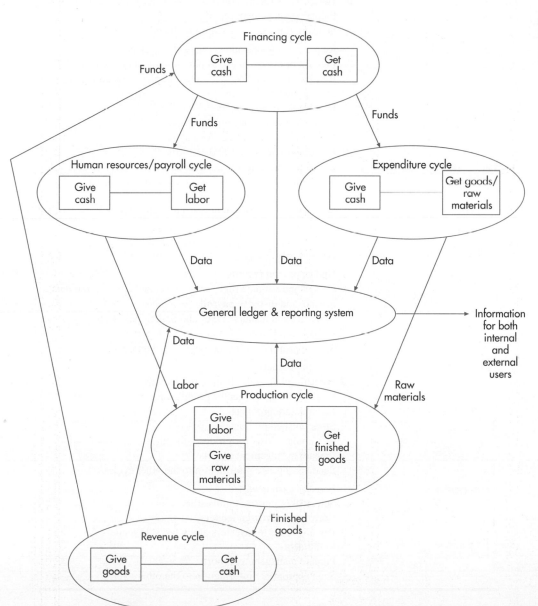

FIGURE 1-2

The AIS and Its Subsystems

These basic give-get exchanges are supported by a number of other business activities. For example, S&S may need to answer a number of customer inquiries and check inventory levels before it can make a sale. Likewise, it may have to check customer credit before a credit sale is made. Accounts receivable will have to be increased each time a credit sale is made and decreased each time a customer payment is received. Table 1-3 lists the major activities in each transaction cycle.

TABLE 1-3 Common Cycle Activities

Transaction Cycle	Major Activities in the Cycle
Revenue	Receive and answer customer inquiries
	Take customer orders and enter them into the AIS
	Approve credit sales
	Check inventory availability
	Initiate back orders for goods out of stock
	Pick and pack customer orders
	Ship goods to customers or perform services
	Bill customers for goods shipped or services performed
	Update (increase) sales and accounts receivable
	Receive customer payments and deposit them in the bank
	Update (reduce) accounts receivable
	Handle sales returns, discounts, allowances, and bad debts
	Prepare management reports
	Send appropriate information to the other cycles
Expenditure	Request that goods and services be purchased
	Prepare, approve, and send purchase orders to vendors
	Receive goods and services and complete a receiving report
	Store goods
	Receive vendor invoices
	Update (increase) accounts payable
	Approve vendor invoices for payment
	Pay vendors for goods and services
	Update (reduce) accounts payable
	Handle purchase returns, discounts, and allowances
	Prepare management reports
	Send appropriate information to the other cycles
Human Resources/Payroll	Recruit, hire, and train new employees
	Evaluate employee performance and promote employees
	Discharge employees
	Update payroll records
	Collect and validate time, attendance, and commission data
	Prepare and disburse payroll
	Calculate and disburse taxes and benefit payments
	Prepare employee and management reports
	Send appropriate information to the other cycles
Production	Design products
	Forecast, plan, and schedule production
	Request raw materials for production
	Manufacture products
	Store finished products
	Accumulate costs for products manufactured
	Prepare management reports
	Send appropriate information to the other cycles
Financing	Forecast cash needs
	Sell stock/securities to investors
	Borrow money from lenders
	Pay dividends to investors and interest to lenders
	Retire debt
	Prepare management reports
	Send appropriate information to the other cycles

Notice that the last activity listed in Table 1-3 for each transaction cycle is "Send appropriate information to the other cycles." Figure 1-2 shows how these various transaction cycles relate to one another and interface with the **general ledger and reporting system**, which is used to generate information for both management and external parties. The general ledger and reporting system is discussed in more depth in Chapter 16.

In many accounting software packages, the various transaction cycles are implemented as separate modules. Not every organization needs to implement every module. Retail stores like S&S, for example, do not have a production cycle and would not implement that module. Moreover, some types of organizations have unique requirements. Financial institutions, for example, have demand deposit and installment-loan cycles that relate to transactions involving customer accounts and loans, respectively. In addition, the nature of a given transaction cycle differs across different types of organizations. For example, the expenditure cycle of a service company, such as a public accounting or a law firm, does not involve processing transactions related to the purchase, receipt, and payment for merchandise that will be resold to customers.

Each transaction cycle can include many different business processes or activities. Each business process can be relatively simple or quite complex. Focus 1-1 shows how Toyota's attention to continuously improving its business processes has helped it become the largest and most profitable automobile manufacturer in the world.

FOCUS 1-1   Improving Business Processes Helps Drive Toyota's Success

Toyota's Georgetown, Kentucky, manufacturing plant, its largest in North America, is the size of 156 football fields, employs 7,000 people, and produces a new car every 55 seconds. Because Toyota produces a high-quality car at a lower cost than its competitors do, it is now the largest automobile manufacturer in the world, a title General Motors had for almost a hundred years.

A major factor in its success is the Toyota Production System (TPS), which is a set of philosophies, principles, and business processes supported by IT. Its goal is to improve continually so Toyota has the most effective and most efficient manufacturing and business processes possible. Toyota willingly shares TPS and its manufacturing and business processes with its suppliers to help them improve their quality and efficiency. It also shares TPS with its competitors, knowing that by the time they duplicate it Toyota will have greatly improved TPS.

The following are some of the principles and business processes on which TPS is built and which Toyota's information systems must support and enable:

- Performance-monitoring software warns assembly line workers of equipment problems. Workers stop production whenever necessary to prevent or correct defects.
- Their just-in-time (JIT) inventory system is one of the most sophisticated in the world. Driverless carts take parts to assembly stations when they are needed so that inventory does not pile up. Suppliers must meet rigid delivery standards. Four hours before they are needed, Toyota software electronically notifies Johnson Controls of exactly what kind of car seats are needed for each car and the exact order in which they must be shipped.

- Continuous improvement is a critical and ongoing process. No process or detail is too small or insignificant to improve. Technology is especially important in the continuous improvement process. This emphasis on continuous improvement creates a culture that values continuous learning and embraces change.
- Electronic displays connected to the manufacturing equipment help workers monitor the assembly line. Information is communicated by light colors (green means the process is operating correctly, yellow means a problem is being investigated, and red means the assembly line has stopped) and by printed messages (which machine malfunctioned, its speed and temperature when it broke down, and who was operating the machine).
- Electronic quality control devices, such as an electronic sensor on a tool or a beam of light, monitor a process. These devices let a computer know when a tool is not used or a required part is not picked up and used at the appropriate time.
- More than half of Toyota's information systems employees work in operations at its plants so they can accompany executives, team leaders, and factory workers when they go to solve assembly line problems.

In summary, Toyota has a very clear and in-depth understanding of the business processes that make it successful, continuously improves those process, and understands the role information systems play in managing, supporting, and facilitating those processes.

Source: Mel Duvall, "What's Driving Toyota?" *Baseline Magazine*, September 5, 2006.

After preparing Tables 1-2 and 1-3 and Figures 1-1 and 1-2, Scott and Susan believe that they understand S&S well enough to begin shopping for an information system. Susan recalled a previous employer that had several separate information systems, because their software was not designed to accommodate the information needs of all managers. She also vividly recalled attending one meeting where she witnessed the negative effects of having multiple systems. The head of marketing had one report on year-to-date sales by product, the production manager had a different report that contained different sales figures, and the controller's report, which was produced by the general ledger system, had yet a third version of year-to-date sales. Over an hour was wasted trying to reconcile those different reports! Susan vowed that she would make sure that S&S did not ever find itself in such a mess. She would make sure that any system selected would have the capability to integrate both financial and nonfinancial data about S&S's various business processes so that everyone could pull information from the same system.

Accounting Information Systems

It has often been said that accounting is the language of business. If that is the case, then an *accounting information system (AIS)* is the intelligence—the information-providing vehicle— of that language.

Accounting is a data identification, collection, and storage process as well as an information development, measurement, and communication process. By definition, accounting is an information system, since an AIS collects, records, stores, and processes accounting and other data to produce information for decision makers. This is illustrated in Figure 1-3.

An AIS can be a paper-and-pencil manual system, a complex system using the latest in IT, or something in between. Regardless of the approach taken, the process is the same. The AIS must collect, enter, process, store, and report data and information. The paper and pencil or the computer hardware and software are merely the tools used to produce the information.

This text does not distinguish an AIS from other information systems. Instead, our viewpoint is that the AIS can and should be the organization's primary information system and that it provides users with the information they need to perform their jobs.

There are six components of an AIS:

1. The *people* who use the system
2. The *procedures and instructions* used to collect, process, and store data
3. The *data* about the organization and its business activities
4. The *software* used to process the data
5. The *information technology infrastructure*, including the computers, peripheral devices, and network communications devices used in the AIS
6. The *internal controls and security measures* that safeguard AIS data

These six components enable an AIS to fulfill three important business functions:

1. Collect and store data about organizational activities, resources, and personnel. Organizations have a number of business processes, such as making a sale or purchasing raw materials, which are repeated frequently.
2. Transform data into information so management can plan, execute, control, and evaluate activities, resources, and personnel. Decision making is discussed in detail later in this chapter.
3. Provide adequate controls to safeguard the organization's assets and data. Control concepts are discussed in detail in Chapters 5–11.

Since accounting data comes from an AIS, AIS knowledge and skills are critical to an accountant's career success. Interacting with an AIS is one of the most important activities that accountants perform. Other important AIS-related activities include designing internal control

FIGURE 1-3

An AIS Processes Data to Produce Information for Decision Makers

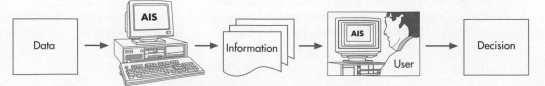

systems and business process improvements, topics covered in detail in the book. Focus 1-2 explains a specialty to designate that certain CPAs have an in-depth knowledge of AIS topics.

How an AIS Can Add Value to an Organization

A well-designed AIS can add value to an organization by:

1. *Improving the quality and reducing the costs of products or services.*   For example, an AIS can monitor machinery so operators are notified immediately when performance falls outside acceptable quality limits. This helps maintain product quality, reduces waste, and lowers costs.
2. *Improving efficiency.*   For example, timely information makes a just-in-time manufacturing approach possible, as it requires constant, accurate, up-to-date information about raw materials inventories and their locations.
3. *Sharing knowledge.*   Sharing knowledge and expertise can improve operations and provide a competitive advantage. For example, CPA firms use their information systems to share best practices and to support communication between offices. Employees can search the corporate database to identify experts to provide assistance for a particular client; thus, a CPA firm's international expertise can be made available to any local client.
4. *Improving the efficiency and effectiveness of its supply chain.*   For example, allowing customers to directly access inventory and sales order entry systems can reduce sales and marketing costs, thereby increasing customer retention rates.
5. *Improving the internal control structure.*   An AIS with the proper internal control structure can protect systems from fraud, errors, system failures, and disasters.
6. *Improving decision making.*   Improved decision making is vitally important and is discussed below in more detail.

FOCUS 1-2   CITP—An IT Specialty Designation for CPAs

The American Institute of Certified Public Accountants (AICPA) offers several specialty designations for CPAs. The CITP (Certified Information Technology Professional) designation reflects the AICPA's recognition of the importance of information technology and its interrelationship with accounting. A CITP possesses a broad range of technological knowledge and understands how organizations use IT to achieve their business objectives.

There are many reasons to earn the CITP certification:

- Because only CPAs can be CITPs, this certification further differentiates you from others in the marketplace.
- It affirms your value as an IT specialist and increases your value to your employer or clients.
- It is a great "calling card" for IT people who want to be leaders in industry, public practice, government, or academia.
- It opens the doors to new technology-related roles and opportunities.
- Automatic membership in the IT Section, which allows you to meet, share best practices, network, and communicate with other CITPs. You can also receive monthly CITP newsletters and other communications, attend monthly CITP Webinars, and access exclusive CITP resources and content on the IT Center Web site.

To qualify for the CITP designation, you must be a CPA and a member of the AICPA. You must earn 100 points in the areas of business experience, lifelong learning, and an optional exam. Candidates must earn a minimum of 15 points, up to a maximum of 75 points, in the area of business experience. The number of points awarded depends on the number of hours spent working in the following areas in the three-year period preceding application for the CITP designation:

- IT Strategic Planning
- Information Systems Management
- Systems Architecture
- Business Applications and E-Business
- Security, Privacy, and Contingency Planning
- Systems Development, Acquisition, and Project Management
- Systems Auditing and Internal Control
- Databases and Database Management

You must also earn a minimum of 30 points, up to a maximum of 70 points, in lifelong learning, which includes continuing education, additional degrees, and obtaining or maintaining other technology-related certifications.

Candidates who have earned at least 60 points in business experience and lifelong learning can earn 40 points by passing an exam that covers the eight previously mentioned topical areas.

Decision making is a complex, multistep activity: identify the problem, collect and interpret information, evaluate ways to solve the problem, select a solution methodology, and implement the solution. An AIS can provide assistance in all phases of decision making. Reports can help to identify potential problems. Decision models and analytical tools can be provided to users. Query languages can gather relevant data to help make the decision. Various tools, such as graphical interfaces, can help the decision maker interpret decision model results, evaluate them, and choose among alternative courses of action. In addition, the AIS can provide feedback on the results of actions.

An AIS can help improve decision making in several ways:

● It can identify situations requiring management action. For example, a cost report with a large variance might stimulate management to investigate and, if necessary, take corrective action.
● It can reduce uncertainty and thereby provide a basis for choosing among alternative actions.
● It can store information about the results of previous decisions, which provides valuable feedback that can be used to improve future decisions. For example, if a company tries a particular marketing strategy and the information gathered indicates that it did not succeed, the company can use that information to select a different marketing strategy.
● It can provide accurate information in a timely manner. For example, Walmart has an enormous database that contains detailed information about sales transactions at each of its stores. It uses this information to optimize the amount of each product carried at each store.
● It analyzes sales data to discover items that are purchased together, and it uses such information to improve the layout of merchandise to encourage additional sales of related items. In a similar vein, Amazon.com uses its database of sales activity to suggest additional books for customers to purchase.

Focus 1-3 discusses how information technology adds value to UPS.

FOCUS 1-3   The Use of Technology by UPS

UPS used to invest heavily in training its employees to perform tasks in less time but spent little money on IT. Today, because of the value added to its business, UPS spends well over $1 billion a year on IT. That is much more than it spends on trucks and about as much as it spends on airplanes. UPS has 4,700 employees devoted to developing and maintaining proprietary software and a Web site that 20 million people visit each day. Its 15 mainframe computers and 9,000 servers allow UPS customers to control each shipment (16 million a day) from the time a delivery order is initiated to the time it arrives at its destination. Here is how the system works:

● Customers use UPS software or the UPS Web site to initiate a delivery. They create, print, and attach labels to their shipment containing detailed sender information and the time the shipment should arrive.
● They schedule a pickup time electronically.
● The UPS system routes the label information to the distribution center closest to the shipment's destination.
● At the distribution center, proprietary software uses the destination, desired arrival time, traffic and weather conditions, and street information (one-way streets, etc.) to create the most efficient delivery route. Drivers have handheld computers with a global positioning system (GPS) that guide their routes.

● The system creates a label that specifies where to put the shipment on the delivery truck so the earliest shipments are nearest the driver. Drivers average 100 pickups and deliveries a day, and boxes loaded out of order can delay the driver up to 30 minutes.
● Customers can use the UPS Web site to reroute or track their shipment. The GPS allows UPS to predict accurately the shipment's approximate arrival time.
● The handheld computer is programmed to beep at the driver if a shipment is delivered to the wrong address or forgotten.

UPS's commitment to IT has produced dramatic results. Recent system improvements allowed drivers to make seven to nine more stops each day, reduced the number of miles UPS drives each year by 1.9 million, and saved over $600 million per year in operating costs.

However, UPS is not congratulating itself on how well it has used IT to improve its business. The UPS system is a work in progress. UPS continues to innovate and find ways to use IT to become even more efficient and better serve the customer.

Source: Corey Dade, "How UPS Went from Low-Tech to an IT Power—and Where It's Headed Next," *The Wall Street Journal,* July 24, 2006, R4.

The AIS and Corporate Strategy

Since most organizations have limited resources, it is important to identify the AIS improvements likely to yield the greatest return. Making a wise decision requires an understanding of the organization's overall business strategy. To illustrate, consider the results of a *CIO* magazine survey of five hundred Chief Information Officers. Asked to identify the three most important skill sets for a CIO, over 75% put strategic thinking and planning on their list.

Figure 1-4 shows three factors that influence the design of an AIS: developments in IT, business strategy, and organizational culture. It is also important to recognize that the design of the AIS can also influence the organization's culture by controlling the flow of information within the organization. For example, an AIS that makes information easily accessible and widely available is likely to increase pressures for more decentralization and autonomy.

IT developments can affect business strategy. For example, the Internet has profoundly affected the way many activities are performed, significantly affecting both strategy and strategic positioning. The Internet dramatically cuts costs, thereby helping companies to implement a low-cost strategy. If every company used the Internet to adopt a low-cost strategy, then the effects might be problematic. Indeed, one possible outcome may be intense price competition among firms, with the likely result that most of the cost savings provided by the Internet get passed on to the industry's customers, rather than being retained in the form of higher profits. Moreover, because every company can use the Internet to streamline its activities, a company is unlikely to gain a sustainable long-term competitive advantage.

Many other technological advances affect company strategy and provide an opportunity to gain a competitive advantage. An example is *predictive analysis*, which uses data warehouses and complex algorithms to forecast future events, based on historical trends and calculated probabilities. Predictive analysis provides an educated guess of what one may expect to see in the near future, allowing companies to make better business decisions and improve their processes. FedEx uses predictive analysis to predict, with 65% to 90% accuracy, how customers respond to price changes and new services. Blue Cross Blue Shield of Tennessee uses a neural-based predictive model to predict the health care that specific patients will need, the severity of illnesses, and organ failures. Stock market analysts are using predictive analysis to predict short-term trends in the stock market.

An organization's AIS plays an important role in helping it adopt and maintain a strategic position. Achieving a close fit among activities requires that data be collected about each activity. It is also important that the information system collect and integrate both financial and nonfinancial data about the organization's activities.

The Role of the AIS in the Value Chain

To provide value to their customers, most organizations perform a number of different activities. Figure 1-5 shows that those activities can be conceptualized as forming a *value chain* consisting of five *primary activities* that directly provide value to customers:

1. *Inbound logistics*   consists of receiving, storing, and distributing the materials an organization uses to create the services and products it sells. For example, an automobile manufacturer receives, handles, and stores steel, glass, and rubber.
2. *Operations*   activities transform inputs into final products or services. For example, assembly line activities convert raw materials into a finished car.

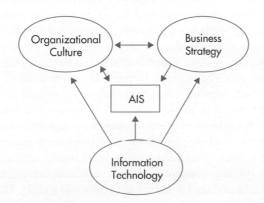

FIGURE 1-4

Factors Influencing Design of the AIS

FIGURE 1-5
The Value Chain

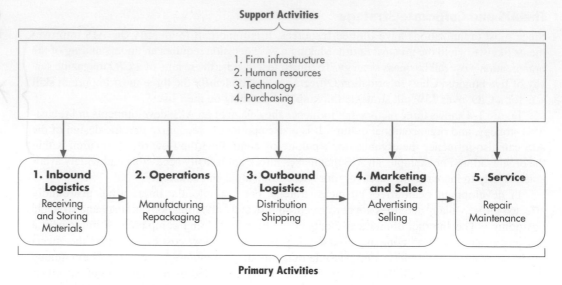

3. *Outbound logistics*   activities distribute finished products or services to customers. An example is shipping automobiles to car dealers.
4. *Marketing and sales*   activities help customers buy the organization's products or services. Advertising is an example of a marketing and sales activity.
5. *Service*   activities provide post-sale support to customers. Examples include repair and maintenance services.

Support activities allow the five primary activities to be performed efficiently and effectively. They are grouped into four categories:

1. *Firm infrastructure*   is the accounting, finance, legal, and general administration activities that allow an organization to function. The AIS is part of the firm infrastructure.
2. *Human resources*   activities include recruiting, hiring, training, and compensating employees.
3. *Technology*   activities improve a product or service. Examples include research and development, investments in IT, and product design.
4. *Purchasing*   activities procure raw materials, supplies, machinery, and the buildings used to carry out the primary activities.

Using IT to redesign supply chain systems yields tremendous benefits and cost savings. For example, Tennessee Valley Authority, a power generator, reengineered its supply chain and created an enterprisewide system that provides up-to-the-minute information, rather than the "current once a day" system that it replaced. The new system replaced 20 smaller and incompatible systems, reduced head count by 89 people, and saved $270 million in its first five years.

An organization's value chain is a part of a larger system called a *supply chain*. As shown in Figure 1-6, a manufacturing organization interacts with its suppliers and distributors. By paying attention to its supply chain, a company can improve its performance by helping the others in the supply chain to improve their performance. For example, S&S can improve its purchasing and inbound logistics activities by implementing a more efficient just-in-time inventory management system that reduces its costs and minimizes the capital tied up in inventory. S&S can reap additional benefits if it links its new systems with its suppliers so they can perform their primary value chain activities more efficiently. For example, by providing more detailed and timely information about its inventory needs, S&S suppliers can more efficiently plan their production schedules. Part of the resultant cost reduction can be passed on to S&S in the form of lower product costs.

The problems created by an ineffective supply chain are illustrated by Limited Brands. Limited experienced explosive growth, including acquisitions of other retail companies such as Victoria's Secret and Abercrombie & Fitch. These acquisitions left Limited with a tangled web of over 60 incompatible information systems. The problems came to a head one night when 400 trailers converged on a distribution center parking lot that could fit only 150 trailers. The trailers blocked traffic along all the highways around the distribution center and caused countless traffic and community

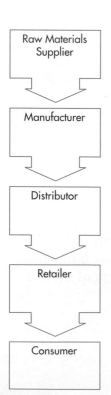

FIGURE 1-6
The Supply Chain

problems. No one in Limited knew where all the trailers came from, what the merchandise was, or where it was to be sent. Chaos reigned for some time, until the merchandise could be routed to stores and other distribution centers. Limited solved many of its problems by installing a new, integrated system that greatly improved its supply chain processes and technologies. Developing the new system was not easy. Limited has over a thousand suppliers and sells its merchandise using various platforms, including retail stores, the Internet, catalogs, and third-party retailers.

Summary and Case Conclusion

Susan and Scott reflected on what they had done to try and understand what decisions S&S would need to make and the information needed to make them. They had begun by obtaining an understanding of S&S's basic business processes and of the key decisions that must be made to operate the business effectively. They followed that with an analysis of the internal and external parties that the AIS would have to interact with and the information the AIS would have to provide them.

Since S&S is a retail merchandising company, its business processes could be described in terms of four basic transaction cycles:

1. The *revenue cycle* encompasses all transactions involving sales to customers and the collection of cash receipts for those sales.
2. The *expenditure cycle* encompasses all transactions involving the purchase of and payment for the merchandise sold by S&S, as well as other services it consumes, such as rent and utilities.
3. The *human resources/payroll cycle* encompasses all the transactions involving the hiring, training, and payment of employees.
4. The *financing cycle* encompasses all transactions involving the investment of capital in the company, borrowing money, payment of interest, and loan repayments.

These four cycles interface with the *general ledger and reporting system*, which consists of all activities related to the preparation of financial statements and other managerial reports.

Scott and Susan will need a well-designed AIS to provide the information they need to effectively plan, manage, and control their business. Their AIS must be able to process data about sales and cash receipts, purchasing and paying for merchandise and services, payroll and tax-related transactions, and acquiring and paying for fixed assets. The company's AIS must also provide the information needed to prepare financial statements.

Fortunately, there are many computer-based accounting packages available for the retail industry. As they begin looking at various software packages, however, Scott and Susan quickly learn that considerable accounting knowledge is required to choose the one that will best fit their business. Because neither has an accounting background, Scott and Susan decide that their next task will be to hire an accountant.

Key Terms

system 4	transaction processing 5	general ledger and reporting
goal conflict 4	give-get exchange 5	system 9
goal congruence 4	business processes or	accounting information
data 4	transaction cycles 7	system (AIS) 10
information 4	revenue cycle 7	predictive analysis 13
information overload 4	expenditure cycle 7	value chain 13
information	production (conversion)	primary activities 13
technology (IT) 4	cycle 7	support activities 14
value of information 4	human resources/payroll	supply chain 14
business process 5	cycle 7	
transaction 5	financing cycle 7	

AIS IN ACTION

Chapter Quiz

1. Data differ from information in which way?
   a. Data are output, and information is input.
   b. Information is output, and data are input.
   c. Data are meaningful bits of information.
   d. There is no difference.

2. Which of the following is NOT a characteristic that makes information useful?
   a. It is reliable.   b. It is timely.   c. It is inexpensive.   d. It is relevant.

3. Which of the following is a primary activity in the value chain?
   a. purchasing   c. post-sales service
   b. accounting   d. human resource management

4. Which transaction cycle includes interactions between an organization and its suppliers?
   a. revenue cycle   c. human resources/payroll cycle
   b. expenditure cycle   d. general ledger and reporting system

5. Which of the following is NOT a means by which information improves decision making?
   a. increases information overload
   b. reduces uncertainty
   c. provides feedback about the effectiveness of prior decisions
   d. identifies situations requiring management action

6. In the value chain concept, upgrading IT is considered what kind of activity?
   a. primary activity   c. service activity
   b. support activity   d. structured activity

7. In which cycle does a company ship goods to customers?
   a. production cycle   c. revenue cycle
   b. financing cycle   d. expenditure cycle

8. Which of the following is a function of an AIS?
   a. reducing the need to identify a strategy and strategic position
   b. transforming data into useful information
   c. allocating organizational resources
   d. automating all decision making

9. A firm, its suppliers, and its customers collectively form which of the following?
   a. supply chain   b. value chain   c. ERP system   d. AIS

10. A report telling how well all approved vendors have performed in the prior 12 months is information that is MOST needed in which business process?
    a. paying vendors   c. selling merchandise
    b. acquiring inventory   d. paying employees

Discussion Questions

1.1. The value of information is the difference between the benefits realized from using that information and the costs of producing it. Would you, or any organization, ever produce information if its expected costs exceeded its benefits? If so, provide some examples. If not, why not?

1.2. Can the characteristics of useful information listed in Table 1-1 be met simultaneously? Or does achieving one mean sacrificing another?

1.3. You and a few of your classmates decided to become entrepreneurs. You came up with a great idea for a new mobile phone application that you think will make lots of money. Your business plan won second place in a local competition, and you are using the $10,000 prize to support yourselves as you start your company.
a. Identify the key decisions you need to make to be successful entrepreneurs, the information you need to make them, and the business processes you will need to engage in.
b. Your company will need to exchange information with various external parties. Identify the external parties, and specify the information received from and sent to each of them.

1.4. How do an organization's business processes and lines of business affect the design of its AIS? Give several examples of how differences among organizations are reflected in their AIS.

1.5. Figure 1-4 shows that organizational culture and the design of an AIS influence one another. What does this imply about the degree to which an innovative system developed by one company can be transferred to another company?

1.6. Figure 1-4 shows that developments in IT affect both an organization's strategy and the design of its AIS. How can a company determine whether it is spending too much, too little, or just enough on IT?

1.7. Apply the value chain concept to S&S. Explain how it would perform the various primary and support activities.

1.8. Information technology enables organizations to easily collect large amounts of information about employees. Discuss the following issues:
a. To what extent should management monitor employees' e-mail?
b. To what extent should management monitor which Web sites employees visit?
c. To what extent should management monitor employee performance by, for example, using software to track keystrokes per hour or some other unit of time? If such information is collected, how should it be used?
d. Should companies use software to electronically "shred" all traces of e-mail?
e. Under what circumstances and to whom is it appropriate for a company to distribute information it collects about the people who visit its Web site?

Problems

1.1. Information technology is continually changing the nature of accounting and the role of accountants. Write a two-page report describing what you think the nature of the accounting function and the accounting information system in a large company will be like in the year 2020.

1.2. The annual report is considered by some to be the single most important printed document that companies produce. In recent years, annual reports have become large documents. They now include such sections as letters to the stockholders, descriptions of the business, operating highlights, financial review, management discussion and analysis, a discussion of company internal controls, segment reporting, inflation data, and the basic financial statements. The expansion has been due in part to a general increase in the degree of sophistication and complexity in accounting standards and disclosure requirements for financial reporting.

The expansion also is reflective of the change in the composition and level of sophistication of users. Current users include not only stockholders but also financial and securities analysts, potential investors, lending institutions, stockbrokers, customers, employees, and—whether the reporting company likes it or not—competitors. Thus, a report that was originally designed as a device for communicating basic financial information now attempts to meet the diverse needs of an ever-expanding audience.

Users hold conflicting views on the value of annual reports. Some argue that they fail to provide enough information, whereas others believe that disclosures in annual reports have expanded to the point where they create information overload. Others argue that the future of most companies depends on acceptance by the investing public and by its customers; therefore, companies should take this opportunity to communicate well-defined corporate strategies.

Required

a. Identify and discuss the basic factors of communication that must be considered in the presentation of the annual report.

b. Discuss the communication problems a corporation faces in preparing the annual report that result from the diversity of the users being addressed.

c. Select two types of information found in an annual report, other than the financial statements and accompanying footnotes, and describe how they are helpful to the users of annual reports.

d. Discuss at least two advantages and two disadvantages of stating well-defined corporate strategies in the annual report.

e. Evaluate the effectiveness of annual reports in fulfilling the information needs of the following current and potential users: shareholders, creditors, employees, customers, and financial analysts.

f. Annual reports are public and accessible to anyone, including competitors. Discuss how this affects decisions about what information should be provided in annual reports. *(CMA Examination, adapted)*

1.3. United Services Automotive Association (USAA) is one of the largest diversified financial services companies in the United States, with close to $75 billion in assets under management. One reason for its success is the use of IT to lower costs and improve customer service. USAA operates one of the most advanced and successful information systems in the world. It communicates with its widely scattered customers, mostly military officers and their families, primarily by e-mail, phone, and its Web site.

Early on, USAA made a strategic choice to become one of the more technology-intensive companies in the world. It views IT as a strategic weapon and uses it in several ways, including the following:

- When customers call from their homes, offices, or cell phones, USAA personnel greet them personally by name. Unlike many diversified companies, a customer representative can handle inquires and transactions about all of USAA's products using a highly integrated database.

- USAA uses its extensive database to keep track of minute details, such as which auto parts are fixed most frequently. It also uses its database to find ways to reduce claims costs. For example, USAA discovered that repair shops would rather charge up to $300 to replace a windshield with punctures than to charge $40 to repair it. USAA began offering to waive the deductible if the owners would repair the windshield rather than replace it.

- USAA spent extensively to develop an image-processing system that digitizes all paper documents sent in by claimants (over 25 million a year). It takes only a few keystrokes for a policy service representative to retrieve pictures of all the documents in a customer's file. The system can sort and prioritize documents so that employees are always working on the most important and urgent tasks.

- USAA offers its customers remote deposit capture using scanning technology. It was the first U.S. bank to implement a remote deposit capture application for the iPhone. The iPhone application allows customers to take pictures of the front and back of each check and submit them electronically for deposit.

- USAA is a world leader in mobile banking. Customers can use their cell phones and other mobile devices to access and execute banking, investment, stock trading, and insurance applications such as filing claims. Customers can also use USAA's two-way text messaging system to send messages and receive text alerts and real-time information. They can also access person-to-person payment applications as well as social networking and personal financial management tools connected to bank accounts. Over 70% of USAA's logins are from cell phone users.

Required

a. Why should USAA collect data on which auto parts are fixed most frequently? What could it do with this data?

b. Even though USAA offered to waive the deductible, the repair shops still managed to convince 95% of the owners to replace rather than repair their damaged windshields. How could USAA use its AIS to persuade more shop owners to repair rather than replace their windows?

c. How does the image-processing system at USAA add value to the organization?

d. How do the remote deposit capture and mobile banking system at USAA add value to the organization?

e. Do an Internet search and find out what other advancements USAA has introduced. Write a brief paragraph on each new application or other newsworthy item you find (maximum limit of three applications or items).

1.4. Matching

Match the description listed in the right column with the information characteristic listed in the left column.

____ **1.** Relevant	a. The report was carefully designed so that the data contained in the report became information to the reader.
____ **2.** Reliable	b. The manager was working one weekend and needed to find some information about production requests for a certain customer. He was able to find the report on the company's network.
____ **3.** Complete	c. The data in a report was checked by two clerks working independently.
____ **4.** Timely	d. An accounts receivable aging report included all customer accounts.
____ **5.** Understandable	e. A report was checked by three different people for accuracy.
____ **6.** Verifiable	f. An accounts receivable aging report is used in credit-granting decisions.
____ **7.** Accessible	g. An accounts receivable aging report was received before the credit manager had to make a decision whether to extend credit to a customer.

1.5. The Howard Leasing Company is a privately held, medium-sized business that purchases school busses and leases them to school districts, churches, charitable organizations, and other businesses. To better serve its customers and, more important, to protect its investment in the busses, Howard operates a large maintenance facility to maintain and repair leased vehicles. Howard's annual sales for last year were $37 million, with a net income of $2.9 million. Howard employs approximately 150 people.

You were recently hired by Howard, and you are eager to prove your worth to the company. Your supervisor just called you into her office and asked you to prepare an accounts receivable aging report as of the end of the year for use in the upcoming audit of the company's financial statements.

Required

a. What is an accounts receivable aging report?

b. Why is an accounts receivable aging report needed for an audit?

c. What is an accounts receivable aging report used for in normal company operations?

d. What data will you need to prepare the report?

e. Where will you collect the data you need to prepare the report?

f. How will you collect the necessary data for the report?

g. What will the report look like (i.e., how will you organize the data collected to create the information your supervisor needs for the audit)? Prepare an accounts receivable aging report in Excel or another spreadsheet package.

h. How will you distribute the report? How many copies will you make? Who should receive the copies? What security features will you implement?

1.6. Based on Walmart's success in the United States, many expected the company to quickly dominate the British market after it bought the Asda grocery chain in 1999. That has not happened; Walmart's market share in groceries is a little more than half that of its biggest competitor, Tesco. Initially, Tesco's sales and net income rose significantly while Walmart's sales and net income increased at a much slower rate. More recently, Walmart has made small gains in market share, and Tesco has had small decreases.

Walmart found out that Tesco is a formidable worldwide competitor. Tesco operates almost 2,400 stores in Britain in four different formats. It has a very successful operation in Central Europe, and it has expanded to the United States with Fresh & Easy stores. In Korea, Tesco's 174 stores are thriving while Walmart gave up after an eight-year effort to succeed and sold its 16 stores.

One of the biggest reasons for Tesco's success is its use of technology. In 1995, Tesco started a loyalty card program, called Clubcard, and over 80% of its shoppers are members. Shoppers fill out an application in the store and receive a plastic card and a key fob in the mail that is scanned before they make a purchase. Tesco gathers massive amounts of data about its customers' 15 million purchases each week. Sales data are analyzed and turned into information that provides Tesco with a significant competitive advantage.

As traditional advertising loses effectiveness, these large stores of data allow Tesco to find new and creative ways to market its products.

Required

a. What kind of information do you think Tesco gathers?

b. How do you think Tesco has motivated over 22 million customers to sign up for its Clubcard program?

c. What can Tesco accomplish with the Clubcard data it collects? Think in terms of strategy and competitive advantage.

d. What are some of the disadvantages to the Clubcard program?

e. Do an Internet search to find out how Tesco is doing in comparison to Walmart and other grocers and retailers. Write a few paragraphs explaining your findings.

1.7. Have you ever imagined having one electronic device that does everything you would ever need? Mobile phone makers in Japan have gone beyond the imagining phase. Cell phones in Japan are becoming more versatile than ever. Newer models of cell phones contain a myriad of applications and can do many of the things that a personal computer (PC) can do. PCs are also able to function as phones. A small but growing number of professionals are trading in their laptops for handheld computers. Cell phone manufacturers in the United States and elsewhere are quickly catching up to their Japanese counterparts.

Required

a. What commercial activities can be done with a cell phone? With a cell phone/PC combination device? What do you do when you're on your cell phone? What do you expect to be doing in five years?

b. How can businesses utilize this technology to attract more customers, sell more products, advertise their products, facilitate the sale of products, and conduct and manage their businesses more efficiently and effectively?

c. What are some problems or drawbacks you can see with using these devices in business?

1.8. Classify each of the following items as belonging in the revenue, expenditure, human resources/payroll, production, or financing cycle.

a. Purchase raw materials

b. Pay off mortgage on a factory

   c. Hire a new assistant controller
   d. Establish a $10,000 credit limit for a new customer
   e. Pay for raw materials
   f. Disburse payroll checks to factory workers
   g. Record goods received from a vendor
   h. Update the allowance for doubtful accounts
   i. Decide how many units to make next month
   j. Complete a picking ticket for a customer order
   k. Record factory employee timecards
   l. Sell concert tickets
   m. Draw on line of credit
   n. Send new employees to a business ethics course
   o. Pay utility bills
   p. Pay property taxes on an office building
   q. Pay federal payroll taxes
   r. Sell a DVD player
   s. Collect payments on customer accounts
   t. Obtain a bank loan
   u. Pay sales commissions
   v. Send an order to a vendor
   w. Put purchased goods into the warehouse

Case 1-1 Ackoff's Management Misinformation Systems

The Web site for this book contains an adaption of Russell L. Ackoff's classic article "Management Misinformation Systems" from *Management Science*. In the article, Ackoff identified five common assumptions about information systems and then explained why he disagreed with them.

Required

Read the five assumptions, contentions, and Ackoff's explanations. For each of the five assumptions, decide whether you agree or disagree with Ackoff's contentions. Prepare a report in which you defend your stand and explain your defense.

AIS IN ACTION SOLUTIONS

Quiz Key

1. Data differ from information in which way?
   a. Data are output, and information is input. [Incorrect. Data are facts and figures that, once organized, can become information. Therefore, data are inputs, and information is output.]
  ▶ b. Information is output, and data are input. [Correct.]
   c. Data are meaningful bits of information. [Incorrect. Information is organized and processed data that provide meaning.]
   d. There is no difference. [Incorrect. There is a difference. Data are unorganized facts and figures. Information is meaningful, organized, and processed data.]

2. Which of the following is NOT a characteristic that makes information useful?
   a. It is reliable. [Incorrect. This is one of the information characteristics listed in Table 1-1 on page 5.]
   b. It is timely. [Incorrect. This is one of the information characteristics listed in Table 1-1 on page 5.]

▶ c. It is inexpensive. [Correct. This is NOT one of the information characteristics listed in Table 1-1 on page 5.]

   d. It is relevant. [Incorrect. This is one of the information characteristics listed in Table 1-1 on page 5.]

3. Which of the following is a primary activity in the value chain?

   a. purchasing [Incorrect. This is a support activity.]

   b. accounting [Incorrect. This is a firm infrastructure support activity.]

▶ c. post-sales service [Correct. Service is a primary activity.]

   d. human resource management [Incorrect. This is a support activity.]

4. Which transaction cycle includes interactions between an organization and its suppliers?

   a. revenue cycle [Incorrect. The revenue cycle involves interactions between an organization and its customers.]

▶ b. expenditure [Correct.]

   c. human resources/payroll cycle [Incorrect. The human resources/payroll cycle involves interactions between an organization and its employees, government, and potential hires.]

   d. general ledger and reporting system [Incorrect. The general ledger and reporting system receives summary information from all cycles.]

5. Which of the following is NOT a means by which information improves decision making?

▶ a. increases information overload [Correct. Decision makers receiving too much information have difficulty incorporating all of the information into their decision framework, and, as a result, decision quality can be reduced rather than improved.]

   b. reduces uncertainty [Incorrect. More reliable information leads to less uncertainty and thus better decisions.]

   c. provides feedback about the effectiveness of prior decisions [Incorrect. Knowledge of effective and ineffective decisions can lead to better decisions in the future.]

   d. identifies situations requiring management action [Incorrect. Identifying the need for management action can lead to improved decision making.]

6. In the value chain concept, upgrading IT is considered what kind of activity?

   a. primary activity [Incorrect. Investing in IT is a support activity.]

   b. support activity [Correct. Technology activities, including investing in IT, are considered a support activity.]

   c. service activity [Incorrect. The value chain includes only primary and support activities. A service activity is a type of primary activity.]

   d. structured activity [Incorrect. The value chain includes only primary and support activities. A structured activity is neither a primary nor a secondary activity.]

7. In which cycle does a company ship goods to customers?

   a. production cycle [Incorrect. The production cycle involves the transformation of raw materials into finished goods.]

   b. financing cycle [Incorrect. The financing cycle deals with interactions between an organization and its lenders and owners.]

▶ c. revenue cycle [Correct. The revenue cycle involves interactions between an organization and its customers, such as shipping them goods.]

   d. expenditure cycle [Incorrect. The expenditure cycle involves interactions between an organization and its suppliers.]

8. Which of the following is a function of an AIS?

   a. reducing the need to identify a strategy and strategic position [Incorrect. An AIS does not reduce the need to identify a strategy. It provides information to executives for the purpose of making strategic decisions.]

▶ b. transforming data into useful information [Correct. This is one of the primary functions of an AIS.]

    c. allocating organizational resources [Incorrect. Decision makers allocate resources, and the purpose of the AIS is to provide information to the decision makers so that they can make the allocation.]

    d. automating all decision making [Incorrect. The AIS provides information to decision makers; it is not designed to automate all decision making.]

9. A firm, its suppliers, and its customers collectively form which of the following?

  ▶ a. supply chain [Correct. The supply chain is made up of the firm, its suppliers, and customers.]

    b. value chain [Incorrect. The value chain is made up of primary and support activities within the firm.]

    c. ERP system [Incorrect. An ERP system integrates all aspects of an organization's activities into one system.]

    d. AIS [Incorrect. The AIS is made up of the human and capital resources within an organization that are responsible for collecting and processing transactions and preparing financial information.]

10. A report telling how well all approved vendors have performed in the prior 12 months is information that is MOST needed in which business process?

    a. paying vendors [Incorrect. To pay a vendor, a company needs to know whether merchandise ordered was received in good condition. They do not need a 12-month history of vendor performance.]

  ▶ b. acquiring inventory [Correct. Companies want to acquire inventory from companies that have performed well in the past. A vendor performance report would disclose whether the vendor shipped inventory on time, whether the inventory was of the requested quality, whether the prices were as agreed upon, etc.]

    c. selling merchandise [Incorrect. A 12-month history of vendor performance is usually not very helpful in trying to sell products to customers. More important would be customer tastes and preferences, customer credit status, etc.]

    d. paying employees [Incorrect. It is very rare for an employee's pay to be based on a 12-month history of vendor performance. More important are hours worked, annual salary, sales figures to calculate commissions, etc.]

Chapter 2

Overview of Transaction Processing and Enterprise Resource Planning Systems

Learning Objectives

After studying this chapter, you should be able to:

1. Describe the four parts of the data processing cycle and the major activities in each.

2. Describe documents and procedures used to collect and process transaction data.

3. Describe the ways information is stored in computer-based information systems.

4. Discuss the types of information that an AIS can provide.

5. Discuss how organizations use enterprise resource planning (ERP) systems to process transactions and provide information.

INTEGRATIVE CASE S&S

The grand opening of S&S is two weeks away. Scott Parry and Susan Gonzalez are working long hours to make the final arrangements for the store opening. Most of the employees have already been hired; training is scheduled for next week.

Susan has ordered inventory for the first month. The store is being remodeled and will have a bright, cheery decor. All seems to be in order—all, that is, except the accounting records.

Like many entrepreneurs, Scott and Susan have not given as much thought to their accounting records as they have to other parts of their business. Recognizing they need qualified accounting help, they hired a full-time accountant, Ashton Fleming. Scott and Susan think Ashton is perfect for the job because of his three

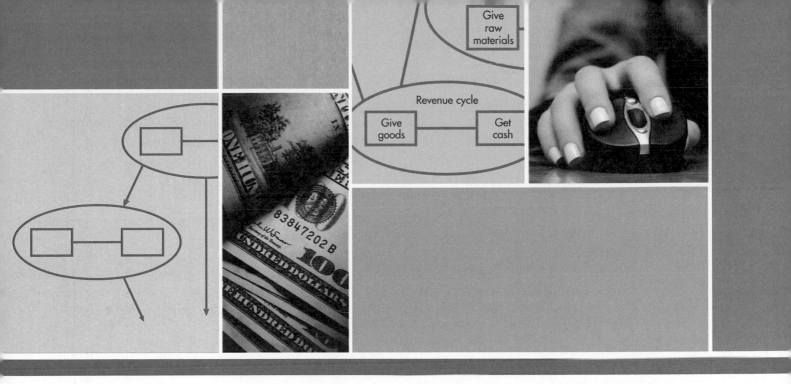

years of experience with a national CPA firm. Ashton is looking forward to working for S&S because he has always wanted to be involved in building a company from the ground up.

During Ashton's first day on the job, Susan gives him the invoices for the inventory she purchased and a folder with their bank loan documentation, with the first payment due after the grand opening. She also hands him a folder containing information on rental payments, utilities, and other expenses. Susan tells Ashton that she and Scott know little about accounting and he will run the accounting end of S&S. She adds that the only thing they have done so far is to open a checking account for S&S and that they have kept the check register updated to monitor their cash flow.

Scott explains that the sales staff is paid a fixed salary and commissions and that all other employees are paid hourly rates. Employees are paid every two weeks, with their first paychecks due next week. Ashton asks Scott what accounting software the company is using. Scott replies that he and Susan have not had time to tackle that aspect yet. Scott and Susan looked at some of the popular packages but quickly realized that they did not know enough about accounting to make an intelligent choice. Scott then tells Ashton that his first task should be to purchase whatever accounting software he thinks will be best for S&S.

After Scott leaves, Ashton feels both excited and a little nervous about his responsibility for creating an AIS for S&S. Although Ashton has audited many companies, he has never organized a company's books and is unsure how to go about it. A million questions run through his head. Here are just a few of them:

1. How should I organize the accounting records so that financial statements can be easily produced?
2. How am I going to collect and process data about all of S&S's transactions?
3. How do I organize all the data that will be collected?

4. How should I design the AIS so that the information provided is reliable and accurate?

5. How can I design procedures to ensure that they meet all government obligations, such as remitting sales, income, and payroll taxes?

Introduction

This chapter is divided into two major sections. The first section discusses the data processing cycle and its role in organizing business activities and providing information to users. It explains how organizations capture and enter data about business activities into their AIS and how companies process data and transform it into useful information. It also discusses basic data storage concepts, showing how data are stored for further use. Finally, information output is discussed, including the different ways information is provided to users.

The second section discusses the role of the information system in modern organizations and introduces the concept of an enterprise resource planning (ERP) system. An ERP can help integrate all aspects of a company's operations with its traditional AIS. This section also describes the significant advantages of an ERP as well as significant challenges that must be overcome to implement an ERP system.

Transaction Processing: The Data Processing Cycle

Accountants and other system users play a significant role in the data processing cycle. For example, they interact with systems analysts to help answer questions such as these: What data should be entered and stored by the organization, and who should have access to them? How should data be organized, updated, stored, accessed, and retrieved? How can scheduled and unanticipated information needs be met? To answer these and related questions, the data processing concepts explained in this chapter must be understood.

One important AIS function is to process company transactions efficiently and effectively. In manual (non-computer-based) systems, data are entered into journals and ledgers maintained on paper. In computer-based systems, data are entered into computers and stored in files and databases. The operations performed on data to generate meaningful and relevant information are referred to collectively as the *data processing cycle*. As shown in Figure 2-1, this process consists of four steps: data input, data storage, data processing, and information output.

Data Input

The first step in processing input is to capture transaction data and enter them into the system. The data capture process is usually triggered by a business activity. Data must be collected about three facets of each business activity:

1. Each activity of interest
2. The resource(s) affected by each activity
3. The people who participate in each activity

FIGURE 2-1
The Data Processing Cycle

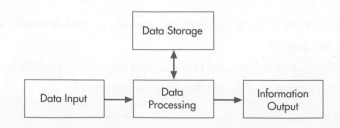

For example, the most frequent revenue cycle transaction is a sale, either for cash or on credit. S&S may find it useful to collect the following data about a sales transaction:

- Date and time the sale occurred
- Employee who made the sale and the checkout clerk who processed the sale
- Checkout register where the sale was processed
- Item(s) sold
- Quantity of each item sold
- List price and actual price of each item sold
- Total amount of the sale
- Delivery instructions
- For credit sales: customer name, customer bill-to and ship-to addresses

Historically, most businesses used paper *source documents* to collect data about their business activities. They later transferred that data into the computer. When the data is entered using computer screens, they often retain the same name and basic format as the paper source document it replaced. Table 2-1 lists some common transaction cycle activities and the source document or form used to capture data about that event. Examples of many of these documents can be found in Chapters 12 through 16. For example, a purchase order, used to request merchandise from suppliers, is shown in Chapter 13.

Turnaround documents are company output sent to an external party, who often adds data to the document, and then are returned to the company as an input document. They are in machine-readable form to facilitate their subsequent processing as input records. An example is a utility bill that is sent to the customer, returned with the customer's payment, and read by a special scanning device when it is returned.

Source data automation devices capture transaction data in machine-readable form at the time and place of their origin. Examples include ATMs used by banks, point-of-sale (POS) scanners used in retail stores, and bar code scanners used in warehouses.

The second step in processing input is to make sure captured data are accurate and complete. One way to do this is to use source data automation or well-designed turnaround documents and data entry screens. Well-designed documents and screens improve accuracy and completeness by providing instructions or prompts about what data to collect, grouping logically related pieces of information close together, using checkoff boxes or pull-down menus to present the available options, and using appropriate shading and borders to clearly separate data items. Data input screens usually list all the data the user needs to enter. Sometimes these screens resemble source documents, and users fill out the screen the same way they would a paper source document.

Users can improve control either by purchasing prenumbered source documents or by having the system automatically assign a sequential number to each new transaction. Prenumbering

TABLE 2-1 Common Business Activities and Source Documents

Business Activity	Source Document
Revenue Cycle	
Take customer order	Sales order
Deliver or ship order	Delivery ticket or bill of lading
Receive cash	Remittance advice or remittance list
Deposit cash receipts	Deposit slip
Adjust customer account	Credit memo
Expenditure Cycle	
Request items	Purchase requisition
Order items	Purchase order
Receive items	Receiving report
Pay for items	Check or electronic funds transfer
Human Resources Cycle	
Collect employee withholding data	W-4 form
Record time worked by employees	Time cards
Record time spent on specific jobs	Job time tickets or time sheet

simplifies verifying that all transactions have been recorded and that none of the documents has been misplaced. (Imagine trying to balance a checkbook if the checks were not prenumbered.)

The third step in processing input is to make sure company policies are followed, such as approving or verifying a transaction. For example, S&S would not want to sell goods to a customer who was not paying his bills or to sell an item for immediate delivery that was out of stock. These problems are prevented by programming the system to check a customer's credit limit and payment history, as well as inventory status, before confirming a customer sale.

Data Storage

A company's data are one of its most important resources. However, the mere existence of relevant data does not guarantee that they are useful. To function properly, an organization must have ready and easy access to its data. Therefore, accountants need to understand how data are organized and stored in an AIS and how they can be accessed. In essence, they need to know how to manage data for maximum corporate use.

Imagine how difficult it would be to read a textbook if it were not organized into chapters, sections, paragraphs, and sentences. Now imagine how hard it would be for S&S to find an invoice if all documents were randomly dumped into file cabinets. Fortunately, information in an AIS is organized for easy and efficient access. This section explains basic data storage concepts and definitions.

LEDGERS   Cumulative accounting information is stored in general and subsidiary ledgers. A *general ledger* contains summary-level data for every asset, liability, equity, revenue, and expense account. A *subsidiary ledger* contains detailed data for any general ledger account with many individual subaccounts. For example, the general ledger has an accounts receivable account that summarizes the total amount owed to the company by all customers. The subsidiary accounts receivable ledger has a separate record for each individual customer, with detailed information such as name, address, purchases, payments, account balance, and credit limit. Subsidiary ledgers are often used for accounts receivable, inventory, fixed assets, and accounts payable.

The general ledger account corresponding to a subsidiary ledger is called a *control account*. The relationship between the general ledger control account and the total of individual subsidiary ledger account balances helps maintain the accuracy of AIS data. Specifically, the sum of all subsidiary ledger account balances should equal the amount in the corresponding general ledger control account. Any discrepancy between them indicates that a recording error has occurred.

CODING TECHNIQUES   Data in ledgers is organized logically using coding techniques. *Coding* is the systematic assignment of numbers or letters to items to classify and organize them.

- With *sequence codes*, items are numbered consecutively to account for all items. Any missing items cause a gap in the numerical sequence. Examples include prenumbered checks, invoices, and purchase orders.
- With a *block code*, blocks of numbers are reserved for specific categories of data. For example, S&S reserved the following numbers for major product categories:

Product Code	Product Type
1000000–1999999	Electric range
2000000–2999999	Refrigerator
3000000–3999999	Washer
4000000–4999999	Dryer

  Users can identify an item's type and model using the code numbers. Other examples include ledger account numbers (blocked by account type), employee numbers (blocked by department), and customer numbers (blocked by region).
- *Group codes*, which are two or more subgroups of digits used to code items, are often used in conjunction with block codes. If S&S uses a seven-digit product code number, the group coding technique might be applied as follows.

Digit Position	Meaning
1–2	Product line, size, style
3	Color
4–5	Year of manufacture
6–7	Optional features

There are four subcodes in the product code, each with a different meaning. Users can sort, summarize, and retrieve information using one or more subcodes. This technique is often applied to general ledger account numbers.

- With *mnemonic codes*, letters and numbers are interspersed to identify an item. The mnemonic code is derived from the description of the item and is usually easy to memorize. For example, Dry300W05 could represent a low end (300), white (W) dryer (Dry) made by Whirlpool (05).

The following guidelines result in a better coding system. The code should:

- Be consistent with its intended use, which requires that the code designer determine desired system outputs prior to selecting the code.
- Allow for growth. For example, don't use a three-digit employee code for a fast-growing company with 950 employees.
- Be as simple as possible to minimize costs, facilitate memorization and interpretation, and ensure employee acceptance.
- Be consistent with the company's organizational structure and across the company's divisions.

CHART OF ACCOUNTS   A great example of coding is the *chart of accounts*, which is a list of the numbers assigned to each general ledger account. These account numbers allow transaction data to be coded, classified, and entered into the proper accounts. They also facilitate the preparation of financial statements and reports, because data stored in individual accounts can easily be summed for presentation.

However, data stored in summary accounts cannot be easily analyzed and reported in more detail. Consequently, it is important that the chart of accounts contain sufficient detail to meet an organization's information needs. To illustrate, consider the consequences if S&S were to use only one general ledger account for all sales transactions. It would be easy to produce reports showing the total amount of sales for a given time period, but it would be very difficult to prepare reports separating cash and credit sales. Indeed, the only way to produce these latter reports would be to go back to original sales records to identify the nature of each sales transaction. If S&S used separate general ledger accounts for cash and credit sales, then reports showing both types of sales could be easily produced. Total sales could also be easily reported by summing each type of sale.

Table 2-2 shows the chart of accounts Ashton developed for S&S. Each account number is three digits long. The first digit represents the major account category and indicates where it appears on S&S's financial statements. Thus, all current assets are numbered in the 100s, non-current assets are numbered in the 200s, and so on.

The second digit represents the primary financial subaccounts within each category. Again, the accounts are assigned numbers to match the order of their appearance in financial statements (in order of decreasing liquidity). Thus, account 120 represents accounts receivable, and account 150 represents inventory.

The third digit identifies the specific account to which the transaction data will be posted. For example, account 501 represents cash sales, and account 502 represents credit sales. Similarly, accounts 101 through 103 represent the various cash accounts used by S&S.

A chart of accounts is tailored to the nature and purpose of an organization. For example, the chart of accounts for S&S indicates that the company is a corporation. In contrast, a partnership would include separate capital and drawing accounts for each partner, instead of common stock and retained earnings. Likewise, because S&S is a retail organization, it has only one type of general ledger inventory account. A manufacturing company, in contrast,

TABLE 2-2 Sample Chart of Accounts for S&S

Account Code	Account Name	Account Code	Account Name
100–199	Current Assets	400–499	Equity Accounts
101	Checking Account	400	Common Stock
102	Savings Account	410	Retained Earnings
103	Petty Cash		
120	Accounts Receivable	500–599	Revenues
125	Allowance for Doubtful Accounts	501	Cash Sales
130	Notes Receivable	502	Credit Sales
150	Inventory	510	Sales Returns & Allowances
160	Supplies	511	Sales Discounts
170	Prepaid Rent	520	Interest Revenue
180	Prepaid Insurance	530	Miscellaneous Revenue
200–299	Noncurrent Assets	600–799	Expenses
200	Land	600	Cost of Goods Sold
210	Buildings	611	Wages Expense
215	Accumulated Depreciation—Buildings	612	Commissions Expense
230	Equipment	613	Payroll Tax Expense
235	Accumulated Depreciation—Equipment	620	Rent Expense
240	Furniture & Fixtures	630	Insurance Expense
245	Accumulated Depreciation—Furniture & Fixtures	640	Supplies Expense
250	Other Assets	650	Bad Debt Expense
		701	Depreciation Expense—Buildings
300–399	Liabilities	702	Depreciation Expense—Equipment
300	Accounts Payable	703	Depreciation Expense—Furniture & Fixtures
310	Wages Payable	710	
321	Employee Income Tax Payable		Income Tax Expense
322	FICA Tax Payable	900–999	
323	Federal Unemployment Tax Payable	910	
324	State Unemployment Tax Payable		Summary Accounts
330	Accrued Interest Payable		Income Summary
360	Other Liabilities		

would have separate general ledger accounts for raw materials, work in process, and finished goods inventories.

Ashton left gaps in S&S's chart of accounts to allow for additional accounts. For example, when S&S has excess cash to invest in marketable securities, a new general ledger account can be created and assigned the number 110. When S&S opens stores in the future, he will add three digits to the chart of accounts to represent each store in the chain, so that S&S can track items in each store.

Subsidiary ledger accounts often have longer account codes than general ledger accounts. At S&S, each account receivable will have a seven-digit code. The first three digits are 120, the code for accounts receivable. The next four digits identify up to 10,000 individual customers.

JOURNALS Transaction data are often recorded in a journal before they are entered into a ledger. A journal entry shows the accounts and amounts to be debited and credited. A *general journal* is used to record infrequent or nonroutine transactions, such as loan payments and end-of-period adjusting and closing entries. A *specialized journal* records large numbers of repetitive transactions such as sales, cash receipts, and cash disbursements.

Table 2-3 is a sample sales journal. All transaction information is recorded in one line, with every entry a debit to accounts receivable and a credit to sales. There is no need to write an explanation of each entry, as is the case with general journal entries. Given the high number of daily sales transactions, the time saved by recording these transactions in a sales journal, rather than in the general journal, is considerable.

The Post Ref column indicates when transactions are posted to the appropriate ledger. In a manual system, ledgers are books; hence, the phrase "keeping the books" refers to the process of maintaining the ledgers.

Figure 2-2 shows how to journalize and post sales transactions. First, each credit sale is recorded in the sales journal. Then each sales journal entry is posted to the appropriate customer account in the accounts receivable subsidiary ledger (note the arrow linking the $1,876.50 sale to KDR Builders in the sales journal to the debit for $1,876.50 in the accounts receivable subsidiary ledger). Periodically, the total of all sales journal entries is posted to the general ledger (note the arrow showing the daily sales journal total of $15,511.00 posted to both the Accounts Receivable and the Credit Sales general ledger accounts).

AUDIT TRAIL Figure 2-2 shows how the posting references and document numbers provide an audit trail. An *audit trail* is a traceable path of a transaction through a data processing system from point of origin to final output, or backwards from from final output to point of origin. It is used to check the accuracy and validity of ledger postings. Observe that the SJ5 posting reference for the $15,511 credit to the sales account in the general ledger refers to page 5 of the sales journal. By checking page 5 of the sales journal, it is possible to verify that $15,511 represents the total credit sales recorded on October 15. Similarly, the posting reference for the $1876.50 debit to the KDR Builders' account in the subsidiary accounts receivable ledger also refers to page 5 of the sales journal as the source of that entry. Furthermore, note that the sales journal lists the invoice numbers for each individual entry. This provides the means for locating and examining the appropriate source documents in order to verify that the transaction occurred and it was recorded accurately.

COMPUTER-BASED STORAGE CONCEPTS An *entity* is something about which information is stored, such as employees, inventory items, and customers. Each entity has *attributes*, or characteristics of interest, that are stored, such as a pay rate and address. Each type of entity possesses the same set of attributes. For example, all employees possess an employee number, pay rate, and home address. The specific values for those attributes will differ. For example, one employee's pay rate might be $12.00 an hour, whereas another's might be $12.25.

TABLE 2-3 Sample Sales Journal

		Sales Journal			Page 5
Date	Invoice Number	Account Debited	Account Number	Post Ref.	Amount
Oct. 15	151	Brown Hospital Supply	120-035	✓	798.00
15	152	Greenshadows Hotel Suites	120-122	✓	1,267.00
15	153	Heathrow Apartments	120-057	✓	5,967.00
15	154	LMS Construction	120-173	✓	2,312.50
15	155	Gardenview Apartments	120-084	✓	3,290.00
15	156	KDR Builders	120-135	✓	1,876.50
		TOTAL	120/502		15,511.00

FIGURE 2-2

Recording and Posting a Credit Sale

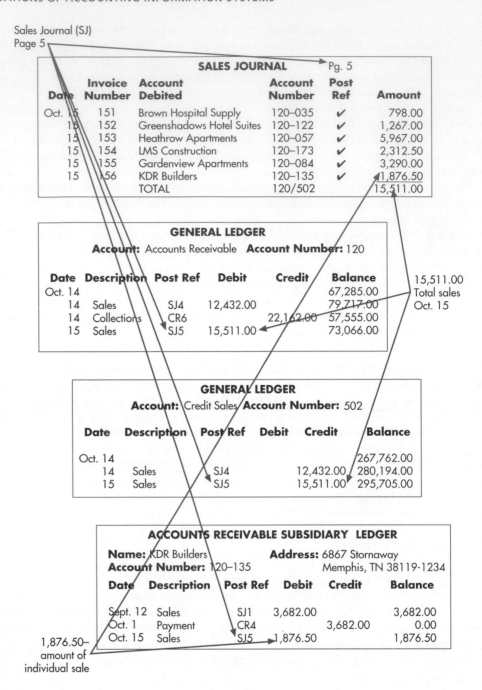

Figure 2-3 shows that computers store data in a *field*. The fields containing data about entity attributes constitute a *record*. In Figure 2-3, each row represents a different record, and each column represents an attribute. Each intersecting row and column in Figure 2-3 is a field within a record, the contents of which are called a *data value*.

A *file* is a group of related records. A *master file,* like a ledger in a manual AIS, stores cumulative information about an organization. The inventory and equipment master files store information about important organizational resources. The customer, supplier, and employee master files store information about important agents with whom the organization interacts.

Master files are permanent; they exist across fiscal periods. However, individual master file records may change frequently. For example, individual customer accounts balances are updated to reflect new sales transactions and payments received. Periodically, new records are added to or removed from a master file, for example, when a new customer is added or a former customer deleted.

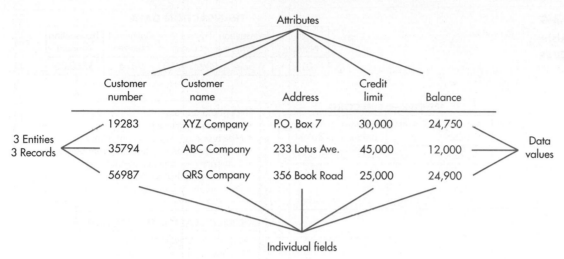

FIGURE 2-3

Data Storage Elements

This accounts receivable file stores information about three separate entities: XYZ Company, ABC Company, and QRS Company. As a result, there are three records in the file. Five separate attributes are used to describe each customer: customer number, customer name, address, credit limit, and balance. There are, therefore, five separate fields in each record. Each field contains a data value that describes an attribute of a particular entity (customer). For example, the data value 19283 is the customer number for the XYZ Company.

A *transaction file* contains records of individual business transactions that occur during a specific time. It is similar to a journal in a manual AIS. For example, S&S will have a daily sales transaction file and a cash receipts file. Both files will update individual customer account balances in the customer master file. Transaction files are not permanent and may not be needed beyond the current fiscal period. However, they are usually maintained for a specified period for backup purposes.

A set of interrelated, centrally coordinated files is referred to as a *database*. For example, the accounts receivable file might be combined with customer, sales analysis, and related files to form a customer database. Chapter 4 discusses database technology.

Data Processing

Once business activity data have been entered into the system, they must be processed to keep the databases current. The four different types of data processing activities, referred to as CRUD, are as follows:

1. *Creating* new data records, such as adding a newly hired employee to the payroll database.
2. *Reading,* retrieving, or viewing existing data.
3. *Updating* previously stored data. Figure 2-4 depicts the steps required to update an accounts receivable record with a sales transaction. The two records are matched using the account number. The sale amount ($360) is added to the account balance ($1,500) to get a new current balance ($1,860).
4. *Deleting* data, such as purging the vendor master file of all vendors the company no longer does business with.

Updating done periodically, such as daily, is referred to as *batch processing*. Although batch processing is cheaper and more efficient, the data are current and accurate only immediately after processing. For that reason, batch processing is used only for applications, such as payroll, that do not need frequent updating and that naturally occur or are processed at fixed time periods.

Most companies update each transaction as it occurs, referred to as *online, real-time processing* because it ensures that stored information is always current, thereby increasing its decision-making usefulness. It is also more accurate because data input errors can be corrected in real time or refused. It also provides significant competitive advantages. For example, FedEx updated its mission statement to include the phrase "Positive control of each package will be maintained by

FIGURE 2-4

The Accounts Receivable File Update Process

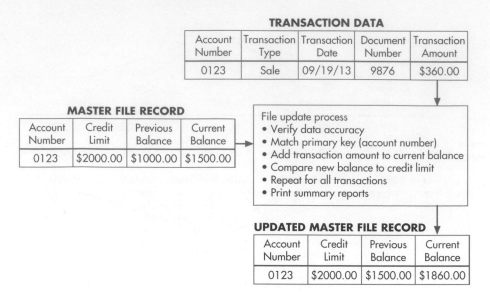

TRANSACTION DATA

Account Number	Transaction Type	Transaction Date	Document Number	Transaction Amount
0123	Sale	09/19/13	9876	$360.00

MASTER FILE RECORD

Account Number	Credit Limit	Previous Balance	Current Balance
0123	$2000.00	$1000.00	$1500.00

File update process
• Verify data accuracy
• Match primary key (account number)
• Add transaction amount to current balance
• Compare new balance to credit limit
• Repeat for all transactions
• Print summary reports

UPDATED MASTER FILE RECORD

Account Number	Credit Limit	Previous Balance	Current Balance
0123	$2000.00	$1500.00	$1860.00

utilizing real-time electronic tracking and tracing systems." With FedEx's system, employees and customers can track the exact location of each package and estimate its arrival time.

A combination of the two approaches is online batch processing, where transaction data are entered and edited as they occur and stored for later processing. Batch processing and online, real-time processing are summarized in Figure 2-5.

Information Output

The final step in the data processing cycle is information output. When displayed on a monitor, output is referred to as "soft copy." When printed on paper, it is referred to as "hard copy." Information is usually presented in one of three forms: a document, a report, or a query response.

Documents are records of transaction or other company data. Some, such as checks and invoices, are transmitted to external parties. Others, such as receiving reports and purchase requisitions, are used internally. Documents can be printed out, or they can be stored as electronic images in a computer. For example, Toys 'R' Us uses electronic data interchange to communicate with its suppliers. Every year it processes over half a million invoices electronically, thereby eliminating paper documents and dramatically reducing costs and errors. This has resulted in higher profits and more accurate information.

Reports are used by employees to control operational activities and by managers to make decisions and to formulate business strategies. External users need reports to evaluate company profitability, judge creditworthiness, or comply with regulatory requirements. Some reports, such as financial statements and sales analyses, are produced on a regular basis. Others are produced on an exception basis to call attention to unusual conditions. For example, S&S could have its system produce a report to indicate when product returns exceed a certain percentage of sales. Reports can also be produced on demand. For example, Susan could produce a report to identify the salesperson who sold the most items during a specific promotional period.

The need for reports should be periodically assessed, because they are often prepared long after they are needed, wasting time, money, and resources. For example, NCR Corporation reduced the number of reports from 1,200 to just over 100. Another company eliminated 6 million pages of reports, a stack four times higher than its 41-story headquarters building. One 25-page report took five days to prepare and sat unread.

A database *query* is used to provide the information needed to deal with problems and questions that need rapid action or answers. A user enters a request for a specific piece of information; it is retrieved, displayed, or analyzed as requested. Repetitive queries are often developed by information systems specialists. One-time queries are often developed by users. Some companies, such as Wal-Mart, allow suppliers to access their databases to help them better serve Wal-Mart's needs. Suppliers can gauge how well a product is selling in every Wal-Mart store in the world and maximize sales by stocking and promoting items that are selling well.

Additional information about system output is contained in Chapters 12 to 16.

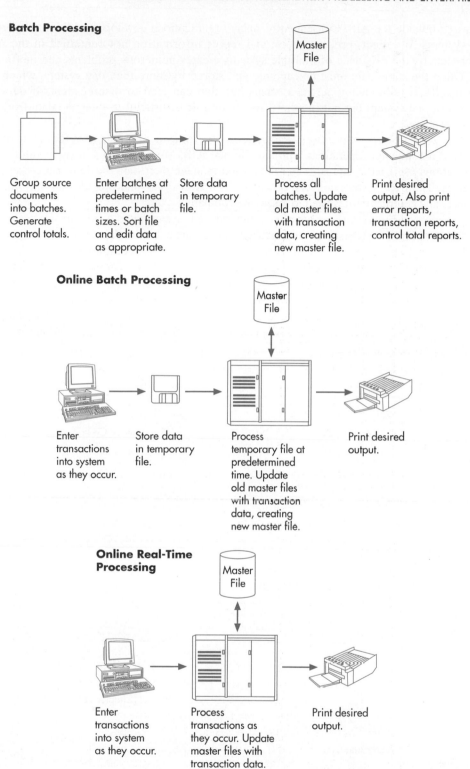

FIGURE 2-5

Batch and Online Processing

Batch Processing

Group source documents into batches. Generate control totals.

Enter batches at predetermined times or batch sizes. Sort file and edit data as appropriate.

Store data in temporary file.

Process all batches. Update old master files with transaction data, creating new master file.

Print desired output. Also print error reports, transaction reports, control total reports.

Master File

Online Batch Processing

Enter transactions into system as they occur.

Store data in temporary file.

Process temporary file at predetermined time. Update old master files with transaction data, creating new master file.

Print desired output.

Master File

Online Real-Time Processing

Enter transactions into system as they occur.

Process transactions as they occur. Update master files with transaction data.

Print desired output.

Master File

Enterprise Resource Planning (ERP) Systems

Traditionally, the AIS has been referred to as a transaction processing system because its only concern was financial data and accounting transactions. For example, when a sale took place, the AIS would record a journal entry showing only the date of the sale, a debit to either cash or accounts receivable, and a credit to sales. Other potentially useful nonfinancial information about the sale, such as the time of day that it occurred, would traditionally be collected and processed outside the AIS. Consequently, many organizations developed additional information systems to collect, process, store, and report information not contained in the AIS. Unfortunately, the existence of multiple systems creates numerous problems and inefficiencies. Often the same data must be captured and stored by more than one system, which not only results in redundancy across systems but also can lead to discrepancies if data are changed in one system but not in others. In addition, it is difficult to integrate data from the various systems.

Enterprise resource planning (ERP) systems overcome these problems as they integrate all aspects of a company's operations with a traditional AIS. Most large and many medium-sized organizations use ERP systems to coordinate and manage their data, business processes, and resources. The ERP system collects, processes, and stores data and provides the information managers and external parties need to assess the company.

As shown in Figure 2-6, a properly configured ERP system uses a centralized database to share information across business processes and coordinate activities. This is important because an activity that is part of one business process often triggers a complex series of activities throughout many different parts of the organization. For example, a customer order may necessitate scheduling additional production to meet the increased demand. This may trigger an order to purchase more raw materials. It may also be necessary to schedule overtime or hire temporary help. Well-designed ERP systems provide management with easy access to up-to-date information about all of these activities in order to plan, control, and evaluate the organization's business processes more effectively.

FIGURE 2-6
Integrated ERP System

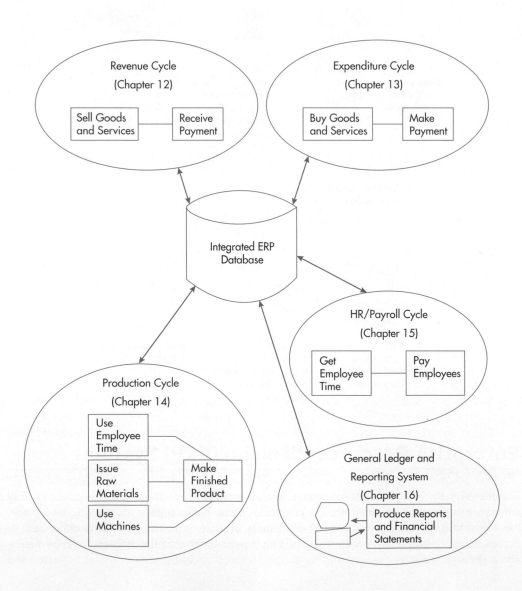

ERP systems are modular, with each module using best business practices to automate a standard business process. This modular design allows businesses to add or delete modules as needed. Typical ERP modules include:

- Financial (general ledger and reporting system)—general ledger, accounts receivable, accounts payable, fixed assets, budgeting, cash management, and preparation of managerial reports and financial statements
- Human resources and payroll—human resources, payroll, employee benefits, training, time and attendance, benefits, and government reporting
- Order to cash (revenue cycle)—sales order entry, shipping, inventory, cash receipts, commission calculation
- Purchase to pay (disbursement cycle)—purchasing, receipt and inspection of inventory, inventory and warehouse management, and cash disbursements
- Manufacturing (production cycle)— engineering, production scheduling, bill of materials, work-in-process, workflow management, quality control, cost management, and manufacturing processes and projects
- Project management—costing, billing, time and expense, performance units, activity management
- Customer relationship management—sales and marketing, commissions, service, customer contact, and call center support
- System tools—tools for establishing master file data, specifying flow of information, access controls, and so on

An ERP system, with its centralized database, provides significant advantages:

- An ERP provides an integrated, enterprise-wide, single view of the organization's data and financial situation. Storing all corporate information in a single database breaks down barriers between departments and streamlines the flow of information.
- Data input is captured or keyed once, rather than multiple times, as it is entered into different systems. Downloading data from one system to another is no longer needed.
- Management gains greater visibility into every area of the enterprise and greater monitoring capabilities. Employees are more productive and efficient because they can quickly gather data from both inside and outside their own department.
- The organization gains better access control. An ERP can consolidate multiple permissions and security models into a single data access structure.
- Procedures and reports are standardized across business units. This standardization can be especially valuable with mergers and acquisitions because an ERP system can replace the different systems with a single, unified system.
- Customer service improves because employees can quickly access orders, available inventory, shipping information, and past customer transaction details.
- Manufacturing plants receive new orders in real time, and the automation of manufacturing processes leads to increased productivity.

ERP systems also have significant disadvantages:

- Cost. ERP hardware, software, and consulting costs range from $50 to $500 million for a Fortune 500 company and upgrades can cost $50 million to $100 million. Midsized companies spend between $10 and $20 million.
- Amount of time required. It can take years to select and fully implement an ERP system, depending on business size, number of modules to be implemented, degree of customization, the scope of the change, and how well the customer takes ownership of the project. As a result, ERP implementations have a very high risk of project failure.
- Changes to business processes. Unless a company wants to spend time and money customizing modules, they must adapt to standardized business processes as opposed to adapting the ERP package to existing company processes. The failure to map current business processes to existing ERP software is a main cause of ERP project failures.
- Complexity. This comes from integrating many different business activities and systems, each having different processes, business rules, data semantics, authorization hierarchies, and decision centers.

- Resistance. Organizations that have multiple departments with separate resources, missions, profit and loss, and chains of command may believe that a single system has few benefits. It also takes considerable training and experience to use an ERP system effectively, and employee resistance is a major reason why many ERP implementations do not succeed. It is not easy to convince employees to change how they do their jobs, train them in new procedures, master the new system, and persuade them to share sensitive information. Resistance, and the blurring of company boundaries, can cause problems with employee morale, accountability, and lines of responsibility.

Reaping the potential benefits of ERP systems and mitigating their disadvantages requires conscious effort and involvement by top management. Top management's commitment to and support for the necessary changes greatly increase the chances of success.

Because ERP systems are complex and expensive, choosing one is not an easy task. In doing so, you must take great care to ensure that the ERP system has a module for every critical company process and that you are not paying for software modules that you do not need. One way to choose a suitable system is to select a package designed for your industry. Although cost is a huge concern, buying too cheaply can cost more in the long run if the system does not meet your needs, because modification costs can be quite high. You can minimize the risk of buying the wrong package by researching the best ERP vendors. There are many ERP vendors, the two largest being SAP and Oracle. Other leading vendors are The Sage Group, Microsoft, and Infor.

Because it is too difficult for most companies to implement ERP software by themselves, they often hire an ERP vendor or a consulting company to do it for them. These firms usually provide three types of services: consulting, customization, and support. For most midsized companies, implementation costs range from the list price of the ERP user licenses to twice that amount. Large companies with multiple sites often spend three to five times the cost of the user license.

Because many processes automatically trigger additional actions in other modules, proper configuration is essential. This requires a sound understanding of all major business processes and their interactions so they can be defined. Examples include setting up cost/profit centers, credit approval policies, and purchase approval rules. In the configuration process, companies balance the way they want the system to operate with the way it lets them operate. If the way an ERP module operates is unacceptable, the company can modify the module. Alternatively, it can use an existing system and build interfaces between it and the ERP system. Both options are time consuming, costly, and result in fewer system integration benefits. In addition, the more customized a system becomes, the more difficult it is to communicate with suppliers and customers. To make configuration easier, ERP vendors are developing built-in "configuration" tools to address most customers' needs for system changes.

The importance of sound internal controls in an ERP cannot be overstated. The integrated nature of ERP systems means that unless every data item is validated and checked for accuracy at the time of initial entry, errors will automatically propagate throughout the system. Thus, data entry controls and access controls are essential. Most managers and employees see and have access to only a small portion of the system. This segregation of duties provides sound internal control. It is important to separate responsibility for custody of assets, authorization of activities that affect those assets, and recording information about activities and the status of organizational assets.

Summary and Case Conclusion

Ashton is aware that Scott and Susan plan to open additional stores in the near future and want to develop a Web site to conduct business over the Internet. Based on this information, Ashton will select an accounting package that will satisfy S&S's current and anticipated future needs. The software should be able to take care of all data processing and data storage tasks. Ashton will also make sure that the software can interface with the source data automation devices he wants to use to capture most data input. The software must be capable of producing a full set of financial reports and be flexible enough to produce other useful information the company will need to be successful. Finally, Ashton realized his next step would be to select the software and produce some documentation of how the system worked.

Key Terms

data processing cycle 26	mnemonic code 29	master file 32
source documents 27	chart of accounts 29	transaction file 33
turnaround documents 27	general journal 31	database 33
source data automation 27	specialized journal 31	batch processing 33
general ledger 28	audit trail 31	online, real-time
subsidiary ledger 28	entity 31	processing 33
control account 28	attribute 31	document 34
coding 28	field 32	report 34
sequence code 28	record 32	query 34
block code 28	data value 32	enterprise resource planning
group code 28	file 32	(ERP) system 36

AIS IN ACTION

Chapter Quiz

1. Which of the following is NOT a step in the data processing cycle?
   a. data collection
   b. data input
   c. data storage
   d. data processing

2. All of the information (name, GPA, major, etc.) about a particular student is stored in the same _____.
   a. file   b. record   c. attribute   d. field

3. Which of the following would contain the total value of all inventory owned by an organization?
   a. source document
   b. general ledger
   c. cash budget

4. Which of the following is most likely to be a general ledger control account?
   a. accounts receivable
   b. petty cash
   c. prepaid rent
   d. retained earnings

5. Which of the following documents is most likely to be used in the expenditure cycle?
   a. sales orders
   b. credit memo
   c. receiving report
   d. job time ticket

6. Which of the following is LEAST likely to be a specialized journal?
   a. sales journal
   b. cash receipts journal
   c. prepaid insurance journal
   d. cash disbursements journal

7. How does the chart of accounts list general ledger accounts?
   a. alphabetical order
   b. chronological order
   c. size order
   d. the order in which they appear in financial statements

8. Which of the following is NOT an advantage of an ERP system?
   a. better access control
   b. standardization of procedures and reports
   c. improved monitoring capabilities
   d. simplicity and reduced costs

9. Records of company data sent to an external party and then returned to the system as input are called _____.
   a. turnaround documents
   b. source data automation documents
   c. source documents
   d. external input documents

10. Recording and processing information about a transaction at the time it takes place is referred to as which of the following?
    a. batch processing
    b. online, real-time processing
    c. captured transaction processing
    d. chart of accounts processing

Discussion Questions

2.1. Table 2-1 lists some of the documents used in the revenue, expenditure, and human resources cycle. What kinds of input or output documents or forms would you find in the production (also referred to as the conversion) cycle?

2.2. With respect to the data processing cycle, explain the phrase "garbage in, garbage out." How can you prevent this from happening?

2.3. What kinds of documents are most likely to be turnaround documents? Do an Internet search to find the answer and to find example turnaround documents.

2.4. The data processing cycle in Figure 2-1 is an example of a basic process found throughout nature. Relate the basic input/process/store/output model to the functions of the human body.

2.5. Some individuals argue that accountants should focus on producing financial statements and leave the design and production of managerial reports to information systems specialists. What are the advantages and disadvantages of following this advice? To what extent should accountants be involved in producing reports that include more than just financial measures of performance? Why?

Problems

2.1. The chart of accounts must be tailored to an organization's specific needs. Discuss how the chart of accounts for the following organizations would differ from the one presented for S&S in Table 2-2.
    a. university
    b. bank
    c. government unit (city or state)
    d. manufacturing company
    e. expansion of S&S to a chain of two stores

2.2. Ollie Mace is the controller of SDC, an automotive parts manufacturing firm. Its four major operating divisions are heat treating, extruding, small parts stamping, and machining. Last year's sales from each division ranged from $150,000 to $3,000,000. Each division is physically and managerially independent, except for the constant surveillance of Sam Dilley, the firm's founder.

The AIS for each division evolved according to the needs and abilities of its accounting staff. Mace is the first controller to have responsibility for overall financial management. Dilley wants Mace to improve the AIS before he retires in a few years so that it will be easier to monitor division performance. Mace decides to redesign the financial reporting system to include the following features:

- It should give managers uniform, timely, and accurate reports of business activity. Monthly reports should be uniform across divisions and be completed by the fifth day of the following month to provide enough time to take corrective actions to affect the next month's performance. Company-wide financial reports should be available at the same time.
- Reports should provide a basis for measuring the return on investment for each division. Thus, in addition to revenue and expense accounts, reports should show assets assigned to each division.

- The system should generate meaningful budget data for planning and decision-making purposes. Budgets should reflect managerial responsibility and show costs for major product groups.

Mace believes that a new chart of accounts is required to accomplish these goals. He wants to divide asset accounts into six major categories, such as current assets and plant and equipment. He does not foresee a need for more than 10 control accounts within each of these categories. From his observations to date, 100 subsidiary accounts are more than adequate for each control account.

No division has more than five major product groups. Mace foresees a maximum of six cost centers within any product group, including both the operating and nonoperating groups. He views general divisional costs as a non-revenue-producing product group. Mace estimates that 44 expense accounts plus 12 specific variance accounts would be adequate.

Required

Design a chart of accounts for SDC. Explain how you structured the chart of accounts to meet the company's needs and operating characteristics. Keep total account code length to a minimum, while still satisfying all of Mace's desires. *(CMA Examination, adapted)*

2.3. An audit trail enables a person to trace a source document to its ultimate effect on the financial statements or work back from financial statement amounts to source documents. Describe in detail the audit trail for the following:
   a. Purchases of inventory
   b. Sales of inventory
   c. Employee payroll

2.4. Your nursery sells various types and sizes of trees, bedding plants, vegetable plants, and shrubs. It also sells fertilizer and potting soil. Design a coding scheme for your nursery.

2.5. Match the following terms with their definitions.

Term	Definition
____ **a.** data processing cycle	1. Contains summary-level data for every asset, liability, equity, revenue, and expense account
____ **b.** source documents	2. Items are numbered consecutively to account for all items; missing items cause a gap in the numerical sequence
____ **c.** turnaround documents	3. Path of a transaction through a data processing system from point of origin to final output, or backwards from final output to point of origin
____ **d.** source data automation	4. List of general ledger account numbers; allows transaction data to be coded, classified, and entered into proper accounts; facilitates preparation of financial statements and reports
____ **e.** general ledger	5. Contents of a specific field, such as "George" in a name field
____ **f.** subsidiary ledger	6. Portion of a data record that contains the data value for a particular attribute, like a cell in a spreadsheet
____ **g.** control account	7. Company data sent to an external party and then returned to the system as input
____ **h.** coding	8. Used to record infrequent or nonroutine transactions

____ i. sequence code

____ j. block code

____ k. group code

____ l. mnemonic code

____ m. chart of accounts

____ n. general journal

____ o. specialized journal

____ p. audit trail

____ q. entity

____ r. attribute

____ s. field

____ t. record

____ u. data value

____ v. master file

____ w. transaction file

____ x. database

____ y. batch processing

____ z. online, real-time processing

9. Characteristics of interest that need to be stored

10. The steps a company must follow to efficiently and effectively process data about its transactions

11. Something about which information is stored

12. Stores cumulative information about an organization; like a ledger in a manual AIS

13. Contains detailed data for any general ledger account with many individual subaccounts

14. Contains records of individual business transactions that occur during a specific time period

15. Updating each transaction as it occurs

16. Devices that capture transaction data in machine-readable form at the time and place of their origin

17. Used to record large numbers of repetitive transactions

18. Set of interrelated, centrally coordinated files

19. Two or more subgroups of digits are used to code items

20. Updating done periodically, such as daily

21. Systematic assignment of numbers or letters to items to classify and organize them

22. Letters and numbers, derived from the item description, are interspersed to identify items; usually easy to memorize

23. Initial record of a transaction that takes place; usually recorded on preprinted forms or formatted screens

24. Fields containing data about entity attributes; like a row in a spreadsheet

25. Sets of numbers are reserved for specific categories of data

26. The general ledger account corresponding to a subsidiary ledger, where the sum of all subsidiary ledger entries should equal the amount in the general ledger account

2.6. For each of the following scenarios, identify which data processing method (batch or online, real-time) would be the most appropriate.
  a. Make an airline reservation
  b. Register for a university course
  c. Prepare biweekly payroll checks
  d. Process an order through an e-commerce Web site
  e. Prepare a daily bank deposit
  f. Preparation of customer bills by a local utility
  g. Accumulate daily costs from a production run of a single automobile part
  h. Identify the replacement drill bit size for a bit broken during a recent production run

2.7. On the following Web sites, you will find several online demonstrations for the SAP and Oracle ERP systems. Visit these Web sites and explore their content by doing the following:

a. The SAP Web site is www.sap.com/solutions. Search the site for corporate videos, and watch two of them. Explore the industries, services, solutions, and platforms that SAP offers. Read several of the articles, such as the ones about customer successes.

b. The Oracle Web site is www.oracle.com/solutions/mid/demo.html. Explore the Web site just as you explored the SAP site.

Required

After viewing the Web sites, and based on your reading of the chapter, write a two-page paper that describes how an ERP can connect and integrate the revenue, expenditure, human resources/payroll, and financing cycles of a business.

2.8. Which of the following actions update a master file and which would be stored as a record in a transaction file?

a. Update customer address change
b. Update unit pricing information
c. Record daily sales
d. Record payroll checks
e. Change employee pay rates
f. Record production variances
g. Record sales commissions
h. Change employee office location
i. Update accounts payable balance
j. Change customer credit limit
k. Change vendor payment discount terms
l. Record purchases

2.9. You were hired to assist Ashton Fleming in designing an accounting system for S&S. Ashton has developed a list of the journals, ledgers, reports, and documents that he thinks S&S needs (see Table 2-4). He asks you to complete the following tasks:

a. Specify what data you think should be collected on each of the following four documents: sales invoice, purchase order, receiving report, employee time card.

TABLE 2-4 Documents, Journals, and Ledgers for S&S

Title	Purpose
Documents	
Sales Invoice	Record cash and credit sales of merchandise
Service Invoice	Record sales of repair services
Delivery Ticket	Record delivery of merchandise to customers
Monthly Statement	Inform customers of outstanding account balances
Credit Memo	Support adjustments to customer accounts for sales returns and allowances and sales discounts; also support write-off of uncollectible accounts
Purchase Order	Order merchandise from vendors
Receiving Report	Record receipt of merchandise from vendors, indicating both quantity and condition of items received
Time Card	Record time worked by employees
Specialized Journals	
Sales	Record all credit sales
Cash Receipts	Record cash sales, payments from customers, and other cash receipts
Purchases	Record all purchases from vendors
Cash Disbursements	Record all cash disbursements
General Journal	Record infrequent, nonroutine transactions; also record adjusting and closing entries
Subsidiary Ledgers	
Accounts Receivable	Maintain details about amounts due from customers
Accounts Payable	Maintain details about amounts due to vendors
Inventory	Maintain details about each inventory item
Fixed Assets	Maintain details about each piece of equipment and other fixed assets
General Ledger	Maintain details about all major asset, liability, equity, revenue, and expense accounts

b. Design a report to manage inventory.

c. Design a report to assist in managing credit sales and cash collections.

d. Visit a local office supply store and identify what types of journals, ledgers, and blank forms for various documents (sales invoices, purchase orders, etc.) are available. Describe how easily they could be adapted to meet S&S's needs.

Case 2-1   Bar Harbor Blueberry Farm

The Bar Harbor Blueberry Farm is a family-owned, 200-acre farm that grows and sells blueberries to grocery stores, blueberry wholesalers, and small roadside stands. Bar Harbor has 25 full-time employees and hires 150 to 200 seasonal workers for the harvest.

For the past six summers, you have picked berries for Bar Harbor. When you graduated, you were hired full-time as the accountant/office manager. Until now, Bar Harbor kept most of its accounting records in a big file box. Jack Phillips, the owner, would like a more organized approach to the farm's

accounting records. He asked you to establish a proper set of books. You decide to start by establishing appropriate journals and ledgers for these transactions.

Presented below are a set of vendor invoices and a few partially completed journals and ledgers. Your job is to record these transactions and update the appropriate ledgers. Be sure to leave a proper audit trail. You may also use Excel, Great Plains, Peachtree, QuickBooks, or another accounting software package of your choosing to complete this problem.

Vendor Invoices

Date	Supplier Invoice	Supplier Name	Supplier Address	Amount
March 7	AJ34	Bud's Soil Prep	PO Box 34	$2,067.85
March 11	14568	Osto Farmers Supply	45 Main	$ 67.50
March 14	893V	Whalers Fertilizer	Route 34	$5,000.00
March 21	14699	Osto Farmers Supply	45 Main	$3,450.37
March 21	10102	IFM Wholesale	587 Longview	$4,005.00
March 24	10145	IFM Wholesale	587 Longview	$ 267.88

Purchases Journal

Page 1

Date	Supplier	Supplier Invoice	Account Number	Post Ref	Amount
March 7	Bud's Soil Prep	AJ34			$2,067.85

General Ledger

Accounts Payable   Account Number: 300

Date	Description	Post Ref	Debit	Credit	Balance
March 1	Balance Forward				$18,735.55

General Ledger

Purchases					Account Number: 605
Date	Description	Post Ref	Debit	Credit	Balance
March 1	Balance Forward				$54,688.49

Accounts Payable Subsidiary Ledger

Account No: 23	Bud's Soil Prep	PO Box 34		Terms: 2/10, Net 30
Date	Description	Debit	Credit	Balance

Account No: 24				Terms: 2/10, Net 30
Date	Description	Debit	Credit	Balance

Account No: 36				Terms: 2/10, Net 30
Date	Description	Debit	Credit	Balance

Account No: 38				Terms: 2/10, Net 30
Date	Description	Debit	Credit	Balance

AIS IN ACTION SOLUTIONS

Quiz Key

1. Which of the following is NOT a step in the data processing cycle?
   ▶ a. data collection [Correct. Data collection is a part of data input and is therefore not a step in the data processing cycle.]
   b. data input [Incorrect. Data input is the first step in the data processing cycle. This is the step where data is captured, collected, and entered into the system.]
   c. data storage [Incorrect. Data storage is the data processing cycle step where data is stored for future use by the company.]
   d. data processing [Incorrect. Data processing is the data processing cycle step where stored data is updated with new input data.]

2. All of the information (name, GPA, major, etc.) about a particular student is stored in the same _____.
   a. file [Incorrect. A file is designed to include information about many students.]
   ▶ b. record [Correct. A record should include all information maintained by the system about a particular entity, such as a student.]
   c. attribute [Incorrect. An attribute is a descriptor or a characteristic of an entity—in this example, the student's major is an attribute.]
   d. field [Incorrect. A field represents a data storage space—in this example, an accounting student would have "Accounting" stored in the major field.]

3. Which of the following would contain the total value of all inventory owned by an organization?
   a. source document [Incorrect. A source document contains data about a particular event or transaction.]
   ▶ b. general ledger [Correct. The general ledger maintains summary information on inventory and every other general ledger account.]
   c. cash budget [Incorrect. A cash budget provides information only on projected cash inflows and outflows.]

4. Which of the following is most likely to be a general ledger control account?
   ▶ a. accounts receivable [Correct. Accounts receivable is typically made up of many individual customer accounts maintained in a subsidiary ledger. The total of all individual customer accounts in the subsidiary ledger is maintained in the accounts receivable control account in the general ledger.]
   b. petty cash [Incorrect. Petty cash is made up of only one account.]
   c. prepaid rent [Incorrect. A subsidiary ledger containing multiple prepaid rent accounts is usually not necessary.]
   d. retained earnings [Incorrect. Retained earnings is typically comprised of only one account.]

5. Which of the following documents is most likely to be used in the expenditure cycle?
   a. sales order [Incorrect. The sales order is a revenue cycle document that captures the information about a customer's order.]
   b. credit memo [Incorrect. A credit memo is a revenue cycle document that is used to give a credit to a customer for damaged or returned goods.]
   ▶ c. receiving report [Correct. A receiving report is an expenditure cycle document that is used to record the receipt of goods from suppliers. Companies pay their suppliers based on the goods received and recorded on the receiving report.]
   d. job time ticket [Incorrect. A job time ticket is a production cycle document that is used to record time spent on specific jobs.]

6. Which of the following is LEAST likely to be a specialized journal?
    a. sales journal [Incorrect. A specialized journal is used to record large numbers of repetitive transactions. Most companies have a large number of sales.]
    b. cash receipts journal [Incorrect. A specialized journal is used to record large numbers of repetitive transactions. Most companies have a large number of cash receipts.]
 ▶ c. prepaid insurance journal [Correct. A specialized journal is used to record large numbers of repetitive transactions, and most companies have very few prepaid insurance transactions.]
    d. cash disbursements journal [Incorrect. A specialized journal is used to record large numbers of repetitive transactions. Most companies have a large number of cash disbursements.]

7. How does the chart of accounts list general ledger accounts?
    a. alphabetical order [Incorrect. General ledger accounts are listed in the order in which they appear in the financial statements, not in alphabetical order.]
    b. chronological order [Incorrect. General ledger accounts are listed in the order in which they appear in the financial statements, not according to the date they were created.]
    c. size order [Incorrect. General ledger accounts are listed in the order in which they appear in the financial statements, not according to their size.]
 ▶ d. the order in which they appear in financial statements [Correct.]

8. Which of the following is NOT an advantage of an ERP system?
    a. better access control [Incorrect. Better access control is an advantage because an ERP can consolidate multiple permissions and security models into a single data access structure.]
    b. standardization of procedures and reports [Incorrect. Standardization of procedures and reports is an advantage because procedures and reports can be standardized across business units and in mergers and acquisitions they can replace the different systems with a single, unified system.]
    c. improved monitoring capabilities [Incorrect. Improved monitoring capabilities are an advantage because management gains greater visibility into every area of the enterprise that allows them to better monitor the organization.]
 ▶ d. simplicity and reduced costs [Correct. ERP systems are quite complex and costly; they do not offer the advantages of simplicity and reduced costs.]

9. Records of company data sent to an external party and then returned to the system as input are called _____ .
 ▶ a. turnaround documents [Correct. For example, a utility bill is sent to a customer, who then returns the bill with payment.]
    b. source data automation documents [Incorrect. Source data automation is the capturing of input data in machine-readable form.]
    c. source documents [Incorrect. Source documents collect data about business activities.]
    d. external input documents [Incorrect. These documents originate from external sources.]

10. Recording and processing information about a transaction at the time it takes place is referred to as which of the following?
    a. batch processing [Incorrect. Batch processing involves processing transactions in groups or batches all at the same time.]
 ▶ b. online, real-time processing [Correct. Online, real-time processing involves processing transactions as they occur.]
    c. captured transaction processing [Incorrect. This is not a recognized transaction processing method.]
    d. chart of accounts processing [Incorrect. The chart of accounts, although typically updated every so often, is not a transaction processing method.]

Chapter 3

Systems Documentation Techniques

Learning Objectives

After studying this chapter, you should be able to:

1. Prepare and use data flow diagrams to understand, evaluate, and document information systems.

2. Prepare and use flowcharts to understand, evaluate, and document information systems.

INTEGRATIVE CASE S&S

What a hectic few months it has been for Ashton Fleming! He helped S&S get started, helped get S&S through its weeklong grand opening, and was swamped with processing all the transactions from the highly successful grand opening. Because of its rapid growth, S&S has outgrown the initial rudimentary AIS that Ashton selected. Lacking time and expertise, Ashton has engaged Computer Applications (CA), a systems consulting firm, to help S&S select and install a new and more powerful AIS.

During Ashton's first meeting with Kimberly Sierra, CA's manager, she asked about S&S's system requirements and management's expectations. Ashton had yet to think through these issues, so he could not answer her specifically. When she asked how S&S's system worked, Ashton plunged into a discussion about the use of various company documents, but Kimberly seemed unable to absorb his detailed explanations. Ashton thought that part of his discussion was helpful, but overall it was irrelevant to the issue at hand.

Ashton came away impressed by CA and Kimberly. He also realized the need to understand S&S's information requirements more clearly. From his days as an auditor, Ashton knew the value of good system documentation in helping unfamiliar users both understand and evaluate a system. Good system documentation would be a big help to him and Kimberly, as well as to Scott and Susan as they evaluate the current and proposed systems.

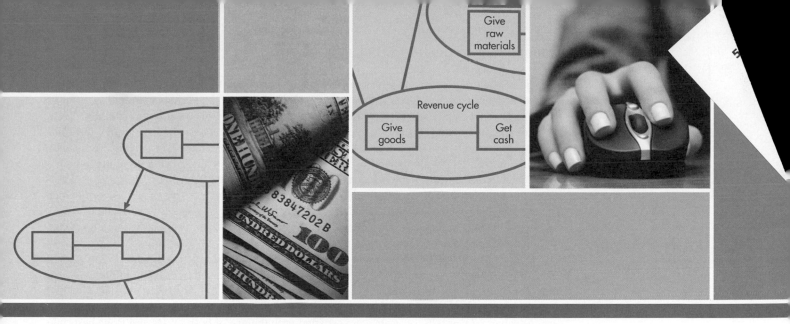

After sharing his conclusions with Susan and Scott, they enthusiastically approved Ashton's plan to document the current and proposed systems. They supported his taking a leadership role in moving toward a new system and were especially interested in diagrams or charts that would document the existing system and help them understand and evaluate it.

Introduction

Documentation encompasses the narratives, flowcharts, diagrams, and other written materials that explain how a system works. This information covers the who, what, when, where, why, and how of data entry, processing, storage, information output, and system controls. Popular means of documenting a system include diagrams, flowcharts, tables, and other graphical representations of information. These are supplemented by a *narrative description* of the system, a written step-by-step explanation of system components and interactions. In this chapter, we explain two common systems documentation tools: data flow diagrams and flowcharts.

Documentation tools are important on the following levels:

1. At a minimum, you must be able to *read* documentation to determine how a system works.
2. You may need to *evaluate* internal control systems documentation to identify strengths and weaknesses and recommend improvements. Or, you may need to evaluate documentation for a proposed system to determine whether it meets the company's needs.
3. More skill is needed to *prepare* internal control documentation or documentation that shows how an existing or proposed system operates.

This chapter discusses the following documentation tools:

1. *Data flow diagram (DFD),* a graphical description of data sources, flows, processes, storage, and destinations
2. *Document flowchart,* a graphical description of the flow of documents and information between departments or areas of responsibility
3. *System flowchart,* a graphical description of the relationship among the input, processing, and output in an information system
4. *Program flowchart,* a graphical description of the sequence of logical operations a computer performs as it executes a program

Accountants use documentation techniques extensively. Auditing standards require that independent auditors understand the automated and manual internal control procedures an entity uses.

One good way to gain this understanding is to use flowcharts to document the internal control system, because such graphic portrayals more readily reveal weaknesses and strengths.

The Sarbanes-Oxley Act (SOX) of 2002 requires an internal control report in public company annual reports that (1) states that management is responsible for establishing and maintaining an adequate internal control structure and (2) assesses the effectiveness of the company's internal controls. SOX also specifies that a company's auditor must evaluate management's assessment of the company's internal control structures and attest to its accuracy. The auditor's attestation should include a specific notation about significant defects or material noncompliance found during internal control tests. This means that both the company and its auditors have to document and test the company's internal controls. To do so, they must be able to prepare, evaluate, and read different types of documentation, such as flowcharts.

Documentation tools are also used extensively in the systems development process. In addition, the team members who develop information systems applications often change, and documentation tools help the new team members get up to speed quickly.

According to one study, 62.5% of information systems professionals use DFDs and 97.6% use flowcharts. Over 92% of users were satisfied with the use of both DFDs and flowcharts and use both.

Documentation is easier to prepare and revise when a software package is used. Once a few basic commands are mastered, users can quickly and easily prepare, store, revise, and print presentation-quality documentation.

The documentation tools in this chapter are used throughout the book. They are also tested on professional examinations, and learning about them better prepares you for these examinations.

Data Flow Diagrams

A *data flow diagram (DFD)* graphically describes the flow of data within an organization. It uses the symbols shown in Figure 3-1 to represent four basic elements: data sources and destinations, data flows, transformation processes, and data stores. For example, Figure 3-2 shows that the input to process C is data flow B, which comes from data source A. The outputs of process C are data flows D and E. Data flow E is sent to data destination J. Process F uses data flows D and G as input and produces data flows I and G as output. Data flow G comes from and returns to data store H. Data flow I is sent to data destination K.

Figure 3-3 assigns specific titles to each of the processes depicted in Figure 3-2. Figures 3-2 and 3-3 will be used to examine the four basic elements of a DFD in more detail.

A *data source* and a *data destination* are entities that send or receive data that the system uses or produces. An entity can be both a source and a destination. They are represented by squares, as illustrated by items A (customer), J (bank), and K (credit manager) in Figure 3-3.

FIGURE 3-1
Data Flow Diagram Symbols

Symbol	Name	Explanation
☐	Data sources and destinations	The people and organizations that send data to and receive data from the system are represented by square boxes. Data destinations are also referred to as *data sinks*.
↗	Data flows	The flow of the data into or out of a process is represented by curved or straight lines with arrows.
○	Transformation processes	The processes that transform data from inputs to outputs are represented by circles. They are often referred to as *bubbles*.
▭	Data stores	The storage of data is represented by two horizontal lines.

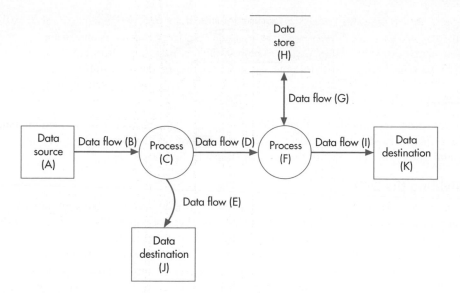

FIGURE 3-2

Basic Data Flow Diagram Elements

A *data flow* is the movement of data among processes, stores, sources and destinations. Data that pass between data stores and a source or destination must go through a data transformation process. Data flows are labeled to show what information is flowing. The only exception is data flow between a process and a data store, such as data flow G in Figure 3-3, because the data flow is usually obvious. In data flow G, data from the accounts receivable file is retrieved, updated, and stored back in the file. Other data flows in Figure 3-3 are B (customer payment), D (remittance data), E (deposit), and I (receivables information).

If two or more data flows move together, a single line is used. For example, data flow B (customer payment) consists of a payment and remittance data. Process 1.0 (process payment) splits them and sends them in different directions. The remittance data (D) is used to update accounts receivable records, and the payment (E) is deposited in the bank. If the data flow separately, two lines are used. For example, Figure 3-4 shows two lines because customer inquiries (L) do not always accompany a payment (B). If represented by the same data flow, the separate elements and their different purposes are obscured, and the DFD is more difficult to interpret.

Processes represent the transformation of data. Figure 3-3 shows that process payment (C) splits the customer payment into the remittance data and the check, which is deposited in the bank. The update receivables process (F) uses remittance (D) and accounts receivable (H) data to update receivable records and send receivables information to the credit manager.

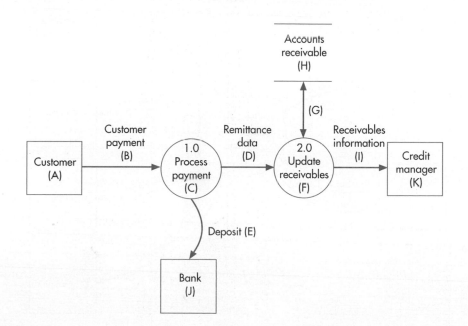

FIGURE 3-3

Data Flow Diagram of Customer Payment Process

FIGURE 3-4

Splitting Customer Payments and Inquiries

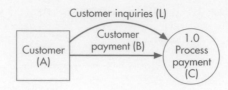

A *data store* is a repository of data. DFDs do not show the physical storage medium (such as a server or paper) used to store the data. As shown in Figure 3-3, data stores (H) are represented by horizontal lines, with the name of the file written inside the lines.

Subdividing the DFD

DFDs are subdivided into successively lower levels to provide ever-increasing amounts of detail, because few systems can be fully diagrammed on one sheet of paper. Also, users have differing needs, and a variety of levels can better satisfy differing requirements.

The highest-level DFD is referred to as a *context diagram* because it provides the reader with a summary-level view of a system. It depicts a data processing system and the entities that are the sources and destinations of system inputs and outputs. For example, Ashton drew Figure 3-5 to document payroll processing procedures at S&S. The payroll processing system receives time card data from different departments and employee data from human resources. The system processes these data and produces (1) tax reports and payments for governmental agencies, (2) employee paychecks, (3) a payroll check deposited in the payroll account at the bank, and (4) payroll information for management.

Ashton used the description of S&S's payroll processing procedures in Table 3-1 to decompose the context diagram into successively lower levels, each with an increasing amount of detail. Read this description and determine the following:

● How many major data processing activities are involved?
● What are the data inputs and outputs of each activity (ignoring all references to people, departments, and document destinations)?

The narrative in Table 3-1 describes five data processing activities:

1. Updating the employee/payroll master file (first paragraph).
2. Handling employee compensation (second, fifth, and sixth paragraphs). Later in this chapter, you will see a breakdown of this activity into smaller parts in a lower-level DFD.
3. Generating management reports (third paragraph).

FIGURE 3-5

Context Diagram for S&S Payroll Processing

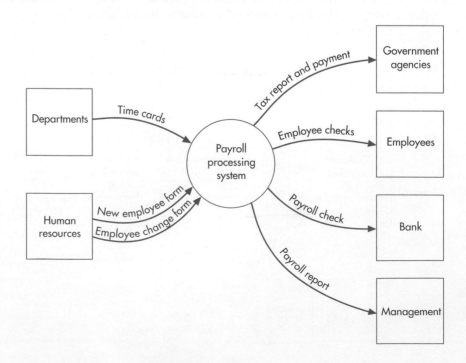

TABLE 3-1 Narrative Description of Payroll Processing at S&S

When employees are hired, they complete a new-employee form. When a change to an employee's payroll status occurs, such as a raise or a change in the number of exemptions, the human resources department completes an employee change form. A copy of these forms is sent to payroll. These forms are used to create or update the records in the employee/payroll file and are then stored in the file. Employee records are stored alphabetically.

Some S&S employees are paid a salary, but most are hourly workers who record their time on time cards. At the end of each pay period, department managers send the time cards to the payroll department. The payroll clerk uses the time card data, data from the employee file (such as pay rate and annual salary), and the appropriate tax tables to prepare a two-part check for each employee. The clerk also prepares a two-part payroll register showing gross pay, deductions, and net pay for each employee. The clerk updates the employee file to reflect each employee's current earnings. The original copy of the employee paychecks is forwarded to Susan. The payroll register is forwarded to the accounts payable clerk. The time cards and the duplicate copies of the payroll register and paychecks are stored by date in the payroll file.

Every pay period, the payroll clerk uses the data in the employee/payroll file to prepare a payroll summary report for Susan so that she can control and monitor labor expenses. This report is forwarded to Susan, with the original copies of the employee paychecks.

Every month, the payroll clerk uses the data in the employee/payroll file to prepare a two-part tax report. The original is forwarded to the accounts payable clerk, and the duplicate is added to the tax records in the payroll file. The accounts payable clerk uses the tax report to prepare a two-part check for taxes and a two-part cash disbursements voucher. The tax report and the original copy of each document are forwarded to Susan. The duplicates are stored by date in the accounts payable file.

The accounts payable clerk uses the payroll register to prepare a two-part check for the total amount of the employee payroll and a two-part disbursements voucher. The original copy of each document is forwarded to Susan, and the payroll register and the duplicates are stored by date in the accounts payable file.

Susan reviews each packet of information she receives, approves it, and signs the checks. She forwards the cash disbursements vouchers to Ashton, the tax reports and payments to the appropriate governmental agency, the payroll check to the bank, and the employee checks to the employees. She files the payroll report chronologically.

Ashton uses the payroll tax and the payroll check cash disbursement vouchers to update the general ledger. He then cancels the journal voucher by marking it "posted" and files it numerically.

4. Paying taxes (fourth paragraph).
5. Posting entries to the general ledger (last paragraph).

The five activities and all data inflows and outflows are shown in Table 3-2.

Ashton exploded his context diagram and created the Level 0 DFD (called level 0 because there are zero meaningful decimal points—1.0, 2.0, etc.) shown in Figure 3-6. Notice that some data inputs and outputs have been excluded from this DFD. For example, in process 2.0, the data inflows and outflows that are not related to an external entity or to another process are not depicted (tax tables and payroll register). These data flows are internal to the "pay employees" activity and are shown on the next DFD level.

TABLE 3-2 Activities and Data Flows in Payroll Processing at S&S

Activities	Data Inputs	Data Outputs
Update employee/payroll file	New employee form Employee change form	Updated employee/payroll file
Pay employees	Time cards Employee/payroll file Tax rates table	Employee checks Payroll register Updated employee/payroll file Payroll check Payroll cash disbursements voucher
Prepare reports	Employee/payroll file	Payroll report
Pay taxes	Employee/payroll file	Tax report Tax payment Payroll tax cash disbursements voucher Updated employee/payroll file
Update general ledger	Payroll tax cash disbursements voucher Payroll cash disbursements voucher	Updated general ledger

FIGURE 3-6

Level 0 DFD for S&S payroll processing

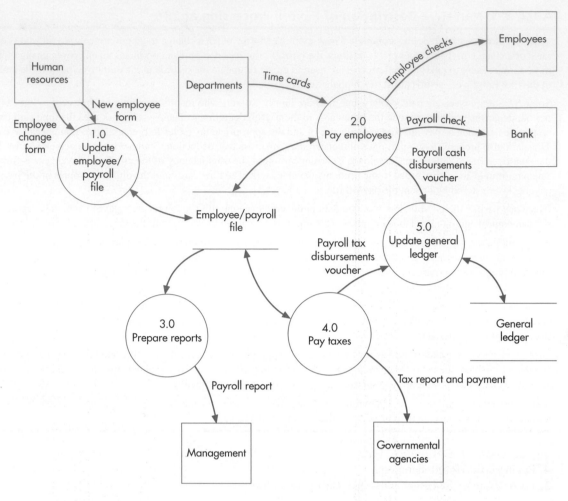

Ashton exploded process 2.0 (pay employees) to create a Level 1 DFD (it has one meaning-ful decimal place—2.1, 2.2, etc.). Figure 3-7 provides more detail about the data processes involved in paying employees, and it includes the tax rates table and the payroll register data flow omitted from Figure 3-6. In a similar fashion, each of the Figure 3-6 processes could be exploded, using a Level 1 DFD, to show a greater level of detail.

Some general guidelines for developing DFDs are shown in Focus 3-1.

FIGURE 3-7

Level 1 DFD for Process 2.0 in S&S Payroll Processing

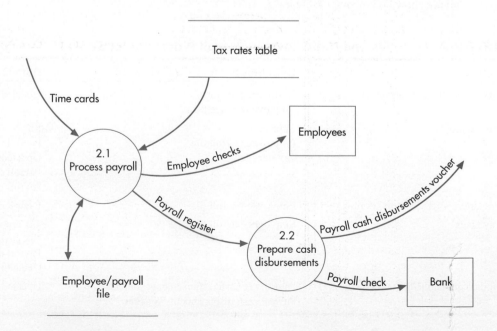

FOCUS 3-1   Guidelines for Drawing a DFD

1. **Understand the system.** Observe organization information flows, and interview the individuals who use and process the data. *[handwritten: Talk to End USER is Key]*

2. **Ignore certain aspects of the system.** A DFD is a diagram of the origins, flow, transformation, storage, and destinations of data. All control processes and actions are ignored. Only very important error paths are included; unimportant error paths are ignored. Determining how the system starts and stops is not shown.

3. **Determine system boundaries.** Determine what to include and exclude. Include all relevant data elements In the DFD, because excluded items will not be considered during system development. *[handwritten: Only looking at payment apply]*

4. **Develop a context diagram.** A context diagram depicts system boundaries. In the diagram's center is a circle with the name of the system. Outside entities the system interacts with directly are in boxes on either side, connected by data flows depicting the data passed between them. DFDs in successively more detail depict data flows in the system.

5. **Identify data flows.** Identify all data flows entering or leaving the system's boundary, including where the data originate and its final destination. A significant movement of information is usually a data flow. All data flows come from and go to a transformation process, a data store (file), or a source or destination. Data flows can move in two directions, shown as a line with arrows on both ends (see G in Figure 3-3).

6. **Group data flows.** A data flow can consist of one or more pieces of datum. Data elements that always flow together should be grouped together and shown as one data flow until they are separated. If the data do not always flow together, show them as separate data flows.

7. **Identify transformation processes.** Place a circle wherever work is required to transform one data flow into another. All transformation processes should have one or more incoming and outgoing data flows.

8. **Group transformation processes.** Transformation processes that are logically related or occur at the same time and place should be grouped together. Never combine unrelated items into a single transformation process. If data are not processed together, or are sometimes processed differently, then separate them.

9. **Identify all files or data stores.** Identify each temporary or permanent data repository, and identify each data flow into and out of it. *[handwritten: Resting spots]*

10. **Identify all data sources and destinations.** Include them on the DFD.

11. **Name all DFD elements.** Except for data flows into or out of data stores (the data store name is usually sufficient to identify the data flow), data elements should be given unique and descriptive names representing what is known about them. Naming data flows first forces you to concentrate on the all-important data flows, rather than on the processes or stores. Processes and data stores typically take their names from the data inflows or outflows. Choose active and descriptive names, such as "update inventory" and "validate transaction," rather than "input data" or "update process." Process names should include action verbs such as *update*, *edit*, *prepare*, *reconcile*, and *record*.

12. **Subdivide the DFD.** A cluttered DFD is hard to read and understand. If you have more than five to seven processes on a page, decompose the context diagram into high level processes. Explode these high-level processes into successively lower-level processes.

13. **Give each process a sequential number.** Giving each process a sequential number (lower to higher) helps readers navigate among the DFD levels.

14. **Repeat the process.** Work through data flows several times. Each subsequent pass helps refine the diagram and identify the fine points. Organize the DFD to flow from top to bottom and from left to right.

15. **Prepare a final copy.** Do not allow data flow lines to cross over each other; if necessary, repeat a data store or destination. Place the name of the DFD, the date prepared, and the preparer's name on each page.

[handwritten notes in margins: What is the Data Cashpmt?; DO #13 first then #12; It was a payment now Its a deposit.; get Validation from Mgr both sign & date process]

Flowcharts

A *flowchart* is an analytical technique used to describe some aspect of an information system in a clear, concise, and logical manner. Flowcharts use a standard set of symbols to describe pictorially the transaction processing procedures a company uses and the flow of data through a system. The symbols used to create flowcharts are shown in Figure 3-8.

Flowcharting was introduced by industrial engineers in the 1950s as a way of (1) recording how business processes are performed and documents flow and (2) analyzing how to improve processes and document flows. Soon internal auditors began using flowcharts in operational audits to better understand their company's business processes. Later, external auditors began using flowcharts to evaluate their clients' internal controls. Flowcharts became even more important when the Sarbanes-Oxley Act required companies to document their business processes and internal controls.

Flowcharts have significant advantages. A pictorial representation is much easier to understand than a narrative description. Both the auditor and the business owner can use the flowchart as a working tool during discussions. For an experienced flowcharter using a computerized drawing tool, flowcharts provide an easy way to capture and record data during interviews, and they can be easily and quickly revised.

Flowcharts do have some disadvantages. Some people do not like or understand them. Many are poorly drawn and therefore not as helpful as they should be. They are time-consuming to prepare if the flowcharter is not trained properly.

Early flowcharts were drawn using a flowcharting template, a piece of hard, flexible plastic on which symbols have been die cut. Most flowcharts are now drawn using a software program such as Visio. Flowcharts can also be drawn using Microsoft Word, Excel, or PowerPoint.

Flowcharting symbols are divided into four categories, as shown in Figure 3-8:

1. *Input/output symbols* represent devices or media that provide input to or record output from processing operations.
2. *Processing symbols* show what types of devices are used to process data or indicate when processing is performed manually.
3. *Storage symbols* represent the devices used to store data.
4. *Flow and miscellaneous symbols* indicate the flow of data, where flowcharts begin or end, where decisions are made, and when to add explanatory notes to flowcharts.

FIGURE 3-8
Common flowcharting symbols

Symbol	Name	Explanation
Input/Output Symbols		
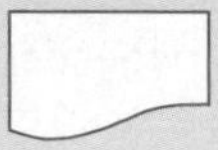	Document	A document or report.
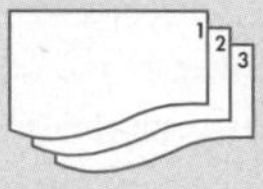	Multiple copies of one document	Illustrated by overlapping the document symbol and printing the document number on the face of the document in the upper right corner
	Input/output; Journal/ledger	Any input or output function on a program flowchart. Also used to represent accounting journals and ledgers in a document flowchart
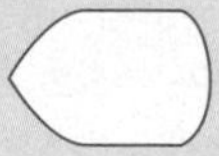	Display	Information displayed by an online output device such as a terminal, monitor, or screen
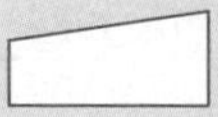	Online keying	Data entry by online devices, such as a terminal or personal computer
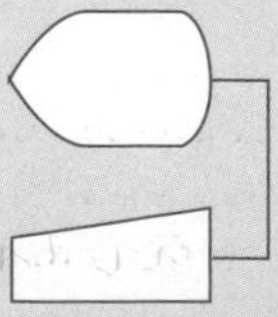	Terminal or personal computer	The display and online keying symbols are used together to represent terminals, personal computers, and other electronic devices capable of both input and output
	Transmittal tape	Manually prepared control totals; used for control purposes to compare to computer-generated totals
Processing Symbols		
	Computer processing	A computer-performed processing function; usually results in a change in data or information
	Manual operation	A processing operation performed manually

FIGURE 3-8
(*continued*)

Symbol	Name	Explanation
	Auxiliary operation	A processing function performed by a device that is not a computer
	Off-line keying	An operation utilizing an off-line keying device (e.g., key to disk, off-line cash register)

Storage Symbols

Symbol	Name	Explanation
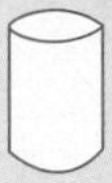	Magnetic disk/drive	Data stored on a magnetic disk or drive
	Magnetic tape	Data stored on a magnetic tape
	File	File of documents manually stored and retrieved; following letters indicate file-ordering sequence: N = numerically, A = alphabetically, D = by date

Flow and Miscellaneous Symbols

Symbol	Name	Explanation
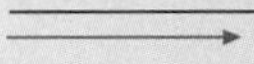	Document or processing flow	Direction of processing or document flow; normal flow is down and to the right
	Data/ information flow	Direction of data/information flow; often used to show data copied from one document to another
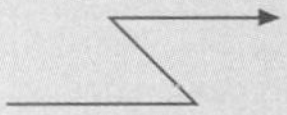	Communication link	Transmission of data from one geographic location to another via communication lines
	On-page connector	Connects the processing flow on the same page; its usage avoids lines crisscrossing a page
	Off-page connector	An entry from, or an exit to, another page
	Terminal	A beginning, end, or point of interruption in a process or program; also used to indicate an external party
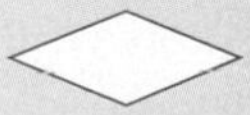	Decision	A decision-making step; used in a program flowchart to show branching to alternative paths
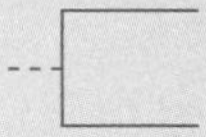	Annotation	Addition of descriptive comments or explanatory notes as clarification

[handwritten margin note:] Don't Label Lines unless decision Yes↓ No→

[handwritten margin note:] IC if so&so is on vacation — does it or Normal process but this could happen

Document Flowcharts

A *document flowchart* illustrates the flow of documents and information among areas of responsibility within an organization. They trace a document from its cradle to its grave, showing where each document originates, its distribution, its purpose, its disposition, and everything that happens as it flows through the system.

A document flowchart is particularly useful in analyzing internal control procedures. Document flowcharts that describe and evaluate internal controls are often referred to as *internal control flowcharts*. They can reveal system weaknesses or inefficiencies, such as inadequate communication flows, unnecessary complexity in document flows, or procedures responsible for causing wasteful delays. Document flowcharts prepared as part of the systems design process should be included in system documentation.

The document flowchart that Ashton developed for the payroll process at S&S, as described in Table 3-1 and 3-2, is shown in Figure 3-9.

General guidelines for preparing flowcharts that are readable, clear, concise, consistent, and understandable are presented in Focus 3-2 (see page 60).

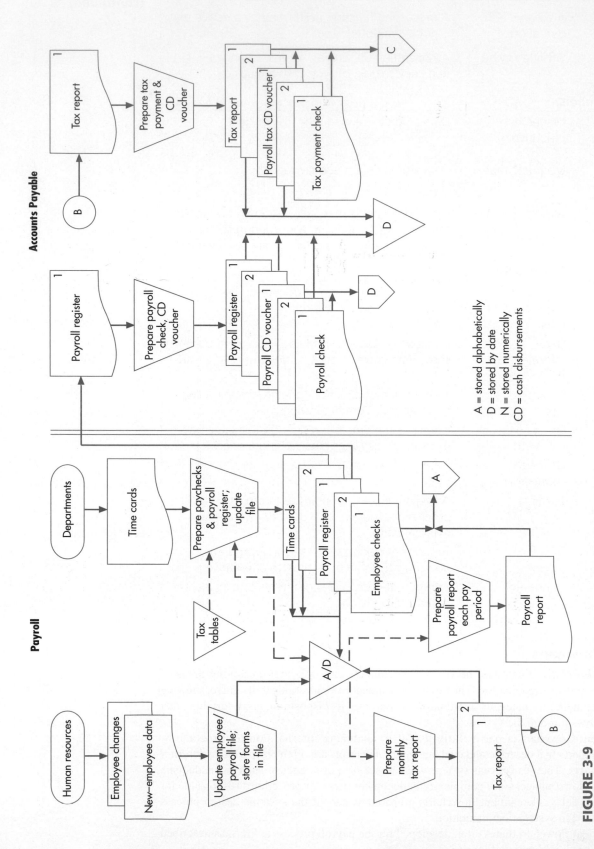

Payroll

Accounts Payable

A = stored alphabetically
D = stored by date
N = stored numerically
CD = cash disbursements

FIGURE 3-9
Document Flowchart of Payroll Processing at S&S

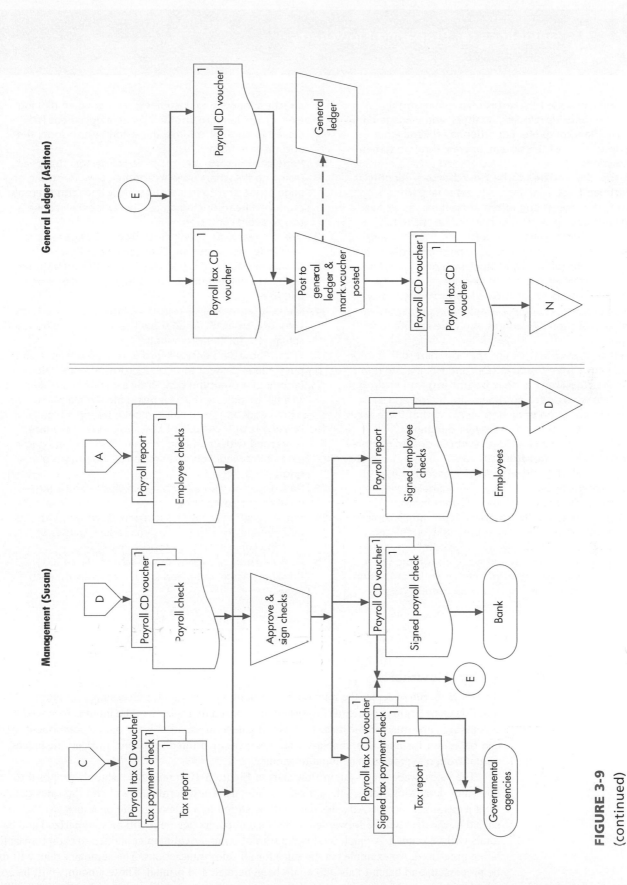

FIGURE 3-9
(continued)

[handwritten: ✱ Cradle to Grave   Application to Payoff of loan]

F**O**CUS 3-2 Guidelines for Preparing Flowcharts

1. **Understand a system before flowcharting it.** Interview users, developers, auditors, and management, or have them complete a questionnaire. Read a narrative description of the system, or walk through system transactions.

2. **Identify the entities to be flowcharted.** Identify departments, job functions, and external parties. Identify documents and information flows, as well as the activities or processes performed on the data.

3. **Divide the flowchart into columns.** When several departments or functions need to be shown, divide the flowchart into columns and label each one. Flowchart the activities of each entity in its respective column.

4. **Flowchart the normal flow of operations.** Ensure that all procedures and processes are in proper order. Identify exception procedures using the annotation symbol.

5. **Organize flowchart.** Design the flowchart so that information flows from top to bottom and from left to right.

6. **Give the flowchart a clear beginning and ending.** Designate where each document originates, and show the final disposition of all documents so that there are no loose ends that leave the reader dangling.

7. **Use standard flowcharting symbols drawn with a template or a computer.**

8. **Clearly label all symbols.** Write a description of the input, process, or output inside the symbol. If the description will not fit, use the annotation symbol.

9. **Multiple copies of documents.** For multiple copies of a document, place document numbers in the top right-hand corner of the symbol. The number should accompany the symbol as it moves through the system.

10. **Manual processing symbol.** Each manual processing symbol should have an input and an output. Do not directly connect two documents, except when moving from one column to another. When a document is moved to another column, it is often best to show the document in both.

11. **Page connectors.** Use off-page connectors to move from one flowchart page to another. Consider using on-page connectors to avoid excess flow lines and thereby produce a neat-looking page. Clearly label all connectors to avoid confusion.

12. **Use arrowheads on all flow lines.** Do not assume the reader will know the direction of the flow.

13. **Multiple pages.** If a flowchart cannot fit on a single page, clearly label the pages as follows: 1 of 3, 2 of 3, and so on.

14. **Show documents or reports in the column where they are created.** Then show them moving to another column for further processing.

15. **Files.** Show data entered into or retrieved from a computer file as passing through a processing operation (a computer program) first. Draw a line from a document to a file to indicate that it is being filed. A manual process is not needed to show a document entering a file.

16. **Draw a rough sketch of the flowchart.** Be more concerned with capturing content than with making a perfect drawing. Few systems can be flowcharted in a single draft.

17. **Redesign the flowchart.** Avoid clutter and a large number of crossed lines.

18. **Verify the flowchart's accuracy.** Review it with the people familiar with the system. Be sure all uses of flowcharting conventions are consistent.

19. **Draw a final copy of the flowchart.** Place the flowchart name, date, and preparer's name on each page.

[handwritten left margin: Interview / Ask - What if - you are out for a week / - what keeps you up at night / - What do you dislike/hate / - Why do you do this]

[handwritten: Use bars to show (SWITCHOFF) to other person or dept]

System Flowcharts

System flowcharts depict the relationships among system input, processing, and output. A system flowchart begins by identifying system inputs and their origins. The input is followed by the processing performed on the data. The resulting new information is the output component, which can be stored for later use, displayed on a screen, or printed on paper. In many instances, the output from one process is an input to another.

The sales processing system flowchart in Figure 3-10 represents Ashton's proposal to capture sales data using state-of-the-art sales terminals. These terminals will edit the sales data and print a customer receipt. All sales data will be stored in a sales data file on a disk. At the end of each day, the data will be forwarded to S&S's computers, where it will be summarized and batch totals will be printed. A batch total is the sum of a numerical item contained in each transaction being processed. An example is total sales for all sales transactions. The summary data will then be processed, and batch totals will again be generated and printed. These amounts will be compared with the batch totals generated prior to processing, and all errors and exceptions will be reconciled. The accounts receivable, inventory, and sales marketing databases and the general ledger will be updated. Users can access the files at any time by using an inquiry processing

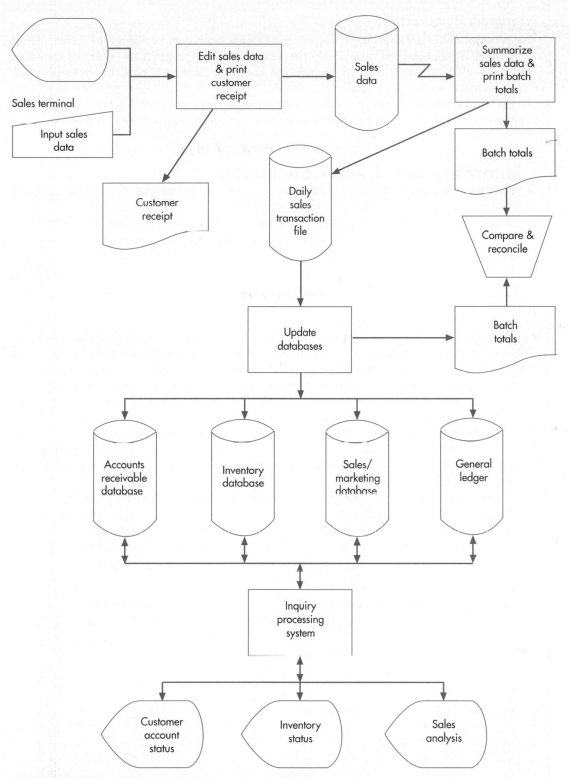

FIGURE 3-10
System Flowchart of Sales Processing at S&S

system. This system will produce standard reports and allow users to access the data needed for special analyses.

System flowcharts are an important systems analysis, design, and evaluation tool. They are universally employed in systems work and provide an immediate form of communication among workers. The system flowchart is an excellent vehicle for describing information flows and procedures within an AIS.

Program Flowcharts

A *program flowchart* illustrates the sequence of logical operations performed by a computer in executing a program. The relationship between system and program flowcharts is shown in Figure 3-11. A program flowchart describes the specific logic used to perform a process shown on a system flowchart.

Program flowcharts employ a subset of the symbols shown in Figure 3-8. Once designed and approved, the program flowchart serves as the blueprint for coding the computer program.

Summary and Case Conclusion

Ashton prepared the DFDs and flowcharts of S&S's payroll processing system (Figures 3-6, 3-7, and 3-9) to document and explain the operation of the existing system. He was pleased to see that Scott and Susan were able to grasp the essence of the system from this documentation. The DFDs indicated the logical flow of data, and the flowcharts illustrated the physical dimensions of the system: The origin and final disposition and the interworkings of the documents in each department were clear.

Susan and Scott agreed that Ashton should document the remainder of the system. The documentation would help all of them understand the current system. It would also help Ashton and the consultants design the new system. In fact, the payroll documentation had already helped them identify a few minor changes they wanted to make in their system. Using the information from Figure 3-9, Susan now understands why the payroll clerk sometimes had to borrow the only copy of the payroll report that was prepared. She thus recommended that a second copy be made and kept in the payroll department. Susan also questioned the practice of keeping all the payroll records in one employee/payroll file. To keep the file from becoming unwieldy, she recommended that it be divided into three files: personal employee data, pay period documentation, and payroll tax data. A discussion with the payroll clerk verified that this approach would make payroll processing easier and more efficient.

Over the next few weeks, Ashton documented the remaining accounting cycles. This process helped him identify inefficiencies and unneeded reports. He also found that some system documents were inadequately controlled. In addition, he got several ideas about how an automated system could help him reengineer the business processes at S&S. By substituting technology for human effort, outdated processes and procedures could be eliminated to make the system more effective.

FIGURE 3-11

Relationship Between System and Program Flowcharts

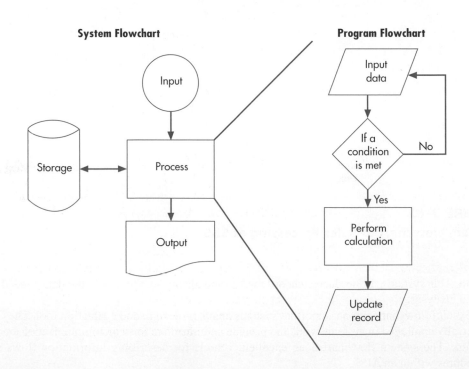

When Ashton completed his analysis and documentation of the current system, Susan and Scott asked him to continue his work in designing a new system. To do that, Ashton must thoroughly understand the information needs of the various employees in the company. Then he can design a new system using the tools that were explained in this chapter. Systems development is discussed in Chapters 20 through 22).

Key Terms

documentation 49	data flow 51	document flowchart 57
narrative description 49	process 51	internal control flowchart 57
data flow diagram (DFD) 50	data store 52	system flowchart 60
data source 50	context diagram 52	program flowchart 62
data destination 50	flowchart 55	

AIS IN ACTION

Chapter Quiz

1. A DFD is a representation of which of the following?
   a. relationship among modules, data, and programs of an AIS
   b. flow of data in an organization
   c. decision rules in a computer program
   d. computer hardware configuration

2. Documentation methods such as DFDs and flowcharts save both time and money, adding value to an organization.
   a. True   b. False

3. Which of the following statements is FALSE?
   a. Flowcharts make use of many symbols.
   b. A flowchart emphasizes the flow of documents or records containing data.
   c. DFDs help convey the timing of events.
   d. Both a and b are false.

4. A DFD consists of the following four basic elements: data sources and destinations, data flows, transformation processes, and data stores. Each is represented on a DFD by a different symbol.
   a. True   b. False

5. Which of the following is NOT one of the guidelines that should be followed in naming DFD data elements?
   a. Process names should include action verbs such as *update*, *edit*, *prepare*, and *record*.
   b. Make sure the names describe all the data or the entire process.
   c. Name only the most important DFD elements.
   d. Choose active and descriptive names.

6. The documentation skills that accountants require vary with their job function. However, they should at least be able to do which of the following?
   a. Read documentation to determine how the system works.
   b. Critique and correct documentation that others prepare.
   c. Prepare documentation for a newly developed information system.
   d. Teach others how to prepare documentation.

7. Which of the following statements is FALSE?
   a. A flowchart is an analytical technique used to describe some aspect of an information system in a clear, concise, and logical manner.
   b. Flowcharts use a standard set of symbols to describe pictorially the flow of documents and data through a system.
   c. Flowcharts are easy to prepare and revise when the designer utilizes a flowcharting software package.
   d. A system flowchart is a narrative representation of an information system.
   e. A program flowchart shows the logic used in computer programs.

8. Which of the following flowcharts illustrates the flow of information among areas of responsibility in an organization?
   a. program flowchart
   b. computer configuration chart
   c. system flowchart
   d. document flowchart

9. Which of the following is NOT one of the recommended guidelines for making flowcharts more readable, clear, concise, consistent, and understandable?
   a. Divide the flowchart into columns with labels.
   b. Flowchart all information flows, especially exception procedures and error routines.
   c. Design the flowchart so that flow proceeds from top to bottom and from left to right.
   d. Show the final disposition of all documents to prevent loose ends that leave the reader dangling.
   e. Make sure that each manual processing symbol has an input and an output.

10. How are data sources and destinations represented in a data flow diagram?
    a. as a square
    b. as a curved arrow
    c. as a circle
    d. as two parallel lines
    e. none of the above

Comprehensive Problem

Accuflow Cash Disbursements Process

SoftData, a vendor, sends an invoice to Accuflow for data warehousing support services. The invoice is sent directly to Megan Waters, the accounts payable clerk, who manually records the invoice in the accounts payable subsidiary ledger. Once the invoice is recorded, it is forwarded to Stan Phillips, the cash disbursements clerk, for processing. Stan prepares a check to pay the invoice and sends the check and invoice to John Sterling, the company treasurer. John approves and signs the check and cancels the invoice. John then mails the check back to SoftData and returns the canceled invoice to Stan for recording in the cash disbursements journal and filing. Once a week, Megan manually posts disbursements from the cash disbursements journal to the accounts payable subsidiary ledger.

Required

Prepare a document flowchart, a context diagram, a level 0 data flow diagram, and a level 1 data flow diagram for the Accuflow cash disbursement process. To maximize learning from this problem, do your best to solve it before looking at the solution at the end of the chapter.

Discussion Questions

3.1. Identify the DFD elements in the following narrative: A customer purchases a few items from a local grocery store. Jill, a salesclerk, enters the transaction in the cash register and takes the customer's money. At closing, Jill gives both the cash and the register tape to her manager.

3.2. Do you agree with the following statement: "Any one of the systems documentation procedures can be used to adequately document a given system"? Explain.

3.3. Compare the guidelines for preparing flowcharts and DFDs. What general design principles and limitations are common to both documentation techniques?

3.4. Your classmate asks you to explain flowcharting conventions using real-world examples. Draw each of the major flowchart symbols from memory, placing them into one of four categories: input/output, processing, storage, and flow and miscellaneous. For each symbol, suggest several uses.

Problems

3.1. Prepare flowcharting segments for each of the following operations:
   a. processing transactions stored on magnetic tape to update a master file stored on magnetic tape
   b. processing transactions stored on magnetic tape to update a database stored on a magnetic disk
   c. converting source documents to magnetic tape using a computer-based optical character reader (OCR)
   d. processing OCR documents online to update a database on magnetic disk
   e. reading data from a magnetic disk into the computer to be printed on a report
   f. using a computer or terminal to key data from source documents to a file stored on a magnetic disk
   g. manually sorting and filing invoices numerically
   h. using a terminal to enter source document data and send it to a remote location where an online processing system records it in a database stored on magnetic disk
   i. a scheduled automatic backup of an internal hard drive to an external hard drive
   j. using a terminal to query customer sales data maintained on a magnetic disk
   k. entering employee hours recorded on time cards in the payroll transaction file maintained on disk and updating wage data maintained on the payroll master file
   l. using a terminal to access a price list maintained on disk to complete a purchase order. An electronic copy of the purchase order is sent to the vendor and a backup copy is printed and filed by vendor name
   m. updating an airline reservation on a Web-based airline reservation system from a home computer

3.2. The Happy Valley Utility Company uses turnaround documents in its computerized customer accounting system. Meter readers are provided with preprinted computer forms, each containing the account number, name, address, and previous meter readings. Each form also contains a formatted area in which the customer's current meter reading can be marked in pencil. After making their rounds, meter readers turn in batches of these documents to the computer data preparation department, where they are processed by a mark-sense document reader that transfers their contents to magnetic tape.

   This magnetic tape file is used as input for two computer runs. The first run sorts the transaction records on the tape into sequential order by customer account number. On the second run, the sorted transaction tape is processed against the customer master file, which is stored on a magnetic disk. Second-run outputs are (1) a printed report listing summary information and any erroneous transactions detected by the computer and (2) customer bills printed in a special OCR-readable font. Bills are mailed, and customers are requested to return the stub portion along with payment.

   Customer payments are received in the mailroom and checked for consistency against the returned remittance stubs. Checks are then sent to the cashier's office. The mailroom provides the computer data preparation department with three sets of records: (1) stubs with compatible amounts, (2) stubs with differing amounts, and (3) a list of amounts received from customers, without stubs. For the latter two types of records, data preparation personnel use a special off-line keying device to prepare corrected stubs. An

OCR document reader reads all the stubs and sends the data to the company's computer. The computer updates the customer master file to post the payment amounts. Two printed outputs from this second process are (1) reports listing erroneous transactions and summary information and (2) past-due customer balances.

Required

a. Draw a system flowchart of the billing operations, commencing with the computer preparation of the meter reading forms and ending with the mailing of customer bills.
b. Draw a system flowchart depicting customer payments processing, starting with the mailroom operations and ending with the two printed reports.

3.3. The Dewey Construction Company processes its payroll transactions to update both its payroll master file and its work-in-process master file in the same computer run. Both files are stored on magnetic disk.

Job time tickets are keyed onto a tape using an off-line key-to-tape encoder. The tape is then processed to update the files. The processing run also produces a payroll register on magnetic tape, employee paychecks and earnings statements, and a printed report listing error transactions and summary information.

Required

Prepare a system flowchart of the process described.

3.4. Prepare a document flowchart to reflect how ANGIC Insurance Company processes its casualty claims. The process begins when the claims department receives a notice of loss from a claimant. The claims department prepares and sends the claimant four copies of a proof-of-loss form on which the claimant must detail the cause, amount, and other aspects of the loss. The claims department also initiates a record of the claim, which is sent with the notice of loss to the data processing department, where it is filed by claim number.

The claimant must fill out the proof-of-loss forms with an adjuster's assistance. The adjuster must concur with the claimant on the estimated amount of loss. The claimant and adjuster each keep one copy of the proof-of-loss form. The adjustor files his copy numerically. The adjustor sends the first two copies to the claims department. Separately, the adjuster submits a report to the claims department, confirming the estimates on the claimant's proof-of-loss form.

The claims department authorizes a payment to the claimant, forwards a copy of the proof-of-loss form to data processing, and files the original proof-of-loss form and the adjuster's report alphabetically. The data processing department prepares payment checks and mails them to the customers, files the proof-of-loss form with the claim record, and prepares a list of cash disbursements, which it transmits to the accounting department.

3.5. Beccan Company is a discount tire dealer operating 25 retail stores in the metropolitan area. The company operates a centralized purchasing and warehousing facility and employs a perpetual inventory system. All purchases of tires and related supplies are placed through the company's central purchasing department to optimize quantity discounts. The tires and supplies are received at the central warehouse and distributed to the retail stores as needed. The perpetual inventory system at the central facility maintains current inventory records, designated reorder points, and optimum order quantities for each type and size of tire and other related supplies. Beccan uses the following five documents in its inventory control system.

- **Retail stores requisition.** The retail stores submit a retail store requisition to the central warehouse when they need tires or supplies. The warehouse shipping clerks fill the orders from inventory and authorize store deliveries.
- **Purchase requisition.** The inventory control clerk prepares a purchase requisition when the quantity on hand for an item falls below the designated reorder point and forwards it to the purchasing department.
- **Purchase order.** The purchasing department prepares a purchase order when items need to be ordered and submits it to an authorized vendor.

- **Receiving report.** The warehouse department prepares a receiving report when ordered items are received from vendors. The receiving clerk indicates the vendor's name and the date and quantity of the shipment received.
- **Invoice.** An invoice is received from vendors, specifying the amounts Beccan owes.

The following departments are involved in Beccan's inventory control system:

- **Inventory control department.** Responsible for the maintenance of all perpetual inventory records, including quantity on hand, reorder point, optimum order quantity, and quantity on order for each item carried.
- **Warehouse department.** Maintains the physical inventory of all items carried in stock. All orders from vendors are received (receiving clerk) and all distributions to retail stores are filled (shipping clerks) in this department.
- **Purchasing department.** Places all orders for items needed by the company.
- **Accounts payable department.** Maintains all open accounts with vendors and other creditors, in addition to processing payments.

Required

a. Prepare a document flowchart that indicates the interaction and use of these documents among all departments at Beccan Company's central facility. It should provide adequate internal control over the receipt, issuance, replenishment, and payment of tires and supplies. You may assume that there are a sufficient number of document copies to ensure that the perpetual inventory system has the necessary basic internal controls.
b. Using the flowcharting conventions discussed in Focus 3-2, critique the instructor provided CMA solution. List all the ways the CMA solution violates those flowcharting guidelines. *(CMA Examination, adapted)*

3.6. As the internal auditor for No-Wear Products, you have been asked to document the company's payroll processing system. Based on your documentation, No-Wear hopes to develop a plan for revising the current system to eliminate unnecessary delays in paycheck processing. The head payroll clerk explained the system:

> The payroll processing system at No-Wear Products is fairly simple. Time data are recorded in each department using time cards and clocks. It is annoying, however, when people forget to punch out at night, and we have to record their time by hand. At the end of the period, our payroll clerks enter the time card data into a payroll file for processing. Our clerks are pretty good—though I've had to make my share of corrections when they mess up the data entry.
>
> Before the payroll file is processed for the current period, human resources sends us personnel changes, such as increases in pay rates and new employees. Our clerks enter this information into the payroll file. Usually, when mistakes get back to us, it's because human resources is recording the wrong pay rate or an employee has left and the department forgets to remove the record.
>
> The data are processed and individual employee paychecks are generated. Several reports are generated for management—though I don't know what they do with them. In addition, the government requires regular federal and state withholding reports for tax purposes. Currently, the system generates these reports automatically, which is nice.

Required

a. Prepare a context diagram and level 0 DFD to document the payroll processing system at No-Wear Products.
b. Prepare a document flowchart to document the payroll processing system at No-Wear Products.

3.7. Ashton Fleming has decided to document and analyze the accounts payable process at S&S so the transition to a computerized system will be easier. He also hopes to improve any weaknesses he discovers in the system. In the following narrative, Ashton explains what happens at S&S:

> Before S&S pays a vendor invoice, the invoice must be matched against the purchase order used to request the goods and the receiving report that the receiving department prepares. Because all three of these documents enter the accounts payable department at different times, a separate alphabetical file is kept for each type of document. The purchase orders that are forwarded from purchasing are stored in a purchase order file. The receiving reports are stored in a receiving report file. When vendor invoices are received, the accounts payable clerk records the amount due in the accounts payable file and files the invoices in the vendor invoice file.
>
> S&S pays all accounts within 10 days to take advantage of early-payment discounts. When it is time to pay a bill, the accounts payable clerk retrieves the vendor invoice, attaches the purchase order and the receiving report, and forwards the matched documents to Ashton Fleming.
>
> Ashton reviews the documents to ensure they are complete, prepares a two-part check, forwards all the documents to Susan, and records the check in the cash disbursements journal.
>
> Susan reviews the documents to ensure that they are valid payables and signs the checks. She forwards the check to the vendor and returns the documents and the check copy to the accounts payable clerk. The clerk files the documents alphabetically in a paid invoice file. At the end of every month, the accounts payable clerk uses the accounts payable ledger to prepare an accounts payable report that is forwarded to Susan. After she is finished with the report, Susan files it chronologically.

Required

a. Prepare a context diagram and a level 0 DFD to document accounts payable processing at S&S.
b. Prepare a document flowchart to document accounts payable processing at S&S.

3.8. Since opening its doors in Hawaii two years ago, Oriental Trading has enjoyed tremendous success. Oriental Trading purchases textiles from Asia and resells them to local retail shops. To keep up with the strong demand, Oriental Trading is expanding its local operations, including a new information system to handle the tremendous increase in purchases.

The following is a summary of your interviews with department supervisors who interact with the acquisition/payment system:

> A purchase requisition is sent from the inventory system to Sky Ishibashi, a purchasing department clerk . Sky prepares a purchase order using the vendor and inventory files and mails it to the vendor. The vendor returns a vendor acknowledgment to Sky indicating receipt of the purchase order. Sky then sends a purchase order notification to Elei Mateaki, an accounts payable clerk.
>
> When the receiving department accepts vendor goods, the inventory system sends Elei a receiving report. Elei also receives invoices from the various vendors. He matches the invoices with the purchase order notification and the receiving report and updates the accounts payable master file. Elei then sends a payment authorization to the accounting department. There, Andeloo Nonu prepares and mails a check to the vendor. When the check is issued, the system automatically updates the accounts payable master file and the general ledger.

Required

a. Develop a context diagram and a level 0 DFD of the acquisition/payment system at Oriental Trading.
b. Prepare a document flowchart to document the acquisition/payment system at Oriental Trading.

3.9. Ashton Fleming has asked you to develop a comprehensive DFD for the cash receipts system. Ashton's narrative of the system follows:

> Customer payments include cash received at the time of purchase and payments received in the mail. At day's end, the treasurer endorses all checks and prepares a

deposit slip for the checks and the cash. A clerk deposits the checks, cash, and deposit slip at the local bank each day. When checks are received as payment for accounts due, a remittance slip is included with the payment. The remittance slips are used to update the accounts receivable file at the end of the day. The remittance slips are stored in a file drawer by date.

Every week, a cash receipts report and an aged trial balance are generated using the accounts receivable ledger. The cash receipts report is sent to Scott and Susan. A copy of the aged trial balance is sent to the credit and collections department.

Required

a. Develop a context diagram and a level 0 DFD for the cash receipts system at S&S.
b. Prepare a document flowchart for the cash receipts system at S&S.

3.10. A mail-order skin and body care company advertises in magazines. Magazine subscribers initiate most orders by completing and sending coupons directly to the company. The firm also takes orders by phone, answers inquiries about products, and handles payments and cancellations of orders. Products that have been ordered are sent either directly to the customer or to the company's regional offices that handle the required distribution. The mail-order company has three basic data files, which contain customer mailing information, product inventory information, and billing information based on invoice number. During the next few years, the company expects to become a multimillion-dollar operation. Recognizing the need to computerize much of the mail-order business, the company has begun the process by calling you.

Required

Draw a context diagram and at least two levels of DFDs for the preceding operations.

3.11. The local college requires that each student complete a registration request form and mail or deliver it to the registrar's office. A clerk enters the request into the system. The system checks the accounts receivable subsystem to ensure that no fees are owed. Next, for each course, the system checks the student transcript to ensure that he or she has completed the course prerequisites. Then the system checks class position availability and adds the student's Social Security number to the class list.

The report back to the student shows the result of registration processing: If the student owes fees, a bill is sent and the registration is rejected. If prerequisites for a course are not fulfilled, the student is notified and that course is not registered. If the class is full, the student request is annotated with "course closed." If a student is accepted into a class, then the day, time, and room are printed next to the course number. Student fees and total tuition are computed and printed on the form. Student fee information is interfaced to the accounts receivable subsystem. Course enrollment reports are prepared for the instructors.

Required

a. Prepare a context diagram and at least two levels of DFDs for this operation.
b. Prepare a document flowchart for this operation.

3.12. Charting, Inc., a new audit client of yours, processes its sales and cash receipts documents in the following manner:

1. *Payment on account.* Each morning a mail clerk in the sales department opens the mail and prepares a remittance advice (showing customer and amount paid) if one is not received. The checks and remittance advices are forwarded to the sales department supervisor, who reviews each check and forwards the checks and remittance advices to the accounting department supervisor.

The accounting department supervisor, who also functions as credit manager (approving new credit and credit limits), reviews all checks for payments on past-due accounts. He forwards the checks and remittance advices to the accounts receivable clerk, who arranges the advices in alphabetical order. The remittance advices are posted directly to the accounts receivable ledger. The checks are endorsed and the total is posted to the cash receipts journal. The remittance advices are filed chronologically. After receiving the cash from the previous day's cash sales, the accounts receivable clerk prepares the daily deposit slip in triplicate. The third copy of the deposit slip is filed by date, and the second copy and the original accompany the bank deposit.

2. *Sales.* Sales clerks prepare sales invoices in triplicate. The original and the second copy are presented to the cashier. The sales clerk retains the third copy in the sales book. When a sale is for cash, the customer pays the sales clerk, who gives the money to the cashier with the invoice copies.

   The cashier approves a credit sale from an approved credit list after the sales clerk prepares the three-part invoice. After receiving the cash or approving the invoice, the cashier validates the original copy of the sales invoice and gives it to the customer. At the end of each day, the cashier recaps the sales and cash received and forwards the cash and the second copy of the sales invoices to the accounts receivable clerk.

   The accounts receivable clerk balances the cash received with cash sales invoices and prepares a daily sales summary. The credit sales invoices are posted to the accounts receivable ledger, and then all invoices are sent to the inventory control clerk in the sales department for posting to the inventory control cards. After posting, the inventory control clerk files all invoices numerically. The accounts receivable clerk posts the daily sales summary to the cash receipts and sales journals and files the sales summaries by date.

   The cash from cash sales is combined with the cash received on account to make up the daily bank deposit.

3. *Bank deposits.* The bank validates the deposit slip and returns the second copy to the accounting department, where the accounts receivable clerk files it by date.

   Monthly bank statements are reconciled promptly by the accounting department supervisor and filed by date.

Required

You recognize weaknesses in the existing system and believe a document flowchart would be beneficial in evaluating the client's internal control in preparing for your examination of the financial statements.

a. Complete the flowchart given in Figure 3-12, for sales and cash receipts of Charting, Inc., by labeling the appropriate symbols and indicating information flows.

b. Using the guidelines for preparing flowcharts in Focus 3-2 and the flowcharting symbols shown in Figure 3-8, critique the flowchart shown in Figure 3-12. List the ways the flowchart violates the guidelines or uses improper symbols. *(CPA Examination, adapted)*

3.13. A partially completed flowchart appears in Figure 3-13. The flowchart depicts the credit sales activities of the Bottom Manufacturing Corporation.

When a customer's purchase order is received, a six-part sales order is prepared and distributed as follows:

Copy 1—Billing copy, to billing department

Copy 2—Shipping copy, to shipping department

Copy 3—Credit copy, to credit department

Copy 4—Stock request copy, to credit department

Copy 5—Customer copy, to customer

Copy 6—Sales order copy, filed in sales order department

When each copy of the sales order reaches the appropriate department or destination, it calls for specific internal control procedures and related documents. Some procedures and related documents are indicated on the flowchart; others are labeled by the letters *a* to *r*.

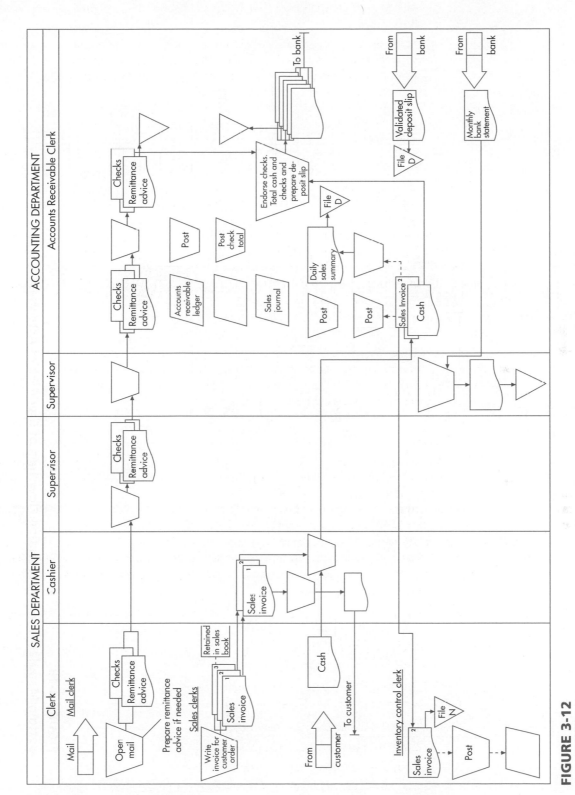

FIGURE 3-12

Charting, Inc., Flowchart for Sales and Cash Receipts

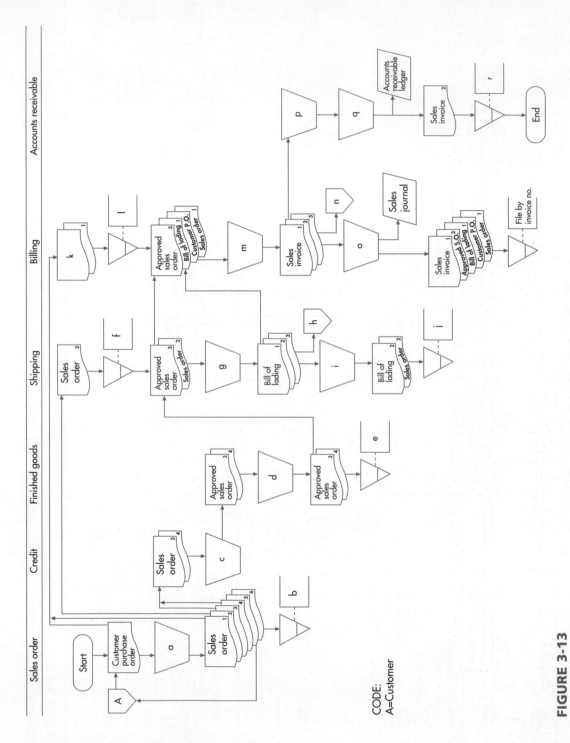

FIGURE 3-13

Bottom Manufacturing Corporation Flowchart of Credit Sales Activities

Required

a. List the procedures or the internal documents that are labeled letters *c* to *r* in the flow-chart of Bottom Manufacturing Corporation's charge sales system. Organize your answer as follows (Note that the explanations of the letters *a* and *b* in the flowchart are entered as examples):

Flowchart Symbol Letter	Procedures or Internal Document
a	Prepare six-part sales order.
b	File by order number.

b. Using the guidelines for preparing flowcharts in Focus 3-2 and the flowcharting symbols shown in Figure 3-8, critique the flowchart shown in Figure 3-13. List the ways the flow-chart violates the guidelines or uses improper symbols. (*CPA Examination, adapted*)

3.14. Prepare a context diagram and a level 0 data flow diagram for each of the following situations.

a. Prepare and file a tax return with the tax owed to the Internal Revenue Service.

b. A customer pays an invoice with a check. Accounts receivable is updated to reflect the payment. The check is recorded and deposited into the bank.

c. A customer places an online order to purchase merchandise. The order is approved, filled, and sent to the customer with an invoice.

d. An inventory request is received by the purchasing department. The purchasing depart-ment prepares and sends a purchase order to the appropriate vendor.

e. A vendor invoice is received, reviewed, and compared against the appropriate purchase order, then paid and filed.

f. A bill of lading for ordered inventory is received from a vendor, recorded, checked against the appropriate purchase order, and filed.

3.15. Melanie is doing a study on various weight-loss plans and needs to determine an individ-ual's weight status by calculating his body mass index. To calculate a person's body mass index, height must be measured in meters and weight measured in kilograms. The index is calculated by dividing a person's weight by the square of his height. The result is then compared to the following scale to determine the person's weight status: Below 18.5 = underweight; 18.5–24.5 = normal weight; over 25.0 = overweight. Five hundred people have agreed to participate in Melanie's study. With so many calculations to perform, she would like a computer program that will do this calculation for her. She decides to prepare a flowchart to help her properly design the computer program.

Required

Prepare a program flowchart to help Melanie program this process.

3.16. Match the flowchart, context diagram, or data flow diagram segments in the right column to an appropriate description in the left column.

1. Statements are prepared and sent to customers from data contained in the accounts receivable data store.

A.

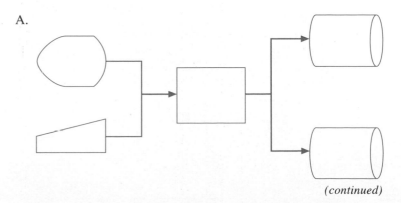

(*continued*)

2. A customer sends a sales invoice to the accounts payable process.

B.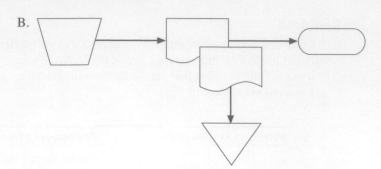

3. A check is manually prepared from data on a vendor invoice.

C.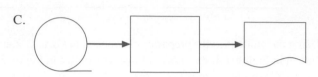

4. The cash receipt process updates the cash receipts data store.

D.

5. A sales invoice is manually prepared and sent to a customer.

E.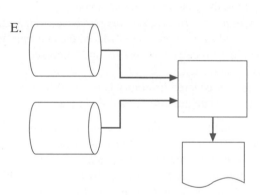

6. A report is prepared from data stored on magnetic tape.

F.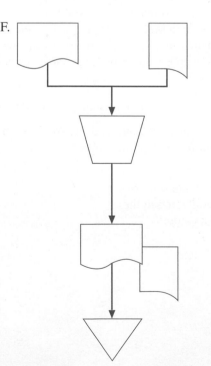

7. Billing data are entered online and used to update the sales order file and the customer master file.

G.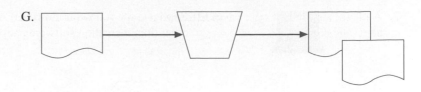

8. Data from a cancelled invoice are used to update the cash disbursements ledger.

H.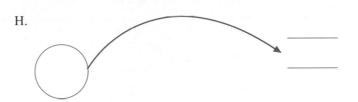

9. A sales order is prepared manually. Copy 1 is sent to the warehouse, and copy 2 is filed.

I.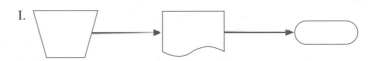

10. An accounts receivable aging report is prepared from the accounts receivable master file and the cash receipts master file, both stored on disk.

J.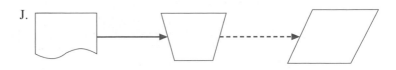

11. An error listing and batch total are compared and filed.

K.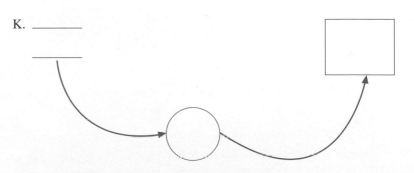

3.17. Replicate the following flowchart in Visio, Microsoft Word, Microsoft Excel, or some other documentation software package.

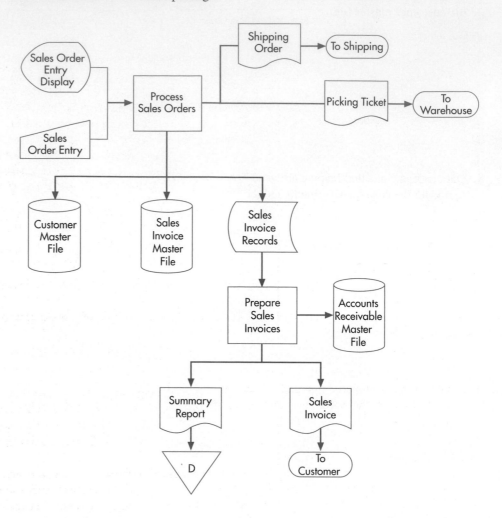

3.18. Replicate the following data flow diagram in Visio, Microsoft Word, Microsoft Excel, or some other documentation software package.

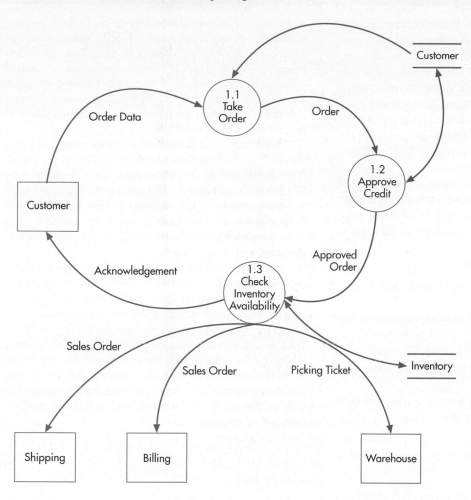

Case 3-1 Dub 5

You are the systems analyst for the Wee Willie Williams Widget Works (also known as Dub 5, which is a shortened version of 5 Ws). Dub 5 has been producing computer keyboard components for more than 20 years and has recently signed an exclusive 10-year contract to provide the keyboards for all Dell personal computers. As the systems analyst, you have been assigned the task of developing a level 0 DFD for Dub 5's order processing system. You have finished gathering all the information you need to develop the first-pass DFD and now want to complete the diagram.

Customer orders, which are all credit sales, arrive via e-mail and by phone. When an order is processed, a number of other documents are prepared. You have diagrammed the overall process and the documents produced, as shown in the context diagram shown below.

The following documents are created:

- Order processing creates a packing slip, which the warehouse uses to fill the order.
- A customer invoice is prepared and sent once the goods have been shipped.
- When orders are not accepted, an order rejection is sent to the customer, explaining why the order cannot be filled.
- A receivables notice, which is a copy of the customer invoice, is sent to the accounting department so accounts receivable records can be updated.

After reviewing your notes, you write the following narrative summary:

When an order comes in, the order processing clerk checks the customer's credit file to confirm credit approval and

ensure that the amount falls within the credit limit. If either of these conditions is not met, the order is sent to the credit department. If an order meets both conditions, the order-processing clerk enters it into the system on a standard order form. The information on the form is used to update the company's customer file (in which the name, address, and other information are stored), and the form is placed in the company's open order file.

When the credit department receives a rejected order, the credit clerk determines why the order has been rejected. If the credit limit has been exceeded, the customer is notified that the merchandise will be shipped as soon as Dub 5 receives payment. If the customer has not been approved for credit, a credit application is sent to the customer along with a notification that the order will be shipped as soon as credit approval is granted.

Before preparing a packing slip, the system checks the inventory records to determine whether the company has the products ordered on hand. If the items are in stock, a packing slip is prepared and sent to the warehouse.

Once notification of shipped goods has been received from the warehouse, a customer invoice is prepared. A copy is filed by the order processing department, another is sent to the customer, and another is sent to the accounting department so that accounts receivables can be updated. A note is placed in the customer file indicating that the invoice has been sent.

From the information presented, complete a Level 0 DFD for order processing and a Level 1 DFD for the credit review process for Dub 5.

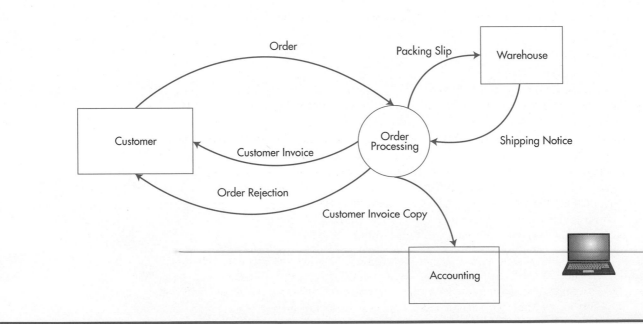

AIS IN ACTION SOLUTIONS

Quiz Key

1. A DFD is a representation of which of the following?
   a. relationship among modules, data, and programs of an AIS [Incorrect. A flowchart represents the relationship among modules, data, and programs.]
   ▶ b. flow of data in an organization [Correct.]
   c. decision rules in a computer program [Incorrect. A DFD is a graphical representation of how data move through an organization. Decision rules are objective statements specific to computer programs.]
   d. computer hardware configuration [Incorrrect. This relates to how various parts of a computer fit together.]

2. Documentation methods such as DFDs and flowcharts save both time and money, adding value to an organization.
   ▶ a. True [Correct. A picture is worth a thousand words: An individual may learn more and learn it more quickly by studying the DFD or flowchart of a system than by reading a narrative description of the same system.]
   b. False [Incorrect]

3. Which of the following statements is FALSE?
   a. Flowcharts make use of many symbols. [Incorrect. The statement is true. See Figure 3-8 for an illustration of the many symbols used in flowcharts.]
   b. A document flowchart emphasizes the flow of documents or records containing data. [Incorrect. The statement is true. The reason it is called a document flowchart is that it shows the flow of documents or records containing data.]
   ▶ c. DFDs help convey the timing of events. [Correct. DFDs show data movement, but not necessarily the timing of the movement.]
   d. Both a and b are false. [Incorrect. As explained above, a and b are true statements.]

4. A DFD consists of the following four basic elements: data sources and destinations, data flows, transformation processes, and data stores. Each is represented on a DFD by a different symbol.
   ▶ a. True [Correct. The four elements of DFDs are illustrated in Figure 3-1.]
   b. False [Incorrect]

5. Which of the following is NOT one of the guidelines that should be followed in naming DFD data elements?
   a. Process names should include action verbs such as *update*, *edit*, *prepare*, and *record*. [Incorrect. Action verbs should be used to name process data elements. See item 11 in Focus 3-1.]
   b. Make sure the names describe all the data or the entire process. [Incorrect. Data element names should reflect what is known about the element. See item 11 in Focus 3-1.]
   ▶ c. Name only the most important DFD elements. [Correct. All data elements should be named, with the exception of data flows into data stores, when the inflows and outflows make naming the data store redundant. See item 11 in Focus 3-1.]
   d. Choose active and descriptive names. [Incorrect. Active and descriptive names should be used in naming data elements. See item 11 in Focus 3-1.]

6. The documentation skills that accountants require vary with their job function. However, all accountants should at least be able to do which of the following?
   ▶ a. Read documentation to determine how the system works. [Correct. All accountants should at least be able to read and understand system documentation.]
   b. Critique and correct documentation that others prepare. [Incorrect. Although senior accountants may critique and correct documentation prepared by junior accountants, at a minimum all accountants need to be able to read and understand documentation.]

    c. Prepare documentation for a newly developed information system. [Incorrect. Some accountants may need to develop internal control documentation, but system developers and analysts normally prepare systems documentation.]

    d. Teach others how to prepare documentation. [Incorrect. Most accountants will not be asked to teach documentation skills.]

7. Which of the following statements is FALSE?

    a. A flowchart is an analytical technique used to describe some aspect of an information system in a clear, concise, and logical manner. [Incorrect. This is the definition of a flowchart given previously in the text.]

    b. Flowcharts use a standard set of symbols to describe pictorially the flow of documents and data through a system. [Incorrect. The symbols used for flowcharting are shown in Figure 3-8.]

    c. Flowcharts are easy to prepare and revise when the designer utilizes a flowcharting software package. [Incorrect. There are a number of good flowcharting software packages that make it easy to draw and modify flowcharts.]

▶ d. A system flowchart is a narrative representation of an information system. [Correct. A flowchart is a graphical rather than a narrative representation of an information system.]

    e. A program flowchart shows the logic used in computer programs. [Incorrect. A program flowchart illustrates program logic and the structure of the program.]

8. Which of the following flowcharts illustrates the flow of information among areas of responsibility in an organization?

    a. program flowchart [Incorrect. A program flowchart documents a computer program.]

    b. computer configuration chart [Incorrect. A computer configuration chart illustrates how computer hardware is arranged and implemented.]

    c. system flowchart [Incorrect. A system flowchart illustrates the relationship among inputs, processes, and outputs of a system, not areas of responsibility.]

▶ d. document flowchart [Correct. A document flowchart traces the life of a document from its cradle to its grave as it works its way through the areas of responsibility within an organization.]

9. Which of the following is NOT one of the recommended guidelines for making flowcharts more readable, clear, concise, consistent, and understandable?

    a. Divide the flowchart into columns with labels. [Incorrect. Dividing the flowchart into columns helps make it more readable, clear, concise, consistent, and understandable. See item 3 in Focus 3-2.]

▶ b. Flowchart all information flows, especially exception procedures and error routines. [Correct. Including all exception procedures and error routines clutters the flowchart and makes it difficult to read and understand. See item 4 in Focus 3-2.]

    c. Design the flowchart so that flow proceeds from top to bottom and from left to right. [Incorrect. Flowcharts should be prepared so that they are read like a book. See item 5 in Focus 3-2.]

    d. Show the final disposition of all documents to prevent loose ends that leave the reader dangling. [Incorrect. All documents should be placed either in a file or sent to another entity. See item 6 in Focus 3-2.]

    e. Make sure that each manual processing symbol has an input and an output. [Incorrect. A manual process must have an input and an output. Without an input, nothing can be processed; and without an output, there is no evidence of processing. See item 10 in Focus 3-2.]

10. How are data sources and destinations represented in a data flow diagram?

▶ a. as a square [Correct. See Figure 3-1.]

    b. as a curved arrow [Incorrect. A curved arrow represents a data flow. See Figure 3-1.]

    c. as a circle [Incorrect. A circle represents a process. See Figure 3-1.]

    d. as two parallel lines [Incorrect. Two parallel lines represent a data store. See Figure 3-1.]

    e. as none of the above [Incorrect. Option a is correct.]

Comprehensive Problem Solution

Flowchart

The first step in preparing a document flowchart is to become familiar with the problem. The next step is to identify the primary actors or major players. In this problem there are three major players: Megan Waters (accounts payable clerk), Stan Phillips (cash disbursement clerk), and John Sterling (treasurer). Since we are documenting Accuflow's cash disbursement process, we are not interested in the internal workings of the vendor, SoftData. As a result, we do not include it as one of our major players. Now that we have identified the major players, we can list their functions in Table 3-3. Note that forwarding to and receiving from the next major player are not considered functions in preparing document flowcharts.

We will now explain, step by step, how to create the document flowchart solution for Accuflow shown in Figure 3-14. To document the functions of the three major players, divide the document flowchart into three columns, one for each player. It is usually best to arrange the columns in the order in which they occur and to use the primary function of the major player as the column name. Because the accounts payable clerk receives the invoice from the vendor, we place her in the first column. After the accounts payable clerk records the invoice, she sends it to the cash disbursements clerk, who prepares a check and sends it to the treasurer. Therefore, the cash disbursements clerk should be in the second column, and the treasurer should be in the last column, as illustrated in Figure 3-14.

Because the process begins with an invoice from an external party (a vendor), a terminal symbol with the term "From Vendor" is placed in the upper left portion of the Accounts Payable Clerk column. Next, a document symbol with the words "Vendor Invoice" printed inside it is placed below the terminal symbol. An arrow representing the document's flow and the order of operations connects the two symbols.

According to the narrative, Megan manually records the invoice in the accounts payable subsidiary ledger. Thus, a manual process symbol with the words "Record Invoice" is placed below the invoice document symbol, and the two symbols are connected with an arrow. Then, a journal/ledger symbol, also called an input/output symbol, is placed to the side of the manual process. Because only information from the invoice is used to update the accounts payable subsidiary ledger, a dotted arrow is used to connect the two symbols. A new vendor invoice symbol is drawn below the record invoice symbol.

Because the vendor invoice moves from the accounts payable clerk to the cash disbursements clerk, the vendor invoice symbol is placed at the top of the cash disbursements column with an arrow connecting the two representations of the same document. We redraw the vendor invoice symbol in the cash disbursements clerk column to make the flowchart easier to read.

To show that the cash disbursement clerk prepares a check to pay the vendor invoice, a manual process symbol with "Prepare Check" inside it is placed next to the vendor invoice. We could have placed it below the invoice symbol but put it beside it to save space. Two document symbols are placed below the manual process for the vendor invoice and the newly prepared check.

The cash disbursements clerk then sends the invoice and check to the treasurer. As a result, the vendor invoice and check appear in the Treasurer column. A manual symbol with "Approve & Sign Check; Cancel Invoice" inside is used to show that the check is signed and the invoice is cancelled. The documents are again shown in the flowchart, this time with new titles (Cancelled Invoice and Signed Check) to show the changed nature of the documents. The treasurer sends the signed check to the vendor, which is illustrated using a terminal symbol with words "To Vendor" written in it.

TABLE 3-3 Accuflow's Table of Functions

Accounts Payable Clerk (Megan Waters)	Cash Disbursements Clerk (Stan Phillips)	Treasurer (John Sterling)
Receives invoice	Prepares check	Approves and signs check
Records invoice	Records cash disbursement	Cancels invoice
Posts cash disbursement	Files cancelled invoice	Mails check

FIGURE 3-14
Accuflow's Document Flowchart

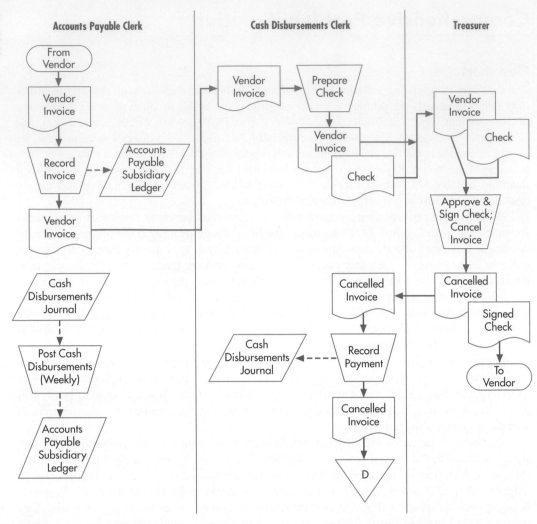

The cancelled invoice is used to record the cash disbursement in the cash disbursements journal, so it is sent back to the middle column (Cash Disbursements). A manual process symbol with "Record Payment" inside it and a dotted arrow are used to show that the disbursement is recorded in the cash disbursements journal, represented by a journal/ledger symbol. To illustrate that the cancelled invoice is filed by date, it is shown, using appropriate arrows, as exiting the record payment manual process and entering a file. A "D" is placed in the file symbol to indicate that the documents are filed by date.

Each week, the accounts payable clerk manually posts entries from the cash disbursements journal to the accounts payable subsidiary ledger. To show this, the cash disbursements journal symbol is reproduced in the accounts payable clerk column, and a manual process symbol with the words "Post Cash Disbursements (Weekly)" is placed under it. Dotted arrows show information from this journal being entered into the accounts payable subsidiary ledger.

This completes the document flowchart for the Accuflow Company's cash disbursements process.

Context Diagram

A context diagram is an overview of the information process being documented. As such, a context diagram includes a single transformation process (circle or bubble) and the data sources and data destinations that send or receive data directly from the transformation process. Thus, the first step in preparing a context diagram is to draw a single circle or bubble and then label it with a name that best describes the process being documented. In this case, "Cash Disbursements System" effectively describes the process (see Figure 3-15).

The next step is to draw and label squares for the entities that either send data to the cash disbursements process or receive data from the cash disbursements process. In this example, there is

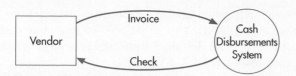

FIGURE 3-15

Accuflow's Context Diagram

a single entity—the vendor that acts as both a source and a destination of data to/from the cash disbursements process. In other processes, an outside entity could be just a source or a destination of data, and there could be more than one source or destination of data.

The last step is to connect the process (circle) with the source/destination (square) with arrows representing data flows. In this case, we have two arrows representing an invoice sent to Accuflow's cash disbursement process and a check sent to the vendor from Accuflow.

Level 0 Data Flow Diagram

In the context diagram, we saw the entire cash disbursements process in one bubble. In a level 0 DFD, we break down the cash disbursements process into its major functions. In reading the narrative, we find the following five primary steps in the cash disbursements process at Accuflow:

1. Receive vendor invoice and record payable
2. Prepare the check
3. Sign and send the check and cancel the invoice
4. Record the cash disbursement
5. Post the cash disbursements to the accounts payable ledger

Each of these processes is represented by a circle or bubble in Figure 3-16. Since this is the level 0 DFD, we assign each of these processes a real number, with the first digit after the decimal point being a zero. We also place the circles in the order that the data should flow in the process. As a result, "Receive and Record Invoice" is assigned process 1.0, "Prepare Check" is assigned process 2.0, "Approve and Sign Check" is 3.0, "Record Cash Disbursement" is 4.0, and "Post Cash Disbursement to Accounts Payable Ledger" is 5.0. This numbering system allows us to

FIGURE 3-16

Accuflow's Level 0 Data Flow Diagram

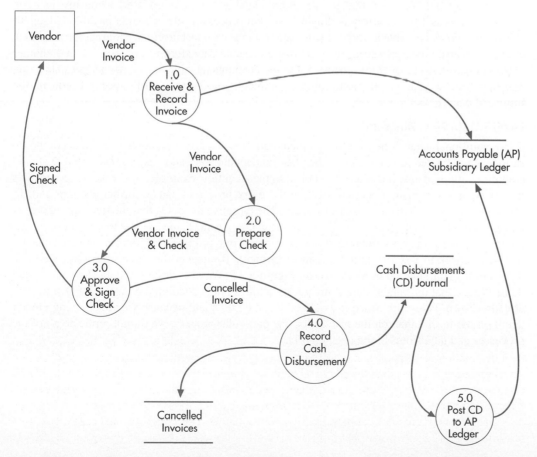

decompose these processes into more detailed subprocesses and still keep a consistent numbering system. Thus, if we needed to decompose process 3.0 to a more detailed level, we could assign subprocess bubbles as 3.1, 3.2, 3.3, etc. We can even provide greater detail by decomposing process 3.1 into subprocesses 3.1.1, 3.1.2, 3.1.3, etc.

Next, we place the data sources and data destinations on the level 0 DFD. Because we had only one data source and destination (i.e., the vendor), we draw a square and label it "Vendor." It is very important that we reconcile back to the context diagram when we prepare the different levels of DFDs. That is, the same data sources and destinations that appeared on the context diagram must also appear on the level 0 DFD. No new data sources and destinations may appear on the level 0 DFD. If, when preparing the level 0 DFD, you discover that a data source/destination is necessary to document the system properly, then you must revise the context diagram with the new data source/destination, because the context diagram should represent the entire process.

Once the data source/destinations and processes are drawn, we then connect them by drawing the arrows between the appropriate symbols. These arrows represent the data moving or flowing from one process to another and from one source or destination to or from a particular process. Accordingly, we have a vendor invoice moving from the vendor to the "Receive and Record Invoice" process and from that process to the "Prepare Check" process. The vendor invoice and a check move from the "Prepare Check" process to the "Approve and Sign Check" process. We also have arrows leaving process 3.0 to represent the signed check being sent to the vendor and the cancelled invoice going to process 4.0, "Record Cash Disbursements."

Some processes require that data be stored. As a result, we also draw any necessary files or data stores. The level 0 DFD is the first time data stores appear in a DFD set. (Note: Data stores should not be represented on a context diagram.) Data store labels should identify the data being sent to or from it. As a result, labeling the data flows to or from data stores is normally unnecessary. Data stores are prepared by drawing two parallel lines and inserting the name of the data store between the parallel lines.

In Figure 3-16 we have three data stores: the cash disbursements journal, accounts payable subsidiary ledger, and the cancelled invoices data store. Because the cash disbursements journal is updated in process 4.0, a data flow is sent from the process 4.0 circle to the cash disbursements journal data store. To show that the accounts payable ledger is updated when invoices are received (process 1.0), an arrow is drawn from that process to the accounts payable ledger. To show that accounts payable is updated with data from the cash disbursements journal (process 5.0), a data flow arrow is drawn from the cash disbursements data store to process 5.0, and another data flow arrow is drawn from process 5.0 to the accounts payable subsidiary ledger data store. The update takes place weekly, but unlike document flowcharts, a DFD does not indicate the timing of data flows.

Level 1 Data Flow Diagram

When additional detail is needed to document data flows, a process bubble may be decomposed further. As indicated in Focus 3-1, to be clear, understandable, and easy to read, a DFD should contain no more than seven process bubbles. In the Accuflow example, we broke the company's data flows into five main processes. Each of these five processes can be further decomposed. To illustrate this, we will decompose process 3.0. The narrative indicates that the treasurer approves and signs the prepared check, sends it to the vendor, and cancels the invoice to prevent duplicate payments. Therefore, we will break down process 3.0 into process 3.1 (approve and sign check), 3.2 (send check to vendor), and 3.3 (cancel invoice). To display the three processes, we draw three circles and label them as shown on Figure 3-17. We also draw the data flows and label them. Notice that the vendor data source/destination is not needed on the level 1 DFD since it is already shown on level 0. Since it would clutter the DFD, and because we are showing greater detail on the level 1 than on the level 0 for one particular process, we do not replicate all of the processes and data stores in the level 0 DFD.

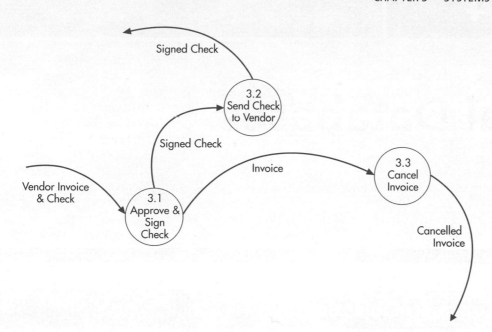

FIGURE 3-17
**Accuflow's Level 1 Data
Flow Diagram**

Chapter 4

Relational Databases

Learning Objectives

After studying this chapter, you should be able to:

1. Explain the importance and advantages of databases, as well as the difference between database systems and file-based legacy systems.

2. Explain the difference between logical and physical views of a database.

3. Explain fundamental concepts of database systems such as DBMS, schemas, the data dictionary, and DBMS languages.

4. Describe what a relational database is and how it organizes data.

5. Create a set of well-structured tables to store data in a relational database.

6. Perform simple queries using the Microsoft Access database.

INTEGRATIVE CASE S&S

S&S is very successful and operates five stores and a popular Web site. Ashton Fleming believes that it is time to upgrade S&S's AIS so that Susan and Scott can easily access the information they need to run their business. Most new AISs are based on a relational database. Since Ashton knows that Scott and Susan are likely to have questions, he prepared a brief report that explains why S&S's new AIS should be a relational database system. His report addresses the following questions:

1. What is a database system, and how does it differ from file-oriented systems?
2. What is a *relational* database system?
3. How do you design a well-structured set of tables in a relational database?
4. How do you query a relational database system?

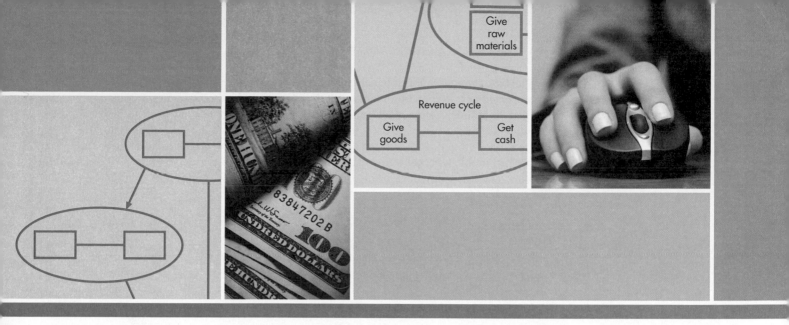

Introduction

Relational databases underlie most modern integrated AISs. This chapter and Chapters 17 through 19 explain how to participate in the design and implementation of a database. This chapter defines a database, with the emphasis on understanding the relational database structure. Chapter 17 introduces two tools accountants use to design databases—entity-relationship diagramming and REA data modeling—and demonstrates how to use them to build an AIS data model. Chapter 18 explains how to implement an REA data model and how to produce the information needed to manage an organization. Chapter 19 discusses advanced data modeling and database design issues.

Files versus Databases

To appreciate the power of databases, it is important to understand how data are stored in computer systems. Figure 4-1 shows a data hierarchy. Information about the attributes of a customer, such as name and address, are stored in fields. All the fields containing data about one entity (e.g., one customer) form a record. A set of related records, such as all customer records, forms a file (e.g., the customer file). A set of interrelated, centrally coordinated files forms a *database*.

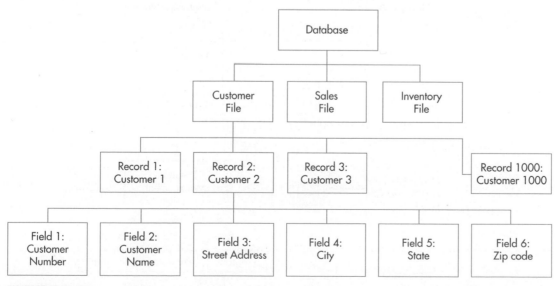

FIGURE 4-1

Basic Elements of Data Hierarchy

Databases were developed to address the proliferation of master files. For many years, companies created new files and programs each time a need for information arose. Bank of America once had 36 million customer accounts in 23 separate systems. This proliferation created problems such as storing the same data in two or more master files, as shown in Figure 4-2. This made it difficult to integrate and update data and to obtain an organization-wide view of data. It also created problems because the data in the different files were inconsistent. For example, a customer's address may have been correctly updated in the shipping master file but not the billing master file.

Figure 4-2 illustrates the differences between file-oriented systems and database systems. In the database approach, data is an organizational resource that is used by and managed for the entire organization, not just the originating department. A *database management system (DBMS)* is the interface between the database and the various application programs. The database, the DBMS, and the application programs that access the database through the DBMS are referred to as the *database system*. The *database administrator (DBA)* is responsible for the database.

Using Data Warehouses for Business Intelligence

In today's fast-paced global economy, management must constantly reevaluate financial and operating performance in light of strategic goals and quickly alter plans as needed. Since strategic decision making requires access to large amounts of historical data, organizations are building separate databases called data warehouses. A *data warehouse* contains both detailed and summarized data for a number of years and is used for analysis rather than transaction processing. It is not unusual for data warehouses to contain hundreds of terabytes of data.

Data warehouses do not replace transaction processing databases; they complement them by providing support for strategic decision making. Since data warehouses are not used for transaction processing, they are usually updated periodically rather than in real time. Whereas transaction processing databases minimize redundancy and maximize the efficiency of updating them to reflect the results of current transactions, data warehouses are purposely redundant to maximize query efficiency.

Using a data warehouse for strategic decision making is often referred to as *business intelligence*. There are two main techniques used in business intelligence: online analytical processing (OLAP) and data mining. *Online analytical processing (OLAP)* is using queries to guide the investigation of hypothesized relationships in data. For example, a manager may analyze

FIGURE 4-2
File-Oriented Systems Versus Database Systems

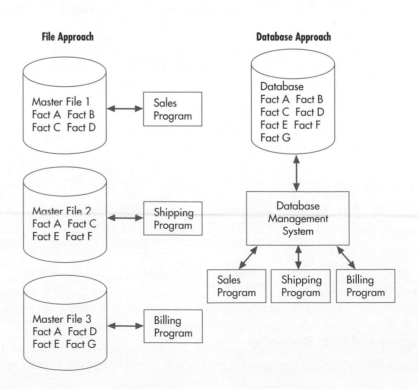

supplier purchases for the last three years. This may be followed by additional queries that "drill down" to lower levels by, for example, grouping purchases by different items and by fiscal periods. *Data mining* is using sophisticated statistical analysis, including artificial intelligence techniques such as neural networks, to "discover" unhypothesized relationships in the data. For example, credit card companies use data mining to identify usage patterns indicative of fraud. Similarly, data mining techniques can identify previously unknown relationships in sales data that can be used in future promotions.

Proper controls are needed to reap significant benefits from data warehousing. Data validation controls are needed to ensure that data warehouse input is accurate. Verifying the accuracy, called scrubbing the data, is often one of the most time-consuming and expensive steps in creating a data warehouse. It is also important to control access to the data warehouse as well as to encrypt the data stored in the data warehouse. Finally, it is important to regularly backup copies of the data warehouse and store them securely.

Bank of America created a customer information database to provide customer service, marketing analysis, and managerial information. It was the largest in the banking industry, with over 600 billion characters of data. It contained all bank data on checking and savings accounts; real estate, consumer, and commercial loans; ATMs; and bankcards. Although the bank spends $14 million a year to maintain the data warehouse, it is worth the cost. Queries that formerly averaged two hours took only five minutes. Minutes after Los Angeles suffered an earthquake, the bank sorted its $28 billion mortgage loan portfolio by Zip code, identified loans in the earthquake area, and calculated its potential loan loss.

The Advantages of Database Systems

Virtually all mainframes and servers use database technology, and database use in personal computers is growing rapidly. Most accountants are involved with databases through data entry, data processing, querying, or auditing. They also develop, manage, or evaluate the controls needed to ensure database integrity. Databases provide organizations with the following benefits:

- *Data integration.*   Master files are combined into large "pools" of data that many application programs access. An example is an employee database that consolidates payroll, personnel, and job skills master files.
- *Data sharing.*   Integrated data are more easily shared with authorized users. Databases are easily browsed to research a problem or obtain detailed information underlying a report. The FBI, which does a good job of collecting data but a poor job of sharing it, is spending eight years and $400 million to integrate data from their different systems.
- *Minimal data redundancy and data inconsistencies.*   Because data items are usually stored only once, data redundancy and data inconsistencies are minimized.
- *Data independence.*   Because data and the programs that use them are independent of each other, each can be changed without changing the other. This facilitates programming and simplifies data management.
- *Cross-functional analysis.*   In a database system, relationships, such as the association between selling costs and promotional campaigns, can be explicitly defined and used in the preparation of management reports.

The Importance of Good Data

Incorrect database data can lead to bad decisions, embarrassment, and angry users. For example:

- A company sent half its mail-order catalogs to incorrect addresses. A manager finally investigated the large volume of returns and customer complaints. Correcting customer address in the database saved the company $12 million a year.
- Valparaiso, Indiana, used the county database to develop its tax rates. After the tax notices were mailed, a huge error was discovered: A $121,900 home was valued at $400 million and caused a $3.1 million property tax revenue shortfall. As a result, the city, the school district, and governmental agencies had to make severe budget cuts.

The Data Warehousing Institute estimates that bad data cost businesses over $600 billion a year in unnecessary postage, marketing costs, and lost customer credibility. It is estimated that over

25% of business data is inaccurate or incomplete. In a recent survey, 53% of 750 information technology (IT) professionals said their companies experienced problems due to poor-quality data.

Managing data gets harder every year: The quantity of data generated and stored doubles every 18 months. To avoid outdated, incomplete, or erroneous data, management needs policies and procedures that ensure clean, or scrubbed, data. The Sarbanes-Oxley Act states that top executives face prosecution and jail time if a company's financial data are not in order. Preventing and detecting bad data are discussed in more detail in Chapters 5 through 11.

Database Systems

Logical and Physical Views of Data

In file-oriented systems, programmers must know the physical location and layout of records. Figure 4-3 shows a *record layout* of an accounts receivable file. Suppose a programmer wants a report showing customer number, credit limit, and current balance. To write the program, she must understand the location and length of the fields needed (i.e., record positions 1 through 10 for customer number) and the format of each field (alphanumeric or numeric). The process becomes more complex if data from several files are used.

Database systems overcome this problem by separating the storage of the data from the use of data elements. The database approach provides two separate views of the data: the physical view and the logical view. The *logical view* is how people conceptually organize and understand the data. For example, a sales manager views all customer information as being stored in a table. The *physical view* refers to how and where data are physically arranged and stored in the computer system.

As shown in Figure 4-4, database management (DBMS) software links the way data are physically stored with each user's logical view of the data. The DBMS allows users to access, query, or update the database without reference to how or where data are physically stored. Separating the logical and physical views of data also means that users can change their logical view of data without changing the way data are physically stored. Likewise, the database administrator can change physical storage to improve system performance without affecting users or application programs.

Schemas

A *schema* describes the logical structure of a database. There are three levels of schemas: the conceptual, the external, and the internal. Figure 4-5 shows the relationships among these three levels. The *conceptual-level schema*, the organization wide view of the *entire* database, lists all data elements and the relationships among them. The *external-level schema* consists of individual user views of portions of the database, each of which is referred to as a *subschema*. The *internal-level schema*, a low-level view of the database, describes how the data are stored and accessed, including record layouts, definitions, addresses, and indexes. Figure 4-5 connects each of the levels with bidirectional arrows to represent schema mappings. The DBMS uses the mappings to translate a user's or a program's request for data (expressed in terms of logical names and relationships) into the indexes and addresses needed to physically access the data.

At S&S, the conceptual schema for the revenue cycle database contains data about customers, sales, cash receipts, sales personnel, cash, and inventory. External subschemas are derived from this schema, each tailored to the needs of different users or programs. Each subschema can prevent access to those portions of the database that do not apply to it. For example,

FIGURE 4-3
Accounts Receivable File Record Layout

Customer Number N	Customer Name A	Address A	Credit Limit N	Balance N
1 10	11 30	31 60	61 68	69 76

A = alphanumeric field
N = numeric field

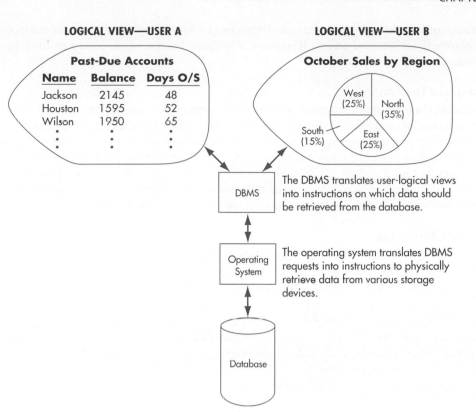

FIGURE 4-4

Function of the DBMS: To Support Multiple Logical Views of Data

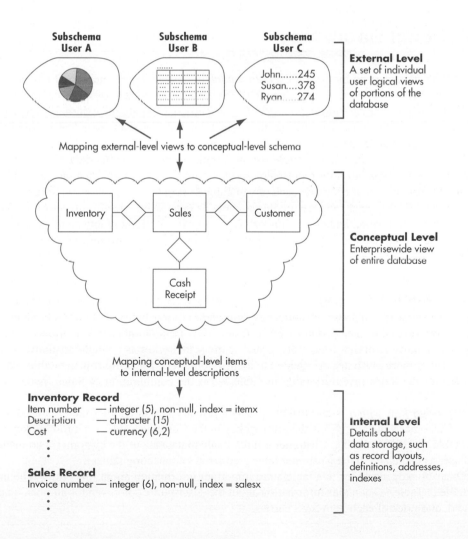

FIGURE 4-5

Three Levels of Schemas

the sales order entry subschema includes data about customer credit limits, current balances, and inventory quantities and prices. It would not include the cost of inventory or bank account balances.

The Data Dictionary

A *data dictionary* contains information about the structure of the database. As shown in Table 4-1, for each data element stored in the database, there is a record in the dictionary describing it. The DBMS maintains the data dictionary, whose inputs include new or deleted data elements and changes in data element names, descriptions, or uses. Outputs include reports for programmers, designers, and users such as (1) programs or reports using a data item, (2) synonyms for the data elements in a file, and (3) data elements used by a user. These reports are used for system documentation, for database design and implementation, and as part of the audit trail.

DBMS Languages

A DBMS has several languages. The *data definition language (DDL)* builds the data dictionary, creates the database, describes logical views for each user, and specifies records or field security constraints. The *data manipulation language (DML)* changes database content, including data element updates, insertions, and deletions. The *data query language (DQL)* contains powerful, easy-to-use commands that enable users to retrieve, sort, order, and display data. A *report writer* simplifies report creation. Users specify the data elements they want printed, and the report writer searches the database, extracts the data elements, and prints them in the user-specified format. The DQL and report writer are available to users. The DDL and DML should be restricted to authorized administrators and programmers.

Relational Databases

A DBMS is characterized by the logical *data model*, or abstract representation of database contents, upon which it is based. As most new DBMSs are relational databases, this chapter focuses primarily on them. The *relational data model* represents conceptual- and external-level schemas as if data are stored in tables like the one shown in Table 4-2. The data are actually stored not in tables, but in the manner described in the internal-level schema.

Each row in a table, called a *tuple* (rhymes with *couple*), contains data about a specific occurrence of the type of entity represented by that table. Each column contains data about an attribute of that entity. For example, each row in Table 4-2 contains data about a particular inventory item that S&S carries, and each column contains data about specific inventory attributes, such as description, color, and price. Similarly, each row in a customer table contains data about a specific customer, and each column contains data about customer attributes, such as name and address.

Types of Attributes

A *primary key* is the database attribute, or combination of attributes, that uniquely identifies a specific row in a table. The primary key in Table 4-2 is Item Number as it uniquely identifies each merchandise item that S&S sells. Usually, the primary key is a single attribute. In some tables, two or more attributes are needed to identify uniquely a specific row in a table. The primary key of the Sales-Inventory table in Table 4-5 is the combination of Sales Invoice # and Item #.

A *foreign key*, *which* is an attribute that is a primary key in another table, is used to link tables. Customer # in Table 4-5 is the primary key in the Customer table and a foreign key in the Sales table. In the Sales table, Customer # links a sale to data about the customer who made the purchase, as contained in the Customer table (see arrows connecting tables).

Other nonkey attributes in a table store important information about that entity. The inventory table in Table 4-2 contains information about the description, color, vendor number, quantity on hand, and price of each item S&S carries.

TABLE 4-1 Example of a Data Dictionary

Data Element Name	Description	Records in Which Contained	Source	Field Length	Field Type	Programs in Which Used	Outputs in Which Contained	Authorized Users	Other Data Names
Customer number	Unique identifier of each customer	A/R record, customer record, sales analysis record	Customer number listing	10	Numeric	A/R update, customer file update, sales analysis update, credit analysis	A/R aging report, customer status report, sales analysis report, credit report	No restrictions	None
Customer name	Complete name of customer	Customer record	Initial customer order	20	Alphanumeric	Customer file update, statement processing	Customer status report, monthly statement	No restrictions	None
Address	Street, city, state, and Zip code	Customer record	Credit application	30	Alphanumeric	Customer file update, statement processing	Customer status report, monthly statement	No restrictions	None
Credit limit	Maximum credit that can be extended to customer	Customer record, A/R record	Credit application	8	Numeric	Customer file update, A/R update, credit analysis	Customer status report, A/R aging report, credit report	D. Dean R. Dalebout H. Heaton	CR_limit
Balance	Balance due from customer on credit purchases	A/R record, sales analysis record	Various sales and payment transactions	8	Numeric	A/R update, sales analysis update, statement processing, credit analysis	A/R aging report, sales analysis report, monthly statement, credit report	G. Burton B. Heninger S. Summers	Cust_bal

TABLE 4-2 Sample Inventory Table for S&S

Item Number	Description	Color	Vendor Number	Quantity on Hand	Price
1036	Refrigerator	White	10023	12	1199
1038	Refrigerator	Almond	10023	7	1299
1039	Refrigerator	Hunter Green	10023	5	1499
2061	Range	White	10011	6	799
2063	Range	Black	10011	5	999
3541	Washer	White	10008	15	499
3544	Washer	Black	10008	10	699
3785	Dryer	White	10019	12	399
3787	Dryer	Almond	10019	8	499

Record: 10 of 10

Designing a Relational Database for S&S, Inc.

In a manual accounting system, S&S would capture sales information on a preprinted sales invoice that provides both a logical and physical view of the data collected. Physical storage of sales invoice data is simple; S&S stores a copy of the invoice in a file cabinet.

Storing the same data in a computer is more complex. Suppose S&S wanted to store five sales invoices (numbered 101 to 105) electronically. On several invoices, a customer buys more than one item. Let us look at the effects of several ways of storing this information.

1: Store All Data in One Uniform Table. S&S could store sales data in one table, as illustrated in Table 4-3. This approach has two disadvantages. First, it stores lots of redundant data. Examine invoice 102 in Table 4-3. Because three inventory items are sold, invoice and customer data (columns 1–9) are recorded three times. Likewise, inventory descriptions and unit prices are repeated each time an item is sold. Because sales volumes are high in a retail store (remember, Table 4-3 represents only five invoices), such redundancy makes file maintenance unnecessarily time-consuming and error-prone.

Second, problems occur when invoice data are stored in one table. The first is called an *update anomaly*, because data value updates are not correctly recorded. Changing a customer's address involves searching the entire table and changing every occurrence of that customer's address. Overlooking even one row creates an inconsistency, because multiple addresses would exist for the same customer. This could result in unnecessary duplicate mailings and other errors.

An *insert anomaly* occurs in our example because there is no way to store information about prospective customers until they make a purchase. If prospective customer data is entered before a purchase is made, the Sales Invoice # column would be blank. However, the sales invoice number is the primary key for Table 4-3 and cannot be blank, as it uniquely identifies the record.

A *delete anomaly* occurs when deleting a row has unintended consequences. If a customer had one purchase of a single item, deleting that row erases all data about that customer.

2: Vary the Number of Columns. An alternative to Table 4-3 is to record sales invoice and customer data once and add additional columns to record each item sold. Table 4-4 illustrates this approach. Although this reduces data redundancy and eliminates some anomalies associated with Table 4-3, it has drawbacks. S&S would have to decide in advance how many item numbers to leave room for in each row (that is, how many columns to put in the table; note in Table 4-4 that to store each additional item requires five additional columns—Item, Quantity, Description, Unit Price, and Extended Amount). If room is left for four items (20 columns), how would data about a sale involving eight items (40 columns) be stored? If room is left for eight items, however, there will be a great deal of wasted space, as is the case for sales invoices 103 and 104.

TABLE 4-3 Example of Storing All Sales Data for S&S in One Table

Sales : Table

Sales Invoice #	Date	Salesperson	Customer #	Invoice Total	Customer Name	Street
101	10/15/2015	J. Buck	151	1447	D. Ainge	123 Lotus Lane
101	10/15/2015	J. Buck	151	1447	D. Ainge	123 Lotus Lane
102	10/15/2015	S. Knight	152	4394	G. Kite	40 Quatro Road
102	10/15/2015	S. Knight	152	4394	G. Kite	40 Quatro Road
102	10/15/2015	S. Knight	152	4394	G. Kite	40 Quatro Road
103	10/15/2015	S. Knight	151	898	D. Ainge	123 Lotus Lane
104	10/15/2015	J. Buck	152	789	G. Kite	40 Quatro Road
105	11/14/2015	J. Buck	153	3994	F. Roberts	401 Excel Way
105	11/14/2015	J. Buck	153	3994	F. Roberts	401 Excel Way
105	11/14/2015	J. Buck	153	3994	F. Roberts	401 Excel Way

Record: 11 of 11

City	State	Item #	Quantity	Description	Unit Price	Extended Amount
Phoenix	AZ	10	2	Television	499	998
Phoenix	AZ	50	1	Microwave	449	449
Mesa	AZ	10	1	Television	499	499
Mesa	AZ	20	3	Freezer	699	2097
Mesa	AZ	30	2	Refrigerator	899	1798
Phoenix	AZ	50	2	Microwave	449	898
Mesa	AZ	40	1	Range	789	789
Chandler	AZ	10	3	Television	499	1497
Chandler	AZ	20	1	Freezer	699	699
Chandler	AZ	30	2	Refrigerator	899	1798

TABLE 4-4 Example of Storing S&S Sales Data by Adding Columns for Each Additional Item Sold

Sales Invoice #	Columns 2-9	Item #	Quantity	Description	Unit Price	Extended Amount	Item #2	Quantity2
101	Same 8	10	2	Television	499	998	50	1
102	columns	10	1	Television	499	499	20	3
103	as in	50	2	Microwave	449	898		
104	Table 4-3	40	1	Range	789	789		
105	above	10	3	Television	499	1497	20	1

Record: |◄ ◄ | 6 | ► ►| ►* | of 6

3. The Solution: A Set of Tables.   The storage problems in Tables 4-3 and 4-4 are solved using a *relational database*. The set of tables in Table 4-5 represent a well-structured relational database.

Basic Requirements of a Relational Database

We now turn to the guidelines used to develop a properly structured relational database.

1. *Every column in a row must be single valued.*   In a relational database, there can only be one value per cell. At S&S, each sale can involve more than one item. On invoice 102, the customer bought a television, a freezer, and a refrigerator. If Item # were an attribute in the Sales table, it would have to take on three values (item numbers 10, 20, and 30). To solve this problem, a Sales-Inventory table was created that lists each item sold on an invoice. The third line in the Sales-Inventory table in Table 4-5 shows invoice 102 and item number 10 (television). The fourth line shows invoice 102 and item 20 (freezer). The fifth line shows invoice 102 and item 30 (refrigerator). This table repeats the invoice number as often as needed to show all the items purchased on a sales invoice.

2. *Primary keys cannot be null.*   A primary key cannot uniquely identify a row in a table if it is null (blank). A non-null primary key ensures that every row in a table represents something and that it can be identified. This is referred to as the ***entity integrity rule***. In the Sales-Inventory table in Table 4-5, no single field uniquely identifies each row. However, the first two columns, taken together, do uniquely identify each row and constitute the primary key.

3. *Foreign keys, if not null, must have values that correspond to the value of a primary key in another table.*   Foreign keys link rows in one table to rows in another table. In Table 4-5, Customer # can link each sales transaction with the customer who participated in that event only if the Sales table Customer # value corresponds to an actual customer number in the Customer table. This constraint, called the ***referential integrity rule***, ensures database consistency. Foreign keys can contain null values. For example, when customers pay cash, Customer # in the sales table can be blank.

4. *All nonkey attributes in a table must describe a characteristic of the object identified by the primary key.*   Most tables contain other attributes in addition to the primary and foreign keys. In the Customer table in Table 4-5, Customer # is the primary key, and customer name, street, city, and state are important facts that describe the customer.

These four constraints produce a well-structured (normalized) database in which data are consistent and redundancy is minimized and controlled. In Table 4-5, having a table for each entity of interest avoids the anomaly problems discussed previously and minimizes redundancy. Redundancy is not eliminated, as certain items, such as Sales Invoice #, appear in more than one table when they are foreign keys. The referential integrity rule ensures that there are no update anomaly problems with the foreign keys.

When data about objects of interest are stored in separate database tables, it is easy to add new data by adding another row to the table. For example, adding a new customer is as simple as adding a new row to the Customer table. Thus, the tables depicted in Table 4-5 are free from insert anomalies.

Relational databases also simplify data deletion. Deleting sales invoice 105, the only sale to customer 153, does not erase all data about that customer, because it is stored in the Customer table. This avoids delete anomalies.

Description2	Unit Price2	Extended Amou	Item #3	Quantity3	Description3	Unit Price3	Extended Amount3
Microwave	449	449					
Freezer	699	2097	30	2	Refrigerator	899	1798
Freezer	699	699	30	2	Refrigerator	899	1798

▶∗ of 6   ◀   ▶

Another benefit of the schema shown in Table 4-5 is that space is used efficiently. The Sales-Inventory table contains a row for each item sold on each invoice. There are no blank rows, yet all sales data are recorded. In contrast, the schema in Table 4-4 results in much wasted space.

Two Approaches to Database Design

One way to design a relational database, called *normalization*, assumes that everything is initially stored in one large table. Rules are followed to decompose that initial table into a set of tables in what is called *third normal form (3NF)*, because they are free of update, insert, and delete anomalies. The details of the normalization process can be found in any database textbook.

In an alternative design approach, called *semantic data modeling*, the designer uses knowledge of business processes and information needs to create a diagram that shows what to include in the database. This diagram is used to create a set of relational tables that are already in 3NF.

Semantic data modeling has significant advantages. First, using a system designer's knowledge of business processes facilitates the efficient design of transaction processing databases. Second, the graphical model explicitly represents the organization's business processes and policies and, by facilitating communication with system users, helps ensure that the new system meets users' actual needs. Chapter 17 introduces two semantic data modeling tools, entity-relationship diagramming and REA modeling, used to design transaction processing databases.

Creating Relational Database Queries

To retrieve stored data, users query databases. This section of the chapter shows you how to query databases using Microsoft Access. If you want to follow along by creating the queries illustrated in this section, download the S&S In-Chapter Database from the text's Web site. When you open the database and select the Create ribbon, the ribbon in the top half of Table 4-6 appears. There are two ways to query the database: create a query in Design view (the "Query Design" button) or use the wizard (the "Query Wizard" button). These options are highlighted in the top half of Table 4-6. In the example shown in Table 4-6, the Design view is used. Clicking on the "Query Design" button produces the Show Table window shown in Table 4-6. The user selects the tables needed to produce the desired information; if more tables than necessary are selected, the query may not run properly.

We will use the tables in Table 4-5 to walk through the steps needed to create and run five queries. This will not make you an expert in querying an Access database, but it will show you how to produce useful information.

Query 1

Query 1 answers two questions: What are the invoice numbers of all sales made to D. Ainge, and who was the salesperson for each sale?

The Sales and Customer tables contain the three items needed to answer this query: Sales Invoice #, Salesperson, and Customer Name. Click the "Query Design" button (see Table 4-6), and select the Sales and Customer tables by double-clicking on their names or by single-clicking

TABLE 4-5 Set of Relational Tables for Storing S&S Sales Data

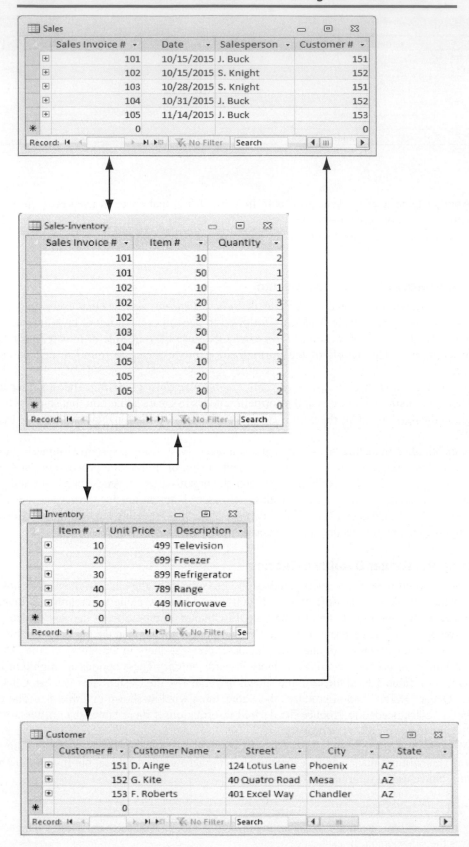

TABLE 4-6 Creating Queries in the Microsoft Access Database

on the name and clicking the Add button. The selected tables appear as shown in Table 4-7. A line between the two tables connects the Customer # fields (the Customer table primary key and the Sales table foreign key). Click on Close to make the Show Table window disappears.

To populate the bottom half of the screen shown in Table 4-7, double-click on Sales Invoice #, Salesperson, and Customer Name or drag and drop them into the Field row. Access automatically checks the box in the Show line, so the item will be shown when the query is run.

Since we only want sales to D. Ainge, enter that in the criteria line of the Customer Name column. Run the query by clicking on the red ! (exclamation) mark on the Query Tools Design ribbon. Table 4-8 shows the tables used, the relationship of the primary and foreign keys between tables, and the query answer. The query answer does not automatically have the title "Ainge Sales." To assign the query a name, save it by selecting File from the Access menu, then Save Object As, and then enter "Ainge Sales" in the first line of the Save As window, making sure the Object select box is set to "Query," and then clicking OK. When the query is rerun, the title shown in Table 4-8 will appear.

TABLE 4-7 Completed Query 1

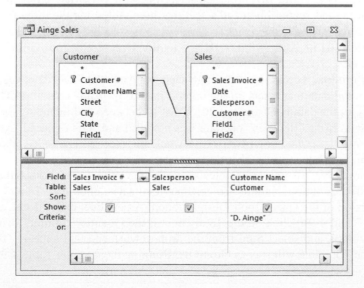

TABLE 4-8 Query 1 Relationships and Query Answer

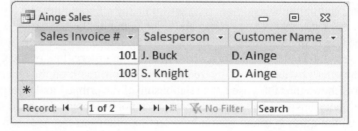

Query 2

Query 2 answers this question: How many televisions were sold in October?

The Sales, Inventory, and Sales-Inventory tables contain the three items needed to answer this query: Date, Inventory Description, and Quantity. Click on the "Query Design" button in the Create ribbon and select the three tables and the three fields, as shown in Table 4-9. Since we want the quantity of televisions sold in October, we add the criteria "Between #10/1/2015# And #10/31/2015#" to the Date field and "Television" to the Description field.

To specify criteria, Access uses operators such as "And" "Or" and "Between." An "And" operator returns the data that meets *all* the criteria linked by "And" operators. The "Between" operator selects all the data in October of 2015; that is, between and including the first and last days of the month. If the "Between" operator was not used and "Or" replaced "And," all televisions sold either on 10/1/2015 or on 10/31/2015 would be selected. The "#" symbol tells Access to look for a date rather than some other type of text.

Since we are only looking for total television sales in October, we uncheck the "Show" box in the Date and Description columns. To generate total sales, click the "Totals" button in the Show/Hide portion of the Query Tools Design ribbon. A new line, called Total, appears (compare Tables 4-7 and 4-9). Click on the Totals line in the Quantity column, then click on the down-arrow symbol, and select Sum from the drop-down menu that appears. The remaining two fields in the Total line will stay as Group By. Running the query in Table 4-9 produces the answer shown.

TABLE 4-9 Completed Query 2 and Answer

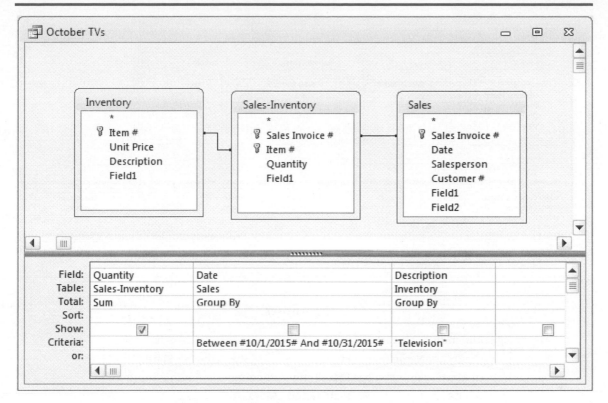

Query Answer

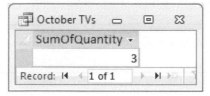

Query 3

Query 3 answers this question: What are the names and addresses of customers buying televisions in October?

This query needs these fields: Date (to select October sales), Description (to select televisions), and Customer Name, Street, City, and State (the information requested). All four tables are used because the Sales-Inventory table is used to move between the Sales and Inventory tables. The query uses the same criteria as Query 2. The date and description data do not need to be displayed, so the boxes in the Show line are unchecked. Running the query produces the answer shown in Table 4-10.

Query 4

Query 4 answers this question: What are the sales invoice numbers, dates, and invoice totals for October sales, arranged in descending order by sale amount?

Since the database does not contain an Invoice Total column, it is calculated as follows:

1. For each invoice, calculate the total sales price of each item sold by multiplying the Quantity field in the Sales-Inventory table by the Unit Price field in the Inventory table. The Sales-Inventory table in Table 4-5 shows that three items were sold on Sales Invoice 102. For item 20, we multiply the quantity (3) by the Unit Price (699), producing 2,097. The same calculation is made for items 10 and 30.
2. Sum the three item totals to get an invoice total.

TABLE 4-10 Completed Query 3 and Answer

Customers TV October

Field:	Customer Name	Street	City	State	Date	Description
Table:	Customer	Customer	Customer	Customer	Sales	Inventory
Sort:						
Show:	✓	✓	✓	✓	☐	☐
Criteria:					Between #10/1/2015# And #10/31/2015#	"Television"
or:						

Query Answer

Customers TV October

Customer Name ▾	Street ▾	City ▾	State ▾
D. Ainge	124 Lotus Lane	Phoenix	AZ
G. Kite	40 Quatro Road	Mesa	AZ

Record: ◄ ◄ 1 of 2 ► ►I ►⊞   No Filter   Search

Query 4 requires the Sales table (Date, Sales Invoice #), Sales-Inventory table (Quantity), and the Inventory table (Unit Price). However, some fields will not appear in columns on the Select Query window. As shown in Table 4-11, three columns are displayed: Sales Invoice #, Date, and Invoice Total, which we will calculate. The other fields are used in the Invoice Total calculations.

To calculate Invoice Total, type "Invoice Total:" in the first blank Field cell, right-click in the cell, and select Build from the pop-up menu that appears. An Expression Builder window (see Table 4-12) appears, where the formula to calculate the invoice total is entered by typing "Sum( )". Between the parentheses, click on the + sign in front of the S&S In-Chapter Database folder in the Expressions Elements box. Then clicking on the + sign in the Tables folder causes the four database tables to appear. Click on the Sales-Inventory table, and the fields in the Sales-Inventory table appear. Double-click on Quantity to put this field in the expression. Note in Table 4-12 that the expression shows the table name and the field name, separated by an exclamation point. To multiply Quantity by Unit Price, type * (the multiplication symbol) and select the Inventory table and the Unit Price field. The formula is now complete, and the screen will appear as shown. To enter the expression into the Select Query window, click on OK.

To complete Query 4, click the Totals button in the Query Tools Design ribbon. Click on the down arrow in the Total row of the Invoice Totals column, and select Expression from the pop-up menu. This tells Access to calculate the indicated expression for all items with the same sales invoice number and date. In the same column, click on the down arrow in the Sort row, and select Descending so that the answer is show in descending Invoice Total order. In the criteria section of the Date column, use the "Between" operator to specify the month of October. Running Query 4 produces the answer shown in Table 4-11.

TABLE 4-11 Completed Query 4 and Answer

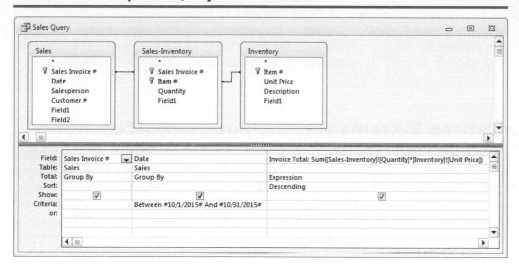

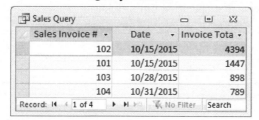

Query Answer

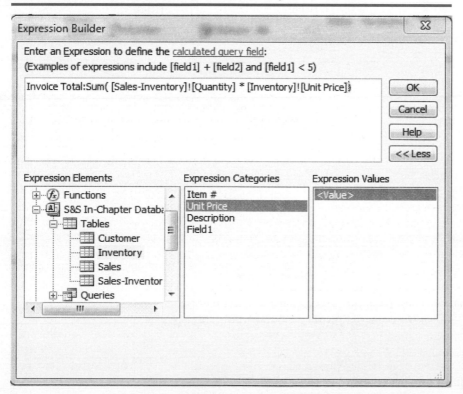

TABLE 4-12 Expression Builder for Query 4

Query 5

Query 5 will answer this question: What are total sales by salesperson?

This query is similar to Query 4, except that we total invoices by salesperson rather than by invoice number. We are also not confining our query to the month of October. Try coming up with the query by yourself. The completed query and the answer are shown in Table 4-13.

Database Systems and the Future of Accounting

Database systems have the potential to alter external reporting significantly. Considerable time and effort are currently invested in defining how companies should summarize and report accounting information to external users. In the future, companies may make a copy of the company's financial database available to external users in lieu of the traditional financial statements. Users would be free to analyze the raw data however they see fit. Focus 4-1 discusses this possibility in more detail.

A significant advantage of database systems is the ability to create ad hoc queries to provide the information needed for decision making. No longer is financial information available only in predefined formats and at specified times. Instead, powerful and easy-to-use relational

TABLE 4-13 Query 5

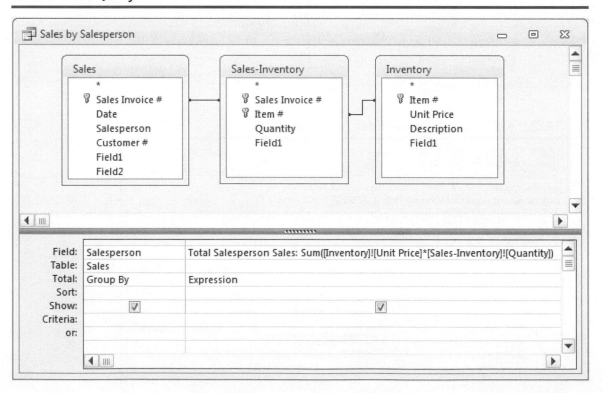

Query Answer

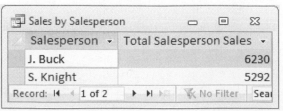

Databases or Financial Statements?

4-1

Although information technology has dramatically changed the way business is conducted, it has had less effect on external reporting. Companies still produce highly aggregated, periodic (quarterly and annual) financial reports of past activities based on historical costs. It is estimated that the average financial database of a large company is over 100 gigabytes. Yet annual reports contain only 100 kilobytes of data. Consequently, users see only a small portion of company data presented in a predefined financial statement format.

Why not replace the annual report with a copy of the company's financial database? Many companies already give suppliers and customers limited access to their databases. Suppliers are given access to inventory data to plan production and deliveries. However, they are not given access to payroll data. Companies could similarly exclude data too sensitive to fall into competitors' hands. This database view could be placed on the Internet for investors, creditors, and other external users. The computing power of PCs makes processing such a database feasible, and external users would get a fuller and timelier picture of the organization's performance.

In such a system, the company's primary financial reporting function would be defining data elements and database structure. Users would be free to aggregate and classify that information using whatever decision model they believed to be appropriate.

Source: Robert K. Elliot, "Confronting the Future: Choices for the Attest Function," *Accounting Horizons* (September 1994): 106–124.

database query languages can find and prepare the information management needs, when they want it.

Relational DBMSs can also accommodate multiple views of the same underlying phenomenon. For example, tables storing information about assets can include columns not only for historical costs but also for current replacement costs and market values. Thus, managers will no longer be forced to look at data in ways predefined by accountants.

Finally, relational DBMSs are capable of integrating financial and operational data. For example, customer satisfaction data could be stored in the database, giving managers a richer set of data for decision making.

Relational DBMSs have the potential to increase the use and value of accounting information. Accountants must understand database systems so they can help design and use the AISs of the future. Such participation is important for ensuring that adequate controls are included in those systems to safeguard the data and ensure the reliability of the information produced.

Summary and Case Conclusion

Ashton prepared a report for Scott and Susan summarizing what he knew about databases. He explained that a database management system (DBMS), the software that makes a database system work, is based on a logical data model that shows how users perceive the way the data are stored. Many DBMSs are based on the relational data model that represents data as being stored in tables. Every row in a relational table has only one data value in each column. Neither row nor column position is significant. These properties support the use of simple, yet powerful, query languages for interacting with the database. Users only need to specify the data they want and do not need to be concerned with how the data are retrieved. The DBMS functions as an intermediary between the user and the database, thereby hiding the complex addressing schemes actually used to retrieve and update the information stored in the database.

After reading Ashton's report, Scott and Susan agreed that it was time to upgrade S&S's AIS and to hire a consulting firm to help select and install the new system. They asked Ashton to oversee the design process to ensure that the new system meets their needs.

Key Terms

database 87	schema 90	relational data model 92
database management system (DBMS) 88	conceptual-level schema 90	tuple 92
	external-level schema 90	primary key 92
database system 88	subschema 90	foreign key 92
database administrator (DBA) 88	internal-level schema 90	update anomaly 94
	data dictionary 92	insert anomaly 94
data warehouse 88	data definition language (DDL) 92	delete anomaly 94
business intelligence 88		relational database 96
online analytical processing (OLAP) 88	data manipulation language (DML) 92	entity integrity rule 96
		referential integrity rule 96
data mining 89	data query language (DQL) 92	normalization 97
record layout 90		semantic data modeling 97
logical view 90	report writer 92	
physical view 90	data model 92	

AIS IN ACTION

Chapter Quiz

1. The relational data model portrays data as being stored in _____.
   a. hierarchies   c. objects
   b. tables   d. files

2. How a user conceptually organizes and understands data is referred to as the _____.
   a. physical view   c. data model view
   b. logical view   d. data organization view

3. What is each row in a relational database table called?
   a. relation   c. anomaly
   b. attribute   d. tuple

4. Which of the following is an individual user's view of the database?
   a. conceptual-level schema   c. internal-level schema
   b. external-level schema   d. logical-level schema

5. Which of the following would managers most likely use to retrieve information about sales during the month of October?
   a. DML   c. DDL
   b. DSL   d. DQL

6. Which of the following attributes would most likely be a primary key?
   a. supplier name   c. supplier Zip code
   b. supplier number   d. supplier account balance

7. Which of the following is a software program that runs a database system?
   a. DQL   c. DML
   b. DBMS   d. DDL

8. The constraint that all primary keys must have non-null data values is referred to as which of the following?
   a. referential integrity rule   c. normalization rule
   b. entity integrity rule   d. relational data model rule

9. The constraint that all foreign keys must have either null values or the value of a primary key in another table is referred to as which of the following?
   a. referential integrity rule
   b. entity integrity rule
   c. foreign key value rule
   d. null value rule

10. Which of the following attributes in the Cash Receipts table (representing payments received from customers) would most likely be a foreign key?
    a. cash receipt number
    b. customer check number
    c. customer number
    d. cash receipt date

Comprehensive Problem

The Butler Financing Company runs a mortgage brokerage business that matches lenders and borrowers. Table 4-14 lists some of the data that Butler maintains on its borrowers and lenders. The data are stored in a spreadsheet that must be manually updated for each new

TABLE 4-14 Butler Financing Company Spreadsheet

Borrower Number	Last Name	First Name	Current Address	Requested Mortgage Amount	Lender Number	Lender Name	Lender Office Address	Property Appraiser Number	Property Appraiser Name
450	Adams	Jennifer	450 Peachtree Rd.	$245,000	13	Excel Mortgage	6890 Sheridan Dr.	8	Advent Appraisers
451	Adamson	David	500 Loop Highway	$124,688	13	Excel Mortgage	6890 Sheridan Dr.	9	Independent Appraisal Service
452	Bronson	Paul	312 Mountain View Dr.	$345,000	14	CCY	28 Buckhead Way	10	Jones Property Appraisers
453	Brown	Marietta	310 Loop Highway	$ 57,090	15	Advantage Lenders	3345 Lake Shore Dr.	10	Jones Property Appraisers
454	Charles	Kenneth	3 Commons Blvd.	$ 34,000	16	Capital Savings	8890 Coral Blvd.	8	Advent Appraisers
455	Coulter	Tracey	1367 Peachtree Rd.	$216,505	13	Excel Mortgage	6890 Sheridan Dr.	8	Advent Appraisers
456	Foster	Harold	678 Loop Highway	$117,090	12	National Mortgage	750 16 St.	9	Independent Appraisal Service
457	Frank	Vernon	210 Bicayne Blvd.	$ 89,000	12	National Mortgage	750 16 St.	10	Jones Property Appraisers
458	Holmes	Heather	1121 Bicayne Blvd.	$459,010	16	Capital Savings	8890 Coral Blvd.	10	Jones Property Appraisers
459	Johanson	Sandy	817 Mountain View Dr.	$ 67,900	15	Advantage Lenders	3345 Lake Shore Dr.	9	Independent Appraisal Service
460	Johnson	James	985 Loop Highway	$ 12,000	12	National Mortgage	750 16 St.	10	Jones Property Appraisers
461	Jones	Holly	1650 Washington Blvd.	$ 67,890	15	Advantage Lenders	3345 Lake Shore Dr.	9	Independent Appraisal Service

borrower, lender, or mortgage. This updating is error-prone, which has harmed the business. In addition, the spreadsheet has to be sorted in many different ways to retrieve the necessary data.

Create a database from Butler's spreadsheet that does not have any of the data anomalies explained in the chapter. To test the database, prepare a query to show which borrowers (both borrower number and name) took out loans from Excel Mortgage and who the appraiser was for each loan.

Discussion Questions

4.1. Contrast the logical and the physical views of data, and discuss why separate views are necessary in database applications. Describe which perspective is most useful for each of the following employees: a programmer, a manager, and an internal auditor. How will understanding logical data structures assist you when designing and using database systems?

4.2. The relational data model represents data as being stored in tables. Spreadsheets are another tool that accountants use to employ a tabular representation of data. What are some similarities and differences in the way these tools use tables? How might an accountant's familiarity with the tabular representation of spreadsheets facilitate or hinder learning how to use a relational DBMS?

4.3. Some people believe database technology may eliminate the need for double-entry accounting. This creates three possibilities: (1) the double-entry model will be abandoned; (2) the double-entry model will not be used directly, but an external-level schema based on the double-entry model will be defined for accountants' use; or (3) the double-entry model will be retained in database systems. Which alternative do you think is most likely to occur? Why?

4.4. Relational DBMS query languages provide easy access to information about the organization's activities. Does this mean that online, real-time processing should be used for all transactions? Does an organization need real-time financial reports? Why or why not?

4.5. Why is it so important to have good data?

4.6. What is a data dictionary, what does it contain, and how is it used?

4.7. Compare and contrast the file-oriented approach and the database approach. Explain the main advantages of database systems.

Problems

4.1. The following data elements comprise the conceptual-level schema for a database:
billing address
cost
credit limit
customer name
customer number
description
invoice number

item number
price
quantity on hand
quantity sold
shipping address
terms

Required

a. Identify three potential users and design a subschema for each. Justify your design by explaining why each user needs access to the subschema data elements.
b. Use Microsoft Access or some other relational database product to create the schema tables. Specify the primary key(s), foreign key(s), and other data for each table. Test your model by entering sample data in each table.

4.2. Most DBMS packages contain data definition, data manipulation, and data query languages. For each of the following, indicate which language would be used and why.

a. A database administrator defines the logical structure of the database.
b. The controller requests a cost accounting report containing a list of all employees being paid for more than 10 hours of overtime in a given week.
c. A programmer develops a program to update the fixed-assets records stored in the database.
d. The human resources manager requests a report noting all employees who are retiring within five years.
e. The inventory serial number field is extended in the inventory records to allow for recognition of additional inventory items with serial numbers containing more than 10 digits.
f. A user develops a program to print out all purchases made during the past two weeks.
g. An additional field is added to the fixed-asset records to record the estimated salvage value of each asset.

4.3. Ashton wants to store the following data about S&S's purchases of inventory:
item number
date of purchase
vendor number
vendor address
vendor name
purchase price
quantity purchased
employee number
employee name
purchase order number
description
quantity on hand
extended amount
total amount of purchase

Required

a. Design a set of relational tables to store this data. Do all of the data items need to be stored in a table? If not, which ones do not need to be stored, and why do they not need to be stored?
b. Identify the primary key for each table.
c. Identify the foreign keys needed in the tables to implement referential integrity.
d. Implement your tables using any relational database product to which you have access.
e. Test your specification by entering sample data in each table.
f. Create a few queries to retrieve or analyze the data you stored.

4.4. Retrieve the S&S In-Chapter Database (in Microsoft Access format) from the text's Web site (or create the tables in Table 4-5 in a relational DBMS product). Write queries to answer the following questions. *Note*: For some questions, you may have to create two queries—one to calculate an invoice total and the second to answer the question asked.

a. How many different kinds of inventory items does S&S sell?

b. How many sales were made during October?

c. What were total sales in October?

d. What was the average amount of a sales transaction?

e. Which salesperson made the largest sale?

f. How many units of each product were sold?

g. Which product was sold most frequently?

4.5. Enter the tables in Table 4-15 into a relational DBMS package. Write queries to answer the following questions. *Note*: For some questions, you may have to create two queries—one to calculate a total and the second to answer the question asked.

a. Which customers (show their names) made purchases from Martinez?

b. Who has the largest credit limit?

c. How many sales were made in October?

d. What were the item numbers, price, and quantity of each item sold on invoice number 103?

e. How much did each salesperson sell?

f. How many customers live in Arizona?

g. How much credit does each customer still have available?

h. How much of each item was sold? (Include the description of each item in your answer.)

i. Which customers still have more than $1,000 in available credit?

j. For which items are there at least 100 units on hand?

TABLE 4-15

Customer

Customer #	Customer Name	City	State	Credit Limit
1000	Smith	Phoenix	AZ	2500
1001	Jones	St. Louis	MO	1500
1002	Jeffries	Atlanta	GA	4000
1003	Gilkey	Phoenix	AZ	5000
1004	Lankford	Phoenix	AZ	2000
1005	Zeile	Chicago	IL	2000
1006	Pagnozzi	Salt Lake City	UT	3000
1007	Arocha	Chicago	IL	1000
0				

Inventory

Item #	Description	Unit Cost	Unit Price	Quantity on Hand
1010	Blender	$14.00	$29.95	200
1015	Toaster	$12.00	$19.95	300
1020	Mixer	$23.00	$33.95	250
1025	Television	$499.00	$699.95	74
1030	Freezer	$799.00	$999.95	32
1035	Refrigerator	$699.00	$849.95	25
1040	Radio	$45.00	$79.95	100
1045	Clock	$79.00	$99.95	300
0			$0.00	

Sales

Invoice Number	Date	Salesperson	Customer N	Amount
101	10/3/2015	Wilson	1000	$1,549.90
102	10/5/2015	Mahomet	1003	$299.95
103	10/5/2015	Jackson	1002	$1,449.80
104	10/15/2015	Drezen	1000	$799.90
105	10/15/2015	Martinez	1005	$849.95
106	10/16/2015	Martinez	1007	$99.95
107	10/29/2015	Mahomet	1002	$2,209.70
108	11/3/2015	Martinez	1000	$779.90
0				0

Sales-Inventory

Invoice Number	Item Numbe	Quantity	Extension
101	1025	1	$699.95
101	1035	1	$849.95
102	1045	3	$299.85
103	1010	1	$29.95
103	1015	1	$19.95
103	1025	2	$1,399.90
104	1025	1	$699.95
104	1045	1	$99.95
105	1035	1	$849.95
106	1045	1	$99.95
107	1030	1	$999.95
107	1035	1	$849.95
107	1040	2	$159.90
107	1045	2	$199.90
108	1025	1	$699.95
108	1045	1	$99.95
0	0	0	

4.6.   The BusyB Company wants to store data about its employee skills. Each employee may possess one or more specific skills, and several employees may have the same skill. Include the following facts in the database:

date hired
date of birth
date skill acquired
employee name
employee number
pay rate
skill name

TABLE 4-16 Database That Needs to Be Extended

Item Number	Description	Quantity on Hand	List Price
10573	19" Monitor	13	$495.00
10574	21" Monitor	8	$949.00
10622	Laser Printer	22	$395.00
10623	Color Laser Printer	5	$699.00
10624	Multi-functional Printer	12	$799.00
		0	

Record: I◄ ◄   ► ►I ►□ ⊠ No Filter   Search

Inventory Table (Item # is primary key)

Customer Number	Name	Street	City	State	Zip Code	Credit Limit	Account Balance
11255	G. Hwang	2993 Main	Mesa	AZ	85281	$4,000.00	$875.00
12971	J. Jackson	466 W. Oak	Tempe	AZ	85286	$5,000.00	$2,588.00
13629	P. Szabo	246 E. Palm	Mesa	AZ	85281	$6,000.00	$3,955.00
15637	S. Martinez	2866 Spring	Tempe	AZ	85287	$5,000.00	$250.00
18229	B. Adams	1744 Apache	Tempe	AZ	85287	$3,000.00	$1,675.00
		0					

Record: I◄ ◄   ► ►I ►□ ⊠ No Filter   Search

Customer Table (Customer # is primary key)

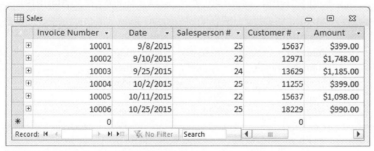

Invoice Number	Date	Salesperson #	Customer #	Amount
10001	9/8/2015	25	15637	$399.00
10002	9/10/2015	22	12971	$1,748.00
10003	9/25/2015	24	13629	$1,185.00
10004	10/2/2015	25	11255	$399.00
10005	10/11/2015	22	15637	$1,098.00
10006	10/25/2015	25	18229	$990.00
		0	0	

Record: I◄ ◄   ► ►I ►□ ⊠ No Filter   Search

Sales Table (Invoice # is primary key)

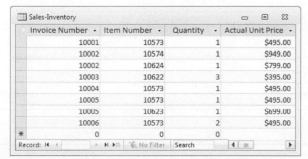

Invoice Number	Item Number	Quantity	Actual Unit Price
10001	10573	1	$495.00
10002	10574	1	$949.00
10002	10624	1	$799.00
10003	10622	3	$395.00
10004	10573	1	$495.00
10005	10573	1	$495.00
10005	10623	1	$699.00
10006	10573	2	$495.00
0	0	0	

Record: I◄ ◄   ► ►I ►□ ⊠ No Filter   Search

Sales-Inventory Line Items Table (Combination of Invoice # and Item # forms primary key)

skill number
supervisor

Required

a. Design a set of relational tables to store these data.
b. Identify the primary key for each table, and identify any needed foreign keys.
c. Implement your schema using any relational DBMS. Specify primary and foreign keys, and enforce referential integrity. Demonstrate the soundness of your design by entering sample data in each table.

4.7. You want to extend the schema shown in Table 4-16 to include information about customer payments. Some customers make installment payments on each invoice. Others write a check to pay for several different invoices. You want to store the following information:
amount applied to a specific invoice
cash receipt number
customer name
customer number
date of receipt
employee processing payment
invoice payment applies to
total amount received

Required

a. Modify the set of tables in Table 4-16 to store this additional data.
b. Identify the primary key for each new table you create.
c. Implement your schema using any relational DBMS package. Indicate which attributes are primary and foreign keys, and enter sample data in each table you create.

4.8. Create relational tables that solve the update, insert, and delete anomalies in Table 4-17.

TABLE 4-17 Invoice Table

Invoice #	Date	Order Date	Customer ID	Customer Name	Item #	Description	Quantity
52	6-19-2015	5-25-2015	201	Johnson	103	Trek 9000	5
52	6-19-2015	5-25-2015	201	Johnson	122	Nimbus 4000	8
52	6-19-2015	5-25-2015	201	Johnson	10	Izzod 3000	11
52	6-19-2015	5-25-2015	201	Johnson	71	LD Trainer	12
57	6-20-2015	6-01-2015	305	Henry	535	TR Standard	18
57	6-20-2015	6-01-2015	305	Henry	115	NT 2000	15
57	6-20-2015	6-01-2015	305	Henry	122	Nimbus 4000	5

4.9. Create relational tables that solve the update, insert, and delete anomalies in Table 4-18.

TABLE 4-18 Purchase Order (PO) Table

Purchase Order #	Purchase Date	Order Part #	Description	Unit Price	Quantity Ordered	Vendor #	Vendor Name	Vendor Address
2	3/9/2015	334	XYZ	$30	3	504	KL Supply	75 Stevens Dr.
2	3/9/2015	231	PDQ	$50	5	504	KL Supply	75 Stevens Dr.
2	3/9/2015	444	YYM	$80	6	504	KL Supply	75 Stevens Dr.
3	4/5/2015	231	PDQ	$50	2	889	Oscan Inc	55 Cougar Cir.

TABLE 4-19 Selected Query Screen for Chapter Comprehensive Problem

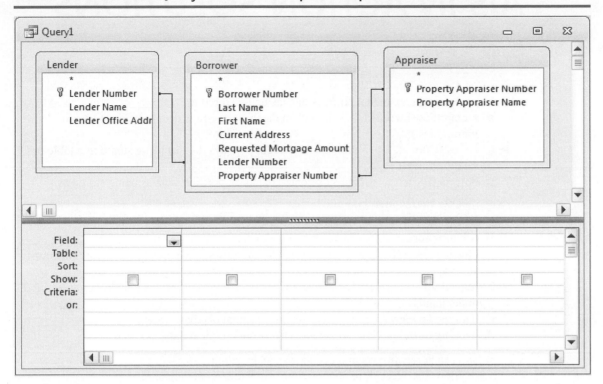

4.10. From the database created in the comprehensive problem, perform queries based on the tables and query grid shown in Table 4-19.
   a. Which borrowers use Advent Appraisers?
   b. What is the average amount borrowed from National Mortgage?
   c. List all of the property appraisers.
   d. List all of the lenders.
   e. List the lenders that lent more than $100,000.
   f. Which borrower requested the largest mortgage?
   g. Which borrower requested the smallest mortgage?

Case 4-1 Research Project

As in all areas of information technology, DBMSs are constantly changing and improving. Research how businesses are using DBMSs, and write a report of your findings. Address the following issues:

1. Which popular DBMS products are based on the relational data model?

2. Which DBMS products are based on a logical model other than the relational data model?

3. What are the relative strengths and weaknesses of the different types (relational versus other logical models) of DBMSs?

AIS IN ACTION SOLUTIONS

Quiz Key

1. The relational data model portrays data as being stored in _____.
   a. hierarchies (Incorrect. A hierarchical database portrays data as being stored in hierarchies.)
   ▶ b. tables (Correct. The relational data model portrays data as being stored in a table or relation format.)
   c. objects (Incorrect. An object-oriented database portrays data as being stored as objects.)
   d. files (Incorrect. The file-based data model portrays data as being stored in files.)

2. How a user conceptually organizes and understands data is referred to as the _____.
   a. physical view (Incorrect. The physical view shows how and where data are physically stored.)
   ▶ b. logical view (Correct. The logical view shows how a user conceptually organizes and understands data.)
   c. data model view (Incorrect. This is not a typical database view.)
   d. data organization view (Incorrect. This is not a typical database view.)

3. What is each row in a relational database table called?
   a. relation (Incorrect. A relation is a table in a relational database.)
   b. attribute (Incorrect. Each column in a relational database is an attribute that describes some characteristic of the entity about which data are stored.)
   c. anomaly (Incorrect. An anomaly is a problem in a database, such as an insert anomaly or a delete anomaly.)
   ▶ d. tuple (Correct. A tuple is also called a row in a relational database.)

4. Which of the following is an individual user's view of the database?
   a. conceptual-level schema (Incorrect. A conceptual-level schema is the organization-wide view of the entire database.)
   ▶ b. external-level schema (Correct. The external-level schema represents an individual user's view of the database.)
   c. internal-level schema (Incorrect. The internal-level schema represents how the data are actually stored and accessed.)
   d. logical-level schema (Incorrect. This is not a schema mentioned in the text.)

5. Which of the following would managers most likely use to retrieve information about sales during the month of October?
   a. DML (Incorrect. DML—data manipulation language—is used for data maintenance.)
   b. DSL (Incorrect. DSL is not a DBMS language.)
   c. DDL (Incorrect. DDL—data definition language—is used to build the data dictionary, create a database, describe logical views, and specify any limitations or constraints on security.)
   ▶ d. DQL (Correct. DQL—data query language—is used to retrieve information from a database.)

6. Which of the following attributes would most likely be a primary key?
    a. supplier name (Incorrect. The primary key must be unique. The same name could be used by multiple entities.)
    ▶ b. supplier number (Correct. A unique number can be assigned as a primary key for each entity.)
    c. supplier Zip code (Incorrect. The primary key must be unique. More than one supplier could reside in the same Zip code.)
    d. supplier account balance (Incorrect. The primary key must be unique. The same account balance, such as a $0.00 balance, could be maintained by multiple entities.)

7. Which of the following is a software program that runs a database system?
    a. DQL (Incorrect. DQL—data query language—is used to retrieve information from a database.)
    ▶ b. DBMS (Correct. A DBMS—database management system—is a software program that acts as an interface between a database and various application programs.)
    c. DML (Incorrect. DML—data manipulation language—is used for data maintenance.)
    d. DDL (Incorrect. DDL—data definition language—is used to build the data dictionary, create a database, describe logical views, and specify any limitations or constraints on security.)

8. The constraint that all primary keys must have non-null data values is referred to as which of the following?
    a. referential integrity rule (Incorrect. The referential integrity rule stipulates that foreign keys must have values that correspond to the value of a primary key in another table or be empty.)
    ▶ b. entity integrity rule (Correct. Every primary key in a relational table must have a non-null value.)
    c. normalization rule (Incorrect. The text does not discuss a normalization rule.)
    d. relational data model rule (Incorrect. The text does not discuss a relational data model rule.)

9. The constraint that all foreign keys must have either null values or the value of a primary key in another table is referred to as which of the following?
    ▶ a. referential integrity rule (Correct. The referential integrity rule stipulates that foreign keys must have values that correspond to the value of a primary key in another table or be empty.)
    b. entity integrity rule (Incorrect. This rule states that every primary key in a relational table must have a non-null value.)
    c. foreign key value rule (Incorrect. The text does not discuss a foreign key value rule.)
    d. null value rule (Incorrect. The text does not discuss a null value rule.)

10. Which of the following attributes in the Cash Receipts table (representing payments received from customers) would most likely be a foreign key?
    a. cash receipt number (Incorrect. A cash receipt number is a good candidate for the primary key of the Cash Receipts table.)
    b. customer check number (Incorrect. Because there is no reason to store customer check numbers in a separate table, it is not a good candidate for a foreign key.)
    ▶ c. customer number (Correct. Customer number would be a foreign key in the Cash Receipts table and would link the Cash Receipts table to the Customer Table.)
    d. cash receipt date (Incorrect. Dates usually are not good candidates for foreign keys. The cash receipt date would likely be an attribute in the Cash Receipts table.)

Comprehensive Problem Solution

Since lender and appraiser data are repeated throughout Table 4-14, the spreadsheet contains update, insert, and delete anomalies. To eliminate anomaly problems and reduce redundancy, we break the spreadsheet into three smaller tables: borrowers (Table 4-20), lenders (Table 4-21), and appraisers (Table 4-22).

TABLE 4-20 Borrower Table

Borrower Number (Primary Key)	Last Name	First Name	Current Address	Requested Mortgage Amount	Lender Number (Foreign Key to Lender Table)	Property Appraiser Number (Foreign Key to Appraiser Table)
450	Adams	Jennifer	450 Peachtree Rd.	$245,000	13	8
451	Adamson	David	500 Loop Highway	$124,688	13	9
452	Bronson	Paul	312 Mountain View Dr.	$345,000	14	10
453	Brown	Marietta	310 Loop Highway	$ 57,090	15	10
454	Charles	Kenneth	3 Commons Blvd.	$ 34,000	16	8
455	Coulter	Tracey	1367 Peachtree Rd.	$216,505	13	8
456	Foster	Harold	678 Loop Highway	$117,090	12	9
457	Frank	Vernon	210 Bicayne Blvd.	$ 89,000	12	10
458	Holmes	Heather	1121 Bicayne Blvd.	$459,010	16	10
459	Johanson	Sandy	817 Mountain View Dr.	$ 67,900	15	9
460	Johnson	James	985 Loop Highway	$ 12,000	12	10
461	Jones	Holly	1650 Washington Blvd.	$ 67,890	15	9

TABLE 4-21 Lender Table

Lender Number (Primary Key)	Lender Name	Lender Office Address
12	National Mortgage	750 16 St.
13	Excel Mortgage	6890 Sheridan Dr.
14	CCY	28 Buckhead Way
15	Advantage Lenders	3345 Lake Shore Dr.
16	Capital Savings	8890 Coral Blvd.

TABLE 4-22 Appraiser Table

Property Appraiser Number (Primary Key)	Property Appraiser Name
8	Advent Appraisers
9	Independent Appraisal Service
10	Jones Property Appraisers

Borrower number, lender number, and appraiser number are the primary keys because each uniquely identifies the rows in their respective tables. The primary keys from the Lender and Appraiser tables are added to the Borrower table as foreign keys so that the Lender and Appraiser tables will have a direct link to the Borrower table.

Creating smaller tables with primary and foreign keys solves the three anomaly problems.

- The insert anomaly is solved because a new lender and appraiser can be added without requiring a borrower.
- The delete anomaly is solved because deleting a borrower that decides not to pursue a mortgage does not delete information about the lender and appraiser.
- The update anomaly is solved because there is only one row in one table to update when a lender moves and changes its address, instead of changing all spreadsheet rows that store the lender address.

After the data are entered into the Microsoft Access tables, we can query the database. The query in Table 4-23, which finds the borrowers and appraisers associated with loans from Excel Mortgage, is created as follows:

- From the Query menu option, select "Create Query in Design view."
- Add all three tables to your Query Design. Access automatically links the primary and foreign keys.
- Select the following fields: Borrower Number, Last Name, First Name, Lender Name, and Property Appraiser Name.
- Specify "Excel Mortgage" as the criteria in the Lender Name column.
- Run the query.

TABLE 4-23 Borrowers with Loans from Excel Mortgage

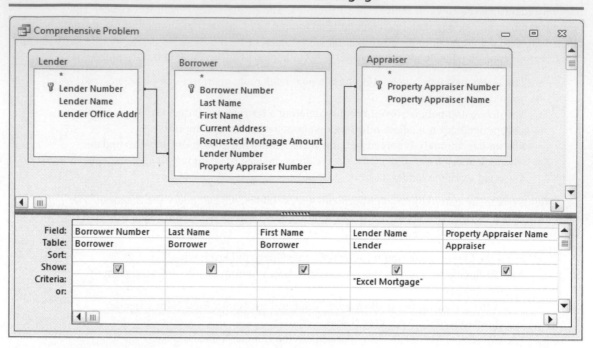

Field:	Borrower Number	Last Name	First Name	Lender Name	Property Appraiser Name
Table:	Borrower	Borrower	Borrower	Lender	Appraiser
Sort:					
Show:	✓	✓	✓	✓	✓
Criteria:				"Excel Mortgage"	
or:					

Query Answer

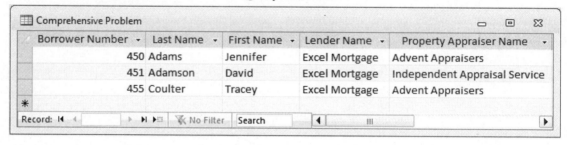

Borrower Number	Last Name	First Name	Lender Name	Property Appraiser Name
450	Adams	Jennifer	Excel Mortgage	Advent Appraisers
451	Adamson	David	Excel Mortgage	Independent Appraisal Service
455	Coulter	Tracey	Excel Mortgage	Advent Appraisers

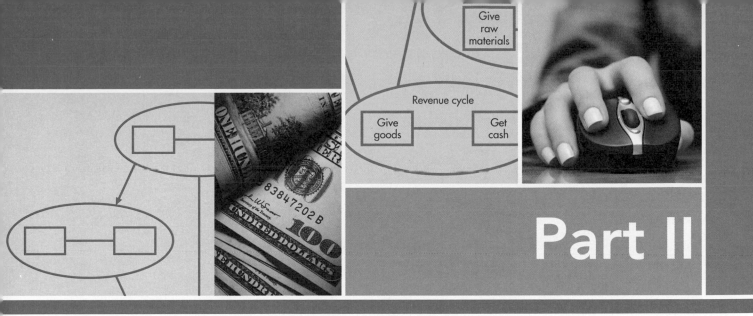

Control and Audit of Accounting Information Systems

Chapter 5

Computer Fraud

INTEGRATIVE CASE NORTHWEST INDUSTRIES

Jason Scott is an internal auditor for Northwest Industries, a forest products company. On March 31, he reviewed his completed tax return and noticed that the federal income tax withholding on his final paycheck was $5 more than the amount indicated on his W-2 form. He used the W-2 amount to complete his tax return and made a note to ask the payroll department what happened to the other $5. The next day, Jason was swamped, and he dismissed the $5 difference as immaterial.

On April 16, a coworker grumbled that the company had taken $5 more from his check than he was given credit for on his W-2. When Jason realized he was not the only one with the $5 discrepancy, he investigated and found that all 1,500 employees had the same $5 discrepancy. He also discovered that the W-2 of Don Hawkins, the payroll programmer, had thousands of dollars more in withholdings reported to the IRS than had been withheld from his paycheck.

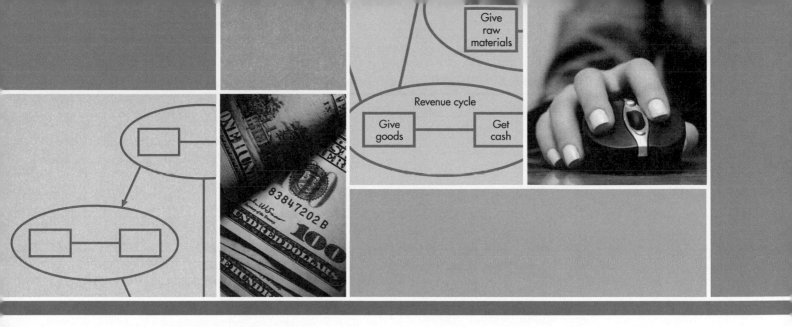

Jason knew that when he reported the situation, management was going to ask questions, such as:

1. What constitutes a fraud, and is the withholding problem a fraud?
2. How was the fraud perpetrated? What motivated Don to commit it?
3. Why did the company not catch these mistakes? Was there a breakdown in controls?
4. How can the company detect and prevent fraud?
5. How vulnerable is the company's computer system to fraud?

Introduction

As accounting information systems grow more complex to meet our escalating needs for information, companies face the growing risk that their systems may be compromised. Recent surveys show that 67% of companies had a security breach, over 45% were targeted by organized crime, and 60% reported financial losses.

The four types of AIS threats a company faces are summarized in Table 5-1.

AIS Threats

Natural and political disasters—such as fires, floods, earthquakes, hurricanes, tornadoes, blizzards, war, and attacks by terrorists—can destroy an information system and cause many companies to fail. For example:

● Terrorist attacks on the World Trade Center in New York City and on the Federal Building in Oklahoma City destroyed or disrupted all the systems in those buildings.
● A flood in Chicago destroyed or damaged 400 data processing centers. Hurricanes on the East coast of the United States have destroyed many computer systems.
● The Mississippi and Missouri rivers overflowed and flooded parts of eight states. Many organizations lost their systems, including the city of Des Moines, Iowa, whose computers were buried under eight feet of water.

TABLE 5-1 Threats to Accounting Information Systems

Threats	Examples
Natural and political disasters	Fire or excessive heat Floods, earthquakes, landslides, hurricanes, tornadoes, blizzards, snowstorms, and freezing rain War and attacks by terrorists
Software errors and equipment malfunctions	Hardware or software failure Software errors or bugs Operating system crashes Power outages and fluctuations Undetected data transmission errors
Unintentional acts	Accidents caused by human carelessness, failure to follow established procedures, and poorly trained or supervised personnel Innocent errors or omissions Lost, erroneous, destroyed, or misplaced data Logic errors Systems that do not meet company needs or cannot handle intended tasks
Intentional acts (computer crimes)	Sabotage Misrepresentation, false use, or unauthorized disclosure of data Misappropriation of assets Financial statement fraud Corruption Computer fraud—attacks, social engineering, malware, etc.

- Earthquakes in Los Angeles and San Francisco destroyed numerous computer systems and severed communication lines. Other systems were damaged by falling debris, water from ruptured sprinkler systems, and dust.
- Attacks on government information systems by foreign countries, espionage agents, and terrorists are widespread. Military contractors and businesses are also targets.

Software errors, operating system crashes, hardware failures, power outages and fluctuations, and undetected data transmission errors constitute a second type of threat. Of special concern are vulnerabilities in Microsoft Windows; in a recent survey, 30% of companies had moved systems off Windows to reduce security risks.

A federal study estimated yearly economic losses due to software bugs at almost $60 billion. More than 60% of companies studied had significant software errors in. For example:

- As a result of tax system bugs, California failed to collect $635 million in business taxes.
- Defective software caused massive power failures that left hundreds of thousands of people and businesses without power.
- A bug in Burger King's software resulted in a $4,334.33 debit card charge for four hamburgers. The cashier accidentally keyed in the $4.33 charge twice, resulting in the overcharge.

A third type of threat, unintentional acts such as accidents or innocent errors and omissions, is the greatest risk to information systems and causes the greatest dollar losses. The Computing Technology Industry Association estimates that human errors cause 80% of security problems. Forrester Research estimates that employees unintentionally create legal, regulatory, or financial risks in 25% of their outbound e-mails.

Unintentional acts are caused by human carelessness, failure to follow established procedures, and poorly trained or supervised personnel. Users lose or misplace data and accidentally erase or alter files, data, and programs. Computer operators and users enter the wrong input or erroneous input, use the wrong version of a program or the wrong data files, or misplace data files. Systems analysts develop systems that do not meet company needs, that leave them vulnerable to attack, or that are incapable of handling their intended tasks. Programmers make logic errors. Examples of unintentional acts include the following:

- A data entry clerk at Mizuho Securities mistakenly keyed in a sale for 610,000 shares of J-Com for 1 yen instead of the sale of 1 share for 610,000 yen. The error cost the company $250 million.
- A programmer made a one-line-of-code error that priced all goods at Zappos, an online retailer, at $49.95 even though some of the items it sells are worth thousands of dollars. The change went into effect at midnight, and by the time it was detected at 6:00 A.M., the company had lost $1.6 million on goods sold far below cost.
- A bank programmer mistakenly calculated interest for each month using 31 days. Before the mistake was discovered, over $100,000 in excess interest was paid.
- A Fannie Mae spreadsheet error misstated earnings by $1.2 billion.
- UPS lost a box of computer tapes containing sensitive information on 3.9 million Citigroup customers.
- Jefferson County, West Virginia released a new online search tool that exposed the personal information of 1.6 million people.
- McAfee, the antivirus software vendor, mistakenly identified svchost.exe, a crucial part of the Windows operating system, as a malicious program in one of its updates. Hundreds of thousands of PCs worldwide had to be manually rebooted—a process that took 30 minutes per machine. A third of the hospitals in Rhode Island were shut down by the error. One company reported that the error cost them $2.5 million.

A fourth threat is an intentional act such as a computer crime, a fraud, or **sabotage**, which is deliberate destruction or harm to a system. Information systems are increasingly vulnerable to attack. Symantec estimates that hackers attack computers more than 8.6 million times per day. It is estimated that Internet fraud cost its victims over $600 million a year. In a recent three-year period, the number of networks that were compromised rose 700%. That is just the tip of the iceberg: Experts believe the actual number of incidents is six times higher because companies tend not to report security breaches.

Consider the case of OpenTable, a restaurant reservation service that did not properly design its **cookie** (data a Web site stores on your computer to identify the Web site to your computer so that you do not have to log on each time you visit the site). An experienced programmer opened an account at OpenTable and, in less than an hour, wrote a program that downloaded most of the company's database. Many other companies have had problems with the same type of system vulnerability.

The seven chapters in Part II focus on control concepts. Fraud is the topic of this chapter. Computer fraud and abuse techniques are the topic of Chapter 6. Chapter 7 explains general principles of control in business organizations and describes a comprehensive business risk and control framework. Chapter 8 introduces five basic principles that contribute to systems reliability and then focuses on security, the foundation on which the other four principles rest. Chapter 9 discusses two of the other four principles of systems reliability: confidentiality and privacy. Chapter 10 discusses the last two principles: processing integrity and availability. Chapter 11 examines the processes and procedures used in auditing computer-based systems.

This chapter discusses fraud in four main sections: an introduction to fraud, why fraud occurs, approaches to computer fraud, and how to deter and detect computer fraud.

Introduction to Fraud

Fraud is gaining an unfair advantage over another person. Legally, for an act to be fraudulent there must be:

1. A *false statement, representation, or disclosure*
2. A *material fact*, which is something that induces a person to act
3. An *intent to deceive*
4. A *justifiable reliance;* that is, the person relies on the misrepresentation to take an action
5. An *injury or loss* suffered by the victim

No one knows the total losses to fraud each year. Income tax fraud (the difference between what taxpayers owe and what they pay) is estimated to be almost $400 billion a year. Fraud in the health care industry is estimated to exceed $100 billion a year. The Association of Certified Fraud Examiners estimates that:

- Fraud and abuse costs the United States $994 billion a year.
- The average organization loses 7% of its annual revenues to fraud.
- The median fraud loss is $175,000. Financial statement fraud is the most costly fraud, with a median loss of $2 million.
- The average fraud lasted two years.
- The most common frauds are corruption and fraudulent billing schemes.
- Small businesses are especially vulnerable, with check tampering and fraudulent billings the most common frauds.
- Frauds are more likely to be detected by a tip than by audits, controls, or other means.
- The industries most commonly victimized were banking and financial services, government, and health care. The largest median losses occurred in manufacturing ($441,000), banking ($250,000), and insurance ($216,000).
- People in accounting departments committed 29% of frauds; executives or upper management committed 18%. Frauds committed by executives were particularly costly, resulting in a median loss of $853,000.
- Most fraudsters are first-time offenders. Only 7% had prior convictions, and only 12% had been previously terminated by an employer for fraud-related conduct.
- Fraud perpetrators often display behavioral traits related to living beyond their means or struggling to overcome financial difficulties. In financial statement fraud, excessive organizational pressure to perform is a particularly strong warning sign.

An estimated 75% to 90% of computer fraud perpetrators are knowledgeable insiders with the requisite access, skills, and resources. Because employees understand a company's system and its weaknesses, they are better able to commit and conceal a fraud. The controls used to protect corporate assets make it more difficult for an outsider to steal from a company. Fraud perpetrators are often referred to as **white-collar criminals.**

Fraud takes two forms: misappropriation of assets and fraudulent financial reporting.

Misappropriation of Assets

Misappropriation of assets is the theft of company assets. Examples include the following:

- Albert Milano, a manager at *Reader's Digest* responsible for processing bills, embezzled $1 million over a five-year period. He forged a superior's signature on invoices for services never performed, submitted them to accounts payable, forged the endorsement on the check, and deposited it in his account. Milano used the stolen funds to buy an expensive home, five cars, and a boat.
- A bank vice president approved $1 billion in bad loans in exchange for $585,000 in kickbacks. The loans cost the bank $800 million and helped trigger its collapse.
- A manager at a Florida newspaper went to work for a competitor after he was fired. The first employer soon realized its reporters were being scooped. An investigation revealed the manager still had an active account and password and regularly browsed its computer files for information on exclusive stories.

The most significant contributing factor in most misappropriations is the absence of internal controls and/or the failure to enforce existing internal controls. A typical misappropriation has the following important elements or characteristics. The perpetrator:

- Gains the trust or confidence of the entity being defrauded.
- Uses trickery, cunning, or false or misleading information to commit fraud.
- Conceals the fraud by falsifying records or other information.
- Rarely terminates the fraud voluntarily.
- Sees how easy it is to get extra money, need or greed impels the person to continue. Some frauds are self-perpetuating; if perpetrators stop, their actions are discovered.
- Spends the ill-gotten gains. Rarely does the perpetrator save or invest the money. Some perpetrators come to depend on the "extra" income, and others adopt a lifestyle that

requires even greater amounts of money. For these reasons, there are no small frauds—only large ones that are detected early.

- Gets greedy and takes ever-larger amounts of money at intervals that are more frequent, exposing the perpetrator to greater scrutiny and increasing the chances the fraud is discovered. The sheer magnitude of some frauds leads to their detection. For example, the accountant at an auto repair shop, a lifelong friend of the shop's owner, embezzled ever-larger sums of money over a seven-year period. In the last year of the fraud, the embezzler took over $200,000. Facing bankruptcy, the owner eventually laid off the accountant and had his wife take over the bookkeeping. When the company immediately began doing better, the wife investigated and uncovered the fraud.
- Grows careless or overconfident as time passes. If the size of the fraud does not lead to its discovery, the perpetrator eventually makes a mistake that does lead to the discovery.

Fraudulent Financial Reporting

The National Commission on Fraudulent Financial Reporting (the Treadway Commission) defined **fraudulent financial reporting** as intentional or reckless conduct, whether by act or omission, that results in materially misleading financial statements. Financial statements are falsified to deceive investors and creditors, increase a company's stock price, meet cash flow needs, or hide company losses and problems. The Treadway Commission studied 450 lawsuits against auditors and found undetected fraud to be a factor in half of them.

Through the years, many highly publicized financial statement frauds have occurred. In each case, misrepresented financial statements led to huge financial losses and a number of bankruptcies. The most frequent "cook the books" schemes involve fictitiously inflating revenues, holding the books open (recognizing revenues before they are earned), closing the books early (delaying current expenses to a later period), overstating inventories or fixed assets, and concealing losses and liabilities.

The Treadway Commission recommended four actions to reduce fraudulent financial reporting:

1. Establish an organizational environment that contributes to the integrity of the financial reporting process.
2. Identify and understand the factors that lead to fraudulent financial reporting.
3. Assess the risk of fraudulent financial reporting within the company.
4. Design and implement internal controls to provide reasonable assurance of preventing fraudulent financial reporting.

The Association of Certified Fraud Examiners found that an asset misappropriation is 17 times more likely than fraudulent financial reporting but that the amounts involved are much smaller. As a result, auditors and management are more concerned with fraudulent financial reporting even though they are more likely to encounter misappropriations. The following section discusses an auditors' responsibility for detecting material fraud.

SAS No. 99: The Auditor's Responsibility to Detect Fraud

Statement on Auditing Standards (SAS) No. 82, *Consideration of Fraud in a Financial Statement Audit*, was adopted in 1997 to clarify the auditor's responsibility to detect fraud. It was revised as SAS No. 99, with the same title, and became effective in December 2002. SAS No. 99 requires auditors to:

- *Understand fraud.*   Because auditors cannot effectively audit something they do not understand, they must understand fraud and how and why it is committed.
- *Discuss the risks of material fraudulent misstatements.*   While planning the audit, team members discuss among themselves how and where the company's financial statements are susceptible to fraud.
- *Obtain information.*   The audit team gathers evidence by looking for fraud risk factors; testing company records; and asking management, the audit committee of the board of

directors, and others whether they know of past or current fraud. Because many frauds involve revenue recognition, special care is exercised in examining revenue accounts.

● *Identify, assess, and respond to risks.* The evidence is used to identify, assess, and respond to fraud risks by varying the nature, timing, and extent of audit procedures and by evaluating carefully the risk of management overriding internal controls.

● *Evaluate the results of their audit tests.* Auditors must evaluate whether identified misstatements indicate the presence of fraud and determine its impact on the financial statements and the audit.

● *Document and communicate findings.* Auditors document and communicate their findings to management and the audit committee.

● *Incorporate a technology focus.* SAS No. 99 recognizes the impact technology has on fraud risks and provides commentary and examples recognizing this impact. It also notes the opportunities auditors have to use technology to design fraud-auditing procedures.

Who Perpetrates Fraud and Why

When researchers compared the psychological and demographic characteristics of white-collar criminals, violent criminals, and the public, they found significant differences between violent and white-collar criminals. They found few differences between white-collar criminals and the public. Their conclusion: Fraud perpetrators look just like you and me.

Some fraud perpetrators are disgruntled and unhappy with their jobs and seek revenge against employers. Others are dedicated, hard-working, and trusted employees. Most have no previous criminal record; they were honest, valued, and respected members of their community.

Computer fraud perpetrators are younger and possess more computer experience and skills. Some are motivated by curiosity, a quest for knowledge, the desire to learn how things work, and the challenge of beating the system. Some view their actions as a game rather than as dishonest behavior. Others commit computer fraud to gain stature in the hacking community.

A large and growing number of computer fraud perpetrators seek to turn their actions into money. Malicious software is a big business and a huge profit engine for the criminal underground, especially for digitally savvy hackers in Eastern Europe. They break into financial accounts and steal money. They sell data to spammers, organized crime, hackers, and the intelligence community. They market malware, such as virus-producing software, to others. Some work with organized crime. A recently convicted hacker was paid $150 for every 1,000 computers he infected with his adware and earned hundreds of thousands of dollars a year.

Cyber-criminals are a top FBI priority because they have moved from isolated and uncoordinated attacks to organized fraud schemes targeted at specific individuals and businesses. They use online payment companies to launder their ill-gotten gains. To hide their money, they take advantage of the lack of coordination between international law enforcement organizations.

The Fraud Triangle

Three conditions are present when fraud occurs: a pressure, an opportunity, and a rationalization. This is referred to as the fraud triangle, and is the middle triangle in Figure 5-1.

PRESSURES A **pressure** is a person's incentive or motivation for committing fraud. Three types of pressures that lead to misappropriations are shown in the Employee Pressure Triangle in Figure 5-1 and are summarized in Table 5-2.

Financial pressures often motivate misappropriation frauds by employees. Examples of such pressures include living beyond one's means, heavy financial losses, or high personal debt. Often, the perpetrator feels the pressure cannot be shared and believes fraud is the best way out of a difficult situation. For example, Raymond Keller owned a grain elevator where he stored grain for local farmers. He made money by trading in commodities and built a lavish house overlooking the Des Moines River. Heavy financial losses created a severe cash shortage and high debt. He asked some farmers to wait for their money, gave others bad checks, and sold grain that did not belong to him. Finally, the seven banks to which he owed over $3 million began to call their loans. When a state auditor showed up unexpectedly, Raymond took his life rather than face the consequences of his fraud.

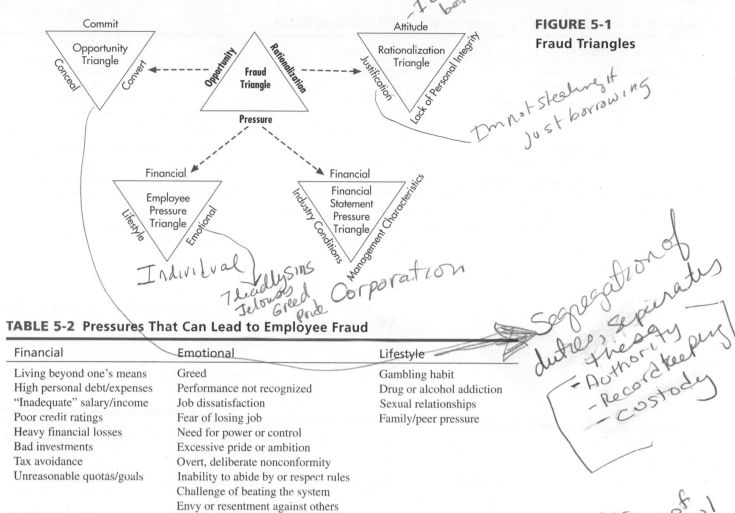

FIGURE 5-1
Fraud Triangles

(handwritten notes: "I deserve better", "I'm not stealing it just borrowing", "Individual", "7 deadly sins Jealousy Greed Pride", "Corporation", "Segregation of duties, separates the acty - Authority - Record keeping - Custody", "Control's - perception of control is sometimes just as good")

TABLE 5-2 Pressures That Can Lead to Employee Fraud

Financial	Emotional	Lifestyle
Living beyond one's means	Greed	Gambling habit
High personal debt/expenses	Performance not recognized	Drug or alcohol addiction
"Inadequate" salary/income	Job dissatisfaction	Sexual relationships
Poor credit ratings	Fear of losing job	Family/peer pressure
Heavy financial losses	Need for power or control	
Bad investments	Excessive pride or ambition	
Tax avoidance	Overt, deliberate nonconformity	
Unreasonable quotas/goals	Inability to abide by or respect rules	
	Challenge of beating the system	
	Envy or resentment against others	

A second type of pressure is emotional. Many employee frauds are motivated by greed. Some employees turn to fraud because they have strong feelings of resentment or believe they have been treated unfairly. They may feel their pay is too low, their contributions are not appreciated, or the company is taking advantage of them. A California accountant, passed over for a raise, increased his salary by 10%, the amount of the average raise. He defended his actions by saying he was only taking what was rightfully his. When asked why he did not increase his salary by 11%, he responded that he would have been stealing 1%.

Other people are motivated by the challenge of "beating the system" or subverting system controls and breaking into a system. When a company boasted that its new system was impenetrable, a team of individuals took less than 24 hours to break into the system and leave a message that the system had been compromised.

A third type of employee pressure is a person's lifestyle. The person may need funds to support a gambling habit or support a drug or alcohol addiction. Some people commit fraud to keep pace with other family members. A plastic surgeon, making $800,000 a year, defrauded his clinic of $200,000 to compete in the family "game" of financial one-upmanship.

Three types of organizational pressures that motivate management to misrepresent financial statements are shown in the Financial Statement Pressure triangle in Figure 5-1 and summarized in Table 5-3. A prevalent financial pressure is a need to meet or exceed earnings expectations to keep a stock price from falling. Managers create significant pressure with unduly aggressive earnings forecasts or unrealistic performance standards or with incentive programs that motivate employees to falsify financial results to keep their jobs or to receive stock options and other incentive payments. Industry conditions such as new regulatory requirements or significant market saturation with declining margins can motivate fraud.

TABLE 5-3 Pressures That Can Lead to Financial Statement Fraud

Management Characteristics	Industry Conditions	Financial
Questionable management ethics, management style, and track record	Declining industry	Intense pressure to meet or exceed earnings expectations
Unduly aggressive earnings forecasts, performance standards, accounting methods, or incentive programs	Industry or technology changes leading to declining demand or product obsolescence	Significant cash flow problems; unusual difficulty collecting receivables, paying payables
Significant incentive compensation based on achieving unduly aggressive goals	New regulatory requirements that impair financial stability or profitability	Heavy losses, high or undiversified risk, high dependence on debt, or unduly restrictive debt covenants
Management actions or transactions with no clear business justification	Significant competition or market saturation, with declining margins	Heavy dependence on new or unproven product lines
Oversensitivity to the effects of alternative accounting treatments on earnings per share	Significant tax changes or adjustments	Severe inventory obsolescence or excessive inventory buildup
Strained relationship with past auditors		Economic conditions (inflation, recession)
Failure to correct errors on a timely basis, leading to even greater problems		Litigation, especially management vs. shareholders
High management/employee turnover		Impending business failure or bankruptcy
Unusual/odd related-party relationships		Problems with regulatory agencies
		High vulnerability to rise in interest rates
		Poor or deteriorating financial position
		Unusually rapid growth or profitability compared to companies in same industry
		Significant estimates involving highly subjective judgments or uncertainties

OPPORTUNITIES   As shown in the Opportunity Triangle in Figure 5-1, **opportunity** is the condition or situation that allows a person or organization to do three things:

1. *Commit the fraud.*   The theft of assets is the most common type of misappropriation. Most instances of fraudulent financial reporting involve overstatements of assets or revenues, understatements of liabilities, or failures to disclose information.

2. *Conceal the fraud.*   To prevent detection when assets are stolen or overstated, perpetrators must keep the accounting equation in balance by inflating other assets or decreasing liabilities or equity. Concealment often takes more effort and time and leaves behind more evidence than the theft or misrepresentation. Taking cash requires only a few seconds; altering records to hide the theft is more challenging and time-consuming.

    One way to hide a theft is to charge the stolen item to an expense account. The perpetrator's exposure is limited to a year or less, because expense accounts are zeroed out at the end of each year. Perpetrators who hide a theft in a balance sheet account must continue the concealment. In a **lapping** scheme, a perpetrator steals the cash or checks customer A mails in to pay its accounts receivable. Later, funds from customer B are used to pay off customer A's balance. Funds from customer C are used to pay off customer B's balance, and so forth. Because the theft involves two asset accounts (cash and accounts receivable), the cover-up must continue indefinitely unless the money is replaced.

    In check **kiting**, cash is created using the lag between the time a check is deposited and the time it clears the bank. Suppose a fraud perpetrator opens accounts in banks A, B, and C. The perpetrator "creates" cash by depositing a $1,000 check from bank B in bank C and withdrawing the funds. If it takes two days for the check to clear bank B, he has created $1,000 for two days. After two days, the perpetrator deposits a $1,000 check from bank A in bank B to cover the created $1,000 for two more days. At the appropriate time, $1,000 is deposited from bank C in bank A. The scheme continues—writing checks and making deposits as needed to keep the checks from bouncing.

3. *Convert the theft or misrepresentation to personal gain.*   In a misappropriation, fraud perpetrators who do not steal cash or use the stolen assets personally must convert them to

a spendable form. For example, employees who steal inventory or equipment sell the items or otherwise convert them to cash. In cases of falsified financial statements, perpetrators convert their actions to personal gain through indirect benefits; that is, they keep their jobs, their stock rises, they receive pay raises and promotions, or they gain more power and influence.

Table 5-4 lists frequently mentioned opportunities. Many opportunities are the result of a deficient system of internal controls, such as deficiencies in proper segregation of duties, authorization procedures, clear lines of authority, proper supervision, adequate documents and records, safeguarding assets, or independent checks on performance. Management permits fraud by inattention or carelessness. Management commits fraud by overriding internal controls or using a position of power to compel subordinates to perpetrate it. The most prevalent opportunity for fraud results from a company's failure to design and *enforce* its internal control system.

Companies who do not perform a background check on potential employees risk hiring a "phantom controller." In one case, the company president stopped by the office one night, saw a light on in the controller's office, and went to see why he was working late. The president was surprised to find a complete stranger at work. An investigation showed that the controller was not an accountant and had been fired from three jobs over the prior eight years. Unable to do the accounting work, he hired someone to do his work for him at night. What he was good at was stealing money—he had embezzled several million dollars.

Other factors provide an opportunity to commit and conceal fraud when the company has unclear policies and procedures, fails to teach and stress corporate honesty, and fails to prosecute those who perpetrate fraud. Examples include large, unusual, or complex transactions; numerous adjusting entries at year-end; questionable accounting practices; pushing accounting principles to the limit; related-party transactions; incompetent personnel, inadequate staffing, rapid turnover of key employees, lengthy tenure in a key job, and lack of training.

Frauds occur when employees build mutually beneficial personal relationships with customers or suppliers, such as a purchasing agent buying goods at an inflated price in exchange for a vendor kickback. Fraud can also occur when a crisis arises and normal control procedures are ignored. A Fortune 500 company had three multimillion-dollar frauds the year it disregarded standard internal control procedures while trying to resolve a series of crises.

TABLE 5-4 Opportunities Permitting Employee and Financial Statement Fraud

Internal Control Factors	Other Factors
Failure to enforce/monitor internal controls	Large, unusual, or complex transactions
Management's failure to be involved in the control system	Numerous adjusting entries at year-end
Management override of controls	Related-party transactions
Managerial carelessness, inattention to details	Accounting department that is understaffed, overworked
Dominant and unchallenged management	Incompetent personnel
Ineffective oversight by board of directors	Rapid turnover of key employees
No effective internal auditing staff	Lengthy tenure in a key job
Infrequent third-party reviews	Overly complex organizational structure
Insufficient separation of authorization, custody, and record-keeping duties	No code of conduct, conflict-of-interest statement, or definition of unacceptable behavior
Too much trust in key employees	Frequent changes in auditors, legal counsel
Inadequate supervision	Operating on a crisis basis
Unclear lines of authority	Close association with suppliers/customers
Lack of proper authorization procedures	Assets highly susceptible to misappropriation
No independent checks on performance	Questionable accounting practices
Inadequate documents and records	Pushing accounting principles to the limit
Inadequate system for safeguarding assets	Unclear company policies and procedures
No physical or logical security system	Failing to teach and stress corporate honesty
No audit trails	Failure to prosecute dishonest employees
Failure to conduct background checks	Low employee morale and loyalty
No policy of annual vacations, rotation of duties	

RATIONALIZATIONS A **rationalization** allows perpetrators to justify their illegal behavior. As shown in the Rationalization Triangle in Figure 5-1, this can take the form of a justification ("I only took what they owed me"), an attitude ("The rules do not apply to me"), or a lack of personal integrity ("Getting what I want is more important than being honest"). In other words, perpetrators rationalize that they are not being dishonest, that honesty is not required of them, or that they value what they take more than honesty and integrity. Some perpetrators rationalize that they are not hurting a real person, but a faceless and nameless computer system or an impersonal company that will not miss the money. One such perpetrator stole no more than $20,000, the maximum loss the insurance company would reimburse.

The most frequent rationalizations include the following:

- I am only "borrowing" it, and I will repay my "loan."
- You would understand if you knew how badly I needed it.
- What I did was not that serious.
- It was for a good cause. (The Robin Hood syndrome: robbing the rich to give to the poor)
- In my very important position of trust, I am above the rules.
- Everyone else is doing it.
- No one will ever know.
- The company owes it to me; I am taking no more than is rightfully mine.

Fraud occurs when people have high pressures; an opportunity to commit, conceal, and convert; and the ability to rationalize away their personal integrity. Fraud is less likely to occur when people have few pressures, little opportunity, and high personal integrity. Usually all three elements of the fraud triangle must be present to some degree before a person commits fraud.

Likewise, fraud can be prevented by eliminating or minimizing one or more fraud triangle elements. Although companies can reduce or minimize some pressures and rationalizations, their greatest opportunity to prevent fraud lies in reducing or minimizing opportunity by implementing a good system of internal controls. This is discussed in Chapters 7 through 10.

Computer Fraud

Computer fraud is any fraud that requires computer technology knowledge to perpetrate, investigate, or prosecute it.. Examples include the following:

- Unauthorized theft, use, access, modification, copying, or destruction of software or data
- Theft of assets by altering computer records
- Theft of computer time
- Theft or destruction of hardware or software
- Use of computer resources to commit a felony
- Intent to obtain information or tangible property illegally using computers

Millions of dollars can be stolen in less than a second, leaving little or no evidence. Therefore, computer fraud can be much more difficult to detect than other types of fraud.

The Rise in Computer Fraud

Computer systems are particularly vulnerable for the following reasons:

- People who break into corporate databases can steal, destroy, or alter massive amounts of data in very little time. One bank lost $10 million in cash in a single day.
- Perpetrators can steal many more assets with much less time and effort.
- Some organizations grant employees, customers, and suppliers access to their system. The number and variety of these access points significantly increase the risks.
- Computer programs need to be modified illegally only once for them to operate improperly for as long as they are in use.
- Personal computers (PCs) are vulnerable to security risks. It is difficult to control physical access to each PC that accesses the network. The more legitimate users there are, the greater the risk of an attack on the network. PC users are generally less aware of the

importance of security and control. Segregation of systems duties is difficult because PCs are located in user departments, and one person may be responsible for both development and operations. PCs and their data can be lost, stolen, or misplaced.

- Computer systems face a number of unique challenges: reliability, equipment failure, environmental dependency (i.e., power, damage from water or fire), vulnerability to electromagnetic interference and interruption, eavesdropping, and misrouting.

As early as 1979, *Time* magazine labeled computer fraud a "growth industry." Most businesses have been victimized by computer fraud. During a one-year period, the estimated dollar losses from unauthorized employee computer fraud and abuse in the United States increased 15-fold, from $181,400 to $2.81 million per incident. A few years ago, it was estimated that U.S. Defense Department computers were attacked more than a half million times per year, with the number of incidents increasing 50% to 100% per year. Defense Department staffers and outside consultants made 38,000 "friendly hacks" on their networks to evaluate security. Almost 70% were successful, and the Defense Department detected only 4% of the attacks; the others went unnoticed. The Pentagon, which has the U.S. government's most advanced hacker-awareness program, detected and reported only 1 in 500 break-ins. The Defense Department estimates that more than 100 foreign spy agencies are working to gain access to U.S. government computers as well as an unknown number of criminal organizations. Recently, a spy network in China hacked into 1,300 government and corporate computers in 103 countries.

The number of incidents, the total dollar losses, and the sophistication of the perpetrators and the schemes used to commit computer fraud are increasing rapidly for several reasons:

1. *Not everyone agrees on what constitutes computer fraud.* Many people, for example, do not believe that copying software constitutes computer fraud. Software publishers think otherwise and prosecute those who make illegal copies. Some people do not think it is a crime to browse someone else's computer files if they do no harm, whereas companies whose data are browsed feel much differently.
2. *Many instances of computer fraud go undetected.* At one time, the FBI estimated that only 1% of computer crime is detected; other estimates are between 5% and 20%.
3. *A high percentage of frauds is not reported.* Many companies believe the adverse publicity would result in copycat fraud and a loss of customer confidence, which could cost more than the fraud itself.
4. *Many networks are not secure.* Dan Farmer, who wrote SATAN (a network security testing tool), tested 2,200 high-profile Web sites at government institutions, banks, and newspapers. Only three sites detected and contacted him.
5. *Internet sites offer step-by-step instructions on how to perpetrate computer fraud and abuse.* For instance, an Internet search found thousands of sites telling how to conduct a "denial of service" attack, a common form of computer abuse.
6. *Law enforcement cannot keep up with the growth of computer fraud.* Because of lack of funding and skilled staff, the FBI investigates only 1 in 15 computer crimes.
7. *Calculating losses is difficult.* It is difficult to calculate total losses when information is stolen, Web sites are defaced, and viruses shut down entire computer systems.

This increase in computer fraud created the need for the cyber sleuths discussed in Focus 5-1.

Computer Fraud Classifications

As shown in Figure 5-2, computer fraud can be categorized using the data processing model.

INPUT FRAUD The simplest and most common way to commit a computer fraud is to alter or falsify computer input. It requires little skill; perpetrators need only understand how the system operates so they can cover their tracks. For example:

- A man opened a bank account in New York and had blank bank deposit slips printed that were similar to those available in bank lobbies, except that his account number was encoded on them. He replaced the deposit slips in the bank lobby with his forged ones. For three days, bank deposits using the forged slips went into his account. The perpetrator withdrew the money and disappeared. He was never found.

Cyber Sleuths

Two forensic experts, disguised as repair people, entered an office after hours. They took a digital photograph of three employee desks, made a copy of each employee's hard drive, and used the photo to leave everything as they found it. When the hard drive copy was analyzed, they found evidence of a fraud and notified the company who had hired them. The company turned the case over to law enforcement for investigation and prosecution.

The forensic experts breaking into the company and copying the data worked for a Big Four accounting firm. The accountants, turned cyber sleuths, specialize in catching fraud perpetrators. Cyber sleuths come from a variety of backgrounds, including accounting, information systems, government, law enforcement, military, and banking.

Cyber sleuths need the following skills:

- **Ability to follow a trail, think analytically, and be thorough.** Fraud perpetrators leave tracks, and a cyber sleuth must think analytically to follow paper and electronic trails and uncover fraud. They must be thorough so they do not miss or fail to follow up on clues.
- **Good understanding of information technology (IT).** Cyber sleuths need to understand data storage, data communications, and how to retrieve hidden or deleted files and e-mails.
- **Ability to think like a fraud perpetrator.** Cyber sleuths must understand what motivates perpetrators,

how they think, and the schemes they use to commit and conceal fraud.

- **Ability to use hacking tools and techniques.** Cyber sleuths need to understand the tools computer criminals use to perpetrate fraud and abuse.

Another way to fight crime is to develop software to examine bank or accounting records for suspicious transactions. Pattern recognition software searches millions of bank, brokerage, and insurance accounts and reviews trillions of dollars worth of transactions each day. Some companies, such as PayPal, use the software to lower their fraud rates significantly.

This software is based on a mathematical principle known as Benford's Law. In 1938, Frank Benford discovered that one can predict the first or second digit in a set of naturally occurring numerical data with surprising accuracy. Benford found that the number 1 is the first digit 31% of the time, compared to only 5% for the number 9. Pattern recognition software uses Benford's Law to examine company databases and transaction records to root out accounting fraud.

Students seeking to find their niche in life should be aware that if playing James Bond sounds appealing, then a career as a computer forensics expert might be the way to go.

- A man used desktop publishing to prepare bills for office supplies that were never ordered or delivered and mailed them to companies across the country. The perpetrator kept the invoice total below $300, an amount that in many companies does not require purchase orders or approvals. A high percentage of the companies paid the bills.
- A Milwaukee woman electronically filed over $13,000 of federal and state income tax refunds for 10 fictitious people.
- An employee at the Veteran's Memorial Coliseum sold customers full-price tickets, entered them as half-price tickets, and pocketed the difference.

FIGURE 5-2

Computer Fraud Classifications

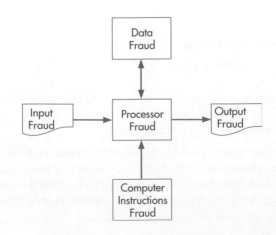

- Railroad employees entered data to scrap over 200 railroad cars. They removed the cars from the railway system, repainted them, and sold them.
- A company providing on-site technical support created exact duplicates of the checks used to pay them, using off-the-shelf scanners, graphics software, and printers. If the double payments were caught, the bank checked their microfiche copies of the two identical checks, assumed a clerical error had occurred, and wrote off the loss as a gesture of maintaining good customer relations.

PROCESSOR FRAUD Processor fraud includes unauthorized system use, including the theft of computer time and services. For example:

- An insurance company installed software to detect abnormal system activity and found that employees were using company computers to run an illegal gambling Web site.
- Two accountants without the appropriate access rights hacked into Cisco's stock option system, transferred over $6.3 million of Cisco stock to their brokerage accounts, and sold the stock. They used part of the funds to support an extravagant lifestyle, including a $52,000 Mercedes-Benz, a $44,000 diamond ring, and a $20,000 Rolex watch.

COMPUTER INSTRUCTIONS FRAUD Computer instruction fraud includes tampering with company software, copying software illegally, using software in an unauthorized manner, and developing software to carry out an unauthorized activity. This approach used to be uncommon because it required specialized programming knowledge. Today, it is more frequent because of the many Web pages that tell users how to create them.

DATA FRAUD Illegally using, copying, browsing, searching, or harming company data constitutes data fraud. It is estimated that, on average, it costs a company $6.6 million, including lost business, to recover from a data breach. The biggest cause of data breaches is employee negligence.

Company employees are much more likely to perpetrate data fraud than outsiders are. A recent study shows that 59% of employees who lost or left a job admitted to stealing confidential company information. Almost 25% of them had access to their former employer's computer system.

In the absence of controls, it is not hard for an employee to steal data. For example, an employee using a small flash drive or an iPod can steal large amounts of data and remove it without being detected. In today's world, you can even buy wristwatches with a USB port and internal memory.

The following are some recent examples of stolen data:

- The office manager of a Wall Street law firm sold information about prospective mergers and acquisitions found in Word files to friends and relatives, who made several million dollars trading the securities.
- A 22-year old Kazakh man broke into Bloomberg's network and stole account information, including that of Michael Bloomberg, the mayor of New York and the founder of the financial news company. He demanded $200,000 in exchange for not using or selling the information. He was arrested in London when accepting the ransom.
- A software engineer tried to steal Intel's new microprocessor plans. Because he could view but not copy or print the plans, he photographed them screen by screen late at night in his office. Unbeknownst to him, one of Intel's controls was to notify security when the plans were viewed after business hours. He was caught red-handed and arrested.
- Cyber-criminals used sophisticated hacking and identity theft techniques to hack into seven accounts at a major online brokerage firm. They sold the securities in those accounts and used the cash to pump up the price of low-priced, thinly traded companies they already owned. Then they sold the stocks in their personal accounts for huge gains. E-trade lost $18 million and Ameritrade $4 million in similar pump-and-dump schemes.
- The U.S. Department of Veterans Affairs was sued because an employee laptop containing the records of 26.5 million veterans was stolen, exposing them to identity theft. Soon thereafter, a laptop with the records of 38,000 people disappeared from a subcontractor's office.

Data can also be changed, damaged, destroyed, or defaced, especially by disgruntled employees and hackers. Vandals broke into the NCAA's Web site before basketball tournament pairings were announced and posted swastikas, racial slurs, and a white-power logo. The Air Force, CIA, and NASA have also been the victims of high-profile Web site attacks. A Computer Security Institute analyst described the problem as "cyberspace vandals with digital spray cans."

Data can be lost as a result of negligence or carelessness. Particularly good sources of confidential data are the hard drives of used computers donated to charity or resold. A professor at a major university bought 10 used computers for his computer forensics class. Using commercially available software, his students found highly confidential data on 8 of the 10 hard drives.

Deleting files does not erase them. Even reformatting a hard drive may not wipe it clean. To erase a hard drive completely, special software must be used. When used computers are to be disposed of, the best way to protect data is to destroy the hard drive.

OUTPUT FRAUD   Unless properly safeguarded, displayed or printed output can be stolen, copied, or misused. A Dutch engineer showed that some monitors emit television-like signals that, with the help of some inexpensive electronic gear, can be displayed on a television screen. Under ideal conditions, the signals can be picked up from monitors two miles away. One engineer set up equipment in the basement of an apartment building and read a monitor on the eighth floor.

Fraud perpetrators use computers to forge authentic-looking outputs, such as a paycheck. A fraud perpetrator can scan a company paycheck, use desktop publishing software to erase the payee and amount, and print fictitious paychecks. Losses to check fraud in the United States total more than $20 billion a year.

Preventing and Detecting Fraud and Abuse

To prevent fraud, organizations must create a climate that makes fraud less likely, increases the difficulty of committing it, improves detection methods, and reduces the amount lost if a fraud occurs. These measures are summarized in Table 5-5 and discussed in Chapters 6 through 10.

TABLE 5-5 Summary of Ways to Prevent and Detect Fraud

Make Fraud Less Likely to Occur
- Create an organizational culture that stresses integrity and commitment to ethical values and competence.
- Adopt an organizational structure, management philosophy, operating style, and risk appetite that minimizes the likelihood of fraud.
- Require oversight from an active, involved, and independent audit committee of the board of directors.
- Assign authority and responsibility for business objectives to specific departments and individuals, encourage them to use initiative to solve problems, and hold them accountable for achieving those objectives.
- Identify the events that lead to increased fraud risk, and take steps to prevent, avoid, share, or accept that risk.
- Develop a comprehensive set of security policies to guide the design and implementation of specific control procedures, and communicate them effectively to company employees.
- Implement human resource policies for hiring, compensating, evaluating, promoting, and discharging employees that send messages about the required level of ethical behavior and integrity.
- Effectively supervise employees, including monitoring their performance and correcting their errors.
- Train employees in integrity and ethical considerations, as well as security and fraud prevention measures.
- Require annual employee vacations and signed confidentiality agreements; periodically rotate duties of key employees.
- Implement formal and rigorous project development and acquisition controls, as well as change management controls.
- Increase the penalty for committing fraud by prosecuting fraud perpetrators more vigorously.

Increase the Difficulty of Committing Fraud
- Develop a strong system of internal controls.
- Segregate the accounting functions of authorization, recording, and custody.
- Implement a proper segregation of duties between systems functions.
- Restrict physical and remote access to system resources to authorized personnel.

TABLE 5-5 Continued

- Require transactions and activities to be authorized by appropriate supervisory personnel. Have the system authenticate the person, and their right to perform the transaction, before allowing the transaction to take place.
- Use properly designed documents and records to capture and process transactions.
- Safeguard all assets, records, and data.
- Require independent checks on performance, such as reconciliation of two independent sets of records, where practical.
- Implement computer-based controls over data input, computer processing, data storage, data transmission, and information output.
- Encrypt stored and transmitted data and programs to protect them from unauthorized access and use.
- When disposing of used computers, destroy the hard drive to keep criminals from mining recycled hard drives.
- Fix software vulnerabilities by installing operating system updates, as well as security and application programs.

Improve Detection Methods

- Create an audit trail so individual transactions can be traced through the system to the financial statements and financial statement data can be traced back to individual transactions.
- Conduct periodic external and internal audits, as well as special network security audits.
- Install fraud detection software.
- Implement a fraud hotline.
- Employ a computer security officer, computer consultants, and forensic specialists as needed.
- Monitor system activities, including computer and network security efforts, usage and error logs, and all malicious actions. Use intrusion detection systems to help automate the monitoring process.

Reduce Fraud Losses

- Maintain adequate insurance.
- Develop comprehensive fraud contingency, disaster recovery, and business continuity plans.
- Store backup copies of program and data files in a secure off-site location.
- Use software to monitor system activity and recover from fraud.

Summary and Case Conclusion

Needing evidence to support his belief that Don Hawkins had committed a fraud, Jason Scott expanded the scope of his investigation. A week later, Jason presented his findings to the president of Northwest. To make his case hit close to home, Jason presented her with a copy of her IRS withholding report and pointed out her withholdings. Then he showed her a printout of payroll withholdings and pointed out the $5 difference, as well as the difference of several thousand dollars in Don Hawkins's withholdings. This got her attention, and Jason explained how he believed a fraud had been perpetrated.

During the latter part of the prior year, Don had been in charge of a payroll program update. Because of problems with other projects, other systems personnel had not reviewed the update. Jason asked a former programmer to review the code changes. She found program code that subtracted $5 from each employee's withholdings and added it to Don's withholdings. Don got his hands on the money when the IRS sent him a huge refund check.

Don apparently intended to use the scheme every year, as he had not removed the incriminating code. He must have known there was no reconciliation of payroll withholdings with the IRS report. His simple plan could have gone undetected for years if Jason had not overheard someone in the cafeteria talk about a $5 difference.

Jason learned that Don had become disgruntled when he was passed over the previous year for a managerial position. He made comments to coworkers about favoritism and unfair treatment and mentioned getting even with the company somehow. No one knew where he got the money, but Don purchased an expensive sports car in April, boasting that he had made a sizable down payment.

When the president asked how the company could prevent this fraud from happening again, Jason suggested the following guidelines:

1. Review internal controls to determine their effectiveness in preventing fraud. An existing control—reviewing program changes—could have prevented Don's scheme had it been followed. As a result, Jason suggested a stricter enforcement of the existing controls.

2. Put new controls into place to detect fraud. For example, Jason suggested a reconciliation of the IRS report and payroll record withholdings.

3. Train employees in fraud awareness, security measures, and ethical issues.

Jason urged the president to prosecute the case. She was reluctant to do so because of the adverse publicity and the problems it would cause Don's wife and children. Jason's supervisor tactfully suggested that if other employees found out that Don was not prosecuted, it would send the wrong message to the rest of the company. The president finally conceded to prosecute if the company could prove that Don was guilty. The president agreed to hire a forensic accountant to build a stronger case against Don and try to get him to confess.

Key Terms

sabotage 123	fraudulent financial	rationalization 130
cookie 123	reporting 125	computer fraud 130
fraud 123	pressure 126	
white-collar criminal 124	opportunity 128	
misappropriation of	lapping 128	
assets 124	kiting 128	

AIS IN ACTION

Chapter Quiz

1. Which of the following is a fraud in which later payments on account are used to pay off earlier payments that were stolen?
   a. lapping
   b. kiting
   c. Ponzi scheme
   d. salami technique

2. Which type of fraud is associated with 50% of all auditor lawsuits?
   a. kiting
   b. fraudulent financial reporting
   c. Ponzi schemes
   d. lapping

3. Which of the following statements is FALSE?
   a. The psychological profiles of white-collar criminals differ from those of violent criminals.
   b. The psychological profiles of white-collar criminals are significantly different from those of the general public.
   c. There is little to no difference between computer fraud perpetrators and other types of white-collar criminals.
   d. Computer fraud perpetrators often do not view themselves as criminals.

4. Which of the following conditions is/are usually necessary for a fraud to occur? (Select all correct answers.)
   a. pressure
   b. opportunity
   c. explanation
   d. rationalization

5. Which of the following is NOT an example of computer fraud?
   a. theft of money by altering computer records
   b. obtaining information illegally using a computer
   c. failure to perform preventive maintenance on a computer
   d. unauthorized modification of a software program

6. Which of the following causes the majority of computer security problems?
    a. human errors   c. natural disasters
    b. software errors   d. power outages

7. Which of the following is NOT one of the responsibilities of auditors in detecting fraud according to SAS No. 99?
    a. Evaluate the results of their audit tests.
    b. Incorporate a technology focus.
    c. Discuss the risks of material fraudulent misstatements.
    d. Catch the perpetrators in the act of committing the fraud.

8. Which of the following control procedures is most likely to deter lapping?
    a. encryption
    b. continual update of the access control matrix
    c. background check on employees
    d. periodic rotation of duties

9. Which of the following is the most important, basic, and effective control to deter fraud?
    a. enforced vacations   c. segregation of duties
    b. logical access control   d. virus protection controls

10. Once fraud has occurred, which of the following will reduce fraud losses? (Select all correct answers.)
    a. insurance   c. contingency plan
    b. regular backup of data and programs d. segregation of duties

Discussion Questions

5.1. Do you agree that the most effective way to obtain adequate system security is to rely on the integrity of company employees? Why or why not? Does this seem ironic? What should a company do to ensure the integrity of its employees?

5.2. You are the president of a multinational company in which an executive confessed to kiting $100,000. What is kiting, and what can your company do to prevent it? How would you respond to the confession? What issues must you consider before pressing charges?

5.3. Discuss the following statement by Roswell Steffen, a convicted embezzler: "For every foolproof system, there is a method for beating it." Do you believe a completely secure computer system is possible? Explain. If internal controls are less than 100% effective, why should they be employed at all?

5.4. Revlon hired Logisticon to install a real-time invoice and inventory processing system. Seven months later, when the system crashed, Revlon blamed the Logisticon programming bugs they discovered and withheld payment on the contract. Logisticon contended that the software was fine and that it was the hardware that was faulty. When Revlon again refused payment, Logisticon repossessed the software using a telephone dial-in feature to disable the software and render the system unusable. After a three-day standoff, Logisticon reactivated the system. Revlon sued Logisticon, charging them with trespassing, breach of contract, and misappropriation of trade secrets (Revlon passwords). Logisticon countersued for breach of contract. The companies settled out of court.

Would Logisticon's actions be classified as sabotage or repossession? Why? Would you find the company guilty of committing a computer crime? Be prepared to defend your position to the class.

5.5. Because improved computer security measures sometimes create a new set of problems—user antagonism, sluggish response time, and hampered performance—some people believe the most effective computer security is educating users about good moral conduct. Richard Stallman, a computer activist, believes software licensing is antisocial because it prohibits the growth of technology by keeping information away from the neighbors. He believes high school and college students should have unlimited access to computers without security measures so that they can learn constructive and civilized behavior. He states that a protected system is a puzzle and, because it is human nature to solve puzzles, eliminating computer security so that there is no temptation to break in would reduce hacking.

Do you agree that software licensing is antisocial? Is ethical teaching the solution to computer security problems? Would the removal of computer security measures reduce the incidence of computer fraud? Why or why not?

Problems

5.1. You were asked to investigate extremely high, unexplained merchandise shortages at a department store chain. You found the following:
   a. The receiving department supervisor owns and operates a boutique carrying many of the same labels as the chain store. The general manager is unaware of the ownership interest.
   b. The receiving supervisor signs receiving reports showing that the total quantity shipped by a supplier was received and then diverts 5% to 10% of each shipment to the boutique.
   c. The store is unaware of the short shipments because the receiving report accompanying the merchandise to the sales areas shows that everything was received.
   d. Accounts Payable paid vendors for the total quantity shown on the receiving report.
   e. Based on the receiving department supervisor's instructions, quantities on the receiving reports were not counted by sales personnel.

Required

Classify each of the five situations as a fraudulent act, a fraud symptom, an internal control weakness, or an event unrelated to the investigation. Justify your answers.
(CIA Examination, adapted)

5.2. A client heard through its hot line that John, the purchases journal clerk, periodically enters fictitious acquisitions. After John creates a fictitious purchase, he notifies Alice, the accounts payable ledger clerk, so she can enter them in her ledger. When the payables are processed, the payment is mailed to the nonexistent supplier's address, a post office box rented by John. John deposits the check in an account he opened in the nonexistent supplier's name.

Required

   a. Define *fraud, fraud deterrence, fraud detection*, and *fraud investigation*.
   b. List four personal (as opposed to organizational) fraud symptoms, or red flags, that indicate the possibility of fraud. Do not confine your answer to this example.
   c. List two procedures you could follow to uncover John's fraudulent behavior.
      (CIA Examination, adapted)

5.3. The computer frauds that are publicly revealed represent only the tip of the iceberg. Although many people perceive that the major threat to computer security is external, the more dangerous threats come from insiders. Management must recognize these problems and develop and enforce security programs to deal with the many types of computer fraud.

Required

Explain how each of the following six types of fraud is committed. Using the format provided, identify a different method of protection for each, and describe how it works.
(CMA Examination, adapted)

Type of Fraud	Explanation	Identification and Description of Protection Methods
a. Input manipulation		
b. Program alteration		
c. File alteration		
d. Data theft		
e. Sabotage		
f. Theft of computer time		

5.4. Environmental, institutional, or individual pressures and opportune situations, which are present to some degree in all companies, motivate individuals and companies to engage in fraudulent financial reporting. Fraud prevention and detection require that pressures and opportunities be identified and evaluated in terms of the risks they pose to a company.

Required

a. Identify two company pressures that would increase the likelihood of fraudulent financial reporting.

b. Identify three corporate opportunities that make fraud easier to commit and detection less likely.

c. For each of the following, identify the external environmental factors that should be considered in assessing the risk of fraudulent financial reporting:
   - The company's industry
   - The company's business environment
   - The company's legal and regulatory environment

d. What can top management do to reduce the possibility of fraudulent financial reporting? *(CMA Examination, adapted)*

5.5. For each of the following independent cases of employee fraud, recommend how to prevent similar problems in the future.

a. Abnormal inventory shrinkage in the audiovisual department at a retail chain store led internal auditors to conduct an in-depth audit of the department. They learned that one customer frequently bought large numbers of small electronic components from a certain cashier. The auditors discovered that they had colluded to steal electronic components by not recording the sale of items the customer took from the store.

b. During an unannounced audit, auditors discovered a payroll fraud when they, instead of department supervisors, distributed paychecks. When the auditors investigated an unclaimed paycheck, they discovered that the employee quit four months previously after arguing with the supervisor. The supervisor continued to turn in a time card for the employee and pocketed his check.

c. Auditors discovered an accounts payable clerk who made copies of supporting documents and used them to support duplicate supplier payments. The clerk deposited the duplicate checks in a bank account she had opened using a name similar to that of the supplier. *(CMA Examination, adapted)*

5.6. An auditor found that Rent-A-Wreck management does not always comply with its stated policy that sealed bids be used to sell obsolete cars. Records indicated that several vehicles with recent major repairs were sold at negotiated prices. Management vigorously assured the auditor that performing limited repairs and negotiating with knowledgeable buyers resulted in better sales prices than the sealed-bid procedures. Further investigation revealed that the vehicles were sold to employees at prices well below market value. Three managers and five other employees pleaded guilty to criminal charges and made restitution.

Required

a. List the fraud symptoms that should have aroused the auditor's suspicion.

b. What audit procedures would show that fraud had in fact occurred? *(CIA Examination, adapted)*

5.7. A bank auditor met with the senior operations manager to discuss a customer's complaint that an auto loan payment was not credited on time. The customer said the payment was made on May 5, its due date, at a teller's window using a check drawn on an account in the bank. On May 10, when the customer called for a loan pay-off balance so he could sell the car, he learned that the payment had not been credited to the loan. On May 12, the customer went to the bank to inquire about the payment and meet with the manager. The manager said the payment had been made on May 11. The customer was satisfied because no late charge would have been assessed until May 15. The manager asked whether the auditor was comfortable with this situation.

The auditor located the customer's paid check and found that it had cleared on May 5. The auditor traced the item back through the computer records and found that the teller had processed the check as being cashed. The auditor traced the payment through the entry records of May 11 and found that the payment had been made with cash instead of a check.

Required

What type of embezzlement scheme is this, and how does it work?

(CIA Examination, adapted)

5.8. Jamison Cardstock did not spend much time or money on internal controls for its cash transactions. The following information reflects Jamison's cash position as of June 30:
- The accounting records show a cash balance of $18,901.62, including undeposited cash receipts.
- A $100 bank statement credit was not recorded in the company's accounting records.
- The bank statement balance was $15,550.
- There were six outstanding checks:

Check Number	Amount
62	$116.25
183	$150.00
284	$253.25
8621	$190.71
8623	$206.80
8632	$145.28

The company cashier embezzled all undeposited cash receipts in excess of the $3,794.41 listed on the following bank reconciliation:

Balance per books, June 30		$18,901.62
Add: Outstanding Checks:		
No. 8621	$190.71	
No. 8623	$206.80	
No. 8632	$145.28	442.79
		$19,344.41
Subtract: Undeposited Receipts		3,794.41
Balance per bank, June 30		$15,550.00
Subtract: Unrecorded Credit		100.00
True Cash, June 30		$15,450.00

Required

a. Prepare a schedule showing how much the cashier embezzled.
b. Describe how the cashier attempted to hide the theft. *(AICPA, adapted)*

5.9. An accountant with the Atlanta Olympic Games was charged with embezzling over $60,000 to purchase a Mercedes-Benz and to invest in a certificate of deposit. Police alleged that he created fictitious invoices from two companies that had contracts with the Olympic Committee: International Protection Consulting and Languages Services. He then wrote checks to pay the fictitious invoices and deposited them into a bank account he had opened under the name of one of the companies. When he was apprehended, he cooperated with police to the extent of telling them of the bogus bank account and the purchase of the Mercedes-Benz and the CD. The accountant was a recent honors graduate from a respected university who, supervisors stated, was a very trusted and loyal employee.

a. How does the accountant fit the profile of a fraudster? How does he not fit the profile?
b. What fraud scheme did he use to perpetrate his fraud?
c. What controls could have prevented his fraud?
d. What controls could have detected his fraud?

5.10. Lexsteel, a manufacturer of steel furniture, has facilities throughout the United States. Problems with the accounts payable system have prompted Lexsteel's external auditor to recommend a detailed study to determine the company's exposure to fraud and to identify ways to improve internal control. Lexsteel's controller assigned the study to Dolores Smith. She interviewed Accounts Payable employees and created the flowchart of the current system shown in Figure 5-3.

Lexsteel's purchasing, production control, accounts payable, and cash disbursements functions are centralized at corporate headquarters. The company mainframe at corporate headquarters is linked to the computers at each branch location by leased telephone lines.

The mainframe generates production orders and the bills of material needed for the production runs. From the bills of material, purchase orders for raw materials are generated and e-mailed to vendors. Each purchase order tells the vendor which manufacturing plant to ship the materials to. When the raw materials arrive, the manufacturing plants produce the items on the production orders received from corporate headquarters.

The manufacturing plant checks the goods received for quality, counts them, reconciles the count to the packing slip, and e-mails the receiving data to Accounts Payable. If raw material deliveries fall behind production, each branch manager can send emergency purchase orders directly to vendors. Emergency order data and verification of materials received are e-mailed to Accounts Payable. Since the company employs a computerized perpetual inventory system, periodic physical counts of raw materials are not performed.

Vendor invoices are e mailed to headquarters and entered by Accounts Payable when received. This often occurs before the branch offices transmit the receiving data. Payments are due 10 days after the company receives the invoices. Using information on the invoice, Data Entry calculates the final day the invoice can be paid, and it is entered as the payment due date.

Once a week, invoices due the following week are printed in chronological entry order on a payment listing, and the corresponding checks are drawn. The checks and payment listing are sent to the treasurer's office for signature and mailing to the payee. The check number is printed by the computer, displayed on the check and the payment listing, and validated as the checks are signed. After the checks are mailed, the payment listing is returned to Accounts Payable for filing. When there is insufficient cash to pay all the invoices, the treasurer retains certain checks and the payment listing until all checks can be paid. When the remaining checks are mailed, the listing is then returned to Accounts Payable. Often, weekly check mailings include a few checks from the previous week, but rarely are there more than two weekly listings involved.

When Accounts Payable receives the payment listing from the treasurer's office, the expenses are distributed, coded, and posted to the appropriate cost center accounts. Accounts Payable processes weekly summary performance reports for each cost center and branch location.

1. Discuss three ways Lexsteel is exposed to fraud, and recommend improvements to correct these weaknesses.
2. Describe three ways in which management information could be distorted, and recommend improvements to correct these weaknesses.
3. Identify and explain three strengths in Lexsteel's procedures. (*CMA Examination, adapted*)

FIGURE 5-3

**Accounts Payable
Procedures at Lexsteel**

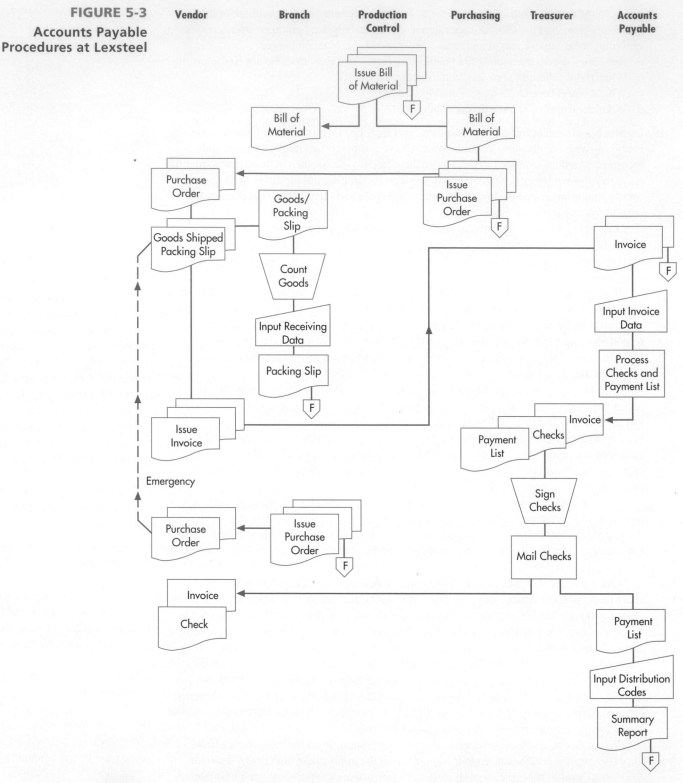

| Vendor | Branch | Production Control | Purchasing | Treasurer | Accounts Payable |

5.11. The Association of Certified Fraud Examiners periodically prepares an article called "What Is Your Fraud IQ?" It consists of 10 or more multiple choice questions dealing with various aspects of fraud. The answers, as well as an explanation of each answer, are provided at the end of the article. Visit the *Journal of Accountancy* site (http://www. journalofaccountancy.com) and search for the articles. Read and answer the questions in three of these articles, and then check your answers.

5.12. Explore the Anti-Fraud and Forensic Accounting portion of the AICPA Web site (www. aicpa.org/InterestAreas/ForensicAndValuation/Resources/ForensicAcctg/Pages/default. aspx), and write a two-page report on the three most interesting things you found on the site.

Case 5-1 David L. Miller: Portrait of a White-Collar Criminal

There is an old saying: Crime doesn't pay. However, for David Miller crime paid for two Mercedes-Benz sedans; a lavish suburban home; a condominium at Myrtle Beach; expensive suits; tailored and monogrammed shirts; diamond, sapphire, ruby, and emerald rings for his wife; and a new car for his father-in-law. Though Miller confessed to embezzling funds from six different employers over a 20-year period, he has never been prosecuted or incarcerated in large part because his employers never turned him in.

Miller was fired from his first employer for stealing $200. After an assortment of odd jobs, he worked as an accountant for a local baker. Miller was caught embezzling funds and paid back the $1,000 he stole. Again, law enforcement was not notified, and he was quietly dismissed.

Several months after Miller started work at Wheeling Bronze, his third victim, the president discovered a $30,000 cash shortfall and several missing returned checks. An extensive search found the canceled checks, with forged signatures, in an outdoor sand pile. Miller confessed to the scheme and was given the choice of repaying the stolen funds or being prosecuted. When Miller's parents mortgaged their home and repaid the stolen money, he escaped prosecution.

Miller's fourth victim was Robinson Pipe Cleaning. When Miller was caught embezzling funds, he again avoided prosecution by promising to repay the $20,000 he stole.

Miller's fifth victim was Crest Industries, where he worked as accountant. He was an ideal employee—dedicated and hard working, doing outstanding work. He was quickly promoted to office manager and soon purchased a new home, car, and wardrobe. Two years later, Crest auditors discovered that $31,000 was missing. Miller had written several checks to himself, recorded them as payments to suppliers, and intercepted and altered the monthly bank statements. With the stolen money, he financed his lifestyle and repaid Wheeling Bronze and Robinson Pipe Cleaning. Once again, Miller tearfully confessed, claiming he had never embezzled funds previously. Miller showed so much remorse that Crest hired a lawyer for him. He promised to repay the stolen money, gave Crest a lien on his house, and was quietly dismissed. Because Crest management did not want to harm Miller's wife and three children, Crest never pressed charges.

Miller's sixth victim was Rustcraft Broadcasting Company. When Rustcraft was acquired by Associated Communications, Miller moved to Pittsburgh to become Associated's new controller. Miller immediately began dipping into Associated's accounts. Over a six-year period, Miller embezzled $1.36 million, $450,000 of that after he was promoted to CFO. Miller circumvented the need for two signatures on checks by asking executives leaving on vacation to sign several checks "just in case" the company needed to disburse funds while he was gone. Miller used the checks to siphon funds to his personal account. To cover the theft, Miller removed the canceled check from the bank reconciliation and destroyed it. The stolen amount was charged to a unit's expense account to balance the company's books.

While working at Associated, Miller bought a new house, new cars, a vacation home, and an extravagant wardrobe. He was generous with tips and gifts. His $130,000 salary could not have supported this lifestyle, yet no one at Associated questioned the source of his conspicuous consumption. Miller's lifestyle came crashing down while he was on vacation and the bank called to inquire about a check written to Miller. Miller confessed and, as part of his out-of-court settlement, Associated received most of Miller's personal property.

Miller cannot explain why he was never prosecuted. His insistence that he was going to pay his victims back usually satisfied his employers and got him off the hook. He believes these agreements actually contributed to his subsequent thefts; one rationalization for stealing from a new employer was to pay back the former one. Miller believes his theft problem is an illness, like alcoholism or compulsive gambling, that is driven by a subconscious need to be admired and liked by others. He thought that by spending money, others would like him. Ironically, he was universally well liked and admired at each job, for reasons that had nothing to do with money. In fact, one Associated coworker was so surprised by the thefts that he said it was like finding out that your brother was an ax murderer. Miller claims he is not a bad person; he never intended to hurt anyone, but once he got started, he could not stop.

After leaving Associated, Miller was hired by a former colleague, underwent therapy, and now believes he has resolved his problem with compulsive embezzlement.

1. How does Miller fit the profile of the average fraud perpetrator? How does he differ? How did these characteristics make him difficult to detect?
2. Explain the three elements of the opportunity triangle (commit, conceal, convert), and discuss how Miller accomplished each when embezzling funds from Associated Communications. What specific concealment techniques did Miller use?
3. What pressures motivated Miller to embezzle? How did Miller rationalize his actions?
4. Miller had a framed T-shirt in his office that said, "He who dies with the most toys wins." What does this tell you about Miller? What lifestyle red flags could have tipped off the company to the possibility of fraud?
5. Why do companies hesitate to prosecute white-collar criminals? What are the consequences of not prosecuting? How could law enforcement officials encourage more prosecution?
6. What could the victimized companies have done to prevent Miller's embezzlement?

Source: Based on Bryan Burrough, "David L. Miller Stole from His Employer and Isn't in Prison," *The Wall Street Journal* (September 19, 1986): 1.

Case 5-2   Heirloom Photo Plans

Heirloom Photos sells a $900 photography plan to rural customers using a commissioned sales force. Rather than pay the price up front, most customers pay $250 down and make 36 monthly payments of $25 each. The $900 plan includes the following:

1. A coupon book good for one free sitting every 6 months for the next 5 years (10 sittings) at any Heirloom-approved photo studio. The customer receives one free 11-by-14-inch black-and-white print. Additional photos or color upgrades can be purchased at the photographer's retail prices.
2. To preserve the 11-by-14-inch photos, the family name is embossed in 24-carat gold on a leather-bound photo album.

The embossed leather album, with a retail value of $300, costs Heirloom $75. Each sitting and free 11-by-14-inch print, with a retail value of $150, costs Heirloom only $50 because photographers are given exclusive rights to all Heirloom customers in a geographic region and have the opportunity to offer customers upgrades to color and/or more pictures.

The commissioned sales staff is paid on the 10th of each month, based upon the prior month's sales. The commission rates are as follows:

Number of plans sold	Commission	Quantity bonus
Fewer than 100	$100 per plan	
101 to 200	$125 per plan	On sale of plan #101, $2,500 is paid to cover the extra $25 on the first 100 sales
More than 200	$150 per plan	On sale of plan #201, $5,000 is paid to cover the extra $25 on the first 200 sales

Over 70% of all agents sell at least 101 plans per year; 40% sell over 200. There is a strong sales surge before year-end as customers purchase plans to give as holiday gifts. About 67% of all agents reach their highest incentive level in late November or December. Heirloom treats the sales staff and the photographers as independent contractors and does not withhold any income or payroll taxes on amounts paid to them.

Salespeople send Heirloom's accounting department the order form, the total payment or the down payment, and the signed note for $650 if the customer finances the transaction. Often, the payment is a hand-written money order. Because many customers live in rural areas, the return address is often a Post Office box, and some customers do not have phones. Heirloom does not perform any credit checks of customers.

Heirloom makes the following entries at the time a new contract is recorded:

To record sale of the contract (assumes contract financed)

Cash	250	
Note Receivable	650	
Sales of Photo Plans		900

To record expenses related to the sale

Album Expense	65	
Embossing/shipping	10	
Sales Expense	130	
Album Inventory		65
Accounts Payable		10
Commissions Payable		130

(Sales expense is estimated using the average cost paid to salespersons in the prior year.)

To record the liability for Photographer Sittings Expense

Photographer Expense	500	
Accrued Liabilities		500

Because the entire cost of the photographer is accrued, the company points to the last entry to show how conservative its accounting is.

After waiting 10 days for the check or money order to clear, Heirloom embosses and ships the album, the photo coupon book, and a payment coupon book with 36 payments of $25. Customers mail a payment coupon and a check or money order to a three-person Receivables Department at headquarters. The Receivables employees open the envelopes, post the payments to the receivables records, and prepare the bank deposit.

The photo coupon book has 10 coupons for photographer sessions, each good for a specific 6-month period. If not used within the 6-month period, the coupon expires.

Each month, the credit manager sends letters and makes phone calls to collect on delinquent accounts. Between 35% and 40% of all customers eventually stop paying on their notes, usually either early in the contract (months 4 to 8) or at the 2-year point (months 22 to 26).

Notes are written off when they are 180 days delinquent. Heirloom's CFO and credit manager use their judgment to adjust the Allowance for Bad Debts monthly. They are confident they can accurately predict the Allowance balance needed at any time, which historically has been about 5% of outstanding receivables.

Agricultural product prices in the area where Heirloom sells its plans have been severely depressed for the second straight year.

Heirloom has been growing quickly and finds that it is continually running short of cash, partly because of the large salaries paid to the two equal owners and their wives. (The wives each receive $100,000 to serve as the treasurer and the secretary; very little, if any, time is required in these duties.) In addition, Heirloom spent large amounts of cash to buy its headquarters, equipment and furnishings, and expensive automobiles for the two owners, their wives, and the four vice presidents.

Heirloom needs to borrow from a local bank for corporate short-term operating purposes. It is willing to pledge unpaid contracts as collateral for a loan. A local bank president is willing to lend Heirloom up to 70% of the value of notes receivable that are not more than 60 days overdue. Heirloom must also provide, by the fifth day of each month, a note receivable aging list for the preceding month and a calculation showing the maximum amount Heirloom may borrow under the agreement.

1. **Figure 5-4** shows the employees and external parties that deal with Heirloom. Explain how Heirloom could defraud the bank and how each internal and external party, except the bank, could defraud Heirloom.

2. What risk factor, unusual item, or abnormality would alert you to each fraud?

3. What control weaknesses make each fraud possible?

4. Recommend one or more controls to prevent or detect each means of committing fraud.

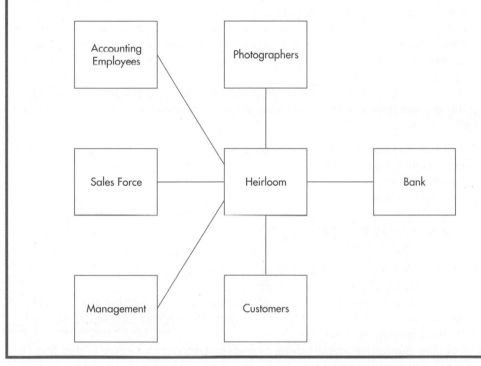

FIGURE 5-4

Internal and External Relationships at Heirloom Photos

AIS IN ACTION SOLUTIONS

Quiz Key

1. Which of the following is a fraud in which later payments on account are used to pay off earlier payments that were stolen?
   ▶ a. lapping (Correct.)
   b. kiting (Incorrect. In a kiting scheme, the perpetrator creates cash by transferring money between banks.)
   c. Ponzi scheme (Incorrect. In a Ponzi scheme, money from new investors is used to pay off earlier investors.)
   d. salami technique (Incorrect. The salami technique involves stealing tiny slices of money over a period of time.)

2. Which type of fraud is associated with 50% of all auditor lawsuits?
   a. kiting (Incorrect. Losses from kiting, a scheme involving bank transfers, are not large enough to be associated with 50% of auditor lawsuits.)

▶ b. fraudulent financial reporting (Correct. Attesting to fraudulent financial statements is the basis of a large percentage of lawsuits against auditors.)

c. Ponzi schemes (Incorrect. Ponzi schemes, in which money from new investors is used to pay off earlier investors, are investment frauds that often do not involve auditors.)

d. lapping (Incorrect. Losses from lapping, in which later payments on account are used to pay off earlier payments that were stolen, are not large enough to be associated with 50% of auditor lawsuits.)

3. Which of the following statements is FALSE?

a. The psychological profiles of white-collar criminals differ from those of violent criminals. (Incorrect. This is a true statement. Psychologically, white-collar criminals are very different than violent criminals.)

▶ b. The psychological profiles of white-collar criminals are significantly different from those of the general public. (Correct. This is false; the psychological profile of white-collar criminals is similar to that of the general public.)

c. There is little to no difference between computer fraud perpetrators and other types of white-collar criminals. (Incorrect. This is a true statement. Although different things can motivate perpetrators of computer fraud, they share many similarities with other types of white-collar criminals.)

d. Computer fraud perpetrators often do not view themselves as criminals. (Incorrect. This is a true statement. Computer fraud perpetrators often do not view what they do as wrong.)

4. Which of the following conditions is/are usually necessary for a fraud to occur? (See the Fraud Triangle in Figure 5-1.)

▶ a. pressure (Correct.)

▶ b. opportunity (Correct.)

c. explanation (Incorrect. An explanation is not one of the three elements of the fraud triangle, as shown in Figure 5-1.)

▶ d. rationalization (Correct.)

5. Which of the following is NOT an example of computer fraud? (See the "Computer Fraud Classifications" section of the chapter.)

a. theft of money by altering computer records (Incorrect. The simplest and most common way to commit a computer fraud is to alter or falsify computer input, such as altering computer records.)

b. obtaining information illegally using a computer (Incorrect. One type of data fraud is using a computer to acquire information illegally.)

▶ c. failure to perform preventive maintenance on a computer (Correct. This is poor management of computer resources, but it is not computer fraud.)

d. unauthorized modification of a software program (Incorrect. Tampering with company software is a type of computer instructions fraud.)

6. Which of the following causes the majority of computer security problems?

▶ a. human errors (Correct. The Computing Technology Industry Association estimates that human errors cause 80% of security problems. These unintentional acts usually are caused by human carelessness, failure to follow established procedures, and poorly trained or supervised personnel.)

b. software errors (Incorrect. Although a federal study estimated yearly economic losses due to software bugs at almost $60 billion a year and revealed that more than 60% of companies studied had significant software errors in the previous year, it is not the main cause of computer security issues.)

c. natural disasters (Incorrect. Natural disasters—such as fires, floods, earthquakes, hurricanes, tornadoes, and blizzards—can destroy an information system and cause a company to fail. When a disaster strikes, many companies are affected at the same time. However, this is not a frequent occurrence and is not the main cause of computer security problems.)

    d. power outages (Incorrect. Massive power failures caused by defective software occasionally occur and leave hundreds of thousands of people and businesses without power, but this is not the main cause of computer security issues.)

7. Which of the following is NOT one of the responsibilities of auditors in detecting fraud according to SAS No. 99?

    a. Evaluate the results of their audit tests. (Incorrect. When an audit is completed, auditors must evaluate whether any identified misstatements indicate the presence of fraud. If they do, the auditor must determine the impact of this on the financial statements and the audit.)

    b. Incorporate a technology focus. (Incorrect. SAS No. 99 recognizes the impact technology has on fraud risks and provides commentary and examples specifically recognizing this impact. It also notes the opportunities the auditor has to use technology to design fraud-auditing procedures.)

    c. Discuss the risks of material fraudulent misstatements. (Incorrect. While planning the audit, team members should discuss among themselves how and where the company's financial statements might be susceptible to fraud.)

▶ d. Catch the perpetrators in the act of committing the fraud. (Correct. SAS No. 99 does not require auditors to witness the perpetrators committing fraud.)

8. Which of the following control procedures is most likely to deter lapping?

    a. encryption (Incorrect. Encryption is used to code data in transit so it cannot be read unless it is decoded. It does not stop employees from lapping accounts receivable payments.)

    b. continual update of the access control matrix (Incorrect. The access control matrix specifies what computer functions employees can perform and what data they can access with a computer. It does not stop employees from lapping accounts receivable payments.)

    c. background check on employees (Incorrect. A background check can help screen out dishonest job applicants, but it does not stop employees from lapping accounts receivable payments.)

▶ d. periodic rotation of duties (Correct. Lapping requires a constant and ongoing cover-up to hide the stolen funds. Rotating duties such that the perpetrator does not have access to the necessary accounting records will most likely result in the fraud's discovery.)

9. Which of the following is the most important, basic, and effective control to deter fraud?

    a. enforced vacations (Incorrect. Enforced vacations will prevent or deter some, but not all, fraud schemes.)

    b. logical access control (Incorrect. Logical access controls will prevent or deter some, but not all, fraud schemes.)

▶ c. segregation of duties (Correct. Segregating duties among different employees is the most effective control for the largest number of fraud schemes, because it makes it difficult for any single employee to both commit and conceal a fraud.)

    d. virus protection controls (Incorrect. Virus protection controls will help prevent some computer-related abuses, but they are unlikely to deter much fraud.)

10. Once fraud has occurred, which of the following will reduce fraud losses? (Select all correct answers.)

▶ a. insurance (Correct. The right insurance will pay for all or a portion of fraud losses.)

▶ b. regular backup of data and programs (Correct. Regular backup helps the injured party recover lost or damaged data and programs.)

▶ c. contingency plan (Correct. A contingency plan helps the injured party restart operations on a timely basis.)

    d. segregation of duties (Incorrect. Segregation of duties is an effective method of deterring fraud but does not help a company recover from fraud once it occurs.)

Chapter 6

Computer Fraud and Abuse Techniques

Learning Objectives

After studying this chapter, you should be able to:

1. Compare and contrast computer attack and abuse tactics.

2. Explain how social engineering techniques are used to gain physical or logical access to computer resources.

3. Describe the different types of malware used to harm computers.

INTEGRATIVE CASE NORTHWEST INDUSTRIES

Northwest Industries wants to expand its service area and has been negotiating to buy Remodeling Products Centers (RPC), a competitor that operates in an area contiguous to Northwest. Jason Scott was part of a team sent to look over RPC's books before the deal was finalized. At the end of their first day, RPC's computer system crashed. The team decided to finish up what work they could and to let RPC's information technology (IT) people get the system up that night.

The next day, RPC's system was still down, so Jason tried to log into Northwest's computer system. It seemed to take forever to access, and then Jason found that system response was rather slow. His manager called the corporate office and found that there was something wrong with Northwest's system. It was assumed that the problem had something to do with communications with RPC's computers.

Jason's team was assigned to do a computer fraud and abuse evaluation of RPC's system while they waited. Since Jason had never participated in such a review, he was told to go back to the hotel where he could get on the Internet and spend the day researching the different ways computer systems could be attacked.

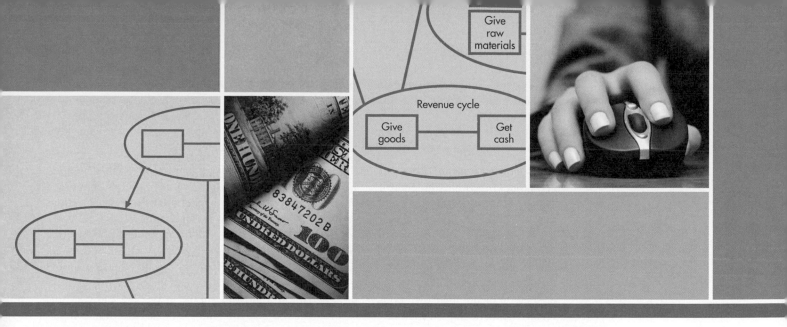

Introduction

Cyber criminals have devised an ever-increasing number of ways to commit computer fraud and abuse. This chapter discusses some of the more common techniques in three sections: computer attacks and abuse, social engineering, and malware. These classifications are not distinct; there is a lot of overlap among the categories. For example, social engineering methods are often used to launch computer attacks.

Computer Attacks and Abuse

All computers connected to the Internet, especially those with important trade secrets or valuable IT assets, are under constant attack from hackers, foreign governments, terrorist groups, disaffected employees, industrial spies, and competitors. These people attack computers looking for valuable data or to harm the computer system. Preventing attacks is a constant battle. On a busy day, large Web hosting farms suffer millions of attack attempts. This section describes some of the more common attack techniques.

Hacking is the unauthorized access, modification, or use of an electronic device or some element of a computer system. Most hackers break into systems using known flaws in operating systems or application programs, or as a result of poor access controls. One software-monitoring company estimates there are over 7,000 known flaws in software released in any given year. The following examples illustrate hacking attacks and the damage they cause:

- Russian hackers broke into Citibank's system and stole $10 million from customer accounts.
- Acxiom manages customer information for credit card issuers, banks, automotive manufacturers, and retailers. Daniel Baas, a systems administrator for a company doing business with Acxiom, exceeded his authorized access, downloaded an encrypted password file, and used a password-cracking program to access confidential identification information. The intrusion cost Acxiom over $5.8 million.
- During the Iraq war, Dutch hackers stole confidential information, including troop movements and weapons information, from 34 military sites. Their offer to sell the information to Iraq was declined, probably because Iraq feared it was a setup.
- A 17-year-old hacker, nicknamed Shadow Hawk, hacked the Bell Laboratories national network, destroyed files valued at $174,000, and copied 52 proprietary software programs worth $1.2 million. He published confidential information—such as telephone numbers, passwords, and instructions on how to breach AT&T's computer security

system—on underground bulletin boards. He was sentenced to nine months in prison and fined $10,000. Like Shadow Hawk, many hackers are young, some as young as 12 and 13.

● A hacker penetrated a software supplier's computer and used its "open pipe" to a bank customer to install a powerful Trojan horse in the bank's computer.

A *botnet*, short for robot network, is a network of powerful and dangerous hijacked computers. *Hijacking* is gaining control of a computer to carry out illicit activities without the user's knowledge. *Bot herders* install software that responds to the hacker's electronic instructions onto unwitting PCs. Bot software is delivered in a variety of ways, including Trojans, e-mails, instant messages, Tweets, or an infected Web site. Bot herders use the combined power of the hijacked computers, called *zombies*, to mount a variety of Internet attacks. Worldwide, there are over 2,000 botnets containing over 10 million computers (10% of online computers), many of them for rent. Bot toolkits and easy-to-use software are available on the Internet showing hackers how to create their own botnets; hacking is now almost as simple as picking and choosing features and clicking on a checkbox. The Mariposa botnet, containing almost 13 million computers in 190 countries, was created by three men without any advanced hacker skills.

Botnets are used to perform a *denial-of-service (DoS) attack*, which is designed to make a resource unavailable to its users. In an e-mail attack, so many e-mails (thousands per second) are received, often from randomly generated false addresses, that the Internet service provider's e-mail server is overloaded and shuts down. Another attack involves sending so many Web page requests that the Web server crashes. An estimated 5,000 denial-of-service attacks occur per week. The Web sites of online merchants, banks, governmental agencies, and news agencies are frequent victims. The following examples illustrate denial-of-service attacks and the damage they cause:

● A DoS attack shut down 3,000 Web sites for 40 hours on one of the busiest shopping weekends of the year.
● CloudNine, an Internet service provider, went out of business after DoS attacks prevented its subscribers and their customers from communicating.
● An estimated 1 in 12 e-mails carried the MyDoom virus at its peak. The virus turned its host into a zombie that attacked Microsoft. Other companies, such as Amazon, Yahoo, CNN, and eBay, have all suffered similar DoS attacks.

Spamming is e-mailing or texting an unsolicited message to many people at the same time, often in an attempt to sell something. An estimated 250 billion e-mails are sent every day (2.8 million per second); 80% are spam and viruses. The Federal Trade Commission estimates that 80% of spam is sent from botnets. Spams are annoying and costly, and 10% to 15% offer products or services that are fraudulent. In retaliation, some spammers are spammed in return with thousands of messages, causing their e-mail service to fail. Such retaliation affects innocent users and can result in the closure of an e-mail account. Spammers scan the Internet for addresses posted online, hack into company databases, and steal or buy mailing lists. An AOL employee stole the names and e-mail addresses of 92 million people and sold them to spammers.

Spammers also stage *dictionary attacks* (also called *direct harvesting attacks*). Spammers use special software to guess addresses at a company and send blank e-mail messages. Messages not returned usually have valid e-mail addresses and are added to spammer e-mail lists. Dictionary attacks are a major burden to corporate e-mail systems and Internet service providers. Some companies receive more dictionary attack e-mail than valid e-mail messages. One day 74% of the e-mail messages that Lewis University received were for nonexistent addresses. Companies use e-mail filtering software to detect dictionary attacks; unfortunately, spammers continue to find ways around the rules used in e-mail filtering software.

A blog (short for We*b log*) is a Web site containing online journals or commentary. Hackers create *splogs* (combination of *sp*am and b*log*) with links to Web sites they own to increase their Google PageRank, which is how often a Web page is referenced by other Web pages. Since Web sites with high PageRanks appear first in search results pages, splogs are created to artificially inflate paid-ad impressions from visitors, to sell links, or to get new sites indexed. Splogs are annoying, waste valuable disk space and bandwidth, and pollute search engine results.

Spoofing is making an electronic communication look as if someone else sent it to gain the trust of the recipient. Spoofing can take various forms, including the following:

- *E-mail spoofing* is making an e-mail appear as though it originated from a different source. Many spam and phishing attacks use special software to create random sender addresses. A former Oracle employee was charged with breaking into the company's computer network, falsifying evidence, and committing perjury for forging an e-mail message to support her charge that she was fired for ending a relationship with the company CEO. Using cell phone records, Oracle lawyers proved that the supervisor who had supposedly fired her and written the e-mail was out of town when the e-mail was written and could not have sent it. The employee was found guilty of forging the e-mail message and faced up to six years in jail.
- *Caller ID spoofing* is displaying an incorrect number (any number the attacker chooses) on a caller ID display to hide the caller's identity.
- *IP address spoofing* is creating Internet Protocol (IP) packets with a forged source IP address to conceal the identity of the sender or to impersonate another computer system. IP spoofing is most frequently used in denial-of-service attacks.
- *Address Resolution Protocol (ARP) spoofing* is sending fake ARP messages to an Ethernet LAN. ARP is a networking protocol for determining a network host's hardware address when only its IP or network address is known. ARP is critical for local area networking as well as for routing internet traffic across gateways (routers). ARP spoofing allows an attacker to associate his *MAC address* (*Media Access Control* address, a hardware address that uniquely identifies each node on a network) with the IP address of another node. Any traffic meant for the intended IP address is mistakenly sent to the attacker instead. The attacker can sniff the traffic and forward it to its intended target, modify the data before forwarding it (called a man-in-the-middle attack), or launch a denial of service attack.
- *SMS spoofing* is using the short message service (SMS) to change the name or number a text message appears to come from. In Australia, a woman got a call asking why she had sent the caller multiple adult message texts every day for the past few months. Neither she nor her mobile company could explain the texts, as her account showed that they were not coming from her phone. When she realized there was no way of blocking the messages, she changed her mobile number to avoid any further embarrassment by association.
- *Web-page spoofing*, also called phishing, is discussed later in the chapter.
- *DNS spoofing* is sniffing the ID of a Domain Name System (the "phone book" of the Internet that converts a domain, or Web site name, to an IP address) request and replying before the real DNS server can.

A *zero-day attack* (or *zero-hour attack*) is an attack between the time a new software vulnerability is discovered and the time a software developer releases a *patch* that fixes the problem. When hackers detect a new vulnerability, they "release it into the wild" by posting it on underground hacker sites. Word spreads quickly, and the attacks begin. It takes companies time to discover the attacks, study them, develop an antidote, release the patch to fix the problem, install the patch on user systems, and update antivirus software. One way software developers minimize the vulnerability window is to monitor known hacker sites so they know about the vulnerability when the hacker community does.

Vulnerability windows last anywhere from hours to forever if users do not patch their system. A national retailing firm employee used the server that clears credit card transactions to download music from an infected Web site. The music contained Trojan horse software that allowed Russian hackers to take advantage of an unpatched, known vulnerability to install software that collected and sent credit card data to 16 different computers in Russia every hour for four months until it was detected.

Cybercrooks take advantage of Microsoft's security update cycle by timing new attacks right before or just after "Patch Tuesday"—the second Tuesday of each month, when the software maker releases its fixes. The term "zero-day Wednesday" describes this strategy.

Cross-site scripting (XSS) is a vulnerability in dynamic Web pages that allows an attacker to bypass a browser's security mechanisms and instruct the victim's browser to execute code thinking it came from the desired Web site. Most attacks use executable JavaScript, although HTML, Flash, or other codes the browser can execute are also used. XSS flaws are the most prevalent flaws in Web applications today and occur anywhere a Web application uses input from a user in the output it generates without validating or encoding it. The likelihood that a site contains XSS vulnerabilities is extremely high. Finding these flaws is not difficult for attackers; there are many free tools available that help hackers find them, create the malicious code, and inject it into a target site. Many prominent sites have had XSS attacks, including Google, Yahoo, Facebook, MySpace, and MediaWiki. In fact, MediaWiki has had to fix over 30 XSS weaknesses to protect Wikipedia.

An example of how XSS works follows. Luana hosts a Web site that Christy frequently uses to store all her financial data. To use the Web site, Christy logs on using her username and password. While searching for vulnerable Web sites, Miles finds that Luana's Web site has an XSS vulnerability. Miles creates a URL to exploit it and sends it to Christy in an e-mail that motivates Christy to click on it while logged into Luana's Web site. The XSS vulnerability is exploited when the malicious script embedded in Miles's URL executes in Christy's browser, as if it came directly from Luana's server. The script sends Christy's session cookie to Miles, who hijacks Christy's session. Miles can now do anything Christy can do. Miles can also send the victim's cookie to another server, inject forms that steal Christy's confidential data, disclose her files, or install a Trojan horse program on her computer. Miles can also use XSS to send a malicious script to her husband Jeremy's computer. Jeremy's browser has no way of knowing that the script should not be trusted; it thinks it came from a trusted source and executes the script.

Miles could also execute XSS by posting a message with the malicious code to a social network. When Brian reads the message, Miles's XSS will steal his cookie, allowing Miles to hijack Brian's session and impersonate him.

Attempting to filter out malicious scripts is unlikely to succeed, as attackers encode the malicious script in hundreds of ways so it looks less suspicious to the user. The best way to protect against XSS is HTML sanitization, which is a process of validating input and only allowing users to input predetermined characters. Companies also try to identify and remove XSS flaws from a Web application. To find flaws, companies review their code, searching for all the locations where input from an HTTP request could enter the HTML output.

A *buffer overflow attack* happens when the amount of data entered into a program is greater than the amount of the memory (the input buffer) set aside to receive it. The input overflow usually overwrites the next computer instruction, causing the system to crash. Hackers exploit this buffer overflow by carefully crafting the input so that the overflow contains code that tells the computer what to do next. This code could open a back door into the system, provide the attacker with full control of the system, access confidential data, destroy or harm system components, slow system operations, and carry out any number of other inappropriate acts. Buffer overflow exploits can occur with any form of input, including mail servers, databases, Web servers, and ftps. Many exploits have been written to cause buffer overflows. The Code Red worm used a buffer overflow to exploit a hole in Microsoft's Internet Information Services.

In an *SQL injection (insertion)* attack, malicious code in the form of an SQL query is inserted into input so it can be passed to and executed by an application program. The idea is to convince the application to run SQL code that it was not intended to execute by exploiting a database vulnerability. It is one of several vulnerabilities that can occur when one programming language is embedded inside another. A successful SQL injection can read sensitive data from the database; modify, disclose, destroy, or limit the availability of the data; allow the attacker to become a database administrator; spoof identity; and issue operating system commands. An SQL injection attack can have a significant impact that is limited only by the attacker's skill and imagination and system controls.

Albert Gonzalez used SQL injection techniques to create a back door on corporate systems. He then used packet sniffing and ARP spoofing attacks to steal data on more than 170 million credit cards. His $200 million fraud was the largest such fraud in history. He was sentenced to 20 years in prison, the harshest computer crime sentence in American history. Like most fraud perpetrators, he spent his ill-gotten gains on a Miami condominium, an expensive car, Rolex watches, and a Tiffany ring for his girlfriend. He threw himself a $75,000 birthday party and stayed in lavish hotels and resorts. He even complained about having to count $340,000 by hand after his currency-counting machine broke.

As shown in Figure 6-1, a *man-in-the-middle (MITM) attack* places a hacker between a client and a host and intercepts network traffic between them. An MITM attack is often called a

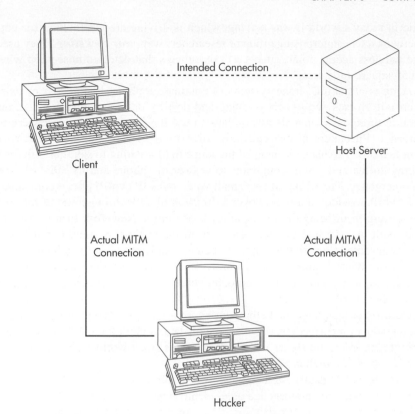

FIGURE 6-1

**A Man-in-the Middle
Cyber Attack**

session hijacking attack. MITM attacks are used to attack public-key encryption systems where sensitive and valuable information is passed back and forth. For example, Linda sniffs and eavesdrops on a network communication and finds David sending his public key to Teressa so that they can communicate securely. Linda substitutes her forged public key for David's key and steps in the middle of their communications. If Linda can successfully impersonate both David and Teressa by intercepting and relaying the messages to each other, they believe they are communicating securely. Once an MITM presence is established, the hacker can read and modify client messages, mislead the two parties, manipulate transactions, and steal confidential data. To prevent MITM attacks, most cryptographic protocols authenticate each communication endpoint. Many of the spoofing techniques discussed in the chapter are used in MITM attacks.

Masquerading or *impersonation* is pretending to be an authorized user to access a system. This is possible when the perpetrator knows the user's ID number and password or uses her computer after she has logged in (while the user is in a meeting or at lunch).

Piggybacking has several meanings:

1. The clandestine use of a neighbor's Wi-Fi network; this can be prevented by enabling the security feature in the wireless network.
2. Tapping into a telecommunications line and electronically latching onto a legitimate user before the user enters a secure system; the legitimate user unknowingly carries the perpetrator into the system.
3. An unauthorized person following an authorized person through a secure door, bypassing physical security controls such as keypads, ID cards, or biometric identification scanners.

Password cracking is penetrating a system's defenses, stealing the file containing valid passwords, decrypting them, and using them to gain access to programs, files, and data. A police officer suspected his wife of an affair and believed the lovers communicated by e-mail. He asked a former police officer to break into his wife's password-protected corporate e-mail account and print her e-mails. The hacker used a wireless access point to penetrate the network and download her e-mail. It took three days to crack her password and confirm the husband's suspicions.

War dialing is programming a computer to dial thousands of phone lines searching for dial-up modem lines. Hackers hack into the PC attached to the modem and access the network to which it is connected. This approach got its name from the movie *War Games*. Much more problematic in today's world is *war driving*, which is driving around looking for unprotected wireless networks. One enterprising group of researchers went *war rocketing*. They used rockets to let loose wireless access points attached to parachutes that detected unsecured wireless networks in a 50-square-mile area.

Phreaking is attacking phone systems to obtain free phone line access or using phone lines to transmit viruses and to access, steal, and destroy data. One telephone company lost $4.5 million in three days when details on how to use its phone lines for free were published on the Internet. Phreakers also break into voice mail systems, as the New York Police Department learned. The hackers changed the voice mail greeting to say that officers were too busy drinking coffee and eating doughnuts to answer the phone and to call 119 (not 911) in case of an emergency. The owner of two small voice-over-IP (VoIP) phone companies hacked into a larger VoIP provider and routed over $1 million of calls through one of his systems. To keep the rerouting from being discovered, they broke into a New York firm's system, set up a server, and made it look like the calls came from many third parties. Other hackers have hijacked calls, rerouted them to their own call centers, and asked callers to identify themselves by divulging confidential information. To protect a system from phreakers, companies use a voice firewall that scans inbound and outbound voice traffic, terminates any suspicious activity, and provides real-time alerts.

Data diddling is changing data before, during, or after it is entered into the system in order to delete, alter, add, or incorrectly update key system data. A clerk for a Denver brokerage altered a transaction to record 1,700 shares of Loren Industries stock worth $2,500 as shares in Long Island Lighting worth more than $25,000.

Data leakage is the unauthorized copying of company data. Ten Social Security employees stole 11,000 Social Security numbers and other identifying information and sold them to identity theft fraudsters. Acxiom suffered a data loss when, over a year and a half, an individual used a company's ftp client to steal 8.2 GB of data. *Podslurping* is using a small device with storage capacity, such as an iPod or Flash drive, to download unauthorized data. Security expert Abe Usher created slurp.exe and copied all document files from his computer in 65 seconds. Usher now makes a version of his program for security audits that does not copy files but generates a report of the information that could have been stolen in a real attack.

The *salami technique* is used to embezzle money a "salami slice" at a time from many different accounts. A disgruntled employee programmed the company computer to increase all production costs by a fraction of a percent and place the excess in the account of a dummy vendor he controlled. Every few months, the fraudulent costs were raised another fraction of a percent. Because all expenses were rising together, no single account would call attention to the fraud. The perpetrator was caught when a teller failed to recognize the payee name on a check the perpetrator was trying to cash. The salami scheme was part of the plot line in several films, including *Superman III, Hackers,* and *Office Space.*

One salami technique has been given a name. In a *round-down fraud*, all interest calculations are truncated at two decimal places and the excess decimals put into an account the perpetrator controls. No one is the wiser, since all the books balance. Over time, these fractions of a cent add up to a significant amount, especially when interest is calculated daily.

Economic espionage is the theft of information, trade secrets, and intellectual property. Losses are estimated to total $250 billion a year, with losses increasing by 323% during one five-year period. Almost 75% of losses are to an employee, former employee, contractor, or supplier. The FBI is investigating about 800 separate incidents of economic espionage at any point in time. Reuters Analytics allegedly broke into the computers of Bloomberg, a competitor, and stole code that helps financial institutions analyze stock market data. Toshiba paid $465 million to Lexar Media as compensation for trade secrets provided by a member of Lexar's board of directors.

Cyber-extortion is threatening to harm a company or a person if a specified amount of money is not paid. The owner of a credit card processor received an e-mail listing his clients as well as their credit card numbers. The e-mail told him to pay $50,000 in six payments, or the data would be sent to his clients. An investigation showed that his system had been successfully penetrated and that customer data had been copied. Not believing the attacker, the owner did nothing. The extortionists released the data, and he spent weeks trying to reassure his irate customers. His efforts were futile; his customers abandoned him, and within six months, he shut down his business. Diana DeGarmo, the runner-up from the third season of *American Idol*, was stalked by an obsessive fan who wanted to "become" Diana. The fan broke into Diana's MySpace account, stole her identity, and sent e-mails to her friends and fans. The fan phoned, e-mailed, and texted Diana more than a hundred times a day. When Diana finally asked her what she wanted, she replied that she wanted $1 million.

Cyber-bullying is using the Internet, cell phones, or other communication technologies to support deliberate, repeated, and hostile behavior that torments, threatens, harasses, humiliates, embarrasses, or otherwise harms another person. Cyber-bullying is especially prevalent among young people; research shows that almost half of all teens and preteens report some form of cyber-bullying. *Sexting* is exchanging explicit text messages and revealing pictures. One particularly degrading form of cyber-bullying is posting or sharing these pictures and messages with people who were never intended to see or read them. Anyone involved in transmitting nude pictures of someone under the age of 18 can be charged with dealing in child pornography. Legislation penalizing cyber-bullying has been passed in many states.

Internet terrorism is the act of disrupting electronic commerce and harming computers and communications. A Massachusetts man hired hackers to attack the WeaKnees.com Web site because WeaKnees turned down a business deal with him. The six-week-long attack used a botnet of 10,000 hijacked computers and caused $2 million in damage.

Internet misinformation is using the Internet to spread false or misleading information. McDonald's spent seven years fighting false accusations on Web sites. After 313 days of testimony and a cost of $16 million, McDonald's won and was awarded $94,000. A Web site mocked the verdict, called its campaign "unstoppable," and set up shop under a new name. Another form of Internet misinformation is pretending to be someone else and posting Web-based messages that damage the reputation of the impersonated person. Even subtler is entering bogus information in legitimate news stories. One young man broke into Yahoo's news pages and replaced the name of an arrested hacker with that of Bill Gates.

Perpetrators also send unsolicited *e-mail threats*. Global Communications sent messages threatening legal action if an overdue amount was not paid within 24 hours. The court action could be avoided by calling an 809 area code (the Caribbean). Callers got a clever recording that responded to the caller's voice. The responses were designed to keep callers on the phone as long as possible because they were being billed at $25 per minute.

Internet auction fraud is using an Internet auction site to defraud another person. According to the FBI, 45% of the complaints they receive are about Internet auction fraud. Internet auction fraud can take several forms. For example, a seller can use a false identity or partner with someone to drive up the bid price. A person can enter a very high bid to win the auction and then cancel his bid, allowing his partner, who has the next highest, and much lower, bid to win. The seller can fail to deliver the merchandise, or the buyer can fail to make the agreed-upon payment. The seller can deliver an inferior product or a product other than the one sold. In a recent case, three art dealers were convicted of casting bids in over 1,100 of each other's eBay auctions to drive up the price of their merchandise over a five-year period. Many of the 120 defrauded consumers paid thousands of dollars more than they would have without the fake bids.

Internet pump-and-dump fraud is using the Internet to pump up the price of a stock and then selling it. Pump-and-dump fraudsters do three things. First, they buy a significant number of shares in small, low-priced, thinly traded penny stocks without driving up their price. Second, they use spam e-mails, texts, Tweets, and Internet postings to disseminate overly optimistic or false information about the company to create a buying frenzy that drives up the stock price. Third, they sell their shares to unsuspecting investors at inflated prices and pocket a handsome profit. Once they stop touting the stock, its price crumbles, and investors lose their money. In a recent fraud, fraudsters quietly acquired shares in 15 thinly traded public companies. They used sophisticated hacking and identity fraud techniques, such as installing keystroke-logging software on computers in hotel business centers and Internet cafes, to gain access to online brokerage accounts. The hackers sold the securities in those accounts, used the money to purchase large quantities of stock of the 15 companies to pump up the share prices of those companies, and sold their stock for a $732,941 profit. The pump-and-dump operation, which was perpetrated in a few hours, cost U.S. brokerage firms an estimated at $2 million.

Companies advertising online pay from a few cents to over $10 for each click on their ads. *Click fraud* is manipulating click numbers to inflate advertising bills. Examples include

(1) companies clicking on a competitor's ad to drive up their advertising costs, (2) Web page owners who get a commission to host a pay-per-click ad clicking to boost commissions, and (3) ad agencies inflating the number of clicks to make an ad campaign appear more effective. Most click fraudsters are cyber criminals who create Web sites with nothing on them but ads and use their botnets to repeatedly click on the ads. As many as 30% of all clicks are not legitimate. That is no small sum, given that total revenues from online advertising exceed $15 billion dollars a year.

Web cramming is offering a free Web site for a month, developing a worthless Web site, and charging the phone bill of the people who accept the offer for months, whether they want to continue using the Web site or not. Web cramming has been in the top ten of online scams for the past few years, and there are no signs that it is going away. Law enforcement has cracked down on this for the past few years with no apparent permanent success.

Software piracy is the unauthorized copying or distribution of copyrighted software. Software piracy usually takes one of three forms: (1) selling a computer with pre-loaded illegal software, (2) installing a single-license copy on multiple machines, and (3) loading software on a network server and allowing unrestricted access to it in violation of the software license agreement.

It is estimated that for every legal software sale, between seven and eight illegal copies are made. Within days of being released, most new software is on the Internet and available free to those who want to download it illegally. An estimated 43% of software is pirated; in some countries, over 90% is pirated. The software industry estimates the economic losses due to software piracy exceed $50 billion a year.

The Business Software Alliance, which files lawsuits against software pirates, found 1,400 copies of unlicensed software at an adult vocational school in Los Angeles and claimed $5 million in damages. Individuals convicted of software piracy are subject to fines of up to $250,000 and jail terms of up to five years. However, they are often given more creative punishments. A Puget Sound student was required to write a 20-page paper on the evils of software piracy and copyright infringement and perform 50 hours of community service wiring schools for Internet usage. Failure to comply would subject him to a $10,000 fine and a copyright infringement lawsuit.

Social Engineering

Social engineering refers to techniques or psychological tricks used to get people to comply with the perpetrator's wishes in order to gain physical or logical access to a building, computer, server, or network—usually to get the information needed to access a system for the purpose of obtaining confidential data. Often, the perpetrator has a conversation with someone to trick, lie to, or otherwise deceive the victim. Often the perpetrator has information, knowledge, authority, or confidence that makes it appear that he belongs or knows what he is doing.

Establishing the following policies and procedures—and training people to follow them—can help minimize social engineering:

1. Never let people follow you into a restricted building.
2. Never log in for someone else on a computer, especially if you have administrative access.
3. Never give sensitive information over the phone or through e-mail.
4. Never share passwords or user IDs.
5. Be cautious of anyone you do not know who is trying to gain access through you.

The remainder of this section discusses various social engineering issues and techniques.

Identity theft is assuming someone's identity, usually for economic gain, by illegally obtaining and using confidential information, such as a Social Security number or a bank account or credit card number. Identity thieves empty bank accounts, apply for credit cards, run up large debts, and take out mortgages and loans. By carefully covering his tracks and having all bills sent to an address he controls, the identity thief can prolong the scheme because the victim will not know what is happening until considerable damage has been caused. Victims can usually prove they are not responsible for the debts or missing funds, but it takes significant time to clean up credit records and restore reputations.

A convicted felon incurred $100,000 of credit card debt, took out a home loan, purchased homes and consumer goods, and filed for bankruptcy in the victim's name. He phoned and mocked his victim because the victim could not do anything, because identity theft was not a crime at the time. The victim spent four years and $15,000 to restore his credit and reputation. The identity thief served a brief sentence for lying while buying a gun and did not have to make restitution. This and similar cases resulted in Congress making identity theft a federal offense in 1998.

Pretexting is using an invented scenario (the pretext) to increase the likelihood that a victim will divulge information or do something. The pretext is more than a just simple lie; it usually involves creating legitimacy in the target's mind that makes impersonation possible. Pretexters conduct a security survey and lull the victim into disclosing confidential information by asking 10 innocent questions before asking the confidential ones. They call help desks and claim to be an employee who has forgotten a password. They call users and say they are testing the system and need a password. They pose as buyers, prospective employees, or salespeople to get plant tours and obtain information that may help them break into the system. They use voice-changing devices to make a male voice sound like a female voice or use spoofing devices to make it appear they are phoning from the intended victim's phone.

The chairwoman of Hewlett-Packard was forced to resign after H-P hired a private investigator to catch H-P directors who had leaked confidential information to reporters. The private investigator pretended to be someone he was not to get private phone records and other confidential information of directors and journalists. As a result, Congress passed a bill making the use of pretexting to obtain a person's phone records illegal.

A hacker tricked a T-Mobile employee into disclosing the information needed to hack into Paris Hilton's phone by answering the question "What is your favorite pet's name?" Tinkerbell, the name of her dog, was well known. The hacker accessed her phone and posted the contents of her address book, notes, and some very embarrassing photos on the Internet.

Posing is creating a seemingly legitimate business (often selling new and exciting products), collecting personal information while making a sale, and never delivering the product. Fraudsters also create Internet job listing sites to collect confidential information.

Phishing is sending an electronic message pretending to be a legitimate company, usually a financial institution, and requesting information or verification of information and often warning of some dire consequence if it is not provided. The recipient is asked to respond to the bogus request or visit a Web page and submit data. The message usually contains a link to a Web page that appears legitimate. The Web page has company logos, familiar graphics, phone numbers, and Internet links that appear to be those of the victimized company. It also has a form requesting everything from a home address to an ATM card's PIN. Phishers are becoming more sophisticated. Early phishing scams sent messages to everyone. Targeted versions of phishing, called spear phishing, have emerged that target known customers of a specific company.

In the early days, each phishing e-mail resulted in tens of thousands of calls to bank call centers, disrupted business, and cost hundreds of thousands of dollars to handle the deluge of calls. An estimated 2 million Americans have been fooled by phishing scams, with yearly losses exceeding $3.2 billion.

It is easy to launch a phishing attack because hackers sell kits that lead people through the process. Some phishing e-mails secretly install software that spies on or hijacks the user's computer. The software captures log-on names or takes pictures of the user's screen when he logs into his financial institution.

The IRS has set up a Web site and an e-mail address (phishing@irs.gov) where people can forward suspicious e-mails that purport to be from the IRS. In a recent IRS phishing attack, e-mail recipients were told that they were due a refund and were directed to a Website that looked just like the IRS Web site and contained forms that looked just like IRS forms. To claim the refund, the taxpayer had to enter confidential information that facilitated identity theft.

Voice phishing, or *vishing*, is like phishing except that the victim enters confidential data by phone. Perpetrators use Voice over Internet Protocol (VoIP) to spoof the legitimate phone number (caller ID shows they are calling their financial institution) and to detect the telephone keystrokes.

To avoid being phished or vished, be highly skeptical of any message that suggests you are the target of illegal activity. Ignore e-mails that request confidential information, and do not call a number given in an unsolicited message. If you are concerned, call the institution using a number you know is valid to ensure that account information has not been tampered with.

Carding refers to activities performed on stolen credit cards, including making a small online purchase to determine whether the card is still valid and buying and selling stolen credit card numbers. Scores of underground Web sites facilitate carding, with some rating the reliability of sellers the same way eBay does. Cyber-criminal gangs run many of the carding sites.

Pharming is redirecting Web site traffic to a spoofed Web site. If you could change XYZ Company's number in the phone book to your phone number, people using the phone book to call XYZ Company would reach you instead. Similarly, each Web site has a unique IP (Internet) address (four groupings of numbers separated by three periods). There is a Domain Name System (think phone book) that converts a domain (Web site) name to an IP address. Pharmers change the IP address in the Domain Name System (DNS) to an IP address they control. Compromised DNS servers are referred to as "poisoned."

Malware can also be used to change a computer's host file (internal DNS) or an Internet service provider's IP addresses. Because most PCs are not as well controlled, they are better targets for pharming than Internet servers. Once these files are poisoned, all subsequent requests to visit that Web site are directed to the spoofed site.

Pharming is a very popular social engineering tool for two reasons. First, it is difficult to detect because the user's browser shows the correct Web site. Antivirus and spyware removal software are currently ineffective protections against pharming. Instead, complicated anti-pharming techniques are required. Second is the ability to target many people at a time through domain spoofing rather than one at a time with phishing e-mails.

A recent pharming attack targeted 65 financial firms, including PayPal, eBay, Discover Card, and American Express. The sophisticated and multi-pronged attack involved thousands of computers, multiple IP addresses in multiple countries, and a flood of fraudulent spam. The two-and-a-half-day pharming attack was so successful, resilient, and hard to correct that it was evident that a professional team planned it. The first e-mail spam contained bogus news that the Australia Prime Minister was struggling for his life after a heart attack. The e-mail contained a link to a newspaper story from *The Australian*. The second e-mail lure had a link to news of a cricket match in Australia. When people clicked on the links, they were redirected to one of five malicious Web sites that infected their computers with pharming malware.

An *evil twin* is a wireless network with the same name (called *Service Set Identifier*, or *SSID*) as a legitimate wireless access point. The hacker produces a wireless signal that is stronger than the legitimate signal or disrupts or disables the legitimate access point by disconnecting it, directing a denial-of-service against it, or creating radio frequency interference around it. Users are unaware that they connect to the evil twin. The perpetrator monitors the traffic looking for confidential information. Hackers also use evil twins to unleash a wide variety of malware and to install software to attack other computers. After a small coffee shop advertised free wireless Internet, there was an increase in identity thefts. The police discovered that a man living next to the coffee shop had set up an evil twin and was stealing confidential information.

Typosquatting, or *URL hijacking*, is setting up similarly named Web sites so that users making typographical errors when entering a Web site name are sent to an invalid site. For example, typing goggle.com instead of google.com might lead to a cyber-squatter site that:

- Tricks the user into thinking she is at the real site because of a copied or a similar logo, Web site layout, or content. These sites often contain advertising that appeals to the person looking for the real domain name. The typosquatter might also be a competitor.
- Is very different from what was wanted. One typosquatter sent people looking for a children's site to a pornographic Web site.
- Distributes malware such as viruses, spyware, and adware.

To stop typosquatting, companies send a cease-and-desist letter to the offender, purchase the Web site address, or file a lawsuit. Google won a case against a Russian typosquatter who registered domain names such as googkle.com and gooigle.com. The lawsuit was decided on three criteria: The domain names were obvious misspellings of google.com, the Russian had no independent claims or interest in the names, and he used the Web sites to infect computers with malware. Google was given possession of the domain names.

To prevent typosquatting, a company (1) tries to obtain all the Web names similar to theirs to redirect people to the correct site, or (2) uses software to scan the Internet and find domains that appear to be typosquatting. Parents can use the same software to restrict access to sites that squat on typos of children's Web sites.

Tabnapping is secretly changing an already open browser tab. Tabnapping begins when a victim is tricked into opening an e-mail link or visiting an infected Web site. The site uses JavaScript to identify a frequently visited site and secretly change the label and contents of the open, but inactive, browser tab. When the victim clicks on the altered tab, it shows that the site has been timed out. When the victim logs back in, the user ID and password are captured and forwarded to the identity thief.

Scavenging, or *dumpster diving*, is gaining access to confidential information by searching documents and records. Some identity thieves search garbage cans, communal trash bins, and city dumps to find information. Oracle Corporation was embarrassed a few years ago when investigators it hired were caught going through the trash of companies that supported its rival, Microsoft. The investigators had paid building janitors $1,200 for the trash. In another instance, Jerry Schneider discovered Pacific Telephone computer operating guides in a trash bin on his way home from high school. Over time, his scavenging activities resulted in a technical library that allowed him to steal $1 million worth of electronic equipment.

In *shoulder surfing*, as its name suggests, perpetrators look over a person's shoulders in a public place to get information such as ATM PIN numbers or user IDs and passwords. Fraudsters also surf from a distance using binoculars or cameras. In South America, a man hid a video camera in some bushes and pointed it at a company president's computer, which was visible through a first-floor window. A significant business acquisition almost fell through because of the information on the videotape. Shoulder surfers can be foiled by blocking the surfer's view of the input device.

In *Lebanese looping*, the perpetrator inserts a sleeve into an ATM that prevents the ATM from ejecting the card. When it is obvious that the card is trapped, the perpetrator approaches the victim and pretends to help, tricking the person into entering her PIN again. Once the victim gives up, the thief removes the card and uses the card and PIN to withdraw as much money as the ATM allows. Lebanese looping is common in any country with a large number of ATMs.

Skimming is double-swiping a credit card in a legitimate terminal or covertly swiping a credit card in a small, hidden, handheld card reader that records credit card data for later use. Commonly committed in retail outlets such as restaurants and carried out by employees with a legitimate reason to possess the victim's cards, skimming losses exceed $1 billion per year. A part-time employee at a gas station skimmed the cards of 80 customers, including the owner, who was a relative, and stole over $200,000.

Chipping is posing as a service engineer and planting a small chip that records transaction data in a legitimate credit card reader. The chip is later removed to access the data recorded on it.

Eavesdropping is listening to private communications or tapping into data transmissions. The equipment needed to set up a wiretap on an unprotected communications line is readily available at local electronics stores. One alleged wiretapping fraud involved Mark Koenig, a 28-year-old telecommunications consultant, and four associates. Federal agents say they pulled crucial data about Bank of America customers from telephone lines and used it to make 5,500 fake ATM cards. Koenig and his friends allegedly intended to use the cards over a long weekend to withdraw money from banks across the country. Authorities were tipped off, and they were apprehended before they could use the cards.

Malware

This section describes *malware*, which is any software that can be used to do harm. A recent study shows that malware is spread using several simultaneous approaches, including file sharing (used in 72% of attacks), shared access to files (42%), e-mail attachments (25%), and remote access vulnerabilities (24%).

Spyware software secretly monitors and collects personal information about users and sends it to someone else. The information is gathered by logging keystrokes, monitoring Web sites visited, and scanning documents on the computer's hard drive. Spyware can also hijack a browser, replacing a computer's home page with a page the spyware creator wants you to visit. Unless the spyware is removed, resetting a browser home page lasts only until the computer is rebooted. Spyware can also hijack search requests, returning results chosen by the spyware rather than the results desired. Spyware infections, of which users are usually unaware, come from the following:

- Downloads such as file-sharing programs, system utilities, games, wallpaper, screensavers, music, and videos.
- Web sites that secretly download spyware. This is called *drive-by downloading*.
- A hacker using security holes in Web browsers and other software.
- Malware masquerading as anti-spyware security software.
- A worm or virus.
- Public wireless networks. At Kinko's in Manhattan, an employee gathered the data needed to open bank accounts and apply for credit cards in the names of the people using Kinko's wireless network.

Spyware is especially problematic for companies with employees who telecommute or remotely access the network. Spyware on these computers record the user's network interactions, copy corporate data, and introduce spyware to the entire organization. A main source of spyware is adult-oriented sites. The computers of people who visit those sites are infected, and when they log onto their corporate systems those infections are passed to their employer's internal network.

Adware is spyware that pops banner ads on a monitor, collects information about the user's Web-surfing and spending habits, and forwards it to the adware creator. Adware companies charge for each computer showing its ads. They increase the number of computers with adware by paying shareware developers to bundle the adware with their software. This allows shareware developers to make money without charging for their software. One company that engages in digital media content sharing offers users a $30 version or a free version. The license agreement for the free software discloses the adware (hence making it "legal" spyware), but most users do not read the agreement and are not aware it is installed. Reputable adware companies claim sensitive or identifying data are not collected. However, there is no way for users to effectively control or limit the data collected and transmitted.

A recent AOL study found that 80% of inspected computers were infected with spyware, each machine containing on average 93 spyware or adware components. Another study estimated that 90% of computers connected to the Internet had spyware, with 90% of the owners unaware of the infection. The best protection against spyware and adware is a good antispyware software package that neutralizes or eliminates it and prevents its installation. One downside is that after the spyware or adware is erased, the free software that was its host may not work. Use multiple anti-spyware programs; unlike antivirus software and firewalls, they won't conflict.

Some malware developers intentionally make their software difficult to uninstall. Malware companies sometimes battle each other over whose software will infect a computer. Some of them have developed *torpedo software* that destroys competing malware, resulting in "malware warfare" between competing developers.

Scareware is software that is often malicious and of little or no benefit that is sold using scare tactics. The most common scare tactic is a dire warning that most computers are infected with viruses, spyware, and other catastrophic problems. Some scareware even warns that a user's job, career, or marriage is at risk. The scareware creators offer a solution—a free computer scan using their fake antivirus software. Accepting the free scan does several things. First, it does not perform a scan. Second, it claims to find dozens of problems and again warns of dire consequences if the computer is not cleaned up. Third, it often introduces into the consumer's computer the very problems that scared the consumer into trying the software. Fourth, it encourages the consumer to buy the fake antivirus software to clean the computer and keep it clean.

Scareware is marketed using spam e-mail and pop-up windows or banners on Web sites, some of which look as though they were placed by big-name corporations. To deceive consumers, the software looks and feels like legitimate security software, the e-mails look like they come from legitimate security software companies, and the pop-ups look like they come from the user's operating system. Scareware scammers also create Web pages about celebrity news and other hot topics that appear at the top of Google search results; clicking on any of the many links on the Web page launches the scareware. Scammers also steal Facebook and Twitter account logons, send messages carrying a tainted Web link to the victim's contacts, and rely on the high trust common to social networks to trick users into launching scareware.

There are tens of thousands of different scareware packages, with the number rising almost 600% in one recent six-month period. In another growth comparison, Microsoft reported that its free Malicious Software Removal Tool cleaned scareware off 7.8 million PCs in one six-month period compared to 5.3 million in the prior six months.

Scareware can be spotted several ways, First, the scare tactics are a big giveaway; legitimate companies will not try to scare you into using their products. A second giveaway is bad English; most scareware comes from countries where English is not the creator's first language.

The Federal Trade Commission sued the perpetrators of a massive scareware scheme that offered fake computer scans that falsely claimed to detect viruses, spyware, system errors, and illegal pornography. They tricked over a million people into spending $1.9 million to buy fake computer security products, including DriveCleaner, XP Antivirus, WinAntivirus, ErrorSafe, and WinFixer.

Like scareware, *ransomware* comes in the form of fake antivirus software. When activated, well-written ransomware locks you out of all your programs and data by encrypting them. That means you can't run your installed security programs and, if it disables your USB ports and DVD drives, you can't load new security programs to combat it. It directs Internet Explorer to the perpetrator's Web site, where the victim is informed that a monetary payment made directly to a bank must be made to have the software removed. Since payments can be traced, ransomware is not as common as other malware. Most ransomware is delivered via a spam e-mail that motivates the recipient to open an infected file. It can also be delivered by Web sites. Keeping Windows updated is crucial to blocking these downloads.

Key logging software records computer activity, such as a user's keystrokes, e-mails sent and received, Web sites visited, and chat session participation. Parents use the software to monitor their children's computer usage, and businesses use it to monitor employee activity. Law enforcement uses it to detect or prevent crime. A Drug Enforcement Administration agent persuaded a federal judge to authorize him to sneak into an Escondido, California, office believed to be a front for manufacturing the drug Ecstasy. Copying the contents of all hard drives and installing keystroke loggers successfully thwarted their plans to distribute Ecstasy.

Fraud perpetrators use key loggers to capture and send confidential information. Over 10,000 unique key logging software programs are available in underground chat rooms; most are free or very cheap. Computers are infected with key logging software when they visit corrupt Web sites or download free software. One enterprising student installed key logging software on his teacher's computer, recorded her typed exams answers, and decoded the keystrokes. He was caught trying to sell exam answers to other students.

A *Trojan horse* is a set of malicious computer instructions in an authorized and otherwise properly functioning program. Unlike viruses and worms, the code does not try to replicate itself. Some Trojan horses give the creator the power to control the victim's computer remotely. Most Trojan horse infections occur when a user runs an infected program received in an e-mail, visits a malicious Web site, or downloads software billed as helpful add-ons to popular software programs. In Israel, companies were sent business proposals on a disk that contained the Trojan. In another case, visitors to an adult site were told to download a special program to see the pictures. This program disconnected them from their Internet service providers and connected them to a service that billed them $2 a minute until they turned off their computers. Over 800,000 minutes were billed, with some phone bills as high as $3,000, before the scam was detected. The HotLan Trojan caused infected computers to sign up for Microsoft Hotmail and Google Gmail accounts and used them for spamming. Over 514,000 Hotmail accounts and 49,000 Gmail accounts were created in a single day. One type of Trojan horse relies on the curiosity of the victim. The attacker creates a malware-infected CD ROM or USB flash drive, gives it a legitimate looking and curiosity piquing label (company logo, accompanied by 4Q Evaluation and Salary Data), leaves it where it can be found (bathroom, desktop, hallway), and waits for a curious employee to try to read the file. The file installs the Trojan on the employee's computer, likely giving the attacker access to the company's internal computer network.

Time bombs and *logic bombs* are Trojan horses that lie idle until triggered by a specified date or time, by a change in the system, by a message sent to the system, or by an event that does not occur. Once triggered, the bomb goes off, destroying programs, data, or both. Disgruntled company insiders who want to get even with their company write many bombs. Anticipating that he would not receive a bonus or new contract, Roger Duronio planted a Trojan horse time bomb at USB PaineWebber. Several weeks after he left the firm, the trigger date of March 4 arrived. His 60 lines of malicious code attacked the company's 2,000 servers and deleted company files just as the stock market opened. The effects were catastrophic. Broker computers were out of commission for days or weeks, depending on how badly the machines were damaged and the existence of branch backup tapes. Some 20% of the computers had no backup tapes, and some servers were never fully restored. Over 400 employees and 200 IBM consultants worked feverishly, at a cost of $3.1 million, to restore the system. Duronio cashed out his IRA and sold UBS stock short, figuring to make a killing when the stock plunged. It never did, and he lost money on his short sale. Duronio was sentenced to eight years in prison.

There are legal uses of time and logic bombs, such as in trial versions of software. The software becomes unusable after a certain amount of time passes or after the software has been used a certain number of times.

A *trap door*, or *back door*, is a way into a system that bypasses normal authorization and authentication controls. Programmers create trap doors so they can modify programs during systems development and then remove them before the system is put into operation. The back door can also be created by a virus or worm or by a disgruntled programmer. Anyone who discovers a trap door can enter the program. Security consultants claim that back doors are frequently discovered in organizations. BackOrifice, Netbus, and SubSeven are tools intruders use to gain remote, back door access to systems with Windows software. Jonathan James, the first juvenile sent to prison for hacking, installed a back door into a Department of Defense server, accessed sensitive e-mails, and captured employee usernames and passwords.

Packet sniffers capture data from information packets as they travel over networks. Captured data are examined to find confidential or proprietary information. In Sweden, Dan Egerstad's packet sniffer looked for key words such as *government*, *military*, *war*, *passport*, and *visa*. He intercepted e-mails from embassies and governments, many with visa and passport data.

Steganography is writing hidden messages in such a way that no one, apart from the sender and intended recipient, suspects their existence. Steganography messages do not attract attention to themselves, whereas an encrypted message arouses suspicion. *Steganography programs* hide data files inside a host file, such as a large image or sound file. The software merges the two files by removing scattered bytes from the host file and replacing them with data from the hidden file. The steganography program password protects the merged file, and the only way to reassemble the hidden file is to key the password into the same steganography program. The host file can still be heard or viewed because human visual and auditory senses are not sensitive enough to pick up the slight decrease in image or sound quality that the hidden file causes. Company employees can merge confidential information with a seemingly harmless file and send it anywhere in the world, where the confidential information is reassembled.

Steganography is used by terrorists, as it is an effective way for a spy to transmit information and receive orders. Some experts believe steganography was one way terrorists communicated in planning the September 11 terrorist attack on the United States. A *USA Today* article alleged that Al-Qaeda operatives sent hundreds of messages hidden in digital photographs sold on eBay.

A *rootkit* conceals processes, files, network connections, memory addresses, systems utility programs, and system data from the operating system and other programs. Rootkits often modify the operating system or install themselves as drivers. A rootkit is used to hide the presence of trap doors, sniffers, and key loggers; conceal software that originates a denial-of-service or an e-mail spam attack; and access user names and log-in information. Unlike viruses and worms, rootkits do not spread to other systems. Rootkit software is readily available on the Internet. Several vendors sell programs that detect rootkits, and security vendors include rootkit detection in their antivirus products. When a rootkit is detected, it is better to reinstall the operating system from scratch rather than spend the time and effort to delete it from the system. In a famous instance of rootkit use, Sony music CDs secretly placed a copy-protection rootkit on Windows computers. The software inadvertently opened security holes that allowed viruses to break in. Sony had to recall all CDs that included the software.

Superzapping is the unauthorized use of special system programs to bypass regular system controls and perform illegal acts, all without leaving an audit trail. The technique derives its name from Superzap, a software utility developed by IBM to handle emergencies. The manager of computer operations at a bank was told to use a Superzap program to correct a problem affecting account balances caused by unanticipated problems in changing from one computer system to another. When he discovered he could use the program to make account changes without the usual controls, audits, or documentation, he moved $128,000 into the accounts of several friends. Because the Superzap program left no evidence of data file changes, he was not detected until a customer complained about a shortage in his account.

A computer *virus* is a segment of self-replicating, executable code that attaches itself to a file or program. During its replication phase, the virus spreads to other systems when the infected file or program is downloaded or opened by the recipient. Newer viruses can mutate each time they infect a computer, making them more difficult to detect and destroy. Many viruses lie dormant for extended periods without causing damage, except to propagate themselves. In one survey, 90% of respondents said their company was infected with a virus during the prior 12 months.

During the attack phase, triggered by some predefined event, viruses destroy or alter data or programs, take control of the computer, destroy the hard drive's file allocation table, delete or rename files or directories, reformat the hard drive, change the content of files, or keep users from booting the system or accessing data on the hard drive. A virus can intercept and change transmissions, display disruptive images or messages, or cause the screen image to change color or disappear. Many viruses automatically send e-mails, faxes, or text messages with the victim's name as the source. As the virus spreads, it takes up space, clogs communications, and hinders system performance. Computer virus symptoms include computers that will not start or execute; unexpected read or write operations; an inability to save files; long program load times; abnormally large file sizes; slow systems operation; incessant pop-ups; and unusual screen activity, error messages, or file names.

A bad virus attack shut down a bank with 200 servers and 10,000 desktop computers for four days. During the downtime, the bank was locked out of its system, and customer accounts could not be accessed. A firm that specializes in fixing virus attacks eventually restored the system. The Sobig virus, written by Russian hackers, infected an estimated 1 of every 17 e-mails several years ago. The virus took months to write and was released in ever-improving versions. A year later, the MyDoom virus infected 1 in 12 e-mails and did $4.75 billion in damages.

Every day, virus creators send an estimated 1 billion virus-infected e-mail messages. The creators are getting good at making them look authentic. One recent virus came in an e-mail that appeared to come from Microsoft—the Microsoft logo and copyright were included in the message window launched by the virus. The e-mail told the recipient to use the attached patch to fix a security flaw in either Microsoft Internet Explorer or Outlook. Instead, opening the attachment downloaded malicious software that installed a back door allowing the perpetrator to control the computer.

It is estimated that viruses and worms cost businesses over $20 billion a year. A computer system can be protected from viruses by following the guidelines listed in Focus 6-1.

A computer *worm* is a self-replicating computer program similar to a virus, with some exceptions:

1. A virus is a segment of code hidden in or attached to a host program or executable file, whereas a worm is a stand-alone program.
2. A virus requires a human to do something (run a program, open a file, etc.) to replicate itself, whereas a worm does not and actively seeks to send copies of itself to other network devices.
3. Worms harm networks (if only by consuming bandwidth), whereas viruses infect or corrupt files or data on a targeted computer.

Worms often reside in e-mail attachments and reproduce by mailing themselves to the recipient's mailing list, resulting in an electronic chain letter. Some recent worms have completely shut down e-mail systems. Worms are not confined to personal computers; thousands of worms infect cell phones each year by jumping from phone to phone over wireless networks.

A worm usually does not live very long, but it is quite destructive while alive. It takes little technical knowledge to create a worm or virus. Many Web sites provide applications that enable unsophisticated users to create worms. One application has been downloaded over 25,000 times.

Focus 6-2 describes an early and destructive worm that affected 6,000 computers in a very short time. More recently, MySpace had to go offline to disable a worm that added over 1 million friends to the hacker's site in less than a day. MySpace profiles were also infected by a worm after viewing

Keeping Your Computers Virus-Free

Here are some practical suggestions for protecting computers from viruses:

- Install reputable and reliable antivirus software that scans for, identifies, and destroys viruses. Use only one antivirus program; multiple programs conflict with each other.
- Do not fall for ads touting free antivirus software; much of it is fake and contains malware. Some hackers create Web sites stuffed with content about breaking news so that the site appears on the first page of search results. Anyone clicking on the link is confronted with a pop-up with a link to fake antivirus software.
- Do not fall for pop-up notices that warn of horrible threats and offer a free scan of your computer. Although no scan actually takes place, the program reports dozens of dangerous infections and tells you to purchase and download their fake antivirus program to clean it up.
- Make sure that the latest versions of the antivirus programs are used. National City Bank in Cleveland, Ohio, installed some new laptops. The manufacturer and the bank checked the laptops for viruses but did not use the latest antivirus software. A virus spread from the laptop hard drives to 300 network servers and 12,000 workstations. It took the bank over two days to eradicate the virus from all bank systems.
- Scan all incoming e-mail for viruses at the server level as well as at users' desktops.

- Do not download anything from an e-mail that uses noticeably bad English, such as terrible grammar and misspelled words. Real companies hire people to produce quality writing. Many viruses come from overseas perpetrators whose first language is not English.
- All software should be certified as virus-free before you load it into the system. Be wary of software from unknown sources: They may be virus bait—especially if their prices or functionality sound too good to be true.
- Deal only with trusted software retailers.
- Some software suppliers use electronic techniques to make tampering evident. Ask whether the software you are purchasing has such protection.
- Check new software on an isolated machine with virus-detection software. Software direct from the publisher has been known to have viruses.
- Have two backups of all files. Data files should be backed up separately from programs to avoid contaminating backup data.
- If you use flash drives or CDs, do not put them in strange machines; they may become infected. Do not let others use those storage devices on your machine. Scan all new files with antiviral software before any data or programs are copied to your machine.

A Worm Run Amok

Within minutes, a rash of unknown users trying to log on crashed Berkeley's computer system. Within hours, computer experts discovered it was invading the *entire* Internet. While scientists attempted to stop the worm, law enforcement and the press investigated it. Information on the perpetrator was scarce until an unidentified phone caller tipped off a *New York Times* writer by inadvertently referring to him as "RTM."

Robert T. Morris acquired a passion for computer security while working with his father, a scientist at Bell Labs. At Harvard, he was recognized for projects that improved Bell Systems' Internet operations and its UNIX operating system. At age 20, Robert's skills in UNIX security were so extensive that he gave an address on computer security to both the National Security Agency and the Naval Research Laboratory.

While Robert was in graduate school at Cornell, the first computer viruses sparked his interest in developing an

undetectable worm that would reach as many computers as possible. Using a bug in the UNIX Sendmail subprogram, Robert developed a worm capable of entering a system without authorization. From his system at Cornell, Robert illegally logged on to an artificial intelligence lab computer at MIT and released his creation. After dinner, Robert attempted to log on, but the computer did not respond. He immediately knew something was wrong. After several attempts to remedy the problem, Robert realized he had made a fatal programming error that allowed the worm to replicate out of control throughout the Internet. Cleaning out the Internet system and recreating the files that the worm destroyed took several months.

Robert was arrested, charged with a felony, convicted, and sentenced to three years' probation, 400 hours of community service, and a $10,000 fine.

a QuickTime video containing malicious software that replaced the links in the user's page with links to a phishing site. The devastating Conficker worm infected 25% of enterprise Window PCs.

Many viruses and worms exploit known software vulnerabilities than can be corrected with a software patch. Therefore, a good defense against them is making sure that all software patches are installed as soon as they are available.

Recent viruses and worms have attacked cell phones and personal electronic devices using text messages, Internet page downloads, and Bluetooth wireless technology. Flaws in Bluetooth applications open the system to attack. *Bluesnarfing* is stealing (snarfing) contact lists, images, and other data using Bluetooth. A reporter for TimesOnline accompanied Adam Laurie, a security expert, around London scanning for Bluetooth-compatible phones. Before a Bluetooth connection can be made, the person contacted must agree to accept the link. However, Laurie has written software to bypass this control and identified vulnerable handsets at an average rate of one per minute. He downloaded entire phonebooks, calendars, diary contents, and stored pictures. Phones up to 90 meters away were vulnerable.

Bluebugging is taking control of someone else's phone to make or listen to calls, send or read text messages, connect to the Internet, forward the victim's calls, and call numbers that charge fees. These attacks will become more popular as phones are used to pay for items purchased. When a hacker wants something, all he has to do is bluebug a nearby phone and make a purchase. To prevent these attacks, a bluetooth device can be set to make it hard for other devices to recognize it. Antivirus software for phones is being developed to deal with such problems.

In the future, many other devices—such as home security systems, home appliances, automobiles, and elevators—will be connected to the Internet and will be the target of viruses and worms.

Table 6-1 summarizes, in alphabetical order, the computer fraud and abuse techniques discussed in the chapter.

TABLE 6-1 Computer Fraud and Abuse Techniques

Technique	Description
Address Resolution Protocol (ARP) spoofing	Sending fake ARP messages to an Ethernet LAN. ARP is a computer networking protocol for determining a network host's hardware address when only its IP or network address is known.
Adware	Software that collects and forwards data to advertising companies or causes banner ads to pop up as the Internet is surfed.
Bluebugging	Taking control of a phone to make calls, send text messages, listen to calls, or read text messages.
Bluesnarfing	Stealing contact lists, images, and other data using Bluetooth.
Botnet, bot herders	A network of hijacked computers. Bot herders use the hijacked computers, called zombies, in a variety of Internet attacks.
Buffer overflow attack	Inputting so much data that the input buffer overflows. The overflow contains code that takes control of the computer.
Caller ID spoofing	Displaying an incorrect number on the recipient's caller ID display to hide the identity of the caller.
Carding	Verifying credit card validity; buying and selling stolen credit cards.
Chipping	Planting a chip that records transaction data in a legitimate credit card reader.
Cross-site scripting (XSS) attack	Exploits Web page security vulnerabilities to bypass browser security mechanisms and create a malicious link that injects unwanted code into a Web site.
Cyber-bullying	Using computer technology to harm another person.
Cyber-extortion	Requiring a company to pay money to keep an extortionist from harming a computer or a person.
Data diddling	Changing data before, during, or after it is entered into the system.
Data leakage	Unauthorized copying of company data.
Denial-of-service attack	An attack designed to make computer resources unavailable to its users. For example, so many e-mail messages that the Internet service provider's e-mail server is overloaded and shuts down.
Dictionary attack	Using software to guess company addresses, send employees blank e-mails, and add unreturned messages to spammer e-mail lists.
DNS spoofing	Sniffing the ID of a Domain Name System (server that converts a Web site name to an IP address) request and replying before the real DNS server.
Eavesdropping	Listening to private voice or data transmissions.

(*Continued*)

TABLE 6-1 Continued

Technique	Description
Economic espionage	The theft of information, trade secrets, and intellectual property.
E-mail threats	Sending a threatening message asking recipients to do something that makes it possible to defraud them.
E-mail spoofing	Making a sender address and other parts of an e-mail header appear as though the e-mail originated from a different source.
Evil twin	A wireless network with the same name as another wireless access point. Users unknowingly connect to the evil twin; hackers monitor the traffic looking for useful information.
Hacking	Unauthorized access, modification, or use of computer systems, usually by means of a PC and a communications network.
Hijacking	Gaining control of someone else's computer for illicit activities.
IP address spoofing	Creating Internet Protocol packets with a forged IP address to hide the sender's identity or to impersonate another computer system.
Identity theft	Assuming someone's identity by illegally obtaining confidential information such as a Social Security number.
Internet auction fraud	Using an Internet auction site to commit fraud.
Internet misinformation	Using the Internet to spread false or misleading information.
Internet terrorism	Using the Internet to disrupt communications and ecommerce.
Internet pump-and-dump fraud	Using the Internet to pump up the price of a stock and then sell it.
Key logger	Using spyware to record a user's keystrokes.
Lebanese looping	Inserting a sleeve into an ATM so that it will not eject the victim's card, pretending to help the victim as a means to discover his or her PIN, and then using the card and PIN to drain the account.
Logic bombs and time bombs	Software that sits idle until a specified circumstance or time triggers it, destroying programs, data, or both.
Malware	Software that can be used to do harm.
Man-in-the-middle (MITM) attack	A hacker placing himself between a client and a host to intercept network traffic; also called *session hijacking*.
Masquerading/impersonation	Accessing a system by pretending to be an authorized user. The impersonator enjoys the same privileges as the legitimate user.
Packet sniffing	Inspecting information packets as they travel the Internet and other networks.
Password cracking	Penetrating system defenses, stealing passwords, and decrypting them to access system programs, files, and data.
Pharming	Redirecting traffic to a spoofed Web site to obtain confidential information.
Phishing	Communications that request recipients to disclose confidential information by responding to an e-mail or visiting a Web site.
Phreaking	Attacking phone systems to get free phone access; using phone lines to transmit viruses and to access, steal, and destroy data.
Piggybacking	1. Clandestine use of someone's Wi-Fi network. 2. Tapping into a communications line and entering a system by latching onto a legitimate user. 3. Bypassing physical security controls by entering a secure door when an authorized person opens it.
Podslurping	Using a small device with storage capacity (iPod, Flash drive) to download unauthorized data from a computer.
Posing	Creating a seemingly legitimate business, collecting personal data while making a sale, and never delivering items sold.
Pretexting	Acting under false pretenses to gain confidential information.
Rootkit	Software that conceals processes, files, network connections, and system data from the operating system and other programs.
Round-down fraud	Truncating interest calculations at two decimal places and placing truncated amounts in the perpetrator's account.
Ransomware	Software that encrypts programs and data until a ransom is paid to remove it.
Salami technique	Stealing tiny slices of money over time.
Scareware	Malicious software of no benefit that is sold using scare tactics.

TABLE 6-1 Continued

Technique	Description
Scavenging/dumpster diving	Searching for confidential information by searching for documents and records in garbage cans, communal trash bins, and city dumps
Sexting	Exchanging explicit text messages and pictures.
Shoulder surfing	Watching or listening to people enter or disclose confidential data.
Skimming	Double-swiping a credit card or covertly swiping it in a card reader that records the data for later use.
SMS spoofing	Using short message service (SMS) to change the name or number a text message appears to come from.
Social engineering	Techniques that trick a person into disclosing confidential information.
Software piracy	Unauthorized copying or distribution of copyrighted software.
Spamming	E-mailing an unsolicited message to many people at the same time.
Splog	A spam blog that promotes Web sites to increase their Google PageRank (how often a Web page is referenced by other pages).
Spyware	Software that monitors computing habits and sends that data to someone else, often without the user's permission.
Spoofing	Making electronic communications look like someone else sent it.
SQL injection attack	Inserting a malicious SQL query in input in such a way that it is passed to and executed by an application program.
Steganography	Hiding data from one file inside a host file, such as a large image or sound file.
Superzapping	Using special software to bypass system controls and perform illegal acts.
Tabnapping	Secretly changing an already open browser tab using JavaScript.
Trap door	A back door into a system that bypasses normal system controls.
Trojan horse	Unauthorized code in an authorized and properly functioning program.
Typosquatting/URL hijacking	Web sites with names similar to real Web sites; users making typographical errors are sent to a site filled with malware.
Virus	Executable code that attaches itself to software, replicates itself, and spreads to other systems or files. Triggered by a predefined event, it damages system resources or displays messages.
Vishing	Voice phishing, in which e-mail recipients are asked to call a phone number that asks them to divulge confidential data.
War dialing	Dialing phone lines to find idle modems to use to enter a system, capture the attached computer, and gain access to its network(s).
War driving/rocketing	Looking for unprotected wireless networks using a car or a rocket.
Web cramming	Developing a free and worthless trial-version Web site and charging the subscriber's phone bill for months even if the subscriber cancels.
Web-page spoofing	Also called *phishing*.
Worm	Similar to a virus; a program rather than a code segment hidden in a host program. Actively transmits itself to other systems. It usually does not live long but is quite destructive while alive.
Zero-day attack	Attack between the time a software vulnerability is discovered and a patch to fix the problem is released.

Summary and Case Conclusion

It took RPC two days to get its system back up to the point that the audit team could continue their work. RPC had been hit with multiple problems at the same time. Hackers had used packet sniffers and eavesdropping to intercept a public key RPC had sent to Northwest. That led to a man-in-the-middle attack, which allowed the hacker to intercept all communications about the pending merger. It also opened the door to other attacks on both systems.

Law enforcement was called in to investigate the problem, and they were following up on three possibilities. The first was that hackers had used the intercepted information to purchase stock in both companies, leak news of the purchase to others via Internet chat rooms, and, once the stock price had been pumped up, to dump the stock of both companies. There did seem to be significant, unusual trading in the two companies' stock in the last few months. The second possibility was hackers exploiting system weaknesses they had found, stealing confidential data on RPC's customers, and causing considerable harm when they were done to cover their tracks. The third possibility was economic espionage and Internet terrorism. They received an anonymous tip that one of Northwest's competitors was behind the attack. It would take weeks or even months to track down all the leads and determine who had caused the problem and why.

Jason's research helped him understand the many ways outside hackers and employees attack systems. He never knew there were so many different things that could be spoofed in systems. He was also intrigued by some of the more technical attacks, such as cross-site scripting, buffer overflow attacks, man-in-the middle attacks, zero-day attacks, and SQL injection. He also found it interesting to learn about all the ways that people use computers to defraud other individuals and companies: Internet terrorism, misinformation, and auction fraud as well as cyber-bullying and cyber-extortion.

Jason was familiar with some of the social engineering techniques he read about, such as pretexting, posing, pharming, and phishing. However, he was unfamiliar with many of the techniques such as Lebanese looping, evil twin, chipping, and typosquatting. He had a similar experience when learning about malware. He was familiar with spyware, adware, Trojan horses, viruses, and key loggers. He learned many new things when he read about scareware, ransomware, steganography, rootkits, and bluebugging.

Jason's research also gave him a perspective on past and future uses of computer fraud and abuse techniques. He learned that many hacker attacks use more than one technique. For example, hackers often send spam e-mails that lure the victim to a Web site that downloads either a keylogger software or code that hijacks the computer and turns it into a botnet zombie or tries to trick the user into disclosing confidential information.

He also learned that hackers take advantage of people who share personal information on social networking sites. For example, a recent worm-based phishing attack targeted Twitter and Facebook users. Users received a message from a friend telling them they could accumulate more friends by clicking on a link. They were prompted to enter their account information, which was used to send the same message to all their friends.

With the harvested personal information that makes them more targeted than before, cyber attacks are increasingly successful in tricking even savvy users into making a mistake. For example, past phishing attacks used a generic spam e-mail message that was obviously bogus. Newer attacks use current-events issues or hot-button topics. Clicking on the accompanying links automatically downloads botware software. Attacks that are even more sophisticated use information about the intended target to make them look legitimate. For example, the e-mail may use stolen information, such as the victim's employer or a friend of family member, to induce them to open an attachment or visit a Web site.

Lastly, Jason learned there is a plethora of fraud software on the market and that hackers compete to make the most easy-to-use tools. In a recent month, six different Web exploit vendors released new products at the same time. As a result, hackers do not need to be programmers; they just need to know to whom they want to target and check a few boxes. For example, with Zeus, one of the most popular and successful data-stealing toolkits, cyber criminals can generate detailed reports on each Web site visited. They can also use the program's powerful search engine to browse through their victims' machines and find detailed information, such as which banks they use. Conversely, the best hackers are more knowledgeable than in the past and use sophisticated technologies. For example, zombies on a botnet used an automated SQL injection attack to compromise over 500,000 Web sites last year, stealing sensitive information and injecting malware into the site.

Key Terms

hacking 149	zombie 150	dictionary attack 150
botnet 150	denial-of-service (DoS)	splog 150
hijacking 150	attack 150	spoofing 151
bot herder 150	spamming 150	e-mail spoofing 151

AIS IN ACTION

Chapter Quiz

1. A set of instructions to increase a programmer's pay rate by 10% is hidden inside an authorized program. It changes and updates the payroll file. What is this computer fraud technique called?
   a. virus
   b. worm
   c. trap door
   d. Trojan horse

2. Which computer fraud technique involves a set of instructions hidden inside a calendar utility that copies itself each time the utility is enabled until memory is filled and the system crashes?
   a. logic bomb
   b. trap door
   c. virus
   d. Trojan horse

3. Interest calculations are truncated at two decimal places, and the excess decimals are put into an account the perpetrator controls. What is this fraud called?
   a. typosquatting
   b. URL hijacking
   c. chipping
   d. round-down fraud

4. A perpetrator attacks phone systems to obtain free phone line access or uses telephone lines to transmit viruses and to access, steal, and destroy data. What is this computer fraud technique called?
   a. phishing
   b. phreaking
   c. pharming
   d. vishing

5. Fraud perpetrators threaten to harm a company if it does not pay a specified amount of money. What is this computer fraud technique called?
   a. cyber-terrorism
   b. blackmailing
   c. cyber-extortion
   d. scareware

6. Techniques used to obtain confidential information, often by tricking people, are referred to as what?
   a. pretexting
   b. posing
   c. social engineering
   d. identity theft

7. What type of software secretly collects personal information about users and sends it to someone else without the user's permission?
   a. rootkit
   b. torpedo software
   c. spyware
   d. malware

8. What type of software conceals processes, files, network connections, memory addresses, systems utility programs, and system data from the operating system and other programs?
   a. rootkit
   b. spyware
   c. malware
   d. adware

9. Which type of computer attack takes place between the time a software vulnerability is discovered and the time software developers release a software patch that fixes the problem?
   a. posing
   b. zero-day attack
   c. evil twin
   d. software piracy

10. Someone redirects a Web site's traffic to a bogus Web site, usually to gain access to personal and confidential information. What is this computer fraud technique called?
    a. vishing
    b. phishing
    c. pharming
    d. phreaking

Discussion Questions

6.1. When U.S. Leasing (USL) computers began acting sluggishly, computer operators were relieved when a software troubleshooter from IBM called. When he offered to correct the problem they were having, he was given a log-on ID and password. The next morning, the computers were worse. A call to IBM confirmed USL's suspicion: Someone had impersonated an IBM repairman to gain unauthorized access to the system and destroy the database. USL was also concerned that the intruder had devised a program that would let him get back into the system even after all the passwords were changed. What techniques might the impostor have employed to breach USL's internal security? What could USL do to avoid these types of incidents in the future?

6.2. What motives do people have for hacking? Why has hacking become so popular in recent years? Do you regard it as a crime? Explain your position.

6.3. The UCLA computer lab was filled to capacity when the system slowed and crashed, disrupting the lives of students who could no longer log into the system or access data to prepare for finals. IT initially suspected a cable break or an operating system failure, but diagnostics revealed nothing. After several frustrating hours, a staff member ran a virus detection program and uncovered a virus on the lab's main server. The virus was eventually traced to the computers of unsuspecting UCLA students. Later that evening, the system was brought back online after infected files were replaced with backup copies. What conditions made the UCLA system a potential breeding ground for the virus? What symptoms indicated that a virus was present?

Problems

6.1. A few years ago, news began circulating about a computer virus named Michelangelo that was set to "ignite" on March 6, the birthday of the famous Italian artist. The virus attached itself to the computer's operating system boot sector. On the magical date, the virus would release itself, destroying all of the computer's data. When March 6 arrived, the virus did minimal damage. Preventive techniques limited the damage to isolated personal and business computers. Though the excitement surrounding the virus was largely illusory, Michelangelo helped the computer-using public realize its systems' vulnerability to outside attack.

Required

a. What is a computer virus? Cite at least three reasons why no system is completely safe from a computer virus.

b. Why do viruses represent a serious threat to information systems? What damage can a virus do to a computer system?

c. How does a virus resemble a Trojan horse?

d. What steps can be taken to prevent the spread of a computer virus?

6.2. The controller of a small business received the following e-mail with an authentic-looking e-mail address and logo:

> From: Big Bank [antifraud@bigbank.com]
> To: Justin Lewis, Controller, Small Business USA
> Subject: Official Notice for all users of Big Bank!

Due to the increased incidence of fraud and identity theft, we are asking all bank customers to verify their account information on the following Web page: www.antifraudbigbank.com
*   Please confirm your account information as soon as possible. Failure to confirm your account information will require us to suspend your account until confirmation is made.*

A week later, the following e-mail was delivered to the controller:

> From: Big Bank [antifraud@bigbank.com]
> To: Justin Lewis, Controller, Small Business USA
> Subject: Official Notice for all users of Big Bank!

Dear Client of Big Bank,
Technical services at Big Bank is currently updating our software. Therefore, we kindly ask that you access the website shown below to confirm your data. Otherwise, your access to the system may be blocked.
web.da-us.bigbank.com/signin/scripts/login2/user_setup.jsp
We are grateful for your cooperation.

Required

a. What should Justin do about these e-mails?

b. What should Big Bank do about these e-mails?

c. Identify the computer fraud and abuse technique illustrated.

6.3. A purchasing department received the following e-mail.

Dear Accounts Payable Clerk,
You can purchase everything you need online—including peace of mind—when you shop using Random Account Numbers (RAN). RAN is a free service for Big Credit Card customers that substitutes a random credit card number in place of your normal credit card number when you make online purchases and payments. This random number provides you with additional security. Before every online purchase, simply get a new number from RAN to use at each new vendor. Sign up for an account at www.bigcreditcard.com. Also, take advantage of the following features:

- *Automatic Form automatically completes a vendor's order form with the RAN, its expiration date, and your shipping and billing addresses.*

- *Set the spending limit and expiration date for each new RAN.*
- *Use RAN once or use it for recurring payments for up to one year.*

Required

Explain which computer fraud and abuse techniques could be prevented using a random account number that links to your corporate credit card.

6.4. Computer Fraud and Abuse Techniques.

Match the Internet-related computer fraud and abuse technique in the left column with the scenario in the right column. Terms on the left may be used once, more than once, or not at all.

____ 1. Adware	a.	Software that monitors and reports a user's computing habits
____ 2. Botnet	b.	A program stored in a Web page that is executed by a Web browser
____ 3. Bot herder	c.	Sending an e-mail instructing the recipient to do something or else suffer adverse consequences
____ 4. Click fraud	d.	Using the Internet to pass off the work of another as your own
____ 5. DoS	e.	E-mailing an unsolicited message to many people at the same time
____ 6. E-mail threats	f.	Creating Web sites with names similar to real Web sites so users making errors while entering a Web site name are sent to a hacker's site
____ 7. Hijacking	g.	An e-mail warning regarding a virus that, in reality, does not exist
____ 8. Internet misinformation	h.	A spam blog that promotes affiliated Web sites to increase their Google PageRank
____ 9. Internet terrorism	i.	Software that collects consumer surfing and purchasing data
____ 10. Key logger	j.	E-mails that look like they came from a legitimate source but are actually from a hacker who is trying to get the user to divulge personal information
____ 11. Pharming	k.	Making an e-mail look like it came from someone else
____ 12. Phishing	l.	Gaining control of a computer to carry out unauthorized illicit activities
____ 13. Spamming	m.	Using the Internet to disrupt communications and e-commerce
____ 14. Splog	n.	Diverting traffic from a legitimate Web site to a hacker's Web site to gain access to personal and confidential information
____ 15. Spyware	o.	A network of hijacked computers
____ 16. Spoofing	p.	Using a legion of compromised computers to launch a coordinated attack on an Internet site
____ 17. Typosquatting	q.	Use of spyware to record a user's keystrokes
	r.	Hackers that control hijacked computers
	s.	Circulating lies or misleading information using the world's largest network
	t.	Overloading an Internet service provider's e-mail server by sending hundreds of e-mail messages per second from randomly generated false addresses
	u.	Inflating advertising revenue by clicking online ads numerous times

6.5. Computer Fraud and Abuse Techniques.

Match the computer fraud and abuse technique in the left column with the scenario in the right column. Terms on the left may be used once, more than once, or not at all.

____ 1. Bluebugging	a.	Intercepting Internet and other network transmissions
____ 2. Bluesnarfing	b.	E-mails instructing a user to call a phone number where they are asked to divulge personal information
____ 3. Eavesdropping	c.	Searching for unprotected wireless networks in a vehicle
____ 4. Evil twin	d.	Gaining access to a protected system by latching onto a legitimate user
____ 5. Packet sniffing	e.	Decoding and organizing captured network data
____ 6. Phreaking	f.	Intercepting and/or listening in on private voice and data transmissions
____ 7. Piggybacking	g.	Deep packet filtering
____ 8. Vishing	h.	Searching for modems on unprotected phone lines in order to access the attached computer and gain access to the network(s) to which it is attached
____ 9. War dialing	i.	Making phone calls and sending text messages using another user's phone without physically holding that phone
____ 10. War driving	j.	Using telephone lines to transmit viruses and to access, steal, and destroy data
	k.	Capturing data from devices that use Bluetooth technology
	l.	Devices that hide IP addresses
	m.	A rogue wireless access point masquerading as a legitimate access point

6.6. Computer Fraud and Abuse Techniques.

Match the computer fraud and abuse technique in the left column with the scenario in the right column. Terms on the left may be used once, more than once, or not at all.

____ 1. Chipping	a.	Illegally obtaining confidential information, such as a Social Security number, about another person so that it can be used for financial gain
____ 2. Data diddling	b.	Searching through garbage for confidential data
____ 3. Data leakage	c.	Covertly swiping a credit card in a card reader that records the data for later use
____ 4. Identity theft	d.	Embezzling small fractions of funds over time
____ 5. Round-down	e.	Inserting a chip that captures financial data in a legitimate credit card reader
____ 6. Salami technique	f.	Copying company data, such as computer files, without permission
____ 7. Scavenging	g.	Concealing data within a large MP3 file
	h.	Use of spyware to record a user's keystrokes
	i.	Altering data during the IPO (Input-Process-Output) cycle
	j.	Placing truncated decimal places in an account controlled by the perpetrator

6.7.   Computer Fraud and Abuse Techniques.

Match the computer fraud and abuse technique in the left column with the scenario in the right column. Terms on the left may be used once, more than once, or not at all.

____ 1. Dictionary attack	a. Special software used to bypass system controls
____ 2. Hacking	b. A segment of executable code that attaches itself to software
____ 3. Logic bomb	c. Capturing and decrypting passwords to gain access to a system
____ 4. Malware	d. Malicious computer code that specifically targets a computer's start-up instructions
____ 5. Masquerading	e. Using a wireless network without permission
____ 6. Password cracking	f. Covertly swiping a credit card in a card reader that records the data for later use
____ 7. Piggybacking	g. Concealing data within a large MP3 file
____ 8. Posing	h. Attack occurring between the discovery of a software vulnerability and the release of a patch to fix the problem
____ 9. Pretexting	i. Entering a system using a back door that bypasses normal system controls
____ 10. Rootkit	j. Using software to guess company addresses, send employees blank e-mails, and add unreturned messages to spammer e-mail lists
____ 11. Shoulder surfing	k. Unauthorized code in an authorized and properly functioning program
____ 12. Skimming	l. Software used to do harm
____ 13. Social engineering	m. A program that can replicate itself and travel over networks
____ 14. Software piracy	n. Pretending to be a legitimate user, thereby gaining access to a system and all the rights and privileges of the legitimate user
____ 15. Steganography	o. Special code or password that bypasses security features
____ 16. Superzapping	p. Unauthorized copying or distribution of copyrighted software
____ 17. Trap door	q. Software that conceals processes, files, network connections, and system data from the operating system and other programs
____ 18. Trojan horse	r. Methods used to trick someone into divulging personal information
____ 19. Virus	s. Software that sits idle until a specified circumstance or time triggers it
____ 20. Worm	t. The act of duplicating software, music, or movies
____ 21. Zero-day attack	u. Acting under false pretenses to gain confidential information
	v. Observing or listening to users as they divulge personal information
	w. Gaining access to a computer system without permission
	x. Creating a seemingly legitimate business, collecting personal information while making a sale, and never delivering the item sold

6.8. Computer Fraud and Abuse Techniques.

Match the computer fraud and abuse technique in the left column with the scenario in the right column. Terms on the left may be used once, more than once, or not at all.

_____	1. Address Resolution Protocol (ARP) spoofing	a.	Inserting a sleeve to trap a card in an ATM, pretending to help the owner and thereby obtaining the PIN, and using the card and PIN to drain the account
_____	2. Buffer overflow attack	b.	A segment of executable code that attaches itself to software
_____	3. Carding	c.	Using a small storage device to download unauthorized data from a computer
_____	4. Caller ID spoofing	d.	Malicious computer code that specifically targets a computer's start-up instructions
_____	5. Cyber-extortion	e.	Malicious software that people are frightened into buying
_____	6. Cyber-bullying	f.	Covertly swiping a credit card in a card reader that records the data for later use
_____	7. Economic espionage	g.	Using the Internet to inflate a stock price so it can be sold for a profit
_____	8. E-mail spoofing	h.	Exchanging explicit messages and pictures by telephone
_____	9. IP address spoofing	i.	Inserting a malicious database query in input in a way that it can be executed by an application program
_____	10. Internet auction fraud	j.	So much input data that storage is exceeded; excess input contains code that takes control of the computer
_____	11. Internet pump-and-dump fraud	k.	Making an electronic communication appear as though it originated from a different source
_____	12. Lebanese looping	l.	Creating packets with a forged address to impersonate another computing system
_____	13. Man-in-the-middle (MITM) attack	m.	Fake computer networking protocol messages sent to an Ethernet LAN to determine a network host's hardware address when only its IP address is known
_____	14. Podslurping	n.	Changing the name or number a text message appears to come from
_____	15. Ransomware	o.	Special code or password that bypasses security features
_____	16. Scareware	p.	A link containing malicious code that takes a victim to a vulnerable Web site. Once there, the victim's browser executes the malicious code embedded in the link.
_____	17. Sexting	q.	Using social networking to harass another person
_____	18. SQL Injection	r.	Displaying an incorrect phone number to hide the caller's identity
_____	19. SMS spoofing	s.	Software that encrypts programs and data until a payment is made to remove it
_____	20. XSS attack	t.	A hacker placing himself between a client and a host to intercept network traffic
_____	21. Tabnapping	u.	A demand for payment to ensure a hacker does not harm a computer
		v.	Theft of trade secrets and intellectual property
		w.	Using a site that sells to the highest bidder to defraud another person
		x.	Verifying credit card validity
		y.	Secretly changing an already open browser tab

6.9. Identify the computer fraud and abuse technique used in each the following actual examples of computer wrongdoing.

a. A teenage gang known as the "414s" broke into the Los Alamos National Laboratory, Sloan-Kettering Cancer Center, and Security Pacific Bank. One gang member appeared in *Newsweek* with the caption "Beware: Hackers at play."

b. Daniel Baas was the systems administrator for a company that did business with Acxiom, who manages customer information for companies. Baas exceeded his authorized access and downloaded a file with 300 encrypted passwords, decrypted the password file, and downloaded Acxiom customer files containing personal information. The intrusion cost Acxiom over $5.8 million.

c. Cyber-attacks left high-profile sites such as Amazon.com, eBay, Buy.com, and CNN Interactive staggering under the weight of tens of thousands of bogus messages that tied up the retail sites' computers and slowed the news site's operations for hours.

d. Susan Gilmour-Latham got a call asking why she was sending the caller multiple adult text messages per day. Her account records proved the calls were not coming from her phone. Neither she nor her mobile company could explain how the messages were sent. After finding no way to block the unsavory messages, she changed her mobile number to avoid further embarrassment by association.

e. A federal grand jury in Fort Lauderdale claimed that four executives of a rental-car franchise modified a computer-billing program to add five gallons to the actual gas tank capacity of their vehicles. Over three years, 47,000 customers who returned a car without topping it off ended up paying an extra $2 to $15 for gasoline.

f. A mail-order company programmer truncated odd cents in sales-commission accounts and placed them in the last record in the commission file. Accounts were processed alphabetically, and he created a dummy sales-commission account using the name of Zwana. Three years later, the holders of the first and last sales-commission accounts were honored. Zwana was unmasked and his creator fired.

g. MicroPatent, an intellectual property firm, was notified that their proprietary information would be broadcast on the Internet if they did not pay a $17 million fee. The hacker was caught by the FBI before any damage was done.

h. When Estonia removed a Russian World War II war memorial, Estonian government and bank networks were knocked offline in a distributed DoS attack by Russian hackers. A counterfeit letter of apology for removing the memorial statue was placed on the Web site of Estonia's prime minister.

i. eBay customers were notified by e-mail that their accounts had been compromised and were being restricted unless they re-registered using an accompanying hyperlink to a Web page that had eBay's logo, home page design, and internal links. The form had a place for them to enter their credit card data, ATM PINs, Social Security number, date of birth, and their mother's maiden name. Unfortunately, eBay hadn't sent the e-mail.

j. A teenager hijacked the eBay.de domain name and several months later the domain name for a large New York ISP. Both hijacked Web sites pointed to a site in Australia.

k. Travelers who logged into the Alpharetta, Georgia, airport's Internet service had personal information stolen and picked up as many as 45 viruses. A hacker had set up a rogue wireless network with the same name as the airport's wireless access network.

l. Criminals in Russia used a vulnerability in Microsoft's server software to add a few lines of Java code to users' copies of Internet Explorer. The code recorded the users' keyboard activities, giving the criminals access to usernames and passwords at many banking Web sites. The attacks caused $420 million in damage.

m. America Online subscribers received a message offering free software. Users who opened the attachments unknowingly unleashed a program hidden inside another program that secretly copied the subscriber's account name and password and forwarded them to the sender.

n. Rajendrasinh Makwana, an Indian citizen and IT contractor who worked at Fannie Mae's Maryland facility, was terminated at 1:00 P.M. on October 24. Before his network access was revoked, he created a program to wipe out all 4,000 of Fannie Mae's servers on the following January 31.

o. A man accessed millions of ChoicePoint files by claiming in writing and on the phone to be someone he was not.

p. A 31-year-old programmer unleashed a Visual Basic program by deliberately posting an infected document to an alt.sex Usenet newsgroup using a stolen AOL account. The program evaded security software and infected computers using the Windows operating system and Microsoft Word. On March 26, the Melissa program appeared on thousands of e-mail systems disguised as an important message from a colleague or friend. The program sent an infected e-mail to the first 50 e-mail addresses on the users' Outlook address book. Each infected computer would infect 50 additional computers, which in turn would infect another 50 computers. The program spread rapidly and exponentially, causing considerable damage. Many companies had to disconnect from the Internet or shut down their e-mail gateways because of the vast amount of e-mail the program was generating. The program caused more than $400 million in damages.

q. Microsoft filed a lawsuit against two Texas firms that produced software that sent incessant pop-ups resembling system warnings. The messages stated "CRITICAL ERROR MESSAGE! REGISTRY DAMAGED AND CORRUPTED" and instructed users to visit a Web site to download Registry Cleaner XP at a cost of $39.95.

r. As many as 114,000 Web sites were tricked into running database commands that installed malicious HTML code redirecting victims to a malicious Web server that tried to install software to remotely control the Web visitors' computers.

s. Zeus records log-in information when the user of the infected computer logs into a list of target Web sites, mostly banks and other financial institutions. The user's data is sent to a remote server where it is used and sold by cyber-criminals. The new version of Zeus will significantly increase fraud losses, given that 30% of Internet users bank online.

t. It took Facebook 15 hours to kill a Facebook application that infected millions of PCs with software that displays a constant stream of pop-up ads. The program posted a "Sexiest Video Ever" message on Facebook walls that looked like it came from a friend. Clicking the link led to a Facebook installation screen, where users allowed the software to access their profiles and walls. Once approved, the application told users to download an updated, free version of a popular Windows video player. Instead, it inserted a program that displayed pop-up ads and links. A week later a "Distracting Beach Babes" message did the same thing.

u. Robert Thousand, Jr. discovered he lost $400,000 from his Ameritrade retirement account shortly after he began receiving a flood of phone calls with a 30-second recording for a sex hotline. An FBI investigation revealed that the perpetrator obtained his Ameritrade account information, called Ameritrade to change his phone number, created several VoIP accounts, and used automated dialing tools to flood the dentist's phones in case Ameritrade called his real number. The perpetrator requested multiple monetary transfers, but Ameritrade would not process them until they reached Thousand to verify them. When the transfers did not go through, the attacker called Ameritrade, gave information to verify that he was Thousand, claimed he had been having phone troubles, and told Ameritrade he was not happy that the transfers had not gone through. Ameritrade processed the transfers, and Thousand lost $400,000.

v. The Internet Crime Complaint Center reports a "hit man" scam. The scammer claims that he has been ordered to assassinate the victim and an associate has been ordered to kill a family member. The only way to prevent the killings is to send $800 so an Islamic expatriate can leave the United States.

w. In an economic stimulus scam, individuals receive a phone call from President Obama telling them to go to a Web site to apply for the funds. To receive the stimulus money, victims have to enter personal identification information, complete an online application, and pay a $28 fee.

6.10. On a Sunday afternoon at a hospital in the Pacific Northwest, computers became sluggish, and documents would not print. Monday morning, the situation became worse when employees logged on to their computers. Even stranger things happened—operating-room doors would not open, pagers would not work, and computers in the intensive care unit shut down. By 10:00 A.M., all 50 IT employees were summoned. They discovered that the hospital was under attack by a botnet that exploited a Microsoft operating system flaw and installed pop-up ads on hospital computers. They got access to the first computer on Sunday and used the hospital's network to spread the infection to other computers. Each infected computer became a zombie that scanned the network looking for new victims. With the network clogged with zombie traffic, hospital communications began to break down. The IT staff tried to halt the attack by shutting off the hospital's Internet connection, but it was too late. The bots were inside the hospital's computer system and infecting other computers faster than they could be cleaned. Monday afternoon IT figured out which malware the bots were installing and wrote a script, which was pushed out hourly, directing computers to remove the bad code. The script helped to slow the bots down a bit.

(*Source:* D. Gage, *Baseline Security* February 6, 2007.)

Required

a. What could the hospital do to stop the attack and contain the damage?
b. Which computer fraud and abuse technique did the hackers use in their attack on the hospital?
c. What steps should the hospital have taken to prevent the damage caused by the attack?

Case 6-1 Shadowcrew

At 9:00 P.M., Andrew Mantovani, cofounder of the group Shadowcrew, received a knock at his door while chatting on his computer. For Mantovani and 27 others, that knock marked the end of Shadowcrew, which provided online marketplaces and discussion forums for identity thieves. Shadowcrew members used the organization's Web site to traffic in stolen Social Security numbers, names, e-mail addresses, counterfeit driver's licenses, birth certificates, and foreign and domestic passports. It also shared best practices for carrying out fraudulent activity. By the time it was shut down, Shadowcrew had trafficked in at least 1.7 million credit cards and it was responsible for more than $4.3 million in fraud losses.

Considered the online equivalent of the Russian Mafia, Shadowcrew operated as a highly sophisticated and hierarchical organization. All users operated under aliases, never revealing their true names or other personal information. Operations and communications were conducted using proxy servers that hid the location and identity of the users. Shadowcrew users were divided into five different roles: administrators, moderators, reviewers, vendors, and members.

Administrators   Shadowcrew administrators were the heads of the organization.

Moderators   A dozen moderators, chosen from the general membership based on proven skill in fraudulent activity, controlled the flow of information.

Reviewers   Reviewers tested the quality of illicit goods (credit cards, passports, etc.) trafficked on the Shadowcrew site. For example, reviewers would run a test called a "dump check" on credit card numbers by hacking into a retailer's cash register system. The fraudster accessed the system through back doors used by technical support personnel to

remotely perform maintenance or repairs. The reviewer would then enter a trivial charge of $1 or $2 to see whether the charge was approved. Reviewers would then write up and post detailed descriptions of the credit cards or other merchandise tested.

Vendors   Vendors managed the sale of stolen data. Prices were posted and products were sold using an auction forum much like eBay. Payments were processed via Western Union money transfers or an electronic currency and were made using a fraud victim's stolen data.

Members   Thousands of people used the Shadowcrew Web site to gather and share information on committing identity fraud. Shadowcrew practiced open registration, but more sensitive discussion areas were password protected, and members needed another trusted member to vouch for them in order to join the forum.

Members could be promoted up the organization by providing quality products or by sharing new or unique tips or techniques for committing fraud. Shadowcrew punished acts of disloyalty. For instance, one disloyal group member had his actual name, address, and phone number posted on the Web site for all to see.

Shadowcrew's demise began when MasterCard informed the United States government that a hundred Web sites promoted and supported identity fraud. The United States Secret Service covertly infiltrated Shadowcrew. Acting as trusted members, agents set up a Virtual Private Network (VPN) over which Shadowcrew leaders could conduct illicit business. The VPN allowed the Secret Service to track the organization's doings and discover the real identities and locations of Shadowcrew users.

It was vital that all arrests occur simultaneously, because any one of the targets could instantly warn the others via Shadowcrew's discussion forum. With the help of the Justice Department, the Homeland Security Department, the Royal Canadian Mounted Police, Europol, and local police departments, authorities simultaneously knocked on the suspects' doors at precisely 9:00 P.M. The operation led to 28 arrests, 21 in the United States. Rather than immediately deactivating the Web site, investigators replaced the home page with the following warning: "Activities by Shadowcrew members are being investigated by the United States Secret Service." Under a picture of hands clutching bars of a jail cell, agents listed the criminal charges that Shadowcrew members faced and called on visitors to turn themselves in: "Contact your local United States Secret Service field office before we contact you!"

(Source: J. McCormick and D. Gage, *Baseline Security*, March 7, 2005.)

1. How did Shadowcrew members conceal their identities? How can average citizens protect their identities while interacting online?
2. How has the Internet made detecting and identifying identity fraudsters difficult?
3. What are some of the most common electronic means of stealing personal information?
4. What is the most common way that fraudsters use personal data?
5. What measures can consumers take to protect against the online brokering of their personal data?
6. What are the most effective means of detecting identity theft?
7. What pieces of personal information are most valuable to identity fraudsters?

AIS IN ACTION SOLUTIONS

Quiz Key

1. A set of instructions to increase a programmer's pay rate by 10% is hidden inside an authorized program. It changes and updates the payroll file. What is this computer fraud technique called?
   a. virus (Incorrect. A virus damages a system using a segment of executable code that attaches itself to software, replicates itself, and spreads to other systems or files.)
   b. worm (Incorrect. A worm is a program that hides in a host program and copies and actively transmits itself directly to other systems.)
   c. trap door (Incorrect. A trap door is entering a system using a back door that bypasses normal system controls.)
   ▶ d. Trojan horse (Correct. Placing unauthorized computer instructions, such as fraudulently increasing an employee's pay, in an authorized and properly functioning program is an example of a Trojan horse.)

2. Which computer fraud technique involves a set of instructions hidden inside a calendar utility that copies itself each time the utility is enabled until memory is filled and the system crashes?
   a. logic bomb (Incorrect. A logic bomb sabotages a system using a program that lies idle until some specified circumstance or a particular time triggers it.)
   b. trap door (Incorrect. A trap door is a means of bypassing normal system controls to enter a system.)
   ▶ c. virus (Correct. A virus damages a system using a segment of executable code that attaches itself to software, replicates itself, and spreads to other systems or files.)
   d. Trojan horse (Incorrect. Placing unauthorized computer instructions, such as fraudulently increasing an employee's pay, in an authorized and properly functioning program is an example of a Trojan horse.)

3. Interest calculations are truncated at two decimal places, and the excess decimals are put into an account the perpetrator controls. What is this fraud called?
   a. typosquatting (Incorrect. Typosquatting is the practice of setting up Web sites with names similar to real Web sites so that users who make typographical errors when typing Web site names are sent to a site filled with malware.)

    b. URL hijacking (Incorrect. URL hijacking is another name for typosquatting, which is explained above.)

    c. chipping (Incorrect. Chipping is planting a chip that records transaction data in a legitimate credit card reader.)

 ▶ d. round-down fraud (Correct.)

4. A perpetrator attacks phone systems to obtain free phone line access or uses telephone lines to transmit viruses and to access, steal, and destroy data. What is this computer fraud technique called?

    a. phishing (Incorrect. Phishing is the practice of sending e-mails requesting recipients to visit a Web page and verify data or fill in missing data. The e-mails and Web sites look like legitimate companies, primarily financial institutions.)

 ▶ b. phreaking (Correct.)

    c. pharming (Incorrect. Pharming is redirecting traffic to a spoofed Web site to gain access to personal and confidential information.)

    d. vishing (Incorrect. Vishing is voice phishing, in which e-mail recipients are asked to call a phone number where they are asked to divulge confidential data.)

5. Fraud perpetrators threaten to harm a company if it does not pay a specified amount of money. What is this fraud technique called?

    a. cyber-terrorism (Incorrect. Cyber-terrorism, or Internet terrorism, is using the Internet to disrupt communications and e-commerce.)

    b. blackmailing (Incorrect. Blackmailing is the extortion of money or something else of value from a person by the threat of exposing a criminal act or discreditable information.)

 ▶ c. cyber-extortion (Correct.)

    d. scareware (Incorrect. Scareware is software of limited or no benefit, often malicious in nature, that is sold using scare tactics. The most common scare tactic is a dire warning that the person's computer is infected with viruses, spyware, or some other catastrophic problem.)

6. Techniques used to obtain confidential information, often by tricking people, are referred to as what?

    a. pretexting (Incorrect. Pretexting is one specific type of social engineering. It involves acting under false pretenses to gain confidential information.)

    b. posing (Incorrect. Posing is one specific type of social engineering in which someone creates a seemingly legitimate business, collects personal information while making a sale, and never delivers the item sold.)

 ▶ c. social engineering (Correct.)

    d. identity theft (Incorrect. Identity theft is a type of social engineering in which one person assumes another's identity, usually for economic gain, by illegally obtaining confidential information, such as a Social Security number.)

7. What type of software secretly collects personal information about users and sends it to someone else without the user's permission?

    a. rootkit (Incorrect. A rootkit is software that conceals processes, files, network connections, and system data from the operating system and other programs.)

    b. torpedo software (Incorrect. Torpedo software is software that destroys competing malware, resulting in "malware warfare" between competing developers.)

 ▶ c. spyware (Correct.)

    d. malware (Incorrect. *Malware* is a general term that applies to any software used to do harm. There is a more specific correct answer to this question.)

8. What type of software conceals processes, files, network connections, memory addresses, systems utility programs, and system data from the operating system and other programs?

 ▶ a. rootkit (Correct.)

    b. spyware (Incorrect. Spyware is software that is used to monitor computing habits and send that data to someone else, often without the computer user's permission.)

    c. malware (Incorrect. Malware is any software that is used to do harm.)

   d. adware (Incorrect. Adware is software used to collect Web-surfing and spending data and forward it to advertising or media organizations. It also causes banner ads to pop up on computer monitors as the Internet is surfed.)

9. Which type of computer attack takes place between the time a software vulnerability is discovered and the time software developers release a software patch that fixes the problem?

   a. posing (Incorrect. Posing is creating a seemingly legitimate business, collecting personal information while making a sale, and never delivering the item sold.)

▶ **b.** zero-day attack (Correct.)

   c. evil twin (Incorrect. An evil twin is a wireless network with the same name as a local wireless access point that unsuspecting people use, allowing hackers to monitor the network's traffic looking for useful information.)

   d. software piracy (Incorrect. Software piracy is the illegal copying of computer software.)

10. Someone redirects a Web site's traffic to a bogus Web site, usually to gain access to personal and confidential information. What is this computer fraud technique called?

   a. vishing (Incorrect. Vishing is voice phishing, in which e-mail recipients are asked to call a phone number where they are asked to divulge confidential data.)

   b. phishing (Incorrect. Phishing is sending e-mails requesting recipients to visit a Web page and verify data or fill in missing data. The e-mails and Web sites look like legitimate companies, primarily financial institutions.)

▶ **c.** pharming (Correct.)

   d. phreaking (Incorrect. Phreaking is attacking phone systems and using telephone lines to transmit viruses and to access, steal, and destroy data.

Chapter 7

Control and Accounting Information Systems

Learning Objectives

After studying this chapter, you should be able to:

1. Explain basic control concepts and explain why computer control and security are important.

2. Compare and contrast the COBIT, COSO, and ERM control frameworks.

3. Describe the major elements in the internal environment of a company.

4. Describe the four types of control objectives that companies need to set.

5. Describe the events that affect uncertainty and the techniques used to identify them.

6. Explain how to assess and respond to risk using the Enterprise Risk Management (ERM) model.

7. Describe control activities commonly used in companies.

8. Describe how to communicate information and monitor control processes in organizations.

INTEGRATIVE CASE SPRINGER'S LUMBER & SUPPLY

Jason Scott, an internal auditor for Northwest Industries, is auditing Springer's Lumber & Supply, Northwest's building materials outlet in Bozeman, Montana. His supervisor, Maria Pilier, asked him to trace a sample of purchase transactions from purchase requisition to cash disbursement to verify that proper control procedures were followed. Jason is frustrated with this task, and for good reasons:

- The purchasing system is poorly documented.
- He keeps finding transactions that have not been processed as Ed Yates, the accounts payable manager, said they should be.

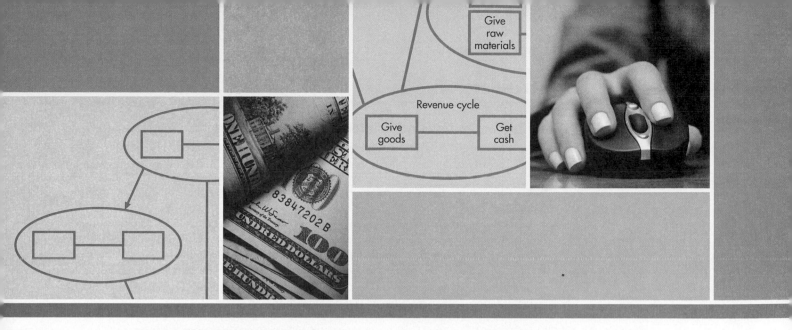

- Purchase requisitions are missing for several items personally authorized by Bill Springer, the purchasing vice president.
- Some vendor invoices have been paid without supporting documents, such as purchase orders and receiving reports.
- Prices for some items seem unusually high, and there are a few discrepancies in item prices between the vendor invoice and the corresponding purchase order.

Yates had a logical answer for every question Jason raised and advised Jason that the real world is not as tidy as the world portrayed in college textbooks. Maria also has some concerns:

- Springer's is the largest supplier in the area and has a near monopoly.
- Management authority is held by the company president, Joe Springer, and his two sons, Bill (the purchasing vice president) and Ted (the controller). Several relatives and friends are on the payroll. Together, the Springers own 10% of the company.
- Lines of authority and responsibility within the company are loosely defined and confusing.
- Maria believes that Ted Springer may have engaged in "creative accounting" to make Springer's one of Northwest's best-performing retail outlets.

After talking to Maria, Jason ponders the following issues:

1. Because Ed Yates had a logical explanation for every unusual transaction, should Jason describe these transactions in his report?
2. Is a violation of control procedures acceptable if management has authorized it?
3. Maria's concerns about Springer's loosely defined lines of authority and possible use of "creative accounting" are matters of management policy. With respect to Jason's control procedures assignment, does he have a professional or an ethical responsibility to get involved?

Introduction

Why Threats to Accounting Information Systems Are Increasing

In most years, more than 60% of organizations experience a major failure in controlling the security and integrity of their computer systems. Reasons for the failures include the following:

- Information is available to an unprecedented number of workers. Chevron, for example, has over 35,000 PCs.
- Information on distributed computer networks is hard to control. At Chevron, information is distributed among many systems and thousands of employees worldwide. Each system and each employee represent a potential control vulnerability point.
- Customers and suppliers have access to each others' systems and data. For example, WalMart allows vendors to access their databases. Imagine the confidentiality problems as these vendors form alliances with WalMart competitors.

Organizations have not adequately protected data for several reasons:

- Some companies view the loss of crucial information as a distant, unlikely threat.
- The control implications of moving from centralized computer systems to Internet-based systems are not fully understood.
- Many companies do not realize that information is a strategic resource and that protecting it must be a strategic requirement. For example, one company lost millions of dollars because it did not protect data transmissions. A competitor tapped into its phone lines and obtained faxes of new product designs.
- Productivity and cost pressures motivate management to forgo time-consuming control measures.

Any potential adverse occurrence is called a *threat* or an event. The potential dollar loss from a threat is called the *exposure* or *impact*. The probability that it will happen is called the *likelihood* of the threat.

Overview of Control Concepts

Internal control is the process implemented to provide reasonable assurance that the following control objectives are achieved:

- Safeguard assets: prevent or detect their unauthorized acquisition, use, or disposition.
- Maintain records in sufficient detail to report company assets accurately and fairly.
- Provide accurate and reliable information.
- Prepare financial reports in accordance with established criteria.
- Promote and improve operational efficiency.
- Encourage adherence to prescribed managerial policies.
- Comply with applicable laws and regulations.

Internal control is a process because it permeates an organization's operating activities and is an integral part of management activities. Internal control provides reasonable assurance—complete assurance is difficult to achieve and prohibitively expensive. In addition, internal control systems have inherent limitations, such as susceptibility to simple errors and mistakes, faulty judgments and decision making, management overrides, and collusion.

Developing an internal control system requires a thorough understanding of information technology (IT) capabilities and risks, as well as how to use IT to achieve an organization's control objectives. Accountants and systems developers help management achieve their control objectives by (1) designing effective control systems that take a proactive approach to eliminating system threats and that detect, correct, and recover from threats when they occur; and (2) making it easier to build controls into a system at the initial design stage than to add them after the fact.

Internal controls perform three important functions:

1. *Preventive controls* deter problems before they arise. Examples include hiring qualified personnel, segregating employee duties, and controlling physical access to assets and information.
2. *Detective controls* discover problems that are not prevented. Examples include duplicate checking of calculations and preparing bank reconciliations and monthly trial balances.
3. *Corrective controls* identify and correct problems as well as correct and recover from the resulting errors. Examples include maintaining backup copies of files, correcting data entry errors, and resubmitting transactions for subsequent processing.

Internal controls are often segregated into two categories:

1. *General controls* make sure an organization's control environment is stable and well managed. Examples include security; IT infrastructure; and software acquisition, development, and maintenance controls.
2. *Application controls* make sure transactions are processed correctly. They are concerned with the accuracy, completeness, validity, and authorization of the data captured, entered, processed, stored, transmitted to other systems, and reported.

Robert Simons, a Harvard business professor, has espoused four levels of control to help management reconcile the conflict between creativity and controls.

1. A *belief system* describes how the company creates value, helps employees understand management's vision, communicates company core values, and inspires employees to live by those values.
2. A *boundary system* helps employees act ethically by setting boundaries on employee behavior. Employees are not told exactly what to do. Instead, they are encouraged to creatively solve problems and meet customer needs while meeting minimum performance standards, shunning off-limit activities, and avoiding actions that might damage their reputation.
3. A *diagnostic control system* measures, monitors, and compares actual company progress to budgets and performance goals. Feedback helps management adjust and fine-tune inputs and processes so future outputs more closely match goals.
4. An *interactive control system* helps managers to focus subordinates' attention on key strategic issues and to be more involved in their decisions. Interactive system data are interpreted and discussed in face-to-face meetings of superiors, subordinates, and peers.

Regrettably, not all organizations have an effective internal control system. For instance, one report indicated that the FBI is plagued by IT infrastructure vulnerabilities and security problems, some of which were identified in an audit 13 years previously. Specific areas of concern were security standards, guidelines, and procedures; segregation of duties; access controls, including password management and usage; backup and recovery controls; and software development and change controls.

The Foreign Corrupt Practices and Sarbanes–Oxley Acts

In 1977, the *Foreign Corrupt Practices Act (FCPA)* was passed to prevent companies from bribing foreign officials to obtain business. Congress incorporated language from an American Institute of Certified Public Accountants (AICPA) pronouncement into the FCPA that required corporations to maintain good systems of internal control. Unfortunately, these requirements were not sufficient to prevent further problems.

In the late 1990s and early 2000s, news stories were reporting accounting frauds at Enron, WorldCom, Xerox, Tyco, Global Crossing, Adelphia, and other companies. When Enron, with $62 billion in assets, declared bankruptcy in December 2001, it was the largest bankruptcy in U.S. history. In June 2002, Arthur Andersen, once the largest CPA firm, collapsed. The Enron bankruptcy was dwarfed when WorldCom, with over $100 billion in assets, filed for bankruptcy in July 2002. In response to these frauds, Congress passed the *Sarbanes–Oxley Act (SOX)* of 2002. SOX applies to publicly held companies and their auditors and was designed to prevent financial statement fraud, make financial reports more transparent, protect investors, strengthen internal controls, and punish executives who perpetrate fraud.

SOX is the most important business-oriented legislation in the last 75 years. It changed the way boards of directors and management operate and had a dramatic impact on CPAs who audit them. The following are some of the most important aspects of SOX:

- *Public Company Accounting Oversight Board (PCAOB).* SOX created the *Public Company Accounting Oversight Board (PCAOB)* to control the auditing profession. The PCAOB sets and enforces auditing, quality control, ethics, independence, and other auditing standards.
- *New rules for auditors.* Auditors must report specific information to the company's audit committee, such as critical accounting policies and practices. Audit partners must be rotated periodically. SOX prohibits auditors from performing certain nonaudit services, such as information systems design and implementation. Audit firms cannot provide services to companies if top management was employed by the auditing firm and worked on the company's audit in the preceding 12 months.
- *New roles for audit committees.* Audit committee members must be on the company's board of directors and be independent of the company. One member of the audit committee must be a financial expert. The audit committee hires, compensates, and oversees the auditors, who report directly to them.
- *New rules for management.* SOX requires the CEO and CFO to certify that (1) financial statements and disclosures are fairly presented, were reviewed by management, and are not misleading; and that (2) the auditors were told about all material internal control weaknesses and fraud. If management knowingly violates these rules, they can be prosecuted and fined. Companies must disclose, in plain English, material changes to their financial condition on a timely basis.
- *New internal control requirements.* Section 404 requires companies to issue a report accompanying the financial statements stating that management is responsible for establishing and maintaining an adequate internal control system. The report must contain management's assessment of the company's internal controls, attest to their accuracy, and report significant weaknesses or material noncompliance.

After SOX was passed, the SEC mandated that management must:

- Base its evaluation on a recognized control framework. The most likely frameworks, formulated by COSO, are discussed in this chapter.
- Disclose all material internal control weaknesses.
- Conclude that a company does not have effective financial reporting internal controls if there are material weaknesses.

Control Frameworks

This section discusses three frameworks used to develop internal control systems.

COBIT Framework

The Information Systems Audit and Control Association (ISACA) developed the *Control Objectives for Information and Related Technology (COBIT)* framework. COBIT consolidates control standards from 36 different sources into a single framework that allows (1) management to benchmark security and control practices of IT environments, (2) users to be assured that adequate IT security and control exist, and (3) auditors to substantiate their internal control opinions and to advise on IT security and control matters.

The framework addresses control from three vantage points:

1. *Business objectives.* To satisfy business objectives, information must conform to seven categories of criteria that map into the objectives established by the Committee of Sponsoring Organizations (COSO; see next section).
2. *IT resources.* These include people, application systems, technology, facilities, and data.
3. *IT processes.* These are broken into four domains: planning and organization, acquisition and implementation, delivery and support, and monitoring and evaluation.

The COBIT framework is shown in Figure 8-1 and discussed in more depth in Chapters 8 through 10.

COSO's Internal Control Framework

The *Committee of Sponsoring Organizations (COSO)* consists of the American Accounting Association, the American Institute of Certified Public Accountants, the Institute of Internal Auditors, the Institute of Management Accountants, and the Financial Executives Institute. In 1992, COSO issued *Internal Control—Integrated Framework (IC)*, which is widely accepted as the authority on internal controls and is incorporated into policies, rules, and regulations used to control business activities.

The five components of the IC framework, summarized in Table 7-1, are part of COSO's newer Enterprise Risk Management framework.

COSO's Enterprise Risk Management Framework

To improve the risk management process, COSO developed a second control framework called *Enterprise Risk Management—Integrated Framework (ERM)*. ERM is the process the board of directors and management use to set strategy, identify events that may affect the entity, assess and manage risk, and provide reasonable assurance that the company achieves its objectives and goals. The basic principles behind ERM are as follows:

- Companies are formed to create value for their owners.
- Management must decide how much uncertainty it will accept as it creates value.
- Uncertainty results in risk, which is the possibility that something negatively affects the company's ability to create or preserve value.
- Uncertainty results in opportunity, which is the possibility that something positively affects the company's ability to create or preserve value.
- The ERM framework can manage uncertainty as well as create and preserve value.

COSO developed Figure 7-1 to illustrate the elements of ERM. The four columns at the top represent the objectives management must meet to achieve company goals. The columns on the right represent the company's units. The horizontal rows are the eight interrelated risk and control components of ERM. The ERM model is three-dimensional. Each of the eight risk and control elements applies to each of the four objectives and to the company and/or one of its subunits. For example, XYZ Company could look at the control activities for the operations objectives in its Pacific Division.

The Enterprise Risk Management Framework versus the Internal Control Framework

The IC framework has been widely adopted as the way to evaluate internal controls, as required by Sarbanes–Oxley. However, it examines controls without looking at the purposes and risks of business processes and provides little context for evaluating the results. Under the IC framework,

TABLE 7-1 Five Interrelated Components of COSO's Internal Control Model

Component	Description
Control environment	The core of any business is its people—their individual attributes, including integrity, ethical values, and competence—and the environment in which they operate. They are the engine that drives the organization and the foundation on which everything rests.
Control activities	Control policies and procedures help ensure that the actions identified by management as necessary to address risks and achieve the organization's objectives are effectively carried out.
Risk assessment	The organization must identify, analyze, and manage its risks. It must set objectives so that the organization is operating in concert.
Information and communication	Information and communication systems capture and exchange the information needed to conduct, manage, and control the organization's operations.
Monitoring	The entire process must be monitored, and modifications made as necessary so the system can change as conditions warrant.

FIGURE 7-1

COSO's Enterprise Risk Management Model

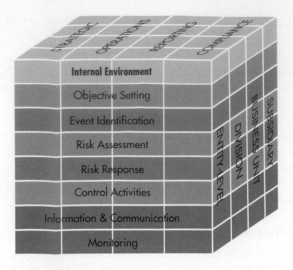

it is hard to know which control systems are most important, whether they adequately deal with risk, and whether important controls are missing.

The more comprehensive ERM framework takes a risk-based rather than a controls-based approach. ERM adds three additional elements to COSO's IC framework: setting objectives, identifying events that may affect the company, and developing a response to assessed risk. As a result, controls are flexible and relevant because they are linked to current organizational objectives. The ERM model also recognizes that risk, in addition to being controlled, can be accepted, avoided, diversified, shared, or transferred.

Because it is more comprehensive, the ERM model will likely become the more widely adopted model. The eight ERM components shown in Figure 7-1 are the topic of the remainder of the chapter.

The Internal Environment

The *internal environment*, or company culture, influences how organizations establish strategies and objectives; structure business activities; and identify, assess, and respond to risk. It is the foundation for all other ERM components. A weak or deficient internal environment often results in breakdowns in risk management and control. It is essentially the same thing as the control environment in the IC framework.

An internal environment consists of the following:

1. Management's philosophy, operating style, and risk appetite
2. The board of directors
3. Commitment to integrity, ethical values, and competence
4. Organizational structure
5. Methods of assigning authority and responsibility
6. Human resource standards
7. External influences

Enron is an example of an ineffective internal environment that resulted in financial failure. Although Enron appeared to have an effective ERM system, its internal environment was defective. Management engaged in risky and dubious business practices, which the board of directors never questioned. Management misrepresented the company's financial condition, lost the confidence of shareholders, and finally filed for bankruptcy.

Management's Philosophy, Operating Style, and Risk Appetite

Collectively, an organization has a philosophy, or shared beliefs and attitudes, about risk that affects policies, procedures, oral and written communications, and decisions. Companies also have a *risk appetite*, which is the amount of risk they are willing to accept to achieve their goals. To avoid undue risk, risk appetite must be in alignment with company strategy.

The more responsible management's philosophy and operating style, and the more clearly they are communicated, the more likely employees will behave responsibly. If management has little concern for internal controls and risk management, then employees are less diligent in achieving control objectives. The culture at Springer's Lumber & Supply provides an example. Maria Pilier found that lines of authority and responsibility were loosely defined and suspected management might have used "creative accounting" to improve company performance. Jason Scott found evidence of poor internal control practices in the purchasing and accounts payable functions. These two conditions may be related; management's loose attitude may have contributed to the purchasing department's inattentiveness to good internal control practices.

Management's philosophy, operating style, and risk appetite can be assessed by answering questions such as these:

- Does management take undue business risks to achieve its objectives, or does it assess potential risks and rewards prior to acting?
- Does management manipulate performance measures, such as net income, so they are seen in a more favorable light?
- Does management pressure employees to achieve results regardless of the methods, or does it demand ethical behavior? In other words, do the ends justify the means?

The Board of Directors

An involved board of directors represents shareholders and provides an independent review of management that acts as a check and balance on its actions. Sarbanes–Oxley requires public companies to have an *audit committee* of outside, independent directors. The audit committee is responsible for financial reporting, regulatory compliance, internal control, and hiring and overseeing internal and external auditors, who report all critical accounting policies and practices to them. Directors should also approve company strategy and review security policies.

Commitment to Integrity, Ethical Values, and Competence

Organizations need a culture that stresses integrity and commitment to ethical values and competence. Ethics pays—ethical standards are good business. Integrity starts at the top, as company employees adopt top management attitudes about risks and controls. A powerful message is sent when the CEO, confronted with a difficult decision, makes the ethically correct choice.

Companies endorse integrity by:

- Actively teaching and requiring it—for example, making it clear that honest reports are more important than favorable ones.
- Avoiding unrealistic expectations or incentives that motivate dishonest or illegal acts, such as overly aggressive sales practices, unfair or unethical negotiation tactics, and bonuses excessively based on reported financial results.
- Consistently rewarding honesty and giving verbal labels to honest and dishonest behavior. If companies punish or reward honesty without labeling it as such, or if the standard of honesty is inconsistent, then employees will display inconsistent moral behavior.
- Developing a written code of conduct that explicitly describes honest and dishonest behaviors. For example, most purchasing agents agree that accepting $5,000 from a supplier is dishonest, but a weekend vacation is not as clear-cut. A major cause of dishonesty comes from rationalizing unclear situations and allowing the criterion of expediency to replace the criterion of right versus wrong. Companies should document that employees have read and understand the code of conduct.
- Requiring employees to report dishonest or illegal acts and disciplining employees who knowingly fail to report them. All dishonest acts should be investigated, and dishonest employees should be dismissed and prosecuted to show that such behavior is not allowed.
- Making a commitment to competence. Companies should hire competent employees with the necessary knowledge, experience, training, and skills.

Organizational Structure

A company's organizational structure provides a framework for planning, executing, controlling, and monitoring operations. Important aspects of the organizational structure include the following:

- Centralization or decentralization of authority
- A direct or matrix reporting relationship
- Organization by industry, product line, location, or marketing network
- How allocation of responsibility affects information requirements
- Organization of and lines of authority for accounting, auditing, and information system functions
- Size and nature of company activities

A complex or unclear organizational structure may indicate serious problems. For example, ESM, a brokerage company, used a multilayered organizational structure to hide a $300 million fraud. Management hid stolen cash in their financial statements using a fictitious receivable from a related company.

In today's business world, hierarchical structures, with layers of management who supervise others, are being replaced with flat organizations of self-directed work teams that make decisions without needing multiple layers of approval. The emphasis is on continuous improvement rather than periodic reviews and appraisals. These organizational structure changes impact the nature and type of controls used.

Methods of Assigning Authority and Responsibility

Management should make sure employees understand entity goals and objectives, assign authority and responsibility for them to departments and individuals, hold them accountable for achieving them, and encourage the use of initiative to solve problems. It is especially important to identify who is responsible for the company's information security policy.

Authority and responsibility are assigned and communicated using formal job descriptions, employee training, operating schedules, budgets, a code of conduct, and written policies and procedures. The *policy and procedures manual* explains proper business practices, describes needed knowledge and experience, explains document procedures, explains how to handle transactions, and lists the resources provided to carry out specific duties. The manual includes the chart of accounts and copies of forms and documents. It is a helpful on-the-job reference for current employees and a useful tool for training new employees.

Human Resources Standards

One of the greatest control strengths is the honesty of employees; one of the greatest control weaknesses is the dishonesty of employees. Human resource policies and practices governing working conditions, job incentives, and career advancement can be a powerful force in encouraging honesty, efficiency, and loyal service. Policies should convey the required level of expertise, competence, ethical behavior, and integrity required. The following policies and procedures are important.

HIRING   Employees should be hired based on educational background, experience, achievements, honesty and integrity, and meeting written job requirements. All company personnel, including cleaning crews and temporary employees, should be subject to hiring policies. Some fraudsters pose as janitors or temporary employees to gain physical access to company computers.

Applicant qualifications can be evaluated using resumes, reference letters, interviews, and background checks. A thorough *background check* includes talking to references, checking for a criminal record, examining credit records, and verifying education and work experience. Many applicants include false information in their applications or resumes. Philip Crosby Associates (PCA) hired John Nelson, MBA, CPA, without conducting a background check. In reality, the CPA designation and his glowing references were phony. Nelson was actually Robert W. Liszewski, who had served an 18-month jail sentence for embezzling $400,000. By the time PCA discovered this, Liszewski had embezzled $960,000 using wire transfers to a dummy corporation, supported by forged signatures on contracts and authorization documents.

Many firms hire companies that specialize in background checks because some applicants buy phony degrees from Web site operators who "validate" the bogus education when employers call. Some applicants even pay hackers to break into university databases and enter fake graduation or grade data.

Compensating, Evaluating and Promoting   Poorly compensated employees are more likely to feel resentment and financial pressures that can motivate fraud. Fair pay and appropriate bonus incentives help motivate and reinforce outstanding employee performance. Employees should be given periodic performance appraisals to help them understand their strengths and weaknesses. Promotions should be based on performance and qualifications.

TRAINING   Training programs should teach new employees their responsibilities; expected levels of performance and behavior; and the company's policies and procedures, culture, and operating style. Employees can be trained by conducting informal discussions and formal meetings, issuing periodic memos, distributing written guidelines and codes of professional ethics, circulating reports of unethical behavior and its consequences, and promoting security and fraud training programs. Ongoing training helps employees tackle new challenges, stay ahead of the competition, adapt to changing technologies, and deal effectively with the evolving environment.

Fraud is less likely to occur when employees believe security is everyone's business, are proud of their company and protective of its assets, and recognize the need to report fraud. Such a culture has to be created, taught, and practiced. Acceptable and unacceptable behavior should be defined. Many computer professionals see nothing wrong with using corporate computer resources to gain unauthorized access to databases and browse them. The consequences of unethical behavior (reprimands, dismissal, and prosecution) should also be taught and reinforced.

MANAGING DISGRUNTLED EMPLOYEES   Some disgruntled employees, seeking revenge for a perceived wrong, perpetrate fraud or sabotage systems. Companies need procedures to identify disgruntled employees and either help them resolve their feelings or remove them from sensitive jobs. For example, a company may choose to establish grievance channels and provide employee counseling. Helping employees resolve their problems is not easy to do, however, because most employees fear that airing their feelings could have negative consequences.

DISCHARGING   Dismissed employees should be removed from sensitive jobs immediately and denied access to the information system. One terminated employee lit a butane lighter under a smoke detector located just outside the computer room. It set off a sprinkler system that ruined most of the computer hardware.

VACATIONS AND ROTATION OF DUTIES   Fraud schemes that require ongoing perpetrator attention are uncovered when the perpetrator takes time off. Periodically rotating employee duties and making employees take vacations can achieve the same results. For example, the FBI raided a gambling establishment and discovered that Roswell Steffen, who earned $11,000 a year, was betting $30,000 a day at the racetrack. The bank where he worked discovered that he embezzled and gambled away $1.5 million over a three-year period. A compulsive gambler, Steffen borrowed $5,000 to bet on a "sure thing" that did not pan out. He embezzled ever-increasing amounts in an effort to win back the money he had "borrowed." Steffen's scheme was simple; he transferred money from inactive accounts to his own account. If anyone complained, Steffen, the chief teller with the power to resolve these types of problems, replaced the money by taking it from another inactive account. When asked, after his arrest, how the fraud could have been prevented, Steffen said the bank could have coupled a two-week vacation with several weeks of rotation to another job function. Had the bank taken these measures, Steffen's embezzlement, which required his physical presence at the bank, would have been almost impossible to cover up.

CONFIDENTIALITY AGREEMENTS AND FIDELITY BOND INSURANCE   All employees, suppliers, and contractors should sign and abide by a confidentiality agreement. Fidelity bond insurance coverage of key employees protects companies against losses arising from deliberate acts of fraud.

PROSECUTE AND INCARCERATE PERPETRATORS   Most fraud is not reported or prosecuted for several reasons:

1. Companies are reluctant to report fraud because it can be a public relations disaster. The disclosure can also reveal system vulnerabilities and attract more fraud or hacker attacks.
2. Law enforcement and the courts are busy with violent crimes and have less time and interest for computer crimes in which no physical harm occurs.

3. Fraud is difficult, costly, and time-consuming to investigate and prosecute.
4. Many law enforcement officials, lawyers, and judges lack the computer skills needed to investigate and prosecute computer crimes.
5. Fraud sentences are often light. A famous example involved C. Arnold Smith, former owner of the San Diego Padres, who was named Mr. San Diego of the Century. Smith was involved in the community and made large political contributions. When investigators discovered he had stolen $200 million from his bank, he pleaded no contest. His sentence was four years of probation. He was fined $30,000, to be paid at the rate of $100 a month for 25 years with no interest. Mr. Smith was 71 at the time. The embezzled money was never recovered.

External Influences

External influences include requirements imposed by stock exchanges, the Financial Accounting Standards Board (FASB), the Public Company Accounting Oversight Board (PCAOB), and the Securities and Exchange Commission (SEC). They also include requirements imposed by regulatory agencies, such as those for banks, utilities, and insurance companies.

Objective Setting

Objective setting is the second ERM component. Management determines what the company hopes to achieve, often referred to as the *corporate* vision or mission. Management sets objectives at the corporate level and then subdivides them into more specific objectives for company subunits. The company determines what must go right to achieve the objectives and establishes performance measures to determine whether they are met.

Strategic objectives, which are high-level goals that are aligned with the company's mission, support it, and create shareholder value, are set first. Management should identify alternative ways of accomplishing the strategic objectives; identify and assess the risks and implications of each alternative; formulate a corporate strategy; and set operations, compliance, and reporting objectives.

Operations objectives, which deal with the effectiveness and efficiency of company operations, determine how to allocate resources. They reflect management preferences, judgments, and style and are a key factor in corporate success. They vary significantly—one company may decide to be an early adopter of technology, another may adopt technology when it is proven, and a third may adopt it only after it is generally accepted.

Reporting objectives help ensure the accuracy, completeness, and reliability of company reports; improve decision making; and monitor company activities and performance. *Compliance objectives* help the company comply with all applicable laws and regulations. Most compliance objectives, and many reporting objectives, are imposed by external entities in response to laws or regulations. How well a company meets its compliance and reporting objectives can significantly impact a company's reputation.

ERM provides reasonable assurance that reporting and compliance objectives are achieved because companies have control over them. However, the only reasonable assurance ERM can provide about strategic and operations objectives, which are sometimes at the mercy of uncontrollable external events, is that management and directors are informed on a timely basis of the progress the company is making in achieving them.

Event Identification

COSO defines an *event* as "an incident or occurrence emanating from internal or external sources that affects implementation of strategy or achievement of objectives. Events may have positive or negative impacts or both." An event represents uncertainty; it may or may not occur. If it does occur, it is hard to know when. Until it occurs, it may be difficult to determine its impact. When it occurs, it may trigger another event. Events may occur individually or concurrently. Management must try to anticipate all possible positive or negative events, determine which are most and least likely to occur, and understand the interrelationship of events.

As an example, consider the implementation of an electronic data interchange (EDI) system that creates electronic documents, transmits them to customers and suppliers, and receives electronic responses in return. A few of the events a company could face are choosing an inappropriate technology, unauthorized access, loss of data integrity, incomplete transactions, system failures, and incompatible systems.

Some techniques companies use to identify events include using a comprehensive list of potential events, performing an internal analysis, monitoring leading events and trigger points, conducting workshops and interviews, using data mining, and analyzing business processes.

Risk Assessment and Risk Response

The risks of an identified event are assessed in several different ways: likelihood, positive and negative impacts, individually and by category, their effect on other organizational units, and on an inherent and a residual basis. *Inherent risk* exists before management takes any steps to control the likelihood or impact of an event. *Residual risk* is what remains after management implements internal controls or some other response to risk. Companies should assess inherent risk, develop a response, and then assess residual risk.

To align identified risks with the company's tolerance for risk, management must take an entity-wide view of risk. They assess a risk's likelihood and impact, as well as the costs and benefits of the alternative responses. Management can respond to risk in one of four ways:

- *Reduce.* Reduce the likelihood and impact of risk by implementing an effective system of internal controls.
- *Accept.* Accept the likelihood and impact of the risk.
- *Share.* Share risk or transfer it to someone else by buying insurance, outsourcing an activity, or entering into hedging transactions.
- *Avoid.* Avoid risk by not engaging in the activity that produces the risk. This may require the company to sell a division, exit a product line, or not expand as anticipated.

Accountants and systems designers help management design effective control systems to reduce inherent risk. They also evaluate internal control systems to ensure that they are operating effectively. They assess and reduce inherent risk using the risk assessment and response strategy shown in Figure 7-2. The first step, event identification, has already been discussed.

Estimate Likelihood and Impact

Some events pose a greater risk because they are more likely to occur. Employees are more likely to make a mistake than to commit fraud, and a company is more likely to be the victim of a fraud than an earthquake. The likelihood of an earthquake may be small, but its impact could destroy a company. The impact of fraud is usually not as great, because most instances of fraud do not threaten a company's existence. Likelihood and impact must be considered together. As either increases, both the materiality of the event and the need to protect against it rise.

Software tools help automate risk assessment and response. Blue Cross Blue Shield of Florida uses ERM software that lets managers enter perceived risks; assess their nature, likelihood, and impact; and assign them a numerical rating. An overall corporate assessment of risk is developed by aggregating all the rankings.

Identify Controls

Management should identify controls that protect the company from each event. Preventive controls are usually superior to detective controls. When preventive controls fail, detective controls are essential for discovering the problem. Corrective controls help recover from any problems. A good internal control system should employ all three.

FIGURE 7-2

Risk Assessment Approach to Designing Internal Controls

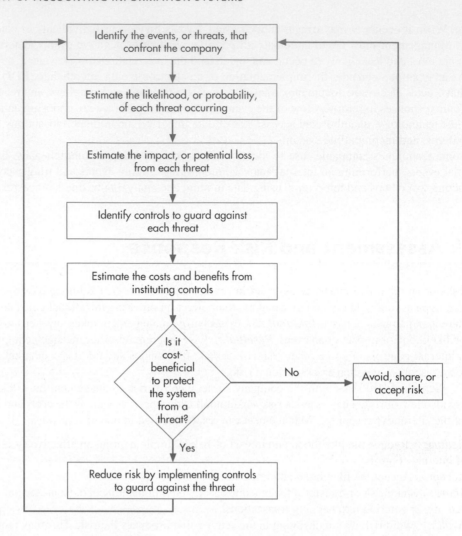

Estimate Costs and Benefits

The objective in designing an internal control system is to provide reasonable assurance that events do not take place. No internal control system provides foolproof protection against all events, because having too many controls is cost-prohibitive and negatively affects operational efficiency. Conversely, having too few controls will not provide the needed reasonable assurance.

The benefits of an internal control procedure must exceed its costs. Benefits, which can be hard to quantify accurately, include increased sales and productivity, reduced losses, better integration with customers and suppliers, increased customer loyalty, competitive advantages, and lower insurance premiums. Costs are usually easier to measure than benefits. A primary cost element is personnel, including the time to perform control procedures, the costs of hiring additional employees to achieve effective segregation of duties, and the costs of programming controls into a computer system.

One way to estimate the value of internal controls involves **expected loss**, the mathematical product of impact and likelihood:

$$\text{Expected loss} = \text{Impact} \times \text{Likelihood}$$

The value of a control procedure is the difference between the expected loss with the control procedure(s) and the expected loss without it.

Determine Cost/Benefit Effectiveness

Management should determine whether a control is cost beneficial. For example, at Atlantic Richfield data errors occasionally required an entire payroll to be reprocessed, at a cost of $10,000. A data validation step would reduce the event likelihood from 15% to 1%, at a cost of $600 per pay period. The cost/benefit analysis that determined that the validation step should be employed is shown in Table 7-2.

TABLE 7-2 Cost/Benefit Analysis of Payroll Validation Procedure

	Without Validation Procedure	With Validation Procedure	Net Expected Difference
Cost to reprocess entire payroll	$10,000	$10,000	
Likelihood of payroll data errors	15%	1%	
Expected reprocessing cost ($10,000 ×likelihood)	$1,500	$100	$1,400
Cost of validation procedure	$0	$600	$(600)
Net expected benefit of validation procedure			$800

In evaluating internal controls, management must consider factors other than those in the expected benefit calculation. For example, if an event threatens an organization's existence, its extra cost can be viewed as a catastrophic loss insurance premium.

Implement Control or Accept, Share, or Avoid the Risk

Cost-effective controls should be implemented to reduce risk. Risks not reduced must be accepted, shared, or avoided. Risk can be accepted if it is within the company's risk tolerance range. An example is a risk with a small likelihood and a small impact. A response to reduce or share risk helps bring residual risk into an acceptable risk tolerance range. A company may choose to avoid the risk when there is no cost-effective way to bring risk into an acceptable risk tolerance range.

Control Activities

Control activities are policies and procedures that provide reasonable assurance that control objectives are met and risk responses are carried out. It is management's responsibility to develop a secure and adequately controlled system. Management establishes a set of procedures to ensure control compliance and enforcement. The information security officer and the operations staff are responsible for ensuring that control procedures are followed.

Controls are much more effective when placed in the system as it is built, rather than as an afterthought. As a result, managers need to involve systems analysts, designers, and end users when designing computer-based control systems. It is important that control activities be in place during the end-of-the-year holiday season, because a disproportionate amount of computer fraud and security break-ins takes place during this time. Some reasons for this are (1) extended employee vacations mean that there fewer people to "mind the store"; (2) students are out of school and have more time on their hands; and (3) lonely counterculture hackers increase their attacks.

Control procedures fall into the following categories:

1. Proper authorization of transactions and activities
2. Segregation of duties
3. Project development and acquisition controls
4. Change management controls
5. Design and use of documents and records
6. Safeguarding assets, records, and data
7. Independent checks on performance

Focus 7-1 discusses how a violation of specific control activities, combined with internal environment factors, resulted in a fraud.

Proper Authorization of Transactions and Activities

Because management lacks the time and resources to supervise each company activity and decision, it establishes policies for employees to follow and then empowers them. This empowerment, called *authorization*, is an important control procedure. Authorizations are often documented by signing, initialing, or entering an authorization code on a document or

F O CUS 7-1   Control Problems in a School District

The audit report for a school district disclosed serious internal control deficiencies. To improve controls, the district (1) selected a new software package, (2) standardized accounting procedures, (3) instituted purchase order procedures, (4) implemented a separation of duties, and (5) created a control system for vending machine cash and inventory.

After the changes, the director noted that middle school fee balances were low and asked the auditors to investigate. The secretary, responsible for depositing student fees daily and sending them to the central office, said the low amount was due to the principal's waiver of fees for students who qualified for free or reduced-cost lunches. The principal denied having waived the fees.

The auditor examined fee cards for each child and found that the daily deposits did not agree with the dates on student fee cards. They also discovered that the secretary was in charge of a faculty welfare fund that was never

audited or examined, nor was it subject to the newly implemented internal controls. Deposits to the fund were checks from the faculty and cash from the vending machines. To perpetrate her $20,000 fraud, the secretary had stolen all the cash from the vending machines, replaced the payee name on vendor checks with her name, and deposited student fees into the faculty welfare fund to cover up the stolen money.

The secretary was immediately discharged. Because the secretary was bonded, the district was able to recover all of its missing funds.

The school district strengthened controls. Internal auditors examine all funds at the schools. Control of faculty welfare funds was transferred to a faculty member. Because the investigation had revealed the secretary's prior criminal record, a background check was required for all future hires.

record. Computer systems can record a *digital signature*, a means of signing a document with data that cannot be forged. Digital signatures are discussed in Chapter 9.

Employees who process transactions should verify the presence of appropriate authorizations. Auditors review transactions to verify proper authorization, as their absence indicates a possible control problem. For example, Jason Scott discovered that some purchases did not have a purchase requisition. Instead, they had been "personally authorized" by Bill Springer, the purchasing vice president. Jason also found that some payments had been authorized without proper supporting documents, such as purchase orders and receiving reports. These findings raise questions about the adequacy of Springer's internal control procedures.

Certain activities or transactions may be of such consequence that management grants *specific authorization* for them to occur. For example, management review and approval may be required for sales in excess of $50,000. In contrast, management can authorize employees to handle routine transactions without special approval, a procedure known as *general authorization*. Management should have written policies on both specific and general authorization for all types of transactions.

Segregation of Duties

Good internal control requires that no single employee be given too much responsibility over business transactions or processes. An employee should not be in a position to commit *and* conceal fraud. Segregation of duties is discussed in two separate sections: segregation of accounting duties and segregation of systems duties.

SEGREGATION OF ACCOUNTING DUTIES As shown in Figure 7-3, effective *segregation of accounting duties* is achieved when the following functions are separated:

- *Authorization*—approving transactions and decisions
- *Recording*—preparing source documents; entering data into online systems; maintaining journals, ledgers, files or databases; and preparing reconciliations and performance reports
- *Custody*—handling cash, tools, inventory, or fixed assets; receiving incoming customer checks; writing checks

If one person performs two of these functions, problems can arise. For example, the city treasurer of Fairfax, Virginia, embezzled $600,000. When residents used cash to pay their taxes, she kept the currency and entered the payments on property tax records, but did not report them

FIGURE 7-3
Separation of Duties

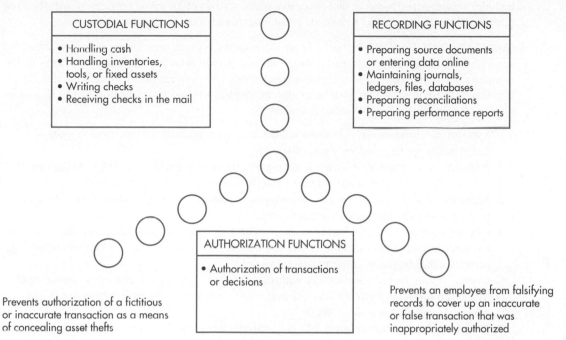

Prevents employees from falsifying records in order to conceal theft of assets entrusted to them

CUSTODIAL FUNCTIONS

- Handling cash
- Handling inventories, tools, or fixed assets
- Writing checks
- Receiving checks in the mail

RECORDING FUNCTIONS

- Preparing source documents or entering data online
- Maintaining journals, ledgers, files, databases
- Preparing reconciliations
- Preparing performance reports

AUTHORIZATION FUNCTIONS

- Authorization of transactions or decisions

Prevents authorization of a fictitious or inaccurate transaction as a means of concealing asset thefts

Prevents an employee from falsifying records to cover up an inaccurate or false transaction that was inappropriately authorized

to the controller. Periodically, she made an adjusting journal entry to bring her records into agreement with those of the controller. When she received checks in the mail that would not be missed if not recorded, she put them in the cash register and stole that amount of cash. Because the treasurer was responsible for both the *custody* of cash receipts and the *recording* of those receipts, she was able to steal cash receipts and falsify the accounts to conceal the theft.

In another example, the utilities director of Newport Beach, California, embezzled $1.2 million. Responsible for authorizing transactions, he forged invoices or easement documents authorizing payments to real or fictitious property owners. Finance department officials gave him the checks to deliver to the property owners. He forged signatures and deposited the checks in his own account. Because he was given *custody* of the checks he authorized, he could *authorize* fictitious transactions and steal the payments.

The payroll director of the Los Angeles Dodgers embezzled $330,000. He credited employees for hours not worked and received a kickback of 50% of the extra compensation. He added fictitious names to the Dodgers payroll and cashed the paychecks. The fraud was discovered while he was ill and another employee performed his duties. Because the perpetrator was responsible for *authorizing* the hiring of employees and for *recording* employee hours, he did not need to prepare or handle the paychecks. The company mailed the checks to the address he specified.

Computers can be programmed to perform one or more of the authorization, custody, and recording functions. Segregation of duties is maintained, except that the computer performs the function. For example, people can pay for gas using a credit or debit card. The computer performs both the custody and the recording function. In addition to better internal control, this better serves the customer by increasing convenience and eliminating lines to pay for the gas.

In a system with effective separation of duties, it is difficult for any single employee to embezzle successfully. Detecting fraud where two or more people are in **collusion** to override controls is more difficult because it is much easier to commit and conceal the fraud. For example, two women at a credit card company colluded. One woman authorized new credit card accounts, and the other wrote off unpaid accounts of less than $1,000. The first woman created a new account for each of them using fictitious data. When the amounts outstanding neared the $1,000 limit, the woman in collections wrote them off. The process would then be repeated. They were caught when a jilted boyfriend seeking revenge reported the scheme to the credit card company.

Employees can collude with other employees, customers, or vendors. The most frequent employee/vendor collusion includes billing at inflated prices, performing substandard work and receiving full payment, payment for nonperformance, duplicate billings, and improperly purchasing more goods from a colluding company. The most frequent employee/customer collusion includes unauthorized loans or insurance payments, receipt of assets or services at unauthorized discount prices, forgiveness of amounts owed, and unauthorized extension of due dates.

SEGREGATION OF SYSTEMS DUTIES   In an information system, procedures once performed by separate individuals are combined. Therefore, any person who has unrestricted access to the computer, its programs, and live data could perpetrate and conceal fraud. To combat this threat, organizations implement *segregation of systems duties*. Authority and responsibility should be divided clearly among the following functions:

1. *Systems administration.*   *Systems administrators* make sure all information system components operate smoothly and efficiently.
2. *Network management.*   *Network managers* ensure that devices are linked to the organization's internal and external networks and that those networks operate properly.
3. *Security management.*   *Security management* makes sure that systems are secure and protected from internal and external threats.
4. *Change management.*   *Change management* is the process of making sure that changes are made smoothly and efficiently and that they do not negatively affect systems reliability, security, confidentiality, integrity, and availability.
5. *Users.*   Users record transactions, authorize data to be processed, and use system output.
6. *Systems analysis.*   *Systems analysts* help users determine their information needs and design systems to meet those needs.
7. *Programming.*   *Programmers* take the analysts' design and create a system by writing the computer programs.
8. *Computer operations.*   *Computer operators* run the software on the company's computers. They ensure that data are input properly, that they are processed correctly, and that output is produced when needed.
9. *Information system library.*   The information system librarian maintains custody of corporate databases, files, and programs in a separate storage area called the *information system library*.
10. *Data control.*   The *data control group* ensures that source data have been properly approved, monitors the flow of work through the computer, reconciles input and output, maintains a record of input errors to ensure their correction and resubmission, and distributes systems output.

Allowing a person to do two or more of these jobs exposes the company to fraud. For example, if a credit union programmer uses actual data to test her program, she could erase her car loan balance during the test. Likewise, if a computer operator has access to programming logic and documentation, he might be able to increase his salary while processing payroll.

Project Development and Acquisition Controls

It is important to have a proven methodology to govern the development, acquisition, implementation, and maintenance of information systems. It should contain appropriate controls for management approval, user involvement, analysis, design, testing, implementation, and conversion. These methodologies are discussed in Chapters 20 through 22.

Important systems development controls include the following:

1. A *steering committee* guides and oversees systems development and acquisition.
2. A *strategic master plan* is developed and updated yearly to align an organization's information system with its business strategies. It shows the projects that must be completed, and it addresses the company's hardware, software, personnel, and infrastructure requirements.
3. A *project development plan* shows the tasks to be performed, who will perform them, project costs, completion dates, and *project milestones*—significant points when progress is reviewed and actual and estimated completion times are compared. Each project is assigned to a manager and team who are responsible for its success or failure.
4. A *data processing schedule* shows when each task should be performed.

5. *System performance measurements* are established to evaluate the system. Common measurements include *throughput* (output per unit of time), *utilization* (percentage of time the system is used), and *response time* (how long it takes the system to respond).

6. A *post-implementation review* is performed after a development project is completed to determine whether the anticipated benefits were achieved.

Some companies hire a *systems integrator* to manage a systems development effort involving its own personnel, its client, and other vendors. These development projects are subject to the same cost overruns and missed deadlines as systems developed internally. For example, Westpac Banking began a five-year, $85 million systems development project to decentralize its systems, create new financial products, and downsize its systems department. Three years and $150 million later, no usable results had been attained, and it was clear the scheduled completion date would not be met. With a runaway on its hands, Westpac fired IBM, the primary software developer, and brought in Accenture to review the project and develop recommendations for salvaging it.

Companies using systems integrators should use the same project management processes and controls as internal projects. In addition, they should:

- *Develop clear specifications.* This includes exact descriptions and system definitions, explicit deadlines, and precise acceptance criteria. Suffolk County, New York, spent 12 months and $500,000 preparing detailed specifications for a $16 million criminal justice system before accepting bids. Only 6 of 22 invited integrators bid on the project because of the county's rigorous cost and quality standards. County officials believe their diligent up-front efforts helped ensure their new system's success and saved the county $3 million.
- *Monitor the project.* Companies should establish formal procedures for measuring and reporting a project's status. The best approach is to divide the project into manageable tasks, assign responsibility for each task, and meet at least monthly to review progress and assess quality.

Change Management Controls

Organizations modify existing systems to reflect new business practices and to take advantage of IT advancements. Those in charge of changes should make sure they do not introduce errors and facilitate fraud. Change management controls are discussed in Chapter 10.

Design and Use of Documents and Records

The proper design and use of electronic and paper documents and records help ensure the accurate and complete recording of all relevant transaction data. Their form and content should be as simple as possible, minimize errors, and facilitate review and verification. Documents that initiate a transaction should contain a space for authorizations. Those that transfer assets need a space for the receiving party's signature. Documents should be sequentially prenumbered so each can be accounted for. An audit trail facilitates tracing individual transactions through the system, correcting errors, and verifying system output. Document, form, and input screen design are discussed in Chapter 22.

Safeguard Assets, Records, and Data

A company must protect its cash and physical assets as well as its information. A reporter for Reuters noticed that Intentia, a Swedish software developer, released its first- and second-quarter earnings reports on Web sites with nearly identical Web addresses. He guessed the third-quarter Web address, found their unreleased numbers, and ran a story on the disappointing results. Intentia filed criminal hacking charges, but they were dismissed. The Swedish Stock Exchange censored Intentia for not protecting its financial information.

Employees are a much greater security risk than outsiders are. They are better able to hide their illegal acts, because they know system weakness better. Almost 50% of companies report that insiders access data without the proper authorization. A software engineer at America Online was charged with selling 92 million e-mail addresses he illegally obtained using another employee's ID and password. An Internet gambling business bought the names and used them to increase company earnings by $10,000 to $20,000 a day. The data theft was not uncovered for a year, until an anonymous tipster informed authorities that the gambling business was reselling the names to spammers selling herbal male enhancement products.

Employees also cause unintentional threats, such as accidentally deleting company data, opening virus-laden e-mail attachments, or trying to fix hardware or software without the appropriate expertise. These can result in crashed networks, corrupt data, and hardware and software malfunctions.

Chapters 8 through 10 discuss computer-based controls that help safeguard assets. In addition, it is important to:

- *Create and enforce appropriate policies and procedures.* All too often, policies and procedures are created but not enforced. A laptop with the names, Social Security numbers, and birthdates of 26.5 million people was stolen from the home of a Veteran Affairs (VA) Department analyst. The VA did not enforce its policies that sensitive data be encrypted and not leave VA offices. The cost to taxpayers of notifying all 26.5 million people and buying them a credit-checking service was $100 million. Two years prior to the theft, an inspector general report identified the inadequate control of sensitive data as a weakness, but it had never been addressed.
- *Maintain accurate records of all assets.* Periodically reconcile the recorded amounts of company assets to physical counts of those assets.
- *Restrict access to assets.* Restricting access to storage areas protects inventories and equipment. Cash registers, safes, lockboxes, and safety deposit boxes limit access to cash and paper assets. Over $1 million was embezzled from Perini Corp. because blank checks were kept in an unlocked storeroom. An employee made out checks to fictitious vendors, ran them through an unlocked check-signing machine, and cashed the checks.
- *Protect records and documents.* Fireproof storage areas, locked filing cabinets, backup files, and off-site storage protect records and documents. Access to blank checks and documents should be limited to authorized personnel. In Inglewood, California, a janitor stole 34 blank checks, wrote checks from $50,000 to $470,000, forged the names of city officials, and cashed them.

Independent Checks on Performance

Independent checks on performance, done by someone other than the person who performs the original operation, help ensure that transactions are processed accurately. They include the following:

- *Top-level reviews.* Management should monitor company results and periodically compare actual company performance to (a) planned performance, as shown in budgets, targets, and forecasts; (b) prior period performance; and (c) competitors' performance.
- *Analytical reviews.* An *analytical review* is an examination of the relationships between different sets of data. For example, as credit sales increase, so should accounts receivable. In addition, there are relationships between sales and accounts such as cost of goods sold, inventory, and freight out.
- *Reconciliation of independently maintained records.* Records should be reconciled to documents or records with the same balance. For example, a bank reconciliation verifies that company checking account balances agree with bank statement balances. Another example is comparing subsidiary ledger totals with general ledger totals.
- *Comparison of actual quantities with recorded amounts.* Significant assets are periodically counted and reconciled to company records. At the end of each clerk's shift, cash in a cash register drawer should match the amount on the cash register tape. Inventory should be periodically counted and reconciled to inventory records.
- *Double-entry accounting.* The maxim that debits equal credits provides numerous opportunities for independent checks. Debits in a payroll entry may be allocated to numerous inventory and/or expense accounts; credits are allocated to liability accounts for wages payable, taxes withheld, employee insurance, and union dues. After the payroll entries, comparing total debits and credits is a powerful check on the accuracy of both processes. Any discrepancy indicates the presence of an error.
- *Independent review.* After a transaction is processed, a second person reviews the work of the first, checking for proper authorization, reviewing supporting documents, and checking the accuracy of prices, quantities, and extensions.

Information and Communication

Information and communication constitute the seventh component of the ERM model. This relates directly to the primary purpose of an AIS, which is to gather, record, process, store, summarize, and communicate information about an organization. This includes understanding how transactions are initiated, data are captured, files are accessed and updated, data are processed, and information is reported. It includes understanding accounting records and procedures, supporting documents, and financial statements. These items provide an *audit trail*, which allows transactions to be traced back and forth between their origination and the financial statements.

According to the AICPA, an AIS has five primary objectives: to identify and record all valid transactions, properly classify transactions, record transactions at their proper monetary value, record transactions in the proper accounting period, and properly present transactions and related disclosures in the financial statements.

Accounting systems generally consist of several subsystems, each designed to process a particular type of transaction using the same sequence of procedures, called accounting cycles. The major accounting cycles and their related control objectives and procedures are detailed in Chapters 12 through 17.

Monitoring

ERM processes must be continuously monitored and modified as needed, and deficiencies must be reported to management. Key methods of monitoring performance include the following:

Perform ERM Evaluations

ERM effectiveness is measured using a formal or a self-assessment ERM evaluation. A team can be formed to conduct the evaluation, or it can be done by internal auditing.

Implement Effective Supervision

Effective supervision involves training and assisting employees, monitoring their performance, correcting errors, and overseeing employees who have access to assets. Supervision is especially important in organizations without responsibility reporting or an adequate segregation of duties.

Use Responsibility Accounting Systems

Responsibility accounting systems include budgets, quotas, schedules, standard costs, and quality standards; reports comparing actual and planned performance; and procedures for investigating and correcting significant variances.

Monitor System Activities

Risk analysis and management software packages review computer and network security measures, detect illegal access, test for weaknesses and vulnerabilities, report weaknesses found, and suggest improvements. Cost parameters can be entered to balance acceptable levels of risk tolerance and cost-effectiveness. Software also monitors and combats viruses, spyware, adware, spam, phishing, and inappropriate e-mails. It blocks pop-up ads, prevents browsers from being hijacked, and validates a phone caller's identity by comparing the caller's voice to a previously recorded voiceprint. Software can help companies recover from malicious actions. One package helped a company recover from a disgruntled employee's rampage. After a negative performance evaluation, the perpetrator ripped cables out of PCs, changed the inventory control files, and edited the password file to stop people from logging on to the network. The software quickly identified the corrupted files and alerted company headquarters. The damage was undone by utility software, which restored the corrupted file to its original status.

All system transactions and activities should be recorded in a log that indicates who accessed what data, when, and from which online device. These logs should be reviewed frequently and used to monitor system activity, trace problems to their source, evaluate employee productivity, control company costs, fight espionage and hacking attacks, and comply with legal requirements. One company used these logs to analyze why an employee had almost zero productivity and found that he spent six hours a day visiting Internet pornography sites.

The Privacy Foundation estimated that one-third of all American workers with computers are monitored, and that number is expected to increase. Companies who monitor system activities should not violate employee privacy. One way to do that is to have employees agree in writing to written policies that include the following:

- The technology an employee uses on the job belongs to the company.
- E-mails received on company computers are not private and can be read by supervisory personnel. This policy allowed a large pharmaceutical company to identify and terminate an employee who was e-mailing confidential drug-manufacturing data to an external party.
- Employees should not use technology to contribute to a hostile work environment.

Track Purchased Software and Mobile Devices

The Business Software Alliance (BSA) tracks down and fines companies that violate software license agreements. To comply with copyrights and protect themselves from software piracy lawsuits, companies should periodically conduct software audits. There should be enough licenses for all users, and the company should not pay for more licenses than needed. Employees should be informed of the consequences of using unlicensed software.

The increasing number of mobile devices should be tracked and monitored, because their loss could represent a substantial exposure. Items to track are the devices, who has them, what tasks they perform, the security features installed, and what software the company needs to maintain adequate system and network security.

Conduct Periodic Audits

External, internal, and network security audits can assess and monitor risk as well as detect fraud and errors. Informing employees of audits helps resolve privacy issues, deters fraud, and reduces errors. Auditors should regularly test system controls and periodically browse system usage files looking for suspicious activities. During the security audit of a health care company, auditors pretending to be computer support staff persuaded 16 of 22 employees to reveal their user IDs and passwords. They also found that employees testing a new system left the company's network exposed to outside attacks. Systems auditing is explained in Chapter 11.

Internal audits assess the reliability and integrity of financial and operating information, evaluate internal control effectiveness, and assess employee compliance with management policies and procedures as well as applicable laws and regulations. The internal audit function should be organizationally independent of accounting and operating functions. Internal audit should report to the audit committee, not the controller or chief financial officer.

One internal auditor noted that a department supervisor took the office staff to lunch in a limousine on her birthday. Wondering whether her salary could support her lifestyle, he investigated and found she set up several fictitious vendors, sent the company invoices from these vendors, and cashed the checks mailed to her. Over a period of several years, she embezzled over $12 million.

Employ a Computer Security Officer and a Chief Compliance Officer

A *computer security officer (CSO)* is in charge of system security, independent of the information system function, and reports to the chief operating officer (COO) or the CEO. The overwhelming tasks related to SOX and other forms of compliance have led many companies to delegate all compliance issues to a *chief compliance officer (CCO)*. Many companies use outside computer consultants or in-house teams to test and evaluate security procedures and computer systems.

Engage Forensic Specialists

Forensic investigators who specialize in fraud are a fast-growing group in the accounting profession. Their increasing presence is due to several factors, most notably SOX, new accounting rules, and demands by boards of directors that forensic investigations be an ongoing part of the financial reporting and corporate governance process. Most forensic investigators received specialized training with the FBI, IRS, or other law enforcement agencies. Investigators with the computer skills to ferret out fraud perpetrators are in great demand. The Association of Certified Fraud Examiners sponsors a Certified Fraud Examiner (CFE) professional certification program. To become a CFE, candidates must pass a two-day exam. Currently there are about 30,000 CFEs worldwide.

Computer forensics specialists discover, extract, safeguard, and document computer evidence such that its authenticity, accuracy, and integrity will not succumb to legal challenges. Computer forensics can be compared to performing an "autopsy" on a computer system to determine whether a crime was committed as well as who committed it, and then marshalling the evidence lawyers need to prove the charges in court. Some of the more common matters investigated are improper Internet usage; fraud; sabotage; the loss, theft, or corruption of data; retrieving "erased" information from e-mails and databases; and figuring out who performed certain computer activities. A Deloitte & Touche forensics team uncovered evidence that helped convict a Giant Supermarket purchasing manager who had accepted over $600,000 in supplier kickbacks.

Install Fraud Detection Software

Fraudsters follow distinct patterns and leave clues behind that can be discovered by fraud detection software. ReliaStar Financial used software from IBM to detect the following:

- A Los Angeles chiropractor submitted hundreds of thousands of dollars in fraudulent claims. The software identified an unusual number of patients who lived more than 50 miles away from the doctor's office and flagged these bills for investigation.
- A Long Island doctor submitted weekly bills for a rare and expensive procedure normally done only once or twice in a lifetime.
- A podiatrist saw four patients and billed for 500 separate procedures.

Neural networks (programs with learning capabilities) can accurately identify fraud. The Visa and MasterCard operation at Mellon Bank uses a neural network to track 1.2 million accounts. It can spot illegal credit card use and notify the owner shortly after the card is stolen. It can also spot trends before bank investigators do. For example, an investigator learned about a new fraud from another bank. When he went to check for the fraud, the neural network had already identified it and had printed out transactions that fit its pattern. The software cost the bank less than $1 million and paid for itself in six months.

Implement a Fraud Hotline

People witnessing fraudulent behavior are often torn between two conflicting feelings. Although they want to protect company assets and report fraud perpetrators, they are uncomfortable blowing the whistle, so all too often they remain silent. This reluctance is stronger if they are aware of whistle-blowers who have been ostracized, been persecuted, or suffered damage to their careers.

SOX mandates a mechanism for employees to report fraud and abuse. A *fraud hotline* is an effective way to comply with the law and resolve whistle-blower conflict. In one study, researchers found that 33% of 212 frauds were detected through anonymous tips. The insurance industry set up a hotline to control $17 billion a year in fraudulent claims. In the first month, more than 2,250 calls were received; 15% resulted in investigative action. The downside of hotlines is that many calls are not worthy of investigation; some are motivated by a desire for revenge, some are vague reports of wrongdoing, and others have no merit.

Summary and Case Conclusion

One week after Jason and Maria filed their audit report, they were summoned to the office of Northwest's director of internal auditing to explain their findings. Shortly thereafter, a fraud investigation team was dispatched to Bozeman to take a closer look at the situation. Six months later, a company newsletter indicated that the Springer family sold its 10% interest in the business and resigned from all management positions. Two Northwest executives were transferred in to replace them. There was no other word on the audit findings.

Two years later, Jason and Maria worked with Frank Ratliff, a member of the high-level audit team. After hours, Frank told them the investigation team examined a large sample of purchasing transactions and all employee timekeeping and payroll records for a 12-month period. The team also took a detailed physical inventory. They discovered that the problems Jason identified—including missing purchase requisitions, purchase orders, and receiving reports, as well as excessive prices—were widespread. These problems occurred in transactions with three large vendors from whom Springer's had purchased several million dollars of inventory. The investigators discussed the unusually high prices with the vendors but did not receive a satisfactory explanation. The county business-licensing bureau revealed that Bill Springer held a majority ownership interest in each of these companies. By authorizing excessive prices to companies he owned, Springer earned a significant share of several hundred thousand dollars of excessive profits, all at the expense of Northwest Industries.

Several Springer employees were paid for more hours than they worked. Inventory was materially overstated; a physical inventory revealed that a significant portion of recorded inventory did not exist and that some items were obsolete. The adjusting journal entry reflecting Springer's real inventory wiped out much of their profits over the past three years.

When confronted, the Springers vehemently denied breaking any laws. Northwest considered going to the authorities but was concerned that the case was not strong enough to prove in court. Northwest also worried that adverse publicity might damage the company's position in Bozeman. After months of negotiation, the Springers agreed to the settlement reported in the newsletter. Part of the settlement was that no public statement would be made about any alleged fraud or embezzlement involving the Springers. According to Frank, this policy was normal. In many fraud cases, settlements are reached quietly, with no legal action taken, so that the company can avoid adverse publicity.

Key Terms

threat 184
exposure 184
impact 184
likelihood 184
internal control 184
preventive control 185
detective control 185
corrective control 185
general control 185
application control 185
belief system 185
boundary system 185
diagnostic control
   system 185
interactive control
   system 185
Foreign Corrupt
   Practices Act 185
Sarbanes–Oxley Act
   (SOX) 185
Public Company Accounting
   Oversight Board
   (PCAOB) 186
Control Objectives for
   Information and Related
   Technology (COBIT) 186

Committee of Sponsoring
   Organizations
   (COSO) 187
Internal Control—Integrated
   Framework (IC) 187
Enterprise Risk
   Management—Integrated
   Framework (ERM) 187
internal environment 188
risk appetite 189
audit committee 189
policy and procedures
   manual 190
background check 190
strategic objective 192
operations objective 192
reporting objective 192
compliance objective 192
event 192
inherent risk 193
residual risk 193
expected loss 194
control activities 195
authorization 195
digital signature 196
specific authorization 196

general authorization 196
segregation of accounting
   duties 196
collusion 197
segregation of systems
   duties 198
systems administrator 198
network manager 198
security management 198
change management 198
systems analyst 198
programmer 198
computer operator 198
information system
   library 198
data control group 198
steering committee 198
strategic master plan 198
project development
   plan 198
project milestone 198
data processing schedule 198
system performance
   measurements 199
throughput 199
utilization 199

AIS IN ACTION

Chapter Quiz

1. COSO identified five interrelated components of internal control. Which of the following is NOT one of those five?
   a. risk assessment
   b. internal control policies
   c. monitoring
   d. information and communication

2. In the ERM model, COSO specified four types of objectives that management must meet to achieve company goals. Which of the following is NOT one of those types?
   a. responsibility objectives
   b. strategic objectives
   c. compliance objectives
   d. reporting objectives
   e. operations objectives

3. Which of the following statements is true?
   a. COSO's enterprise risk management framework is narrow in scope and is limited to financial controls.
   b. COSO's internal control integrated framework has been widely accepted as the authority on internal controls.
   c. The Foreign Corrupt Practices Act had no impact on internal accounting control systems.
   d. It is easier to add controls to an already designed system than to include them during the initial design stage.

4. All other things being equal, which of the following is true?
   a. Detective controls are superior to preventive controls.
   b. Corrective controls are superior to preventive controls.
   c. Preventive controls are equivalent to detective controls.
   d. Preventive controls are superior to detective controls.

5. Which of the following statements about the control environment is FALSE?
   a. Management's attitudes toward internal control and ethical behavior have little impact on employee beliefs or actions.
   b. An overly complex or unclear organizational structure may be indicative of problems that are more serious.
   c. A written policy and procedures manual is an important tool for assigning authority and responsibility.
   d. Supervision is especially important in organizations that cannot afford elaborate responsibility reporting or are too small to have an adequate separation of duties.

6. To achieve effective segregation of duties, certain functions must be separated. Which of the following is the correct listing of the accounting-related functions that must be segregated?
   a. control, recording, and monitoring
   b. authorization, recording, and custody
   c. control, custody, and authorization
   d. monitoring, recording, and planning

7. Which of the following is NOT an independent check?
   a. bank reconciliation
   b. periodic comparison of subsidiary ledger totals to control accounts
   c. trial balance
   d. re-adding the total of a batch of invoices and comparing it with your first total

8. Which of the following is a control procedure relating to both the design and use of documents and records?
   a. locking blank checks in a drawer
   b. reconciling the bank account
   c. sequentially prenumbering sales invoices
   d. comparing actual physical quantities with recorded amounts

9. Which of the following is the correct order of the risk assessment steps discussed in this chapter?
   a. Identify threats, estimate risk and exposure, identify controls, and estimate costs and benefits.
   b. Identify controls, estimate risk and exposure, identify threats, and estimate costs and benefits.
   c. Estimate risk and exposure, identify controls, identify threats, and estimate costs and benefits.
   d. Estimate costs and benefits, identify threats, identify controls, and estimate risk and exposure.

10. Your current system is deemed to be 90% reliable. A major threat has been identified with an impact of $3,000,000. Two control procedures exist to deal with the threat. Implementation of control A would cost $100,000 and reduce the likelihood to 6%. Implementation of control B would cost $140,000 and reduce the likelihood to 4%. Implementation of both controls would cost $220,000 and reduce the likelihood to 2%. Given the data, and based solely on an economic analysis of costs and benefits, what should you do?
    a. Implement control A only.
    b. Implement control B only.
    c. Implement both controls A and B.
    d. Implement neither control.

Discussion Questions

7.1. Answer the following questions about the audit of Springer's Lumber & Supply.
   a. What deficiencies existed in the internal environment at Springer's?
   b. Do you agree with the decision to settle with the Springers rather than to prosecute them for fraud and embezzlement? Why or why not?
   c. Should the company have told Jason and Maria the results of the high-level audit? Why or why not?

7.2. Effective segregation of duties is sometimes not economically feasible in a small business. What internal control elements do you think can help compensate for this threat?

7.3. One function of the AIS is to provide adequate controls to ensure the safety of organizational assets, including data. However, many people view control procedures as "red tape." They also believe that instead of producing tangible benefits, business controls create resentment and loss of company morale. Discuss this position.

7.4. In recent years, Supersmurf's external auditors have given clean opinions on its financial statements and favorable evaluations of its internal control systems. Discuss whether it is necessary for this corporation to take any further action to comply with the Sarbanes–Oxley Act.

7.5. When you go to a movie theater, you buy a prenumbered ticket from the cashier. This ticket is handed to another person at the entrance to the movie. What kinds of irregularities is the theater trying to prevent? What controls is it using to prevent these irregularities? What remaining risks or exposures can you identify?

7.6. Some restaurants use customer checks with prenumbered sequence codes. Each food server uses these checks to write up customer orders. Food servers are told not to destroy any customer checks; if a mistake is made, they are to void that check and write a new one. All voided checks are to be turned in to the manager daily. How does this policy help the restaurant control cash receipts?

7.7. Compare and contrast the following three frameworks: COBIT, COSO Integrated Control, and ERM.

7.8. Explain what an event is. Using the Internet as a resource, create a list of some of the many internal and external factors that COSO indicated could influence events and affect a company's ability to implement its strategy and achieve its objectives.

7.9. Explain what is meant by objective setting, and describe the four types of objectives used in ERM.

7.10. Discuss several ways that ERM processes can be continuously monitored and modified so that deficiencies are reported to management.

Problems

7.1. You are an audit supervisor assigned to a new client, Go-Go Corporation, which is listed on the New York Stock Exchange. You visited Go-Go's corporate headquarters to become acquainted with key personnel and to conduct a preliminary review of the company's accounting policies, controls, and systems. During this visit, the following events occurred:

a. You met with Go-Go's audit committee, which consists of the corporate controller, treasurer, financial vice president, and budget director.

b. You recognized the treasurer as a former aide to Ernie Eggers, who was convicted of fraud several years ago.

c. Management explained its plans to change accounting methods for depreciation from the accelerated to the straight-line method. Management implied that if your firm does not concur with this change, Go-Go will employ other auditors.

d. You learned that the financial vice president manages a staff of five internal auditors.

e. You noted that all management authority seems to reside with three brothers, who serve as chief executive officer, president, and financial vice president.

f. You were told that the performance of division and department managers is evaluated on a subjective basis, because Go-Go's management believes that formal performance evaluation procedures are counterproductive.

g. You learned that the company has reported increases in earnings per share for each of the past 25 quarters; however, earnings during the current quarter have leveled off and may decline.

h. You reviewed the company's policy and procedures manual, which listed policies for dealing with customers, vendors, and employees.

i. Your preliminary assessment is that the accounting systems are well designed and that they employ effective internal control procedures.

j. Some employees complained that some managers occasionally contradict the instructions of other managers regarding proper data security procedures.

k. After a careful review of the budget for data security enhancement projects, you feel the budget appears to be adequate.

l. The enhanced network firewall project appeared to be on a very aggressive implementation schedule. The IT manager mentioned that even if he put all of his personnel on the project for the next five weeks, he still would not complete the project in time. The manager has mentioned this to company management, which seems unwilling to modify the schedule.

m. Several new employees have had trouble completing some of their duties, and they do not appear to know who to ask for help.

n. Go-Go's strategy is to achieve consistent growth for its shareholders. However, its policy is not to invest in any project unless its payback period is no more than 48 months and yields an internal rate of return that exceeds its cost of capital by 3%.

o. You observe that company purchasing agents wear clothing and exhibit other paraphernalia from major vendors. The purchasing department manager proudly displays a picture of himself holding a big fish on the deck of a luxury fishing boat that has the logo of a major Go-Go vendor painted on its wheelhouse.

Required

The information you have obtained suggests potential problems relating to Go-Go's internal environment. Identify the problems, and explain them in relation to the internal environment concepts discussed in this chapter.

7.2. Explain how the principle of separation of duties is violated in each of the following situations. Also, suggest one or more procedures to reduce the risk and exposure highlighted in each example.

a. A payroll clerk recorded a 40-hour workweek for an employee who had quit the previous week. He then prepared a paycheck for this employee, forged her signature, and cashed the check.

b. While opening the mail, a cashier set aside, and subsequently cashed, two checks payable to the company on account.

c. A cashier prepared a fictitious invoice from a company using his brother-in-law's name. He wrote a check in payment of the invoice, which the brother-in-law later cashed.

d. An employee of the finishing department walked off with several parts from the storeroom and recorded the items in the inventory ledger as having been issued to the assembly department.

e. A cashier cashed a check from a customer in payment of an account receivable, pocketed the cash, and concealed the theft by properly posting the receipt to the customer's account in the accounts receivable ledger.

f. Several customers returned clothing purchases. Instead of putting the clothes into a return bin to be put back on the rack, a clerk put the clothing in a separate bin under some cleaning rags. After her shift, she transferred the clothes to a gym bag and took them home.

g. A receiving clerk noticed that four cases of MP3 players were included in a shipment when only three were ordered. The clerk put the extra case aside and took it home after his shift ended.

h. An insurance claims adjuster had check-signing authority of up to $6,000. The adjuster created three businesses that billed the insurance company for work not performed on valid claims. The adjuster wrote and signed checks to pay for the invoices, none of which exceeded $6,000.

i. An accounts payable clerk recorded invoices received from a company that he and his wife owned and authorized their payment.

j. A cashier created false purchase return vouchers to hide his theft of several thousand dollars from his cash register.

k. A purchasing agent received a 10% kickback of the invoice amount for all purchases made from a specific vendor.

7.3. The following description represents the policies and procedures for agent expense reimbursements at Excel Insurance Company.

Agents submit a completed expense reimbursement form to their branch manager at the end of each week. The branch manager reviews the expense report to determine whether the claimed expenses are reimbursable based on the company's expense reimbursement policy and reasonableness of amount. The company's policy manual states that agents are to document any questionable expense item and that the branch manager must approve in advance expenditures exceeding $500.

After the expenses are approved, the branch manager sends the expense report to the home office. There, accounting records the transaction, and cash disbursements prepares the expense reimbursement check. Cash disbursements sends the expense reimbursement checks to the branch manager, who distributes them to the agents.

To receive cash advances for anticipated expenses, agents must complete a Cash Advance Approval form. The branch manager reviews and approves the Cash Advance Approval form and sends a copy to accounting and another to the agent. The agent submits the copy of the Cash Advance Approval form to the branch office cashier to obtain the cash advance.

At the end of each month, internal audit at the home office reconciles the expense reimbursements. It adds the total dollar amounts on the expense reports from each branch, subtracts the sum of the dollar totals on each branch's Cash Advance Approval form, and compares the net amount to the sum of the expense reimbursement checks issued to agents. Internal audit investigates any differences.

Required

Identify the internal control strengths and weaknesses in Excel's expense reimbursement process. Look for authorization, recording, safeguarding, and reconciliation strengths and weaknesses. (*CMA Examination, adapted*)

7.4. The Gardner Company, a client of your firm, has come to you with the following problem. It has three clerical employees who must perform the following functions:
   a. Maintain the general ledger
   b. Maintain the accounts payable ledger
   c. Maintain the accounts receivable ledger
   d. Prepare checks for signature
   e. Maintain the cash disbursements journal
   f. Issue credits on returns and allowances
   g. Reconcile the bank account
   h. Handle and deposit cash receipts

Assuming equal abilities among the three employees, the company asks you to assign the eight functions to them to maximize internal control. Assume that these employees will perform no accounting functions other than the ones listed.

Required

   a. List four possible unsatisfactory pairings of the functions.
   b. State how you would distribute the functions among the three employees. Assume that with the exception of the nominal jobs of the bank reconciliation and the issuance of credits on returns and allowances, all functions require an equal amount of time. (*CPA Examination, adapted*)

7.5. During a recent review, ABC Corporation discovered that it has a serious internal control problem. It is estimated that the impact associated with this problem is $1 million and that the likelihood is currently 5%. Two internal control procedures have been proposed to deal with this problem. Procedure A would cost $25,000 and reduce likelihood to 2%; procedure B would cost $30,000 and reduce likelihood to 1%. If both procedures were implemented, likelihood would be reduced to 0.1%.

Required

   a. What is the estimated expected loss associated with ABC Corporation's internal control problem before any new internal control procedures are implemented?
   b. Compute the revised estimate of expected loss if procedure A were implemented, if procedure B were implemented, and if both procedures were implemented.
   c. Compare the estimated costs and benefits of procedure A, procedure B, and both procedures combined. If you consider only the estimates of cost and benefit, which procedure(s) should be implemented?

    d. What other factors might be relevant to the decision?

    e. Use the Goal Seek function in Microsoft Excel to determine the likelihood of occurrence without the control and the reduction in expected loss if the net benefit/cost is 0. Do this for procedure A, procedure B, and both procedures together.

7.6. The management at Covington, Inc., recognizes that a well-designed internal control system provides many benefits. Among the benefits are reliable financial records that facilitate decision making and a greater probability of preventing or detecting errors and fraud. Covington's internal auditing department periodically reviews the company's accounting records to determine the effectiveness of internal controls. In its latest review, the internal audit staff found the following eight conditions:

    1. Daily bank deposits do not always correspond with cash receipts.

    2. Bad debt write-offs are prepared and approved by the same employee.

    3. There are occasional discrepancies between physical inventory counts and perpetual inventory records.

    4. Alterations have been made to physical inventory counts and to perpetual inventory records.

    5. There are many customer refunds and credits.

    6. Many original documents are missing or lost. However, there are substitute copies of all missing originals.

    7. An unexplained decrease in the gross profit percentage has occurred.

    8. Many documents are not approved.

Required

For each of the eight conditions detected by the Covington internal audit staff:

a. Describe a possible cause of the condition.

b. Recommend actions to be taken and/or controls to be implemented that would correct the condition. (*CMA, adapted*)

7.7. Consider the following two situations:

    1. Many employees of a firm that manufactures small tools pocket some of the tools for their personal use. Because the quantities taken by any one employee are immaterial, the individual employees do not consider the act as fraudulent or detrimental to the company. The company is now large enough to hire an internal auditor. One of the first things she did was to compare the gross profit rates for industrial tools to the gross profit for personal tools. Noting a significant difference, she investigated and uncovered the employee theft.

    2. A manufacturing firm's controller created a fake subsidiary. He then ordered goods from the firm's suppliers, told them to ship the goods to a warehouse he rented, and approved the vendor invoices for payment when they arrived. The controller later sold the diverted inventory items, and the proceeds were deposited to the controller's personal bank account. Auditors suspected something was wrong when they could not find any entries regarding this fake subsidiary office in the property, plant, and equipment ledgers or a title or lease for the office in the real-estate records.

Required

For the situations presented, describe the recommendations the internal auditors should make to prevent similar problems in the future. (*CMA, adapted*)

7.8. Tralor Corporation manufactures and sells several different lines of small electric components. Its internal audit department completed an audit of its expenditure processes. Part of the audit involved a review of the internal accounting controls for payables, including the controls over the authorization of transactions, accounting for transactions, and the protection of assets. The auditors noted the following items:

    1. Routine purchases are initiated by inventory control notifying the purchasing department of the need to buy goods. The purchasing department fills out a prenumbered purchase order and gets it approved by the purchasing manager. The original of the five-part purchase order goes to the vendor. The other four copies are for purchasing, the user department, receiving for use as a receiving report, and accounts payable.

2. For efficiency and effectiveness, purchases of specialized goods and services are negotiated directly between the user department and the vendor. Company procedures require that the user department and the purchasing department approve invoices for any specialized goods and services before making payment.

3. Accounts payable maintains a list of employees who have purchase order approval authority. The list was updated two years ago and is seldom used by accounts payable clerks.

4. Prenumbered vendor invoices are recorded in an invoice register that indicates the receipt date, whether it is a special order, when a special order is sent to the requesting department for approval, and when it is returned. A review of the register indicated that there were seven open invoices for special purchases, which had been forwarded to operating departments for approval over 30 days previously and had not yet been returned.

5. Prior to making entries in accounting records, the accounts payable clerk checks the mathematical accuracy of the transaction, makes sure that all transactions are properly documented (the purchase order matches the signed receiving report and the vendor's invoice), and obtains departmental approval for special purchase invoices.

6. All approved invoices are filed alphabetically. Invoices are paid on the 5th and 20th of each month, and all cash discounts are taken regardless of the terms.

7. The treasurer signs the checks and cancels the supporting documents. An original document is required for a payment to be processed.

8. Prenumbered blank checks are kept in a locked safe accessible only to the cash disbursements department. Other documents and records maintained by the accounts payable section are readily accessible to all persons assigned to the section and to others in the accounting function.

Required

Review the eight items listed, and decide whether they represent an internal control strength or weakness.

a. For each internal control strength you identified, explain how the procedure helps achieve good authorization, accounting, or asset protection control.

b. For each internal control weakness you identified, explain why it is a weakness and recommend a way to correct the weakness. (*CMA, adapted*)

7.9. Lancaster Company makes electrical parts for contractors and home improvement retail stores. After their annual audit, Lancaster's auditors commented on the following items regarding internal controls over equipment:

1. The operations department that needs the equipment normally initiates a purchase requisition for equipment. The operations department supervisor discusses the proposed purchase with the plant manager. If there are sufficient funds in the requesting department's equipment budget, a purchase requisition is submitted to the purchasing department once the plant manager is satisfied that the request is reasonable.

2. When the purchasing department receives either an inventory or an equipment purchase requisition, the purchasing agent selects an appropriate supplier and sends them a purchase order.

3. When equipment arrives, the user department installs it. The property, plant, and equipment control accounts are supported by schedules organized by year of acquisition. The schedules are used to record depreciation using standard rates, depreciation methods, and salvage values for each type of fixed asset. These rates, methods, and salvage values were set 10 years ago during the company's initial year of operation.

4. When equipment is retired, the plant manager notifies the accounting department so the appropriate accounting entries can be made.

5. There has been no reconciliation since the company began operations between the accounting records and the equipment on hand.

Required

Identify the internal control weaknesses in Lancaster's system, and recommend ways to correct them. (*CMA, adapted*)

7.10. The Langston Recreational Company (LRC) manufactures ice skates for racing, figure skating, and hockey. The company is located in Kearns, Utah, so it can be close to the Olympic Ice Shield, where many Olympic speed skaters train.

Given the precision required to make skates, tracking manufacturing costs is very important to management so it can price the skates appropriately. To capture and collect manufacturing costs, the company acquired an automated cost accounting system from a national vendor. The vendor provides support, maintenance, and data and program backup service for LRC's system.

LRC operates one shift, five days a week. All manufacturing data are collected and recorded by Saturday evening so that the prior week's production data can be processed. One of management's primary concerns is how the actual manufacturing process costs compare with planned or standard manufacturing process costs. As a result, the cost accounting system produces a report that compares actual costs with standards costs and provides the difference, or variance. Management focuses on significant variances as one means of controlling the manufacturing processes and calculating bonuses.

Occasionally, errors occur in processing a week's production cost data, which requires the entire week's cost data to be reprocessed at a cost of $34,500. The current risk of error without any control procedures is 8%. LRC's management is currently considering a set of cost accounting control procedures that is estimated to reduce the risk of the data errors from 8% to 3%. This data validation control procedure is projected to cost $1,000 per week.

Required

a. Perform a cost/benefit analysis of the data validation control procedures.
b. Based on your analysis, make a recommendation to management regarding the control procedure.
c. The current risk of data errors without any control procedures is estimated to be 8%. The data control validation procedure costs $1,000 and reduces the risk to 3%. At some point between 8% and 3% is a point of indifference—that is, Cost of reprocessing the data without controls = Cost of processing the data with the controls + Cost of controls. Use a spreadsheet application such as Excel Goal Seek to find the solution.

7.11. Spring Water Spa Company is a 15-store chain in the Midwest that sells hot tubs, supplies, and accessories. Each store has a full-time, salaried manager and an assistant manager. The sales personnel are paid an hourly wage and a commission based on sales volume.

The company uses electronic cash registers to record each transaction. The salesperson enters his or her employee number at the beginning of his/her shift. For each sale, the salesperson rings up the order by scanning the item's bar code, which then displays the item's description, unit price, and quantity (each item must be scanned). The cash register automatically assigns a consecutive number to each transaction. The cash register prints a sales receipt that shows the total, any discounts, the sales tax, and the grand total.

The salesperson collects payment from the customer, gives the receipt to the customer, and either directs the customer to the warehouse to obtain the items purchased or makes arrangements with the shipping department for delivery. The salesperson is responsible for using the system to determine whether credit card sales are approved and for approving both credit sales and sales paid by check. Sales returns are handled in exactly the reverse manner, with the salesperson issuing a return slip when necessary.

At the end of each day, the cash registers print a sequentially ordered list of sales receipts and provide totals for cash, credit card, and check sales, as well as cash and credit card returns. The assistant manager reconciles these totals to the cash register tapes, cash in the cash register, the total of the consecutively numbered sales invoices, and the return slips. The assistant manager prepares a daily reconciled report for the store manager's review.

Cash sales, check sales, and credit card sales are reviewed by the manager, who prepares the daily bank deposit. The manager physically makes the deposit at the bank and files the validated deposit slip. At the end of the month, the manager performs the bank reconciliation. The cash register tapes, sales invoices, return slips, and reconciled report are mailed daily to corporate headquarters to be processed with files from all the other stores. Corporate headquarters returns a weekly Sales and Commission Activity Report to each store manager for review.

Required

Please respond to the following questions about Spring Water Spa Company's operations:

a. The fourth component of the COSO ERM framework is risk assessment. What risk(s) does Spring Water face?

b. Identify control strengths in Spring Water's sales/cash receipts system.

c. The sixth component of the COSO ERM framework deals with control activities. What control activities do these strengths fall under?

d. What problems were avoided or risks mitigated by the controls identified in question b?

e. How might Spring Water improve its system of controls?

7.12. PriceRight Electronics (PEI) is a small wholesale discount supplier of electronic instruments and parts. PEI's competitive advantage is its deep-discount, three-day delivery guarantee, which allows retailers to order materials often to minimize in-store inventories. PEI processes its records with stand-alone, incompatible computer systems except for integrated enterprise resource planning (ERP) inventory and accounts receivable modules. PEI decided to finish integrating its operations with more ERP modules, but because of cash flow considerations, this needs to be accomplished on a step-by-step basis.

It was decided that the next function to be integrated should be sales order processing to enhance quick response to customer needs. PEI implemented and modified a commercially available software package to meet PEI's operations. In an effort to reduce the number of slow-paying or delinquent customers, PEI installed Web-based software that links to the Web site of a commercial credit rating agency to check customer credit at the time of purchase. The following are the new sales order processing system modules:

- *Sales*. Sales orders are received by telephone, fax, e-mail, Web site entry, or standard mail. They are entered into the sales order system by the Sales department. If the order does not cause a customer to exceed his credit limit, the system generates multiple copies of the sales order.

- *Credit*. When orders are received from new customers, the system automatically accesses the credit rating Web site and suggests an initial credit limit. On a daily basis, the credit manager reviews new customer applications for creditworthiness, reviews the suggested credit limits, and accepts or changes the credit limits in the customer database. On a monthly basis, the credit manager reviews the accounts receivable aging report to identify slow-paying or delinquent accounts for potential revisions to or discontinuance of credit. As needed, the credit manager issues credit memos for merchandise returns based on requests from customers and forwards copies of the credit memos to Accounting for appropriate account receivable handling.

- *Warehousing*. Warehouse personnel update the inventory master file for inventory purchases and sales, confirm availability of materials to fill sales orders, and establish back orders for sales orders that cannot be completed from stock on hand. Warehouse personnel gather and forward inventory to Shipping and Receiving along with the corresponding sales orders. They also update the inventory master file for merchandise returned to Receiving.

- *Shipping and receiving*. Shipping and Receiving accepts inventory and sales orders from Warehousing, packs and ships the orders with a copy of the sales order as a packing slip, and forwards a copy of the sales order to Billing. Customer inventory returns are unpacked, sorted, inspected, and sent to Warehousing.

- *Accounting*. Billing prices all sales orders received, which is done approximately 5 days after the order ships. To spread the work effort throughout the month, customers are placed in one of six 30-day billing cycles. Monthly statements, prepared by Billing, are sent to customers during the cycle billing period. Outstanding carry-forward balances reported by Accounts Receivable and credit memos prepared by the credit manager are included on the monthly statement. Billing also prepares electronic sales and credit memos for each cycle. Electronic copies of invoices and credit memos are forwarded to Accounts Receivable for entry into the accounts receivable master file by customer account. An aging report is prepared at the end of each month and forwarded to the credit manager. The general accounting office staff access the accounts receivable master file that reflects total charges and credits processed through the accounts receivable system for each cycle. General accounting runs a query to compare this information to the electronic sales and credit memo and posts the changes to the general ledger master file.

Required

a. Identify the internal control strengths in PEI's system.
b. Identify the internal control weaknesses in PEI's system, and suggest ways to correct them.

Case 7-1 The Greater Providence Deposit & Trust Embezzlement

Nino Moscardi, president of Greater Providence Deposit & Trust (GPD&T), received an anonymous note in his mail stating that a bank employee was making bogus loans. Moscardi asked the bank's internal auditors to investigate the transactions detailed in the note. The investigation led to James Guisti, manager of a North Providence branch office and a trusted 14-year employee who had once worked as one of the bank's internal auditors. Guisti was charged with embezzling $1.83 million from the bank using 67 phony loans taken out over a three-year period.

Court documents revealed that the bogus loans were 90-day notes requiring no collateral and ranging in amount from $10,000 to $63,500. Guisti originated the loans; when each one matured, he would take out a new loan, or rewrite the old one, to pay the principal and interest due. Some loans had been rewritten five or six times.

The 67 loans were taken out by Guisti in five names, including his wife's maiden name, his father's name, and the names of two friends. These people denied receiving stolen funds or knowing anything about the embezzlement. The fifth name was James Vanesse, who police said did not exist. The Social Security number on Vanesse's loan application was issued to a female, and the phone number belonged to a North Providence auto dealer.

Lucy Fraioli, a customer service representative who cosigned the checks, said Guisti was her supervisor and she thought nothing was wrong with the checks, though she did not know any of the people. Marcia Perfetto, head teller, told police she cashed checks for Guisti made out to four of the five persons. Asked whether she gave the money to Guisti when he gave her checks to cash, she answered, "Not all of the time," though she could not recall ever having given the money directly to any of the four, whom she did not know.

Guisti was authorized to make consumer loans up to a certain dollar limit without loan committee approvals, which is a standard industry practice. Guisti's original lending limit was $10,000, the amount of his first fraudulent loan. The dollar limit was later increased to $15,000 and then increased again to $25,000. Some of the loans, including the one for $63,500, far exceeded his lending limit. In addition, all loan applications should have been accompanied by the applicant's credit history report, purchased from an independent credit rating firm. The loan taken out in the fictitious name would not have had a credit report and should have been flagged by a loan review clerk at the bank's headquarters.

News reports raised questions about why the fraud was not detected earlier. State regulators and the bank's internal auditors failed to detect the fraud. Several reasons were given for the failure to find the fraud earlier. First, in checking for bad loans, bank auditors do not examine all loans and generally focus on loans much larger than the ones in question. Second, Greater Providence had recently dropped its computer services arrangement with a local bank in favor of an out-of-state bank. This changeover may have reduced the effectiveness of the bank's control procedures. Third, the bank's loan review clerks were rotated frequently, making follow-up on questionable loans more difficult.

Guisti was a frequent gambler and used the embezzled money to pay gambling debts. The bank's losses totaled $624,000, which was less than the $1.83 million in bogus loans, because Guisti used a portion of the borrowed money to repay loans as they came due. The bank's bonding company covered the loss.

The bank experienced other adverse publicity prior to the fraud's discovery. First, the bank was fined $50,000 after pleading guilty to failure to report cash transactions exceeding $10,000, which is a felony. Second, bank owners took the bank private after a lengthy public battle with the State Attorney General, who alleged that the bank inflated its assets and overestimated its capital surplus to make its balance sheet look stronger. The bank denied this charge.

1. How did Guisti commit the fraud, conceal it, and convert the fraudulent actions to personal gain?
2. Good internal controls require that the custody, recording, and authorization functions be separated. Explain which of those functions Guisti had and how the failure to segregate them facilitated the fraud.
3. Identify the preventive, detective, and corrective controls at GPD&T, and discuss whether they were effective.
4. Explain the pressures, opportunities, and rationalizations that were present in the Guisti fraud.

5. Discuss how Greater Providence Deposit & Trust might improve its control procedures over the disbursement of loan funds to minimize the risk of this type of fraud. In what way does this case indicate a lack of proper segregation of duties?

6. Discuss how Greater Providence might improve its loan review procedures at bank headquarters to minimize its fraud risk. Was it a good idea to rotate the assignments of loan review clerks? Why or why not?

7. Discuss whether Greater Providence's auditors should have been able to detect this fraud.

8. Are there any indications that the internal environment at Greater Providence may have been deficient? If so, how could it have contributed to this embezzlement?

Source: John Kostrezewa, "Charge: Embezzlement," *Providence Journal-Bulletin* (July 31, 1988): F-1.

AIS IN ACTION SOLUTIONS

Quiz Key

1. COSO identified five interrelated components of internal control. Which of the following is NOT one of those five?
   a. risk assessment (Incorrect. The organization must be aware of and deal with the risks it faces.)
   ▶ b. internal control policies (Correct. Internal control policies are NOT one of COSO's five components of internal control. However, control environment and control activities are two of the five internal control framework components.)
   c. monitoring (Incorrect. The entire internal control process must be monitored, and modifications made as necessary.)
   d. information and communication (Incorrect. The primary purpose of an AIS is to process and communicate information about an organization, and these activities are an essential part of an internal control system.)

2. In the ERM model, COSO specified four types of objectives that management must meet to achieve company goals. Which of the following is NOT one of those types?
   ▶ a. responsibility objectives (Correct. Responsibility objectives are NOT one of the objectives in COSO's ERM model.)
   b. strategic objectives (Incorrect. Strategic objectives are high-level goals aligned with the company's mission and are one of the objectives in COSO's ERM model.)
   c. compliance objectives (Incorrect. Compliance objectives help the company comply with all applicable laws and regulations and are one of the objectives in COSO's ERM model.)
   d. reporting objectives (Incorrect. Reporting objectives help ensure the accuracy, completeness, and reliability of internal and external reports and are one of the objectives in COSO's ERM model.)
   e. operations objectives (Incorrect. Operations objectives deal with the effectiveness and efficiency of operations and are one of the objectives in COSO's ERM model.)

3. Which of the following statements is true?
   a. COSO's enterprise risk management framework is narrow in scope and is limited to financial controls. (Incorrect. The ERM framework incorporates all kinds of internal controls, not just financial controls, and provides an all-encompassing focus on the broader subject of enterprise risk management.)
   ▶ b. COSO's internal control integrated framework has been widely accepted as the authority on internal controls. (Correct. The internal control integrated framework is the accepted authority on internal controls and is incorporated into policies, rules, and regulations that are used to control business activities.)

    c. The Foreign Corrupt Practices Act had no impact on internal accounting control systems. (Incorrect. The Foreign Corrupt Practices Act specifically requires corporations to maintain good systems of internal accounting control.)

    d. It is easier to add controls to an already designed system than to include them during the initial design stage. (Incorrect. The opposite is true: It is easier to include internal controls at the initial design stage than after the system is already designed.)

4. All other things being equal, which of the following is true?

    a. Detective controls are superior to preventive controls. (Incorrect. The reverse is true—preventive controls are superior to detective controls. Preventive controls keep an error or irregularity from occurring. Detective controls uncover an error or irregularity after the fact.)

    b. Corrective controls are superior to preventive controls. (Incorrect. The reverse is true—preventive controls are superior to corrective controls. Preventive controls keep an error or irregularity from occurring. Corrective controls fix an error after the fact.)

    c. Preventive controls are equivalent to detective controls. (Incorrect. Preventive controls keep an error or irregularity from occurring. Detective controls uncover an error or irregularity after the fact.)

  ▶ d. Preventive controls are superior to detective controls. (Correct. With respect to controls, it is always of utmost importance to prevent errors from occurring.)

5. Which of the following statements about the control environment is FALSE?

  ▶ a. Management's attitudes toward internal control and ethical behavior have little impact on employee beliefs or actions. (Correct. This statement is false. Management's attitude toward internal control is critical to the organization's effectiveness and success. They set the "tone at the top" that other employees follow.)

    b. An overly complex or unclear organizational structure may be indicative of problems that are more serious. (Incorrect. This is a true statement. Management may intentionally build overly complex or unclear organizational structures to hide fraud or errors.)

    c. A written policy and procedures manual is an important tool for assigning authority and responsibility. (Incorrect. This is a true statement. A written policy and procedures manual explains proper business practices, describes the knowledge and experience needed by key personnel, and lists the resources provided to carry out specific duties.)

    d. Supervision is especially important in organizations that cannot afford elaborate responsibility reporting or are too small to have an adequate separation of duties. (Incorrect. This is a true statement. In many organizations, effective supervision takes the place of more expensive controls. Effective supervision involves training and assisting employees, monitoring their performance, correcting errors, and safeguarding assets by overseeing employees who have access to them.)

6. To achieve effective segregation of duties, certain functions must be separated. Which of the following is the correct listing of the accounting-related functions that must be segregated?

    a. control, recording, and monitoring (Incorrect. See Figure 7-3.)

  ▶ b. authorization, recording, and custody (Correct. See Figure 7-3.)

    c. control, custody, and authorization (Incorrect. See Figure 7-3.)

    d. monitoring, recording, and planning (Incorrect. See Figure 7-3.)

7. Which of the following is NOT an independent check?

    a. bank reconciliation (Incorrect. A bank reconciliation is an independent check, as are top-level reviews, analytical reviews, reconciling two independently maintained sets of records, comparisons of actual quantities with recorded amounts, double-entry accounting, and independent reviews.)

    b. periodic comparison of subsidiary ledger totals to control accounts (Incorrect. A periodic comparison of subsidiary ledger totals to control accounts is an independent check, as are top-level reviews, analytical reviews, reconciling two independently maintained sets of records, comparisons of actual quantities with recorded amounts, double-entry accounting, and independent reviews.)

    c. trial balance (Incorrect. A trial balance is an independent check, as are top-level reviews, analytical reviews, reconciling two independently maintained sets of records,

comparisons of actual quantities with recorded amounts, double-entry accounting, and independent reviews.)
▶ d. re-adding the total of a batch of invoices and comparing it with your first total (Correct. One person performing the same procedure twice using the same documents, such as re-adding invoice batch totals, is not an independent check because it does not involve a second person, a second set of documents or records, or a second process.)

8. Which of the following is a control procedure relating to both the design and use of documents and records?
   a. locking blank checks in a drawer (Incorrect. Locking blank checks in a drawer is not a control procedure related to the design of documents.)
   b. reconciling the bank account (Incorrect. Reconciling the bank account is not a control procedure related to the design of documents.)
   ▶ c. sequentially prenumbering sales invoices (Correct. Designing documents so that they are sequentially prenumbered and then using them in order is a control procedure relating to both the design and use of documents.)
   d. comparing actual physical quantities with recorded amounts (Incorrect. Comparing actual quantities to recorded amounts is not a control procedure related to the design of documents.)

9. Which of the following is the correct order of the risk assessment steps discussed in this chapter?
   ▶ a. Identify threats, estimate risk and exposure, identify controls, and estimate costs and benefits. (Correct. See Figure 7-2.)
   b. Identify controls, estimate risk and exposure, identify threats, and estimate costs and benefits. (Incorrect. See Figure 7-2.)
   c. Estimate risk and exposure, identify controls, identify threats, and estimate costs and benefits. (Incorrect. See Figure 7-2.)
   d. Estimate costs and benefits, identify threats, identify controls, and estimate risk and exposure. (Incorrect. See Figure 7-2.)

10. Your current system is deemed to be 90% reliable. A major threat has been identified with an impact of $3,000,000. Two control procedures exist to deal with the threat. Implementation of control A would cost $100,000 and reduce the likelihood to 6%. Implementation of control B would cost $140,000 and reduce the likelihood to 4%. Implementation of both controls would cost $220,000 and reduce the likelihood to 2%. Given the data, and based solely on an economic analysis of costs and benefits, what should you do?
   a. Implement control A only. (Incorrect. Control procedure A provides a net benefit of only $20,000, whereas control procedure B provides a net benefit of $40,000.)
   ▶ b. Implement control B only. (Correct. Control procedure B provides a net benefit of $40,000. Procedure A and the combination of A and B provide a benefit of only $20,000.)
   c. Implement both controls A and B. (Incorrect. The combination of procedures A and B provides a net benefit of only $20,000, whereas control procedure B provides a net benefit of $40,000.)
   d. Implement neither control. (Incorrect. Both controls provide a net benefit. Control procedure B provides a net benefit of $40,000. Procedure A and the combination of A and B each provide a net benefit of $20,000.)

Expected loss = Impact × Likelihood ($300,000 = $3,000,000 × 10%)

Control Procedure	Likelihood	Impact	Revised Expected Loss	Reduction in Expected Loss	Cost of Control(s)	Net Benefit (Cost)
A	0.06	$3,000,000	$180,000	$120,000	$100,000	$20,000
B	0.04	$3,000,000	$120,000	$180,000	$140,000	$40,000
Both	0.02	$3,000,000	$ 60,000	$240,000	$220,000	$20,000

Chapter 8

Information Systems Controls for System Reliability— Part 1: Information Security

Learning Objectives

After studying this chapter, you should be able to:

1. Discuss how the COBIT framework can be used to develop sound internal control over an organization's information systems.

2. Explain the factors that influence information systems reliability.

3. Describe how a combination of preventive, detective, and corrective controls can be employed to provide reasonable assurance about information security.

INTEGRATIVE CASE NORTHWEST INDUSTRIES

Jason Scott's next assignment is to review the internal controls over Northwest Industries' information systems. Jason realizes that the Committee of Sponsoring Organizations (COSO) Enterprise Risk Management (ERM) framework does not specifically address information technology. A friend who is an information systems auditor for a major international audit firm tells him that the Control Objectives for Information and Related Technology (COBIT) framework developed by ISACA (formerly the Information Systems Audit and Control Association, but now goes by its acronym only) discusses internal controls and governance issues related to information systems. It also provides specific suggestions for how to audit information systems controls and identifies those information systems controls most directly relevant to achieving compliance with the requirements of the Sarbanes-Oxley Act.

Jason obtains a copy of the COBIT framework and is impressed by its thoroughness. He finds particularly helpful the report that explains how specific information technology (IT) controls relate to Sarbanes-Oxley, and he decides that he will begin his review of Northwest Industries' accounting system by focusing on the controls designed

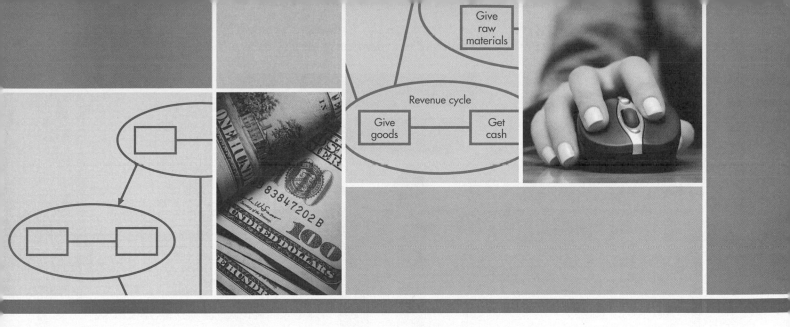

to provide reasonable assurance about information security. He writes down the following questions that will guide his investigation:

1. What controls does Northwest Industries employ to prevent unauthorized access to its accounting system?
2. How can successful and unsuccessful attempts to compromise the company's accounting system be detected in a timely manner?
3. What procedures are in place to respond to security incidents?

Introduction

Today, every organization relies on information technology. Management wants assurance that the information produced by its accounting system is reliable. It also wants to know that its investment in information technology is cost-effective. Although the COSO and COSO-ERM frameworks provide broad coverage of internal controls, neither specifically addresses controls over information technology. The COBIT framework developed by ISACA fills that void. COBIT presents a comprehensive view of the controls necessary for systems reliability.

Figure 8-1 summarizes the COBIT framework. It shows that achieving the organization's business and governance objectives requires adequate controls over IT resources to ensure that information provided to management satisfies seven key criteria:

1. *Effectiveness*—the information must be relevant and timely.
2. *Efficiency*—the information must be produced in a cost-effective manner.
3. *Confidentiality*—sensitive information must be protected from unauthorized disclosure.
4. *Integrity*—the information must be accurate, complete, and valid.
5. *Availability*—the information must be available whenever needed.
6. *Compliance*—controls must ensure compliance with internal policies and with external legal and regulatory requirements.
7. *Reliability*—management must have access to appropriate information needed to conduct daily activities and to exercise its fiduciary and governance responsibilities.

Figure 8-1 shows 34 generic IT processes that must be properly managed and controlled in order to produce information that satisfies the seven criteria listed above. Those processes are grouped into four basic management activities, which COBIT refers to as *domains*:

1. *Plan and Organize (PO).* Figure 8-1 lists 10 important processes for properly designing and managing an organization's information systems.

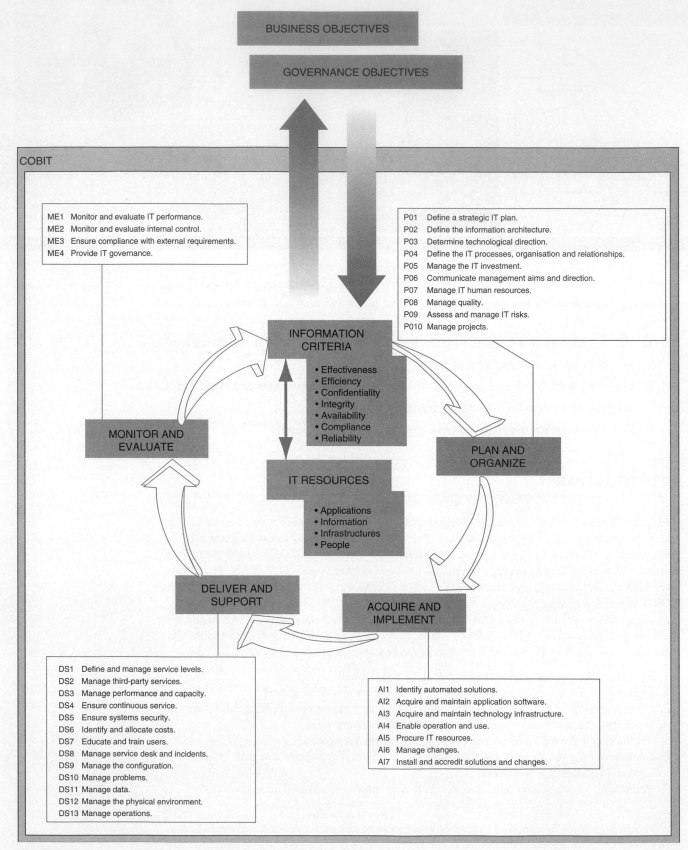

FIGURE 8-1

Overview of the COBIT Framework

(*Source:* Figure 23 in COBIT 4.1, IT Governance Institute, p. 26; note: adapted to use American spelling)

2. *Acquire and Implement (AI).*   Figure 8-1 lists seven fundamental processes for obtaining and installing technology solutions.
3. *Deliver and Support (DS).*   Figure 8-1 lists 13 critical processes for effectively and efficiently operating information systems and providing the information management needs to run the organization.
4. *Monitor and Evaluate (ME).*   Figure 8-1 lists four essential processes for assessing the operation of an organization's information systems.

Note the circle of arrows in Figure 8-1, which indicates that effective operation, control, and governance of an information system is an ongoing process. Management develops plans to organize information resources to provide the information it needs. It then authorizes and oversees efforts to acquire (or build internally) the desired functionality. Management then performs a number of activities to ensure that the resulting system actually delivers the desired information. Finally, there is a need for constant monitoring and evaluation of performance against the established criteria. The entire cycle constantly repeats, as management modifies existing plans and procedures or develops new ones to respond to changes in business objectives and new developments in information technology.

COBIT specifies 210 detailed control objectives for these 34 processes to enable effective management of an organization's information resources. It also describes specific audit procedures for assessing the effectiveness of those controls and suggests metrics that management can use to evaluate performance. This comprehensiveness is one of the strengths of COBIT and underlies its growing international acceptance as a framework for managing and controlling information systems. External auditors, however, may be concerned only with a subset of the issues covered by COBIT, specifically those that most directly pertain to the accuracy of an organization's financial statements and compliance with the Sarbanes-Oxley (SOX) Act. Consequently, ISACA issued a document entitled "IT Control Objectives for Sarbanes-Oxley, 2nd Edition" that discusses the portions of COBIT most directly relevant for compliance with SOX and provides guidance for assessing the adequacy of those controls. In addition, the Trust Services Framework developed jointly by the American Institute of Certified Public Accountants and the Canadian Institute of Chartered Accountants classifies information systems controls into five categories that most directly pertain to systems reliability (and the reliability of an organization's financial statements):

1. *Security*—access to the system and its data is controlled and restricted to legitimate users.
2. *Confidentiality*—sensitive organizational information (e.g., marketing plans, trade secrets) is protected from unauthorized disclosure.
3. *Privacy*—personal information about customers is collected, used, disclosed, and maintained only in compliance with internal policies and external regulatory requirements and is protected from unauthorized disclosure.
4. *Processing Integrity*—data are processed accurately, completely, in a timely manner, and only with proper authorization.
5. *Availability*—the system and its information are available to meet operational and contractual obligations.

The Trust Services framework is not a substitute for COBIT, because it addresses only a subset of the issues covered by COBIT. We adopt it to guide our discussion of IT controls in this text, however, because it provides a useful means for consolidating COBIT's control objectives to focus on a specific aspect of IT governance that has become especially relevant because of SOX: systems reliability. For example, the various audit issues and control objectives pertaining to information security occur in all four COBIT domains (PO, AI, DS, and ME), and the same holds true for confidentiality, privacy, processing integrity, and availability. We will identify the specific subsections of COBIT that pertain to the topics discussed in the text by using COBIT two-letter domain abbreviations followed by the number of a specific control objective. For example, COBIT control objective DS 5.5 discusses the need to regularly test and evaluate the effectiveness of information security controls.

Figure 8-2 shows how the five fundamental Trust Services principles contribute to the overall objective of systems reliability. Note the importance of information security. Security procedures restrict system access to authorized users only, thereby protecting the confidentiality of

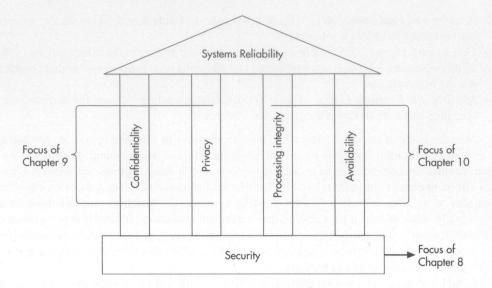

sensitive organizational data and the privacy of personal information collected from customers. Security procedures protect information integrity by preventing submission of unauthorized or fictitious transactions and preventing unauthorized changes to stored data or programs. Finally, security procedures provide protection against a variety of attacks, including viruses and worms, thereby ensuring that the system is available when needed. Thus, as Figure 8-2 shows, information security is the foundation of systems reliability. Consequently, this chapter focuses on the Trust Services principle of information security. Chapter 9 discusses the IT controls relevant to protecting the confidentiality of an organization's intellectual property and the private information it collects about its customers and business partners. Chapter 10 then covers the IT controls designed to ensure the integrity and availability of the information produced by an organization's accounting system.

Two Fundamental Information Security Concepts

1 Security Is a Management Issue, Not a Technology Issue

Section 302 of SOX requires the CEO and the CFO to certify that the financial statements fairly present the results of the company's activities. The accuracy of an organization's financial statements depends upon the reliability of its information systems. As Figure 8-2 shows, information security is the foundation for systems reliability. Consequently, information security is management's responsibility. Therefore, although information security is a complex technical subject, it is first and foremost a management issue, not an information technology issue.

The importance of management's role in information security is reflected in the fact that COBIT's first detailed security control objective (DS 5.1) calls for information security to be managed at the highest appropriate level. Indeed, as Table 8-1 shows, the active involvement and support of senior management is necessary in every facet of information security. Management involvement is especially important in the planning stage (steps 1–4 in Table 8-1). Recall that COSO stresses the importance of the "tone at the top" for creating a good internal environment; in the same manner, senior management's attitudes and behaviors are critical to shaping the organization's security culture. The identification and valuation of information resources also requires management's input; just as senior management does not have the necessary knowledge to select which firewall or encryption software to purchase, information security professionals cannot accurately assess the value of the organization's information. Although information security professionals can identify and estimate the risk of various threats, only senior management can properly assess their impact and select the appropriate risk response. Finally, employees are more likely to comply with policies and procedures when they know that senior management fully supports them.

TABLE 8-1 Management's Role in Information Security

Activity	Management's Role
1. Create and foster a pro-active "security-aware" culture.	COSO stresses the importance of management's operating philosophy and ethics in creating a "tone at the top" conducive to building a sound internal environment. The same principle applies to information security. Every employee must practice "safe" computing. This will only occur if senior management demonstrates, by example, that information security is important. Management must also provide the time and resources for security awareness training for all employees. The COBIT framework recognizes the importance of senior management involvement in and support for creating a "security-aware" culture by devoting several sections (PO 4, PO 7, and DS 7) to the various aspects of hiring, training, and properly managing the employees who work in the IT function.
2. Inventory and value the organization's information resources.	COBIT control objective PO 2.3 indicates that organizations need to identify and place a value on all their information resources (hardware, software, and information). Management must provide the time and funding necessary to perform this task. Moreover, only management possesses the breadth of understanding needed to accurately determine the value of specific information resources.
3. Assess risks and select a risk response.	It is generally not possible to totally eliminate all risk. Therefore, COBIT section PO 9 discusses the importance of developing a risk management program involving risk mitigation strategies that reduce residual risk to an acceptable level. The previous chapter explained the four possible responses to risk (reduce, accept, share, or avoid) and the process for choosing a specific response. Although systems professionals possess knowledge about the technical merits of each potential security investment and the risks of various threats, senior managers must also participate in this process to ensure that all relevant organizational factors are considered so that the funds invested in information security reflect the organization's risk appetite.
4. Develop and communicate security plans, policies, and procedures.	COBIT section PO 6 stresses the need for management to develop and communicate an enterprise-wide IT control framework. A key component of that framework is an enterprise-wide security plan. Without such a plan, the organization will most likely end up purchasing a mishmash of security products that do not protect every information system resource. COBIT control objective DS 5.2 notes that management must then translate the organization's information security plan into a set of policies and procedures and communicate those policies and procedures to all employees. To be effective, this communication must involve more than just handing people a written document and asking them to sign an acknowledgment that they received and read it. Instead, employees must receive regular, periodic reminders about security policies and training on how to comply with them. Only the active support and involvement of top management can ensure that information security training and communication is taken seriously.
5. Acquire and deploy information security technologies and products.	COBIT sections DS 5, DS 11, DS 12, and DS 13 identify a number of specific actions that are necessary to protect an organization's information resources. Management must provide the resources to implement those control activities.
6. Monitor and evaluate the effectiveness of the organization's information security program.	Information security is a moving target. Advances in information technology create new threats and alter the risks associated with existing threats. Therefore, COBIT section ME 2 indicates that effective control over information systems involves a continuous cycle of developing policies to address identified threats, communicating those policies to all employees, implementing specific control procedures to mitigate risk, monitoring performance, and taking corrective actions in response to identified problems. Often, the necessary corrective actions involve the modification of existing policies and the development of new ones, thereby beginning the entire cycle anew (refer to Figure 8-1). Senior management needs to be involved in this process to ensure that security policies remain consistent with and support the organization's business strategy. Finally, for security policies to be effective, there need to be sanctions associated with their violation. Therefore, senior management must support enforcing sanctions against employees who violate security policies.

2 Defense-in-Depth and the Time-Based Model of Information Security

The idea of *defense-in-depth* is to employ multiple layers of controls in order to avoid having a single point of failure. For example, many organizations use not only firewalls but also multiple authentication methods (passwords, tokens, and biometrics) to restrict access. The use of overlapping, complementary, and redundant controls increases overall effectiveness because if one control fails or gets circumvented, another may function as planned.

Defense-in-depth typically involves the use of a combination of preventive, detective, and corrective controls. The role of preventive controls is to limit actions to specified individuals in accordance with the organization's security policy. However, auditors have long recognized that preventive controls can never provide 100% protection. Given enough time and resources, any preventive control can be circumvented. Consequently, it is necessary to supplement preventive controls with methods for detecting incidents and procedures for taking corrective remedial action.

Detecting a security breach and initiating corrective remedial action must be timely, because once preventive controls have been breached, it takes little time to destroy, compromise, or steal the organization's economic and information resources. Therefore, the goal of the *time-based model of security* is to employ a combination of detective and corrective controls that identify an information security incident early enough to prevent the loss or compromise of information. This objective can be expressed in a formula that uses the following three variables:

P = the time it takes an attacker to break through the organization's preventive controls

D = the time it takes to detect that an attack is in progress

C = the time it takes to respond to the attack

Those three variables are then evaluated as follows: If $P > D + C$, then the organization's security procedures are effective. Otherwise, security is ineffective.

The time-based model of security provides a means for management to identify the most cost-effective approach to improving security by comparing the effects of additional investments in preventive, detective, or corrective controls. For example, management may be considering the investment of an additional $100,000 to enhance security. One option might be the purchase of a new firewall that would increase the value of P by 10 minutes. A second option might be to upgrade the organization's intrusion detection system in a manner that would decrease the value of D by 12 minutes. A third option might be to invest in new methods for responding to information security incidents so as to decrease the value of C by 30 minutes. In this example, the most cost-effective choice would be to invest in additional corrective controls that enable the organization to respond to attacks more quickly.

Although the time-based model of security provides a sound theoretical basis for evaluating and managing an organization's information security practices, it should be viewed as a strategic tool and not as a precise mathematical formula. One problem is that it is hard, if not impossible, to derive accurate, reliable measures of the parameters P, D, and C. In addition, even when those parameter values can be reliably calculated, new IT developments can quickly diminish their validity. For example, discovery of a major new vulnerability can effectively reduce the value of P to zero. Consequently, the time-based model of security is best used as a high-level framework for strategic analysis. For tactical and daily management of security, most organizations follow the principle of defense-in-depth and employ multiple preventive, detective, and corrective controls.

Understanding Targeted Attacks

Before we discuss the preventive, detective, and corrective controls that can be used to mitigate the risk of systems intrusions, it is helpful to understand the basic steps criminals use to attack an organization's information system:

1. *Conduct reconnaissance.*   Bank robbers usually do not just drive up to a bank and attempt to rob it. Instead, they first study their target's physical layout to learn about the controls it has in place (alarms, number of guards, placement of cameras, etc.). Similarly, computer attackers begin by collecting information about their target. Perusing an organization's financial statements, SEC filings, Web site, and press releases can yield much valuable information. The objective of this initial reconnaissance is to learn as much as possible about the target and to identify potential vulnerabilities.

2. *Attempt social engineering.*   Why go through all the trouble of trying to break into a system if you can get someone to let you in? Attackers will often try to use the information

obtained during their initial reconnaissance to "trick" an unsuspecting employee into granting them access, a process referred to as *social engineering*. Social engineering can take place in countless ways, limited only by the creativity and imagination of the attacker. Social engineering attacks often take place over the telephone. One common technique is for the attacker to impersonate an executive who cannot obtain remote access to important files. The attacker calls a newly hired administrative assistant and asks that person to help obtain the critical files. Another common ruse is for the attacker to pose as a clueless temporary worker who cannot log onto the system and calls the help desk for assistance. Social engineering attacks can also take place via e-mail. An attack known as *spear phishing* involves sending e-mails purportedly from someone that the victim knows, or should know. The spear phishing e-mail asks the victim to click on an embedded link, which contains a Trojan horse program that enables the attacker to obtain access to the system. Yet another social engineering tactic is to spread USB drives in the targeted organization's parking lot. An unsuspecting or curious employee who picks up the drive and plugs it into their computer will load a Trojan horse program that enables the attacker to gain access to the system.

3. *Scan and map the target*. If an attacker cannot successfully penetrate the target system via social engineering, the next step is to conduct more detailed reconnaissance to identify potential points of remote entry. The attacker uses a variety of automated tools to identify computers that can be remotely accessed and the types of software they are running.
4. *Research*. Once the attacker has identified specific targets and knows what versions of software are running on them, the next step is to conduct research to find known vulnerabilities for those programs and learn how to take advantage of those vulnerabilities.
5. *Execute the attack* and obtain unauthorized access to the system.
6. *Cover tracks*. After penetrating the victim's information system, most attackers will try to cover their tracks and create "back doors" that they can use to obtain access if their initial attack is discovered and controls are implemented to block that method of entry.

Now that we have a basic understanding of how criminals attack an organization's information system, we can proceed to methods for mitigating the risk that such attacks will be successful. The following sections discuss the major types of preventive, detective, and corrective controls listed in Table 8-2 that can be used to provide information security through defense-in-depth.

Preventive Controls

This section discusses the preventive controls listed in Table 8-2 that organizations commonly use to restrict access to information resources.

TABLE 8-2 Commonly Used Information Security Controls

Type of Control	Examples
Preventive	• Training
	• User access controls (authentication and authorization)
	• Physical access controls (locks, guards, etc.)
	• Network access controls (firewalls, intrusion prevention systems, etc.)
	• Device and software hardening controls (configuration options)
Detective	• Log analysis
	• Intrusion detection systems
	• Security testing and audits
	• Managerial reports
Corrective	• Computer incident response teams (CIRT)
	• Chief information security officer (CISO)
	• Patch management

Training

People play a critical role in information security. Employees must understand and follow the organization's security policies. Thus, training is a critical preventive control. Indeed, its importance is reflected in the fact that one of the 34 top-level control processes in the COBIT framework, DS 7, focuses exclusively on the need to train both users and systems professionals.

All employees should be taught why security measures are important to the organization's long-run survival. They also need to be trained to follow safe computing practices, such as never opening unsolicited e-mail attachments, using only approved software, not sharing passwords, and taking steps to physically protect laptops. Training is especially needed to educate employees about social engineering attacks. For example, employees should be taught never to divulge passwords or other information about their accounts or their workstation configurations to anyone who contacts them by telephone, e-mail, or instant messaging and claims to be part of the organization's information systems security function. Employees also need to be trained not to allow other people to follow them through restricted access entrances. This social engineering attack, called *piggybacking*, can take place not only at the main entrance to the building but also at any internal locked doors, especially to rooms that contain computer equipment. Piggybacking may be attempted not only by outsiders but also by other employees who are not authorized to enter a particular area. Piggybacking often succeeds because many people feel it is rude to not let another person come through the door with them or because they want to avoid confrontations. Role-playing exercises are particularly effective for increasing sensitivity to and skills for dealing with social engineering attacks.

Security awareness training is important for senior management, too, because in recent years many social engineering attacks, such as spear phishing, have been targeted at them. Training of information security professionals is also important. New developments in technology continuously create new security threats and make old solutions obsolete. Therefore, it is important for organizations to support continuing professional education for their security specialists.

However, an organization's investment in security training will be effective only if management clearly demonstrates that it supports employees who follow prescribed security policies. This is especially important for combating social engineering attacks, because countermeasures may sometimes create embarrassing confrontations with other employees. For example, one of the authors heard an anecdote about a systems professional at a major bank who refused to allow a person who was not on the list of authorized employees to enter the room housing the servers that contained the bank's key financial information. The person denied entry happened to be a new executive who was just hired. Instead of reprimanding the employee, the executive demonstrated the bank's commitment to and support for strong security by writing a formal letter of commendation for meritorious performance to be placed in the employee's performance file. It is this type of visible top management support for security that enhances the effectiveness of all security policies. Top management also needs to support the enforcement of sanctions, up to and including termination, against employees who willfully violate security policies. Doing so not only sends a strong message to other employees but also may sometimes lessen the consequences to the organization if the employee had engaged in illegal behavior.

User Access Controls

COBIT control objective DS 5.3 stresses the importance of being able to uniquely identify everyone who accesses the organization's information system and track the actions that they perform. There are two related but distinct types of user access controls that accomplish that objective. Authentication controls restrict who can access the organization's information system. Authorization controls limit what those individuals can do once they have been granted access.

AUTHENTICATION CONTROLS *Authentication* is the process of verifying the identity of the person or device attempting to access the system. The objective is to ensure that only legitimate users can access the system.

Three types of credentials can be used to verify a person's identity:

1. Something they know, such as passwords or personal identification numbers (PINs)
2. Something they have, such as smart cards or ID badges

FOCUS 8-1   The Debate Over Passwords

To be effective, passwords must satisfy a number of requirements:

- **Length.** The strength of a password is directly related to its length. Most security experts recommend that strong passwords include at least eight characters.
- **Multiple character types.** Using a mixture of upper- and lowercase alphabetic, numeric, and special characters greatly increases the strength of the password.
- **Randomness.** Passwords should not be words found in dictionaries. Nor should they be words with either a preceding or following numeric character (such as 3Diamond or Diamond3). They must also not be related to the employee's personal interests or hobbies; special-purpose password-cracking dictionaries that contain the most common passwords related to various topics are available on the Internet. For example, the password Ncc1701 appears, at first glance, to fit the requirements of a strong password because it contains a mixture of upper- and lowercase characters and numbers. But *Star Trek* fans will instantly recognize it as the designation of the starship *Enterprise*. Consequently, Ncc1701 and many variations on it (changing which letters are capitalized, replacing the number 1 with the ! symbol, etc.) are included in most password-cracking dictionaries and, therefore, are quickly compromised.
- **Changed frequently.** Passwords should be changed at regular intervals. Most users should change their passwords at least every 90 days; users with access to sensitive information should change their passwords more often, possibly every 30 days.

Most important, passwords must be kept secret to be effective. However, a problem with strong passwords, such as dX%m8K#2, is that they are not easy to remember.

Consequently, when following the requirements for creating strong passwords, people tend to write those passwords down. This weakens the value of the password by changing it from something they know to something they have—which can then be stolen and used by anyone.

These problems have led some information security experts to conclude that the attempt to enforce the use of strong passwords is counterproductive. They note that a major component of help desk costs is associated with resetting passwords that users forgot. Consequently, they argue for abandoning the quest to develop and use strong passwords and to rely on the use of dual-factor authentication methods, such as a combination of a smart card and a simple PIN, instead.

Other information security experts disagree. They note that operating systems can now accommodate passwords that are longer than 15 characters. This means that users can create strong, yet easy-to-remember, passphrases, such as Ilove2gosnorkelinginHawaiidoU?. Such long passphrases dramatically increase the effort required to crack them by brute-force guessing of every combination. For example, an eight-character password consisting solely of lower- and uppercase letters and numerals has 62^8 possible combinations, but a 20-character passphrase has 62^{20} possible combinations. This means that passphrases do not need to be changed as frequently as passwords. Therefore, some information security experts argue that the ability to use the same passphrase for long periods of time, coupled with the fact that it is easier to remember a long passphrase than a strong password, should dramatically cut help desk costs while improving security. However, it remains to be seen whether users will balk at having to enter long passphrases, especially if they need to do so frequently because they are required to use passphrase-protected screen savers.

3. Some physical characteristic (referred to as a ***biometric identifier***), such as their fingerprints or voice

Passwords are probably the most commonly used authentication method, and also the most controversial. Focus 8-1 discusses some of the requirements for creating strong passwords as well as the ongoing debate about their continued use in the future.

Individually, each authentication method has its limitations. Passwords can be guessed, lost, written down, or given away. Physical identification techniques (cards, badges, USB devices, etc.) can be lost, stolen, or duplicated. Even biometric techniques are not yet 100% accurate, sometimes rejecting legitimate users (for example, voice recognition systems may not recognize an employee who has a cold) and sometimes allowing access to unauthorized people. Moreover, some biometric techniques, such as fingerprints, carry negative connotations that may hinder their acceptance. There are also security concerns about storage of the biometric information itself. Biometric templates, such as the digital representation of an individual's fingerprints or voice, must be stored somewhere. The compromising of those templates would create serious, lifelong problems for the donor because biometric characteristics, unlike passwords or physical tokens, cannot be replaced or changed.

Although none of the three basic authentication credentials, by itself, is foolproof, the use of two or all three types in conjunction, a process referred to as *multifactor authentication*, is quite effective. For example, requiring a user both to insert a smart card in a card reader and enter a password provides much stronger authentication than using either method alone. In some situations, using multiple credentials of the same type, a process referred to as *multimodal authentication*, can also improve security. For example, many online banking sites use several things that a person knows (password, user ID, and recognition of a graphic image) for authentication. Similarly, because most laptops now are equipped with a camera and a microphone, plus a fingerprint reader, it is possible to employ multimodal biometric authentication involving a combination of face, voice, and fingerprint recognition to verify identity. Both multifactor authentication and multimodal authentication are examples of applying the principle of defense-in-depth.

It is important to authenticate not only people, but also every device attempting to connect to the network. Every workstation, printer, or other computing device needs a network interface card (NIC) to connect to the organization's internal network. Each NIC has a unique identifier, referred to as its media access control (MAC) address. Therefore, an organization can restrict network access to only corporate-owned devices by comparing the device's MAC to a list of recognized MAC addresses. There exists software, however, that can be used to change a device's MAC address, thereby enabling malicious users to "spoof" their device's identity. Therefore, a stronger way to authenticate devices involves the use of digital certificates that employ encryption techniques to assign unique identifiers to each device. Digital certificates and encryption are discussed in Chapter 9.

AUTHORIZATION CONTROLS   *Authorization* is the process of restricting access of authenticated users to specific portions of the system and limiting what actions they are permitted to perform. For example, a customer service representative should not be authorized to access the payroll system. In addition, that employee should be permitted only to read, but not to change, the prices of inventory items.

Authorization controls are often implemented by creating an *access control matrix* (Figure 8-3). Then, when an employee attempts to access a particular information systems resource, the system performs a *compatibility test* that matches the user's authentication credentials against the access control matrix to determine whether that employee should be allowed to access that resource and perform the requested action. It is important to regularly update the access control matrix to reflect changes in job duties due to promotions or transfers. Otherwise, over time an employee may accumulate a set of rights and privileges that is incompatible with proper segregation of duties.

It is possible to achieve even greater control and segregation of duties by using business process management systems to embed authorization into automated business processes, rather than relying on a static access control matrix. For example, authorization can be granted only to perform a specific task for a specific transaction. Thus, a particular employee may be permitted to access credit information about the customer who is currently requesting service, but simultaneously prevented from "browsing" through the rest of the customer file. In addition, business process management systems enforce segregation of duties because employees can perform only the specific tasks that the system has assigned them. Employees cannot delete tasks from their

FIGURE 8-3
Example of an Access Control Matrix

User	Files			Programs			
User ID	A	B	C	1	2	3	4
NHale	0	0	1	0	0	0	0
JPJones	0	2	0	0	0	0	1
BArnold	1	1	0	1	1	0	0
....	....	....	....	....	....	....	....

Codes for File Access:
0 = No Access
1 = Read/display only
2 = Read/display and update
3 = Read/display, update, create, and delete

Codes for Program Access:
0 = No Access
1 = Execute

assigned task list, and the system sends reminder messages until the task is completed—two more measures that further enhance control. Business process management software also can instantly route transactions that require specific authorization (such as a credit sale above a certain amount) electronically to a manager for approval. The transaction cannot continue until authorization is granted, but because the need for such approval is indicated and granted or denied electronically, this important control is enforced without sacrificing efficiency.

Like authentication controls, authorization controls can and should be applied not only to people but also to devices. For example, including MAC addresses or digital certificates in the access control matrix makes it possible to restrict access to the payroll system and payroll master files to only payroll department employees and only when they log in from their desktop or assigned laptop computer. After all, why would a payroll clerk need to log in from a workstation located in the warehouse or attempt to establish dial-in access from another country? Applying authentication and authorization controls to both humans and devices is another way in which defense-in-depth increases security.

Physical Access Controls

It is absolutely essential to control physical access to information resources. A skilled attacker needs only a few minutes of unsupervised direct physical access in order to bypass existing information security controls. For example, an attacker with unsupervised direct physical access can install a keystroke logging device that captures a user's authentication credentials, thereby enabling the attacker to subsequently obtain unauthorized access to the system by impersonating a legitimate user. Someone with unsupervised physical access could also insert special "boot" disks that provide direct access to every file on the computer and then copy sensitive files to a portable device such as a USB drive or an iPod. Alternatively, an attacker with unsupervised physical access could simply remove the hard drive or even steal the entire computer. Given this wide range of potential threats associated with unsupervised physical access, it should not be surprising that another of COBIT's 34 top-level control objectives, DS 12, focuses specifically on physical access controls.

Physical access control begins with entry points to the building itself. Ideally, there should only be one regular entry point that remains unlocked during normal office hours. Fire codes usually require additional emergency exits, but these should not permit entry from the outside and should be connected to an alarm system that is automatically triggered whenever the fire exit is opened. In addition, either a receptionist or a security guard should be stationed at the main entrance to verify the identity of employees. Visitors should be required to sign in and be escorted by an employee wherever they go in the building.

Once inside the building, physical access to rooms housing computer equipment must also be restricted. These rooms should be securely locked and all entry/exit monitored by closed-circuit television systems. Multiple failed access attempts should trigger an alarm. Rooms housing servers that contain especially sensitive data should supplement regular locks with stronger technologies—card readers, numeric keypads, or various biometric devices, such as iris or retina scanners, fingerprint readers, or voice recognition. Focus 8-2 describes an especially elaborate set of physical access controls referred to as a *man-trap*.

Access to the wiring used in the organization's LANs also needs to be restricted in order to prevent wiretapping. That means that cables and wiring should not be exposed in areas accessible to casual visitors. Wiring closets containing telecommunications equipment need to be securely locked. If wiring closets are shared with other tenants of an office building, the organization should place its telecommunications equipment inside locked steel cages to prevent unauthorized physical access by anyone else with access to that wiring closet. Wall jacks not in current use should be physically disconnected from the network to prevent someone from just plugging in their laptop and attempting to access the network.

Physical access controls must be cost-effective. This requires the involvement of top management in planning physical access security controls to ensure that all information system resources are properly valued and that the nature and combination of access controls reflect the value of the assets being protected.

Laptops, cell phones, and PDA devices require special attention. Laptop theft is a large problem. The major cost is not the price of replacing the laptop, but rather the loss of the confidential information it contains and the costs of notifying those affected. Often, companies also

F O CUS 8-2 | Controlling Physical Access with Man-Traps

Financial institutions, defense contractors, and various intelligence agencies store especially valuable data. Therefore, they often need to employ much more elaborate physical access control measures to their data centers than those used by most other organizations. One such technique involves the use of specially designed rooms called man-traps. These rooms typically contain two doors, each of which uses multiple authentication methods to control access. For example, entry to the first door may require that the person both insert an ID card or smart card into a reader and enter an identification code into a keypad. Successful authentication opens the first door and provides access to the entrance room. Once inside the room, the first door automatically closes behind the person, locks, and cannot be opened from inside the room. The other door, which opens into the data center, is also locked. Thus, the person is now trapped in this small room (hence the name *man-trap*). The only way out is to successfully pass a second set of authentication controls that restrict access through the door leading to the data center. Typically, this involves multifactor authentication that includes a biometric credential. Failure to pass this second set of tests leaves the person in the room until members of the security staff arrive.

have to pay for credit-monitoring services for customers whose personal information was lost or stolen. There may even be class action lawsuits and fines by regulatory agencies.

To deal with the threat of laptop theft, employees should be trained to always lock their laptops to an immovable object. This is necessary even when in the office, as there have been cases where thieves disguised as cleaning crews have stolen laptops and other equipment during working hours. Ideally, sensitive information should not be stored on laptops. If it is, security experts suggest that it be encrypted during storage to minimize the likelihood that a thief will be able to access it. Some organizations are also installing special software on laptops that sends a message to a security server whenever the laptop connects to the Internet. Then, if the laptop is lost or stolen, its location can be identified the next time it is connected to the Internet. The security server can also send a reply message that permanently erases all information stored on the laptop.

Cell phones and PDAs also increasingly store confidential information and therefore need the same types of controls that are used for laptops. It is also important to restrict access to network printers, because they often store document images on their hard drives. There have been cases where intruders have stolen the hard drives in those printers, thereby gaining access to sensitive information.

Network Access Controls

Most organizations provide employees, customers, and suppliers with remote access to their information systems. Usually this access occurs via the Internet, but some organizations still maintain their own proprietary networks or provide direct dial-up access by modem. Many organizations also provide wireless access to their systems. We now discuss the various methods that can be used to satisfy COBIT control objective DS 5.10 to control remote access to information resources.

PERIMETER DEFENSE: ROUTERS, FIREWALLS, AND INTRUSION PREVENTION SYSTEMS   Figure 8-4 shows the relationship between an organization's information system and the Internet. A device called a *border router* connects an organization's information system to the Internet. Behind the border router is the main *firewall*, which is either a special-purpose hardware device or software running on a general-purpose computer. The *demilitarized zone (DMZ)* is a separate network that permits controlled access from the Internet to selected resources, such as the organization's e-commerce Web server. Together, the border router and firewall act as filters to control which information is allowed to enter and leave the organization's information system. To understand how they function, it is first necessary to briefly discuss how information is transmitted on the Internet.

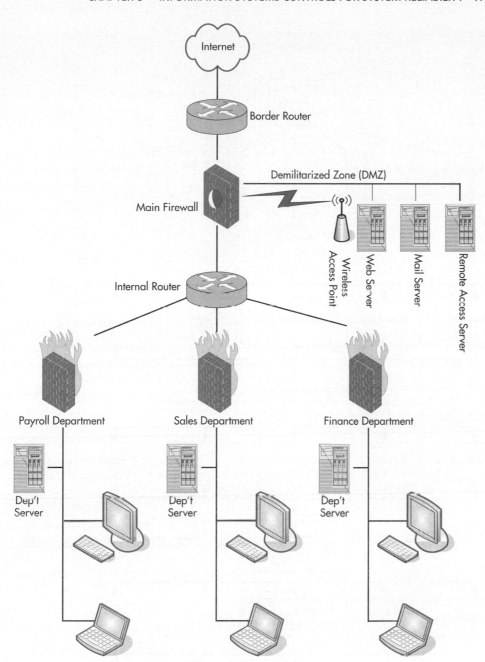

FIGURE 8-4

Example Organizational Network Architecture

Overview of TCP/IP and Routers. Information traverses the Internet and internal local area networks in the form of packets. Thus, the documents and files on your computer are not sent intact to a printer or a colleague. Instead, they are first divided into packets, and those packets are then sent over the local area network, and perhaps the Internet, to their destination. The device receiving those packets must then reassemble them to recreate the original document or file. Well-defined rules and procedures called protocols dictate how to perform all these activities. Figure 8-5 shows how two important protocols, referred to as TCP/IP, govern the process for transmitting information over the Internet. The *Transmission Control Protocol (TCP)* specifies the procedures for dividing files and documents into packets to be sent over the Internet and the methods for reassembly of the original document or file at the destination. The *Internet Protocol (IP)* specifies the structure of those packets and how to route them to the proper destination.

The structure of IP packets facilitates their efficient transmission over the Internet. Every IP packet consists of two parts: a header and a body. The header contains the packet's origin and destination addresses, as well as information about the type of data contained in the body of the packet. The IP protocol prescribes the size of the header and the sequence of information fields

FIGURE 8-5
Functions of TCP/IP Protocols

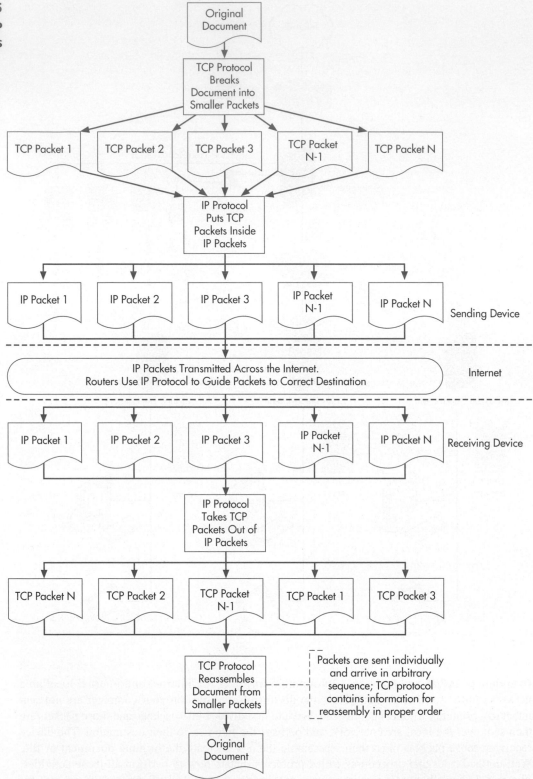

in it. For example, in IP version 4, which is still commonly used in North America, the 13th through 16th bytes in the header *always* contain the IP address of the source of the packet, and the 17th through 20th bytes *always* contain the destination address. This well-defined structure makes it easy for computers to decide where to send each packet that arrives.

Special-purpose devices called **routers** are designed to read the destination address fields in IP packet headers to decide where to send (route) the packet next. The current version of the IP protocol, IPv4, uses 32-bit-long addresses. Those addresses consist of four 8-bit numbers separated by periods. When users type a URL in their browser, that name is translated into the appropriate address. For example, the Acme Manufacturing Company's publicly accessible Web server might have an IP address of 135.22.74.10, but anyone wishing to visit the site can enter the URL of www.acme.com in their browser instead of that IP address. An organization's border router checks the contents of the destination address field of every packet it receives. If the address is not that of the organization, the packet is forwarded on to another router on the Internet. If the destination address matches that of the organization, the packet undergoes one or more tests before being allowed in.

Controlling Access by Filtering Packets.   A set of rules, called an *access control list (ACL)*, determines which packets are allowed entry and which are dropped. Border routers typically perform *static packet filtering*, which screens individual IP packets based solely on the contents of the source and/or destination fields in the IP packet header. Typically, the border router's ACL identifies source and destination addresses that should not be permitted to enter the organization's internal network. The function of the border router is to quickly identify and drop certain types of packets and to pass all other packets to the firewall, where they will be subjected to more detailed testing before being allowed to enter the organization's internal network. Thus, most rules in the border router's ACL focus on dropping packets. The last rule in the ACL, however, usually specifies that any packet not dropped because of the preceding rules should be passed on to the firewall.

Like the border router, firewalls use ACLs to determine what to do with each packet that arrives. A major difference, however, is that firewalls are designed to permit entry only to those packets that meet specific conditions. Thus, unlike border routers, the final rule in a firewall ACL usually specifies that any packet not allowed entry by any of the previous rules in the ACL should be dropped. Note, however, that firewalls do not block *all* traffic, but only filter it. That is why all the firewalls in Figure 8-4 have holes in them—to show that certain kinds of traffic can pass through.

To filter packets, firewalls use more sophisticated techniques than border routers do. For example, most firewalls employ stateful packet filtering. Whereas static packet filtering examines each IP packet in isolation, *stateful packet filtering* creates and maintains a table in memory that lists all established connections between the organization's computers and the Internet. The firewall consults this table to determine whether an incoming packet is part of an ongoing communication initiated by an internal computer. Stateful packet filtering enables the firewall to reject specially crafted attack packets that would have passed a simple static packet filter by pretending to be a response to an internally initiated request, when in fact no such preceding request occurred.

Deep Packet Inspection.   Stateful packet filtering is still limited to examining only information in the IP packet header, however. Essentially, this is the same thing as trying to screen mail simply by looking at the destination and return addresses on the envelope. Such a process is fast and can catch patently undesirable packages (e.g., businesses may not want to accept mail from casinos or pornographic magazines), but its effectiveness is limited. Undesirable mail can get through if the IP address is not on the list of unacceptable sources or if the sender purposely disguises the true source address. Clearly, control over incoming mail would be more effective if each envelope or package were opened and inspected.

Similarly, firewalls that examine the data in the body of an IP packet can provide more effective access control than those that look only at information in the IP header. Thus, a Web application firewall can better protect an organization's e-commerce Web server by examining the contents of incoming packets to ensure that they contain only HTML code. The firewall can even restrict the types of commands permitted. For example, requests for data using the HTML "get" command would be allowed, but requests to upload data to the Web server using the HTML "put" command would be blocked to prevent an attacker from defacing the Web site.

This process of examining the data contents of a packet is called *deep packet inspection*. The added control provided by deep packet inspection, however, comes at the cost of speed: It takes more time to examine the body of an IP packet, which could contain more than a thousand bytes of data, than to examine only the 20 bytes in the header of an IPv4 packet.

Deep packet inspection is the heart of a new type of security technology called *intrusion prevention systems (IPS)* that monitors *patterns* in the traffic flow, rather than only inspecting individual packets, to identify and automatically block attacks. This is important because examining a pattern of traffic is often the only way to identify undesirable activity. For example, a firewall performing deep packet inspection would permit incoming packets that contained allowable HTML commands to connect to TCP port 80 on the organization's e-commerce Web server and block all other incoming packets. Such a firewall would dutifully pass or block packets, and perhaps record its decisions in a log. An IPS, in contrast, could identify a sequence of packets attempting to connect to various TCP ports on the e-commerce Web server as being an indicator of an attempt to scan and map the Web server (step 3 in a targeted attack). The IPS would not only block the offending packets, but also notify a security administrator that an attempted scan was in progress. Thus, IPSs provide the opportunity for real-time response to attacks.

An IPS consists of a set of sensors and a central monitor unit that analyzes the data collected. Sensors must be installed in several places to effectively monitor network traffic. A sensor located just inside the main firewall can monitor all incoming traffic. Placing another sensor outside the main firewall provides a means to monitor the number of attempted intrusions that were successfully blocked by the firewall, which may provide early warning that the organization is being targeted. Additional sensors inside each internal firewall can be used to monitor the effectiveness of policies concerning employee access to information resources.

IPSs use several different techniques to identify undesirable traffic patterns. The simplest approach is to compare traffic patterns to a database of signatures of known attacks. Another approach involves developing a profile of "normal" traffic and using statistical analysis to identify packets that do not fit that profile. Most promising is the use of rule bases that specify acceptable standards for specific types of traffic and that drop all packets that do not conform to those standards. The beauty of this approach is that it blocks not only known attacks, for which signatures already exist, but also any new attacks that violate the standards.

Although IPSs are a promising addition to the arsenal of security products, they are relatively new and, therefore, not without problems. As mentioned earlier, deep packet inspection slows overall throughput. In addition, there is the danger of false alarms, which results in blocking legitimate traffic. Nevertheless, a great deal of research is being undertaken to improve the intelligence of IPSs, and they are likely to become an important part of an organization's security toolkit. IPSs will not, however, replace the need for firewalls. Instead, they are a complementary tool and provide yet another layer of perimeter defense.

Using Defense-in-Depth to Restrict Network Access.   The use of multiple perimeter filtering devices is more efficient and effective than relying on only one device. Thus, most organizations use border routers to quickly filter out obviously bad packets and pass the rest to the main firewall. The main firewall does more detailed checking, using either stateful packet filtering or deep packet inspection. The IPS then monitors the traffic passed by the firewall to identify and block suspicious network traffic patterns that may indicate that an attack is in progress.

Figure 8-4 illustrates one other dimension of the concept of defense-in-depth: the use of multiple internal firewalls to segment different departments within the organization. Recall that many security incidents involve employees, not outsiders. Internal firewalls help to restrict what data and portions of the organization's information system particular employees can access. This not only increases security but also strengthens internal control by providing a means for enforcing segregation of duties.

Finally, an especially effective way to achieve defense-in-depth is to integrate physical and remote access control systems. For example, if an organization uses keypads, card or badge readers, or biometric identifiers to control and log physical access to the office, that data should be considered when applying remote access controls. This would identify situations likely to represent security breaches, such as when an employee who supposedly is inside the office is simultaneously trying to log into the system remotely from another geographically distant location.

SECURING DIAL-UP CONNECTIONS   Many organizations still permit employees to remotely access the organizational network by dialing in with a modem. It is important to verify the identity of users attempting to obtain dial-in access. The *Remote Authentication Dial-In User Service (RADIUS)* is a standard method for doing that. Dial-in users connect to a remote access server and submit their log-in credentials. The remote access server passes those credentials to the RADIUS server, which performs compatibility tests to authenticate the identity of that user. Note that Figure 8-4 shows the remote access server located in the DMZ. Thus, only *after* the user has been authenticated is access to the internal corporate network granted. This subjects dial-in users to the same controls applied to traffic coming in from the untrusted Internet.

Modems, however, are cheap and easy to install, so employees are often tempted to install them on their desktop workstations without seeking permission or notifying anyone that they have done so. This creates a huge hole in perimeter security, because the incoming connection is not filtered by the main firewall. Moreover, when employees install modems, they seldom configure any strong authentication controls. Consequently, a single unauthorized ("rogue") modem connected to an employee's desktop workstation creates a "back door" through which attackers can often easily compromise an otherwise well-protected system. Therefore, either information security or internal audit staff must periodically check for the existence of rogue modems. The most efficient and effective way to do this is to use *war dialing* software, which calls every telephone number assigned to the organization to identify those which are connected to modems. (Hackers do this also, to identify targets). Any rogue modems discovered by war dialing should be disconnected, with sanctions applied to the employees responsible for installing them.

SECURING WIRELESS ACCESS   Many organizations also provide wireless access to their information systems. Wireless access is convenient and easy, but it also provides another venue for attack and extends the perimeter that must be protected. For example, a number of companies have experienced security incidents in which intruders obtained unauthorized wireless access to the organization's corporate network from a laptop while sitting in a car parked outside the building.

It is not enough to monitor the parking lot, because wireless signals can often be picked up miles away. Figure 8-4 shows that to secure wireless access, all wireless access points (the devices that accept incoming wireless communications and permit the sending device to connect to the organization's network) should be located in the DMZ. This treats all wireless access as though it were coming in from the Internet and forces all wireless traffic to go through the main firewall and any intrusion prevention systems that are used to protect the perimeter of the internal network. In addition, the following procedures need to be followed to adequately secure wireless access:

- Turn on available security features. Most wireless equipment is sold and installed with these features disabled. For example, the default installation configuration for most wireless routers does not turn on encryption.
- Authenticate all devices attempting to establish wireless access to the network *before* assigning them an IP address. This can be done by treating incoming wireless connections as attempts to access the network from the Internet and routing them first through a RADIUS server or other authentication device.
- Configure all authorized wireless devices to operate only in infrastructure mode, which forces the device to connect only to wireless access points. (Wireless devices can also be set to operate in ad hoc mode, which enables them to communicate directly with any other wireless device. This is a security threat because it creates peer-to-peer networks with little or no authentication controls.) In addition, predefine a list of authorized MAC addresses, and configure wireless access points to accept connections only if the device's MAC address is on the authorized list.
- Use noninformative names for the access point's address, which is called a service set identifier (SSID). SSIDs such as "payroll," "finance," or "R&D" are more obvious targets to attack than devices with generic SSIDs such as "A1" or "X2."
- Reduce the broadcast strength of wireless access points, locate them in the interior of the building, and use directional antennas to make unauthorized reception off-premises more difficult. Special paint and window films can also be used to contain wireless signals within a building.
- Encrypt all wireless traffic.

However, as is the case with modems, it is easy and inexpensive for employees to set up unauthorized wireless access points in their offices. Therefore, information security or internal audit staff must periodically test for the existence of such rogue access points, disable any that are discovered, and appropriately discipline the employees responsible for installing them.

Device and Software Hardening Controls

Routers, firewalls, and intrusion prevention systems are designed to protect the network perimeter. However, just as many homes and businesses supplement exterior door locks and alarm systems with locked cabinets and safes to store valuables, an organization can enhance information system security by supplementing preventive controls on the network perimeter with additional preventive controls on the workstations, servers, printers, and other devices (collectively referred to as *endpoints)* that comprise the organization's network. Three areas deserve special attention: (1) endpoint configuration, (2) user account management, and (3) software design.

1 ENDPOINT CONFIGURATION   Endpoints can be made more secure by modifying their configurations. Default configurations of most devices typically turn on a large number of optional settings that are seldom, if ever, used. Similarly, default installations of many operating systems turn on many special-purpose programs, called *services*, that are not essential. Turning on unnecessary features and extra services makes it more likely that installation will be successful without the need for customer support. This convenience, however, comes at the cost of creating security weaknesses. Every program that is running represents a potential point of attack because it probably contains flaws, called *vulnerabilities*, that can be exploited to either crash the system or take control of it. Therefore, any optional programs and features that are not used should be disabled. Tools called *vulnerability scanners* can be used to identify unused and, therefore, unnecessary programs that represent potential security threats. This process of modifying the default configuration of endpoints to eliminate unnecessary settings and services is called *hardening*.

In addition to hardening, every endpoint needs to be running antivirus and firewall software that is regularly updated. IPS may also be installed to prevent unauthorized attempts to change the configuration of a specific device. COBIT control objective DS 5.7 recognizes that it is especially important to harden and properly configure every device used to protect the network (firewalls, IPS, routers, etc.), to make them resistant to tampering.

2 USER ACCOUNT MANAGEMENT   COBIT control objective DS 5.4 stresses the need to carefully manage all user accounts, especially those accounts that have unlimited (administrative) rights on that computer. Administrative rights are needed in order to install software and alter most configuration settings. These powerful capabilities make accounts with administrative rights prime targets for attackers. In addition, many vulnerabilities affect only accounts with administrative rights. Therefore, employees who need administrative powers on a particular computer should be assigned two accounts: one with administrative rights and another that has only limited privileges. These employees should be trained to log in under their limited account to perform routine daily duties and to log in to their administrative account only when they need to perform some action, such as installing new software, that requires administrative rights. It is especially important that the employee use a limited regular user account when browsing the Web or reading e-mail. This way, if the user visits a compromised Web site or opens an infected e-mail, the attacker will acquire only limited rights on the machine. Although the attacker can use other tools to eventually obtain administrative rights on that machine, other security controls might detect and thwart such attempts to escalate privileges before they can be completed. Finally, it is important to change the default passwords on all administrative accounts that are created during initial installation of any software or hardware because those account names and their default passwords are publicly available on the Internet and thus provide attackers with an easy way to compromise a system.

3 SOFTWARE DESIGN   As organizations have increased the effectiveness of their perimeter security controls, attackers have increasingly targeted vulnerabilities in application programs. Buffer overflows, SQL injection, and cross-site scripting are common examples of attacks against the software running on Web sites. These attacks all exploit poorly written software that does not thoroughly check user-supplied input prior to further processing. Consider the common task of soliciting user input such as name and address. Most programs set aside a fixed amount of memory, referred to as a buffer, to hold user input. However, if the program does not carefully check the size of data being input, an attacker may enter many times the amount of data that was anticipated and overflow the buffer. The excess data may be written to an area of memory normally used to store and execute commands. In such cases, an attacker may be able to take control of the machine by sending carefully crafted commands in the excess data. Similarly, SQL injection attacks occur whenever Web application software that interfaces with a database server does not filter user input, thereby permitting an attacker to embed SQL commands within a data entry request and have those commands executed on the database server. Cross-site scripting attacks occur when Web application software does not carefully filter user input before returning any of that data to the browser, in which case the victim's browser will execute any embedded malicious script.

The common theme in all of these attacks is the failure to "scrub" user input to remove potentially malicious code. Therefore, programmers must be trained to treat all input from external users as untrustworthy and to carefully check it before performing further actions. Poor programming techniques affect not only internally created code but also software purchased from third parties. Consequently, several sections of the COBIT framework are devoted to control objectives for application software. Section AI 2 specifies the need to carefully design security into all new applications. Section AI 7 stresses the importance of thoroughly testing new applications before deployment. Sections DS 1 and DS 2 enumerate specific control objectives that should be followed when contracting with vendors.

Detective Controls

As noted earlier, preventive controls are never 100% effective in blocking all attacks. Therefore, COBIT control objective DS 5.5 stresses that organizations also need to implement controls designed to detect intrusions in a timely manner. Detective controls enhance security by monitoring the effectiveness of preventive controls and detecting incidents in which preventive controls have been successfully circumvented. This section discusses the four types of detective controls listed in Table 8-2: log analysis, intrusion detection systems, managerial reports, and security testing.

Log Analysis

Most systems come with extensive capabilities for logging who accesses the system and what specific actions each user performed. These logs form an audit trail of system access. Like any other audit trail, logs are of value only if they are routinely examined. *Log analysis* is the process of examining logs to identify evidence of possible attacks.

It is especially important to analyze logs of failed attempts to log on to a system and failed attempts to obtain access to specific information resources. For example, Figure 8-6 presents a portion of security log from a computer running the Windows operating system that shows that a user named "rjones" unsuccessfully tried to log onto a computer named "payroll server." The goal of log analysis is to determine the reason for this failed log-on attempt. One possible explanation is that rjones is a legitimate user who forgot his or her password. Another possibility is that rjones is a legitimate user but is not authorized to access the payroll server. Yet another possibility is that this may represent an attempted attack by an external intruder.

It is also important to analyze changes to the logs themselves (i.e., "to audit the audit trail"). Logs records are routinely created whenever the appropriate event occurs. However, log records are not normally deleted or updated. Therefore, finding such changes to a log file indicate that the system has likely been compromised.

Logs need to be analyzed regularly to detect problems in a timely manner. This is not easy, because logs can quickly grow in size. Another problem is that many devices produce logs with proprietary formats, making it hard to correlate and summarize logs from different devices. Software tools such as log management systems and security information management systems attempt to address these issues by converting vendor-specific log formats into common representations and producing reports that correlate and summarize information from multiple sources. Nevertheless, log analysis ultimately requires human judgment to interpret the reports and identify situations that are not "normal".

FIGURE 8-6
Example of a System Log

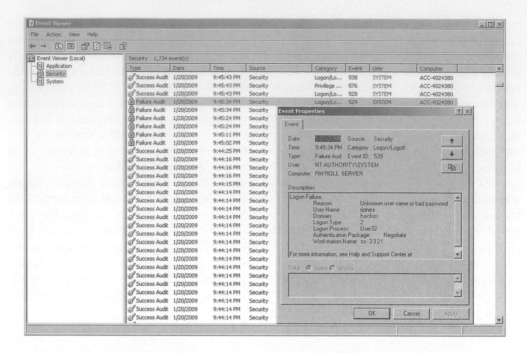

Intrusion Detection Systems

Intrusion detection systems (IDSs) consist of a set of sensors and a central monitoring unit that create logs of network traffic that was permitted to pass the firewall and then analyze those logs for signs of attempted or successful intrusions. Like an IPS, an IDS functions by comparing observed traffic to a database of signatures of known attacks or to a model of "normal" traffic on a particular network. In addition, an IDS can be installed on a specific device to monitor unauthorized attempts to change that device's configuration. The main difference between an IDS and an IPS is that the former only produces a warning alert when it detects a suspicious pattern of network traffic, whereas the latter not only issues an alert but also automatically takes steps to stop a suspected attack.

Managerial Reports

COBIT sections ME 1 and ME 2 address the need for management to monitor and evaluate both system performance and controls. The COBIT framework provides management guidelines that identify critical success factors associated with each control objective and suggests key performance indicators that management can use to monitor and assess control effectiveness. For example, the COBIT management guidelines suggest that key performance indicators relevant to DS 5, information security, include such things as:

1. Number of incidents with business impact
2. Percentage of users who do not comply with password standards
3. Percentage of cryptographic keys compromised and revoked

Nevertheless, despite its importance, surveys indicate that many organizations fail to regularly monitor security. This is clearly an area where accountants can help by using the COBIT framework to design security effectiveness scorecards and encouraging management to regularly review such reports.

Security Testing

COBIT control objective DS 5.5 notes the need to periodically test the effectiveness of existing security procedures. We already discussed the use of vulnerability scanners to identify potential weaknesses in system configuration. Penetration testing provides a more rigorous way to test the effectiveness of an organization's information security. A *penetration test* is an *authorized* attempt by either an internal audit team or an external security consulting firm to break into the organization's information system. These teams try everything possible to compromise a company's system. Because there are numerous potential attack vectors, penetration tests almost always succeed. Thus, their value is not so much in demonstrating that a system *can* be broken into, but in identifying where additional protections are most needed to increase the time and effort required to compromise the system.

Corrective Controls

Detecting attempted and successful intrusions is not enough. Organizations also need procedures to undertake timely corrective actions. Many corrective controls, however, rely on human judgment. Consequently, their effectiveness depends to a great extent on proper planning and preparation. That is why COBIT control objective DS 5.6 prescribes the need to define and communicate characteristics of security incidents to facilitate their proper classification and treatment. In addition, COBIT sections DS 8 and DS 10 outline specific control objectives for effectively managing incidents and problems. This section discusses three particularly important corrective controls listed in Table 8-2: (1) establishment of a computer incident response team, (2) designation of a specific individual, typically referred to as the Chief Information Security Officer (CISO), with organization-wide responsibility for information security, and (3) an well-designed patch management system

Computer Incident Response Team

A key component to being able to respond to security incidents promptly and effectively is the establishment of a *computer incident response team (CIRT)* responsible for dealing with major incidents. The CIRT should include not only technical specialists but also senior operations management, because some potential responses to security incidents have significant economic consequences. For example, it may be necessary to temporarily shut down an e-commerce server. The decision to do so is too important to leave to the discretion of IT security staff; only operations management possesses the breadth of knowledge to properly evaluate the costs and benefits of such an action, and only it should have the authority to make that decision.

The CIRT should lead the organization's incident response process through the following four steps:

1. *Recognition* that a problem exists. Typically, this occurs when an IPS or IDS signals an alert or as a result of log analysis by a systems administrator.
2. *Containment* of the problem. Once an intrusion is detected, prompt action is needed to stop it and to contain the damage.
3. *Recovery.* Damage caused by the attack must be repaired. This may involve restoring data from backup and reinstalling corrupted programs. We will discuss backup and disaster recovery procedures in more detail in Chapter 10.
4. *Follow-up.* Once recovery is in process, the CIRT should lead the analysis of how the incident occurred. Steps may need to be taken to modify existing security policy and procedures to minimize the likelihood of a similar incident occurring in the future. An important decision that needs to be made is whether to attempt to catch and punish the perpetrator. If the organization decides that it wants to prosecute the attacker(s), it needs to immediately involve forensic experts to ensure that all possible evidence is collected and maintained in a manner that makes it admissible for use in court.

Communication is vital throughout all four steps in the incident response process. Therefore, multiple methods of notifying members of the CIRT are necessary. For example, IPSs and IDSs might be configured to send e-mail alerts. However, if the system goes down or is compromised, the e-mail alerts may not work. Traditional telephones and cell phones provide good alternative channels for sending the initial alerts and subsequent communications.

It is also important to practice the incident response plan, including the alert process. It is much better to discover a gap in the plan during a practice run than when a real incident occurs. Regular practice helps identify the need for change in response to technological changes. For example, many organizations are switching from a traditional telephone system to one based on voice-over IP (VoIP). This can save considerable money, but it also means that if the computer network goes down, so, too, does the phone system. This side effect may not be noticed until the incident response plan is practiced.

Chief Information Security Officer (CISO)

COBIT control objective PO 4.8 specifies that responsibility for information security be assigned to someone at an appropriate senior level. One way to satisfy this objective is to create the position of chief information security officer (CISO), who should be independent of other information systems functions and should report to either the chief operating officer (COO) or the CEO. The CISO must understand the company's technology environment and work with the CIO to design, implement, and promote sound security policies and procedures. The CISO should also be an impartial assessor and evaluator of the IT environment. Accordingly, the CISO should have responsibility for ensuring that vulnerability and risk assessments are performed regularly and that security audits are carried out periodically. The CISO also needs to work closely with the person in charge of physical security, because unauthorized physical access can allow an intruder to bypass the most elaborate logical access controls. To facilitate integrating physical and information security, some organizations have created a new position, the chief security officer (CSO), who is in charge of both functions.

Patch Management

COBIT control objective DS 5.9 stresses the need to fix known vulnerabilities by installing the latest updates to both security programs (e.g., antivirus and firewall software) and to operating systems and other applications programs in order to protect the organization from viruses and other types of malware. This is important because the number of reported vulnerabilities rises each year. A primary cause of the rise in reported vulnerabilities is the ever-increasing size and complexity of software. Many widely used programs now contain millions of lines of code. This means that even if 99.99% of the code is "bug-free," there are still 100 possible vulnerabilities for each million lines of code. Hackers and security consulting firms constantly search for vulnerabilities in widely used software. Once a vulnerability has been identified, the next step is to explore and document how to take advantage of it to compromise a system. The set of instructions for taking advantage of a vulnerability is called an *exploit*. Although the creation of an exploit takes considerable skill, once an exploit is published on the Internet it can be easily used by anyone who runs that code.

The widespread availability of many exploits and their ease of use make it important for organizations to take steps to quickly correct known vulnerabilities in software they use. A *patch* is code released by software developers that fixes a particular vulnerability. *Patch management* is the process for regularly applying patches and updates to all software used by the organization. This is not as straightforward as it sounds. Patches represent modifications to already complex software. Consequently, patches sometimes create new problems because of unanticipated side effects. Therefore, organizations need to carefully test the effect of patches prior to deploying them; otherwise, they run the risk of crashing important applications. Further complicating matters is the fact that there are likely to be multiple patches released each year for each software program used by an organization. Thus, organizations may face the task of applying hundreds of patches to thousands of machines every year. This is one area where intrusion prevention systems (IPSs) hold great promise. If an IPS can be quickly updated with the information needed to respond to new vulnerabilities and block new exploits, the organization can use the IPS to buy the time needed to thoroughly test patches before applying them.

Security Implications of Virtualization and the Cloud

Recently, many organizations have embraced virtualization and cloud computing to enhance both efficiency and effectiveness. *Virtualization* takes advantage of the power and speed of modern computers to run multiple systems simultaneously on one physical computer. This cuts hardware costs, because fewer servers need to be purchased. Fewer machines mean lower maintenance costs. Data center costs also fall because less space needs to be rented, which also reduces utility costs.

Cloud computing takes advantage of the high bandwidth of the modern global telecommunication network to enable employees to use a browser to remotely access software (software as a service), data storage devices (storage as a service), hardware (infrastructure as a service), and entire application environments (platform as a service). The arrangement is referred to as a "private," "public," or "hybrid" cloud depending upon whether the remotely accessed resources are entirely owned by the organization, a third party, or a mix of the two, respectively. Cloud computing can potentially generate significant cost savings. For example, instead of purchasing, installing, and maintaining separate copies of software for each end user, an organization can purchase one copy, install it on a central server, and pay for the right of a specified number of employees to simultaneously use a browser to remotely access and use that software. Public clouds actually eliminate the need for making major capital investments in IT, with organizations purchasing (and expensing) their use of computing resources on a pay-for-use or subscription basis. In addition to reducing costs, the centralization of computing resources with cloud computing (whether public, private, or hybrid) makes it easier to change software and hardware, thereby improving flexibility.

Virtualization and cloud computing alter the risk of some information security threats. For example, unsupervised physical access in a virtualization environment exposes not just one device but the entire virtual network to the risk of theft or destruction and compromise. Similarly, compromising a cloud provider's system may provide unauthorized access to multiple systems. Moreover, in cloud computing authentication often relies solely on passwords. Thus, the only thing protecting one cloud customer's data from unauthorized access by another cloud customer is the strength of the passwords used to sign onto the system. Public clouds also raise concerns about the other aspects of systems reliability (confidentiality, privacy, processing integrity, and availability) because the organization is outsourcing control of its data and computing resources to a third party.

Although virtualization and cloud computing can increase the risk of some threats, they also offer the opportunity to significantly improve overall security. For example, implementing strong access controls in the cloud or over the server that hosts a virtual network provides good security over all the systems contained therein. The important point is that all of the controls discussed previously in this chapter remain relevant in the context of virtualization and cloud computing. Strong user access controls, ideally involving the use of multifactor authentication, and physical access controls are essential. Virtual firewalls, IPS, and IDS need to be deployed to isolate virtual machines and cloud customers from one another. The need for timely detection of problems continues to exist, as does the need for corrective controls such as patch management. Thus, virtualization and cloud computing can have either positive or negative effects on the overall level of information security, depending upon how well the organization or the cloud provider implements the various layers of preventive, detective, and corrective controls.

Summary and Case Conclusion

Jason Scott finished his review of the company's information systems security procedures and prepared an interim report for his supervisor. The report began by explaining that security was one of five principles of systems reliability. Because absolute security is not practical, the report noted that Northwest Industries' goal should be to adopt the time-based model of security and employ a combination of detective and corrective controls that would allow the company to detect and respond to attacks in less time than it would take an intruder to break through its preventive controls and successfully attack the system. In addition, the report pointed out the value of deploying redundant, overlapping controls to provide layers of defense-in-depth.

Jason's report then described and evaluated the various security procedures in place at Northwest Industries. Physical access to the company's office is limited to one main entrance, which is staffed at all times by a security guard. All visitors have to sign in at the security desk and are escorted at all times by an employee. Access to rooms with computing equipment requires insertion of an employee badge in a card reader plus entry of a PIN in a keypad lock on the door. Remote access controls include a main firewall that performs stateful packet filtering and additional internal firewalls that segregate different business functions from one another. The information security staff regularly scans all equipment for vulnerabilities and makes sure that every employee's workstation is running a current version of the company's A-V software as well as a firewall. To improve security awareness, all employees attend monthly hour-long workshops that cover a different current security issue each month. The company uses intrusion detection systems, and top management receives monthly reports on the effectiveness of system security. Corrective controls include a computer incident response team and quarterly practice of an incident response plan.

Jason's report concluded by emphasizing that information security is primarily a management issue, not an IT issue. Jason explained how management's attitude and philosophy about security are critical determinants of an organization's overall security. He noted that when top management considers information security to be an integral part of the organization's processes, similar to quality, security is more likely to be proactive and effective. In contrast, if top management considers information security to be primarily an issue of compliance with regulatory requirements, security is more likely to be reactive in nature and less effective.

Jason's supervisor was pleased with his interim report. She asked Jason to continue his review of the company's information systems by examining two of the other principles of systems reliability in the AICPA's Trust Services framework: confidentiality and privacy.

Key Terms

defense-in-depth   223
time-based model of
    security   224
social engineering   225
authentication   226
biometric identifier   227
multifactor
    authentication   228
multimodal
    authentication   228
authorization   228
access control
    matrix   228
compatibility test   228
border router   230
firewall   230

demilitarized zone
    (DMZ)   230
Transmission Control
    Protocol (TCP)   231
Internet Protocol (IP)   231
routers   232
access control list
    (ACL)   233
static packet filtering   233
stateful packet filtering   233
deep packet inspection   233
intrusion prevention system
    (IPS)   234
Remote Authentication
    Dial-In User Service
    (RADIUS)   234

war dialing   235
endpoints   236
vulnerabilities   236
vulnerability scanners   236
hardening   236
log analysis   237
intrusion detection system
    (IDS)   238
penetration test   238
computer incident response
    team (CIRT)   239
exploit   240
patch   240
patch management   240
virtualization   240
cloud computing   241

AIS IN ACTION

Chapter Quiz

1. Which of the following statements is true?
   a. The concept of defense-in-depth reflects the fact that security involves the use of a few sophisticated technical controls.
   b. Information security is necessary for protecting confidentiality, privacy, integrity of processing, and availability of information resources.

   c. The time-based model of security can be expressed in the following formula: $P < D + C$

   d. Information security is primarily an IT issue, not a managerial concern.

2. Which of the following is a preventive control?
   a. training
   b. log analysis
   c. CIRT
   d. virtualization

3. The control procedure designed to restrict what portions of an information system an employee can access and what actions he or she can perform is called _____.
   a. authorization
   b. authentication
   c. intrusion prevention
   d. intrusion detection

4. A weakness that an attacker can take advantage of to either disable or take control of a system is called a(n) _____.
   a. exploit
   b. patch
   c. vulnerability
   d. attack

5. Which of the following is a corrective control designed to fix vulnerabilities?
   a. virtualization
   b. patch management
   c. penetration testing
   d. authorization

6. Which of the following is a detective control?
   a. hardening endpoints
   b. physical access controls
   c. penetration testing
   d. patch management

7. A firewall that implements perimeter defense by examining only information in the packet header of a single IP packet in isolation is using a technique referred to as

   _____.
   a. deep packet inspection
   b. static packet filtering
   c. stateful packet filtering
   d. single packet inspection

8. Which of the following techniques is the most effective way to protect the perimeter?
   a. deep packet inspection
   b. static packet filtering
   c. stateful packet filtering
   d. All of the above are equally effective.

9. Which of the following combinations of credentials is an example of multifactor authentication?
   a. voice recognition and a fingerprint reader
   b. a PIN and an ATM card
   c. a password and a user ID
   d. all of the above

10. Modifying default configurations to turn off unnecessary programs and features to improve security is called _____.
    a. user account management
    b. defense-in-depth
    c. vulnerability scanning
    d. hardening

Discussion Questions

8.1. Explain why an organization would want to use all of the following information security controls: firewalls, intrusion prevention systems, intrusion detection systems, and a CIRT.

8.2. What are the advantages and disadvantages of having the person responsible for information security report directly to the chief information officer (CIO), who has overall responsibility for all aspects of the organization's information systems?

8.3. Reliability is often included in service level agreements (SLAs) when an organization is outsourcing. The toughest thing is to decide how much reliability is enough. Consider an application such as e-mail. If an organization outsources its e-mail to a cloud provider, what is the difference between 95%, 99%, 99.99%, and 99.9999% reliability?

8.4. What is the difference between authentication and authorization?

8.5. What are the limitations, if any, of relying on the results of penetration tests to assess the overall level of security?

8.6. Security awareness training is necessary to teach employees "safe computing" practices. The key to effectiveness, however, is that it changes employee behavior. How can organizations maximize the effectiveness of their security awareness training programs?

8.7. What is the relationship between COSO, COBIT, and the AICPA's Trust Services frameworks?

Problems

8.1. Match the following terms with their definitions:

Term	Definition
____ 1. Vulnerability	a. Code that corrects a flaw in a program
____ 2. Exploit	b. Verification of claimed identity
____ 3. Authentication	c. The firewall technique that filters traffic by comparing the information in packet headers to a table of established connections
____ 4. Authorization	d. A flaw or weakness in a program
____ 5. Demilitarized zone (DMZ)	e. A test that determines the time it takes to compromise a system
____ 6. Deep packet inspection	f. A subnetwork that is accessible from the Internet but separate from the organization's internal network
____ 7. Router	g. The device that connects the organization to the Internet
____ 8. Social engineering	h. The rules (protocol) that govern routing of packets across networks
____ 9. Firewall	i. The rules (protocol) that govern the division of a large file into packets and subsequent reassembly of the file from those packets
____ 10. Hardening	j. An attack that involves deception to obtain access
____ 11. CIRT	k. A device that provides perimeter security by filtering packets
____ 12. Patch	l. The set of employees assigned responsibility for resolving problems and incidents
____ 13. Virtualization	m. Restricting the actions that a user is permitted to perform
____ 14. Transmission Control Protocol (TCP)	n. Improving security by removal or disabling of unnecessary programs and features
____ 15. Static packet filtering	o. A device that uses the Internet Protocol (IP) to send packets across networks
____ 16. Border router	p. A detective control that identifies weaknesses in devices or software
____ 17. Vulnerability scan	q. A firewall technique that filters traffic by examining the packet header of a single packet in isolation
____ 18. Penetration test	r. The process of applying code supplied by a vendor to fix a problem in that vendor's software
____ 19. Patch management	s. Software code that can be used to take advantage of a flaw and compromise a system

Term	Definition
____ **20.** Cloud computing	t. A firewall technique that filters traffic by examining not just packet header information but also the contents of a packet
	u. The process of running multiple machines on one physical server
	v. An arrangement whereby a user remotely accesses software, hardware, or other resources via a browser.

8.2. Install and run the latest version of the Microsoft Baseline Security Analyzer (MBSA) on your home computer or laptop. Write a report explaining the weaknesses identified by the tool and how to best correct them. Attach a copy of the MBSA output to your report.

8.3. The following table lists the actions that various employees are permitted to perform:

Employee	Permitted Actions
Able	Check customer account balances
	Check inventory availability
Baker	Change customer credit limits
Charley	Update inventory records for sales and purchases
Denise	Add new customers
	Delete customers whose accounts have been written off as uncollectible
	Add new inventory items
	Remove discontinued inventory items
Ellen	Review audit logs of employee actions

Complete the following access control matrix so that it enables each employee to perform those specific activities:

Employee	Customer Master file	Inventory Master File	Payroll Master File	System Log Files
Able				
Baker				
Charley				
Denise				
Ellen				

Use the following codes:

0 = No access

1 = Read-only access

2 = Read and modify records

3 = Read, modify, create, and delete records

8.4. Which preventive, detective, and/or corrective controls would best mitigate the following threats?

a. An employee's laptop was stolen at the airport. The laptop contained personal information about the company's customers that could potentially be used to commit identity theft.

b. A salesperson successfully logged into the payroll system by guessing the payroll supervisor's password.

c. A criminal remotely accessed a sensitive database using the authentication credentials (user ID and strong password) of an IT manager. At the time the attack occurred, the IT manager was logged into the system at his workstation at company headquarters.

d. An employee received an e-mail purporting to be from her boss informing her of an important new attendance policy. When she clicked on a link embedded in the e-mail to view the new policy, she infected her laptop with a keystroke logger.

e. A company's programming staff wrote custom code for the shopping cart feature on its Web site. The code contained a buffer overflow vulnerability that could be exploited when the customer typed in the ship-to address.

f. A company purchased the leading "off-the-shelf" e-commerce software for linking its electronic storefront to its inventory database. A customer discovered a way to directly access the back-end database by entering appropriate SQL code.

g. Attackers broke into the company's information system through a wireless access point located in one of its retail stores. The wireless access point had been purchased and installed by the store manager without informing central IT or security.

h. An employee picked up a USB drive in the parking lot and plugged it into his laptop to "see what was on it." As a result, a keystroke logger was installed on that laptop.

i. Once an attack on the company's Web site was discovered, it took more than 30 minutes to determine who to contact to initiate response actions.

j. To facilitate working from home, an employee installed a modem on his office workstation. An attacker successfully penetrated the company's system by dialing into that modem.

k. An attacker gained access to the company's internal network by installing a wireless access point in a wiring closet located next to the elevators on the fourth floor of a high-rise office building that the company shared with seven other companies.

8.5. What are the advantages and disadvantages of the three types of authentication credentials (something you know, something you have, and something you are)?

8.6. a. Apply the following data to evaluate the time-based model of security for the XYZ Company. Does the XYZ Company satisfy the requirements of the time-based model of security? Why?
   • Estimated time for attacker to successfully penetrate system = 25 minutes
   • Estimated time to detect an attack in progress and notify appropriate information security staff = 5 minutes (best case) to 10 minutes (worst case)
   • Estimated time to implement corrective actions = 6 minutes (best case) to 20 minutes (worst case)

   b. Which of the following security investments to you recommend? Why?
   1. Invest $50,000 to increase the estimated time to penetrate the system by 4 minutes
   2. Invest $50,000 to reduce the time to detect an attack to between 2 minutes (best case) and 6 minutes (worst case)
   3. Invest $50,000 to reduce the time required to implement corrective actions to between 4 minutes (best case) and 14 minutes (worst case)

8.7. Explain how the following items individually and collectively affect the overall level of security provided by using a password as an authentication credential.
   a. Length
   b. Complexity requirements (which types of characters are required to be used: numbers, alphabetic, case-sensitivity of alphabetic, special symbols such as $ or !)
   c. Maximum password age (how often password must be changed)
   d. Minimum password age (how long a password must be used before it can be changed)
   e. Maintenance of password history (how many prior passwords the system remembers to prevent reselection of the same password when the user is required to change passwords)
   f. account lockout threshold (how many failed log-in attempts are allowed before the account is locked)
   g. time frame during which account lockout threshold is applied (i.e., if lockout threshold is five failed log-in attempts, the time frame is the period during which those five failures must occur: within 15 minutes, 1 hour, 1 day, etc.).
   h. account lockout duration (how long the account remains locked after the user exceeds the maximum allowable number of failed log-in attempts)

8.8. The chapter briefly discussed the following three common attacks against applications:
   a. Buffer overflows
   b. SQL injection
   c. Cross-site scripting

Required

Research each of these three attacks, and write a report explaining in detail how each attack actually works and describing suggested controls for reducing the risks that these attacks will be successful.

8.9. Physical security is extremely important. Read the article "19 Ways to Build Physical Security into a Data Center," which appeared in the November 2005 issue of *CSO Magazine* (you can find the article at www.csoonline.com/read/110105/datacenter.html). Which methods would you expect almost any major corporation to use? Which might likely be justified only at a financial institution?

Case 8-1 Costs of Preventive Security

Firewalls are one of the most fundamental and important security tools. You are likely familiar with the software-based host firewall that you use on your laptop or desktop. Such firewalls should also be installed on every computer in an organization. However, organizations also need corporate-grade firewalls, which are usually, but not always, dedicated special-purpose hardware devices. Conduct some research to identify three different brands of such corporate-grade firewalls, and write a report that addresses the following points:

- Cost
- Technique (deep packet inspection, static packet filtering, or stateful packet filtering)
- Ease of configuration and use

Case 8-2 Developing an Information Security Checklist

Obtain a copy of COBIT (available at www.isaca.org), and read section DS 5. Design a checklist for assessing each of the 11 detailed information security control objectives. The checklist should contain questions to which a yes response represents a control strength, a no response represents a control weakness, plus a possible N/A response. Provide a brief reason for asking each question. Organize your checklist as follows:

Question	Yes	No	N/A	Reason for asking
1. Is there regular security awareness training?				Training is one of the most important preventive controls because many security incidents happen due to either human error or social engineering.

AIS IN ACTION SOLUTIONS

Quiz Key

1. Which of the following statements is true?
   a. The concept of defense-in-depth reflects the fact that security involves the use of a few sophisticated technical controls. (Incorrect. The concept of defense-in-depth is based on the idea that, given enough time and resources, any single control, no matter how sophisticated, can be overcome—therefore, the use of redundant, overlapping controls maximizes security.)

▸ b. Information security is necessary for protecting confidentiality, privacy, integrity of processing, and availability of information resources. (Correct. As Figure 8-2 shows, security is the foundation for achieving the other four components of system reliability.)

c. The time-based model of security can be expressed in the following formula: $P < D + C$ (Incorrect. The formula is $P > D + C$.)

d. Information security is primarily an IT issue, not a managerial concern. (Incorrect. Security is primarily a managerial issue because only management can choose the most appropriate risk response to protect the organization's information resources.)

2. Which of the following is a preventive control?

▸ a. training (Correct. Training is designed to prevent employees from falling victim to social engineering attacks and unsafe practices such as clicking on links embedded in e-mail from unknown sources.)

b. log analysis (Incorrect. Log analysis involves examining a record of events to discover anomalies. Thus, it is a detective control.)

c. CIRT (Incorrect. The purpose of a computer incident response team is to respond to and remediate problems and incidents. Thus, it is a corrective control.)

d. virtualization (Incorrect. Virtualization involves using one physical computer to run multiple virtual machines. It is primarily a cost-control measure, not an information security control procedure.)

3. The control procedure designed to restrict what portions of an information system an employee can access and what actions he or she can perform is called _____.

a. authentication (Incorrect. Authentication is the process of verifying a user's identity to decide whether or not to grant that person access.)

▸ b. authorization (Correct. Authorization is the process of controlling what actions—read, write, delete, etc.—a user is permitted to perform.)

c. intrusion prevention (Incorrect. Intrusion prevention systems monitor patterns in network traffic to identify and stop attacks.)

d. intrusion detection (Incorrect. Intrusion detection is a detective control that identifies when an attack has occurred.)

4. A weakness that an attacker can take advantage of to either disable or take control of a system is called a(n) _____.

a. exploit (Incorrect. An exploit is the software code used to take advantage of a weakness.)

b. patch (Incorrect. A patch is code designed to fix a weakness.)

▸ c. vulnerability (Correct. A vulnerability is any weakness that can be used to disable or take control of a system.)

d. attack (Incorrect. An attack is the action taken against a system. To succeed, it exploits a vulnerability.)

5. Which of the following is a corrective control designed to fix vulnerabilities?

a. virtualization (Incorrect. Virtualization involves using one physical computer to run multiple virtual machines. It is primarily a cost-control measure, not an information security control procedure.)

▸ b. patch management (Correct. Patch management involves replacing flawed code that represents a vulnerability with corrected code, called a patch.)

c. penetration testing (Incorrect. Penetration testing is detective control.)

d. authorization (Incorrect. Authorization is a preventive control used to restrict what users can do.)

6. Which of the following is a detective control?

a. Endpoint hardening (Incorrect. Hardening is a preventive control that seeks to eliminate vulnerabilities by reconfiguring devices and software.)

b. Physical access controls (Incorrect. Physical access controls are a preventive control designed to restrict access to a system.)

▸ c. Penetration testing (Correct. Penetration testing is a detective control designed to identify how long it takes to exploit a vulnerability.)

    d. Patch management (Incorrect. Patch management is a corrective control that fixes vulnerabilities.)

7. A firewall that implements perimeter defense by examining only information in the packet header of a single IP packet in isolation is using a technique referred to as _____.

    a. deep packet inspection (Incorrect. Deep packet inspection examines the contents of the data in the body of the IP packet, not just the information in the packet header.)

  ▶ **b.** static packet filtering (Correct. Static packet filtering examines the headers of individual IP packets.)

    c. stateful packet filtering (Incorrect. Stateful packet filtering examines not only the headers of individual IP packets but also a state table to determine whether incoming packets are part of an already established connection.)

    d. single packet inspection (Incorrect. There is no such thing.)

8. Which of the following techniques is the most effective way to protect the perimeter?

  ▶ **a.** deep packet inspection (Correct. Deep packet inspection examines the contents of the data in the body of the IP packet, not just the information in the packet header. This is the best way to catch malicious code.)

    b. static packet filtering (Incorrect. Static packet filtering examines the headers of individual IP packets. It can be fooled by attacks that pretend to be sending a response to earlier outbound messages.)

    c. stateful packet filtering (Incorrect. Stateful packet filtering maintains information about "state" or connections initiated by the organization, but it examines only the information in the packet header. Therefore, it cannot detect malware in the payload of a message.)

    d. All of the above are equally effective (Incorrect. Choices b and c are less effective than choice a.)

9. Which of the following combinations of credentials is an example of multifactor authentication?

    a. voice recognition and a fingerprint reader (Incorrect. This is a combination of two biometric credentials and is an example of multimodal authentication.)

  ▶ **b.** a PIN and an ATM card (Correct. The PIN is something a person knows, the ATM card is something the person has.)

    c. password and a user ID (Incorrect. These are both things a person knows and thus represent an example of multimodal authentication.)

    d. all of the above (Incorrect. Only choice b is correct.)

10. Modifying default configurations to turn off unnecessary programs and features to improve security is called _____.

    a. user account management (Incorrect. User account management is a preventive control that limits what a user can do.)

    b. defense-in-depth (Incorrect. Defense-in-depth is the general security principle of using multiple overlapping controls to protect a system.)

    c. vulnerability scanning (Incorrect. Vulnerability scanning is a detective control designed to identify weaknesses.)

  ▶ **d.** hardening (Correct. This is the definition of hardening.)

Chapter 9

Information Systems Controls for Systems Reliability—Part 2: Confidentiality and Privacy

INTEGRATIVE CASE NORTHWEST INDUSTRIES

Jason Scott was preparing for his meeting with the company's chief information security officer (CISO). Although Jason was satisfied that Northwest Industries' computer security policies and procedures provided the company with adequate protection against intrusions, he was concerned about other aspects of systems reliability. In particular, he wanted to learn what Northwest Industries was doing to address the following issues:

1. Protecting the confidentiality of sensitive corporate information, such as marketing plans and trade secrets
2. Protecting the privacy of personal information collected from customers

Jason planned to use his interview with the CISO to obtain a general understanding of the company's information systems controls. He then planned to follow up by collecting evidence about the effectiveness of those controls.

Introduction

Chapter 8 discussed information security, which is the fundamental principle of systems reliability. This chapter covers two other important principles of reliable systems in the Trust Services Framework: preserving the confidentiality of an organization's intellectual property and protecting

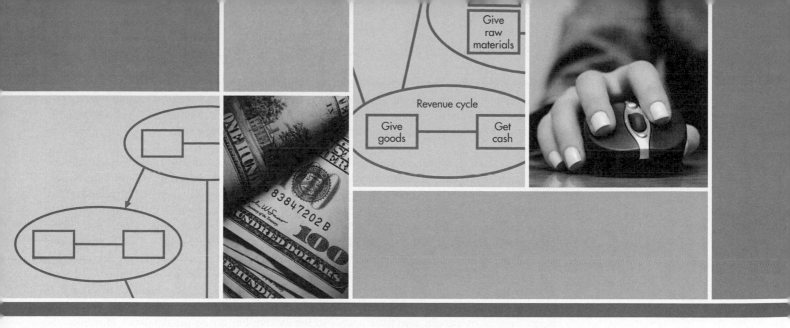

the privacy of personal information it collects from customers. We also discuss the topic of encryption in detail, because it is a critical tool to protecting both confidentiality and privacy.

Preserving Confidentiality

Organizations possess a myriad of sensitive information, including strategic plans, trade secrets, cost information, legal documents, and process improvements. This intellectual property often is crucial to the organization's long-run competitive advantage and success. Consequently, preserving the confidentiality of the organization's intellectual property, and similar information shared by its business partners, has long been recognized as a basic objective of information security. This section discusses the actions that must be taken to preserve confidentiality: (1) identification and classification of the information to be protected, (2) encryption of sensitive information, (3) controlling access to sensitive information, and (4) training.

Identification and Classification of Information to be Protected

The first step to protect the confidentiality of intellectual property and other sensitive business information is to identify where such information resides and who has access to it. This sounds easy, but undertaking a thorough inventory of every digital and paper store of information is both time-consuming and costly because it involves examining more than just the contents of the organization's financial systems. For example, manufacturing firms typically employ large-scale factory automation. Those systems contain instructions that may provide significant cost advantages or product quality enhancements over those of competitors and, therefore, must be protected from unauthorized disclosure or tampering.

After the information that needs to be protected has been identified, the next step, as discussed in the Control Objectives for Information and Related Technology (COBIT) control objective PO 2.3, is to classify the information in terms of its value to the organization. Information classification is not a task to be delegated solely to information systems professionals; to properly recognize the information's value, the process also needs input from senior management. Once the information has been classified, the appropriate set of controls can be deployed to protect it.

Protecting Confidentiality with Encryption

Encryption (to be discussed later in this chapter) is an extremely important and effective tool to protect confidentiality. It is the only way to protect information in transit over the Internet. It is also a necessary part of defense-in-depth to protect information stored on Web sites or in a public cloud. For example, many accounting firms have created secure portals that they use to share sensitive audit, tax, or consulting information with clients. The security of such portals, however, is limited by the strength of the authentication methods used to restrict access. In most cases, this involves only single factor authentication via a password. Encrypting the client's data that is stored on the portal provides an additional layer of protection in the event of unauthorized access to the portal. Similarly, encrypting information stored in a public cloud protects it from unauthorized access by employees of the cloud service provider or by anyone else who is using that same cloud.

Encryption, however, is not a panacea. Some sensitive information, particularly "knowhow" such as process shortcuts, may not be stored digitally and, therefore, cannot be protected by being encrypted. In addition, encryption protects information only in specific situations. For example, full disk encryption protects the information stored on a laptop in the event that it is lost or stolen. The person who steals or finds such a laptop will not be able to read any of the encrypted information, *unless* he or she can log on as the legitimate owner. That is why strong authentication is also needed. In addition, the information on the laptop is decrypted whenever the owner has logged on, which means that anyone who can sit down at the keyboard can view the sensitive information. Therefore, physical access controls are also needed. Similarly, in enterprise systems, encrypting information while it is stored in the database protects it from being viewed by people who have access to the system but not to the database. However, the database has to decrypt the information in order to process it; therefore, anyone who can log on to the database can potentially see confidential information. That is why strong access controls are also needed. In summary, sensitive information is exposed in plain view whenever it is being processed by a program, displayed on a monitor, or included in printed reports. Consequently, protecting confidentiality requires application of the principle of defense-in-depth: supplementing encryption with access controls and training.

Controlling Access to Sensitive Information

Chapter 8 discussed how organizations use authentication and authorization controls to restrict access to information systems that contain sensitive information. *Information rights management (IRM)* software provides an additional layer of protection to specific information resources, offering the capability not only to limit access to specific files or documents, but also to specify the actions (read, copy, print, download to USB devices, etc.) that individuals who are granted access to that resource can perform. Some IRM software even has the capability to limit those privileges to a specific period of time and to remotely erase protected files. Either the creator of the information or the person responsible for managing it must assign the access rights. To access an IRM-protected resource, a person must first authenticate to the IRM server, which then downloads code containing the access-limiting instructions to that person's computer.

COBIT control objectives DS 12.2 and DS 12.3 address physical access controls, which are also important in preventing someone with unsupervised access from quickly downloading and copying gigabytes of confidential information onto a USB drive, an iPod, a cell phone, or other portable device. It is especially important to restrict access to rooms that contain printers, digital copiers, and fax machines because such devices typically possess large amounts of RAM, which may store any confidential information that was printed. Laptops and workstations should run password-protected screen savers automatically after a few minutes of inactivity, to prevent unauthorized viewing of sensitive information. Screen protection devices that limit the distance and angle from which information on a laptop or workstation monitor can be seen are also useful.

In addition, COBIT control objective DS 11.4 addresses the importance of controlling the *disposal* of information resources. Printed reports and microfilm containing confidential information should be shredded before being thrown out. Special procedures are needed to destroy information stored on magnetic and optical media. Using built-in operating system commands to delete that information is insufficient, because many utility programs exist that can recover such deleted files. Frequently, people who have purchased used computers, cell phones, digital copy machines, and other devices discover information that the previous owner thought had been deleted. Proper disposal of computer media requires use of special software designed to "wipe" the media clean by repeatedly overwriting the disk or drive with random patterns of data. Probably the safest alternative is to physically destroy (e.g., by incineration) magnetic and optical media that have been used to store extremely sensitive data.

Today, organizations constantly exchange information with their business partners and customers. Therefore, protecting confidentiality also requires controls over outbound communications. One tool for accomplishing that is *data loss prevention (DLP)* software, which works like antivirus programs in reverse, blocking outgoing messages (whether e-mail, IM, or other means) that contain key words or phrases associated with the intellectual property or other sensitive data the organization wants to protect. DLP software is a preventive control. It can and should be supplemented by embedding code called a *digital watermark* in documents. The digital watermark is a detective control that enables an organization to identify confidential information that has been disclosed. When an organization discovers documents containing its digital watermark on the Internet, it has evidence that the preventive controls designed to protect its sensitive information have failed. It should then investigate how the compromise occurred and take appropriate corrective action.

Access controls designed to protect confidentiality must be continuously reviewed and modified to respond to new threats created by technological advances. For example, the incorporation of digital cameras in cell phones makes it possible for visitors to surreptitiously capture confidential information. Consequently, many organizations now prohibit visitors from using cell phones while touring manufacturing facilities or other areas likely to contain confidential information. Because camera phones are so easy to hide, most organizations also require that visitors always be escorted by employees to further reduce the risk that the visitors photograph sensitive information.

Telephone conversations are another area affected by advances in technology. In the past, wiretaps were the only serious threat to the confidentiality of telephone conversations, and the difficulty of setting them up meant that the risk of that threat was relatively low. The use of voice-over-the-Internet (VoIP), however, means that telephone conversations are now routed as packets over the Internet. This means that VoIP telephone conversations are as vulnerable to interception as any other information sent over the Internet. Therefore, VoIP conversations about sensitive topics should be encrypted.

Virtualization and cloud computing also affect the risk of unauthorized access to sensitive or confidential information. An important control in virtual environments, including internally managed "private" clouds, is to use virtual firewalls to restrict access between different virtual machines that coexist on the same physical server. In addition, virtual machines that store highly sensitive or confidential data should not be hosted on the same physical server with virtual machines that are accessible via the Internet because of the risk that a skilled attacker might be able to break out of the latter and compromise the former. With public clouds, the data is stored elsewhere, and access occurs over the Internet via browsers. Therefore, all communication between users and the cloud must be encrypted. Browser software, however, often contains numerous vulnerabilities. Consequently, highly sensitive and confidential data probably should not be stored in a public cloud because of lack of control over where that information is actually stored and because of the risk of unauthorized access by other cloud customers, who may include competitors, or even by employees of the cloud provider.

Training

Training is arguably the most important control for protecting confidentiality. Employees need to know what information they can share with outsiders and what information needs to be protected. They also need to be taught how to protect confidential data. For example, employees need to know how to use encryption software. They also need to learn to always log out of applications before leaving their laptop or workstation unattended, to prevent other employees from obtaining unauthorized access to that information. Employees also need to know how to code reports they create to reflect the importance of the information contained therein so that other employees will know how to handle those reports. They also need to be taught not to leave reports containing sensitive information in plain view on their desks when they leave.

Training is particularly important concerning the proper use of e-mail, instant messaging (chat), and blogs because it is impossible to control the subsequent distribution of information once it has been sent or posted through any of those methods. For example, it is important to teach employees not to routinely use the "reply all" option with e-mail because doing so may disclose sensitive information to people who should not see it. Employees also need to be taught how to participate in discussions at conferences or professional education courses so that they do not inadvertently disclose information that might compromise their employer's competitive advantage. Employees often do not realize the importance of information they possess, such as time-saving steps or undocumented features they have discovered when using a particular software program. Therefore, it is important for management to inform employees who will attend external training courses, trade shows, or conferences whether they can discuss such information or whether it should be protected because it provides the company a cost savings or quality improvement advantage over its competitors.

With proper training, employees can play an important role in protecting the confidentiality of an organization's information and enhance the effectiveness of related controls. For example, if employees understand their organization's data classification scheme, they may recognize situations in which sensitive information has not been properly protected and proactively take appropriate corrective actions. Training in how to protect the confidentiality of an organization's intellectual property can also enhance its efforts to protect the privacy of personal information it collects from its customers.

Privacy

The Trust Services framework privacy principle is closely related to the confidentiality principle, differing primarily in that it focuses on protecting personal information about customers rather than organizational data. Consequently, the controls that need to be implemented to protect privacy are the same ones used to protect confidentiality: identification of the information that needs to be protected, encryption, access controls, and training.

Privacy Controls

As is the case for confidential information, the first step to protect the privacy of personal information collected from customers is to identify what information is collected, where it is stored, and who has access to it. It is then important to implement controls to protect that information because incidents involving the unauthorized disclosure of customers' personal information, whether intentional or accidental, can be costly. For example, the Massachusetts Data Security Law (201 CMR 17.00) fines companies $5,000 per record for data breaches. Governments may also restrict the daily business operations of companies that suffer a breach. For example, after Citibank's online credit card application in Taiwan was hacked and personal customer data compromised in November 2003, the Taiwanese government imposed a one-month moratorium on issuing new credit cards and a three-month suspension of the online application, until Citibank's online security could be independently verified.

Encryption is a fundamental control for protecting the privacy of personal information that organizations collect from their customers. That information needs to be encrypted both while it is in transit over the Internet and while it is in storage (indeed, the Massachusetts law mandates encryption of personal information at all times, whether in transit or in storage). Encrypting customers' personal information not only protects it from unauthorized disclosure, but also can save organizations money. Many states have passed data breach notification laws that require organizations to notify customers after any event, such as the loss or theft of a laptop or portable media device, that may have resulted in the unauthorized disclosure of customer personal information. This can be expensive for businesses that have hundreds of thousands or millions of customers. The costly notification requirement is usually waived, however, if the lost or stolen customer information was encrypted.

However, customers' personal information is not encrypted during processing or when it is displayed either on a monitor or in a printed report. Consequently, as with confidentiality, protecting customers' privacy requires supplementing encryption with access controls and training. Strong authentication and authorization controls restrict who can access systems that contain customers' personal information and the actions the users can perform once they are granted access. It is especially important to prevent programmers from having access to personal information, such as credit card numbers, telephone numbers, and Social Security numbers. In developing new applications, programmers often have to use "realistic" data to test the new system. It is tempting, and easy, to provide them with a copy of the data in the organization's transaction processing system. Doing so, however, gives programmers access to customers' personal information. To protect privacy, organizations should run *data masking* programs that replace customers' personal information with fake values (e.g., replace a real Social Security number with a different set of numbers that have the same characteristics, such as 123-45-6789) before sending that data to the program development and testing system.

Organizations also need to train employees on how to manage and protect personal information collected from customers. This is especially important for medical and financial information. Obviously, intentional misuse of such information can have serious negative economic consequences, including significant declines in stock prices. Unintentional disclosure of such personal information can also create costly problems, however. For example, someone denied health or life insurance because of improper disclosure of personal information is likely to sue the organization that was supposed to restrict access to that data.

Privacy Concerns

Two major privacy-related concerns are spam and identity theft.

SPAM   *Spam* is unsolicited e-mail that contains either advertising or offensive content. Spam is a privacy-related issue because recipients are often targeted as a result of unauthorized access to e-mail address lists and databases containing personal information. The volume of spam is overwhelming many e-mail systems. Spam not only reduces the efficiency benefits of e-mail but also is a source of many viruses, worms, spyware programs, and other types of malware. To deal with this problem, the U.S. Congress passed the Controlling the Assault of Non-Solicited Pornography and Marketing (CAN-SPAM) Act in 2003. CAN-SPAM provides both criminal and civil penalties for violations of the law. CAN-SPAM applies to commercial e-mail, which is defined as any e-mail that has the primary purpose of advertising or promotion. This covers much of the legitimate e-mail that many organizations send to their customers, suppliers, and, in the case of nonprofit organizations, their donors. Thus, organizations need to be sure to follow CAN-SPAM's guidelines or risk sanctions. Key provisions include the following:

- The sender's identity must be clearly displayed in the header of the message.
- The subject field in the header must clearly identify the message as an advertisement or solicitation.
- The body of the message must provide recipients with a working link that can be used to opt out of future e-mail. After receiving an opt-out request, organizations have 10 days to implement steps to ensure they do not send any additional unsolicited e-mail to that address. This means that organizations need to assign someone responsibility for processing opt-out requests.
- The body of the message must include the sender's valid postal address. Although not required, best practice would be to also include full street address, telephone, and fax numbers.
- Organizations should not send commercial e-mail to randomly generated addresses, nor should they set up Web sites designed to "harvest" e-mail addresses of potential customers. Experts recommend that organizations redesign their own Web sites to include a visible means for visitors to opt in to receive e-mail, such as checking a box.

IDENTITY THEFT   Another privacy-related issue that is of growing concern is identity theft. *Identity theft* is the unauthorized use of someone's personal information for the perpetrator's benefit. Often, identity theft is a financial crime, in which the perpetrator obtains loans or opens new credit cards in the victim's name and sometimes loots the victim's bank accounts. However, a growing portion of identity theft cases involve fraudulently obtaining medical care and services. Medical identity theft can have life-threatening consequences because of errors it may create in the victim's medical records, such as changing information about drug allergies or prescriptions. It may even cause victims to lose their insurance coverage if the thief has used up their annual or lifetime cap for coverage of a specific illness.

Focus 9-1 discusses the steps that individuals should take to minimize the risk of identity theft. Organizations, however, also have a role to play in preventing identity theft. Customers entrust them with personal information. Organizations economically benefit from having access to that information. Therefore, organizations have an ethical and moral obligation to implement controls to protect the personal information that they collect from and about their customers.

FOCUS 9-1 Protecting Yourself from Identity Theft

Victims of identity theft often spend much time and money to recover from it. Fortunately, there are a number of simple steps you can take to minimize your risk of becoming a victim of identity theft.

- Shred all documents that contain personal information, especially unsolicited credit card offers, before discarding them. Cross-cut shredders are much more effective than strip-cut shredders.
- Never send personal information (Social Security number, passport number, etc.) in unencrypted e-mail.
- Beware of e-mail, telephone, and print requests to "verify" personal information that the requesting party should already possess. For example, credit card companies will never need to ask you for the three- or four-digit security code on your card. Similarly, the IRS will never e-mail you asking you to send personally identifying information in response to an audit.
- Do not carry your Social Security card with you. Be wary of requests to reveal the last four digits of your Social Security number. The first three and middle two digits are assigned based on the location and date you applied for a Social Security number and, therefore, can be discovered through research, but the last four digits are assigned randomly.

- Print only your initials and last name, rather than your full name, on checks. This prevents a thief from knowing how you sign your name.
- Limit the amount of other information (address and phone number) preprinted on checks, and consider totally eliminating such information.
- Do not place outgoing mail containing checks or personal information in your mailbox for pickup.
- Do not carry more than a few blank checks with you.
- Use special software to thoroughly clean any digital media prior to disposal, or physically destroy the media. It is especially important to thoroughly erase or destroy hard drives (for computers, printers, *and* copy machines) prior to donating or disposing of obsolete equipment because they likely contain information about online financial transactions.
- Monitor your credit reports regularly.
- File a police report as soon as you discover that your purse or wallet was lost or stolen.
- Make photocopies of driver's licenses, passports, and credit cards. Store this information, along with the telephone numbers of all your credit cards, in a safe location to facilitate notifying appropriate authorities in the case that those documents are lost or stolen.
- Immediately cancel any stolen or lost credit cards.

Privacy Regulations and Generally Accepted Privacy Principles

Concerns about spam, identity theft, and protecting individual privacy have resulted in numerous government regulations. In addition to state disclosure laws, a number of federal regulations, including the Health Insurance Portability and Accountability Act (HIPAA), the Health Information Technology for Economic and Clinical Health Act (HITECH), and the Financial Services Modernization Act (commonly referred to as the Gramm–Leach–Bliley Act, representing the names of its three Congressional sponsors), impose specific requirements on organizations to protect the privacy of their customers' personal information. Many other countries also have regulations concerning the use and protection of customers' personal information.

To help organizations cost-effectively comply with these myriad requirements, the American Institute of Certified Public Accountants (AICPA) and the Canadian Institute of Chartered Accountants (CICA) jointly developed a framework called *Generally Accepted Privacy Principles (GAPP)*. GAPP identifies and defines the following 10 internationally recognized best practices for protecting the privacy of customers' personal information:

1. *Management.* Organizations need to establish a set of procedures and policies for protecting the privacy of personal information they collect from customers, as well as information about their customers obtained from third parties such as credit bureaus. They should assign responsibility and accountability for implementing those policies and procedures to a specific person or group of employees.
2. *Notice.* An organization should provide notice about its privacy policies and practices at or before the time it collects personal information from customers, or as soon as practicable thereafter. The notice should clearly explain what information is being collected, the reasons for its collection, and how the information will be used.
3. *Choice and consent.* Organizations should explain the choices available to individuals and obtain their consent prior to the collection and use of their personal information. The

nature of the choices offered differs across countries. In the United States, the default policy is called opt-out, which allows organizations to collect personal information about customers unless the customer explicitly objects. In contrast, the default policy in Europe is opt-in, meaning that organizations cannot collect personally identifying information unless customers explicitly give them permission to do so. However, even in the United States, GAPP recommends that organizations follow the opt-in approach and obtain explicit positive consent prior to collecting and storing sensitive personal information, such as financial or health records, political opinions, religious beliefs, and prior criminal history.

4. *Collection.*   An organization should collect only the information needed to fulfill the purposes stated in its privacy policies. One particular issue of concern is the use of cookies on Web sites. A *cookie* is a text file created by a Web site and stored on a visitor's hard disk. Cookies store information about what the user has done on the site. Most Web sites create multiple cookies per visit in order to make it easier for visitors to navigate to relevant portions of the Web site. It is important to note that cookies are text files, which means that they cannot "do" anything besides store information. They do, however, contain personal information that may increase the risk of identity theft and other privacy threats. Browsers can be configured to not accept cookies, and GAPP recommends that organizations employ procedures to accede to such requests and not surreptitiously use cookies.

5. *Use and retention.*   Organizations should use customers' personal information only in the manner described in their stated privacy policies and retain that information only as long as it is needed to fulfill a legitimate business purpose. This means that organizations need to create retention policies and assign someone responsibility for ensuring compliance with those policies.

6. *Access.*   An organization should provide individuals with the ability to access, review, correct, and delete the personal information stored about them.

7. *Disclosure to third parties.*   Organizations should disclose their customers' personal information to third parties only in the situations and manners described in the organization's privacy policies and only to third parties who provide the same level of privacy protection as does the organization which initially collected the information. This principle has implications for using cloud computing, because storing customers' personal information in the cloud may make it accessible to the cloud provider's employees; hence such information should be encrypted at all times.

8. *Security.*   An organization must take reasonable steps to protect its customers' personal information from loss or unauthorized disclosure. Indeed, it is not possible to protect privacy without adequate information security. Therefore, organizations must use the various preventive, detective, and corrective controls discussed in Chapter 8 to restrict access to their customers' personal information. However, achieving an acceptable level of information security is not sufficient to protect privacy. It is also necessary to train employees to avoid practices that can result in the unintentional or inadvertent breach of privacy. One sometimes overlooked issue concerns the disposal of computer equipment. It is important to follow the suggestions presented in the section on protecting confidentiality for properly erasing all information stored on computer media. Perhaps one of the most famous incidents of failing to properly erase information on a hard drive involved the disposal of an obsolete personal computer by a British bank. It was sold at an auction; the buyer found that it contained personal information about the financial affairs of Paul McCartney. E-mail presents a second threat vector to consider. For example, in 2002 drug manufacturer Eli Lilly sent an e-mail about its antidepressant drug Prozac to 669 patients. However, because it used the cc: function to send the message to all patients, the e-mails revealed the identities of other patients. A third often overlooked area concerns the release of electronic documents. Just as special procedures are used to black out (redact) personal information on paper documents, organizations should train employees to use procedures to remove such information on electronic documents in a manner that prevents the recipient of the document from recovering the redacted information.

9. *Quality.*   Organizations should maintain the integrity of their customers' personal information and employ procedures to ensure that it is reasonably accurate. Providing customers with a way to review the personal information stored by the organization (GAPP principle 6) can be a cost-effective way to achieve this objective.

10. *Monitoring and enforcement.*   An organization should assign one or more employees to be responsible for ensuring compliance with its stated privacy policies. Organizations must also periodically verify that their employees are complying with stated privacy policies. In addition, organizations should establish procedures for responding to customer complaints, including the use of a third-party dispute resolution process.

In summary, GAPP shows that protecting the privacy of customers' personal information requires first implementing a combination of policies, procedures, and technology, then training everyone in the organization to act in accordance with those plans, and subsequently monitoring compliance. Only senior management possesses the authority and the resources to accomplish this, which reinforces the fact that all aspects of systems reliability are, at bottom, a managerial issue and not just an IT issue. Because accountants and auditors serve as trusted advisors to senior management, they too need to be knowledgeable about these issues.

Encryption

Encryption is a preventive control that can be used to protect both confidentiality and privacy. Encryption protects data that is being sent over the Internet and it provides one last barrier that must be overcome by an intruder who has obtained unauthorized access to stored information. As we will see later, encryption also strengthens authentication procedures and plays an essential role in ensuring and verifying the validity of e-business transactions. Therefore, it is important for accountants, auditors, and systems professionals to understand encryption.

As shown in Figure 9-1, *encryption* is the process of transforming normal content, called *plaintext,* into unreadable gibberish, called *ciphertext. Decryption* reverses this process,

FIGURE 9-1

Steps in the Encryption and Decryption Process

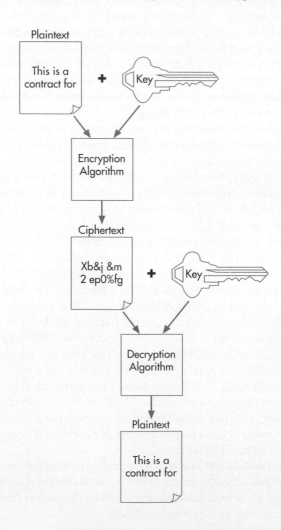

transforming ciphertext back into plaintext. Both encryption and decryption involve use of a key and an algorithm. Computers represent both plaintext and ciphertext as a series of binary digits (0s and 1s). The key is also a string of binary digits of a fixed length; for example, a 128-bit key consists of a string of 128 0s and 1s. The algorithm is a formula for combining the key and the text. Most documents are longer than the key, so the encryption process begins by dividing the plaintext into blocks, each block being of equal length to the key. Then the algorithm is applied to the key and the block of plaintext. For example, if a 128-bit key is being used, the computer first divides the document or file into 128-bit-long blocks and then combines each block with the key in the manner specified by the algorithm (for example, by adding them). The result is a ciphertext version of the document or file, equal in size to the original. To reproduce the original document, the computer first divides the ciphertext into 128-bit blocks and then applies the decryption key to each block.

Factors that Influence Encryption Strength

Three important factors determine the strength of any encryption system: (1) key length, (2) encryption algorithm, and (3) policies for managing the cryptographic keys.

KEY LENGTH Longer keys provide stronger encryption by reducing the number of repeating blocks in the ciphertext. This makes it harder to spot patterns in the ciphertext that reflect patterns in the original plaintext. For example, a 24-bit key encrypts plaintext in blocks of 24 bits. In English, each letter is represented by 8 bits. Thus, a 24-bit key encrypts English plaintext in chunks of three letters. This makes it easy to use information about relative word frequencies, such as the fact that *the* is one of the most common three-letter words in English, to "guess" that the most commonly recurring pattern of 24 bits in the ciphertext probably represents the English word *the* and proceed to "break" the encryption. That's why most encryption keys are at least 256 bits long (corresponding to 42 English letters), and are often 1024 bits or longer.

ENCRYPTION ALGORITHM The nature of the algorithm used to combine the key and the plaintext is important. A strong algorithm is difficult, if not impossible, to break by using brute-force guessing techniques. Secrecy is not necessary for strength. Indeed, the procedures used by the most accepted and widely used encryption algorithms are publicly available. Their strength is due not to the secrecy of their procedures, but to the fact that they have been rigorously tested and demonstrated to resist brute-force guessing attacks. Therefore, organizations should not attempt to create their own "secret" encryption algorithm, but instead should purchase products that use widely accepted standard algorithms whose strength has been proven.

POLICIES FOR MANAGING CRYPTOGRAPHIC KEYS CoBiT control objective DS 5.8 stresses the importance of sound practices for managing cryptographic keys. Indeed, this is often the most vulnerable aspect of encryption systems. No matter how long the keys are, or how strong an encryption algorithm is, if the keys have been compromised, the encryption can be easily broken. Therefore, cryptographic keys must be stored securely and protected with strong access controls. Best practices include not storing cryptographic keys in a browser or any other file that other users of that system can readily access and using a strong (and long) passphrase to protect the keys.

Organizations must also have a way to decrypt the data in the event that the employee who encrypted it is no longer present. One way to do this is to use encryption software that creates a built-in master key that can be used to decrypt anything encrypted by that software. An alternative is a process called *key escrow,* which involves making copies of all encryption keys used by employees and storing those copies securely. Organizations also need sound policies and procedures for issuing and revoking keys. Keys should be issued only to employees who handle sensitive data and, therefore, need the ability to encrypt it. It is also important to promptly revoke (cancel) keys when an employee leaves or when there is reason to believe the key has been compromised and to notify everyone who has relied upon those keys that they are no longer valid.

Types of Encryption Systems

There are two basic types of encryption systems. *Symmetric encryption systems* use the same key both to encrypt and to decrypt. DES and AES are examples of symmetric encryption systems. *Asymmetric encryption systems* use two keys. One key, called the *public key,* is widely distributed and available to everyone; the other, called the *private key,* is kept secret and known only to the owner of that pair of keys. Either the public or private key can be used to encrypt, but only the other key can decrypt the ciphertext. RSA and PGP are examples of asymmetric encryption systems.

Symmetric encryption is much faster than asymmetric encryption, but it has two major problems. First, both parties (sender and receiver) need to know the shared secret key. This means that the two parties need to have some method for securely exchanging the key that will be used to both encrypt and decrypt. E-mail is not a solution, because anyone who can intercept the e-mail would know the secret key. Thus, some other method of exchanging keys is needed. Although this could be done by telephone, postal mail, or private delivery services, such techniques quickly become cost-prohibitive, particularly for global communications. The second problem is that a separate secret key needs to be created for use by each party with whom the use of encryption is desired. For example, if company A wants to encrypt information it shares with companies B and C, but prevent B and C from having access to the other's information, it needs to create two encryption keys, one for use with company B and the other for use with company C. Otherwise, if Company A shared only one common secret key with both B and C, either company could decrypt any information to which it obtained access, even if intended for the other company. Thus, secure management of keys quickly becomes more complex as the number of participants in a symmetric encryption system increases.

Asymmetric encryption systems solve these problems. It does not matter who knows the public key, because any text encrypted with it can be decrypted only by using the corresponding private key. Therefore, the public key can be distributed by e-mail or even be posted on a Web site so that anyone who wants to can send encrypted information to the owner of that public key. Also, any number of parties can use the same public key to send encrypted messages because only the owner of the corresponding private key can decrypt the messages. In addition, information can be encrypted with the private key and then decrypted with the corresponding public key. Since only one party possesses the private key, asymmetric encryption systems make it possible to prove who created a document, thereby providing a means for creating legally binding electronic agreements.

The main drawback to asymmetric encryption systems is speed. Asymmetric encryption is much (thousands of times) slower than symmetric encryption, making it impractical for use to exchange large amounts of data over the Internet. Consequently, e-business uses both types of encryption systems. Symmetric encryption is used to encode most of the data being exchanged, and asymmetric encryption is used to safely send the symmetric key to the recipient for use in decrypting the ciphertext. In addition, as will be discussed later, asymmetric encryption is also used in combination with a process called hashing to create digital signatures.

Hashing

Hashing is a process that takes plaintext of any length and transforms it into a short code called a *hash*. For example, the SHA-256 algorithm creates a 256-bit hash, regardless of the size of the original plaintext. As Table 9-1 shows, hashing differs from encryption in two important aspects. First, encryption always produces ciphertext similar in length to the original plaintext, but hashing always produces a hash that is of a fixed short length, regardless of the length of the original

TABLE 9-1 Comparison of Hashing and Encryption

Hashing	Encryption
1. One-way function (cannot reverse, or "unhash").	1. Reversible (can decrypt back to plaintext).
2. Any size input yields same fixed-size output. For example, SHA-256 hashing algorithm produces a 256-bit hash for each of the following: + a one-sentence document + a one-page document + a ten-page document	2. Output size approximately the same as input size. For example: + a one-sentence document becomes a one-sentence encrypted document + a one-page document becomes a one-page encrypted document + a ten-page document becomes a ten-page encrypted document

plaintext. The second difference is that encryption is reversible, but hashing is not. Given the decryption key and the algorithm, ciphertext can be decrypted back into the original plaintext. In contrast, it is not possible to transform a hash back into the original plaintext, because hashing throws away information. For example, using SHA-256 to hash a 10,000-character document produces a string of 256 bits. There is no way to recover the 79,744 bits that were discarded and convert the short 256-bit hash back into the original document.

Hashing algorithms have another interesting property: They use every bit in the original plaintext to calculate the hash value. Therefore, changing any character in the document being hashed, such as replacing a 1 with a 7, adding or removing a single space, or even switching from upper- to lowercase produces a different hash value. This property of hashing algorithms provides a means to verify that the contents of a message have not been altered.

Digital Signatures

An important issue for business transactions has always been *nonrepudiation,* or how to create legally binding agreements that cannot be unilaterally repudiated by either party. Traditionally, this has been accomplished by signing contracts and other documents and then making photo-copies so that each party can retain an identical copy. Today, however, many business transactions occur digitally using the Internet. How can businesses obtain the same level of assurance about the enforceability of a digital transaction that a signed original or photocopy provides for a paper-based transaction? The answer is to use both hashing and asymmetric encryption to create a digital signature.

As Figure 9-2 shows, a *digital signature* is a hash of a document (or file) that is encrypted using the document creator's private key. Digital signatures provide proof about two important issues: (1) that a copy of a document or file has not been altered, and (2) who created the original version of a digital document or file. Thus, digital signatures provide assurance that someone cannot enter into a digital transaction and then subsequently deny they had done so and refuse to fulfill their side of the contract.

How do digital signatures provide this assurance? First, remember that an important property of a hash is that it reflects every bit in a document. Therefore, if two hashes are identical, it means that two documents or files are identical. Consequently, just as a photocopy can be compared to an original to verify that it has not been altered, comparing a hash of a document on one computer to a hash of a document on another computer provides a way to determine whether two documents are identical. Second, remember that in asymmetric encryption systems, something encrypted with a private key can only be decrypted with the corresponding public key. Therefore, if something can be decrypted with an entity's public key, it must have been encrypted with the corresponding private key, which proves that it had to have been encrypted by the owner of that pair of public and private keys.

Let us now see how both of these facts work together to provide nonrepudiation. For example, a supplier receives a purchase order along with a digital signature of that purchase order from a customer. The supplier can hash its copy of the purchase order using the same hashing algorithm that the customer used to create its digital signature. The supplier can then use the customer's public key to decrypt the digital signature, thereby producing a hash of some document that must have existed in the customer's information system. If the hash resulting from decrypting the customer's digital signature matches the hash of the purchase order in the supplier's possession, it proves that (1) the supplier's copy of the purchase order is an exact copy of a purchase order that exists on some other system (otherwise, the two hashes would not match) and (2) that

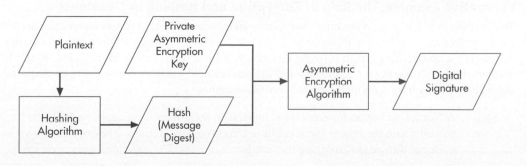

FIGURE 9-2

Creating a Digital Signature

the purchase order must have existed on the *customer's* information system (otherwise, decrypting the digital signature with the customer's public key would not have produced the hash).

One question still remains, however. Successfully using a public key to decrypt a document or file proves that it was created by the party possessing the corresponding private key. But how can the recipient be sure of the other party's identity? Returning to our prior example, how can a supplier know that the public key purportedly belonging to a customer really belongs to a legitimate customer and not to a criminal who created that pair of public and private keys? For that matter, how does the supplier obtain the customer's public key? The answers to these questions involve the use of digital certificates and a public key infrastructure.

Digital Certificates and Public Key Infrastructure

A *digital certificate* is an electronic document that contains an entity's public key and certifies the identity of the owner of that particular public key. Thus, digital certificates function like the digital equivalent of a driver's license or passport. Just as passports and drivers licenses are issued by a trusted independent party (the government) and employ mechanisms such as holograms and watermarks to prove that they are genuine, digital certificates are issued by an organization called a *certificate authority* and contain the certificate authority's digital signature to prove that they are genuine. Digital certificates intended for e-business use are typically issued by commercial certificate authorities, such as Thawte and VeriSign. These certificate authorities charge a fee to issue a pair of public and private keys and collect evidence to verify the claimed identity of the person or organization purchasing those keys and the corresponding digital certificate.

This system for issuing pairs of public and private keys and corresponding digital certificates is called a *public key infrastructure (PKI)*. The entire PKI system hinges on trusting the certificate authorities that issue the keys and certificates. The AICPA's Trust Services framework contains a list of criteria that can be used to evaluate the overall reliability of a particular certificate authority. One important factor concerns the procedures the certificate authority uses to verify the identity of an applicant for a digital certificate. Several classes of digital certificates exist. The cheapest, and least trustworthy, may involve nothing more than verifying the applicant's e-mail address. The most expensive certificates may require verification of the applicant's identity through use of credit reports and tax returns. Digital certificates are valid for only a specified period of time. Thus, a second important criterion for assessing the reliability of a certificate authority is the procedures it uses to update certificates and revoke expired digital certificates.

Digital certificates provide a mechanism for securely obtaining and verifying the validity of another party's public key. Organizations can store their digital certificates on their Web sites. Browsers are designed to automatically obtain a copy of a Web site's digital certificate to acquire the site's public key. (You can manually examine the contents of a Web site's digital certificate by double-clicking on the lock icon that appears in your browser window when you visit a Web site). Browsers also are designed to automatically check the validity of a Web site's digital certificate. Recall that a digital certificate is signed by the issuing certificate authority. All browsers come preloaded with the public keys of widely recognized certificate authorities. (In Internet Explorer, you can view the list of certificate authorities trusted by your browser by opening your browser, selecting Internet Options on the Tools menu, then moving to the Content tab and then clicking the Publishers button). The browser uses that key to decrypt the certificate authority's digital signature, which yields a hash of the digital certificate. The browser then creates its own hash of the digital certificate; if the two hashes match, the certificate is valid.

Illustrative Example: The Role of Encryption and Hashing in E-Business

To illustrate how hashing, symmetric encryption, and asymmetric encryption techniques are all used together in an e-business transaction, Figure 9-3 uses the example of Northwest Industries submitting a competitive bid to provide services to a local government agency. The example assumes that both Northwest Industries and the government agency have previously acquired digital certificates from a mutually trusted certificate authority.

Step 1.   A Northwest Industries employee connects to the government agency's Web site and clicks on the button for submitting bids on open contracts. *The browser moves to a secure Web page displaying the familiar lock icon. The browser software on the*

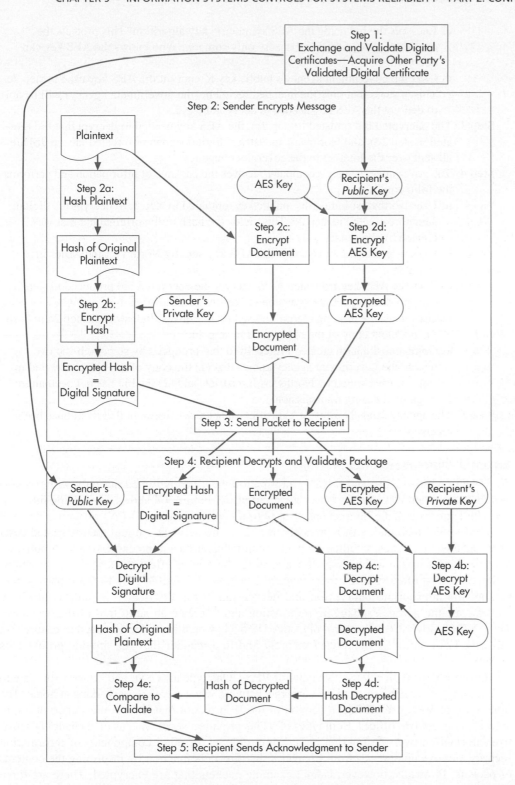

FIGURE 9-3

Using Encryption and Hashing for E-Business

employee's computer obtains the Web site's digital certificate, verifies its validity, and opens it to get the agency's public key. The government Web site software follows similar steps to acquire Northwest Industries' public key.

Step 2. The employee clicks a button to attach and submit the company's bid. *Behind the scenes, the encryption software performs the following actions:*

    a. Uses a hashing algorithm, such as SHA-256, to create a hash of the bid.

    b. Encrypts the hash using Northwest Industries' private key. This creates a digital signature for the bid.

   c. Encrypts the bid using the AES symmetric key algorithm. This protects the confidentiality of the bid, because only someone who knows the AES key can decrypt it.

   d. Uses the government agency's public key to encrypt the AES key used in step 2c. This ensures that only the intended recipient (the government agency) will be able to decrypt the AES key needed to decrypt the bid.

Step 3. The encrypted bid (created in step 2c), the AES key needed to decrypt that bid (created in step 2d), and Northwest Industries' digital signature (created in step 2b) are all sent over the Internet to the government agency.

Step 4. The government agency's computer receives the package of information and performs the following steps:

   a. Uses Northwest Industries' public key, obtained in step 1, to decrypt the digital signature created in step 2b. This yields the hash of the original bid that was created by the sender.

   b. Uses its private key to decrypt the AES key sent by Northwest Industries in step 2d.

   c. Uses the AES key from step 4b to decrypt the encrypted bid produced in step 2c. This produces a plaintext version of Northwest Industries' bid.

   d. Uses the same hashing algorithm used by Northwest Industries in step 2a to hash the plaintext copy of the bid created in step 4c.

   e. Compares the hash created in step 4d to that produced by step 4a. If the two match, the government agency knows that (1) the copy of the bid it recreated in step 4c was created by Northwest Industries, and (2) the bid has not been altered or garbled during transmission.

Step 5. The agency sends Northwest Industries an acknowledgement that its bid has been received.

Virtual Private Networks (VPNs)

To protect confidentiality and privacy, information must be encrypted not only within a system, but also when it is in transit over the Internet. As Figure 9-4 shows, encrypting information while it traverses the Internet creates a *virtual private network (VPN)*, so named because it provides the functionality of a privately owned secure network without the associated costs of leased telephone lines, satellites, and other communication equipment. Using VPN software to encrypt information while it is in transit over the Internet in effect creates private communication channels, often referred to as *tunnels*, which are accessible only to those parties possessing the appropriate encryption and decryption keys. VPNs also include controls to authenticate the parties exchanging information and to create an audit trail of the exchange. Thus, VPNs satisfy CobiT control objective DS 5.11, which identifies the need to ensure that sensitive information is exchanged securely and in a manner that can provide proof of its authenticity.

Organizations typically use two types of VPNs. One type uses SSL and browser software to give employees remote access to the corporate network when traveling or working at home. The other type of VPN uses IPSec, a version of the IP protocol that incorporates encryption, to securely connect two offices. Both types of VPNs provide a secure means of exchanging sensitive information over the Internet but create problems for other components of information security. For example, recall from Chapter 8 that firewalls function by inspecting the contents of packets. Firewalls, however, cannot examine packets that are encrypted. There are three

FIGURE 9-4
Virtual Private Networks (VPNs)

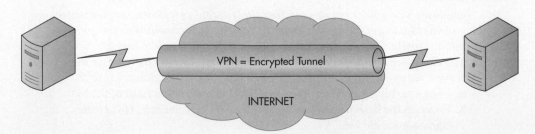

commonly used approaches to dealing with this problem. One is to configure the firewall to send encrypted packets to a computer in the DMZ that decrypts them; that computer then sends the decrypted packets back through the firewall for filtering before being allowed into the internal network. Although this approach allows the firewall to screen all incoming packets, it means that sensitive information is unencrypted both in the DMZ and within the internal network. A second approach is to configure the main firewall to allow encrypted packets to enter the internal network and decrypt them only at their final destination. Although this approach protects the confidentiality of sensitive information until it reaches the appropriate destination, it creates potential holes in access controls because not all incoming packets are filtered by the firewall. The third approach is to have the firewall also function as the VPN termination point, decrypting all incoming traffic and then inspecting the content. This approach is costly, creates a single point of failure (if the firewall goes down, so too does the VPN), and means that sensitive information is not encrypted while traveling on the internal corporate network. Thus, organizations must choose which systems reliability objective is more important: confidentiality (privacy) or security. Unfortunately, this type of dilemma is not limited to firewalls; antivirus programs, intrusion prevention systems, and intrusion detection systems also have difficulty in dealing with encrypted packets. This necessity of making trade-offs among different components of systems reliability is another reason that information security and controls is a managerial concern, and not just an IT issue.

Summary and Case Conclusion

Jason Scott reviewed what he had learned about Northwest Industries' information systems controls to protect confidentiality and privacy. Confidential information about business plans and personal information collected from customers was encrypted both in storage and whenever it was transmitted over the Internet. Employee laptops were configured with VPN software so that they could securely access the company's information systems when they worked at home or while traveling on business. Northwest Industries employed a key escrow system to manage the encryption keys; Jason had tested and verified that it worked as planned. The CISO had used GAPP to develop procedures to protect personal information collected from customers. Jason verified that employees received detailed training on how to handle such information when initially hired and attended mandatory "refresher" courses every six months. Multifactor authentication was used to control access to the company's databases. Jason also verified that Northwest Industries digitally signed transactions with its business partners and required customers to digitally sign all orders that exceeded $10,000.

Based on his report, Jason's supervisor and the CIO were satisfied with Northwest Industries' measures to protect confidentiality and privacy. They asked Jason next to examine the controls in place to achieve the remaining two principles of systems reliability in the AICPA's Trust Services framework: processing integrity and availability.

Key Terms

information rights
  management (IRM) 252
data loss prevention (DLP)
  252
digital watermark 253
data masking 254
spam 255
identity theft 255
cookie 257
encryption 258

plaintext 258
ciphertext 258
decryption 258
key escrow 259
symmetric encryption
  systems 259
asymmetric encryption
  systems 259
public key 259
private key 260

hashing 260
hash 260
nonrepudiation 261
digital signature 261
digital certificate 262
certificate authority 262
public key infrastructure
  (PKI) 262
virtual private network
  (VPN) 264

AIS IN ACTION

Chapter Quiz

1. Which of the following statements is true?
   a. Encryption is sufficient to protect confidentiality and privacy.
   b. Cookies are text files that only store information. They cannot perform any actions.
   c. The controls for protecting confidentiality are not effective for protecting privacy.
   d. All of the above are true.

2. A digital signature is _____.
   a. created by hashing a document and then encrypting the hash with the signer's private key
   b. created by hashing a document and then encrypting the hash with the signer's public key
   c. created by hashing a document and then encrypting the hash with the signer's symmetric key
   d. none of the above

3. Able wants to send a file to Baker over the Internet and protect the file so that only Baker can read it and can verify that it came from Able. What should Able do?
   a. Encrypt the file using Able's public key, and then encrypt it again using Baker's private key.
   b. Encrypt the file using Able's private key, and then encrypt it again using Baker's private key.
   c. Encrypt the file using Able's public key, and then encrypt it again using Baker's public key.
   d. Encrypt the file using Able's private key, and then encrypt it again using Baker's public key.

4. Which of the following statements is true?
   a. Encryption and hashing are both reversible (can be decoded).
   b. Encryption is reversible, but hashing is not.
   c. Hashing is reversible, but encryption is not.
   d. Neither hashing nor encryption is reversible.

5. Confidentiality focuses on protecting _____.
   a. personal information collected from customers
   b. a company's annual report stored on its Web site
   c. merger and acquisition plans
   d. all of the above

6. Which of the following statements about obtaining consent to collect and use a customer's personal information is true?
   a. The default policy in Europe is opt-out, but in the United States the default is opt-in.
   b. The default policy in Europe is opt-in, but in the United States the default is opt-out.
   c. The default policy in both Europe and the United States is opt-in.
   d. The default policy in both Europe and the United States is opt-out.

7. One of the ten Generally Accepted Privacy Principles concerns security. According to GAPP, what is the nature of the relationship between security and privacy?
   a. Privacy is a necessary, but not sufficient, precondition to effective security.
   b. Privacy is both necessary and sufficient to effective security.
   c. Security is a necessary, but not sufficient, precondition to protect privacy.
   d. Security is both necessary and sufficient to protect privacy.

8. Which of the following statements is true?
   a. Symmetric encryption is faster than asymmetric encryption and can be used to provide nonrepudiation of contracts.
   b. Symmetric encryption is faster than asymmetric encryption but cannot be used to provide nonrepudiation of contracts.

  c. Asymmetric encryption is faster than symmetric encryption and can be used to provide nonrepudiation of contracts.

  d. Asymmetric encryption is faster than symmetric encryption but cannot be used to provide nonrepudiation of contracts.

9. Which of the following statements is true?
  a. VPNs protect the confidentiality of information while it is in transit over the Internet.
  b. Encryption limits firewalls' ability to filter traffic.
  c. A digital certificate contains that entity's public key.
  d. All of the above are true.

10. Which of the following can organizations use to protect the privacy of a customer's personal information when giving programmers a realistic data set with which to test a new application?
  a. digital signature
  b. digital watermark
  c. data loss prevention
  d. data masking

Discussion Questions

9.1. From the viewpoint of the customer, what are the advantages and disadvantages to the opt-in versus the opt-out approaches to collecting personal information? From the viewpoint of the organization desiring to collect such information?

9.2. What risks, if any, does offshore outsourcing of various information systems functions pose to satisfying the principles of confidentiality and privacy?

9.3. Should organizations permit personal use of e-mail systems by employees during working hours?

9.4. What privacy concerns might arise from the use of biometric authentication techniques? What about the embedding of radio frequency identification (RFID) tags in products such as clothing? What other technologies might create privacy concerns?

9.5. What do you think an organization's duty or responsibility to protect the privacy of its customers' personal information should be? Why?

9.6. Assume you have interviewed for a job online and now receive an offer of employment. The job requires you to move across the country. The company sends you a digital signature along with the contract. How does this provide you with enough assurance to trust the offer so that you are willing to make the move?

Problems

9.1. Match the terms with their definitions:

____ 1. Virtual private network (VPN)	a. A hash encrypted with the creator's private key
____ 2. Data loss prevention (DLP)	b. A company that issues pairs of public and private keys and verifies the identity of the owner of those keys
____ 3. Digital signature	c. A secret mark used to identify proprietary information
____ 4. Digital certificate	d. An encrypted tunnel used to transmit information securely across the Internet
____ 5. Data masking	e. Replacing real data with fake data
____ 6. Symmetric encryption	f. Unauthorized use of facts about another person to commit fraud or other crimes

____	7. Spam	g.	The process of turning ciphertext into plaintext
____	8. Plaintext	h.	Unwanted e-mail
____	9. Hashing	i.	A document or file that can be read by anyone who accesses it
____	10. Ciphertext	j.	Used to store an entity's public key, often found on Web sites
____	11. Information rights management	k.	A procedure to filter outgoing traffic to prevent confidential information from leaving
____	12. Certificate authority	l.	A process that transforms a document or file into a fixed-length string of data
____	13. Nonrepudiation	m.	A document or file that must be decrypted to be read
____	14. Digital watermark	n.	A copy of an encryption key stored securely to enable decryption if the original encryption key becomes unavailable
____	15. Asymmetric encryption	o.	An encryption process that uses a pair of matched keys, one public and the other private; either key can encrypt something, but only the other key in that pair can decrypt
____	16. Key escrow	p.	An encryption process that uses the same key to both encrypt and decrypt
		q.	The inability to unilaterally deny having created a document or file or having agreed to perform a transaction
		r.	Software that limits what actions (read, copy, print, etc.) that users granted access to a file or document can perform.

9.2. Cost-effective controls to provide confidentiality require valuing the information that is to be protected. This involves classifying information into discrete categories. Propose a minimal classification scheme that could be used by any business, and provide examples of the type of information that would fall into each of those categories.

9.3. Download a hash calculator from the course web site that can create hashes for both files and text input. Use it to create SHA-256 (or any other hash algorithm your instructor assigns) hashes for the following:
   a. A document that contains this text: "Congratulations! You earned an A+"
   b. A document that contains this text: "Congratulations! You earned an A−"
   c. A document that contains this text: "Congratulations! You earned an a−"
   d. A document that contains this text: "Congratulations! You earned an A+" (this message contains two spaces between the exclamation point and the capital letter Y).
   e. Make a copy of the document used in step a, and calculate its hash value.
   f. Hash any multiple-page text file on your computer.

9.4. Accountants often need to print financial statements with the words "CONFIDENTIAL" or "DRAFT" appearing in light type in the background.
   a. Create a watermark with the word "CONFIDENTIAL" in a Word document. Print out a document that displays that watermark.
   b. Create the same watermark in Excel, and print out a spreadsheet page that displays that watermark.
   c. Can you make your watermark "invisible" so that it can be used to detect whether a document containing sensitive information has been copied to an unauthorized location? How? How could you use that "invisible" watermark to detect violation of copying policy?

9.5. Create a spreadsheet to compare current monthly mortgage payments versus the new monthly payments if the loan were refinanced, as shown:

Refinancing Calculator

Instructions: Only enter data into borderless cells; DO NOT enter data into cells with borders

Current loan amount	500000
Current term (years)	30

Current interest rate	5%
Current monthly payment	$2,684.11
New Loan amount	400000
New Loan term (years)	25
New interest rate	4.50%
New monthly payment	$2,223.33

Required

a. Restrict access to the spreadsheet by encrypting it.

b. Further protect the spreadsheet by limiting users to the ability to select and enter data only in the six cells without borders.

Hint: The article "Keeping Secrets: How to Protect Your Computer from Snoops and Spies," by Theo Callahan in the July 2007 issue of the *Journal of Accountancy* explains how to do this using Excel 2003. Review the article, and then use Excel's built-in help function to learn how to do this with later versions of Excel.

9.6. Research the information rights management software that may be available for your computer. What are its capabilities for limiting access rights? Write a report of your findings.

Optional: If you can download and install IRM software from Microsoft, use it to prevent anyone from being able to copy or print your report.

9.7. The principle of confidentiality focuses on protecting an organization's intellectual property. The flip side of the issue is ensuring that employees respect the intellectual property of other organizations. Research the topic of software piracy and write a report that explains the following:

a. What software piracy is

b. How organizations attempt to prevent their employees from engaging in software piracy

c. How software piracy violations are discovered

d. The consequences to both individual employees and to organizations who commit software piracy

9.8. Practice encryption.

Required

a. Use your computer operating system's built-in encryption capability to encrypt a file. Create another user account on your computer, and log in as that user. Which of the following actions can you perform?

   1. Open the file
   2. Copy the file to a USB drive
   3. Move the file to a USB drive
   4. Rename the file
   5. Delete the file

b. TruCrypt is one of several free software programs that can be used to encrypt files stored on a USB drive. Download and install a copy of TruCrypt (or another program recommended by your professor) from the course web site. Use it to encrypt some files on a USB drive. Compare its functionality to that of the built-in encryption functionality provided by your computer's operating system.

9.9. Research the problem of identity theft and write a report that explains the following:

a. Whether the problem of identity theft is increasing or decreasing

b. What kind of identity theft protection services or insurance products are available. Compare and contrast at least two products

9.10. Certificate authorities are an important part of a public key infrastructure (PKI). Research at least two certificate authorities, and write a report that explains the different types of digital certificates that they offer.

9.11. Obtain a copy of COBIT (available at www.isaca.org), and read the control objectives that relate to encryption (DS5.8 and DS5.11). What are the essential control procedures that organizations should implement when using encryption?

Case 9-1 Protecting Privacy of Tax Returns

The department of taxation in your state is developing a new computer system for processing individual and corporate income-tax returns. The new system features direct data input and inquiry capabilities. Taxpayers are identified by Social Security number (for individuals) and federal tax identification number (for corporations). The new system should be fully implemented in time for the next tax season.

The new system will serve three primary purposes:

1. Tax return data will automatically input into the system either directly (if the taxpayer files electronically) or by a clerk at central headquarters scanning a paper return received in the mail.
2. The returns will be processed using the main computer facilities at central headquarters. Processing will include four steps:
   a. Verifying mathematical accuracy
   b. Auditing the reasonableness of deductions, tax due, and so on, through the use of edit routines, which also include a comparison of current and prior years' data
   c. Identifying returns that should be considered for audit by department revenue agents
   d. Issuing refund checks to taxpayers

3. Inquiry services. A taxpayer will be allowed to determine the status of his or her return or get information from the last three years' returns by calling or visiting one of the department's regional offices or by accessing the department's Web site and entering his or her Social Security number.

The state commissioner of taxation and the state attorney general are concerned about protecting the privacy of personal information submitted by taxpayers. They want to have potential problems identified *before* the system is fully developed and implemented so that the proper controls can be incorporated into the new system.

Required

Describe the potential privacy problems that could arise in each of the following three areas of processing, and recommend the corrective action(s) to solve each problem identified:

a. Data input
b. Processing of returns
c. Data inquiry

(CMA examination, adapted)

Case 9-2 Generally Accepted Privacy Principles

Obtain the practitioner's version of Generally Accepted Privacy Principles from the AICPA's Web site (www.aicpa.org). Use it to answer the following questions:

1. What is the difference between confidentiality and privacy?
2. How many categories of personal information exist? Why?
3. In terms of the principle of choice and consent, what does GAPP recommend concerning opt-in versus opt-out?
4. Can organizations outsource their responsibility for privacy?
5. What does principle 1 state concerning top management's and the board of directors' responsibility for privacy?
6. What does principle 1 state concerning the use of customers' personal information when organizations test new applications?
7. Obtain a copy of your university's privacy policy statement. Does it satisfy GAPP criterion 2.2.3? Why?

8. What does GAPP principle 3 say about the use of cookies?
9. What are some examples of practices that violate management criterion 4.2.2?
10. What does management criterion 5.2.2 state concerning retention of customers' personal information? How can organizations satisfy this criterion?
11. What does management criterion 5.2.3 state concerning the disposal of personal information? How can organizations satisfy this criterion?
12. What does management criterion 6.2.2 state concerning access? What controls should organizations use to achieve this objective?
13. According to GAPP principle 7, what should organizations do if they wish to share personal information they collect with a third party?
14. What does GAPP principle 8 state concerning the use of encryption?
15. What is the relationship between GAPP principles 9 and 10?

AIS IN ACTION SOLUTIONS

Quiz Key

1. Which of the following statements is true?
    a. Encryption is sufficient to protect confidentiality and privacy. (Incorrect. Encryption is not sufficient, because sensitive information cannot be encrypted at all times—it must be decrypted during processing, when displayed on a monitor, or included in a printed report.)
    ▶ b. Cookies are text files that only store information. They cannot perform any actions. (Correct. Cookies are text files, not executable programs. They can, however, store sensitive information, so they should be protected.)
    c. The controls for protecting confidentiality are not effective for protecting privacy. (Incorrect. The same set of controls—encryption, access controls, and training—can be used to protect both confidentiality and privacy.)
    d. All of the above are true. (Incorrect. Statements a and c are false.)

2. A digital signature is _____.
    ▶ a. created by hashing a document and then encrypting the hash with the signer's private key (Correct. Creating a hash provides a way to verify the integrity of a document, and encrypting it with the signer's private key provides a way to prove that the sender created the document.)
    b. created by hashing a document and then encrypting the hash with the signer's public key (Incorrect. Anyone could encrypt something with the signer's public key. Therefore, this process cannot be used to prove who created a document.)
    c. created by hashing a document and then encrypting the hash with the signer's symmetric key (Incorrect. A symmetric key is possessed by more than one party, so encrypting something with it does not provide a means to prove who created a document).
    d. none of the above (Incorrect. Only choices b and c are incorrect; choice a is correct.)

3. Able wants to send a file to Baker over the Internet and protect the file so that only Baker can read it and can verify that it came from Able. What should Able do?
    a. Encrypt the file using Able's public key, and then encrypt it again using Baker's private key. (Incorrect. Able does not know Baker's private key.)
    b. Encrypt the file using Able's private key, and then encrypt it again using Baker's private key. (Incorrect. Able does not know Baker's private key.)
    c. Encrypt the file using Able's public key, and then encrypt it again using Baker's public key. (Incorrect. Baker does not know Able's private key and therefore cannot decrypt the file encrypted with Able's public key.)
    ▶ d. Encrypt the file using Able's private key, and then encrypt it again using Baker's public key. (Correct. Encrypting it with Baker's public key means that only Baker can decrypt it. Then, Baker can use Able's public key to decrypt the file—if the result is understandable, it had to have been created by Able and encrypted with Able's private key.)

4. Which of the following statements is true?
    a. Encryption and hashing are both reversible (can be decoded). (Incorrect. Hashing is irreversible.)
    ▶ b. Encryption is reversible, but hashing is not. (Correct. Encryption can be reversed to decrypt the ciphertext, but hashing cannot be reversed.)
    c. Hashing is reversible, but encryption is not. (Incorrect. Hashing is irreversible, but encryption is reversible.)
    d. Neither hashing nor encryption is reversible. (Incorrect. Encryption is reversible, a process called decryption.)

5. Confidentiality focuses on protecting _____.
    a. personal information collected from customers (Incorrect. Protecting customers' personal information relates to the principle of privacy.)

> **b.** a company's annual report stored on its Web site (Incorrect. A company's annual report is meant to be available to the public.)
>
> ▶ **c.** merger and acquisition plans (Correct. Merger and acquisition plans are sensitive information that should not be made public until the deal is consummated.)
>
> **d.** all of the above (Incorrect. Statements a and b are false.)

6. Which of the following statements about obtaining consent to collect and use a customer's personal information is true?
   a. The default policy in Europe is opt-out, but in the United States the default is opt-in. (Incorrect. The default policy in Europe is opt-in, and in the United States it is opt-out.)
   ▶ **b.** The default policy in Europe is opt-in, but in the United States the default is opt-out. (Correct.)
   c. The default policy in both Europe and the United States is opt-in. (Incorrect. The default policy in Europe is opt-in, and in the United States it is opt-out.)
   d. The default policy in both Europe and the United States is opt-out. (Incorrect. The default policy in Europe is opt-in and in the U.S. it is opt-out.)

7. One of the ten Generally Accepted Privacy Principles concerns security. According to GAPP, what is the nature of the relationship between security and privacy?
   a. Privacy is a necessary, but not sufficient, precondition to effective security. (Incorrect. Security is one of the ten criteria in GAPP because you need security in order to have privacy. Security alone, however, is not enough—that is why there are nine other criteria in GAPP.)
   b. Privacy is both necessary and sufficient to effective security. (Incorrect. Security is one of the ten criteria in GAPP because you need security in order to have privacy. Security alone, however, is not enough—that is why there are nine other criteria in GAPP.)
   ▶ **c.** Security is a necessary, but not sufficient, precondition to protect privacy. (Correct.)
   d. Security is both necessary and sufficient to protect privacy. (Incorrect. Security is one of the ten criteria in GAPP because you need security in order to have privacy. Security alone, however, is not enough—that is why there are nine other criteria in GAPP.)

8. Which of the following statements is true?
   a. Symmetric encryption is faster than asymmetric encryption and can be used to provide nonrepudiation of contracts. (Incorrect. Symmetric encryption cannot be used for nonrepudiation because both parties share the key, so there is no way to prove who created and encrypted a document.)
   ▶ **b.** Symmetric encryption is faster than asymmetric encryption but cannot be used to provide nonrepudiation of contracts. (Correct. Symmetric encryption is faster than asymmetric encryption, but it cannot be used for nonrepudiation; the key is shared by both parties, so there is no way to prove who created and encrypted a document.)
   c. Asymmetric encryption is faster than symmetric encryption and can be used to provide nonrepudiation of contracts. (Incorrect. Symmetric encryption is faster than asymmetric encryption.)
   d. Asymmetric encryption is faster than symmetric encryption but cannot be used to provide nonrepudiation of contracts. (Incorrect. Symmetric encryption is faster than asymmetric encryption. Also, asymmetric encryption can be used to provide nonrepudiation, because encrypting a contract with the creator's private key proves that the encrypter did indeed create the contract.)

9. Which of the following statements is true?
   a. VPNs protect the confidentiality of information while it is in transit over the Internet. (Incorrect. This statement is true, but so are the others.)
   b. Encryption limits firewalls' ability to filter traffic. (Incorrect. This statement is true—firewalls cannot apply their rules to encrypted packets—but so are the others.)
   c. A digital certificate contains that entity's public key. (Incorrect. This statement is true, but so are the others.)
   ▶ **d.** All of the above are true. (Correct. All three statements are true.)

10. Which of the following can organizations use to protect the privacy of a customer's personal information when giving programmers a realistic data set with which to test a new application?
    a. digital signature (Incorrect. A digital signature is used for nonrepudiation. However, because it is an encrypted hash, it cannot be used to test programming logic.)
    b. digital watermark (Incorrect. A digital watermark is used to identify proprietary data, but it does not protect privacy.)
    c. data loss prevention (Incorrect. Data loss prevention is designed to protect confidentiality by filtering outgoing messages to prevent sensitive data from leaving the company.)
    ▶ d. data masking (Correct. Masking replaces actual values with fake ones, but the result is still the same type of data, which can then be used to test program logic.)

Chapter 10

Information Systems Controls for Systems Reliability—Part 3: Processing Integrity and Availability

Learning Objectives

After studying this chapter, you should be able to:

1. Identify and explain controls designed to ensure processing integrity.

2. Identify and explain controls designed to ensure systems availability.

INTEGRATIVE CASE   NORTHWEST INDUSTRIES

Jason Scott began his review of Northwest Industries' processing integrity and availability controls by meeting with the CFO and the CIO. The CFO mentioned that she had just read an article about how spreadsheet errors had caused several companies to make poor decisions that cost them millions of dollars. She wanted to be sure that such problems did not happen to Northwest Industries. She also stressed the need to continue to improve the monthly closing process so that management would have more timely information. The CIO expressed concern about the company's lack of planning for how to continue business operations in the event of a major natural disaster such as the recent floods in the Midwest, which had forced several small businesses to close. Jason thanked them for their input and set about collecting evidence about the effectiveness of Northwest Industries' procedures for ensuring processing integrity and availability.

Introduction

The previous two chapters discussed the first three principles of systems reliability identified in the Trust Services Framework: security, confidentiality, and privacy. This chapter addresses the remaining two principles of reliable systems: processing integrity and availability. We conclude with a discussion of the importance of controlling changes to systems to ensure that the

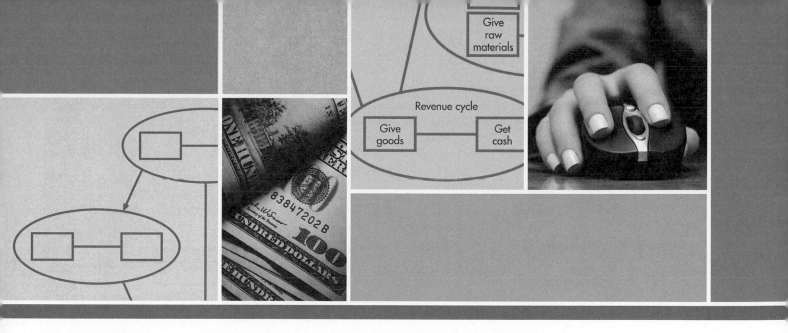

new system continues to satisfy all five principles of systems reliability identified in the Trust Services Framework.

Processing Integrity

The Processing Integrity principle of the Trust Services Framework states that a reliable system is one that produces information that is accurate, complete, timely, and valid. As discussed in COBIT control objective DS 11.1, this requires controls over the input, processing, and output of data. Table 10-1 presents the six basic categories of application controls discussed in the COBIT framework for ensuring processing integrity.

TABLE 10-1 Application Controls Discussed in COBIT to Ensure Processing Integrity

Process Stage and COBIT Category	Threats/Risks	Controls
Input: • AC1—Source Data Preparation and Authorization • AC2—Source Data Collection and Entry • AC3—Accuracy, Completeness, and Authenticity Checks	Data that is: • Invalid • Unauthorized • Incomplete • Inaccurate	Forms design, cancellation and storage of documents, authorization and segregation of duties controls, visual scanning, data entry controls
Processing: • AC4—Processing Integrity and Validity	Errors in output and stored data	Data matching, file labels, batch totals, cross-footing and zero-balance tests, write-protection mechanisms, database processing integrity controls
Output: • AC5—Output Review, Reconciliation and Error Handling • AC6—Transaction Authenticity and Integrity	• Use of inaccurate or incomplete reports • Unauthorized disclosure of sensitive information • Loss, alteration, or disclosure of information in transit	Reviews and reconciliations, encryption and access controls, parity checks, message acknowledgement techniques

Input Controls

The phrase "garbage in, garbage out" highlights the importance of input controls. If the data entered into a system are inaccurate, incomplete, or invalid, the output will be too. Consequently, source documents should be prepared only by authorized personnel acting within their authority. In addition, forms design, cancellation and storage of source documents, and automated data entry controls are needed to verify the validity of input data.

FORMS DESIGN   Source documents and other forms should be designed to minimize the chances for errors and omissions. Two particularly important forms design controls involve sequentially prenumbering source documents and using turnaround documents.

1. All source documents should be sequentially prenumbered. Prenumbering improves control by making it possible to verify that no documents are missing. (To understand this, consider the difficulty you would have in balancing your checking account if none of your checks were numbered.) When sequentially prenumbered source data documents are used, the system should be programmed to identify and report missing or duplicate source documents.
2. A *turnaround document* is a record of company data sent to an external party and then returned by the external party to the system as input. Turnaround documents are prepared in machine-readable form to facilitate their subsequent processing as input records. An example is a utility bill that a special scanning device reads when the bill is returned with a payment. Turnaround documents improve accuracy by eliminating the potential for input errors when entering data manually.

CANCELLATION AND STORAGE OF SOURCE DOCUMENTS   Source documents that have been entered into the system should be canceled so they cannot be inadvertently or fraudulently reentered into the system. Paper documents should be defaced, for example, by stamping them "paid." Electronic documents can be similarly "canceled" by setting a flag field to indicate that the document has already been processed. *Note:* Cancellation does *not* mean disposal. Original source documents (or their electronic images) should be retained for as long as needed to satisfy legal and regulatory requirements and provide an audit trail.

DATA ENTRY CONTROLS   Source documents should be scanned for reasonableness and propriety before being entered into the system. However, this manual control must be supplemented with automated data entry controls, such as the following:

● A *field check* determines whether the characters in a field are of the proper type. For example, a check on a field that is supposed to contain only numeric values, such as a U.S. Zip code, would indicate an error if it contained alphabetic characters.
● A *sign check* determines whether the data in a field have the appropriate arithmetic sign. For example, the quantity-ordered field should never be negative.
● A *limit check* tests a numerical amount against a fixed value. For example, the regular hours-worked field in weekly payroll input must be less than or equal to 40 hours. Similarly, the hourly wage field should be greater than or equal to the minimum wage.
● A *range check* tests whether a numerical amount falls between predetermined lower and upper limits. For example, a marketing promotion might be directed only to prospects with incomes between $50,000 and $99,999.
● A *size check* ensures that the input data will fit into the assigned field. For example, the value 458,976,253 will not fit in an eight-digit field.
● A *completeness check* on each input record determines whether all required data items have been entered. For example, sales transaction records should not be accepted for processing unless they include the customer's shipping and billing addresses.
● A *validity check* compares the ID code or account number in transaction data with similar data in the master file to verify that the account exists. For example, if product number 65432 is entered on a sales order, the computer must verify that there is indeed a product 65432 in the inventory database.
● A *reasonableness test* determines the correctness of the logical relationship between two data items. For example, overtime hours should be zero for someone who has not worked the maximum number of regular hours in a pay period.

- Authorized ID numbers (such as employee numbers) can contain a *check digit* that is computed from the other digits. For example, the system could assign each new employee a nine-digit number, then calculate a tenth digit from the original nine and append that calculated number to the original nine to form a ten-digit ID number. Data entry devices can then be programmed to perform *check digit verification* by using the first nine digits to calculate the tenth digit each time an ID number is entered. If an error is made in entering any of the ten digits, the calculation made on the first nine digits will not match the tenth, or check digit.

The preceding data entry tests are used for both batch processing and online real-time processing. Additional data input controls differ for the two processing methods.

ADDITIONAL BATCH PROCESSING DATA ENTRY CONTROLS

- Batch processing works more efficiently if the transactions are sorted so that the accounts affected are in the same sequence as records in the master file. For example, accurate batch processing of sales transactions to update customer account balances requires that the transactions first be sorted by customer account number. A *sequence check* tests whether a batch of input data is in the proper numerical or alphabetical sequence.
- An error log that identifies data input errors (date, cause, problem) facilitates timely review and resubmission of transactions that cannot be processed.
- *Batch totals* summarize important values for a batch of input records. The following are three commonly used batch totals:
  1. A *financial total* sums a field that contains monetary values, such as the total dollar amount of all sales for a batch of sales transactions.
  2. A *hash total* sums a nonfinancial numeric field, such as the total of the quantity ordered field in a batch of sales transactions.
  3. A *record count* is the number of records in a batch.

These batch totals are calculated and stored by the system when data is initially entered. They will be recalculated later to verify that all input was processed correctly.

ADDITIONAL ONLINE DATA ENTRY CONTROLS

- *Prompting*, in which the system requests each input data item and waits for an acceptable response, ensures that all necessary data are entered (i.e., prompting is an online completeness check).
- *Closed-loop verification* checks the accuracy of input data by using it to retrieve and display other related information. For example, if a clerk enters an account number, the system could retrieve and display the account name so that the user could verify that the correct account number had been entered.
- A transaction log includes a detailed record of all transactions, including a unique transaction identifier, the date and time of entry, and who entered the transaction. If an online file is damaged, the transaction log can be used to reconstruct the file. If a malfunction temporarily shuts down the system, the transaction log can be used to ensure that transactions are not lost or entered twice.

Processing Controls

Controls are also needed to ensure that data is processed correctly. Important processing controls include the following:

- *Data matching.*   In certain cases, two or more items of data must be matched before an action can take place. For example, before paying a vendor, the system should verify that information on the vendor invoice matches information on both the purchase order and the receiving report.
- *File labels.*   File labels need to be checked to ensure that the correct and most current files are being updated. Both external labels that are readable by humans and internal labels that are written in machine-readable form on the data recording media should be used. Two important types of internal labels are header and trailer records. The *header record* is located at the beginning of each file and contains the file name, expiration date, and other

identification data. The *trailer record* is located at the end of the file and contains the batch totals calculated during input. Programs should be designed to read the header record *prior* to processing, to ensure that the correct file is being updated. Programs should also be designed to read the information in the trailer record *after* processing, to verify that all input records have been correctly processed.

- *Recalculation of batch totals.* Batch totals should be recomputed as each transaction record is processed, and the total for the batch should then be compared to the values in the trailer record. Any discrepancies indicate a processing error. Often, the nature of the discrepancy provides a clue about the type of error that occurred. For example, if the recomputed record count is smaller than the original, one or more transaction records were not processed. Conversely, if the recomputed record count is larger than the original, either additional unauthorized transactions were processed, or some transaction records were processed twice. If a financial or hash total discrepancy is evenly divisible by 9, the likely cause is a *transposition error*, in which two adjacent digits were inadvertently reversed (e.g., 46 instead of 64). Transposition errors may appear to be trivial but can have enormous financial consequences. For example, consider the effect of misrecording the interest rate on a loan as 6.4% instead of 4.6%.

- *Cross-footing and zero-balance tests.* Often totals can be calculated in multiple ways. For example, in spreadsheets a grand total can be computed either by summing a column of row totals or by summing a row of column totals. These two methods should produce the same result. A *cross-footing balance test* compares the results produced by each method to verify accuracy. A *zero-balance test* applies this same logic to control accounts. For example, the payroll clearing account is debited for the total gross pay of all employees in a particular time period. It is then credited for the amount of all labor costs allocated to various expense categories. The payroll clearing account should have a zero balance after both sets of entries have been made; a nonzero balance indicates a processing error.

- *Write-protection mechanisms.* These protect against overwriting or erasing of data files stored on magnetic media. Write-protection mechanisms have long been used to protect master files from accidentally being damaged. Technological innovations also necessitate the use of write-protection mechanisms to protect the integrity of transaction data. For example, radio frequency identification (RFID) tags used to track inventory need to be write-protected so that unscrupulous customers cannot change the price of merchandise.

- *Concurrent update controls.* Errors can occur when two or more users attempt to update the same record simultaneously. *Concurrent update controls* prevent such errors by locking out one user until the system has finished processing the transaction entered by the other.

Output Controls

Careful checking of system output provides additional control over processing integrity. Important output controls include the following:

- *User review of output.* Users should carefully examine system output to verify that it is reasonable, that it is complete, and that they are the intended recipients.
- *Reconciliation procedures.* Periodically, all transactions and other system updates should be reconciled to control reports, file status/update reports, or other control mechanisms. In addition, general ledger accounts should be reconciled to subsidiary account totals on a regular basis. For example, the balance of the inventory control account in the general ledger should equal the sum of the item balances in the inventory database. The same is true for the accounts receivable, capital assets, and accounts payable control accounts.
- *External data reconciliation.* Database totals should periodically be reconciled with data maintained outside the system. For example, the number of employee records in the payroll file can be compared with the total number of employees in the human resources database to detect attempts to add fictitious employees to the payroll database. Similarly, inventory on hand should be physically counted and compared to the quantity on hand recorded in the database.

● *Data transmission controls.*   Organizations also need to implement controls designed to minimize the risk of data transmission errors. Whenever the receiving device detects a data transmission error, it requests the sending device to retransmit that data. Generally, this happens automatically, and the user is unaware that it has occurred. For example, the Transmission Control Protocol (TCP) discussed in Chapter 8 assigns a sequence number to each packet and uses that information to verify that all packets have been received and to reassemble them in the correct order. Two other common data transmission controls are checksums and parity bits.

1. *Checksums.*   When data are transmitted, the sending device can calculate a hash of the file, called a *checksum*. The receiving device performs the same calculation and sends the result to the sending device. If the two hashes agree, the transmission is presumed to be accurate. Otherwise, the file is resent.

2. *Parity bits.*   Computers represent characters as a set of binary digits called bits. Each bit has two possible values: 0 or 1. Many computers use a seven-bit coding scheme, which is more than enough to represent the 26 letters in the English alphabet (both upper- and lowercase), the numbers 0 through 9, and a variety of special symbols ($, %, &, etc.). A **parity bit** is an extra digit added to the beginning of every character that can be used to check transmission accuracy. Two basic schemes are referred to as *even parity* and *odd parity.* In even parity, the parity bit is set so that each character has an even number of bits with the value 1; in odd parity, the parity bit is set so that an odd number of bits in the character have the value 1. For example, the digits 5 and 7 can be represented by the seven-bit patterns 0000101 and 0000111, respectively. An even parity system would set the parity bit for 5 to 0, so that it would be transmitted as 00000101 (because the binary code for 5 already has two bits with the value 1). The parity bit for 7 would be set to 1 so that it would be transmitted as 10000111 (because the binary code for 7 has 3 bits with the value 1). The receiving device performs **parity checking**, which entails verifying that the proper number of bits are set to the value 1 in each character received.

Illustrative Example: Credit Sales Processing

We now use a credit sale to illustrate how many of the application controls that have been discussed actually function. The following transaction data are used: sales order number, customer account number, inventory item number, quantity sold, sale price, and delivery date. If the customer purchases more than one product, there will be multiple inventory item numbers, quantities sold, and prices associated with each sales transaction. Processing these transactions includes the following steps: (1) entering and editing the transaction data; (2) updating the customer and inventory records (the amount of the credit purchase is added to the customer's balance; for each inventory item, the quantity sold is subtracted from the quantity on hand); and (3) preparing and distributing shipping and/or billing documents. Examples for both batch and online processing are presented.

BATCH PROCESSING INTEGRITY CONTROLS   Figure 10-1 shows the application controls that should be applied at each step of processing a batch of credit sales transactions:

1. *Prepare batch totals.*   The sum of all sales amounts is calculated as a financial total and recorded on batch control forms that accompany each group of sales documents.

2. *Deliver the transactions to the computer operations department for processing.*   Each batch is checked for proper authorization and recorded in a control log.

3. *Enter the transaction data into the system.*   As data are entered, the system performs several preliminary validation tests. Check digit verification identifies transactions with invalid account numbers or invalid inventory item numbers. Field checks verify that the quantity ordered and price fields contain only numbers and that the date field follows the correct MM/DD/YYYY format. A sequence check on sales order numbers and reconciliation of the batch totals calculated in step 1 verifies that no transactions are missing.

A control report lists all data entry errors. Data entry errors that occurred because an operator read a source document incorrectly or accidentally struck the wrong key can usually be corrected immediately after being detected. Incorrect source data, such as an

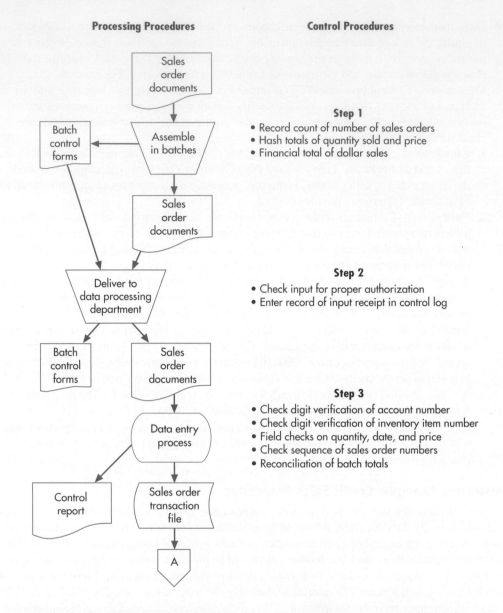

FIGURE 10-1

Application Controls in Batch Processing of Credit Sales

Processing Procedures

Sales order documents

Batch control forms → Assemble in batches

Sales order documents

Deliver to data processing department

Batch control forms   Sales order documents

Data entry process

Control report   Sales order transaction file

A

Control Procedures

Step 1
- Record count of number of sales orders
- Hash totals of quantity sold and price
- Financial total of dollar sales

Step 2
- Check input for proper authorization
- Enter record of input receipt in control log

Step 3
- Check digit verification of account number
- Check digit verification of inventory item number
- Field checks on quantity, date, and price
- Check sequence of sales order numbers
- Reconciliation of batch totals

unauthorized sales transaction or an invalid account number, are more problematic and should be returned to the sales department for correction.

4. *Sort and edit the transaction file.* The transaction file is now sorted by customer account number. Additional validation checks are performed, including sign checks that both the quantity ordered and price fields contain positive numbers, and a range check on promised delivery dates to verify that it is not earlier than the date of the order nor later than the company's advertised policies. Rejected transactions are listed on a control report along with the computed batch totals. Data control reconciles the batch totals, investigates and corrects any errors, and submits the corrected transactions for processing.

5. *Update the master files.* The sales transaction file is processed against customer (accounts receivable) and inventory databases or master files. The operator reads the external label, and the program reads the internal header record to ensure that the correct master file is being updated. Sales transactions with customer numbers or item numbers that do not exist in the corresponding master file are not processed; instead, they are entered on an error report. After a sales transaction is processed, a sign check is performed to ensure that the quantity-on-hand field in the inventory master record is not negative. Tests are also performed to ensure that sales prices fall within normal ranges, that the order does not exceed the customer's credit limit, and that the quantity ordered is reasonable given the nature of the item and the customer's order history. Redundant data checks—for example, comparing inventory item number and description—are used to ensure that the correct master file

Processing Procedures   **Control Procedures**   **FIGURE 10-1 Continued**

Step 4
- Sequence check on account number
- Limit checks on quantity and price
- Range check on delivery date
- Completeness test on entire record
- Reconciliation of batch totals
- Review errors identified by edit checks
- Investigation and correction of erroneous input

Step 5
- Security of master files in file library
- Protection of master files with file labels
- Maintenance of backup copies of master files
- Validity check of customer account number
- Validity check of inventory item number
- Sign check of inventory quantity on hand
- Limit check of sale amount versus credit limit
- Range check on sale price
- Reasonableness test of quantity ordered
- Redundant data check on customer data
- Redundant data check on inventory data

Step 6
- Reconciliation of batch totals
- Review of errors identified by edit checks
- Investigation and correction of erroneous input
- Distribution of billing and shipping documents
- Recording of output distribution in control log
- Return of master files to file library

Step 7
- Visual inspection of output
- Reconciliation of batch totals

record is updated. The total change in customer balances is computed; this financial total is compared to the total sales amount of all transactions that were processed.

6. *Prepare and distribute output.*   Outputs include billing and/or shipping documents and a control report. The control report contains batch totals accumulated during the file update run and a list of transactions rejected by the update program.

7. *User review.*   Users in the shipping and billing departments perform a limited review of the documents for incomplete data or other obvious deficiencies. They also compare the system-generated batch totals to those calculated in step 1 to verify that all transactions were processed.

ONLINE PROCESSING INTEGRITY CONTROLS   Online real-time processing records each credit sales transaction individually as it occurs (Figure 10-2). This enables more timely detection and correction of errors. The various application controls discussed in this chapter are applied at each stage (input, processing, output) of online transaction processing, as follows.

Online Data Entry Controls

- When an employee accesses the online system, logical access controls confirm the identity of the data entry device (personal computer, terminal) and the validity of the employee's user ID number and password.

FIGURE 10-2

Application Controls in Online Processing of Credit Sales

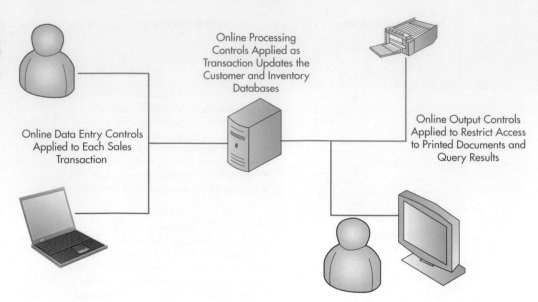

Online Data Entry Controls Applied to Each Sales Transaction

Online Processing Controls Applied as Transaction Updates the Customer and Inventory Databases

Online Output Controls Applied to Restrict Access to Printed Documents and Query Results

- A compatibility test ensures that the employee is authorized to perform that task.
- The system automatically assigns the transaction the next sequential sales order number and the current date as the date of the invoice.
- The system prompts for all required input (completeness test). After each prompt, the system waits for a response.
- Each response is tested using one or more of the following controls: validity checks (valid customer and inventory numbers), field and sign checks (only positive, numeric characters in the quantity, date, and price fields), and limit or range checks (delivery date versus current date).
- When the customer number is entered, the system retrieves the corresponding customer name from the database and displays it on the screen (closed-loop verification). The operator visually examines the customer name. If it matches the name on the sales order document, the operator signals the system to proceed with the transaction. If not, the operator rechecks the customer number and enters the correct value.
- When the inventory item number is entered, the system and the operator go through the same procedures as they do with the customer number.

Online Processing Controls. Because the file update program accesses the customer and inventory database records, it performs additional input validation tests by comparing data in each transaction record with data in the corresponding database record. These tests often include the following:

- Validity checks on the customer and inventory item numbers
- Sign checks on inventory-on-hand balances (after subtracting quantities sold)
- Limit checks that compare each customer's total amount due with the credit limit
- Range checks on the sale price of each item sold relative to the permissible range of prices for that item
- Reasonableness tests on the quantity sold of each item relative to normal sales quantities for that customer and that item

Online Output Controls. Outputs of this process include billing and/or shipping documents and a control report. The following output controls are used:

- Billing and shipping documents are forwarded electronically only to preauthorized users.
- Users in the shipping and billing departments perform a limited review of the documents by visually inspecting them for incomplete data or other obvious errors.
- The control report is sent automatically to its intended recipients, or the recipients can query the system for the report. If they query the system, logical access controls confirm the identity of the device making the query and the validity of the user's ID number and password.

FOCUS 10-1   Ensuring the Processing Integrity of Electronic Voting

Electronic voting may eliminate some of the types of problems that occur with manual or mechanical voting. For example, electronic voting software could use limit checks to prevent voters from attempting to select more candidates than permitted in a particular race. A completeness check would identify a voter's failure to make a choice in every race, and closed-loop verification could then be used to verify whether that was intentional. (This would eliminate the "hanging chad" problem created when voters fail to punch out the hole completely on a paper ballot.)

Nevertheless, there are concerns about electronic voting, particularly its audit trail capabilities. At issue is the ability to verify that only properly registered voters did indeed vote and that they voted only once. Although no one disagrees with the need for such authentication, there is debate over whether electronic voting machines can create adequate audit trails without risking the loss of voters' anonymity.

There is also debate about the overall security and reliability of electronic voting. Some security experts suggest that election officials should adopt the methods used by the state of Nevada to ensure that electronic gambling machines operate honestly and accurately, which include the following:

- **Access to the source code.** The Nevada Gaming Control Board keeps copies of all software. It is illegal for casinos to use any unregistered software. Similarly, security experts recommend that the government should keep copies of the source code of electronic voting software.
- **Hardware checks.** Frequent on-site spot checks of the computer chips in gambling machines are made to verify compliance with the Nevada Gaming Control Board's records. Similar tests should be done to voting machines.
- **Tests of physical security.** The Nevada Gaming Control Board extensively tests how machines react to stun guns and large electric shocks. Voting machines should be similarly tested.
- **Background checks.** All gambling machine manufacturers are carefully scrutinized and registered. Similar checks should be performed on voting machine manufacturers, as well as election software developers.

The preceding example illustrated the use of application controls to ensure the integrity of processing business transactions. Focus 10-1 explains the importance of processing integrity controls in nonbusiness settings, too.

Processing Integrity Controls in Spreadsheets

Most organizations have thousands of spreadsheets that are used to support decision making. The importance of spreadsheets to financial reporting is reflected in the fact that the ISACA document *IT Control Objectives for Sarbanes-Oxley* contains a separate appendix that specifically addresses processing integrity controls that should be used in spreadsheets. Yet, because spreadsheets are almost always developed by end users, they seldom contain adequate application controls. Therefore, it is not surprising that many organizations have experienced serious problems caused by spreadsheet errors. For example, an August 17, 2007, article in *CIO Magazine*[1] describes how spreadsheet errors caused companies to lose money, issue erroneous dividend payout announcements, and misreport financial results.

These kinds of costly mistakes could have been prevented by careful testing of spreadsheets before use. Although most spreadsheet software contains built-in "audit" features that can easily detect common errors, spreadsheets intended to support important decisions need more thorough testing to detect subtle errors. Nevertheless, a survey of finance professionals[2] indicates that only 2% of firms use multiple people to examine every spreadsheet cell, which is the only reliable way to effectively detect spreadsheet errors. It is especially important to check for *hardwiring*, where formulas contain specific numeric values (e.g., sales tax = 8.5% × A33), instead of referencing a cell that contains the current value for that variable (e.g., sales tax = A8 × A33). The problem with hardwiring is that the spreadsheet initially produces correct answers, but when the hardwired variable (e.g., the sales tax rate in the preceding example) changes, the formula may not be corrected.

---

[1] Thomas Wailgum, "Eight of the Worst Spreadsheet Blunders," *CIO Magazine* (August 2007), available at www.cio.com/article/131500/Eight_of_the_Worst_Spreadsheet_Errors
[2] Raymond R. Panko, "Controlling Spreadsheets," *Information Systems Control Journal-Online* (2007): Volume 1. Accessible at www.isaca.org/publications

Availability

Interruptions to business processes due to the unavailability of systems or information can cause significant financial losses. Consequently, COBIT section DS 4 addresses the importance of ensuring that systems and information are available for use whenever needed. The primary objective is to minimize the risk of system downtime. It is impossible, however, to completely eliminate the risk of downtime. Therefore, organizations also need controls designed to enable quick resumption of normal operations after an event disrupts system availability. Table 10-2 summarizes the key controls related to these two objectives.

Minimizing Risk of System Downtime

Organizations can undertake a variety of actions to minimize the risk of system downtime. COBIT control objective DS 13.5 identifies the need for preventive maintenance, such as cleaning disk drives and properly storing magnetic and optical media, to reduce the risk of hardware and software failure. The use of redundant components provides *fault tolerance*, which is the ability of a system to continue functioning in the event that a particular component fails. For example, many organizations use *redundant arrays of independent drives (RAID)* instead of just one disk drive. With RAID, data is written to multiple disk drives simultaneously. Thus, if one disk drive fails, the data can be readily accessed from another.

COBIT section DS 12 addresses the importance of locating and designing the data centers housing mission-critical servers and databases so as to minimize the risks associated with natural and human-caused disasters. Common design features include the following:

- Raised floors provide protection from damage caused by flooding.
- Fire detection and suppression devices reduce the likelihood of fire damage.
- Adequate air-conditioning systems reduce the likelihood of damage to computer equipment due to overheating or humidity.
- Cables with special plugs that cannot be easily removed reduce the risk of system damage due to accidental unplugging of the device.
- Surge-protection devices provide protection against temporary power fluctuations that might otherwise cause computers and other network equipment to crash.
- An *uninterruptible power supply (UPS)* system provides protection in the event of a prolonged power outage, using battery power to enable the system to operate long enough to back up critical data and safely shut down. (However, it is important to regularly inspect and test the batteries in a UPS to ensure that it will function when needed.)
- Physical access controls reduce the risk of theft or damage.

Training can also reduce the risk of system downtime. Well-trained operators are less likely to make mistakes and will know how to recover, with minimal damage, from errors they do commit. That is why COBIT control objective DS 13.1 stresses the importance of defining and documenting operational procedures and ensuring that IT staff understand their responsibilities.

System downtime can also occur because of computer malware (viruses and worms). Therefore, it is important to install, run, and keep current antivirus and anti-spyware programs. These programs should be automatically invoked not only to scan e-mail, but also any removable

TABLE 10-2 Availability: Objectives and Key Controls

Objective	Key Controls
1. To minimize risk of system downtime	• Preventive maintenance • Fault tolerance • Data center location and design • Training • Patch management and antivirus software
2. Quick and complete recovery and resumption of normal operations	• Backup procedures • Disaster recovery plan (DRP) • Business continuity plan (BCP)

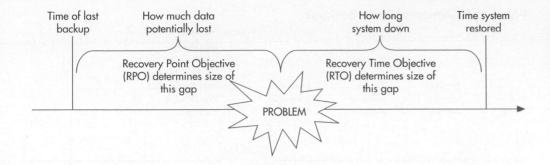

FIGURE 10-3

Relationship of Recovery Point Objective and Recovery Time Objective

computer media (CDs, DVDs, USB drives, etc.) that are brought into the organization. A patch management system provides additional protection by ensuring that vulnerabilities that can be exploited by malware are fixed in a timely manner.

Recovery and Resumption of Normal Operations

The preventive controls discussed in the preceding section can minimize, but not entirely eliminate, the risk of system downtime. Hardware malfunctions, software problems, or human error can cause data to become inaccessible. That's why backup procedures are necessary. A ***backup*** is an exact copy of the most current version of a database, file, or software program that can be used in the event that the original is no longer available. Natural disasters or terrorist acts can destroy not only data but also the entire information system. That's why organizations also need disaster recovery and business continuity plans.

An organization's backup procedures and disaster recovery and business continuity plans reflect management's answers to two fundamental questions:

1. How much data are we willing to recreate from source documents (if they exist) or potentially lose (if no source documents exist)?
2. How long can the organization function without its information system?

Figure 10-3 shows the relationship between these two questions. When a problem occurs, data about everything that has happened since the last backup is lost unless it can be reentered into the system. Thus, management's answer to the first question determines the organization's ***recovery point objective (RPO)***, which represents the maximum amount of data that the organization is willing to potentially lose. The answer to the second question determines the organization's ***recovery time objective (RTO)***, which represents the length of time that the organization is willing to attempt to function without its information system.

For some organizations, the answer to both questions is close to zero. Airlines and financial institutions, for example, cannot operate without their information systems, nor can they afford to lose information about transactions. For such organizations, the goal is not quick recovery from problems, but resiliency. The solution is to employ real-time mirroring. ***Real-time mirroring*** involves maintaining two copies of the database at two separate data centers at all times and updating both copies in real-time as each transaction occurs. In the event that something happens to one data center, the organization can immediately switch all daily activities to the other.

For other organizations, however, acceptable RPO and RTO may be measured in hours or even days. Achieving those goals requires data backup procedures plus disaster recovery and business continuity plans.

DATA BACKUP PROCEDURES   Data backup procedures are designed to deal with situations where information is not accessible because the relevant files or databases have become corrupted as a result of hardware failure, software problems, or human error, but the information system itself is still functioning. Several different backup procedures exist. A *full backup* is an exact copy of the entire database. Full backups are time-consuming, so most organizations only do full backups weekly and supplement them with daily partial backups. Figure 10-4 compares the two types of daily partial backups:

1. An ***incremental backup*** involves copying only the data items that have changed since the last partial backup. This produces a set of incremental backup files, each containing the

FIGURE 10-4

Comparison of
Incremental and
Differential Daily
Backups

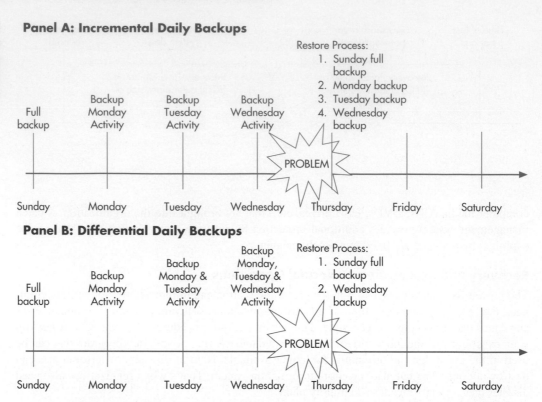

Panel A: Incremental Daily Backups

Restore Process:
1. Sunday full backup
2. Monday backup
3. Tuesday backup
4. Wednesday backup

Full backup — Backup Monday Activity — Backup Tuesday Activity — Backup Wednesday Activity — PROBLEM

Sunday   Monday   Tuesday   Wednesday   Thursday   Friday   Saturday

Panel B: Differential Daily Backups

Restore Process:
1. Sunday full backup
2. Wednesday backup

Full backup — Backup Monday Activity — Backup Monday & Tuesday Activity — Backup Monday, Tuesday & Wednesday Activity — PROBLEM

Sunday   Monday   Tuesday   Wednesday   Thursday   Friday   Saturday

results of one day's transactions. Restoration involves first loading the last full backup and then installing each subsequent incremental backup in the proper sequence.

2. A *differential backup* copies all changes made since the last full backup. Thus, each new differential backup file contains the cumulative effects of all activity since the last full backup. Consequently, except for the first day following a full backup, daily differential backups take longer than incremental backups. Restoration is simpler, however, because the last full backup needs to be supplemented with only the most recent differential backup, instead of a set of daily incremental backup files.

No matter which backup procedure is used, multiple backup copies should be created. One copy can be stored on-site, for use in the event of relatively minor problems, such as failure of a hard drive. In the event of a more serious problem, such as a fire or flood, any backup copies stored on-site will likely be destroyed or inaccessible. Therefore, a second backup copy needs to be stored off-site. These backup files can be transported to the remote storage site either physically (e.g., by courier) or electronically. In either case, the same security controls need to be applied to backup files as are used to protect the original copy of the information. This means that backup copies of sensitive data should be encrypted both in storage and during electronic transmission. Access to backup files also needs to be carefully controlled and monitored.

It is also important to periodically practice restoring a system from its backups. This verifies that the backup procedure is working correctly and that the backup media (tape or disk) can be successfully read by the hardware in use.

Backups are retained for only a relatively short period of time. For example, many organizations maintain only several months of backups. Some information, however, must be stored much longer. An *archive* is a copy of a database, master file, or software that is retained indefinitely as an historical record, usually to satisfy legal and regulatory requirements. As with backups, multiple copies of archives should be made and stored in different locations. Unlike backups, archives are seldom encrypted because their long retention times increase the risk of losing the decryption key. Consequently, physical and logical access controls are the primary means of protecting archive files.

What media should be used for backups and archives, tape or disk? Disk backup is faster, and disks are less easily lost. Tape, however, is cheaper, easier to transport, and more durable. Consequently, many organizations use both media. Data are first backed up to disk, for speed, and then transferred to tape.

Special attention needs to be paid to backing up and archiving e-mail, because it has become an important repository of organizational behavior and information. Indeed, e-mail often contains solutions to specific problems. E-mail also frequently contains information relevant to lawsuits. It may be tempting for an organization to consider a policy of periodically deleting all e-mail, to prevent a plaintiff's attorney from finding a "smoking gun" and to avoid the costs of finding the e-mail requested by the other party. Most experts, however, advise against such policies, because there are likely to be copies of the e-mail stored in archives outside the organization. Therefore, a policy of regularly deleting all e-mail means that the organization will not be able to tell its side of the story; instead, the court (and jury) will only read the e-mail created by the other party to the dispute. There have also been cases where the courts have fined organizations millions of dollars for failing to produce requested e-mail. Therefore, organizations need to back up and archive important e-mail while also periodically purging the large volume of routine, trivial e-mail.

DISASTER RECOVERY AND BUSINESS CONTINUITY PLANNING   Backups are designed to mitigate problems when one or more files or databases become corrupted because of hardware, software, or human error. Disaster recovery and business continuity plans are designed to mitigate more serious problems.

A *disaster recovery plan (DRP)* outlines the procedures to restore an organization's IT function in the event that its data center is destroyed by a natural disaster or act of terrorism. Organizations have three basic options for replacing their IT infrastructure, which includes not just computers, but also network components such as routers and switches, software, data, Internet access, printers, and supplies. The first option is to contract for use of a *cold site*, which is an empty building that is prewired for necessary telephone and Internet access, plus a contract with one or more vendors to provide all necessary equipment within a specified period of time. A cold site still leaves the organization without the use of its information system for a period of time, so it is appropriate only when the organization's RTO is one day or more. A second option is to contract for use of a *hot site*, which is a facility that is not only prewired for telephone and Internet access but also contains all the computing and office equipment the organization needs to perform its essential business activities. A hot site typically results in an RTO of hours.

A problem with both cold and hot sites is that the site provider typically oversells its capacity, under the assumption that at any one time only a few clients will need to use the facility. That assumption is usually warranted. In the event of a major disaster, such as Hurricane Katrina, that affects all organizations in a geographic area, however, some organizations may find that they cannot obtain access to their cold or hot site. Consequently, a third infrastructure replacement option for organizations with a very short RTO is to establish a second data center as a backup and use it to implement real-time mirroring.

A *business continuity plan (BCP)* specifies how to resume not only IT operations, but all business processes, including relocating to new offices and hiring temporary replacements, in the event that a major calamity destroys not only an organization's data center but also its main headquarters. Such planning is important, because more than half of the organizations without a DRP and a BCP never reopen after being forced to close down for more than a few days because of a disaster. Thus, having both a DRP and a BCP can mean the difference between surviving a major catastrophe such as Hurricane Katrina or 9/11 and going out of business. Focus 10-2 describes how planning helped NASDAQ survive the complete destruction of its offices in the World Trade Center on September 11, 2001.

Simply having a DRP and a BCP, however, is not enough. Both plans must be well documented. The documentation should include not only instructions for notifying appropriate staff and the steps to take to resume operations, but also vendor documentation of all hardware and software. It is especially important to document the numerous modifications made to default configurations, so that the replacement system has the same functionality as the original. Failure to do so can create substantial costs and delays in implementing the recovery process. Detailed operating instructions are also needed, especially if temporary replacements have to be hired. Finally, copies of all documentation need to be stored both on-site and off-site so that it is available when needed.

Periodic testing and revision are probably the most important components of effective disaster recovery and business continuity plans. Most plans fail their initial test because it is impossible

Thanks to its effective disaster recovery and business continuity plans, NASDAQ was up and running six days after the
September 11, 2001, terrorist attack that destroyed the twin
towers of the World Trade Center. NASDAQ'S headquarters
were located on the 49th and 50th floors of One Liberty
Plaza, just across the street from the World Trade Center.
When the first plane hit, NASDAQ'S security guards immediately evacuated personnel from the building. Most of the
employees were out of the building by the time the second
plane crashed into the other tower. Although employees were
evacuated from the headquarters and the office in Times
Square had temporarily lost telephone service, NASDAQ was
able to relocate to a backup center at the nearby Marriott
Marquis hotel. Once there, NASDAQ executives went through
their list of priorities: first, their employees; next, the physical
damage; and last, the trading industry situation.

Effective communication became essential in determining
the condition of these priorities. NASDAQ attributes much of
its success in communicating and coordinating with the rest
of the industry to its dress rehearsals for Y2K. While preparing for the changeover, NASDAQ had regular nationwide
teleconferences with all the exchanges. This helped it organize similar conferences after the 9/11 attack. NASDAQ had

already planned for one potential crisis, and this proved
helpful in recovering from a different, unexpected, crisis. By
prioritizing and teleconferencing, the company was able to
quickly identify problems and the traders who would need
extra help before NASDAQ could open the market again.

NASDAQ'S extremely redundant and dispersed systems
also helped it quickly reopen the market. Executives carried
more than one mobile phone so that they could continue
to communicate in the event one carrier lost service. Every
trader was linked to two of NASDAQ's 20 connection centers located throughout the United States. The centers are
connected to each other using two separate paths and
sometimes two distinct vendors. Servers are kept in different
buildings and have two network topologies. In addition
to Manhattan and Times Square, NASDAQ had offices in
Maryland and Connecticut. This decentralization allowed
it to monitor the regulatory processes throughout the days
following the attack. It also lessened the risk of losing all
NASDAQ'S senior management.

NASDAQ also invested in interruption insurance to help
defer the costs of closing the market. All of this planning
and foresight saved NASDAQ from losing what could have
been tens of millions of dollars.

to fully anticipate everything that could go wrong. The time to discover such problems is not during an actual emergency, but rather in a setting in which weaknesses can be carefully and thoroughly analyzed and appropriate changes in procedures made. Therefore, disaster recovery and
business continuity plans need to be tested on at least an annual basis to ensure that they accurately reflect recent changes in equipment and procedures. It is especially important to test the
procedures involved in the transfer of actual operations to cold or hot sites. Finally, DRP and
BCP documentation needs to be updated to reflect any changes in procedures made in response
to problems identified during tests of those plans.

EFFECTS OF VIRTUALIZATION AND CLOUD COMPUTING A virtual machine is just a collection of
software files. Therefore, if the physical server hosting that machine fails, the files can be
installed on another host machine within minutes. Thus, virtualization significantly reduces the
time needed to recover (RTO) from hardware problems. Note that virtualization does not
eliminate the need for backups; organizations still need to create periodic "snapshots" of desktop
and server virtual machines and then store those snapshots on a network drive so that the
machines can be recreated. Virtualization can also be used to support real-time mirroring in
which two copies of each virtual machine are run in tandem on two separate physical hosts.
Every transaction is processed on both virtual machines. If one fails, the other picks up without
any break in service.

Cloud computing has both positive and negative effects on availability. Cloud computing
typically utilizes banks of redundant servers in multiple locations, thereby reducing the risk that
a single catastrophe could result in system downtime and the loss of all data. However, if a public cloud provider goes out of business, it may be difficult, if not impossible, to retrieve any data
stored in the cloud. Therefore, a policy of making regular backups and storing those backups
somewhere other than with the cloud provider is critical. In addition, accountants need to assess
the long-run financial viability of a cloud provider before their organization commits to outsource any of its data or applications to a public cloud.

Change Control

COBIT sections AI 6, AI 7, and DS 9 address different aspects of the critically important topic of change control. Organizations constantly modify their information systems to reflect new business practices and to take advantage of advances in information technology. *Change control* is the formal process used to ensure that modifications to hardware, software, or processes do not reduce systems reliability. In fact, good change control often results in overall *better* operating performance: careful testing prior to implementation reduces the likelihood of making changes that cause system downtime, and thorough documentation facilitates quicker "trouble-shooting" and resolution of any problems that do occur. Companies with a good change control process are also less likely to suffer financial or reputational harm from security incidents.

Effective change control procedures require regularly monitoring for unauthorized changes and sanctioning anyone who intentionally introduces such changes. Other principles of a well-designed change control process include the following:

- All change requests should be documented and follow a standardized format that clearly identifies the nature of the change, the reason for the request, the date of the request, and the outcome of the request.
- All changes should be approved by appropriate levels of management. Approvals should be clearly documented to provide an audit trail. Managers should consult with the CISO or other IT managers about the effects of the proposed changes on systems reliability.
- To assess the impact of the proposed change on all five principles of systems reliability, changes should be thoroughly tested prior to implementation in a separate, nonproduction environment, not the system actually used for daily business processes. (Virtualization technology can be used to reduce the costs of creating a separate testing and development system). As data from old files and databases are entered into new data structures, conversion controls are needed to ensure that the new data storage media are free of errors. The old and new systems should be run in parallel at least once and the results compared to identify discrepancies. Internal auditors should review data conversion processes for accuracy.
- All documentation (program instructions, systems descriptions, backup and disaster recovery plans, etc.) should be updated to reflect authorized changes to the system.
- "Emergency" changes or deviations from standard operating policies must be documented and subjected to a formal review and approval process as soon after implementation as practicable. All emergency changes need to be logged to provide an audit trail.
- "Backout" plans need to be developed for reverting to previous configurations in case approved changes need to be interrupted or abandoned.
- User rights and privileges must be carefully monitored *during* the change process to ensure that proper segregation of duties is maintained.

Probably the most important change control is adequate monitoring and review by top management to ensure that proposed and implemented changes are consistent with the organization's multiyear strategic plan. The objective of this oversight is to make certain that the organization's information system continues to effectively support its strategy. Many organizations create IT steering committees to perform this important monitoring function.

Summary and Case Conclusion

Jason's report assessed the effectiveness of Northwest Industries' controls designed to ensure processing integrity. To minimize data entry, and the opportunity for mistakes, Northwest Industries mailed turnaround documents to customers, which were returned with their payments. All data entry was done online, with extensive use of input validation routines to ensure the accuracy of the information entering the system. Managers reviewed output for reasonableness, and the accuracy of key components of financial reports was regularly cross-validated with independent sources. For example, inventory was counted quarterly, and the results of the physical counts were reconciled to the quantities stored in the system.

Jason was concerned about the effectiveness of controls designed to ensure systems availability, however. He noted that although Northwest Industries had developed a disaster recovery and business continuity plan, those plans had not been reviewed or updated for three years. Of even greater concern was the fact that many portions of the plan, including arrangements for a cold site located in California, had never been tested. Jason's biggest concern, however, related to backup procedures. All files were backed up weekly, on Saturdays, onto DVDs, and incremental backups were made each night, but no one had ever practiced restoring the data. In addition, the backups were not encrypted, and one copy was stored on-site in the main server room on a shelf by the door.

Jason also documented evidence of weaknesses related to change control. One point of concern was the finding that "emergency" changes made during the past year were not documented. Another was the fact that in order to save money, Northwest Industries gave programmers access to its transaction processing system to make changes, rather than using a separate testing and development system.

Jason concluded his report with specific recommendations to address the weaknesses he had found. He recommended that Northwest Industries immediately test its backup restoration procedures and encrypt its backup files. Jason also recommended testing the DRP and BCP plans. Another recommendation was to purchase a server that would use virtualization software to create a testing and development system and restrict programmers' access to only that virtual system. Finally, he suggested the CIO should assign someone to update the documentation to record the effects of "emergency changes" made during the past year and implement procedures to ensure that all future changes be documented. Jason felt confident that once those recommendations were implemented, management could be reasonably assured that Northwest Industries' information systems had satisfied the AICPA's Trust Services framework criteria and principles for systems reliability.

Key Terms

turnaround document 276	header record 277	recovery point objective
field check 276	trailer record 278	(RPO) 285
sign check 276	transposition error 278	recovery time objective
limit check 276	cross-footing balance	(RTO) 285
range check 276	test 278	real-time mirroring 285
size check 276	zero-balance test 278	incremental backup 285
completeness check 276	concurrent update	differential backup 286
validity check 276	controls 278	archive 286
reasonableness test 276	checksum 279	disaster recovery plan
check digit 277	parity bit 279	(DRP) 287
check digit verification 277	parity checking 279	cold site 287
sequence check 277	fault tolerance 284	hot site 287
batch totals 277	redundant arrays of	business continuity plan
financial total 277	independent drives	(BCP) 287
hash total 277	(RAID) 284	change control 289
record count 277	uninterruptible power supply	
prompting 277	(UPS) 284	
closed-loop verification 277	backup 285	

AIS IN ACTION

Chapter Quiz

1. Which of the following measures the amount of data that might be potentially lost as a result of a system failure?
   a. recovery time objective (RTO)
   b. recovery point objective (RPO)
   c. disaster recovery plan (DRP)
   d. business continuity plan (BCP)

2. Which data entry application control would detect and prevent entry of alphabetic characters as the price of an inventory item?
   a. field check
   b. limit check
   c. reasonableness check
   d. sign check

3. Which of the following controls would prevent entry of a nonexistent customer number in a sales transaction?
   a. field check
   b. completeness check
   c. validity check
   d. batch total

4. Which disaster recovery strategy involves contracting for use of a physical site to which all necessary computing equipment will be delivered within 24 to 36 hours?
   a. virtualization
   b. cold site
   c. hot site
   d. data mirroring

5. Which of the following statements is true?
   a. Incremental daily backups are faster to perform than differential daily backups, but restoration is slower and more complex.
   b. Incremental daily backups are faster to perform than differential daily backups, and restoration is faster and simpler.
   c. Differential daily backups are faster to perform than incremental daily backups, but restoration is slower and more complex.
   d. Differential daily backups are faster to perform than incremental daily backups, and restoration is faster and simpler.

6. Information that needs to be stored securely for 10 years or more would most likely be stored in which type of file?
   a. backup
   b. archive
   c. encrypted
   d. log

7. Which of the following is an example of the kind of batch total called a hash total?
   a. the sum of the purchase amount field in a set of purchase orders
   b. the sum of the purchase order number field in a set of purchase orders
   c. the number of completed documents in a set of purchase orders
   d. all of the above

8. Which of the following statements is true?
   a. "Emergency" changes need to be documented once the problem is resolved.
   b. Changes should be tested in a system separate from the one used to process transactions.
   c. Change controls are necessary to maintain adequate segregation of duties.
   d. All of the above are true.

9. Which of the following provides detailed procedures to resolve the problems resulting from a flash flood that completely destroys a company's data center?
   a. backup plan
   b. disaster recovery plan (DRP)
   c. business continuity plan (BCP)
   d. archive plan

10. Which of the following is a control that can be used to verify the accuracy of information transmitted over a network?
    a. completeness check
    b. check digit
    c. parity bit
    d. size check

Discussion Questions

10.1. Two ways to create processing integrity controls in Excel spreadsheets are to use the built-in Data Validation tool or to write custom code with IF statements. What are the relative advantages and disadvantages of these two approaches?

10.2. What is the difference between using check digit verification and using a validity check to test the accuracy of an account number entered on a transaction record?

10.3. For each of the three basic options for replacing IT infrastructure (cold sites, hot sites, and real-time mirroring), give an example of an organization that could use that approach as part of its DRP. Be prepared to defend your answer.

10.4. Use the numbers 10–19 to show why transposition errors are always divisible by 9.

10.5. What are some business processes for which an organization might use batch processing?

10.6. Why do you think that surveys continue to find that a sizable percentage of organizations either do not have formal disaster recovery and business continuity plans or have not tested and revised those plans for more than a year?

Problems

10.1. Match the following terms with the appropriate definition or example:

____	**1.** Business continuity plan (BCP)	a. A file used to store information for long periods of time
____	**2.** Completeness check	b. A plan that describes how to resume IT functionality after a disaster
____	**3.** Hash total	c. An application control that verifies that the quantity ordered is greater than 0
____	**4.** Incremental daily backup	d. A control that counts the number of odd or even bits in order to verify that all data were transmitted correctly
____	**5.** Archive	e. An application control that tests whether a customer is 18 or older
____	**6.** Field check	f. A daily backup plan that copies all changes since the last full backup
____	**7.** Sign check	g. A disaster recovery plan that contracts for use of an alternate site that has all necessary computing and network equipment, plus Internet connectivity
____	**8.** Change control	h. A disaster recovery plan that contracts for use of another company's information system
____	**9.** Cold site	i. A disaster recovery plan that contracts for use of an alternate site that is prewired for Internet connectivity but has no computing or network equipment
____	**10.** Limit check	j. An application control that ensures that a customer's ship-to address is entered in a sales order
____	**11.** Zero-balance test	k. An application control that involves use of an account that should not have a balance after processing
____	**12.** Recovery point objective (RPO)	l. An application control that involves comparing the sum of a set of columns to the sum of a set of rows
____	**13.** Recovery time objective (RTO)	m. A measure of the length of time that an organization is willing to function without its information system
____	**14.** Record count	n. A measure of the amount of data that an organization is willing to reenter or possibly lose in the event of a disaster
____	**15.** Validity check	o. A batch total that does not have any intrinsic meaning
____	**16.** Check digit verification	p. A batch total that represents the number of transactions processed

_____ **17.** Closed-loop verification

q. An application control that validates the correctness of one data item in a transaction record by comparing it to the value of another data item in that transaction record

_____ **18.** Parity checking

r. An application control that verifies that an account number entered in a transaction record matches an account number in the related master file

_____ **19.** Reasonableness test

s. A plan that describes how to resume business operations after a major calamity, such as Hurricane Katrina, that destroys not only an organization's data center but also its headquarters

_____ **20.** Financial total

t. A data entry application control that verifies the accuracy of an account number by recalculating the last number as a function of the preceding numbers

_____ **21.** Turnaround document

u. A daily backup procedure that copies only the activity that occurred on that particular day

v. A data entry application control that could be used to verify that only numeric data are entered into a field

w. A plan to ensure that modifications to an information system do not reduce its security

x. A data entry application control in which the system displays the value of a data item and asks the user to verify that the system has accessed the correct record

y. A batch total that represents the total dollar value of a set of transactions

z. A document sent to an external party and subsequently returned so that preprinted data can be scanned rather than manually reentered.

10.2. Excel Problem

Enter the following data into a spreadsheet, and then perform the following tasks:

Employee Number	Pay Rate	Hours Worked	Gross Pay	Deductions	Net Pay
12355	10.55	38	400.90	125.00	275.90
2178g	11.00	40	440.00	395.00	45.00
24456	95.00	90	8550.00	145.00	8405.00
34567	10.00	40	400.00	105.00	505.00

a. Calculate examples of these batch totals:
   • A hash total
   • A financial total
   • A record count

b. Assume the following rules govern normal data:
   • Employee numbers are five digits in length and range from 10000 through 99999.
   • Maximum pay rate is $25, and minimum is $9.
   • Hours worked should never exceed 40.
   • Deductions should never exceed 40% of gross pay.

Give a specific example of an error or probable error in the data set that each of the following controls would detect:
   • Field check
   • Limit check
   • Reasonableness test
   • Cross-footing balance test

c. Create a control procedure that would prevent, or at least detect, each of the errors in the data set.

10.3. Excel Problem

The Moose Wings Cooperative Flight Club owns a number of airplanes and gliders. It serves fewer than 2,000 members, who are numbered sequentially from the founder, Tom Eagle (0001), to the newest member, Jacques Noveau (1368). Members rent the flying machines by the hour, and all must be returned on the same day. The following six records were among those entered for the flights taken on September 1, 2010:

Member #	Flight Date MM/DD/YY	Plane Used*	Takeoff Time	Landing Time
1234	09/10/10	G	6:25	8:46
4111	09/01/10	C	8:49	10:23
1210	09/01/10	P	3:42	5:42
0023	09/01/10	X	1:59	12:43
012A	09/01/10	P	12:29	15:32
0999	09/01/10	L	15:31	13:45

*C = Cessna, G = Glider, L = Lear Jet, P = Piper Cub

Required

a. Identify and describe any errors in the data.
b. For each of the five data fields, suggest one or more input edit controls that could be used to detect input errors.
c. Enter the data in a spreadsheet, and create appropriate controls to prevent or at least detect the input errors.
d. Suggest other controls to minimize the risk of input errors.

(SMAC adapted)

10.4. The first column in Table 10-3 lists transaction amounts that have been summed to obtain a batch total. Assume that all data in the first column are correct. Cases A through D each contain an input error in one record, along with a batch total computed from that set of records.

Required

For each case (a through d), compute the difference between the correct and erroneous batch totals, and explain how this difference could help identify the cause of the error.

TABLE 10-3 Data for Problem 10.4

	Correct Transactions	Case A	Case B	Case C	Case D
	$3,630.62	$3,630.62	$3,630.62	$3,630.62	$3,630.62
	1,484.86	1,484.86	1,484.86	1,484.86	1,484.86
	1,723.46	1,723.46	1,723.46	1,723.46	1,723.46
	9,233.25	9,233.25	9,233.25	9,233.25	9,233.25
	123.45	123.45	123.45	123.45	123.45
	7,832.44	7,832.44	1,832.44	7,832.44	7,832.44
	2,398.33	2,398.33	2,398.33	2,398.33	2,398.33
	3,766.24	3,766.24	3,766.24	3,766.24	3,766.24
	4,400.00	4,400.00	4,400.00	−4,400.00	4,400.00
	2,833.00	2,833.00	2,833.00	2,833.00	2,833.00
	1,978.95	1,987.95	1,978.95	1,978.95	1,978.95
	654.32	654.32	654.32	654.32	9,876.23
	9,876.23	9,876.23	9,876.23	9,876.23	2,138.10
	2,138.10	2,138.10	2,138.10	2,138.10	5,533.99
	5,533.99	5,533.99	5,533.99	5,533.99	
Batch total	$57,607.24	$57,616.24	$51,607.24	$48,807.24	$56,952.92

10.5. Excel Problem

Create a spreadsheet with the following columns:

- Plaintext character
- ASCII code (seven bits, binary number)
- First bit
- Second bit
- Third bit
- Fourth bit
- Fifth bit
- Sixth bit
- Seventh bit
- Number of bits with value = 1
- Parity bit for odd parity coding
- Parity bit for even parity coding

Required

a. Enter a-e, A-E, 0-9, ?, !,%, &, and ; in the plaintext column.

b. The ASCII column should convert the plaintext character to the binary code used by your computer.

c. The next seven columns should each display one bit of the ASCII code, beginning with the leftmost digit. (*Hint:* Excel provides text functions that can select individual characters from a string.)

d. The tenth column should sum the number of bits that have the value 1. (*Hint:* The text functions used to populate columns 3–9 return a text string that you will need to convert to a numeric value.)

e. Column 11 should have a 1 if the number in column 10 is odd, and 0 if the number in column 10 is even.

f. Column 12 should have a 1 if the number in column 10 is even, and a 0 if the number in column 10 is odd.

10.6. The ABC Company is considering the following options for its backup plan:

1. Daily full backups:
   - Time to perform backup = 60 minutes
   - Size of backup = 50 GB
   - Time to restore from backup = 30 minutes
2. Weekly full backups plus daily incremental backup:
   - Same requirements as option 1 to do a full backup on Friday, plus
   - Time to perform daily backup = 10 minutes
   - Size of daily backup = 10 GB
   - Time to restore each daily backup file = 5 minutes
3. Weekly full backups plus daily differential backup:
   - Same requirements as option 1 to do a full backup on Friday, plus
   - Time to perform daily backup = 10 minutes first day, growing by 5 minutes each day thereafter
   - Size of daily backup = 10 GB first day, growing by 10 GB each day
   - Time to restore differential backup file = 5 minutes first day, increasing by 2 minutes each subsequent day

   Which approach would you recommend? Why?

10.7. Which control(s) would best mitigate the following threats?

a. The hours-worked field in a payroll transaction record contained the value 400 instead of 40. As a result, the employee received a paycheck for $6,257.24 instead of $654.32.

b. The accounts receivable file was destroyed because it was accidentally used to update accounts payable.

c. During processing of customer payments, the digit 0 in a payment of $204 was mistakenly typed as the letter "O." As a result, the transaction was not processed correctly, and the customer erroneously received a letter that the account was delinquent.

d. A salesperson mistakenly entered an online order for 50 laser printers instead of 50 laser printer toner cartridges.

e. A 20-minute power brownout caused a mission-critical database server to crash, shutting down operations temporarily.

f. A fire destroyed the data center, including all backup copies of the accounts receivable files.

g. After processing sales transactions, the inventory report showed a negative quantity on hand for several items.

h. A customer order for an important part did not include the customer's address. Consequently, the order was not shipped on time, and the customer called to complain.

i. When entering a large credit sale, the clerk typed in the customer's account number as 45982 instead of 45892. That account number did not exist. The mistake was not caught until later in the week, when the weekly billing process was run. Consequently, the customer was not billed for another week, delaying receipt of payment.

j. A visitor to the company's Web site entered 400 characters into the five-digit Zip code field, causing the server to crash.

k. Two traveling sales representatives accessed the parts database at the same time. Salesperson A noted that there were still 55 units of part 723 available and entered an order for 45 of them. While salesperson A was keying in the order, salesperson B, in another state, also noted the availability of 55 units for part 723 and entered an order for 33 of them. Both sales reps promised their customer next-day delivery. Salesperson A's customer, however, learned the next day that the part would have to be back-ordered. The customer canceled the sale and vowed to never again do business with the company.

l. The warranty department manager was upset because special discount coupons were mailed to every customer who had purchased the product within the past three years, instead of to only those customers who had purchased the product within the past three months.

m. The clerk entering details about a large credit sale mistakenly typed in a nonexistent account number. Consequently, the company never received payment for the items.

n. A customer filled in the wrong account number on the portion of the invoice being returned with payment. Consequently, the payment was credited to another customer's account.

o. A batch of 73 time sheets was sent to the payroll department for weekly processing. Somehow, one of the time sheets did not get processed. The mistake was not caught until payday, when one employee complained about not receiving a paycheck.

p. Sunspot activity resulted in the loss of some data being sent to the regional office. The problem was not discovered until several days later, when managers attempted to query the database for that information.

10.8. MonsterMed Inc. (MMI) is an online pharmaceutical firm. MMI has a small systems staff that designs and writes MMI's customized software. The data center is installed in the basement of its two-story headquarters building. The data center is equipped with halon-gas fire suppression equipment and an uninterruptible power supply system.

The computer operations staff works a two-shift schedule, five days per week. MMI's programming staff, located in the same building, has access to the data center and can test new programs and program changes when the operations staff is not available. Programmers make changes in response to oral requests by employees using the system. Because the programming staff is small and the work demands have increased, systems and programming documentation is developed only when time is available. Backups are made whenever time permits. The backup files are stored in a locked cabinet in the data center. Unfortunately, due to several days of heavy rains, MMI's building recently experienced serious flooding that destroyed not only the computer hardware but also all the data and program files that were on-site.

Required

a. Identify at least five weaknesses in MonsterMed Inc.'s backup and DRP procedures.
b. Evaluate change controls at MonsterMed Inc.

(CMA exam, adapted)

10.9. Excel Problem

Create data validation rules in a spreadsheet to perform each of the following controls:
a. Limit check—that values in the cell are < 70
b. Range check—that values in the cell are between 15 and 65
c. Sign check—that values in the cell are positive
d. Field check—that values in a cell are only numeric
e. Size check—that the cell accepts no more than 40 characters of text
f. Reasonableness check—that the cell's value is less than 75% of the cell to its left
g. Validity check—that a value exists in a list of allowable values

10.10. Excel Problem

Creating and testing check digits.

Required

a. Create a spreadsheet that will take as input a five-digit account number, and calculate a check digit using this formula: (5 × left-most digit + 4 × next digit + 3 × third digit + 2 × fourth digit + fifth digit) modulus division by 7. (Modulus division returns the remainder—for example: 11 modulus division by 3 = 2). The check digit then becomes the sixth (right-most) digit in the account number. Your spreadsheet should look like this:

Check digits—creation and use

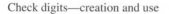

a. Creating check digits   Formula = (5x left-most digit + 4x next digit + 3x third digit + 2x fourth digit + fifth digit) mod 7

Raw account#	First digit	Second digit	Third digit	Fourth digit	Fifth digit	Check digit calculation	Actual account #
12345	1	2	3	4	5	0	123450
12346	1	2	3	4	6	1	123461
12347	1	2	3	4	7	2	123472
12348	1	2	3	4	8	3	123483
12349	1	2	3	4	9	4	123494
12350	1	2	3	5	0	4	123504
12351	1	2	3	5	1	5	123515
12352	1	2	3	5	2	6	123526
12353	1	2	3	5	3	0	123530

b. Add another panel to the spreadsheet that takes as input a six-digit account number and uses the check digit formula in part a to test whether or not the account number is valid. Your solution should look like this:

b. Testing check digits

Account number	First digit	Second digit	Third digit	Fourth digit	Fifth digit	Check digit	Valid? (Y/N)
123530	1	2	3	5	3	0	Y
123534	1	2	3	5	3	4	N

10.11. For each of the following scenarios, determine whether the company's current backup procedures enable it to meet its recovery objectives, and explain why:
a. Scenario 1:
   • Recovery point objective = 24 hours
   • Daily backups at 3:00 A.M., process takes 2 hours
   • Copy of backup tapes picked up daily at 8:00 A.M. for storage off-site

b. Scenario 2: Company makes daily incremental backups Monday through Saturday at 7:00 P.M. each night. Company makes full backup weekly, on Sunday at 1:00 P.M.
   - Recovery time objective = 2 hours
   - Time to do full backup = 3 hours
   - Time to restore from full backup = 1 hour
   - Time to make incremental daily backup = 1 hour
   - Time to restore each incremental daily backup = 30 minutes
c. Scenario 3: Company makes daily differential backups Monday through Friday at 8:00 P.M. each night. Company makes full backup weekly, on Saturdays, at 8:00 A.M.
   - Recovery time objective = 6 hours
   - Time to do full backup = 4 hours
   - Time to restore from full backup = 3 hours
   - Time to do differential daily backups = 1 hour on Monday, increasing by 30 minutes each successive day
   - Time to restore differential daily backup = 30 minutes for Monday, increasing by 15 minutes each successive day

Case 10-1 • Ensuring Systems Availability

The *Journal of Accountancy* (available at www.aicpa.org) has published a series of articles that address different aspects of disaster recovery and business continuity planning:

1. J. A. Gerber and E. R. Feldman, "Is Your Business Prepared for the Worst?" *Journal of Accountancy* (April 2002): 61–64.
2. E. McCarthy, "The Best-Laid Plans," *Journal of Accountancy* (May 2004): 46–54.
3. R. Myers, "Katrina's Harsh Lessons," *Journal of Accountancy* (June 2006): 54–63.
4. S. Phelan and M. Hayes, "Before the Deluge—and After," *Journal of Accountancy* (April 2003): 57–66.

Required

Read one or more of these articles that your professor assigns, plus section DS 4 of COBIT version 4.1 (available at www.isaca.org), to answer the following questions:

1. What does COBIT suggest as possible metrics for evaluating how well an organization is achieving the objective of DS 4? Why do you think that metric is useful?

2. For each article assigned by your professor, complete the following table, summarizing what each article said about a specific COBIT control objective (an article may not address all 10 control objectives in DS 4):

COBIT Control Objective	Points Discussed in Article
DS 4.1	
DS 4.2	
DS 4.3	
DS 4.4	
DS 4.5	
DS 4.6	
DS 4.7	
DS 4.8	
DS 4.9	
DS 4.10	

Case 10-2 Change Controls

Read section AI 6 in version 4.1 of COBIT (available at www. isaca.org), and answer the following questions:

1. What is the purpose of each detailed control objective—why is it important?
2. How is each of the suggested metrics useful?

AIS IN ACTION SOLUTIONS

Quiz Key

1. Which of the following measures the amount of data that might be potentially lost as a result of a system failure?
   a. recovery time objective (RTO) (Incorrect. The RTO measures the time that an organization may have to function without its information system.)
   ▶ b. recovery point objective (RPO) (Correct. The RPO measures the time between the last data backup and the occurrence of a problem.)
   c. disaster recovery plan (DRP) (Incorrect. A DRP specifies the procedures to restore IT operations.)
   d. business continuity plan (BCP) (Incorrect. A BCP specifies the procedures to resume business processes.)

2. Which data entry application control would detect and prevent entry of alphabetic characters as the price of an inventory item?
   ▶ a. field check (Correct. Field checks test whether data are numeric or alphabetic.)
   b. limit check (Incorrect. A limit check compares an input value against a fixed number.)
   c. reasonableness check (Incorrect. A reasonableness check compares two data items to determine whether the values of both are reasonable.)
   d. sign check (Incorrect. A sign check determines whether a numeric field is positive or negative.)

3. Which of the following controls would prevent entry of a nonexistent customer number in a sales transaction?
   a. field check (Incorrect. A field check tests only whether data are numeric or alphabetic.)
   b. completeness check (Incorrect. A completeness check would ensure that a customer number was entered, but it does not test whether the customer number exists.)
   ▶ c. validity check (Correct. A validity check compares a customer number entered into a transaction record against the customer numbers that exist in the master file or database.)
   d. batch total (Incorrect. A batch total is used to verify completeness of data entry.)

4. Which disaster recovery strategy involves contracting for use of a physical site to which all necessary computing equipment will be delivered within 24 to 36 hours?
   a. virtualization (Incorrect. Virtualization is a strategy to make better use of resources by running multiple virtual machines on one physical host. It is not a disaster recovery strategy.)
   ▶ b. cold site (Correct.)
   c. hot site (Incorrect. A hot site is an infrastructure replacement strategy which contracts for use of a physical site that contains all necessary computer and network equipment.)

    d. data mirroring (Incorrect. Data mirroring is a fault-tolerant backup strategy in which the organization maintains a second data center and all transactions are processed on both systems as they occur.)

5. Which of the following statements is true?
   ▶ **a.** Incremental daily backups are faster to perform than differential daily backups, but restoration is slower and more complex. (Correct.)
      b. Incremental daily backups are faster to perform than differential daily backups, and restoration is faster and simpler. (Incorrect. Incremental daily backups produce separate backup files for each day since the last full backup, making restoration more complex.)
      c. Differential daily backups are faster to perform than incremental daily backups, but restoration is slower and more complex. (Incorrect. Differential daily backups are slower than incremental daily backups, but restoration is faster and simpler because only the most recent differential daily backup and the last full backup files are required.)
      d. Differential daily backups are faster to perform than incremental daily backups, and restoration is faster and simpler. (Incorrect. Differential daily backups are slower to perform than incremental daily backups.)

6. Information that needs to be stored securely for 10 years or more would most likely be stored in which type of file?
      a. backup (Incorrect. Backups are for short-term storage; archives are for long-term storage.)
   ▶ **b.** archive (Correct.)
      c. encrypted (Incorrect. Long-term retention uses archives, which are usually not encrypted.)
      d. log (Incorrect. A log is part of an audit trail.)

7. Which of the following is an example of the kind of batch total called a hash total?
      a. the sum of the purchase amount field in a set of purchase orders (Incorrect. This is an example of a financial total.)
   ▶ **b.** the sum of the purchase order number field in a set of purchase orders (Correct. The sum of purchase order numbers has no intrinsic meaning.)
      c. the number of completed documents in a set of purchase orders (Incorrect. This is an example of a record count.)
      d. all of the above (Incorrect. Choices a and c are incorrect.)

8. Which of the following statements is true?
      a. "Emergency" changes need to be documented once the problem is resolved. (Incorrect. This statement is true, but so are b and c.)
      b. Changes should be tested in a system separate from the one used to process transactions. (Incorrect. This statement is true, but so are a and c.)
      c. Change controls are necessary to maintain adequate segregation of duties. (Incorrect. This statement is true, but so are a and b.)
   ▶ **d.** All of the above are true. (Correct.)

9. Which of the following provides detailed procedures to resolve the problems resulting from a flash flood that completely destroys a company's data center?
      a. backup plan (Incorrect. Backup plans focus solely on making a duplicate copy of files in the event that the original becomes corrupted because of hardware malfunctions, software problems, or human error.)
   ▶ **b.** disaster recovery plan (DRP) (Correct. A DRP focuses on restoring an organization's IT functionality.)
      c. business continuity plan (BCP) (Incorrect. A BCP focuses on restoring not only IT, but all aspects business processes.)
      d. archive plan (Incorrect. An archive plan deals with long-term retention of data.)

10. Which of the following is a control that can be used to verify the accuracy of information transmitted over a network?
    a. completeness check (Incorrect. A completeness check is a data input control to ensure that all necessary data are entered.)
    b. check digit (Incorrect. A check digit is a data input control designed to detect miskeying of account numbers.)
    ▶ c. parity bit (Correct. A parity bit is a communications control that counts the number of bits in order to verify the integrity of data sent and received.)
    d. size check (Incorrect. A size check is a data input control to ensure that the amount of data entered does not exceed the space set aside for it. Size checks are especially important for programs that accept input from users, because they can prevent buffer overflow attacks.)

Chapter 11

Auditing Computer-Based Information Systems

Learning Objectives

After studying this chapter, you should be able to:

1. Describe the scope and objectives of audit work, and identify the major steps in the audit process.

2. Identify the objectives of an information system audit, and describe the four-step approach necessary for meeting these objectives.

3. Design a plan for the study and evaluation of internal control in an AIS.

4. Describe computer audit software, and explain how it is used in the audit of an AIS.

5. Describe the nature and scope of an operational audit.

INTEGRATIVE CASE SEATTLE PAPER PRODUCTS

Seattle Paper Products (SPP) is modifying its sales department payroll system to change the way it calculates sales commissions. Under the old system, commissions were a fixed percentage of dollar sales. The new system is considerably more complex, with commission rates varying according to the product sold and the total dollar volume of sales.

Jason Scott was assigned to use audit software to write a parallel simulation test program to calculate sales commissions and compare them with those generated by the new system. Jason obtained the necessary payroll system documentation and the details on the new sales commission policy and prepared his program.

Jason used the sales transaction data from the last payroll period to run his program. To his surprise, his calculations were $5,000 less than those produced by SPP's new program. Individual differences existed for about half of the company's salespeople. Jason double-checked his program code but could not locate any errors. He

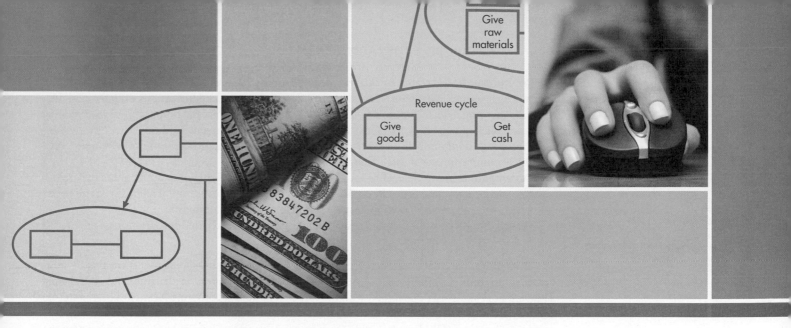

selected a salesperson with a discrepancy and calculated the commission by hand. The result agreed with his program. He reviewed the new commission policy with the sales manager, line by line, and concluded that he understood the new policy completely. Jason is now convinced that his program is correct and that the error lies with SPP's new program. He is now asking himself the following questions:

1. How could a programming error of this significance be overlooked by experienced programmers who thoroughly reviewed and tested the new system?
2. Is this an inadvertent error, or could it be a fraud?
3. What can be done to find the error in the program?

Introduction

This chapter focuses on auditing an accounting information system (AIS). *Auditing* is the systematic process of obtaining and evaluating evidence regarding assertions about economic actions and events in order to determine how well they correspond with established criteria. The results of the audit are then communicated to interested users. Auditing requires careful planning and the collection, review, and documentation of audit evidence. In developing recommendations, the auditor uses established criteria, such as the principles of control described in previous chapters, as a basis for evaluation.

Many organizations in the United States employ internal auditors to evaluate company operations. Governments employ auditors to evaluate management performance and compliance with legislative intent. The Department of Defense employs auditors to review the financial records of companies with defense contracts. Publicly held companies hire external auditors to provide an independent review of their financial statements.

This chapter is written from the perspective of an internal auditor. *Internal auditing* is an independent, objective assurance and consulting activity designed to add value and improve organizational effectiveness and efficiency, including assisting in the design and implementation of an AIS. Internal auditing helps an organization accomplish its objectives by bringing a systematic, disciplined approach to evaluate and improve the effectiveness of risk management, control, and governance processes.

There are several different types of internal audits:

1. A *financial audit* examines the reliability and integrity of financial transactions, accounting records, and financial statements.

2. An *information systems*, or *internal control*, **audit** reviews the controls of an AIS to assess its compliance with internal control policies and procedures and its effectiveness in safeguarding assets. The audits usually evaluate system input and output; processing controls; backup and recovery plans; system security; and computer facilities.
3. An *operational* **audit** is concerned with the economical and efficient use of resources and the accomplishment of established goals and objectives.
4. A *compliance audit* determines whether entities are complying with applicable laws, regulations, policies, and procedures. These audits often result in recommendations to improve processes and controls used to ensure compliance with regulations.
5. An *investigative audit* examines incidents of possible fraud, misappropriation of assets, waste and abuse, or improper governmental activities.

In contrast, external auditors are responsible to corporate shareholders and are mostly concerned with gathering the evidence needed to express an opinion on the financial statements. They are only indirectly concerned with the effectiveness of a corporate AIS. However, external auditors are required to evaluate how audit strategy is affected by an organization's use of information technology (IT). External auditors may need specialized skills to (1) determine how the audit will be affected by IT, (2) assess and evaluate IT controls, and (3) design and perform both tests of IT controls and substantive tests.

Despite the distinction between internal and external auditing, many of the internal audit concepts and techniques discussed in this chapter also apply to external audits.

The first section of this chapter provides an overview of auditing and the steps in the auditing process. The second section describes a methodology and set of techniques for evaluating internal controls in an AIS and conducting an information system audit. The third section discusses the computer software and other techniques for evaluating the reliability and integrity of information in an AIS. Finally, operational audits of an AIS are reviewed.

The Nature of Auditing

Overview of the Audit Process

All audits follow a similar sequence of activities. Audits may be divided into four stages: planning, collecting evidence, evaluating evidence, and communicating audit results. Figure 11-1 is an overview of the auditing process and lists many of the procedures performed within each of these stages.

AUDIT PLANNING   Audit planning determines why, how, when, and by whom the audit will be performed. The first step is to establish the audit's scope and objectives. For example, an audit of a publicly held corporation determines whether its financial statements are presented fairly. In contrast, an internal audit may examine a specific department or a computer application. It may focus on internal controls, financial information, operating performance, or some combination of the three.

An audit team with the necessary experience and expertise is formed. They become familiar with the auditee by conferring with supervisory and operating personnel, reviewing system documentation, and reviewing prior audit findings.

An audit is planned so the greatest amount of audit work focuses on the areas with the highest risk factors. There are three types of audit risk:

1. *Inherent risk* is the susceptibility to material risk in the absence of controls. For example, a system that employs online processing, networks, databases, telecommunications, and other forms of advanced technology has more inherent risk than a batch processing system.
2. *Control risk* is the risk that a material misstatement will get through the internal control structure and into the financial statements. A company with weak internal controls has a higher control risk than one with strong controls. Control risk can be determined by reviewing the control environment, testing internal controls, and considering control weaknesses identified in prior audits and evaluating how they have been rectified.

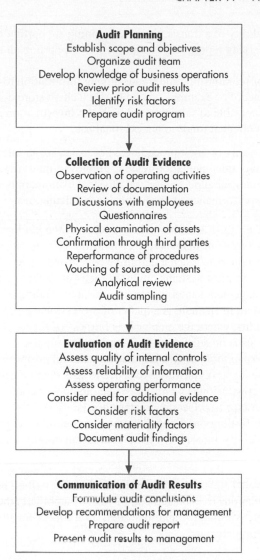

FIGURE 11-1

Overview of the Auditing Process

3. *Detection risk* is the risk that auditors and their audit procedures will fail to detect a material error or misstatement.

To conclude the planning stage, an audit program is prepared to show the nature, extent, and timing of the procedures needed to achieve audit objectives and minimize audit risks. A time budget is prepared, and staff members are assigned to perform specific audit steps.

COLLECTION OF AUDIT EVIDENCE   Most audit effort is spent collecting evidence. Because many audit tests cannot be performed on all items under review, they are often performed on a sample basis. The following are the most common ways to collect audit evidence:

- *Observation* of the activities being audited (e.g., watching how data control personnel handle data processing work as it is received)
- *Review of documentation* to understand how a particular process or internal control system is supposed to function
- *Discussions* with employees about their jobs and about how they carry out certain procedures
- *Questionnaires* that gather data
- *Physical examination* of the quantity and/or condition of tangible assets, such as equipment and inventory
- *Confirmation* of the accuracy of information, such as customer account balances, through communication with independent third parties
- *Reperformance* of calculations to verify quantitative information (e.g., recalculating the annual depreciation expense)

- *Vouching* for the validity of a transaction by examining supporting documents, such as the purchase order, receiving report, and vendor invoice supporting an accounts payable transaction
- *Analytical review* of relationships and trends among information to detect items that should be further investigated. For example, an auditor for a chain store discovered that one store's ratio of accounts receivable to sales was too high. An investigation revealed that the manager was diverting collected funds to her personal use.

A typical audit has a mix of audit procedures. For example, an internal control audit makes greater use of observation, documentation review, employee interviews, and reperformance of control procedures. A financial audit focuses on physical examination, confirmation, vouching, analytical review, and reperformance of account balance calculations.

EVALUATION OF AUDIT EVIDENCE   The auditor evaluates the evidence gathered and decides whether it supports a favorable or unfavorable conclusion. If inconclusive, the auditor performs sufficient additional procedures to reach a definitive conclusion.

Because errors exist in most systems, auditors focus on detecting and reporting those that significantly impact management's interpretation of the audit findings. Determining *materiality*, what is and is not important in an audit, is a matter of professional judgment. Materiality is more important to external audits, where the emphasis is fairness of financial statement, than to internal audits, where the focus is on adherence to management policies.

The auditor seeks **reasonable assurance** that no material error exists in the information or process audited. Because it is prohibitively expensive to seek complete assurance, the auditor has some risk that the audit conclusion is incorrect. When inherent or control risk is high, the auditor must obtain greater assurance to offset the greater uncertainty and risks.

In all audit stages, findings and conclusions are documented in audit working papers. Documentation is especially important at the evaluation stage, when conclusions must be reached and supported.

COMMUNICATION OF AUDIT RESULTS   The auditor submits a written report summarizing audit findings and recommendations to management, the audit committee, the board of directors, and other appropriate parties. Afterwards, auditors often do a follow-up study to ascertain whether recommendations were implemented.

The Risk-Based Audit Approach

The following internal control evaluation approach, called the risk-based audit approach, provides a framework for conducting information system audits:

1. *Determine the threats (fraud and errors) facing the company.*   This is a list of the accidental or intentional abuse and damage to which the system is exposed.
2. *Identify the control procedures that prevent, detect, or correct the threats.*   These are all the controls that management has put into place and that auditors should review and test, to minimize the threats.
3. *Evaluate control procedures.*   Controls are evaluated two ways:
   a. A *systems review* determines whether control procedures are actually in place.
   b. *Tests of controls* are conducted to determine whether existing controls work as intended.
4. *Evaluate control weaknesses to determine their effect on the nature, timing, or extent of auditing procedures.*   If the auditor determines that control risk is too high because the control system is inadequate, the auditor may have to gather more evidence, better evidence, or more timely evidence. Control weaknesses in one area may be acceptable if there are *compensating controls* in other areas.

The risk-based approach provides auditors with a clearer understanding of the fraud and errors that can occur and the related risks and exposures. It also helps them plan how to test and evaluate internal controls, as well as how to plan subsequent audit procedures. The result is a sound basis for developing recommendations to management on how the AIS control system should be improved.

Information Systems Audits

The purpose of an information systems audit is to review and evaluate the internal controls that protect the system. When performing an information systems audit, auditors should ascertain that the following six objectives are met:

1. Security provisions protect computer equipment, programs, communications, and data from unauthorized access, modification, or destruction.
2. Program development and acquisition are performed in accordance with management's general and specific authorization.
3. Program modifications have management's authorization and approval.
4. Processing of transactions, files, reports, and other computer records is accurate and complete.
5. Source data that are inaccurate or improperly authorized are identified and handled according to prescribed managerial policies.
6. Computer data files are accurate, complete, and confidential.

Figure 11-2 depicts the relationship among these six objectives and information systems components. Each of these objectives is discussed in detail in the following sections. Each description includes an audit plan to accomplish each objective, as well as the techniques and procedures to carry out the plan.

Objective 1: Overall Security

Table 11-1 uses the risk-based approach to present a framework for auditing overall computer security. It shows that overall system security threats include accidental or intentional damage to system assets; unauthorized access, disclosure, or modification of data and programs; theft; and interruption of crucial business activities.

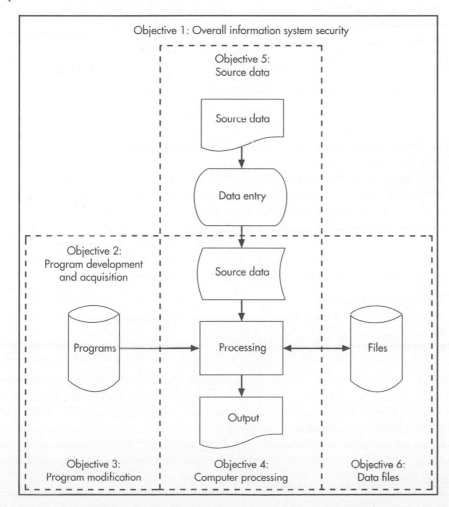

FIGURE 11-2

Information Systems Components and Related Audit Objectives

TABLE 11-1 Framework for Audit of Overall Computer Security

Types of Errors and Fraud

- Theft of or accidental or intentional damage to hardware
- Loss, theft, or unauthorized access to programs, data, and other system resources
- Loss, theft, or unauthorized disclosure of confidential data
- Unauthorized modification or use of programs and data files
- Interruption of crucial business activities

Control Procedures

- Information security/protection plan
- Limiting of physical access to computer equipment
- Limiting of logical access to system using authentication and authorization controls
- Data storage and transmission controls
- Virus protection procedures
- File backup and recovery procedures
- Fault-tolerant systems design
- Disaster recovery plan
- Preventive maintenance
- Firewalls
- Casualty and business interruption insurance

Audit Procedures: System Review

- Inspect computer sites
- Review the information security/protection and disaster recovery plans
- Interview information system personnel about security procedures
- Review physical and logical access policies and procedures
- Review file backup and recovery policies and procedures
- Review data storage and transmission policies and procedures
- Review procedures employed to minimize system downtime
- Review vendor maintenance contracts
- Examine system access logs
- Examine casualty and business interruption insurance policies

Audit Procedures: Tests of Controls

- Observe and test computer-site access procedures
- Observe the preparation of and off-site storage of backup files
- Test assignment and modification procedures for user IDs and passwords
- Investigate how unauthorized access attempts are dealt with
- Verify the extent and effectiveness of data encryption
- Verify the effective use of data transmission controls
- Verify the effective use of firewalls and virus protection procedures
- Verify the use of preventive maintenance and an uninterruptible power supply
- Verify amounts and limitations on insurance coverage
- Examine the results of disaster recovery plan test simulations

Compensating Controls

- Sound personnel policies, including segregation of incompatible duties
- Effective user controls

Control procedures to minimize these threats include developing an information security/protection plan, restricting physical and logical access, encrypting data, protecting against viruses, implementing firewalls, instituting data transmission controls, and preventing and recovering from system failures or disasters.

Systems review procedures include inspecting computer sites; interviewing personnel; reviewing policies and procedures; and examining access logs, insurance policies, and the disaster recovery plan.

Auditors test security controls by observing procedures, verifying that controls are in place and work as intended, investigating errors or problems to ensure they were handled correctly, and examining any tests previously performed. For example, one way to test logical access controls is to try to break into a system. During a U.S. government security audit, auditors used agency terminals to gain unauthorized access to its computer system, disable its security-checking procedures, and control the system from the terminal. The security breakdown was possible because of poor administrative controls and inadequate security software.

Sound personnel policies and effective segregation of incompatible duties can partially compensate for poor computer security. Good user controls will also help, provided that user personnel can recognize unusual system output. Because it is unlikely these controls can compensate indefinitely for poor computer security, auditors should strongly recommend that security weaknesses be corrected.

Objective 2: Program Development and Acquisition

The auditor's role in systems development should be limited to an independent review of systems development activities. To maintain objectivity, auditors should not help develop the system.

Two things can go wrong in program development: (1) inadvertent programming errors due to misunderstanding system specifications or careless programming and (2) unauthorized instructions deliberately inserted into the programs.

These problems can be controlled by requiring management and user authorization and approval, thorough testing, and proper documentation.

During systems review, auditors should discuss development procedures with management, system users, and information system personnel. They should also review the policies, procedures, standards, and documentation listed in Table 11-2.

TABLE 11-2 Framework for Audit of Program Development

Types of Errors and Fraud

- Inadvertent programming errors or unauthorized program code

Control Procedures

- Review of software license agreements
- Management authorization for program development and software acquisition
- Management and user approval of programming specifications
- Thorough testing of new programs, including user acceptance tests
- Complete systems documentation, including approvals

Audit Procedures: System Review

- Independent review of the systems development process
- Review of systems development/acquisition policies and procedures
- Review of systems authorization and approval policies and procedures
- Review of programming evaluation standards
- Review of program and system documentation standards
- Review of test specifications, test data, and test results
- Review of test approval policies and procedures
- Review of acquisition of copyright license agreement policies and procedures
- Discussions with management, users, and information system personnel regarding development procedures

Audit Procedures: Tests of Controls

- Interview users about their systems acquisition/development and implementation involvement
- Review minutes of development team meetings for evidence of involvement
- Verify management and user sign-off approvals at development milestone points
- Review test specifications, test data, and systems test results
- Review software license agreements

Compensating Controls

- Strong processing controls
- Independent processing of test data by auditor

To test systems development controls, auditors should interview managers and system users, examine development approvals, and review development team meeting minutes. The auditor should review all documentation relating to the testing process to make sure all program changes were tested. The auditor should examine the test specifications and the test data and evaluate the test results. Auditors should ascertain how unexpected test result problems were resolved.

Strong processing controls may compensate for inadequate development controls if auditors obtain persuasive evidence of compliance with processing controls, using techniques such as independent test data processing. If this evidence is not obtained, auditors may have to conclude that a material internal control weakness exists and that the risk of significant threats in application programs is unacceptably high.

Objective 3: Program Modification

Table 11-3 presents a framework for auditing changes to application programs and system software. The same threats that occur during program development occur during program modification. For example, a programmer assigned to modify his company's payroll system inserted a command to erase all company files if he was terminated. When he was fired, the system crashed and erased key files.

TABLE 11-3 Framework for Audit of Program Modifications

Types of Errors and Fraud
- Inadvertent programming errors or unauthorized program code

Control Procedures
- List program components to be modified
- Management authorization and approval of program modifications
- User approval of program change specifications
- Thorough test of program changes, including user acceptance tests
- Complete program change documentation, including approvals
- Separate development, test, and production versions of programs
- Changes implemented by personnel independent of users and programmers
- Logical access controls

Audit Procedures: System Review
- Review program modification policies, standards, and procedures
- Review documentation standards for program modification
- Review final documentation of program modifications
- Review program modification testing and test approval procedures
- Review test specifications, test data, and test results
- Review test approval policies and procedures
- Review programming evaluation standards
- Discuss modification policies and procedures with management, users, and systems personnel
- Review logical access control policies and procedures

Audit Procedures: Tests of Controls
- Verify user and management signoff approval for program changes
- Verify that program components to be modified are identified and listed
- Verify that program change test procedures and documentation comply with standards
- Verify that logical access controls are in effect for program changes
- Observe program change implementation
- Verify that separate development, test, and production versions are maintained
- Verify that changes are not implemented by user or programming personnel
- Test for unauthorized or erroneous program changes using a source code comparison program, reprocessing, and parallel simulation

Compensating Controls
- Independent audit tests for unauthorized or erroneous program changes
- Strong processing controls

When a program change is submitted for approval, a list of all required updates should be compiled and approved by management and program users. All program changes should be tested and documented. During the change process, the developmental program must be kept separate from the production version. After the modified program is approved, the production version replaces the developmental version.

During systems review, auditors should discuss the change process with management and user personnel. The policies, procedures, and standards for approving, modifying, testing, and documenting the changes should be examined. All final documentation materials for program changes, including test procedures and results, should be reviewed. The procedures used to restrict logical access to the developmental program should be reviewed.

An important part of tests of controls is to verify that program changes were identified, listed, approved, tested, and documented. The auditor should verify that separate development and production programs are maintained and that changes are implemented by someone independent of the user and programming functions. The development program's access control table is reviewed to verify that only authorized users had access to the system.

Auditors should test programs on a surprise basis to guard against an employee inserting unauthorized program changes after the audit is completed and removing them prior to the next audit. There are three ways auditors test for unauthorized program changes:

1. After testing a new program, auditors keep a copy of its source code. Auditors use a *source code comparison program* to compare the current version of the program with the source code. If no changes were authorized, the two versions should be identical; any differences should be investigated. If the difference is an authorized change, auditors examine program change specifications to ensure that the changes were authorized and correctly incorporated.
2. In the *reprocessing* technique, auditors reprocess data using the source code and compare the output with the company's output. Discrepancies in the output are investigated.
3. In *parallel simulation*, the auditor writes a program instead of using the source code, compares the outputs, and investigates any differences. Parallel simulation can be used to test a program during the implementation process. For example, Jason used this technique to test a portion of SPP's new sales department payroll system.

For each major program change, auditors observe testing and implementation, review authorizations and documents, and perform independent tests. If this step is skipped and program change controls subsequently prove to be inadequate, it may not be possible to rely on program outputs.

If program change controls are deficient, a compensating control is source code comparison, reprocessing, or parallel simulation performed by the auditor. Sound processing controls, independently tested by the auditor, can partially compensate for such deficiencies. However, if the deficiencies are caused by inadequate restrictions on program file access, the auditor should strongly recommend actions to strengthen the organization's logical access controls.

Objective 4: Computer Processing

Table 11-4 provides a framework for auditing the processing of transactions, files, and related computer records to update files and databases and to generate reports.

During computer processing, the system may fail to detect erroneous input, improperly correct input errors, process erroneous input, or improperly distribute or disclose output. Table 11-4 shows the control procedures to detect and prevent these threats and the systems review and tests of controls used to understand the controls, evaluate their adequacy, and test whether they function properly.

Auditors periodically reevaluate processing controls to ensure their continued reliability. If they are unsatisfactory, user and source data controls may be strong enough to compensate. If not, a material weakness exists, and steps should be taken to eliminate the control deficiencies.

Several specialized techniques are used to test processing controls, each of which has its own advantages and disadvantages. No technique is effective for all circumstances; all are more appropriate in some situations and less so in others. Auditors should not disclose which technique they use, because doing so may lessen their effectiveness. Each of these procedures is now explained.

TABLE 11-4 Framework for Audit of Computer Processing Controls

Types of Errors and Fraud

- Failure to detect incorrect, incomplete, or unauthorized input data
- Failure to properly correct errors flagged by data editing procedures
- Introduction of errors into files or databases during updating
- Improper distribution or disclosure of computer output
- Intentional or unintentional inaccuracies in reporting

Control Procedures

- Data editing routines
- Proper use of internal and external file labels
- Reconciliation of batch totals
- Effective error correction procedures
- Understandable operating documentation and run manuals
- Competent supervision of computer operations
- Effective handling of data input and output by data control personnel
- Preparation of file change listings and summaries for user department review
- Maintenance of proper environmental conditions in computer facility

Audit Procedures: System Review

- Review administrative documentation for processing control standards
- Review systems documentation for data editing and other processing controls
- Review operating documentation for completeness and clarity
- Review copies of error listings, batch total reports, and file change lists
- Observe computer operations and data control functions
- Discuss processing and output controls with operators and information system supervisors

Audit Procedures: Tests of Controls

- Evaluate adequacy of processing control standards and procedures
- Evaluate adequacy and completeness of data editing controls
- Verify adherence to processing control procedures by observing computer and data control operations
- Verify that application system output is properly distributed
- Reconcile a sample of batch totals; follow up on discrepancies
- Trace a sample of data edit routines errors to ensure proper handling
- Verify processing accuracy of sensitive transactions
- Verify processing accuracy of computer-generated transactions
- Search for erroneous or unauthorized code via analysis of program logic
- Check accuracy and completeness of processing controls using test data
- Monitor online processing systems using concurrent audit techniques
- Recreate selected reports to test for accuracy and completeness

Compensating Controls

- Strong user controls and effective controls of source data

PROCESSING TEST DATA   One way to test a program is to process a hypothetical set of valid and invalid transactions. The program should process all valid transactions correctly and reject all invalid ones. All logic paths should be checked by one or more test transactions. Invalid data include records with missing data, fields containing unreasonably large amounts, invalid account numbers or processing codes, nonnumeric data in numeric fields, and records out of sequence.

The following resources are helpful when preparing test data:

- A list of actual transactions
- The test transactions the company used to test the program
- A *test data generator*, which prepares test data based on program specifications

In a batch processing system, the company's program and a copy of relevant files are used to process the test data. Results are compared with the predetermined correct output; discrepancies indicate processing errors or control deficiencies to be investigated.

In an online system, auditors enter test data and then observe and log the system's response. If the system accepts erroneous test transactions, the auditor reverses the effects of the transactions, investigates the problem, and recommends that the deficiency be corrected.

Processing test transactions has two disadvantages. First, the auditor must spend considerable time understanding the system and preparing the test transactions. Second, the auditor must ensure that test data do not affect company files and databases. The auditor can reverse the effects of the test transactions or process the transactions in a separate run using a copy of the file or database. However, a separate run removes some of the authenticity obtained from processing test data with regular transactions. Because the reversal procedures may reveal the existence and nature of the auditor's test to key personnel, it can be less effective than a concealed test.

CONCURRENT AUDIT TECHNIQUES   Because transactions can be processed in an online system without leaving an audit trail, evidence gathered after data is processed is insufficient for audit purposes. In addition, because many online systems process transactions continuously, it is difficult to stop the system to perform audit tests. Thus, auditors use *concurrent audit techniques* to continually monitor the system and collect audit evidence while live data are processed during regular operating hours. Concurrent audit techniques use *embedded audit modules*, which are program code segments that perform audit functions, report test results, and store the evidence collected for auditor review. Concurrent audit techniques are time-consuming and difficult to use but are less so if incorporated when programs are developed.

Auditors commonly use five concurrent audit techniques.

1. An *integrated test facility (ITF)* inserts fictitious records that represent a fictitious division, department, customer, or supplier in company master files. Processing test transactions to update them will not affect actual records. Because fictitious and actual records are processed together, company employees are unaware of the testing. The system distinguishes ITF records from actual records, collects information on the test transactions, and reports the results. The auditor compares processed data with expected results to verify that the system and its controls operate correctly. In a batch processing system, the ITF eliminates the need to reverse test transactions. ITF effectively tests online processing systems, because test transactions can be submitted frequently, processed with actual transactions, and traced through every processing stage without disrupting regular processing operations. The auditor must take care not to combine dummy and actual records during the reporting process.
2. In the *snapshot technique*, selected transactions are marked with a special code. Audit modules record these transactions and their master file records before and after processing and store the data in a special file. The auditor reviews the data to verify that all processing steps were properly executed.
3. *System control audit review file (SCARF)* uses embedded audit modules to continuously monitor transaction activity, collect data on transactions with special audit significance, and store it in a SCARF file or *audit log*. Transactions recorded include those exceeding a specified dollar limit, involving inactive accounts, deviating from company policy, or containing write-downs of asset values. Periodically, the auditor examines the audit log to identify and investigate questionable transactions.
4. *Audit hooks* are audit routines that notify auditors of questionable transactions, often as they occur. State Farm's use of audit hooks, including how the company detected a major fraud, is explained in Focus 11-1.
5. *Continuous and intermittent simulation (CIS)* embeds an audit module in a database management system (DBMS) that examines all transactions that update the database using criteria similar to those of SCARF. If a transaction has special audit significance, the CIS module independently processes the data (in a manner similar to parallel simulation), records the results, and compares them with those obtained by the DBMS. When discrepancies exist, they are stored in an audit log for subsequent investigation. If the discrepancies are serious, the CIS may prevent the DBMS from executing the update.

ANALYSIS OF PROGRAM LOGIC   If auditors suspect that a program contains unauthorized code or serious errors, a detailed analysis of program logic may be necessary. This is time-consuming and requires proficiency in the appropriate programming language, so it should be used as a last

The State Farm Life Insurance Company computer system has a host computer in Bloomington, Illinois, and smaller computers in regional offices. The system processes more than 30 million transactions per year for over 4 million individual policies worth more than $7 billion.

This online, real-time system updates files and databases as transactions occur. Paper audit trails have virtually vanished, and documents supporting changes to policyholder records have been eliminated or are held only a short time before disposition.

Because anyone with access and a working knowledge of the system could commit fraud, the internal audit staff was asked to identify all the ways fraud was possible. They brainstormed ways to defraud the system and interviewed system users, who provided extremely valuable insights.

Auditors implemented 33 embedded audit hooks to monitor 42 different types of transactions. One audit hook monitors unusual transactions in transfer accounts, which are clearing accounts for temporarily holding funds that are to be credited to multiple accounts.

The audit hooks have been very successful. One employee fraudulently processed a loan on her brother's life insurance policy, forged her brother's signature, and cashed the check. To conceal the fraud, she had to repay the loan before the annual status report was sent to her brother. She used a series of fictitious transactions involving a transfer account. The fraud was uncovered almost immediately when the transfer account audit hook recognized the first of these fictitious transactions and notified the auditor. Within a month of the notification, the case had been investigated and the employee terminated.

Source: Linda Marie Leinicke, W. Max Rexroad, and John D. Ward, "Computer Fraud Auditing: It Works," *Internal Auditor* (August 1990).

resort. Auditors analyze development, operating, and program documentation as well as a printout of the source code. They also use the following software packages:

- *Automated flowcharting programs* interpret source code and generate a program flowchart.
- *Automated decision table programs* interpret source code and generate a decision table.
- *Scanning routines* search a program for all occurrences of specified items.
- *Mapping programs* identify unexecuted program code. This software could have uncovered the program code that an unscrupulous programmer inserted to erase all computer files when he was terminated.
- *Program tracing* sequentially prints all program steps executed when a program runs, intermingled with regular output so the sequence of program execution events can be observed. Program tracing helps detect unauthorized program instructions, incorrect logic paths, and unexecuted program code.

Objective 5: Source Data

An *input controls matrix* is used to document the review of source data controls. The matrix in Figure 11-3 shows the control procedures applied to each input record field.

The data control function should be independent of other functions, maintain a data control log, handle errors, and ensure the overall efficiency of operations. It is usually not economically feasible for small businesses to have an independent data control function. To compensate, user department controls must be stronger with respect to data preparation, batch control totals, edit programs, restrictions on physical and logical access, and error-handling procedures. These procedures should be the focus of the auditor's systems review and tests of controls when there is no independent data control function.

Although source data controls may not change often, how strictly they are applied may change, and auditors should regularly test them. The auditor tests the system by evaluating source data samples for proper authorization, reconciling batch controls, and evaluating whether data edit errors were resolved and resubmitted for processing.

If source data controls are inadequate, user department and data processing controls may compensate. If not, auditors should recommend that source data control deficiencies be corrected.

Table 11-5 shows the internal controls that prevent, detect, and correct inaccurate or unauthorized source data. It also shows the system review and tests of control procedures auditors use. In an online system, the source data entry and processing functions are one operation. Therefore, source data controls are integrated with processing controls in Table 11-4.

Record Name: Employee Weekly Time Report / Input Controls	Employee number	Last name	Department number	Transaction code	Week ending (date)	Regular hours	Overtime hours	Comments
Financial totals								
Hash totals	✓				✓	✓		
Record counts								Yes
Cross-footing balance								No
Visual inspection								All fields
Check digit verification	✓							
Prenumbered forms								No
Turnaround document								No
Edit program								Yes
Sequence check	✓							
Field check	✓	✓			✓	✓		
Sign check								
Validity check	✓	✓	✓	✓				
Limit check					✓	✓		
Reasonableness test					✓	✓		
Completeness check			✓	✓	✓	✓		
Overflow procedure								
Other:								

FIGURE 11-3
Input Controls Matrix

Objective 6: Data Files

The sixth objective concerns the accuracy, integrity, and security of data stored on machine-readable files. Table 11-6 summarizes the errors, controls, and audit procedures for this objective. If file controls are seriously deficient, especially with respect to physical or logical access or to backup and recovery procedures, the auditor should recommend they be rectified.

TABLE 11-5 Framework for Audit of Source Data Controls

Types of Errors and Fraud

- Inaccurate or unauthorized source data

Control Procedures

- Effective handling of source data input by data control personnel
- User authorization of source data input
- Preparation and reconciliation of batch control totals
- Logging the receipt, movement, and disposition of source data input
- Check digit verification
- Key verification
- Use of turnaround documents
- Data editing routines
- User department review of file change listings and summaries
- Effective procedures for correcting and resubmitting erroneous data

Audit Procedures: System Review

- Review documentation about data control function responsibilities
- Review administrative documentation for source data control standards
- Review authorization methods and examine authorization signatures
- Review documentation to identify processing steps and source data content and controls
- Document source data controls using an input control matrix
- Discuss source data controls with data control personnel, system users, and managers

(Continued)

TABLE 11-5 Continued

Audit Procedures: Tests of Controls

- Observe and evaluate data control department operations and control procedures
- Verify proper maintenance and use of data control log
- Evaluate how error log items are dealt with
- Examine source data for proper authorization
- Reconcile batch totals and follow up on discrepancies
- Trace disposition of errors flagged by data edit routines

Compensating Controls

- Strong user and data processing controls

TABLE 11-6 Framework for Audit of Data File Controls

Types of Errors and Fraud

- Destruction of stored data due to errors, hardware or software malfunctions, and intentional acts of sabotage or vandalism
- Unauthorized modification or disclosure of stored data

Control Procedures

- Storage of data in a secure file library and restriction of physical access to data files
- Logical access controls and an access control matrix
- Proper use of file labels and write-protection mechanisms
- Concurrent update controls
- Data encryption for confidential data
- Virus protection software
- Off-site backup of all data files
- Checkpoint and rollback procedures to facilitate system recovery

Audit Procedures: System Review

- Review documentation for file library operation
- Review logical access policies and procedures
- Review standards for virus protection, off-site data storage, and system recovery procedures
- Review controls for concurrent updates, data encryption, file conversion, and reconciliation of master file totals with independent control totals
- Examine disaster recovery plan
- Discuss file control procedures with managers and operators

Audit Procedures: Tests of Controls

- Observe and evaluate file library operations
- Review records of password assignment and modification
- Observe and evaluate file-handling procedures by operations personnel
- Observe the preparation and off-site storage of backup files
- Verify the effective use of virus protection procedures
- Verify the use of concurrent update controls and data encryption
- Verify completeness, currency, and testing of disaster recovery plans
- Reconcile master file totals with separately maintained control totals
- Observe the procedures used to control file conversion

Compensating Controls

- Strong user and data processing controls
- Effective computer security controls

The auditing-by-objectives approach is a comprehensive, systematic, and effective means of evaluating internal controls. It can be implemented using an audit procedures checklist for each objective. The checklist helps auditors reach a separate conclusion for each objective and suggests compensating controls as appropriate. Each of the six checklists should be completed for each significant application.

Audit Software

Computer-assisted audit techniques (CAATS) refer to audit software, often called *generalized audit software (GAS)*, that uses auditor-supplied specifications to generate a program that performs audit functions, thereby automating or simplifying the audit process. Two of the most popular software packages are Audit Control Language (ACL) and Interactive Data Extraction and Analysis (IDEA). CAATS is ideally suited for examining large data files to identify records needing further audit scrutiny.

The U.S. government discovered that computer-assisted audit techniques are a valuable tool in reducing massive federal budget deficits. The software is used to identify fraudulent Medicare claims and pinpoint excessive charges by defense contractors. The General Accounting Office (GAO) cross-checked figures with the IRS and discovered that thousands of veterans lied about their income to qualify for pension benefits. Some 116,000 veterans who received pensions based on need did not disclose $338 million in income from savings, dividends, or rents. More than 13,600 underreported income; one did not report income of over $300,000. When the Veterans Administration (VA) notified beneficiaries that their income would be verified with the IRS and the Social Security Administration, pension rolls dropped by more than 13,000, at a savings of $9 million a month. The VA plans to use the same system for checking income levels of those applying for medical care. If their income is found to be above a certain level, patients will be required to make copayments.

In another example, a new tax collector in a small New England town requested a tax audit. Using CAATS, the auditor accessed tax collection records for the previous four years, sorted them by date, summed collections by month, and created a report of monthly tax collections. The analysis revealed that collections during January and July, the two busiest months, had declined by 58% and 72%, respectively. Auditors then used CAATS to compare each tax collection record with property records. They identified several discrepancies, including one committed by the former tax collector, who used another taxpayer's payment to cover her own delinquent tax bills. The former tax collector was arrested for embezzlement.

To use CAATS, auditors decide on audit objectives, learn about the files and databases to be audited, design the audit reports, and determine how to produce them. This information is recorded on specification sheets and entered into the system. The CAATS program uses the specifications to produce an auditing program. The program uses a copy of the company's live data (to avoid introducing any errors) to perform the auditing procedures and produce the specified audit reports. CAATS cannot replace the auditor's judgment or free the auditor from other phases of the audit. For example, the auditor must still investigate items on exception reports, verify file totals against other sources of information, and examine and evaluate audit samples.

CAATS are especially valuable for companies with complex processes, distributed operations, high transaction volumes, or a wide variety of applications and systems.

The following are some of the more important uses of CAATS:

- Querying data files to retrieve records meeting specified criteria
- Creating, updating, comparing, downloading, and merging files
- Summarizing, sorting, and filtering data
- Accessing data in different formats and converting the data into a common format
- Examining records for quality, completeness, consistency, and correctness
- Stratifying records, selecting and analyzing statistical samples
- Testing for specific risks and identifying how to control for that risk
- Performing calculations, statistical analyses, and other mathematical operations
- Performing analytical tests, such as ratio and trend analysis, looking for unexpected or unexplained data patterns that may indicate fraud

- Identifying financial leakage, policy noncompliance, and data processing errors
- Reconciling physical counts to computed amounts, testing clerical accuracy of extensions and balances, testing for duplicate items
- Formatting and printing reports and documents
- Creating electronic work papers

Operational Audits of an AIS

The techniques and procedures used in operational audits are similar to audits of information systems and financial statements. The basic difference is audit scope. An information systems audit is confined to internal controls and a financial audit to systems output, whereas an operational audit encompasses all aspects of systems management. In addition, objectives of an operational audit include evaluating effectiveness, efficiency, and goal achievement.

The first step in an operational audit is audit planning, during which the scope and objectives of the audit are established, a preliminary system review is performed, and a tentative audit program is prepared. The next step, evidence collection, includes the following activities:

- Reviewing operating policies and documentation
- Confirming procedures with management and operating personnel
- Observing operating functions and activities
- Examining financial and operating plans and reports
- Testing the accuracy of operating information
- Testing controls

At the evidence evaluation stage, the auditor measures the system against one that follows the best systems management principles. One important consideration is that the results of management policies and practices are more significant than the policies and practices themselves. That is, if good results are achieved through policies and practices that are theoretically deficient, then the auditor must carefully consider whether recommended improvements would substantially improve results. Auditors document their findings and conclusions and communicate them to management.

The ideal operational auditor has audit training and experience as well as a few years' experience in a managerial position. Auditors with strong auditing backgrounds but weak management experience often lack the perspective necessary to understand the management process.

Summary and Case Conclusion

Jason is trying to determine how his parallel simulation program generated sales commission figures that were higher than those generated by SPP's program. Believing that this discrepancy meant there was a systematic error, he asked to review a copy of SPP's program.

The program was lengthy, so Jason used a scanning routine to search the code for occurrences of "40000," because that was the point at which the commission rate changes, according to the new policy. He discovered a commission rate of 0.085 for sales in excess of $40,000, whereas the policy called for only 0.075. Some quick calculations confirmed that this error caused the differences between the two programs.

Jason's audit manager met with the embarrassed development team, who acknowledged and corrected the coding error.

The audit manager called Jason to congratulate him. He informed Jason that the undetected programming error would have cost over $100,000 per year in excess sales commissions. Jason was grateful for the manager's praise and took the opportunity to point out deficiencies in the development team's programming practices. First, the commission rate table was embedded in the program code; good programming practice requires that it be stored in a separate table to be used by the program when needed. Second, the incident called into question the quality of SPP's program development and testing practices. Jason asked whether a more extensive operational audit of those practices was appropriate. The audit manager agreed it was worth examining and promised to raise the issue at his next meeting with Northwest's director of internal auditing.

Key Terms

auditing   303
internal auditing   303
financial audit   303
information systems audit
   304
internal control audit   304
operational audit   304
compliance audit   304
investigative audit   304
inherent risk   304
control risk   304
detection risk   305
materiality   306
reasonable assurance   306
systems review   306
tests of control   306

compensating controls   306
source code comparison
   program   311
reprocessing   311
   parallel simulation   311
test data generator   312
concurrent audit techniques
   313
embedded audit modules
   313
integrated test facility (ITF)
   313
snapshot technique   313
system control audit review
   file (SCARF)   313
audit log   313

audit hooks   313
continuous and intermittent
   simulation (CIS)   313
automated flowcharting
   programs   314
automated decision table
   programs   314
scanning routines   314
mapping programs   314
program tracing   314
input controls matrix   314
computer-assisted audit
   techniques (CAATS)
   317
generalized audit software
   (GAS)   317

AIS IN ACTION

Chapter Quiz

1. Which of the following is a characteristic of auditing?
   a. Auditing is a systematic, step-by-step process.
   b. Auditing involves the collection and review of evidence.
   c. Auditing involves the use of established criteria to evaluate evidence.
   d. All of the above are characteristics of auditing.

2. Which of the following is NOT a reason an internal auditor should participate in internal control reviews during the design of new systems?
   a. It is more economical to design controls during the design stage than to do so later.
   b. It eliminates the need for testing controls during regular audits.
   c. It minimizes the need for expensive modifications after the system is implemented.
   d. It permits the design of audit trails while they are economical.

3. Which type of audit involves a review of general and application controls, with a focus on determining whether there is compliance with policies and adequate safeguarding of assets?
   a. information systems audit   c. operational audit
   b. financial audit   d. compliance audit

4. At what step in the audit process do the concepts of reasonable assurance and materiality enter into the auditor's decision process?
   a. planning   c. evidence evaluation
   b. evidence collection   d. they are important in all three steps.

5. What is the four-step approach to internal control evaluation that provides a logical framework for carrying out an audit?
   a. inherent risk analysis   c. tests of controls
   b. systems review   d. risk-based approach to auditing

6. Which of the following procedures is NOT used to detect unauthorized program changes?
   a. source code comparison   c. reprocessing
   b. parallel simulation   d. reprogramming code

7. Which of the following is a concurrent audit technique that monitors all transactions and collects data on those that meet certain characteristics specified by the auditor?
   a. integrated test facility
   b. snapshot techniques
   c. SCARF
   d. audit hooks

8. Which of the following is a computer technique that assists an auditor in understanding program logic by identifying all occurrences of specific variables?
   a. mapping program
   b. program tracing
   c. automated flowcharting
   d. scanning routine

9. Which of the following is a computer program written especially for audit use?
   a. GAS
   b. CATAS
   c. ITF
   d. CIS

10. The focus of an operational audit is on which of the following?
    a. reliability and integrity of financial information
    b. all aspects of information systems management
    c. internal controls
    d. safeguarding assets

Discussion Questions

11.1. Auditing an AIS effectively requires that an auditor have some knowledge of computers and their accounting applications. However, it may not be feasible for every auditor to be a computer expert. Discuss the extent to which auditors should possess computer expertise in order to be effective auditors.

11.2. Should internal auditors be members of systems development teams that design and implement an AIS? Why or why not?

11.3. Berwick Industries is a fast-growing corporation that manufactures industrial containers. The company has a sophisticated AIS that uses advanced technology. Berwick's executives have decided to pursue listing the company's securities on a national stock exchange, but they have been advised that their listing application would be stronger if they were to create an internal audit department.

At present, no Berwick employees have auditing experience. To staff its new internal audit function, Berwick could (a) train some of its computer specialists in auditing, (b) hire experienced auditors and train them to understand Berwick's information system, (c) use a combination of the first two approaches, or (d) try a different approach. Which approach would you support, and why?

11.4. The assistant finance director for the city of Tustin, California, was fired after city officials discovered that she had used her access to city computers to cancel her daughter's $300 water bill. An investigation revealed that she had embezzled a large sum of money from Tustin over a long period. She was able to conceal the embezzlement for so long because the amount embezzled always fell within a 2% error factor used by the city's internal auditors. What weaknesses existed in the audit approach? How could the audit plan be improved? What internal control weaknesses were present in the system? Should Tustin's internal auditors have discovered this fraud earlier?

11.5. Lou Goble, an internal auditor for a large manufacturing enterprise, received an anonymous note from an assembly-line operator who has worked at the company's West Coast factory for the past 15 years. The note indicated that there are some fictitious employees on the payroll as well as some employees who have left the company. He offers no proof or names. What computer-assisted audit technique could Lou use to substantiate or refute the employee's claims? *(CIA Examination, adapted)*

11.6. Explain the four steps of the risk-based audit approach, and discuss how they apply to the overall security of a company.

11.7. Compare and contrast the frameworks for auditing program development/acquisition and for auditing program modification.

Problems

11.1. You are the director of internal auditing at a university. Recently, you met with Issa Arnita, the manager of administrative data processing, and expressed the desire to establish a more effective interface between the two departments. Issa wants your help with a new computerized accounts payable system currently in development. He recommends that your department assume line responsibility for auditing suppliers' invoices prior to payment. He also wants internal auditing to make suggestions during system development, assist in its installation, and approve the completed system after making a final review.

Required

Would you accept or reject each of the following? Why?
a. The recommendation that your department be responsible for the preaudit of suppliers' invoices
b. The request that you make suggestions during system development
c. The request that you assist in the installation of the system and approve the system after making a final review
   (CIA Examination, adapted)

11.2. As an internal auditor for the Quick Manufacturing Company, you are participating in the audit of the company's AIS. You have been reviewing the internal controls of the computer system that processes most of its accounting applications. You have studied the company's extensive systems documentation. You have interviewed the information system manager, operations supervisor, and other employees to complete your standardized computer internal control questionnaire. You report to your supervisor that the company has designed a successful set of comprehensive internal controls into its computer systems. He thanks you for your efforts and asks for a summary report of your findings for inclusion in a final overall report on accounting internal controls.

Required

Have you forgotten an important audit step? Explain. List five examples of specific audit procedures that you might recommend before reaching a conclusion.

11.3. As an internal auditor, you have been assigned to evaluate the controls and operation of a computer payroll system. To test the computer systems and programs, you submit independently created test transactions with regular data in a normal production run.

Required

List four advantages and two disadvantages of this technique.
(CIA Examination, adapted)

11.4. You are involved in the audit of accounts receivable, which represent a significant portion of the assets of a large retail corporation. Your audit plan requires the use of the computer, but you encounter the following reactions:
a. The computer operations manager says the company's computer is running at full capacity for the foreseeable future and that the auditor will not be able to use the system for audit tests.
b. The scheduling manager suggests that your computer program be stored in the computer program library so that it can be run when computer time becomes available.
c. You are refused admission to the computer room.

d. The systems manager tells you that it will take too much time to adapt the auditor's computer audit program to the computer's operating system and that company programmers will write the programs needed for the audit.

Required

For each situation, state how the auditor should proceed with the accounts receivable audit. *(CIA Examination, adapted)*

11.5. You are a manager for the CPA firm of Dewey, Cheatem, and Howe (DC&H). While reviewing your staff's audit work papers for the state welfare agency, you find that the test data approach was used to test the agency's accounting software. A duplicate program copy, the welfare accounting data file obtained from the computer operations manager, and the test transaction data file that the welfare agency's programmers used when the program was written were processed on DC&H's home office computer. The edit summary report listing no errors was included in the working papers, with a notation by the senior auditor that the test indicates good application controls. You note that the quality of the audit conclusions obtained from this test is flawed in several respects, and you decide to ask your subordinates to repeat the test.

Required

Identify three existing or potential problems with the way this test was performed. For each problem, suggest one or more procedures that might be performed during the revised test to avoid flaws in the audit conclusions.

11.6. You are performing an information system audit to evaluate internal controls in Aardvark Wholesalers' (AW) computer system. From an AW manual, you have obtained the following job descriptions for key personnel:

> *Director of information systems:* Responsible for defining the mission of the information systems division and for planning, staffing, and managing the IS department.
>
> *Manager of systems development and programming:* Reports to director of information systems. Responsible for managing the systems analysts and programmers who design, program, test, implement, and maintain the data processing systems. Also responsible for establishing and monitoring documentation standards.
>
> *Manager of operations:* Reports to director of information systems. Responsible for management of computer center operations, enforcement of processing standards, and systems programming, including implementation of operating system upgrades.
>
> *Data entry supervisor:* Reports to manager of operations. Responsible for supervision of data entry operations and monitoring data preparation standards.
>
> *Operations supervisor:* Reports to manager of operations. Responsible for supervision of computer operations staff and monitoring processing standards.
>
> *Data control clerk:* Reports to manager of operations. Responsible for logging and distributing computer input and output, monitoring source data control procedures, and custody of programs and data files.

Required

a. Prepare an organizational chart for AW's information systems division.
b. Name two positive and two negative aspects (from an internal control standpoint) of this organizational structure.
c. What additional information would you require before making a final judgment on the adequacy of AW's separation of functions in the information systems division?

11.7. Robinson's Plastic Pipe Corporation uses a data processing system for inventory. The input to this system is shown in Table 11-7. You are using an input controls matrix to help audit the source data controls.

TABLE 11-7 Parts Inventory Transaction File

Field Name	Field Type
Item number	Numeric
Description	Alphanumeric
Transaction date	Date
Transaction type	Alphanumeric
Document number	Alphanumeric
Quantity	Numeric
Unit cost	Monetary

Required

Prepare an input controls matrix using the format and input controls shown in Figure 11-3; however, replace the field names shown in Figure 11-3 with those shown in Table 11-7. Place checks in the matrix cells that represent input controls you might expect to find for each field.

11.8. As an internal auditor for the state auditor's office, you are assigned to review the implementation of a new computer system in the state welfare agency. The agency is installing an online computer system to maintain the state's database of welfare recipients. Under the old system, applicants for welfare assistance completed a form giving their name, address, and other personal data, plus details about their income, assets, dependents, and other data needed to establish eligibility. The data are checked by welfare examiners to verify their authenticity, certify the applicant's eligibility for assistance, and determine the form and amount of aid.

Under the new system, welfare applicants enter data on the agency's Web site or give their data to clerks, who enter it using online terminals. Each applicant record has a "pending" status until a welfare examiner can verify the authenticity of the data used to determine eligibility. When the verification is completed, the examiner changes the status code to "approved," and the system calculates the aid amount.

Periodically, recipient circumstances (income, assets, dependents, etc.) change, and the database is updated. Examiners enter these changes as soon as their accuracy is verified, and the system recalculates the recipient's new welfare benefit. At the end of each month, payments are electronically deposited in the recipient's bank accounts.

Welfare assistance amounts to several hundred million dollars annually. You are concerned about the possibilities of fraud and abuse.

Required

a. Describe how to employ concurrent audit techniques to reduce the risks of fraud and abuse.
b. Describe how to use computer audit software to review the work welfare examiners do to verify applicant eligibility data. Assume that the state auditor's office has access to other state and local government agency databases.

11.9. Melinda Robinson, the director of internal auditing at Sachem Manufacturing Company, believes the company should purchase software to assist in the financial and procedural audits her department conducts. Robinson is considering the following software packages:

- A generalized audit software package to assist in basic audit work, such as the retrieval of live data from large computer files. The department would review this information using conventional audit investigation techniques. The department could perform criteria selection, sampling, basic computations for quantitative analysis, record handling, graphical analysis, and print output (i.e., confirmations).
- An ITF package that uses, monitors, and controls dummy test data processed by existing programs. It also checks the existence and adequacy of data entry and processing controls.
- A flowcharting package that graphically presents the flow of information through a system and pinpoints control strengths and weaknesses.

· A parallel simulation and modeling package that uses actual data to conduct the same tests using a logic program developed by the auditor. The package can also be used to seek answers to difficult audit problems (involving many comparisons) within statistically acceptable confidence limits.

Required

a. Without regard to any specific computer audit software, identify the general advantages of using computer audit software.
b. Describe the audit purpose facilitated and the procedural steps followed when using the following:

   · Generalized audit software
   · Integrated test facility
   · Flowcharting
   · Parallel simulation and modeling

   (CMA Examination, adapted)

11.10.   The fixed-asset master file at Thermo-Bond includes the following data items:

Asset number	Date of retirement (99/99/2099 for assets still in service)
Description	Depreciation method code
Type code	Depreciation rate
Location code	Useful life (years)
Date of acquisition	Accumulated depreciation at beginning of year
Original cost	Year-to-date depreciation

Required

Explain how generalized audit software can be used in a financial audit of Thermo-Bond's fixed assets.

11.11.   You are auditing the financial statements of a cosmetics distributor that sells thousands of individual items. The distributor keeps its inventory in its distribution center and in two public warehouses. At the end of each business day, it updates its inventory file, whose records contain the following data:

Item number	Cost per item
Item description	Date of last purchase
Quantity-on-hand	Date of last sale
Item location	Quantity sold during year

You will use audit software to examine inventory data as of the date of the distributor's physical inventory count. You will perform the following audit procedures:

1. Observe the distributor's physical inventory count at year-end and test a sample for accuracy.
2. Compare the auditor's test counts with the inventory records.
3. Compare the company's physical count data with the inventory records.
4. Test the mathematical accuracy of the distributor's final inventory valuation.
5. Test inventory pricing by obtaining item costs from buyers, vendors, or other sources.
6. Examine inventory purchase and sale transactions on or near the year-end date to verify that all transactions were recorded in the proper accounting period.
7. Ascertain the propriety of inventory items located in public warehouses.
8. Analyze inventory for evidence of possible obsolescence.
9. Analyze inventory for evidence of possible overstocking or slow-moving items.
10. Test the accuracy of individual data items listed in the distributor's inventory master file.

Required

Describe how an audit software package and a copy of the inventory file can help you perform each auditing procedure.

(AICPA Examination, adapted)

11.12. Which of the following should have the primary responsibility to detect and correct data processing errors? Explain why that function should have primary responsibility and why the others should not.
   a. The data processing manager
   b. The computer operator
   c. The corporate controller
   d. The independent auditor

   (CPA Examination, adapted)

Case 11-1   Preston Manufacturing

You are performing a financial audit of the general ledger accounts of Preston Manufacturing. As transactions are processed, summary journal entries are added to the general ledger file at the end of the day. At the end of each day, the general journal file is processed against the general ledger control file to compute a new current balance for each account and to print a trial balance.

The following resources are available as you complete the audit:

- Your firm's generalized computer audit software
- A copy of the general journal file for the entire year
- A copy of the general ledger file as of fiscal year-end (current balance = year-end balance)
- A printout of Preston's year-end trial balance listing the account number, account name, and balance of each account on the general ledger control file

Create an audit program for Preston Manufacturing. For each audit step, list the audit objectives and the procedures you would use to accomplish the audit program step.

General Journal

Field Name	Field Type
Account number	Numeric
Amount	Monetary
Debit/credit code	Alphanumeric
Date (MM/DD/YY)	Date
Reference document type	Alphanumeric
Reference document number	Numeric

General Ledger Control

Field Name	Field Type
Account number	Numeric
Account name	Alphanumeric
Beginning balance/year	Monetary
Beg-bal-debit/credit code	Alphanumeric
Current balance	Monetary
Cur-bal-debit/credit code	Alphanumeric

AIS IN ACTION SOLUTIONS

Quiz Key

1. Which of the following is a characteristic of auditing?
   a. Auditing is a systematic, step-by-step process. (Incorrect. While this is true, it is not the only correct answer.)
   b. Auditing involves the collection and review of evidence. (Incorrect. While this is true, it is not the only correct answer.)
   c. Auditing involves the use of established criteria to evaluate evidence. (Incorrect. While this is true, it is not the only correct answer.)

▶ **d.** All of the above are characteristics of auditing. (Correct. Auditing is a systematic, step-by-step process that involves the collection and review of evidence and uses established criteria to evaluate evidence.)

2. Which of the following is NOT a reason an internal auditor should participate in internal control reviews during the design of new systems?
   a. It is more economical to design controls during the design stage than to do so later. (Incorrect. Internal audit should participate in internal control reviews because it is far less expensive to design controls during systems design than to try and implement controls after the system has been designed.)
   ▶ **b.** It eliminates the need for testing controls during regular audits. (Correct. Even if the auditor participates in internal control reviews, the auditor will still have to test controls to determine whether they are in place and working as intended.)
   c. It minimizes the need for expensive modifications after the system is implemented. (Incorrect. Internal auditors should participate in internal control reviews because it reduces the likelihood of post-system-implementation modifications.)
   d. It permits the design of audit trails while they are economical. (Incorrect. Internal auditors should participate in internal control reviews because their participation in systems design does facilitate the design of effective audit trails.)

3. Which type of audit involves a review of general and application controls, with a focus on determining if there is compliance with policies and adequate safeguarding of assets?
   ▶ **a.** information systems audit (Correct. An information systems audit reviews general and application controls, with a focus on determining whether there is compliance with policies and adequate safeguarding of assets.)
   b. financial audit (Incorrect. A financial audit examines the reliability of accounting records.)
   c. operational audit (Incorrect. An operational audit is concerned with the efficient use of resources and the accomplishment of entity objectives.)
   d. compliance audit (Incorrect. A compliance audit is concerned with reviewing whether an entity is meeting prescribed policies, rules, and laws.)

4. At what step in the audit process do the concepts of reasonable assurance and materiality enter into the auditor's decision process?
   a. planning (Incorrect. Although materiality and reasonable assurance enter into the auditor's decision process during planning, they are also important in other steps in the audit process.)
   b. evidence collection (Incorrect. Although materiality and reasonable assurance enter into the auditor's decision process during evidence collection, they are also important in other steps in the audit process.)
   c. evidence evaluation (Incorrect. Although materiality and reasonable assurance enter into the auditor's decision process during evidence evaluation, they are also important in other steps in the audit process.)
   ▶ **d.** They are important in all three steps. (Correct. Materiality and reasonable assurance are important when the auditor plans an audit and when the auditor collects and evaluates evidence.)

5. What is the four-step approach to internal control evaluation that provides a logical framework for carrying out an audit?
   a. inherent risk analysis (Incorrect. Inherent risk is the susceptibility to material risk in the absence of controls.)
   b. systems review (Incorrect. Systems review involves reviewing system documentation and interviewing appropriate personnel to determine whether the necessary procedures are in place.)
   c. tests of controls (Incorrect. Tests of controls are conducted to determine whether control policies and procedures are satisfactorily followed.)

▶ **d.** risk-based approach to auditing (Correct. The risk-based audit approach is a four-step approach to carrying out an audit. The four steps are determining threats, identifying control procedures, evaluating control procedures, and evaluating weaknesses.)

6. Which of the following procedures is NOT used to detect unauthorized program changes?
   a. source code comparison (Incorrect. Source code comparison is used to detect unauthorized program changes by thoroughly testing a newly developed program and keeping a copy of its source code.)
   b. parallel simulation (Incorrect. To use parallel simulation to detect unauthorized program changes, an auditor writes a version of the program, reprocesses the company's data, compares the results to the company's results, and investigates any differences.)
   c. reprocessing (Incorrect. To use reprocessing to detect unauthorized program changes, the auditor verifies the integrity of an application program, saves it, and on a surprise basis uses the program to reprocess data and compare that output with the company's output.)
   ▶ **d.** reprogramming code (Correct. Reprogramming code is not used to test for unauthorized program changes.)

7. Which of the following is a concurrent audit technique that monitors all transactions and collects data on those that meet certain characteristics specified by the auditor?
   a. integrated test facility (Incorrect. An integrated test facility inserts a dummy company or division into a computer system to test transaction data without affecting real data.)
   b. snapshot techniques (Incorrect. The snapshot technique records the content of both a transaction record and a related master file record before each processing step.)
   ▶ **c.** SCARF (Correct. System control audit review file is a concurrent audit technique that embeds audit modules into application software to monitor continuously all transaction activity.)
   d. audit hooks (Incorrect. An audit hook is a concurrent audit technique that embeds audit routines into application software to flag certain kinds of transactions that might be indicative of fraud.)

8. Which of the following is a computer technique that assists an auditor in understanding program logic by identifying all occurrences of specific variables?
   a. mapping program (Incorrect. Mapping programs are activated during regular processing and provide information about portions of the application program that were not executed.)
   b. program tracing (Incorrect. Program tracing is a technique used to determine application program logic in order to test program controls.)
   c. automated flowcharting (Incorrect. Automated flowcharting interprets source code and generates a flowchart of that program.)
   ▶ **d.** scanning routine (Correct. Scanning routine software programs search for particular variable names or specific characters.)

9. Which of the following is a computer program written especially for audit use?
   ▶ **a.** GAS (Correct. Generalized audit software is a software program written especially for audit uses, such as testing data files. Examples are ACL and IDEA.)
   b. CATAS (Incorrect. CATAS has no meaning in information systems auditing. Computer-assisted audit techniques (CAATS) is the name given to all computer-assisted techniques used to audit computers.)
   c. ITF (Incorrect. An integrated test facility places a small set of fictitious records in master files. Transactions are processed for these records, and the actual and expected results are compared.)
   d. CIS (Incorrect. Continuous and intermittent simulation embeds an audit module in a DBMS that examines all transactions that update the database.)

10. The focus of an operational audit is on which of the following?
    a. reliability and integrity of financial information (Incorrect. A financial audit examines the reliability and integrity of financial information.)
    ▶ b. all aspects of information systems management (Correct. An operational audit is concerned with all aspects of information systems management.)
    c. internal controls (Incorrect. The focus of an operational audit is much broader than just internal controls.)
    d. safeguarding assets (Incorrect. The focus of an operational audit is much broader than just the safeguarding of assets.)

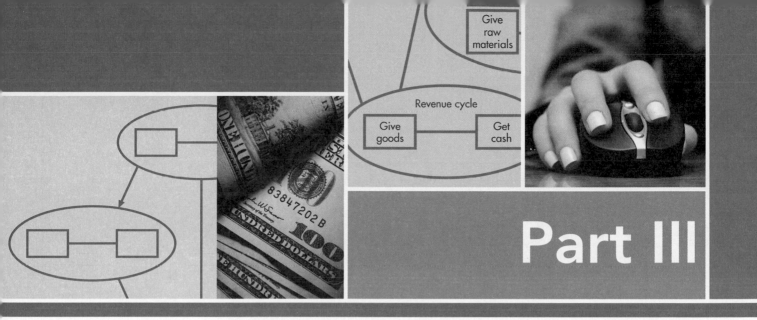

Accounting Information Systems Applications

Chapter 12

The Revenue Cycle: Sales to Cash Collections

Learning Objectives

After studying this chapter, you should be able to:

1. Describe the basic business activities and related information processing operations performed in the revenue cycle.

2. Discuss the key decisions that need to be made in the revenue cycle, and identify the information needed to make those decisions.

3. Identify major threats in the revenue cycle, and evaluate the adequacy of various control procedures for dealing with those threats.

INTEGRATIVE CASE ALPHA OMEGA ELECTRONICS

Alpha Omega Electronics (AOE) manufactures a variety of inexpensive consumer electronic products, including calculators, digital clocks, radios, pagers, toys, games, and small kitchen appliances. AOE's primary customers are retail stores, but the company has recently begun selling in bulk to Internet storefronts. Figure 12-1 shows a partial organization chart for AOE.

Linda Spurgeon, president of AOE, called an executive meeting to discuss two pressing issues. First, AOE has been steadily losing market share for the past three years. Second, cash flow problems have necessitated increased short-term borrowing. At the executive meeting, Trevor Whitman, vice president of marketing, explained that one reason for AOE's declining market share is that competitors are apparently providing better customer service. When Linda asked for specifics, however, Trevor admitted that his opinion was based on recent conversations with two major customers. He also admitted that he could not readily identify AOE's 10 most profitable customers. Linda then asked Elizabeth Venko, the controller, about AOE's cash flow problems. The most recent accounts receivable aging schedule indicated a significant increase in the

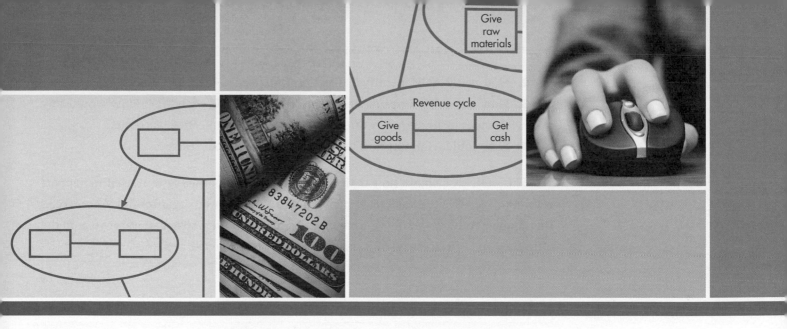

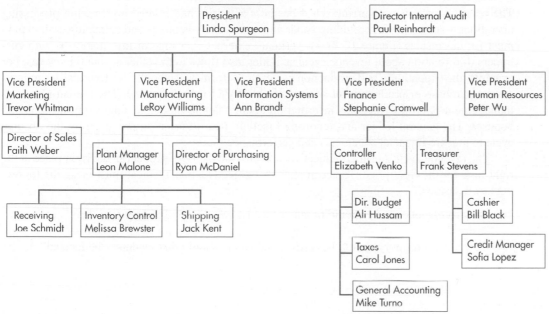

FIGURE 12-1

Partial Organization
Chart for Alpha
Omega Electronics

President
Linda Spurgeon

Director Internal Audit
Paul Reinhardt

Vice President
Marketing
Trevor Whitman

Vice President
Manufacturing
LeRoy Williams

Vice President
Information Systems
Ann Brandt

Vice President
Finance
Stephanie Cromwell

Vice President
Human Resources
Peter Wu

Director of Sales
Faith Weber

Plant Manager
Leon Malone

Director of Purchasing
Ryan McDaniel

Controller
Elizabeth Venko

Treasurer
Frank Stevens

Receiving
Joe Schmidt

Inventory Control
Melissa Brewster

Shipping
Jack Kent

Dir. Budget
Ali Hussam

Cashier
Bill Black

Taxes
Carol Jones

Credit Manager
Sofia Lopez

General Accounting
Mike Turno

number of past-due customer accounts. Consequently, AOE has had to increase its
short-term borrowing because of delays in collecting customer payments. In addition,
the Best Value Company, a retail chain that has been one of AOE's major customers,
recently went bankrupt. Elizabeth admitted that she is unsure whether AOE will be
able to collect the large balance due from Best Value.

Linda was frustrated with the lack of detailed information regarding both issues.
She ended the meeting by asking Elizabeth and Trevor to work with Ann Brandt, vice
president of information systems, to develop improved reporting systems so that AOE
could more closely monitor and take steps to improve both customer service and cash
flow management. Specifically, Linda asked Elizabeth, Trevor, and Ann to address the
following issues:

1. How could AOE improve customer service? What information does marketing
   need to perform its tasks better?

2. How could AOE identify its most profitable customers and markets?

3. How can AOE improve its monitoring of credit accounts? How would any changes in credit policy affect both sales and uncollectible accounts?

4. How could AOE improve its cash collection procedures?

The AOE case shows how deficiencies in the information system used to support revenue cycle activities can create significant problems for an organization. As you read this chapter, think about how a well-designed information system can improve both the efficiency and effectiveness of an organization's revenue cycle activities.

Introduction

The *revenue cycle* is a recurring set of business activities and related information processing operations associated with providing goods and services to customers and collecting cash in payment for those sales (Figure 12-2). The primary external exchange of information is with customers. Information about revenue cycle activities also flows to the other accounting cycles. For example, the expenditure and production cycles use information about sales transactions to initiate the purchase or production of additional inventory to meet demand. The human resources management/payroll cycle uses information about sales to calculate sales commissions and bonuses. The general ledger and reporting function uses information produced by the revenue cycle to prepare financial statements and performance reports.

The revenue cycle's primary objective is to provide the right product in the right place at the right time for the right price. To accomplish that objective, management must make the following key decisions:

● To what extent can and should products be customized to individual customers' needs and desires?
● How much inventory should be carried, and where should that inventory be located?

FIGURE 12-2
The Context Diagram of the Revenue Cycle

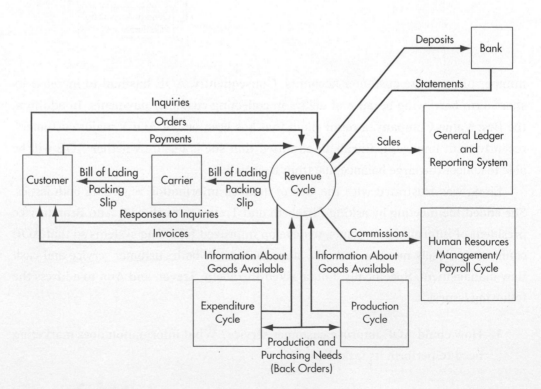

- How should merchandise be delivered to customers? Should the company perform the shipping function itself or outsource it to a third party that specializes in logistics?
- What are the optimal prices for each product or service?
- Should credit be extended to customers? If so, what credit terms should be offered? How much credit should be extended to individual customers?
- How can customer payments be processed to maximize cash flow?

The answers to those questions guide how an organization performs the four basic revenue cycle activities depicted in Figure 12-3:

1. Sales order entry
2. Shipping
3. Billing
4. Cash collections

This chapter explains how an organization's information system supports each of those activities. We begin by describing the design of the revenue cycle information system and the basic controls necessary to ensure that it provides management with reliable information. We

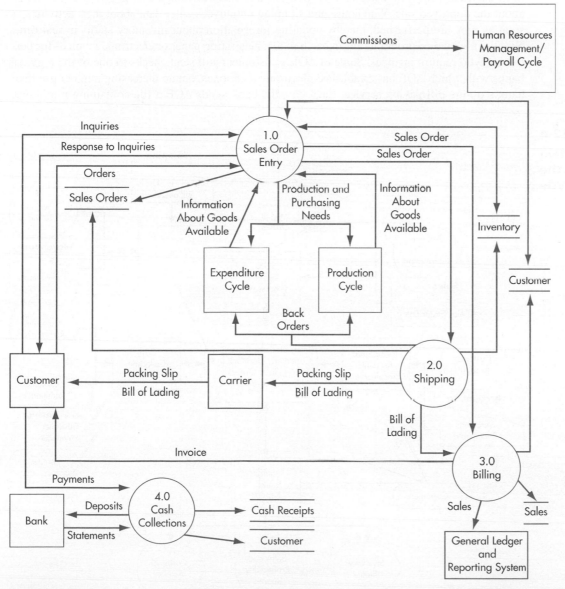

FIGURE 12-3

Level 0 Data Flow Diagram: Revenue Cycle

then discuss in detail each of the four basic revenue cycle activities. For each activity, we, describe how the information needed to perform and manage those activities is collected, processed, and stored. We also explain the controls necessary to ensure not only the reliability of that information but also the safeguarding of the organization's resources.

Revenue Cycle Information System

Like most large organizations, AOE uses an enterprise resource planning (ERP) system. Figure 12-4 shows the portion of the ERP system that supports AOE's revenue cycle business activities.

Process

AOE's online sales order processing system receives customer orders via the Internet from various retail Web sites. Using their laptops, salespeople enter orders when calling on customers. The sales department enters customer orders received over the telephone, by fax, or by mail. Regardless of how an order is initially received, the system quickly verifies customer creditworthiness, checks inventory availability, and notifies the warehouse and shipping departments about the approved sale. Warehouse and shipping employees enter data about their activities as soon as they are performed, thereby updating information about inventory status in real time. Nightly, the invoice program runs in batch mode, generating paper or electronic invoices for customers who require invoices. Some of AOE's customers still send checks to one of the regional banks with which AOE has established electronic lockboxes, but an increasing number use their bank's online bill paying service. Each day, the bank sends AOE a file containing remittance

FIGURE 12-4

Overview of ERP System Design to Support the Revenue Cycle

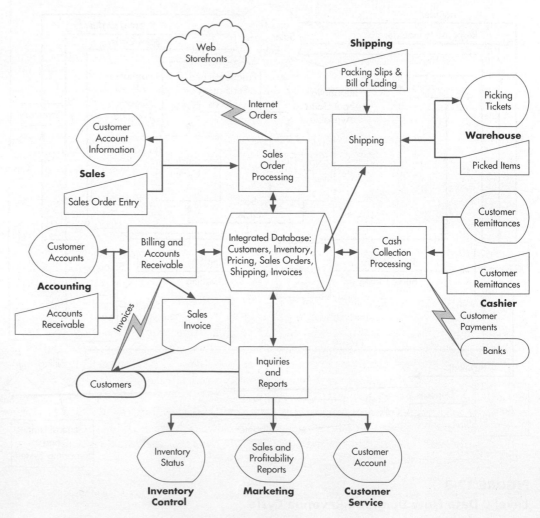

data, which the cashier uses to update the company's cash account balances and the accounts receivable clerk uses to update customer accounts.

Threats and Controls

Figure 12-4 shows that all revenue cycle activities depend on the integrated database that contains information about customers, inventory, and pricing. Therefore, the first general threat listed in Table 12-1 is inaccurate or invalid master data. Errors in customer master data could result in shipping merchandise to the wrong location, delays in collecting payments because of sending invoices to the wrong address, or making sales to customers that exceed their credit limits. Errors in inventory master data can result in failure to timely fulfill customer orders due to unanticipated shortages of inventory, which may lead to loss of future sales. Errors in pricing master data can result in customer dissatisfaction due to overbilling or lost revenues due to underbilling.

As Table 12-1 shows, one way to mitigate the threat of inaccurate or invalid master data is to use the various processing integrity controls discussed in Chapter 10 to minimize the risk of data input errors. It is also important to restrict access to that data and configure the system so that only authorized employees can make changes to master data. This requires changing the default configurations of employee roles in ERP systems to appropriately segregate incompatible duties. For example, sales order entry staff should not be able to change master pricing data or customer credit limits. Similarly, the person who maintains customer account information should not be able to process cash collections from customers or issue credit memos to authorize writing off sales as uncollectible. However, because such preventive controls can never be 100% effective, Table 12-1 also indicates that an important detective control is to regularly produce a report of all changes to master data and review them to verify that the database remains accurate.

A second general threat in the revenue cycle is unauthorized disclosure of sensitive information, such as pricing policies or personal information about customers. Table 12-1 shows that one way to mitigate the risk of this threat is to configure the system to employ strong access controls that limit who can view such information. It is also important to configure the system to limit employees' ability to use the system's built-in query capabilities to access only those specific tables and fields relevant to performing their assigned duties. In addition, sensitive data should be encrypted in storage to prevent IT employees who do not have access to the ERP system from using operating system utilities to view sensitive information. The organization should also design its Web sites to use SSL to encrypt information requested from customers while that information is in transit over the Internet.

A third general threat in the revenue cycle concerns the loss or destruction of master data (see Table 12-1). The best way to mitigate the risk of this threat is to employ the backup and disaster recovery procedures that were discussed in Chapter 10. A best practice is to implement the ERP system as three separate instances. One instance, referred to as production, is used to process daily activity. A second is used for testing and development. A third instance should be maintained as an online backup to production system to provide near real-time recovery.

Accurate master data enables management to better use an ERP system's extensive reporting capabilities to monitor performance (see threat 4 in Table 12-1). Accountants should use their knowledge about the underlying business processes to design innovative measures that provide management with insights beyond those provided by traditional financial statements. For example, companies have always closely monitored sales trends. Additional information is needed, however, to identify the causes of changes in that measure. Metrics such as revenue margin[1] can provide such information. Revenue margin equals gross margin minus all expenses incurred to generate sales, including payroll, salesforce-related travel, customer service and support costs, warranty and repair costs, marketing and advertising expenses, and distribution and delivery expenses. Thus, revenue margin integrates the effects of changes in both productivity and customer behavior. Growth in revenue margin indicates that customers are satisfied (as reflected in repeat sales), productivity is increasing (reflected in reduced costs per sale), or both. Conversely, a declining revenue margin indicates problems with customer retention, productivity, or both. Revenue margin is a metric to evaluate overall performance of revenue cycle activities. As we will see in the following sections, accountants can help managers design detailed reports and metrics that are relevant to evaluating each business activity.

---

[1]The concept of revenue margin was developed by James B. Hangstefer in "Revenue Margin: A Better Way to Measure Company Growth," in *Strategic Finance* (July 2000): pp. 40–45.

TABLE 12-1 Threats and Controls in the Revenue Cycle

Activity	Threat	Controls (first number refers to the corresponding threat)
General issues throughout entire revenue cycle	1. Inaccurate or invalid master data 2. Unauthorized disclosure of sensitive information 3. Loss or destruction of data 4. Poor performance	1.1 Data processing integrity controls 1.2 Restriction of access to master data 1.3 Review of all changes to master data 2.1 Access controls 2.2 Encryption 3.1 Backup and disaster recovery procedures 4.1 Managerial reports
Sales order entry	5. Incomplete/inaccurate orders 6. Invalid orders 7. Uncollectible accounts 8. Stockouts or excess inventory 9. Loss of customers	5.1 Data entry edit controls (see Chapter 10) 5.2 Restriction of access to master data 6.1 Digital signatures or written signatures 7.1 Credit limits 7.2 Specific authorization to approve sales to new customers or sales that exceed a customer's credit limit 7.3 Aging of accounts receivable 8.1 Perpetual inventory control system 8.2 Use of bar-codes or RFID 8.3 Training 8.4 Periodic physical counts of inventory 8.5 Sales forecasts and activity reports 9.1 CRM systems, self-help Web sites, and proper evaluation of customer service ratings
Shipping	10. Picking the wrong items or the wrong quantity 11. Theft of inventory 12. Shipping errors (delay or failure to ship, wrong quantities, wrong items, wrong addresses, duplication)	10.1 Bar-code and RFID technology 10.2 Reconciliation of picking lists to sales order details 11.1 Restriction of physical access to inventory 11.2 Documentation of all inventory transfers 11.3 RFID and bar-code technology 11.4 Periodic physical counts of inventory and reconciliation to recorded quantities 12.1 Reconciliation of shipping documents with sales orders, picking lists, and packing slips 12.2 Use RFID systems to identify delays 12.3 Data entry via bar-code scanners and RFID 12.4 Data entry edit controls (if shipping data entered on terminals) 12.5 Configuration of ERP system to prevent duplicate shipments
Billing	13. Failure to bill 14. Billing errors 15. Posting errors in accounts receivable 16. Inaccurate or invalid credit memos	13.1 Separation of billing and shipping functions 13.2 Periodic reconciliation of invoices with sales orders, picking tickets, and shipping documents 14.1 Configuration of system to automatically enter pricing data 14.2 Restriction of access to pricing master data 14.3 Data entry edit controls 14.4 Reconciliation of shipping documents (picking tickets, bills of lading, and packing list) to sales orders 15.1 Data entry controls 15.2 Reconciliation of batch totals 15.3 Mailing of monthly statements to customers 15.4 Reconciliation of subsidiary accounts to general ledger 16.1 Segregation of duties of credit memo authorization from both sales order entry and customer account maintenance 16.2 Configuration of system to block credit memos unless there is either corresponding documentation of return of damaged goods or specific authorization by management

TABLE 12-1 (Continued)

Activity	Threat	Controls (first number refers to the corresponding threat)
Cash collections	17. Theft of cash 18. Cash flow problems	17.1 Separation of cash handling function from accounts receivable and credit functions 17.2 Regular reconciliation of bank account with recorded amounts by someone independent of cash collections procedures 17.3 Use of EFT, FEDI, and lockboxes to minimize handling of customer payments by employees 17.4 Prompt, restrictive endorsement of all customer checks 17.5 Having two people open all mail likely to contain customer payments 17.6 Use of cash registers 17.7 Daily deposit of all cash receipts 18.1 Lockbox arrangements, EFT, or credit cards 18.2 Discounts for prompt payment by customers 18.3 Cash flow budgets

Sales Order Entry

The revenue cycle begins with the receipt of orders from customers. The sales department, which reports to the vice president of marketing (refer to Figure 12-1), typically performs the sales order entry process, but increasingly customers are themselves entering much of this data through forms on a company's Web site storefront.

Figure 12-5 shows that the sales order entry process entails three steps: taking the customer's order, checking and approving customer credit, and checking inventory availability. Figure 12-5

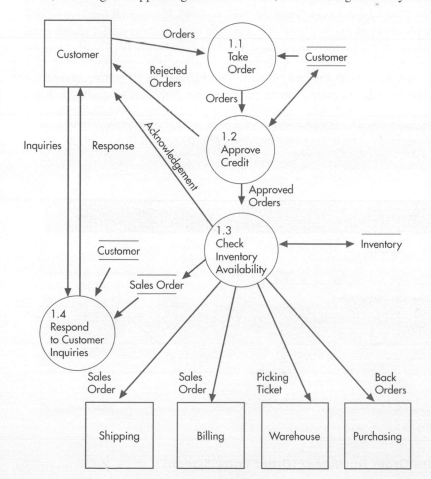

FIGURE 12-5

Level 1 Data Flow Diagram: Sales Order Entry

also includes an important related event that may be handled either by the sales order department or by a separate customer service department (which typically also reports to the vice president of marketing): responding to customer inquiries.

Taking Customer Orders

Customer order data are recorded on a sales order document. In the past, organizations used paper documents; today, as Figure 12-6 shows, the *sales order* document is usually an electronic form displayed on a computer monitor screen (interestingly, many ERP systems continue to refer to these data entry screens as documents). Examination of Figure 12-6 reveals that the sales order contains information about item numbers, quantities, prices, and other terms of the sale.

PROCESS   In the past, customer orders were entered into the system by employees. Increasingly, organizations seek to leverage IT to have customers do more of the data entry themselves. One way to accomplish this is to have customers complete a form on the company's Web site. Another is for customers to use *electronic data interchange (EDI)* to submit the order electronically in a format compatible with the company's sales order processing system. Both techniques improve efficiency and cut costs by eliminating the need for human involvement in the sales order entry process.

Besides cutting costs, Web sites also provide opportunities to increase sales. One technique, used by many Internet retailers, is to use sales history information to create marketing messages tailored to the individual customer. For example, once an Amazon.com customer selects a book, the Web site suggests related books that other customers have purchased when they bought the one the customer has already selected. Amazon.com and other Internet retailers also use sales history data to create customized electronic coupons that they periodically send to customers to encourage additional purchases. Another technique involves the use of interactive sales order entry systems that allow customers to customize products to meet their exact needs. For example, visitors to Dell Computer's Web site can try numerous combinations of components and features until they find a configuration that meets their needs at a price they can afford. Such interactive sales order entry systems not only increase sales, but also help improve cash flow in two ways. First, because many sales are built to order, less capital needs to be tied up in carrying a large inventory of finished goods. Second, the build to order model allows companies to collect all or part of the payment in advance, possibly even before they have to pay for the raw materials.

The effectiveness of a Web site depends largely on its design, however. Therefore, companies should regularly review records of customer interaction on their Web sites to quickly identify

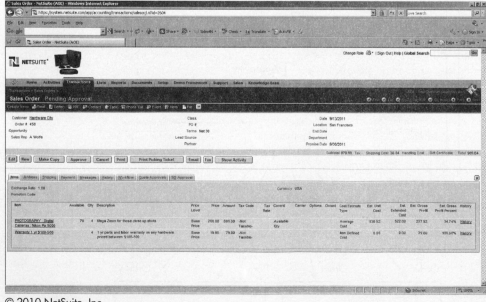

© 2010 NetSuite, Inc.

FIGURE 12-6

Example of a Sales Order Document (Order Entry Screen)

potential problems. A hard-to-use Web site may actually hurt sales by frustrating customers and creating ill will. Conversely, a well-designed Web site can provide useful insights. For example, when managers at National Semiconductor noticed a marked increase in customer interest in the company's new heat sensors, they ramped up production so that the company was able to satisfy increased demand for those products.

Like AOE, many companies continue to employ a sales staff in addition to using a Web site storefront, because of the benefits associated with face-to-face contact with existing and prospective business customers. Information technology provides many opportunities to improve sales force efficiency and effectiveness, a process referred to as sales force automation. Storing promotional information online is cheaper than printing and mailing those materials to sales representatives. E-mail and instant messaging (IM) reduce the costs and time it takes to inform sales staff of pricing changes and sales promotions. Both techniques also can be used to provide sales staff with last-minute reminders about a particular customer's special needs and interests and to enable management to quickly approve special deals. E-mail and IM also reduce the need for salespeople to return to the home office, thereby increasing the proportion of time they can spend with customers. Technology also enhances the quality of sales presentations. Laptop computers enable salespeople to make multimedia presentations, which improves their ability to demonstrate and explain the capabilities and features of complex technical products.

THREATS AND CONTROLS   A basic threat during sales order entry is that important data about the order will be either missing or inaccurate (threat 5 in Table 12-1). This not only creates inefficiencies (someone will have to call the customer back and reenter the order in the system), but also may negatively affect customer perceptions and, thereby, adversely affect future sales. ERP systems use a variety of data entry edit controls to mitigate this threat. For example, completeness checks can ensure that all required data, such as both shipping and billing addresses, are entered. Automatic lookup of reference data already stored in the customer master file, such as customer addresses, prevents errors by eliminating data entry. To illustrate, examine the sales order entry screen depicted in Figure 12-6. In the header section (the top portion of the screen), the salesperson need only enter the name of the customer in the sold-to and ship-to fields, and the system pulls the rest of the information from the customer master file. In the detail section (the lower portion of the figure), the salesperson needs to enter only the item number and quantity ordered, and the rest of the information is pulled from the inventory and pricing master files. Note that by looking up the reference data, the ERP system is necessarily performing a validity check of the customer name and inventory item number entered by the salesperson. ERP systems should also be configured to perform reasonableness tests to compare the quantity ordered with item numbers and past sales history.

Of course, all of these built-in controls presuppose that the master data is accurate, which is why Table 12-1 also indicates the need to restrict access to the integrated database (control 5.2) to prevent unauthorized changes that could destroy the integrity of the data. In addition, all of these data entry edit controls need to be incorporated on Web sites to ensure that customers accurately and completely enter all required data and in the EDI system used to accept electronic orders from customers.

A second threat associated with the sales order entry activity concerns the legitimacy of orders (threat 6 in Table 12-1). If a company ships merchandise to a customer and the customer later denies having placed the order, there is a potential loss of assets. For paper-based transactions, the legitimacy of customer orders is established by the customer's signature. As explained in Chapter 9, digital signatures provide similar assurance of legitimacy and the evidence to support nonrepudiation for electronic transactions.

Finally, accountants can help managers to better monitor sales activity by using their knowledge about business processes to design reports that focus on key performance drivers. For example, reports that break down sales by salesperson, region, or product provide a means to evaluate sales order entry efficiency and effectiveness. Reports that show marginal profit contribution by product, distribution channel, region, salesperson, or customer can provide additional insights.

Credit Approval

Most business-to-business sales are made on credit. Therefore, another revenue cycle threat listed in Table 12-1 (threat 7) is the possibility of making sales that later turn out to be uncollectible. Requiring proper authorization for each credit sale diminishes this threat.

For existing customers with well-established payment histories, a formal credit check for each sale is usually unnecessary. Instead, management gives sales staff general authorization to approve orders from customers in good standing, meaning those without past-due balances, provided that such sales do not increase the customer's total account balance beyond their credit limit. A *credit limit* is the maximum allowable account balance that management wishes to allow for a customer based on that customer's past credit history and ability to pay. Thus, for existing customers, credit approval simply involves checking the customer master file to verify the account exists, identifying the customer's credit limit, and verifying that the amount of the order plus any current account balance does not exceed this limit. This can be done automatically by the system.

The system can also automatically flag orders that require specific authorization because they exceed a customer's preapproved credit limit. For such cases, and for sales to new customers, Table 12-1 shows that someone other than the sales representative should specifically approve extension of credit (control 7.2). This is especially important if the sales staff is paid on commission because their motivation is to make sales, not focus on collectability. The organization chart for AOE (see Figure 12-1) shows how most companies segregate these duties. The credit manager, who sets credit policies and approves the extension of credit to new customers and the raising of credit limits for existing customers, is independent of the marketing function. To enforce this segregation of duties in ERP systems, sales order entry clerks should be granted read-only access to information about individual customer credit limits; the ability to actually change credit limits should be granted only to the credit manager. Figure 12-7 shows some of the information the system makes available to help the credit manager decide whether to adjust a customer's credit limit. The quality of those decisions depends upon maintaining accurate and current information about account balances, sales, and customer remittances.

To be effective, credit approval must occur *before* the goods are released from inventory and shipped to the customer. Nevertheless, problems will occur, and some customers will end up not paying off their accounts. Therefore, careful monitoring of accounts receivable is extremely important. A useful report for doing this is an *accounts receivable aging report*, which lists customer account balances by length of time outstanding (Figure 12-8). The information provided by such reports is useful for projecting the timing of future cash inflows related to sales, deciding whether to increase the credit limit for specific customers, and for estimating bad debts.

FIGURE 12-7

Sample Inquiry Screen for Checking Customer Credit

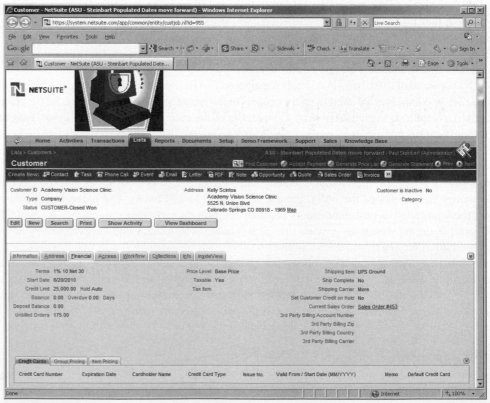

© 2010 NetSuite, Inc.

Customer	Amount	Current	1–30 Days Past Due	31–60 Days Past Due	61–90 Days Past Due	Over 90 Days Past Due
Able						
Invoice 221	$ 3,450	$ 3,450				
Invoice 278	2,955	2,955				
Total	$ 6,405	$ 6,405				
Baker						
Invoice 178	$ 4,500			$ 4,500		
Invoice 245	2,560	2,560				
Total	$ 7,060	$ 2,560		$ 4,500		
Other Accounts	$ 185,435	$ 137,935	$ 28,500	$ 5,500	$ 2,500	$ 11,000
Totals	$ 198,900	$ 146,900	$ 28,500	$ 10,000	$ 2,500	$ 11,000

FIGURE 12-8

Example of an Accounts Receivable Aging Report

Management needs to regularly review the accounts receivable aging report because prompt attention to customers who fall behind in their payments can minimize losses. Such a report could have enabled AOE to spot problems with the Best Value Company earlier, so that it could have stopped making additional credit sales. In addition, reports that show trends in bad debt expense can help management decide whether changes are needed in credit policies.

Checking Inventory Availability

In addition to checking a customer's credit, salespeople also need to determine whether sufficient inventory is available to fill the order, so that customers can be informed of the expected delivery date.

PROCESS   Figure 12-9 shows an example of the information typically available to the sales order staff: quantity on hand, quantity already committed to other customers, and quantity available. If sufficient inventory is available to fill the order, the sales order is completed, and the

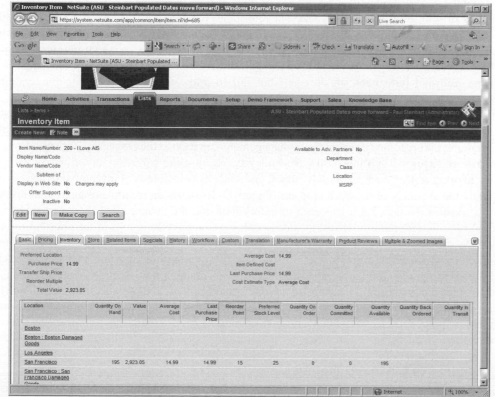

FIGURE 12-9

Sample Inquiry Screen for Checking Inventory Availability

© 2010 NetSuite, Inc.

quantity-available field in the inventory file for each item ordered is reduced by the amount ordered. The shipping, inventory control, and billing departments are then notified of the sale, and an acknowledgment may be sent to the customer. If there is not sufficient inventory on hand to fill the order, a *back order* for those items must be created. In manufacturing companies, creating a back order involves notifying the production department to initiate the production of the requested items. In retail companies, the purchasing department would be notified about the need to order the required items.

Once inventory availability has been determined, the system then generates a *picking ticket* that lists the items and quantities of each item that the customer ordered. The picking ticket authorizes the inventory control function to release merchandise to the shipping department. Although traditionally a paper document, picking tickets today are often electronic forms that may be displayed on portable handheld devices or on monitors built into forklifts. To improve efficiency, the picking ticket often lists the items by the sequence in which they are stored in the warehouse, rather than in the order listed on the sales order.

THREATS AND CONTROLS   Accurate inventory records are important to prevent both stockouts and excess inventory (threat 8 in Table 12-1). Stockouts may result in lost sales if customers are not willing to wait and instead purchase from another source. Conversely, excess inventory increases carrying costs and may even require significant markdowns that reduce profitability. Frequent markdowns can change a company's image to that of a discount retailer, thereby conditioning customers to expect price cuts.

Integrated ERP systems, like the one depicted in Figure 12-4, facilitate the use of the perpetual inventory method, which reduces the risk of unexpected stockouts or excessive inventories. However, the accuracy of the perpetual inventory records requires careful data entry during performance of revenue cycle activities. In particular, shipping and sales clerks must correctly record the quantity of items removed from inventory and delivered to customers. This task is particularly error-prone in retail establishments. For example, when customers purchase multiple items with the same price, such as different flavors of yogurt or soft drinks, the checkout clerks at supermarkets may scan only one item and then enter the total quantity purchased. Although this will generate the correct total sales amount, it will introduce errors into the inventory records. The recorded quantity-on-hand for the one item that was physically scanned will be too low, and the recorded quantity-on-hand for the other flavors of that item will be too high. Proper handling of sales returns is another task that contributes to inaccurate inventory records, particularly in retail establishments. In clothing stores, for example, when a customer returns a wrong-sized item and exchanges it for another, the clerks should enter the exchange into the system. Often, especially during extremely busy sales periods, the clerks simply make the exchange and put the returned item back on the shelf but fail to make the proper entry in the system. Consequently, the system's records for both items are inaccurate.

Replacing bar codes with RFID tags can eliminate many of these problems because the data entry occurs automatically. For situations where use of RFID tags is uneconomical or not practical, training and regular reminders from management can reduce the frequency of the undesired behavior (control 8.3 in Table 12-1). Nevertheless, because the behaviors described above are likely to occur during particularly busy times, periodic physical counts of inventory are necessary to verify the accuracy of recorded amounts. Figure 12-10 shows an example of a physcial inventory worksheet. Notice that it lists each inventory item and the quantity that should be on hand, according to system records. It also includes a column to record the results of the physical count.

Sales forecasts (control 8.5 in Table 12-1) are another tool to help companies better predict inventory needs and thereby reduce the risk of stockouts or carrying excess inventory. Accountants can also prepare reports that enable sales managers to identify the need to adjust those forecasts. For example, reports about the frequency and size of back orders can identify items for which forecasts need to be adjusted to better avoid stockouts. Conversely, reports that break down sales by item can identify slow-moving products in time to prevent excessive stockpiling.

Responding to Customer Inquiries

Besides processing customer orders, as Figure 12-5 shows, the sales order entry process also includes responding to customer inquiries. Sometimes these inquiries precede an order, and often they occur after orders have been placed. In either case, responding to customer inquiries

FIGURE 12-10

Example of Physical Inventory Worksheet

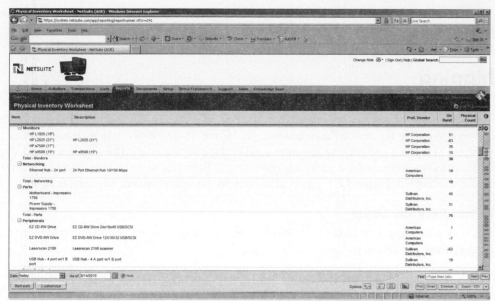

promptly and accurately is extremely important to a company's long-run success. The objective is to retain customers (threat 9 in Table 12-1). This is important because a general marketing rule of thumb is that it costs at least five times as much to attract and make a sale to a new customer as it does to make a repeat sale to an existing customer. Retention requires more than merely satisfying customers. It requires creating loyalty. Research indicates that if customer satisfaction is rated on a 1-to-5 scale, with 5 representing completely satisfied and 1 representing completely dissatisfied, customers who rated their satisfaction level at 5 were many times more likely to make repeat purchases than were customers who rated their satisfaction level only at 4. Moreover, that same research indicates that the key to generating total satisfaction, and thereby retaining customers, is the quality and nature of the post-sale customer contacts.

Customer service is so important that many companies use special software packages, called **customer relationship management (CRM) systems**, to support this vital process. CRM systems help organize detailed information about customers to facilitate more efficient and more personalized service. CRM systems also help generate additional sales. For example, after responding to a customer inquiry, a customer service representative can use information about customer preferences and transaction history to suggest other products that may be of interest to the customer. Detailed data about customer requirements and business practices can also be used to proactively contact customers about the need to reorder.

Many customer inquiries are routine, however. Consequently, companies can and should use IT to automate the response to common requests, such as questions about account balances and order status, so that sales order and customer service representatives can concentrate their time and effort on handling the more complex, nonroutine inquiries. For example, Web sites provide a cost-effective alternative to traditional toll-free telephone customer support, automating that process with a list of frequently asked questions (FAQs). Discussion boards can also be provided so that customers can share information and useful tips with one another. Web sites also enable customers to use PINs to directly access their account information and to check on the status of orders. These techniques can significantly reduce customer service costs. Wells Fargo, for example, found that customers with online access to their accounts made 40% fewer calls to the customer service department than did customers without such access. It is impossible, however, to anticipate every question customers may ask. Therefore, Web sites designed to provide customer service should include an instant messaging or chat feature to enable customers to obtain real-time expert assistance and advice for dealing with special issues the FAQ list does not satisfactorily address. Finally, it is important for accountants to design reports that will assist managers in *properly* evaluating the performance of customer service representatives by incorporating both internal and external measures (control 9.1). Failure to include both types of data can result in reports that cause dysfunctional behavior. For example, reports that use only internal data, such as number of inquiries handled per unit of time, may encourage customer service representatives to try to maximize their efficiency at the expense of satisfying customers. Conversely, relying solely on customer satisfaction ratings removes incentives to be efficient.

Shipping

The second basic activity in the revenue cycle (circle 2.0 in Figure 12-3) is filling customer orders and shipping the desired merchandise. As Figure 12-11 shows, this process consists of two steps: (1) picking and packing the order and (2) shipping the order. The warehouse and shipping departments perform these activities, respectively. Both functions include custody of inventory and, as shown in Figure 12-1, report ultimately to the vice president of manufacturing.

Pick and Pack the Order

The first step in filling a customer order involves removing the correct items from inventory and packaging them for delivery.

PROCESS   The picking ticket generated by the sales order entry process triggers the pick and pack process. Warehouse workers use the picking ticket to identify which products, and the quantity of each product, to remove from inventory. Warehouse workers record the quantities of each item actually picked, either on the picking ticket itself (if a paper document is used) or by entering the data into the system (if electronic forms are used). The inventory is then transferred to the shipping department.

AOE, like many companies, has made significant investments in automated warehouse systems consisting of computers, bar-code scanners, conveyer belts, and communications technology. The goal of such investments is to reduce the time and cost of moving inventory into and out of the warehouse while also improving the accuracy of perpetual inventory systems. Wireless technology, in particular, increases warehouse productivity by eliminating the need for workers to repeatedly return to a centralized dispatch center to receive printed instructions. For example, JCPenney equips its forklifts with radio-frequency data communication (RFDC) terminals to provide drivers with information about which items to pick next and where they are located. At Corporate Express, an office supplies distributor in Broomfield, Colorado, warehouse workers wear headsets and listen to computer-synthesized voice instructions about what to items to pick and package for delivery. The company reports that the oral instructions result in fewer mistakes than occur when drivers try to read a small terminal screen in dim light.

Radio-frequency identification (RFID) tags improve the efficiency and accuracy of tracking inventory movement. With bar codes, the item or box must be positioned properly so that the bar code can be read by the scanner. Switching to an RFID tag eliminates this need to align items

FIGURE 12-11

Level 1 Data Flow Diagram: Shipping

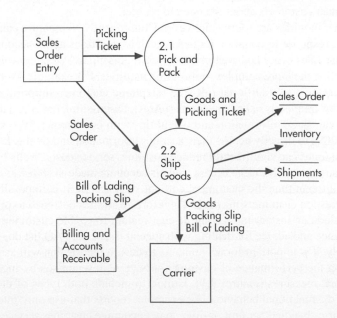

with scanners; instead, the tags can be read as the inventory moves throughout the warehouse. In addition, each RFID tag can store detailed information to facilitate properly storage and routing of the inventory item. For companies that handle large volumes of merchandise, such as Federal Express and UPS, RFID's ability to reduce by even a few seconds the time it takes to process each package can field enormous cost savings.

Automated warehouse systems not only cut costs and improve efficiency in handling inventory but also can allow for more customer-responsive shipments. For example, manufacturers can use bar-code and RFID systems in their warehouses to facilitate packing and shipping related items (e.g., matching shirts and ties) together. The cartons can then be either bar-coded or RFID-tagged so that retailers can quickly check in the merchandise and move it to the selling floor. These services not only save retailers time and money but also help improve turnover, thereby increasing the manufacturer's sales.

THREATS AND CONTROLS   One potential problem is the risk of picking the wrong items or in the wrong quantity (threat 10 in Table 12-1). The automated warehousing technologies described earlier can minimize the chance of such errors. Bar-code and RFID scanners, in particular, virtually eliminate errors when they are used by the system to automatically compare the items and quantities picked by warehouse workers with the information on sales orders.

Another threat involves the theft of inventory. Theft losses can be extremely large, and the perpetrators can be either outsiders or employees. In addition to a loss of assets, theft also makes inventory records inaccurate, which can lead to problems in filling customer orders. Table 12-1 lists several control procedures that can reduce the risk of inventory theft. First, inventory should be kept in a secure location to which physical access is restricted (control 11.1). Second, all inventory transfers within the company should be documented. Inventory should be released to shipping employees based only on approved sales orders. Both warehouse and shipping employees should sign the document accompanying the goods (or make the appropriate acknowledgment of the transfer online) at the time the goods are transferred from inventory to shipping. This procedure facilitates tracking the cause of any inventory shortages, and the accountability provided encourages employees to prepare and maintain accurate records. The use of wireless communications technologies and RFID tags can provide real-time tracking of inventory in transit, which may help reduce theft. Finally, recorded amounts of inventory should be periodically reconciled with physical counts of inventory on hand (control 11.4), and the employees responsible for inventory custody should be held accountable for any shortages.

As with the other steps in the revenue cycle, accountants can help managers better monitor performance by designing useful reports. Note that the order-picking process does not involve any direct interaction with customers. Therefore, reports that focus on efficiency, using only internally generated measures such as orders filled per unit of time, are sufficient.

Ship the Order

After the merchandise has been removed from the warehouse, it is shipped to the customer.

PROCESS   The shipping department should compare the physical count of inventory with the quantities indicated on the picking ticket and with the quantities indicated on the sales order. Discrepancies can arise either because the items were not stored in the location indicated on the picking ticket or because the perpetual inventory records were inaccurate. In such cases, the shipping department needs to initiate the back ordering of the missing items and enter the correct quantities shipped on the packing slip.

After the shipping clerk counts the goods delivered from the warehouse, the sales order number, item number(s), and quantities are entered using online terminals. This process updates the quantity-on-hand field in the inventory master file. It also produces a packing slip and multiple copies of the bill of lading. The *packing slip* (see Figure 12-12) lists the quantity and description of each item included in the shipment. The *bill of lading* is a legal contract that defines responsibility for the goods in transit. It identifies the carrier, source, destination, and any special shipping instructions, and it indicates who (customer or vendor) must pay the carrier (see Figure 12-13). A copy of the bill of lading and the packing slip accompany the shipment. If the customer is to pay the shipping charges, this copy of the bill of lading may serve as a *freight bill*, to indicate the amount the customer should pay to the carrier. In other cases, the freight bill is a separate document.

FIGURE 12-12
Example of a Packing Slip

Packing Slip

Order Date	Order #
9/13/2011	458

AOE
2431 Bradford Lane
San Francisco CA 94403
US

Ship To
Hardware City 4742 Mesa Drive Mesa AZ 85284 United States

Ship Date	Ship Via	Tracking #
9/15/2011	UPS Ground	

Item	Description	Order	B/O	Shipped
Nikon Pix 5000	Mega Zoom for those close up shots	4		4
Warranty 1 yr $100–500	1 yr parts and labor warranty on any hardware priced between $100–500	4		4

AOE **Customer Return Form**

Ship Returns To
2431 Bradford Lane San Francisco CA 94493 US

R.A. #	Customer	Order #
	Hardware City	458

Item	Quantity	Reason for Returning

One important decision that needs to be made when filling and shipping customer orders concerns the choice of delivery method. Traditionally, many companies have maintained their own truck fleets for deliveries. Large companies such as General Motors have even assigned entire departments to this function. Increasingly, however, manufacturers are outsourcing this function to commercial carriers such as Ryder System, Inc., Schneider Logistics, and YRC. Outsourcing deliveries reduces costs and allows manufacturers to concentrate on their core business activity (the production of goods). Selecting the proper carrier, however, requires collecting and monitoring information about carrier performance (e.g., percentage of on-time deliveries and damage claims).

Another important decision concerns the location of distribution centers. Increasingly, many customers are asking suppliers and manufacturers to deliver products only when needed. Consequently, suppliers and manufacturers must use logistics software tools to identify the optimal locations to store inventory in order to minimize the total amount of inventory carried and to meet each customer's delivery requirements. Logistics software also helps optimize daily activities, such as how to most efficiently use 17 available trucks to make 300 deliveries to various locations in one metropolitan area.

Globalization adds further complexity to outbound logistics. The efficiency and effectiveness of different distribution methods, such as trucking or rail, differ around the world. Taxes and

STRAIGHT BILL OF LADING—SHORT FORM	Not Negotiable.	

Shipper's No. _____

Carrier _____   Carrier's No. _____

RECEIVED, subject to the classifications and tariffs in effect on the date of the issue of this Bill of Lading.

at_____20_____ from _____

the property described below, in apparent good order, except as noted (contents and condition of contents of packages unknown), marked, consigned, and destined as indicated below, which said carrier (the word carrier being understood throughout this contract as meaning any person or corporation in possession of the property under the contract) agrees to carry to its usual place of delivery at said destination, if on its route, otherwise to deliver to another carrier on the route to said destination. It is mutually agreed, as to each carrier of all or any of said property over all or any portion of said route to destination, and as to each party at any time interested in any or all of said property, that every service to be performed hereunder shall be subject to all terms and conditions of the Uniform Domestic Straight Bill of Lading set forth (1) in Uniform Freight Classification in effect on the date hereof, if this is a rail or a rail-water shipment, or (2) in the applicable motor carrier classification or tariff if this is a motor carrier shipment.

  Shipper hereby certifies that he is familiar with all the terms and conditions of the said bill of lading, including those on the back thereof, set forth in the classification or tariff which governs the transportation of this shipment, and the said terms and conditions are hereby agreed to by the shipper and accepted for himself and his assigns.

Consigned to _____

(Mail or street address of consignee—For purposes of notification only.)

Destination _____ State _____ Zip Code _____ County _____

Delivery Address ★ _____

(★ To be filled in only when shipper desires and governing tariffs provide for delivery thereat.)

Route _____

Delivering Carrier _____   Car or Vehicle Initials _____   No. _____

No. Packages	Kind of Package, Description of Articles, Special Marks, and Exceptions	*Weight (Sub. to Cor.)	Class or Rate	Check Column	Subject to Section 7 of Conditions of applicable bill of lading, if this shipment is to be delivered to the consignee without recourse on the consignor, the consignor shall sign the following statement.
					The carrier shall not make delivery of this shipment without payment of freight and all other lawful charges.
					(Signature of Consignor.)
					If charges are to be prepaid, write or stamp here, "To Be Prepaid."

*If the shipment moves between two ports by a carrier by water, the law requires that the bill of lading shall state whether it is "carrier's or shipper's weight."

NOTE—Where the rate is dependent on value, shippers are required to state specifically in writing the agreed or declared value of the property.

The agreed or declared value of the property is hereby specifically stated by the shipper to be not exceeding

per

Received $ _____ to apply in prepayment of the charges on the property described hereon.

Agent or Cashier

Per _____

amount prepaid

Charges advanced:
$

†"The fiber boxes used for this shipment conform to the specifications set forth in the box maker's certificate thereon, and all other requirements of Uniform Freight Classification."

†Shipper's imprint in lieu of stamp; not a part of bill of lading approved by the Interstate Commerce Commission.

_____ Shipper, per _____   _____ Agent, Per _____

Permanent post office address of shipper, _____   _____

FIGURE 12-13
Sample Bill of Lading

regulations in various countries can also affect distribution choices. Therefore, an organization's information system must include logistics software that can maximize the efficiency and effectiveness of its shipping function.

THREATS AND CONTROLS   Table 12-1 indicates that shipping errors are a potential problem (threat 11). Regular reconciliation of information about shipments with sales orders (control 11.1) enables timely detection of delay or failure to ship goods to customers. In addition, RFID systems can provide real-time information on shipping status and thus provide additional information about possible delays. If the seller learns that a shipment is going to be late, prompt notification can help the customer revise its plans accordingly. The cost of providing such notifications is minimal, especially if done via e-mail or IM, but the effort is likely to significantly improve customer satisfaction and loyalty.

Shipping the wrong items or quantities of merchandise and shipping to the wrong location can cause customer dissatisfaction, resulting in the loss of future sales. Shipping errors may also result in the loss of assets if customers do not pay for goods erroneously shipped. To minimize the risk of shipping errors, ERP systems like the one depicted in Figure 12-4 should be configured to compare the quantities and item numbers entered by shipping employees to the information on the sales order and to display a warning about any discrepancies so that the problem can be corrected prior to shipment. Of course, the effectiveness of this control depends upon the accuracy of the information collected about outgoing shipments. To reduce data entry errors by shipping employees, bar codes and RFID tags should be used whenever possible (control 12.3). If shipping data must be entered manually at a terminal, application controls such as field checks, limit or range checks, and completeness tests are necessary.

Duplicate shipments result in increased costs associated with shipping and then processing the return of merchandise. To mitigate this threat, ERP systems should be configured to "block" the line items on sales orders once shipping documents are printed (control 12.5), to prevent using that same sales order to authorize another shipment of the same goods to the same customer. Companies that still use paper documents can reduce the risk of duplicate shipments by sequentially prenumbering all shipping documents, requiring that they be matched with the supporting sales order and picking ticket, and then marking those documents in a manner that prevents their reuse.

Billing

The third basic activity in the revenue cycle (circle 3.0 in Figure 12-3) involves billing customers. Figure 12-14 shows that this involves two separate, but closely related, tasks: invoicing and updating accounts receivable, which are performed by two separate units within the accounting department.

Invoicing

Accurate and timely billing for shipped merchandise is crucial. The invoicing activity is just an information processing activity that repackages and summarizes information from the sales order entry and shipping activities. It requires information from the shipping department identifying the items and quantities shipped and information about prices and any special sales terms from the sales department.

FIGURE 12-14
Level 1 Data Flow Diagram: Billing Process

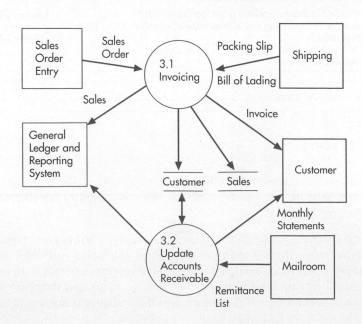

PROCESS   The basic document created in the billing process is the *sales invoice* (Figure 12-15), which notifies customers of the amount to be paid and where to send payment. Like many companies, AOE still prints paper invoices that it mails to many of its smaller customers. Larger customers, however, receive invoices via EDI. EDI not only eliminates printing and postage costs, but also the labor involved in performing those tasks. For companies that generate hundreds of thousands of sales invoices annually, saving even a few seconds per invoice can yield significant cost reductions. EDI invoices and online bill payment also benefit customers by reducing their time and costs, which should increase both satisfaction and loyalty.

In fact, a well-designed accounting system can entirely eliminate the need to create and store invoices, at least with customers that have sophisticated systems of their own. To understand this concept, reexamine the information included in a typical sales invoice (see Figure 12-13). The invoice indicates the quantity of each item sold and the price charged for that item; but the price is usually set at the time the order is placed, and the actual quantity sold is known at the time the merchandise is shipped to the customer. Thus, the selling company's accounting system already contains all the information needed to calculate the amount of the sale at the time the goods are shipped. Indeed, invoices are often printed in a batch process without any manual data entry. Conversely, the buyer knows the price at the time the order is placed and knows the quantity purchased when the goods are received. Consequently, if both companies have accurate transaction processing systems, it may be possible to establish an agreement in which the buyer will

FIGURE 12-15

Example of a Sales Invoice

Invoice

Date	Invoice #
9/16/2011	3091380

AOE
2431 Bradford Lane
San Francisco, CA
99403

Bill To	Ship To
Hardware City 35 Appliance Way Phoenix AZ 85201 United States	Hardware City 4742 Mesa Drive Mesa AZ 85284 United States

Terms	Due Date	PO #	Sales Rep	Ship Via	Tracking Numbers
Net 30	10/16/2011		JKL	UPS Ground	

Item	Qty	Description	Price	Amount
Nikon Pix 5000	4	Mega Zoom for those close up shots	200.00	800.00
Warranty 1 yr $100–500	4	1 yr parts and labor warranty on any hardware priced between $100–500	19.95	79.80

Subtotal		879.80
Shipping Cost (UPS Ground)		30.04
Total		$909.84

automatically remit payments within a specified number of days after receiving the merchandise. The seller sends an electronic notification, usually via e-mail, when the goods are shipped and the customer sends an electronic acknowledgment when the goods are received. Ford is just one of many companies that have established such relationships with their major suppliers. Note that the seller can still monitor and determine accounts receivable by reconciling shipments to customer remittances because accounts receivable represents all shipments for which the seller has not yet been paid. The attraction of such invoiceless billing is that it saves both the seller and buyer considerable amounts of time and money by eliminating the need to perform a traditional business process (invoicing) that does not provide any new information.

An integrated ERP system also provides the opportunity to merge the billing process with the sales and marketing function by using data about a customer's past purchase history to send information about related products and services. Such customized advertising may generate additional sales with little if any incremental costs.

THREATS AND CONTROLS   One threat associated with the invoicing process is a failure to bill customers (threat 13 in Table 12-1), which results in the loss of assets and erroneous data about sales, inventory, and accounts receivable. Segregating the shipping and billing functions is an important control to reduce the risk that this occurs intentionally. Otherwise, an employee performing both functions could ship merchandise to friends without billing them. To reduce the risk of unintentional failure to bill, ERP systems need to be configured to regularly compare sales orders, picking tickets, and shipping documents with sales invoices to produce reports of shipments for which an invoice has not been created. (For invoiceless systems, this control involves matching sales orders to shipping documents). Management needs to regularly review such reports and take corrective action. In paper-based systems, prenumbering all documents and periodically accounting for them identifies shipments that have not been invoiced.

Billing errors, such as pricing mistakes and billing customers for items not shipped or on back order, represent another potential threat. Overbilling can result in customer dissatisfaction, and underbilling results in the loss of assets. Pricing mistakes can be avoided by having the system retrieve the appropriate data from the pricing master file and by restricting the ability of employees to make changes to that data. If employees must enter billing data manually, the use of the data entry edit controls discussed in chapter 10 can minimize errors. Mistakes involving quantities shipped can be caught by reconciling the quantities listed on the packing slips with those on the sales order.

Maintain Accounts Receivable

The accounts receivable function, which reports to the controller, performs two basic tasks: It uses the information on the sales invoice to debit customer accounts and subsequently credits those accounts when payments are received.

PROCESS   The two basic ways to maintain accounts receivable are the open-invoice and the balance-forward methods. The two methods differ in terms of when customers remit payments, how those payments are applied to update the accounts receivable master file, and the format of the monthly statement sent to customers. Under the *open-invoice method*, customers typically pay according to each invoice. Usually, two copies of the invoice are mailed to the customer, who is requested to return one copy with the payment. This copy is a turnaround document called a *remittance advice*. Customer payments are then applied against specific invoices. In contrast, under the *balance-forward method,* customers typically pay according to the amount shown on a monthly statement, rather than by individual invoices. The *monthly statement* lists all transactions, including both sales and payments, that occurred during the past month and informs customers of their current account balances (Figure 12-16). The monthly statement often has a tear-off portion containing preprinted information, including the customer's name, account number, and balance. Customers are asked to return this stub, which serves as a remittance advice, with payment. Remittances are applied against the total account balance, rather than against specific invoices.

One advantage of the open-invoice method is that it is conducive to offering discounts for prompt payment, as invoices are individually tracked and aged. It also results in a more uniform flow of cash collections throughout the month. A disadvantage of the open-invoice method is the added complexity required to maintain information about the status of each individual invoice

FIGURE 12-16

Example of a Monthly Statement

MONTHLY STATEMENT Alpha Omega Electronics 2431 Bradford Lane San Francisco, CA 99403						March 2011	

Hardware City

35 Appliance Way

Phoenix, AZ 85201

Invoice Number	Date	Current	Past Due 1–30	Past Due 31–60	Past Due 61–90	Past Due Over 90
34567	3/20/2011	4292.50				
34591	3/27/2011	2346.50				
	Totals	6639.00				
		Total Amount Due	6639.00			

Please detach here and return with remittance

Bill date	03/31/2011
Account number	73256
Payment due	04/10/2011
Total amount due	6639.00
Amount enclosed	☐

Pay To: AOE
PO Box 7341
San Francisco, CA 99403-7341

for each customer. Consequently, the open-invoice method is typically used by business whose customers are primarily other businesses, because the number of individual transactions is relatively small and the dollar value of those transactions is high. Companies with large numbers of customers who make many small purchases each month, such as utility companies, credit card issuers (e.g., Citibank), or national retail chains (e.g., Sears and JCPenney) typically use the balance-forward method. For them, this method is more efficient and reduces costs by avoiding the need to process cash collections for each individual sale. It is also more convenient for the customer to make one monthly remittance.

Many companies that use the balance-forward method use a process called cycle billing to prepare and mail monthly statements to their customers. Under *cycle billing*, monthly statements are prepared for subsets of customers at different times. For example, the customer master file might be divided into four parts, and each week monthly statements would be prepared for one-fourth of the customers. Cycle billing produces a more uniform flow of cash collections throughout the month and reduces the time that the computer system is dedicated to printing monthly statements. Cycle billing can significantly affect processing requirements. Consider the case of a utility company serving several million customers in a large metropolitan area. If it prepared monthly statements for all its customers at the same time, and it took 10 seconds to print out each one, its printers would be tied up for several days.

Image processing technology can further improve the efficiency and effectiveness of managing customer accounts. The digital images of customer remittances and invoices can be stored electronically and then be easily retrieved, manipulated, and integrated with other images and data to produce various types of output. Doing so provides employees fast access to all documents relating to a customer and eliminates the time wasted searching through file cabinets for lost paperwork. If a customer needs a duplicate copy of a monthly statement or an invoice to replace a lost original, it can be retrieved, printed, and faxed while the employee is talking to the customer on the phone. Image processing also can facilitate resolving customer complaints, because the same image can be viewed simultaneously by more than one person. Thus, a customer account representative and a credit manager could both review an image of a document in question while discussing the problem with the customer on the telephone. Image processing also reduces the space and cost associated with storing paper documents. The savings in this area can be substantial: One optical disk can store up to 20,000 documents, in a fraction of the space.

Adjustments to a customer's account are sometimes necessary. For example, customer accounts may be credited to reflect either the return of items or allowances granted for damaged goods. To credit a customer's account for returned goods, the credit manager must obtain information from the receiving dock that the goods were actually returned and placed back in inventory. Upon notification from the receiving department that the goods have been returned, the credit manager issues a *credit memo* (Figure 12-17), which authorizes the crediting of the customer's account. If the damage to the goods is minimal, the customer may agree to keep them for a price reduction. In such cases, the credit manager issues a credit memo to reflect the amount that should be credited to the customer's account. A copy of the credit memo is sent to accounts receivable to authorize an adjustment to the customer's account balance; another copy is sent to the customer.

After repeated attempts to collect payment have failed, it may be necessary to write off a customer's account. In such cases, the credit manager issues a credit memo to authorize the write-off. Unlike the cases involving damaged or returned goods, however, a copy of the credit memo used to authorize the write-off of an account is not sent to the customer.

THREATS AND CONTROLS   Errors in maintaining customer accounts (threat 15 in Table 12-1) can lead to the loss of future sales and also may indicate possible theft of cash. The data entry edit checks discussed in Chapter 10 can minimize the risk of errors in maintaining customer accounts. For example, validity checks and closed-loop verification can ensure that the correct customer account is being updated, and field checks can ensure that only numeric data is entered for sales and payments. Customer payments are often processed in batches, so batch totals can provide an additional means to detect posting errors. Specifically, the sum of all customer

FIGURE 12-17
Example of a Credit Memo

						11121
		CREDIT MEMORANDUM				
		Alpha Omega Electronics				
		2431 Bradford Lane				
		San Francisco, CA 99403				

Credit To:	Hardware City			Date	April 7, 2011
	35 Appliance Way				
	Phoenix, AZ 85201			Salesperson	FRM

Apply To Invoice Number	Date	Customer's Order No.
34603	April 1, 2011	7413

Quantity	Item Number	Description	Unit Price	Amount
3	4120	PCS	85.00	255 00

Reason Credit Issued:	Units damaged during shipment.
	Returned on April 6, 2011

Received By:	ALZ	Authorized By:	PJS

We Credit Your Account For This Amount	255 00

payments processed should equal the change to the total of all customer account balances. To ensure that all remittances were processed, the number of customer accounts updated should be compared with the number of checks received. These reconciliations should be performed by someone other than the individual involved in processing the original transactions because (1) it is easier to catch someone else's mistakes than one's own, and (2) it provides a means to identify possible cases of fraud. Mailing monthly account statements to every customer (control 15.3) provides an additional independent review of posting accuracy because customers will complain if their accounts have not been properly credited for payments they remitted. Traditionally, another important control to verify the accuracy of updates to accounts receivable involved reconciling the subsidiary accounts receivable records with the general ledger. After customer payments are processed, the sum of all individual customer account balances (the accounts receivable subsidiary file) should equal the total balance of the accounts receivable control account in the general ledger. If the two are not equal, an error in posting has probably occurred, and all transactions just entered should be reexamined. ERP systems, however, typically are configured so that postings to general ledger control accounts can occur only through the subsidiary ledger and are only made by the system itself. Although this eliminates the possibility of discrepancies between the subsidiary and general ledger arising from data entry errors, configuration errors are still possible.

Another threat listed in Table 12-1 is that an employee may issue credit memos to write-off account balances for friends or to cover up the theft of cash or inventory. Proper segregation of duties (control 16.1) can reduce the risk of this threat. To prevent employees making sales to friends that are then written off, the ERP system should be configured so that the person who can issue credit memos does not also have rights to enter sales orders or to maintain customer accounts. The system should also be configured to match all credit memos to sales invoices. In addition, the system should be configured to block credit memos for which there does not exist validated documentation that the goods have been returned by the customer (control 16.2). Blocking forces specific managerial review and approval of cases where the company agrees to let the customer both keep the merchandise and receive credit.

Cash Collections

The final step in the revenue cycle is collecting and processing payments from customers (circle 4.0 in Figure 12-3).

Process

Because cash and customer checks can be stolen so easily, it is important to take appropriate measures to reduce the risk of theft. As discussed more fully in the section on controls, this means that the accounts receivable function, which is responsible for recording customer remittances, should not have physical access to cash or checks. Instead, the cashier, who reports to the treasurer (see Figure 12-1), handles customer remittances and deposits them in the bank.

How then, does the accounts receivable function identify the source of any remittances and the applicable invoices that should be credited? One method involves mailing the customer two copies of the invoice and requesting that one be returned with the payment. This remittance advice is then routed to accounts receivable, and the actual customer payment is sent to the cashier. An alternative solution is to have mailroom personnel prepare a *remittance list*, which is a document identifying the names and amounts of all customer remittances, and send it to accounts receivable. Yet another alternative is to photocopy all customer remittances and send the copies to accounts receivable while forwarding the actual remittances to the cashier for deposit.

Managing cash flow is important to overall profitability, as the AOE case showed. Therefore, companies are continually seeking ways to speed up the receipt of payments from customers. Focus 12-1 describes how imaging technology can improve cash flow in situations where customers send payments directly to the company.

Using Image Processing Technology to Speed Cash Collections

Image-scanning software offers an opportunity to improve the efficiency of the internal processing of customer payments and reduce the time it takes to access those funds. Scanners can detect the presence of any metal objects, such as coins or staples, in envelopes containing payments from customers. Envelopes without such items can be opened mechanically and their contents (customer checks) run through a high-speed imaging device that automatically applies remittances to the corresponding customer account. Only envelopes containing staples or coins need to be processed manually.

By using Remote Deposit Capture software, businesses can more quickly get access to funds remitted by customers. The software creates an encrypted file of customer checks that have been scanned. Then, instead of physically depositing the customer checks with its bank, the company electronically transmits the encrypted file of check images. The bank decrypts the file and notifies the company electronically when the checks have cleared. This process shaves at least one day off the clearing process and also saves the company the time and expense associated with physically depositing the checks.

Another way to speed up the processing of customer payments involves the use of a lockbox arrangement with a bank. A *lockbox* is a postal address to which customers send their remittances. The participating bank picks up the checks from the Post Office box and deposits them in the company's account. The bank then sends the remittance advices, an electronic list of all remittances, and photocopies of all checks to the company. Having customers send payments to a lockbox eliminates the delay associated with processing customer remittances before depositing them. Cash flow can be further improved by selecting several banks around the country to maintain lockboxes, with the locations chosen to minimize the time customer checks are in the mail. Similarly, establishing lockbox arrangements with foreign banks reduces the time it takes to collect payments from sales to international customers.

Information technology can provide additional efficiencies in the use of lockboxes. In an *electronic lockbox* arrangement, the bank electronically sends the company information about the customer account number and the amount remitted as soon as it receives and scans those checks. This method enables the company to begin applying remittances to customer accounts before the photocopies of the checks arrive.

Lockbox arrangements, however, eliminate only those delays that are associated with internal processing of remittances mailed directly to the company. With *electronic funds transfer (EFT)*, customers send their remittances electronically to the company's bank and thus eliminate the delay associated with the time the payment is in the mail system. EFT also reduces the time lag before the bank makes the deposited funds available to the company. EFT is usually accomplished through the banking system's Automated Clearing House (ACH) network.

EFT, however, involves only the transfer of funds. To properly credit customer accounts, companies also need additional data about each remittance, such as invoice numbers and discounts taken. Although every bank can do EFT through the ACH system, not every bank possesses the EDI capabilities necessary to process the related remittance data. Consequently, many companies have had to separate the EFT and EDI components of processing customer payments, as shown in the top panel of Figure 12-18. This complicates the seller's task of properly crediting customer accounts for payments because information about the total amount of funds received arrives separately from information about the invoices that payment should be applied against. Similarly, the customer's task is complicated by the need to send information about the payment to two different parties.

Financial electronic data interchange (FEDI) solves these problems by integrating the exchange of funds (EFT) with the exchange of the remittance data (EDI). As shown in the lower panel of Figure 12-18, the customer sends both remittance data and funds transfer instructions together. Similarly, the seller receives both pieces of information simultaneously. Thus, FEDI completes the automation of both the billing and cash collections processes. To fully reap the

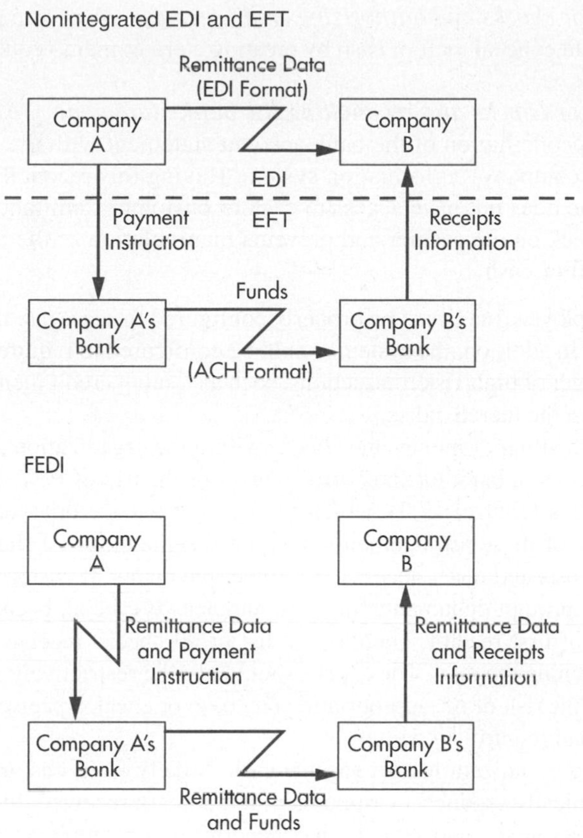

Nonintegrated EDI and EFT

FIGURE 12-18
EFT and FEDI

benefits of FEDI, however, requires that both the selling company and its customers use banks that are capable of providing EDI services.

Companies can also speed the collection process by accepting credit cards or procurement cards (a special type of credit card that will be discussed in Chapter 13). The benefit is that the card issuer usually transfers the funds within two days of the sale. This benefit must be weighed against the costs of accepting such cards, which typically range from 2% to 4% of the gross sales price.

Threats and Controls

The primary objective of the cash collections function is to safeguard customer remittances. Special control procedures must be utilized because cash is so easy to steal (threat 17 in Table 12-1). Segregation of duties is the most effective control procedure for reducing the risk of such theft. Employees who have physical access to cash should not have responsibility for recording or authorizing any transactions involving its receipt. Specifically, the following pairs of duties should be segregated:

1. *Handling cash or checks and posting remittances to customer accounts.*   A person performing both of these duties could commit the special type of embezzlement called *lapping* that was discussed in Chapter 5. Therefore, only the remittance data should be sent to the accounts receivable department, with customer payments being sent to the cashier. Such an arrangement establishes two mutually independent control checks. First, the total credits to accounts receivable recorded by the accounting department should equal the total debit to cash representing the amount deposited by the cashier. Second, the copy of the remittance list that is sent to the internal audit department can be compared with the validated deposit slips and bank statements to verify that all checks the organization received were deposited. Finally, the monthly statements mailed to customers provide another layer of control, because customers would notice the failure to properly credit their accounts for payments remitted.

2. *Handling cash or checks and authorizing credit memos.* A person performing both of these duties could conceal theft of cash by creating a credit memo equal to the amount stolen.

3. *Handling cash or checks and reconciling the bank statement.* An important detective control is reconciliation of the bank account statement with the balance of cash recorded in the company's information system. Having this reconciliation performed by someone who does not have access to cash or customer remittances provides an independent check on the cashier and prevents manipulation of the bank statement to conceal the theft of cash.

In ERP systems, employee roles must be properly configured to segregate these combinations of incompatible duties. In addition, the system should be configured to require specific approval by an appropriate manager of high-risk transactions, such as issuing credit memos without requiring the customer to return the merchandise.

In general, the handling of money and checks within the organization should be minimized. The optimal methods are a bank lockbox arrangement or the use of EFT, FEDI, or credit cards for customer payments (control 17.3), which totally eliminates employee access to customer payments. The costs of these arrangements must be weighed against the benefits of reduced internal processing costs and faster access to customer payments. If customer payments must be processed internally, prompt documentation of remittances is crucial, because the risk of loss is greatest at the time of first receipt. Therefore, a list of all checks received should be prepared *immediately* after opening the mail. The checks should also be restrictively endorsed at that time. To further minimize the risk of misappropriating any cash or checks received, two people should open all incoming mail (control 17.5).

Retail stores and organizations that receive cash directly from customers should use cash registers that automatically produce a written record of all cash received. In these situations, customers also can play a role in controlling cash collections. For example, many stores use signs to inform customers that their purchase is free if they fail to get a receipt or that receipts marked with a red star entitle them to a discount. Such policies encourage customers to watch that employees actually ring up the cash sale and do so correctly.

All customer remittances should be deposited, intact, in the bank each day (control 17.7). Daily deposits reduce the amount of cash and checks at risk of theft. Depositing all remittances intact, and not using any of them for miscellaneous expenditures, facilitates reconciliation of the bank statement with the records of sales, accounts receivable, and cash collections. ERP systems should be configured to require that all cash collections transactions be processed through an approved list of bank accounts.

Finally, as the AOE case illustrated, cash flow problems are a serious concern (threat 18 in Table 12-1). The use of lockbox arrangements, EFT, credit cards, and offering discounts for early payment can speed up cash collections. However, the best control procedure to reduce the risk of unanticipated cash shortfalls is to use a *cash flow budget* (Figure 12-19), which provides estimates of cash inflows (projected collections from sales) and outflows (outstanding payables). A cash flow budget can alert an organization to a pending short-term cash shortage, thereby enabling it to plan ahead to secure short-term loans at the best possible rates. Conversely, an organization that knows a surplus of cash is pending can take steps to invest those excess funds

FIGURE 12-19

Sample Cash Flow Budget

	January	February	March	April
Beginning Balance	10,000	11,000	8,000	8,000
Projected Cash Receipts:				
Cash Sales	7,000	8,500	8,000	9,000
Collections on Account	26,000	29,000	28,000	30,000
Total Cash Available (A)	43,000	48,500	44,000	47,000
Projected Cash Disbursements (B)	(32,000)	(41,000)	(39,000)	(36,000)
Projected Ending Cash Balance (C = A − B)	11,000	7,500	5,000	11,000
Desired Minimum Balance (D)	8,000	8,000	8,000	8,000
Amount Needed to Borrow	0	500	3,000	0
Ending Balance	11,000	8,000	8,000	11,000

to earn the best possible returns. Regular monitoring of a cash flow budget would have helped AOE avoid the need for short-term borrowing at unfavorable rates.

Summary and Case Conclusion

An organization's accounting system should be designed to maximize the efficiency and effectiveness with which the four basic revenue cycle activities (sales order entry, shipping, billing, and cash collections) are performed. It must also incorporate adequate internal control procedures to mitigate such threats as uncollectible sales, billing errors, and lost or misappropriated inventory and cash. Control procedures also are needed to ensure that the information provided for decision making is both accurate and complete. Finally, to facilitate strategic decision making, the accounting system should be designed to accommodate the integration of internally generated data with data from external sources.

At the next executive meeting, Elizabeth summarized the proposals that she, Trevor, and Ann developed to provide the information needed to better manage customer relationships and cash flows. Among the recommendations were the following:

1. Equip the sales force with wireless-enabled pen-based laptop computers. Trevor Whitman, vice president of marketing, believes that AOE will still need its sales staff to visit existing customers to identify which additional products can be profitably carried. Sales staff also will continue to make cold calls on prospective customers to try to convince them to carry AOE's products. As they walk down store aisles, sales representatives can check off the items that need to be restocked and then write in the appropriate quantities. When the order is complete, they can transmit the order back to headquarters. The system can check the customer's credit status and inventory availability and confirm orders within minutes, including an estimated delivery date. After the customer approves the order, the system will immediately update all affected files so that current information about inventory status is available to other sales representatives.
2. Improve warehouse and shipping efficiency by replacing bar codes with RFID tags.
3. Improve billing process efficiency by increasing the number of customers who agree to participate in invoiceless sales relationships and, when possible, by using EDI to transmit invoices to those customers who still require them.
4. In an effort to improve customer service, periodically survey customers about their satisfaction with AOE's products and performance.
5. Improve the efficiency of cash collections by encouraging all customers to use EFT. In addition, encourage EDI-capable customers to move to FEDI so that AOE receives both the funds and remittance data together.

Linda Spurgeon approved these proposals. She then asked Elizabeth and Ann to turn their attention to solving several problems related to AOE's expenditure cycle business activities.

Key Terms

revenue cycle   332
sales order   337
electronic data interchange (EDI)   337
credit limit   340
accounts receivable aging report   341
back order   342
picking ticket   342
customer relationship management (CRM) systems   343
packing slip   345
bill of lading   345
sales invoice   349
open-invoice method   350
remittance advice   350
balance-forward method   350
monthly statement   350
cycle billing   351
credit memo   352
remittance list   353
lockbox   354
electronic lockbox   354
electronic funds transfer (EFT)   354
financial electronic data interchange (FEDI)   354
cash flow budget   356

AIS IN ACTION

Chapter Quiz

1. Which activity is part of the sales order entry process?
   a. setting customer credit limits
   b. preparing a bill of lading
   c. checking customer credit
   d. approving sales returns

2. Which document often accompanies merchandise shipped to a customer?
   a. picking ticket
   b. packing slip
   c. credit memo
   d. sales order

3. Which method is most likely used when a company offers customers discounts for prompt payment?
   a. open-invoice method
   b. balance-forward method
   c. accounts receivable aging method
   d. cycle billing method

4. Which of the following techniques is the most efficient way to process customer payments and update accounts receivable?
   a. EFT
   b. CRM
   c. FEDI
   d. ACH

5. Which of the following revenue cycle activities can potentially be eliminated by technology?
   a. sales order entry
   b. shipping
   c. billing
   d. cash collections

6. The integrated database underlying an ERP system results in which of the following general threats to the revenue cycle?
   a. inaccurate or invalid master data
   b. unauthorized disclosure of sensitive information
   c. loss or destruction of data
   d. all of the above

7. Which document is used to authorize the release of merchandise from inventory control (warehouse) to shipping?
   a. picking ticket
   b. packing slip
   c. shipping order
   d. sales invoice

8. Which of the following provides a means both to improve the efficiency of processing customer payments and also to enhance control over those payments?
   a. CRM
   b. lockboxes
   c. aging accounts receivable
   d. EDI

9. For good internal control, who should approve credit memos?
   a. credit manager
   b. sales manager
   c. billing manager
   d. controller

10. For good internal control over customer remittances, the mailroom clerk should separate the checks from the remittance advices and send the customer payments to which department?
    a. billing
    b. accounts receivable
    c. cashier
    d. sales

Discussion Questions

12.1. Customer relationship management systems hold great promise, but their usefulness is determined by the amount of personal data customers are willing to divulge. To what extent do you think concerns about privacy-related issues affect the use of CRM systems?

12.2. Some products, such as music and software, can be digitized. How does this affect each of the four main activities in the revenue cycle?

12.3. Many companies use accounts receivable aging schedules to project future cash inflows and bad-debt expense. Review the information typically presented in such a report (see Figure 12-8). Which specific metrics can be calculated from those data that might be especially useful in providing early warning about looming cash flow or bad-debt problems?

12.4. Table 12-1 suggests that restricting physical access to inventory is one way to reduce the threat of theft. How can information technology help accomplish that objective?

12.5. Invoiceless pricing has been adopted by some large businesses for business-to-business transactions. What are the barriers, if any, to its use in sales to consumers?

12.6. The use of some form of electronic "cash" that would provide the same kind of anonymity for e-commerce that cash provides for traditional physical business transactions has been discussed for a long time. What are the advantages and disadvantages of electronic cash to customers? To businesses? What are some of the accounting implications of using electronic cash?

Problems

12.1. Match the term in the left column with its definition in the right column.

___ **1.** CRM system	a. Document used to authorize reducing the balance in a customer account
___ **2.** Open-invoice method	b. Process of dividing customer account master file into subsets and preparing invoices for one subset at a time
___ **3.** Credit memo	c. System that integrates EFT and EDI information
___ **4.** Credit limit	d. System that contains customer-related data organized in a manner to facilitate customer service, sales, and retention
___ **5.** Cycle billing	e. Electronic transfer of funds
___ **6.** FEDI	f. Method of maintaining accounts receivable that generates one payment for all sales made the previous month
___ **7.** Remittance advice	g. Method of maintaining customer accounts that generates payments for each individual sales transaction
___ **8.** Lockbox	h. Maximum possible account balance for a customer
___ **9.** Back order	i. Electronic invoicing
___ **10.** Picking ticket	j. Post Office box to which customers send payments
___ **11.** Bill of lading	k. Document used to indicate stockouts exist
	l. Document used to establish responsibility for shipping goods via a third party
	m. Document that authorizes removal of merchandise from inventory
	n. Turnaround document returned by customers with payments

12.2. What internal control procedure(s) would provide protection against the following threats?

   a. Workers on the shipping dock steal goods, claiming that the inventory shortages reflect errors in the inventory records.

   b. An employee posts the sales amount to the wrong customer account because he incorrectly keys the customer account number into the system.

   c. An employee makes a credit sale to a customer who is already four months behind in making payments on his account.

   d. An employee authorizes a credit memo for a sales return when the goods were never actually returned.

   e. An employee writes off a customer's accounts receivable balance as uncollectible to conceal the theft of subsequent cash payments from that customer.

   f. Customers are billed for the quantity ordered, but the quantity shipped is actually less because some items have been back ordered.

   g. The mailroom clerk steals checks and then endorses them for deposit into the clerk's personal bank account.

   h. The cashier steals funds by cashing several checks from customers.

   i. A waiter steals cash by destroying the customer sales ticket for customers who paid cash.

   j. Goods are shipped to a customer, but that customer is not billed.

   k. A business loses sales because of stockouts of several products for which the computer records indicated there was adequate quantity on hand.

   l. A business experiences unauthorized disclosure of the buying habits of several well-known customers.

   m. A business loses all information about amounts owed by customers in New York City because the master database for that office was destroyed in a fire.

   n. The company's Web site is unavailable for seven hours because of a power outage.

   o. Customers' credit card numbers are intercepted and stolen while being sent to the company's Web site.

   p. A sales clerk sells a $7,000 wide-screen TV to a friend and alters the price to $700.

   q. A shipping clerk who is quitting to start a competing business copies the names of the company's 500 largest customers and offers them lower prices and better terms if they purchase the same product from the clerk's new company.

   r. A fire in the office next door damages the company's servers and all optical and magnetic media in the server room. The company immediately implements its disaster recovery procedures and shifts to a backup center several miles away. The company has made full daily backups of all files and has stored a copy at the backup center. However, none of the backup copies are readable.

12.3. For good internal control, which of the following duties can be performed by the same individual?

   1. Approving changes to customer credit limits

   2. Sales order entry

   3. Shipping merchandise

   4. Billing customers

   5. Depositing customer payments

   6. Maintaining accounts receivable

   7. Issuing credit memos

   8. Reconciling the organization's bank accounts

   9. Checking inventory availability

12.4. Excel Project. (*Hint:* For help on steps b and c, see the article "Dial a Forecast," by James A. Weisel, in the December 2006 issue of the *Journal of Accountancy*. The *Journal of Accountancy* is available in print or online at the AICPA's Web site: www.aicpa.org.

Required

a. Create a 12-month cash flow budget in Excel using the following assumptions:
   - Initial sales of $5 million, with forecasted monthly growth of 1%
   - 40% of each month's sales for cash; 30% collected the following month; 20% collected 2 months later; 8% collected 3 months later; and 2% never collected
   - Initial cash balance of $350,000

b. Add a "spinner" to your spreadsheet that will enable you to easily change forecasted monthly sales growth to range from 0.5% to 1.5% in increments of 0.1%.

c. Add a scroll bar to your spreadsheet that will let you modify the amount of initial sales to vary from $4 million to $6 million in increments of $100,000.

d. Design appropriate data entry and processing controls to ensure spreadsheet accuracy.

12.5. For each of the following activities, identify the data that must be entered by the employee performing that activity, and list the appropriate data entry controls:

a. A sales order entry clerk takes a customer order.

b. A shipping clerk completes a bill of lading for shipment of an order to a customer.

12.6. Create a questionnaire checklist that can be used to evaluate controls for each of the four basic activities in the revenue cycle (sales order entry, shipping, billing, and cash collections).

Required

a. For each control issue, write a Yes/No question such that a "No" answer represents a control weakness. For example, one question might be, "Are customer credit limits set and modified by a credit manager with no sales responsibility?"

b. For each Yes/No question, write a brief explanation of why a "No" answer represents a control weakness.

12.7. O'Brien Corporation is a midsized, privately owned industrial instrument manufacturer supplying precision equipment to manufacturers in the Midwest. The corporation is ten years old and uses an integrated ERP system. The administrative offices are located in a downtown building, and the production, shipping, and receiving departments are housed in a renovated warehouse a few blocks away.

Customers place orders on the company's Web site, by fax, or by telephone. All sales are on credit, FOB destination. During the past year, sales have increased dramatically, but 15% of credit sales have had to written off as uncollectible, including several large online orders to first-time customers who denied ordering or receiving the merchandise.

Customer orders are picked and sent to the warehouse, where they are placed near the loading dock in alphabetical sequence by customer name. The loading dock is used both for outgoing shipments to customers and for receipt of incoming deliveries. There are 10 to 20 incoming deliveries every day, from a variety of sources.

The increased volume of sales has resulted in a number of errors in which customers were sent the wrong items. There have also been some delays in shipping because items that supposedly were in stock could not be found in the warehouse. Although a perpetual inventory is maintained, there has been no physical count of inventory for two years. When an item is missing, the warehouse staff writes the information down in a log book. Once a week, the warehouse staff uses the log book to update the inventory records.

The system is configured to prepare the sales invoice only after shipping employees enter the actual quantities sent to a customer, thereby ensuring that customers are billed only for items actually sent and not for anything on back order.

Required

Identify at least three weaknesses in O'Brien Corporation's revenue cycle activities. Describe the problem resulting from each weakness. Recommend control procedures that should be added to the system to correct the weakness. *(CMA Examination, adapted)*

12.8. Parktown Medical Center, Inc., is a small health care provider owned by a publicly held corporation. It employs seven salaried physicians, ten nurses, three support staff, and three clerical workers. The clerical workers perform such tasks as reception, correspondence, cash receipts, billing, and appointment scheduling. All are adequately bonded.

Most patients pay for services rendered by cash or check on the day of their visit. Sometimes, however, the physician who is to perform the respective services approves credit based on an interview. When credit is approved, the physician files a memo with one of the clerks to set up the receivable using data the physician generates.

The servicing physician prepares a charge slip that is given to one of the clerks for pricing and preparation of the patient's bill. At the end of the day, one of the clerks uses the bills to prepare a revenue summary and, in cases of credit sales, to update the accounts receivable subsidiary ledger.

The front office clerks receive cash and checks directly from patients and give each patient a prenumbered receipt. The clerks take turns opening the mail. The clerk who opens that day's mail immediately stamps all checks "for deposit only." Each day, just before lunch, one of the clerks prepares a list of all cash and checks to be deposited in Parktown's bank account. The office is closed from 12 noon until 2:00 P.M. for lunch. During that time, the office manager takes the daily deposit to the bank. During the lunch break the clerk who opened the mail that day uses the list of cash receipts and checks to update patient accounts.

The clerks take turns preparing and mailing monthly statements to patients with unpaid balances. One of the clerks writes off uncollectible accounts only after the physician who performed the respective services believes the account will not pay and communicates that belief to the office manager. The office manager then issues a credit memo to write off the account, which the clerk processes.

The office manager supervises the clerks, issues write-off memos, schedules appointments for the doctors, makes bank deposits, reconciles bank statements, and performs general correspondence duties.

Additional services are performed monthly by a local accountant who posts summaries prepared by the clerks to the general ledger, prepares income statements, and files the appropriate payroll forms and tax returns.

Required

Identify at least three control weaknesses at Parktown. Describe the potential threat and exposure associated with each weakness, and recommend how to best correct them. *(CPA Examination, adapted)*

12.9. Figure 12-20 on pages 364 and 365 depicts the activities performed in the revenue cycle by the Newton Hardware Company.

Required

a. Identify at least seven weaknesses in Newton Hardware's revenue cycle. Explain the resulting threat, and suggest methods to correct the weakness.
b. Identify ways to use IT to streamline Newton's revenue cycle activities. Describe the control procedures required in the new system.
   (CPA Examination, adapted)

12.10. The Family Support Center is a small charitable organization. It has only four full-time employees: two staff, an accountant, and an office manager. The majority of its funding comes from two campaign drives, one in the spring and one in the fall. Donors make pledges over the telephone. Some donors pay their pledge by credit card during the telephone campaign, but many prefer to pay in monthly installments by check. In such cases, the donor pledges are recorded during the telephone campaign, and the donors are then mailed pledge cards. Donors mail their contributions directly to the charity. Most donors send a check, but occasionally some send cash. Most donors return their pledge card with their check or cash donation, but occasionally the Family Support Center receives anonymous cash donations. The procedures used to process donations are as follows:

Sarah, a staff member who has worked for the Family Support Center for 12 years, opens all mail. She sorts the donations from the other mail and prepares a list of all donations, indicating the name of the donor (or anonymous), amount of the donation, and the pledge number (if the donor returned the pledge card). Sarah then sends the list, cash, and checks to the accountant.

The accountant enters the information from the list into the computer to update the Family Support Center's files. The accountant then prepares a deposit slip (in duplicate) and deposits all cash and checks into the charity's bank account at the end of each day. No funds are left on the premises overnight. The validated deposit slip is then filed by date. The accountant also mails an acknowledgment letter thanking each donor. Monthly, the accountant retrieves all deposit slips and uses them to reconcile the Family Support Center's bank statement. At this time, the accountant also reviews the pledge files and sends a follow-up letter to those people who have not yet fulfilled their pledges.

Each employee has a computer workstation that is connected to the internal network. Employees are permitted to surf the Web during lunch hours. Each employee has full access to the charity's accounting system, so that anyone can fill in for someone else who is out sick or on vacation. Each Friday, the accountant makes a backup copy of all computer files. The backup copy is stored in the office manager's office.

Required

a. Identify two major control weaknesses in the Family Support Center's cash receipts procedures. For each weakness you identify, suggest a method to correct that weakness. Your solution must be specific—*identify which specific employees should do what. Assume that no new employees can be hired.*

b. Describe the IT control procedures that should exist in order to protect the Family Support Center from loss, alteration, or unauthorized disclosure of data.

12.11. Match the threats in the first column to the appropriate control procedures in the second column (more than one control may address the same threat).

Threat	**Applicable Control Procedures**
___ **1.** Uncollectible sales	a. Restricted access to master data
___ **2.** Mistakes in shipping orders to customers	b. Encryption of customer information while in storage
___ **3.** Crediting customer payments to the wrong account	c. Backup and disaster recovery procedures
___ **4.** Theft of customer payments	d. Digital signatures
___ **5.** Theft of inventory by employees	e. Physical access controls on inventory
___ **6.** Excess inventory	f. Segregation of duties of handling cash and maintaining accounts receivable
___ **7.** Reduced prices for sales to friends	g. Reconciliation of packing lists with sales orders
___ **8.** Orders later repudiated by customers who deny placing them	h. Reconciliation of invoices with packing lists and sales orders
___ **9.** Failure to bill customers	i. Use of bar codes or RFID tags
___**10.** Errors in customer invoices	j. Periodic physical counts of inventory
___**11.** Cash flow problems	k. Perpetual inventory system
___**12.** Loss of accounts receivable data	l. Use of either EOQ, MRP, or JIT inventory control system
___**13.** Unauthorized disclosure of customer personal information	m. Lockboxes or electronic lockboxes
___**14.** Failure to ship orders to customers	n. Cash flow budget
	o. Mailing of monthly statements to customers
	p. Credit approval by someone not involved in sales
	q. Segregation of duties of shipping and billing
	r. Periodic reconciliation of prenumbered sales orders with prenumbered shipping documents

FIGURE 12-20

Newton Hardware Company Revenue Cycle Procedures

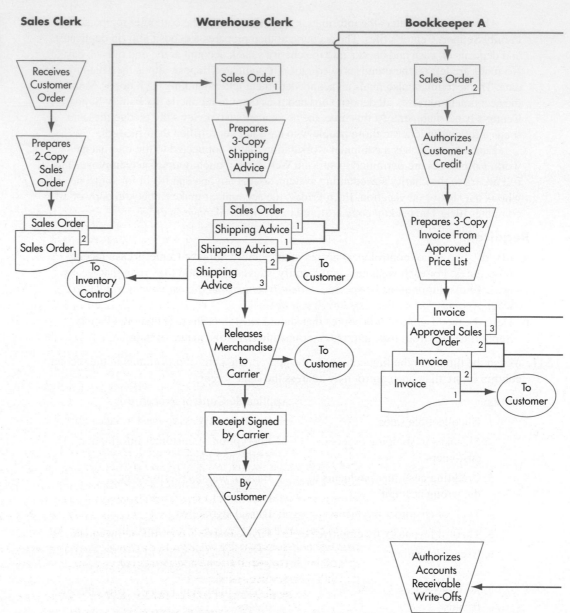

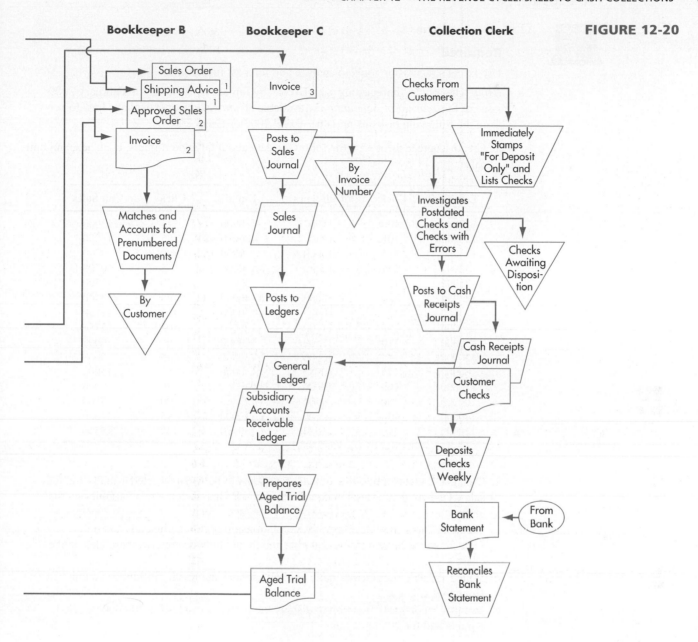

FIGURE 12-20

12.12. Excel Problem

Required

Use Excel's regression tools to analyze and forecast future sales.

(*Hint:* The article "Forecasting with Excel," by James A. Weisel in the February 2009 issue of the *Journal of Accountancy* (available at www.aicpa.org) explains how to perform the following tasks using either Excel 2003 or Excel 2007.)

a. Create a spreadsheet with the following data about targeted e-mails, click ads, and unit sales:

E-mails	Clicks	Unit Sales	E-mails	Clicks	Unit Sales
150000	100	12000	130000	125	13000
155000	105	12500	100000	85	12000
125000	75	10000	110000	100	9000
130000	150	14000	120000	135	10000
135000	125	12500	130000	140	13500
120000	100	10000	140000	125	13400
125000	125	10900	130000	115	12750
130000	135	11500	120000	105	12750
130000	110	12500	100000	95	10000
120000	95	10500	130000	145	9000
100000	75	10750	150000	150	15000
110000	100	10000	140000	120	12000
100000	80	9500	125000	100	13500
140000	130	13500	110000	95	11000
120000	110	11500	130000	140	13500

b. Create a scattergraph to illustrate the relationship between targeted e-mails and unit sales. Display the regression equation and the R^2 between the two variables on the chart.

c. Create a scattergraph to illustrate the relationship between click ads and unit sales. Display the regression equation and the R^2 between the two variables on the chart.

d. Which variable (targeted e-mails or click ads) has the greater influence on unit sales? How do you know?

e. Use the "=Forecast" function to display the forecasted sales for 200,000 targeted e-mails and for 200 click ads.

12.13. Give two specific examples of nonroutine transactions that may occur in processing cash receipts and updating accounts receivable. Also, specify the control procedures that should be in place to ensure the accuracy, completeness, and validity of those transactions.

Case 12-1 Research Project: Impact of IT on Revenue Cycle Activities, Threats, and Controls

Search popular business and technology magazines (*Business Week, Forbes, Fortune, CIO*, etc.) to find an article about an innovative use of IT to improve one or more activities in the revenue cycle. Write a report that:

   a. Explains how IT can be used to change revenue cycle activities.

   b. Discusses the control implications. Refer to Table 12-1, and explain how the new procedure changes the threats and appropriate control procedures for mitigating those threats.

AIS IN ACTION SOLUTIONS

Quiz Key

1. Which activity is part of the sales order entry process?
   a. setting customer credit limits (Incorrect. The credit department, not the sales department, sets credit limits.)
   b. preparing a bill of lading (Incorrect. This occurs as part of the shipping process.)
   ▶ **c.** checking customer credit (Correct. Checking customer credit and inventory availability are two key parts of the sales order entry process.)
   d. approving sales returns (Incorrect. Someone outside the sales department should approve all returns.)

2. Which document often accompanies merchandise shipped to a customer?
   a. picking ticket (Incorrect. The picking ticket is used by warehouse workers to fill the order. If a copy of the picking ticket is used as a packing slip, it is referred to as a packing slip.)
   ▶ **b.** packing slip (Correct. This document specifies what is being shipped.)
   c. credit memo (Incorrect. A credit memo is used to adjust a customer's account balance for sales returns, allowances, or write-offs.)
   d. sales order (Incorrect. This is a source document created during sales order entry.)

3. Which method is most likely used when a company offers customers discounts for prompt payment?
   ▶ **a.** open-invoice method (Correct. The open-invoice method provides a means to offer discounts because it facilitates aging each invoice to verify whether a discount should be granted.)
   b. balance-forward method (Incorrect. The balance-forward method does not facilitate tracking the age of individual invoices and thus is difficult to use to offer discounts for early payment of individual invoices.)
   c. accounts receivable aging method (Incorrect. Aging of accounts receivable is a control measure designed to timely detect potential uncollectible accounts.)
   d. cycle billing method (Incorrect. Cycle billing is a method of smoothing the timing of cash receipts by billing different subsets of the customer file each week.)

4. Which of the following techniques is the most efficient way to process customer payments and update accounts receivable?
   a. EFT (Incorrect. EFT deals only with the transfer of funds. It does not include remittance information necessary to update accounts receivable.)
   b. CRM (Incorrect. CRM stands for "customer relationship management.")
   ▶ **c.** FEDI (Correct. FEDI integrates EFT, for processing customer payments, with EDI, for processing related remittance data to update accounts receivable.)
   d. ACH (Incorrect. ACH stands for "Automated Clearing House," the private communications network used by financial institutions to transfer funds.)

5. Which of the following revenue cycle activities can potentially be eliminated by technology?
   a. sales order entry (Incorrect. IT may change how sales orders are entered, but the sales process must always begin with taking the customer's order.)
   b. shipping (Incorrect. The product must always be shipped to the customer. The manner may change, particularly for products that can be digitized, but there is still a shipping process.)
   ▶ c. billing (Correct. The use of integrated ERP systems makes printing invoices superfluous, because both the seller and customer already know all the information included in the invoice. Some large manufacturers have already moved to invoiceless systems with their major suppliers.)
   d. cash collections (Incorrect. IT may change how the funds are received, but sellers will always need to collect payments from customers.)

6. The integrated database underlying an ERP system results in which of the following general threats to the revenue cycle?
   a. inaccurate or invalid master data (Incorrect. Table 12-1 shows that this is not the only general threat to the revenue cycle.)
   b. unauthorized disclosure of sensitive information (Incorrect. Table 12-1 shows that this is not the only general threat to the revenue cycle.)
   c. loss or destruction of data (Incorrect. Table 12-1 shows that this is not the only general threat to the revenue cycle.)
   ▶ d. all of the above (Correct.)

7. Which document is used to authorize the release of merchandise from the inventory control (warehouse) to shipping?
   ▶ a. picking ticket (Correct. A picking ticket is generated by sales order entry to authorize removal of inventory to be shipped to the customer.)
   b. packing slip (Incorrect. The packing slip accompanies the shipment and lists the contents of the shipment.)
   c. shipping order (Incorrect. A shipping order is an internal document used to record what was shipped when the shipping function is performed in-house; a bill of lading serves the same purpose when a third-party common carrier is used to deliver merchandise.)
   d. sales invoice (Incorrect. A sales invoice documents the terms of the sale and requests payment.)

8. Which of the following provides a means to both improve the efficiency of processing customer payments and also enhance control over those payments?
   a. CRM (Incorrect. CRM stands for "customer relationship management" and is a process used to improve customer satisfaction and retention.)
   ▶ b. lockboxes (Correct. The use of lockboxes eliminates the delays involved in processing customer payments and then depositing them. It also improves control because customer payments are not directly handled by any employees.)
   c. aging accounts receivable (Incorrect. Aging accounts receivable is an important control for managing customer accounts, but not for processing payments.)
   d. EDI (Incorrect. EDI stands for "electronic data interchange." It is used to exchange documents, but not to process customer payments.)

9. For good internal control, who should approve credit memos?
   ▶ a. credit manager (Correct. This is the credit manager's function.)
   b. sales manager (Incorrect. The same person who authorizes sales should not also authorize credit memos to adjust customer accounts for those sales.)
   c. billing manager (Incorrect. The billing manager is in charge of invoicing customers and should not have authority to reduce accounts receivable by issuing credit memos.)
   d. controller (Incorrect. The controller is responsible for the recording function and should not also be able to authorize changes to accounts via credit memos.)

10. For good internal control over customer remittances, the mailroom clerk should separate the checks from the remittance advices and send the customer payments to which department?
    a. billing (Incorrect. Billing creates invoices but should not be involved in processing payments from customers.)
    b. accounts receivable (Incorrect. Accounts receivable performs the recording function and should not also have physical custody of assets.)
    ▶ c. cashier (Correct. This is the cashier's job. The cashier function has custody of cash accounts.)
    d. sales (Incorrect. The sales department authorizes release of merchandise and should not also have custody of assets.)

Chapter 13

The Expenditure Cycle: Purchasing to Cash Disbursements

Learning Objectives

After studying this chapter, you should be able to:

1. Explain the basic business activities and related information processing operations performed in the expenditure cycle.

2. Discuss the key decisions to be made in the expenditure cycle, and identify the information needed to make those decisions.

3. Identify major threats in the expenditure cycle, and evaluate the adequacy of various control procedures for dealing with those threats.

INTEGRATIVE CASE ALPHA OMEGA ELECTRONICS

Although the new enterprise resource planning (ERP) system at Alpha Omega Electronics (AOE) has enabled the company to slash its costs associated with purchasing and accounts payable, Linda Spurgeon, AOE's president, is convinced that additional improvements are needed. She is particularly concerned about issues recently raised by LeRoy Williams, vice president of manufacturing for AOE. LeRoy is upset because several production runs were delayed at the Wichita plant because components that AOE's inventory records indicated as being in stock actually were not on hand. There were also delays at the Dayton plant because suppliers either did not deliver components on time or delivered substandard products.

Linda asked Elizabeth Venko, the controller, and Ann Brandt, AOE's vice president of information systems, for some recommendations on how AOE's new ERP system could help solve these problems. Specifically, she asked Elizabeth and Ann to address the following issues:

1. What must be done to ensure that AOE's inventory records are current and accurate to avoid unexpected components shortages like those experienced at the Wichita plant?

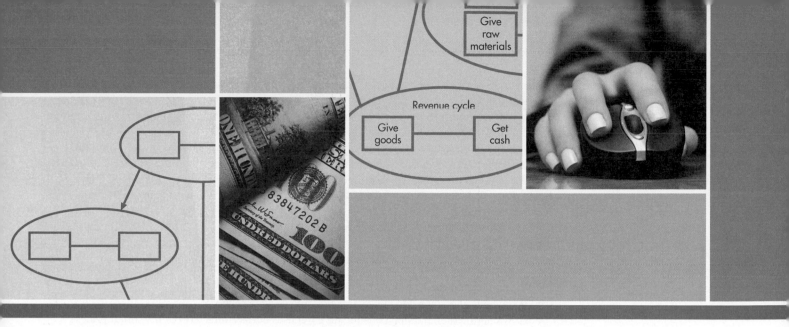

2. How could the problems at the Dayton plant be avoided in the future? What can be done to ensure timely delivery of quality components?
3. Is it possible to reduce AOE's investment in materials inventories?
4. How could the information system provide better information to guide planning and production?
5. How could IT be used to further reengineer expenditure cycle activities?

As this case reveals, deficiencies in the information system used to support expenditure cycle activities can create significant financial problems for an organization. Current and accurate information about inventories, suppliers, and the status of outstanding purchase orders is crucial for managing the expenditure cycle effectively. As you read this chapter, think about how to solve AOE's problems with its expenditure cycle activities.

Introduction

The *expenditure cycle* is a recurring set of business activities and related information processing operations associated with the purchase of and payment for goods and services (Figure 13-1). This chapter focuses on the acquisition of raw materials, finished goods, supplies, and services.

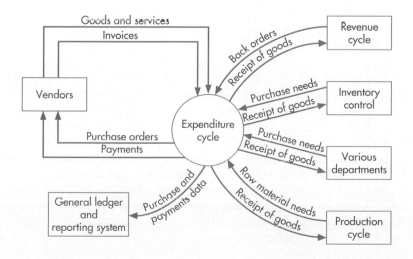

FIGURE 13-1

Context Diagram of the Expenditure Cycle

Chapters 13 and 14 address two other special types of expenditures: the acquisition of fixed assets and labor services, respectively.

In the expenditure cycle, the primary external exchange of information is with suppliers (vendors). Within the organization, information about the need to purchase goods and materials flows to the expenditure cycle from the revenue and production cycles, inventory control, and various departments. Once the goods and materials arrive, notification of their receipt flows back to those sources from the expenditure cycle. Expense data also flow from the expenditure cycle to the general ledger and reporting function for inclusion in financial statements and various management reports.

The primary objective in the expenditure cycle is to minimize the total cost of acquiring and maintaining inventories, supplies, and the various services the organization needs to function. To accomplish this objective, management must make the following key decisions:

● What is the optimal level of inventory and supplies to carry?
● Which suppliers provide the best quality and service at the best prices?
● How can the organization consolidate purchases across units to obtain optimal prices?
● How can information technology (IT) be used to improve both the efficiency and accuracy of the inbound logistics function?
● How can the organization maintain sufficient cash to take advantage of any discounts suppliers offer?
● How can payments to vendors be managed to maximize cash flow?

The answers to those questions guide how an organization performs the four basic expenditure cycle activities depicted in Figure 13-2:

1. Ordering materials, supplies, and services
2. Receiving materials, supplies, and services
3. Approving supplier invoices
4. Cash disbursements

This chapter explains how an organization's information system supports each of those activities. We begin by describing the design of the expenditure cycle information system and the basic controls necessary to ensure that it provides management with reliable information to assess operational efficiency and effectiveness. We then discuss in detail each of the four basic expenditure cycle activities. For each activity, we describe how the information needed to perform and manage those activities is collected, processed, and stored. We also explain the controls necessary to ensure not only the reliability of that information but also the safeguarding of the organization's resources.

Expenditure Cycle Information System

As Table 13-1 shows, the activities in the expenditure cycle are mirror images of the basic activities performed in the revenue cycle.

These close linkages between the buyer's expenditure cycle activities and the seller's revenue cycle activities have important implications for the design of both parties' accounting information systems. Specifically, by applying new IT developments to reengineer expenditure cycle activities, companies create opportunities for suppliers to reengineer their revenue cycle activities. Conversely, using IT to redesign a company's revenue cycle can create opportunities for customers to modify their own expenditure cycles. In fact, the changes in one company's operations may *necessitate* corresponding changes in the operations of other companies with which it does business. For example, the major automobile manufacturers and many large retailers, such as Walmart, require their suppliers to transmit invoices via electronic data interchange (EDI), or they will not do business with them. Consequently, those suppliers must modify their accounting information systems to incorporate the use of EDI.

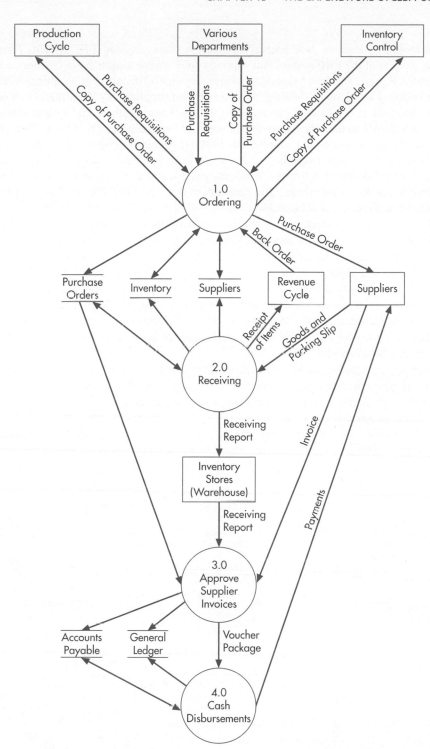

FIGURE 13-2

Level 0 Data Flow Diagram for the Expenditure Cycle

TABLE 13-1 Comparison of Revenue and Expenditure Cycle Activities

Revenue Cycle Activity	Expenditure Cycle Activity
Sales order entry—process orders from customers	Ordering of materials, supplies, and services—send orders to suppliers
Shipping—deliver merchandise or services to customers (outbound logistics)	Receiving—receive merchandise or services from suppliers (inbound logistics)
Billing—send invoices to customers	Processing invoices—review and approve invoices from suppliers
Cash collections—process payments from customers	Cash disbursements—process payments to suppliers

Process

Like most large organizations, AOE uses an enterprise resource planning (ERP) system. Figure 13-3 shows the portion of the ERP system that supports AOE's expenditure cycle business activities.

Although Figure 13-3 shows that AOE's inventory control department has primary responsibility for ensuring an adequate quantity of materials and supplies, any department can submit a request to purchase items. Once a purchase request has been approved, the system searches the inventory master file to identify the preferred supplier for that item. The system then creates a purchase order that is sent to the supplier via EDI. (If necessary, paper copies are printed and mailed.) The receiving department has access to the open purchase order file so that it can plan for and verify the validity of deliveries. Accounts payable is notified of orders so that it can plan for pending financial commitments. The department that generated the purchase requisition is also notified that its request has been approved.

Major suppliers send electronic notification of coming deliveries, which enables AOE to plan to have adequate staffing to process incoming shipments at its warehouses. When a shipment arrives, the receiving dock workers use the inquiry processing system to verify that an order is expected from that supplier. Most suppliers bar-code or RFID tag their products to facilitate the counting of the goods. Receiving dock workers inspect the goods and use an online terminal to enter information about the quantity and condition of items received. The exact time of the delivery also is recorded to help evaluate vendor performance. The system checks that data against the open purchase order, and any discrepancies are immediately displayed on the screen so that they can be resolved.

Upon transfer of the goods to the warehouse, the inventory stores clerk verifies the count of the items and enters that data in the system. For suppliers who do not send invoices, the system automatically schedules a payment according to the terms agreed upon when the order was placed. Accounts payable clerks enter information from suppliers who send EDI, and sometimes paper, invoices. The system then compares the supplier invoice with the information contained in the purchase order and receiving report to ensure accuracy and validity. For purchases

FIGURE 13-3

Overview of ERP System Design to Support the Expenditure Cycle

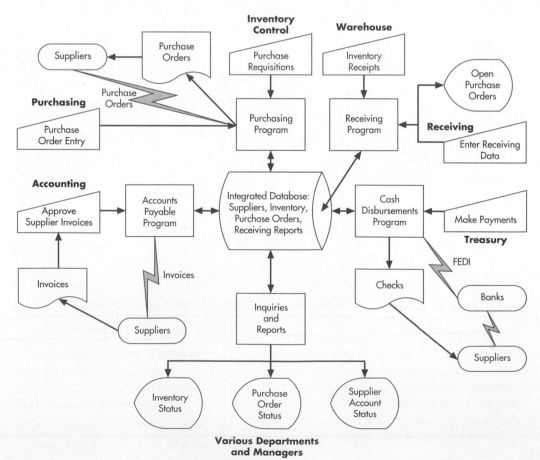

of supplies or services that do not usually involve purchase orders and receiving reports, the invoice is sent to the appropriate supervisor for approval. The supplier invoice itself is also checked for mathematical accuracy. The system automatically schedules invoices for payment by due date.

AOE, like most companies, uses batch processing to pay its suppliers. Each day, the treasurer uses the inquiry processing system to review the invoices that are due and approves them for payment. AOE makes payments to some of its larger suppliers using FEDI but still prints paper checks for many of its smaller suppliers. When an EFT payment is authorized or a check is printed, the system updates the accounts payable, open-invoice, and general ledger files. For each supplier, the totals of all vouchers are summed, and that amount is subtracted from the balance field in that supplier's master file record. The relevant purchase orders and receiving reports are flagged to mark that those transactions have been paid. The invoices that are paid are then deleted from the open-invoice file. A remittance advice is prepared for each supplier, which lists each invoice being paid and the amounts of any discounts or allowances taken. For payments made by EFT, the remittance data accompany the EFT payment as part of the FEDI package. For payments made by check, the printed remittance advice accompanies the signed check. After all disbursement transactions have been processed, the system generates a summary journal entry, debiting accounts payable and crediting cash, and posts that entry to the general ledger.

The cashier reviews checks against the supporting documents and then signs them. Checks above a specified amount also require a second signature by the treasurer or another authorized manager. The cashier then mails the signed checks and remittance advices to the suppliers. EFT transactions are also performed by the cashier and reviewed by the treasurer.

The easy access to up-to-date, accurate information enables managers to closely monitor performance. However, the quality of decisions depends upon the accuracy of the information in the database. We now discuss the general threats associated with the expenditure cycle activities and explain the controls that can mitigate them.

Threats and Controls

Figure 13-3 shows that all expenditure cycle activities depend on the integrated database that contains information about suppliers, inventory, and purchasing activities. Therefore, the first general threat listed in Table 13-2 is inaccurate or invalid master data. Errors in the supplier master data could result in ordering from unapproved suppliers, purchasing materials of inferior quality, untimely deliveries, sending payments to the wrong address, and fraudulent disbursements to fictitious suppliers. Errors in the inventory master data can result in production delays due to unanticipated shortages of key materials or unnecessary purchases and excess inventory. Errors in the purchasing master data can result in unauthorized purchases and failure to take advantage of negotiated discounts.

Table 13-2 shows that one way to mitigate the threat of inaccurate or invalid master data is to employ the data processing integrity controls described in Chapter 10. It is also important to restrict access to expenditure cycle master data and configure the system so that only authorized employees can make changes to master data. This requires changing the default configurations of employee roles in ERP systems to appropriately segregate incompatible duties. For example, consider the situation where an accounts payable clerk enters the name of a supplier who is not currently on the list of approved suppliers. The default configuration of many ERP systems would result in a prompt query as to whether the clerk wants to create a new supplier record. This violates proper segregation of duties by permitting the person responsible for recording payments to suppliers to also authorize the creation of new accounts. Similarly, the default configurations of many ERP systems permit accounts payable staff not only to read the prices of various products and the current balances owed to suppliers but also to change the values of those data items. These examples are just some of the many configuration settings that need to be reviewed to ensure proper segregation of duties. However, because such preventive controls can never be 100% effective, Table 13-2 also indicates that an important detective control is to regularly produce a report of all changes to master data and review them to verify that the database remains accurate (control 1.3).

A second general threat in the expenditure cycle is unauthorized disclosure of sensitive information, such as banking information about suppliers and special pricing discounts offered

TABLE 13-2 Threats and Controls in the Expenditure Cycle

Activity	Threat	Controls (first number refers to the corresponding threat)
General issues throughout entire expenditure cycle	1. Inaccurate or invalid master data 2. Unauthorized disclosure of sensitive information 3. Loss or destruction of data 4. Poor performance	1.1 Data processing integrity controls 1.2 Restriction of access to master data 1.3 Review of all changes to master data 2.1 Access controls 2.2 Encryption 3.1 Backup and disaster recovery procedures 4.1 Managerial reports
Ordering	5. Inaccurate inventory records 6. Purchasing items not needed 7. Purchasing at inflated prices 8. Purchasing goods of inferior quality 9. Unreliable suppliers 10. Purchasing from unauthorized suppliers 11. Kickbacks	5.1 Perpetual inventory system 5.2 Bar coding or RFID tags 5.3 Periodic physical counts of inventory 6.1 Perpetual inventory system 6.2 Review and approval of purchase requisitions 6.3 Centralized purchasing function 7.1 Price lists 7.2 Competitive bidding 7.3 Review of purchase orders 7.4 Budgets 8.1 Purchasing only from approved suppliers 8.2 Review and approval of purchases from new suppliers 8.3 Holding purchasing managers responsible for rework and scrap costs 8.4 Tracking and monitoring product quality by supplier 9.1 Requiring suppliers to possess quality certification (e.g., ISO 9000) 9.2 Collecting and monitoring supplier delivery performance data 10.1 Maintaining a list of approved suppliers and configuring the system to permit purchase orders only to approved suppliers 10.2 Review and approval of purchases from new suppliers 10.3 EDI-specific controls (access, review of orders, encryption, policy) 11.1 Requiring purchasing agents to disclose financial and personal interests in suppliers 11.2 Training employees in how to respond to offers of gifts from suppliers 11.3 Job rotation and mandatory vacations 11.4 Supplier audits
Receiving	12. Accepting unordered items 13. Mistakes in counting 14. Verifying receipt of services 15. Theft of inventory	12.1 Requiring existence of approved purchase order prior to accepting any delivery 13.1 Do not inform receiving employees about quantity ordered 13.2 Require receiving employees to sign receiving report 13.3 Incentives 13.4 Document transfer of goods to inventory 13.5 Use of bar-codes and RFID tags 13.6 Configuration of the ERP system to flag discrepancies between received and ordered quantities that exceed tolerance threshold for investigation 14.1 Budgetary controls 14.2 Audits 15.1 Restriction of physical access to inventory 15.2 Documentation of all transfers of inventory between receiving and inventory employees 15.3 Periodic physical counts of inventory and reconciliation to recorded quantities 15.4 Segregation of duties: custody of inventory versus receiving
Approving supplier invoices	16. Errors in supplier invoices 17. Mistakes in posting to accounts payable	16.1 Verification of invoice accuracy 16.2 Requiring detailed receipts for procurement card purchases 16.3 ERS 16.4 Restriction of access to supplier master data 16.5 Verification of freight bill and use of approved delivery channels 17.1 Data entry edit controls 17.2 Reconciliation of detailed accounts payable records with the general ledger control account

TABLE 13-2 Continued

Activity	Threat	Controls (first number refers to the corresponding threat)
Cash disbursements	18. Failure to take advantage of discounts for prompt payment 19. Paying for items not received 20. Duplicate payments 21. Theft of cash 22. Check alteration 23. Cash flow problems	18.1 Filing of invoices by due date for discounts 18.2 Cash flow budgets 19.1 Requiring that all supplier invoices be matched to supporting documents that are acknowledged by both receiving and inventory control 19.2 Budgets (for services) 19.3 Requiring receipts for travel expenses 19.4 Use of corporate credit cards for travel expenses 20.1 Requiring a complete voucher package for all payments 20.2 Policy to pay only from original copies of supplier invoices 20.3 Cancelling all supporting documents when payment is made 21.1 Physical security of blank checks and check-signing machine 21.2 Periodic accounting of all sequentially numbered checks by cashier 21.3 Access controls to EFT terminals 21.4 Use of dedicated computer and browser for online banking 21.5 ACH blocks on accounts not used for payments 21.6 Separation of check-writing function from accounts payable 21.7 Requiring dual signatures on checks greater than a specific amount 21.8 Regular reconciliation of bank account with recorded amounts by someone independent of cash disbursements procedures 21.9 Restriction of access to supplier master file 21.10 Limiting the number of employees with ability to create one-time suppliers and to process invoices from one-time suppliers 21.11 Running petty cash as an imprest fund 21.12 Surprise audits of petty cash fund 22.1 Check protection machines 22.2 Use of special inks and papers 22.3 "Positive Pay" arrangements with banks 23.1 Cash flow budget

by preferred suppliers. Table 13-2 shows that one way to mitigate the risk of this threat is to configure the system to employ strong access controls that limit who can view such information. It is also important to configure the system to limit employees' ability to use the system's built-in query capabilities to specific tables and fields. In addition, sensitive data should be encrypted in storage to prevent IT employees who do not have access to the ERP system from using operating system utilities to view sensitive information. Information exchanged with suppliers over the Internet should also be encrypted during transmission.

As Table 13-2 shows, a third general threat in the expenditure cycle concerns the loss or destruction of master data. The best way to mitigate the risk of this threat is to employ the backup and disaster recovery procedures that were discussed in Chapter 10. A best practice is to implement the ERP system as three separate instances. One instance, referred to as *production*, is used to process daily activity. A second is used for testing and development. A third instance should be maintained as an online backup to the production system to provide near real-time recovery.

Accurate master data enable management to better use an ERP system's extensive reporting capabilities to monitor performance. Because inventory represents a sizable investment of working capital, reports that help manage inventory are especially valuable. A key measure to evaluate inventory management is inventory turnover, which is the ratio of cost of goods sold divided by inventory on hand. Consider the following example: annual sales are $500 million, and annual cost of goods sold total $360 million. An inventory turnover ratio of 1 means that the company is effectively carrying a year's supply of inventory, tying up $360 million. Improving the inventory turnover ratio to 3 would reduce that unprofitable investment to $120 million, thereby freeing up $240 million that could be used for other purposes.

Accountants need to understand how business activities are performed in order to design other reports that can help management better manage inventory. For example, it is useful to monitor the percentage of requisitions that are filled from inventory on hand. For critical items, this should be close to 100% to avoid stockouts and delays in filling customer orders. For most items, however, such a high fill rate is undesirable because it requires carrying too much inventory. Other reports can help management identify the relative importance of various inventory items. For example, it may be useful to classify items along several dimensions, such as frequency of purchase, frequency of use or resale, and contribution to profitability. Items that are frequently purchased and used and that make a significant contribution to profitability are of high importance and should be managed so as to maintain high fill rates. In contrast, management may wish to consider eliminating items that are seldom purchased, infrequently used, and that do not contribute much to profitability. As we will see in the following sections, accountants can help managers by designing a variety of detailed reports and metrics that are relevant to evaluating each business activity in the expenditure cycle.

Ordering Materials, Supplies and Services

The first major business activity in the expenditure cycle (circle 1.0 in Figure 13-2) is ordering inventory, supplies, or services. This involves first identifying what, when, and how much to purchase, and then choosing from which supplier to purchase.

Identifying What, When, and How Much to Purchase

As the introductory case showed, inaccurate inventory records can create significant problems for organizations. Therefore, accountants and systems professionals need to understand best practices for managing inventory.

PROCESS   The traditional approach to managing inventory is to maintain sufficient stock so that production can continue without interruption even if inventory use is greater than expected or if suppliers are late in making deliveries. This traditional approach is often called the *economic order quantity (EOQ)* approach because it is based on calculating an optimal order size to minimize the sum of ordering, carrying, and stockout costs. *Ordering costs* include all expenses associated with processing purchase transactions. *Carrying costs* are those associated with holding inventory. *Stockout costs* are those that result from inventory shortages, such as lost sales or production delays.

Actual application of the EOQ approach varies depending on the type of item. For high-cost or high-use items, such as the computer chips and displays AOE uses, all three types of costs are included in the formula. For low-cost or low-usage items, such as the screws and springs AOE uses to assemble its products, ordering and carrying costs are usually ignored, and the sole objective is to maintain sufficient inventory levels. The EOQ formula is used to calculate *how much* to order. The *reorder point* specifies *when* to order. Companies typically set the reorder point based on delivery time and desired levels of safety stock to handle unexpected fluctuations in demand.

The traditional EOQ approach to inventory control often results in carrying significant amounts of inventory. The money invested in carrying inventory earns nothing. Consequently, in recent years many large U.S. manufacturing companies, including Xerox, Ford, Motorola, NCR, Intel, McDonnell Douglas, and Delco Electronics, have minimized or even eliminated the amount of inventory on hand by adopting either materials requirements planning or just-in-time inventory management systems.

Materials requirements planning (MRP) seeks to reduce required inventory levels by improving the accuracy of forecasting techniques to better schedule purchases to satisfy production needs. For example, the production planning department of a company using MRP would prepare a detailed schedule specifying the quantities of each finished product to manufacture in a specified time period, such as the next three months, based on sales forecast data. This schedule and the engineering specifications for each product identify the quantities of raw materials, parts, and supplies needed in production and the point in time when they will be needed. Thus, MRP systems reduce uncertainties about when raw materials are needed and therefore enable companies to carry less inventory.

A *just-in-time (JIT) inventory system* attempts to minimize, if not totally eliminate, finished goods inventory by purchasing and producing goods only in response to actual, rather than forecasted, sales. Consequently, JIT systems are characterized by frequent deliveries of small amounts of materials, parts, and supplies directly to the specific locations that require them when they are needed, rather than by infrequent bulk deliveries to a central receiving and storage facility. Therefore, a factory using a JIT system will have multiple receiving docks, each assigned to accept deliveries of items needed at nearby work centers.

A major difference between MRP and JIT systems is production scheduling. MRP systems schedule production to meet forecasted sales, thereby creating an "optimal" quantity of finished goods inventory. JIT systems schedule production in response to customer demands, thereby virtually eliminating finished goods inventory, but they require carrying sufficient quantities of raw materials in order to quickly adjust production in response to consumer demand. Both MRP and JIT systems can reduce costs and improve efficiency. Choosing between them depends, in part, on the types of products a company sells. MRP systems are more effectively used with products that have predictable patterns of demand, such as consumer staples. For such items, companies can plan purchases to minimize stockouts (with the resultant lost sales) while simultaneously minimizing the risk of overstocking and the subsequent costs of marking down or scrapping the excess inventory. In contrast, JIT inventory systems are especially useful for products that have relatively short life cycles and for which demand cannot be accurately predicted, such as toys associated with specific movies. In such cases, it is important that the business be able to quickly speed up production to meet unanticipated demand as well as to quickly stop production to avoid accumulating large inventories that must be marked down for clearance because the product is no longer in demand.

A request to purchase goods or supplies is triggered either by the inventory control function or when employees notice a shortage of materials. The advanced inventory control systems used in large manufacturing companies, such as IBM and Ford, automatically generate purchase requests when the quantity of an item on hand falls below its reorder point. In small companies, however, the employees who use the items note when stock is running low and request that it be reordered. Moreover, even in large companies, office supplies, such as copier paper and pencils, are often ordered by the employees who use those items when they notice that stock is running low.

Regardless of its source, the need to purchase goods or supplies often results in the creation of a ***purchase requisition*** that identifies the requisitioner; specifies the delivery location and date needed; identifies the item numbers, descriptions, quantity, and price of each item requested; and may suggest a supplier. The person approving the purchase requisition indicates the department number and account number to which the purchase should be charged.

Figure 13-4 shows a typical purchase requisition data entry screen used in ERP systems. Minimizing the amount of data that must be manually entered improves both efficiency and accuracy. Thus, in Figure 13-4, the employee initiating the purchase request needs to complete

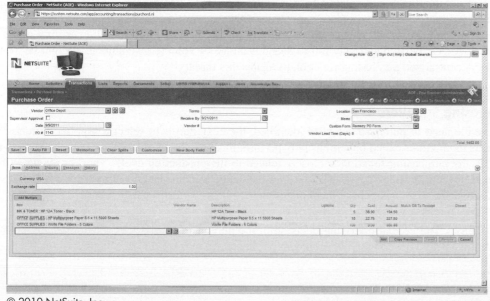

FIGURE 13-4

Purchase Requisition Data Entry Screen

only the supplier (vendor), date required, and location (where to ship the merchandise) fields in the header section (the top of the screen) and the item number and quantity requested in the details section. The system then pulls up all the other relevant information from the related master files. You probably noticed the similarity in design to the sales order entry data entry screen (see Figure 12-6). This is intentional; it makes it easier for employees to learn how to perform new job duties arising from promotions or transfers.

THREATS AND CONTROLS   One threat is that inaccurate inventory records can result in stockouts that lead to lost sales or to carrying excess inventory that increases costs. To reduce the risk of these problems, the perpetual inventory method should be used to ensure that information about inventory stocks is always current. However, data entry errors can result in inaccurate perpetual inventory records because even expert typists do make mistakes. Therefore, using information technology to eliminate the need for manual data entry can improve the accuracy of perpetual inventory records.

Bar-coding is one option, but it is not a panacea. Errors can still occur if employees attempt to save time by scanning one item and then manually entering the quantity. For example, a grocery store orders 12 varieties of a private-brand soda, the receiving clerk may scan only one can and then manually enter the number purchased. Since the flavors are all priced the same, the amount of the purchase is correctly calculated. The perpetual inventory records will be incorrect, however, because the exact count of the flavors purchased is not correctly recorded.

Affixing RFID tags to individual products eliminates the problems just discussed because the reader automatically records each item. RFID technology is also more efficient than bar codes because there is no need for a human to align the bar code on the product with the reader. However, RFID technology is more expensive than bar-coding and cannot be used for every type of product (e.g., liquids).

It is also important to periodically count inventory on hand and investigate any discrepancies between those counts and the perpetual inventory records (control 5.3 in Table 13-2). One annual physical inventory count will generally not be sufficient to maintain accurate inventory records, especially for MRP and JIT systems. Instead, an *ABC cost analysis* should be used to classify items according to their importance: The most critical items (A items) should be counted most frequently, and the least critical items (C items) can be counted less often. If such interim counts reveal significant discrepancies with inventory records, a comprehensive count of all inventory should be immediately undertaken. This approach might have alerted management at AOE's Wichita plant in the chapter introductory case about shortages of key components early enough to avoid production delays.

Another threat is purchasing items that are not currently needed. Accurate perpetual inventory records (control 6.1) ensure the validity of purchase requisitions that the inventory control system automatically generates. Supervisors need to review and approve purchase requisitions that individual employees initiate. A related problem is multiple purchases of the same item by different subunits of the organization. As a result, the organization may be carrying a larger inventory than desired and may fail to take advantage of volume discounts that might be available. A centralized purchasing function mitigates this threat.

Choosing Suppliers

Once the need to purchase has been identified, the next step is to select a supplier. Purchasing agents (sometimes called buyers) usually perform this task. In manufacturing companies such as AOE, the purchasing function is closely related to the production cycle. Thus, as Figure 12-1 shows, Ryan McDaniel, the head of the purchasing department at AOE, reports directly to LeRoy Williams, the vice president of manufacturing.

PROCESS   The crucial operating decision in the purchasing activity is selecting suppliers for inventory items. Several factors should be considered in making this decision:

- Price
- Quality of materials
- Dependability in making deliveries

Note that properly evaluating suppliers requires more than just maintaining data about purchase prices. Companies also incur costs, such as rework and scrap, related to the quality of the products purchased. There are also costs associated with supplier delivery performance (such as the problems described in the introductory case at AOE's Dayton plant). Supplier dependability is especially important for companies that use JIT systems because late deliveries can bring the entire system to a halt.

Once a supplier has been selected for a product, the supplier's identity should become part of the product inventory master record to avoid repeating the supplier selection process for every subsequent order. (In some cases, however, such as for the purchase of high-cost and low-usage items, management may explicitly want to reevaluate all potential suppliers each time that product is ordered.) A list of potential alternative suppliers for each item should also be maintained, in case the primary supplier is out of stock of a needed item.

A *purchase order* (Figure 13-5) is a document or electronic form that formally requests a supplier to sell and deliver specified products at designated prices. It is also a promise to pay and becomes a contract once the supplier accepts it. The purchase order includes the names of the supplier and purchasing agent, the order and requested delivery dates, the delivery location and shipping method, and information about the items ordered. Frequently, several purchase orders are generated to fill one purchase requisition, because different vendors may be the preferred suppliers for the various items requested. The quantity ordered may also differ from that requested, to allow the purchaser to take advantage of quantity discounts.

Many companies maintain special purchasing arrangements with important suppliers. A *blanket purchase order* is a commitment to purchase specified items at designated prices from a particular supplier for a set time period, often one year. Blanket purchase orders reduce the buyer's uncertainty about reliable sources of raw materials and help the supplier plan its capacity and operations more effectively.

The major cost driver in the purchasing function is the number of purchase orders processed. Thus, finding ways to reduce the number of orders processed and to streamline the steps involved can yield significant savings. Using EDI is one way to improve the purchasing process. EDI reduces costs by eliminating the clerical work associated with printing and mailing paper documents.

FIGURE 13-5

Example of a Purchase Order (items in bold are pre-printed)

Alpha Omega Electronics				**No. 2463**

Billing Address: 2431 Bradford Lane
San Francisco, CA 94403
(314) 467-2341

Reference the above number on all invoices and shipping documents

PURCHASE ORDER

To: Best Office Supply
4567 Olive Blvd.
Dayton, OH 33422-1234

Ship To: AOE, Inc.
1735 Sandy Dr.
Dayton, OH 33421–2243

Vendor Number: 121	**Order Date:** 07/03/2011	**Requisition Number:** 89010	**Buyer:** Fred Mozart	**Terms:** 1/10, n/30

F.O.B. Destination	**Ship Via:** Your choice	**Delivery Date:** 07/15/2011	**Remarks:**	

Item	**Item Number**	**Quantity**	**Description**	**Unit Price**
1	32047	15 boxes	Xerox 4200 paper, 20 wt., 10 ream box	$33.99
2	80170	5 boxes	Moore 2600 continuous form, 20 lb.	$31.99
3	81756	20 boxes	CD cases, box of 10	$ 6.49
4	10407	100	700 MB CDs, 1 box	$19.99

Approved by: *Susan Beethoven*

The time between recognizing the need to reorder an item and subsequently receiving it also is reduced. Consequently, the risk of running out of stock is diminished, which can significantly increase profitability. In the past, EDI was expensive because it required the use of proprietary third-party networks and software. However, the development of standards for EDI over the Internet (EDINT) has drastically cut the costs of EDI. An example is AS2, which is a protocol that governs the secure electronic exchange of documents such as purchase orders.

Vendor-managed inventory programs provide another means of reducing purchase and inventory costs. A *vendor-managed inventory* program essentially outsources much of the inventory control and purchasing function: Suppliers are given access to sales and inventory data and are authorized to automatically replenish inventory when stocks fall to predetermined reorder points. This arrangement cuts carrying costs by reducing the amount of inventory on hand and lowers processing costs by eliminating the need to generate and exchange formal purchase orders.

Reverse auctions provide yet another technique to reduce purchasing-related expenses. In reverse auctions, suppliers compete with one another to meet demand at the lowest price. Although reverse auctions can yield significant cost savings, because the primary focus is on price, they are probably best suited to the purchase of commodity items rather than critical components for which quality, vendor reliability, and delivery performance are important.

One other way to reduce purchasing-related costs is to conduct a pre-award audit. Pre-award audits are typically used for large purchases that involve formal bids by suppliers. The internal auditor visits each potential supplier who has made the final cut in the contracting process to verify the accuracy of its bid. Pre-award audits often identify simple mathematical errors in complex pricing formulas and other discrepancies that, when corrected, can provide considerable savings.

EDI, vendor-managed inventory, reverse auctions, and pre-award audits are techniques for reducing the purchasing-related costs of raw materials and finished goods inventory. New IT developments can also change how companies account for their inventory. Traditionally, most companies have used the LIFO, FIFO, or weighted-average approaches to allocate costs to inventory and cost of goods sold. RFID, however, provides the capability to track individual inventory items. Thus, RFID makes it possible for companies to more accurately account for actual inventory-related costs by switching to the specific identification method for accounting for inventories.

THREATS AND CONTROLS Table 13-2 lists five threats to placing orders with suppliers. One (threat 7) involves purchasing items at inflated prices. The cost of purchased components represents a substantial portion of the total cost of many manufactured products. Therefore, companies strive to secure the best prices for the items they purchase. Several procedures can help ensure that companies do not pay too much for specific products. Price lists for frequently purchased items should be stored in the computer and consulted when orders are made. The prices of many low-cost items can be readily determined from catalogs. Competitive, written bids should be solicited for high-cost and specialized products (control 7.2). Purchase orders should be reviewed to ensure that these policies have been followed.

Budgets (control 7.4) are also helpful in controlling purchasing expenses. Purchases should be charged to an account that is the responsibility of the person or department approving the requisition. Actual costs should be compared periodically with budget allowances. To facilitate control, these reports should highlight any significant deviations from budgeted amounts for further investigation (the principle of management by exception).

In attempting to obtain the lowest possible prices, another threat is purchasing inferior-quality products. Substandard products can result in costly production delays. Moreover, the costs of scrap and rework often result in higher total production costs than if higher-quality, more expensive materials had been initially purchased. Through experience, buyers often learn which suppliers provide the best-quality goods at competitive prices. Such informal knowledge should be incorporated into formal control procedures so that it is not lost when a particular employee leaves the company. One best practice is to establish lists of approved suppliers known to provide goods of acceptable quality (control 8.1). Purchase orders should be reviewed to ensure that only these approved suppliers are being used. In addition, the accounting information system should collect detailed product quality data. For example, AOE can measure the quality of a supplier's products by tracking how often its items fail to pass inspection in the receiving department and the amount of production that has to be reworked or scrapped because of substandard materials. The purchasing manager should regularly review that data to maintain and revise the list of approved suppliers. Finally, purchasing managers should be held responsible for the total cost of purchases, which includes not only the purchase price but also the quality-related costs of rework and scrap. Doing this requires designing the system to track the latter costs so that they can be allocated back to the purchasing department.

As the introductory case demonstrated, another potential problem is unreliable performance by suppliers (threat 9 in Table 13-2). One way to reduce the risk of problems with supplier dependability is to require that suppliers be certified as meeting international quality standards such as ISO 9000. However, the accounting information system should also be designed to capture and track information about supplier performance (control 9.2). For example, AOE can track actual delivery dates versus those promised. Indeed, the ERP system can be configured to automatically generate reports of purchase orders that have been not been delivered within the promised time period.

Purchasing from unauthorized suppliers (threat 10) can result in numerous problems. Items may be of inferior quality or overpriced. The purchase may even cause legal problems. Various government agencies, such as the Office of Foreign Assets Control and the Bureau of Industry and Security in the Department of Commerce, maintain lists of individuals and companies with whom it is illegal to transact business. Payments to entities on such lists can result in substantial fines and, sometimes, imprisonment. Consequently, all purchase orders should be reviewed to ensure that only approved suppliers are used. It is especially important to restrict access to the approved supplier list and to periodically review the list for any unauthorized changes. ERP systems should be configured to prevent issuing purchase orders to suppliers not in the approved master file.

Using EDI for purchase orders requires additional control procedures. Access to the EDI system should be controlled and limited to authorized personnel through the use of passwords, user IDs, access control matrices, and physical access controls. Procedures to verify and authenticate EDI transactions also are needed. Most EDI systems are programmed to send an acknowledgment for each transaction, which provides a rudimentary accuracy check. Further protection against transmission problems, which can result in the loss of orders, is provided by time-stamping and numbering all EDI transactions. Companies should maintain and periodically review a log of all EDI transactions to ensure that all have been processed and that established policies are being followed. Encryption can ensure the privacy of EDI transactions, which is especially important for competitive bids. Digital signatures should be used to ensure the authenticity of transactions.

Numerous policy-related threats also arise with EDI, each of which must be covered in the trading agreement. Examples of these types of issues include the following:

● At what point in the process can the order be canceled?
● Which party is responsible for the cost of return freight if contract terms are not followed?
● Which party is responsible for errors in bar codes, RFID tags, and labels?
● What happens if errors in the purchasing company's sales system cause additional errors in the amount of goods that suppliers provide?
● Can suppliers ship more inventory than ordered if doing so reduces total freight costs because it results in a full, rather than partial, truckload?

Table 13-2 shows that *kickbacks*, which are gifts from suppliers to purchasing agents for the purpose of influencing their choice of suppliers, are another threat. For the kickback to make economic sense, the supplier must find some way to recover the money spent on the bribe. This usually is accomplished by inflating the price of subsequent purchases or by substituting goods of inferior quality. Even if neither of these problems occurs, kickbacks impair the buyer's objectivity.

To prevent kickbacks, companies should prohibit purchasing agents from accepting any gifts from potential or existing suppliers. (Trinkets that are clearly of inconsequential value may be allowed.) These policies should apply not only to gifts of tangible goods, but also to services. For example, meeting planners should be informed that it is against company policy to accept frequent-traveler points from hotels for booking the company's meetings there. Training employees how to respond to unsolicited "gifts" from suppliers (control 11.2) is also important, because many kickback schemes are initiated when unethical vendors send such "tokens of appreciation,"

FOCUS 13-1   Supplier Audits: A Means to Control Purchasing

Supplier audits may be one of the best tools for assessing the effectiveness of expenditure cycle controls. It entails having an internal auditor visit a supplier's office to check its records. The objective is to identify suppliers likely to be associated with problems such as kickbacks. Red flags that indicate potential problems include:

1. A large percentage of the supplier's gross sales was to the company conducting the supplier audit.
2. The supplier's pricing methods differ from standard industry practice.
3. The supplier does not own the equipment it rents, but is itself renting that equipment from a third party.

4. Entertainment expenses are high in terms of a percentage of the supplier's gross sales.
5. The supplier submits altered or fictitious third-party invoices.
6. The supplier's address on its invoices is fictitious.

Supplier audits can yield substantial returns. One company recovered more than $250,000 for such problems as duplicate billings. Supplier audits also often uncover violations of the company's conflict of interest policy. Interestingly, many suppliers support the idea of supplier audits, because the process gives them a "good excuse" for not offering purchasing agents gifts or entertainment.

usually in the form of cash, to unwary employees. Once the employee accepts the gift, the supplier threatens to disclose the payment to a supervisor unless the employee makes additional purchases from that vendor.

Job rotation is another important control to reduce the risk of kickbacks: Purchasing agents should not deal with the same suppliers indefinitely, because doing so increases the risk that they may succumb to the constant temptations offered by an unethical vendor. If the organization is too small to rotate job duties across different purchasing agents, it should periodically conduct a detailed audit of the purchasing agent's activities. Purchasing agents should also be required to take their allotted vacation time each year, because many frauds are discovered when the perpetrator is absent and unable to continue covering up the illicit activity. Finally, purchasing agents should be required to sign annual conflict of interest statements, disclosing any financial interests they may have in current or potential suppliers.

Kickbacks are difficult to prevent, so detective controls are also necessary. Focus 13-1 discusses one particularly effective detection control: the supplier audit.

Receiving

The second major business activity in the expenditure cycle (circle 2.0 in Figure 13-2) is the receipt and storage of ordered items. The receiving department is responsible for accepting deliveries from suppliers. It usually reports to the warehouse manager, who in turn reports to the vice president of manufacturing. The inventory stores department, which also reports to the warehouse manager, is responsible for storage of the goods. Information about the receipt of ordered merchandise must be communicated to the inventory control function to update the inventory records.

Process

When a delivery arrives, a receiving clerk compares the purchase order number referenced on the supplier's packing slip with the open purchase order file to verify that the goods were ordered. The receiving clerk then counts the quantity of goods delivered. Before routing the inventory to the warehouse or factory, the receiving clerk also should examine each delivery for signs of obvious damage.

The *receiving report* documents details about each delivery, including the date received, shipper, supplier, and purchase order number (Figure 13-6). For each item received, it shows the item number, description, unit of measure, and quantity. The receiving report also contains space to identify the persons who received and inspected the goods as well as for remarks concerning the

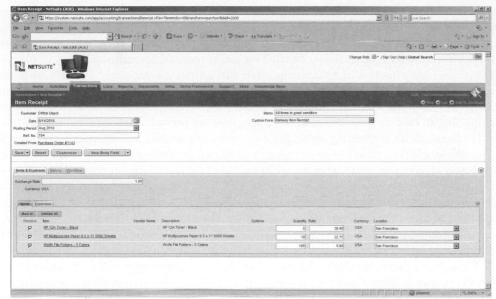

FIGURE 13-6

Example of a Receiving Report Data Entry Screen

© 2010 NetSuite, Inc.

quality of the items received. A receiving report is typically not used to document the receipt of services, such as advertising and cleaning. Instead, receipt of such services is usually documented by supervisory approval of the supplier's invoice.

The three possible exceptions to this process are (1) receiving a quantity of goods different from the amount ordered, (2) receiving damaged goods, or (3) receiving goods of inferior quality that fail inspection. In all three cases, the purchasing department must resolve the situation with the supplier. Usually the supplier will give the buyer permission to correct the invoice for any discrepancies in quantity. In the case of damaged or poor-quality goods, a document called a debit memo is prepared after the supplier agrees to take back the goods or to grant a price reduction. The *debit memo* records the adjustment being requested. One copy of the debit memo is sent to the supplier, who subsequently creates and returns a credit memo in acknowledgment. The accounts payable department is notified and adjusts the account balance owed to that supplier. A copy of the debit memo accompanies the goods to the shipping department to authorize their return to the supplier.

Counting and recording inventory deliveries is a labor-intensive task. One way for companies such as AOE to improve the efficiency of this process is to require suppliers to bar-code or affix RFID tags to their products. Either approach streamlines the counting of items received but does not eliminate the need to inspect the quality.

EDI and satellite technology provide another way to improve the efficiency of inbound logistics. EDI advance shipping notices inform companies when products have been shipped. By using shipping companies whose trucks are equipped with data terminals linked to satellites, a business can track the exact location of all incoming shipments and ensure that adequate staff will be there to unload the trucks. Truck drivers also can be directed to pull up to specific loading docks closest to the place where the goods will be used.

Finally, audits may identify opportunities to cut freight costs. For example, many companies have negotiated significant savings with specific carriers. The success of such arrangements depends on suppliers using the designated carriers. Periodic audits can verify this. Internal auditors should also verify the accuracy of freight bills and invoices to ensure that suppliers are not billing for transportation costs that they are supposed to pay.

Threats and Controls

Accepting delivery of unordered goods (threat 12) results in costs associated with unloading, storing, and later returning those items. The best control procedure to mitigate this threat is to instruct the receiving department to accept only deliveries for which there is an approved purchase order. Therefore, the receiving department needs access to the open purchase orders file.

Another threat is making mistakes in counting items received. Correctly counting the quantity received is crucial for maintaining accurate perpetual inventory records. It also ensures that the company pays only for goods actually received. To encourage the receiving clerk to accurately count what was delivered, many companies design the inquiry processing system so that receiving-dock workers do not see the quantity ordered (control 13.1). (If paper documents are still used, the quantity-ordered field is blacked out on the receiving department's copy of the purchase order.) Nevertheless, the receiving clerk still knows the expected quantity of goods because suppliers usually include a packing slip with each order. Consequently, there is a temptation to do just a quick visual comparison of quantities received with those indicated on the packing slip, to quickly route the goods to where they are needed. Therefore, companies must clearly communicate to receiving clerks the importance of carefully and accurately counting all deliveries. An effective means of communication is to require receiving clerks not only to record the quantity received but also to sign the receiving report (or enter their employee ID numbers in the system). Such procedures indicate an assumption of responsibility, which usually results in more diligent work. Some companies also offer bonuses to receiving clerks for catching discrepancies between the packing slip and actual quantity received before the delivery person leaves. An additional control is to require the inventory control function, or the appropriate user department, to count the items transferred from receiving and then hold that department responsible for any subsequent shortages. Wherever feasible, use of bar codes and RFID tags can significantly reduce accidental mistakes in counting. Finally, the ERP system should be configured to automatically flag discrepancies between receiving counts and order quantities that exceed a predetermined tolerance level so that they can be promptly investigated.

Thus far, the discussion has centered on the purchase of inventory items. Different procedures are needed to control the purchase of services, such as painting or maintenance work. The major challenge in this area is establishing that the services were actually performed (threat 14), which may be difficult. For example, visual inspection can indicate whether a room has been painted; it does not reveal, however, whether the walls were appropriately primed, unless the inspection was done during the painting process, which may not always be feasible.

One way to control the purchase of services is to hold the appropriate supervisor responsible for all such costs incurred by that department. The supervisor is required to acknowledge receipt of the services, and the related expenses are then charged to accounts for which he or she is responsible. Actual versus budgeted expenses should be routinely compared and any discrepancies investigated.

It is difficult to prevent fraudulent billing for services. Therefore, detective controls are also needed. One of the most effective techniques is for the internal audit function to periodically conduct detailed reviews of contracts for services, including audits of supplier records, as discussed in Focus 13-1.

Theft of inventory is another threat. Several control procedures can be used to safeguard inventory against loss. First, inventories should be stored in secure locations with restricted access. Second, all transfers of inventory within the company should be documented. For example, both the receiving department and the inventory stores department should acknowledge the transfer of goods from the receiving dock into inventory. Similarly, both the inventory stores and the production departments should acknowledge the release of inventory into production. This documentation provides the necessary information for establishing responsibility for any shortages, thereby encouraging employees to take special care to record all inventory movements accurately. Third, it is important to periodically count the inventory on hand and to reconcile those counts with the inventory records.

Finally, proper segregation of duties (control 15.4) can further help minimize the risk of inventory theft. Employees who are responsible for controlling physical access to inventory should not be able to adjust inventory records without review and approval. Neither the employees responsible for custody of inventory nor those authorized to adjust inventory records should be responsible for the receiving or shipping functions.

Approving Supplier Invoices

The third main activity in the expenditure cycle is approving supplier invoices for payment (circle 3.0 in Figure 13-2).

Process

The accounts payable department approves supplier invoices for payment. A legal obligation to pay suppliers arises at the time goods are received. For practical reasons, however, most companies record accounts payable only after receipt and approval of the supplier's invoice. This timing difference is usually not important for daily decision making, but it does require making appropriate adjusting entries to prepare accurate financial statements at the end of a fiscal period.

When a supplier's invoice is received, the accounts payable department is responsible for matching it with a corresponding purchase order and receiving report. This combination of the supplier invoice and associated supporting documentation creates what is called a *voucher package*. Figure 13-7 shows an example of a data entry screen for approving a supplier invoice. Once the approver has verified that the company received what it had ordered, the invoice is approved for payment.

There are two ways to process supplier invoices, referred to as nonvoucher or voucher systems. In a *nonvoucher system*, each approved invoice (along with the supporting documentation) is posted to individual supplier records in the accounts payable file and is then stored in an open-invoice file. When a check is written to pay for an invoice, the voucher package is removed from the open-invoice file, the invoice is marked paid, and then the voucher package is stored in the paid-invoice file. In a *voucher system*, an additional document called a disbursement voucher is also created when a supplier invoice is approved for payment. The *disbursement voucher* identifies the supplier, lists the outstanding invoices, and indicates the net amount to be paid after deducting any applicable discounts and allowances.

Voucher systems offer three advantages over nonvoucher systems. First, they reduce the number of checks that need to be written, because several invoices may be included on one disbursement voucher. Second, because the disbursement voucher is an internally generated document, it can be prenumbered to simplify tracking all payables. Third, because the voucher provides an explicit record that a vendor invoice has been approved for payment, it facilitates separating the time of invoice approval from the time of invoice payment. This makes it easier to schedule both activities to maximize efficiency.

The accounts payable process, which matches vendor invoices to purchase orders and receiving reports, is a prime candidate for automation. Large global companies can process over a million vendor invoices each year. Processing efficiency can be improved by requiring suppliers to submit invoices electronically, by EDI, and having the system automatically match those invoices to the appropriate purchase orders and receiving reports. Only those vendor invoices that fail this matching process need be processed manually.

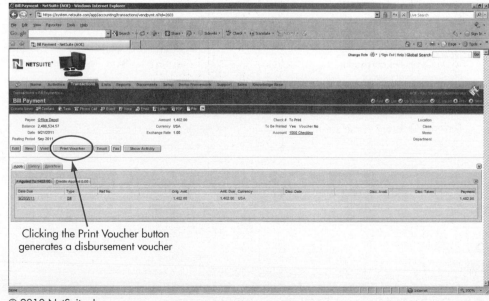

Clicking the Print Voucher button generates a disbursement voucher

FIGURE 13-7

Example of Supplier Invoice Approval Screen

© 2010 NetSuite, Inc.

Another option is to eliminate vendor invoices. After all, for most recurring purchases, companies know the prices of goods and services at the time they are ordered. Thus, as soon as receipt of the goods or services is verified, all the information required to pay the supplier is already known. This "invoiceless" approach is called *evaluated receipt settlement (ERS)*. ERS replaces the traditional three-way matching process (vendor invoice, receiving report, and purchase order) with a two-way match of the purchase order and receiving report (Figure 13-8). ERS saves time and money by reducing the number of documents that need to be matched and, hence, the number of potential mismatches. In fact, ERS systems are often configured to automate the two-way matching process and automatically generate payments; manual review is necessary only when there are discrepancies between the receiving report and purchase order. ERS also saves suppliers the time and expense of generating and tracking invoices. This is an example

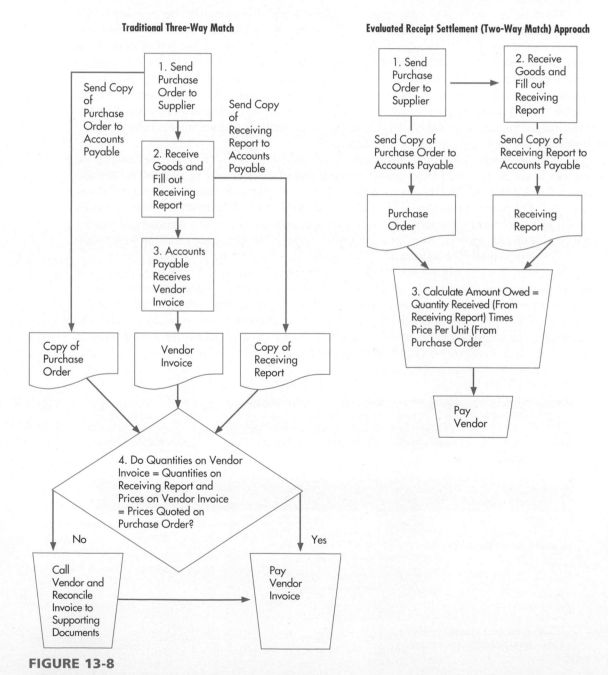

FIGURE 13-8

Comparison of Traditional Three-Way Match for Accounts Payable with the Two-Way Match used by Evaluated Receipt Settlement (ERS) Systems

of how improvements in one company's expenditure cycle processes provide benefits to another company's revenue cycle processes.

Noninventory purchases for supplies provide perhaps the biggest opportunity to improve the efficiency of accounts payable and cash disbursements. Noninventory purchases typically account for a large proportion of accounts payable transactions but represent a small percentage of the total dollar value of all purchases. For example, an AICPA-sponsored survey found that over 60% of all invoices processed by accounts payable departments were for amounts under $2,000. Procurement cards provide one way to eliminate the need for accounts payable to process many such small invoices. A *procurement card* is a corporate credit card that employees can use only at designated suppliers to purchase specific kinds of items. Spending limits can be set for each card. In addition, the account numbers on each procurement card can be mapped to specific general ledger accounts, such as office supplies. Procurement cards simplify accounts payable because the company receives one monthly statement that summarizes noninventory purchases by account category. Procurement cards also improve the efficiency of the cash disbursement process because the company only has to make one payment for all noninventory purchases during a given time period, instead of making separate payments to various suppliers. Finally, as Focus 13-2 shows, dramatic improvements can often result from reengineering the accounts payable process itself.

Threats and Controls

Table 13-2 indicates that one threat is errors on supplier invoices, such as discrepancies between quoted and actual prices charged or miscalculations of the total amount due. Consequently, the mathematical accuracy of vendor invoices must be verified and the prices and quantities listed therein compared with those indicated on the purchase order and receiving report. For procurement

FOCUS 13-2   Applying Manufacturing Process Improvement Principles to Accounts Payable

Medtronic, Inc., a global medical technology company, is demonstrating that process improvement principles originally developed to improve manufacturing activities can also be successfully adopted to improve the accounts payable function. Like many manufacturers, Medtronic had successfully used both Six Sigma and Lean principles to streamline its work-flow activities and improve product quality. Six Sigma is a philosophy that focuses on improving quality by reducing mistakes. Lean analysis seeks to improve efficiency by eliminating bottlenecks and redundancies. Medtronic decided to try to apply these same techniques used in manufacturing to its accounts payable function. The initial motivation for doing so was the insight that financial transactions, just like manufacturing a product, involved moving an item (e.g., a vendor invoice) through a sequence of steps.

Medtronic initiated a series of intensive 5-day projects, called *kaizen*, to apply Six Sigma and Lean principles to improve accounts payable. On day 1, a team consisting of accounts payable employees and manufacturing process improvement experts carefully studied how vendor invoices were processed, beginning with the time when mail was first opened all the way through printing and mailing checks. On day 2, the team measured the time it took to perform each step of the process and the volume of transactions passing through each step. On days 3 and 4, the team diagrammed

the physical flow of all accounts payable documentation. They then rearranged cubicles and desks and added new wheeled carts and paper bins to slash the physical distance a vendor invoice traveled from 1,464 to 165 feet. They also modified the image-scanning process to be able to merge all vendor invoices (those for inventory purchases, with associated purchase orders, and those without purchase orders) into one queue. On day 5, the team walked the entire department through the reengineered workflow process.

Medtronic's application of process improvement techniques yielded a dramatic improvement in the efficiency and effectiveness of its accounts payable function:

● The time required to open the mail and to sort, process, and record vendor invoices dropped from 3 days to 1 day.
● The number of invoices for which discounts for prompt payment were taken increased by 15%.
● Payment processing times were cut by 50%.

It is important to note that these benefits were obtained with the same employees who had been working in accounts payable prior to the reengineering effort. This shows that when companies are seeking to improve results, they should focus first on fixing the process, rather than on replacing the people who perform it.

card purchases, users should be required to keep receipts and verify the accuracy of the monthly statement. Adopting the ERS approach eliminates the potential for errors in vendor invoices because companies pay by matching counts of what they receive with prices quoted when the goods were ordered. However, the use of ERS makes it important to control access to the supplier master file and monitor all changes made to it because the supplier master file now contains information about the prices of the various items being purchased. Upon entry of data about the quantity of goods received, the system uses those prices to establish the amount to be paid to suppliers. Thus, unauthorized changes to those prices can result in overpayments to suppliers.

Even with ERS, freight expenses require special consideration because their complexity creates numerous opportunities for mistakes to occur. The best way to reduce freight-related threats is to provide the purchasing and accounts payable staffs with adequate training on transportation practices and terminology. For example, if the purchase contract says "full freight allowed," then the supplier is responsible for the freight costs. When the purchasing organization is responsible for freight expenses, using a designated carrier for all incoming shipments can reduce costs. The discounts will only be realized, however, if suppliers comply with requests to use that carrier. Therefore, an important detective control is to capture data on all incoming carriers, so that reports identifying suppliers who fail to comply with shipping instructions can be prepared.

Mistakes in recording and posting payments to suppliers (threat 17) result in additional errors in financial and performance reports that, in turn, can contribute to poor decision making. The data entry and processing controls to ensure processing integrity that were discussed in Chapter 10 are necessary to prevent these types of problems. One such control is to compare the difference in supplier account balances with the total amount of invoices processed—before and after processing checks. The total of all supplier account balances (or unpaid vouchers) also should be reconciled periodically with the amount of the accounts payable control account in the general ledger.

Cash Disbursements

The final activity in the expenditure cycle is paying suppliers (circle 4.0 in Figure 13-2).

Process

The cashier, who reports to the treasurer, is responsible for paying suppliers. This segregates the custody function, performed by the cashier, from the authorization and recording functions, performed by the purchasing and accounts payable departments, respectively. Payments are made when accounts payable sends the cashier a voucher package. Although many payments continue to be made by check, the use of EFT and FEDI is increasing.

Threats and Controls

Failing to take advantage of purchase discounts for prompt payment (threat 18) can be costly. For example, a 1% discount for paying within 10 days instead of 30 days represents a savings of 18% annually. Proper filing can significantly reduce the risk of this threat. Approved invoices should be filed by due date, and the system should be designed to track invoice due dates and print a periodic list of all outstanding invoices. A cash flow budget that indicates expected cash inflows and outstanding commitments also can help companies plan to utilize available purchase discounts. The information in this budget comes from a number of sources. Accounts receivable provides projections of future cash collections. The accounts payable and open purchase order files indicate the amount of current and pending commitments to suppliers, and the human resources function provides information about payroll needs.

Another threat is paying for goods not received. The best control to prevent this threat is to compare the quantities indicated on the vendor invoice with the quantities entered by the inventory control person, who accepts the transfer of those goods from the receiving department. Many companies require the inventory control department to verify the quantities on the receiving report before it can be used to support payment of a supplier invoice. Verification that services (e.g., cleaning or painting) were performed in the manner billed is more difficult. Therefore, most companies rely on budgetary controls and careful review of departmental expenses to indicate potential problems that need investigation.

Reimbursement of employees' travel and entertainment expenses warrants special attention because this is an area in which fraud often occurs and technological trends have made it easier for employees to submit fraudulent claims. For example, most airlines now encourage travelers to print their boarding passes at home. This saves the traveler time at check-in, but it also reduces the value of a boarding pass as supporting documentation for a claimed expense because the document can be altered by the traveler or printed but never used. Consequently, many organizations require employees to submit additional evidence to prove that they actually took a trip, such as a conference agenda that identifies attendees. Another potential threat is for an employee to book multiple flights or hotels, cancel all but the cheapest ones, but submit a reimbursement claim for the most expensive option. The best way to prevent this problem is to require all employees to use corporate credit cards for travel, as this ensures that the organization will receive a complete audit trail of all charges *and* credits to the account.

Duplicate payments (threat 20) can happen for a variety of reasons. It may be a duplicate invoice that was sent after the company's check was already in the mail, or it may have become separated from the other documents in the voucher package. Although the supplier usually detects a duplicate payment and credits the company's account, it can affect a company's cash flow needs. In addition, the financial records will be incorrect, at least until the duplicate payment is detected.

Several related control procedures can mitigate this threat. First, invoices should be approved for payment only when accompanied by a complete voucher package (purchase order and receiving report). Second, only the original copy of an invoice should be paid. Most duplicate invoices that suppliers send clearly indicate that they are not originals. Payment should never be authorized for a photocopy of an invoice. Third, when the check to pay for an invoice is signed, the invoice and the voucher package should be canceled (marked "paid") in a manner that would prevent their resubmission. Although ERS eliminates vendor invoices entirely, it is still important to mark all receiving reports as paid to avoid duplicate payments.

Probably the most serious threat associated with the cash disbursements function is theft or misappropriation of funds (threat 21). Because cash is the easiest asset to steal, access to cash, blank checks, and the check-signing machine should be restricted. Checks should be sequentially numbered and periodically accounted for by the cashier.

Electronic funds transfer (EFT), either by itself or as part of FEDI, requires additional control procedures. Strict access controls over all outgoing EFT transactions are important. Passwords and user IDs should be used to specifically identify and monitor each employee authorized to initiate EFT transactions. The location of the originating terminal should also be recorded. EFT transactions above a certain threshold should require real-time supervisory approval. There should also be limits on the total dollar amount of transactions allowed per day per individual. All EFT transmissions should be encrypted to prevent alteration. In addition, all EFT transactions should be time-stamped and numbered to facilitate subsequent reconciliation. Special programs, called *embedded audit modules*, can be designed into the system to monitor all transactions and identify any that possess specific characteristics. A report of those flagged transactions then can be given to management and internal audit for review and, if necessary, more detailed investigation.

Online banking transactions require constant monitoring. Timely detection of suspicious transactions and prompt notification of the bank are necessary for recovering any funds that are fraudulently disbursed. A serious threat is that keystroke-logging software could infect the computer used for online banking and provide criminals with the organization's banking credentials. The best way to mitigate this threat is to designate a specific computer to be used for online banking, to restrict access to that computer to the treasurer or whoever is responsible for authorizing payments, and to use that computer only for online banking and no other activity. Companies should also consider placing Automated Clearing House (ACH) blocks, which instruct banks to not allow ACH debits (outflows) from specific accounts. For example, if a company makes all payments to its suppliers only from its main operating checking account, it may wish to instruct the bank to block all ACH debits from any of its other bank accounts.

Fraudulent disbursements, particularly the issuance of checks to fictitious suppliers, are a common type of fraud. Proper segregation of duties (control 21.6) can significantly reduce the risk of this threat. The accounts payable function should authorize payment, including the assembling of a voucher package; however, only the treasurer or cashier should sign checks. To ensure that checks are sent to the intended recipients, the cashier should mail the signed checks rather than return them to accounts payable. The cashier also should cancel all documents in the voucher package to prevent their being resubmitted to support another disbursement. Checks in excess of a certain amount, such as $5,000 to $10,000, should require two signatures, thereby providing yet another independent review of the expenditure. Finally, someone who did not participate in processing either cash collections or disbursements should reconcile all bank accounts. This control provides an independent check on accuracy and prevents someone from misappropriating cash and then concealing the theft by adjusting the bank statement.

Access to the approved supplier list should be restricted, and any changes to that list should be carefully reviewed and approved. It is especially important to restrict the ability to create one-time suppliers and process invoices so that the same employee cannot both create a new supplier and issue a check to that supplier.

When possible, expenditures should be made by check or EFT. Nevertheless, it is often more convenient to pay for minor purchases, such as coffee or pencils, in cash. A petty cash fund, managed by an employee who has no other cash-handling or accounting responsibilities, should be established to handle such expenditures. The petty cash fund should be set up as an imprest fund. An *imprest fund* has two characteristics: it is set at a fixed amount, such as $100, and it requires vouchers for every disbursement. At all times, the sum of cash plus vouchers should equal the preset fund balance. When the fund balance gets low, the vouchers are presented to accounts payable for replenishment. After accounts payable authorizes this transaction, the cashier then writes a check to restore the petty cash fund to its designated level. As with the supporting documents used for regular purchases, the vouchers used to support replenishment of the petty cash fund should be canceled at the time the fund is restored to its preset level.

The operation of an imprest petty cash fund technically violates the principle of segregation of duties, because the same person who has custody of the cash also authorizes disbursements from the fund and maintains a record of the fund balance. The threat of misappropriation is more than offset, however, by the convenience of not having to process small miscellaneous purchases through the normal expenditure cycle. Moreover, the risk of misappropriation can be mitigated by having the internal auditor make periodic unannounced counts of the fund balance and vouchers and by holding the person in charge of the petty cash fund responsible for any shortages discovered during those surprise audits.

Theft can also occur through check alteration (threat 22). Check-protection machines can reduce the risk of this threat by imprinting the amount in distinctive colors, typically a combination of red and blue ink. Using special inks that change colors if altered and printing checks on special papers that contain watermarks can further reduce the probability of alteration. Many banks also provide special services to help protect companies against fraudulent checks. One such service, called Positive Pay, involves sending a daily list of all legitimate checks to the bank, which will then clear only checks appearing on that list. Finally, bank reconciliations are an important detective control for identifying check fraud. If done in a timely manner, they facilitate recovery from banks. Indeed, many banks will cover bad-check losses only if a company notifies them promptly of any such checks it discovers.

Finally, it is important to plan and monitor expenditures in order to avoid cash flow problems (threat 23). A cash flow budget (see Chapter 12) is the best control to mitigate this threat.

Summary and Case Conclusion

The basic business activities performed in the expenditure cycle include ordering materials, supplies, and services; receiving materials, supplies, and services; approving supplier invoices for payment; and paying for goods and services.

The efficiency and effectiveness of these activities can significantly affect a company's overall performance. For example, deficiencies in requesting and ordering necessary inventory and supplies can create production bottlenecks and result in lost sales due to stockouts of popular items. Problems in the procedures related to receiving and storing inventory can result in a company's paying for items it never received, accepting delivery and incurring storage costs for unordered items, and experiencing a theft of inventory. Problems in approving supplier invoices for payment can result in overpaying suppliers or failing to take available discounts for prompt payment. Weaknesses in the cash disbursement process can result in the misappropriation of cash.

IT can help improve the efficiency and effectiveness with which expenditure cycle activities are performed. In particular, EDI, bar-coding, RFID, and EFT can significantly reduce the time and costs associated with ordering, receiving, and paying for goods. Proper control procedures, especially segregation of duties, are needed to mitigate various threats such as errors in performing expenditure cycle activities and the theft of inventory or cash.

At the next executive meeting, Ann Brandt and Elizabeth Venko presented to Linda Spurgcon their recommendations for improving AOE's expenditure cycle business activities. Ann indicates that LeRoy Williams's plan to conduct more frequent physical counts of key raw materials components will increase the accuracy of the database and reduce the likelihood of future stockouts at the Wichita plant. She also designed a query to produce a daily supplier performance report that will highlight any negative trends before they become the types of problems that disrupted production at the Dayton plant. Ann also indicated that it would be possible to link AOE's inventory and production planning systems with major suppliers to better manage AOE's inventory levels.

Elizabeth Venko stated that she was working to increase the number of suppliers who either bar-code or RFID tag their shipments. This would improve both the efficiency and accuracy of the receiving process and also the accuracy of AOE's inventory records, thereby providing possible additional reductions in inventory carrying costs. In addition, Elizabeth wants to encourage more suppliers to either send invoices via EDI or agree to ERS, which should improve the efficiency and accuracy of processing invoices and reduce the costs associated with handling and storing paper invoices. Concurrently, Elizabeth plans to increase EFT as much as possible to further streamline the cash disbursements process and reduce the costs associated with processing payments by check.

As the meeting draws to a close, LeRoy Williams asks if Elizabeth and Ann can meet with him to explore additional ways to improve how AOE's new system tracks manufacturing activities.

Key Terms

expenditure cycle 371	purchase requisition 379	voucher package 387
economic order quantity (EOQ) 378	purchase order 381	nonvoucher system 387
	blanket purchase order 381	voucher system 387
reorder point 378	vendor-managed inventory 382	disbursement voucher 387
materials requirements planning (MRP) 378	kickbacks 383	evaluated receipts settlement (ERS) 388
just-in-time (JIT) inventory system 378	receiving report 384	procurement card 389
	debit memo 385	imprest fund 392

AIS IN ACTION

Chapter Quiz

1. Which of the following inventory control methods is most likely to be used for a product such as lumber (1 × 2's, 2 × 4's, etc.) for which sales can be reliably forecast?
   - a. JIT
   - b. EOQ
   - c. MRP
   - d. ABC

2. Which of the following matches is performed in evaluated receipt settlement (ERS)?
   a. the vendor invoice with the receiving report
   b. the purchase order with the receiving report
   c. the vendor invoice with the purchase order
   d. the vendor invoice, the receiving report, and the purchase order

3. Which of the following is true?
   a. ERS systems involve a three-way match of purchase orders, receiving reports, and supplier invoices.
   b. Setting up petty cash as an imprest fund violates segregation of duties.
   c. The EOQ formula is used to identify when to reorder inventory.
   d. A voucher package usually includes a debit memo.

4. Which document is used to establish a contract for the purchase of goods or services from a supplier?
   a. vendor invoice
   b. purchase requisition
   c. purchase order
   d. disbursement voucher

5. Which method would provide the greatest efficiency improvements for the purchase of noninventory items such as miscellaneous office supplies?
   a. bar-coding
   b. EDI
   c. procurement cards
   d. EFT

6. Which of the following expenditure cycle activities can be eliminated through the use of IT or reengineering?
   a. ordering goods
   b. approving vendor invoices
   c. receiving goods
   d. cash disbursements

7. What is the best control procedure to prevent paying the same invoice twice?
   a. Segregate check-preparation and check-signing functions.
   b. Prepare checks only for invoices that have been matched to receiving reports and purchase orders.
   c. Require two signatures on all checks above a certain limit.
   d. Cancel all supporting documents when the check is signed.

8. For good internal control, who should sign checks?
   a. cashier
   b. accounts payable
   c. purchasing agent
   d. controller

9. Which of the following procedures is designed to prevent the purchasing agent from receiving kickbacks?
   a. maintaining a list of approved suppliers and requiring all purchases to be made from suppliers on that list
   b. requiring purchasing agents to disclose any financial investments in potential suppliers
   c. requiring approval of all purchase orders
   d. prenumbering and periodically accounting for all purchase orders

10. Which document is used to record adjustments to accounts payable based on the return of unacceptable inventory to the supplier?
    a. receiving report
    b. credit memo
    c. debit memo
    d. purchase order

Discussion Questions

13.1. In this chapter and in Chapter 12, the controller of AOE played a major role in evaluating and recommending ways to use IT to improve efficiency and effectiveness. Should the company's chief information officer make these decisions instead?

Should the controller be involved in making these types of decisions? Why or why not?

13.2. Companies such as Walmart have moved beyond JIT to vendor-managed inventory (VMI) systems. Discuss the potential advantages and disadvantages of this arrangement. What special controls, if any, should be developed to monitor VMI systems?

13.3. Procurement cards are designed to improve the efficiency of small noninventory purchases. What controls should be placed on their use? Why?

13.4. In what ways can you apply the control procedures discussed in this chapter to paying personal debts (e.g., credit card bills)?

13.5. Should every company switch from the traditional three-way matching process (purchase orders, receiving reports, and supplier invoices) to the two-way match (purchase orders and receiving reports) used in evaluated receipt settlement (ERS)? Why or why not?

13.6. Should companies allow purchasing agents to start their own businesses that produce goods the company frequently purchases? Why? Would you change your answer if the purchasing agent's company were rated by an independent service, such as *Consumer Reports*, as providing the best value for price? Why?

Problems

13.1. Which internal control procedure would be most cost-effective in dealing with the following expenditure cycle threats?
   a. A purchasing agent orders materials from a supplier that he partially owns.
   b. Receiving-dock personnel steal inventory and then claim the inventory was sent to the warehouse.
   c. An unordered supply of laser printer paper delivered to the office is accepted and paid for because the "price is right." After all of the laser printers are jammed, however, it becomes obvious that the "bargain" paper is of inferior quality.
   d. The company fails to take advantage of a 1% discount for promptly paying a vendor invoice.
   e. A company is late in paying a particular invoice. Consequently, a second invoice is sent, which crosses the first invoice's payment in the mail. The second invoice is submitted for processing and also paid.
   f. Inventory records show that an adequate supply of copy paper should be in stock, but none is available on the supply shelf.
   g. The inventory records are incorrectly updated when a receiving-dock employee enters the wrong product number at the terminal.
   h. A clerical employee obtains a blank check and writes a large amount payable to a fictitious company. The employee then cashes the check.
   i. A fictitious invoice is received and a check is issued to pay for goods that were never ordered or delivered.
   j. The petty cash custodian confesses to having "borrowed" $12,000 over the last five years.
   k. A purchasing agent adds a new record to the supplier master file. The company does not exist. Subsequently, the purchasing agent submits invoices from the fake company for various cleaning services. The invoices are paid.
   l. A clerk affixes a price tag intended for a low-end flat-panel TV to a top-of-the-line model. The clerk's friend then purchases that item, which the clerk scans at the checkout counter.

13.2. Match the terms in the left column with their appropriate definition in the right column.

Terms

_____ 1. Economic order quantity

_____ 2. Materials requirements planning (MRP)

_____ 3. Just-in-time (JIT) inventory system

_____ 4. Purchase requisition

_____ 5. Imprest fund

_____ 6. Purchase order

_____ 7. Kickbacks

_____ 8. Procurement card

_____ 9. Blanket purchase order

_____ 10. Evaluated receipts settlement (ERS)

_____ 11. Disbursement voucher

_____ 12. Receiving report

_____ 13. Debit memo

_____ 14. Vendor-managed inventory

_____ 15. Voucher package

_____ 16. Nonvoucher system

_____ 17. Voucher system

Definitions

a. A document that creates a legal obligation to buy and pay for goods or services

b. The method used to maintain the cash balance in petty cash account

c. The time to reorder inventory triggered when the quantity on hand falls to a predetermined level

d. A document used to authorize a reduction in accounts payable because merchandise has been returned to a supplier

e. An inventory control system that triggers production based upon actual sales

f. An inventory control system that triggers production based on forecasted sales

g. A document used only internally to initiate the purchase of materials, supplies, or services

h. A process for approving supplier invoices based on a two-way match of the receiving report and purchase order

i. A process for approving supplier invoices based on a three-way match of the purchase order, receiving report, and supplier invoice

j. A method of maintaining accounts payable in which each supplier invoice is tracked and paid for separately

k. A method of maintaining accounts payable that generates one check to pay for a set of invoices from the same supplier

l. Combination of a purchase order, receiving report, and supplier invoice that all relate to the same transaction

m. A document used to list each invoice being paid by a check

n. An inventory control system that seeks to minimize the sum of ordering, carrying, and stockout costs

o. A system whereby suppliers are granted access to point-of-sale (POS) and inventory data in order to automatically replenish inventory levels

p. An agreement to purchase set quantities at specified intervals from a specific supplier

q. A document used to record the quantities and condition of items delivered by a supplier

r. A special-purpose credit card used to purchase supplies

s. A fraud in which a supplier pays a buyer or purchasing agent in order to sell its products or services

13.3. Excel Project: Using Benford's Law to Detect Potential Disbursements Fraud.

Required

a. Read the article "Using Spreadsheets and Benford's Law to Test Accounting Data," by Mark G. Simkin in the *ISACA Journal*, Vol. 1, 2010, available at www.isaca.org.

b. Follow the steps in the article to analyze the following set of supplier invoices:

Invoice Number	Amount	Invoice Number	Amount
2345	$7,845	2360	$8,256
2346	$2,977	2361	$1,863
2347	$1,395	2362	$3,375
2348	$3,455	2363	$6,221
2349	$7,733	2364	$1,799
2350	$1,455	2365	$1,450
2351	$6,239	2366	$7,925
2352	$2,573	2367	$2,839
2353	$1,862	2368	$1,588
2354	$1,933	2369	$2,267
2355	$7,531	2370	$7,890
2356	$4,400	2371	$7,945
2357	$5,822	2372	$1,724
2358	$7,925	2373	$9,311
2359	$2,100	2374	$4,719

Hint: You may need to use the VALUE function to transform the results of using the LEFT function to parse the lead digit in each invoice amount.

13.4. Match the threats in the left column to appropriate control procedures in the right column. More than one control may be applicable.

Threat

_____ 1. Failing to take available purchase discounts for prompt payment

_____ 2. Recording and posting errors in accounts payable

_____ 3. Paying for items not received

_____ 4. Kickbacks

_____ 5. Theft of inventory

_____ 6. Paying the same invoice twice

_____ 7. Stockouts

_____ 8. Purchasing items at inflated prices

_____ 9. Misappropriation of cash

_____ 10. Purchasing goods of inferior quality

_____ 11. Wasted time and cost of returning unordered merchandise to suppliers

_____ 12. Accidental loss of purchasing data

Control Procedure

a. Accept only deliveries for which an approved purchase order exists.

b. Document all transfers of inventory.

c. Restrict physical access to inventory.

d. File invoices by due date.

e. Maintain a cash budget.

f. Conduct an automated comparison of total change in cash to total changes in accounts payable.

g. Adopt a perpetual inventory system.

h. Require purchasing agents to disclose financial or personal interests in suppliers.

i. Require purchases to be made only from approved suppliers.

j. Restrict access to the supplier master data.

k. Restrict access to blank checks.

l. Issue checks only for complete voucher packages (receiving report, supplier invoice, and purchase order).

Threat	Control Procedure
_____ 13. Disclosure of sensitive supplier information (e.g., banking data)	m. Cancel or mark "Paid" supporting documents in voucher package when check is issued.
	n. Carry out a regular backup of expenditure cycle database.
	o. Train employees in how to properly respond to gifts or incentives offered by suppliers.
	p. Hold purchasing managers responsible for costs of scrap and rework.
	q. Ensure that someone other than the cashier reconciles bank accounts.

13.5. Use Table 13-2 to create a questionnaire checklist that can be used to evaluate controls for each of the basic activities in the expenditure cycle (ordering goods, receiving, approving supplier invoices, and cash disbursements).

Required

a. For each control issue, write a Yes/No question such that a "No" answer represents a control weakness. For example, one question might be "Are supporting documents, such as purchase orders and receiving reports, marked 'paid' when a check is issued to the vendor?"

b. For each Yes/No question, write a brief explanation of why a "No" answer represents a control weakness.

13.6. Excel Project

a. Expand the cash flow budget you created in Problem 12.4 to include a row for expected cash outflows equal to 77% of the current month's sales.

b. Also add a row to calculate the amount of cash that needs to be borrowed in order to maintain a minimum cash balance of $50,000 at the end of each month.

c. Add another row to show the cash inflow from borrowing.

d. Add another row to show the cumulative amount borrowed.

e. Add another row to show the amount of the loan that can be repaid, being sure to maintain a minimum ending balance of $50,000 each month.

f. Add appropriate data validation controls to ensure spreadsheet accuracy.

13.7. For each of the following activities, identify the data that must be entered by the employee performing that activity, and list the appropriate data entry controls:

a. Purchasing agent generating a purchase order

b. Receiving clerk completing a receiving report

13.8. The following list identifies several important control features. For each control, (1) describe its purpose, and (2) explain how it could be best implemented in an integrated ERP system.

a. Cancellation of the voucher package by the cashier after signing the check

b. Separation of duties of approving invoices for payment and signing checks

c. Prenumbering and periodically accounting for all purchase orders

d. Periodic physical count of inventory

e. Requiring two signatures on checks for large amounts

f. Requiring that a copy of the receiving report be routed through the inventory stores department prior to going to accounts payable

g. Requiring a regular reconciliation of the bank account by someone other than the person responsible for writing checks

h. Maintaining an approved supplier list and checking that all purchase orders are issued only to suppliers on that list

13.9. For good internal control, which of the following duties can be performed by the same individual?

1. Approve purchase orders

2. Negotiate terms with suppliers

3. Reconcile the organization's bank account

4. Approve supplier invoices for payment

5. Cancel supporting documents in the voucher package

6. Sign checks

7. Mail checks

8. Request inventory to be purchased

9. Inspect quantity and quality of inventory received

13.10. Last year the Diamond Manufacturing Company purchased over $10 million worth of office equipment under its "special ordering" system, with individual orders ranging from $5,000 to $30,000. Special orders are for low-volume items that have been included in a department manager's budget. The budget, which limits the types and dollar amounts of office equipment a department head can requisition, is approved at the beginning of the year by the board of directors. The special ordering system functions as follows.

Purchasing A purchase requisition form is prepared and sent to the purchasing department. Upon receiving a purchase requisition, one of the five purchasing agents (buyers) verifies that the requester is indeed a department head. The buyer next selects the appropriate supplier by searching the various catalogs on file. The buyer then phones the supplier, requests a price quote, and places a verbal order. A prenumbered purchase order is processed, with the original sent to the supplier and copies to the department head, receiving, and accounts payable. One copy is also filed in the open requisition file. When the receiving department verbally informs the buyer that the item has been received, the purchase order is transferred from the open to the filled file. Once a month, the buyer reviews the unfilled file to follow up on open orders.

Receiving The receiving department gets a copy of each purchase order. When equipment is received, that copy of the purchase order is stamped with the date, and, if applicable, any differences between the quantity ordered and the quantity received are noted in red ink. The receiving clerk then forwards the stamped purchase order and equipment to the requisitioning department head and verbally notifies the purchasing department that the goods were received.

Accounts Payable Upon receipt of a purchase order, the accounts payable clerk files it in the open purchase order file. When a vendor invoice is received, it is matched with the applicable purchase order, and a payable is created by debiting the requisitioning department's equipment account. Unpaid invoices are filed by due date. On the due date, a check is prepared and forwarded to the treasurer for signature. The invoice and purchase order are then filed by purchase order number in the paid invoice file.

Treasurer Checks received daily from the accounts payable department are sorted into two groups: those over and those under $10,000. Checks for less than $10,000 are machine signed. The cashier maintains the check signature machine's key and signature plate and monitors its use. Both the cashier and the treasurer sign all checks over $10,000.

Required

a. Describe the weaknesses relating to purchases and payments of "special orders" by the Diamond Manufacturing Company.

    b. Recommend control procedures that must be added to overcome weaknesses identified in part a.

    c. Describe how the control procedures you recommended in part b should be modified if Diamond reengineered its expenditure cycle activities to make maximum use of current IT (e.g., EDI, EFT, bar-code scanning, and electronic forms in place of paper documents). *(CPA Examination, adapted)*

13.11. The ABC Company performs its expenditure cycle activities using its integrated ERP system as follows:

- Employees in any department can enter purchase requests for items they note as either out of stock or in small quantity.
- The company maintains a perpetual inventory system.
- Each day, employees in the purchasing department process all purchase requests from the prior day. To the extent possible, requests for items available from the same supplier are combined into one larger purchase order to obtain volume discounts. Purchasing agents use the Internet to compare prices in order to select suppliers. If an Internet search discovers a potential new supplier, the purchasing agent enters the relevant information in the system, thereby adding the supplier to the approved supplier list. Purchase orders above $10,000 must be approved by the purchasing department manager. EDI is used to transmit purchase orders to most suppliers, but paper purchase orders are printed and mailed to suppliers who are not EDI capable.
- Receiving department employees have read-only access to outstanding purchase orders. Usually, they check the system to verify existence of a purchase order prior to accepting delivery, but sometimes during rush periods they unload trucks and place the items in a corner of the warehouse where they sit until there is time to use the system to retrieve the relevant purchase order. In such cases, if no purchase order is found, the receiving employee contacts the supplier to arrange for the goods to be returned.
- Receiving department employees compare the quantity delivered to the quantity indicated on the purchase order. Whenever a discrepancy is greater than 5%, the receiving employee sends an e-mail to the purchasing department manager. The receiving employee uses an online terminal to enter the quantity received before moving the material to the inventory stores department.
- Inventory is stored in a locked room. During normal business hours, an inventory employee allows any employee wearing an identification badge to enter the storeroom and remove needed items. The inventory storeroom employee counts the quantity removed and enters that information in an online terminal located in the storeroom.
- Occasionally, special items are ordered that are not regularly kept as part of inventory, from a specialty supplier who will not be used for any regular purchases. In these cases, an accounts payable clerk creates a one-time supplier record.
- All supplier invoices (both regular and one-time) are routed to accounts payable for review and approval. The system is configured to perform an automatic three-way match of the supplier invoice with the corresponding purchase order and receiving report.
- Each Friday, approved supplier invoices that are due within the next week are routed to the treasurer's department for payment. The cashier and treasurer are the only employees authorized to disburse funds, either by EFT or by printing a check. Checks are printed on dedicated printer located in the treasurer's department, using special stock paper that is stored in a locked cabinet accessible only to the treasurer and cashier. The paper checks are sent to accounts payable to be mailed to suppliers.
- Monthly, the treasurer reconciles the bank statements and investigates any discrepancies with recorded cash balances.

Required

Identify weaknesses in ABC's expenditure cycle procedures, explain the resulting problems, and suggest how to correct those problems.

13.12. Alden, Inc., has hired you to review its internal controls for the purchase, receipt, storage, and issuance of raw materials. You observed the following:

- Raw materials, which consist mainly of high-cost electronic components, are kept in a locked storeroom. Storeroom personnel include a supervisor and four clerks. All are well trained, competent, and adequately bonded. Raw materials are removed from the storeroom only upon written or oral authorization by a production supervisor.
- No perpetual inventory records are kept; hence, the storeroom clerks do not keep records for goods received or issued. To compensate, the storeroom clerks perform a physical inventory count each month.
- After the physical count, the storeroom supervisor matches the quantities on hand against a predetermined reorder level. If the count is below the reorder level, the supervisor enters the part number on a materials requisition list that is sent to the accounts payable clerk. The accounts payable clerk prepares a purchase order for each item on the list and mails it to the supplier from whom the part was last purchased.
- The storeroom clerks receive the ordered materials upon their arrival. The clerks count all items and verify that the counts agree with the quantities on the bill of lading. The bill of lading is then initialed, dated, and filed in the storeroom to serve as a receiving report.

Required

a. Describe the weaknesses that exist in Alden's expenditure cycle.
b. Suggest control procedures to overcome the weaknesses noted in part a.
c. Discuss how those control procedures would be best implemented in an integrated ERP system using the latest developments in IT.
(CPA Examination, adapted)

Case 13-1 Research Project: Impact of Information Technology on Expenditure Cycle Activities, Threats, and Controls

Search popular business and technology magazines (*Business Week, Forbes, Fortune, CIO,* etc.) to find an article about an innovative use of IT that can be used to improve one or more activities in the expenditure cycle. Write a report that:
a. Explains how IT can be used to change expenditure cycle activities.

b. Discusses the control implications. Refer to Table 13-2, and explain how the new procedure changes the threats and appropriate control procedures for mitigating those threats.

AIS IN ACTION SOLUTIONS

Quiz Key

1. Which of the following inventory control methods is most likely to be used for a product such as lumber (1 × 2's, 2 × 4's, etc.) for which sales can be reliably forecast?
   a. JIT (Incorrect. JIT seeks to minimize inventory by making purchases only after sales. It is used to primarily for products for which it is hard to forecast demand. Lumber is an example of a product for which demand can be forecast rather accurately.)
   b. EOQ (Incorrect. EOQ represents the optimal amount of inventory to purchase to minimize the sum of ordering, carrying, and stockout costs.)
   ▶ c. MRP (Correct. MRP forecasts sales and uses that information to purchase inventory to meet anticipated needs. Demand for lumber can be forecast rather accurately, including

seasonal fluctuations (increased demand due to construction during spring, summer, and fall and reduced demand during winter).

    d. ABC (Incorrect. ABC is a method for stratifying inventory according to importance and scheduling more frequent inventory counts for the more important items.)

2. Which of the following matches is performed in evaluated receipt settlement (ERS)?
    a. the vendor invoice with the receiving report (Incorrect. ERS eliminates the vendor invoice.)
    ▶ **b.** the purchase order with the receiving report (Correct. ERS eliminates the vendor invoice and schedules payments based on matching the purchase order and receiving report.)
    c. the vendor invoice with the purchase order (Incorrect. ERS eliminates the vendor invoice.)
    d. the vendor invoice, the receiving report, and the purchase order (Incorrect. ERS eliminates the vendor invoice.)

3. Which of the following is true?
    a. ERS systems involve a three-way match of purchase orders, receiving reports, and supplier invoices. (Incorrect. ERS systems eliminate supplier invoices and rely upon a two-way match of purchase orders and receiving reports.)
    ▶ **b.** Setting up petty cash as an imprest fund violates segregation of duties. (Correct. Technically, setting up petty cash as an imprest fund violates segregation of duties because the same person has custody of the asset—cash—authorizes its disbursement, and maintains records.)
    c. The EOQ formula is used to identify when to reorder inventory. (Incorrect. The EOQ formula is used to determine how much to order. The reorder point identifies when to reorder inventory.)
    d. A voucher package usually includes a debit memo. (Incorrect. Voucher packages consist of the purchase order, receiving report, and vendor invoice, if one is received; debit memos are used to record adjustments of accounts payable.)

4. Which document is used to establish a contract for the purchase of goods or services from a supplier?
    a. vendor invoice (Incorrect. The vendor invoice is a bill.)
    b. purchase requisition (Incorrect. A purchase requisition is an internal document.)
    ▶ **c.** purchase order (Correct. A purchase order is an offer to buy goods.)
    d. disbursement voucher (Incorrect. A disbursement voucher is used to specify which accounts to debit when paying vendor invoices.)

5. Which method would provide the greatest efficiency improvements for the purchase of noninventory items such as miscellaneous office supplies?
    a. bar-coding (Incorrect. Bar-coding improves accuracy of counting inventory items. The biggest efficiency-realted problem with non-inventory purchases is the time and effort required to generate a purchase order, create a voucher package, and make payments for a large number of small-dollar amount purchases.)
    b. EDI (Incorrect. EDI is seldom used for miscellaneous purchases.)
    ▶ **c.** procurement cards (Correct. Procurement cards were designed specifically for purchase of noninventory items.)
    d. EFT (Incorrect. EFT improves the efficiency of payments, but does not improve the efficiency of ordering and approving supplier invoices.)

6. Which of the following expenditure cycle activities can be eliminated through the use of IT or reengineering?
    a. ordering goods (Incorrect. Even with vendor-managed inventory, the vendor's system must initiate the ordering process.)
    ▶ **b.** approving vendor invoices (Correct. ERS systems eliminate vendor invoices.)
    c. receiving goods (Incorrect. Ordered goods must always be received and moved to the appropriate location.)

    d. cash disbursements (Incorrect. IT can change the method used to make cash disbursements, such as by EFT instead of by check, but the function must still be performed.)

7. What is the best control procedure to prevent paying the same invoice twice?
   a. Segregate check-preparation and check-signing functions. (Incorrect. This is a good control procedure, but its purpose is to ensure that payments are valid.)
   b. Prepare checks only for invoices that have been matched to receiving reports and purchase orders. (Incorrect. This is a good control procedure, but its purpose is to ensure that organizations pay only for goods ordered and received.)
   c. Require two signatures on all checks above a certain limit. (Incorrect. This is a good control procedure, but its purpose is to better control large outflows of cash.)
   ▶ d. Cancel all supporting documents when the check is signed. (Correct. This ensures that the supporting documents cannot be resubmitted to pay the same invoice again.)

8. For good internal control, who should sign checks?
   ▶ a. cashier (Correct. The cashier is responsible for managing cash and reports to the treasurer.)
   b. accounts payable (Incorrect. Accounts payable maintains vendor records.)
   c. purchasing agent (Incorrect. The purchasing agent authorizes acquisition of goods.)
   d. controller (Incorrect. The controller is in charge of accounting, the record-keeping function.)

9. Which of the following procedures is designed to prevent the purchasing agent from receiving kickbacks?
   a. maintaining a list of approved suppliers and requiring all purchases to be made from suppliers on that list (Incorrect. The purpose of this control is to minimize the risk of purchasing inferior goods at inflated prices or violating regulations.)
   ▶ b. requiring purchasing agents to disclose any financial investments in potential suppliers (Correct. The purpose of such disclosure is to minimize the risk of conflicts of interest that could result in kickbacks.)
   c. requiring approval of all purchase orders (Incorrect. This control is designed to ensure that only goods that are really needed are ordered and that they are ordered from approved vendors.)
   d. prenumbering and periodically accounting for all purchase orders (Incorrect. This control procedure is designed to ensure that all valid purchase orders are recorded.)

10. Which document is used to record adjustments to accounts payable based on the return of unacceptable inventory to the supplier?
    a. receiving report (Incorrect. This document records quantities of goods received.)
    b. credit memo (Incorrect. This document is used in the revenue cycle to adjust a customer's account.)
    ▶ c. debit memo (Correct. This document is used to adjust accounts payable.)
    d. purchase order (Incorrect. This document establishes a legal obligation to purchase goods.)

Chapter 14

The Production Cycle

Learning Objectives

After studying this chapter, you should be able to:

1. Describe the major business activities and related information processing operations performed in the production cycle.

2. Identify major threats in the production cycle and evaluate the adequacy of various control procedures for dealing with those threats.

3. Explain how a company's cost accounting system can help it achieve its manufacturing goals.

4. Discuss the key decisions that must be made in the production cycle and identify the information required to make those decisions.

INTEGRATIVE CASE   ALPHA OMEGA ELECTRONICS

LeRoy Williams, vice president for manufacturing at Alpha Omega Electronics (AOE), is concerned about problems associated with the company's change in strategic mission. Two years ago, AOE's top management decided to shift the company from its traditional position as a low-cost producer of consumer electronic products to a product differentiation strategy. Since then, AOE has increased the variety of sizes, styles, and features within each of its product lines.

To support this shift in strategic focus, AOE has invested heavily in factory automation. Top management also endorsed LeRoy's decision to adopt lean manufacturing techniques, with the goal of dramatically reducing inventory levels of finished goods. AOE's cost accounting system has not been changed, however. For example, manufacturing overhead is still allocated based on direct labor hours, even though automation has drastically reduced the amount of direct labor used to manufacture a product. Consequently, investments in new equipment and machinery have resulted in

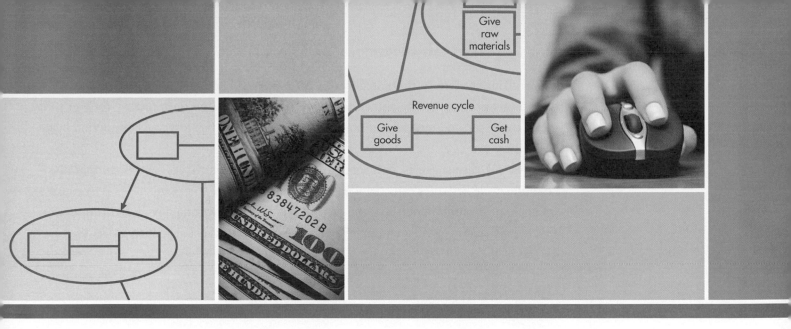

dramatic increases in manufacturing overhead rates. This situation has created the following problems:

1. Production supervisors complain that the accounting system makes no sense and that they are being penalized for making investments that improve overall efficiency. Indeed, according to the system, some products now cost more to produce using state-of-the-art equipment than they did before the new equipment was purchased. Yet the new equipment has increased production capacity while simultaneously reducing defects.

2. The marketing and product design executives have all but dismissed the system's product cost figures as useless for setting prices or determining the potential profitability of new products. Indeed, some competitors have begun to price their products below what AOE's cost accounting system says it costs to produce that item.

3. Although a number of steps have been taken to improve quality, the cost accounting system does not provide adequate measures to evaluate the effect of those steps and to indicate areas that need further improvement. Indeed, LeRoy is frustrated by his inability to quantify the effects of the quality improvements that have occurred.

4. Performance reports continue to focus primarily on financial measures. Line managers in the factory, however, complain that they need more accurate and timely information on physical activities, such as units produced, defect rates, and production time.

5. LeRoy is frustrated because the move to lean manufacturing was successful in markedly reducing inventory levels this past year, but the traditional GAAP-based financial reports show that this has significantly lowered profitability.

LeRoy has expressed these concerns to Linda Spurgeon, AOE's president, who agrees that the problems are serious. Linda then called a meeting with LeRoy; Ann Brandt, AOE's vice president of information systems; and Elizabeth Venko, AOE's controller. At the meeting, Elizabeth and Ann agreed to study how to modify the cost accounting system to more accurately reflect AOE's new production processes. To begin this project, LeRoy agreed to take Elizabeth and Ann on a factory tour so that they could see and understand how the new technology has affected production cycle activities.

As this case suggests, deficiencies in the information system used to support production cycle activities can create significant problems for an organization. As you read this chapter, think about how the introduction of new technology in the production cycle may require corresponding changes in a company's cost accounting system.

Introduction

The **production cycle** is a recurring set of business activities and related information processing operations associated with the manufacture of products. Figure 14-1 shows how the production cycle is linked to the other subsystems in a company's information system. The revenue cycle information system (see Chapter 12) provides the information (customer orders and sales forecasts) used to plan production and inventory levels. In return, the production cycle information system sends the revenue cycle information about finished goods that have been produced and are available for sale. Information about raw materials needs is sent to the expenditure cycle information system (see Chapter 13) in the form of purchase requisitions. In exchange, the expenditure cycle system provides information about raw material acquisitions and also about other expenditures included in manufacturing overhead. Information about labor needs is sent to the human resources cycle (see Chapter 15), which in return provides data about labor costs and availability. Finally, information about the cost of goods manufactured is sent to the general ledger and reporting information system (see Chapter 16).

Figure 14-2 depicts the four basic activities in the production cycle: product design, planning and scheduling, production operations, and cost accounting. Although accountants are involved primarily in the fourth step, cost accounting, they also must understand the other three processes to be able to design reports that provide management with the information needed to manage the production cycle activities of a modern manufacturing company. For example, one popular approach to improving manufacturing performance, called Six Sigma, begins with careful measurement and analysis of current processes in order to find ways to improve them. Accountants should participate in such efforts by helping to design accurate measures; their ability to do so, however, requires that they understand the production activities being measured.

This chapter explains how an organization's information system supports each of the production cycle activities. We begin by describing the design of the information system and the basic controls necessary to ensure that it provides management with reliable information to assess the efficiency and effectiveness of production cycle activities. We then discuss in detail

FIGURE 14-1

Context Diagram of the Production Cycle

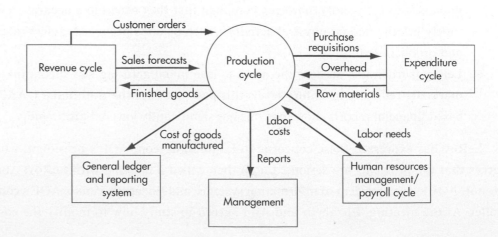

FIGURE 14-2

**Level 0 Data Flow
Diagram of the
Production Cycle**

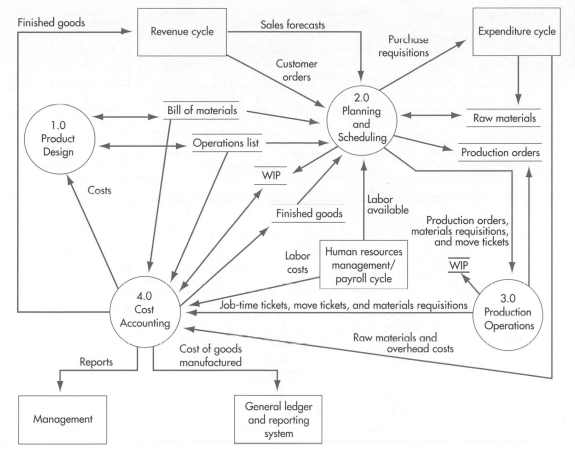

each of the four basic production cycle activities. For each activity, we describe how the information needed to perform and manage those activities is collected, processed, and stored. We also explain the controls necessary to ensure not only the reliability of that information but also the safeguarding of the organization's resources.

Production Cycle Information System

Figure 14-3 presents the portion of the enterprise resource planning (ERP) that supports an organization's production cycle.

Process

Notice how the production cycle information system integrates both operational and financial data from many sources. The engineering department is responsible for developing product specifications. The bill of materials file stores information about product components, and the operations list file contains information about how to manufacture each product. To develop those specifications, engineering accesses both files to examine the design of similar products. It also accesses the general ledger and inventory files for information about the costs of alternative product designs. The sales department enters information about sales forecasts and customer orders. The production planning department uses that information, plus data about current inventory levels, to develop the master production schedule and create new records in the production order file to authorize the production of specific goods. At the same time, new records are added to the work-in-process file to accumulate cost data. Materials requisitions are sent to the inventory stores department to authorize the release of raw materials. The computer-integrated manufacturing (CIM) interface sends detailed instructions to factory workstations. The CIM interface also collects cost and operational data that is used to update the work-in-process and production order files, respectively.

FIGURE 14-3
Overview of ERP System Design to Support the Production Cycle

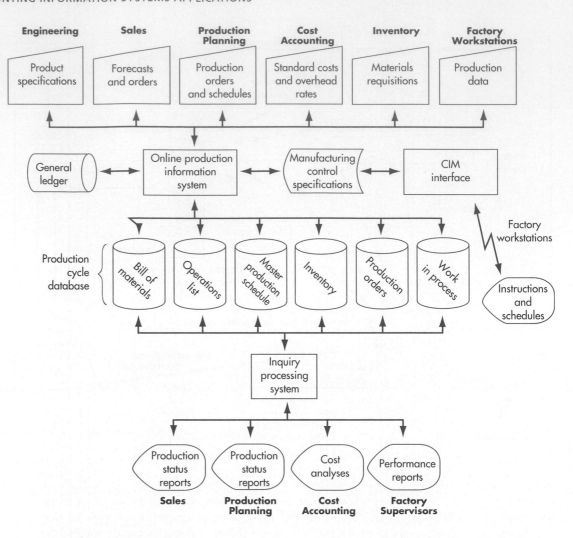

Threats and Controls

As Figure 14-3 shows, the production cycle activities depend on and update the integrated database that contains master data about product specifications and inventory (both finished goods and raw materials). Therefore, the first threat listed in Table 14-1 is the risk of inaccurate or invalid master data. Inaccurate data about factory operations can result in incorrect costing of products and valuation of inventory. Inaccurate inventory records can result in either failure to timely manufacture finished goods or unnecessary production. Errors in product specifications (bills of materials and operations lists) can result in poorly designed products. The various processing integrity controls discussed in Chapter 10 can reduce the risk of inaccurate data entry. It is also important to restrict access to production cycle master data. Enforcing proper access controls and segregation of duties requires that the controller or CFO review and suggest appropriate configuration of user rights in integrated ERP systems. The default installation of such systems typically provides every employee with far too much power. Therefore, it is important to modify user permissions to ensure that employees are assigned only those privileges necessary to perform their specified job duties. In addition to multifactor authentication of employees, location-based access controls on devices should also be used. For example, the system should be programmed to reject any attempts to alter inventory records from a terminal located in the engineering department. Finally, logs of all activities, especially any actions involving managerial approval, such as requests for additional raw materials or overtime, should be recorded and maintained for later review as part of the audit trail.

Another threat is the unauthorized disclosure of production information, such as trade secrets and process improvements that provide a company with a competitive advantage. The various access controls discussed earlier provide one way to mitigate this threat. In addition, sensitive data, such as the precise procedures to follow in manufacturing a given product, should be

TABLE 14-1 Threats and Controls in the Production Cycle

Activity	Threat	Controls (first number refers to the corresponding threat)
General issues throughout entire production cycle	1. Inaccurate or invalid master data 2. Unauthorized disclosure of sensitive information 3. Loss or destruction of data	1.1 Data processing integrity controls 1.2 Restriction of access to master data 1.3 Review of all changes to master data 2.1 Access controls 2.2 Encryption 3.1 Backup and disaster recovery procedures
Product design	4. Poor product design resulting in excess costs	4.1 Accounting analysis of costs arising from product design choices 4.2 Analysis of warranty and repair costs
Planning and scheduling	5. Over- and underproduction	5.1 Production planning systems 5.2 Review and approval of production schedules and orders 5.3 Restriction of access to production orders and production schedules
Production operations	6. Theft of inventory 7. Theft of fixed asset 8. Poor performance 9. Suboptimal investment in fixed assets 10. Loss of inventory or fixed assets due to fire or other disasters 11. Disruption of operations	6.1 Physical access control 6.2 Documention of all inventory movement 6.3 Segregation of duties—custody of assets from recording and authorization of removal 6.4 Restriction of access to inventory master data 6.5 Periodic physical counts of inventory and reconciliation of those counts to recorded quantities 7.1 Physical inventory of all fixed assets 7.2 Restriction of physical access to fixed assets 7.3 Maintaining detailed records of fixed assets, including disposal 8.1 Training 8.2 Performance reports 9.1 Proper approval of fixed asset acquisitions, including use of requests for proposals to solicit multiple competitive bids 10.1 Physical safeguards (e.g., fire sprinklers) 10.2 Insurance 11.1 Backup and disaster recovery plans
Cost accounting	12. Inaccurate cost data 13. Inappropriate allocation of overhead costs 14. Misleading reports	12.1 Source data automation 12.2 Data processing integrity controls 13.1 Time-driven activity based costing 14.1 Innovative performance metrics (e.g., throughput)

encrypted both while in storage and during transmission over the Internet to manufacturing plants and business partners.

The third general threat listed in Table 14-1 is the loss or alteration of production data. The production cycle database must be protected from either intentional or accidental loss or damage. As discussed in Chapter 10, regular backing up of all data files is imperative. Additional copies of key master files, such as open production orders and raw materials inventory, should be stored off-site. To reduce the possibility of accidental erasure of important files, all disks and tapes should have both external and internal file labels.

Now that we have provided an overview of the production cycle information system, let us examine each of the basic activities depicted in Figure 14-2 in more detail.

Product Design

The first step in the production cycle is product design (circle 1.0 in Figure 14-2). The objective is to create a product that meets customer requirements in terms of quality, durability, and functionality while simultaneously minimizing production costs. These criteria often conflict with one another, making product design a challenging task.

Process

The product design activity creates two outputs. The first, a **bill of materials** (Figure 14-4), specifies the part number, description, and quantity of each component used in a finished product. The second is an *operations list* (Figure 14-5), which specifies the sequence of steps to follow in making the product, which equipment to use, and how long each step should take.

Tools such as product life-cycle management (PLM) software can help improve the efficiency and effectiveness of the product design process. PLM software consists of three key components: computer-aided design (CAD) software to design new products, digital manufacturing software that simulates how those products will be manufactured, and product data management software that stores all the data associated with products. CAD software enables manufacturers to design and test virtual 3-D models of products, thereby eliminating the costs associated with creating and destroying physical prototypes. CAD software facilitates collaboration by design teams dispersed around the globe and eliminates the costs associated with exchanging static copies of product designs. Digital manufacturing software allows companies to determine labor, machine, and process requirements to optimally produce items in different facilities across the globe in order to minimize costs. Product data management software provides easy access to detailed engineering specifications and other product data to facilitate product redesign, modification, and post-sale maintenance. Although PLM can dramatically improve both the efficiency and effectiveness of product design, Focus 14-1 shows that reaping its full benefits requires careful supervision by senior management.

Threats and Controls

Poor product design (threat 4 in Table 14-1) drives up costs in several ways. Using too many unique components when producing similar products increases the costs associated with purchasing and maintaining raw materials inventories. It also often results in inefficient production processes because of excessive complexity in changing from the production of one product to another. Poorly designed products are also more likely to incur high warranty and repair costs.

To mitigate this threat, accountants should participate in the product design activity because 65% to 80% of product costs are determined at this stage of the production process. Accountants can analyze how the use of alternative components and changes to the production process affect costs. In addition, accountants can use information from the revenue cycle about repair and warranty costs associated with existing products to identify the primary causes of product failure and suggest opportunities to redesign products to improve quality.

FIGURE 14-4

Example of a Bill of Materials

Finished Product: DVD Player		
Part Number	Description	Quantity
105	Control Unit	1
125	Back Panel	1
148	Side Panel	2
155	Top/Bottom Panel	2
173	Timer	1
195	Front Panel	1
199	Screw	6

FIGURE 14-5

Example of an Operations List

Operations List for: Create Side Panel			
Operation Number	Description	Machine Number	Standard Time (minutes:seconds)
105	Cut to shape	ML15-12	2:00
106	Corner cut	ML15-9	3:15
124	Turn and shape	S28-17	4:00
142	Finish	F54-5	7:10
155	Paint	P89-1	9:30

The potential benefits of PLM software are enormous. For example, General Motors estimates that it costs approximately $500,000 to run crash tests with real cars and hopes that CAD software can reduce the number of such tests by 85%. As Airbus learned, however, PLM software also has pitfalls. In 2006 it announced that production of the A380 superjumbo airliner would be delayed by up to two years, costing Airbus approximately $6 billion in lost profits. The problem? Use of different versions of the same CAD software by design teams in Germany and France resulted in incompatibilities between the front and rear fuselages. Each A380 contains over 300 miles of wires and more than 40,000 connectors to power everything in both the customer cabin and the cockpit. When workers tried to assemble the front and rear fuselages, they discovered that the wiring could not be properly connected.

How could using two editions of the same software create such problems? The answer is that each version treated drawings in different ways, resulting in different models. Engineers using the older version at the German plant had

to manually tinker with the drawings to indicate where conduits should be placed, whereas the newer version of the software used at the French plant did this automatically. In addition, many technical notes containing key information about product specifications and units of measurement were lost when drawings were converted between the two versions of the software.

The experience of Airbus is not unique. A survey found that almost 50% of companies using CAD software had to redesign products because of incompatibilities between CAD software used by different design teams. Airbus executives did not force engineers at different plants to use the same versions of CAD software. This decision initially saved money by avoiding the need to purchase new software and the associated time and costs of retraining engineers. But those short-term savings were more than offset by the subsequent loss of profits due to production delays. This underscores the importance of management involvement and support whenever companies implement complex software such as PLM.

Planning and Scheduling

The second step in the production cycle is planning and scheduling (circle 2.0 in Figure 14-2). The objective is to develop a production plan efficient enough to meet existing orders and anticipated short-term demand while minimizing inventories of both raw materials and finished goods.

Production Planning Methods

Two common methods of production planning are manufacturing resource planning and lean manufacturing. **Manufacturing resource planning (MRP-II)** is an extension of materials resource planning (discussed in Chapter 13) that seeks to balance existing production capacity and raw materials needs to meet forecasted sales demands. MRP-II systems are often referred to as *push manufacturing*, because goods are produced in expectation of customer demand.

Just as MRP-II is an extension of MRP inventory control systems, *lean manufacturing* extends the principles of just-in-time inventory systems (discussed in Chapter 13) to the entire production process. The goal of lean manufacturing is to minimize or eliminate inventories of raw materials, work in process, and finished goods. Lean manufacturing is often referred to as *pull manufacturing*, because goods are produced in response to customer demand. Theoretically, lean manufacturing systems produce only in response to customer orders. In practice, however, most lean manufacturing systems develop short-run production plans. For example, Toyota develops monthly production plans so that it can provide a stable schedule to its suppliers. This strategy enables the suppliers to plan their production schedules so that they can deliver their products to Toyota at the exact time they are needed.

Thus, both MRP-II and lean manufacturing systems plan production in advance. They differ, however, in the length of the planning horizon. MRP-II systems may develop production plans for up to 12 months in advance, whereas lean manufacturing systems use much shorter planning horizons. If demand for a company's product is predictable and the product has a long life cycle, then an MRP-II approach may be justified. In contrast, a lean manufacturing approach may be more appropriate if a company's products are characterized by short life cycles, unpredictable demand, and frequent markdowns of excess inventory.

Key Documents and Forms

Information about customer orders, sales forecasts, and inventory levels of finished goods is used to determine production levels. The result is a ***master production schedule (MPS)***, which specifies how much of each product is to be produced during the planning period and when that production should occur (Figure 14-6). Although the long-range part of the MPS may be modified in response to changes in market conditions, production plans for many products must be frozen a few weeks in advance to provide sufficient time to procure the necessary raw materials, supplies, and labor resources.

The complexity of scheduling increases dramatically as the number of factories grows. For example, large manufacturing companies such as Intel and General Motors must coordinate production at many different plants in different countries. Some of those plants produce basic components, and others assemble the final products. The production information system must coordinate these activities to minimize bottlenecks and the buildup of partially completed inventories.

The MPS is used to develop a detailed timetable that specifies daily production and to determine whether raw materials need to be purchased. To do this, it is necessary to "explode" the bill of materials to determine the immediate raw materials requirements for meeting the production goals listed in the MPS (Table 14-2). These requirements are compared with current inventory levels, and if additional materials are needed, purchase requisitions are generated and sent to the purchasing department to initiate the acquisition process.

Figure 14-2 shows that the planning and scheduling activity produces three other documents: production orders, materials requisitions, and move tickets. A **production order** authorizes the manufacture of a specified quantity of a particular product. It lists the operations that need to be performed, the quantity to be produced, and the location where the finished product should be delivered. It also collects data about each of those activities (Figure 14-7). A ***materials requisition*** authorizes the removal of the necessary quantity of raw materials from the storeroom to the factory location where they will be used. This document contains the production order number, date of issue, and, based on the bill of materials, the part numbers and quantities of all necessary raw materials (Figure 14-8). Subsequent transfers of raw materials throughout the factory are documented on ***move tickets***, which identify the parts being transferred, the location to which they are transferred, and the time of transfer (Figure 14-9 shows an example of an inventory transfer data entry screen).

FIGURE 14-6

Sample of a Master Production Schedule (MPS)

MASTER PRODUCTION SCHEDULE								
Product Number	120			**Description:**		DVD Player		
Lead time:[a]	**Week Number**							
1 week	**1**	**2**	**3**	**4**	**5**	**6**	**7**	**8**
Quantity on hand	500	350[b]	350	300	350	300	450	300
Scheduled production	150[c]	300	250	300	250	400	250	300
Forecasted sales	300	300	300	250	300	250	400	250
Net available	350[d]	350	300	350	300	450	300	350

[a]*Time to manufacture product (1 week for DVD player).*
[b]*Ending quantity on hand (net available) from prior week.*
[c]*Calculated by subtracting quantity on hand from sum of this week's and next week's forecasted sales, plus a 50-unit buffer stock. For example, begin week 1 with 500 units. Projected sales for weeks 1 and 2 total 600 units. Adding 50-unit desired buffer inventory yields 650 units needed by end of week 1. Subtracting beginning inventory of 500 units results in planned production of 150 units during week 1.*
[d]*Beginning quantity on hand plus scheduled production less forecasted sales.*

TABLE 14-2 Example of "Exploding" a Bill of Materials

COMPONENTS IN EACH DVD PLAYER

	Part No.	Description	Quantity	Number of DVD Players	Total Requirements
Step 1: Multiply the component requirements for ONE product by the number of products to be produced next period (from the MPS).	105	Control Unit	1	2,000	2,000
	125	Back Panel	1	2,000	2,000
	148	Side Panel	4	2,000	8,000
	173	Timer	1	2,000	2,000
	195	Front Panel	1	2,000	2,000
	199	Screw	6	2,000	12,000
	135	Top Panel	1	2,000	2,000
	136	Bottom Panel	1	2,000	2,000

COMPONENTS IN EACH CD PLAYER

Part No.	Description	Quantity	Number of CD Players	Total Requirements
103	Control Unit	1	3,000	3,000
120	Front Panel	1	3,000	3,000
121	Back Panel	1	3,000	3,000
173	Timer	1	3,000	3,000
190	Side Panel	4	3,000	12,000
199	Screw	4	3,000	12,000
135	Top Panel	1	3,000	3,000
136	Bottom Panel	1	3,000	3,000

	Part No.	DVD Player	CD Player	Total
Step 2: Calculate total component requirements by summing products.	103	0	3,000	3,000
	105	2,000	0	2,000
	120	0	3,000	3,000
	121	0	3,000	3,000
	125	2,000	0	2,000
	148	8,000	0	8,000
	173	2,000	3,000	5,000
	190	0	12,000	12,000
	195	2,000	0	2,000
	199	12,000	12,000	24,000
	135	2,000	3,000	5,000
	136	2,000	3,000	5,000

	Part No.	Week 1	Week 2	Week 3	Week 4	Week 5	Week 6
Step 3: Repeat steps 1 and 2 for each week during planning horizon.	103	3,000	2,000	2,500	3,000	2,500	3,000
	105	2,000	2,000	2,500	2,500	2,000	3,000
	120	3,000	2,000	2,500	3,000	2,500	3,000
	121	3,000	2,000	2,500	3,000	2,500	3,000
	125	2,000	2,000	2,500	2,500	2,000	3,000
	148	8,000	8,000	10,000	10,000	8,000	12,000
	173	5,000	4,000	5,000	5,500	4,500	6,000
	190	12,000	12,000	10,000	12,000	10,000	12,000
	195	2,000	2,000	2,500	2,500	2,000	3,000
	199	24,000	20,000	25,000	27,000	22,000	30,000
	135	5,000	5,000	5,000	5,000	5,000	5,000
	136	5,000	5,000	5,000	5,000	5,000	5,000

FIGURE 14-7
Sample Production Order for Alpha Omega Electronics

4587

Alpha Omega Engineering

PRODUCTION ORDER

Order No. 2289	Product No. 4430	Description: Cabinet Side Panel		Production Quantity 1000
Approved by: *PJS*	Release Date: 02/24/2011	Issue Date: 02/25/2011	Completion Date: 03/09/2011	Deliver to: Assembly Department

Work Station No.	Product Operation No.	Quantity	Operation Description	Start Date & Time		Finish Date & Time	
MH25	100	1,003	Transfer from stock	02/28	0700	02/28	0800
ML15-12	105	1,003	Cut to shape	02/28	0800	02/28	1000
ML15-9	106	1,002	Corner cut	02/28	1030	02/28	1200
S28-17	124	1,002	Turn & shape	02/28	1300	02/28	1700
F54-5	142	1,001	Finish	03/01	0800	03/01	1100
P89-1	155	1,001	Paint	03/01	1300	03/02	1300
QC94	194	1,001	Inspect	03/02	1400	03/02	1600
MH25	101	1,000	Transfer to assembly	03/02	1600	03/02	1700

Explanation of numbers in Quantity column:
1. *Total of 1,003 sheets of raw material used to produce 1,000 good panels and 3 rejected panels.*
2. *One panel not cut to proper shape, thus only 1,002 units had operations 106 and 124 performed on them.*
3. *One panel not properly turned and shaped; hence only 1,001 panels finished, painted, and received final inspection.*
4. *One panel rejected during final inspection; thus only 1,000 good panels transferred to assembly department.*

Notice that many of the documents used in the production cycle track the movement and usage of raw materials. The use of bar-coding and RFID tags provides opportunities to improve the efficiency and accuracy of these materials handling activities by eliminating the need for manual entry of data. RFID also facilitates locating specific inventory because the scanning devices are not limited to reading only those items that are directly in line-of-sight. This can be especially useful in large warehouse and storage facilities, where items may get moved around to make room for new shipments.

Finally, accurate production plannning requires integrating information about customer orders (from the revenue cycle) with information about purchases from suppliers (from the expenditure cycle), along with information about labor availability (from the HR/payroll cycle). Figure 14-10 illustrates how an ERP system provides this integration. The system first checks inventory on hand to determine how much needs to be produced to fill the new order. It then

FIGURE 14-8
Sample Materials Requisition for Alpha Omega Electronics

No. 2345

MATERIALS REQUISITION

Issued To: Assembly	Issue Date: 08/15/2011	Production Order Number: 62913

Part Number	Description	Quantity	Unit Cost $	Total Cost $
115	Calculator Unit	2,000	2.95	5,900.00
135	Lower Casing	2,000	.45	900.00
198	Screw	16,000	.02	320.00
178	Battery	2,000	.75	1,500.00
136	Upper Casing	2,000	.80	1,600.00
199	Screw	12,000	.02	240.00
Issued by: **AKL**				10,460.00
Received by: *GWS*		Costed by: *ZBD*		

Note: Cost information is entered when the materials requisition is turned in to the cost accounting department. Other information, except for signatures, is printed by the system when the document is prepared.

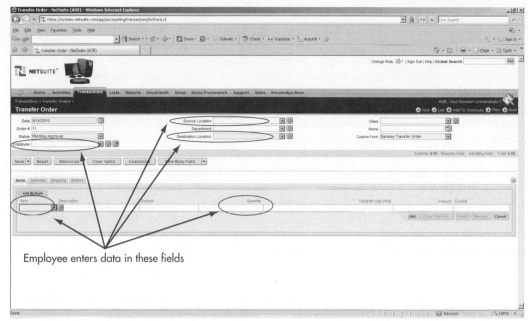

© 2010 NetSuite, Inc.

FIGURE 14-9

Example of Inventory Transfer Screen

calculates labor needs and determines whether there is a need to schedule overtime or hire temporary help in order to meet the promised fill date. At the same time, information in the bill of materials is used to determine what components, if any, need to be ordered. Any necessary purchase orders are sent to suppliers via electronic data interchange (EDI). The master production schedule is then adjusted to include the new order. Notice how this sharing of information across the revenue, production, and expenditure cycles in the manner just described enables companies to efficiently manage inventories by timing their purchases to meet actual customer demand.

Threats and Controls

Table 14-1 shows that the primary threat in the planning and scheduling activity is over- or underproduction. Overproduction can result in a supply of goods in excess of short-run demands, thereby creating potential cash flow problems because resources are tied up in

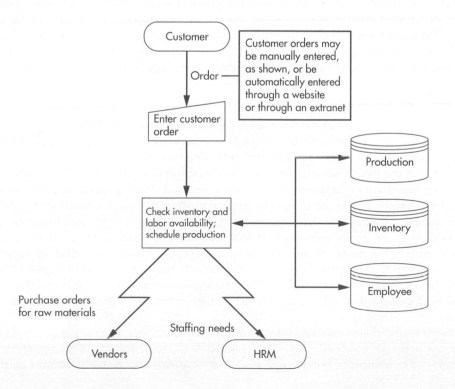

FIGURE 14-10

Illustration of How ERP Systems Integrate Production Cycle Information with Data from Other Cycles

inventory. Overproduction also increases the risk of carrying inventory that becomes obsolete. Conversely, underproduction can result in lost sales and customer dissatisfaction because of lack of availability of desired items. These threats are especially important for companies that produce new, innovative products, such as current fashion clothing, because the demand for such products is much more volatile than the demand for staples and commodities, such as food or office supplies.

Production planning systems can reduce the risk of over- and underproduction. Improvement requires accurate and current sales forecasts and data about inventory stocks, information that the revenue and expenditure cycle systems can provide. In addition to improved forecasts, information about production performance, particularly concerning trends in total time to manufacture each product, should be regularly collected. These data sources should be used periodically to review and adjust the master production schedule.

Proper approval and authorization of production orders is another control to prevent over- or underproduction of specific items. The risk of unauthorized production orders can be reduced by restricting access to the production scheduling program. Careful review and approval also ensures that the correct production orders are released.

Production Operations

The third step in the production cycle is the actual manufacture of products (circle 3.0 in Figure 14-2). The manner in which this activity is accomplished varies greatly across companies, differing according to the type of product being manufactured and the degree of automation used in the production process.

Using various forms of information technology (IT) in the production process, such as robots and computer-controlled machinery, is referred to as **computer-integrated manufacturing (CIM)**. CIM can significantly reduce production costs. For example, Northrop Grumman Corporation once used 16,000 sheets of paper to record shop-floor work instructions related to the manufacture of plane fuselages. Installation of online terminals at each assembly station eliminated that paper flow and improved efficiency, reducing costs by 30%.

Accountants need not be experts on every facet of CIM, but they must understand how it affects both operations and cost accounting. One operational effect of CIM is a shift from mass production to custom-order manufacturing. For example, every Northrop Grumman product is assembled to order. Each product, however, can use any of about 256,000 separate components. Thus, CIM requires redesign of inventory management systems and work flows to facilitate quick changes in production. As we will discuss in the final section of this chapter, such flexibility in manufacturing operations also has implications for the design of cost accounting systems.

Threats and Controls

Theft of inventories (threat 6) and fixed assets (threat 7) are major concerns (see Table 14-1). In addition to the loss of assets, thefts also result in overstated asset balances, which can lead to erroneous analyses of financial performance and underproduction.

To reduce the risk of inventory loss, physical access to inventories should be restricted, and all internal movements of inventory should be documented. Thus, materials requisitions should be used to authorize the release of raw materials to production. Both the inventory control clerk and the production employee receiving the raw materials should sign the requisition to acknowledge release of the goods to production. Requests for additional materials in excess of the amounts specified in the bill of materials should be documented and authorized by supervisory personnel. Move tickets should be used to document subsequent movement of inventory through various stages of the production process. The return of any materials not used in production also should be documented. Wherever feasible, RFID tags or bar codes should be used to automate the tracking of inventories.

Proper segregation of duties is important to safeguard inventory. Maintaining physical custody of the raw materials and finished goods inventories is the responsibility of the inventory stores department. Department or factory supervisors have primary responsibility for work-in-process inventories. The authorization function, represented by the preparation of production orders, materials requisitions, and move tickets, is the responsibility of the production planners or, increasingly, of the production information system itself. RFID equipment, bar-code scanners, and online terminals can be used to record movement of inventory, thereby maintaining accurate perpetual inventory records. Consequently, proper access controls and compatibility tests are important to ensure that only authorized personnel have access to those records (control 6.4). Finally, an employee without any custodial responsibility should periodically count inventory on hand. Any discrepancies between these physical counts and recorded amounts should be investigated.

Similar controls are needed to safeguard fixed assets. First, all fixed assets must be identified and recorded (control 7.1) so that managers can be assigned responsibility and accountability for fixed assets under their control. RFID tags provide a cost-effective way to monitor the location of fixed assets. As with inventory, security measures should be in place to control physical access to fixed assets. Because manufacturing machinery and equipment are often replaced before they are completely worn out, it is important to formally approve and accurately record their sale or disposal. A report of all fixed-asset transactions should be printed periodically and sent to the controller, who should verify that each transaction was properly authorized and executed. The cost accounting system also needs to maintain accurate records of acquisition cost, any improvements, and depreciation in order to properly calculate the gain or loss arising from such transactions.

Poor performance is another threat to production operations. Training is one way to mitigate this threat. Indeed, surveys of manufacturing companies report a direct relationship between time spent on training and overall productivity. It is also important to regularly prepare and review reports on performance in order to identify when additional training is needed.

Another threat associated with production cycle activities is suboptimal investment in fixed assets. Overinvesting in fixed assets can create excess costs; underinvestment can impair productivity. Both problems reduce profitability. Thus, proper authorization of fixed-asset transactions is important.

Acquisitions of fixed assets represent a special type of expenditure and follow the same basic processes (order the fixed asset, receive it, and pay for it) and control procedures discussed in Chapter 13. Nonetheless, the size of most fixed-asset transactions necessitates some modifications of the processes used to acquire inventory and miscellaneous supplies. A supervisor or manager, who provides details about expected cash flows and other costs and benefits of the proposed expenditure, should first recommend large capital expenditures. All such recommendations should be reviewed by a senior executive or by an executive committee and the various projects ranked by priority. Smaller capital expenditures (e.g., those costing $10,000 or less) usually can be purchased directly out of departmental budgets, which avoids a formal approval process. Holding managers accountable for their department's return on the fixed assets provides additional incentive to control such expenditures.

Another difference is that orders for machinery and equipment almost always involve a formal request for competitive bids by potential suppliers. A document called a **request for proposal (RFP)**, which specifies the desired properties of the asset, is sent to each prospective supplier. The capital investments committee should review the responses and select the best bid. Once a supplier has been selected, the acquisition of the asset may be handled through the regular expenditure cycle process, as described in Chapter 13. Specifically, a formal purchase order is prepared, receipt of the asset is formally documented using a receiving report, and a disbursement voucher is used to authorize payment to the supplier. The same set of processing controls and edit checks employed for other purchases also should be used for fixed-asset acquisitions (for details, refer back to the discussion in Chapter 13).

Another threat noted in Table 14-1 is that both inventories and fixed assets are subject to loss due to fire or other disasters. Physical safeguards, such as fire suppression systems, are designed to prevent such disasters. However, because preventive controls are never 100% effective, organizations also need to purchase adequate insurance to cover such losses and provide for replacement of those assets.

A related concern is disruption of production activities (threat 11). The high level of automation in production cycle activities means that disasters, such as the power outages experienced in California in recent years, not only interrupt the functioning of information systems but can also disrupt manufacturing activities. Backup power sources, such as generators, and uninterruptible power supply devices should be acquired to ensure that critical equipment and machinery is not damaged by sudden unexpected loss of power and that important production processes can continue on schedule. Companies also need to investigate the disaster preparedness of key suppliers and identify alternative sources for critical components. This is especially important for companies that practice lean manufacturing; they maintain low inventories of both raw materials and finished goods, so any disruptions to either their manufacturing activities or those of their suppliers can quickly result in lost sales.

Cost Accounting

The final step in the production cycle is cost accounting (circle 4.0 in Figure 14-2). The three principal objectives of the cost accounting system are (1) to provide information for planning, controlling, and evaluating the performance of production operations; (2) to provide accurate cost data about products for use in pricing and product mix decisions; and (3) to collect and process the information used to calculate the inventory and cost of goods sold values that appear in the company's financial statements.

Process

To successfully accomplish the first objective, the cost accounting system must be designed to collect real-time data about the performance of production activities so that management can make timely decisions. To accomplish the other two objectives, the cost accounting system must classify costs by various categories and then assign those costs to specific products and organizational units. This requires careful coding of cost data during collection, because often the same costs may be allocated in multiple ways, for several different purposes. For example, factory supervisory costs may be assigned to departments for performance evaluation purposes but to specific products for pricing and product mix decisions.

Most companies use either job-order or process costing to assign production costs. **Job-order costing** assigns costs to specific production batches, or jobs, and is used when the product or service being sold consists of discretely identifiable items. For example, construction companies use job-order costing for each house being built. Similarly, public accounting and law firms use job-order costing to account for the costs of individual audits or cases, respectively. AOE currently uses job-order costing.

In contrast, **process costing** assigns costs to each process, or work center, in the production cycle, and then calculates the average cost for all units produced. Process costing is used when similar goods or services are produced in mass quantities and discrete units cannot be readily identified. For example, breweries accumulate the costs associated with the various processes (e.g., mashing, primary fermentation, filtering, and bottling) in producing a batch of a particular kind of beer and then compute the average total unit cost for that product. Similarly, mutual funds accumulate the costs associated with handling customer deposits and withdrawals and then compute the per-unit costs of those transactions.

The choice of job-order or process costing affects only the method used to *assign* costs to products, not the methods used to collect that data. Let us now examine how data about raw materials used, labor hours expended, machine operations performed, and manufacturing overhead are collected.

RAW MATERIALS USAGE DATA When production is initiated, the issuance of a materials requisition triggers a debit to work in process for the raw materials sent to production. If additional materials are needed, another debit is made to work in process. Conversely, work in process is credited for any materials not used and returned to inventory. Many raw materials are bar-coded so that usage data can be collected by scanning the products when released from, or returned to, inventory. Increasingly, manufacturers are using RFID tags to further improve the efficiency of tracking materials usage. In fact, if RFID tags are applied to individual products, companies may, if they desire, adopt the specific identification method for tracking inventory. It is difficult, however, to use bar codes or RFID tags for some items, such as liquids. Inventory clerks and factory workers must use online terminals to enter usage data for such items.

DIRECT LABOR COSTS   In the past, AOE and other manufacturers used a paper document called a *job-time ticket* to collect data about labor activity. This document recorded the amount of time a worker spent on each specific job task. Now, as shown in Figure 14-3, workers enter this data using online terminals at each factory workstation. To further improve the efficiency of this process, AOE is considering switching to coded identification cards, which workers would run through a badge reader or bar-code scanner when they start and finish any task. The time savings associated with using bar-coding to automate data collection can be significant. For example, Consolidated Diesel Company found that using bar-code scanners to capture data about materials usage and labor operations saved about 12 seconds per workstation, per activity. Although this may not seem like much, when multiplied by the hundreds of workstations and multiple activities performed daily by hundreds of employees, the change resulted in a permanent 15% increase in productivity.

MACHINERY AND EQUIPMENT USAGE   As companies implement CIM to automate the production process, an ever larger proportion of product costs relate to the machinery and equipment used to make that product. Data about machinery and equipment usage are collected at each step in the production process, often in conjunction with data about labor costs. For example, when workers record their activities at a particular workstation, the system can also record information identifying the machinery and equipment used and the duration of such use. Until recently, this data was collected by wiring the factory so that each piece of equipment was linked to the computer system. This limited the ability to quickly and easily redesign the layout of the shop floor to improve production efficiency. Consequently, many manufacturing companies are replacing such wired connections with wireless technology. Doing so enables them to use new 3-D simulation software to evaluate the effects of modifying shop-floor layout and workflow and to easily and quickly implement beneficial changes.

MANUFACTURING OVERHEAD COSTS   Manufacturing costs that are not economically feasible to trace directly to specific jobs or processes are considered **manufacturing overhead.** Examples include the costs of water, power, and other utilities; miscellaneous supplies; rent, insurance, and property taxes for the factory plant; and the salaries of factory supervisors. Most of these costs are collected by the expenditure cycle information system (see Chapter 13), with the exception of supervisory salaries, which are processed by the human resources cycle information system (see Chapter 15).

Accountants can play a key role in controlling overhead costs by carefully assessing how changes in product mix affect total manufacturing overhead. They should go beyond merely collecting such data, however, and identify the underlying factors that drive the changes in total costs. This information then can be used to adjust production plans and factory layout to maximize efficiency and profitability. As the AOE case illustrates, to do this effectively requires that the cost accounting system be redesigned to collect and report costs in a manner consistent with the production planning techniques of the company. For example, lean manufacturing emphasizes working in teams and seeks to maximize the efficiency and synergy of all teams involved in making a particular product. Consequently, Elizabeth Venko realizes that collecting and reporting labor variances at the individual or team level may create dysfunctional incentives to maximize local performance at the expense of plantwide performance. Therefore, she plans to redesign AOE's cost accounting system so that it collects and reports costs in a manner that highlights the *joint* contributions of all teams that make a particular product.

Threats and Controls

As the AOE case illustrated, inaccurate cost data (threat 12 in Table 14-1) can diminish the effectiveness of production scheduling and undermine management's ability to monitor and control manufacturing operations. For example, inaccurate cost data can result in inappropriate decisions about which products to make and how to set current selling prices. Errors in inventory records can lead to either over- or underproduction of goods. Overstated fixed assets increase expenses through extra depreciation and higher property taxes. Understated fixed assets also can cause problems; for example, inaccurate counts of the number of personal computers in use can cause a company to unknowingly violate software license requirements. Inaccuracies in financial statements and managerial reports can distort analyses of past performance and the desirability of future investments or changes in operations.

The best control procedure to ensure that data entry is accurate is to automate data collection using RFID technology, bar-code scanners, badge readers, and other devices. When this is not feasible, online terminals should be used for data entry and should employ the various data entry edit controls discussed in chapter 10. For example, check digits and closed-loop verification should be used to ensure that information about the raw materials used, operations performed, and employee number is entered correctly. Validity checks, such as comparing part numbers of raw materials to those listed in the bill of materials file, provide further assurance of accuracy. Finally, to verify the accuracy of database records, periodic physical counts of inventories and fixed assets should be made and compared with recorded quantities.

Accurate cost data are not sufficient, however. As the AOE case showed, poorly designed cost accounting systems misallocate costs to products (threat 13) and produce misleading reports about production cycle activities (threat 14), both of which can lead to erroneous decisions and frustration. The following two subsections explain how activity-based costing systems and innovative performance metrics can mitigate these problems.

IMPROVED CONTROL WITH ACTIVITY-BASED COSTING SYSTEMS   Traditional cost systems use volume-driven bases, such as direct labor or machine hours, to apply overhead to products. Many overhead costs, however, do not vary directly with production volume. Purchasing costs, for example, vary with the number of purchase orders processed. Similarly, receiving costs vary with the number of shipments from suppliers. Setup and materials handling costs vary with the number of different batches that are run, not with the total number of units produced. Thus, allocating these types of overhead costs to products based on output volume overstates the costs of products manufactured in large quantities. It also understates the costs of products manufactured in small batches.

In addition, allocating overhead based on direct labor input can distort costs across products. As investments in factory automation increase, the amount of direct labor used in production decreases. Consequently, the amount of overhead charged per unit of labor increases dramatically. As a result, small differences in the amount of labor used to produce two products can result in significant differences in product costs.

Activity-based costing[1] can refine and improve cost allocations under both job-order and process cost systems. It attempts to trace costs to the activities that create them, such as grinding or polishing, and only subsequently allocates those costs to products or departments. An underlying objective of activity-based costing is to link costs to corporate strategy. Corporate strategy results in decisions about what goods and services to produce. Activities must be performed to produce these goods and services, which in turn incur costs. Thus, corporate strategy determines costs. Consequently, by measuring the costs of basic activities, such as materials handling or processing purchase orders, activity-based costing provides information to management for evaluating the consequences of strategic decisions.

Activity-based costing systems differ from conventional cost accounting systems in three important ways:

1. Activity-based cost systems attempt to directly trace a larger proportion of overhead costs to products. Advances in IT make this feasible. For example, RFID technology and bar-coding facilitate tracking the exact quantities of miscellaneous parts used in each product or process stage. When implementing activity-based costing systems, accountants observe production operations and interview factory workers and supervisors to obtain a better understanding of how manufacturing activities affect costs.
2. Activity-based cost systems use a greater number of cost pools to accumulate indirect costs (manufacturing overhead). Whereas most traditional cost systems lump all overhead costs together, activity-based costing systems distinguish three separate categories of overhead:
   - **Batch-related overhead**.   Examples include setup costs, inspections, and materials handling. Activity-based cost systems accumulate these costs for a batch and then allocate them to the units produced in that batch. Thus, products produced in large quantities have lower batch-related overhead costs per unit than products produced in small quantities.

---

[1]In this section, we provide an overview of activity-based costing, its effects on the cost accounting system, and its benefits. For additional details on the mechanics of activity-based costing, see any cost accounting textbook.

- **Product-related overhead.** These costs are related to the diversity of the company's product line. Examples include research and development, expediting, shipping and receiving, environmental regulations, and purchasing. Activity-based cost systems try to link these costs to specific products when possible. For example, if a company produces three product lines, one of which generates hazardous waste, an activity-based cost system would charge only that one set of products for all the costs of complying with environmental regulations. Other costs, such as purchasing raw materials, might be allocated across products based on the relative number of purchase orders required to make each product.
- **Companywide overhead.** This category includes such costs as rent or property taxes. These costs apply to all products. Thus, activity-based cost systems typically allocate them using departmental or plant rates.

3. Activity-based cost systems attempt to rationalize the allocation of overhead to products by identifying cost drivers. A **cost driver** is anything that has a cause-and-effect relationship on costs. For example, the number of purchase orders processed is one cost driver of purchasing department costs; that is, the total costs of processing purchase orders (e.g., purchasing department salaries, postage) vary directly with the number of purchase orders that are processed. As in this example, cost drivers in activity-based cost systems are often nonfinancial variables. In contrast, traditional costing systems often use financial variables, such as dollar volume of purchases, as the bases for allocating manufacturing overhead.

ERP systems make it easier to implement activity-based costing because they provide detailed information about the steps required to process a transaction. For example, the time (and therefore the cost) of requisitioning the raw materials needed to manufacture a product depends upon the number of components in the finished product. Accountants and engineers can observe and calculate the average time it takes to retrieve one component from inventory. That time measure can then be multiplied by the number of line items in a production order (automatically recorded by the ERP system) to calculate the materials requisition costs for each different finished product.

Proponents of activity-based costing argue that it provides two important benefits: More accurate cost data result in better product mix and pricing decisions, and more detailed cost data improve management's ability to control and manage total costs.

Better Decisions   Traditional cost systems tend to apply too much overhead to some products and too little to others, because too few cost pools are used. This leads to two types of problems, both of which AOE experienced. First, companies may accept sales contracts for some products at prices below their true cost of production. Consequently, although sales increase, profits decline. Second, companies may overprice other products, thereby inviting new competitors to enter the market. Ironically, if more accurate cost data were available, companies would find that they could cut prices to keep competitors out of the market and still make a profit on each sale. Activity-based cost systems avoid these problems because overhead is divided into three categories and applied using cost drivers that are causally related to production. Therefore, product cost data are more accurate.

Activity-based costing also makes better use of production data to improve product design. For example, the costs associated with processing purchase orders can be used to calculate the purchasing-related overhead associated with each component used in a finished product. Engineering can use this information, along with data on relative usage of components across products, to identify unique components that could be replaced by lower-cost, more commonly used parts.

Finally, activity-based cost data improve managerial decision making by providing information about the costs associated with specific activities, instead of classifying those costs by financial statement category. Table 14-3 shows an example of how this rearrangement of data can improve managerial analysis by focusing attention on key processes. Notice how the traditional cost report draws attention to the fact that travel and software costs are above budget. The activity-based cost report, in contrast, shows which *activities* (training, testing, maintenance and systems analysis) are running over budget, and which are not.

Improved Cost Management   Proponents argue that another advantage of activity-based costing is that it clearly measures the results of managerial actions on overall profitability. Whereas

TABLE 14-3 Comparison of Reports Based on Activity-Based and Traditional Cost Systems

TRADITIONAL COST REPORTS, BASED ON GENERAL LEDGER ACCOUNT CATEGORIES		
	Budget	Actual	Variance
Salaries	$386,000	$375,000	$11,000
Computer software	845,000	855,000	(10,000)
Travel	124,000	150,000	(26,000)
Supplies	25,000	20,000	5,000
Total	$1,380,000	$1,400,000	($20,000)

ACTIVITY-BASED COSTING ANALYSIS		
	Budget	Actual	Variance
Systems analysis	$200,000	$210,000	($10,000)
Coding	440,000	400,000	40,000
Testing	235,000	250,000	(15,000)
Maintenance	250,000	275,000	(25,000)
User support	90,000	50,000	40,000
Reports	87,000	75,000	12,000
Training	78,000	140,000	(62,000)
Total	$1,380,000	$1,400,000	($20,000)

traditional cost systems only measure spending to acquire resources, activity-based cost systems measure both the amount spent to acquire resources and the consumption of those resources. This distinction is reflected in the following formula:

$$\text{Cost of activity capability} = \text{Cost of activity used} + \text{Cost of unused capacity}$$

To illustrate, consider the receiving function at a manufacturing firm such as AOE. The total monthly employee cost in the receiving department, including salaries and benefits, represents the cost of providing this function—receiving shipments from suppliers. Assume that the salary expense of the receiving department is $100,000, and assume that the number of employees is sufficient to handle 500 shipments. The cost per shipment would be $200. Finally, assume that 400 shipments are actually received. The activity-based cost system would report that the cost of the receiving activity used is $80,000 ($200 × 400 shipments) and that the remaining $20,000 in salary expense represents the cost of unused capacity.

In this way, performance reports that activity-based cost systems generate help direct managerial attention to how policy decisions made in one area affect costs in another area. For example, a purchasing department manager may decide to increase the minimum size of orders to obtain larger discounts for bulk purchases. This would reduce the number of incoming shipments that the receiving department must handle, thereby increasing its unused capacity. Similarly, actions taken to improve the efficiency of operations, such as requiring vendors to send products in bar-coded containers, increase practical capacity and create additional unused capacity. In either case, activity-based cost performance reports highlight this excess capacity for managerial attention. Management can then try to improve profitability by applying that unused capacity to other revenue-generating activities.

IMPROVED CONTROL WITH INNOVATIVE PERFORMANCE METRICS Modern approaches to production, such as lean manufacturing, differ significantly from traditional mass production. One major difference is a marked reduction in inventory levels of finished goods, because production is scheduled in response to customer demand instead of projections based on prior years. Although this is beneficial in the long run, it often creates a short-term decline in reported profitability. The reason: Traditional financial accounting treats inventory as an asset. Thus, the costs of producing inventory are not recognized until the products are sold. When a company switches from mass production to lean manufacturing, it reduces existing inventory levels, with the result that costs incurred in prior periods to create that inventory are now expensed. In addition, because lean manufacturing seeks to minimize the creation of additional inventories, almost all labor and overhead costs are expensed in the current period, instead of being allocated to inventory and thereby treated as an asset and deferred to future periods. The combined effect of these changes often results in a marked increase in expenses in the year of transitioning to lean accounting. Although this effect is only temporary, it can create significant concern among managers, particularly if their performance evaluations are based primarily on the company's reported financial statements.

To address these problems, CPAs who work for and with companies that have adopted lean manufacturing techniques advocate supplementing traditional financial reports based on GAAP with additional reports based on lean accounting[2] principles. One suggested change involves assigning costs to product lines instead of departments. For example, all the costs incurred to design, produce, sell, deliver, process customer payments, and provide postsales support are grouped by product. Another change involves reporting overhead costs as a separate item, rather than including them in the calculation of the cost of goods sold. Lean-accounting reports also identify the change in inventory as a separate expense item, to more clearly reveal the effect of inventory levels on reported profits.

In addition to changing the structure of performance reports, accountants should also develop and refine new measures designed to focus on issues important to production cycle managers. Two particularly important issues are the level of usable output produced per unit of time and measures of quality control.

Throughput: A Measure of Production Effectiveness   Throughput represents the number of good units produced in a given period of time. It consists of three factors, each of which can be separately controlled, as shown in the following formula[3]:

$$\text{Throughput} = (\text{Total units produced/Processing time}) \times (\text{Processing time/Total time})$$
$$\times (\text{Good units/Total units})$$

Productive capacity, the first term in the formula, shows the maximum number of units that can be produced using current technology. Productive capacity can be increased by improving labor or machine efficiency, by rearranging the factory-floor layout to expedite the movement of materials, or by simplifying product design specifications. *Productive processing time*, the second term in the formula, indicates the percentage of total production time used to manufacture the product. Productive processing time can be improved by improving maintenance to reduce machine downtime or by more efficient scheduling of material and supply deliveries to reduce wait time. *Yield*, the third term in the formula, represents the percentage of good (nondefective) units produced. Using better-quality raw materials or improving worker skills can improve yield.

Quality Control Measures   Information about quality costs can help companies determine the effects of actions taken to improve yield and identify areas for further improvement. Quality control costs can be divided into four areas:

1. *Prevention costs* are associated with changes to production processes designed to reduce the product defect rate.
2. *Inspection costs* are associated with testing to ensure that products meet quality standards.
3. *Internal failure costs* are associated with reworking, or scrapping, products identified as being defective prior to sale.
4. *External failure costs* result when defective products are sold to customers. They include such costs as product liability claims, warranty and repair expenses, loss of customer satisfaction, and damage to the company's reputation.

---

[2]The introductory material in this section is based on an article by Karen M. Kroll, "The Lowdown on Lean Accounting," *Journal of Accountancy* (July 2004): 69–76.

[3]This formula was developed by Carole Cheatham in "Measuring and Improving Throughput," *Journal of Accountancy* (March 1990): 89–91.

The ultimate objective of quality control is to "get it right the first time" by manufacturing products that meet customer specifications. This often requires trade-offs among the four quality cost categories. For example, increasing prevention costs can lower inspection costs as well as internal and external failure costs. Many companies have found, however, that increased spending to prevent defects reduces total manufacturing costs. In addition, improved quality control can also help companies become "greener." For example, when the Subaru plant in Indiana redesigned its manufacturing process, it reduced the amount of electricity required to produce a car by 14% and totally eliminated waste sent to landfills.

Summary and Case Conclusion

The production cycle consists of four basic activities: product design, production planning and scheduling, production operations, and cost accounting. Companies are continually investing in IT to improve the efficiency of the first three activities. However, for a business to reap the full benefit of these changes, corresponding modifications must also be made to the cost accounting system. In addition, accountants need to modify financial reports and develop new measures that more accurately reflect and measure manufacturing performance.

After completing her tour of the factory, Elizabeth Venko was convinced that some major changes were required in AOE's cost accounting system. For example, although AOE's production operations were highly automated, manufacturing overhead was still being allocated based on direct labor hours. This resulted in distorted product costs due to small differences in the amount of direct labor used to assemble each item. Elizabeth decided that the solution was to do more than merely change the allocation base. Instead, AOE would implement activity-based costing. A number of different pools would be used to accumulate overhead costs, and the appropriate cost drivers would be identified for use in assigning those costs to specific products. Based on her research, including conversations with a controller at another company that had recently implemented an activity-based costing system, Elizabeth believed that these changes would solve AOE's problems with product pricing and mix decisions and more accurately reflect the effects of investments in factory automation.

Elizabeth also decided that three other major changes were needed in the reports the production cycle information system produced. First, data about all the costs associated with quality control, not just those involving rework and scrap, should be collected and reported. Second, performance reports should include nonfinancial measures, such as throughput, in addition to financial measures. Third, lean accounting principles, rather than GAAP, could be used to create financial reports intended for internal use. She discussed with LeRoy the likely behavioral effects of these changes. They agreed that identifying the different components of quality control costs should encourage continued investments that would be likely to improve the overall yield rate. Further, separately showing the effect of changes in inventory levels on profits would make it easier to reward efforts to reduce inventory levels. They also agreed on the need to closely monitor the effects of any new performance reports and make appropriate modifications to them.

Ann Brandt realized that Elizabeth's proposed changes would necessitate a redesign of AOE's production cycle database. In addition, the desire for more timely and accurate information would require additional investments in RFID technology to replace the use of bar codes wherever feasible.

Elizabeth and Ann presented their plans at the next executive meeting. LeRoy Williams was satisfied that the changes would indeed address his complaints about AOE's current production cycle information system. Linda Spurgeon supported the proposal and agreed to fund the necessary changes. She then told Elizabeth and Ann that their next task was to look at ways to improve AOE's HR and payroll process.

Key Terms

production cycle 406	production order 412	request for proposal (RFP)
bill of materials 410	materials requisition 412	417
operations list 410	move ticket 412	job-order costing 418
manufacturing resource	computer-integrated	process costing 418
planning (MRP-II) 411	manufacturing (CIM) 416	activity-based costing 420
lean manufacturing 411	job-time ticket 419	cost driver 421
master production schedule	manufacturing overhead 419	throughput 424
(MPS) 412		

AIS IN ACTION

Chapter Quiz

1. Most costs are locked in at which stage in the production cycle?
   a. product design
   b. production planning
   c. production operations
   d. cost accounting

2. Which of the following is an advantage of bar-coding over RFID?
   a. speed
   b. accuracy
   c. cost
   d. safety

3. Which document lists the components needed to manufacture a specific product?
   a. operations list
   b. master production schedule
   c. bill of materials
   d. production order

4. Which document captures information about labor used in production?
   a. move ticket
   b. job time ticket
   c. operations list
   d. bill of materials

5. An increase in which component of quality costs is most likely to result in a decrease in the other three components?
   a. prevention costs
   b. inspection costs
   c. internal failure costs
   d. external failure costs

6. Activity-based costing can be used to refine which of the following?
   a. job-order costing
   b. process costing
   c. both job-order and process costing
   d. neither job-order nor process costing

7. Which system is most likely to be used by a company that mass-produces large batches of standard items in anticipation of customer demand?
   a. MRP-II
   b. lean manufacturing
   c. activity-based costing
   d. throughput

8. The development of an MPS would be most effective in preventing which of the following threats?
   a. recording and posting errors
   b. loss of inventory
   c. production of poor-quality goods
   d. excess production

9. Which control procedure is probably *least* effective in reducing the threat of inventory loss?
   a. limiting physical access to inventory
   b. documenting all transfers of inventory within the company

   c. regular materials usage reports that highlight variances from standards
   d. periodically counting inventory and investigating any discrepancies between those counts
      and recorded amounts

10. What is the number of good units produced in a given period of time called?
    a. productive capacity   c. yield
    b. productive processing time   d. throughput

Discussion Questions

14.1. When activity-based cost reports indicate that excess capacity exists, management should
      either find alternative revenue-enhancing uses for that capacity or eliminate it through
      downsizing. What factors influence management's decision? What are the likely behav-
      ioral side effects of each choice? What implications do those side effects have for the
      long-run usefulness of activity-based cost systems?

14.2. Why should accountants participate in product design? What insights about costs can
      accountants contribute that differ from the perspectives of purchasing managers and
      engineers?

14.3. Some companies have eliminated the collection and reporting of detailed analyses on
      direct labor costs broken down by various activities. Instead, first-line supervisors are
      responsible for controlling the total costs of direct labor. The justification for this argu-
      ment is that labor costs represent only a small fraction of the total costs of producing a
      product and are not worth the time and effort to trace to individual activities. Do you
      agree or disagree with this argument? Why?

14.4. Typically, McDonald's produces menu items in advance of customer orders based on
      anticipated demand. In contrast, Burger King produces menu items only in response to
      customer orders. Which system (MRP-II or lean manufacturing) does each company use?
      What are the relative advantages and disadvantages of each system?

14.5. Some companies have switched from a "management by exception" philosophy to a
      "continuous improvement" viewpoint. The change is subtle, but significant. Continuous
      improvement focuses on comparing actual performance to the ideal (i.e., perfection).
      Consequently, all variances are negative (how can you do better than perfect?). The
      largest variances indicate the areas with the greatest amount of "waste," and, correspond-
      ingly, the greatest opportunity for improving the bottom line. What are the advantages
      and disadvantages of this practice?

Problems

14.1. Match the terms in the left column with their definitions from the right column:

_____ 1. Bill of materials   a. A factor that causes costs to change

_____ 2. Operations list   b. A measure of the number of good units produced in a
                                        period of time

_____ 3. Master production   c. A list of the raw materials used to create a finished
         schedule   product

_____ 4. Lean manufacturing   d. A document used to authorize removal of raw materials
                                        from inventory

_____ 5. Production order   e. A cost accounting method that assigns costs to products
                                        based on specific processes performed

_____ 6. Materials requisition   f. A cost accounting method that assigns costs to specific
                                        batches or production runs and is used when the product
                                        or service consists of uniquely identifiable items

_____ 7. Move ticket

    g. A cost accounting method that assigns costs to each step or work center and then calculates the average cost for all products that passed through that step or work center

_____ 8. Job-time ticket

    h. A document that records labor costs associated with manufacturing a product

_____ 9. Job-order costing

    i. A document that tracks transfer of inventory from one work center to another

_____10. Cost driver

    j. A document that authorizes manufacture of a finished good

_____11. Throughput

    k. A document that lists the steps required to manufacture a finished good

_____12. Computer-integrated manufacturing

    l. A document that specifies how much of a finished good is to be produced during a specific time period

    m. A production planning technique that is an extension of the just-in-time inventory control method

    n. A production planning technique that is an extension of the materials requirement planning inventory control method

    o. A term used to refer to the use of robots and other IT techniques as part of the production process

14.2. What internal control procedure(s) would best prevent or detect the following problems?

a. A production order was initiated for a product that was already overstocked in the company's warehouse.

b. A production employee stole items of work-in-process inventory.

c. The "rush-order" tag on a partially completed production job became detached from the materials and lost, resulting in a costly delay.

d. A production employee entered a materials requisition form into the system in order to steal $300 worth of parts from the raw materials storeroom.

e. A production worker entering job-time data on an online terminal mistakenly entered 3,000 instead of 300 in the "quantity-completed" field.

f. A production worker entering job-time data on an online terminal mistakenly posted the completion of operation 562 to production order 7569 instead of production order 7596.

g. A parts storeroom clerk issued parts in quantities 10% lower than those indicated on several materials requisitions and stole the excess quantities.

h. A production manager stole several expensive machines and covered up the loss by submitting a form to the accounting department indicating that the missing machines were obsolete and should be written off as worthless.

i. The quantity-on-hand balance for a key component shows a negative balance.

j. A factory supervisor accessed the operations list file and inflated the standards for work completed in his department. Consequently, future performance reports show favorable budget variances for that department.

k. A factory supervisor wrote off a robotic assembly machine as being sold for salvage but actually sold the machine and pocketed the proceeds.

l. Overproduction of a slow-moving product resulted in excessive inventory that had to eventually be marked down and sold at a loss.

14.3. Use Table 14-1 to create a questionnaire checklist that can be used to evaluate controls for each of the basic activities in the production cycle (product design, planning and scheduling, production operations, and cost accounting).

Required

a. For each control issue, write a Yes/No question such that a "No" answer represents a control weakness.

b. For each Yes/No question, write a brief explanation of why a "No" answer represents a control weakness.

14.4. You have recently been hired as the controller for a small manufacturing firm that makes high-definition televisions. One of your first tasks is to develop a report measuring throughput.

Required

Describe the data required to measure throughput and the most efficient and accurate method of collecting that data.

14.5. The Joseph Brant Manufacturing Company makes athletic footwear. Processing of production orders is as follows: At the end of each week, the production planning department prepares a master production schedule (MPS) that lists which shoe styles and quantities are to be produced during the next week. A production order preparation program accesses the MPS and the operations list (stored on a permanent disk file) to prepare a production order for each shoe style that is to be manufactured. Each new production order is added to the open production order master file stored on disk.

Each day, parts department clerks review the open production orders and the MPS to determine which materials need to be released to production. All materials are bar-coded. Factory workers work individually at specially designed U-shaped work areas equipped with several machines to assist them in completely making a pair of shoes. Factory workers scan the bar codes as they use materials. To operate a machine, the factory workers swipe their ID badge through a reader. This results in the system automatically collecting data identifying who produced each pair of shoes and how much time it took to make them.

Once a pair of shoes is finished, it is placed in a box. The last machine in each work cell prints a bar-code label that the worker affixes to the box. The completed shoes are then sent to the warehouse.

Required

a. Prepare a data flow diagram of all operations described.
b. What control procedures should be included in the system?

14.6. The XYZ Company's current production processes have a scrap rate of 15% and a return rate of 3%. Scrap costs (wasted materials) are $12 per unit; warranty/repair costs average $60 per unit returned. The company is considering the following alternatives to improve its production processes:

- Option A: Invest $400,000 in new equipment. The new process will also require an additional $1.50 of raw materials per unit produced. This option is predicted to reduce both scrap return rates by 40% from current levels.
- Option B: Invest $50,000 in new equipment, but spend an additional $3.20 on higher-quality raw materials per unit produced. This option is predicted to reduce both scrap and return rates by 90% from current levels.
- Option C: Invest $2 million in new equipment. The new process will require no change in raw materials. This option is predicted to reduce both scrap and return rates by 50% from current levels.

Required

a. Assume that current production levels of 1 million units will continue. Which option do you recommend? Why?
b. Assume that all of the proposed changes will increase product quality such that production will jump to 1.5 million units. Which option do you recommend? Why?

 14.7. Excel Problem

Required

a. Create the following spreadsheet (next page):

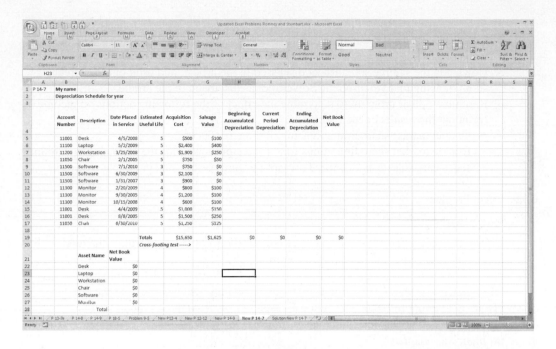

b. Create formulas to calculate the following:
   - Accumulated depreciation (all assets use the straight-line method; all assets acquired any time during the year get a full year's initial depreciation)
   - Current year's depreciation (straight-line method, full amount for initial year in which asset acquired)
   - Ending accumulated depreciation
   - Net book value at end of period
   - Current year in the cell to the right of the phrase "Depreciation schedule for year"
   - Column totals for acquisition cost, beginning depreciation, current depreciation, ending accumulated depreciation, net book value
   - In the cell to the right of the arrow following the text "Cross-footing test," create a formula that checks whether the sum of the net book value column equals the sum of acquisition costs minus the sum of ending accumulated depreciation. If the two values match, the formula should display the text "Okay"; otherwise, it should display the text "Error."

c. Create a table at the bottom of your worksheet that consists of two columns: (1) asset name (values should be chair, desk, laptop, monitor, software, and workstation); and (2) net book value (create a formula to calculate this number), assuming that the current date is 06/30/2011. Then:
   - Create a formula that sums the total net book values for all classes of assets.
   - In the cell to the right of the total net book values for all asset classes, create a formula that compares the total net book values for all classes of assets to the sum of all net book values in the top portion of the spreadsheet. The formula should return "Okay" if the two totals match or "Error: Sum of net book values by asset class does not equal sum of all net book values" if the two totals do not equal one another.

d. Enter your name in row 1 in the cell to the right of the text "Name."

14.8. Excel Problem

Task: Use Excel and the Solver add-in to explore the effect of various resource constraints on the optimal product mix.

a. Read the article "Boost Profits With Excel," by James A. Weisel in the December 2003 issue of the *Journal of Accountancy* (available online at the AICPA's Web site, www. aicpa.org).

b. Download the sample spreadsheet discussed in the article, and print out the screen-shots showing that you used the Solver tool as discussed in the article.

c. Rerun the Solver program to determine the effect of the following actions on income (print out the results of each option):
   • Double market share limitations for all three products
   • Double market share limitations for all three products plus the following constraint: sauce case sales cannot exceed 50% of the sum of soup and casserole case sales

14.9. Excel Problem

Required

Create the spreadsheet shown in Figure 14-11. Write formulas to calculate the total depreciation expense and to display the correct values in the following three columns: Age, Depreciation Rate, and Depreciation Expense. (*Hint*: You will need to use the VLOOKUP and MATCH functions to do this. You may also want to read the article "Double-Teaming In Excel," by Judith K. Welch, Lois S. Mahoney, and Daniel R. Brickner, in the November 2005 issue of the *Journal of Accountancy*, from which this problem was adapted.)

FIGURE 14-11

Spreadsheet for Problem 14-9

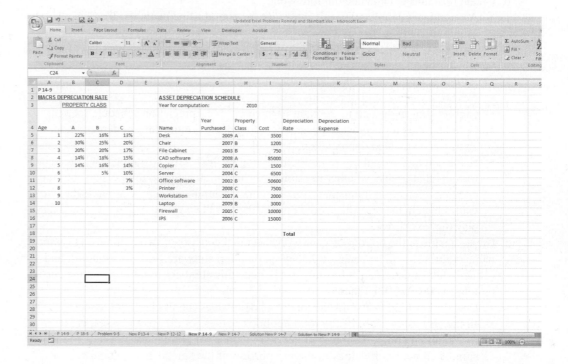

Case 14-1 The Accountant and CIM

Examine issues of the *Journal of Accountancy*, *Strategic Finance*, and other business magazines for the past three years to find stories about current developments in factory automation. Write a brief report that discusses the accounting implications of one development: how it affects the efficiency and accuracy of data collection and any new opportunities for improving the quality of performance reports. Also discuss how the development affects the risks of various production cycle threats and the control procedures used to mitigate those risks.

AIS IN ACTION SOLUTIONS

Quiz Key

1. Most costs are locked in at which stage in the production cycle?
   ▶ a. product design (Correct. Decisions made during product design determine the majority of costs.)
   b. production planning (Incorrect. Decisions made during product design determine the majority of costs.)
   c. production operations (Incorrect. Decisions made during product design determine the majority of costs.)
   d. cost accounting (Incorrect. Decisions made during product design determine the majority of costs.)

2. Which of the following is an advantage of bar-coding over RFID?
   a. speed (Incorrect. RFID technology can read information from multiple items at the same time, whereas bar-code scanners can read only one item at a time. In addition, employees spend time aligning the bar codes on each item with the reader.)
   b. accuracy (Incorrect. In certain applications, RFID is more accurate than bar-coding. For example, in retail stores, when checking out items that are similar but not identical—for example, different flavors of soda—clerks frequently enter the bar code for one item and then enter a quantity of, say, 7, rather than scanning the bar codes of each item; an RFID reader, in contrast, would identify which seven specific products were sold.)
   ▶ c. cost (Correct. Bar-coding is currently less expensive than RFID.)
   d. safety (Incorrect. There is no difference in the safety of bar-coding and RFID.)

3. Which document lists the components needed to manufacture a specific product?
   a. operations list (Incorrect. This document lists the sequence of steps to manufacture the product.)
   b. master production schedule (Incorrect. This document is used to plan production activities.)
   ▶ c. bill of materials (Correct. The bill of materials lists the components of a finished product.)
   d. production order (Incorrect. This document authorizes production activities.)

4. Which document captures information about labor used in production?
   a. move ticket (Incorrect. The move ticket documents movement of materials.)
   ▶ b. job-time ticket (Correct. The job-time ticket records time spent on each activity.)
   c. operations list (Incorrect. The operations list specifies the sequence of steps to manufacture a product.)
   d. bill of materials (Incorrect. The bill of materials identifies the components used to manufacture a product.)

5. An increase in which component of quality costs is most likely to result in a decrease in the other three components?

   ▶ a. prevention costs (Correct. Increases in prevention costs often reduce the time and cost of inspecting products, as well as the proportion of defective products.)

   b. inspection costs (Incorrect. Increases in inspection costs do not necessarily reduce the other three quality control costs.)

   c. internal failure costs (Incorrect. Increases in internal failure costs do not have any effect on prevention or inspection costs.)

   d. external failure costs (Incorrect. Increases in external failure costs do not reduce other components of quality costs.)

6. Activity-based costing can be used to refine which of the following?

   a. job-order costing (Incorrect. Activity-based costing can be used with either job-order or process costing.)

   b. process costing (Incorrect. Activity-based costing can be used with either job-order or process costing.)

   ▶ c. both job-order and process costing (Correct. Activity-based costing can be used with either job-order or process costing.)

   d. neither job-order nor process costing (Incorrect. Activity-based costing can be used with either job-order or process costing.)

7. Which system is most likely to be used by a company that mass-produces large batches of standard items in anticipation of customer demand?

   ▶ a. MRP-II (Correct. MRP-II is a push form of manufacturing that is appropriate for mass production of standardized items for which demand is predictable.)

   b. lean manufacturing (Incorrect. Lean manufacturing seeks to minimize inventories by producing only in response to customer orders.)

   c. activity-based costing (Incorrect. Activity-based costing is a cost allocation system, not a production planning technique.)

   d. throughput (Incorrect. Throughput is a measure of efficiency.)

8. The development of an MPS would be most effective in preventing which of the following threats?

   a. recording and posting errors (Incorrect. Data validation and processing controls would best minimize recording and posting errors.)

   b. loss of inventory (Incorrect. Access controls and frequent physical counts of inventory would best reduce the risk of inventory theft.)

   c. production of poor-quality goods (Incorrect. Product design addresses this issue.)

   ▶ d. excess production (Correct. An MPS schedules production to satisfy demand and, therefore, reduces the chance of overproduction.)

9. Which control procedure is probably *least* effective in reducing the threat of inventory loss?

   a. limiting physical access to inventory (Incorrect. Physical access controls are an important method for reducing the risk of inventory theft.)

   b. documenting all transfers of inventory within the company (Incorrect. Adequate documentation is an important control to reduce the risk of inventory theft.)

   ▶ c. regular materials usage reports that highlight variances from standards (Correct. Although variances could indicate theft, they are more likely to reflect changes in efficiency.)

   d. periodically counting inventory and investigating any discrepancies between those counts and recorded amounts (Incorrect. Periodic counts of inventory are an important control for reducing the risk of inventory theft.)

10. What is the number of good units produced in a given period of time called?
    a. productive capacity (Incorrect. Productive capacity is a component of throughput that represents the total number of units, both good and bad, produced per unit of time.)
    b. productive processing time (Incorrect. Productive processing time is the component of throughput that measures the proportion of time actually spent producing output.)
    c. yield (Incorrect. Yield is the component of throughput that measures the proportion of good units produced per batch.)
    ▶ d. throughput (Correct. Throughput is the measure of the number of good units produced per unit of time.)

Chapter 15

The Human Resources Management and Payroll Cycle

Learning Objectives

After studying this chapter, you should be able to:

1. Describe the major business activities and related information processing operations performed in the human resources management (HRM)/payroll cycle.

2. Discuss the key decisions to be made in the HRM/payroll cycle and identify the information needed to make those decisions.

3. Identify the major threats in the HRM/payroll cycle and evaluate the adequacy of various internal control procedures for dealing with them.

INTEGRATIVE CASE ALPHA OMEGA ELECTRONICS

Like many companies, AOE did not fully implement all modules of its new enterprise resource planning (ERP) system at the same time. It focused first on integrating the revenue and expenditure cycles with the production cycle while continuing to use its existing payroll and HRM systems. Thus, like many companies, AOE currently has separate HRM and payroll systems. The payroll system, which is under the accounting department's control, produces employee paychecks and maintains the related records as required by government regulations. The payroll system uses batch processing: Hourly employees are paid biweekly; salaried employees and those on commission are paid monthly. The HRM system, which the human resources department runs, maintains files on employee job history, skills, and benefits; these files are updated weekly. Each system maintains its own separate files, sometimes storing the same data, such as pay rates, in different formats. This practice makes it difficult for accounting personnel to prepare reports that combine HRM and payroll data.

Peter Wu, the new vice president for human resources at AOE, wants to address several problems with AOE's payroll and HRM activities. Payroll processing costs have

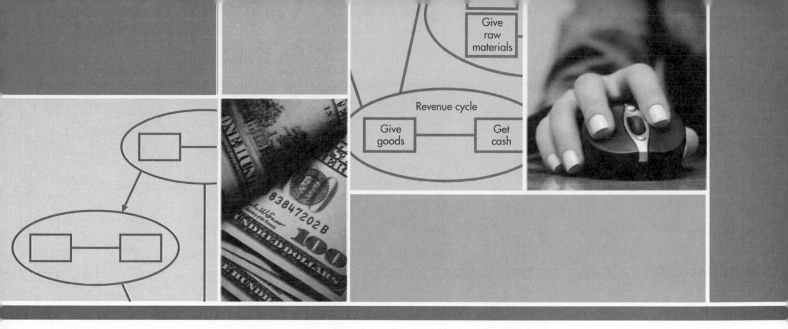

risen, and employees are unhappy with the lengthy delays required to obtain information about their benefits and retirement plans. In addition, the current HRM system makes it difficult to accurately track employee skill development, which impedes evaluating the effectiveness of AOE's investment in training and continuing education. Consequently, employees find it difficult and time-consuming to obtain approval to attend professional training classes. In addition, managers have tended to hire externally to meet new staffing needs, rather than promoting or transferring existing employees. These practices have hurt employee morale. Peter thinks that implementing the payroll and HRM modules of the ERP system will solve these problems.

Peter meets with Elizabeth Venko and Ann Brandt to discuss the process of migrating from AOE's current stand-alone payroll and HRM systems to integration of those functions in the new ERP system. Elizabeth and Ann agree that such a conversion would improve both the efficiency of payroll processing and the effectiveness of HR management. They begin developing a detailed timetable for the system conversions. As you read this chapter, think about the relationships between HRM and payroll activities and how an integrated database can make both functions more efficient and effective.

Introduction

The *human resources management (HRM)/payroll cycle* is a recurring set of business activities and related data processing operations associated with effectively managing the employee workforce. The more important tasks include the following:

1. Recruiting and hiring new employees
2. Training
3. Job assignment
4. Compensation (payroll)
5. Performance evaluation
6. Discharge of employees due to voluntary or involuntary termination

Tasks 1 and 6 are performed only once for each employee, whereas tasks 2 through 5 are performed repeatedly for as long as an employee works for the company. In most companies, these six activities are split between two separate systems. Task 4, compensating employees, is the

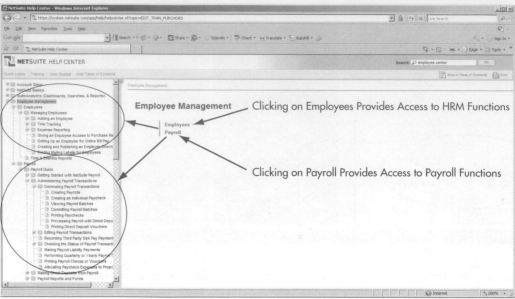

© 2010 NetSuite, Inc.

payroll system's primary function. (In addition, as discussed in Chapter 14, the payroll system also allocates labor costs to products and departments for use in product pricing and mix decisions.) The HRM system performs the other five tasks. In many companies, these two systems are organizationally separate: The HRM system is usually the responsibility of the director of human resources, whereas the controller manages the payroll system. However, as Figure 15-1 shows, ERP systems integrate the two sets of activities.

This chapter focuses primarily on the payroll system, because accountants have traditionally been responsible for this function. We begin by describing the design of the integrated HRM/payroll system and discuss the basic controls necessary to ensure that it provides management with reliable information and complies with government regulations. We then describe in detail each of the basic payroll cycle activities. We conclude with a discussion of options for outsourcing both payroll and HRM functions.

HRM/Payroll Cycle Information System

Figure 15-2 depicts the portion of an ERP system that supports the HRM/payroll cycle. The HRM-related activities (information about hiring, firing, transfers, training, etc.) and the collection of information about the use of employee time occur daily. The actual processing of payroll, however, occurs only periodically because in most organizations employees are paid on a weekly, biweekly, or monthly basis rather than every day. Thus, payroll is one application that continues to be processed in batch mode.

Overview of HRM Process and Information Needs

Organizational success depends on skilled and motivated employees because their knowledge and skills affect the quality of the goods and services provided to customers. Indeed, in professional service organizations, such as accounting and law firms, employees' knowledge and skills *are* the principal component of the company's product, and labor costs represent the major expense incurred in generating revenues. Even in manufacturing firms, where direct labor costs represent only a fraction of total direct costs, employees are a key cost driver in that the quality of their work affects both overall productivity and product defect rates. Thus, it is not surprising to find that some stock analysts believe that employee skills and knowledge may be worth several times the value of a company's tangible assets such as inventory, property, and equipment.

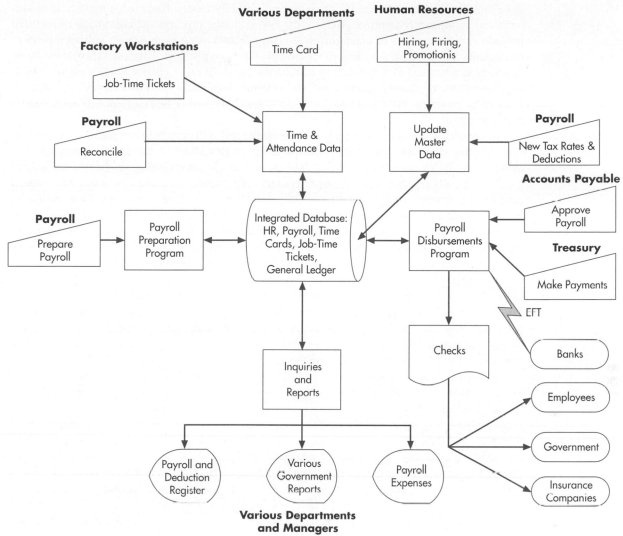

FIGURE 15-2

Portion of ERP System That Supports Human Resources Management and Payroll

To effectively utilize the organization's employees, the HRM/payroll system must collect and store the information managers need to answer the following kinds of questions:

- How many employees does the organization need to accomplish its strategic plans?
- Which employees possess specific skills?
- Which skills are in short supply? Which skills are in oversupply?
- How effective are current training programs in maintaining and improving employee skill levels?
- Is overall performance improving or declining?
- Are there problems with turnover, tardiness, or absenteeism?

The HRM/payroll master database (Figure 15-2) provides some of the information needed to answer those questions. However, it typically contains only descriptive information, such as which employees possess which skills and who has attended various training programs. Although such information enables managers to make staffing-related decisions, it does not help leverage the specific knowledge and expertise possessed by its employees.

To more effectively use employees' knowledge and skills, many organizations have invested in knowledge management systems. *Knowledge management systems* not only serve as a directory identifying the areas of expertise possessed by individual employees, but also capture and store that knowledge so that it can be shared and used by others. Knowledge management systems can significantly improve productivity. For example, professional consulting firms often provide similar services to many different clients. Knowledge management software enables consultants to store their solutions to specific problems in a shared database. Oftentimes, those solutions can be used as a template to address the needs of other clients. Such reuse of knowledge saves time on future engagements. Access to the shared database also enables employees to learn from geographically dispersed colleagues who have had prior experience in addressing a particular issue.

Recognizing the value of employees' knowledge and skills can help companies better understand the true costs associated with excessive turnover. In addition to the direct expenses associated with the hiring process (advertising, background checks, interviewing candidates, etc.), there are also the costs associated with hiring temporary help, training new employees, and the reduced productivity of new employees until they fully learn how to perform their tasks. Thus, estimates place the total costs to replace an employee at about 1.5 times the annual salary. Consequently, organizations that experience below-industry-average turnover rates reap considerable cost savings compared to rivals with higher turnover rates. For example, consider two companies, each with 1,500 employees earning on average $40,000. One company experiences 20% annual turnover, the other only 5%. The company with 20% annual turnover would incur costs of $18 million (300 employees times $60,000) to replace employees, compared to only $4.5 million for the company experiencing only 5% annual turnover. Of course, some turnover will always occur and may even be desirable. For example, professional consulting organizations have traditionally encouraged some level of turnover because they believe it provides an important source of new ideas. The key is to control and manage turnover rates so that they are not excessive.

Employee morale is also important. Low employee morale creates financial costs when it results in turnover. Conversely, there is increasing evidence that high employee morale provides financial benefits. For example, Sears collected detailed data on employee satisfaction, actual behavior, and customer satisfaction. Statistical analysis revealed that employee attitudes about their jobs and the company significantly predicted how they behaved with customers, which in turn affected customer satisfaction as measured by repeat sales. Sears' results are not isolated; research has found a positive correlation between employee attitudes and financial performance, particularly in highly competitive industries[1]. Thus, it is not surprising that many companies are monitoring employee attitudes. Focus 15-1 describes some of the methods companies use to better understand employees' job-related concerns and how they use that information to improve working conditions and morale.

Threats and Controls

Figure 15-2 shows that all HRM/payroll cycle activities depend on the integrated database that contains information about employees, payroll, and use of employee time. Therefore, the first general threat listed in Table 15-1 is inaccurate or invalid master data. Inaccurate employee master data could result in over- or understaffing. It can also create inefficiencies due to assigning employees to perform tasks for which they are not fully qualified. Inaccurate payroll master data that results in errors in paying employees can create significant morale issues. In addition, the organization may incur fines for errors made in paying payroll taxes. Errors in data about use of employee time can result in inaccurate performance evaluations and mistakes in calculating the costs of the organization's products and services.

One way to mitigate the threat of inaccurate or invalid master data is to use the various processing integrity controls discussed in Chapter 10 to minimize the risk of data input errors. It is also important to restrict access to that data and configure the system so that only authorized employees can make changes to master data. This requires changing the default configurations of employee roles in ERP systems to appropriately segregate incompatible duties. For example, consider the situation where a payroll clerk types in the name of an employee who is not currently in the database. The default configurations of most integrated ERP systems would respond by asking

[1] Alex Edmans, "Does the Stock Market Fully Value Intangibles? Employee Satisfaction and Equity Prices," (June 2010), SSRN.com/abstract=985735; Rajiv D. Banker and Raj Mashruwala, "The Moderating Role of Competition in the Relationship between Nonfinancial Measures and Future Financial Performance," Contemporary Accounting Research (24:3, Fall 2007): pp. 763–793.

FOCUS 15-1 The Value of Understanding Employee Jobs and Attitudes

A growing number of companies, including Walt Disney, Continental Airlines, Sysco, and Amazon.com, periodically require some of their upper-level executives to spend time in the trenches to better understand job duties and pressures. The experience can help executives identify needed changes in working conditions. For example, when the CEO of Loews Hotels assumed the roles of bellman, pool attendant, and housekeeper at a Florida hotel, he found that the company's polyester uniform caused him to sweat profusely. He immediately ordered that the style and material be altered for all employees. Immersion experiences also enable top executives to better empathize with rank-and-file workers. For example, after the vice president of DaVita Inc., a major provider of dialysis treatment, spent three days working in one of the company's clinics, she understood how physically demanding and stressful the work is. She also personally experienced how the need to respond to life-threatening emergencies can result in delays in completing corporate-mandated reports. As a result of these experiences, the vice president now strives to ensure that new initiatives and changes in procedures are implemented in a manner that does not interfere with clinic technicians' primary patient care responsibilities.

Executive immersion experiences are important because there is a growing body of evidence that employees who have positive attitudes contribute to improved profitability by being more willing to take initiative, to step in when needed to help fulfill customer requests, and to promote the company when not at work. Thus, it is not surprising to find that many companies regularly survey employees to learn about their concerns. These new surveys replace traditional questions about job satisfaction with ones specially designed to better reveal employees' true attitudes about their job, coworkers, and managers. The answers can help managers take specific steps to improve employee morale and motivation. For example, such surveys informed the manager of a fast food franchise in Houston that some employees were unhappy because they were assigned too few hours to work but that others were unhappy because they had to work too many hours. The manager now makes a point to review work schedules for the following month early enough to accommodate employees' desires as much as possible. As with executive immersion experience, follow-through on such survey data is critical because if companies do not act on feedback obtained from employees by these methods, employee morale and performance drop sharply.

TABLE 15-1 Threats and Controls in the Payroll/HRM Cycle

Activity	Threat	Controls (first number refers to the corresponding threat)
General issues throughout entire HRM/ payroll cycle	1. Inaccurate or invalid master data 2. Unauthorized disclosure of sensitive information 3. Loss or destruction of data 4. Hiring unqualified or larcenous employees 5. Violations of employment laws	1.1 Data processing integrity controls 1.2 Restriction of access to master data 1.3 Review of all changes to master data 2.1 Access controls 2.2 Encryption 3.1 Backup and disaster recovery procedures 4.1 Sound hiring procedures, including verification of job applicants' credentials, skills, references, and employment history 4.2 Criminal background investigation checks of all applicants for finance-related positions 5.1 Thorough documentation of hiring, performance evaluation, and dismissal procedures 5.2 Continuing education on changes in employment laws
Update payroll master data	6. Unauthorized changes to payroll master data 7. Inaccurate updating of payroll master data	6.1 Segregation of duties: HRM department updates master data, but only payroll department issues paychecks 6.2 Access controls 7.1 Data processing integrity controls 7.2 Regular review of all changes to master payroll data
Validate time and attendance data	8. Inaccurate time and attendance data	8.1 Source data automation for data capture 8.2 Biometric authentication 8.3 Segregation of duties (reconciliation of job-time tickets to time cards) 8.4 Supervisory review

(Continued)

TABLE 15-1 (*Continued*)

Activity	Threat	Controls (first number refers to the corresponding threat)
Prepare payroll	9. Errors in processing payroll	9.1 Data processing integrity controls: batch totals, cross-footing of the payroll register, use of a payroll clearing account and a zero-balance check 9.2 Supervisory review of payroll register and other reports 9.3 Issuing earnings statements to employees 9.4 Review of IRS guidelines to ensure proper classification of workers as either employees or independent contractors
Disburse payroll	10. Theft or fraudulent distribution of paychecks	10.1 Restriction of physical access to blank payroll checks and the check signature machine 10.2 Restriction of access to the EFT system 10.3 Prenumbering and periodically accounting for all payroll checks and review of all EFT direct deposit transactions 10.4 Require proper supporting documentation for all paychecks 10.5 Use of a separate checking account for payroll, maintained as an imprest fund 10.6 Segregation of duties (cashier versus accounts payable; check distribution from hiring/firing; independent reconciliation of the payroll checking account) 10.7 Restriction of access to payroll master database 10.8 Verification of identity of all employees receiving paychecks 10.9 Redepositing unclaimed paychecks and investigating cause
Disburse payroll taxes and miscellaneous deductions	11. Failure to make required payments 12. Untimely payments 13. Inaccurate payments	11.1 Configuration of system to make required payments using current instructions from IRS (Publication Circular E) 12.1 Same as 11.1 13.1 Processing integrity controls 13.2 Supervisory review of reports 13.3 Employee review of earnings statement

whether the clerk wants to create a new employee record. This violates segregation of duties by permitting the person who does the recording (payroll) to also authorize the creation of new accounts. Similarly, the default configurations of many systems permit payroll staff not only to read but also to change the salary information in the employee payroll master file. These examples are just some of the many areas that the controller or CFO needs to review to ensure that various users are assigned only those privileges necessary to perform their specified job duties. Although the procedures for modifying configurations vary across different software packages, knowing what changes need to be made requires only a sound understanding of proper segregation of duties for different business processes. However, since such preventive controls can never be 100% effective, Table 15-1 also indicates that an important detective control is to regularly produce a report of all changes to master data and review them to verify that the database remains accurate.

A second general threat in the HRM/payroll cycle is unauthorized disclosure of sensitive information, such as salary and performance evaluations for individual employees. Such disclosures can create morale problems if employees learn that their pay differs significantly from coworkers. In addition, unauthorized disclosure of performance evaluations or reasons for firing an employee may subject the organization to lawsuits. The best control procedure for reducing the risk of unauthorized disclosure of payroll data is using multifactor authentication and physical security controls to restrict access to HRM/payroll master data to only those employees who need such access to perform their jobs. It is also important to configure the system to limit employees' ability to use the system's built-in query capabilities to indirectly infer sensitive information. For example, queries about salary averages should be allowed only if the query set is sufficiently large. Otherwise, someone could infer another employee's salary by writing a query that calculates the average salary for two people: the query writer and the employee of interest. Encrypting the database (control 2.2) provides additional protection by making the information unintelligible to anyone who succeeds in obtaining unauthorized access to the database. Encryption also prevents information technology (IT) employees who do not have access to the ERP system from using operating system utilities to view sensitive information.

A third general threat in the HRM/payroll cycle concerns the loss or destruction of master data. The best way to mitigate the risk of this threat is to employ the backup and disaster recovery procedures that were discussed in Chapter 10.

A fourth general threat in the HRM/payroll cycle is hiring unqualified or larcenous employees. Hiring unqualified employees can increase production expenses, and hiring a larcenous employee can result in the theft of assets. Both problems are best dealt with by appropriate hiring procedures. Skill qualifications for each open position should be stated explicitly in the position control report. Candidates should be asked to sign a statement on the job application form that confirms the accuracy of the information being submitted and provides their consent to a thorough background check of their credentials and employment history. Independent verification of an applicant's credentials is important because resumes often contain false or embellished information. For example, in November 2008 the *Wall Street Journal* reported a number of cases where resumes for senior executives at companies contained information that could not be verified. To reduce the risk of hiring larcenous employees, organizations should hire a professional firm to perform thorough background checks of all applicants for positions that involve access to financial data and assets, to identify applicants with a prior criminal record.

The fifth general threat in the HRM/payroll cycle is violation of applicable laws and regulations concerning the proper hiring and dismissal of employees. The government imposes stiff penalties on firms that violate provisions of employment law. In addition, organizations can also be subject to civil suits by alleged victims of employment discrimination. Table 15-1 shows that the best control procedure to mitigate these potential problems is to carefully document all actions relating to advertising for, recruiting, and hiring new employees and to the dismissal of employees; this will demonstrate compliance with the applicable government regulations. Continued training to keep current with employment law is also important.

Payroll Cycle Activities

Figure 15-3 presents a context diagram of the payroll system. It shows that there are five major sources of inputs to the payroll system. The HRM department provides information about hirings, terminations, and pay-rate changes due to raises and promotions. Employees initiate changes in their discretionary deductions (e.g., contributions to retirement plans). The various departments provide data about actual hours employees work. Government agencies provide tax rates and instructions for meeting regulatory requirements. Similarly, insurance companies and other organizations provide instructions for calculating and remitting various withholdings.

Figure 15-3 shows that checks (which may be electronic) are the payroll system's principal output. Employees receive individual *paychecks* in compensation for their services. A *payroll check* is sent to the bank to transfer funds from the company's regular accounts to its payroll account. Checks also are issued to government agencies, insurance companies, and other organizations to meet company obligations (e.g., taxes, insurance premiums). In addition, the payroll system produces a variety of reports, which we discuss later, for internal and external use.

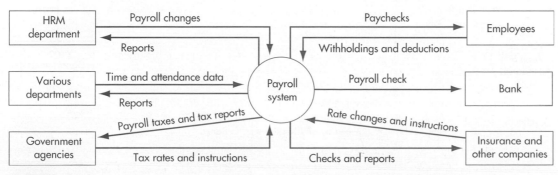

FIGURE 15-3

Context Diagram of the Payroll Portion of the HRM/Payroll Cycle

Figure 15-4 shows the basic activities performed in the payroll cycle. We now discuss each of those activities. For each activity, we describe how the information needed to perform and manage the activity is collected, processed, and stored. We also explain the controls necessary to ensure not only the reliability of that information but also the safeguarding of the organization's resources.

Update Payroll Master Database

The first activity in the HRM/payroll cycle involves updating the payroll master database to reflect various types of internally initiated changes: new hires, terminations, changes in pay rates, or changes in discretionary withholdings (circle 1.0 in Figure 15-4). In addition, periodically the master data needs to be updated to reflect changes in tax rates and deductions for insurance.

PROCESS   Figure 15-2 shows that the HRM department is responsible for updating the payroll master database for internally initiated changes related to employment, whereas the payroll department updates information about tax rates and other payroll deductions when it receives notification of changes from various government units and insurance companies. Although payroll is processed in batch mode, the HRM department has online access to update the payroll master database so that all payroll changes are entered in a timely manner and are properly reflected in the next pay period. Records of employees who quit or are fired should not be deleted immediately, however, because some year-end tax reports, including W-2 forms, require data about all employees who worked for the organization at any time during the year.

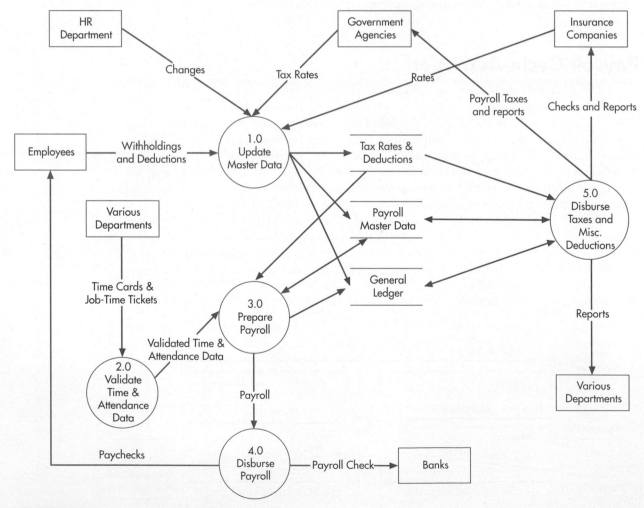

FIGURE 15-4
Level 0 Data Flow Diagram for the Payroll Cycle

THREATS AND CONTROLS   Unauthorized changes to payroll master data (threat 6 in Table 15-1) can result in increased expenses from unjustified payments to employees. Proper segregation of duties is the key control procedure for dealing with this threat. As shown in Figure 15-2, only the HRM department should be able to update the payroll master file for hirings, firings, pay raises, and promotions. HRM department employees in turn should not directly participate in payroll processing or paycheck distribution. This segregation of duties prevents someone with access to paychecks from creating fictitious employees or altering pay rates and then intercepting those fraudulent checks. In addition, all changes to the payroll master file should be reviewed and approved by someone other than the person recommending the change. To facilitate this review, the system should be configured to produce a report listing all payroll-related changes and send the report to each affected department supervisor for review.

Controlling access to the payroll system (control 6.2) is also important. The system should be configured to compare user IDs and passwords with an access control matrix that (1) defines what actions each employee is allowed to perform and (2) confirms what files each employee is allowed to access.

Another threat is inaccurate updating of payroll master data, which can result in errors in paying employees and fines for not remitting proper amounts of payroll taxes to the government. To mitigate this threat, appropriate processing integrity controls discussed in Chapter 10, such as validity checks on employee number and reasonableness tests for the changes being made, should be applied to all payroll change transactions. In addition, having department managers review reports of all changes to employees in their department provides a timely way to detect errors.

Validate Time and Attendance Data

The second step in the payroll cycle is to validate each employee's time and attendance data (circle 2.0 in Figure 15-4).

PROCESS   How employee time and attendance data is collected differs depending on the employee's pay status. For employees paid on an hourly basis, many companies use a *time card* to record the employee's daily arrival and departure times. Employees who earn a fixed salary (e.g., managers and professional staff) seldom record their labor efforts on time cards. Instead, their supervisors informally monitor their presence on the job.

As discussed in Chapter 14, manufacturing companies also use job-time tickets to record detailed data about how employees use their time (i.e., which jobs they perform). The job-time ticket data are used to allocate labor costs among various departments, cost centers, and production jobs. Professionals in such service organizations as accounting, law, and consulting firms similarly track the time they spend performing various tasks and for which clients, recording that data on *time sheets* (see Figure 15-5 for an example of a data entry screen to track time). Their employers use the time sheets to assign costs and accurately bill clients for services provided.

Sales staff often are paid either on a straight commission or on a salary plus commission basis. This requires the staff to carefully record the amount of their sales. In addition, some sales staff are paid bonuses for exceeding targets. An increasing number of companies in the United States are extending such incentive bonuses to employees other than sales staff, to motivate employees to improve their productivity and work quality. For example, Nucor Corporation, one of the largest steel producers in the United States, pays its steelworkers an hourly rate set at approximately 60% of the industry average, plus a bonus based on the tons of steel they produce and ship. Companies have long used stock options to reward executives; in recent years, many companies have extended this practice to their nonexecutive employees as well. The argument is that stock options motivate employees to actively look for ways to improve service and cut costs so that the value of their compensation package rises.

Using incentives, commissions, and bonuses requires linking the payroll system and the information systems of sales and other cycles to collect the data used to calculate bonuses. Moreover, the bonus/incentive schemes must be properly designed with realistic, attainable goals that can be objectively measured. It is also important that goals be congruent with corporate objectives and that managers monitor goals to ensure that they continue to be appropriate. Indeed, poorly designed incentive pay schemes can result in undesirable behavior. For example, Sears Automotive experienced unintended negative effects from implementing a new incentive plan in

© 2010 NetSuite, Inc.

the early 1990s that paid its repair staff a commission based on the amount of parts sold and number of hours worked. The intent was to focus employees' attention on how their efforts affected the company's bottom line. The result, however, was a scandal in which it was alleged that Sears employees recommended unnecessary repairs to boost their own pay. The alleged abuses reduced public trust in Sears Automotive and led to lower revenues. Although Sears discontinued use of this incentive system, it took years to fully regain the consumer trust it had lost. Besides the possibility of creating unintended and undesirable behaviors, poorly designed incentive pay schemes can also run afoul of legal, tax, and regulatory requirements. Thus, as Focus 15-2 explains, accountants should be involved in reviewing a company's compensation practices.

THREATS AND CONTROLS   The main threat to this payroll activity is inaccurate time and attendance data. Inaccuracies in time and attendance records can result in increased labor expenses and erroneous labor expense reports. Moreover, inaccuracies can either hurt employee morale (if paychecks are incorrect or missing) or result in payments for labor services not rendered.

Source data automation can reduce the risk of *unintentional* errors in collecting time and attendance data. For example, badge readers can be used to collect job-time data for production employees and automatically feed the data to the payroll processing system. Using technology to capture time and attendance data can also improve productivity and cut costs. For example, the retail chain Meijer, Inc., installed fingerprint readers at its cash registers so that employees could log in and immediately begin working. The company estimates that this eliminated several minutes of wasted time spent walking from the time clock in the back of the store to the register. Saving a few minutes per employee may not sound dramatic, but when multiplied across thousands of employees in an industry with a profit margin of less than 1%, the effect on the bottom line can be significant. Source data automation can also be used to collect time and attendance data for professional service staff. For example, AT&T's internal service staff uses touch-tone telephones to log in time spent on various tasks, thereby eliminating the use of paper time sheets. Various data processing integrity checks discussed in Chapter 10, such as a limit check on hours worked and a validity check on employee number, ensure the accuracy of that information.

Information technology can also reduce the risk of *intentional* inaccuracies in time and attendance data. For example, some manufacturing companies now use biometric authentication techniques (control 8.2), such as hand scans, to verify the identity of the employee who is clocking in and out of work. The objective is to prevent an employee from leaving work early but having a friend falsely record that person as being at work. Segregation of duties is also important. Time card data, used for calculating payroll, should be reconciled to the job-time ticket data, used for

FOCUS 15-2   Accountants and Compensation Policies

Recent revelations of multimillion-dollar bonuses and large severance packages for top executives of companies with declining financial performance have created the impression that some top executives are more concerned about their own compensation than shareholders' interests. As a result, regulators and Congress have begun to scrutinize executive compensation practices more closely. In particular, the use of stock options attracted a great deal of attention. The Financial Accounting Standards Board (FASB) issued new rules requiring that stock options be expensed, and the major U.S. stock exchanges now require companies to obtain shareholder approval of all equity-based compensation.

In the past, top executives often were involved indirectly in crafting their own compensation packages by hiring the consultants who designed those packages. Now, in response to recent scandals, the role of board compensation committees is increasing. Accountants can help these committees improve their company's compensation plans by providing advice concerning the financial and tax effects of proposed changes in executive compensation. One area where accounting expertise can be especially helpful is in identifying the

appropriate metrics to use when linking compensation to performance. To be useful, those metrics need to be linked to the factors most important to a particular company's success. Obviously, this varies from company to company. For example, the key measures for a retail organization such as Walmart or Home Depot will be different from those used by an insurance company such as Prudential, which will differ from those that are important to a basic manufacturer such as Alcoa.

Accountants can also help board compensation committees comply with legal and regulatory requirements. For example, members of compensation committees may not understand all the details of tax regulations, such as the Employee Retirement Income Security Act (ERISA), which limit the allowable differences between benefit packages offered to executives and those made available to other employees. Accountants can review proposed changes for compliance with such rules. Finally, accountants can help companies improve shareholder relations by suggesting the best ways to go beyond minimum disclosure rules concerning executive compensation without revealing information vital to continued competitive success.

costing and managerial purposes, by someone not involved in generating that data. The total time spent on all tasks, as recorded on the job-time tickets, should not exceed the attendance time indicated on an employee's time card. Conversely, all time spent at work should be accounted for on the job-time tickets.

In addition, requiring departmental supervisors to review and approve time cards and job-time tickets (see Figure 15-6, which illustrates one way to implement control 8.4) provides a

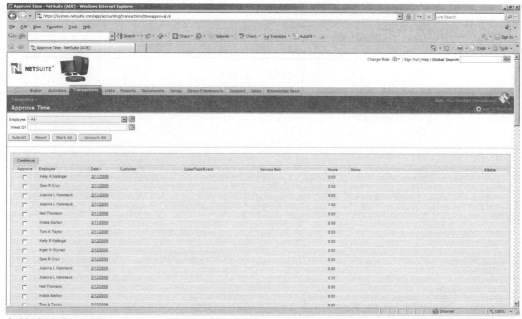

FIGURE 15-6

Example of Supervisory Approval of Time Worked Screen

detective control on the accuracy of time and attendance data. Supervisory review is particularly important for employees who telecommute. Analysis of system logs can provide assurance that telecommuters are truly working the amount of time for which they are getting paid and that they are not operating a personal business on the side, using company-provided assets.

Prepare Payroll

The third step in the payroll cycle is preparing payroll (circle 3.0 in Figure 15-4).

PROCESS   Figure 15-7 shows the sequence of activities in processing payroll. First, payroll transaction data is edited, and the validated transactions are then sorted by employee number. If the organization is processing payrolls from several divisions, each of these payroll transaction files must also be merged. The sorted payroll transactions file is then used to prepare employee paychecks. For each employee, the payroll master file record and corresponding transaction record are read, and gross pay is calculated. For hourly employees, the number of hours worked is multiplied by the wage rate, and then any applicable premiums for overtime or bonuses are

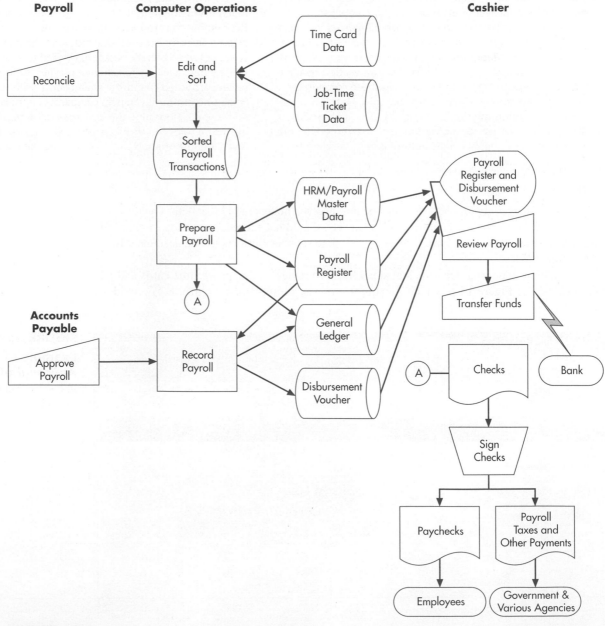

FIGURE 15-7
Flowchart of Payroll Batch Processing

added. For salaried employees, gross pay is a fraction of the annual salary, where the fraction reflects the length of the pay period. For example, salaried employees paid monthly would receive one-twelfth of their annual salary each pay period. Any applicable commissions, bonuses, and other incentives are also included in calculating gross pay.

Next, all payroll deductions are summed, and the total is subtracted from gross pay to obtain net pay. Payroll deductions fall into two broad categories: payroll tax withholdings and voluntary deductions. The former includes federal, state, and local income taxes, as well as Social Security taxes. Voluntary deductions include contributions to a pension plan; premiums for group life, health, and disability insurance; union dues; and contributions to various charities.

Once net pay is calculated, the year-to-date fields for gross pay, deductions, and net pay in each employee's record in the payroll master file are updated. Maintaining accurate cumulative earnings records is important for two reasons. First, because Social Security tax withholdings and other deductions have cutoffs, the company must know when to cease deductions for individual employees. Second, this information is needed to ensure that the appropriate amounts of taxes and other deductions are remitted to government agencies, insurance companies, and other organizations (such as the United Way). This information also must be included in the various reports filed with those agencies.

Next, the payroll and deduction registers are created. The *payroll register* lists each employee's gross pay, payroll deductions, and net pay in a multicolumn format. It also serves as the supporting documentation to authorize transferring funds to the organization's payroll check ing account. The *deduction register* lists the miscellaneous voluntary deductions for each employee. Figure 15-8 presents examples of these two reports.

Finally, the system prints employee paychecks (or facsimiles, in the case of direct deposit). These also typically include an *earnings statement,* which lists the amount of gross pay, deductions, and net pay for the current period and year-to-date totals for each category.

As each payroll transaction is processed, the system also allocates labor costs to the appropriate general ledger accounts by checking the code on the job-time ticket record. The system maintains a running total of these allocations until all employee payroll records have been processed. These totals, and the column totals in the payroll register, form the basis for the summary journal entry, which is posted to the general ledger after all paychecks have been printed.

The payroll system also produces a number of detailed reports. Table 15-2 describes the content of the most common reports. Some of these are for internal use, but many are required by various government agencies. Consequently, as Figure 15-9 shows, the HRM/payroll portion of ERP systems provides extensive support for meeting the reporting requirements of federal, state, and local governments.

Alpha Omega Electronics				PAYROLL REGISTER				Period Ended 12/03/2011		
					Deductions					
Employee No.	Name	Hours	Pay Rate	Gross Pay	Fed. Tax	FICA	State Tax	Misc.	Net Pay
37884	Jarvis	40.0	6.25	250.00	35.60	18.75	16.25	27.60	151.80
37885	Burke	43.6	6.50	295.10	42.40	22.13	19.18	40.15	171.24
37886	Lincoln	40.0	6.75	270.00	39.20	20.25	17.55	27.90	165.10
37887	Douglass	44.2	7.00	324.10	46.60	24.31	21.07	29.62	202.50

Alpha Omega Electronics				DEDUCTION REGISTER			Period Ended 12/03/2011	
		Miscellaneous Deductions						
Employee No.	Name	Health Ins.	Life Ins.	Retirement	Union Dues	Savings Bond	Total Misc.
37884	Jarvis	10.40	5.50	7.50	4.20	0.00	27.60
37885	Burke	11.60	5.50	8.85	4.20	10.00	40.15
37886	Lincoln	10.40	5.20	8.10	4.20	0.00	27.90
37887	Douglass	10.20	5.50	9.72	4.20	0.00	29.62

FIGURE 15-8

Examples of Payroll and Deduction Registers

TABLE 15-2 Contents and Purpose of Commonly Generated HRM/Payroll Reports

Report Name	Contents	Purpose
Cumulative earnings register	Cumulative year-to-date gross pay, net pay, and deductions for each employee	Used for employee information and annual payroll reports
Workforce inventory	List of employees by department	Used in preparing labor-related reports for government agencies
Position control report	List of each authorized position, job qualifications, budgeted salary, and position status (filled or vacant)	Used in planning future workforce needs
Skills inventory report	List of employees and current skills	Useful in planning future workforce needs and training programs
Form 941	Employer's quarterly federal tax return (showing all wages subject to tax and amounts withheld for income tax and FICA)	Filed quarterly to reconcile monthly tax payments with total tax liability for the quarter
Form W-2	Report of wages and withholdings for each employee	Sent to each employee for use in preparing individual tax returns; due by January 31
Form W-3	Summary of all W-2 forms	Sent to federal government along with a copy of all W-2 forms; due by February 28
Form 1099-Misc.	Report of income paid to independent contractors	Sent to recipients of income for use in filing their income tax returns; due by January 31
Various other reports to government agencies	Data on compliance with various regulatory provisions, state and local tax reports, etc.	To document compliance with applicable regulations

FIGURE 15-9

Screenshot Showing Typical ERP System Support for Payroll-Related Reports Required for Federal, State, and Local Governments

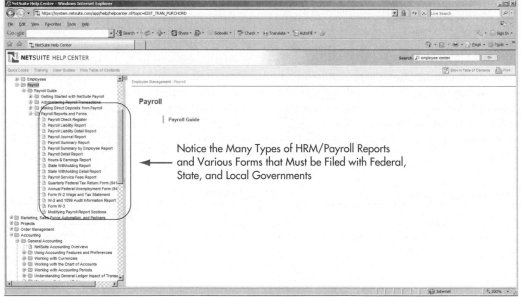

© 2010 NetSuite, Inc.

THREATS AND CONTROLS   The complexity of payroll processing, especially the various tax law requirements, makes it susceptible to errors (threat 9 in Table 15-1). Errors obviously can hurt employee morale, particularly if paychecks are late. In addition to incorrect payroll expense records and reports, processing errors can lead to penalties if the errors result in failure to remit the proper amount of payroll taxes due the government. Similarly, failure to accurately accurately garnishments on employees' wages and remit those funds to the appropriate party can also lead to financial penalties.

Table 15-1 lists three types of data processing integrity controls that can mitigate the threat of payroll errors:

1. *Batch totals.*   Even advanced HRM/payroll systems will continue to use batch processing for payroll. Consequently, batch totals should be calculated at the time of data entry and then

checked against comparable totals calculated during each stage of processing. Hash totals of employee numbers, for example, are particularly useful. If the original and subsequent hash totals of employee numbers agree, it means that (1) all payroll records have been processed, (2) data input was accurate, and (3) no bogus time cards were entered during processing. If the batch totals do not agree, the organization has timely evidence of a payroll error (most likely a failure to generate a paycheck for an employee) so that the problem can be promptly corrected.

2. *Cross-footing the payroll register.*   The total of the net pay column should equal the total of gross pay less total deductions. If it does not, an error occurred in processing that needs to be promptly investigated and corrected.

3. *A payroll clearing account.*   The *payroll clearing accoun*t is a general ledger account that is used in a two-step process to check the accuracy and completeness of recording payroll costs and their subsequent allocation to appropriate cost centers. First, the payroll clearing account is debited for the amount of gross pay; cash is credited for the amount of net pay, and the various withholdings are credited to separate liability accounts. Second, the cost accounting process distributes labor costs to various expense categories and credits the payroll clearing account for the sum of these allocations. The amount credited to the payroll clearing account should equal the amount that was previously debited when net pay and the various withholdings were recorded. This particular internal check is an example of a *zero-balance check* (discussed in Chapter 10), because the payroll clearing account should equal zero once both entries have been posted.

In addition, supervisory review of the payroll register and other reports serves as a detective control to identify payroll processing errors. Issuing employees an earnings statement provides another layer of detective controls, because employees are likely to report obvious errors.

It is also important to properly classify workers as either employees or independent contractors, because misclassification can cause companies to owe substantial back taxes, interest, and even penalties. This issue often arises when department managers attempt to circumvent a general hiring freeze by using independent contractors. The HRM department always should review any decisions to hire temporary or outside help. The IRS provides a checklist of questions that can be used to determine whether a worker should be classified as an employee or an independent contractor.

Disburse Payroll

The next step is the actual disbursement of paychecks to employees (circle 4.0 in Figure 15-4). Most employees are paid either by check or by direct deposit of the net pay amount into their personal bank account. Unlike cash payments, both methods provide a means to document the amount of wages paid.

PROCESS   After paychecks have been prepared, accounts payable reviews and approves the payroll register. A disbursement voucher is then prepared to authorize the transfer of funds from the company's general checking account to its payroll bank account. The disbursement voucher is then used to update the general ledger.

After reviewing the payroll register and disbursement voucher, the cashier then prepares and signs a check (or initiates an EFT transaction) transferring funds to the company's payroll bank account. If the organization still issues paper checks, the cashier also reviews, signs, and distributes the employee paychecks. The cashier promptly redeposits any unclaimed paychecks in the company's bank account. A list of unclaimed paychecks is then sent to the internal audit department for further investigation.

Direct deposit is one way to improve the efficiency and reduce the costs of payroll processing. Employees who are paid by direct deposit generally receive a copy of the paycheck indicating the amount deposited along with an earnings statement. The payroll system must generate a series of payroll deposit files, one for each bank through which payroll deposits are made. Each file contains a record for each employee whose account is maintained at a particular bank. Each record includes the employee's name, Social Security number, bank account number, and net pay amount. These files are sent electronically, using electronic data interchange (EDI), to each participating bank. The funds are then electronically transferred from the employer's bank account to the employee's account. Direct deposit thus eliminates the need for the cashier to sign individual payroll checks. The cashier does, however, still have to authorize the release of funds from the organization's regular checking account.

Direct deposit provides savings to employers by eliminating the cost of purchasing, processing, and distributing paper checks. It also reduces bank fees and postage expenses. Consequently, most companies now offer their employees the option of direct deposit payment and encourage them to elect this form of payment. Some employees, however, may not have bank accounts and, therefore, cannot elect direct deposit. Organizations can still eliminate the need to issue paper payroll checks by paying such employees with payroll debit cards. Employees can use payroll debit cards to make purchases and can withdraw available cash at ATM machines. Payroll debit cards are stored value cards that cannot be overdrawn, but they can be replenished with additional funds each payday.

THREATS AND CONTROLS   As Table 15-1 indicates, another major threat in the payroll process is the theft of paychecks or the issuance of paychecks to fictitious or terminated employees. This can result in increased expenses and the loss of cash.

Applying to payroll the controls related to other cash disbursements, discussed in Chapter 13, can mitigate this threat. Specifically:

- Access to blank payroll checks and to the check signature machine should be restricted. Similarly, ability to authorize electronic funds transfer (EFT) transactions should be restricted and controlled through the use of strong multifactor authentication.
- All payroll checks should be sequentially prenumbered and periodically accounted for. If payroll is made via direct deposit, all EFT transactions should be reviewed.
- The cashier should sign all payroll checks only when supported by proper documentation (the payroll register and disbursement voucher).

In addition, payroll checks should not be drawn on the organization's regular bank account. Instead, for control purposes, a separate payroll bank account should be used (control 10.5). Doing so limits the company's loss exposure to the amount of cash in the separate payroll account. It also makes it easier to reconcile payroll and to detect paycheck forgery. Like petty cash, the payroll account should be operated as an imprest fund. Each payday, the amount of the check written (or EFT funds transfer) to replenish the payroll checking account should equal the amount of net pay for that period. Thus, when all paychecks have been cashed, the payroll account should have a zero balance. A separate payroll checking account also makes it easier to spot any fraudulent checks when the account is reconciled. As with the other cash disbursements discussed in Chapter 13, segregation of duties is another important control. Thus, accounts payable has responsibility for recording payroll, but the cashier is responsible for distributing paychecks. It is also important that the person who distributes paychecks or authorizes EFT transactions for direct deposit has no other HRM-related duties. To see why this segregation of duties is so important, assume that the person responsible for hiring and firing employees also distributes paychecks. This combination of duties could enable that person to conveniently forget to report an employee's termination and subsequently keep that employee's future paychecks. In addition, the payroll bank account should be reconciled by someone who performs no other payroll or HRM duties.

Use of multifactor authentication and other controls to restrict access to the payroll master database (control 10.7) reduces the risk of creating checks for non-existent employees. In addition, the person responsible for distributing paychecks should be required to positively identify each person picking up a paycheck. Further control is provided by having the internal audit department periodically observe, on a surprise basis, the paycheck distribution process to verify that all paychecks are picked up by valid employees.

Special procedures should be used to handle unclaimed paychecks because they indicate the possibility of a problem, such as a nonexistent or terminated employee. Unclaimed paychecks should be returned to the treasurer's office for prompt redeposit. They should then be traced back to time records and matched against the employee payroll master file to verify that they are indeed legitimate.

Calculate and Disburse Employer-Paid Benefits Taxes and Voluntary Employee Deductions

The final payroll activity is to calculate and remit payroll taxes and employee benefits to the appropriate government or other entity (circle 5.0 in Figure 15-4).

PROCESS   Employers must pay Social Security taxes in addition to the amounts withheld from employee paychecks. Federal and state laws also require employers to contribute a specified percentage of each employee's gross pay, up to a maximum annual limit, to federal and state unemployment compensation insurance funds.

In addition to mandatory tax-related disbursements, employers are responsible for ensuring that other funds deducted from employee paychecks are correctly calculated and remitted in a timely manner to the appropriate entity. Such deductions include court-ordered payments for alimony, child support, or bankruptcy. Many employers also contribute some or all of the amounts to pay for their employees' health, disability, and life insurance premiums as well as making matching contributions to retirement plans.

Many employers also offer their employees *flexible benefit plans,* under which each employee chooses some minimum coverage in medical insurance, retirement plans, and charitable contributions. Flexible benefit plans place increased demands on a company's HRM/payroll system. For example, the HRM staff of a large company with thousands of employees can spend a considerable amount of time just responding to 401(k) plan inquiries. Moreover, employees want to be able to make changes in their investment decisions on a timely basis. Organizations can satisfy employee demands for such services without increasing costs by providing access to HRM/payroll information on the company's intranet.

THREATS AND CONTROLS   The primary threats in this activity are failing to make the necessary remittances, untimely remittances, or errors in those remittances (threats 11-13 in Table 15-1). These problems can result in fines from government agencies and employee complaints if the errors adversely affect their retirement or other benefits.

Circular E, *Employer's Tax Guide*, published by the IRS, provides detailed instructions about an employer's obligations for withholding and remitting payroll taxes and for filing various reports. To mitigate the threats of omitted or untimely remittances, the information in Circular E should be used to configure the payroll system to automatically disburse the funds when payroll is processed. Processing integrity controls, such as cross-footing checks and batch totals, minimize the risk of inaccuracies. Regular supervisory review of payroll reports provides a detective control. In addition, providing employees with earnings statements enables them to timely detect and report any problems.

Outsourcing Options: Payroll Service Bureaus and Professional Employer Organizations

In an effort to reduce costs, many organizations are outsourcing their payroll and HRM functions to payroll service bureaus and professional employer organizations. A *payroll service bureau* maintains the payroll master data for each of its clients and process payroll for them. A *professional employer organization (PEO)* not only processes payroll but also provides HRM services such as employee benefit design and administration. Because they provide a narrower range of services, payroll service bureaus are generally less expensive than PEOs.

When organizations outsource payroll processing, they send time and attendance data along with information about personnel changes to the payroll service bureau or PEO at the end of each pay period. The payroll service bureau or PEO then uses that data to prepare employee paychecks, earnings statements, and a payroll register. The payroll processing service also periodically produces employee W-2 forms and other tax-related reports.

Payroll service bureaus and PEOs are especially attractive to small and midsized businesses for the following reasons:

- *Reduced costs.*   Payroll service bureaus and PEOs benefit from the economies of scale associated with preparing paychecks for a large number of companies. They can charge fees that are typically less than the cost of doing payroll in-house. A payroll service bureau or PEO also saves money by eliminating the need to develop and maintain the expertise required to comply with the constantly changing tax laws.
- *Wider range of benefits.*   PEOs pool the costs of administering benefits across all their clients. Consequently, a PEO enables smaller companies to offer the same wide range of benefits that large companies typically provide.

- **Freeing up of computer resources.**   A payroll service bureau or PEO eliminates one or more AIS applications (payroll and benefits management). The freed-up computing resources can then be used to improve service in other areas, such as sales order entry.

As the basis for competitive advantage increasingly hinges on employees' skills and knowledge, the effective and efficient management of the payroll and HRM functions becomes increasingly important. Outsourcing may provide a way to reduce costs. However, companies need to be sure to carefully monitor service quality to ensure that the outsourced system effectively integrates HRM and payroll data in a manner that supports effective management of employees.

Summary and Case Conclusion

The HRM/payroll cycle information system consists of two related, but separate, subsystems: HRM and payroll. The HRM system records and processes data about the activities of recruiting, hiring, training, assigning, evaluating, and discharging employees. The payroll system records and processes data used to pay employees for their services.

The HRM/payroll system must be designed to comply with a myriad of government regulations related to both taxes and employment practices. In addition, adequate controls must exist to prevent (1) overpaying employees due to invalid (overstated) time and attendance data and (2) disbursing paychecks to fictitious employees. These two threats can be best minimized by proper segregation of duties, specifically by having the following functions performed by different individuals:

1. Authorizing and making changes to the payroll master file for such events as hirings, firings, and pay raises
2. Recording and verifying time worked by employees
3. Preparing paychecks
4. Distributing paychecks
5. Reconciling the payroll bank account

Although the HRM and payroll systems have traditionally been separated, many companies, including AOE, are trying to integrate them to manage their human resources more effectively and to provide employees with better benefits and service. Elizabeth Venko and Ann Brandt showed Peter Wu how AOE's new ERP system would facilitate integrating these two functions. Peter was impressed with how easily he could retrieve data about employee skills and attendance at training classes from this database. He agreed that this would satisfy the needs of department managers for quick and easy access to such information. Peter also realized that the HRM staff could similarly use this query capability to provide quick response to employee requests for information about their benefits, deductions, or retirement plans. He was even more impressed when Elizabeth and Ann explained that another recently implemented add-on feature would also allow employees to make direct changes in their retirement savings allocations, medical plan choices, and other benefit options. Peter realized that freeing the HRM staff from these routine clerical tasks would allow them to devote more time to helping him organize the information needed to make strategic decisions, such as planning for future workforce needs, career counseling, employee development, and negotiations with service providers to improve benefits.

Elizabeth explained that payroll processing itself could continue to be performed in batch mode, because there is no need for online processing (employees would continue to be paid only at periodic intervals). However, she wants to require employees to either sign up for direct deposit of their paychecks or receive payroll debit cards, thereby eliminating the need to issue paychecks. An access control matrix would be created to maintain adequate segregation of duties in the new system and protect the integrity of the HRM/payroll database. For example, only HRM employees would add new employees, and only from terminals located in the HRM department.

Linda Spurgeon was pleased with Elizabeth and Ann's work on improving the company's HRM/payroll systems. She indicated that their next task would be to work with Stephanie Cromwell, AOE's chief financial officer, to improve the financial closing process and to help develop reports that would provide better insight into AOE's performance.

Key Terms

human resource management (HRM)/payroll cycle 435	time sheet 443	flexible benefit plans 451
knowledge management systems 437	payroll register 447	payroll service bureau 451
	deduction register 447	professional employer
time card 443	earnings statement 447	organization (PEO) 451
	payroll clearing account 449	

AIS IN ACTION

Chapter Quiz

1. Traditionally, accountants have been most involved with which portion of the HRM/ payroll cycle?
   a. hiring
   b. payroll
   c. training
   d. performance evaluation

2. Which of the following statements is true?
   a. Financial statements report the value of employee knowledge and skills.
   b. Turnover and absenteeism are costly.
   c. All employees must fill out time cards.
   d. Default configurations of ERP packages typically provide good segregation of duties.

3. Which document lists the current amount and year-to-date totals of gross pay, deductions, and net pay for one employee?
   a. payroll register
   b. time card
   c. paycheck
   d. earnings statement

4. Online processing is most useful for which of these tasks?
   a. preparing payroll checks
   b. reconciling job-time tickets and time cards
   c. paying payroll tax obligations
   d. making changes in employee benefit choices

5. Use of a payroll service bureau or a PEO provides which of the following benefits?
   a. fewer staff needed to process payroll
   b. lower cost of processing payroll
   c. less need for developing and maintaining payroll tax expertise
   d. all of the above

6. Which control procedure would be most effective in detecting the failure to prepare a paycheck for a new employee *before* paychecks are distributed?
   a. validity checks on the employee number on each time card
   b. record counts of time cards submitted and time cards processed
   c. zero-balance check
   d. use of a separate payroll bank account

7. Which department should have responsibility for authorizing pay-rate changes?
   a. timekeeping
   b. payroll
   c. HRM
   d. accounting

8. To maximize effectiveness of internal controls over payroll, which of the following persons should be responsible for distributing employee paychecks?
   a. departmental secretary
   b. payroll clerk
   c. controller
   d. departmental supervisor

9. Where should unclaimed paychecks be returned?
   a. HRM department
   c. payroll department
   b. cashier
   d. absent employee's supervisor

10. Which of the following is an important supporting document to authorize the transfer of funds to the payroll bank account?
    a. earnings statement
    c. payroll register
    b. time card
    d. W-2 form

Discussion Questions

15.1. This chapter noted many of the benefits that can arise by integrating the HRM and payroll databases. Nevertheless, many companies maintain separate payroll and HRM information systems. Why do you think this is so? (*Hint*: Think about the differences in employee background and the functions performed by the HRM and payroll departments.)

15.2. Some accountants have advocated that a company's human assets be measured and included directly in the financial statements. For example, the costs of hiring and training an employee would be recorded as an asset that is amortized over the employee's expected term of service. Do you agree or disagree? Why?

15.3. You are responsible for implementing a new employee performance measurement system that will provide factory supervisors with detailed information about each of their employees on a weekly basis. In conversation with some of these supervisors, you are surprised to learn they do not believe these reports will be useful. They explain that they can already obtain all the information they need to manage their employees simply by observing the shop floor. Comment on that opinion. How could formal reports supplement and enhance what the supervisors learn by direct observation?

15.4. One of the threats associated with having employees telecommute is that they may use company-provided resources (laptop, printer, etc.) for a side business. What are some other threats? What controls can mitigate the risk of these threats?

15.5. How would you respond to the treasurer of a small charity who tells you that the organization does not use a separate checking account for payroll because the benefits are not worth the extra monthly service fee?

15.6. This chapter discussed how the HR department should have responsibility for updating the HRM/payroll database for hiring, firing, and promotions. What other kinds of changes may need to be made? What controls should be implemented to ensure the accuracy and validity of such changes?

Problems

15.1. Match the terms in the left column with the appropriate definition from the right column.

____ 1. Payroll service bureau

a. A list of each employee's gross pay, payroll deductions, and net pay in a multicolumn format

____ 2. Payroll clearing account

b. Used to record the activities performed by a salaried professional for various clients

____ 3. Earnings statement

c. Used to record time worked by an hourly-wage employee

____ 4. Payroll register

d. An organization that processes payroll and provides other HRM services

___ **5.** Time card
     e. An organization that processes payroll

___ **6.** Time sheet
     f. A list of all the deductions for each employee

     g. A document given to each employee that shows gross pay, net pay, and itemizes all deductions both for the current pay period and for the year-to-date

     h. Special general ledger account used for payroll processing

15.2. What internal control procedure(s) would be most effective in preventing the following errors or fraudulent acts?

a. An inadvertent data entry error caused an employee's wage rate to be overstated in the payroll master file.

b. A fictitious employee payroll record was added to the payroll master file.

c. During data entry, the hours worked on an employee's time card for one day were accidentally entered as 80 hours, instead of 8 hours.

d. A computer operator used an online terminal to increase her own salary.

e. A factory supervisor failed to notify the HRM department that an employee had been fired. Consequently, paychecks continued to be issued for that employee. The supervisor pocketed and cashed those paychecks.

f. A factory employee punched a friend's time card in at 1:00 P.M. and out at 5:00 P.M. while the friend played golf that afternoon.

g. A programmer obtained the payroll master file and increased his salary.

h. Some time cards were lost during payroll preparation; consequently, when paychecks were distributed, several employees complained about not being paid.

i. A large portion of the payroll master file was destroyed when the disk pack containing the file was overwritten when used as a scratch file for another application.

j. The organization was fined $5,000 for making a late quarterly payroll tax payment to the IRS.

15.3. You have been hired to evaluate the payroll system for the Skip-Rope Manufacturing Company. The company processes its payroll in-house. Use Table 15-1 as a reference to prepare a list of questions to evaluate Skip-Rope's internal control structure as it pertains to payroll processing for its factory employees. Each question should be phrased so that it can be answered with either a yes or a no; all "no" answers should indicate potential internal control weaknesses. Include a third column listing the potential problem that could arise if that particular control were not in place. *(CPA Examination, adapted)*

15.4. Although most medium and large companies have implemented sophisticated payroll and HRM systems like the one described in this chapter, many smaller companies still maintain separate payroll and HRM systems that employ many manual procedures. Typical of such small companies is the Kowal Manufacturing Company, which employs about 50 production workers and has the following payroll procedures:

• The factory supervisor interviews and hires all job applicants. The new employee prepares a W-4 form (Employee's Withholding Exemption Certificate) and gives it to the supervisor. The supervisor writes the hourly rate of pay for the new employee in the corner of the W-4 form and then gives the form to the payroll clerk as notice that a new worker has been hired. The supervisor verbally advises the payroll department of any subsequent pay raises.

• A supply of blank time cards is kept in a box near the entrance to the factory. All workers take a time card on Monday morning and fill in their names. During the week they record the time they arrive and leave work by punching their time cards in the time clock located near the main entrance to the factory. At the end of the week the workers drop the time cards in a box near the exit. A payroll clerk retrieves the completed time cards from the box on Monday morning. Employees are automatically removed from the payroll master file when they fail to turn in a time card.

• The payroll checks are manually signed by the chief accountant and then given to the factory supervisor, who distributes them to the employees. The factory supervisor arranges for delivery of the paychecks to any employee who is absent on payday.

• The payroll bank account is reconciled by the chief accountant, who also prepares the various quarterly and annual tax reports.

Required

a. Identify weaknesses in current procedures, and explain the threats that they may allow to occur.
b. Suggest ways to improve the Kowal Manufacturing Company's internal controls over hiring and payroll processing.
   (CPA Examination, adapted)

15.5. Arlington Industries manufactures and sells engine parts for large industrial equipment. The company employs over 1,000 workers for three shifts, and most employees work overtime when necessary. Figure 15-10 depicts the procedures followed to process payroll. Additional information about payroll procedures follows:

- The HRM department determines the wage rates of all employees. The process begins when a form authorizing the addition of a new employee to the payroll master file is sent to the payroll coordinator for review and approval. Once the information about the new employee is entered in the system, the computer automatically calculates the overtime and shift differential rates for that employee.
- A local accounting firm provides Arlington with monthly payroll tax updates, which are used to modify the tax rates.
- Employees record their time worked on time cards. Every Monday morning, the previous week's time cards are collected from a bin next to the time clock, and new time cards are left for employees to use. The payroll department manager reviews the time cards to ensure that hours are correctly totaled; the system automatically determines whether overtime has been worked or a shift differential is required.
- The payroll department manager performs all the other activities depicted in Figure 15-10.
- The system automatically assigns a sequential number to each payroll check. The checks are stored in a box next to the printer for easy access. After the checks are printed, the payroll department manager uses an automatic check-signing machine to sign the checks. The signature plate is kept locked in a safe. After the checks have been signed, the payroll manager distributes the paychecks to all first-shift employees. Paychecks for the other two shifts are given to the shift supervisor for distribution.
- The payroll master file is backed up weekly, after payroll processing is finished.

Required

a. Identify and describe at least three weaknesses in Arlington Industries' payroll process.
b. Identify and describe at least two different areas in Arlington's payroll processing system where controls are satisfactory.
   (CMA Examination, adapted)

15.6. Excel Problem

Objective: Learn how to find and correct errors in complex spreadsheets used for payroll.

Required (Continues on next two pages)

(a) Read the article "Ferret Out Spreadsheet Errors" by Mark G. Simkin, in the *Journal of Accountancy* (February 2004). You can find a copy online by accessing www.aicpa.org.
(b) Download the worksheet referenced in the article.
(c) Disable data validation on the hours worked column in order to input the following erroneous data:

- Change hours worked for Adams to 400.
- Change hours worked for Englert to 4.
- Change hours worked for Hartford to –40.
- Create a chart like that shown in Exhibit 2 of the article. Which of the errors are easily found by the chart? What are the strengths and limitations of creating such charts to detect errors? Print out your chart and save your work.

(d) Create the three data validation rules described in the article (Exhibits 4–7 in the article illustrate how to create the first rule). Print out screen shots of how you create

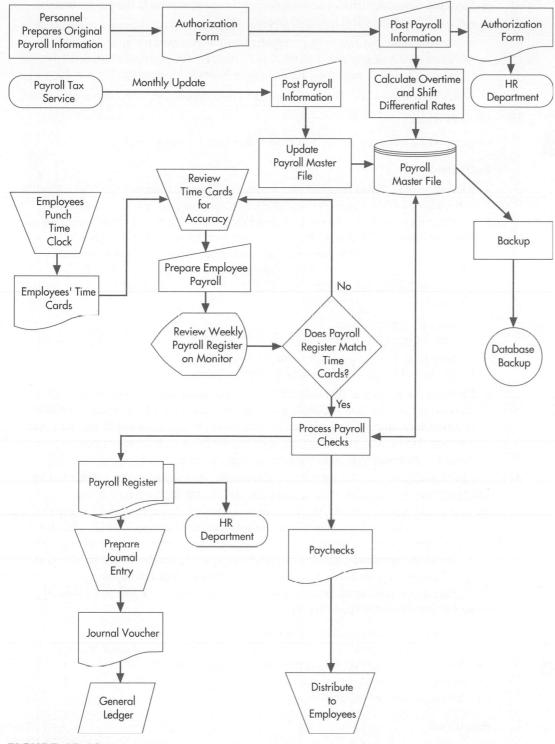

FIGURE 15-10

Arlington Industries Flowchart for Problem 15.4

each rule, and save your work. (*Note:* The article "Block That Spreadsheet Error" by Theo Callahan, in the *Journal of Accountancy* (August 2002) provides additional examples of data validation rules.)

(e) Follow the instructions for using the formula auditing tool. Print out a screen shot showing use of the tool to circle invalid data (yours should be similar to Exhibit 9 in the article).

(f) Follow the article's instructions to run the "trace precedents" audit tool. Print screen shots that show the results, and save your work. How useful is this tool? What are its limitations, if any?

(g) Enter the following data for new employees (insert new rows in the proper order to maintain the alphabetical listing of employees):

- Name = Able, pay rate = 11.11, regular hours = 40, overtime hours = 5
- Name = Easton, pay rate = 10.00, regular hours = 40, overtime hours = 0
- Name = Johnson, pay rate = 12.00, regular hours = 35, overtime hours = 10

Which audit tests and validation rules change? Why? Print screen shots, and save your work.

15.7. Excel Problem

Objective: Learn how to use the VLOOKUP function for payroll calculations.

Required

a. Read the article "Make Excel a Little Smarter" by Lois S. Mahoney and Charles Kelliher in the *Journal of Accountancy* (July 2003). You can find a copy at www.aicpa.org.
b. Read the section titled "Data in Different Places," and create the spreadsheet illustrated in Exhibit 6. Print a screen shot of your work, and save your spreadsheet.
c. Create a formula that calculates total bonuses. Also create a cell entry that indicates what that number represents. Print a screen shot of your work, and save it.
d. Add the following data validation controls to your spreadsheet, including explanatory error messages. Save your work.

- Sales must be positive.
- Sales cannot exceed 125.
- Amount of bonus must be non-negative.
- Amount of bonus cannot exceed 20% of unit sales.

e. Modify your worksheet by placing the sales data and resulting bonus on a different worksheet from the bonus table. Name your table array, and modify the VLOOKUP function accordingly. Then add another employee: Johnson, who sold 150 units. Print a screen shot of your new worksheet showing the bonuses for each employee, including Johnson. Save your work.

15.8. The local community feels that secondary school education is a necessity and that lack of education leads to a number of social problems. As a result, the local school board has decided to take action to reverse the rising dropout rate. The board has voted to provide funds to encourage students to remain in school and earn their high school diplomas. The idea is to treat secondary education like a job and pay students. The board, however, could not agree on the details for implementing this new plan. Consequently, you have been hired to devise a system to compensate students for staying in school and earning a diploma.

As you devise your compensation scheme, be sure it meets the following general control objectives for the payroll cycle:

- All transactions are properly authorized.
- Everyone is assigned to do productive work, and they do it efficiently and effectively.
- All transactions are accurately recorded and processed.
- Accurate records are maintained.
- All disbursements are proper.

Required

Write a proposal that addresses these five questions:

a. How should the students be compensated (e.g., for attendance, grades)?
b. How and by whom will the payments be authorized?
c. How will the payments be processed?
d. How should the payments be made (e.g., in cash or other means)?
e. When will the payments be made?

(Adapted from Carol F. Venable, "Development of Diversity Awareness and Critical Thinking," Proceedings of the Lilly Conference on Excellence in College and University Teaching—West (Lake Arrowhead, Calif., March 1995); and American Accounting Association Teaching and Curriculum Demonstration Session (Orlando, Fla., August 1995). Reprinted with permission of Dr. Carol Venable.)

15.9. What is the purpose of each of the following control procedures (i.e., what threats is it designed to mitigate)?

    a. Comparison of a listing of current and former employees to the payroll register.

    b. Reconciliation of labor costs (based on job-time ticket data) with payroll (based on time card data).

    c. Direct deposit of paychecks.

    d. Validity checks on Social Security numbers of all new employees added to the payroll master file.

    e. Cross-footing the payroll register.

    f. Limit checks on hours worked for each time card.

    g. Use of a fingerprint scanner for employees to record the time they started and the time they quit working each day.

    h. Encryption of payroll data both when it is electronically sent to a payroll service bureau and while at rest in the HR/payroll database.

    i. Establishing a separate payroll checking account and funding it as an imprest account.

    j. Comparison of hash totals of employee numbers created prior to transmitting time-worked data to payroll provider with hash totals of employee numbers created by payroll provider when preparing paychecks.

    k. Periodic reports of all changes to payroll database sent to each department manager.

    l. Providing employees with earnings statements every pay period.

15.10. Excel Problem

Objective: Learn how to use text and array formulas to locate potential payroll problems.

Required

    a. Download the spreadsheet for this problem from the course Web site.

    b. In column I, under the label "Ghost Employee?" write a function that compares the employee# in the time cards column to the employee# in the payroll master data column and displays the message: "Time card employee# does not exist in master data" for any employee in the time cards column who is not listed in the payroll master data column. The function should leave the cell blank if the employee# in the time cards worksheet does exist in the payroll master file worksheet. (*Hint:* Use the ISNA and MATCH functions.)

    c. In column L, titled "Invalid SSN?" write a function to identify invalid Social Security numbers. Assume that Social Security numbers that begin with the digit 9 or that have the digits 00 for the middle two numbers are invalid. Your function should display a message that flags either of these two conditions or that displays nothing otherwise. (*Hint:* There are text functions that examine specific portions of a string, such as the left three characters, and there are also functions that convert text to numeric values.)

    d. In column P, titled "Missing Paycheck?" write a function to check whether a time card exists for each employee in the master payroll data section of the worksheet. The formula should either return the message "No paycheck created for this employee" or display nothing.

Case 15-1 Research Report: HRM/Payroll Opportunities for CPAs

Payroll has traditionally been an accounting function, and some CPAs have provided payroll processing services to their clients. Today, CPAs are finding additional new lucrative opportunities to provide not only payroll processing but also various HR services. Write a brief report that compares the provision of payroll and HR services by CPAs with that of national payroll providers. Perform the following research to collect the data for your report:

1. Read the articles "Be an HR Resource for Your Clients," by Michael Hayes and "Hired Help: Finding the Right Consultant," by Joanne Sammer, both of which were published in the November 2006 issue of the *Journal of Accountancy*.

2. Contact a local CPA firm that provides payroll and HR services, and find out what types of services they perform and what types of clients they serve.

AIS IN ACTION SOLUTIONS

Chapter Quiz Key

1. Traditionally, accountants have been most involved with which portion of the HRM/payroll cycle?
    a. hiring (Incorrect. This has traditionally been handled by the HR department.)
    ▶ b. payroll (Correct. The payroll system has traditionally been the part of the HRM/payroll system used by accountants.)
    c. training (Incorrect. This has traditionally been handled by the HR department.)
    d. performance evaluation (Incorrect. This has traditionally been handled by supervisors.)

2. Which of the following statements is true?
    a. Financial statements report the value of employee knowledge and skills. (Incorrect. Costs associated with acquiring the use of employees' skills and knowledge have traditionally been recognized as an expense on the income statement.)
    ▶ b. Turnover and absenteeism are costly. (Correct. Turnover costs 1.5 times the departing employee's salary, and absenteeism increases overtime and short-term hiring costs.)
    c. All employees must fill out time cards. (Incorrect. Hourly employees typically fill out time cards to record hours worked. Salaried professionals, however, do not because their periodic pay is a set fraction of their annual salary. Salaried employees in professional services firms, however, do record the time spent performing various activities for different clients on time sheets so that their employers can accurately assign costs and bill clients for services rendered.)
    d. Default configurations of ERP packages typically provide good segregation of duties. (Incorrect. Default configurations of ERP systems typically provide users with far too much authority.)

3. Which document lists the current amount and year-to-date totals of gross pay, deductions, and net pay for one employee?
    a. payroll register (Incorrect. The payroll register lists this information for all employees.)
    b. time card (Incorrect. Time cards collect data about time worked during a specific pay period.)
    c. paycheck (Incorrect. The paycheck is a means of transferring funds.)
    ▶ d. earnings statement (Correct. The earnings statement attached to each paycheck provides the information listed.)

4. Online processing is most useful for which of these tasks?
    a. preparing payroll checks (Incorrect. Because paychecks are issued only periodically, batch processing is appropriate.)
    b. reconciling job-time tickets and time cards (Incorrect. Because this occurs only when payroll is calculated, batch processing is appropriate.)
    c. paying payroll tax obligations (Incorrect. Payment is periodic, so batch processing is appropriate.)
    ▶ d. making changes in employee benefit choices (Correct. Employees want to be able to have access to this information and make changes whenever desired.)

5. Use of a payroll service bureau or a PEO provides which of the following benefits?
    ▶ a. fewer staff needed to process payroll (Incorrect. Outsourcing not only typically reduces staffing requirements, but also lowers costs (answer b) and reduces the need for in-house expertise (answer c).)
    b. lower cost of processing payroll (Incorrect. Outsourcing usually not only reduces costs, but also requires fewer staff (answer a) and reduces the need for in-house expertise (answer c).)

    c. less need for developing and maintaining payroll tax expertise (Incorrect. Outsourcing does reduce the need to maintain in-house payroll tax expertise, but it also provides the benefits listed in answers a and b.)

    d. all of the above (Correct.)

6. Which control procedure would be most effective in detecting the failure to prepare a paycheck for a new employee before paychecks are distributed?

    a. validity checks on the employee number on each time card (Incorrect. This control is designed to ensure that only valid employees are paid.)

    ▶ b. record counts of time cards submitted and time cards processed (Correct. Batch totals, such as record counts, would identify failure to process all transaction records.)

    c. zero-balance check (Incorrect. This control is designed to verify the accuracy of payroll disbursements.)

    d. use of a separate payroll bank account (Incorrect. This control is designed to limit the amount of cash that could be lost as a result of forged or altered paychecks.)

7. Which department should have responsibility for authorizing pay-rate changes?

    a. timekeeping (Incorrect. Timekeeping is a recording function.)

    b. payroll (Incorrect. Payroll calculates the pay for the current period and should not also authorize changes.)

    ▶ c. HRM (Correct. HRM has no other role in the payroll process.)

    d. accounting (Incorrect. Accounting maintains records related to payroll and should not authorize changes in pay rates.)

8. To maximize effectiveness of internal controls over payroll, which of the following persons should be responsible for distributing employee paychecks?

    ▶ a. departmental secretary (Correct. This person has no other payroll duties so cannot conceal theft of paychecks.)

    b. payroll clerk (Incorrect. The payroll clerk prepares and records the checks and so could create checks for nonexistent employees and cash them.)

    c. controller (Incorrect. The controller is in charge of the recording function and should not have custody of checks.)

    d. departmental supervisor (Incorrect. The supervisor authorizes payment by reviewing time cards and should not also have custody of assets.)

9. Where should unclaimed paychecks be returned?

    a. HRM department (Incorrect. Unclaimed checks should be returned to the cashier for redeposit.)

    ▶ b. cashier (Correct. This permits funds to be quickly redeposited.)

    c. payroll department (Incorrect. Unclaimed checks should be returned to the cashier for redeposit.)

    d. absent employee's supervisor (Incorrect. Unclaimed checks should be returned to the cashier for redeposit.)

10. Which of the following is an important supporting document to authorize the transfer of funds to the payroll bank account?

    a. earnings statement (Incorrect. This is the stub attached to each paycheck, providing the employee with YTD information about pay and various deductions.)

    b. time card (Incorrect. This document records time worked.)

    ▶ c. payroll register (Correct. This document summarizes the amount to be paid to each employee and is sent to the accounts payable department for use in preparing a disbursement voucher to authorize the transfer of funds to the payroll account.)

    d. W-2 form (Incorrect. This is a year-end statement given to each employee summarizing net pay, taxes withheld, and other deductions.)

Chapter 16

General Ledger and Reporting System

INTEGRATIVE CASE ALPHA OMEGA ELECTRONICS

Linda Spurgeon, president and CEO of Alpha Omega Electronics (AOE), is not satisfied with the reporting capabilities of AOE's new enterprise resource planning (ERP) system. Although the monthly closing process now takes less than two days, the system only provides management with timely information about the firm's financial performance. Linda wants a report that integrates financial information with operational measures about how the firm is doing. She is also concerned about how to prepare AOE to transition from U.S. Generally Accepted Accounting Principles (GAAP) to International Financial Reporting Standards (IFRS) and about satisfying the SEC's new requirements to begin submitting financial information using XBRL.

Linda calls a meeting with Stephanie Cromwell, AOE's chief financial officer, Elizabeth Venko, AOE's controller, and Ann Brandt, AOE's vice president of information

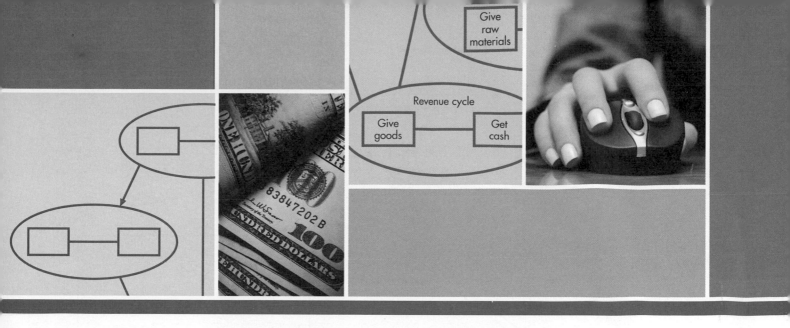

systems, to discuss these issues. Stephanie mentions that she has been reading about something called a balanced scorecard that might provide the kind of multidimensional report Linda desires. Ann and Elizabeth agree to research the balanced scorecard and investigate how AOE's new ERP system could be configured to produce one. Stephanie asks them to also look at how AOE could make better use of the reporting and graphing capabilities of its new ERP system. In addition, they will report back on what needs to be done to prepare for IFRS and to use XBRL. As you read this chapter, think about how both technological and regulatory changes affect the design and operation of an organization's general ledger and reporting systems.

Introduction

This chapter discusses the information processing operations involved in updating the general ledger and preparing reports that summarize the results of an organization's activities. As shown in Figure 16-1, the general ledger and reporting system plays a central role in a company's accounting information system. Its primary function is to collect and organize data from the following sources:

- Each of the accounting cycle subsystems described in Chapters 12 through 15 provides information about regular transactions. (Only the principal data flows from each subsystem are depicted, to keep the figure uncluttered.)
- The treasurer provides information about financing and investing activities, such as the issuance or retirement of debt and equity instruments and the purchase or sale of investment securities.
- The budget department provides budget numbers.
- The controller provides adjusting entries.

Figure 16-2 shows the basic activities performed in the general ledger and reporting cycle. The first three activities represent the basic steps in the accounting cycle, which culminate in the production of the traditional set of financial statements. The fourth activity indicates that, in addition to financial reports for external users, an organization's accounting system produces a variety of reports for internal management.

We begin by describing the design of a typical general ledger and reporting system and discuss the basic controls necessary to ensure that it provides management and various external stakeholders with reliable information. We then discuss in detail each of the basic general ledger and reporting cycle activities depicted in Figure 16-2. For each activity, we describe

FIGURE 16-1

Context Diagram of the General Ledger and Reporting System

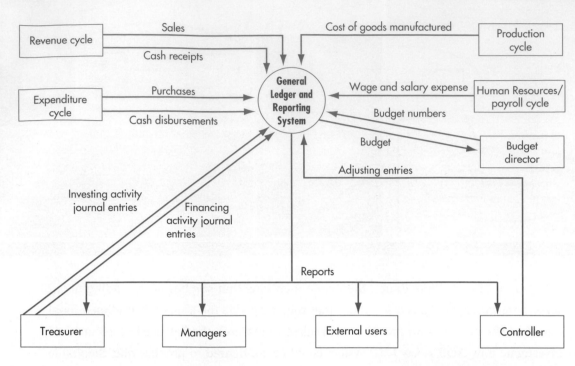

how the information needed to perform and manage the activity is collected, processed, and stored. We also explain the controls necessary to ensure not only the reliability of that information but also the safeguarding of the organization's resources. In addition, we discuss the impact of regulatory and technological changes, such as the proposed switch from GAAP to IFRS and the SEC's mandate to use XBRL for electronic filing, on the design and operation of the general ledger and reporting system. We also explore how tools such as responsibility accounting, balanced scorecards, and well-designed graphs can improve the quality of information provided to managers.

FIGURE 16-2

Level 0 Data Flow Diagram of the General Ledger and Reporting Cycle

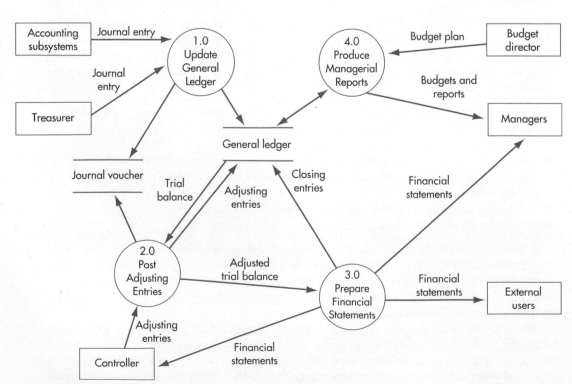

General Ledger and Reporting System

Figure 16-3 shows the typical design of an online general ledger and reporting system.

Process

The centralized database must be organized in a manner that facilitates meeting the varied information needs of both internal and external users. Managers need timely detailed information about the results of operations in their particular area of responsibility. Investors and creditors want periodic financial statements and timely updates to help them assess the organization's performance. Various government agencies also mandate specific information requirements. To satisfy these multiple needs, the general ledger and reporting system not only produces periodic reports but also supports online inquiries.

Threats and Controls

Figure 16-3 shows that all general ledger and reporting cycle activities depend on the integrated database. Therefore, the first general threat listed in Table 16-1 is inaccurate or invalid general ledger data. Inaccurate general ledger data can result in misleading reports that cause managers to make erroneous decisions. Similarly, errors in financial statements provided to creditors, investors, and government agencies can cause those stakeholders to make wrong decisions. In addition, errors in financial statements and reports provided to external stakeholders can also result in fines and negative reactions from the capital markets.

One way to mitigate the threat of inaccurate or invalid general ledger data is to use the various processing integrity controls discussed in Chapter 10 to minimize the risk of data input errors when the treasurer and controller make direct journal entries. It is also important to restrict access to the general ledger and configure the system so that only authorized employees can make changes to master data. Thus, multifactor authentication should be used to restrict access to

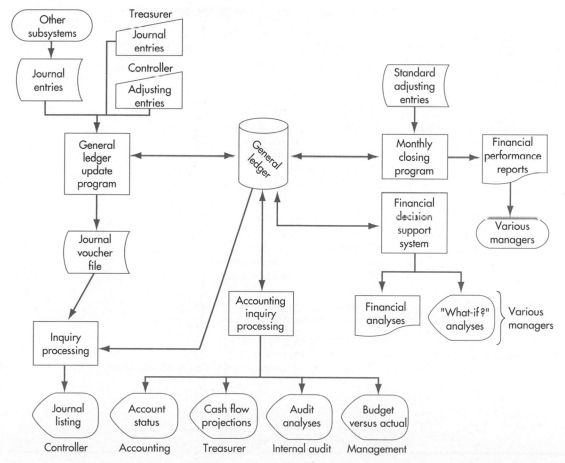

FIGURE 16-3

Typical Design of Online General Ledger and Reporting System

the general ledger. In addition, authorization controls (an access control matrix and compatibility tests) should also be used to limit the functions that each legitimate user may perform. For example, most managers should be given read-only access to the general ledger, as depicted at the bottom of Figure 16-3. Otherwise, an unscrupulous manager can conceal theft of assets or poor performance by altering the information in the general ledger. In addition, the access control matrix should also be designed to limit the functions that can be performed at various terminals. Adjusting entries, for example, should be allowed only from terminals in the controller's office. However, because such preventive controls can never be 100% effective, Table 16-1 also indicates that an important detective control is to regularly produce a report of all changes to the general ledger and review them to verify that the database remains accurate.

A second general threat in the general ledger and reporting cycle is unauthorized disclosure of financial information. In particular, it is important not to prematurely release financial statements; doing so is likely to result in fines from various regulatory agencies and possible shareholder lawsuits. The best control procedure for reducing the risk of unauthorized disclosure of financial statements is to use multifactor authentication and physical security controls to restrict access to the general ledger to only those employees who need such access to perform their jobs. Encrypting the database provides additional protection by making the information unintelligible to anyone who succeeds in obtaining unauthorized access to the database. Encryption also prevents IT employees who do not have access to the ERP system from using operating system utilities to view sensitive information. In addition, general ledger data should be encrypted when it is being transmitted over the Internet to other corporate offices, analysts, or government agencies.

A third general threat in the general ledger and reporting cycle concerns the loss or destruction of master data. The best way to mitigate the risk of this threat is to employ the backup and disaster recovery procedures that were discussed in Chapter 10.

TABLE 16-1 Threats and Controls in the General Ledger and Reporting System

Activity	Threat	Controls (first number refers to the corresponding threat)
General issues throughout entire general ledger and reporting cycle	1. Inaccurate or invalid general ledger data 2. Unauthorized disclosure of financial statement 3. Loss or destruction of data	1.1 Data processing integrity controls 1.2 Restriction of access to general ledger 1.3 Review of all changes to general ledger data 2.1 Access controls 2.2 Encryption 3.1 Backup and disaster recovery procedures
Update general ledger	4. Inaccurate updating of general ledger 5. Unauthorized journal entries	4.1 Data entry processing integrity controls 4.2 Reconciliations and control reports 4.3 Audit trail creation and review 5.1 Access controls 5.2 Reconciliations and control reports 5.3 Audit trail creation and review
Post adjusting entries	6. Inaccurate adjusting entries 7. Unauthorized adjusting entries	6.1 Data entry processing integrity controls 6.2 Spreadsheet error protection controls 6.3 Standard adjusting entries 6.4 Reconciliations and control reports 6.5 Audit trail creation and review 7.1 Access controls 7.2 Reconciliations and control reports 7.3 Audit trail creation and review
Prepare financial statements	8. Inaccurate financial statements 9. Fraudulent financial reporting	8.1 Processing integrity controls 8.2 Use of packaged software 8.3 Training and experience in applying IFRS and XBRL 8.4 Audits 9.1 Audits
Produce managerial reports	10. Poorly designed reports and graphs	10.1 Responsibility accounting 10.2 Balanced scorecard 10.3 Training on proper graph design

Update General Ledger

As shown in Figure 16-2, the first activity in the general ledger system (circle 1.0) is updating the general ledger.

Process

Updating consists of posting journal entries that originate from two sources:

1. *Accounting subsystems.*   Each of the accounting subsystems described in Chapters 12 through 15 creates a journal entry to update the general ledger. In theory, the general ledger could be updated for each individual transaction. In practice, however, the various accounting subsystems usually update the general ledger by means of summary journal entries that represent the results of all transactions that occurred during a given period of time (day, week, or month). For example, the revenue cycle subsystem would generate a summary journal entry debiting accounts receivable and cash and crediting sales for all sales made during the update period. Similarly, the expenditure cycle would generate summary journal entries to record the purchase of supplies and inventories and to record cash disbursements in payment for those purchases.

2. *Treasurer.*   The treasurer's office provides information for journal entries to update the general ledger for nonroutine transactions such as the issuance or retirement of debt, the purchase or sale of investment securities, or the acquisition of treasury stock. Figure 16-4 shows an example of a typical journal entry screen for an ERP system.

Figure 16-3 shows that the individual journal entries used to update the general ledger are stored in the *journal voucher file.* The journal voucher file contains the information that would be found in the general journal in a manual accounting system: the date of the journal entry, the accounts debited and credited, and the amounts. Note, however, that the journal voucher file is a by-product of, not an input to, the posting process. As we will explain later, the journal voucher file forms an important part of the audit trail, providing evidence that all authorized transactions have been accurately and completely recorded.

Threats and Controls

Table 16-1 shows that two related threats at this stage are inaccurate and unauthorized journal entries to update the general ledger. Both can lead to poor decision making based on erroneous information in financial performance reports.

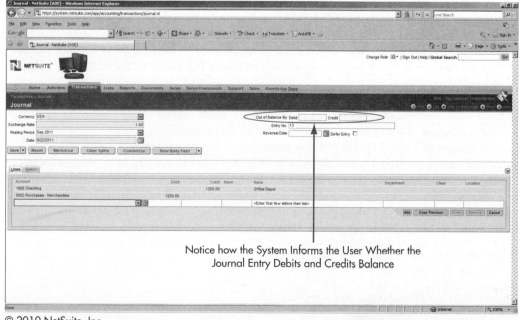

© 2010 NetSuite, Inc.

Notice how the System Informs the User Whether the
Journal Entry Debits and Credits Balance

FIGURE 16-4
Example of Journal Entry Input Screen

As Figure 16-3 shows, there are two sources of journal entries for updating the general ledger: summary journal entries from the other AIS cycles and direct entries made by the treasurer. The former are themselves the output of a series of processing steps, each of which was subject to a variety of application control procedures designed to ensure accuracy and completeness, as described in the preceding four chapters. Consequently, the primary input edit control for summary journal entries from the other cycles is configuring the system to verify that the entries represent activity for the most recent time period.

Journal entries made by the treasurer, however, are original data entry. Consequently, the following types of input edit and processing controls are needed to ensure that they are accurate and complete:

1. A *validity check* to ensure that general ledger accounts exist for each account number referenced in a journal entry.
2. *Field (format) checks* to ensure that the amount field in the journal entry contains only numeric data.
3. A *zero-balance check* to verify that total debits equal total credits in a journal entry.
4. A *completeness test* to ensure that all pertinent data are entered, especially the source of the journal entry.
5. *Closed-loop verification* matching account numbers with account descriptions, to ensure that the correct general ledger account is being accessed.
6. A *sign check* of the general ledger account balance, once updating is completed, to verify that the balance is of the appropriate nature (debit or credit).
7. Calculating *run-to-run totals* to verify the accuracy of journal voucher batch processing. (The computer calculates the new balance of the general ledger account, based on its beginning balance and the total debits and credits applied to that account, then compares that with the actual account balance in the updated general ledger. Any discrepancies indicate a processing error that must be investigated.)

Strong access controls, including multifactor authentication and compatibility tests based on access control matrices, reduce the risk of unauthorized journal entries. In addition to these preventive controls, Table 16-1 lists two types of detective controls that should be used to identify inaccurate and unauthorized journal entries: reconciliations and control reports, and maintenance of an adequate audit trail.

RECONCILIATIONS AND CONTROL REPORTS   Reconciliations and control reports can detect whether any errors were made during the process of updating the general ledger. One form of reconciliation is the preparation of a trial balance. The **trial balance** is a report that lists the balances for all general ledger accounts (see Figure 16-5). Its name reflects the fact that if all activities have been properly recorded, the total of all debit balances in various accounts should equal the total of all credit balances; if not, a posting error has occurred.

Another important reconciliation is comparing the general ledger control account balances to the total balance in the corresponding subsidiary ledger. For example, the sum of the balances of individual customer accounts should equal the amount of the accounts receivable control account in the general ledger. If these two totals do not agree, the difference must be investigated and corrected. It is also important to examine all transactions occurring near the end of an accounting period to verify that they are recorded in the proper time period.

At the end of a fiscal period it is also important to verify that any temporary "suspense" or "clearing" accounts have zero balances. Clearing and suspense accounts provide a means to ensure that the general ledger is always in balance. To illustrate how these types of special accounts are used, assume that one clerk is responsible for recording the release of inventory to customers and that another clerk is responsible for recording the billing of customers. The first clerk would make the following journal entry:

    Unbilled shipments   x x x
       Inventory   x x x

The second clerk would make this entry:

    Accounts receivable   x.xx
       Unbilled shipments   x.xx

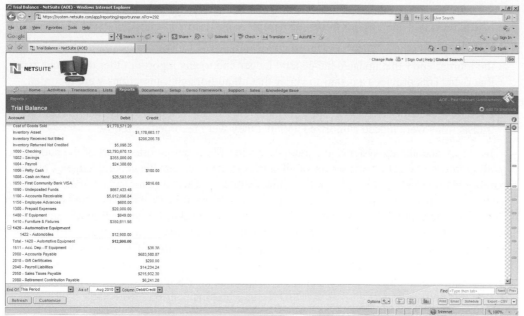

FIGURE 16-5

Example Portion of Trial Balance

© 2010 NetSuite, Inc.

Once both entries have been completed, the special clearing account, unbilled shipments, should have a zero balance. If not, an error has been made and must be investigated and corrected.

Figure 16-6 is an example of one of the many kinds of control reports that ERP systems provide to help identify the source of any errors that occurred in the general ledger update process. Listing journal vouchers by general account number facilitates identifying the cause of errors affecting a specific general ledger account. Listing the journal vouchers by numerical sequence, date, and account number can indicate the absence of any journal entry postings. These reports often include totals to show whether total debits and credits posted to the general ledger were equal.

THE AUDIT TRAIL   The *audit trail* is a traceable path that shows how a transaction flows through the information system to affect general ledger account balances. It is an important detective

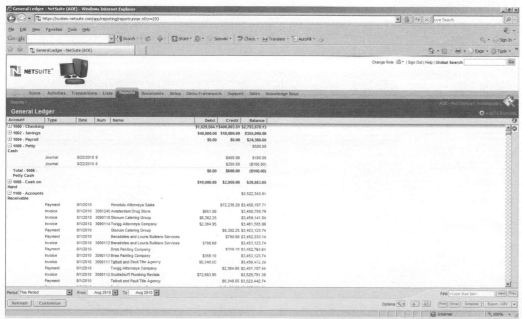

FIGURE 16-6

Example of Control Report Providing Details About Changes to a General Ledger Account Balance

© 2010 NetSuite, Inc.

control that provides evidence about the causes of changes in general ledger account balances. A properly designed audit trail provides the ability to perform the following tasks:

1. Trace any transaction from its original source document (whether paper or electronic) to the journal entry that updated the general ledger and to any report or other document using that data. This provides a means to verify that all authorized transactions were recorded.
2. Trace any item appearing in a report back through the general ledger to its original source document (whether paper or electronic). This provides a means to verify that all recorded transactions were indeed authorized and that they were recorded correctly.

In legacy accounting systems, the journal voucher file is an important part of the audit trail, providing information about the source of all entries made to update the general ledger. The same capability is provided by the business workflow features in ERP systems, which make it easy to trace every step performed in processing a transaction. The usefulness of the audit trail depends on its integrity. Therefore, it is important to periodically make backups of all audit trail components and to control access to them to ensure that they cannot be altered. Thus, as Figure 16-7 shows, access to the audit trail is typically restricted to managers. In addition, ERP systems provide built-in tools to ensure the integrity of the audit trail. SAP, for example, creates prenumbered records (called documents) for every action that is performed. These documents cannot be deleted; thus, enabling this built-in feature ensures that SAP creates and maintains a secure audit trail.

Post Adjusting Entries

The second activity in the general ledger system is posting various adjusting entries (circle 2.0 in Figure 16-2).

Process

Adjusting entries originate from the controller's office, after the initial trial balance has been prepared. Adjusting entries fall into five basic categories:

1. *Accruals* are entries made at the end of the accounting period to reflect events that have occurred but for which cash has not yet been received or disbursed. Examples include the recording of interest revenue earned and wages payable.

FIGURE 16-7

Illustration of How Access to Audit Trail is Restricted to Managers

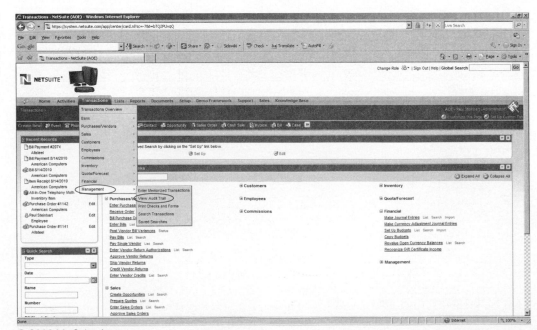

© 2010 NetSuite, Inc.

2. *Deferrals* are entries made at the end of the accounting period to reflect the exchange of cash prior to performance of the related event. Examples include recognizing advance payments from customers as a liability and recording certain payments (e.g., rent, interest, and insurance) as prepaid assets.

3. *Estimates* are entries that reflect a portion of expenses expected to occur over a number of accounting periods. Examples include depreciation and bad-debt expenses.

4. *Revaluations* are entries made to reflect either differences between the actual and recorded value of an asset or a change in accounting principle. Examples include a change in the method used to value inventory, reducing the value of inventory to reflect obsolescence, or adjusting inventory records to reflect the results noted during a physical count of inventory.

5. *Corrections* are entries made to counteract the effects of errors found in the general ledger.

As shown in Figure 16-3, information about these adjusting entries is also stored in the journal voucher file. After all adjusting entries have been posted, an adjusted trial balance is prepared. The adjusted trial balance serves as the input to the next step in the general ledger and financial reporting cycle, the preparation of financial statements.

Threats and Controls

As Table 16-1 shows, inaccurate and unauthorized adjusting journal entries are threats that need to be addressed because they can produce erroneous financial statements that lead to poor decisions. To reduce the risk of erroneous input, the same types of data entry processing integrity controls discussed earlier to prevent the threat of erroneous journal entries by the treasurer should also be applied to adjusting journal entries made by the controller. Often, however, adjusting journal entries are calculated in spreadsheets. Therefore, it is also important to employ the various spreadsheet error protection controls discussed in Chapter 10 to minimize the risk of mistakes. Additional control is provided by creating a standard adjusting entry file for recurring adjusting entries made each period, such as depreciation expense. A standard adjusting entry file improves input accuracy by eliminating the need to repeatedly key in the same types of journal entries. It also reduces the risk of forgetting to make a recurring adjusting entry, thereby ensuring input completeness.

Strong access controls reduce the risk of unauthorized adjusting entries. In addition to the preceding preventive controls, periodic reconciliations and audit trails provide a means to detect unauthorized or inaccurate adjusting entries.

Prepare Financial Statements

The third activity in the general ledger and reporting system is preparing financial statements (circle 3.0 in Figure 16-2).

Process

Most organizations "close the books" to produce financial statements both monthly and annually. A closing journal entry zeroes out all revenue and expense accounts in the adjusted trial balance and transfers the net income (or loss) to retained earnings. The income statement summarizes performance for a period of time (usually either a month or a year). The balance sheet presents information about the organization's assets, liabilities, and equity at a point in time. The statement of cash flows provides information about how the organization's operating, investing, and financing activities affected its cash balance. We now discuss two important recent regulatory and technological developments that are likely to significantly affect the process of preparing financial statements: the proposed upcoming change from U.S. GAAP to IFRS and the mandatory use of XBRL to submit reports to the SEC.

TRANSITION FROM GAAP TO IFRS   In 2010, the SEC reaffirmed its commitment to decide in 2011 whether it will require American companies to switch from U.S.-based Generally Accepted Accounting Principles (GAAP) to International Financial Reporting Standards (IFRS) as the basis for preparing financial statements. Although the switch to IFRS will not likely occur until 2015 at the earliest, companies need to begin planning for the transition now because it will likely require extensive changes to their general ledger and reporting systems.

IFRS differs from GAAP in several ways that affect the design of a company's general ledger and reporting systems. One major difference concerns accounting for fixed assets. Under GAAP, most major fixed assets are recorded and depreciated on a composite basis. For example, the entire cost of a new corporate headquarters building would be recorded as one asset and depreciated over its estimated useful life, which, for buildings, is typically 40 years. In contrast, IFRS generally requires componentization of fixed assets, to recognize the fact that different elements (components) may have different economic lives. In terms of a corporate headquarters building, that would mean that the costs of the roof and of the heating and air conditioning systems would be recorded separately from the building itself, because they are not likely to last 40 years. Componentization will require companies to dig through their databases to identify and disaggregate the costs of many fixed assets. For large companies that may have tens of thousands of fixed assets, componentization will be a major undertaking that carries the risk of classification and recording errors as they change the structure of their general ledgers.

Another difference involves accounting for research and development (R&D) costs. IFRS permits capitalization of development costs at an earlier stage of the process than does GAAP. Consequently, American companies may need to improve the way that they collect and record R&D related costs so that they can properly decide which costs must be expensed and which can be capitalized. At a minimum, this process will require creating additional fields in data records to capture information about the stage of the R&D process when costs were incurred. In turn, this will necessitate careful modification and testing of existing programs to ensure that they correctly process the redesigned transaction records.

A third difference is that IFRS does not permit use of the last-in first-out (LIFO) method of accounting for inventory. Consequently, companies that use LIFO will have to modify their cost accounting systems and the calculations used to value inventory. Those changes will need to be carefully reviewed and tested to minimize the risk of errors.

XBRL: REVOLUTIONIZING THE REPORTING PROCESS *XBRL* stands for e**X**tensible **B**usiness **R**eporting **L**anguage; it is a special programming language designed specifically to facilitate the communication of business information. Beginning in June 2009, the SEC required the 500 largest U.S. public companies to use XBRL when submitting their filings. By June 2011 all public companies will have to use XBRL.

To understand the revolutionary nature of XBRL, examine Figure 16-8. The top portion shows that prior to XBRL, preparers had to manually create reports in various formats for different users. Although those reports were then sent electronically to users, the recipients then had to reenter the data into their own systems in order to manipulate it. The entire process was inefficient and prone to error.

The bottom portion of Figure 16-8 shows how XBRL improves the reporting process. Preparers encode the data and transmit it electronically in various formats to users, who can directly analyze it. Thus, XBRL saves time and reduces the chances for data entry errors.

Without XBRL, electronic documents, regardless of format (text, HTML, PDF, etc.) were essentially just digital versions of paper reports. Humans could read the data, but computers could not automatically process it until the recipient manually entered it in the appropriate format. XBRL changes that by encoding information about what a particular data item means so that other computer programs can understand what to do with it. To illustrate, Figure 16-9 shows how XBRL can annotate a number in a spreadsheet to indicate that it represents sales for a particular time period, following U.S. GAAP and measured in U.S. dollars. (The top portion of Figure 16-9 shows the spreadsheet that most users would see; the XBRL code in the bottom portion is intended for use by software, although it can be viewed by programmers, auditors, or anyone who needs or wants to see it).

XBRL Process and Terminology Figure 16-10 provides a high-level view of the basic steps in preparing and delivering XBRL reports. The XBRL file containing the tagged data that is delivered to users is called an *instance document*. The instance document contains facts about specific financial statement line items, including their values and contextual information such as the measurement unit (dollars, euros, yuans, etc.) and whether the value is for a specific point in time (e.g., a balance sheet item) or a period of time (e.g., an income statement item). Each specific data item in an XBRL document is called an *element*. An element's specific value is displayed in an instance document between tags. Angle brackets are used to identify tags. Two tags are used

FIGURE 16-8
How XBRL Transforms the Reporting Process

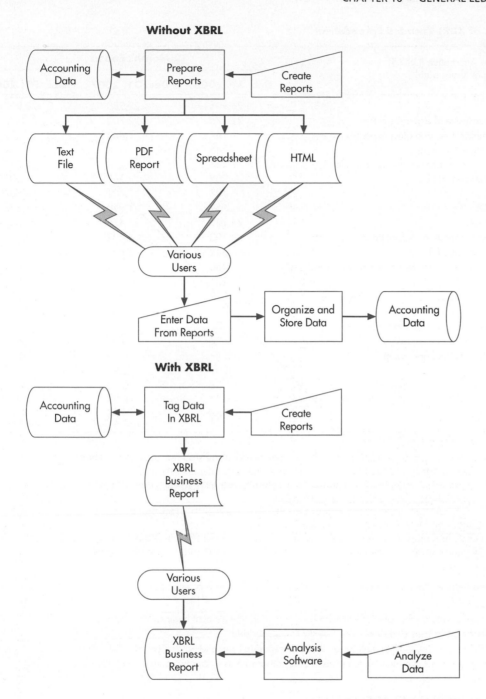

Without XBRL

With XBRL

for each element. The first tag presents the element name inside a pair of angle brackets; the second tag also uses a pair of angle brackets but precedes the element name with a slash. For example, the XBRL code *2590* indicates that value of the element called Net Sales equals 2590. Additional information is needed to properly interpret that value, such as the monetary units used to measure net sales and the time period during which those sales occurred. That context information is also presented in the instance document between tags. For example, the XBRL code *ISO 4217:USD* indicates that items are being measured in U.S. dollars, and *P1Y 2011-12-31* indicates that sales are being reported for the 1-year period ending December 31, 2011.

An instance document is created by applying a taxonomy to a set of data. A *taxonomy* is a set of files that defines the various elements and the relationships between them. One part of the taxonomy is called the *schema,* which is a file that contains the definitions of every element that could appear in an instance document. The following are some of the basic attributes used to define each element:

- A unique identifying *name* used by the software
- A *description* that can be used to correctly interpret the element

Panel A: Portion of XBRL-Encoded Spreadsheet

Statement Of Income Alternative (USD $) (in Millions, except per share data)	12 Months Ended		
	Dec. 31, 2008	Dec. 31, 2007	Dec. 31, 2006
Sales (Q)	26,901	29,280	28,950
Cost of goods sold (exclusive of expenses below)	22,175	22,803	21,955
Selling, general administrative, and other expenses	1,167	1,444	1,372
Research and development expenses	246	238	201
Provision for depreciation, depletion, and amortization	1,234	1,244	1,252
Restructuring and other charges (D)	939	268	507
Interest expense (V)	407	401	384
Other income, net (O)	−59	−1,920	−236
Total costs and expenses	26,109	24,478	25,435
Income from continuing operations before taxes on income	792	4,802	3,515
Provision for taxes on income (T)	342	1,623	853
Income from continuing operations before minority interests' share	450	3,179	2,662
Minority interests	221	365	436
Income from continuing operations (Statement [Line Items])	229	2,814	2,226
(Loss) income from discontinued operations (B)	−303	-250	22
Net (Loss) Income (Statement [Line Items])	−74	2,564	2,248
Income from continuing operations (Basic:)	0.28	3.27	2.56
(Loss) income from discontinued operations (Basic:)	−0.37	−0.29	0.03
Net (loss) income (Basic:)	−0.09	2.98	2.59
Income from continuing operations (Diluted:)	0.28	3.23	2.54
(Loss) income from discontinued operations (Diluted:)	−0.37	−0.28	0.03
Net (loss) income (Diluted:)	−0.09	2.95	2.57

Panel B: Portion of XBRL Code

```
<us-gaap:ResearchAndDevelopmentExpense contextRef="eol_0001193125-09-029469_STD_p12m_20061231_0"
    decimals="-6" unitRef="USD">201000000</us-gaap:ResearchAndDevelopmentExpense>
<us-gaap:RestructuringCharges contextRef="eol_0001193125-09-029469_STD_p12m_20061231_0" decimals="-6"
    unitRef="USD">507000000</us-gaap:RestructuringCharges>
<us-gaap:SalesRevenueGoodsNet contextRef="eol_0001193125-09-029469_STD_p12m_20061231_0" decimals="-6"
    unitRef="USD">28950000000</us-gaap:SalesRevenueGoodsNet>
<us-gaap:SellingGeneralAndAdministrativeExpense contextRef="eol_0001193125-09-029469_STD_p12m_20061231_0"
    decimals="-6" unitRef="USD">1372000000</us-gaap:SellingGeneralAndAdministrativeExpense>
```

Explanation:

The spreadsheet shows that the company had sales of $28,950,000,000 for the year ended December 31, 2006. The XBRL code reveals that:

• The number 28950 appearing on the spreadsheet is based on us-gaap (the element begins with <usgaap: SalesRevenueGoodsNet and closes with </us-gaap:SalesRevenueGoodsNet>).
• The context is the SEC Edgar Online filing (eol) for a 12-month period (p12m) ending on December 31, 2006.
• The numbers on the spreadsheet are rounded to the nearest million (decimals = -6, raw value = 28950000000).
• The value is in U.S. dollars ("USD").

FIGURE 16-9 Example of an XBRL Report

• The element's *data type* (monetary unit, text, date, etc.)
• The element's normal *balance type* (debit or credit)
• The element's *period type* (one point in time, called an instant, or a period of time, called a duration)

Attribute information is enclosed within tags. Thus, to continue our example, the schema would contain the following portion of a definition of the *Net Sales* element:

<element name="NetSales" description="Sales net of returns and allowances" type=monetaryItemType balance="credit" periodType="duration" </element>

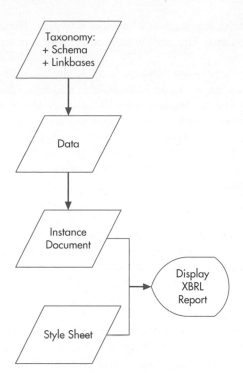

FIGURE 16-10

Electronic Reporting with XBRL

The taxonomy also includes a set of files called *linkbases,* which define the relationships among elements. Important linkbases include the following:

- The *Reference* linkbase identifies relevant authoritative pronouncements (e.g., U.S.-GAAP, IFRS) for that element.
- The *Calculation* linkbase specifies how to combine elements (e.g., that "Current Assets" equals the sum of Cash, Accounts Receivable, and Inventory).
- The *Definition* linkbase indicates hierarchical relationships among elements (e.g., that "Current Assets" is a subset of "Assets").
- The *Presentation* linkbase describes how to group elements (e.g., Assets, Liabilities, and Equities).
- The *Label* linkbase associates human-readable labels with elements.

As Figure 16-10 shows, the information in an XBRL taxonomy is used to tag the data and create an instance document. The same taxonomy is usually used to create a set of separate instance documents, one for each reporting year. Instance documents, however, contain only the data values.. Another document, called the *style sheet,* provides the instructions on how to appropriately display the content of an instance document, either on a computer screen or in a printed report.

The benefits of XBRL are not limited to its use for external reporting. Internal reporting will also benefit because data can be exported from the basic ERP system in a format that managers can import directly into a variety of applications, saving time and eliminating the errors arising from having to manually reenter data.

The Accountant's Role Accountants can, and should, play a major role in all phases of producing XBRL reports, beginning with the selection of an appropriate taxonomy. To ensure comparability across XBRL reports produced by different organizations, standard taxonomies have been developed for many different countries and industries. Accountants use their knowledge of the organization's business practices plus general accounting principles to select the standard taxonomy that best fits the organization. They then map each data item in the organization's accounting system to its corresponding element in the taxonomy.

However, standard taxonomies cannot cover every possible situation. Sometimes, an organization needs to record financial information in a different manner or level of detail to reflect its unique way of doing business. In such cases, accountants can create new tags to more accurately present information about the organization's business activities. These new tags create what is called an *extension taxonomy.* This ability to modify XBRL is why it is referred to as an *extensible* language.

Accountants are also likely to use software to apply the taxonomy (and any extensions) to tag their organization's data, create instance documents, and then validate those instance documents before they are submitted. Accountants will also typically participate in creating style sheets to ensure that the information is displayed appropriately.

Not only do accountants use XBRL; as Focus 16-1 explains, the accounting profession played a major role in its creation. XBRL is a work in process. You should bookmark and regularly visit both the xbrl.org and sec.gov Web sites to stay abreast of continued developments in this important reporting tool.

Threats and Controls

Table 16-1 shows that one threat is the creation of inaccurate financial statements. The data processing integrity controls for journal entries discussed earlier combined with the use of packaged software (e.g., an ERP system) to produce the financial statements minimizes the risk numerical errors in the data. However, because both IFRS and XBRL require numerous judgments about how to classify information, there is a risk that financial statements may not accurately represent the results of operations. For example, mistakes in componentizing fixed assets can result in inaccurate depreciation expenses for IFRS financial statements. XBRL standard taxonomies offer many fine-grained choices (e.g., more than 20 elements define the concept "Cash and Cash Equivalents"), which can result in selecting an inappropriate tag unless the person doing the mapping has extensive knowledge both about the organization's business practices and the XBRL taxonomies. Unnecessarily creating taxonomy extensions instead of using a standard tag is another potential problem. Training and experience will likely reduce the risk of making such mistakes. In addition, an independent external audit is necessary as a detective control.

Fraudulent financial reporting (threat 9) is another potential problem. Financial statement fraud often involves journal entries by upper-level management that cause the organization's financial statements to either overstate revenues or understate liabilities. It is difficult to prevent

FOCUS 16-1   The Accounting Profession's Role in XBRL

The origins of XBRL can be traced back to the early 1990s. At that time, a software engineer named Jon Bosak recognized that a critical shortcoming of HTML is its inability to describe the content of the data being presented. Bosak convinced the World Wide Web Consortium (W3C) to sponsor the development of a language with this capability. That project resulted in Bosak and two other software engineers creating a programming language called XML, which stands for extensible markup language. XML is a general-purpose tool that can tag any data with identifying markers.

XML was a step in the right direction. Charlie Hoffman, a CPA who worked for a local accounting firm in Tacoma, Washington realized, however, that XML did not go far enough to be a general-purpose language for communicating financial information. What was needed was the ability not only to identify each piece of data but also how to process it and how to relate it to other data items. Hoffman started work on adding the desired capabilities to XML but realized that the project required additional support. He sought and obtained the AICPA's help to pursue the

development of a prototype set of XML-enhanced financial statements.

As the work progressed, the results were shared with major software companies, who recognized the value of such a common business language and joined the project. Eventually, many leading software companies, and important user groups, cooperated in the venture with the AICPA. The result: XBRL. The continued development and maintenance of XBRL is now overseen by a nonprofit international organization (XBRL International). Vendors are currently working on making a wide range of financial and decision support software capable of supporting XBRL. Industry-specific coding taxonomies have been developed in many countries. XBRL is on its way to becoming the global computer language for communicating financial data. And it all started with one CPA who was looking for a better way to disseminate financial data on the Internet!

Postscript: In December 2006, the AICPA formally recognized Charlie Hoffman's pioneering work in developing XBRL with a special achievement award.

such journal entries because upper-level management inherently has the ability to override most internal controls. Therefore, the best control to mitigate the threat of financial statement fraud is an independent review (audit) of all special journal entries to the general ledger (i.e., all entries other than the summary journal entries automatically generated by the various cycles discussed in Chapters 12 to 15). Although Statement of Auditing Standards number 99 requires external auditors to "test the appropriateness of journal entries recorded in the general ledger and other adjustments," internal auditors should also regularly review all adjustments to the general ledger. To be effective, however, such testing requires proper configuration of the accounting system, so that every change to general ledger accounts is captured and recorded as part of the audit trail.

Produce Managerial Reports

The final activity in the general ledger and reporting system (circle 4.0 in Figure 16-2) is to produce various managerial reports, including budgets.

Process

ERP systems like the one depicted in Figure 16-3 can produce a number of budgets to help managers plan and evaluate performance. An operating budget depicts planned revenues and expenditures for each organizational unit. A capital expenditures budget shows planned cash inflows and outflows for each capital project. Cash flow budgets compare estimated cash inflows from operations with planned expenditures and are used to determine borrowing needs.

In addition to budgets, the inquiry processing capabilities of ERP systems enable managers to easily create an almost unlimited number of performance reports. For example, sales can be broken down by products, by salesperson, and by customer. Displaying the data in graphs can help managers quickly identify important trends and relationships, as well as areas in need of more detailed analysis. Accountants should understand how to use the flexible reporting and graphing capabilities of ERP systems so that they can add value by suggesting alternative ways to organize and analyze data about business processes.

Threats and Controls

Poorly designed reports and graphs (threat 10 in Table 16-1) can cause managers to make biased or erroneous decisions. The following subsections discuss three important controls to mitigate that threat: the use of responsibility accounting and flexible budgets to design performance reports, the balanced scorecard, and understanding the principles of proper graph design.

RESPONSIBILITY ACCOUNTING AND FLEXIBLE BUDGETING   To properly evaluate performance, reports should highlight the results that can be directly controlled by the person or unit being evaluated. *Responsibility accounting* does this by producing a set of correlated reports that break down the organization's overall performance by the specific subunits which can most directly control those activities, as shown in Figure 16-11. Note how each report shows actual costs and variances from budget for the current month and the year to date, but only for those items that the manager of that subunit controls. Note also the hierarchical nature of the reports: The total cost of each individual subunit is displayed as a single line item on the next-higher-level report.

It is also important to design the budget so that its content matches the nature of the unit being evaluated. For example, the performance reports depicted in Figure 16-11 focus on costs, because production departments are usually treated as cost centers. In contrast, sales departments are often evaluated as revenue centers. Consequently, their performance reports should compare actual to forecasted sales, broken down by appropriate product and geographic categories. Similarly, reports for departments that are treated as profit centers should include both revenues and expenses.

No matter which basis is used to prepare a unit's budgetary performance report, the method used to calculate the budget standard is crucial. The easiest approach is to establish fixed targets for each unit, store those figures in the database, and compare actual performance with those preset values. A major drawback to this approach is that the budget number is static and does not reflect unforeseen changes in the operating environment. Consequently, individual managers may be penalized or rewarded for factors beyond their control. For example, assume that the

FIGURE 16-11

Sample Set of Reports to Illustrate Responsibility Accounting

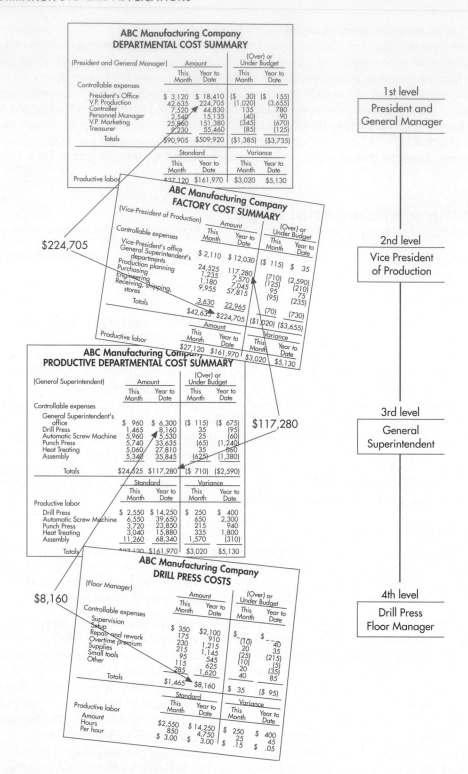

budgeted amounts in Figure 16-11 for the general superintendent are based on planned output of 2,000 units. If, however, actual production is 2,200 units because of greater-than-anticipated sales, then the negative variances for each expense category may indicate not inefficiency, but rather the increased level of output.

A *flexible budget,* in which the budgeted amounts vary in relation to some measure of organizational activity, mitigates such problems. In terms of our previous example, flexible budgeting would entail dividing the budget for each line item in the general superintendent's department into its fixed and variable cost components. In this way, budget standards would be automatically adjusted for any unplanned increases (or decreases) in production. Thus, any differences between these adjusted standards and actual costs can more appropriately be interpreted.

TABLE 16-2 Example of a Balanced Scorecard

Dimension Goals	Measure	Target	Current Period	Prior Period
FINANCIAL				
New revenue streams	Sales of new products (000s)	104	103	100
Improve profitability	Return on equity (%)	12.5%	12.6%	12.2%
Positive cash flow	Cash from operations (000s)	156	185	143
CUSTOMER				
Improve satisfaction	Rating (0–100)	95	93	92
Be a preferred supplier	Percentage of key customers' electronics purchases made from us	20%	20%	18%
INTERNAL OPERATIONS				
Service quality	Orders filled without error (%)	98%	97%	95%
Speed of delivery	Order cycle time (days)	10.4	10.5	11.2
Process efficiency	Defect rate	1.0%	1.1%	1.05%
INNOVATION AND LEARNING				
New products	Number of new products	4	4	3
Employee learning	Personnel attending advanced training courses (%)	10%	25%	9%

THE BALANCED SCORECARD[1]   As the chapter opening case illustrated, one problem with the reports produced by many accounting systems is that the reports too narrowly focus on just one dimension of performance: that reflected in the financial statements. Balanced scorecards attempt to solve that problem. A *balanced scorecard* is a report that provides a multidimensional perspective of organizational performance. As shown in Table 16-2, a balanced scorecard contains measures reflecting four perspectives of the organization: financial, customer, internal operations, and innovation and learning. The financial section contains lagging indicators of past performance, whereas the other three sections provide leading indicators about likely future performance. For each dimension, the balanced scorecard shows the organization's goals and specific measures that reflect performance in attaining those goals. Together, the four dimensions of the balanced scorecard provide a much more comprehensive overview of organizational performance than that provided by financial measures alone. Let us now examine Table 16-2 to see how the four parts of the balanced scorecard reflect key aspects of an organization's strategy and important causal relationships between various measures.

AOE's top management, like many companies, agreed on three key financial goals: increased revenue streams through sales of new products, increased profitability as reflected in return on equity, and maintaining adequate cash flow to meet obligations. As shown in Table 16-2, specific measures and targets were developed to track the attainment of those goals. Both the choice of key metrics and the setting of target values are important management decisions. Many organizations make the mistake of setting targets that reflect industry benchmark values. The problem with such an approach is that the organization's aspirations and, hence, its performance are limited by its competitors' performance. Although industry benchmarks may provide a useful reference point, management should set targets that take into consideration the organization's unique strengths and weaknesses.

For every organization, customers are the key to achieving financial goals. Accordingly, the customer perspective of AOE's balanced scorecard contains two key goals: Improve customer satisfaction and become the preferred supplier for key customers. In turn, meeting those customer-oriented goals requires efficiently and effectively performing internal business processes. Consequently, the internal operations perspective portion of AOE's balanced scorecard focuses on those activities most likely to directly affect customer perceptions: service quality, speed of delivery, and process efficiency. Finally, AOE's top management acknowledged the

---

[1]This section is based on two articles by Robert S. Kaplan and David P. Norton: "The Balanced Scorecard—Measures That Drive Performance," *Harvard Business Review* (January–February 1992): 71–79; and "Using the Balanced Scorecard as a Strategic Management System," *Harvard Business Review* (January–February 1996): 75–85. Additional information about the balanced scorecard can be found at www.balancedscorecard.org.

importance of developing new products and training its workforce to continuously improve service and results. Therefore, measures of those two items are included in the innovation and learning perspective of AOE's balanced scorecard.

Note that the preceding discussion implied a number of hypotheses about cause-and-effect relationships. For example, increased employee training is expected to improve service quality, as reflected in the percentage of customer orders filled correctly. In turn, improved service quality is expected to result in increased customer satisfaction and in more purchases from key customers. Finally, increased customer satisfaction is expected to result in improved profitability and cash flow. Thus, the measures in the innovation and learning, internal operations, and customer perspective portions of the balanced scorecard can be thought of as leading indicators of financial measures of the organization's strategy. Analyzing trends in the actual measures allows AOE's management to test the validity of those hypotheses. If improvements in one perspective do not generate expected improvements in other areas in subsequent time periods, top management must reevaluate and probably revise hypotheses about the determinants of organizational success. Indeed, this ability to test and refine strategy is one of the major benefits the balanced scorecard provides.

Accountants and systems professionals should participate in the development of a balanced scorecard. Top management's role is to specify the goals to be pursued in each dimension. Accountants and information systems professionals can then help management choose the most appropriate measures for tracking achievement of those goals. In addition, they can provide input concerning the feasibility of collecting the data that would be required to implement various proposed measures.

Although the balanced scorecard was initially developed as a strategic management tool, it can also be used as a vehicle to better manage enterprise risk by incorporating appropriate risk-based goals and measures in the various dimensions. For example, an organization might want to increase information security awareness among employees. One way to motivate attention to that objective is to explicitly list increased security awareness as one of the goals in the Innovation and Learning section of the scorecard and then measure employee knowledge about security best practices. Similarly, listing reduced inventory shrinkage as one of the Internal Operations Process goals and measuring it can help focus attention on reducing the risk of employee theft. External threats, such as loss of market share, can likewise be addressed by including appropriate measures (e.g., sales to repeat customers, number of new customers) in the Customer and Financial sections of the balanced scorecard. Thus, the balanced scorecard can be used as one tool to monitor and evaluate an organization's controls and risk management program.

PRINCIPLES OF PROPER GRAPH DESIGN   Well-designed graphs make it easy to identify and understand trends and relationships. Poorly designed graphs, however, can impair decision making by misdirecting attention, hiding important changes in the data, or causing erroneous initial impressions.

Although many types of graphs exist, bar charts are the most common type used to display trends in financial data. Therefore, we will focus on some basic principles that make bar charts easy to read. Figure 16-12 illustrates the following principles of good graph design:

1. Use a title that summarizes the basic message.
2. Include data values with each element to facilitate mental calculations and analyses.

FIGURE 16-12

Example of a Well-Designed Graph

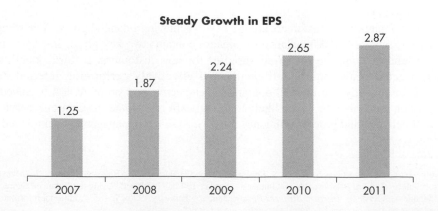

Steady Growth in EPS

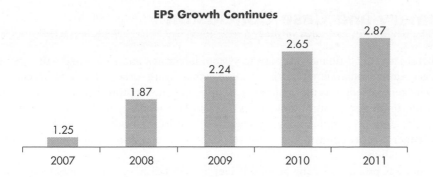

FIGURE 16-13

Example of a Poorly Designed Graph: Vertical Axis Does Not Begin at Zero

3. Use 2-D, instead of 3-D, bars because that makes it easier to accurately assess the magnitude of changes and trends.

However, graphs not only must be easy to read but also must lead to accurate interpretations of the underlying data. The following two principles are essential for properly designing bar charts of financial data so that they are accurately interpreted:

1. *Begin the vertical axis at zero.*   Doing so ensures that the depicted magnitude of change in the data *accurately* reflects the actual change in the data. Beginning at a value other than zero, by contrast, magnifies the visual appearance of a trend. To see the importance of this rule, compare Figure 16-12, which follows this principle, to Figure 16-13, which does not. Exception: Beginning the vertical axis at a value other than zero may be useful if there is a need to monitor minor fluctuations in the data. For example, a day trader may need to quickly identify small changes in stock prices.
2. *For graphs that depict time-series data, order the x-axis chronologically from left to right.*   This principle is illustrated in Figure 16-12. Otherwise, the viewer may form an erroneous initial impression of the nature of the change in the data. For example, the initial visual impression created by Figure 16-14 is that of a declining trend.

The rules for proper graph design are simple, but they are easy to violate. Sometimes, such violations are created automatically by the software program used to create the graph. For example, many financial spreadsheets display the data in reverse chronological order, with the most recent year's data in the column immediately to the right of the descriptive labels. In this case, selecting the data and using the spreadsheet's built-in charting functions automatically produces a graph in which the *x*-axis is in reverse chronological order. Other times, however, violations occur because of deliberate choices made by the graph designer. Regardless of the reason, violating the principles of proper graph design can result in graphs that mislead viewers. Therefore, it is important for accountants and information systems professionals to understand the principles for properly designing graphs so that they can avoid inadvertently creating misleading graphs and identify and correct any such graphs they encounter.

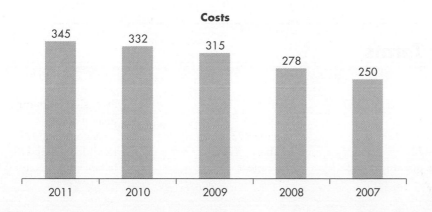

FIGURE 16-14

Example of a Poorly Designed Graph: X-Axis in Reverse Chronological Order

Summary and Case Conclusion

The general ledger and financial reporting system integrates and summarizes the results of the various accounting subsystems for the revenue, expenditure, production, and human resources cycles. The general ledger is the central master file in the accounting system. Consequently, it is important to implement control procedures to ensure its accuracy and security. Important controls include data processing integrity checks of the journal voucher records posted to the general ledger, access controls, an adequate audit trail, and appropriate backup and disaster recovery procedures.

The outputs produced by the general ledger system fall into two primary categories: financial statements and managerial reports. The former are prepared periodically in accordance with regulatory frameworks (GAAP or IFRS) and are distributed to both internal and external users. The latter are prepared for internal use only and therefore often include comparisons between actual and budgeted performance. The usefulness of these reports, whether presented in the form of tables or graphs, is affected by how well they are designed.

Organizations must provide information to a wide variety of users, including government agencies, industry analysts, financial institutions, and individual decision makers. XBRL provides a mechanism for improving the efficiency of generating such information, as well as for using information obtained from external sources. Elizabeth Venko and Ann Brandt proposed that AOE purchase special software designed to create XBRL documents from data in AOE's system. Linda Spurgeon approved their request.

Elizabeth and Ann also explained that AOE's new integrated transaction processing database provides much of the data needed to create a balanced scorecard. They told Linda that they could help her design a balanced scorecard that included metrics that would reflect AOE's strategic goals. Elizabeth also suggested that managers should be trained on how to design graphs properly to depict accurately key performance trends. Linda and Stephanie agreed with those suggestions. They asked Elizabeth and Ann to to oversee the development of some classes in graph design. Finally, Linda approved Elizabeth and Ann's request for two accountants and two IS staff to be assigned to begin work on reconfiguring AOE's new ERP system to generate financial statements in accordance with IFRS.

This chapter concludes our examination of the various cycles in an integrated accounting system. This chapter and the previous four explained how an accounting system should be designed: (1) to process transactions for accountability purposes, (2) to maintain adequate controls to ensure the integrity of the organization's data and the safeguarding of its assets, and (3) to provide information to support decision making. One other theme that appears throughout this book is the need for accountants to move beyond the traditional role of scorekeeper and actively seek to add value to their organization. Accountants should participate in decisions about adopting new technology and implementing new information systems because they have the training to properly evaluate the relative costs and benefits, as well as the economic risks, underlying such investments. Effectively participating in decisions concerning technology, however, requires accountants not only to keep abreast of current accounting developments but also to stay informed about advances in IT. Thus, as an accountant, you must make a commitment to lifelong learning. We wish you well in this endeavor.

Key Terms

journal voucher file 467	element 472	extension taxonomy 476
audit trail 469	taxonomy 473	responsibility
trial balance 468	schema 473	accounting 477
XBRL 472	linkbases 475	flexible budget 478
instance document 472	style sheet 475	balanced scorecard 479

AIS IN ACTION

Chapter Quiz

1. From where do adjusting entries usually come?
    a. treasurer
    b. controller
    c. various accounting cycle subsystems, such as sales order entry
    d. unit managers

2. Preparing performance reports that contain data only about items that a specific organizational unit controls is an example of which of the following?
    a. flexible budget system   c. closing the books
    b. responsibility accounting system d. management by exception

3. The definition of an XBRL element, including such information as whether its normal account balance is a debit or a credit, is found in which of the following?
    a. linkbase   c. schema
    b. instance document   d. style sheet

4. Which of the following shows the implied linkages among the portions of the balanced scorecard?
    a. Financial → Internal → Innovation and learning → Customer
    b. Innovation and learning → Internal → Customer → Financial
    c. Customer → Financial → Internal → Innovation and learning
    d. Internal → Customer → Innovation and learning → Financial

5. Which of the following XBRL documents contains the actual data values for a company's net income for a particular year?
    a. style sheets   c. linkbases
    b. schema   d. instance document

6. The number of orders shipped per warehouse worker each day is a metric that would most likely appear in which part of the balanced scorecard?
    a. innovation and learning   c. internal operations
    b. customer   d. financial

7. Which of the following is an important part of the audit trail?
    a. journal vouchers   c. trial balance
    b. flexible budgets   d. data warehouse

8. An adjusting journal entry to record interest revenue that has been earned but not yet received is an example of which of the following?
    a. accrual   c. estimate
    b. deferral   d. revaluation

9. Which of the following is designed primarily to improve the efficiency of financial reporting?
    a. XML   c. IFRS
    b. XBRL   d. the balanced scorecard

10. Which of the following graph design principles is most important for ensuring that financial data are accurately interpreted?
    a. including a title that summarizes the point of the graph
    b. attaching data values to specific elements in the graph
    c. starting the y-axis of the graph at zero
    d. using different colors for different variables

Discussion Questions

16.1. Although XBRL facilitates the electronic exchange of financial information, some external users do not think it goes far enough. They would like access to the entire general ledger, not just to XBRL-tagged financial reports that summarize general ledger accounts. Should companies provide external users with such access? Why or why not?

16.2. How can responsibility accounting and flexible budgets improve morale?

16.3. Why is the audit trail an important control?

16.4. The balanced scorecard measures organizational performance along four dimensions. Is it possible that measures on the customer, internal operations, and innovation and learning dimensions could be improving without any positive change in the financial dimension? If so, what are the implications of such a pattern?

16.5. Do you think that mandatory standards should be developed for the design of graphs of financial data that are included in annual reports and other periodic communications to investors? Why or why not?

Problems

16.1. Match the term in the left column with its appropriate definition from the right column:

____	**1.** Journal voucher file	a. An individual financial statement item
____	**2.** Instance document	b. Evaluating performance based on controllable costs
____	**3.** XBRL element	c. Evaluating performance by computing standards in light of actual activity levels
____	**4.** Balanced scorecard	d. The set of journal entries that updated the general ledger
____	**5.** XBRL extension taxonomy	e. A set of files that defines XBRL elements and specifies the relationships among them
____	**6.** Audit trail	f. A multidimensional performance report
____	**7.** XBRL taxonomy	g. A file that defines relationships among XBRL elements
____	**8.** XBRL linkbase	h. A file that defines the attributes of XBRL elements
____	**9.** XBRL schema	i. A detective control that can be used to trace changes in general ledger account balances back to source documents
____	**10.** XBRL style sheet	j. A file that explains how to display an XBRL instance document
____	**11.** Responsibility accounting	k. A file that contains specific data values for a set of XBRL elements for a specific time period or point in time
____	**12.** Flexible budget	l. A file containing a set of customized tags to define new XBRL elements that are unique to a specific organization

16.2. Which control procedure would be most effective in addressing the following problems?

a. When entering a journal entry to record issuance of new debt, the treasurer inadvertently transposes two digits in the debit amount.

b. The spreadsheet used to calculate accruals had an error in a formula. As a result, the controller's adjusting entry was for the wrong amount.

c. The controller forgot to make an adjusting entry to record depreciation.

d. A sales manager tipped off friends that the company's financial results, to be released tomorrow, were unexpectedly good.

   e. The general ledger master file is stored on disk. For some reason, the disk is no longer readable. It takes the accounting department a week to reenter the past month's transactions from source documents in order to create a new general ledger master file.

   f. The controller sent a spreadsheet containing a preliminary draft of the income statement to the CFO by e-mail. An investor intercepted the e-mail and used the information to sell his stock in the company before news of the disappointing results became public.

   g. A company's XBRL business report was incorrect because the controller selected the wrong element from the taxonomy.

   h. Instead of a zero, an employee entered the letter o when typing in data values in an XBRL instance document.

16.3. Explain the components of an audit trail for verifying changes to accounts payable. Your answer should specify how those components can be used to verify the accuracy, completeness, and validity of all purchases, purchase returns, purchase discounts, debit memos, and cash disbursements.

16.4. As manager of a local pizza parlor, you want to develop a balanced scorecard so you can more effectively monitor the restaurant's performance.

Required

   a. Propose at least two goals for each dimension, and explain why those goals are important to the overall success of the pizza parlor. One goal should be purely performance oriented, and the other should be risk related.

   b. Suggest specific measures for each goal developed in part a.

   c. Explain how to gather the data needed for each measure developed in part b.

16.5. Use Table 16-1 to create a questionnaire checklist that can be used to evaluate controls in the general ledger and reporting cycle.

   a. For each control issue, write a Yes/No question such that a "No" answer represents a control weakness. For example, one question might be "Is access to the general ledger restricted?"

   b. For each Yes/No question, write a brief explanation of why a "No" answer represents a control weakness.

16.6. Visit the SEC website (www.sec.gov), and explore what is available in terms of interactive data (the SEC's term for XBRL reports). Use the SEC's viewer software, and examine the annual reports for two companies.

16.7. Obtain the annual report of a company assigned by your professor. Read the management discussion and analysis section, and develop a balanced scorecard that reflects that company's vision, mission, and strategy. Create both performance-oriented and risk-based goals and measures for each section of the balanced scorecard.

16.8. Excel Problem. Objective: Practice graph design principles.

Required (continues on next page)

Use the data in Table 16-3 to create the following graphs:

   a. Sales

   b. Sales and Gross Margin

   c. Earnings per Share

TABLE 16-3 Data for Problem 16-8

	2010	2009	2008	2007	2006
Sales	598,000	640,000	575,000	560,000	530,000
Cost of Goods Sold	350,000	400,000	375,000	330,000	300,000
Gross Margin	248,000	240,000	200,000	230,000	230,000
Earnings Per Share	12.52	12.10	11.95	11.66	10.50

Which principles of graph design, if any, did you have to manually implement to override the default graphs created by Excel?

16.9. Excel Problem

Objective: Create pivot tables for what-if analysis.

Required

Read the article "Make Excel an Instant Know-It-All" by Roberta Ann Jones in the March 2004 issue of the *Journal of Accountancy* (available at www.aicpa.org).
a. Follow the instructions in the article to create a spreadsheet with pivot tables.
b. Print out a report that shows sales by month for each salesperson.
c. Assume that Brown and David are in sales group 1 and that the other three salespeople are in sales group 2. Print out a report that shows monthly sales for each group.

16.10. Excel Problem

Objective: How to do what-if analysis with graphs.

Required

a. Read the article "Tweaking the Numbers," by Theo Callahan in the June 2001 issue of the *Journal of Accountancy* (available at www.aicpa.org). Follow the instructions in the article to create a spreadsheet with graphs that do what-if analysis.
b. Now create a spreadsheet to do graphical what-if analysis for the "cash gap." Cash gap represents the number of days between when a company has to pay its suppliers and when it gets paid by its customers. Thus,

$$\text{Cash gap} = \text{Inventory days on hand} + \text{Receivables collection period} - \text{Accounts payable period}$$

The purpose of your spreadsheet is to display visually what happens to cash gap when you "tweak" policies concerning inventory, receivables, and payables. Thus, you will create a spreadsheet that looks like Figure 16-15.

c. Set the three spin buttons to have the following values:

	Spin Button for Inventory	Spin Button for Receivables	Spin Button for Payables
Linked cell	C2	C3	C4
Maximum	120	120	90
Minimum	0	30	20
Value	30	60	20
Small change	10	10	10

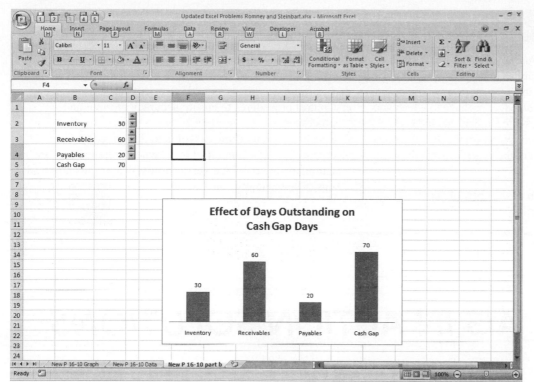

FIGURE 16-15

Spreadsheet for Problem 16-10, part b

Case16-1 Keeping Current with XBRL

Like IT in general, XBRL is continually evolving. Visit xbrl.org to identify developments in the standard, the use of XBRL by companies and regulatory agencies, and XBRL-related products that have come out during the past twelve months. Write a report summarizing your findings.

Case16-2 Evaluating a General Ledger Package

Accounting magazines such as *Journal of Accountancy* and *Strategic Finance* periodically publish reviews of accounting software. Obtain a copy of a recent software review article, and read its comments about a general ledger package to which you have access. Using the software, write a report that indicates whether, and why, you agree or disagree with the review's opinions about the following features of the general ledger package:

a. Ease of installation
b. Flexibility in the initial setup of the chart of accounts and during subsequent modifications
c. Frequency of updates from subsystems (sales, cash receipts, etc.)
d. Control procedures available to restrict access
e. Control procedures to ensure accuracy of input and processing
f. Report flexibility (how easy it is to design reports, etc.)
g. Adequacy of the audit trail (e.g., what reference data are automatically provided versus how much of the audit trail has to be manually constructed)

AIS IN ACTION SOLUTIONS

Quiz Key

1. From where do adjusting entries usually come?
   a. treasurer (Incorrect. Adjusting entries are entered by the controller after the trial balance has been prepared. The treasurer makes regular journal entries to record financing activities, such as issuing or retiring debt.)
   ▶ b. controller (Correct. Adjusting entries are entered by the controller after the trial balance has been prepared.)
   c. various accounting cycle subsystems, such as sales order entry (Incorrect. Subsystems send summary regular journal entries, not adjusting entries, to the general ledger.)
   d. unit managers (Incorrect. Unit managers should not make any journal entries.)

2. Preparing performance reports that contain data only about items that a specific organizational unit controls is an example of which of the following?
   a. flexible budget system (Incorrect. Flexible budgets adjust targets based on actual inputs.)
   ▶ b. responsibility accounting system (Correct. This is the essence and purpose of responsibility accounting.)
   c. closing the books (Incorrect. Closing the books is a process performed at the end of a fiscal period to prepare financial statements.)
   d. management by exception (Incorrect. Management by exception is a reporting technique that focuses on unusual variations from standards.)

3. The definition of an XBRL element, including such information as whether its normal account balance is a debit or a credit, is found in which of the following?
   a. linkbase (Incorrect. The linkbase files in the taxonomy provide information about relationships among elements.)
   b. instance document (Incorrect. The instance document contains the value of an element and contextual information, but not its full definition.)
   ▶ c. schema (Correct. The schema file in the taxonomy contains definitions of XBRL elements.)
   d. style sheet (Incorrect. The style sheet specifies how to display an instance document on either a computer screen or on a printed report.)

4. Which of the following shows the implied linkages among the portions of the balanced scorecard?

   a. Financial → Internal → Innovation and learning → Customer (Incorrect.)

   ▶ b. Innovation and learning → Internal → Customer → Financial (Correct. The theory underlying the balanced scorecard is that learning and innovation will improve internal measures of performance, which will in turn improve customer satisfaction, which will then be reflected in better financial performance.)

   c. Customer → Financial → Internal → Innovation and learning (Incorrect.)

   d. Internal → Customer → Innovation and learning → Financial (Incorrect.)

5. Which of the following XBRL documents contains the actual data values for a company's net income for a particular year?

   a. style sheets (Incorrect. Style sheets provide information about how to display the information in an instance document.)

   b. schema (Incorrect. Schemas define elements of financial statements, such as net income, but do not provide actual data values for those elements.)

   c. linkbases (Incorrect. Linkbases describe relationships among taxonomy elements.)

   ▶ d. instance document (Correct. An instance document contains specific values for financial statement elements.)

6. The number of orders shipped per warehouse worker each day is a metric that would most likely appear in which part of the balanced scorecard?

   a. innovation and learning (Incorrect. The proposed metric is a measure of process efficiency and, therefore, would appear in the internal operations section of the balanced scorecard.)

   b. customer (Incorrect. The proposed metric is a measure of process efficiency and, therefore, would appear in the internal operations section of the balanced scorecard.)

   ▶ c. internal operations (Correct.)

   d. financial (Incorrect. The proposed metric is a measure of process efficiency and, therefore, would appear in the internal operations section of the balanced scorecard.)

7. Which of the following is an important part of the audit trail?

   ▶ a. journal vouchers (Correct. Journal vouchers provide information concerning the source of changes to the general ledger accounts.)

   b. flexible budgets (Incorrect. Flexible budgets are a performance evaluation tool.)

   c. trial balance (Incorrect. The trial balance is a step in the preparation of financial statements.)

   d. data warehouse (Incorrect. A data warehouse is used for business intelligence.)

8. An adjusting journal entry to record interest revenue that has been earned but not yet received is an example of which of the following?

   ▶ a. accrual (Correct.)

   b. deferral (Incorrect. A deferral would involve postponing recognition of an event for which cash has already been exchanged in advance of performing the event.)

   c. estimate (Incorrect. An estimate is an entry used to record the results of judgmental analysis.)

   d. revaluation (Incorrect. A revaluation entry is used to correct a prior error.)

9. Which of the following is designed primarily to improve the efficiency of financial reporting?

   a. XML (Incorrect. XML is a general-purpose language but is not designed for financial reporting.)

   ▶ b. XBRL (Correct. The eXtensible Business Reporting Language was developed, in part, by accountants to facilitate business reporting.)

   c. IFRS (Incorrect. IFRS is an alternative to GAAP.)

   d. the The balanced scorecard (Incorrect. The balanced scorecard is a multidimensional performance report.)

10. Which of the following graph design principles is most important for ensuring that financial data is accurately interpreted?
    a. including a title that summarizes the point of the graph (Incorrect. This principle improves readability but is not specifically designed to ensure that the graph is accurately interpreted.)
    b. attaching data values to specific elements in the graph (Incorrect. This principle facilitates making mental calculations but is not specifically designed to ensure that the graph is accurately interpreted.)
    ▶ c. starting the *y*-axis of the graph at zero (Correct. Starting the *y*-axis at zero accurately depicts the magnitude of changes in the data.)
    d. using different colors for different variables (Incorrect. This principle improves readability but is not specifically designed to ensure that the graph is accurately interpreted.)

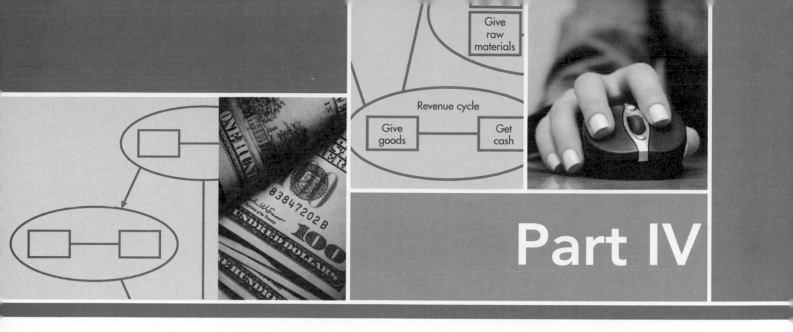

Part IV

The REA Data Model

Chapter 17

Database Design Using the REA Data Model

Learning Objectives

After studying this chapter, you should be able to:

1. Discuss the steps for designing and implementing a database system.

2. Use the REA data model to design an AIS database.

3. Draw an REA diagram of an AIS database.

4. Read an REA diagram and explain what it reveals about the business activities and policies of the organization being modeled.

INTEGRATIVE CASE FRED'S TRAIN SHOP

Fred Smith is frustrated. Business in his model train shop is booming. But the simple accounting software that he uses to run the business has only limited reporting capabilities. Consequently, he often has to manually review transaction data to prepare custom reports. The process is time-consuming and prone to error. For example, Fred spent the past weekend poring over sales records for the prior three months to try to identify which combinations of items were most frequently purchased together. He plans to use the information to offer a special sales promotion but is concerned about the quality of his analysis.

At lunch, Fred explains his frustrations to his CPA, Paul Stone. Paul mentions that he has just completed a training course on database design. He suggests that he could create a relational database for Fred that would interface with his accounting software and that would provide Fred with the ability to easily design reports to analyze his business. Fred likes the idea and hires Paul to design a relational database for his train store.

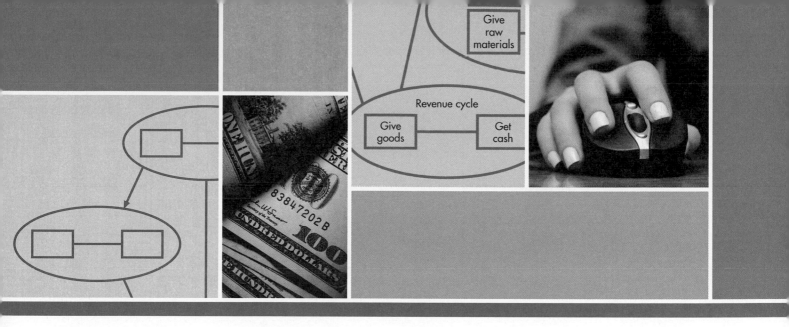

Introduction

Chapter 4 covered the fundamental principles of relational databases. The three chapters in this section will teach you how to design and document a relational database for an accounting information system. You will see that there is much more to building a database than simply learning the syntax of how to use a particular database management system (DBMS). Building accurate databases requires a great deal of careful planning and design *before* you even sit down at the computer.

This chapter introduces the topic of data modeling, one aspect of database design that accountants should understand. We discuss entity-relationship (E-R) diagrams and the REA accounting model and demonstrate how to use these tools to build a data model of an AIS. Then we discuss how such REA models can also serve as a source of documentation about an organization's business activities and policies. Chapter 18 will explain how to implement an REA data model in a database and how to query the resulting database to retrieve information needed to effectively manage an organization's business activities. Chapter 19 concludes this three-chapter section by examining a number of advanced data modeling and database design issues.

Database Design Process

Figure 17-1 shows the five basic steps in database design. The first stage (systems analysis) consists of initial planning to determine the need for and feasibility of developing a new system. This stage includes preliminary judgments about the proposal's technological and economic feasibility. It also involves identifying user information needs, defining the scope of the proposed new system, and using information about the expected number of users and transaction volumes to make preliminary decisions about hardware and software requirements. The second stage (conceptual design) includes developing the different schemas for the new system at the conceptual, external, and internal levels. The third stage (physical design) consists of translating the internal-level schema into the actual database structures that will be implemented in the new system. This is also the stage when new applications are developed. The fourth stage (implementation and conversion) includes all the activities associated with transferring data from existing systems to the new database AIS, testing the new system, and training employees how to use it. The final stage is using and maintaining the new system. This includes carefully monitoring system performance and user satisfaction to determine the need for making system enhancements and modifications. Eventually, changes in business strategies and practices or significant new developments in information technology prompt the company to begin investigating the

FIGURE 17-1

Data Modeling in the Database Design Process

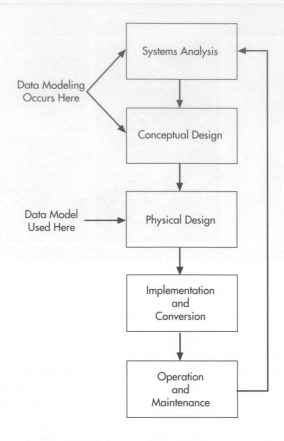

feasibility of developing a new system, and the entire process starts again (note the arrow returning to the systems analysis stage).

Accountants can and should participate in every stage of the database design process, although the level of their involvement is likely to vary across stages. During the systems analysis phase, accountants help evaluate project feasibility and identify user information needs. In the conceptual design stage, accountants participate in developing the logical schemas, designing the data dictionary, and specifying important controls. Accountants with good database skills may directly participate in implementing the data model during the physical design stage. During the implementation and conversion stage, accountants should be involved in testing the accuracy of the new database and the application programs that will use that data, as well as assessing the adequacy of controls. Finally, many accountants are regular users of the organization's database and sometimes even have responsibility for its management.

Accountants may provide the greatest value to their organizations by taking responsibility for data modeling. **Data modeling** is the process of defining a database so that it faithfully represents all aspects of the organization, including its interactions with the external environment. As shown in Figure 17-1, data modeling occurs during both the systems analysis and conceptual design stages of database design. Next, we discuss two important tools that accountants can use to perform data modeling: entity-relationship diagramming and the REA data model.

Entity-Relationship Diagrams[1]

An *entity-relationship (E-R) diagram* is a graphical technique for portraying a database schema. It is called an E-R diagram because it shows the various *entities* being modeled and the important *relationships* among them. An *entity* is anything about which the organization wants

---

[1]The material in this section is based on P. Chen, "The Entity Relationship Model—Toward a Unified View of Data," *Transactions on Database Systems* (March 1976, 1:1): 9–36.

to collect and store information. For example, Fred's Train Shop's database would include entities for employees, customers, suppliers, inventory, and for business events such as sales to customers and deliveries from suppliers. In a relational database, separate tables would be created to store information about each distinct entity; in an object-oriented database, separate classes would be created for each distinct entity.

In an E-R diagram, entities are depicted as rectangles. Unfortunately, however, there are no industry standards for other aspects of E-R diagrams. Some data modelers and authors use diamonds to depict relationships (Figure 17-2, panel A) whereas others do not (Figure 17-2, panel B). Sometimes the attributes associated with each entity are depicted as named ovals connected to each rectangle (Figure 17-2, panel C), whereas other times the attributes associated with each entity are listed in a separate table (Figure 17-2, panel D). In this book, we will be creating E-R diagrams with a large number of entities and relationships. Therefore, to reduce clutter and improve readability, we omit the diamonds for relationships and list the attributes associated with each entity in a separate table. Thus, our diagrams look like panels B and D in Figure 17-2.

E-R diagrams can be used to represent the contents of any kind of database. For example, the E-R diagram of an intramural sports database might include students, teams, and leagues as entities, whereas an E-R diagram for a school might include students, teachers, and courses as entities. In this book, our focus is on databases designed to support an organization's business activities. Consequently, we will show how E-R diagrams can be used not only to design databases but also to document and understand existing databases and to redesign business processes. Business process management is covered in Part V; in this chapter we focus on using E-R diagrams for database design and for understanding the contents of existing databases.

As noted, E-R diagrams can include many different kinds of entities and relationships among those entities. An important step in database design, therefore, entails deciding which entities need to be modeled. The REA data model is useful for making that decision.

FIGURE 17-2
E-R Diagram Variations

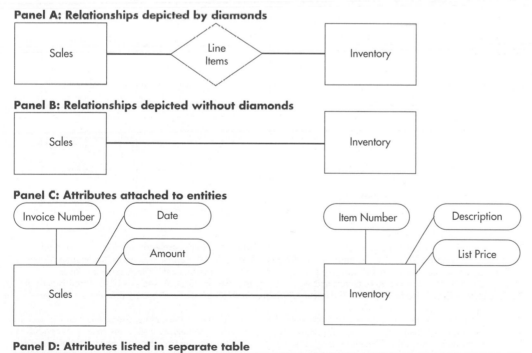

Entity Name	Attributes
Sales	Invoice number, date, amount
Inventory	Item number, description, list price

The REA Data Model[2]

The *REA data model* was developed specifically for use in designing AIS. The REA data model focuses on the business semantics underlying an organization's value-chain activities. It provides guidance for database design by identifying what entities should be included in the AIS database and by prescribing how to structure relationships among the entities in that database. REA data models are usually depicted in the form of E-R diagrams. Consequently, in the remainder of this chapter and throughout the book, we will refer to E-R diagrams developed according to the REA data model as REA diagrams.

Three Basic Types of Entities

The REA data model is so named because it classifies entities into three distinct categories: the *r*esources the organization acquires and uses, the *e*vents (business activities) in which the organization engages, and the *a*gents participating in these events.[3] Figure 17-3 provides examples of these three types of entities.

Resources are those things that have economic value to the organization. Figure 17-3 includes two resource entities: cash and inventory. *Events* are the various business activities about which management wants to collect information for planning or control purposes.[4] There are two event entities in Figure 17-3: Sales and Receive Cash. *Agents* are the people and organizations that participate in events and about whom information is desired for planning, control, and evaluation purposes. Figure 17-3 includes two types of agent entities: Employees and Customers.

FIGURE 17-3

Basic Elements of an REA Diagram

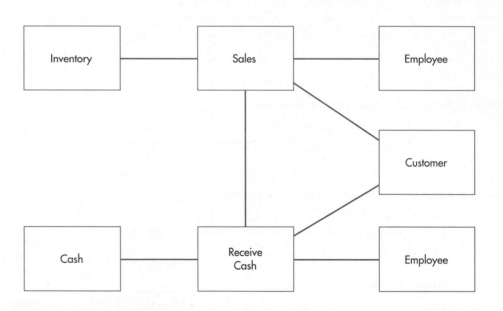

[2]The material in this section is adapted from William E. McCarthy, "An Entity-Relationship View of Accounting Models," *The Accounting Review* (October 1979): 667–686; William E. McCarthy, "The REA Accounting Model: A Generalized Framework for Accounting Systems in a Shared Data Environment," *The Accounting Review* (July 1982): 554–578; and Guido L. Geerts and W. E. McCarthy, "An Ontological Analysis of the Primitives of the Extended-REA Enterprise Information Architecture," *International Journal of Accounting Information Systems* 3(March 2002): 1–16.

[3]Some REA data modelers have proposed a fourth type of entity, which they call locations. Stores and warehouses would be examples of this fourth type of entity. However, such "location" entities are usually also resources controlled by the organization. Therefore, the authors of this text see no compelling reason to create yet another type of entity and model locations as resources. If an organization does not want or need to store information about locations except to identify where an event occurred, location can be an attribute for each event.

[4]The discussion of events in this section is based on the work of Julie Smith David, "Three 'Events' That Define an REA Methodology for Systems Analysis, Design, and Implementation," Working Paper, Arizona State University, August 1997, and Guido L. Geerts and W. E. McCarthy, "An Ontological Analysis of the Primitives of the Extended-REA Enterprise Information Architecture," *International Journal of Accounting Information Systems* 3 (March 2002): 1–16.

Structuring Relationships: The Basic REA Template

The REA data model prescribes a basic pattern for how the three types of entities (resources, events, and agents) should relate to one another. Figure 17-4 presents this basic pattern. The essential features of the pattern are as follows:

1. Each event is linked to at least one resource that it affects.
2. Each event is linked to at least one other event.
3. Each event is linked to at least two participating agents.

RULE 1: EVERY EVENT ENTITY MUST BE LINKED TO AT LEAST ONE RESOURCE ENTITY   Events *must* be linked to at least one resource that they affect. Some events, such as the one labeled "Get Resource A" in Figure 17-4, increase the quantity of a resource. Common examples of such "Get" events include the receipt of goods from a supplier (which increases the quantity on hand of inventory) and the receipt of payment from a customer (which increases the amount of cash). Other events, such as the one labeled "Give Resource B" in Figure 17-4, directly decrease the quantity of a resource. Common examples of such "Give" events include paying suppliers and selling merchandise, which decrease the amount of cash and quantity on hand of inventory, respectively.

Relationships that affect the quantity of a resource are sometimes referred to as *stockflow* relationships because they represent either an inflow or outflow of that resource. Not every event directly alters the quantity of a resource, however. For example, orders from customers represent commitments that will eventually result in a future sale of merchandise, just as orders to suppliers represent commitments that will eventually result in the subsequent purchase of inventory. For simplicity, Figure 17-4 does not include any such commitment events. Organizations do, however, need to track the effects of such commitments, both to provide better service and for planning purposes. For example, customer orders reduce the quantity available of the specific inventory items being ordered. Sales staff need to know this information to be able to properly respond to subsequent customer inquiries and orders. Manufacturing companies may use information about customer orders to plan production. Later in the chapter we will see how to add commitment events to the basic pattern shown in Figure 17-4.

RULE 2: EVERY EVENT ENTITY MUST BE LINKED TO AT LEAST ONE OTHER EVENT ENTITY
Figure 17-4 also shows that the Get Resource A event is linked to the Give Resource B event in what is labeled as an economic duality relationship. Such give-to-get duality relationships reflect

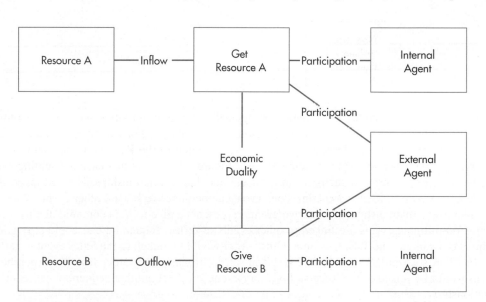

FIGURE 17-4
Standard REA Template

The names on the lines describe the nature of the relationship. Agents participate in events. The economic duality relationship between the "get" event and the "give" event reflects the fact that organizations must give up one resource (e.g., cash) in order to get some other resource (e.g., inventory). The stockflow relationships between an event and a resource represent either inflows or outflows of a resource.

FIGURE 17-5

An AIS Viewed as a Set of Give-to-get Exchanges

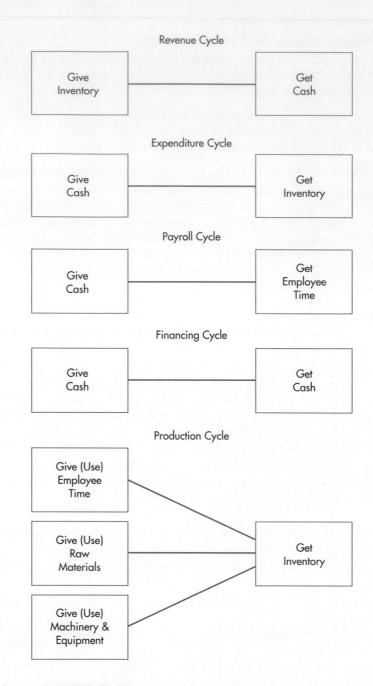

the basic business principle that organizations typically engage in activities that use up resources only in the hopes of acquiring some other resource in exchange. For example, the Sales event, which requires giving up (decreasing) inventory, is related to the Receive Cash event, which involves getting (increasing) the amount of cash. Figure 17-5 shows that each accounting cycle can be described in terms of such give-to-get economic duality relationships. The bottom portion of the figure also shows that sometimes one event can be linked to several other events.

Not every relationship between two events represents a give-to-get economic duality, however. Commitment events are linked to other events to reflect sequential cause–effect relationships. For example, the Take Customer Order event would be linked to the Sales event to reflect the fact that such orders precede and result in sales. Similarly, the Order Inventory (purchase) event would be linked to the Receive Inventory event to reflect another sequential cause–effect relationship.

RULE 3: EVERY EVENT ENTITY MUST BE LINKED TO AT LEAST TWO PARTICIPATING AGENTS For accountability, organizations need to be able to track the actions of employees. Organizations also need to monitor the status of commitments and economic duality exchanges engaged in with outside parties. Thus, Figure 17-4 shows each event linked to two participating agent entities. For events that involve transactions with external parties, the internal agent is the employee who is responsible for the resource affected by that event, and the external agent is the outside party to the transaction. For internal events, such as the transfer of raw materials from the storeroom to production, the internal agent is the employee who is giving up responsibility for or custody of the resource, and the external agent is the employee who is receiving custody of or assuming responsibility for that resource.

Developing an REA Diagram

This chapter focuses on developing an REA diagram for a single business cycle. In the next chapter we will learn how to integrate REA diagrams for individual business cycles to create one enterprise-wide REA diagram.

Developing an REA diagram for a specific business cycle consists of the following three steps:

1. Identify the events about which management wants to collect information.
2. Identify the resources affected by each event and the agents who participate in those events.
3. Determine the cardinalities of each relationship.

Let us follow these three steps to see how Paul developed Figure 17-6 to model the revenue cycle of Fred's Train Shop.

Step 1: Identify Relevant Events
The first step in developing an REA model of a single business cycle is to identify the events of interest to management. At a minimum, every REA model must include the two events that

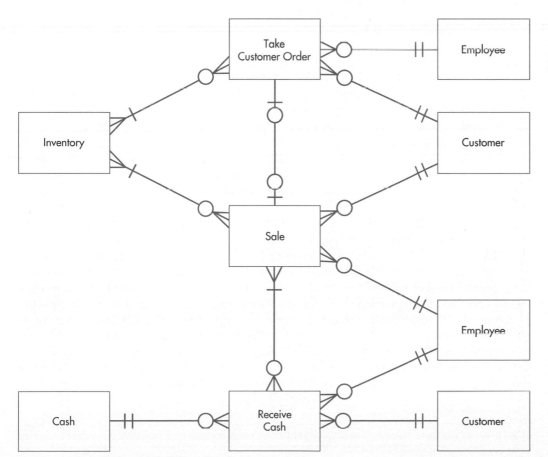

FIGURE 17-6

Partial REA Diagram for Fred's Train Shop Revenue Cycle

represent the basic give-to-get economic exchange performed in that particular business cycle (see Figure 17-5). Usually there are other events that management is interested in planning, controlling, and monitoring; they also need to be included in the REA model.

A solid understanding of activities performed in each business cycle (see Chapters 12–16) is needed to identify which events comprise the basic give-to-get economic duality relationships. For example, Chapter 12 explained that the revenue cycle typically consists of four sequential activities:

1. Take customer orders
2. Fill customer orders
3. Bill customers
4. Collect payment from customers

Analysis of the first activity, taking customer orders, indicates that it does not involve either the acquisition of resources from or provision of resources to an external party. It is only a commitment to perform such actions in the future. The second activity, fill customer orders, does reduce the organization's stock of a resource that has economic value (inventory) by delivering it to an external party (the customer). Thus, it represents an example of the prototypical Give Resource event depicted in Figure 17-4. The third activity, billing customers, involves the exchange of information with an external party but does not directly increase or reduce the quantity of any economic resource. Finally, analysis of the fourth activity, collect payments from customers, indicates that it results in an increase in the organization's supply of an economic resource (the entity labeled "Cash" in Figure 17-6) as a result of receiving it from an external party (the customer). Thus, it is an example of the prototypical Get Resource event depicted in Figure 17-4. Consequently, analysis of the basic business activities performed in the revenue cycle indicates that the basic give-to-get economic exchange consists of two events: fill customer orders (usually referred to as the Sales event) and collect payments from customers (often called the Receive Cash event).

In drawing an REA diagram for an single business cycle, it is useful to divide the paper into three columns, one for each type of entity. Use the left column for resources, the center column for events, and the right column for agents. Readability is further enhanced if the event entities are drawn from top to bottom corresponding to the sequence in which they occur. Thus, Paul begins to draw Figure 17-6 by placing the Sales event entity above the Receive Cash event entity in the center column of the paper.[5]

After the economic exchange events are identified, it is necessary to determine which other business activities should be represented as events in the REA model. This, too, requires understanding what each activity entails because only those activities that involve the acquisition of new information need to be included in the model. Returning to our example, Paul notes that the economic duality of Sales and Receive Cash accurately reflects most in-store sales transactions in which the customer selects one or more items and pays for them. Sometimes, however, customers call the store and ask if specific items can be set aside for pickup later that week. To ensure that he reorders popular items on a timely basis, Fred needs not only to set those items aside but also to record such orders in the system. Therefore, Paul decides to add the commitment event Take Customer Order to the REA diagram, placing it above the Sales event because customer orders precede the Sales event.

Paul then considers the other revenue cycle business activity, billing customers. He knows that in-store sales are paid for immediately and, therefore, do not involve a separate "billing" step. But Fred also sells model trains to shopping centers, hotels, and other institutions that want to set up seasonal displays for their customers. Such sales are made on credit, and Fred does subsequently prepare and mail invoices to those customers. However, printing and mailing invoices does not directly increase or decrease any economic resource. Nor does the billing activity represent a commitment to a future economic exchange: The customer's legal obligation to pay arises from the delivery of the merchandise, not from the printing of an invoice. Consequently, as noted in Chapters 12 and 13, many organizations are beginning to realize that billing is a non-value-added activity that can be eliminated entirely. Moreover, the activity of printing an invoice does not add any new information to the database. The prices and quantities

---

[5]Placement conventions, such as the use of columns and sequential ordering of events, are not *required* to use the REA model to design a database. We suggest these rules only because following them often simplifies the process of drawing an REA diagram and produces REA diagrams that are easy to read.

of items sold were recorded at the time of the sale, at which time the terms of payment were also agreed upon. Thus, the billing activity is simply an information processing event that merely *retrieves* information from the database, similar to writing a query or printing an internal report. Since such information retrieval events do not alter the contents of the database, they need not be modeled as events in an REA diagram. For all the foregoing reasons, Paul realizes that he does not need to include a billing event in his revenue cycle REA diagram for Fred's Train Shop.

But what about accounts receivable? If there is no billing event, how can Fred's Train Shop monitor this balance sheet item? The solution lies in understanding that accounts receivable is merely a timing difference between the two components of the basic economic exchange in the revenue cycle: sales and the receipt of payment. In other words, accounts receivable simply equals all sales for which customers have not yet paid. Consequently, accounts receivable can be calculated and monitored by simply collecting information about Sales and Receive Cash events. The next chapter will illustrate several different ways for extracting information about accounts receivable from a database built using the REA data model.

Finally, notice that there are no events that pertain to the entry of data. The reason for this is that the REA data model is used to design transaction processing databases. The objective is to model the basic value-chain business activities of an organization: what it does to generate revenues and how it spends cash and uses its other resources. Entering data about those events and about the resources and agents associated with them is not usually considered a primary value-chain activity. Thus, just like writing queries and printing reports, data entry activities are not considered important events about which detailed data needs to be collected. Moreover, as discussed in the preceding five chapters, there is a continuous trend to use technology to eliminate routine clerical information processing activities, including data entry. Thus, it is possible to conceive of business events (such as the sale of merchandise) being performed without the need for any separate data entry activities. Indeed, much data entry already occurs as a by-product of performing the business events that are included in the REA diagram. For example, whenever a sale, purchase, receipt of cash, or payment occurs, information about that event is entered in the database. Thus, what gets modeled in the REA diagram is the business event (e.g., the sale transaction) and the facts that management wants to collect about that event, not the entry of that data.

Step 2: Identify Resources and Agents

Once the relevant events have been specified, the resources that are affected by those events need to be identified. This involves answering three questions:

1. What economic resource is reduced by the "Give" event?
2. What economic resource is acquired by the "Get" event?
3. What economic resource is affected by a commitment event?

Again, a solid understanding of business processes makes it easy to answer these questions. To continue our example, Paul has observed that the Sales event involves giving inventory to customers and that the Receive Cash event involves obtaining payments (whether in the form of money, checks, credit card, or debit card) from customers. Therefore, he adds an Inventory resource entity to the REA diagram and links it to the Sales event entity. The Inventory entity stores information about each product that Fred sells. Then Paul adds a Cash resource entity to the diagram. Although organizations typically use multiple accounts to track cash and cash equivalents (e.g., operating checking account, petty cash, and short-term investments), these are all summarized in one balance sheet account called Cash. Similarly, the Cash resource contains information about every individual cash account. Thus, in a relational database, the "cash" table would contain a separate row for each specific account (e.g., petty cash, checking account, etc.). Paul then links the "Cash" resource entity to the Receive Cash event entity. Finally, the Take Customer Order event involves setting aside merchandise for a specific customer. To maintain accurate inventory records, and to facilitate timely reordering to avoid stockouts, each Take Customer Order event should result in reducing the quantity available of that particular inventory item. Therefore, Paul adds a link between the Inventory resource entity and the Take Customer Order event entity in the REA diagram he is developing for Fred's Train Shop revenue cycle.

In addition to specifying the resources affected by each event, it is also necessary to identify the agents who participate in those events. There will always be at least one internal agent (employee) and, in most cases, an external agent (customer or vendor) who participate in each event. In the case of Fred's Train Shop's revenue cycle, a customer and a salesperson participate in each sales event. The customer and a cashier are the two agents participating in each Receive Cash event. Both the salesperson and the cashier are employees of Fred's. Thus, both revenue cycle economic exchange events involve the same two general types of agents: employees (the internal party) and customers (the external party). The Take Customer Order event also involves both customers and employees. Therefore, Paul adds both types of agents to the diagram and draws relationships to indicate which agents participated in which events. To reduce clutter, he sometimes links one copy of a particular agent entity to two adjacent event entities.[6]

Step 3: Determine Cardinalities of Relationships

The final step in drawing an REA diagram for one transaction cycle is to add information about relationship cardinalities. *Cardinalities* describe the nature of the relationship between two entities by indicating how many instances of one entity can be linked to each specific instance of another entity. Consider the relationship between the customer agent entity and the sales event entity. Each entity in an REA diagram represents a set. For example, the Customer entity represents the set of the organization's customers, and the Sales entity represents the set of individual sales transactions that occur during the current fiscal period. Each individual customer or sales transaction represents a specific instance of that entity. Thus, in a relational database, each row in the "Customer" table would store information about a particular customer, and each row in the "Sales" table would store information about a specific sales transaction. Cardinalities define how many sales transactions (instances of the Sales entity) can be associated with each customer (instance of the Customer entity) and, conversely, how many customers can be associated with each sales transaction.

No universal standard exists for representing information about cardinalities in REA diagrams. In this text, we use the graphical "crow's feet" notation style for representing cardinality information because it is becoming increasingly popular and is used by many software design tools. Table 17-1 explains the meaning of the symbols used to represent cardinality information, and Focus 17-1 compares the notation used in this book with other commonly used conventions.

TABLE 17-1 Graphical Symbols for Representing Cardinality Information

Symbol	Cardinalities	Example	Meaning
—O⊦—	Minimum = 0; Maximum = 1	Entity A —O⊦— Entity B	Each instance of entity A may or may not be linked to any instances of entity B, but can be linked to at most one instance of entity B.
—⊦⊦—	Minimum = 1; Maximum = 1	Entity A —⊦⊦— Entity B	Each instance of entity A must be linked to an instance of entity B, and can only be linked to at most one instance of entity B.
—O≺—	Minimum = 0; Maximum = many	Entity A —O≺— Entity B	Each instance of entity A may or may not be linked to any instances of entity B, but could be linked to more than one instance of entity B.
—⊦≺—	Minimum = 1; Maximum = many	Entity A —⊦≺— Entity B	Each instance of entity A must be linked to at least one instance of entity B, but can be linked to many instances of entity B.

---

[6]Deciding how many copies of the same entity to include in an REA diagram is a matter of personal taste. Including too many copies clutters the diagram with redundant rectangles, but too few copies can result in a confusing tangled web of lines connecting entities to one another.

Alternative Methods to Represent Cardinality Information

A number of different notations exist for depicting minimum and maximum cardinalities. Some of the more common alternatives to the crow's feet used in this text are shown here.

Notation	Explanation	Example
(Min, Max)	A pair of alphanumeric characters inside parentheses: (0,1) means minimum = 0, maximum = 1 (1,1) means minimum = 1; maximum = 1 (0,N) means minimum = 0; maximum = many (1,N) means minimum = 1; maximum = many	Entity A — (0, 1) (1, N) — Entity B Each instance of entity A must be linked to at least one instance of entity B but may be linked to many instances of entity B; each instance of entity B may or may not be linked to an instance of entity A but can only be linked to at most one instance of entity A. Note: *Some authors and consultants flip which side of the relationship the cardinality pair appears on!*
UML	One or two alphanumeric characters separated by two periods: 0..1 means minimum = 0; maximum = 1 1 means minimum = 1; maximum = 1 * means minimum = 0; maximum = many 1 * means minimum = 1; maximum = many	Entity A — 1 1..* — Entity B Each instance of entity A must be linked to at least one instance of entity B but may be linked to many instances of entity B; each instance of entity B must be linked to an instance of entity A but can only be linked to at most one instance of entity A.
Maximums only (Microsoft Access)	One alphanumeric character to represent the maximum cardinality in that relationship: 1 means 1; the infinity symbol (∞) means many	Entity A — 1 ∞ — Entity B Each instance of entity A may be linked to many instances of entity B; each instance of entity B can only be linked to at most one instance of entity A.

As shown in Table 17-1, cardinalities are represented by the pair of symbols next to an entity. The four rows in Table 17-1 depict the four possible combinations of minimum and maximum cardinalities. The **minimum cardinality** can be either zero (0) or one (1), depending upon whether the relationship between the two entities is optional (the minimum cardinality is zero; see rows one and three) or mandatory (the minimum cardinality is one, as in rows two and four). The **maximum cardinality** can be either one or many (the crow's feet symbol), depending upon whether each instance of entity A can be linked to at most one instance (as in the top two rows) or potentially many instances of entity B (as in the bottom two rows).

Let us now use the information in Table 17-1 to interpret some of the cardinalities in Figure 17-6. Look first at the Sale-Customer relationship. The minimum and maximum cardinalities next to the Customer entity are both one. This pattern is the same as that in row two in Table 17-1. Thus, the minimum cardinality of one next to the Customer entity in Figure 17-6 indicates that each sale transaction (entity A) *must* be linked to some specific customer (entity B). The maximum cardinality of one means that each sale transaction can be linked to at most *only one* specific customer. This reflects normal business practices: only one legally identifiable customer (which could be an individual or a business) is held responsible for a sale and its subsequent payment. Now look at the cardinality pair next to the Sale entity: as in row three in Table 17-1, the minimum cardinality is zero, and the maximum cardinality is many. The zero minimum cardinality means that the relationship is optional: A customer does not have to be associated with any specific sale transaction. This allows Fred's Train Shop to enter information about prospective customers to whom it can send advertisements before they have ever purchased anything. The maximum cardinality is many, indicating that a specific customer may, and Fred hopes will, be associated with multiple sale transactions (i.e., become a loyal customer who makes repeated purchases from Fred's Train Shop). Now notice that the cardinality pairs next to the Inventory entity in Figure 17-6 have a minimum of one and a maximum of many for every relationship. This is the same pattern as in row four in Table 17-1. This means that every customer order or sale transaction *must* involve at least one inventory item (you cannot sell "nothing") but *may* involve multiple different items (e.g., a customer could purchase both a locomotive and a rail car in the same transaction). Finally, notice that the cardinality pair next to the Sale entity in its relationship with the Take Customer Order entity is like the pattern in row one of Table 17-1. The minimum cardinality of zero reflects the fact that an order may not *yet* have been turned into an actual sale transaction. The maximum cardinality of one indicates that Fred's Train Shop fills all customer orders in full rather than making a number of partial deliveries.

You should be able to interpret the rest of Figure 17-6 by following the same process just presented by comparing the cardinality pairs next to each entity to the four patterns in Table 17-1. Let us now examine what the various types of relationships mean and what they reveal about an organization's business practices.

THREE TYPES OF RELATIONSHIPS   Three basic types of relationships between entities are possible, depending on the *maximum* cardinality associated with each entity (the minimum cardinality does not matter):

1. *A one-to-one (1:1) relationship* exists when the maximum cardinality for each entity in that relationship is 1 (see Figure 17-7, panel A).

FIGURE 17-7

Examples of Different Types of Relationships

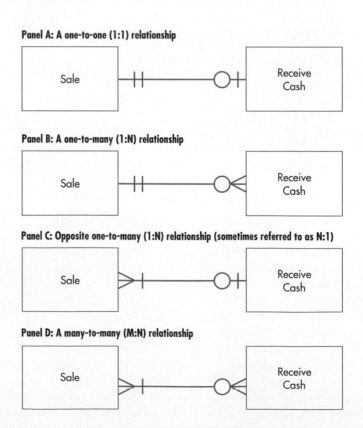

Panel A: A one-to-one (1:1) relationship

Panel B: A one-to-many (1:N) relationship

Panel C: Opposite one-to-many (1:N) relationship (sometimes referred to as N:1)

Panel D: A many-to-many (M:N) relationship

2. *A one-to-many (1:N) relationship* exists when the maximum cardinality of one entity in the relationship is 1 and the maximum cardinality for the other entity in that relationship is many (see Figures 17-7, panels B and C).

3. *A many-to-many (M:N) relationship* exists when the maximum cardinality for both entities in the relationship is many (Figure 17-7, panel D).

Figure 17-7 shows that any of these possibilities *might* describe the relationship between the Sales and Receive Cash events. The data modeler or database designer cannot arbitrarily choose which of these three possibilities to use when depicting various relationships. Instead, the cardinalities *must* reflect the organization's business policies. Let us now examine what each of the possibilities depicted in Figure 17-7 means. Figure 17-7, panel A, depicts a one-to-one (1:1) relationship between the Sales and Receive Cash events. The maximum cardinality of 1 associated with the Receive Cash entity means that each Sales event (transaction) can be linked to *at most* one Receive Cash event. This would be appropriate for an organization that had a business policy of not allowing customers to make installment payments. At the same time, the maximum cardinality of 1 associated with each Sale event means that each payment a customer submits is linked to *at most* one sales event. This would be appropriate for an organization that had a business policy of requiring customers to pay for each sales transaction separately. Thus, the 1:1 relationship depicted in Figure 17-7, panel A, represents the typical revenue cycle relationship for business-to-consumer retail sales: Customers must pay, in full, for each sales transaction before they are allowed to leave the store with the merchandise they purchased. Note that it does not matter *how* customers pay for each sales transaction (i.e., with cash, check, credit card, or debit card). Regardless of the method used, there is one, and only one, payment linked to each sales transaction and, conversely, every sales transaction is linked to one, and only one, payment from a customer (payments made by debit and credit cards also involve the card issuer; for simplicity, that transfer agent is not included in Figure 17-6). If management is interested in tracking the frequency of how customers choose to pay, payment method might be recorded as an attribute of the Receive Cash event.

Panels B and C of Figure 17-7 depict two ways that one-to-many (1:N) relationships can occur. Panel B shows that each Sales event may be linked to *many* Receive Cash events. This indicates that the organization has a business policy that allows customers to make installment payments *to the selling organization*. If the customer uses a third-party source of credit, the selling organization receives *one* payment in full from that third party for that particular sales transaction; the customer may be making installment payments to the credit agency, but those payments would not be modeled in an REA diagram for the selling organization. (Think about it: The selling organization has no way of tracking when one of its customers pays a portion of a credit card bill or makes a monthly payment on a bank loan). The situation depicted in Figure 17-7, panel B, does not, however, mean that *every* sales transaction is paid for in installments: The maximum cardinality of N simply means that some sales transactions may be paid in installments. Panel B of Figure 17-7 also shows that each Receive Cash event is linked to *at most* one Sale event. This indicates that the organization has a business policy that requires customers to pay for each sales transaction separately and are not allowed to build up an account balance over a period of time. Thus, Figure 17-7, panel B, represents the revenue cycle of an organization that probably sells big-ticket items. Should a customer return and make another purchase, a separate set of installment payments would be created in order to separately track how much has been paid for each sales transaction.

Figure 17-7, panel C, shows another type of 1:N relationship between the Sale and Receive Cash events. In this case, each Sale event can be linked to *at most* one Receive Cash event. This indicates that the organization has a business policy that does not permit customers to make installment payments. Figure 17-7, panel C, also shows that each Receive Cash event *may* be linked to many different Sale events. This indicates the existence of a business policy allowing customers to make a number of purchases during a period of time (e.g., a month) and then pay off those purchases with one payment. The situation depicted in Figure 17-7, panel C, is quite common, especially for business-to-business sales of nondurable goods.

Figure 17-7, panel D, depicts a many-to-many (M:N) relationship between the Sale and Receive Cash events. It shows that each Sales event may be linked to *one or more* Receive Cash events and that each Receive Cash event may in turn be linked to *one or more* Sale events. This reflects an organization that has business policies that allow customers to make installment payments and also permits customers to accumulate a balance representing a set of sales transactions over a period of time. Keep in mind, however, that maximum cardinalities of N do not represent mandatory practices: Thus, for the relationship depicted in panel D, some sales transactions may be paid in full in one payment and some customers may pay for each sales transaction separately. The situation depicted in Figure 17-7, panel D, is quite common.

BUSINESS MEANING OF CARDINALITIES   As noted, the choice of cardinalities is not arbitrary, but reflects facts about the organization being modeled and its business practices. This information is obtained during the systems analysis and conceptual design stages of the database design process. Thus, Paul Stone had to clearly understand how Fred's Train Shop conducts its business activities to ensure that Figure 17-6 was correct.

Let us now examine Figure 17-6 to see what it reveals about Fred's Train Shop's revenue cycle processes. First, note that all of the agent–event relationships are 1:N. This is typical for most organizations: A particular agent often participates in many events. For example, organizations expect that over time a given employee will repeatedly perform a particular task. Organizations also desire their customers to make repeat orders and purchases, just as they typically place orders with the same suppliers. However, for accountability purposes, events are usually linked to a specific internal agent and a specific external agent; hence, the maximum cardinality on the agent side of the agent–event relationships in Figure 17-6 is always 1. If, however, a particular event required the cooperation of a team of employees, the maximum cardinality on the agent side of the relationship would be many.

The minimum cardinalities associated with the agent–event relationships in Figure 17-6 also reflect typical business processes followed by most organizations. The figure shows that each event *must* be linked to an agent (a sale must involve a customer, a payment must come from a customer, etc.); hence the minimum cardinality of 1 on the agent side of the relationship. In contrast, Figure 17-6 shows that the minimum cardinality on the event side of the agent–event relationship is 0. There are several reasons why a particular agent need not have participated in any events. The organization may wish to store information about potential customers and alternate suppliers with whom it has not yet conducted any business. Information about newly hired employees will exist in the database prior to their first day on the job. Finally, there is a fundamental difference in the nature of agent entities and event entities. Organizations usually desire to maintain information about agents indefinitely but typically store information only about events that have occurred during the current fiscal year. Thus, agent entities are analogous to master files, whereas event entities are analogous to transaction files. At the end of a fiscal year, the contents of event entities are typically archived, and the next fiscal year begins with no instances of that event. Thus, at the beginning of a new fiscal year, agents are not linked to any current events.

Figure 17-6 depicts M:N relationships between the inventory resource and the various events that affect it. This is the typical situation for organizations, like Fred's Train Shop, that sell mass-produced items. Most organizations track such inventory by an identifier such as part number, item number, or stock-keeping unit (SKU) number and do not attempt to track each physical instance of that product. When a sale occurs, the system notes which product number(s) were sold. Thus, the same inventory item may be linked to many different sales events. For example, Fred's Train Shop uses product number 15734 to refer to a particular model of a steam locomotive. At a given point in time, it may have five of those locomotives in stock. If, during the course of a weekend, five different customers each purchased one of those locomotives, the system would link product number 15734 to five separate sales events. Hence, the maximum cardinality on the event side of the relationship is many. Of course, Fred's Train Shop, like most organizations, permits (and desires) that customers purchase many different products at the same time. For example, a customer who purchases a steam locomotive (product number 15734) may also purchase a box of curved track (product number 3265). Thus, the system would link one sales event to multiple inventory items; hence the maximum cardinality on the inventory side of the relationship is also many.

But what if an organization sells unique, one-of-a-kind inventory, such as original artwork? Such items can only be sold one time; consequently, the maximum cardinality on the event side of the inventory–sales event would be 1. The maximum cardinality on the inventory side of the relationship would still be many, however, because most organizations will be happy to sell as many different one-of-a-kind items as a customer wants and can afford to buy.

The minimum cardinalities on each side of the inventory–event relationships depicted in Figure 17-6 also reflect typical business practices. Fred's Train Shop, like many retail organizations, only sells physical inventory. Therefore, every order or sales event *must* be linked to at least one inventory item; hence, the minimum cardinality on the inventory side of the inventory–event relationships is 1. The minimum cardinality on the event side of those relationships, however, is 0, for the same reasons that it is 0 in agent–event relationships.

Now consider the relationship between the cash resource and the Receive Cash event. Figure 17-6 depicts this as being a 1:N relationship, which reflects a best practice followed by most organizations with good internal controls. Each cash receipt from a customer is deposited into one cash account, usually the organization's general checking account. The treasurer subsequently transfers money from that account to other cash accounts (e.g., payroll, checking, investments, etc.) as necessary. The minimum cardinalities on each side of this relationship are also typical. Each customer payment must be deposited into some account; hence the minimum cardinality is 1 on the resource side of the relationship. Conversely, the minimum cardinality on the event side of the relationship is 0 for the same reasons that it is 0 in the agent–event and inventory–event relationships as discussed previously.

Finally, let us examine the event–event relationships depicted in Figure 17-6. Fred's Train Shop ships each business customer order individually and waits until all items are in stock before filling an order. Thus, each order is linked to only one sales transaction and each sales transaction is related to only one order. Therefore, Paul has modeled the relationship between the Take Customer Order and Sales events as being 1:1. The minimum cardinality on the sales side of the relationship is 0, meaning that orders may exist which are not linked to sales. This reflects the temporal sequence between the two events: Orders precede sales, so at any given point in time, Fred's Train Shop may have orders that it has not yet filled. Fred's Train Shop does not, however, require that every sale be preceded by an order; indeed, while many sales to corporate customers are preceded by orders, walk-in sales to consumers are not. Therefore, Paul Stone has modeled the minimum cardinality on the order side of the sales–order relationship as 0.

Paul also has learned that Fred's Train Shop extends credit to its business customers and mails them monthly statements listing all unpaid purchases. He also has found out that many business customers send Fred one check to cover all their purchases during a given time period. Thus, one Receive Cash event could be linked to many different Sale events. However, Fred's Train Shop also allows its business customers to make installment payments on large purchases; thus, a given Sale event could be connected to more than one Receive Cash event. That is why Paul has modeled the relationship between the Sale and Receive Cash events as being many-to-many.

Because Fred's Train Shop extends credit to some of its customers, at any point in time there can be Sale events that are not yet linked to any Receive Cash events. Therefore, Figure 17-6 shows the minimum cardinality on the Receive Cash side of the relationship as 0. Paul also has learned that Fred's Train Shop never requires customers to pay in advance for special orders. Thus, every Receive Cash event must be linked to a previous Sale event; consequently, Figure 17-6 shows the minimum cardinality on the sales side of the Sale–Receive Cash relationship is 1.

UNIQUENESS OF REA DIAGRAMS   The preceding discussion indicates that each organization will have its own unique REA diagram. At a minimum, because business practices differ across companies, so will relationship cardinalities. In fact, an REA diagram for a given organization will have to change to reflect changes to existing business practices. For example, if Fred's Train Shop decides to begin making partial shipments to fill customer orders, then Figure 17-6 would have to be changed to show the relationship between the Take Customer Order and Sales events as being 1:N, instead of the 1:1 relationship currently depicted. Similarly, if Fred's Train Shop also decided to adopt a policy of combining several orders from one customer into one large shipment, then Figure 17-6 would have to be modified to depict the relationship between those two events as being M:N. Sometimes, differences in business practices can result in different

Data modeling is not an easy task, as Hewlett-Packard learned when it began designing a new database for its accounting and finance function. A major problem was that the same term meant different things to different people. For example, accounting used the term *orders* to refer to the total dollar amount of orders per time period, whereas the sales department used the term to refer to individual customer orders. Moreover, such confusions existed even within the accounting and finance function. For example, the reporting group used the term *product* to refer to any good currently sold to customers. Thus, the primary key for this entity was product number. In contrast, the forecasting group used the term *product* to refer to any good that was often still in the planning stage and had no product number assigned yet.

To solve these problems, Hewlett-Packard asked the different user groups to actively participate in the data modeling process. The first step was to convince all users of the need for and benefits of creating a data model for their function. Then it was necessary to carefully define the scope of the modeling effort. Hewlett-Packard found that the time

invested in these early steps was worthwhile, because it facilitated the activities of clarifying definitions and developing attribute lists that took place later in the process. The latter activity was an iterative affair that included many revisions. Documentation was critical to this process. Each member of the modeling team and user groups had copies of the proposed lists, which made it easier to spot inconsistencies in definitions.

Hewlett-Packard credits the data modeling approach as contributing significantly to the project's overall success. Data modeling allowed the participants to concentrate first on understanding the essential business characteristics of the new system, instead of getting bogged down in specifying the contents of relational database tables. This helped them to identify and resolve conflicting viewpoints early in the process and paved the way for eventual acceptance of the resulting system. The key step, however, was in getting the different user groups to actively participate in the data modeling process. Otherwise, the resulting data model would not have been as accurate or widely accepted.

entities being modeled. For example, if Fred's Train Shop only made sales to walk-in customers and did not take any orders from businesses, then Figure 17-6 would not need to include the Take Customer Order commitment event.

Although the development of the REA diagram for Fred's Train Shop's revenue cycle may seem to have been relatively straightforward and intuitive, data modeling is usually a complex and repetitive process. Frequently, data modelers develop an initial REA diagram that reflects their understanding of the organization's business processes, only to learn when showing it to intended users that they had omitted key dimensions or misunderstood some operating procedures. Thus, it is not unusual to erase and redraw portions of an REA diagram several times before finally producing an acceptable model. One common source of misunderstanding is the use of different terminology by various subsets of the intended user groups. Focus 17-2 highlights the importance of involving the eventual users of the system in the data modeling process so that terminology is consistent.

Summary and Case Conclusion

The database design process has five stages: systems analysis, conceptual design, physical design, implementation and conversion, and operation and maintenance. Because of their extensive knowledge of transaction processing requirements and general business functions, accountants should actively participate in every stage.

One way to perform the activities of systems analysis and conceptual design is to build a data model of the AIS. The REA accounting data model is developed specifically for designing a database to support an AIS. The REA model classifies entities into three basic categories: resources, events, and agents. An REA model can be documented in the form of an entity-relationship (E-R) diagram, which depicts the entities about which data are collected as rectangles and represents the important relationships between entities by connecting lines. The cardinalities of the relationships depicted in REA diagrams specify the minimum and maximum number of times an instance of one entity can be linked to an instance of the other entity participating in that relationship. Cardinalities also provide information about the basic business policies an organization follows.

Developing an REA diagram involves three steps. First, identify the basic events of interest (any activity about which management wants to collect information in order to plan, control, and evaluate performance). Second, identify the resources affected by and the agents who participate in those events. Third, use knowledge about the organization's business practices to add relationship cardinality information to the diagram.

Paul Stone followed these steps to develop an REA diagram for Fred's Train Shop's revenue cycle. He interviewed Fred to understand the store's business policies and used his general knowledge of revenue cycle activities to draw Figure 17-6. Paul showed the diagram to Fred and explained what each portion represents. Fred indicated that the diagram correctly reflects his store's revenue cycle activities. Paul then explained that he will proceed to use the model to design a relational database that Fred can use to automate the analyses he currently does by hand.

Key Terms

data modeling 494	agents 496	one-to-many (1:N)
entity-relationship (E-R)	cardinalities 502	relationship 505
diagram 494	minimum cardinality 503	many-to-many (M:N)
entity 495	maximum	relationship 505
REA data model 496	cardinality 503	
resources 496	one-to-one (1:1)	
events 496	relationship 504	

AIS IN ACTION

Chapter Quiz

1. Accounts Receivable would appear in an REA diagram as an example of which kind of entity?
   a. resource
   b. event
   c. agent
   d. none of the above

2. Which of the following is NOT likely to be depicted as an entity in the REA data model?
   a. customers
   b. sales
   c. invoices
   d. delivery trucks

3. In most cases, the relationship between agent entities and event entities is
   a. 1:1
   b. 1.:N
   c. M:N
   d. 0:N

4. If customers pay for each sales transaction with a separate check and are not permitted to make installment payments on any sales, then the relationship between the Sales and Receive Cash events would be modeled as being which of the following?

   a. 1:1
   b. 1:N

   c. M:N
   d. 0:N

5. Which of the following most accurately models the sales of low-cost, mass-produced items by a retail store?

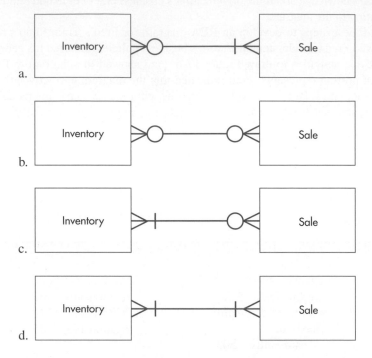

6. Data modeling occurs during which stages of database design?
   a. systems analysis and physical design
   b. systems analysis and conceptual design
   c. conceptual design and implementation and conversion
   d. physical design and implementation and conversion

7. A company has five different cash accounts (checking, money market, petty cash, payroll, and investments). It deposits all payments received from customers into its checking account. Which of the following accurately depicts the relationship between the Cash entity and the Receive Cash event?

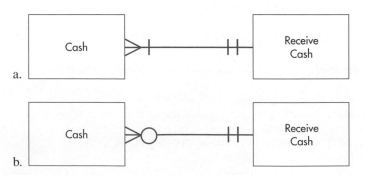

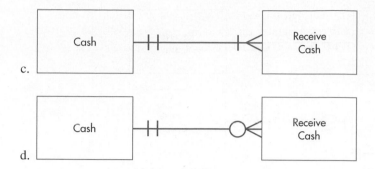

8. EZ Construction Company builds residential houses. It sells only homes that it built. Most of its homes are sold to individuals, but sometimes an investor may purchase several homes and hold them for subsequent resale. Which of the following is the correct way to model the relationship between Sale and Inventory for EZ Construction Company?

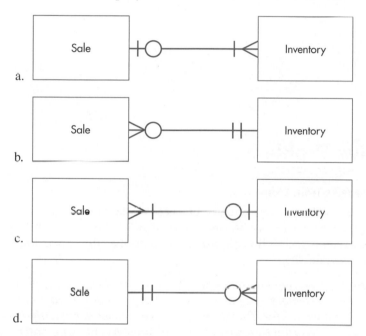

9. Which of the following statements about the REA data model is true?
   a. Every event must be linked to at least two agents.
   b. Every resource must be linked to at least one agent.
   c. Every event must be linked to at least two resources.
   d. Every agent must be linked to at least two events.

10. A business operates by always collecting payments for the entire amount of the sale from customers in advance. It then orders the items from its suppliers, and when they all arrive it ships the entire order to the customer. Which of the following describes the relationship between the Sales and Receive Cash events for this company?

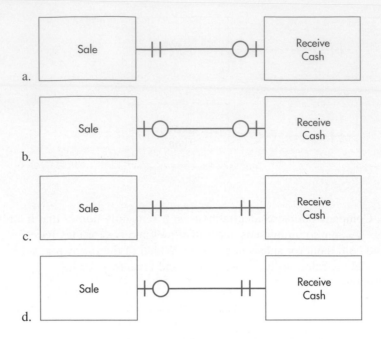

Comprehensive Problem

Expenditure Cycle for Fred's Train Shop

In order for Fred to sell trains and train accessories, he first needs to have inventory to sell. Thus, as part of his overall engagement, Paul Stone has also prepared an REA model for the expenditure cycle of Fred's Train Shop. The following paragraph describes the expenditure cycle business processes of Fred's Train Shop:

> Fred deals with more than one supplier and often places orders for multiple items at the same time. Fred takes inventory and places orders every Monday. Fred's suppliers strive to provide outstanding service. Therefore, they never consolidate multiple orders into one shipment, but always ship merchandise the day after receiving an order. Usually, Fred's suppliers can fill his entire order in one shipment. Occasionally, however, a supplier may be temporarily out of stock of a particular item. In such cases, the supplier ships as much of the order as possible and then ships the out-of-stock item separately as soon as it becomes available. Fred pays for each order in full at one time; that is, he does not make partial payments on orders received. Some suppliers offer discount terms for early payments; Fred always takes advantage of such offers, paying individual invoices, in full, on the appropriate date. Suppliers who do not offer such discounts send Fred monthly statements listing all orders placed the prior month. Fred pays the entire balance indicated on the statement in one check by the specified due date.

Required

Prepare an REA diagram for Fred's Train Shop's expenditure cycle.

Discussion Questions

17.1. Why is it not necessary to model activities such as entering information about customers or suppliers, mailing invoices to customers and recording invoices received from suppliers as events in an REA diagram?

17.2. The basic REA template includes links between two events and links between events and resources and between events and agents. Why do you think the basic REA template does not include direct links between (a) two resources, (b) two agents, or (c) between resources and agents?

17.3. How can REA diagrams help an auditor understand a client's business processes?

17.4. Which parts of Figure 17-6 would accurately depict almost every organization's revenue cycle? Which parts would change?

17.5. What is the relationship between the things that would be represented as resources in an REA diagram and the different categories of assets found on an organization's balance sheet? (*Hint:* Are there any assets that would not be modeled as resources? Are there any resources in an REA diagram that are not listed as assets on a balance sheet?)

17.6. How would accounts payable be reflected in an REA diagram? Why?

17.7. What are the five stages of the database design process? In which stages should accountants participate? Why?

17.8. What is the difference between an Entity-Relationship (E-R) diagram and an REA diagram?

Problems

17.1. Joe's is a small ice-cream shop located near the local university's baseball field. Joe's serves walk-in customers only. The shop carries 26 flavors of ice cream. Customers can buy cones, sundaes, or shakes. When a customer pays for an individual purchase, a sales transaction usually includes just one item. When a customer pays for a family or group purchase, however, a single sales transaction includes many different items. All sales must be paid for at the time the ice cream is served. Joe's maintains several banking accounts but deposits all sales receipts into its main checking account.

Required

Draw an REA diagram, complete with cardinalities, for Joe's revenue cycle.

17.2. Joe, the owner of the ice-cream shop, purchases ice cream from two vendors. Over the years, he has developed good relationships with both vendors so that they allow Joe to pay them biweekly for all purchases made during the preceding two-week period. Joe calls in ice-cream orders on Mondays and Thursdays. The orders are delivered the next day. Joe buys ice-cream toppings from one of several local stores and pays for each such purchase at the time of sale with a check from the company's main checking account.

Required

Draw an REA diagram, complete with cardinalities, for Joe's expenditure cycle.

17.3. Sue's Gallery sells original paintings by local artists. All sales occur in the store. Sometimes customers purchase more than one painting. Individual customers must pay for purchases in full at the time of sale. Corporate customers, such as hotels, however, may pay in installments if they purchase more than 10 paintings. Although Sue's Gallery has several bank accounts, all sales monies are deposited intact into the main checking account.

Required

Draw an REA diagram for the gallery's revenue cycle. Be sure to include cardinalities.

17.4. Sue's Gallery only purchases finished paintings (it never commissions artists). It pays each artist 50% of the agreed price at the time of purchase, and the remainder after the painting is sold. All purchases are paid by check from Sue's main checking account.

Required

Draw an REA diagram, complete with cardinalities, of the gallery's expenditure cycle.

17.5. Develop a data model of Fred's Train Shop's expenditure cycle activities related to the acquisition of office equipment and other fixed assets. Fred sometimes orders multiple pieces of equipment. Vendors usually ship the entire order but sometimes are out of stock of some items. In such cases, they immediately ship to Fred what they have in stock and then send a second shipment when they obtain the other items. Conversely, several orders placed within a short time period with the same vendor might be filled with one delivery. Assume that Fred makes installment payments for most fixed-asset acquisitions but occasionally pays for some equipment in full at the time of purchase.

Required

Draw an REA diagram of your data model. Be sure to include cardinalities.

17.6. Provide an example (in terms of companies with which you are familiar) for each of the business situations described by the following relationship cardinalities:

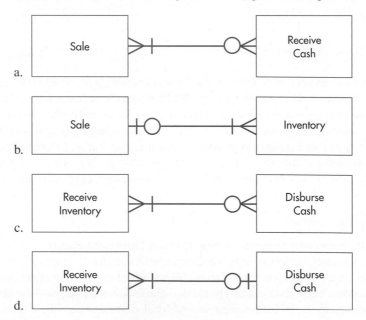

a.
b.
c.
d.

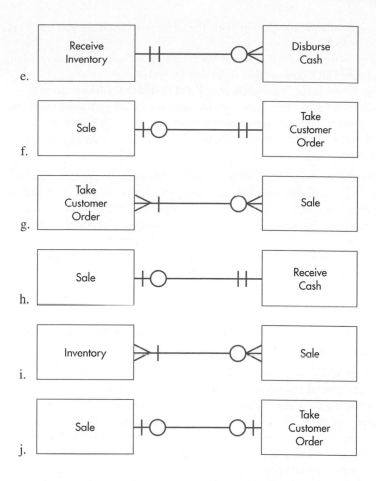

17.7. Model the cardinalities of the following business policies:
   a. The relationship between the Sale and Receive Cash events for installment sales.
   b. The relationship between the Sale and Receive Cash events at a convenience store.
   c. The Take Customer Order–Sale relationship in a situation when occasionally several shipments are required to fill an order because some items were out of stock
   d. The Sale–Inventory relationship for a custom homebuilder.
   e. The relationship between the Sale and Receive Cash events for Dell computers, which requires customers to pay the entire amount of their purchase in advance, prior to Dell shipping the merchandise.
   f. The relationship between the Sale and Receive Cash events for a retail store that has some in-store sales paid in full by customers at the time of the sale but that also makes some in-store sales to customers on credit, billing them later and permitting them to make installment payments.
   g. The relationship between the Receive Inventory and Disburse Cash events in the case where suppliers require payment in advance, in full.
   h. The relationship between the Call on Customers event (i.e., the visit by a salesperson to a potential customer) and the Take Customer Order event for a business that is only conducted door-to-door (e.g., kitchen knives, certain books, etc.) so that the only way

to order the items is when a salesperson visits the customer. (*Hint:* do you think every call results in an order?)

i. The relationship between the Call on Customers and Take Customer Orders events for a manufacturer which also accepts orders on its Web site.

j. The relationship between the Receive Inventory and Disburse Cash events for a company which receives monthly bills from its suppliers for all purchases made the previous month; some suppliers require payment of the entire bill, in full, within 30 days or they will not accept any subsequent orders, but other suppliers accept installment payments.

17.8. The Computer Warehouse sells computer hardware, software, and supplies (such as paper). Individual customers just walk into the store, select merchandise, and must pay for their purchases in full before leaving the store. Corporate customers, however, call in orders in advance, so that the items are waiting to be picked up. Corporate customers may charge their purchases to their account. The Computer Warehouse mails corporate customers monthly statements that summarize all purchases made the prior month. Corporate customers pay the entire balance, as listed on the monthly statement, with one check or EFT transaction.

Required

Draw an REA diagram of the Computer Warehouse's revenue cycle, complete with cardinalities.

17.9. The Computer Warehouse purchases its inventory from more than a dozen different vendors. Orders are placed via telephone, fax, or on the supplier's Web site. Most orders are delivered the next day. Most orders are filled completely in one shipment, but sometimes a supplier is out of stock of a particular item. In such situations, the bulk of the order is shipped immediately and the out-of-stock item is shipped separately as soon as it arrives (such shipments of back orders are never combined with any new orders placed by the Computer Warehouse). The Computer Warehouse pays for some of its purchases COD but usually pays by the 10th of the month for all purchases made the prior month. None of its suppliers allow it to make installment payments.

Required

Draw an REA diagram of the Computer Warehouse's expenditure cycle, complete with cardinalities.

17.10. Stan's Southern Barbeque Supply Store orders mass-produced barbecue products from various suppliers. Stan's maintains information about a contact person at each supplier along with all required address information. Each purchase order has the order number, date, tax, and total. Purchase orders also contain the following information for each product ordered: stock number, description, and price. The manager of Stan's places orders by fax several times a day, whenever he notices that an item is running low. Some suppliers fill each individual order separately. Others, however, consolidate orders and fill all of them in one weekly delivery. Stan's suppliers never make partial shipments; if they are out of stock of a certain item, they wait until they obtain that item and then ship the entire order. Some suppliers require payment at the time of delivery, but others send Stan's a monthly statement detailing all purchases during the current period. Two suppliers allow Stan's to make installment payments for any individual purchase orders that exceed $20,000.

Required

Draw an REA diagram with cardinalities for the expenditure cycle of Stan's Southern Barbeque Supply Store.

Case17-1 REA Data Modeling Extension

An important analytical and problem-solving skill is the ability to adapt and transfer patterns learned in one setting to other situations. This chapter explained how to develop an REA diagram for a business that sells tangible inventory. Yet some businesses provide only a service. For example, the following narrative describes Sparky's Amusement Park's revenue cycle.

Sparky's Amusement Park is an entertainment park run by recent college graduates. It caters to young people and others who are young at heart. The owners are very interested in applying what they have learned in their information systems and marketing classes to operate a park better than any other in the area.

To accomplish these goals, guests of the park are given a personal "membership card" as they enter. This card will be used to identify each guest. Assume that a new card is issued each time a guest comes to the park. As a result, the system does not have to track one person over a period of time.

As at other parks, guests pay a flat fee for the day and then are able to ride all of the attractions (such as a double-looping roller coaster and the merry-go-round) for no extra charge. The owners, however, want to track the rides each guest takes and the attractions the guests use. They plan to have guests swipe their membership card through a computerized card reader, which automatically enters information into the computer system. This should allow the owners to gather data about the following:

● Number of people who use each piece of equipment. (How many people rode the Ferris wheel today?)
● Number of times each piece of equipment is operated daily.
● Times of day the attraction is busy or slow. (When was the carousel the busiest?)
● Number of attractions each guest uses. (How many different pieces of equipment did customer 1122 ride?)
● Number of rides each guest enjoys. (How many different rides did customer 1122 enjoy? Did each guest go on any rides more than once?)

Required

Draw an REA diagram for Sparky's *revenue* cycle only. Be sure to include cardinalities. State any assumptions you had to make.

(This problem is adapted from one developed for classroom use by Dr. Julie Smith David at Arizona State University.)

AIS IN ACTION SOLUTIONS

Quiz Key

1. Accounts Receivable would appear in an REA diagram as an example of which kind of entity?
   a. resource (Incorrect. Accounts Receivable is not a resource as defined in the REA model, but simply equals the difference between the Sales and Receive Cash events.)
   b. event (Incorrect. Accounts Receivable is not an event, but represents the difference between two events.)
   c. agent (Incorrect. Agents are people or organizations.)
   ▶ d. none of the above (Correct. Accounts Receivable would not appear as an entity in an REA diagram because it represents the difference between two events.)

2. Which of the following is NOT likely to be depicted as an entity in the REA data model?
   a. customers (Incorrect. Customers are an agent entity.)
   b. sales (Incorrect. Sales are an event entity.)

▶ c. invoices (Correct. Invoices are paper outputs of a database—they do not meet the definition of being either a resource, an event, or an agent and, therefore, are not modeled as an entity in a REA diagram.)

d. delivery trucks (Incorrect. Delivery trucks are an economic resource entity.)

3. In most cases, the relationship between agent entities and event entities is

a. 1:1 (Incorrect. Over time, agents can participate in many events.)

▶ b. 1:N (Correct. Over time, agents usually participate in many events. Usually, for accountability purposes, an event is linked to only one specific internal agent and one specific external agent. Occasionally, a complex task may be linked to a team of internal agents, but this is not the norm.)

c. M:N (Incorrect. This pattern may occasionally occur, but it is not the norm.)

d. 0:N (Incorrect. There is no such thing as a 0:N relationship.)

4. If customers pay for each sales transaction with a separate check and are not permitted to make installment payments on any sales, then the relationship between the Sale and Receive Cash events would be modeled as being which of the following?

▶ a. 1:1 (Correct. Each sales transaction is linked to only one payment (no installments) and each payment is linked to only one sales transaction (separate checks).)

b. 1:N (Incorrect. This indicates that each sale event could be linked to multiple cash receipts, implying installment payments.)

c. M:N (Incorrect. This not only indicates the possibility of installment payments but also the use of one check to pay for multiple sales.)

d. 0:N (Incorrect. There is no such thing as a 0:N relationship.)

5. Which of the following most accurately models the sales of low-cost, mass-produced items by a retail store?

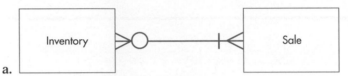

a.

(Incorrect. This indicates that every inventory item must be linked to at least one sale, but that a sales transaction may consist of no inventory.)

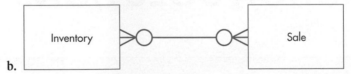

b.

(Incorrect. This shows that a sales transaction can consist of no inventory items.)

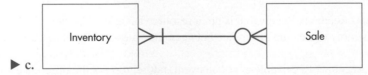

▶ c.

(Correct. Each sale must involve at least one item of inventory, but possibly many; conversely, each inventory item may not be linked to any sales transaction, but a given item could be linked to many sale events.)

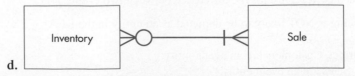

d.

(Incorrect. This says that every inventory item must be linked to at least one sales transaction—this is not true at the beginning of a fiscal year and also precludes storing information about new products prior to their being sold.)

6. Data modeling occurs during which stages of database design?
   a. system analysis and physical design (Incorrect. Data modeling occurs during the system analysis and conceptual design stages of the database design process.)
   ▶ b. system analysis and conceptual design (Correct.)
   c. conceptual design and implementation and conversion (Incorrect. Data modeling occurs during the system analysis and conceptual design stages of the database design process.)
   d. physical design and implementation and conversion (Incorrect. Data modeling occurs during the system analysis and conceptual design stages of the database design process.)

7. A company has five different cash accounts (checking, money market, petty cash, payroll, and investments). It deposits all payments received from customers into its checking account. Which of the following accurately depicts the relationship between the cash entity and the receive cash event?

   a.

   (Incorrect. This says that every Cash account must be linked to at least one Receive Cash event and that a Receive Cash event could be linked to multiple cash accounts.)

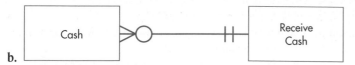

   b.

   (Incorrect. Same problems as in a.)

   c.

   (Incorrect. This says that every Cash account must be linked to at least one Receive Cash event, which is not true: At the beginning of a new fiscal year, there are no Receive Cash events and four of the company's five Cash accounts never directly receive funds collected from customers.)

   ▶ d.

   (Correct. This shows that some Cash accounts may not be linked to any Receive Cash events, whereas others may be linked to many events. Conversely, this shows that each Receive Cash event must be linked to a Cash account, and to only one Cash account.)

8. EZ Construction Company builds residential houses. It sells only homes that it has built. Most of its homes are sold to individuals, but sometimes an investor may purchase several homes and hold them for subsequent resale. Which of the following is the correct way to model the relationship between Sales and Inventory for EZ Construction Company?

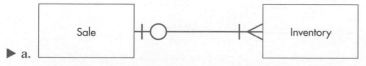

   ▶ a.

   (Correct. Each sale must involve at least one home from inventory but could involve many; conversely, each home may or may not be sold (yet) but can be sold at most one time.)

b.

(Incorrect. This shows that a sale can only involve at most one home from inventory and it shows that a given home can be sold multiple times.)

c.

(Incorrect. This shows that a sale could involve no homes or at most one home, and it shows that every home must be sold but could be sold more than once.)

d.

(Incorrect. This shows that every home must be sold and it also shows that a sale could involve no homes.)

9.   Which of the following statements about the REA data model is true?
  ▶ **a.** Every event must be linked to at least two agents. (Correct.)
  b. Every resource must be linked to at least two agents. (Incorrect. Resources and agents are not usually directly linked to one another.)
  c. Every event must be linked to at least two resources. (Incorrect. Every event must be linked to at least one resource.)
  d. Every agent must be linked to at least two events. (Incorrect. Some agents may only need to be linked to one event.)

10.   A business operates by always collecting payments for the entire amount of the sale from customers in advance. It then orders the items from its suppliers, and when they all arrive it ships the entire order to the customer. Which of the following describes the relationship between the sales and Receive Cash events for this company?

a.

(Incorrect. This shows that a Sale event might not be linked to any Receive Cash events, which means that the merchandise is delivered prior to the customer's payment. Another problem is that this shows that every Receive Cash event must be linked to a Sale event, but the company receives payment prior to delivering the merchandise.)

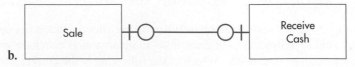

b.

(Incorrect. Same problems as in a.)

c.

(Incorrect. This shows that every Receive Cash event must be linked to a Sale event, but this is not true because the company receives cash prior to shipping the merchandise.)

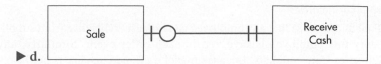

► d.

(Correct. This shows that each Sale event must be linked to a prior Receive Cash event but that a Receive Cash event may not (yet) be linked to any Sale event.)

Comprehensive Problem Solution

REA Diagram of Expenditure Cycle for Fred's Train Shop

To create an entity-relationship diagram using the REA model, follow the three basic steps outlined in the chapter.

1 Identify Events

As explained in the chapter, the first step is to identify all relevant events or transactions using the basic "give-to-get" exchange. After talking to Fred about how he buys the inventory he needs, Paul identifies three basic events that occur:

1. Order Inventory.
2. Receive Inventory.
3. Pay for Inventory, which Paul decides to call "Disburse Cash."

2 Identify Resources and Agents

Next, identify the resources involved with these events. Paul determines that there are two resources involved with these events:

1. Inventory
2. Cash

Then identify the agents or people needed to make these events happen, remembering that there are usually two agents for each event, one internal to Fred's store (i.e., an employee) and one external to Fred's store (i.e., the supplier). Paul lists the following agents as being involved in the Order Inventory event:

1. Purchasing Clerk
2. Supplier

The following are the agents involved in the Receive Inventory event:

3. Receiving Clerk
4. Supplier

The following are the agents involved in the Disburse Cash event:

5. Supplier
6. Cashier

3 Determine Cardinalities of Relationships

After all events, resources, and agents are identified, the next step is to determine how all of these entities interact by determining the cardinalities of all of the relationships between and among the entities. The involves three steps:

1. Specify cardinalities of event–agent relationships.
2. Specify cardinalities of event–resource relationships.
3. Specify cardinalities of event–event relationships.

1 Event–Agent Relationship Cardinalities

After talking with Fred, Paul understands that any employee can order merchandise from suppliers. However, one and only one employee is involved in each order event. Similarly, any employee can check in deliveries from suppliers. Because model train merchandise is not heavy or bulky, each delivery is checked in by only one employee. Fred, or his wife, signs all checks to suppliers, and only one signature is ever required. Thus, the *maximum* cardinality on the agent side of relationships between events and internal agents (employees) is always 1. Obviously, an employee must participate in each event: There must be some employee who places an order, there must be some employee who checks in a delivery, and either Fred or his wife must sign each check. Thus, the *minimum* cardinality on the agent side of relationships between events and internal agents is also 1.

Orders, receipts of inventory, and payments all involve suppliers. Each event must be linked to a particular supplier: A purchase order must identify and be sent to a supplier, a delivery comes from some supplier, and a payment is made to some identifiable supplier. Moreover, each event can be linked to *only one* supplier: Each order is placed with a *specific* supplier, each delivery comes from a *specific* supplier, and each payment is made to a *specific* supplier (e.g., each check is made payable to one, and only one, supplier). Thus, the minimum and maximum cardinalities on the agent side of relationships between events and external agents is 1.

Paul also knows that information about both internal and external agents is maintained indefinitely but that information about events is maintained only for the current fiscal year. Therefore, at the beginning of each fiscal period, no internal agent and no external agent is linked to any order, inventory receipt, or payment events. Thus, the *minimum* cardinality on the event side of relationships between events and agents is 0. During the course of the year, however, the same employee may place many different orders or may check in many different deliveries of merchandise. In addition, both Fred and his wife will sign many different checks that are sent to suppliers. Conversely, during the year many orders may be placed with the same supplier; many deliveries may be received from the same supplier; and many payments may be made to the same supplier. Thus, the *maximum* cardinality on the event side of relationships between events and agents is N.

2 Event–Resource Relationship Cardinalities

Each order must involve at least one inventory item but could be for many different items. Similarly, each delivery of merchandise from a supplier must involve at least one inventory item but may include many different items. Consequently, Paul depicts the minimum cardinality as 1 and the maximum cardinality as N on the inventory side of all relationships between the inventory resource and various events.

Information about inventory is maintained indefinitely, but only orders and inventory receipts that occurred during the current fiscal year are maintained in the database. Thus, at the beginning of each fiscal year the inventory entity is not linked to any order or receive inventory events. During the course of the year, however, a particular inventory item may be ordered and received many times. Thus, Paul depicts the minimum cardinality as 0 and the maximum cardinality as N on the event side of all relationships between the Inventory resource and various events affecting it.

Each payment must be made from some general ledger cash account. In addition, each payment can be made from only one specific account. For example, a check can be linked to either the operating checking account or the payroll checking account, but it cannot be linked to both accounts. Therefore, Paul sets the minimum and maximum cardinalities to 1 on the resource side of the relationship between the Cash resource and the Disburse Cash event.

Information about the various cash accounts in the general ledger (operating checking, payroll, investment, etc.) is maintained indefinitely, but the Disburse Cash event entity contains information only about payments made during the current fiscal year. Therefore, at the beginning of each fiscal year, the cash resource is not linked to any Disburse Cash events. During the course of the year, however, a given cash account may be linked to many different Disburse Cash events. Thus, the minimum cardinality is 0 and the maximum cardinality is N on the event side of the relationship between the Cash resource and the Disburse Cash event.

3 Event–Event Relationship Cardinalities

Orders occur before deliveries. Some orders, however, may include items that are out of stock; when that happens, the merchandise in stock is sent immediately, and one or more additional shipments are made for any items that the supplier had to back order. Thus, one order can be linked to multiple Receive Inventory events. Consequently, Paul assigns a minimum cardinality of 0 and a maximum cardinality of N on the Receive Inventory side of the relationship between the Order Inventory and Receive Inventory events.

Fred's employees have been trained to accept only deliveries for which a valid purchase order exists. Thus, each Receive Inventory event must be linked to an order. Fred's suppliers never consolidate multiple orders into one delivery; thus, each Receive Inventory event can be linked to at most one order event. Therefore, Paul depicts the minimum and maximum cardinalities on the Order Inventory side of the relationship between the Receive Inventory and Order Inventory events as both being 1.

Often, Fred pays for deliveries in the following month. Thus, there may be Receive Inventory events that are not yet linked to any Disburse Cash events. Fred always pays for deliveries in full; he never makes installment payments. Therefore, each Receive Inventory event is linked to at most one Disburse Cash event. Consequently, Paul assigns a minimum cardinality of 0 and a maximum cardinality of 1 to the Disburse Cash side of the relationship between the Receive Inventory and Disburse Cash events.

Fred's only pays for deliveries after the merchandise has been received and inspected. Thus, every Disburse Cash event must be linked to a preceding Receive Inventory event. Oftentimes, Fred or his wife will write one check to pay for several deliveries received during the preceding month. Therefore, Paul draws the minimum cardinality as 1 and the maximum cardinality as N on the Receive Inventory side of the relationship between the Receive Inventory and Disburse Cash events.

After completing the three steps, Paul produced the following REA diagram of the expenditure cycle of Fred's Train Shop.

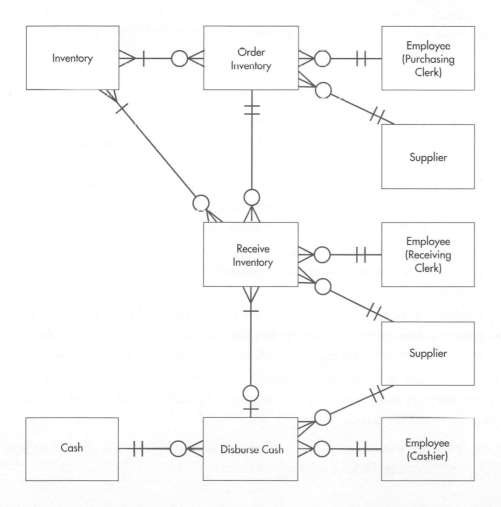

Chapter 18

Implementing an REA Model in a Relational Database

INTEGRATIVE CASE **FRED'S TRAIN SHOP**

Paul Stone shows Fred the set of REA diagrams that he has developed to model the business activities for the revenue, expenditure, and payroll cycles of Fred's Train Shop. Fred verifies that Paul has correctly represented his company's business processes. He then says that although the diagrams "look nice," he wondered why Paul has spent so much time developing them, instead of building Fred the database he had promised. Paul responds that the time spent up front in thoroughly understanding Fred's Train Shop's business processes is necessary to properly design a database that will satisfy Fred's needs.

Paul asks Fred whether he has a database program. Fred replies that a relational database was part of the "business applications" he had purchased as part of an office productivity package. Fred says that although he knows how to use the program, he has not been able to figure out how to import data to it from his AIS and store it in a manner that will allow him to analyze his store's business activities. Paul says that he will do so by following these steps:

1. First, he will integrate the separate REA diagrams he has developed into a single, comprehensive enterprise-wide data model.

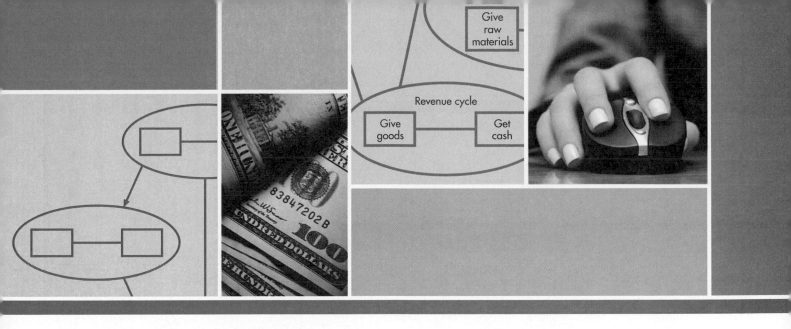

2. Second, he will use the integrated data model to design a set of relational database tables.

3. Third, he will show Fred how he can query the resulting database to generate both traditional financial statements as well as any custom performance reports.

Introduction

The previous chapter introduced the topic of REA data modeling and explained how to develop REA diagrams for an individual business cycle. This chapter shows how to implement an REA diagram in a database. We focus on relational databases because they are commonly used to support transaction processing systems and are likely to be familiar to most business students. Nevertheless, REA data modeling is not limited for use only in designing relational databases, but can also be used to design object- oriented databases.

We begin by showing how to integrate separate REA diagrams developed for individual business cycles into a single, comprehensive enterprise-wide data model. Next, we explain how to implement the resulting model in a relational database. We then describe how to use the REA diagram to query the database to produce traditional financial statements as well as a variey of management reports.

Integrating REA Diagrams Across Cycles

Figures 18-1 ,18-2, and 18-3 present REA diagrams of Fred's Train Shop's revenue, expenditure, and payroll cycles, respectively. These separate diagrams should be integrated to provide a single comprehensive enterprise-wide model of the organization. Doing so requires understanding what the cardinalities in each separate diagram reveal about the organization's business policies and activities. Figure 18-1 and Figure 18-2 were explained in Chapter 17, so we focus here on Figure 18 3.

Figure 18-3 depicts the payroll portion of Fred's Train Shop's HR/payroll cycle activities. The basic economic exchange involves acquiring the use of each employee's time and skills in exchange for which the employee receives a paycheck. Like many small businesses, Fred's Train Shop uses an electronic time clock to record the hours worked by each employee each day. Thus, each Time Worked event records the time an employee began and ended working on a specific day. Each such event must be linked to a particular employee and his or her supervisor; each employee or supervisor, however, may be linked to many different events. Similarly, a paycheck

FIGURE 18-1
Fred's Train Shop Revenue Cycle

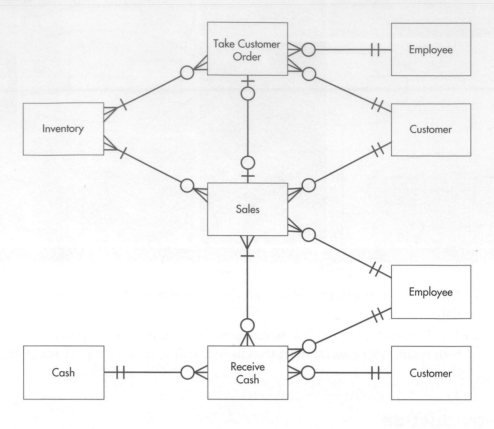

FIGURE 18-2
Fred's Train Shop Expenditure Cycle

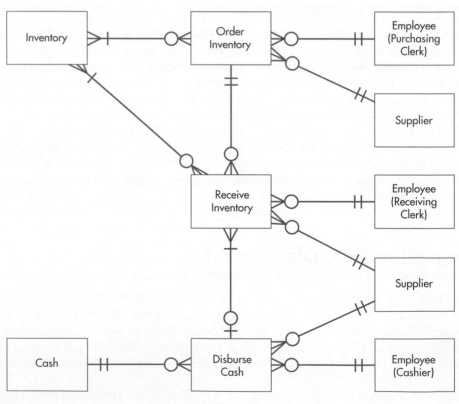

is issued to a particular employee and signed by a particular cashier, but each employee and cashier may be associated with many different Disburse Cash events over time. Hence, Figure 18-3 depicts the relationships between agents and events as being 1:N. The minimum cardinality on the agent side of those relationships is always 1, because each event *must* be linked to a specific employee. (For example, Fred would not want to issue a paycheck and leave the payee

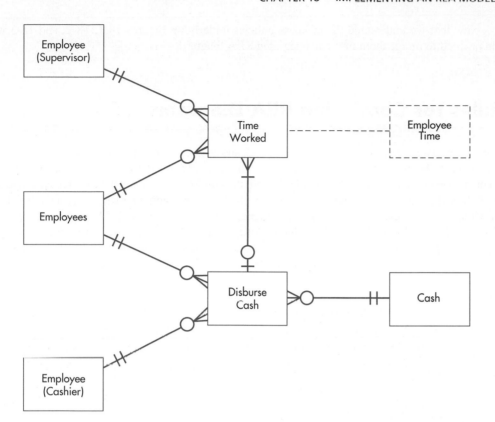

FIGURE 18-3

Fred's Train Shop Payroll Cycle

name blank.) The minimum cardinality on the event side of the relationships is always 0 in order to accommodate storing data about new employees prior to their beginning work and because the event entities are empty at the beginning of each new fiscal year.

The relationship between the Time Worked and Disburse Cash events reflects the basic economic exchange of getting the use of an employee's time and paying for it. Figure 18-3 shows that the relationship between these two events is 1:N. This is because Fred's Train Shop, like most businesses, pays employees periodically but records their time worked daily. Thus, each Disburse Cash event is linked to many daily Time Worked events. Like most businesses, however, Fred's Train Shop does not divide one day into two different pay periods, nor does it pay employees in installments; thus, each Time Worked event is linked to only 1 Disburse Cash event. The minimum cardinalities on each side of the relationship reflect the normal business practice of paying employees after they have worked, rather than in advance.

The Employee Time entity requires some explanation. It represents the fact that the resource being acquired by the Time Worked event is the use of an employee's skills and knowledge for a particular period of time. Time, however, is different from inventory, cash, and other tangible resources, as well as from intangible resources like trade secrets or other forms of intellectual property, in that it cannot be stored. In addition, there are only a few relevant attributes about employee time: the hours worked and how that time was used. Every organization needs to monitor how much time each employee works, in order to calculate payroll. The Time Worked event, which is an example of a "Get" resource event, serves this purpose. Chapter 19 will discuss how some organizations, such as manufacturers and professional services firms (e.g., law firms, consulting organizations, and accounting firms) also collect detailed records of how employees use their time, which is an example of a "Give" resource event, in order to properly bill clients for those services. These two events (Time Worked and Time Used) capture all of the information about employee time that is practical to collect and monitor. Consequently, the Employee Time resource entity is almost never implemented in an actual database. Therefore, it is depicted with dotted lines in Figure 18-3.

Finally, the cardinalities of the relationship between the cash disbursement event and the cash resource are identical to those in the expenditure cycle (Figure 18-2): Each check or electronic funds transfer must be linked to at least one cash account and can be linked to only one cash account, whereas the same cash account may be linked to many disbursement events.

Now that we understand the business policies underlying Figures 18-1, 18-2, and 18-3 we can proceed to merge them into one integrated REA diagram.

Rules for Combining REA Diagrams

You have probably noticed that Figures 18-1, 18-2, and 18-3 each contain some of the same entities. For example, the inventory resource appears in both Figures 18-1 and 18-2. The cash disbursements event appears in both Figures 18-2 and 18-3. Both the employee agent and the cash resource appear in all three diagrams. Such redundancies provide the basis for combining REA diagrams depicting individual business cycles into a single, comprehensive, enterprise-wide REA model. Figure 18-4 shows such a model for Fred's Train Shop. Notice that the integrated diagram merges multiple copies of resource and event entities but retains multiple copies of agent entities. This maximizes the legibility of the comprehensive REA diagram by avoiding the need to have relationship lines cross one another. Let us now examine how to combine redundant resource and event entities.

Merging Redundant Resource Entities

Recall that REA diagrams for individual business cycles are built around basic give-to-get economic exchanges. Such economic duality relationships explain why a resource is either acquired

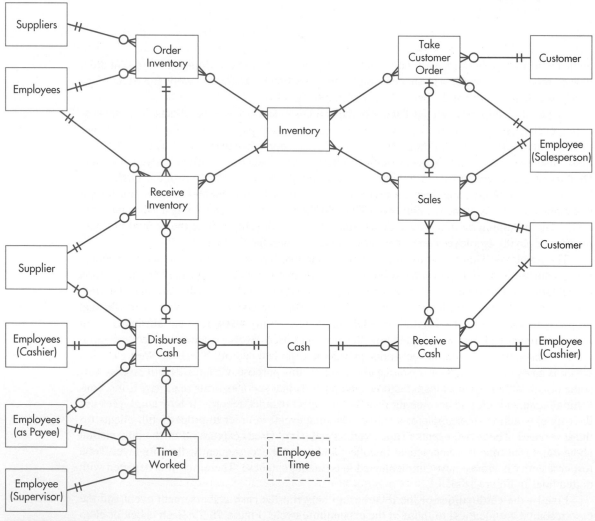

FIGURE 18-4

Integrated REA Diagram for Fred's Train Shop

or disposed of. They provide only a part of the story about each resource, however. For example, Figure 18-1 shows that inventory is reduced (the Sales event) in exchange for cash (the Receive Cash event). But Figure 18-1 does not show how that inventory was initially acquired. Nor does it show how the organization uses the cash it receives from customers. Conversely, Figure 18-2 shows how inventory was acquired (the Receive Inventory event) by giving up cash (the Disburse Cash event). Yet, Figure 18-2 does not show what the organization does with the inventory or how it acquired the cash used to pay suppliers.

Thus, REA diagrams for individual business cycles provide only partial information about the resources controlled by an organization. The complete picture would show how each resource is acquired and how it is used. As shown in Figure 18-4, this can be done by redrawing an REA diagram to place common resources between the events that affect them. Doing so reflects another important duality that must be depicted in a complete REA model of any organization: Every resource must be connected to at least one event that increases that resource and to at least one event that decreases it.

Merging Redundant Event Entities

REA diagrams for individual business cycles may include some events that also appear in the REA diagrams of another cycle. For example, Figures 18-2 and 18-3 both contain the Disburse Cash event entity. As was the case with resources, merging these multiple occurrences of the same event improves the legibility of the resulting comprehensive REA diagram. Thus, Figure 18-4 shows that the Disburse Cash event is linked to both the Receive Inventory and the Time Worked events.

Close examination of Figure 18-4 reveals an important difference, however, between merging redundant events and merging redundant resources: Merging redundant resources does not affect any cardinalities, but merging redundant events alters the minimum cardinalities associated with the other events that are related to the merged event. Thus, in Figure 18-4 the cardinalities between the inventory resource and each of the four events to which it is related are the same as those depicted in Figures 18-1 and 18-2. In contrast, the cardinalities between the Disburse Cash event and the other events with which it is linked are different in Figure 18-4 than in Figures 18-2 and 18-3.

The reason for this difference lies in the underlying semantics about the nature of the relationship between the merged entity and other entities. An instance of a resource entity can, and usually is, linked to multiple events. For example, a given inventory item carried by Fred's Train Shop can be linked not only to a Receive Inventory event, when it is acquired from a supplier, but also to a Sales event, when it is sold to a customer. In other words, the resource entity is linked to event entities in one business cycle *and* to event entities in the other cycle. Because both links are possible, none of the cardinalities in the individual REA diagrams needs to change.

The situation is different when merging an event across business cycles. The event that appears in both individual business cycle REA diagrams may be linked to *either* an event that is part of one business cycle *or* to an event that is part of another cycle *but cannot be linked to both* events. For example, in Figure 18-4, a particular Disburse Cash event (i.e., a particular check or EFT transaction) could be associated with a prior receipt of inventory from a supplier or with time worked by an employee, but the same check (or EFT transaction) cannot be used *both* to pay a supplier for receipt of inventory *and* to pay an employee for working the previous week. Consequently, the minimum cardinality associated with the other events *must* be 0 in the integrated REA diagram, regardless of what it was in each of the individual transaction cycle REA diagrams. To understand why, recall that a minimum of 1 means that each instance of that entity has to be associated with at least one instance of the other entity. In terms of cash disbursements in Figure 18-4, retaining the minimum 1 with the Time Worked event, for example, would mean that every cash disbursement must be linked to a time card transaction—which is clearly not true, because Fred may make a cash disbursement to pay a supplier. For similar reasons, the minimum cardinality from the Disburse Cash event to the Receive Inventory event must also be 0.

Merging two transaction cycles on a common event may also affect the minimum cardinalities between the merged event and the agents participating in that event. For example, in Figure 18-4 the minimum cardinality between the Disburse Cash event and the Supplier entity is now 0, instead of 1, as it was in Figure 18-2. The reason is that a given check (cash disbursement) may be written *either* to a supplier as payee or to an employee as payee, but the same check *cannot* be written to *both* agents simultaneously. That is why the minimum cardinality between the Disburse Cash event and the Employee (payee) agent is also 0. Thus, whenever a merged event involves different agents in each of the individual business cycles being merged, the minimum cardinalities between that event and those agents change from the usual 1 to 0, because the event may now be linked to either of the two types of agents, but not both.

Validating the Accuracy of Integrated REA Diagrams

Chapter 17 presented three basic principles for drawing REA diagrams for individual business cycles; the preceding discussion for combining such diagrams into a single, enterprise-wide model adds two more rules. Thus, a correctly drawn, integrated REA diagram must satisfy these five rules:

1. Every event must be linked to at least one resource.
2. Every event must be linked to two agents who participate in that event.
3. Every event that involves the disposition of a resource must be linked to an event that involves the acquisition of a resource. (This reflects the economic duality underlying "give-to-get" economic exchanges.)
4. Every resource must be linked to at least one event that increments that resource and to at least one event that decrements that resource.
5. If event A can be linked to more than one other event, but cannot be linked simultaneously to all of those other events, then the REA diagram should show that event A is linked to a minimum of 0 of each of those other events.

Notice that these five rules can be used not only to develop an integrated REA diagram but also as "check figures" to validate the accuracy of a completed REA diagram. Technically, Figure 18-4 is not complete because rule 4 is not satisfied for the Employee Time resource. We will correct this shortcoming in Chapter 19. For now, let us ignore it and proceed to the next step in the database design process: implementation of an REA data model in a relational database.

Implementing an REA Diagram in a Relational Database

Once an REA diagram has been developed, it can be used to design a well-structured relational database. In fact, creating a set of tables from an REA diagram automatically results in a well-structured relational database that is not subject to the update, insert, and delete anomaly problems discussed in Chapter 4.

There are three steps to implementing an REA diagram in a relational database:

1. Create a table for each *distinct* entity in the diagram and for each many-to-many relationship.
2. Assign attributes to appropriate tables.
3. Use foreign keys to implement one-to-one and one-to-many relationships.

Recall that even though REA diagrams for different organizations may include the same entities, differences in business policies are likely and will result in differences in relationship cardinalities. For example, the REA diagram for one organization may show a 1:1 relationship between the Sales and Receive Cash events, whereas the REA diagram for another organization may model that same pair of events as being involved in a M:N relationship. Thus, the design of a database (number of tables, placement of attributes) is specific to the organization being modeled.

Step 1: Create Tables for Each Distinct Entity and M:N Relationship

A properly designed relational database has a table for each distinct entity and for each many-to-many relationship in an REA diagram. Figure 18-4 has 13 distinct entities, but as previously discussed, one, Employee Time, will not be implemented in the database. The remaining 12 distinct entities that are depicted in Figure 18-4 need to be implemented as tables in a relational database. Seven tables will represent the event entities in the diagram: Order Inventory, Receive Inventory, Disburse Cash, Time Worked, Take Customer Order, Sales, and Receive Cash. There are two tables for resource entities: Inventory and Cash. Three tables are needed to implement the distinct agent entities: Employees, Customers, and Suppliers (supervisors are labeled separately to make the diagram easier to read, but are themselves employees).

Figure 18-4 also depicts five M:N relationships. Three are from the revenue cycle: Take Customer Orders–Inventory, Sales–Inventory, and Sales–Receive Cash. Two others are from the expenditure cycle: Inventory–Order Inventory and Inventory–Receive Inventory. Therefore, the 17 tables listed in Table 18-1 must be created to accurately implement Figure 18-4 in a

TABLE 18-1 Table Names and Attribute Placement for Figure 18-4

		Attributes	
TABLES	Primary Key	Foreign Keys	Other Attributes
Order Inventory	Purchase order number	Supplier number, employee number	Date, time, reason
Receive Inventory	Receiving report number	Supplier number, employee number, purchase order number, check number	Date, time, remarks, vendor invoice number
Disburse Cash	Check number	Supplier number, employee number (payee), employee number (signer), account number	Amount, description, date
Take Customer Order	Sales order number	Customer number, employee number	Date, time, special remarks
Sales	Invoice number	Customer number, employee number, sales order number	Date, time, invoice sent (Y/N)
Receive Cash	Remittance number	Customer number, employee number, account number	Date, time, method of payment
Time Worked	Timecard number	Employee number, supervisor number, paycheck number	Date, time in, time out
Inventory	Product number		Description, list price, standard cost, beginning quantity-on-hand, beginning quantity-available, reorder quantity, reorder point
Cash	Account number		Beginning-balance, type of account
Employees	Employee number		Name, date hired, date of birth, pay rate, job title
Customers	Customer number		Name, address[a], beginning account balance, credit limit
Suppliers	Supplier number		Name, address[a], beginning account balance, performance rating
Order Inventory—Inventory	Purchase order number, product number		Quantity ordered, actual unit cost
Receive Inventory—Inventory	Receiving report number, product number		Quantity received, condition
Take Customer Order—Inventory	Sales order number, product number		Quantity ordered
Sales—Inventory	Invoice number, product number		Quantity sold, actual sale price
Sales—Receive Cash	Invoice number, remittance number		Amount applied to invoice

[a]Actually, only the street address and Zip code would be stored in these tables. In both tables Zip code would be a foreign key. Zip code would also be the primary key of an "address table," which would also include city and state as other attributes.

relational data base. Notice that the suggested table names in Table 18-1 correspond to the names of entities in the REA diagram or, in the case of tables for M:N relationships, are hyphenated concatenations of the entities involved in the relationship. This makes it easier to verify that all necessary tables have been created and also makes it easier to use the REA diagram as a guide when querying the database.

Step 2: Assign Attributes to Each Table[1]

The next step is to determine which attributes should be included in each table. The database designer needs to interview users and management to identify which facts need to be included in the database. The database designer must use the REA diagram to help determine in which table(s) to place those facts, depending upon whether that fact is a primary key or is just a descriptive attribute.

IDENTIFY PRIMARY KEYS   As explained in Chapter 4, every table in a relational database must have a primary key, consisting of an attribute, or combination of attributes, that uniquely identifies each row in that table. Companies often create numeric identifiers for specific resources, events, and agents. These numeric identifiers are good candidates for primary keys. For example, Table 18-1 shows that Fred's Train Shop uses invoice number as the primary key of the sales table and customer number as the primary key of the customer table.

Usually the primary key of a table representing an entity is a single attribute. The primary key for M:N relationship tables, however, always consists of two attributes that represent the primary keys of each entity linked in that relationship. For example, the primary key of the sales–inventory table consists of both the invoice number (the primary key of the sales entity) and product number (the primary key of the inventory entity). Such multiple-attribute primary keys are called *concatenated keys*.

ASSIGN OTHER ATTRIBUTES TO APPROPRIATE TABLES   Additional attributes besides the primary key are included in each table to satisfy transaction processing requirements and management's information needs. As discussed in Chapter 4, any other attribute included in a relational database table must either be a fact about the object represented by the primary key or a foreign key. Thus, information about customers, such as their name and address, belongs in the customer table, because those attributes describe the object represented by the primary key (customer number) of the customer table; those attributes do not belong in the sales table, because they do not describe some property of the object represented by the primary key (invoice number) of that table.

Table 18-1 shows some of the attributes that Paul Stone has assigned to the various tables he has created to implement Figure 18-4 in a relational database. Some of these attributes, such as the date of each sale and the amount remitted by a customer, are necessary for complete and accurate transaction processing and the production of financial statements and managerial reports. Other attributes are stored because they facilitate the effective management of an organization's resources, events, and agents. For example, Fred can use data about the time of day when each sales transaction occurs to design staff work schedules.

Table 18-1 also includes other attributes in some of the M:N relationship tables. Let us examine the placement of these attributes in some of the M:N tables to see why they must be stored in those particular tables. Consider first the Sales–Receive Cash table. Recall that Fred's Train Shop allows its customers to make multiple purchases on credit and to make installment payments on their outstanding balances. Thus, one customer payment may need to be applied to several different invoices (sales transactions). Therefore, the attribute "amount applied" cannot be placed in the Receive Cash table because it could take on more than one value (one for each invoice being paid), thereby violating the basic requirement of relational databases that every attribute in every row be single-valued (i.e., the requirement that every table be a flat file). Nor can the attribute "amount applied" be placed in the Sales table, because the possibility of installment payments also creates a situation in which that attribute can have multiple values (i.e., one

---

[1]As explained in Chapter 17, some designers prefer to include attributes as part of the REA diagram itself. We choose to list them in a separate table to reduce the clutter on the diagram.

entry for each installment payment related to that particular sale). Thus, analysis of the underlying business process indicates that the attribute "amount applied" is a fact about both a specific customer payment (remittance) and a specific sales transaction and, therefore, belongs in the M:N table linking those two events.

Now examine the Sales–Inventory table. Each row in this table contains information about a line item in an invoice. Although many customers of Fred's Train Shop buy just one of each kind of product it sells, some sales to customers involve larger quantities. For example, a department store may buy five identical coal cars (product number 31125) for its window display. Consequently, Fred's Train Shop must record the quantity sold of each item. Each sales event, however, may include more than one inventory item. Thus, the attribute "quantity sold" may have several values on a single sales invoice, one for each different item (product number) sold. Consequently, the attribute "quantity sold" cannot be placed in the Sales table, because there can be more than one "quantity sold" value associated with a given invoice number. In addition, recall that Fred's Train Shop, like most retail stores, tracks inventory by kinds of items, each of which is identified by product number, not by specific identification. Therefore, a given item, such as an orange diesel locomotive, product number 14887, may be sold as part of many different sales transactions. Consequently, "quantity sold" cannot be an attribute in the Inventory table because it can take on multiple values. Instead, the preceding analysis makes it clear that the attribute "quantity sold" pertains to a specific product number on a specific sales invoice. Therefore, it belongs in the M:N relationship table that links the inventory and sales entities.

Price and Cost Data   In Table 18-1, notice that information about prices and costs are stored as an attribute in several different tables. For example, the Inventory table stores the suggested list price for the item, which generally remains constant for a given fiscal period. The Sales table stores the actual sales price, which varies during the course of the year as a result of sales promotions. Similarly, the standard and actual purchase costs of each item are stored in different tables. The general rule is that time-independent data should be stored as an attribute of a resource or agent, but data that varies across time should be stored with event entities or M:N relationships that link a resource and an event.

Cumulative and Calculable Data   Notice that Table 18-1 does not contain cumulative data, such as "quantity-on-hand" in the inventory table, or calculable data, such as "total amount of sale" in the sales table. The reason is that neither type of data item is needed because those values can be derived from other attributes that are stored. For example, the quantity-on-hand of a given inventory item equals the quantity-on-hand at the beginning of the current fiscal period (an attribute of the Inventory table) plus the total quantity purchased this period (which is itself calculated by summing the quantity received attribute in the Inventory–Receive Inventory table) minus the total quantity sold (which is calculated by summing the quantity sold attribute in the Sales–Inventory table) in this period. Similarly, the total amount of a sales transaction can be calculated by multiplying the quantity sold by the actual sale price of each item sold and summing that result for every row in the Sales–Inventory table that has the same invoice number.

Step 3: Use Foreign Keys to Implement 1:1 and 1:N Relationships

Although 1:1 and 1:N relationships also can be implemented as separate tables, it is usually more efficient to implement them by means of foreign keys. Recall from Chapter 4 that a foreign key is an attribute of one entity that is itself the primary key of another entity. For example, the attribute "customer number" might appear in both the customer and the Sales tables. It would be the primary key of the Customer table, but a foreign key in the Sales table.

USING FOREIGN KEYS TO IMPLEMENT 1:1 RELATIONSHIPS   In a relational database, 1:1 relationships between entities can be implemented by including the primary key of either entity as a foreign key in the table representing the other entity. For purposes of designing a well-structured database, the choice of which table to place the foreign key in is arbitrary. Careful analysis of the minimum cardinalities of the relationship, however, may suggest which approach is likely to be more *efficient*.

Consider the case of a 1:1 relationship between sales and customer payments (see Figure 17-7, panel A). The minimum cardinality for the Receive Cash event is 0, indicating the existence of credit sales, and the minimum cardinality for the Sale event is 1, indicating that customer payments only occur after a sale has been made (e.g., there are no advance deposits). In this case, including invoice number (the primary key of the sales event) as a foreign key in the Receive Cash event may be more efficient because then only that one table would have to be accessed and updated when processing each customer payment. Moreover, for 1:1 relationships between two sequential events, including the primary key of the event that occurs first as a foreign key in the event that occurs second may improve internal control, because the employee given access to update the table containing data about the second event need not access the table used to store information about the first event. However, the internal control benefits of doing this must be weighed against a possible increase in difficulty of querying the database.

USING FOREIGN KEYS TO IMPLEMENT 1:N RELATIONSHIPS As with 1:1 relationships, 1:N relationships also should be implemented in relational databases with foreign keys. There is only one way to do this: The primary key of the entity that can be linked to multiple instances of the other entity *must* become a foreign key in that other entity. Thus, in Table 18-1, the primary keys of the Salesperson and Customer tables are included as foreign keys in the Sales table. Similarly, the primary keys of the Cash, Customer, and Cashier tables are included as foreign keys in the Receive Cash table. Reversing this procedure would violate one of the fundamental rules of relational database design. For example, placing invoice number as a foreign key in the Customer table would not work because it can have more than one value (i.e., a given customer may be, and one hopes is, associated with multiple invoice numbers because of participation in many sales transactions).

Note that this is why M:N relationships *must* be implemented as separate tables: Since each entity can be linked to multiple occurrences of the entity on the other side of the relationship, it is not possible to make either entity's primary key a foreign key in the other entity. Consider the M:N relationship between the Sales event and the Inventory resource. Each Sales event may be linked to many different inventory items. Therefore, product number cannot be used as a foreign key in the Sales table because it would be multivalued. Conversely, each product may be involved in many different sales transactions. Therefore, invoice number cannot be used as a foreign key in the Inventory table because it would be multivalued. Thus, the only way to link the Sales and Inventory tables is to create a new table which has separate rows for each actual combination of invoice number and product number. Notice that in the resulting M:N table a particular invoice number (e.g., 787923) will appear in many different rows, one for each different item that was part of that sales transaction. Conversely, a particular product number (e.g., 12345) will appear in many different rows, once for each different sales transaction in which it was sold. Thus, neither attribute, by itself, uniquely identifies a given row. However, there will be only one row that contains the combination of a particular invoice number and product number (e.g., invoice number 787923 and product number 12345); thus, both attributes together can serve as a primary key for the M:N table.

Completeness Check

The list of attributes that users and management want included in the database provides a means to check and validate the implementation process. Every attribute in that list should appear in at least one table, as either a primary key or "other" attribute.

Checking this list against the table column names may reveal not only the fact that a particular attribute has not been assigned to the appropriate table in the database but may even indicate the need to modify the REA diagram itself. For example, when Paul Stone double-checked the list of desired attributes, he found that he did not have any table in which to place the attribute "product discussed during sales call." In such a situation, the database designer needs to revisit users and management to understand the purpose for collecting that particular attribute. In this case, Fred explains that he plans to have one of his employees call on corporate customers to set up sample displays. Fred wants to collect information about such demonstrations to evaluate their effectiveness.

Paul realizes that this necessitates creating another event entity, Call on Customers, which would be linked to both the Customer and Employee agent tables, the Inventory table, and the Take Customer Order table (see Figure 19-1 on p. 548). The primary key of this new event would be "appointment number." Employee number and customer number would be foreign keys in the table, which would also include attributes for the date and time of the demonstration, along with a text field for comments. Because each demonstration could involve multiple items and each item could be demonstrated in many different calls, there would be a M:N relationship between the Call on Customer event and the Inventory table. The set of rows in that table with the same appointment number would identify which products were shown during a particular sales call. Some calls would result in orders, but others would not. In addition, some orders would occur without any sales call (e.g., because the customer saw an advertisement). Therefore, the minimum cardinality is 0 on each side of the relationship between the Call on Customer and Take Customer Order events. The maximum cardinality on each side of the relationship is 1 to simplify tracking the effect of sales calls.

Paul's need to modify his REA diagram to accommodate additional facts is not unusual. Indeed, it is often useful to create tables and assign attributes to them even before completely finishing an REA diagram. This helps clarify exactly what each entity represents, which often resolves dilemmas about the correct cardinalities for various relationships. The database designer can then modify and refine the REA diagram to include additional entities and relationships to accommodate other facts that are supposed to be in the database but that have not yet been assigned to existing tables.

Once all attributes have been assigned to tables, the basic requirements for designing well-structured relational databases that were discussed in Chapter 4 can be used as a final accuracy check:

1. Every table must have a primary key.
2. Other nonkey attributes in each table must be either a fact about the thing designated by the primary key or foreign keys used to link that table to another table.
3. Every attribute in every table is single-valued (i.e., each table is a flat file).

Note how the set of relational tables listed in Table 18-1 satisfy these three basic requirements. Moreover, they also correspond to Figure 18-4 and, therefore, reflect Fred's Train Shop's business policies. This correspondence also facilitates using the REA diagram to guide the design of queries and reports to retrieve and display information about the organization's business activities.

Using REA Diagrams to Retrieve Information from a Database

Thus far, we have shown how to use the REA data model to guide the design of an AIS that will efficiently store information about an organization's business activities. In this section we refer to Figure 18-4 and Table 18-1 to show how to use completed REA diagrams to facilitate the retrieval of that information to evaluate performance.

Creating Journals and Ledgers

At first glance, it may appear that a number of elements found in traditional AIS, such as journals, ledgers, and information about receivables and payables, are missing. We will see that such information, although not explicitly represented as entities in an REA diagram, can be obtained through appropriate queries. These queries need only be created once and can then be stored and rerun whenever desired.

DERIVING JOURNALS FROM QUERIES Journals provide a chronological listing of transactions. In a relational database designed according to the REA data model, event entities store information about transactions. Thus, the information normally found in a journal is contained in the tables used to record data about events. For example, the Sales and Sales–Inventory tables contains information about a particular sales transaction. Thus, a sales journal can be produced by writing a query that references both tables to calculate the amount of sales made during a given period.

Doing so, however, would not necessarily create the traditional sales journal because it would produce a list of *all* sales transactions, including both credit and cash sales. Traditionally, however, sales journals record only *credit* sales. In a relational database built on the REA model, such as the one in Figure 18-4, customer payments are recorded in the Receive Cash event table. Consequently, a query to produce a traditional sales journal (i.e., listing only those sales made on credit) would have to also include both the Receive Cash and the Sales–Receive Cash tables.

A database built on the REA model would create a row in the Sales table for each sale of merchandise to a customer and a row in the Receive Cash table to record receipt of payment from a customer. For cash sales, both rows would have the same values in the date and customer number columns. Therefore, the logic of a query to produce a traditional sales journal would restrict the output to display only those sales that are *not* linked to a corresponding customer payment event (i.e., the same customer number appears in both tables and the amount of the Receive Cash event equals the amount of the sale) that occurred *on the same day* as the Sale event. (Rows in the Receive Cash table with dates later than the date of the corresponding sales transaction represent payments on credit sales.) Similar processes can be followed to write queries to produce other special journals, such as all credit purchases or all cash disbursements not related to payroll.

LEDGERS   Ledgers are master files that contain cumulative information about specific accounts. In a relational database designed according to the REA data model, resource entities contain permanent information that is carried over from one fiscal year to the next. Thus, much of the information about an organization's assets that is traditionally recorded in ledgers is stored in resource tables in an REA-based relational database. For example, each row in the Equipment resource table would contain information about a specific piece or class of machinery, such as its acquisition cost, useful life, depreciation method, and estimated salvage value. Similarly, each row in the Cash resource table contains information about a specific account that holds the organization's cash and cash equivalents, and each row in the Inventory resource table stores information about a specific inventory item.

Each of these resource accounts is affected by increment and decrement events: Equipment is purchased and used; cash is received and disbursed; inventory is purchased and sold. Thus, queries to display the current cumulative balance for these accounts must reference not only the appropriate table for that resource entity but also the event tables that affect it. For example, a query to display the current balance in a specific bank account would reference not only the Cash resource table, to identify the account number and the balance as of the beginning of the current fiscal period, but also the Receive Cash and Disburse Cash tables, to find the inflows and outflows affecting that account during the current fiscal period.

Generating Financial Statements

A completed REA diagram can also be used to guide the writing of queries to produce the information that would be included in financial statements. Many financial statement accounts, such as Cash, Inventory, and Fixed Assets, are represented as resources in the REA model. An important exception, however, is claims: Figure 18-4 includes neither an entity called Accounts Receivable nor one called Accounts Payable. As explained in Chapter 17, the reason is that both of these accounts merely represent an imbalance between two related events. Accounts receivable represents sales transactions for which customer payments have not yet been received, and accounts payable represents purchases from suppliers that have not yet been paid for. Therefore, neither accounts receivable nor accounts payable needs to be explicitly stored as separate tables in an REA database. Instead, those claims can be derived from a set of queries against the relevant agent and event tables. For example, three queries can be used to calculate total Accounts Receivable. First, sum the total beginning balances in every customer account. Second, calculate total new sales this period by writing a query against the M:N Sales–Inventory relationship table to sum the product of quantity sold times unit price. Third, determine the total cash received from customers this period by summing the amount column in the Receive Cash table. Total Accounts Receivable equals beginning Accounts Receivable (query 1) plus new sales (query 2) minus cash receipts (query 3). Note that these steps yield total Accounts Receivable. A similar set of queries will produce total Accounts Payable.

Creating Managerial Reports

The REA data model facilitates creating a wide variety of managerial reports because it integrates nonfinancial and financial data. For example, Table 18-1 shows that the Sales table in Figure 18-4 includes an attribute to record the *time* that the sale occurred. Fred can use this data to track sales activity during different times of the day to better plan staffing needs at the train shop. Other useful nonfinancial attributes could be included in other tables. For example, the Customer table could be modified to include an attribute that identifies whether a customer has an indoor or outdoor train layout. If Fred can collect this information from his customers, he may be able to better target his advertising to meet each individual customer's interests. In addition, Table 18-1 can be modified easily to integrate data from external sources. For example, to better evaluate the creditworthiness of business customers, Fred may decide to collect information from a credit rating agency, such as Dun & Bradstreet. This information could be added to the database by creating an additional column in the Customer table to store the customer's credit rating. A similar process could be used to store information about suppliers that could be used in the vendor selection process.

Summary and Case Conclusion

REA diagrams for individual business cycles depict basic give-to-get economic duality relationships but usually provide only a partial view of resources, showing either how they are acquired or how they are used, but not both. Therefore, individual business cycle REA diagrams need to be combined in order to provide a comprehensive enterprise-wide data model. This is usually done by merging resource and event entities that appear in two or more individual REA diagrams. Merging two or more REA diagrams that contain the same resource entity does not require any changes to the cardinality pairs in the individual diagrams. Merging two or more diagrams that contain a common event entity, however, often requires changing the minimum cardinalities associated with the other events to 0, to reflect the fact that the merged event may be connected to any one of several different events, but not to all of them simultaneously. The minimum cardinalities associated with the agents participating in those merged events may also have to be changed to 0.

A data model documented in an REA diagram can be implemented in a relational DBMS in three steps. First, create tables for all unique entities and M:N relationships in the REA diagram. Second, assign primary keys and nonkey attributes to each table. Third, use foreign keys to implement 1:1 and 1:N relationships.

Paul Stone follows these steps to implement a database AIS for Fred's Train Shop based on Figure 18-4. He first creates separate tables for each of the 12 distinct entities and 5 M:N relationships in the figure. Next, Paul identifies primary keys for each table and uses some of them as foreign keys to implement the 1:1 and 1:N relationships in Figure 18-4. He then assigns the remaining attributes that Fred wants to monitor to the appropriate tables. Paul then demonstrates how easy it is to write queries to retrieve a variety of managerial reports and financial statements from the relational DBMS. Fred is quite impressed and immediately begins to use the new system to provide detailed information about the business activities of Fred's Train Shop.

Key Terms

concatenated keys 532

AIS IN ACTION

Chapter Quiz

1. Which of the following types of entities *must* become a separate table in a relational database?
   a. resources
   b. events
   c. agents
   d. all of the above

2. How many tables are needed to implement an REA data model that has seven distinct enities, three M:N relationships, and five 1:N relationships in a relational database?
   a. 7   c. 12
   b. 10   d. 15

3. Which type of relationship cardinality *must* be implemented in a relational database as a separate table?
   a. 1:1 relationship   c. M:N relationship
   b. 1:N relationship   d. all of the above

4. Combining two REA diagrams typically does NOT involve merging which type of entity?
   a. resources   c. agents
   b. events   d. all of the above

5. Which of the following elements of a traditional AIS can be derived from queries of an REA database?
   a. journals   c. claims (receivables and payables)
   b. ledgers   d. all of the above

6. Which of the following tables would most likely have a concatenated primary key?
   a. Inventory   c. Inventory–Sales
   b. Sales   d. none of the above

7. An REA diagram contains four instances of the Employee entity. How many tables does this require in a relational database?
   a. 1   c. 3
   b. 2   d. 4

8. A business orders mass-produced merchandise frequently throughout the year. In which table should the attribute "quantity ordered" appear?
   a. Order Inventory   c. Order Inventory–Inventory
   b. Inventory   d. none of the above

9. Which of the following statements is true only about an integrated REA data model?
   a. Every event must be linked to at least two agents.
   b. Every increment (Get) event must be linked to a decrement (Give) event.
   c. Every resource must be linked to at least one increment event and at least one decrement event.
   d. Every resource must be linked to at least one agent.

10. In a relational database designed according to the REA data model, information traditionally stored in ledgers can be obtained by querying which of the following?
    a. resources
    b. events
    c. M:N relationship tables between resources and events
    d. all of the above

Comprehensive Problem

Trailspan Travel Club

The Trailspan Travel Club markets travel books across the United States and Canada. Members of the travel club place orders online through Trailspan's Web site, over the phone by calling an 800 number, or by mail. Online orders are entered into the club computer system automatically. Telephone and mail orders are entered into Trailspan's computer system by the club's sales representatives. Once the orders have been entered, an order notification is sent to the shipping department. A shipping clerk retrieves the ordered items from inventory and then packs and ships each order. Trailspan only ships complete orders; if an item is temporarily out of stock, it notifies the customer that the entire shipment will be delayed. Once an order has been shipped, the computer system sends an invoice to the member and sends a notification to accounts receivable. Members who do not pay within 30 days are charged 6% interest on their outstanding balance. When making payments, members may pay part or all of their remaining balance. A clerk in the cash receipts department processes all cash receipts and makes deposits into the company's bank account.

When a particular inventory item meets its reorder point, Trailspan's computer system generates a purchase order and the purchasing agent sends the purchase order to the appropriate vendor. Suppliers fill each order individually; sometimes, however, they are out of stock of an item. In such cases, they immediately ship what is in stock and then make a second delivery for items that they had to back order. Once an inventory order is received by the receiving clerk, it is counted and sent to inventory. The cash disbursements clerk pays all vendor invoices individually as they become due to take advantage of any purchase discounts.

Required

a. Prepare an integrated REA diagram for the revenue and expenditure cycles of Trailspan Travel Club.

b. Prepare a set of tables to implement your data model in a relational database. Assign every attribute mentioned in the narrative to the appropriate table(s).

Discussion Questions

18.1. How would the process of generating a cash disbursements journal from the REA data model presented in Figure 18-4 and Table 18-1 differ from the process for creating a sales journal?

18.2. Why take the time to develop separate REA diagrams for each business cycle if the ultimate objective is to combine them into one integrated enterprise-wide data model? Why not just focus on the integrated model from the start?

18.3. Building separate tables for every relationship (1:1, 1:N, and M:N) does not violate any of the rules for building a well-structured database. Why then do you think that REA data modelers recommend building separate tables only for M:N relationships and using foreign keys to implement 1:1 and 1:N relationships?

18.4. Assume that there exists a 1:1 relationship between the Receive Inventory and Disburse Cash events. How does the manner in which the relationship between the two events is implemented (i.e., in which table a foreign key is placed) affect the process used to record payments made to suppliers?

18.5. Refer to Figure 18-4 and Table 18-1. How would you determine the amount of cash that Fred's Train Shop has at any point in time?

18.6. Why does Figure 18-4 show only one cash disbursement entity if Fred's Train Shop uses a general operating checking account for purchases of inventory, supplies, and operating expenses such as rent but also uses a separate checking account for payroll?

18.7. Examine Figure 18-4 and Table 18-1. Why do the Inventory, Customers, and Suppliers tables all have an attribute that contains data about the balance at the beginning of the current fiscal period?

Problems

18.1. Refer to Problems 17.1 and 17.2 for information about the revenue and expenditure cycle activities for Joe's ice-cream shop in order to draw an integrated REA diagram of both cycles.

18.2. Develop a set of tables to implement the integrated REA diagram you developed in Problem 18.1 for Joe's ice-cream shop in a relational database. Specify a primary key for each table, and suggest at least one other attribute that should be included in each table.

18.3. Refer to Problems 17.3 and 17.4 for information about the revenue and expenditure cycle activities of Sue's Gallery in order to draw an integrated REA diagram of both cycles.

18.4. Develop a set of tables to implement the integrated REA diagram you developed in Problem 18.3 for Sue's Gallery in a relational database. Specify a primary key for each table, and suggest at least one other attribute that should be included in each table.

18.5. The following tables and attributes exist in a relational database:

Table	Attributes
Vendor	Vendor #, name, street address, city, state
Purchases	P.O. #, date, amount, vendor #, purchasing agent #
Inventory Receipts	Receiving report #, date, receiving clerk #, remarks, P.O. #
Cash Disbursed	Check #, date, amount
Inventory Receipts–Cash Disbursed	Check #, receiving report #, amount applied to invoice

Required

Draw an REA diagram for this database. State any additional assumptions you need to make about cardinalities.

18.6. Refer to Problems 17.8 and 17.9 for information about the revenue and expenditure cycles for the Computer Warehouse and use that information to draw an integrated REA diagram for both cycles.

18.7. Develop a set of tables to implement the integrated REA diagram you developed in Problem 18.6 for the Computer Warehouse in a relational database. Specify a primary key for each table, and suggest at least one other attribute that should be included in each table.

18.8. Explain how to calculate the total amount of accounts payable.

18.9. Refer to Figure 18.4 and Table 18-1 to write the query logic needed to answer the following questions. (Optional: If requested by your instructor, write your queries in SQL or a Query-By-Example graphical interface.) Some answers may require more than one query—try to write the most efficient queries possible.
a. Accounts payable for all suppliers in Arizona
b. Total amount of sales to a customer named Smith
c. Total wage expense
d. Total wages payable
e. Net increase (decrease) in quantity-on-hand for a particular inventory item
f. The proportion of sales made to walk-in customers (i.e., no order)
g. The salesperson who made the largest amount of sales in October
h. The salesperson who made the most sales in October
i. The most popular item, in terms of total units sold

18.10. Refer to Problem 17.10 and develop a set of tables to implement the REA diagram you developed for Stan's Southern Barbeque Supply Store. Identify the primary and foreign keys for each table, and don't forget to address any M:N relationships.

Case 18-1 Practical Database Design

Hands-on practice in database design is important. Use a relational DBMS to implement the integrated REA data model presented in this chapter, or one of the integrated data models from the homework problems, or a model provided by your instructor. Then, perform the following tasks:

1. Write a query to calculate total accounts receivable.
2. Write a query to calculate accounts receivable for a specific customer.
3. Create a sales invoice form that references the appropriate tables and inputs data about attributes into the proper tables.
4. Write queries to calculate as many financial statement items as possible from the data model you implement.
5. Design appropriate input controls to ensure the validity of data entered in the form created in step 3.

AIS IN ACTION SOLUTIONS

Quiz Key

1. Which of the following types of entities *must* become a separate table in a relational database?
   a. resources (Incorrect. All three types of entities become separate tables.)
   b. events (Incorrect. All three types of entities become separate tables.)
   c. agents (Incorrect. All three types of entities become separate tables.)
   ▶ d. all of the above (Correct. All three types of entities become separate tables.)

2. How many tables are needed to implement an REA data model that has seven distinct enities, three M:N relationships, and five 1:N relationships in a relational database?
   a. 7 (Incorrect. There must be 10 tables, one for each distinct entity and one for each M:N relationship.)
   ▶ b. 10 (Correct. There must be 10 tables, one for each distinct entity and one for each M:N relationship.)
   c. 12 (Incorrect. There must be 10 tables, one for each distinct entity and one for each M:N relationship.)
   d. 15 (Incorrect. There must be 10 tables, one for each distinct entity and one for each M:N relationship.)

3. Which type of relationship cardinality *must* be implemented in a relational database as a separate table?
   a. 1:1 relationship (Incorrect. Only M:N relationships must be implemented as separate tables in a relational database. Foreign keys can be used to implement 1:N and 1:1 relationships.)
   b. 1:N relationship (Incorrect. Only M:N relationships must be implemented as separate tables in a relational database. Foreign keys can be used to implement 1:N and 1:1 relationships.)
   ▶ c. M:N relationship (Correct. Only M:N relationships must be implemented as separate tables in a relational database. Foreign keys can be used to implement 1:N and 1:1 relationships.)
   d. All of the above (Incorrect. Only M:N relationships must be implemented as separate tables in a relational database. Foreign keys can be used to implement 1:N and 1:1 relationships.)

4. Combining two REA diagrams typically does not involve merging which type of entity?
   a. resources (Incorrect. Combining two REA diagrams often involves merging resource entities that appear on both individual diagrams.)

      b. events (Incorrect. Combining two REA diagrams often involves merging event entities that appear on both individual diagrams.)

▶ c. agents (Correct. Combining two REA diagrams often involves merging resource and event entities that appear on both individual diagrams but usually retains multiple copies of agent entities to minimize the number of criss-crossing relationships.)

      d. all of the above (Incorrect. Combining two REA diagrams often involves merging resource and event entities that appear on both individual diagrams, but not agent entities.)

5. Which of the following elements of a traditional AIS can be derived from queries of an REA database?

      a. journals (Incorrect. Journals, ledgers, and claims can all be derived from queries of an REA database.)

      b. ledgers (Incorrect. Journals, ledgers, and claims can all be derived from queries of an REA database.)

      c. claims (receivables and payables) (Incorrect. Journals, ledgers, and claims can all be derived from queries of an REA database.)

▶ d. all of the above (Correct. Journals, ledgers, and claims can all be derived from queries of an REA database.)

6. Which of the following tables would most likely have a concatenated primary key?

      a. Inventory (Incorrect. Although any entity may have a concatenated key, few do except for M:N relationships, which must have concatenated primary keys.)

      b. Sales (Incorrect. Although any entity may have a concatenated key, few do except for M:N relationships, which must have concatenated primary keys.)

▶ c. Inventory–Sales (Correct. Although any entity may have a concatenated key, few do except for M:N relationships, which must have concatenated primary keys.)

      d. none of the above (Incorrect. Although any entity may have a concatenated key, few do except for M:N relationships, which must have concatenated primary keys.)

7. An REA diagram contains four instances of the Employee entity. How many tables does this require in a relational database?

▶ a. 1 (Correct. Multiple occurrences of the same entity in an REA diagram improve readability, but only one table is needed for each distinct entity.)

      b. 2 (Incorrect. Multiple occurrences of the same entity in an REA diagram improve readability, but only one table is needed for each distinct entity.)

      c. 3 (Incorrect. Multiple occurrences of the same entity in an REA diagram improve readability, but only one table is needed for each distinct entity.)

      d. 4 (Incorrect. Multiple occurrences of the same entity in an REA diagram improve readability, but only one table is needed for each distinct entity.)

8. A business orders mass-produced merchandise frequently throughout the year. In which table should the attribute "quantity ordered" appear?

      a. Order Inventory (Incorrect. The attribute "quantity ordered" is a fact about a specific order for a specific item. It cannot appear in the Order Inventory table because a purchase order can include more than one inventory item. It cannot be included in the Inventory table because a given item can be ordered many times.)

      b. Inventory (Incorrect. The attribute "quantity ordered" is a fact about a specific order for a specific item. It cannot appear in the Order Inventory table because a purchase order can include more than one inventory item. It cannot be included in the Inventory table because a given item can be ordered many times.)

▶ c. Order Inventory–Inventory (Correct. The attribute "quantity ordered" is a fact about a specific order for a specific item. It cannot appear in the Order Inventory table because a purchase order can include more than one inventory item. It cannot be included in the Inventory table because a given item can be ordered many times.)

      d. none of the above (Incorrect. M:N relationships have concatenated primary keys that consist of the primary key of each entity participating in that relationship.)

9. Which of the following statements is true only about an integrated REA data model?

      a. Every event must be linked to at least two agents. (Incorrect. This is true of any REA model.)

b. Every increment (Get) event must be linked to a decrement (Give) event. (Incorrect. This is true of any REA diagram.)

▶ c. Every resource must be linked to at least one increment event and at least one decrement event. (Correct. This is a unique feature of, and is the reason for, integrating multiple REA diagrams.)

d. Every resource must be linked to at least one agent. (Incorrect. This is not true of any REA diagram.)

10. In a relational database designed according to the REA data model, information traditionally stored in ledgers can be obtained by querying which of the following?

a. resources (Incorrect. To obtain the information traditionally found in a ledger often involves querying not only resource tables but also event tables and any M:N relationships between those two entities.)

b. events (Incorrect. To obtain the information traditionally found in a ledger often involves querying not only resource tables but also event tables and any M:N relationships between those two entities.)

c. M:N relationship tables between resources and events (Incorrect. To obtain the information traditionally found in a ledger often involves querying not only resource tables but also event tables and any M:N relationships between those two entities.)

▶ d. all of the above (Correct. To obtain the information traditionally found in a ledger often involves querying not only resource tables but also event tables and any M:N relationships between those two entities.)

Comprehensive Problem Solution

Part a Prepare an integrated REA diagram for Trailspan Travel Club's revenue and expenditure cycles.

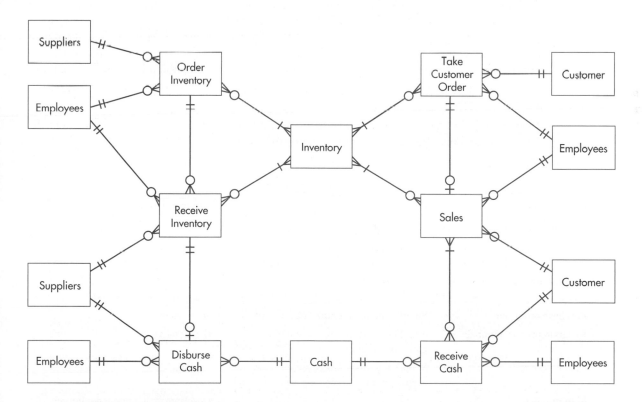

Explanation of Relationships and Cardinalities

The relationships between the agent and event entities are all modeled as 1:N with 0 minimums on the event side and 1 minimums on the agent side. This reflects standard practice: Every event must involve at least one agent, but a given agent may or may not be involved in any particular event. Moreover, for accountability purposes, every event is linked to only one specific internal and one specific external agent, but both types of agents may be linked to many different events.

The cardinalities of the relationships between the Cash resource and the Disburse Cash and Receive Cash events are also standard. Each event must be linked to a cash account (hence the minimum of 1) and for accountability purposes is linked to only one cash account (hence the maximum of 1). Conversely, some cash accounts may never be linked to any Disburse Cash or Receive Cash events (hence the minimum cardinality is 0), but other cash accounts may be linked to many such events (hence the maximum cardinality is N).

The cardinalities of the relationships between the Inventory resource and the four events that affect it are also standard for retail organizations that sell mass-produced goods: They are all M:N. This reflects the fact that a given product number may be linked to many different events, and any given event may involve multiple products. The minimums are 0 going to the event entities for two reasons: (1) to allow the organization to add information about new products prior to engaging in any transactions involving those products and (2) because the event tables are empty at the beginning of each new fiscal year. The minimum cardinalities are 1 in the reverse direction because every event must involve at least one inventory item.

The relationship between the Order Inventory and Receive Inventory events is 1:N because Trailspan's suppliers sometimes are out of items ordered and therefore must make more than one delivery to fill a particular order. Trailspan's suppliers do not hold and aggregate its orders, however, which is why each Receive Inventory event is linked to at most one Order event. The minimum cardinalities reflect the fact that orders precede deliveries from suppliers.

The relationship between the Receive Inventory and Disburse Cash events is 1:1 because Trailspan's policy is to pay for each vendor invoice separately, in order to take advantage of discounts for prompt payment. Thus, it cuts separate checks for each delivery received, and each check pays for only one specific delivery. The minimum cardinalities reflect the fact that Trailspan does not pay for its purchases in advance.

The relationship between Take Customer Orders and Sales is 1:1 because Trailspan fills each customer order separately but does not do so until it can completely fill each order. The minimum cardinalities reflect the fact that orders precede sales.

The relationship between the Sales and Receive Cash events is M:N because Trailspan allows its customers to make installment payments on any given sale and also allows them to periodically pay for multiple sales transactions that occurred during the prior months. The minimum cardinalities reflect the fact that Trailspan does not require customers to ever pay in advance for sales.

Part b Prepare tables for each entity. The following tables must be created to implement the REA diagram developed in part a into a relational database.

Table	Primary Key	Foreign Keys	Other Attributes
Employee	Employee number		Name, address, data hired
Customer	Customer number		Name, address, credit limit, account balance beginning current period
Supplier	Supplier number		Name, address, account balance beginning current period
Order Inventory	Purchase order number	Supplier number, employee number	Date, comments
Receive Inventory	Receiving report number	Supplier number, employee number, purchase order number	Remarks, vendor's invoice number
Disburse Cash	Check number	Supplier number, employee number, account number, receiving report number	Amount, description
Inventory	Item number		Description, list price, beginning quantity-on-hand, beginning quantity-available

Cash	Account number		Balance beginning current period, type of account
Take Customer Order	Sales order number	Customer number, employee number	Date, comments
Sale	Invoice number	Customer number, employee number, sales order number	Date, time
Receive Cash	Remittance number	Customer number, employee number, account number	Date, total amount
Inventory—Order Inventory	Item number, purchase order number		Quantity ordered
Inventory—Receive Inventory	Item number, receiving report number		Quantity received, condition
Inventory—Take Customer Order	Item number, sales order number		Quantity ordered, price
Inventory—Sales	Item number, invoice number		Quantity sold
Sales—Receive Cash	Invoice number, remittance number		Amount applied to invoice

Special Topics in REA Modeling

INTEGRATIVE CASE PAUL STONE, CONSULTING

Paul Stone has enjoyed designing a database for Fred's Train Shop so much that he decides he wants to do similar work for other local businesses. First, however, he realizes that he needs to acquire some additional skills. Although he feels confident of his ability to model the activities of retail businesses like Fred's Train Shop, Paul knows that he needs to learn more about how to model other types of businesses, such as manufacturing businesses and businesses that provide services.

Paul begins searching the Internet for information about data modeling and database design. He finds a link to a workshop on REA data modeling that is being offered by the American Accounting Association. After reading about it, Paul is certain that it is exactly what he is looking for. He registers for the class. He then prepares a list of questions about the situations that he wants to learn how to model:

1. How do you model the revenue cycle activities of a business that provides services, such as computer or automotive repairs? What about a business that rents items instead of selling them?

2. How do you model the production cycle activities of a manufacturer?

3. How do you integrate payroll activities with other HR processes, such as hiring and training employees?

4. How do you model financing transactions, such as the issuance of stock or debt?

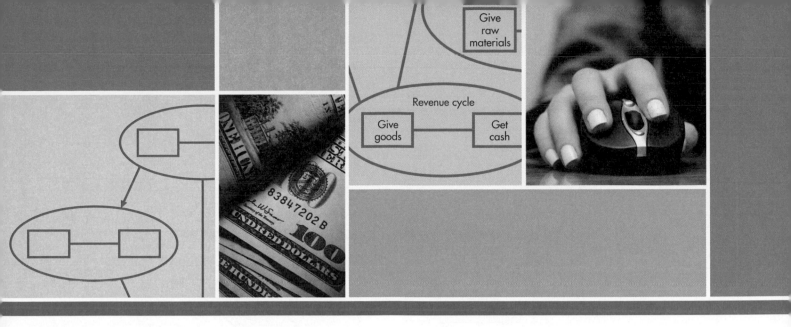

Introduction

The previous two chapters introduced the topic of REA data modeling and explained how to implement an REA model in a relational database. Both chapters focused primarily on the revenue and expenditure cycle activities for a typical retail organization. This chapter extends those basic concepts to a variety of other types of businesses and business cycles. We begin by examining more complex models of the revenue and expenditure cycles, including some additional activities typically performed by manufacturers and distributors and other special situations. Then we discuss several additions to the basic REA model. Next we explain how to model basic business activities in the production, HR, and financing cycles. We conclude by presenting a comprehensive integrated REA model that incorporates many of the topics presented in this chapter.

Additional Revenue and Expenditure Cycle Modeling Topics

Figures 19-1 and 19-2 present REA diagrams that include additional events for the revenue and expenditure cycles, respectively. Tables 19-1 and 19-2 show how to implement these models in a relational database.

Additional Revenue Cycle Events and Attribute Placement

Many of the entities and relationships depicted in Figure 19-1 have already been discussed in previous chapters, so we will focus only on those aspects that are new. Figure 19-1 separates the warehouse activity of filling an order from the activity of actually shipping or delivering that order to the customer. Thus, each instance of the Fill Customer Order event represents the picking and packing of an order by a warehouse employee. The meaning of the cardinality pairs between that event and the inventory resource and participating agents should be understood from discussions in the previous two chapters. The relationship between the Take Customer Order and Fill Customer Order events is represented as being one-to-many (1:N). The minimum cardinalities reflect the fact that two events occur sequentially. The maximum cardinalities reflect the fact that sometimes the company may be out of stock of one or more items that were ordered. Therefore, it may take multiple warehouse activities to completely fill a particular order. Each customer order has to be individually picked and packed, however. The relationship between the Fill Customer Order and Ship Order events is 1:1. The minimum cardinalities reflect the fact that the two events are sequential. The maximum cardinalities are typical best practices followed by most companies. Once all the items that were ordered and in stock have been picked

FIGURE 19-1

**Extended Partial
Revenue Cycle REA
Diagram**

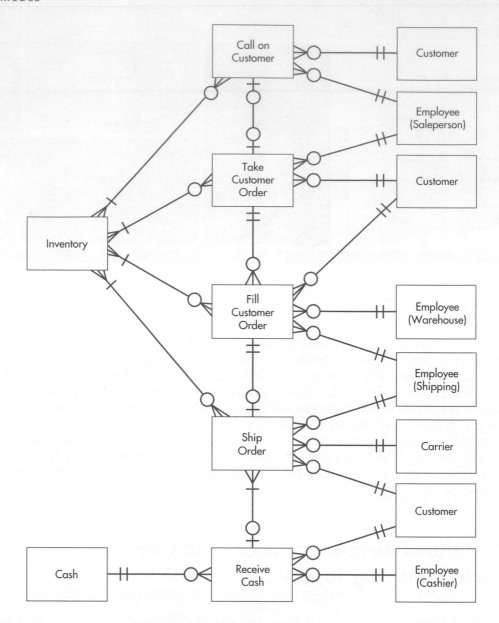

and packed, that entire package is shipped intact to the customer. Note that the Ship Order event occurs when the merchandise is given to the customer (i.e., it is the Sale event). Thus, if formal sales invoices are prepared, there would be a separate invoice for each filled order. For proper accountability each Ship Order event is linked to one, and only one, Fill Customer Order event. It is true that oftentimes many different orders are placed on the same truck or railroad car. However, producing accurate financial records requires tracking each individual "shipment" (sale) on that truckload/carload separately.

Table 19-1 shows that the primary key of the Ship Order event is the shipment number. The bill of lading number is another attribute, but it is not the primary key because it may be null for deliveries made using the company's own trucks. Sales invoice number is another attribute of the shipment event. It is not the primary key, however, because as discussed in Chapters 12 and 13, many companies are moving to eliminate the printing of paper invoices and even the creation of electronic ones. Moreover, even when invoices are still used, they may not be generated at the time the merchandise is shipped. Therefore, if invoice number were the primary key, information about the shipment could not be recorded until the invoice was generated. For companies that do still use invoices, however, the invoice number attribute serves an important internal control function: Examination of the value of this attribute provides an easy means of verifying whether

TABLE 19-1 Attributes for Relational Tables in Figure 19-1

Table Name	Primary Key	Foreign Keys	Other Attributes
Inventory	Product number		Description, unit standard cost, unit list price, weight, reorder point, beginning quantity-on-hand
Cash	General ledger account number		Name, beginning balance
Call on customer	Call number	Customer number, salesperson employee number	Date, time, purpose
Take customer order	Sales order number	Customer number, salesperson employee number, call number	Date, time, terms, desired delivery date
Fill customer order	Picking ticket number	Sales order number, customer number, warehouse employee number, shipping employee number	Date, time, comments
Ship order	Shipment number	Picking ticket number, customer number, shipping employee number, carrier number, remittance number	Date, time, bill-of-lading number, invoice number
Receive cash	Remittance number	Customer number, employee number, cash account number	Date, time, amount received
Employees	Employee number		Name, date hired, date of birth, number of dependents, pay rate, other tax/withholding information, job title
Customers	Customer number		Name, address, credit limit, beginning balance
Carriers	Carrier number		Name, contact phone
Inventory– Call on Customers	Product number, call number		Comments
Inventory– Take Customer Order	Product number, sales order number		Quantity ordered, price per unit
Inventory Fill Order	Product number, picking ticket number		Quantity picked
Inventory–Ship Order	Product number, shipment number		Quantity shipped

all shipments have indeed been billed and recorded (a null value means that an invoice has not yet been prepared).

Also notice that Table 19-1 shows that information about prices and costs is stored in several places. The Inventory table contains information about the standard (list) price and standard cost of each item because those values are typically constant for the entire fiscal year. The Inventory–Take Customer Order table, however, contains information about not only the quantity ordered but also the actual price and accounting cost assigned to each item. This reflects the fact that companies may change prices several times during the year. Thus, although the list price is constant, the actual sales price depends on when the sale occurs. Similarly, although the standard cost for each item is constant during the year, the calculated cost of goods sold (which may be determined using either FIFO, LIFO, weighted-average, or specific identification) will vary throughout the year, especially if a perpetual inventory system is used.

Additional Expenditure Cycle Events and Attribute Placement

Most of the entities and relationships depicted in Figure 19-2 have been explained in the previous two chapters. The one new entity is the Request Inventory event. Many larger organizations want to formally approve requests to purchase goods; the Request Inventory event provides a way to collect data about such activities. Each instance of this event represents a request to

FIGURE 19-2

Extended REA Diagram for Expenditure Cycle

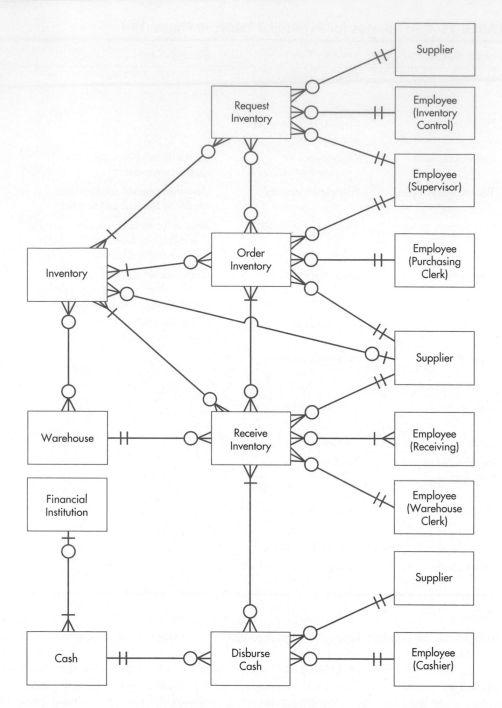

purchase one or more items. The M:N relationship between the Request Inventory and the Order Inventory events has a minimum cardinality of 0 in both directions. The 0 minimum associated with the Order Inventory event reflects the fact that requests occur before actual orders; in addition, some requests are denied and thus are never linked to an order. The 0 minimum associated with the Request Inventory event reflects the fact that some orders are generated automatically by the inventory control system, rather than as a result of a specific request. The maximum associated with the Order Inventory event is many because some requests may be for several different items, each of which may be normally obtained from different sources. Separate purchase orders are needed for each different supplier. Therefore, an approved request may be linked to several different orders. The maximum cardinality associated with the Request Inventory event is many to reflect the common practice of combining different requests for items provided by the same supplier into one larger order to obtain better terms.

Table 19-2 shows that cost information is stored in several tables. Standard cost is stored as an attribute of the Inventory table because it is the same for all units of a given inventory

TABLE 19-2 Attributes for Relational Tables in Figure 19-2

Table Name (Entity)	Primary Key	Foreign Keys	Other Attributes
Inventory	Product number		Description, unit standard cost, unit list price, weight, reorder point, beginning quantity-on-hand
Warehouse	Warehouse number		Name, address, capacity
Financial institution	Institution number		Name, contact phone
Cash	General ledger account number	Financial institution number	Name, beginning balance
Request inventory	Purchase requisition number	Supplier number, inventory control employee number, supervisor employee number	Date, reason
Order inventory	Purchase order number	Supplier number, purchasing clerk employee number, supervisor employee number	Date, comments
Receive inventory	Receiving report number	Warehouse number, supplier number, warehouse employee number	Date, time, remarks, vendor's invoice number
Disburse cash	Check number	Supplier number, employee number, cash account number	Date, amount, memo
Suppliers	Supplier number		Name, contact phone, rating, beginning balance
Employees	Employee number		Name, date hired, date of birth, number of dependents, pay rate, other tax/withholding information, job title
Inventory–Request_Inventory	Product number, purchase requisition number		Quantity requested
Inventory–Order_Inventory	Product number, purchase order number		Quantity ordered, cost per unit
Inventory–Receive_Inventory	Product number, receiving report number		Quantity received, condition
Inventory–Warehouse	Product number, warehouse number		Quantity stored
Request_Inventory–Order_Inventory	Purchase requisition number, purchase order number		
Order_Inventory–Receive_Inventory	Purchase order number, receiving report number		
Receive_Inventory–Disburse_Cash	Receiving report number, check number		Amount applied to invoice
Receive_Inventory–Employee	Receiving report number, employee number		
Inventory–Supplier	Product number, supplier number		Type (preferred, alternate)

item for a fiscal year. In contrast, the actual cost of inventory is stored in the Inventory–Order_Inventory table. This reflects the fact that purchase prices can vary over time. By storing the cost of each order with the quantity purchased, the system can calculate the actual cost of ending inventory and the cost of goods sold according to any accepted inventory valuation method (LIFO, FIFO, weighted-average, or specific identification). If, on the other hand, actual cost were stored as an attribute of the Inventory table, it would necessitate using the weighted-average method because all units of a given inventory item would be assigned the same cost. In addition, cost data would be available only in this format; it would be impossible to

FIGURE 19-3

Partial Revenue Cycle for Sale of Services

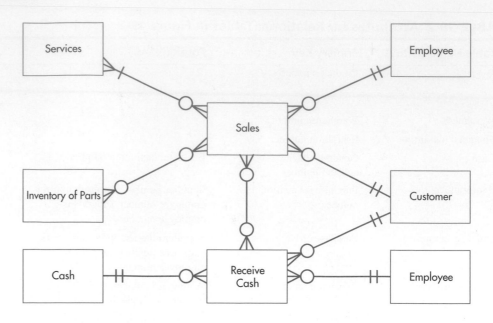

compute alternative values for inventory because the detailed data about the cost associated with each purchase would not be stored in the database.

Sale of Services

Thus far, all our modeling examples have focused on businesses that sell tangible inventory. Businesses like automotive repair shops, however, generate revenue from both the sale of products and the provision of services. Figure 19-3 presents a partial REA model of the revenue cycle for such a company.

The Services entity in Figure 19-3 contains information about the organization's revenue-generating activities. Each row identifies a specific type of service the company provides. For example, the Services table for an automotive repair shop might include individual rows for oil changes and brake replacement. Each row would include information about the standard ("book") time it should take to complete the service and the standard (regular) price charged for that type of repair.

Figure 19-3 includes relationships between the Sales event and both the Services and Inventory Resource entities. The nature of the cardinality of those relationships depends on the specific business, but usually both relationships will be modeled as being M:N because most businesses provide the same types of services to many different customers, using standard mass-produced parts. The minimum and maximum cardinalities in Figure 19-3 are typical for businesses like automotive and appliance repairs. For such businesses, every sales transaction must involve at least one specific type of service but may include several services (e.g., a customer may require an oil change and brake repairs). However, some repair services, such as fixing a flat tire, may not involve the use of any identifiable inventory parts, requiring only labor.

Acquisition of Intangible Services

In addition to purchasing inventory, equipment, and buildings, organizations also acquire various intangible services, such as Internet access, telephone service, and utilities. Figure 19-4 shows how to model such activities.

The basic give-to-get economic exchange involves acquiring various services and paying for them. Payments for those services are included in the Disburse Cash table. A separate event, Acquire Services, is used to collect data about the acquisition of those services. This event entity stores information about the actual amount of the service consumed and the actual price charged. In Figure 19-4, this event is linked to a resource labeled "General and Administrative Services" that reflects the financial accounting treatment for these items. That

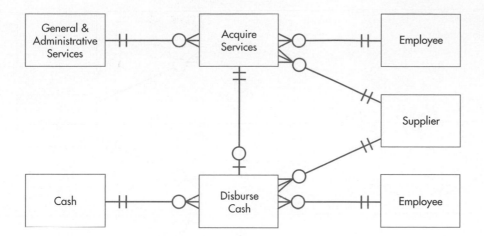

FIGURE 19-4

Partial Expenditure Cycle for Acquisition of Services

resource entity includes information about the intangible resource, such as the length of the contract, if any, its starting date, the budgeted cost for that service, the budgeted or standard amount to be provided each period, and a description of any limitations or special requirements associated with its use.

The relationship between the acquisition event and the resource entity is modeled as 1:N in Figure 19-4 because in most cases each service (telephone, electricity, etc.) is acquired separately, usually from a different supplier. The relationship between the Acquire Services and Disburse Cash events is modeled as 1:1 to reflect the common situation in which the organization obtains the use of a specific service for a particular period of time and makes a payment each month for the services it acquired and used that month.

Digital Assets

What about digital assets? Companies that sell software, music, or digital photographs over the Internet give up a digital copy of those resources, but not the actual resource itself. How does this affect the REA models of the revenue and expenditure cycles? It doesn't. Such companies still need to collect information about their purchase of and payment for those digital assets, as well as tracking orders for and delivery of those digital assets, along with receipt of payments from their customers. Those companies also need an Inventory table so that customers can see what digital products are available for sale. The structure of that Inventory table is almost identical to that of mass-produced merchandise. The only difference is that because sales involve only a digital copy of the resource, there is no need for attributes such as quantity-on-hand, quantity-available, reorder point, and standard reorder quantity. However, the Inventory table will still include information about the standard list price of each item and its description.

Rental Transactions

Some businesses generate revenue through rental transactions, rather than sales. Thus, the basic give-to-get economic exchange involves the temporary use of a resource in return for both the receipt of cash and the subsequent return of the resource being rented. Figure 19-5 shows how to model such transactions.

Businesses that rent equipment or other resources want to track each physical item separately. Therefore, the primary key for the Rental Inventory table is some kind of unique serial number, rather than a part number. Each Rent Item event records information about the rental of one specific item, such as the date and time it was rented, the rental price, and any specific terms of the agreement. If a customer rents multiple items, the system treats this as a set of rental events, each for one particular inventory item. This facilitates tracking the status of each piece of Rental Inventory. For example, a query to determine whether an item is still outstanding needs to reference only the Rental and Return events; in contrast, if the rental of five items had been recorded as one event, then the preceding query would also have to include the M:N relationship table linking the Rental event and Rental Inventory entity. (Note: This is transparent to the

FIGURE 19-5

Partial Revenue Cycle for Rental Transactions

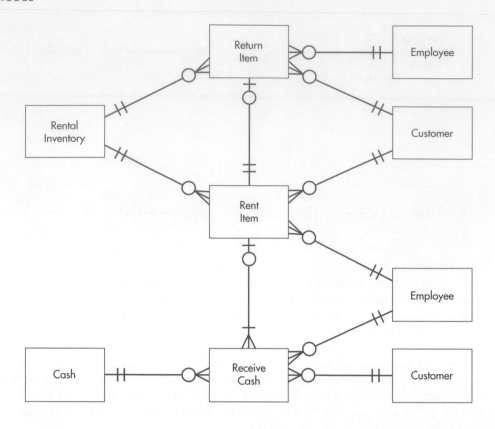

customer. The customer simply completes the required paperwork and pays the specified amount and neither knows, nor cares, that the system created several rows in the database, instead of one, to record the transaction.)

Figure 19-5 shows that the Rent Item event is linked to both the Receive Cash and Return Item events. Examine the relationship from the Rent Item to the Receive Cash event. The minimum cardinality of 1 reflects the fact that customers typically pay first, prior to taking possession of the item. The maximum cardinality is many because there may be additional charges imposed when the item is returned. The cardinality pair associated with the Rent Item event has a 0 minimum and 1 maximum because the Receive Cash event occurs first and is linked to one, and only one, specific rental event. The relationship between the Rent Item and Return Item events is 1:1 to reflect the fact that the rental of each specific item is individually tracked, as is its return; moreover, each item rented can be returned at most one time. The minimum cardinalities on each side of the relationship reflect the temporal sequence of the two events (i.e., an item is rented before it is returned).

Organizations sometimes rent, rather than purchase, resources. For example, many organizations rent office spaces and warehouses. The basic economic give-to-get exchange involves payments to the supplier for the right to use a resource for a specific period of time. Information about the Payment event is included in the Disburse Cash table. A separate Rent Resource event may be created to represent the acquisition of the resource, because that event will probably collect information about different attributes than those that are relevant to the receipt of inventory. Although it is rented and not owned, the resource itself would also be included in the model as a separate entity because organizations will likely need to maintain much of the same kind of information (e.g., location, description, etc.) about rented resources as they do for resources that are owned. Rented and owned resources may be represented in separate entities, however, because each may contain a number of attributes not relevant to the other (e.g., information about rental contract terms, acquisition cost, depreciation method, etc.). In addition, if the rented resource must be returned (e.g., rental of equipment), then another event will need to be included in the REA diagram to record that activity. In that case, the Rent Resource event would be linked to two events: Disburse Cash and the Return of the resource, forming a mirror image of the REA model of the renting organization's revenue cycle activities discussed earlier.

Additional REA Features

Figures 19-1 and 19-2 depict several new additional elements of REA data models not discussed in the prior two chapters: employee roles, M:N agent–event relationships, locations, and relationships between resources and agents.

Employee Roles

Figure 19-1 and 19-2 identified the role played by an employee (e.g., salesperson, warehouse clerk, etc.). This information enriches the REA diagram and can be used to verify whether job functions are properly segregated. However, Tables 19-1 and 19-2 still show that there is only one employee entity. Information about job roles is simply another attribute (job title) in the employee table.

M:N Agent–Event Relationships

Figure 19-2 depicts the relationship between the Receive Inventory event and employees as being M:N. This reflects the fact that many deliveries are so large that several employees must work together to unload and store the items. M:N agent–event relationships occur whenever an activity is performed by more than one employee, yet management wants to retain the ability to monitor each individual's performance.

Locations

Figure 19-2 introduces two new entities: Warehouses and Financial Institutions. These entities store information about the location where resources are stored and where certain events take place. Many companies have multiple warehouses. The cardinality pairs linking the Warehouse and Inventory entities reflect several common situations. A warehouse can, occasionally, be empty but usually stores many different inventory items. Conversely, the same inventory items may be stored in several different warehouses. Sometimes companies may also want to maintain information about inventory that they do not normally carry.

Note also that linking the Receive Inventory event to the Warehouse entity makes it possible to evaluate performance at different locations. Events, such as Receive Inventory, can only occur at a specific location; conversely, many events can occur at the same location. Therefore, Figure 19-2 depicts the relationship between Warehouses and Receive Inventory as 1:N.

Examination of Table 19-2 shows that the Financial Institution entity clarifies the nature of the Cash entity. Each row in the Cash table corresponds to a specific general ledger account that is aggregated in the balance sheet under the heading "Cash and Cash equivalents." The cardinality pairs associated with the Financial Institution and Cash entities reflect common business practices. A specific cash account can only be located at one financial institution and some accounts, such as "Petty Cash," are not on deposit anywhere. Companies also typically only keep information about financial institutions with which they have accounts but may have more than one account at the same financial institution.

Relationships Between Resources and Agents

Figure 19-2 also includes a M:N relationship between the Inventory entity (a Resource) and the Supplier entity (an Agent). This relationship reflects the common best practice of identifying preferred and alternative suppliers for specific inventory items. Similar relationships between resources and employees can be used to model responsibility and accountability.

Production Cycle REA Model

Figure 19-6 is a data model for the basic production cycle activities of a manufacturing company and Table 19-3 lists the tables required to implement that model in a relational database, along with the placement of various attributes. Accurate product cost management and performance evaluation of production cycle activities requires collecting detailed information about the use of

FIGURE 19-6

Partial REA Diagram for Production Cycle

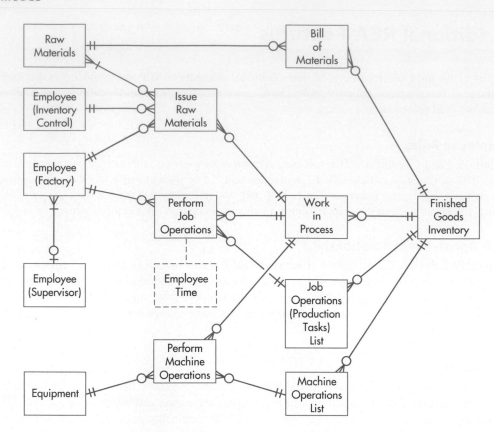

raw materials, labor, and machinery to produce finished products. Thus, there are four main events of interest included in a typical production cycle REA diagram:

1. Issuance of raw materials
2. Use of labor in production
3. Use of machinery and equipment in production
4. Production of new finished products, represented by the work-in-process event

Additional Entities—Intellectual Property

Figure 19-6 includes three special types of entities—the Bill of Materials, the Job Operations List, and the Machine Operations List—that store important portions of a manufacturing company's intellectual property. The Bill of Materials entity contains information about the raw materials used to make a finished product. As Table 19-3 shows, this includes data about the *standard* quantity of each raw material that should be used to make that product. Thus, the bill of materials can be thought of as the list of ingredients in a recipe. By itself, however, such a list is not sufficient to manufacture a product—instructions concerning how to combine those components, including the proper sequence of steps, are also needed. The Job Operations List entity stores the instructions concerning labor activities, and the Machine Operations List entity stores the instructions for actions to be performed using various pieces of equipment. Both entities also store data about the *standard* time it should take to perform those operations.

Figure 19-6 shows 1:N relationships between the Bill of Materials entity and both the Raw Materials and Finished Goods inventory entities. Each row in the Bill of Materials entity specifies how much of a specific raw material is needed to make a particular finished good; thus, each row represents the information that would be found on one line of a Bill of Materials list. This reflects the fact that the same raw material (e.g., 12-gauge wire) may be used in five different products, with a different amount used to make each product. The relationship between the Raw Materials entity and the Issue Raw Materials event is M:N because the same raw materials can be related to many different events of issuing that raw material; conversely, often all of the different materials needed to manufacture a product are issued at the same time; hence, one Issue Raw Materials event can be linked to many different lines in the Raw Materials table.

TABLE 19-3 Attributes for Relational Tables in Figure 19-6

Table Name (Entity)	Primary Key	Foreign Keys	Other Attributes
Raw materials[a]	RM item number		Description, standard unit cost, reorder point, beginning quantity on hand
Employees	Employee number		Name, date hired, date of birth, number of dependents, pay rate, other tax/withholding informatio, job title
Equipment	Equipment ID number		Description, acquisition cost, depreciation method, depreciation life, salvage value
Issue raw materials	RM issue number	Inventory control employee number, factory employee number, WIP job number	Date, time, comments
Perform job operations	Job operation number	Employee number, WIP job number, job operations list number	Date, time started, time finished
Perform machine operations	Machine operation number	Equipment ID number, WIP job number, machine operations list number	Date, time started, time finished
Bill of materials	Bill of materials number	Finished good product number, raw materials item number	Standard quantity needed
Work in process	WIP job number	Finished good product number	Date/time started, date/time completed, target completion date, quantity ordered, quantity produced, production order number
Job operations list	Job operations list number	Finished good product number	Instructions, standard time for operation
Machine operations list	Machine operations list number	Finished good product number	Instructions, standard time for operation
Finished goods inventory[a]	Product number		Description, unit standard cost, unit list price, weight, beginning quantity-on-hand
Raw materials–issue raw materials	RM item number, RM issue number		Quantity issued

[a]Some organizations may combine Finished Goods and Raw Materials into one inventory table.

The relationships between the Finished Goods Inventory resource and both the Job Operations List and Machine Operations List entities are 1:N. This reflects the fact that each row in the list entities represents information about a specific activity required to make a specific product. For example, there would be separate rows for polishing brass for each product that included brass parts; each row would store information about the standard time it should take to polish the brass when making a particular product. Often, multiple steps are required to make a single product. Thus, one finished good would be linked to many different rows in the Job Operations List and Machine Operations List entity tables.

Figure 19-6 also includes an entity labeled "Employee Time". As explained in Chapter 18, this entity is seldom instantiated as a table in a relational database. Hence, it is represented with dashed lines in Figure 19-6.

Production Cycle Events

Data about *actual* raw materials used in production is stored in the Issue Raw Materials entity. Similarly, information about the *actual* labor and machine operations performed, including the actual amount of time each activity took, is stored in the Perform Job Operations and Perform Machine Operations entities, respectively. Performance can be evaluated by comparing the data in these three event entities with the information about standards that is stored in the corresponding information entities (Bill of Materials, Job Operations List, and Machine Operations List).

The Perform Job Operations event entity is an example of a Give Resource event: It records the use of employee time. Each row in that table records information about how much time an employee spent working on a particular job. Thus, there can be many rows in this table for each employee every day. For example, on July 7, employee 727 may spend three hours on WIP job 2234, two hours on WIP job 2235, and three hours on WIP job 2236. Collecting this kind of detailed information about how factory employees use their time enables manufacturing companies to accurately assign labor costs to different production batches and product lines.

The Perform Machine Operations event is similar to the Perform Job Operations event, except that it records information about the use of a specific piece of machinery or equipment. This information is useful not only to assign costs to products but also for scheduling maintenance. Note that the Perform Machine Operations event is *not* used to record depreciation. Depreciation expenses seldom correspond to actual use of the equipment. Depreciation is not modeled as an event in the REA diagram because it is an accounting concept that arbitrarily allocates the cost of an acquired resource to different fiscal periods. Periodic depreciation is simply a calculation based on a formula (depreciation method) and a set of assumptions (estimated useful life, salvage value, etc.). Information about the formula and assumptions is stored in the resource entity for use in calculating periodic depreciation charges, but the calculation process itself is not an event, just as the processes of calculating the total amount of a particular sales transaction or the amount of an employee's paycheck are not modeled as events.

Figure 19-6 models the relationships between the Perform Job Operations event and the Job Operations List entity, and between the Perform Machine Operations event and the Machine Operations List entity, as being 1:N. The list entities store information about the standard time it should take to perform each individually identifiable activity; the operations events record the actual time used to perform that activity. Thus, each actual event can be linked to only one entry in the standards table, but each entry in the standards table is likely to be linked to many actual performances of that activity.

The Work-in-Process entity is used to collect and summarize data about the raw materials, labor, and machine operations used to produce a batch of goods. The relationships between Work-in-Process and those three event entities are all 1:N, reflecting the fact that each production run may involve a number of raw materials issuances, labor operations, and machine operations. Each of those activities, however, is linked to a specific production run. These links reflect an internal give-to-get exchange that is the essence of the production cycle: Raw materials, labor, and equipment are all used in order to produce finished goods inventory. Thus, three Give Resource events are related to one Get Resource event.

New REA Feature

Notice that Figure 19-6 differs from previous REA diagrams in that it shows only one agent associated with the Perform Job Operations (and Perform Machine Operations) events. These internal events differ from the other events discussed throughout this book in that they do not involve an exchange or transfer of resources. Instead, they represent the consumption or use of individual resources, such as a specific employee's time or the use of a specific piece of equipment. Therefore, the event is linked to that agent (employee or piece of machinery) for which management wants to collect information for product costing and performance evaluation purposes.

Figure 19-6 also depicts a 1:N relationship between employees and supervisors. This reflects the typical situation where each employee is assigned to a specific supervisor, but each supervisor is responsible for many employees. In contrast, a matrix style of organization, where each employee reports to several supervisors, would be modeled as an M:N relationship between factory employees and supervisors. Relationships between internal agents may be created to model lines of responsibility. Relationships between internal and external agents can also occur. For example, some organizations that primarily provide services, such as banks and insurance companies, may assign customers to specific employees who are responsible for effectively managing the overall quality of the ongoing association with each customer. Relationships between external agents are rare but may sometimes be implemented to satisfy the requirements for a well-structured database. For example, if an insurance company needed to collect and maintain detailed information about each of a customer's dependents, it could do so by creating a separate entity called "Dependents" and establishing a 1:N relationship between that entity and the Customer entity.

Combined HR/Payroll Data Model

Figure 19-7 integrates payroll and HR activities. The Time Worked event is necessary to calculate payroll. The Time Used event is used for cost accounting, to properly assign labor costs (in manufacturing companies, this event entity is often called "Job Operations"). All of the other events represent important HR activities.

HR Cycle Entities

Notice that in Figure 19-7 the Employee entity is linked to almost every other entity in the diagram, reflecting the importance of employees to the organization. The Employee entity stores much of the data typically found in the employee (payroll) master file: name, date hired, date of birth, pay rate, job title, supervisor, number of dependents, withholding allowances, and information about any voluntary deductions, such as 401(k) plans.

The Skills entity contains data about the different job skills of interest to the organization. There would be a row in this table for each major job skill. For example, a software developer may list different programming languages and application programs in this table. The relationship between Skills and Employees is modeled as being M:N because one employee may possess a number of job skills (i.e., one programmer may be proficient in several different languages) and, conversely, several employees may possess the same skill.

The Training event entity represents the various workshops, training programs, and other opportunities provided for employees to develop and maintain their skills. Thus, this entity stores data that can be used to evaluate the effectiveness and cost of training and development efforts. The relationship between the Employees and Training entities is M:N, because a given employee will, over time, attend numerous training courses and, conversely, several employees may attend the same specific training class. The relationship between the Skills and Training entities is 1:N, because each course is designed to develop a specific skill, but each skill may be taught many different times.

The Recruiting event entity stores data about activities performed to notify the public of job openings. The data recorded in this entity are useful for documenting compliance with employment laws and also for evaluating the effectiveness of various methods used to announce job opportunities.

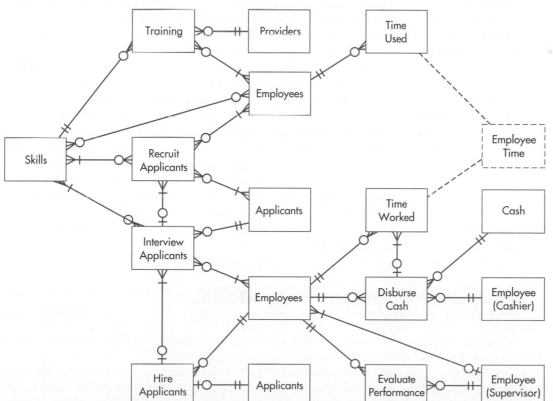

FIGURE 19-7

Integrated REA Diagram for HRM/Payroll Cycles

The M:N relationship between Skills and Recruiting reflects the fact that each advertisement may seek several specific skills and that, over time, there may be several advertisements for a given skill. The relationship between the Recruiting event and Job Applicants is modeled as being M:N because many people typically apply for each job opening, but a given individual may also respond to more than one recruiting event. Also, more than one employee may participate in each recruiting event, and, over time, a given employee may participate in many such events.

The Interview event stores detailed data about each job interview. It is linked to the Hire Employees event in a 1:N relationship. This reflects the fact that the Hiring event occurs only once but may result from either one or a number of preceding interviews.

Tracking Employees' Time

The section on the Production Cycle discussed the use of a Perform Job Operations event to track how factory workers spent their time so that labor costs can be allocated to products. Professional services firms, such as law firms, consulting organizations, and accounting firms, similarly need to track how their members use their time in order to accurately bill each client. Figure 19-7 uses the Time Used event for this purpose. The structure of this table is similar to that of the Perform Job Operations table described earlier (we use a different name here because "perform job operations" has a manufacturing connotation). Thus, each row in this table includes the following attributes: the employee, the job (client) to which that employee's time should be charged, a description of the task performed (e.g., prepare will, telephone consultation, court appearance, etc.), and the time when that task was started and ended. Information about the nature of the task needs to be collected in order to evaluate performance and because sometimes the rate billed for a particular employee may vary depending on the task being performed.

It is instructive to compare the information provided by the Time Used event to that provided by linking specific business events to the employee agent who performed that task. Regular event–agent relationships, such as that between sales and employees, collect data that can be used to answer such questions as "How much did salesperson X sell this week?" or "How many sales did each salesperson make?" In contrast, the Time Used event provides the information needed to answer such questions as "How much time did a particular salesperson spend calling on customers, as opposed to providing customer service support via the telephone?" Each instance of a regular event entity (e.g., each row in the Call on Customer, Sales, or Provide Customer Support tables) captures data about discrete activities, such as a particular sales transaction. In contrast, each row in the Time Used event captures data about what an employee did during a block of time. Hence, each row in the Time Used table can, and often is, linked to many rows in a Business Event table. For example, employee 007 may spend five hours making sales calls to customers, during which time she visited five customers. That would be represented as one row in the Track Time Used table, but five separate rows in the call on customer table. Thus, there is a 1:N relationship between the two types of events. It is not necessary to link the Time Used entity to specific business events, however, but doing so facilitates evaluating performance at a very detailed level (i.e., to answer questions such as during which block of time on which days of the week is a particular salesperson most effective).

Not every organization collects detailed data about their employees' use of time, in which case there is no need for a Time Used entity. Moreover, even when such an event is included, the resource that is used (Employee Time) is seldom implemented as a table in the database because there are no meaningful attributes to describe it. Hence, the resource entity "Employee Time" is depicted with dashed lines in Figure 19-7.

Financing Activities Data Model

Most organizations issue stock and debt to finance their operations. Figure 19-8 is an REA diagram of these two financing activities.

The event Issue Debt is a special kind of cash receipt; hence, it is connected to the Cash resource entity. It is often modeled as a separate event entity distinct from "Receive Cash" because it contains different attributes from those associated with cash receipts that arise from

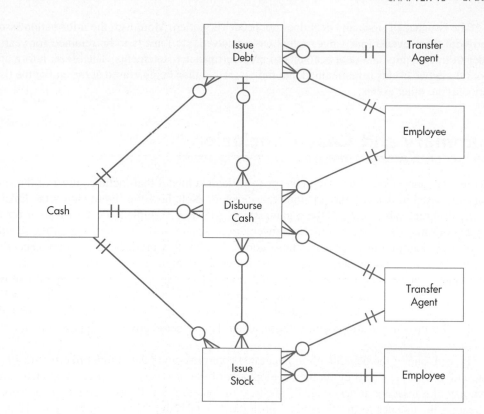

FIGURE 19-8
**Partial Financing
Activities Diagram**

the Sales event, such as the face amount of debt issued, total amount received, date issued, maturity date, and interest rate. Usually, most companies do not deal directly with individual creditors. Instead, they sell their debt instruments through a financial intermediary, which is depicted in Figure 19-8 as the Transfer Agent. The transfer agent maintains the necessary information about individual creditors, to properly direct both the periodic interest payments and eventual repayment of principal. Therefore, each occurrence of an Issue Debt event contains data about the *aggregate* amount received from issuing a set of debt instruments. For example, the issuance of $10,000,000 of 5% bonds, which were ultimately purchased by several thousand different individuals for a total of $9,954,000, constitutes one Issue Debt event.

Debt-related payments (whether periodic interest payments or repayment of principal at maturity) are cash disbursements. Usually, the organization writes one check for the total amount of interest owed for a particular bond or note and sends that to the transfer agent, who then handles the distribution of individual checks to each creditor. Thus, to continue our example, the company would send $125,000 to the transfer agent to make the first quarterly payment on that $10,000,000 of bonds. The transfer of funds would be recorded as *one* row in the Disburse Cash table. Note that if a company has issued different series of bonds at different points in time, it would normally make separate transfers of funds to the transfer agent for payments linked to each debt issue. Thus, Figure 19-8 shows each Disburse Cash event linked to a maximum of 1 Issue Debt events. The minimum cardinality is 0 because a particular Disburse Cash event may be linked to either an Issue Debt event or an Issue Stock event.

Equity transactions are modeled in a manner similar to debt transactions. The Issue Stock event is a special kind of cash receipt associated with the issuance of stock, and the dividend payments are another type of cash disbursement. As with debt, most companies do not deal directly with individual stockholders. Thus, Figure 19-8 shows that both types of equity transactions involve participation by an employee (the treasurer) and the external transfer agent. The relationship between the Disburse Cash and Issue Stock events is modeled as being M:N because each stock issuance may be linked to many dividend payments and, conversely, a particular dividend payment may be related to multiple different issuances of stock (i.e., *all* shareholders, regardless of which issue they bought, will receive a portion of each dividend). The minimum cardinalities are 0 in both directions because there is a temporal sequence between the two events and because a given Disburse Cash event might be linked to an Issue Debt event instead of to an Issue Stock event.

The issuance of stock and debt does not occur very often. Moreover, the information associated with these events (par value, actual cash received, etc.) needs to be retained for years in order to track equity and debt accounts to prepare financial statements. Therefore, information about these two events is maintained indefinitely, rather than being erased at the end of the fiscal period as are other events.

Summary and Case Conclusion

Figure 19-9 presents an integrated enterprise-wide data model that includes most of the situations discussed in this and the previous two chapters. Note how the figure shows the linkages among different subsystems of the organization's AIS. For example, a customer order for finished goods may, if there is insufficient inventory on hand to fill the order, trigger the scheduling of a production run to produce those goods. In turn, this production run may necessitate ordering additional raw materials. Enterprise Resource Planning (ERP) systems are designed to automatically trigger these types of related actions across subsystems by linking each subsystem to a common enterprise-wide database. Thus, even though the databases used in many ERP systems may not be explicitly based on the REA data model, a model like that depicted in Figure 19-9 provides useful documentation about the business activities supported by the ERP system.

Indeed, one of the benefits of an integrated enterprise-wide data model like Figure 19-9 is that auditors can use it to guide the development of queries to validate the completeness and accuracy of transaction processing. To illustrate the possibilities, let us examine the process for validating the updates to the sales account in the general ledger. Referring to Figure 19-9, the first step would be writing queries against the data model for the revenue cycle. One such query would sum the amount of all sales during the time period of interest. Other queries would link the Sales and Take Customer Order tables to verify the completeness and validity of all recorded sales. Additional queries could be written to trace sales to specific customers and sales staff. In fact, the number of such cross-table links that can be easily generated is limited only by the auditor's imagination. In addition, the system can be configured to create extensive log files that make it possible to identify who authorized a transaction. Thus, integrated data models make it possible to write a set of queries that creates a rich, complex audit trail of an organization's business activities.

An integrated enterprise-wide data model like that depicted in Figure 19-9 can also significantly improve the support provided for managerial decision making. Managers can write queries to assess operational efficiency. For example, queries that link the "Use Employee Time" event to various other events can provide information about the relative productivity of various employees. Moreover, the REA model's inherent flexibility makes it easy to collect new information items to evaluate performance, often simply by adding new attributes to existing tables. As Focus 19-1 explains, this flexibility not only facilitates managerial decisions, but can also provide tax benefits.

Creating an integrated, enterprise-wide data model also facilitates the amalgamation of financial and nonfinancial information in the same database, which can improve internal reporting. Traditionally, internal reports have focused primarily on financial performance measures. Effective management of an organization, however, requires measuring performance on multiple dimensions because no single measure is sufficient. Instead, top management must have reports that provide a multidimensional perspective on performance. An integrated, enterprise-wide data model like that depicted in Figure 19-9 facilitates the development of multidimensional performance reports, such as the balanced scorecard discussed in Chapter 16.

Paul Stone reflects on what he has learned at the REA workshop. He realizes that although a number of different types of businesses and transactions were covered, he is likely to encounter clients with yet other situations. Nevertheless, he feels confident that he now understands a wide enough variety of situations that he can use that knowledge to develop solutions to enable him to model almost any type of business activity he is likely to encounter. After all, as a CPA, Paul's entire career has involved continuous learning and refinement of his skills.

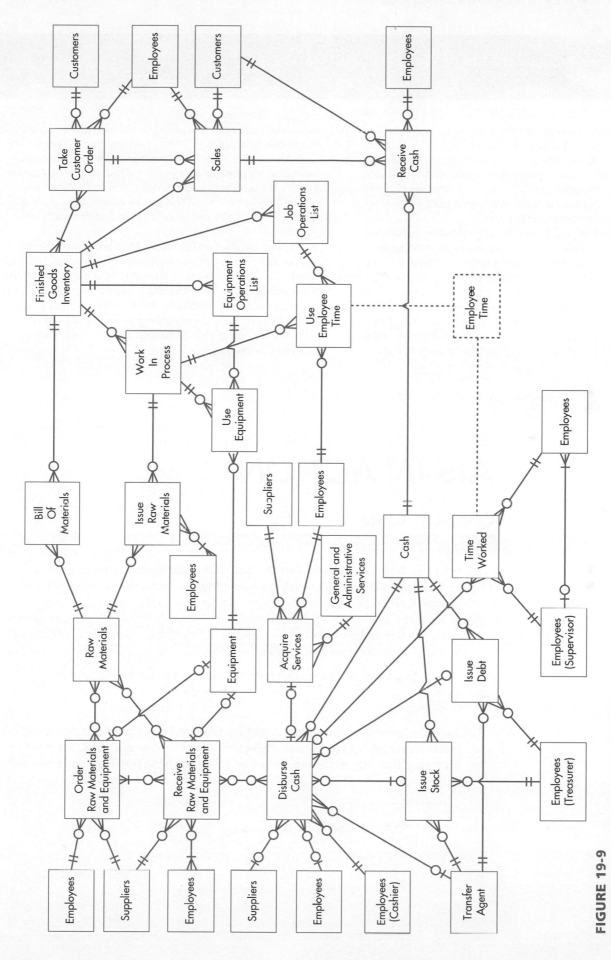

FIGURE 19-9
Integrated, Enterprise-wide REA Diagram

FOCUS 19-1   Tax Benefits of Well-Designed Databases

A well-designed database efficiently and effectively supports an organization's transaction processing requirements while also providing management with easy access to the information it needs to plan, control, and evaluate performance. A properly designed database can also yield tax benefits. This can be illustrated easily when considering business travel and entertainment expenses.

The IRS generally allows organizations to deduct 50% of the meals and entertainment expenses incurred when dealing with customers or prospective customers. Many organizations simply accumulate all meal and entertainment expenses in one general ledger account. This makes it easy to calculate the tax deduction at the end of the year: Just multiply the total amount in the meals and entertainment account by 50%. Although this approach is simple, efficient, and logical, it can cause an organization to miss out on

additional tax deductions. The IRS has established several exceptions in which meals and entertainment expenses are 100% deductible. To take advantage of these exceptions, organizations need to design their databases to be able to identify tax-relevant characteristics of specific meals and entertainment expenses. This can be as simple as adding another attribute to the table used to record those expenses.

Is it worth the effort? Consider the following examples: (a) Four tickets to an NBA game, plus refreshments, can cost over $400; (b) four tickets to a concert by a major symphony with dessert and coffee afterwards can cost over $300. When you multiply such examples by the number of times your sales staff entertains clients during the course of a year, the potential tax benefits of deducting an additional 50% of such costs can be huge.

AIS IN ACTION

Chapter Quiz

1. Which of the following represents the "get" side of the basic give-to-get economic exchange for a business that rents equipment and machinery for use by others?
   a. Rent Equipment
   b. Receive Cash
   c. Return Rented Equipment
   d. Return Rented Equipment and Receive Cash

2. Which resource in the HR/payroll cycle is seldom implemented in a database?
   a. skills   c. applicants
   b. employee time   d. cash disbursements

3. Joe's Computers makes service calls to repair computer equipment. Some calls involve only labor charges, and others involve both labor and parts. Which of the following correctly models the relationship between the Service Calls event and Parts Inventory?

   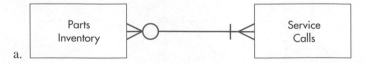

   a.

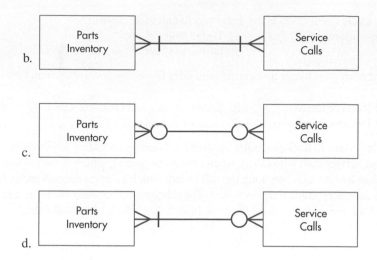

b.

c.

d.

4. Which entity contains information about the components used to manufacture a particular product?
    a. Inventory
    b. Job Operations List
    c. Bill of Materials
    d. Machine Operations List

5. Which of the following production cycle events involves the *acquisition* of a resource (i.e., is a Get event)?
    a. Perform Machine Operations
    b. Perform Job Operations
    c. Work in Process
    d. Issue Raw Materials

6. Acme Manufacturing tracks information about customer calls by sales representative. Although many calls involve demonstrations of products, some are purely to build relationships. What is the correct way to model the relationship between Inventory and the Call on Customers event?

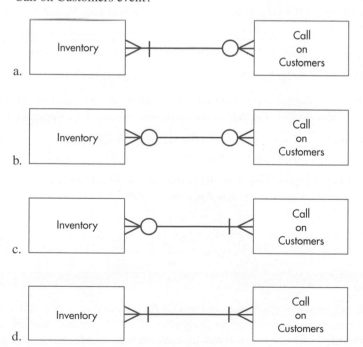

a.

b.

c.

d.

7. Which production cycle event collects the data used to calculate payroll?
   a. Perform Job Operations
   b. Time Worked
   c. Time Used
   d. Disburse Cash

8. The give-to-get economic exchange associated with debt financing involves which two events?
   a. Issue Debt and Receive Cash
   b. Issue Debt and Disburse Cash
   c. Receive Cash and Disburse Cash
   d. none of the above

9. Acme manufacturing wants to track post-sales customer service by collecting information about each customer service call: who called, when the call happened, which customer service representative handled the call, how long the call lasted, which sales transaction prompted the call, and which inventory items were discussed. The relationship between the Sales and Post-sales Service Call events should most likely be modeled as which of the following?
   a. 1:1
   b. 1:N
   c. M:N
   d. 0:N

10. Which of the following additions to the basic REA template are sometimes needed?
    a. relationships between two resources
    b. relationships between two agents
    c. relationships between a resource and an agent
    d. all of the above

Discussion Questions

19.1. Often it takes several sales calls to obtain the first order from a new customer. Why then does Figure 19-1 depict the relationship between the Call on Customer and Take Customer Orders events as being 1:1?

19.2. How could an automobile dealer model the use of loaner cars, which it gives to customers for free whenever they drop off a vehicle for maintenance that will take longer than one day to complete?

19.3. In what situations would you expect to model a relationship between an agent and a resource?

19.4. Why is depreciation not represented as an event in the REA data model?

19.5. How would you model the acquisition of a digital asset, such as the purchase of software online (the software is downloaded and then installed on the purchaser's computer)?

19.6. How are the similarities and differences between the purchase of services, such as telephone service, and the purchase of raw materials reflected in an REA data model?

19.7. How would you modify the expenditure cycle REA diagram depicted in Figure 19-4 to include the return of defective products to suppliers for credit?

Problems

19.1. We-Fix-Computers, Inc., provides spare parts and service for a wide variety of computers. Customers may purchase parts to take home for do-it-yourself repairs, or they may bring their systems in for repair, in which case they pay for both the parts and the labor associated with the type of service required. Some services do not include any new parts, just a labor charge for that service. Individual customers must pay for all parts purchases in full at the time of sale. Individual customers must pay 50% down when they bring their computers in for servicing and pay the balance at pickup. Corporate customers, however, are billed monthly for all sales (parts or service). Although We-Fix-Computers, Inc., has several different banking accounts, all sales are deposited intact into its main checking account.

We-Fix-Computers, Inc. purchases its inventory of parts from more than a dozen different vendors. Orders are usually delivered the next day; sometimes, however, suppliers ship only partial orders. We-Fix-Computers pays for some of its purchases COD, but usually pays by the 10th of the month for all purchases made the prior month. None of its suppliers allows it to make installment payments.

Required

Draw an integrated REA diagram for We-Fix-Computers' revenue and expenditure cycles.

19.2. The Mesa Veterinary Hospital is run by Dr. Brigitte Roosevelt. She has two employees in the office and has asked you to develop a database to help better track her data. Dr. Roosevelt currently uses her personal computer only for word processing, but she is interested in also using it to maintain pet histories and accounting information. She is excited about the transition and is counting on you to help her through the process. She describes her daily activities as follows:

> When new customers come to Mesa Veterinary Hospital, the "owners" of the pets are required to complete an introductory form. This form includes the following:
>
> • Owner name
> • Address
> • Day phone
> • Night phone
>
> They are also required to provide the following information about each pet, as some people own many pets:
>
> • Pet name
> • Breed
> • Color
> • Birth date
>
> Dr. Roosevelt would like to enter this information once, and then have the system retrieve it for all subsequent visits.
>
> When customers call to make appointments, one of the office clerks asks what kind of services they require (e.g., is it a routine exam, a surgery, etc.). Dr. Roosevelt sees only one pet during each appointment. If she is going to see one owner's two pets, then two separate appointments are necessary (but scheduled back-to-back). For each appointment, Dr. Roosevelt records the pet's weight, notes the reason for the appointment, and records her diagnosis. Depending on the diagnosis, the doctor will possibly prescribe any number of medications to cure the pet. Owners are charged $25 for each appointment and must pay additionally for any medications prescribed for their pets. Dr. Roosevelt requires all pets to be brought back for another examination prior to refilling any prescriptions. Customers must pay for services and medication in full at the conclusion of their visits.

You also learn that Dr. Roosevelt orders drugs and medications from several different suppliers. She places orders weekly, on Fridays. Suppliers usually make one shipment to fill each order, but sometimes have to make additional shipments if they are currently out of stock of one or more items. In such cases, they always ship the back-ordered item as soon as they receive it from the manufacturer; they never combine such back orders with subsequent orders by Dr. Roosevelt. Suppliers bill Dr. Roosevelt monthly and expect payment in full by the 15th of the following month. A few suppliers do permit Dr. Roosevelt to make installment payments. The prices charged by suppliers for a given product may change several times during the year, so it is important to accurately store the cost of each item each time it is purchased.

Dr. Roosevelt concludes the interview by requesting that in addition to the facts mentioned, she wants the system to store the following attributes:

- Number of pets owned by each customer
- Total charge for the appointment
- Prescription price
- Drug name

- Length of appointment
- Diagnosis
- Date of appointment
- Service requested

Required

a. Given this brief overview, draw an integrated REA diagram for the Mesa Veterinary Hospital and include cardinalities.

b. As directed by your instructor, either draw the tables necessary to implement the integrated REA diagram you developed for the Mesa Veterinary Hospital or build the tables in a relational DBMS to which you have access. Be sure to include all attributes from the narrative plus the additional ones explicitly listed by Dr. Roosevelt at the conclusion of the interview. Create additional attributes only if necessary.

(This problem is adapted from one created by Dr. Julie Smith David for classroom use at Arizona State University.)

19.3. Your university hires you to implement a database system for the library network. You have interviewed several librarians, and the following summarizes these discussions:

- The library's main goal is to provide students and professors with access to books and other publications. The library, therefore, maintains an extensive collection of materials that are available to anyone with a valid university identification card.

- The standard procedure for lending materials is that the student or faculty member comes to one of the three campus libraries and locates the book or journal on the shelves.

- Each book is assigned three unique numbers. First, the book is assigned a number by the publisher, called the International Standard Book Number (ISBN). This number allows the publishers to track each title and the number changes with each new edition. The second number is the Dewey decimal number, which is assigned to the title and written on the outside spine of the book. This number is used to organize the library shelves and is thus helpful to the students and faculty. It is therefore critical that this number be available to users on the online inquiry screens. The last number is a university book ID number. A different number is assigned to every book that is received so the library can track all copies of each book. This number is different from the other two numbers such that if the library has three copies of one book, each will have a unique university book ID number.

- When students or faculty check out books, the system must be able to track the specific copy that is being borrowed. Each book has a magnetic strip inserted in its spine, which is used as a security measure. If someone tries to take a book without checking it out, an alarm sounds.

- In general, students and faculty have equal clout in the library. Both are able to check out most books and to check out several books at one time. No one is allowed to remove periodicals from any library. The length of time that the book may be borrowed varies, however, depending on who checks it out. Students are allowed to check out a book for several weeks; faculty may borrow books for several months.

- When patrons check out books, they take their materials to the circulation desk. At that time, the librarian scans in each item's university book ID number and the borrower's ID number. The system records a separate loan event for each book being checked out, assigning each a separate loan number. At this time, each book's due date is calculated and marked on a slip located inside each book's front cover. Simultaneously, the magnetic strip is deactivated so the book may be removed from the library.

- After borrowers check out a book, they are expected to return it by its due date. In reality, everyone is allowed 30 days after the due date recorded on the checkout slip before the book is officially overdue. At that point, the book must be returned, and the borrower is assessed a $10 fine. If the book is permanently lost, then the borrower is fined $75 for the book's replacement. All fines must be paid in cash, in full. Students are not allowed to enroll for subsequent semesters until all library fines are paid; they also do not receive a diploma until all library fines are paid. Faculty must pay all outstanding fines by June 30 of each year.

- When a book is returned, the return must be entered into the system, and a unique return number is used to log the transaction. At that time, the loan record is updated to show that the book has been returned.

The following attributes have been identified as critical for the new system:

University book ID	Borrower phone number	Type of borrower (faculty or student)
Book publisher	Cash account number	
Due date	Librarian name	Librarian college degree
Loan number	Book status (on the shelf or checked out)	Actual return date
Checkout date		Borrower ID
Borrower name	Borrower's fine balance owed	Library borrowed from
Book title		Librarian number
Fine receipt number	ISBN number	Account balance
Amount received	Book return number	Total number of books in a specific library
Library name	Dewey decimal number	
Amount of fine	Borrower address	Loan status (still outstanding, or returned)
Default library where book is shelved	Book copyright date	
	Borrower e-mail address	Author name

Required

a. Draw an REA diagram for the library system. Remember to include cardinalities.
b. As directed by your instructor, either create the tables on paper that would be required to implement your REA diagram or actually build those tables in a relational DBMS to which you have access. Only use the attributes listed, unless others are absolutely necessary.

(This problem is adapted from one developed by Dr. Julie Smith David for classroom use at Arizona State University.)

19.4. The XYZ Company sells tools and parts to automotive repair shops. Shops call in orders; all orders received by noon are delivered the same day. Between 12:00 and 1:00, the system prints out schedules. From 1:00 to 5:00, drivers make deliveries according to the printed schedules. Typically, each driver makes between 25 and 30 deliveries each day. Each delivery is signed for by a repair shop manager; the portable laptop then uses wireless communications to transmit information about the delivery back to the XYZ company and the information is recorded as another row in the sales event table. The XYZ Company uses its own trucks to make local deliveries to its customers. It wants to track information about the use of those trucks: which employee drove which truck, to which customers did a particular truck make deliveries, which deliveries are made on which days, what was the starting and stopping mileage each day?

Required

a. Draw a partial REA diagram of the XYZ Company's revenue cycle to model these events: Taking Customer Orders, Deliveries, and the Use of Vehicles. Be sure to include cardinalities.
b. Create a set of tables (either on paper or in a relational DBMS to which you have access) to implement the REA model you developed for the XYZ Company.

19.5. Assume that Stained Glass Artistry, a new shop that specializes in making stained glass artwork, has hired you to design an integrated database that will provide the owners with the accounting information they need to effectively manage the business. Stained Glass Artistry makes a wide variety of stained glass windows for sale in its store.

A unique job order is assigned to each production run, which includes creating multiple copies of the same basic design. When raw materials are issued to employees, the issuance is documented on a prenumbered raw material issue form. The different kinds of glass needed for the product, and other materials such as copper foil or lead, are issued at one time, so that employees can efficiently produce the design.

Creating a piece of stained glass art involves several different steps, including cutting, foiling, and soldering. The owners want to track how much time each employee spends each day performing each of those various tasks.

The owners have developed raw material and direct labor standards for each design they offer. They want their AIS to track actual costs and standard costs so that they can generate reports that provide price and quantity variance information.

The owners also have provided you with the following list of facts that they want stored in the database. (*Note:* You must create appropriate primary keys for each table; this is the list of other attributes.)

Attributes in Standard Glass Artistry AIS

Date hired	Time started task	Time completed task
Style of glass	Quantity on hand	Color of glass
(name or description)	Quantitity to be produced	Actual cost of design
Design name	Standard quantity of glass	Quantity issued
Standard hours to	to use in design	Standard cost of design
make design	Date design produced	Date of birth
Wage rate	Employee name	Standard cost of glass

Required

a. Draw an integrated REA diagram for Stained Glass Artistry. Include both minimum and maximum cardinalities.
b. Create the set of relational tables required to implement your REA diagram for Stained Glass Artistry in a relational database.

19.6. Bernie's Pet Store sells pet food, toys, and supplies. Bernie, the owner, is the only person who places orders with suppliers. He is also the only person who writes checks. Suppliers ship each order individually; if they are out of an item, they back order it and ship it separately as soon as it arrives. Bernie pays each supplier monthly for all purchases made the previous month. Suppliers do not allow him to make installment payments.

Bernie has eight employees, each of whom can check in materials received from suppliers and sell merchandise to customers. Bernie pays his employees weekly from a separate checking account used only for payroll purposes.

All sales are made in-store and are paid for immediately by cash, check, or credit card.

When employees are not working the cash register or checking in merchandise, they restock shelves and clean up the premises. Bernie does not want to track each *individual* restock or clean-up event, but does want to know how much time each employee spends each day doing those tasks. He also wants to track how much time each employee spends each day receiving inventory and how much time they spend working at the cash register. He wants to be able to write queries that would show time spent by job task (restocking, cleaning, receiving, or sales) for each employee. It is not practical, however, to try to measure the time spent on individual tasks (e.g., Bernie does not want employees to track the time they start and finished unloading a shipment from supplier X, then repeat for supplier Y; similarly, he does not want to track how long it takes to ring up each individual customer at the cash register). All he wants is to know how much time each day (e.g., 3.75 hours) each employee spent performing each different type of job.

Required

Draw an integrated REA diagram for Bernie's Pet Shop. Be sure to include both payroll processing and the ability to track how employees use their time.

19.7. At Big Time University (BTU) students are allowed to purchase two basketball tickets for each home game. Each ticket contains the date of the game, and the seat information, such as section, row, and individual seat number. Students pay for each game individually; that is, student sporting event passes are not used at BTU. BTU deposits the proceeds from each game into its bank.

Required

a. Prepare an REA diagram with cardinalities for the revenue cycle for BTU's basketball games. State any assumptions you may have to make concerning BTU's business policies and practices.

b. Implement your model in a set of relational tables. Be sure to specify primary keys, foreign keys, and identify at least one other attribute that should be included in each table.

19.8. Small contractors often rent special equipment for specific jobs. They need to track the equipment that is rented, when it is returned, and payments made to the rental company.

Required

a. Draw a partial REA diagram for the acquisition, payment, and return of rental equipment. Be sure to include cardinalities and state any assumptions you made when specifying those cardinalities.

b. Create a set of tables (either on paper or in a relational DBMS to which you have access) to implement the REA model you developed.

Case19-1 Practical Database Assignment

This case involves creating a database from an integrated REA diagram and then using the REA diagram to guide the writing of queries to prepare financial statements.

Required

a. Create the tables necessary to implement Figure 19-9 in a relational database. Be sure to include primary keys and other relevant attributes in each table.

b. Write the query, or set of queries, necessary to generate as many elements of financial statements as possible. For example, write the query or set of queries that would be used to calculate the amount of cash on hand, the total of accounts receivable, the total value of raw materials inventory on hand, etc.

AIS IN ACTION SOLUTIONS

Quiz Key

1. Which of the following represents the "get" side of the basic give-to-get economic exchange for a business that rents equipment and machinery?
   a. Rent Equipment (Incorrect. The Give event (Rent Equipment) is linked to two Get events: Return Rented Equipment and Receive Cash.)
   b. Receive Cash (Incorrect. The Give event (Rent Equipment) is linked to two Get events: Return Rented Equipment and Receive Cash.)

 c. Receive Cash (Incorrect. The Give event (Rent Equipment) is linked to two Get events: Return Rented Equipment and Receive Cash.)

▶ d. Return Rented Equipment and Receive Cash (Correct. The Give event (Rent Equipment) is linked to two Get events: Return Rented Equipment and Receive Cash.)

2. Which resource in the HR/payroll cycle is seldom implemented in a database?
 a. skills (Incorrect. Information about skills is important to record.)
 ▶ b. employee time (Correct. The employee time represents the right to use an employee's time—but time is a noninventoriable asset and is consumed when it is acquired, so this resource is seldom if ever implemented as a table in a database.)
 c. applicants (Incorrect. Applicants are agents and information about them must be recorded.)
 d. cash disbursements (Incorrect. Cash disbursements is an event about which information must be recorded.)

3. Joe's Computers makes service calls to repair computer equipment. Some calls involve only labor charges, and others involve both labor and parts. Which of the following correctly models the relationship between the Service Calls event and Parts Inventory?

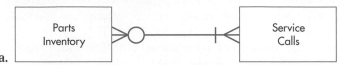

 a. (Incorrect. This shows that every part must be linked to use on at least one service call.)

 b. (Incorrect. This shows that every part must be linked to at least one service call and that every service call must involve use of at least one part.)

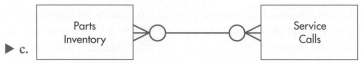

 ▶ c. (Correct. This shows that some parts may not be linked to any service call, but others could be linked to many service calls. It also shows that some service calls do not involve the use of any parts, although other service calls may involve the use of multiple parts.)

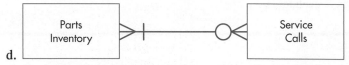

 d. (Incorrect. This shows that every service call must involve the use of at least one part.)

4. Which entity contains information about the components used to manufacture a particular product?
 a. Inventory (Incorrect. The Bill of Materials entity stores the list of ingredients (components) used to manufacture a given product.)
 b. Job Operations List (Incorrect. The Job Operations list entity identifies the steps required to manufacture the product, but the list of components used is stored in the Bill of Materials entity.)
 ▶ c. Bill of Materials (Correct. The Bill of Materials entity stores the list of components used to manufacture a given product.)
 d. Machine Operations List (Incorrect. The Machine Operations List entity stores the steps and processes involving machinery used to manufacture a product.)

5. Which of the following production cycle events involves the *acquisition* of a resource (i.e., is a Get event)?
 a. Perform Machine Operations (Incorrect. The Perform Machine Operations event records information about the use of machinery and equipment; i.e., it is a Give event.)

    b. Perform Job Operations (Incorrect. The Perform Job Operations event records information about the use of labor to manufacture a product; i.e., it is a Give event.)

▶ **c.** Work in Process (Correct. The Work in Process event collects and aggregates all the costs associated with creating a finished product.)

    d. Issue Raw Materials (Incorrect. The Issue Raw Materials event records information about the raw materials used to manufacture a product; it is an example of a Give event.)

6. Acme manufacturing tracks information about customer calls by sales representative. Although many calls involve demonstrations of products, some are purely to build relationships. What is the correct way to model the relationship between Inventory and the Call on Customer event?

    a.

    (Incorrect. This shows that every call must involve demonstration of at least one product.)

▶ **b.**

    (Correct. This shows that a call may not involve the demonstration of any products, although it could demonstrate multiple products. At the same time, it correctly shows that some products may not be linked to any sales calls, whereas others may be linked to many different sales calls.)

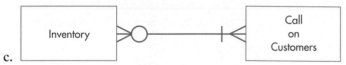

    c.

    (Incorrect. This shows that every product must be linked to a sales call.)

    d.

    (Incorrect. This both shows that every product must be linked to a sales call and that every sales call must involve the demonstration of at least one product.)

7. Which production cycle event collects data used to calculate payroll?

    a. Perform Job Operations (Incorrect. The Perform Job Operations event collects data about the use of labor; it is used to calculate product costs.)

▶ **b.** Time Worked (Correct. This event captures the acquisition of time from employees, in return for which they must be paid.)

    c. Time Used (Incorrect. This event collects data about the use of labor; it is used to calculate product costs.)

    d. Disburse Cash (Incorrect. This event records the paying of wages, but not their calculation.)

8. The give-to-get economic exchange associated with debt financing involves which two events?

    a. Issue Debt and Receive Cash (Incorrect. The Issue Debt is a special instance of the Receive Cash Event.)

▶ **b.** Issue Debt and Disburse Cash (Correct. Issuing debt results in receipt of cash and subsequent repayments of that debt.)

    c. Receive Cash and Disburse Cash (Incorrect. The Issue Debt event is used to record the facts about borrowing events, which differ from the facts collected about cash receipts for sales.)

    d. none of the above (Incorrect.)

9. Acme manufacturing wants to track post-sales customer service by collecting information about each customer service call: who called, when the call happened, which customer service representative handled the call, how long the call lasted, which sales transaction prompted the call, and which inventory items were discussed. The relationship between the Sales and Post-sales Service Call events should most likely be modeled as which of the following?

    a. 1:1 (Incorrect. Some customers may make more than one service call related to a specific sales transaction and they may also discuss several sales transactions during the same service call.)

    b. 1:N (Incorrect. Some customers may make more than one service call related to a specific sales transaction and they may also discuss several sales transactions during the same service call.)

▶ c. M:N (Correct. Some customers may make more than one service call related to a specific sales transaction and they may also discuss several sales transactions during the same service call).

    d. 0:N (Incorrect. There is no such thing as a 0:N relationship).

10. Which of the following additions to the basic REA template are sometimes needed?

    a. relationships between two resources (Incorrect. This chapter introduced an example of this to model location information, but it also introduced examples of relationships between two agents and between a resource and an agent).

    b. The relationship between two agents (Incorrect. This chapter introduced an example of this to model information about supervisors, but it also introduced examples of relationships between two resources and between a resource and an agent).

    c. The relationship between a resource and an agent (Incorrect. This chapter introduced an example of this to model responsibility for a resource, but it also introduced examples of relationships between two resources and between two agents).

▶ d. All of the above (Correct. Examples of each of the above were introduced in this chapter.)

Appendix: Extending the REA Model to Include Information About Policies[1]

Chapters 17–19 have explained how the REA model can be used to describe the contents of a database used to support an organization's transaction processing requirements. The various REA diagrams presented in those three chapters depicted the actual resources, events, and agents involved in carrying out the organization's business processes. The basic rules presented for developing an REA diagram are designed to ensure the accurate recording of things that exist, the events that occurred, and the specific agents who participated in those events. The REA model can be extended to also explicitly represent information about an organization's business policies. Doing so provides the opportunity to model information about such things as standards and internal controls. This Appendix provides a brief introduction to this topic.

Extending the REA model to incorporate information about policies that represent what should, could, or must happen involves the use of two new data modeling concepts: Type and Group entities. Type entities are used to depict "is-a-kind-of" relationships and Group entities are used to represent "is-a-member-of" relationships. Figure 19A-1 shows that both kinds of entities exist at the policy level and that they are mapped to entities at the operational level. For example, each individual sales transaction represents a specific type of sale (Internet, In-store, Mail Order, etc.). Similarly, each individual employee is linked to one, and only one, specific class of employees (buyers, cashiers, salespeople, etc.); in other words, each individual employee is a type of employee. In addition, Figure 19A-1 shows that employees are also assigned to (members of) specific divisions in the organization.

Type and Group entities are similar in that both are abstractions that represent sets of objects. They differ in terms of semantics and attributes. Type entities contain attributes that apply to every individual entity of that type. For example, Figure 19A-1 shows that the Employee Type entity contains the attributes Role, Base Pay, and Salary Range and the Sales Type entity contains attributes about whether to charge for shipping, sales tax, etc. In contrast, Group entities contain attributes that apply to the set as a whole and are often derived values. Thus, Table 19A-1 shows that the Group entity called Division contains attributes such as average salary and the number of employees, which represent properties of the entire set that are calculated from the values of every entity that belongs to that group.

The attributes of Type entities provide a way to specify policy information (e.g., valid salary ranges, shipping charges, etc.) so that the system can enforce and validate adherence to the organization's business policies. For example, an individual employee's salary can be compared to the permissible salary range for that class of employee. Similarly, the system can decide whether to collect sales tax on a particular sales transaction by checking the stated policy for that type of

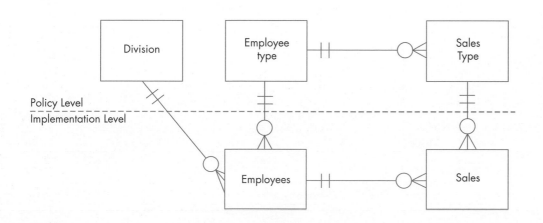

FIGURE 19A-1

Extending the REA Model to Include Policy-Level Information

---

[1]The material in this Appendix is based on the article, "Policy-Level Specification in REA Enterprise Information Systems" by Guido L. Geerts and William E. McCarthy, in the *Journal of Information Systems* 20:2 (Fall 2006): 37–63.

TABLE 19A-1 Policy-Level Entities and Relationships

Policy Level Entities	Primary Key	Foreign Keys	Other Attributes
Division	Division number		Budgeted sales this period
Employee type	Employee type number		Role description, permissible salary range
Sales type	Sales type number	Employee type number	Venue (Internet, mail-order, in-store, etc.), collect sales tax (Y/N)

Operational Level Entities	Primary Key	Foreign Keys	Other Attributes
Employees	Employee number	Division number, employee type number	Name, date hired, salary, etc.
Sales	Invoice number	Employee number, sales type number	Date, time, comments

sale. The attributes of Group entities provide a way to represent budgetary information, such as sales goals for each division, in a manner that facilitates creating reports that compare actual results (data stored in the operational-level entities) with plans (data stored in the policy-level entities).

Finally, Figure 19A-1 also shows that there can be relationships among Type entities. This provides another means to specify business policies and internal controls. For example, including Employee Type as an attribute in the Sales Type entity provides a mechanism for specifying that only sales staff can make sales to customers; similar linkages can be used to specify that only buyers can order inventory from suppliers, that only cashiers can write checks, and so on.

The objective of this Appendix was to provide an introduction to how the REA model can be extended to incorporate information about organizational policies and internal controls. If you take a database course, you will learn more about abstractions like Type and Group entities and the concepts of typification, generalization, and aggregation. You may also learn more about policy-level REA issues on your own, by reading the article cited as the reference source for this Appendix.

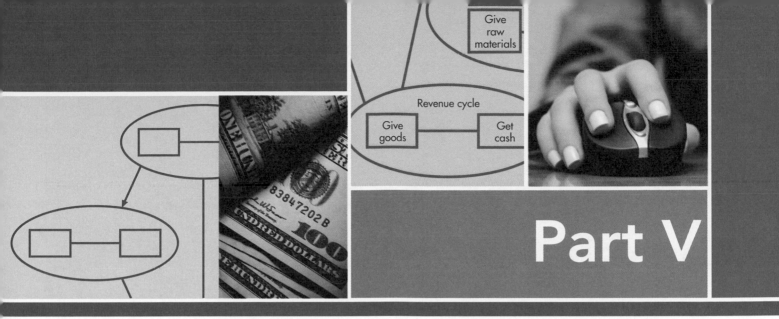

Part V

The Systems Development Process

Introduction to Systems Development and Systems Analysis

Learning Objectives

After studying this chapter, you should be able to:

1. Explain the five phases of the systems development life cycle.

2. Discuss the people involved in systems development and the roles they play.

3. Explain the importance of systems development planning and describe planning techniques.

4. Discuss the various types of feasibility analysis and calculate economic feasibility.

5. Explain why system changes trigger behavioral reactions, what form this resistance to change takes, and how to avoid or minimize the resulting problems.

6. Discuss the key issues and steps in systems analysis.

INTEGRATIVE CASE SHOPPERS MART

Ann Christy is the new controller of Shoppers Mart, a rapidly growing chain of discount stores. To assess how she can better serve Shoppers Mart, she held meetings with top management and visited with store managers and employees. Her findings are as follows:

1. Store managers cannot obtain information other than what is contained in periodic, preformatted reports. If they request information from several functional areas, the system bogs down.

2. Because timely information about product sales is not available, stores are often out of popular items and overstocked with products customers are not buying.

3. Management is concerned about losing market share to rivals with better prices and selection. The current system cannot provide the information management needs to solve this problem.

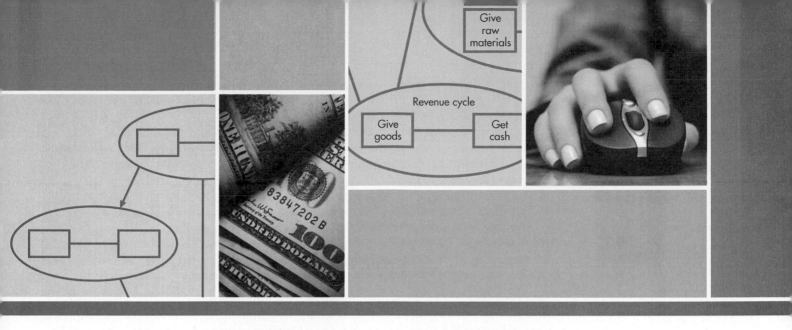

Ann is convinced that Shoppers Mart needs a new information system that is flexible, efficient, and responsive to user needs. Ann knows the new system will not be successful without management's complete support. Before asking for approval and funding for the new system, Ann met with systems development to ask the following questions:

1. What process must be followed to obtain and implement a new system?
2. What planning is necessary to ensure the system's success? Who will be involved, and how? Do special committees need to be formed? What resources are needed? How should the planning be documented?
3. How will employees react to a new system? What problems might this change cause, and how can they be minimized?
4. How should the new system be "sold" to top management? How can expected costs and benefits be quantified to determine whether the system will be cost-effective?

Introduction

Because we live in a highly competitive and ever-changing world, at any given time most organizations are improving or replacing their information systems. It is estimated that each year corporate America spends over $300 billion on more than 200,000 software projects. Companies change their systems for the following reasons:

- *Changes in user or business needs.* Increased competition, business growth or consolidation, downsizing operations, mergers and divestitures, or new regulations can alter an organization's structure and purpose. To remain responsive, the system must change.
- *Technological changes.* As technology advances and becomes less costly, organizations adopt new technologies. For example, a New York utility downsized from a mainframe to a client/server system and eliminated 100 clerical positions. The new system does much more than the old one, including handling workflow management, user contact, database queries, automatic cash processing, and voice/data integration.
- *Improved business processes.* Many companies change their systems to improve inefficient business processes. At Nashua, an office supply manufacturer, processing a customer's telephone order took two days because three separate systems had to be accessed. The new system requires three minutes.

- *Competitive advantage.* Companies invest heavily in technology to increase the quality, quantity, and speed of information; to improve products or services; to lower costs; and to provide other competitive advantages.
- *Productivity gains.* Information systems can automate clerical tasks, decrease task performance time, and provide employees with specialized knowledge. Carolina Power and Light eliminated 27% of its information systems staff with a system that significantly outperformed the old one.
- *Systems integration.* Organizations with incompatible systems integrate them to remove incompatibilities and to consolidate databases. The U.S. Department of Defense is trying to integrate over 700 separate systems.
- *Systems age and need to be replaced.* As systems age and are updated numerous times, they become less stable and eventually need to be replaced. Focus 20-1 describes how the Internal Revenue Service is trying to replace its aged information system.

Developing quality, error-free software is a difficult, expensive, and time-consuming task. Most software development projects deliver less, cost more, and take longer than expected. A study by Standish Group found that 70% of software development projects were late, 54% were over budget, 66% were unsuccessful, and 30% were canceled before completion. An American Management Systems study revealed that 75% of all large systems are not used, are not used as intended, or generate meaningless reports or inaccurate data. Nike implemented a forecasting system that did not work and had to take a multimillion-dollar inventory write-down. The system told Nike to order $90 million of shoes that did not sell, while it had $100 million of orders on popular models that it could not meet.

Skipping or skimping on systems development processes cause runaways that consume time and money and produce no usable results, as illustrated by the following examples:

- Pacific Gas & Electric pulled the plug on a system that was five years in development. It was a financial disaster with no usable product.
- When jeweler Shane Co. upgraded its enterprise resource planning (ERP) system, cost and deadline overruns pushed the cost from $10 million to over $36 million and caused inventory problems that, combined with a faltering economy, resulted in bankruptcy.

F⊙CUS 20-1 The IRS Attempts to Replace Its Aging Information System

The IRS recognizes that it needs to modernize its 40-year-old system to provide better customer service, improve compliance with the nation's tax laws, and reduce the volume of paper tax returns. The system processes and stores all taxpayer records and takes in over $2 *trillion* a year.

Critics claim the fragile and antiquated system has been updated so many times that a software meltdown is a very real possibility. In a worst-case scenario, the IRS would not know who had paid taxes, hundreds of billions of dollars of revenue would not be collected, and the government would have to borrow money to meet its obligations, throwing the financial markets into a panic.

The need to modernize is no secret; the IRS has been trying for some time. Years ago, the IRS spent $3.3 billion on an upgrade effort that failed. More recently, the IRS embarked on an $8 billion effort called the Business Systems Modernization (BSM) program. This program involves more than 20,000 major

tasks and scores of organizations and is one of the largest and most complex information system challenges in history. At the same time, the IRS is trying to change its management culture and the way it is organized; some critics claim both are more out of date than its information system.

The IRS cannot change the entire system at once; instead, it will occur in stages over 15 to 20 years. The effort has been compared to rebuilding all New York City buildings, streets, sewers, and communication and transportation systems, all while its inhabitants do not notice the changes as they go about their daily lives.

How is the IRS doing? Reports are not encouraging. The BSM spent almost $4 million on a project that was canceled. The effort has had a number of significant cost overruns, management delays, performance shortfalls, and missed project completion dates. One report indicates the project runs a "significant risk of not succeeding."

- California's Department of Motor Vehicles attempted to overhaul its system. Developed in 1965, it was so difficult to maintain that it took 18 programmers working an entire year to add a Social Security number file to the drivers' license and vehicle registration system. After seven years, $44 million, and not a single usable application, the project was canceled.

This chapter discusses five topics. The first is the systems development life cycle, the process followed to obtain and implement a new accounting information system (AIS). The second is the planning activities needed during development. The third is preparing a feasibility analysis. The fourth is the behavioral aspects of change that must be dealt with to implement a new system. The fifth topic is systems analysis, the first step in the systems development life cycle.

Systems Development

This section discusses the systems development life cycle and the people involved in systems development.

The Systems Development Life Cycle

Ann Christy asked the manager of systems development to explain the process Shoppers Mart uses to design and implement a new system. He sketched the five-step *systems development life cycle (SDLC)* shown in Figure 20-1 and briefly explained here.

SYSTEMS ANALYSIS   The first step in systems development is *systems analysis,* where the information needed to purchase, develop, or modify a system is gathered. To better use limited resources, development requests are screened and prioritized. If a decision is made to move forward, the nature and scope of the proposed project is identified, the current system is surveyed

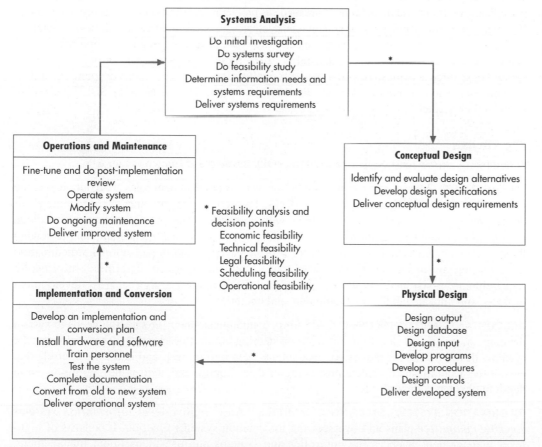

FIGURE 20-1

The Systems Development Life Cycle

Throughout the life cycle, planning must be done and behavioral aspects of change must be considered.

to identify its strengths and weaknesses, and the feasibility of the proposed project is determined. If the proposed project is feasible, the information needs of system users and managers are identified and documented. These needs are used to develop and document the systems requirements that are used to select or develop a new system. A systems analysis report is prepared and submitted to the information systems steering committee.

CONCEPTUAL DESIGN   During *conceptual design*, the company decides how to meet user needs. The first task is to identify and evaluate appropriate design alternatives, such as buying software, developing it in-house, or outsourcing system development to someone else. Detailed specifications outlining what the system is to accomplish and how it is to be controlled are developed. This phase is complete when conceptual design requirements are communicated to the information systems steering committee.

PHYSICAL DESIGN   During *physical design*, the company translates the broad, user-oriented conceptual design requirements into the detailed specifications used to code and test computer programs, design input and output documents, create files and databases, develop procedures, and build controls into the new system. This phase is complete when the results of the physical system design are communicated to the information systems steering committee.

IMPLEMENTATION AND CONVERSION   All the elements and activities of the system come together in the *implementation and conversion* phase. An implementation and conversion plan is developed and followed, new hardware and software are installed and tested, employees are hired and trained or existing employees relocated, and processing procedures are tested and modified. Standards and controls for the new system are established and system documentation completed. The organization converts to the new system and dismantles the old one, makes needed adjustments, and conducts a post-implementation review to detect and correct design deficiencies. When the operational system is delivered, system development is complete. A final report is prepared and sent to the information systems steering committee.

OPERATIONS AND MAINTENANCE   During *operations and maintenance,* the new system is periodically reviewed and modifications are made as problems arise or as new needs become evident. Eventually, a major modification or system replacement is necessary, and the SDLC begins again.

In addition to these five phases, three activities (planning, managing behavioral reactions to change, and assessing the ongoing feasibility of the project) are performed throughout the life cycle. These three activities, as well as systems analysis, are discussed in this chapter. The different approaches to obtaining an AIS are discussed in chapter 21. The last four SDLC phases are explained in chapter 22.

The Players

A number of people must cooperate to successfully develop and implement an AIS.

MANAGEMENT   Management's most important systems development roles are to emphasize the importance of involving users in the process, to provide support and encouragement for development projects, and to align systems with corporate strategies. Other key roles include establishing system goals and objectives, selecting system department leadership and reviewing their performance, establishing policies for project selection and organizational structure, and participating in important system decisions. User management determine information requirements, assist analysts with cost and benefit estimates, assign staff to development projects, and allocate funds for development and operation.

ACCOUNTANTS AND OTHER USERS   AIS users communicate their information needs to system developers. As project development team or steering committee members, they help manage systems development. As requested, accountants help design, test, and audit the controls that ensure the accurate and complete processing of data. Control and audit issues are discussed in depth in chapters 5 through 11.

INFORMATION SYSTEMS STEERING COMMITTEE   An executive-level *information systems steering committee* plans and oversees the information systems function. It consists of high-level management, such as the controller and systems and user-department management. The steering committee sets AIS policies; ensures top-management participation, guidance, and control; and facilitates the coordination and integration of systems activities.

PROJECT DEVELOPMENT TEAM Each development project has a team of systems analysts and specialists, managers, accountants, and users to guide its development. Team members plan each project, monitor it to ensure timely and cost-effective completion, make sure proper consideration is given to the human element, and communicate project status to top management and the steering committee. They should communicate frequently with users and hold regular meetings to consider ideas and discuss progress so that there are no surprises upon project completion. A team approach usually produces better results and facilitates user acceptance of the system.

SYSTEMS ANALYSTS AND PROGRAMMERS *Systems analysts* study existing systems, design new ones, and prepare the specifications used by computer programmers. Analysts interact with employees throughout the organization to bridge the gap between the user and technology. Analysts are responsible for ensuring that the system meets user needs.

Computer programmers write programs using the specifications developed by the analysts. They also modify and maintain existing computer programs.

EXTERNAL PLAYERS Customers, vendors, external auditors, and governmental entities play a role in systems development. For example, Walmart vendors are required to implement and use electronic data interchange (EDI).

Planning Systems Development

This section discusses the planning performed throughout the SDLC (see Figure 20-1).

Imagine that you built a two-bedroom house. Over the years, you add two bedrooms, a bathroom, a family room, a recreation room, a deck, a two-car garage and expand the kitchen. Without a long-range plan, your house will end up as a poorly organized and costly patchwork of rooms surrounding the original structure. This scenario also applies to an AIS; the result is a costly and poorly integrated system that is difficult to operate and maintain.

Planning has distinct advantages. It enables the system's goals and objectives to correspond to the organization's overall strategic plan. Systems are more efficient, subsystems are coordinated, and there is a sound basis for selecting new applications for development. The company remains abreast of the ever-present changes in information technology (IT). Duplication, wasted effort, and cost and time overruns are avoided. The system is less costly and easier to maintain. Finally, management is prepared for resource needs, and employees are prepared for the changes that will occur.

When development is poorly planned, a company must often return to a prior phase and correct errors and design flaws, as shown in Figure 20-2. This is costly and results in delays, frustration, and low morale.

Two systems development plans are needed:

1. *Project development plan.* A *project development plan,* prepared by the project team, contains a cost/benefit analysis, developmental and operational requirements (people, hardware, software, and financial), and a schedule of the activities required to develop and operate the new application.
2. *Master plan.* A long-range *master plan,* prepared by the information systems steering committee, specifies what the system will consist of, how it will be developed, who will develop it, how needed resources will be acquired, and where the AIS is headed. It describes the status of projects in process, prioritizes planned projects, describes the criteria used for prioritization, and provides development timetables. Projects with the highest priority are developed first. A three-year planning horizon is common, with the plan updated quarterly or monthly. Table 20-1 shows the master plan components at Shoppers Mart.

As explained in Focus 20-2, inadequate planning was one reason why Electronic Data Systems (EDS) lost a significant amount of money in its contract with the U.S. military.

Planning Techniques

PERT and the Gantt charts are techniques for scheduling and monitoring systems development activities. The *program evaluation and review technique (PERT)* requires that all activities and

FIGURE 20-2

Reasons for Returning to a Prior SDLC Phase

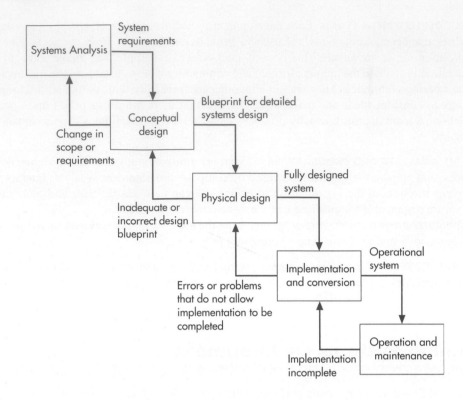

the precedent and subsequent relationships among them be identified. The activities and relationships are used to draw a PERT diagram, which is a network of arrows and nodes representing project activities that require an expenditure of time and resources and the completion and initiation of activities. Completion time estimates are made, and the *critical path*—the path requiring the greatest amount of time—is determined. If any activity on the critical path is delayed, then the whole project is delayed. If possible, resources can be shifted to critical path activities to reduce project completion time.

A *Gantt chart* (Figure 20-3) is a bar chart with project activities on the left-hand side and units of time across the top. For each activity, a bar is drawn from the scheduled starting date to the ending date, thereby defining expected project completion time. As activities are completed, they are recorded on the Gantt chart by filling in the bar; thus, at any time it is possible to determine which activities are on schedule and which are behind. The primary advantage of the Gantt chart is the ability to show graphically the entire schedule for a large, complex project, including

TABLE 20-1 Components of the Master Plan at Shoppers Mart

Organizational goals and objectives	Status of systems being developed
Company mission statement and goals	Proposed systems priorities
Information systems strategic plan and goals	Approved systems development
Organizational constraints	Proposals under consideration
Organizational approach to AIS	Development timetables and schedules
Organizational and AIS priorities	Forecast of future developments
Inventory and assessments	Forecasts of information needs
Current systems	Technological forecasts
Approved systems	Environmental/regulatory forecasts
Current hardware	Audit and control requirements
Current software	External user needs
Current AIS staff	
Assessment of strengths and weaknesses	

 **FOCUS 20-2   EDS Loses Billions in Its Contract with the Navy**

The U.S. military hired Electronic Data Systems (EDS) to develop a secure network to link 350,000 computers at 4,000 Navy sites. The $10 billion contract resulted in significant headaches and estimated losses of $1.7 billion. EDS made the following mistakes:

- With little military experience, EDS did not plan for their delays and requests. Congress delayed the project for 18 months by asking for network-performance tests EDS was not used to handling. EDS also failed to plan for the 200 technical hurdles the military imposed.
- EDS did not verify Navy estimates, such as the 5,000 software programs to be installed on the new PCs; in reality, there were 67,000. EDS underestimated cost and time requirements to customize individual computers. They also had to revamp the Navy's old software before it could be installed.
- EDS did not plan and coordinate project tasks. When EDS went to Navy bases to install the computers, they did not

have proper military clearances and some sailors and officers were busy or overseas.
- EDS did not give the Navy adequate instructions. EDS could not complete an order without a service member's rank, but EDS did not tell the Navy to send the rank.
- EDS did not track computer inventory. Some servicemen ordered PCs and then changed their orders to laptops. EDS did not require them to cancel the first order, so two computers were prepared. Duplicate and incomplete orders sat in warehouses for months.

To get the project back on track, EDS made some changes Rather than installing computers at many different locations simultaneously, it installed computers at the largest bases first, reused expensive hardware, installed the warehoused computers before buying new ones, and customized computers by job function rather than by individual.

progress to date and status. A disadvantage is that the charts do not show the relationships among project activities.

Feasibility Analysis

As shown in Figure 20-1, a *feasibility study* (or business case) is prepared during systems analysis and updated as necessary during the SDLC. The extent varies; for a large-scale system, it is generally extensive, whereas one for a desktop system might be informal. The feasibility study is prepared with input from management, accountants, systems personnel, and users.

FIGURE 20-3
Sample Gantt chart

PROJECT PLANNING CHART

Project Number ___01 - 650___
Project Name ___Labor Cost Analysis Module___
Project Leader ___J. Flaherty___

Page __1__ of __1__
Prepared by ___S. Doe___
Date ___12 / 09 / 2013___

No.	ACTIVITY Name	WEEK STARTING
1-1	Organize implementation team	11/17
1-2	Prepare system support procedures	
1-3	Develop conversion plan	
1-4	Develop testing plan	
2-1	Prepare program specifications	
2-2	Revise system documentation	
2-3	Perform programming tasks	
3-1	System test	
4-1	Install system support procedures	
5-1	Acceptance test	
6-1	Conversion	

Week starting columns: 11/17, 11/24, 12/1, 12/8, 12/15, 12/22, 12/29, 1/5, 1/12, 1/19, 1/26, 2/2, 2/9, 2/16, 2/23, 3/2, 3/9, 3/16, 3/23, 3/30

At major decision points, the steering committee reassess feasibility to decide whether to terminate a project, proceed unconditionally, or proceed if specific problems are resolved. Early go/no-go decisions are particularly important because each subsequent SDLC step requires more time and monetary commitments. The further along a development project is, the less likely it is to be canceled if a proper feasibility study has been prepared and updated.

Although uncommon, systems have been scrapped after implementation because they did not work or failed to meet an organization's needs. Bank of America, for example, hired a software firm to replace a 20-year-old system used to manage billions of dollars in institutional trust accounts. After two years of development, the new system was implemented despite warnings that it was not adequately tested. Ten months later the system was scrapped, top executives resigned, and the company took a $60 million write-off. The company lost 100 institutional accounts with $4 billion in assets. Focus 20-3 describes a Blue Cross/Blue Shield project that was scrapped after six years and a $120 million investment.

There are five important aspects to be considered during a feasibility study:

1. *Economic feasibility.* Will system benefits justify the time, money, and resources required to implement it?
2. *Technical feasibility.* Can the system be developed and implemented using existing technology?
3. *Legal feasibility.* Does the system comply with all applicable federal and state laws, administrative agency regulations, and contractual obligations?
4. *Scheduling feasibility.* Can the system be developed and implemented in the time allotted?
5. *Operational feasibility.* Does the organization have access to people who can design, implement, and operate the proposed system? Will people use the system?

Economic feasibility is now discussed in greater depth. Ann's feasibility analysis for Shoppers Mart is shown in Table 20-8 at the end of this chapter.

Capital Budgeting: Calculating Economic Feasibility

During systems design, alternative approaches to meeting system requirements are developed. Too often, companies overspend on technology because IT costs and payoffs are not measured and evaluated like other corporate investments. Merrill Lynch overcame significant philosophical and bureaucratic obstacles to implement a return-on-investment program for IT

F O CUS
20-3   Blue Cross/Blue Shield Abandons Runaway

Blue Cross/Blue Shield of Massachusetts had high hopes for its new information system. After six years and $120 million, however, the System 21 project was behind schedule and way over budget.

Although system failures of this magnitude are unusual, KPMG found that 35% of major information system projects become a runaway—a project that is millions of dollars over budget and months or years behind schedule. Other surveys show that almost every Fortune 200 company has had at least one runaway.

One reason for the problems was that Blue Cross hired an independent contractor to develop the software but neglected to appoint an in-house person to coordinate and manage the project. Nor did management establish a firm set of priorities regarding essential features and the sequence of application development.

The developers presented claims processing software to Blue Cross, but managers and users were not happy and requested numerous changes. As a result, the whole project was delayed. This led to ever-increasing cost overruns. By the time System 21 was launched, Blue Cross had fallen far behind its competitors' ability to process an ever-swelling paperwork load. During the six-year period, it lost 1 million subscribers and came close to bankruptcy.

Blue Cross learned a painful lesson. It abandoned the system it spent six years building and turned its hardware over to EDS. Fortunately, although the system died, the patient survived.

expenditures. Merrill Lynch now requires a 15% cash return on equity investment within five years, and all IT purchases are made by business, finance, and IT professionals working together.

Many organizations now use capital budgeting return-on-investment techniques to evaluate the economic merits of the alternatives. In a ***capital budgeting model,*** benefits and costs are estimated and compared to determine whether the system is cost beneficial. Benefits and costs that are not easily quantifiable are estimated and included. If they cannot be accurately estimated, they are listed, and their likelihood and expected impact on the organization evaluated. Tangible and intangible benefits include cost savings, improved customer service, productivity increases, improved data processing, better decision making, greater management control, increased job satisfaction, and increased employee morale. Initial outlay and operating costs are shown in Table 20-2. Between 65% and 75% of yearly systems-related expenditures are for maintaining current systems.

The following are three commonly used capital budgeting techniques:

1. *Payback period.*   The ***payback period*** is the number of years required for the net savings to equal the initial cost of the investment. The project with the shortest payback period is usually selected.
2. *Net present value (NPV).*   All estimated future cash flows are discounted back to the present, using a discount rate that reflects the time value of money. The initial outlay costs are deducted from the discounted cash flows to obtain the ***net present value (NPV)***. A positive NPV indicates the alternative is economically feasible. The highest positive NPV is usually selected.
3. *Internal rate of return (IRR).*   The ***internal rate of return (IRR)*** is the effective interest rate that results in an NPV of zero. A project's IRR is compared with a minimum acceptable rate to determine acceptance or rejection. The proposal with the highest IRR is usually selected.

Payback, NPV, and IRR are illustrated in the feasibility analysis shown in Table 20-8.

TABLE 20-2 Initial Outlay and Operating Costs

Hardware
  Central processing unit
  Peripherals
  Communications hardware
  Special input/output devices
  Replacement, upgrade, expansion costs

Software
  Application, system, general-purpose, utility,
    and communications software
  Updated versions of software
  Application software design, programming,
    modification, testing, and documentation

Staff
  Supervisors
  Analysts and programmers
  Computer operators
  Input (data conversion) personnel
  Hiring, training, and relocating staff
  Consultants

Supplies and overhead
  Preprinted forms
  Data storage devices
  Supplies (paper, toner)
  Utilities and power

Maintenance/backup
  Hardware/software maintenance
  Backup and recovery operations
  Power supply protection

Documentation
  Systems documentation
  Training program documentation
  Operating standards and procedures

Site preparation
  Air-conditioning, humidity, dust controls
  Physical security (access)
  Fire and water protection
  Cabling, wiring, and outlets
  Furnishings and fixtures

Installation
  Freight and delivery charges
  Setup and connection fees

Conversion
  Systems testing
  File and data conversions
  Parallel operations

Financial
  Finance charges
  Legal fees
  Insurance

Behavioral Aspects of Change

Individuals participating in systems development are change agents who are continually confronted by resistance to change. The *behavioral aspects of change* are crucial, because the best system will fail without the support of the people it serves. Niccolo Machiavelli discussed resistance to change over 400 years ago:[1]

> *It must be considered that there is nothing more difficult to carry out, nor more doubtful of success, nor more dangerous to handle, than to initiate a new order of things. For the reformer has enemies in all those who could profit by the old order, and only lukewarm defenders in all those who could profit by the new order. This lukewarmness arises partly from fear of their adversaries, who have the laws in their favor, and partly from the incredulity of mankind, who do not truly believe in anything new until they have had an actual experience of it.*

Organizations must be sensitive to and consider the feelings and reactions of persons affected by change. This section discusses the type of behavioral problems that can result from change.

Why Behavioral Problems Occur

An individual's view of change, as either good or bad, usually depends on how that individual is personally affected by it. Management views change positively if it increases profits or reduces costs. Employees view the same change as bad if their jobs are terminated or adversely affected.

To minimize adverse behavioral reactions, one must understand why resistance takes place. Some of the more important factors include the following:

- *Fear.* People fear the unknown, losing their jobs, losing respect or status, failure, technology and automation, and the uncertainty accompanying change.
- *Top management support.* Employees who sense a lack of top-management support for change wonder why they should endorse it.
- *Experience with prior changes.* Employees who had a bad experience with prior changes are more reluctant to cooperate.
- *Communication.* Employees are unlikely to support a change unless the reasons behind it are explained.
- *Disruptive nature of change.* Requests for information and interviews are distracting and place additional burdens on people, causing negative feelings toward the change that prompted them.
- *Manner in which change is introduced.* Resistance is often a reaction to the methods of instituting change rather than to change itself. The rationale used to sell the system to top management may not be appropriate for lower-level employees. The elimination of menial tasks and the ability to advance and grow are often more important to users than are increasing profits and reducing costs.
- *Biases and emotions.* People with emotional attachments to their duties or coworkers may not want to change if those elements are affected.
- *Personal characteristics and background.* Generally speaking, the younger and more highly educated people are, the more likely they are to accept change. Likewise, the more comfortable people are with technology, the less likely they are to oppose changes.

How People Resist Change

Behavioral problems begin when people find out a change is being considered. Initial resistance is often subtle, manifested by failure to provide developers with information, tardiness, or subpar performance. Major behavioral problems often occur when the new system is implemented and the change becomes a reality. Focus 20-4 explains the resistance the U.S. Department of Defense experienced.

Resistance often takes one of three forms: aggression, projection, or avoidance.

---

[1]Niccolo Machiavelli, *The Prince*, translated by Luigi Rice, revised by E.R.P. Vincent (New York: New American Library, 1952).

 **Resistance to Change at the Department of Defense**

The U.S. Department of Defense (DOD) has a budget of $417 billion, 3.3 million employees, and over $1 trillion in assets. It also has one of the most antiquated and inefficient information systems in the world and cannot produce accurate accounting information or get a clean audit. Only a few of their 4,000 systems communicate effectively with other systems. Most systems require data that are transferred between systems to be manually reentered.

The DOD has been trying to modernize its AIS for over 20 years, at a cost of over $35 billion. After three notable failures, it is trying a fourth time. The Business Management Modernization Project's (BMMP) goal is to integrate DOD systems and business processes and produce a user-transparent system. Unfortunately, many people would rather not see the DOD realize this transparency. Past reforms failed because system developers could not break through the barriers DOD agencies created to protect their processes, procedures, and chains of command.

Users resist integration because what is optimal for one user is often suboptimal for the DOD. Government bureaucrats resist because an integrated, transparent system will reveal many unnecessary or obsolete programs that further personal agendas. For example, managers are often promoted for their ability to generate, receive funding for, and operate programs, regardless of their effectiveness. Senators and congressional representatives resist because a new system could adversely affect their ability to steer spending to constituents and thereby get reelected.

To overcome these behavioral problems, the DOD is trying to convince the armed forces to rid themselves of their "program protection" mindset. In one notable success, the Air Force now promotes personnel based on actions that improve the Air Force as a whole, rather than on actions that defend a specific turf or program.

AGGRESSION *Aggression* is behavior that destroys, cripples, or weakens system effectiveness, such as increased error rates, disruptions, or deliberate sabotage. After one organization introduced an online AIS, data input devices had honey poured on them, were run over by forklifts, or had paper clips inserted in them. Employees also entered erroneous data into the system. In another organization, disgruntled workers punched in to an unpopular supervisor's department and worked in other areas. This adversely affected the supervisor's performance evaluation because he was charged for hours that did not belong to him.

PROJECTION *Projection* is blaming the new system for everything that goes wrong. The system becomes the scapegoat for all real and imagined problems and errors. If these criticisms are not controlled or answered, system integrity can be damaged or destroyed.

AVOIDANCE *Avoidance* is ignoring a new AIS in the hope that the problem (the system) will eventually go away. Davis Controls, a struggling manufacturer, processed its orders using e-mail, but pertinent information was frequently lost or forgotten. Davis invested $300,000 in software that efficiently captured customer information, properly handled purchase orders, helped managers make better daily decisions, and made it possible to process four times as many transactions. Employees avoided it, even though the CEO explained the system's benefits and told them the company's survival and their jobs were at stake. Finally, the CEO disabled the uncooperative employees' e-mail accounts and terminated the employees who continued to avoid the system.

Preventing Behavioral Problems

The human element, which is often the most significant problem a company encounters in implementing a system, can be improved by observing the following guidelines:

- *Obtain management support.* Appoint a champion who can provide resources and motivate others to assist and cooperate with systems development.
- *Meet user needs.* It is essential that the system satisfy user needs.
- *Involve users.* Those affected by the system should participate in its development by making suggestions and helping make decisions. To avoid misunderstandings, users

should be told which suggestions are being used and how, and which are not and why. Participation is ego enhancing, challenging, and intrinsically satisfying. Users who participate in development are more knowledgeable, better trained, and more committed to using the system.

- *Allay fears, and stress new opportunities.*   Users are vitally interested in how system changes affect them personally. Address their concerns and provide assurances (to the extent possible) that job losses and responsibility shifts will not occur—for example, through relocation, attrition, and early retirement. If employees are terminated, provide severance pay and outplacement services. Emphasize that the system may provide advancement opportunities and greater job satisfaction because the job has become more interesting and challenging.
- *Avoid emotionalism.*   When logic vies with emotion, it rarely stands a chance. Emotional issues should be allowed to cool, handled in a nonconfrontational manner, or sidestepped.
- *Provide training.*   Effective use and support is not possible if users do not understand the system. User training needs are often underestimated.
- *Reexamine performance evaluation.*   Performance standards and criteria should be reevaluated to ensure that they are congruent with the new system.
- *Keep communication lines open.*   Everyone affected by systems development should have an attitude of trust and cooperation. If employees become hostile, it is difficult to change their attitude and to implement the system. As soon as possible, employees should be told what changes are being made and why and be shown how the new system benefits them. This helps employees identify with the company's efforts and feel they are key players in the company's future goals and plans. It also helps prevent rumors and misunderstandings. Employees should be told whom they can contact if they have questions or concerns.
- *Test the system.*   The system should be properly tested prior to implementation to minimize initial bad impressions.
- *Keep the system simple, and humanize it.*   Avoid complex systems that cause radical changes. Make the change as simple as possible by conforming to existing organizational procedures. The new system is unlikely to be accepted if individuals believe the computer is controlling them or has usurped their positions.
- *Control users' expectations.*   A system is sold too well if users have unrealistic expectations of its capabilities and performance. Be realistic when describing the merits of the system.

These guidelines are time-consuming and expensive, and workers may skip them to speed systems development and installation. However, the problems caused by not following the guidelines are usually more expensive and time-consuming to fix than to prevent.

Systems Analysis

When a new or improved system is needed, a written *request for systems development* is prepared. The request describes the current problems, the reasons for the change, the proposed system's objectives, and its anticipated benefits and costs. The five steps in the analysis phase and their objectives are shown in Figure 20-4 and discussed in this section.

Initial Investigation

An *initial investigation* is conducted to screen the requests for systems development. The exact nature of the problem(s) must be determined. In some instances, the perceived problem is not the real problem. A government accountant once asked a consultant to develop an AIS to produce the information he needed regarding fund expenditures and available funds. An investigation showed that the system provided the information and he did not understand the reports he received.

FIGURE 20-4
Steps in Systems Analysis

Step	Objectives

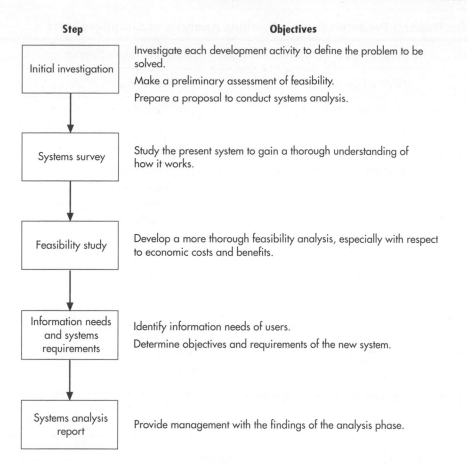

Initial investigation
Investigate each development activity to define the problem to be solved.
Make a preliminary assessment of feasibility.
Prepare a proposal to conduct systems analysis.

Systems survey
Study the present system to gain a thorough understanding of how it works.

Feasibility study
Develop a more thorough feasibility analysis, especially with respect to economic costs and benefits.

Information needs and systems requirements
Identify information needs of users.
Determine objectives and requirements of the new system.

Systems analysis report
Provide management with the findings of the analysis phase.

The project's scope (what it should and should not accomplish) is determined. Scope creep (adding additional requirements to the scope after it has been agreed to) is a real problem. Because of scope creep, a plan to have Census Bureau employees compile and transmit 2010 census information to headquarters with handheld computers was scrapped after two years of work. After spending $595 million on handhelds, the Census Bureau reverted back to pen-and-paper census taking.

A new AIS is useful when problems result from lack of information, inaccessibility of data, and inefficient data processing. A new AIS is not the answer to organizational problems. Likewise, if a manager lacks organizational skills, or if failure to enforce existing procedures causes control problems, a new AIS is not the answer. The initial investigation should also determine a project's viability and preliminary costs and benefits, and it should recommend whether to initiate the project as proposed, modify it, or abandon it.

A *proposal to conduct systems analysis* is prepared for approved projects. The project is assigned a priority and added to the master plan. Table 20-3 shows the information contents of a proposal to conduct systems analysis.

Systems Survey

A *systems survey* is an extensive study of the current AIS that has the following objectives:

- Gain an understanding of company operations, policies, procedures, and information flow; AIS strengths and weaknesses; and available hardware, software, and personnel.
- Make preliminary assessments of current and future processing needs, and determine the extent and nature of the changes needed.
- Develop working relationships with users, and build support for the AIS.
- Collect data that identify user needs, conduct a feasibility analysis, and make recommendations to management.

TABLE 20-3 Table of Contents for Reports Prepared During Systems Analysis at Shoppers Mart

Proposal to Conduct Systems Analysis	Systems Survey Report	Systems Analysis Report
Table of Contents	Table of Contents	Table of Contents
I. Executive Summary	I. Executive Summary	I. Executive Summary
II. System Problems and Opportunities	II. System Goals and Objectives	II. System Goals and Objectives
III. Goals and Objectives of Proposed System	III. System Problems and Opportunities	III. System Problems and Opportunities
IV. Project Scope	IV. Current System Operations	IV. Project Scope
V. Anticipated Costs and Benefits	A. Policies, Procedures, and Practices Affecting System	V. Relationship of Project to Overall Strategic Information Systems Plan
VI. Participants in Development Project	B. System Design and Operation (Intended and Actual)	VI. Current System Operations
VII. Proposed System Development Tasks and Work Plan	C. System Users and Their Responsibilities	VII. User Requirements
VIII. Recommendations	D. System Outputs, Inputs, and Data Storage	VIII. Feasibility Analysis
	E. System Controls	IX. System Constraints
	F. System Strengths, Weaknesses, and Constraints	X. Recommendations for New System
	G. Costs to Operate System	XI. Proposed Project Participants and Work Plan
	V. User Requirements Identified	XII. Summary
		XIII. Approvals
		XIV. Appendix of Documents, Tables, Charts, Glossary

Data about the current AIS is gathered from employees and from documentation such as organizational charts and procedures manuals. External sources include consultants, customers and suppliers, industry associations, and government agencies. The advantages and disadvantages of four common methods of gathering data are summarized here and in Table 20-4.

An *interview* gathers answers to "why" questions. Care must be taken to ensure that personal biases, self-interest, or a desire to say what the employee thinks the interviewer wants to hear does not produce inaccurate information. Ann's Shoppers Mart interviews were successful because of her approach and preparation. For each interview, Ann made an appointment, explained the purpose beforehand, indicated the amount of time needed, and arrived on time. Before each session, Ann studied the interviewee's responsibilities and listed points she wanted to cover. Ann put each interviewee at ease by being friendly, courteous, and tactful. Her questions dealt with the person's responsibilities, how she interacted with the AIS, how the system might be improved, and the person's information needs. Ann let the interviewee do most of the talking and paid special attention to nonverbal communication, because subtle overtones and body language can be as significant as direct responses to questions. Ann took notes, augmented them with detailed impressions shortly after the interview, and asked permission to tape especially important interviews.

Questionnaires are used when the amount of information to be gathered is small and well defined, is obtained from many people or from those who are located elsewhere, or is intended to verify data from other sources. Questionnaires take relatively little time to administer, but developing a quality questionnaire can be challenging and requires significant time and effort.

Observation is used to verify information gathered using other approaches and to determine how a system actually works, rather than how it should work. It is difficult to interpret observations because people may change their normal behavior or make mistakes when they know they are being observed. Identifying what is to be observed, estimating how long it will take, obtaining permission, and explaining what will be done and why can maximize the effectiveness of observation. The observer should not make value judgments and should document notes and impressions as soon as possible.

TABLE 20-4 Advantages and Disadvantages of Data-Gathering Methods

	Advantages	Disadvantages
Interviews	Can answer "why" questions Interviewer can probe and follow up Questions can be clarified Builds positive relationships with interviewee Builds acceptance and support for new system	Time-consuming Expensive Personal biases or self-interest may produce inaccurate information
Questionnaires	Can be anonymous Not time-consuming Inexpensive Allows more time to think about responses	Does not allow in-depth questions or answers Cannot follow up on responses Questions cannot be clarified Impersonal; does not build relationships Difficult to develop Often ignored or completed superficially
Observation	Can verify how system actually works, rather than how it should work Results in greater understanding of the system	Time-consuming Expensive Difficult to interpret properly Observed people may alter behavior
Systems Documentation	Describes how system should work Written form facilitates review, analysis	Time-consuming May not be available or easy to find

Systems documentation describes how the AIS is intended to work. Throughout the survey, the project team should be alert to differences between intended and actual systems operation as they provide important insights into problems and weaknesses.

Systems analysis work is documented so it can be used throughout the development project. Documentation consists of questionnaire copies, interview notes, memos, document copies, and models. *Physical models* illustrate *how* a system functions by describing document flow, computer processes performed, the people performing them, and the equipment used. *Logical models* focus on essential activities (*what* is being done) and the flow of information, not on the physical processes of transforming and storing data. Table 20-5 lists analysis and design tools and techniques used to create an AIS and identifies the chapter where each is discussed.

Once data gathering is complete, the team evaluates the AIS's strengths and weaknesses to develop ideas for designing and structuring the new AIS. When appropriate, strengths are retained and weaknesses corrected.

The systems survey culminates with a *systems survey report*. Table 20-3 shows the table of contents for the Shoppers Mart systems survey report. The report is supported by documentation such as memos, interview and observation notes, questionnaire data, file and record layouts and

TABLE 20-5 Systems Analysis and Design Tools and Techniques

CASE (chapter 21)	Gantt charts (chapter 20)
Data dictionary (chapter 4)	PERT charts (chapter 20)
Data flow diagrams (chapter 3)	Prototyping (chapter 21)
Document flowcharts (chapter 3)	REA data models (chapter 17)
E-R diagrams (chapter 17)	Record layouts (chapter 4)
Forms design checklist (chapter 22)	System flowcharts (chapter 3)

descriptions, input and output descriptions, copies of documents, E-R diagrams, flowcharts, and data flow diagrams.

Feasibility Study

At this point, the thorough feasibility analysis discussed earlier in the chapter is conducted to determine the project's viability. The feasibility analysis is updated regularly as the project proceeds and costs and benefits become clearer.

Information Needs and Systems Requirements

Once a project is deemed feasible, the company identifies the information needs of users and documents systems requirements. Table 20-6 is an example of systems requirements.

Determining information needs is a challenging process because of the sheer quantity and variety of information that must be specified. In addition, it may be difficult for employees to articulate their information needs, or they may identify them incorrectly. According to *CIO* magazine, 70% of project failures are due to insufficient, inaccurate, or outdated systems requirements. Figure 20-5 is a humorous view of the types of communication problems associated with this process.

TABLE 20-6 Possible Contents of System Requirements

Processes	Business process descriptions, including what is to be done and by whom
Data elements	The name, size, format, source, and significance of required data elements
Data structure	How the data elements will be organized into logical records
Outputs	Description of the purpose, frequency, and distribution of system outputs
Inputs	Description of contents, source, and person responsible for system inputs
Documentation	How the new system and each subsystem will operate
Constraints	Deadlines, schedules, security requirements, staffing limitations, and statutory or regulatory requirements
Controls	Controls to ensure the accuracy and reliability of inputs, outputs, and processing
Reorganizations	Organizational reorganization needed to meet users' information needs, such as increasing staff levels and adding new job functions

FIGURE 20-5

Communications Problems in Systems Analysis and Design

1.
As proposed by
user management

2.
As sold to
top management

3.
As planned by project
development team

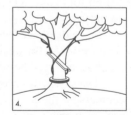
4.
As approved by
the steering committee

5.
As designed by
the senior analyst

6.
As written by
the applications programmers

7.
As installed at
the user's site

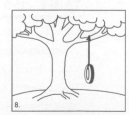
8.
What the users
actually needed

When Corning Corporation investigated the ophthalmic pressings it manufactures, it found that 35% of its drafting documents contained errors. Drafting errors are increasingly more expensive to correct at each subsequent manufacturing stage: $250 before toolmakers cut the tools, $20,000 before production begins, and $100,000 after the tools are sold. Several corrective actions reduced the error rates from 35% to 0.2%. The same cost relationships exist in systems development; error correction costs increase as development proceeds through the SDLC.

System objectives, such as those shown in Table 20-7, are the elements most vital to an AIS's success. It is difficult for a system to satisfy every objective. For example, designing adequate internal controls is a trade-off between the objectives of economy and reliability.

Because organizational constraints make it difficult to develop all AIS components simultaneously, the system is divided into modules that are developed and installed independently. When changes are needed, only the affected module is changed. The modules must be properly integrated into a workable system.

A system's success often depends on the ability to cope with organizational constraints. Common constraints include governmental agency requirements, management policies, lack of qualified staff, user capabilities and attitudes, technology, and limited finances. To maximize system performance, these constraints must be minimized.

The following four strategies are used to determine AIS requirements:

1. *Ask users what they need.*   This is the simplest and fastest strategy, but many people do not understand their needs. They know their job but may be unable to break it down into the individual information elements they use. It is sometimes better to ask what decisions they make and what processes they are involved in and then design systems to address their answers. Users must think beyond current information needs so that new systems do not simply replicate current information in improved formats.
2. *Analyze external systems.*   If a solution already exists, do not "reinvent the wheel."
3. *Examine existing systems.*   Determine if existing modules are used as intended, may be augmented by manual tasks, or may be avoided altogether. This approach helps determine whether a system can be modified or must be replaced.
4. *Create a prototype.*   When it is difficult to identify requirements, a developer can quickly rough out a system for users to critique. Users identify what they like and dislike about the system and request changes. This iterative process of looking at what is developed and improving it continues until users agree on their needs. Prototyping is discussed in Chapter 21.

TABLE 20-7 AIS Objectives

Usefulness	Information output should help management and users make decisions.
Economy	System benefits should exceed the cost.
Reliability	System should process data accurately and completely.
Availability	Users should be able to access the system at their convenience.
Timeliness	Crucial information is produced first, less important items as time permits.
Customer service	Customer service must be courteous and efficient.
Capacity	System capacity must be sufficient to handle periods of peak operation and future growth.
Ease of use	System should be user-friendly.
Flexibility	System should be able to accommodate reasonable requirement changes.
Tractability	System is easily understood and it facilitates problem solving and future development.
Auditability	Auditability is built into the system from the beginning.
Security	Only authorized users are granted access to or allowed to change system data.

Detailed AIS requirements that explain exactly what the system is to produce are created and documented. The requirements are supported by sample input and output forms, as well as charts, so users can conceptualize the system. A nontechnical summary of important user requirements and development efforts to date is often prepared for management. The project team meets with the users, explains the requirements, and obtains their approval. When an agreement is reached, user management signs the system requirements documents to indicate approval.

Systems Analysis Report

The concluding step in systems analysis is preparing a *systems analysis report* to summarize and document analysis activities. The Shoppers Mart systems analysis report, shown in Table 20-3, shows the information typically contained in the report.

A go/no-go decision is made up to three times during systems analysis: first, during the initial investigation, to determine whether to conduct a systems survey; second, at the end of the feasibility study, to determine whether to proceed to the information requirements phase; third, at the completion of the analysis phase, to decide whether to proceed to conceptual systems design. The remaining phases in the SDLC are discussed in the next two chapters.

Summary and Case Conclusion

After an extensive analysis of Shoppers Mart's current system and core business processes, Ann Christy has proposed some changes. She has asked the corporate office to produce daily sales data for each store to help them adapt quickly to customer needs and to help suppliers avoid stockouts and overstocking. Shoppers Mart will coordinate buying at the corporate office to minimize inventory levels and negotiate lower wholesale prices. Stores will electronically send daily orders to the corporate office. Based on store orders and warehouse inventory, the corporate office will send purchase orders to suppliers. Suppliers will process orders and ship goods to regional warehouses or directly to the stores the day orders are received. Each store will have the flexibility to respond to local sales trends and conditions by placing local orders. Accounts payable will be centralized so payments can be made electronically.

Ann reviews the proposed system with the legal department and the AIS staff. She is told it complies with all legal considerations and is technologically feasible. Top management and the information systems steering committee will decide how to allocate time and resources for the project and will communicate all staff assignments to systems management and personnel.

Ann's team conducts an economic feasibility study (see Table 20-8) and determines that the project makes excellent use of funds. The team estimates that initial outlay costs for the system are $5 million. The team estimates recurring operating costs and expected savings for years 1 through 6, which are expected to rise from year to year. Ann calculates the net annual savings and then calculates the after-tax cash savings for each year.

The $5 million system can be depreciated over its six-year expected life. Because the company does not have to pay taxes on the $1 million depreciation in year 1, it ends up saving an additional $340,000. Finally, Ann calculates the net savings for each year.

Ann uses Shoppers Mart's 10% cost of capital rate to calculate the NPV of the investment, which is over $3 million. The internal rate of return is a lofty 25%, and payback occurs in the fourth year. Ann realizes how advantageous it would be for the company to borrow the money (at a 10% interest rate) to produce a 25% return.

Ann presents the system to management and describes its objectives. Challenges to her estimates are plugged into her spreadsheet model to show their effect. Even the stiffest challenges to Ann's numbers show a positive return. Top management votes to support the new system, requests some changes, and tells Ann to proceed.

Ann has found management's enthusiastic support crucial to the system's success. Several employees with vested interests in the current system are critical of her ideas. Some employees remember the problems Shoppers Mart had when the current system was implemented years ago. Ann concludes that people resisting the new system are afraid of the change's effect on them personally. To counter negative behavioral reactions, Ann takes great pains to explain how the new system would benefit employees individually and how it will affect the company as a whole.

TABLE 20-8 Economic Feasibility of Shoppers Mart's New Information System

	Initial Outlay	Year 1	Year 2	Year 3	Year 4	Year 5	Year 6
Initial outlay costs							
Hardware	$2,000,000						
Software	400,000						
Training	200,000						
Site preparation	200,000						
Initial systems design	2,000,000						
Conversion	200,000						
Total initial outlays	$5,000,000						
Recurring costs							
Hardware expansion			$260,000	$300,000	$340,000	$380,000	$400,000
Software			150,000	200,000	225,000	250,000	250,000
Systems maintenance		$60,000	120,000	130,000	140,000	150,000	160,000
Personnel costs		500,000	800,000	900,000	1,000,000	1,100,000	1,300,000
Communication charges		100,000	160,000	180,000	200,000	220,000	250,000
Overhead		300,000	420,000	490,000	560,000	600,000	640,000
Total costs		$960,000	$1,910,000	$2,200,000	$2,465,000	$2,700,000	$3,000,000
Savings							
Clerical cost savings		$600,000	$1,200,000	$1,400,000	$1,600,000	$1,800,000	$2,000,000
Working capital savings		900,000	1,200,000	1,500,000	1,500,000	1,500,000	1,500,000
Profits from sales increases			500,000	900,000	1,200,000	1,500,000	1,800,000
Warehousing efficiencies			400,000	800,000	1,200,000	1,600,000	2,000,000
Total savings		$1,500,000	$3,300,000	$4,600,000	$5,500,000	$6,400,000	$7,300,000
Savings minus recurring costs		$540,000	$1,390,000	$2,400,000	$3,035,000	$3,700,000	$4,300,000
Less income taxes (34% rate)		(183,600)	(472,600)	(816,000)	(1,031,900)	(1,258,000)	(1,462,000)
Cash savings (net of tax)		$356,400	$917,400	$1,584,000	$2,003,100	$2,442,000	$2,838,000
Savings on taxes due to depreciation deduction		340,000	544,000	326,400	195,500	195,500	98,600
Net savings	($5,000,000)	$696,400	$1,461,400	$1,910,400	$2,198,600	$2,637,500	$2,936,600

Payback occurs in the fourth year when the savings net of taxes of $6,266,800 exceed the costs of $5,000,000.

Net present value (interest rate of 10%):   **Depreciation** on initial investment of $5,000,000:

	($5,000,000)		Tax Rate 34%			
696,400 × 0.9091 =	633,097		Year	Rate (%)	Depreciation	Tax Savings
1,461,400 × 0.8265 =	1,207,847		1	20.00	$1,000,000	$340,000
1,910,400 × 0.7513 =	1,435,284		2	32.00	1,600,000	544,000
2,198,600 × 0.6830 =	1,501,644		3	19.20	960,000	326,400
2,637,500 × 0.6209 =	1,637,624		4	11.50	575,000	195,500
2,936,600 × 0.5645 =	1,657,711		5	11.50	575,000	195,500
Net present value is	$3,073,207		6	5.80	290,000	98,600
Internal rate of return is	25.04%					

With management's approval, she assures employees they will not lose their jobs and that all affected employees will be retrained. She involves the two most vocal opponents in planning activities, and they soon become two of the new system's biggest advocates.

Ann invites the managers of all affected departments to be on a steering committee. A master plan for developing the system is formulated, and the system is broken down into manageable projects. The projects are prioritized, and project teams are formed to begin work on the highest-priority projects. Documentation standards are developed and approved.

Key Terms

AIS IN ACTION

Chapter Quiz

1. Which of the following is NOT a reason why companies make changes to their AIS?
   a. gain a competitive advantage
   b. increase productivity
   c. keep up with business growth
   d. downsize company operations
   e. All of the above are reasons why companies change an AIS.

2. Which of the following is the planning technique that identifies implementation activities and their relationships, constructs a network of arrows and nodes, and then determines the critical path through the network?
   a. Gantt chart
   b. PERT diagram
   c. physical model
   d. data flow diagram

3. The purchasing department is designing a new AIS. Who is best able to determine departmental information requirements?
   a. steering committee
   b. controller
   c. top management
   d. purchasing department

4. Which of the following is the correct order of the steps in systems analysis?
   a. initial investigation, determination of information needs and system requirements, feasibility study, system survey
   b. determination of information needs and system requirements, system survey, feasibility study, initial investigation
   c. system survey, initial investigation, determination of information needs and system requirements, feasibility study
   d. initial investigation, system survey, feasibility study, determination of information needs and system requirements

5. Which of the following is the long-range planning document that specifies what the system will consist of, how it will be developed, who will develop it, how needed resources will be acquired, and its overall vision?
   a. steering committee agenda
   b. master plan
   c. systems development life cycle
   d. project development plan

6. Resistance is often a reaction to the methods of instituting change rather than to change itself.
   a. true
   b. false

7. Increased error rates, disruptions, and sabotage are examples of which of the following?
   a. aggression
   b. avoidance
   c. projection
   d. payback

8. What is often the most significant problem a company encounters in designing, developing, and implementing a system?
   a. the human element
   b. technology
   c. legal challenges
   d. planning for the new system

9. Determining whether the organization has access to people who can design, implement, and operate the proposed system is referred to as which of the following?
   a. technical feasibility
   b. operational feasibility
   c. legal feasibility
   d. scheduling feasibility
   e. economic feasibility

10. Which of the following is NOT one of the tangible or intangible benefits a company might obtain from a new system?
    a. cost savings
    b. improved customer service and productivity
    c. improved decision making
    d. improved data processing
    e. All are benefits of a new system.

Comprehensive Problem

Riverbend Software Support Administrators (RSSA) provides online and telephone help desk services. Because RSSA's labor costs have steadily increased, it is outsourcing its call center. RSSA's executive-level committee, who oversees the information systems (IS) function, selected a project development team to create a system to move the help desk and manage it from corporate headquarters.

Two incidents delayed the help desk conversion date by 15 days. A server was damaged when an unidentified employee put a hot coffee pot on it, and several backup tapes were found floating in a restroom sink.

The five-year contract requires an initial payment of $1,750,000 and yearly payments of $525,000. Each year, the contract will save $750,000 in salary, benefits, and equipment costs. There is a $150,000 one-time charge for breaking the current call center's building lease, but doing so will save $360,000 a year. RSSA's cost of capital is 11%.

Required

a. What is the executive-level committee commonly called, who typically serves on it, and what is its primary function?
b. Who typically serves on the project development team?
c. What steps would the development team take during system analysis?
d. Why do you think the server and data tapes were damaged?
e. Calculate the following capital budgeting metrics for RSSA's outsourcing plan:
   1. payback period
   2. net present value (NPV)
   3. internal rate of return (IRR)

Discussion Questions

20.1. The approach to long-range AIS planning described in this chapter is important for large organizations with extensive investments in computer facilities. Should small organizations with far fewer information systems employees attempt to implement planning programs? Why or why not? Be prepared to defend your position to the class.

20.2. You are a consultant advising a firm on the design and implementation of a new system. Management has decided to let several employees go after the system is implemented. Some have many years of company service. How would you advise management to communicate this decision to the affected employees? To the entire staff?

20.3. While reviewing a list of benefits from a computer vendor's proposal, you note an item that reads, "Improvements in management decision making—$50,000 per year." How would you interpret this item? What influence should it have on the economic feasibility and the computer acquisition decision?

20.4. For the following, discuss which data-gathering method(s) are most appropriate and why:
  a. Examining the adequacy of internal controls in the purchase requisition procedure
  b. Identifying the controller's information needs
  c. Determining how cash disbursement procedures are actually performed
  d. Surveying employees about the move to a total quality management program
  e. Investigating an increase in uncollectible accounts

20.5. The following problems occurred in a manufacturing firm. What questions should you ask to understand the problem?
  • Customer complaints about product quality have increased.
  • Accounting sees an increase in the number and dollar value of bad-debt write-offs.
  • Operating margins have declined each of the past four years because of higher-than-expected production costs from idle time, overtime, and reworking products.

20.6. Give some examples of systems analysis decisions that involve a trade-off between each of the following pairs of objectives:
  a. economy and usefulness
  b. economy and reliability
  c. economy and customer service
  d. simplicity and usefulness
  e. simplicity and reliability
  f. economy and capacity
  g. economy and flexibility

20.7. For years, Jerry Jingle's dairy production facilities have led the state in sales volume, but recent declines worry him. Customers are satisfied with his products but are troubled by the dairy's late deliveries and incomplete orders. Production employees (not the cows) are concerned about bottlenecks in milk pasteurization and homogenization due to poor job scheduling, mix-ups in customers' orders, and improperly labeled products. How should Jerry address the problems? What data-gathering techniques would be helpful at this early stage?

20.8. A manufacturing firm needed a specialized software program to identify and monitor cost overruns. After an extensive analysis, the company purchased prepackaged software and assigned three programmers to modify it to meet its individual circumstances and processes. After six months of work, during final testing, the company told the programmers to stop all work until further notice. While reading the software vendor's sales agreement, the manufacturing manager found a clause stating that the software could not be changed without the prior written consent of the vendor. The firm had to pay the software vendor an additional fee so it could use the modified software in its manufacturing process. Which aspect(s) of feasibility did the manufacturing firm fail to consider prior to purchasing the software?

20.9. Ajax Manufacturing installed a new bar-code-based inventory tracking system in its warehouse. To close the books each month on a timely basis, the six people who work in the warehouse must scan each item in a 36-hour period while still performing their normal duties. During certain months, when inventory expands to meet seasonal demands, the scan takes as many as 30 hours to complete. In addition, the scanners do not accurately record some inventory items that require low operating temperatures. A recent audit brought to management's attention that the inventory records are not always accurate. Which aspect(s) of feasibility did Ajax fail to consider prior to installing the inventory tracking system?

Problems

20.1. How do you get a grizzled veteran police officer who is used to filling out paper forms to use a computer to process his arrests and casework—especially when he has little or no experience using a computer? That was the problem facing the Chicago Police Department when it decided to implement a relational database system. The system is capable of churning through massive amounts of data to give officers the information they need to fight crime more effectively.

Initially, the department rolled out the case component of the CLEAR (Citizen Law Enforcement Analysis and Reporting) system that provided criminal history and arrest records. The officers hated it, complaining that the system was not user-friendly, that approval from supervisors was complex and involved multiple screens, and that they did not feel properly trained on the system. After listening to the officers' complaints for a year, the department clearly had to do something. *(Adapted from Todd Datz, "No Small Change," CIO (February 15, 2004): 66–72)*

Required

a. Identify as many system analysis and design problems as you can.
b. What could the department have done differently to prevent the officers' complaints?
c. What principles of system analysis and design were violated in this case?

20.2. Mary Smith is the bookkeeper for Dave's Distributing Company, a distributor of soft drinks and juices. Because the company is rather small, Mary performs all daily accounting tasks herself. Dave, the owner of the company, supervises the warehouse/delivery and front office staff, but he also spends much of his time jogging and skiing.

For several years, profits were good, and sales grew faster than industry averages. Although the accounting system was working well, bottlers were pressuring Dave to computerize. With a little guidance from a CPA friend and with no mention to Mary, Dave bought a new computer system and some accounting software. Only one day was required to set up the hardware, install the software, and convert the files. The morning the vendor installed the computer system, Mary's job performance changed dramatically. Although the software company provided two full days of training, Mary resisted learning the new system. As a result, Dave decided she should run both the manual and computer systems for a month to verify the new system's accuracy.

Mary continually complained that she lacked the time and expertise to update both systems by herself. She also complained that she did not understand how to use the new computer system. To keep accounts up to date, Dave spent two to three hours a day running the new system himself. Dave found that much of the time spent running the system was devoted to identifying discrepancies between the computer and manual results. When the error was located, it was usually in the manual system. This significantly increased Dave's confidence in the new system.

At the end of the month, Dave was ready to scrap the manual system, but Mary said she was not ready. Dave went back to skiing and jogging, and Mary went on with the manual system. When the computer system fell behind, Dave again spent time catching it up. He also worked with Mary to try to help her understand how to operate the computer system.

Months later, Dave was very frustrated because he was still keeping the computer system up to date and training Mary. He commented, "I'm sure Mary *knows* how to use the system, but she doesn't seem to *want* to. I can do all the accounting work on the computer in two or three hours a day, but she can't even do it in her normal eight-hour workday. What should I do?"

Required

a. What do you believe is the real cause of Mary's resistance to computers?
b. What events may have contributed to the new system's failure?
c. In retrospect, how should Dave have handled the accounting system computerization?
d. At what point in the decision-making process should Mary have been informed? Should she have had some say in whether the computer was purchased? If so, what should have been the nature of her input? If Mary had not agreed with Dave's decision to acquire the computer, what should Dave have done?
e. A hard decision must be made regarding Mary. Significant efforts have been made to train her, but they have been unsuccessful. What would you recommend at this point? Should she be fired? Threatened with the loss of her job? Moved somewhere else in the business? Given additional training?

20.3. Wright Company's information system was developed in stages over the past five years. During the design process, department heads specified the information and reports they needed. By the time development began, new department heads were in place, and they requested additional reports. Reports were discontinued only when requested by a department head. Few reports were discontinued, and a large number are generated each period.

Management, concerned about the number of reports produced, asked internal auditing to evaluate system effectiveness. They determined that more information was generated than could be used effectively and noted the following reactions:

- Many departments did not act on reports during peak activity periods. They let them accumulate in the hope of catching up later.
- Some had so many reports they did not act at all or misused the information.
- Frequently, no action was taken until another manager needed a decision made. Department heads did not develop a priority system for acting on the information.
- Department heads often developed information from alternative, independent sources. This was easier than searching the reports for the needed data.

Required

a. Explain whether each reaction is a functional or dysfunctional behavioral response.
b. Recommend procedures to eliminate dysfunctional behavior and prevent its recurrence. *(CMA Examination, adapted)*

20.4. The controller of Tim's Travel (TT) is deciding between upgrading the company's existing computer system or replacing it with a new one. Upgrading the four-year-old system will cost $97,500 and extend its useful life for another seven years. The book value is $19,500, although it would sell for $24,000. Upgrading will eliminate one employee at a salary of $19,400; the new computer will eliminate two employees. Annual operating costs are estimated at $15,950 per year. Upgrading is expected to increase profits 3.5% above last year's level of $553,000.

The BetaTech Company has quoted a price of $224,800 for a new computer with a useful life of seven years. Annual operating costs are estimated to be $14,260. The average processing speed of the new computer is 12% faster than that of other systems in its price range, which would increase TT's profits by 4.5%.

Tim's present tax rate is 35%, and the cost of financing is 11%. After seven years, the salvage value, net of tax, would be $12,000 for the new computer and $7,500 for the present system. For tax purposes, computers are depreciated over five full years (six calendar years; a half year the first and last years), and the depreciation percentages are as follows:

Year	Percent (%)
1	20.00
2	32.00
3	19.20
4	11.52
5	11.52
6	5.76

Required

Using a spreadsheet package, prepare an economic feasibility analysis to determine whether TT should rehabilitate the old system or purchase the new computer. As part of the analysis, compute the after-tax cash flows for years 1 through 7 and the payback, NPV, and IRR of each alternative.

20.5. Rossco is considering the purchase of a new computer with the following estimated costs: initial systems design, $54,000; hardware, $74,000; software, $35,000, one-time initial training, $11,000; system installation, $20,000; and file conversion, $12,000. A net reduction of three employees is expected, with average yearly salaries of $40,000. The system will decrease average yearly inventory by $150,000. Annual operating costs will be $30,000 per year.

The expected life of the machine is four years, with an estimated salvage value of zero. The effective tax rate is 40%. All computer purchase costs will be depreciated using the straight-line method over its four-year life. Rossco can invest money made available from the reduction in inventory at its cost of capital of 11%. All cash flows, except for the initial investment and start-up costs, are at the end of the year. Assume 365 days in a year.

Required

Use a spreadsheet to perform a feasibility analysis to determine whether Rossco should purchase the computer. Compute the following as part of the analysis: initial investment, after-tax cash flows for years 1 through 4, payback period, net present value, and internal rate of return.

20.6. A recently completed feasibility study to upgrade XYZ's computer system shows the following benefits. Compensation figures in parentheses include wages, benefits, and payroll taxes.

1. Production
   a. Market forecasts, which take two $400 person-days a month, will be more accurate with software making the calculations.
   b. Effective inventory control will prevent part stockouts and reduce inventory by $1,000,000. XYZ's cost of capital is 20%.
   c. Detailed evaluations of plan changes will increase production flexibility, reduce sales losses, and eliminate two clerks ($75,000 each).

2. Engineering
   a. Computerized updating of bills of material and operations lists will save 40% of an engineer's ($100,000) and 25% of a clerk's ($60,000) time.
   b. Computerized calculations of labor allocations, rates, and bonus details will save 40% of a clerk's ($80,000) time.

3. Sales. Improved reporting will enable the five-person sales staff to react more quickly to the market, producing a $10,000 per person sales increase.

4. Marketing. Revised reports and an improved forecasting system will increase net income by $50,000.

5. Accounting
   a. Quickly determining new product costs will save 30% of the accountant's ($100,000) time.
   b. An incentive earnings system will save 40% of the payroll clerk's ($60,000) time.

Required

As a board member, which of the benefits can you defend as relevant to the system's cost justification? Calculate how much XYZ will save with the new system.

(SMAC Examination, adapted)

20.7. The following list presents specific project activities and their scheduled starting and completion times:

Activity	Starting Date	Ending Date
A	Jan. 5	Feb. 9
B	Jan. 5	Jan. 19
C	Jan. 26	Feb. 23
D	Mar. 2	Mar. 23
E	Mar. 2	Mar. 16
F	Feb. 2	Mar. 16
G	Mar. 30	Apr. 20
H	Mar. 23	Apr. 27

Required

a. Using a format similar to that in Figure 20-3, prepare a Gantt chart for this project. Assume that each activity starts on a Monday and ends on a Friday.
b. Assume that today is February 16 and that activities A and B have been completed, C is half completed, F is a quarter completed, and the other activities have not commenced. Record this information on your Gantt chart. Is the project behind schedule, on schedule, or ahead of schedule? Explain.
c. Discuss the relative merits of the Gantt chart and PERT as project planning and control tools.

20.8. Recent years have brought an explosive growth in electronic communication. Laptops, netbooks, e-readers, personal digital assistants, sophisticated cell phones, fax machines, e-mail, teleconferencing, office productivity software, and sophisticated management information systems have changed the way information is received, processed, and transmitted. With the decreasing costs of computer equipment and the increasing power of automation, the full impact of computerization has yet to be felt. Although the development of computer applications is directed at being user friendly or user oriented, the integration of computers into the organization has had both positive and negative effects on employees.

Required

a. Describe the benefits companies and employees receive from electronic communications.
b. Discuss the organizational impact of introducing new electronic communication systems.
c. Explain (1) why an employee might resist the introduction of electronic communication systems and (2) the steps an organization can take to alleviate this resistance.
(CMA Examination, adapted)

20.9. PWR manufactures precision nozzles for fire hoses. Ronald Paige, an engineer, started the corporation and it has experienced steady growth. Reporting to Ronald are six vice presidents representing marketing, production, research and development, information services, finance, and human resources. The information services department was established last year when PWR began developing a new information system consisting of a server connected to each employee's personal computer. The PCs can download and upload data to the server. PWR is still designing and developing applications for its new system. Ronald received a letter from the external auditor and called a meeting with his vice presidents to review the recommendation that PWR form an information systems steering committee.

Required

    a. Explain why the auditors would recommend an information systems steering committee, and discuss its specific responsibilities. What advantages can the committee offer PWR?

    b. Identify the PWR managers most likely to serve on the committee. *(CMA Examination, adapted)*

20.10. Businesses often modify or replace their financial information system to keep pace with their growth and take advantage of improved IT. This requires a substantial time and resource commitment. When an organization changes its AIS, a systems analysis takes place.

Required

    a. Explain the purpose and reasons for surveying an organization's existing system.

    b. Explain the activities commonly performed during systems analysis.

    c. Systems analysis is often performed by a project team composed of a systems analyst, a management accountant, and other knowledgeable and helpful people. What is the management accountant's role in systems analysis? *(CMA Examination, adapted)*

20.11. Don Richardson, JEM Corporation's vice president of marketing, is part of a management team that for several months has been discussing plans to develop a new line of business. Rumors about the major organizational changes that may be required to implement the strategic plan have been circulating for months.

    Several employees who are anxious about the expected changes confronted Don. The sales manager said, "It is imperative that we speak to you right away. The employees are very apprehensive about the proposed changes, and their job performance has slacked off." The accounting manager added, "That's right. My staff are asking me all sorts of questions about this new line of business, and I don't have any answers for them. They're not buying the 'We will make an official announcement soon' line any longer. I suspect that some of them are already looking for jobs in case the department changes phase out their positions."

    Implementing organizational change is one of the most demanding assignments an executive faces. It has been suggested that every change requires three steps: unfreezing the current situation, implementing the change, and refreezing the effected change. This view, however, lacks the specific details needed by an operating manager who must initiate the change.

Required

    a. Explain why employees resist organizational change.

    b. Discuss ways JEM Corporation can alleviate employee resistance to change. *(CMA Examination, adapted)*

20.12. Remnants, Inc., with headquarters in St. Louis, manufactures designer clothing. The company markets and services its products by region, with each functioning as a profit center. Each region has a manager, an accounting department, a human resources department, and several area offices to market and service the products. Each area office has sales, service, and administrative departments whose managers report to an area manager.

    The New York area office departed from the standard organizational structure by establishing a branch office to market and service the firm's products in Boston. A branch manager who reports directly to the New York area manager heads the local office.

    The Boston branch manager is encouraging the New York area manager to consider a new information system to handle the local branch's growing information needs. The New York area manager and the eastern region manager want to establish a project team with employees from the region, area, and branch office. The team will assess the information needs at the Boston branch office and develop system recommendations. The following employees have been appointed to the project team, with Keith Nash as chairperson:

Eastern Region Office
Kurt Johnson, Budget Supervisor
Sally Brown, Training Director

New York Area Office
Keith Nash, Administrative Director

Boston Branch
Heidi Meyer, Branch and Sales Manager
Bobby Roos, Assistant Branch and Service Manager
Joe Gonzalez, Salesperson
Juana Martinez, Serviceperson

Required

a. Project team members contribute their skills to help accomplish a given objective. Characteristics of group members can influence the functioning and effectiveness of a project team. Identify some of these characteristics.
b. Given the team's composition, what sources of conflict can you see arising among its members? Do you think the group will succeed in its objective to develop an IS for the Boston branch office? Why or why not?
c. What contribution would a budget supervisor make in a project team?

20.13.   Managers at some companies face an ongoing systems development crisis: IS departments develop systems that businesses cannot or will not use. At the heart of the problem is a "great divide" that separates the world of business and the world of IS. Few departments seem able or ready to cross this gap.

One reason for the crisis is that many companies are looking for ways to improve existing, out-of-date systems or to build new ones. Another is the widespread use of PC-based systems that have spawned high user expectations that IS departments are not meeting. Users seek more powerful applications than are available on many older systems.

The costs of the great divide can be devastating. An East Coast chemical company spent over $1 million on a budgeting and control system that was never used. The systems department's expertise was technical excellence, not budgets. As a result, the new system completely missed the mark when it came to meeting business needs. A Midwestern bank used an expensive computer-aided software engineering (CASE) tool to develop a system that users ignored because there had been no design planning. A senior analyst for the bank said, "They built the system right; but unfortunately they didn't build the right system."

Required

a. What is the great divide in the systems development process? What causes the gap?
b. What would you suggest to solve this information crisis?
c. Discuss the role a systems designer, business manager, and end user can take to narrow the great divide.
d. Who plays the most vital role in the effective development of the system?

20.14.   Joanne Grey, a senior consultant, and David Young, a junior consultant, are conducting a systems analysis for a client to determine the feasibility of integrating and automating clerical functions. Joanne had previously worked for the client, but David was a recent hire.

The first morning on the job, Joanne directed David to interview a departmental supervisor and learn as much as possible about department operations. David introduced himself and said, "Your company has hired us to study how your department works so we can make recommendations on how to improve its efficiency and lower its cost. I would like to interview you to determine what goes on in your department."

David questioned the supervisor for 30 minutes but found him to be uncooperative. David gave Joanne an oral report on how the interview went and what he learned about the department.

Required

Describe several flaws in David's approach to obtaining information. How should this task have been performed?

Case 20-1 Audio Visual Corporation

Audio Visual Corporation (AVC) manufactures and sells visual display equipment. Headquartered in Boston, it has seven sales offices with nearby warehouses that carry its inventory of new equipment and replacement parts. AVC has a departmentalized manufacturing plant with assembly, maintenance, engineering, scheduling, and cost accounting departments as well as several component parts departments.

When management decided to upgrade its AIS, they installed a mainframe at headquarters and local area networks at each sales office. The IS manager and four systems analysts were hired shortly before they integrated the new computer and the existing AIS. The other IS employees have been with the company for years.

During its early years, AVC had a centralized decision-making organization. Top management formulated all plans and directed all operations. As the company expanded, decision making was decentralized, although data processing was highly centralized. Departments coordinated their plans with the corporate office but had the freedom to develop their own sales programs. However, information problems developed, and the IS department was asked to improve the company's information processing system once the new equipment was installed.

Before acquiring the new computer, the systems analysts studied the existing AIS, identified its weaknesses, and designed applications to solve them. In the 18 months since the new equipment was acquired, the following applications were redesigned or developed: payroll, production scheduling, financial statement preparation, customer billing, raw materials usage, and finished goods inventory. The departments affected by the changes were rarely consulted until the system was operational.

Recently the president stated, "The systems people are doing a good job, and I have complete confidence in their work. I talk to them frequently, and they have encountered no difficulties in doing their work. We paid a lot of money for the new equipment, and the systems people certainly cost enough, but the new equipment and new IS staff should solve all our problems."

Two additional conversations regarding the new AIS took place.

BILL TAYLOR, IS MANAGER AND JERRY ADAMS, PLANT MANAGER

JERRY: Bill, you're trying to run my plant for me. I'm the manager, and you keep interfering. I wish you would mind your own business.

BILL: You've got a job to do, and so do I. As we analyzed the information needed for production scheduling and by top management, we saw where we could improve the workflow. Now that the system is operational, you can't reroute work and change procedures, because that would destroy the value of the information we're processing. And while I'm on that subject, we can't trust the information we're getting from production. The documents we receive from production contain a lot of errors.

JERRY: I'm responsible for the efficient operation of production. I'm the best judge of production efficiency. The system you installed reduced my workforce and increased the workload of the remaining employees, but it hasn't improved anything. In fact, it might explain the high error rate in the documents.

BILL: This new computer cost a lot of money, and I'm trying to make sure the company gets its money's worth.

JERRY ADAMS, PLANT MANAGER AND TERRY WILLIAMS, HUMAN RESOURCES MANAGER

JERRY: My best production assistant, the one I'm grooming to be a supervisor, told me he was thinking of quitting. When I asked why, he said he didn't enjoy the work anymore. He's not the only one who is unhappy. The supervisors and department heads no longer have a voice in establishing production schedules. This new computer system took away the contribution we made to company planning and direction. We're going back to when top management made all the decisions. I have more production problems now than I ever had. It boils down to my management team's lack of interest. I know the problem is in my area, but I thought you could help me.

TERRY: I have no recommendations, but I've had similar complaints from purchasing and shipping. We should explore your concerns during tomorrow's plant management meeting.

ANSWER THE FOLLOWING QUESTIONS:

1. Identify the problems the new computer system created, and discuss what caused them.
2. How could AVC have avoided the problems? How can they prevent them in the future?

(CMA Examination, adapted)

AIS IN ACTION SOLUTIONS

Quiz Key

1. Which of the following is NOT a reason why companies make changes to their AIS?
   a. gain a competitive advantage [AIS changes can help a company increase the quality, quantity, and speed of information, which leads to improved decision making and a greater competitive advantage.]
   b. increase productivity [Using computers in an AIS can automate repetitive tasks, which allows more work to be done in the same amount of time. This increases productivity.]
   c. keep up with business growth [As a company grows, its old system will likely not be able to handle the increase in demand and thus will require changes to the AIS to accommodate the growth.]
   d. downsize company operations [A smaller company requires a smaller AIS. For instance, downsizing may prompt a company to move from centralized decision making to decentralized decision making. As a result, the AIS would most likely shift from using a mainframe computer to a set of networked workstations.]
   ▶ e. All of the above are reasons why companies change an AIS. [Correct.]

2. Which of the following is the planning technique that identifies implementation activities and their relationships, constructs a network of arrows and nodes, and then determines the critical path through the network?
   a. Gantt chart [Incorrect. A Gantt chart is a bar chart that displays dates and stages of completion for each project task. See Figure 20-3.]
   ▶ b. PERT diagram [Correct.]
   c. physical model [Incorrect. A physical model illustrates how a system functions. It describes document flows, computer processes, equipment used, and other physical elements of the system.]
   d. data flow diagram [Incorrect. A data flow diagram is used to document a system with four basic symbols—i.e., squares, circles, parallel lines, and arrows.]

3. The purchasing department is designing a new AIS. Who is best able to determine departmental information requirements?
   a. steering committee [Incorrect. The steering committee is a high-level executive committee that oversees the function of the information system; they probably do not understand the purchasing department's information requirements.]
   b. controller [Incorrect. The controller is the manager of the accounting department and probably does not understand all of the purchasing department's information requirements.]
   c. top management [Incorrect. Top management in such cases should provide direction and resources, not detailed analysis of the purchasing department's information requirements.]
   ▶ d. purchasing department [Correct. The people who will actually be using the new system are in the best position to determine the system's information requirements.]

4. Which of the following is the correct order of the steps in systems analysis?
   a. initial investigation, determination of information needs and system requirements, feasibility study, system survey [Incorrect. See Figure 20-4.]
   b. determination of information needs and system requirements, system survey, feasibility study, initial investigation [Incorrect. See Figure 20-4.]
   c. system survey, initial investigation, determination of information needs and system requirements, feasibility study [Incorrect. See Figure 20-4.]
   ▶ d. initial investigation, system survey, feasibility study, determination of information needs and system requirements [Correct. See Figure 20-4.]

5. Which of the following is the long-range planning document that specifies what the system will consist of, how it will be developed, who will develop it, how needed resources will be acquired, and its overall vision?
    a. steering committee agenda [Incorrect. The steering committee's agenda would involve discussing all aspects of the information system, not just system development.]
    ▶ b. master plan [Correct.]
    c. systems development life cycle [Incorrect. The systems development life cycle is not a long-range planning document but a conceptual framework that applies to systems development in general.]
    d. project development plan [Incorrect. The project development plan is used for individual projects. It includes such items as cost/benefit analyses, developmental and operational requirements, and a schedule of activities for developing and operating the new system.]

6. Resistance is often a reaction to the methods of instituting change rather than to change itself.
    ▶ a. true [Correct. Although change is generally difficult, the way change is instituted can either facilitate the change or hinder the change.]
    b. false [Incorrect.]

7. Increased error rates, disruptions, and sabotage are examples of which of the following?
    ▶ a. aggression [Correct. These are classic symptoms of aggression as a reaction to change.]
    b. avoidance [Incorrect. Avoidance is best illustrated by the statement that if a person does not use the new system, maybe it will go away.]
    c. projection [Incorrect. Projection refers to blaming all problems on the new system.]
    d. payback [Incorrect. Payback is an economic feasibility metric.]

8. What is often the most significant problem a company encounters in designing, developing, and implementing a system?
    ▶ a. the human element [Correct. A system will fail without the support of the people it is designed to serve—for a variety of reasons, including fear of change, poor communication and training, disruption of work, and lack of top-management support.]
    b. technology [Incorrect. The technology a system employs is normally tested for functionality prior to its implementation in a new system.]
    c. legal challenges [Incorrect. With proper system planning and design, systems can meet all laws and regulations.]
    d. planning for the new system [Incorrect. Proper planning can actually prevent problems from occurring.]

9. Determining whether the organization has access to people who can design, implement, and operate the proposed system is referred to as which of the following?
    a. technical feasibility [Incorrect. Technical feasibility refers to whether the system can be developed and implemented with existing technology.]
    ▶ b. operational feasibility [Correct. Operational feasibility refers to whether the organization and its people can actually design, implement, and operate the system.]
    c. legal feasibility [Incorrect. Legal feasibility refers to whether the system complies with all applicable laws and regulations.]
    d. scheduling feasibility [Incorrect. Scheduling feasibility refers to whether the system can be analyzed, planned, designed, and implemented in the time allocated.]
    e. economic feasibility [Incorrect. Economic feasibility refers to whether the system's benefits outweigh its costs.]

10. Which of the following is NOT one of the tangible or intangible benefits a company might obtain from a new system?
    a. cost savings [Although this answer is correct, there are other correct answers. Automated systems can reduce clerical costs, as well as other related costs.]

    b. improved customer service and productivity [Although this answer is correct, there are other correct answers. New systems can integrate data from several sources to provide fast, reliable information to assist customers and increase productivity.]

    c. improved decision making [Although this answer is correct, there are other correct answers. Better information greatly increases the likelihood of better decisions.]

    d. improved data processing [Although this answer is correct, there are other correct answers. Better-designed systems using newer technology improve data processing and reduce the likelihood of human error.

▶ **e.** All are benefits of a new system. [Correct.]

Comprehensive Problem Solution

a. *What is the executive-level committee commonly called, who typically serves on it, and what is its primary function?*

An information systems steering committee, which plans and oversees the IS function, consists of high-level management people, such as the controller and systems and user-department management. The committee sets IS policies; ensures top-management participation, guidance, and control; and facilitates the coordination and integration of systems activities.

b. *Who typically serves on the project development team?*

The project development team includes systems analysts, systems specialists, managers, accountants, systems auditors, and users.

c. *What steps would the development team take during system analysis?*

RSSA's development team will do an initial assessment of management's plans for moving the help desk. They will survey the existing system to determine what it does, what the company should continue to use, and what should be changed for the new system. They will complete a feasibility analysis to determine the technical, operational, legal, scheduling, and economic feasibility of the new system. Then the team will determine the system's information needs and requirements. Lastly, the team will prepare a systems analysis report.

d. *Why do you think the server and data tapes were damaged?*

Change is usually difficult for people and organizations. When operations are outsourced, employees can lose their jobs. Apparently, some employees exhibited aggressive behavior toward the new system.

e. *Calculate the following capital budgeting metrics for RSSA's outsourcing plan:*

    1. payback period
    2. net present value (NPV)
    3. internal rate of return (IRR)

Table 20-9 summarizes the cash spent or saved each year of RSSA's proposed project. The initial contract payment and the lease cancellation penalty occur at the beginning of the project, referred to as year 0. For simplicity's sake, we assume cash flows take place at the end of the year. For years 1 through 5, the $525,000 expenditure for operations, the $750,000 personnel savings, and the $360,000 lease cancellation savings are entered. The last line of Table 20-9 shows the net cash flows for each period, which are total cash inflows less total cash outflows.

1 Payback

The payback period is when cash inflows equal cash outflows. Table 20-10, which shows cumulative net cash flow totals, indicates that breakeven occurs during year 4. To determine how far into year 4, divide year-3 negative cumulative cash flows of $145,000 by year-4 net cash flows of $585,000. It took 25% of the year (145,000/585,000), or 3.25 years, to get to payback.

2 Net present value

Payback period does not take into consideration the time value of money (a dollar received today is worth more than the same dollar received a year from now). The net present value (NPV) techniques takes the time value of money into consideration by using the company's cost of capital, called its discount rate. This rate is the company's average cost of borrowing capital.

Net present value is calculated by multiplying each year's net cash flow by a discount factor calculated using the formula $1/(1+r)n$, where r = the company's discount rate and n = the number of time periods between time 0 and the designated cash flow. For example, if the cash flow occurred at the end of year 4, n would equal 4. The discount factor is calculated for each time period and multiplied by the net cash flow for that period. When all net cash flows have been discounted to their present value, they are totaled to determine the project's NPV.

As a practical matter, most people do not use the formula to make the calculations, but rather use a business calculator or the NFV function in Microsoft Excel.

Projects with a positive NPV earn an estimated return in excess of the company's discount rate and are financially feasible. Projects with a negative NPV are usually rejected. As shown in Table 20-11, RSSA's NPV is $262,100 and the project would likely be acceptable to management.

3 Internal rate of return

The NPV calculation does not calculate an estimated rate of return. This limitation is resolved by calculating an internal rate of return (IRR), which is the discount rate that produces a NPV of zero. Calculating an IRR is a trial-and-error process of changing the discount rate until NPV equals zero. Because this is so tedious, IRR is usually calculated using a business calculator or the IRR function in a spreadsheet program. The internal rate of return for this project is 16.35% (rounded).

TABLE 20-9 Cash Flows for RSSA

Year	0	1	2	3	4	5
CASH OUTFLOWS						
Initial Contract	−$1,750,000					
Lease Cancellation Penalty	−$150,000					
Center Operations Cost		−$525,000	−$525,000	−$525,000	−$525,000	−$525,000
Total Cash Outflows	−$1,900,000	−$525,000	−$525,000	−$525,000	−$525,000	−$525,000
CASH INFLOWS						
Personnel Savings		$750,000	$750,000	$750,000	$750,000	$750,000
Lease Cancellation Savings		$360,000	$360,000	$360,000	$360,000	$360,000
Total Cash Inflows	$0	$1,110,000	$1,110,000	$1,110,000	$1,110,000	$1,110,000
NET CASH FLOWS	−$1,900,000	$585,000	$585,000	$585,000	$585,000	$585,000

TABLE 20-10 Payback for RSSA's Proposed Project

Year	0	1	2	3	4	5
Net Cash Flows	−$1,900,000	$585,000	$585,000	$585,000	$585,000	$585,000
Cumulative Cash Flows	−$1,900,000	−$1,315,000	−$730,000	−$145,000	$440,000	$1,025,000
Payback	3.25 years or 3 years, 3 months					

TABLE 20-11 The Net Present Value of RSSA's Proposed Project

NET CASH FLOWS	−$1,900,000	$585,000	$585,000	$585,000	$585,000	$585,000
Present Value Factors	1	0.9009	0.8116	0.7312	0.6587	0.5935
Present Value Amounts	−$1,900,000	$527,027	$474,786	$427,752	$385,340	$347,198
Net Present Value	$262,103					
IRR	16.35%					

AIS Development Strategies

INTEGRATIVE CASE SHOPPERS MART

Ann Christy is elated that the system Shoppers Mart (SM) so badly needed was approved and that she and her team have accurately assessed company needs. Now Ann needs to determine whether to purchase the software, develop it in-house, or outsource system development and operation. More specifically, she needs answers to these questions:

1. Can Ann buy the software she needs? If so, how should she buy hardware and software and select a vendor?

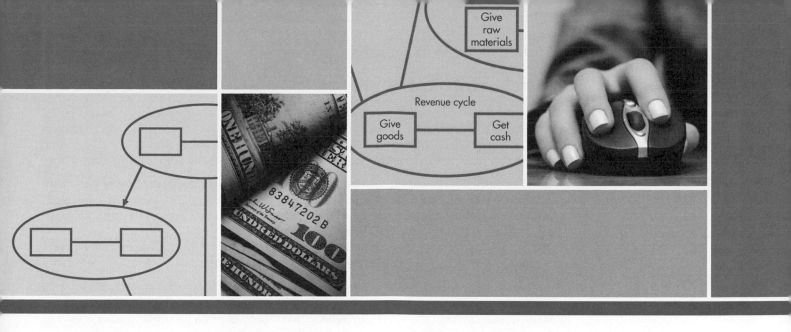

2. How do companies develop software in-house? Is this the best approach for SM?

3. How extensively should SM use end-user-developed software?

4. Should SM improve its existing system or redesign its business processes and develop a system to support them?

5. Is outsourcing the information system a viable alternative to obtain a new system? Do the benefits of outsourcing outweigh its risks?

6. If SM decides to develop the system in-house, should it use prototyping or computer-assisted software engineering?

Ann decided to investigate design alternatives to determine the best course of action for Shoppers Mart.

Introduction

Companies have experienced the following difficulties when developing an AIS:

- Development requests are so numerous that projects are backlogged for years.
- Users discover that the new AIS does not meet their needs. This occurs because users find it hard to visualize how the AIS will operate by reviewing design documentation and because developers who do not understand business or user needs find it hard to make meaningful suggestions for improvement.
- Development takes so long the system no longer meets company needs. Fannie Mae spent eight years and $100 million developing the world's largest loan accounting system. Unfortunately, it no longer met many of Fannie Mae's needs.
- Users do not adequately specify their needs because they do not know what they need or they cannot communicate the needs to systems developers.
- Changes are difficult to make after requirements are frozen. If users keep changing requirements, the AIS may take forever to finish.

In this chapter, you learn three ways to obtain an information system: purchasing software, developing software in-house, and hiring a company to develop and operate the system. You also learn three ways to improve the development process: business process redesign, prototyping, and computer-aided software engineering tools.

Purchasing Software

In the early days of computers, it was difficult to buy software that met user needs. That is no longer the case. A Deloitte & Touche survey found that most chief information officers expect to replace their current systems with commercially available packages. Consider the following examples:

- Hard Rock Café purchased customer relationship software and mailed promotional offers to 225,000 customers. A year later, profits from the increased traffic paid for the new system.
- WellPoint Health Networks installed payroll, benefits, and human resources software so employees could manage their benefits, saving $400,000 a year.
- Pacific Gas & Electric responded to California's power deregulation by spending three years and $204 million installing the largest customer information system in the utility industry.

Canned software is sold to users with similar requirements. *Turnkey systems* are software and hardware sold as a package. The vendor installs the system and the user "turns on the key." Many turnkey systems are written by vendors who specialize in a particular industry, such as doctors, auto repair shops, restaurants, and retail stores.

A major problem with canned software is that it may not meet all of a company's information needs. This is overcome by modifying the software. About 90% of Dow Chemical's software has been modified to match its business processes. The rest was written in-house. It is best when the vendor modifies the software, as unauthorized modifications may not be supported by the vendor and may make the program unreliable.

Companies can rent software from *application service providers (ASPs)*, who deliver software over the Internet. This provides scalability as the business grows and global access to information. It automates software upgrades, allows companies to focus on core financial competencies rather than information technology (IT) issues, and can reduce software costs and administrative overhead.

Companies that buy AIS software follow the normal systems development life cycle (SDLC) except for the following:

- During conceptual systems design, companies determine whether software that meets AIS requirements is available and, if so, whether to buy it or create their own.
- Some physical design and implementation and conversion steps can be omitted. For example, the company usually does not need to design, code, and test program modules or document the computer program.

Selecting a Vendor

Hardware, service, maintenance, and other AIS resource decisions can be made independently of the decision to make or purchase software, although they may depend on the software decision.

Vendors are found by referrals, at conferences, in industry magazines, on the Internet, or in the phone book. Choosing must be done carefully because vendors with little experience, insufficient capital, or a poor product go out of business and leave their customers and products with no support or recourse. Problems can occur even when established vendors are selected. For example, when Texas selected IBM to consolidate data centers across the state, service levels dropped dramatically, and routine tasks took far too long to perform. The problem was attributed to poor project requirements and selecting the vendor with the lowest bid. IBM almost lost the contract after it failed to back up critical systems.

Acquiring Hardware and Software

Companies that buy large or complex systems send vendors a *request for proposal (RFP)*, asking them to propose a system that meets their needs by a specified date. The best proposals are investigated to verify that company requirements can be met. Using an RFP is important because it:

1. *Saves time.*   The same information is provided to all vendors, eliminating repetitive interviews and questions.
2. *Simplifies the decision-making process.*   All responses are in the same format and based on the same information.
3. *Reduces errors.*   The chances of overlooking important factors are reduced.

4. *Avoids potential for disagreement.*   Both parties possess the same expectations, and pertinent information is captured in writing.

RFPs for exact hardware and software specifications have lower total costs and require less time to prepare and evaluate, but they do not permit the vendor to recommend alternative technology. Requesting a system that meets specific performance objectives and requirements leaves technical issues to the vendor but is harder to evaluate and often results in more costly bids.

The more information a company provides vendors, the better their chances of receiving a system that meets its requirements. Vendors need detailed specifications, including required applications, inputs and outputs, files and databases, frequency and methods of file updating and inquiry, and unique requirements. It is essential to distinguish mandatory requirements from desirable features.

Evaluating Proposals and Selecting a System

Proposals that lack important information, fail to meet minimum requirements, or are ambiguous are eliminated. Proposals passing this preliminary screening are compared with system requirements to determine whether all mandatory requirements are met and how many desirable requirements are met. Top vendors are invited to demonstrate their system using company-supplied data to measure system performance and validate vendor's claims. Table 21-1 presents hardware, software, and vendor evaluation criteria.

TABLE 21-1 Hardware, Software, and Vendor Evaluation Criteria

Hardware evaluation	Are hardware costs reasonable, based on capabilities and features?
	Are processing speed and capabilities adequate for the intended use?
	Are secondary storage capabilities adequate?
	Are the input and output speeds and capabilities adequate?
	Is the system expandable?
	Is the hardware based on old technology that will soon to be out-of-date?
	Is the hardware available now? If not, when?
	Is the hardware compatible with existing hardware, software, and peripherals?
	How do performance evaluations compare with competitors?
	What are the availability and cost of support and maintenance?
	What warranties come with the system?
	Is financing available (if applicable)?
Software evaluation	Does the software meet all mandatory specifications?
	How well does the software meet desirable specifications?
	Will program modifications be required to meet company needs?
	Does the software have adequate control capabilities?
	Is the performance (speed, accuracy, reliability) adequate?
	How many companies use the software? Are they satisfied?
	Is documentation adequate?
	Is the software compatible with existing software?
	Was the software demonstration/test drive adequate?
	Does the software have an adequate warranty?
	Is the software flexible, easily maintained, and user-friendly?
	Is online inquiry of files and records possible?
	Will the vendor keep the package up to date?
Vendor evaluation	How long has the vendor been in business?
	Is the vendor financially stable and secure?
	How experienced is the vendor with the hardware and software?
	Does the vendor stand behind its products? How good is its warranty?
	Does the vendor regularly update its products?
	Does the vendor provide financing?
	Will the vendor put promises in a contract?
	Will the vendor supply a list of customer references?
	Does the vendor have a reputation for reliability and dependability?
	Does the vendor provide timely support and maintenance?
	Does the vendor provide implementation and installation support?
	Does the vendor have high-quality, responsive, and experienced personnel?
	Does the vendor provide training?

System performance can be compared several ways. A ***benchmark problem*** is an input, processing, and output task typical of what the new AIS will perform. ***Point scoring*** assigns a weight to each evaluation criterion based on its importance. For each criterion, vendors are scored based on how well their proposals meet the requirement, and the weighted score totals are compared. In Table 21-2, vendor 3 offers the best system because its system scored 190 points more than vendor 2 did.

A ***requirement costing*** estimates the cost of purchasing or developing unavailable features. Total AIS costs, which is the cost of acquiring the system and the cost of developing the unavailable features, provides an equitable basis for comparing systems.

Because neither point scoring nor requirements costing is totally objective, the final choice among vendor proposals is not clear-cut. Point scoring weights and scores are assigned subjectively, and dollar estimates of costs and benefits are not included. Requirement costing overlooks intangible factors such as reliability and vendor support.

Once the best AIS is identified, the software is thoroughly test-driven, other users are contacted to determine their satisfaction with the choice, vendor personnel are evaluated, and proposal details are confirmed to verify that the best AIS on paper is the best in practice. The lessons Geophysical Systems learned from its vendor selection highlight the importance of a thorough vendor evaluation (see Focus 21-1).

TABLE 21-2 Point Scoring Evaluation of Vendor Proposals

		Vendor 1		Vendor 2		Vendor 3	
Criterion	Weight	Score	Weighted Score	Score	Weighted Score	Score	Weighted Score
Hardware compatibility	60	6	360	7	420	8	480
Hardware speed	30	6	180	10	300	5	150
Memory expansion	60	5	300	7	420	8	480
Hardware current	30	9	270	9	270	6	180
Software compatibility	90	7	630	7	630	9	810
Online inquiry capabilities	40	9	360	10	400	8	320
Controls	50	7	350	6	300	9	450
Positive references	40	10	400	8	320	6	240
Documentation	30	9	270	8	240	7	210
Easily maintained; updated regularly	50	7	350	8	400	9	450
Network capabilities	50	8	400	7	350	8	400
Vendor support	70	6	420	9	630	10	700
Totals			**4,290**		**4,680**		**4,870**

 **A Software Purchase That Went Awry**

Geophysical Systems Corporation (GSC) developed a sonar device to analyze the production potential of oil and gas discoveries. GSC needed software to analyze the data generated by the sonar device and paid Seismograph Service $20 million to create it. When the Seismograph system could not accurately process the massive volume of data and perform the complex computations needed, GSC clients canceled their contracts. GSC went from yearly sales of $40 million and profits of $6 million to filing for bankruptcy two years later.

GSC sued, claiming Seismograph's system did not perform as promised and that Seismograph knew that before it began development. The jury awarded GSC $48 million for lost profits and the cost of the computer system. Seismograph appealed, claiming its system did work and that GSC's decline resulted from a slump in oil prices.

GSC's experience is common; many systems development projects do not produce the intended results.

Development by In-House Information Systems Departments

Organizations develop *custom software* when doing so provides a significant competitive advantage. There is little benefit to a custom-written payroll or accounts receivable system, whereas there may be significant benefits to sophisticated, just-in-time inventory management or product manufacturing software.

The hurdles that must be overcome to develop quality software are the significant amounts of time required, the complexity of the system, poor requirements, insufficient planning, inadequate communication and cooperation, lack of qualified staff, and poor top management support.

Custom software is created in-house or by an outside company hired to write the software or assemble it from its inventory of program modules. When using an outside developer, a company maintains control over the development process as follows:

- Carefully select a developer that has experience in the company's industry and an in-depth understanding of how the company conducts its business.
- Sign a contract that rigorously defines the relationship between the company and the developer, places responsibility for meeting system requirements on the developer, and allows the project to be discontinued if key conditions are not met.
- Plan the project in detail and frequently monitor each step in the development.
- Communicate frequently and effectively.
- Control all costs and minimize cash outflows until the project is accepted.

There is no single right answer to the build-or-buy decision. Different companies come to different conclusions. After developing its own software, Gillette decided to purchase canned software when possible to gain a greater competitive advantage from deciding *how* software should be used rather than determining *what* software should be used and then creating it. If canned software does not meet all of Gillette's needs, it is modified using high-level development tools.

Pepsi moved in the opposite direction. It bought most of its mainframe software but, after moving to a client/server architecture, it could not find software sophisticated enough to meet its needs. Although Pepsi still buys software when it can find it, it has created most of its software.

Chapter 20 discusses in more depth the process used to develop custom software.

End-User-Developed Software

After the automobile was introduced, a famous sociologist predicted that the automobile market would not exceed 2 million cars because only that many people would be willing to serve as chauffeurs. It was once predicted that the telephone system would collapse because the geometric growth in calls would require everyone to be telephone operators. Instead, equipment was developed that automated operator functions.

After the introduction of computers, an expert claimed that the demand for information systems would grow so astronomically that almost everyone would have to become a programmer. Does this sound familiar? The solution is to help end users meet their own information needs. As with telephones, technology is being developed to automate much of the process for us. Just as most people have learned to drive automobiles, so will inexpensive PCs, a wide variety of powerful and inexpensive software, increased computer literacy, easier-to-use programming tools, and the Internet allow most organizations and people to meet their information needs.

End-user computing (EUC) is the hands-on development, use, and control of computer-based information systems by users. EUC is people using IT to meet their information needs rather than relying on systems professionals. For example, a savings and loan in California wanted a system to track loan reserve requirements. When the information systems (IS) department said the system would take 18 months to develop, the loan department used a PC and a database program to develop a functional program in one day. Enhancing the program took several more days. The loan department not only cut the development time from 18 months to a few days, but also got the exact information it needed because users developed the system themselves.

The following are examples of appropriate end-user development:

- Retrieving information from company databases to produce simple reports or to answer one-time queries
- Performing "what-if," sensitivity, or statistical analyses
- Developing applications using software such as a spreadsheet or a database system
- Preparing schedules, such as depreciation schedules and loan amortizations

End-user development is inappropriate for complex systems, such as those that process a large number of transactions or update database records. Therefore, it is not used for processing payroll, accounts receivables and payables, general ledger, or inventory.

As end users meet their information needs, they realize they can use computers to meet more and more information needs. Increased access to data also creates many new uses and information needs. The result is a tremendous ongoing growth in end-user computing.

The growth in end-user computing has altered the information system staff's role. They continue to develop and maintain transaction processing systems and companywide databases. In addition, they provide users with technical advice and operational support and make as much information available to end users as possible. Although this has created more work for the IS staff, it is counterbalanced by a decreased demand for traditional services. If the trend in end-user computing continues, it will represent 75% to 95% of all information processing by the end of the next decade.

Advantages and Disadvantages of End-User Computing

End-user computing offers the following advantages:

- *User creation, control, and implementation.* Users, rather than the IS department, control the development process. Users decide whether a system should be developed and what information is important. This ownership helps users develop better systems.
- *Systems that meet user needs.* Systems that are developed by end users are more likely to meet user needs. Users discover flaws that IS people do not catch. Many of the user-analyst-programmer communication problems in traditional program development are avoided.
- *Timeliness.* Much of the lengthy delay inherent in traditional systems development is avoided, such as time-consuming cost/benefit analyses, detailed requirements definitions, and the delays and red tape of the approval process.
- *Freeing up of systems resources.* The more information needs users meet, the more time the IS department can spend on other development and maintenance activities. This reduces both the visible and the invisible backlog of systems development projects.
- *Versatility and ease of use.* Most end-user computing software is easy to understand and use. Users can change the information they produce or modify their application any time their requirements change. With a laptop computer, employees can complete work at home, on a plane—almost anywhere.

However, there are significant drawbacks to end-user computing and to eliminating the involvement of analysts or programmers in the development process.

- *Logic and development errors.* With little experience in systems development, end users are more likely to make errors and less likely to recognize when errors have occurred. They may solve the wrong problem, poorly define system requirements, apply an inappropriate analytical method, use the wrong software, use incomplete or outdated information, use faulty logic, or incorrectly use formulas or software commands. An oil and gas company developed a complex spreadsheet that showed that a proposed acquisition was profitable. When their CPA firm tested the model and agreed with it, a board of directors meeting was scheduled to propose the acquisition. Shortly before the meeting, a presenter tested the model so that he could understand how it worked and answer tough questions. He discovered formulas that distorted the projections, so he called in the creator and the CPA firm. The corrected formulas showed a significant loss on the acquisition. The board presentation was canceled, and the spreadsheet creator and CPA firm were fired.
- *Inadequately tested applications.* Users are less likely to test their applications rigorously, either because they do not recognize the need to do so or because of the difficulty or time involved. One Big Four CPA firm found that 90% of the spreadsheet models it tested had at least one calculation error.

- *Inefficient systems.*   Most end users are not programmers nor are they trained in systems development. As a result, their systems are not always efficient. One bank clerk spent three weeks developing a program that examined each cell in a spreadsheet and changed its value to zero if it was a negative amount. When the 60-page program began returning a "too many nested ifs" error message, the clerk called in a consultant. Within five minutes, the consultant developed a finished application using a built-in spreadsheet function.
- *Poorly controlled and documented systems.*   Many end users do not implement controls to protect their systems. User-created systems are often poorly documented because the user considers the task boring or unimportant. Users fail to realize that without documentation, others cannot understand how their system works.
- *System incompatibilities.*   Companies that add end-user equipment without considering the technological implications have a diversity of hardware and software that is difficult to support or network. Aetna Life & Casualty spent over $1 billion a year on IT to gain a competitive advantage. The result was 50,000 PCs from a few dozen manufacturers, 2,000 servers, 19 incompatible e-mail systems, and 36 different communications networks. Aetna finally realized it needed to shift its emphasis from owning the latest technology to the effective use of technology. Aetna standardized its systems and now uses only a few different PCs, Microsoft software, two e-mail systems, and one network. The result is compatibility across all systems and significantly less cost.
- *Duplication of systems and data; wasted resources.*   End users are typically unaware that other users have similar information needs, resulting in duplicate systems. Inexperienced users may take on more development than they are able to accomplish. Both of these problems end up wasting time and resources.
- *Increased costs.*   A single PC purchase is inexpensive; buying hundreds or thousands is costly. So is updating the hardware and software every few years. End-user computing has a high opportunity cost if it diverts users' attention from their primary jobs. It also increases time and data demands on corporate information systems.

It is possible to achieve the proper balance between the benefits and risks of end-user systems by training users, using systems analysts as advisers, and requiring user-created systems to be reviewed and documented prior to use.

Managing and Controlling End-User Computing

Organizations must manage and control end-user computing. Giving the IS department control discourages end-user computing and eliminates its benefits. However, if the organization maintains no controls over end users, such as what end-user computing tools are purchased or how they are used, it is likely to lead to significant problems. It is best to provide enough guidance and standards to control the system yet allow users the flexibility they need.

A *help desk* supports and controls end-user activities. The 60 help desk analysts and technicians at Schering-Plough handle 9,000 calls a month. Front-line analysts use expert system software to find scripted answers to user questions. Second-line technicians handle queries that are more complicated. Other companies use multimedia software with animation or videos to help staffers walk callers through a complicated process.

Help desk duties include resolving problems, disseminating information, evaluating new hardware and software products and training end users how to use them, assisting with application development, and providing technical maintenance and support. Help desks also develop and implement standards for hardware and software purchases, documentation, application testing, and security. Lastly, the help desk controls access to and sharing of corporate data among end users, while ensuring that the data are not duplicated and that access to confidential data remains restricted.

Outsourcing the System

Outsourcing is hiring an outside company to handle all or part of an organization's data processing activities. In mainframe outsourcing agreements, outsourcers buy client computers, hire the client's IS employees, operate and manage the system on the client's site, or migrate the system to the outsourcer's computers. Many outsourcing contracts are in effect for up to 10 years and cost millions of dollars a year. In a client/server or a PC outsourcing agreement, a service, function, or segment of business is outsourced. Most Fortune 500 companies outsource their PC support function. Royal Dutch Shell, the international oil company, has 80,000 PCs worldwide and outsources its installation, maintenance, training, help desk, and technical support.

Outsourcing was initially used for standardized applications such as payroll and accounting or by companies who wanted a cash infusion from selling their hardware. In 1989, Eastman Kodak surprised the business world by hiring IBM to run its data processing operations, DEC to run its telecommunications functions, and Businessland to run its PC operations. Kodak retained its IS strategic planning and development role, but outsourcers performed the implementation and operation responsibilities. The results were dramatic. Computer expenditures fell 90%. Operating expenses decreased 10% to 20%. Annual IS savings during the 10-year agreement were expected to be $130 million. Several years later, Xerox signed what was then the largest outsourcing deal in history: a $3.2 billion, 10-year contract with EDS to outsource its computing, telecommunications, and software management in 19 countries.

The success of Kodak and Xerox motivated others to outsource their systems. In one survey, some 73% of companies outsourced some or all of their information systems, and most outsourced to several companies to increase flexibility, foster competition, and reduce costs. Most companies do not, however, outsource strategic IT management, business process management, or IT architecture.

Many smaller companies outsource. One company with annual revenues of $1 million outsources all accounting functions to a local CPA. Whenever they want, the owners can view all their transactions on the CPA's Web site and produce a myriad of reports. They also outsourced all IT processes, including Web site design and maintenance.

Advantages and Disadvantages of Outsourcing

There are a number of significant advantages to outsourcing:

- *A business solution.* Outsourcing is a viable strategic and economic business solution that allows companies to concentrate on core competencies. Kodak focused on what it does best and left data processing to qualified computer companies. Kodak treats its outsourcers as partners and works closely with them to meet strategic and operational objectives.
- *Asset utilization.* Organizations improve their cash position and reduce expenses by selling assets to an outsourcer. Health Dimension outsourced data processing at its four hospitals so it could use its limited monetary resources to generate revenue.
- *Access to greater expertise and better technology.* Del Monte Foods turned to outsourcing because the cost and time involved in staying at the cutting edge of technology were rising significantly.
- *Lower costs.* IBM outsources programming to Chinese companies, whose labor costs are 30% of those in the United States. Outsourcers lower costs by standardizing user applications, buying hardware at bulk prices, splitting development and maintenance costs between projects, and operating at higher volumes. Continental Bank will save $100 million during its 10-year contract. However, Occidental Petroleum rejected outsourcing as costing more than internal AIS development and operation.
- *Less development time.* Experienced industry specialists develop and implement systems faster and more efficiently than in-house staff. Outsourcers also help cut through systems development politics.
- *Elimination of peaks-and-valleys usage.* Seasonal businesses require significant computer resources part of the year, and little the rest of the year. From January to March, W. Atlee Burpee's computers operated at 80% capacity processing seed and gardening orders and at 20% the rest of the time. Outsourcing cut Burpee's processing costs in half by paying based on how much the system is used.
- *Facilitation of downsizing.* Companies that downsize often have an unnecessarily large AIS function. General Dynamics downsized dramatically because of reductions in defense industry spending. It signed a $3 billion, 10-year outsourcing contract even though its IS function was rated number one in the aerospace industry. It sold its data centers to CSC for $200 million and transferred 2,600 employees to CSC.

However, not all outsourcing experiences have been successful. Between 25% and 50% of outsourcing agreements fail or are major disappointments. In one survey, company executives labeled 17% of them disasters and almost 50% were brought back in-house. There have been a number of significant outsourcing failures, including the problems EDS has had with its U.S. Navy contract (see Focus 20-2). Another is JPMorgan Chase's cancellation of its $5 billion, seven-year deal with IBM.

Outsourcing failures are caused by failure to prepare properly, lukewarm company buy-in, blind imitation of competitors, thinking that outsourcing will solve deeper problems, shifting responsibility for a bad process to someone else, and entering into ill-defined agreements that do not meet expectations. Finally, many companies do not realize that systems development is a more complex management challenge when performed by outsiders.

Companies that outsource often experience some of the following drawbacks:

- *Inflexibility.*   Many contracts are for 10 years. If a company is dissatisfied or has structural changes, the contract is difficult or costly to break. Before they merged, Integra Financial and Equimark had contracts with different outsourcers. Canceling one of them cost $4.5 million.
- *Loss of control.*   A company runs the risk of losing control of its system and its data. For that reason, Ford's outsourcing agreement prevents CSC from working with other automobile manufacturers.
- *Reduced competitive advantage.*   Companies may lose sight of how their AIS produces competitive advantages. Outsourcers are not as motivated as their clients to meet competitive challenges. Companies can mitigate this problem by outsourcing standard business processes (payroll, cash disbursements, etc.) and customizing those that provide competitive advantages.
- *Locked-in system.*   It is expensive and difficult to reverse outsourcing. A company may have to buy new equipment and hire a new data processing staff, often at prohibitive costs. When Blue Cross of California decided to end its agreement, it knew virtually nothing about its system and could not afford to discharge EDS. In contrast, LSI Logic brought its system back in-house at significant dollar and personnel savings when it installed an enterprise resource planning (ERP) system.
- *Unfulfilled goals.*   Critics claim some outsourcing benefits, such as increased efficiency, are a myth. USF&G canceled its $100 million contract with Cigna Information Services after 18 months when Cigna could not make the system work properly.
- *Poor service.*   Common complaints are that responsiveness to changing business conditions is slow or nonexistent and migration to new technologies is poorly planned.
- *Increased risk.*   Outsourcing business processes can expose a company to significant operational, financial, technology, strategy, personnel, legal, and regulatory risks.

Business Process Management

As organizations seek to improve their information systems and comply with legal and regulatory reforms, they are paying greater attention to their business processes. *Business process reengineering (BPR)* is a drastic, one-time-event approach to improving and automating business processes. However, it has had a low success rate. With further improvements, BPR has evolved into *business process management (BPM),* a systematic approach to continuously improving and optimizing an organization's business processes. BPM is a more gradual and ongoing business process improvement that is supported and enabled by technology. As a result, BPM is a good way to introduce both a human and a technological change capability into an organization.

Some of the important principles underlying BPM are the following:

- *Business processes can produce competitive advantages.*   Innovative processes that help business respond to changing consumer, market, and regulatory demands faster than competitors create competitive advantages. Good business process design is vital to an organization's success. For example, if a competitive bidding process is time sensitive and requires coordination between multiple functions, a poorly designed bid process can handicap the process so much that effective and profitable bids are not prepared.

- *Business processes must be managed end to end.* BPM views business processes as strategic organizational assets that should be understood, managed, and improved. Even if each part of a multi-functional business process functions well independently, the entire process may be suboptimal if there is inadequate communication and coordination among functional units (sales, production, etc). Managing business processes from inception to completion can control such problems. A process owner is designated, performance standards are set, and control and monitoring processes are established.
- *Business processes should be agile.* Organizations must continuously improve and adapt their business processes to compete. This requires flexibility and business process automation technology that supports rapid modifications.
- *Business processes must be aligned with organizational strategy and needs.* To be effective and efficient, a company must align its business processes with its business strategy.

Business process management systems (BPMS) automate and facilitate business process improvements. A BPMS can improve communication and collaboration, automate activities, and integrate with other systems and with other partners in the value chain. Some people claim that BPMS is the bridge between IT and business. Many companies worldwide are successfully implementing BPMS-based processes.

Like enterprise resource planning (ERP) systems, BPMS are enterprise-wide systems that support corporate activities. However, ERP systems are data-centered and BPMS are process-centered. Most manufactures of ERP systems are now integrating BPM into their systems.

A BPMS has the following four major components:

- A process engine to model and execute applications, including business rules
- Business analytics to help identify and react to business issues, trends, and opportunities
- Collaboration tools to remove communication barriers
- A content manager to store and secure electronic documents, images, and other files

Internal Controls in a Business Process Management System

A BPMS can improve internal controls. In event-based (as opposed to process-based) systems, users are granted access only to certain activity types. When authorization is granted using other parameters, such as dollar amounts, system developers have to include complex and expensive authorization restrictions. A BPMS uses the organization's business process rules to determine the correct person to perform a task and authorizes that person to perform it.

Segregation of duties can also be improved in a BPMS. In many event-based systems, the procedures for obtaining management approvals lengthen the business process and add additional costs. BPMS reduces the delays and costs by instantaneously transferring items needing approval to the manager. Within a few minutes, the manager can inspect and authorize the electronic form and transfer it to the next step in the process. BPMS have several other innovative authorization mechanisms, such as delegating authority to co-managers and creating a pool of authorizing managers to reduce bottlenecks when managers are overburdened or unavailable.

Application controls are also strengthened by a BPMS. In event-based systems, users identify what actions must be done, such as billing a customer when goods are shipped. If the action is not taken, an error occurs, such as doing something twice, not doing it at all, or doing the wrong thing. A BPMS uses a proactive process management approach that eliminates such problems. Users do not have to decide whether to take action and then decide which action is correct. The BPMS, using the company's business rules, decides what action must take place and forwards the task to the appropriate person's task list, where it remains until it is executed. The person gets an e-mail informing them that the task awaits their attention. This process prevents errors because it prevents procedures from being circumvented, prevents users from performing a different action, prevents items from being removed from the task list before they are accomplished, and sends additional reminder messages until the task is performed.

Another control advantage of BPMS is its built-in audit trail. The process monitoring and tracking systems, which document and link all actions and process steps in the order they occur in a process log, make it easy to track everything that takes place. This allows the auditor to continuously audit the business processes while they are active and afterward.

Prototyping

Prototyping is a systems design approach in which a simplified working model of a system is developed. Developers who use prototyping still go through the SDLC discussed in Chapter 20, but prototyping allows them to condense and speed up some analysis and design tasks. Prototyping helps capture user needs and helps developers and users make conceptual and physical design decisions.

UNUM Life Insurance wanted to use image processing to link systems and users. When top management had a hard time getting middle managers to understand how the system would work and the issues involved in the change, they had a prototype prepared. After using it, the managers grasped the possibilities and issues. Up to that point, they thought image processing meant replacing file cabinets.

As shown in Figure 21-1, a prototype is developed using four steps. The first is to meet with users to agree on the size and scope of the system and to decide what the system should and should not include. Developers and users also determine decision-making and transaction processing outputs, as well as the inputs and data needed to produce the outputs. The emphasis is on *what* output should be produced rather than *how* it should be produced. The developer must ensure that users' expectations are realistic and that their basic information requirements can be met. The designer uses the information requirements to develop cost, time, and feasibility estimates for alternative AIS solutions.

The second step is to develop an initial prototype. The emphasis is on low cost and rapid development. Nonessential functions, controls, exception handling, input validation, and processing speed are ignored in the interests of simplicity, flexibility, and ease of use. Users need to see and use tentative data entry screens, menus, and source documents; respond to prompts; query the system; judge response times; and issue commands. The developer demonstrates the finished prototype and asks users to provide feedback on what they like and dislike, which is much easier to do than imagining what they want in a system. Even a simple system that is not fully functional demonstrates features better than diagrams, drawings, or verbal explanations.

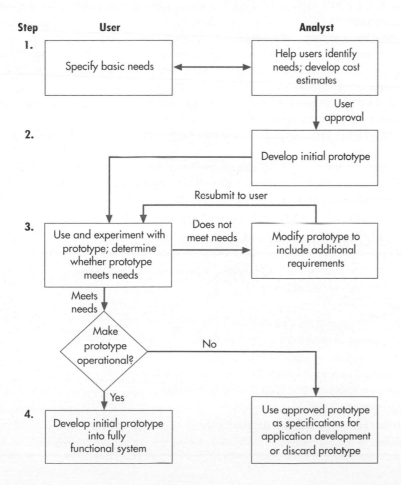

FIGURE 21-1

The Steps for Developing a System from a Prototype

In the third step, developers use the feedback to modify the system and return it to the users. Trial usage and modification continues until users are satisfied that the system meets their needs. A typical prototype goes through four to six iterations.

The fourth step is to use the system. An approved prototype is typically used in one of two ways. Half of all prototypes are turned into fully functional systems, referred to as *operational prototypes*. To make the prototype operational, the developer incorporates the things ignored in step one, provides backup and recovery, and integrates the prototype with other systems. *Nonoperational (throwaway) prototypes* are used several ways. System requirements identified during prototyping can be used to develop a new system. The prototype can be used as the initial prototype for an expanded system designed to meet the needs of many different users. When an unsalvageable prototype is discarded, the company potentially saves itself years of development work and lots of money by avoiding the traditional SDLC process.

When to Use Prototyping

Prototyping is appropriate when there is a high level of uncertainty, it is unclear what questions to ask, the AIS cannot be clearly visualized, or there is a high likelihood of failure. Good candidates for prototyping include decision support systems, executive information systems, expert systems, and information retrieval systems. Prototyping is less appropriate for large or complex systems that serve major organizational components or cross organizational boundaries or for developing standard AIS components, such as accounts receivable or inventory management. Table 21-3 shows the conditions that make prototyping an appropriate design methodology.

Advantages of Prototyping

Prototyping has the following advantages:

- *Better definition of user needs.*   Prototyping generally requires intensive involvement from end users, resulting in well-defined user needs.
- *Higher user involvement and satisfaction.*   Because users' requirements are met, there is less risk that the AIS will not be used. Early user involvement helps to build a climate of acceptance rather than skepticism and criticism.
- *Faster development time.*   Prototypes are often functioning after a few days or weeks, allowing users to immediately evaluate the system. John Hancock Mutual Life Insurance developed an executive information system prototype in one month, as described in Focus 21-2.
- *Fewer errors.*   The users test each version of the prototype, so errors are detected and eliminated early. It is also easier to identify and terminate infeasible systems before a great deal of time and expense is incurred.
- *More opportunity for changes.*   Users can suggest changes until the system is exactly what they want.
- *Less costly.*   Prototype systems can be developed for 20% of the cost of traditional systems. One utility company claimed a 13-to-1 improvement in development time over traditional methods when prototyping was used to develop 10 major applications.

TABLE 21-3 Conditions That Favor the Use of Prototyping

Users' needs are not understood, change rapidly, or evolve as the system is used.

System requirements are hard to define.

System inputs and outputs are not known.

The task to be performed is not well structured.

Designers are uncertain about what technology to use.

The system is crucial and needed quickly.

The risk associated with developing the wrong system is high.

User reactions are especially important development considerations.

Many design strategies must be tested.

The design staff has little experience developing the system or application.

The system will be used infrequently (processing efficiency is not a major concern).

FOCUS 21-2 Prototyping at John Hancock

John Hancock Mutual Life Insurance was dissatisfied with the traditional development process. Too often, after development the typical user reaction was, "I may have said this is what I wanted, but it isn't." To counter this problem, Hancock used prototyping to develop an executive information system (EIS) that would obtain data quickly and easily from the existing system.

The development team included IBM consultants, users, systems analysts, and programmers. The prototyping process was highly interactive, and continual user involvement eliminated many misunderstandings. Programming started immediately, preparing sample screens for the first user interviews. Developers showed the users how the system would work and gave them a chance to try the screens. Almost immediately, users could determine whether what they said they wanted was what they needed.

The EIS prototype, which took a month to build, allowed top management to query current and historical financial data and measurements. Top managers who were skeptical when the project began were impressed by how much the team was able to accomplish in a single month.

Disadvantages of Prototyping

Prototyping has the following disadvantages:

- *Significant user time.* Users must devote significant time to working with the prototype and providing feedback. It may require more involvement and commitment than users are willing to give.
- *Less efficient use of system resources.* Prototype development does not always achieve resource efficiency, sometime resulting in poor performance and reliability as well as high maintenance and support costs.
- *Inadequate testing and documentation.* Developers may shortchange testing and documentation because users are testing the prototype during development.
- *Negative behavioral reactions.* These can occur when requests for improvements are not made, there are too many iterations, or a prototype that users are invested in is thrown away.
- *Never-ending development.* This occurs when prototyping is not managed properly and the prototype is never completed due to recurring iterations and revision requests.

Computer-Aided Software Engineering

Computer-aided software (or systems) engineering (CASE) is an integrated package of tools that skilled designers use to help plan, analyze, design, program, and maintain an information system. CASE software typically has tools for strategic planning, project and system management, database design, screen and report layout, and automatic code generation. Many companies use CASE tools. Florida Power's $86 million customer information system was created using Accenture's CASE tool.

CASE tools provide a number of important advantages:

- *Improved productivity.* CASE can generate bug-free code from system specifications and can automate repetitive tasks. A programmer at Baptist Medical System used CASE to develop a system in one week that was estimated to take four months. Sony reported that CASE increased their productivity by 600%.
- *Improved program quality.* CASE tools simplify the enforcement of structured development standards, check the internal accuracy of the design, and detect inconsistencies.
- *Cost savings.* Savings of 80% to 90% are reported. At DuPont, an application estimated to require 27 months at a cost of $270,000 was finished in 4 months for $30,000. Over 90% of the code was generated directly from design specifications.
- *Improved control procedures.* CASE tools encourage system controls, security measures, and system auditability and error-handling procedures early in the design process.

- *Simplified documentation.*   CASE automatically documents the system as the development progresses.

Some of the more serious problems with CASE technology include the following:

- *Incompatibility.*   Some CASE tools do not interact effectively with other systems.
- *Cost.*   CASE technology is expensive, putting it out of the reach of many small companies.
- *Unmet expectations.*   A Deloitte & Touche survey indicated that only 37% of CIOs using CASE believe they achieved the expected benefits.

Summary and Case Conclusion

A company can use different strategies to obtain a new AIS. First, as the quality and quantity of vendor-written software increases, more companies are purchasing it. Second, IS departments develop the software or allow end users to develop it. Third, some companies buy software and modify it themselves or ask the vendor to modify it so it meets company needs. Fourth, companies outsource data processing activities.

There are many ways to speed up or improve the development process. One way is business process management, which is a systematic approach to continuously improving and optimizing an organization's business processes.

A second way is to design a prototype, a simplified working model of a system. A prototype is quickly and inexpensively built and is given to users to "test drive" so they can decide what they like and dislike about the system. Their reactions and feedback are used to modify the system, which is again given to the users to test. This iterative process of trial usage and modification continues until the users are satisfied that the system adequately meets their needs.

A third way to improve the development process is to use CASE tools to plan, analyze, design, program, and maintain an information system. They are also used to enhance the efforts of managers, users, and programmers in understanding information needs.

Ann has considered the different strategies and eliminated several of them. She has decided against outsourcing because she believes her team can do a better and faster job developing the system than an outsourcer could. Ann does not think prototyping would be effective because Shoppers Mart needs a large and complex system that would serve the needs of many users in many functional areas. Ann has narrowed her options down to purchasing a system or designing one in-house. If Shoppers Mart develops its own software, Ann will investigate the various CASE and BPMS packages on the market to see whether they will add value to the development process.

No matter which approach she chooses, Ann wants to facilitate as much end-user development as is practical and useful. Ann will make the final decision during the conceptual design phase (Chapter 22). To gather the information she needs to decide whether to purchase software, Ann prepares and sends an RFP to vendors asking them to propose software and hardware to meet the company's needs identified during systems analysis.

Key Terms

canned software   614
turnkey systems   614
application service provider (ASP)   614
request for proposal (RFP)   614
benchmark problem   616
point scoring   616
requirement costing   616

custom software   617
end-user computing (EUC)   617
help desk   619
outsourcing   619
business process reengineering (BPR)   621
business process management (BPM)   621

business process management system (BPMS)   622
prototyping   623
operational prototype   624
nonoperational (throwaway) prototype   624
computer-aided software (or systems) engineering (CASE)   625

AIS IN ACTION

Chapter Quiz

1. Which of the following is NOT one of the difficulties accountants have experienced using the traditional systems development life cycle?
   a. AIS development projects are backlogged for years.
   b. Changes are usually not possible after requirements have been frozen.
   c. The AIS that is developed may not meet their needs.
   d. All are difficulties with the SDLC.

2. Companies that buy rather than develop an AIS must still go through the systems development life cycle.
   a. true   b. false

3. Which of the following statements is FALSE?
   a. As a general rule, companies should buy rather than develop software if they can find a package that meets their needs.
   b. As an AIS increases in size and complexity, there is a greater likelihood that canned software can be found that meets user needs.
   c. A company should not attempt to develop its own custom software unless experienced, in-house programming personnel are available and the job can be completed less expensively on the inside.
   d. As a general rule, a company should develop custom software only when it will provide a significant competitive advantage.

4. When a company is buying large and complex systems, vendors are invited to submit systems for consideration. What is such a solicitation called?
   a. request for quotation   c. request for proposal
   b. request for system   d. good-faith estimate

5. To compare system performance, a company can create a data processing task with input, processing, and output jobs. This task is performed on the systems under consideration, and the processing times are compared. The AIS with the lowest time is the most efficient. What is this process called?
   a. benchmarking   c. point scoring
   b. requirements costing   d. performance testing

6. Which of the following statements is true?
   a. Because the AIS is so crucial, companies never outsource parts of the AIS.
   b. Most mainframe outsourcing contracts are for two to three years and cost thousands of dollars a year.
   c. Outsourcers often buy the client's computers and hire all or most of its information systems employees.
   d. Only companies struggling to survive and wanting a quick infusion of cash from selling their hardware use outsourcing.

7. Which of the following is NOT a benefit of outsourcing?
   a. It offers a great deal of flexibility because it is relatively easy to change outsourcers.
   b. It can provide access to the expertise and special services provided by outsourcers.
   c. It allows companies to move to a more sophisticated level of computing at a reasonable cost.
   d. It is a cost-effective way to handle the peaks and valleys found in seasonal businesses.

8. Which of the following is a true statement with respect to prototyping?
   a. In the early stages of prototyping, system controls and exception handling may be sacrificed in the interests of simplicity, flexibility, and ease of use.
   b. A prototype is a scaled-down, first-draft model that is quickly and inexpensively built and given to users to evaluate.

    c. The first step in prototyping is to identify system requirements.

    d. All of the statements are true.

9. Which of the following is NOT an advantage of prototyping?

    a. better definition of user needs

    b. adequately tested and documented systems

    c. higher user involvement and satisfaction

    d. faster development time

10. When is it most appropriate to use prototyping?

    a. when there is little uncertainty about the AIS

    b. when it is clear what users' needs are

    c. when the final AIS cannot be clearly visualized because the decision process is still unclear

    d. when there is a very low likelihood of failure

Chapter Case   Freedom from Telemarketers—the Do Not Call List

In 1991, telemarketers placed 18 million calls per day; by 2003, it was 104 million. President Bush announced the Do Not Call Registry by saying, "Unwanted telemarketing calls are intrusive, they are annoying, and they're all too common. When Americans are sitting down to dinner, or a parent is reading to his or her child, the last thing they need is a call from a stranger with a sales pitch." Congress appropriated $18.1 million to fund the program, which made it a federal offense for telemarketers to call anyone of the list. Within 72 hours, more than 10 million phone numbers were added to the Do Not Call list when people accessed the donotcall.gov Web site or called the toll-free number. The Do Not Call Registry was hailed as one the most successful IT projects in the history of government.

Identify the benefits and risks of the FTC purchasing a prewritten software system, developing the system in-house, and outsourcing the system to an external vendor. What approach do you think the FTC should have used?

(Source: Adapted from Alice Dragoon, "How the FTC Rescued the Dinner Hour," *CIO* (June 1, 2004): 59–64.)

Discussion Questions

21.1. What is the accountant's role in the computer acquisition process? Should the accountant play an active role, or should all the work be left to computer experts? In what aspects of computer acquisition might an accountant provide a useful contribution?

21.2. In a Midwest city of 45,000, a computer was purchased, and in-house programmers began developing programs. Four years later, only one incomplete and poorly functioning application had been developed, none of the software met users' minimum requirements, and the hardware and the software frequently failed. Why do you think the city was unable to produce quality, workable software? Would the city have been better off purchasing software? Could the city have found software that met its needs? Why or why not?

21.3. You are a systems consultant for Ernst, Price, and Deloitte, CPAs. At your country club's annual golf tournament, Frank Fender, an automobile dealer, describes a proposal from Turnkey Systems and asks for your opinion. The system will handle inventories, receivables, payroll, accounts payable, and general ledger accounting. Turnkey personnel would install the $40,000 system and train Fender's employees. Identify the major themes you would touch on in responding to Fender. Identify the advantages and disadvantages of using a turnkey system to operate the organization's accounting system.

21.4. Sara Jones owns a rapidly growing retail store that faces stiff competition due to poor customer service, late and error-prone billing, and inefficient inventory control. For the company's growth to continue, its AIS must be upgraded, but Sara is not sure what the company wants the AIS to accomplish. Sara has heard about prototyping but does not know what it is or whether it would help. How would you explain prototyping to Sara? Include an explanation of its advantages and disadvantages as well as when its use is appropriate.

21.5. Clint Grace has been in business over 30 years and has definite ideas about how his ten retail stores should be run. He is financially conservative and is reluctant to make expenditures that do not have a clear financial payoff. Store profitability has declined sharply, and customer dissatisfaction is high. Store managers never know how much inventory is on hand and when purchases are needed until a shelf is empty. Clint asks you to determine why profitability has declined and to recommend a solution. You determine that the current AIS is inefficient and unreliable and that company processes and procedures are out of date. You believe the solution is to redesign the systems and business processes using BPM. What are some challenges you might face in redesigning the system? How will you present your recommendations to Clint?

Problems

21.1. Don Otno has been researching software options but cannot decide among three alternatives. Don started his search at Computers Made Easy (CME) and almost wished he had looked no further. Steve Young, the manager of CME, appeared knowledgeable and listened attentively to Don's problems, needs, and concerns. Steve had software and hardware that would, with a few exceptions, meet Don's needs. Don could start using the system almost immediately. The system's price was unexpectedly reasonable.

At Custom Designed Software (CDS), Don left convinced that they could produce exactly what he needed. Cost and time estimates were not established, but CDS assured him that the cost would be reasonable and that the software would be complete in a few months.

At Modified Software Unlimited (MSU), the owner said that customized software was very good but expensive and that canned software was inexpensive but rarely met more than a few needs. The best of both worlds could be achieved by having MSU modify the package that came closest to meeting Don's needs.

Don returned to CME and asked Steve about customized and modified software. Steve expressed enough concerns about both that Don came full circle—to thinking canned software was best. That night, Don realized he could not make an objective decision. He was swayed by whichever vendor he was talking with at the time. The next morning he called you for help.

Required

a. List the advantages and disadvantages of each vendor's approach.
b. Recommend a course of action for Don, and support your decision.

21.2. A federal agency signed a 15-month contract for $445,158 for a human resources/payroll system. After 28 months and no usable software, the agency canceled the contract and withheld payment for poor performance. A negotiated settlement price of $970,000 was agreed on. The project experienced the following problems:

• The contractor did not understand what software was desired. The RFP did not have fully developed user requirements or system specifications, and user requirements were never adequately defined and frozen. Changes delayed completion schedules and caused disagreements about whether new requirements were included in the original scope of work.
• The contract did not specify systems requirements or performance criteria, and the terminology was vague. The contract was amended 13 times to add or delete requirements and to reimburse the contractor for the extra costs resulting from agency-caused delays. The amendments increased the cost of the contract to $1,037,448.

- The contractor complained of inexcusable agency delays, such as taking too much time to review items submitted for approval. The agency blamed the delays on the poor quality of the documentation under review.
- The agency did not require each separate development phase to be approved before work continued. When the agency rejected the general system design, the contractor had to scrap work already completed.

Required

a. What caused the problems? How could the agency have better managed the systems development project? What could the contractor have done differently?

b. Can we conclude from this case that organizations should not have custom software written for them? Explain your answer.

21.3. Wong Engineering Corp (WEC) operates in 25 states and three countries. WEC faced a crucial decision: choosing network software that would maximize functionality, manageability, and end-user acceptance of the system. WEC developed and followed a four-step approach:

Step 1. Develop evaluation criteria. WEC organized a committee that interviewed users and developed the following evaluation criteria:
- Ease of use
- Scope of vendor support
- Ease of network management and administration
- Cost, speed, and performance
- Ability to access other computing platforms
- Security and control
- Fault tolerance and recovery abilities
- Ability to connect workstations to the network
- Global naming services
- Upgrade and enhancement options
- Vendor stability

WEC organized the criteria into the following four categories and prioritized them. Criteria vital to short-term and long-term business goals were given a 5. "Wish list" criteria were weighted a 3. Inapplicable criteria were given a 1.
1. Business criteria: overall business, economic, and competitive issues
2. Operational criteria: tactical issues and operating characteristics
3. Organizational criteria: networks' impact on the information systems structure
4. Technical criteria: hardware, software, and communications issues

Step 2. Define the operating environment. Several data-gathering techniques were used to collect information from which an information systems model was developed. The model revealed the need to share accounting, sales, marketing, and engineering data at three organizational levels: district, division, and home office. District offices needed access to centralized financial information to handle payroll. WEC needed a distributed network that allowed users throughout the organization to access company data.

Step 3. Identify operating alternatives. Using the criteria from step 1, committee members evaluated each package and then compared notes during a roundtable discussion.

Step 4. Test the software. The highest-scoring products were tested, and the product that fit the organization's needs the best was selected.

Required

a. Discuss the committee's role in the selection process. How should committee members be selected? What are the pros and cons of using a committee to make the selection?

b. What data-gathering techniques could WEC use to assess user needs? To select a vendor?

c. What is the benefit of analyzing the operating environment before selecting the software? What data-gathering techniques help a company understand the operating environment?

d. In selecting a system using the point-scoring method, how should the committee resolve scoring disputes? List at least two methods.

e. Should a purchase decision be made on the point-scoring process alone? What other procedure(s) should the committee employ in making the final selection?

21.4. Mark Mitton, the liaison to the IS department, has eliminated all but the best three systems. Mark developed a list of required features, carefully reviewed each system, talked to other users, and interviewed appropriate systems representatives. Mark used a point-scoring system to assign weights to each requirement. Mark developed Table 21-4 to help him select the best system.

Required

a. Use a spreadsheet to develop a point-scoring matrix and determine which system Mark should select.

b. Susan Shelton did not agree with Mark's weightings and suggested the following changes:

Flexibility	60
Reputation and reliability	50
Quality of support utilities	10
Graphics capability	10

TABLE 21-4 An Evaluation Matrix

		System		
Selection Criteria	Weight	1	2	3
Software				
Fulfillment of business needs	100	6	8	9
Acceptance in marketplace	30	6	7	6
Quality of documentation	50	7	9	8
Quality of warranty	50	4	8	7
Ease of use	80	7	6	5
Control features	50	9	7	9
Flexibility	20	4	5	9
Security features	30	4	4	8
Modularity	30	8	5	4
Integration with other software	30	8	9	6
Quality of support utilities	50	9	8	5
Vendor				
Reputation and reliability	10	3	9	6
Experience with similar systems	20	5	5	6
Installation assistance	70	9	4	6
Training assistance	35	4	8	6
Timeliness of maintenance	35	5	4	4
Hardware				
Internal memory size (RAM)	70	5	6	8
Hard-drive capacity	40	9	9	5
Graphics capabilities	50	7	7	8
Processing speed	30	8	8	5
Overall performance	40	9	4	4
Expandability	50	7	2	5
Support for network technology	30	3	4	7

When the changes are made, which vendor should Mark recommend?

c. Mark's manager suggested the following changes to Susan's weightings:

Reputation and reliability	90
Installation assistance	40
Experience with similar systems	40
Training assistance	65
Internal memory size	10

Will the manager's changes affect the decision about which system to buy?

d. What can you conclude about point scoring from the changes made by Susan and Mark's manager? Develop your own weighting scale to evaluate the software packages. What other selection criteria would you use? Be prepared to discuss your results with the class.

e. What are the weaknesses of the point-scoring method?

21.5. Nielsen Marketing Research (NMR), with operations in 29 countries, produces and disseminates marketing information. Nielsen has been the primary supplier of decision support information for more than 70 years. NMR's most recognizable product is the Nielsen television ratings. Nielsen is one of the largest users of computer capacity in the United States. Its information system consistently ranks above average in efficiency for its industry. NMR hired IBM to evaluate outsourcing its information processing. NMR wanted to know whether outsourcing would allow it to concentrate on giving its customers value-added services and insights, increase its flexibility, promote rapid growth, and provide it with more real-time information.

Required

What are the benefits and risks of outsourcing for NMR? Do the benefits outweigh the risks? Explain your answer.

21.6. A large organization had 18 months to replace its old customer information system with a new one that could differentiate among customer levels and provide appropriate products and services on demand. The new system, which cost $1 million and was installed by the IS staff on time, did not work properly. Complex transactions were error-prone, some transactions were canceled and others were put on hold, and the system could not differentiate among customers. The system was finally shut down, and transactions were processed manually. New IS management was hired to build a new system and mend the strained relationship between operations and IS.

So what went wrong? IS couldn't—or wouldn't—say no to all the requests for systems enhancements. Eager to please top management, IS management ignored the facts and assured them they could build a scalable system that was on time and on budget. Another big mistake was a strict project schedule with little flexibility to deal with problems and unforeseen challenges. Developers never spoke up about any glitches they encountered along the way. More than a dozen people (including the CIO) lost their jobs because of their roles in this disaster.

Required

a. What could IS management have done differently to make this project successful?

b. What in-house development issues are demonstrated in this case?

c. How could the in-house issues have been addressed to prevent the system's failure?

21.7. Meredith Corporation publishes books and magazines, owns and operates television stations, and has a real estate marketing and franchising service. Meredith has 11 different systems that do not communicate with each other. Management wants an executive information system that provides them with the correct and timely information they need to make good business decisions. Meredith has decided to use prototyping to develop the system.

Required

   a. Identify three questions you would ask Meredith personnel to determine systems requirements. What information are you attempting to elicit from each question?
   b. Explain how prototyping works. What would system developers do during the iterative process? Why would you want the fewest iterations possible?
   c. Would you want the prototype to be operational or nonoperational? Why? If it were an operational prototype, what would have to happen? If it were a nonoperational prototype, how could the prototype be used?
   d. Suppose the company decides the prototype system is not practical, abandons it, and takes some other approach to solving its information problem. Does that mean prototyping is not a valid systems development approach? Explain your answer.

21.8. Norcom, a division of a large manufacturer, needed a new distribution and customer service system. The project was estimated to take 18 months and cost $5 million. The project team consisted of 20 business and IT staff members. After two years, the CIO was fired, and the company hired a CIO with expertise in saving troubled projects. The new CIO said three grave errors were committed.

   1. IT picked the wrong software using a very naïve request for proposal process.
   2. IT did not formulate a project plan.
   3. No one "owned" the project. The IT staff assumed the users owned the project, the users believed the IT staff owned it, and management believed the vendor owned it.

   The CIO developed a 2,000-line plan to rescue the project. Three months later, the system failed, even with IT staff and consultants working on it day and night. The failed system was to have been the company's preeminent system, but it could not even process customer orders correctly, resulting in complaints about late shipments and receiving the wrong goods.

   After three years and $4 million, the new CIO polled the staff anonymously. Only two said the project could be saved, and they had staked their careers on the project. The message that the project was not worth saving was very hard for the CIO to give. It was likewise hard for the division president to receive it; he could not accept the idea of killing a project that cost so much money. He finally accepted the decision and all the ramifications involved, including corporate IT taking control of all IT operations at his division.

Required

   a. List the primary components of an RFP.
   b. Identify possible components or deficiencies in Norcom's RFP that could have led the new CIO to claim that it was naïve or insufficient.
   c. Identify possible approaches Norcom could have used to evaluate RFP responses.

21.9. Quickfix is rapidly losing business, and management wants to redesign its computer repair processes and procedures to decrease costs and increase customer service. Currently, a customer needing help calls one of five regional service centers. A customer service representative records the relevant customer information, finds the closest qualified technician, and calls the technician's cell phone to see whether the repair fits into his or her schedule. If not, the representative finds the next closest technician. When a technician is located, customer repair information is provided over the phone. The technician calls the customer and arranges to pick up the computer and replace it with a loaner. Making these arrangements takes one to two days and sometimes more if technicians are not available or do not promptly return calls.

   If a broken computer cannot be quickly repaired, it is sent to a repair depot. These repairs take another four to seven days. If problems arise, it can take up to two weeks for an item to be repaired. When a customer calls to see whether the computer is ready, the service representative calls the technician to find out the status and calls the customer back. The repair process usually takes five phone calls between the customer, the service representative, and the technician.

There are several problems with this process that have led to a significant drop in business: (1) it is time-consuming; (2) it is inconvenient for a customer to have a computer removed, a new one installed, and then the old one reinstalled; and (3) service representatives do not have immediate access to information about items being repaired. Quickfix decides to use BPM principles to redesign its business processes.

Required

a. Identify the repair processes that occur, and decide which should be redesigned.
b. Describe how the repair process can be redesigned to solve the problems identified.
c. What benefits can Quickfix achieve by redesigning the repair process?

21.10. Search written materials, the Internet, and electronic databases for successful and failed information system implementations. Prepare an oral or written summary of a successful and a failed implementation. Include the approach used to acquire or develop the system.

Case 21-1 Professional Salon Concepts

Steve Cowan owns Professional Salon Concepts (PSC), a hair salon products distribution company. After working for his father, a barber and beauty salon products distributor, he started his own business selling Paul Mitchell products. Business was poor until Steve conducted a free seminar demonstrating how to successfully use his products. He left with a $1,000 order and a decision to sell to salons that allowed him to demonstrate his products.

Steve's strategy paid off as PSC grew to 45 employees, 3,000 customers, and sales of $7 million. PSC carries 1,000 products, compared with 10,000 for most distributors. The smaller product line allows PSC to achieve a 24-hour order turnaround, compared to over two days for the competition. Steve occasionally has to work late packing orders and driving them to the UPS hub a few towns away so he can meet the 2:00 A.M. deadline.

After buying a computer and installing a $3,000 accounting package, Steve thought everything was going great until Terri Klimko, a consultant from a PSC supplier, stopped by. Terri asked the following questions to find out how well he knew his business:

- Do you know exactly how much you ship each month and to whom?
- Do you know how much each customer bought, by supplier?
- Can you rank your customer sales?
- Can you break your sales down by product?
- Do you know how the profit per client breaks down into product lines?
- Do you know how revenues per salesperson vary over the days of the week?

When Steve answered no to each question, Terri told him that people who cannot answer the questions were losing money. Upset, Steve terminated the session by politely dismissing Terri. Although unimpressed with Terri's advice,

Steve was impressed with her and they were soon married. Shortly afterwards she joined the company.

Steve asked Terri to help the salons become more profitable. She developed a template to help salon owners determine how much each hairstylist brings in per client, how many clients receive extra services, and which clients buy hair products. The Cowans soon became more like partners to their customers than trainers. If a salon had employee problems, the Cowans would help settle it. If a salon needed help with a grand opening, they lent a hand. The more PSC products the salons bought, the more time the Cowans gave.

PSC sold turnkey systems and support services at cost to help salons answer Terri's questions. Unfortunately, PSC's computer could not answer those same questions. Steve asked consultant Mike Fenske for help. Mike entered all of PSC's raw data into a database and wrote a program to produce the desired information. The system worked but had problems. It was so slow that accounts payable and purchasing information was handled manually, it did not answer Terri's growing list of questions, and only a few months of detailed information were available at a time. To alleviate these problems, Steve hired Mike as the company controller.

After reading an industry report, Steve realized it was time to purchase a new system. Steve and Mike decided to evaluate and select the software themselves and rely on the vendor for installation help. They spent months researching software and attending demonstrations before settling on a $20,000 system. The vendor began installing the system and training PSC personnel.

Three days prior to conversion, Steve met a distributor who described how his system met his detailed accounting and customer reporting needs as well as his inventory management and order fulfillment needs. Steve was so impressed that they stopped the conversion, went to North Dakota to check out the distributor's system, and flew to Minneapolis to visit DSM, the software developer.

DSM did a great job of demonstrating the software and provided Steve and Mike with great references. The only hitch was DSM's inability to demonstrate two features that were particularly important: adjusting orders automatically to reflect outstanding customer credits and back orders, and determining the least expensive way to pack and ship each order. DSM's salespeople assured them that those features would be up and running by the time the package was delivered to PSC.

Their economic feasibility analysis showed $234,000 in yearly savings:

$144,000	Most PSC orders consist of several boxes, 95% of which are sent COD. The old PSC system had no way to prepare orders for multiple-box shipments; a five-box order required five sales invoices and five COD tickets. The new system allowed PSC to generate one sales order and ship one box COD and the other four by regular delivery. Not having to ship every box COD would save $144,000 a year.
$50,000	PSC paid a CPA firm $50,000 a year to prepare its financial statements. The new software would prepare the statements automatically.
$40,000	Because the old system did not have credit-managing capabilities, it was hard to detect past-due accounts. Earlier detection of past-due accounts would result in faster collections, fewer lost customers, and fewer write-offs.
Unknown	The major reason for acquiring the system was to improve customer service by making more detailed customer information available.

After estimated annual maintenance costs of $10,000, there was an annual return on investment of $224,000. Because the system would pay for itself in less than a year, Steve bought it and wrote off his $20,000 investment in the other system.

When DSM installed the software, Steve found out that the promised features were not available and that there was no immediate plan to add them. Although Steve and Mike were upset, they had to shoulder some of the blame for not insisting on the two features before signing the deal. They found a program that automatically determined the cheapest way to pack and ship an order. DSM agreed to pay half of the $10,000 cost to integrate it into the program. DSM offered to create the module to reflect customer credits and back orders for another $20,000, but Steve declined. These problems pushed the conversion date back several months.

PSC spent three months preparing to implement the new system. Training PSC employees to use the new system was particularly important. Adding a customer to the database required only one screen with the old system, the new software required six screens. Employees were taught to shout "Fire!" when they had a problem they could not handle. Mike or a DSM programmer explained the error and how to correct it. During implementation, the new system was tested for glitches by processing real data. Looking back, Mike admits three

months were not nearly enough for the training and testing. They should have used twice as much time to identify and eliminate glitches.

When PSC converted to the new system, telephone operators were confronted with situations they had not been trained to handle. Soon everyone was yelling "Fire!" at the same time. In less than one hour, so many operators were waiting for help that the programmers stopped explaining the correct procedures and simply ran from operator to operator correcting problems. Mistakes were repeated numerous times, and the situation intensified. Some employees, frustrated by their inability to work the new system, broke down and cried openly.

In the warehouse, Steve was not having much fun either. On a normal day, PSC has 200 to 300 boxes ready for 3:30 P.M. shipment. On conversion day, a lone box sat ready to go. Facing the first default on his 24-hour turnaround promise, Steve, Terri, Mike, and a few others stayed past midnight packing and loading boxes on trucks. They barely made it to the UPS hub on time.

The next day, order entry and shipping proceeded more smoothly, but Steve could not retrieve data to monitor sales. That did not make him feel too kindly about his $200,000 system or DSM. It took Steve weeks to figure out how to get data to monitor sales. When he did, he was horrified that sales had dropped 15%. They had focused so hard on getting the system up and running that they took their eyes off the customers. To make matters worse, Steve could not get information on sales by customer, salesperson, or product, nor could he figure out why or where sales were falling.

Things quickly improved after "Hell Week." Orders were entered just as quickly, and warehouse operations improved thanks to the integrated add-in program. The new system provided pickers with the most efficient path to follow and told them which items to pack in which boxes based on destination and weight. The system selected a carrier and printed labels for the boxes. Order turnaround time was shaved to 20 minutes from five hours.

Months after the system was installed, it still did not do everything Steve needed, including some things the old system did. Nor did it answer all of Terri's questions. Steve is confident, however, that the system will eventually provide PSC with a distinct competitive advantage. He is negotiating with DSM to write the credit and back-order module.

Steve believes the step up to the new system was the right move for his growing company. With the exceptions of taking the DSM salesperson's word and not taking enough time to practice with the system, Steve feels PSC did as good a job as it could have in selecting, installing, and implementing a new system.

Required

1. Do you agree that PSC did a good job selecting, installing, and implementing the new system? If so, why? Or do you feel PSC could have done a better job? If so, what did it do wrong, and what should it have done differently?
2. How could PSC have avoided the missing features problem?

(continued)

3. How could PSC have avoided conversion and reporting problems?

4. Evaluate Steve's economic feasibility analysis. Do you agree with his numbers and his conclusions?

5. How could PSC's customers use the new multibox shipping approach to defraud PSC?

6. How would you rate the service PSC received from DSM? What did it do well, and what did it do poorly?

(Source: Adapted from David H. Freeman, "Computer Upgrade: To Hell and Back," *INC. Technology* (June 15, 1994): 46–53.)

AIS IN ACTION SOLUTIONS

Quiz Key

1. Which of the following is NOT one of the difficulties accountants have experienced using the traditional systems development life cycle?
   a. AIS development projects are backlogged for years. [Incorrect. This is one of the difficulties accountants have experienced using the traditional SDLC, but there is more than one correct answer.]
   b. Changes are usually not possible after requirements have been frozen. [Incorrect. This is one of the difficulties accountants have experienced using the traditional SDLC, but there is more than one correct answer.]
   c. The AIS that is developed may not meet their needs. [Incorrect. This is one of the difficulties accountants have experienced using the traditional SDLC, but there is more than one correct answer.]
   ▶ d. All are difficulties with the SDLC. [Correct.]

2. Companies that buy rather than develop an AIS must still go through the systems development life cycle.
   ▶ a. true [Correct. Purchasing a system still requires a company to follow the systems development life cycle of analyzing, designing (conceptual and physical), and implementing a new system. Otherwise, the company risks not purchasing the right system for its needs.]
   b. false [Incorrect.]

3. Which of the following statements is FALSE?
   a. As a general rule, companies should buy rather than develop software if they can find a package that meets their needs. [Incorrect. This is a true statement, not a false statement. Purchasing software is generally less expensive than developing software in-house.]
   ▶ b. As an AIS increases in size and complexity, there is a greater likelihood that canned software can be found that meets user needs. [Correct. This is a false statement. Large and complex systems need greater customization than smaller systems and thus are less likely to lend themselves to the one-size-fits-all approach of canned software.]
   c. A company should not attempt to develop its own custom software unless experienced, in-house programming personnel are available and the job can be completed less expensively on the inside. [Incorrect. This is a true statement, not a false statement. Skilled in-house programmers and the promise of lower costs are essential if companies decide to develop their own custom software.]

   d. As a general rule, a company should develop custom software only when it will provide a significant competitive advantage. [Incorrect. This is a true statement, not a
   false statement. According to Arthur Little, companies should pursue custom software
   only when it provides a distinct competitive advantage.]

4. When a company is buying large and complex systems, vendors are invited to submit
   systems for consideration. What is such a solicitation called?
   a. request for quotation [Incorrect. A request for quotation asks for dollar bids on
   proposed systems or their components.]
   b. request for system [Incorrect. A request for system is not the terminology used to refer
   to inviting vendors to submit systems for consideration.]
▶ **c.** request for proposal [Correct. A request for proposal invites vendors to propose solutions to a company's needs.]
   d. good-faith estimate [Incorrect. A good-faith estimate provides a vendor's best guess on
   the cost of a proposal based on reliable parameters.]

5. To compare system performance, a company can create a data processing task with input,
   processing, and output jobs. This task is performed on the systems under consideration
   and the processing times are compared. The AIS with the lowest time is the most efficient. What is this process called?
▶ **a.** benchmarking [Correct. Benchmarking measures system performance by comparing
   processing times.]
   b. requirements costing [Incorrect. Requirement costing estimates the costs of purchasing
   or developing features that are not present in a particular AIS.]
   c. point scoring [Incorrect. Point scoring measures system performance by comparing
   each system based on weighted criteria.]
   d. performance testing [Incorrect. Performance testing is a general term applied to many
   types of comparison testing.]

6. Which of the following statements is true?
   a. Because the AIS is so crucial, companies never outsource parts of the AIS. [Incorrect.
   AIS functions are routinely outsourced.]
   b. Most mainframe outsourcing contracts are for two to three years and cost thousands of
   dollars a year. [Incorrect. Most mainframe outsourcing contracts are longer term (aver-
   aging 10 years) and cost hundreds of thousands to millions of dollars.]
▶ **c.** Outsourcers often buy the client's computers and hire all or most of its information
   systems employees. [Correct. Many large outsourcing deals involve purchasing the
   client's hardware and hiring the client's employees.]
   d. Only companies struggling to survive and wanting a quick infusion of cash from selling their hardware use outsourcing. [Incorrect. Many large and financially sound companies use outsourcing as a way to decrease costs and become even more profitable.]

7. Which of the following is NOT a benefit of outsourcing?
▶ **a.** It offers a great deal of flexibility because it is relatively easy to change outsourcers.
   [Correct. This is not a benefit of outsourcing. Because contracts are long term, outsourcers can be very inflexible, as well as difficult and costly to change.]
   b. It can provide access to the expertise and special services provided by outsourcers.
   [Incorrect. This is a benefit of outsourcing. Many companies cannot afford to retain
   information systems expertise on their payroll; therefore, outsourcing provides a less
   expensive way to acquire that expertise.]
   c. It allows companies to move to a more sophisticated level of computing at a reasonable cost. [Incorrect. This is a benefit of outsourcing. Many companies cannot afford
   to maintain the most effective and sophisticated hardware; therefore, outsourcing provides a less expensive way to gain access to that hardware.]
   d. It is a cost-effective way to handle the peaks and valleys found in seasonal businesses.
   [Incorrect. This is a benefit of outsourcing. For companies in cyclical industries, outsourcing provides an effective way to meet company needs during the busy times and
   to lower costs during the slow times of their business cycle.]

8. Which of the following is a true statement with respect to prototyping?
    a. In the early stages of prototyping, system controls and exception handling may be sacrificed in the interests of simplicity, flexibility, and ease of use. [Incorrect. This is a true statement. Prototyping provides simplicity, flexibility, and ease of use by sacrificing controls and exception handling. However, this is not the only true statement.]
    b. A prototype is a scaled-down, first-draft model that is quickly and inexpensively built and given to users to evaluate. [Incorrect. This is a true statement. Prototypes are essentially rough-draft models. However, this is not the only true statement.]
    c. The first step in prototyping is to identify system requirements. [Incorrect. This is a true statement. The first step in prototyping is to identify system requirements. However, this is not the only true statement.]
    ▶ d. All of the statements are true. [Correct.]

9. Which of the following is NOT an advantage of prototyping?
    a. better definition of user needs [Incorrect. This is an advantage of prototyping. Because users can test-drive the model, they can give better feedback to the developers regarding their needs and requirements.]
    ▶ b. adequately tested and documented systems [Correct. This is not an advantage of prototyping. Because prototypes are developed so quickly, developers often neglect documentation and a full testing before the system becomes operational.]
    c. higher user involvement and satisfaction [Incorrect. This is an advantage of prototyping. Prototyping success depends on high user involvement, which generally leads to greater user satisfaction.]
    d. faster development time [Incorrect. This is an advantage of prototyping. Prototypes can be developed in a matter of days or weeks, whereas a more traditional approach can take a year or longer.]

10. When is it most appropriate to use prototyping?
    a. when there is little uncertainty about the AIS [Incorrect. Prototyping is more effective when there is substantial uncertainty about how an AIS should work.]
    b. when it is clear what users' needs are [Incorrect. Prototyping is more effective when users are uncertain of their needs and benefit from working on models to help them identify and solidify their needs.]
    ▶ c. when the final AIS cannot be clearly visualized because the decision process is still unclear [Correct. Prototyping is more effective when there is substantial uncertainty about how an AIS should work, look, and feel.]
    d. when there is a very low likelihood of failure [Incorrect. Prototyping is the most effective when there is substantial uncertainty about whether a new system will work.]

Chapter Case Solution

Identify the benefits and risks of the three courses of action facing the FTC: purchasing a prewritten software system, developing the system in-house, and outsourcing the system to an external vendor.

Purchasing Software

The primary benefit of purchasing software is greater availability and lower cost; because the product is sold to many companies, it can be sold at a lower price. The downside is that because the software is designed for as wide an audience as possible, it may not meet all the needs of the purchaser. In addition, software support is a problem if the vendor goes out of business.

Developing the System In-House

The primary benefit of in-house development is that the system should meet the entity's needs. The drawbacks are that it occupies significant time and resources, it is usually a very complex process, and problems—such as poor requirements planning, insufficient staff, poor top-management support, inadequate communication, and a lack of cooperation between the developers and users—can easily derail a project.

Outsourcing the System

Outsourcing allows entities to devote time and resources to their core competencies instead of diverting attention to systems development. It also gives companies access to expertise at a much lower cost. Outsourcing can save 15% to 30% in overall systems development costs because of quicker development time, smoothing usage peaks and valleys, and facilitating corporate restructuring (downsizing). The risks involve a loss of control over the project, inflexible outsourcing contracts, and poor service. Entities can also lose their competitive advantage by not maintaining proprietary systems.

What the FTC Did

Given the short timeframe to implement such a large task, the Federal Trade Commission could not have built this system on its own. Instead, they outsourced it to AT&T, which had the expertise and staff to handle the system's analysis, design, and implementation. With AT&T's help, the project became one of the government's most successful IT projects.

Chapter 22

Systems Design, Implementation, and Operation

After studying this chapter, you should be able to:

1. Discuss the conceptual systems design process and the activities in this phase.

2. Discuss the physical systems design process and the activities in this phase.

3. Discuss the systems implementation and conversion process and the activities in this phase.

4. Discuss the systems operation and maintenance process and the activities in this phase.

INTEGRATIVE CASE SHOPPERS MART

Ann Christy received permission to develop a new AIS (Chapter 20 conclusion) for Shoppers Mart (SM). Ann is concerned because many development projects bog down during the design and implementation phases, and she does not want a runaway project that she cannot control. She wants to plan the rest of the project so that it is completed correctly, and her first task is to determine what type of system will best meet SM's needs. She scheduled a meeting with the head of systems development to discuss the following questions:

1. Should her team develop what it considers the best approach to meeting SM's needs, or should they develop several approaches?

2. How can she ensure that system output will meet user needs? When and how should input be captured, and who should capture it? Where should AIS data be stored, and how should it be organized and accessed?

3. How should SM convert from its current to its new AIS? How much time and effort will be needed to maintain the new AIS? In what capacity should Ann's accounting staff participate?

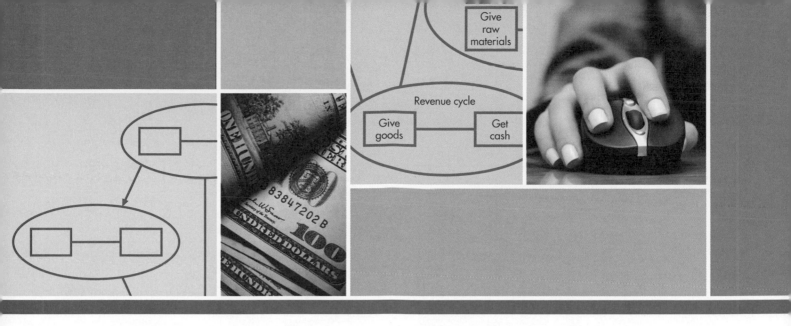

Introduction

Effective systems analysis and design can help developers correctly define business problems and create a system to solve those problems. As discussed in Chapter 20, system requirements are defined during systems analysis. This chapter discusses the other four systems development life cycle (SDLC) steps (see Figure 20-1): conceptual systems design, physical systems design, systems implementation and conversion, and operation and maintenance. Chapter 21 discusses how some SDLC steps can be shortened or made more effective.

Conceptual Systems Design

In *conceptual systems design,* the developer creates a general framework for implementing user requirements and solving the problems identified in the analysis phase. Figure 22-1 shows the conceptual design steps: evaluating design alternatives, preparing design specifications, and preparing the conceptual systems design report.

Evaluate Design Alternatives

There are many ways to design an AIS, so systems designers must make many design decisions. For example, should SM mail hard-copy purchase orders, use electronic data interchange (EDI), or enter orders over the Internet? Should SM have a large centralized mainframe and database or distribute computer power to the stores using a network of servers and PCs? Should data entry be by keyboard, optical character recognition, point-of-sale devices, barcodes, radio-frequency identification (RFID) tags, the Internet, or some combination?

There are many ways SM can approach the systems development process. It can purchase software, ask in-house information systems (IS) staff to develop it, or hire an outside company to develop and manage the system. The company could modify existing software or redesign its business processes and develop software to support the new processes. These conceptual design alternatives are discussed in Chapter 21.

The following standards should be used to evaluate design alternatives: (1) how well it meets organizational and system objectives, (2) how well it meets user needs, (3) whether it is economically feasible, and (4) how advantages weigh against disadvantages. The steering committee evaluates the alternatives and selects the one that best meets the organization's needs.

Table 22-1 summarizes design considerations and alternatives.

FIGURE 22-1
Conceptual Systems
Design Activities

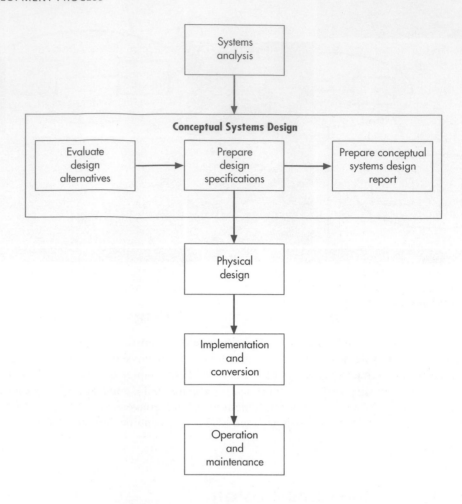

TABLE 22-1 Design Considerations and Alternatives

Design Considerations	Design Alternatives
Communications channels	Telephone, Internet, cable, fiber optics, or satellite
Communications network	Centralized, decentralized, distributed, or local area
Data storage medium	Tape, disk, hard drive, CD, or paper
Data storage structure	Files or database
File organization and access	Random, sequential, or indexed-sequential access
Input medium	Keying, optical character recognition (OCR), magnetic ink character recognition (MICR), point-of-sale (POS), EDI, or voice
Input format	Source document, turnaround document, source data automation, or screen
Operations	In-house or outsourcing
Output and update frequency	Instantaneous, hourly, daily, weekly, or monthly
Output medium	Paper, screen, voice, CD, or microfilm
Output scheduling	Predetermined times or on demand
Output format	Narrative, table, graph, file, or electronic
Printed output format	Preprinted forms or system-generated forms
Processing mode	Manual, batch, or real time
Processor	Personal computer, server, or mainframe
Software acquisition	Canned, custom, or modified
Transaction processing	Batch or online

Prepare Design Specifications and Reports

Once a design alternative is selected, *conceptual design specifications* are created for the following elements:

1. *Output.* Because the system is designed to meet user information needs, output specifications are prepared first. To evaluate store sales, SM must decide (a) how often to produce a sales analysis report, (b) what the report should contain, (c) what it will look like, and (d) whether it is a hard-copy or screen (or both) output.
2. *Data storage.* Data storage decisions include which data elements must be stored to produce the sales report, how they should be stored, and what type of file or database to use.
3. *Input.* Input design considerations include which sales data to enter, sale location and amount, and where, when, and how to collect the data.
4. *Processing procedures and operations.* Design considerations include how to process the input and stored data to produce the sales report, and in which sequence the processes must be performed.

A *conceptual systems design report* summarizes conceptual design activities, guides physical design activities, communicates how all information needs will be met, and helps the steering committee assess feasibility. The main component is a description of one or more recommended system designs. Table 22-8, in the chapter summary, shows what this report contains.

Physical Systems Design

During *physical systems design*, the broad, user-oriented AIS requirements of conceptual design are translated into detailed specifications that are used to code and test the computer programs. Figure 22-2 shows the physical system design phases that are described below in detail.

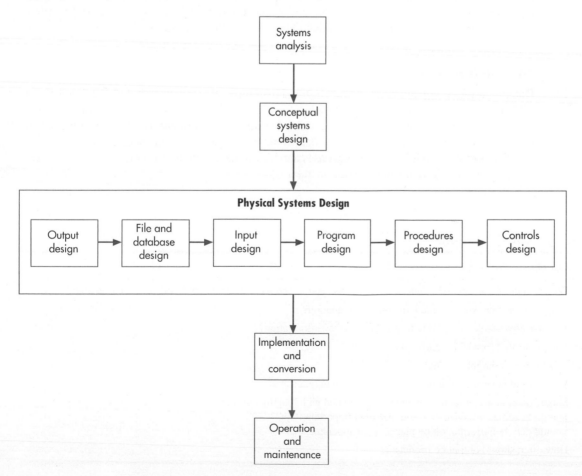

FIGURE 22-2

Physical Systems Design Activities

Failing to take sufficient time on conceptual and physical design can cause problems. A rush to implement an enterprise resource planning (ERP) package at Overstock.com caused early design problems. The result was a mistake-laden Oracle implementation. The ERP package was out-of-sync with the accounting software, causing the order tracking system to go down for a week. Ultimately, five years of earnings had to be restated, with revenue reduced by $12.9 million and increased losses of $10.3 million.

Output Design

The objective of output design is to determine the nature, format, content, and timing of reports, documents, and screen displays. Tailoring the output to user needs requires cooperation between users and designers. Important output design considerations are summarized in Table 22-2.

Output usually fits into one of the following four categories:

1. *Scheduled reports* have a prespecified content and format and are prepared on a regular basis. Examples include monthly performance reports, weekly sales analyses, and annual financial statements.
2. *Special-purpose analysis reports* have no prespecified content or format and are not prepared on a regular schedule. They are prepared in response to a management request to evaluate an issue, such as which of three new products would provide the highest profits.
3. *Triggered exception reports* have a prespecified content and format but are prepared only in response to abnormal conditions. Excessive absenteeism, cost overruns, inventory shortages, and situations requiring immediate corrective action trigger such reports.
4. *Demand reports* have a prespecified content and format but are prepared only on request. Both triggered exception reports and demand reports can be used effectively to facilitate the management process.

Designers often prepare sample outputs and ask users to evaluate whether they are complete, relevant, and useful. Unacceptable output is modified and reviewed again as many times as necessary to make it acceptable. To avoid expensive time delays later in the SDLC, many organizations require users to sign a document stating that the output form and content are acceptable.

File and Database Design

Data in various company units should be stored in compatible formats to help avoid the problem AT&T faced: 23 business units, a jumble of incompatible systems and data formats, and an inability to communicate and share data with other units. AT&T spent five years creating a "single view" of each customer so customer data could be shared across business units.

Chapter 4 discusses files and databases and how to design them. Important file and database design considerations are summarized in Table 22-3.

TABLE 22-2 Output Design Considerations

Consideration	Concern
Use	Who will use the output, why and when do users need it, and what decisions will they make based on it?
Medium	Use paper, screen, voice, e-mail, or some combination?
Format	Will narrative, table, or graphic format best convey information?
Preprinted	Use preprinted forms? Turnaround documents?
Location	Where should output be sent?
Access	Who should have access to hard-copy and screen output?
Detail	Should a summary or table of contents be included with lengthy output? Should headings organize data and highlight important items? Should detailed information be placed in an appendix?
Timeliness	How often should output be produced?

TABLE 22-3 File and Database Design Considerations

Consideration	Concern
Medium	Store data on hard drive, disk, CD, tape, or paper?
Processing mode	Use manual, batch, or real-time processing?
Maintenance	What procedures are needed to maintain data effectively?
Size	How many records will be stored in the database, how large will they be, and how fast will the number of records grow?
Activity level	What percentage of the records will be updated, added, or deleted each year?

Input Design

Input design considerations include what types of data will be input and the optimal input method. Considerations for input design are shown in Table 22-4.

FORM DESIGN   Although systems are moving away from paper documents and toward source data automation, forms design is still an important topic. Forms design principles are summarized in Table 22-5.

COMPUTER SCREEN DESIGN   It is more efficient to enter data directly into the computer than onto paper for subsequent entry. Computer input screens are most effective when these procedures are followed:

- Organize the screen so data can be entered quickly, accurately, and completely. Minimize data input by retrieving as much data as possible from the system. For example, entering a customer number could cause the system to retrieve the customer's name, address, and other key information.
- Enter data in the same order as displayed on paper forms that capture the data.
- Group logically related data together. Complete the screen from left to right and top to bottom.
- Design the screen so users can jump from one data entry location to another or use a single key to go directly to screen locations.
- Make it easy to correct mistakes. Clear and explicit error messages that are consistent across all screens are essential. There should be a help feature to provide online assistance.
- Restrict the data or the number of menu options on a screen to avoid clutter.

Program Design

Program development, one of the most time-consuming SDLC activities, takes place in the eight steps shown below. Step 1 is part of the systems analysis phase. Step 2 begins in

TABLE 22-4 Input Design Considerations

Consideration	Concern
Medium	Enter data using a keyboard, OCR, MICR, POS terminal, barcodes, RFID tags, EDI, or voice input?
Source	Where do data originate (computer, customer, remote location, etc.), and how does that affect data entry?
Format	What format (source or turnaround document, screen, source data automation) efficiently captures the data with the least effort and cost?
Type	What is the nature of the data?
Volume	How much data are to be entered?
Personnel	What are data entry operators' abilities, functions, and expertise? Is additional training necessary?
Frequency	How often must data be entered?
Cost	How can costs be minimized without adversely affecting efficiency and accuracy?
Error detection and correction	What errors are possible, and how can they be detected and corrected?

TABLE 22-5 Principles of Good Forms Design

General Considerations
- Are preprinted data used as much as possible?
- Are the weight and grade of the paper appropriate for the planned use?
- Do bold type, lines, and shading highlight different parts of the form?
- Is the form a standard size?
- Is the form size consistent with filing, binding, or mailing requirements?
- If the form is mailed, will the address show in a window envelope?
- Are copies printed in different colors to facilitate proper distribution?
- Do clear instructions explain how to complete the form?

Introduction
- Does the form name appear at the top in bold type?
- Is the form consecutively prenumbered?
- Is the company name and address preprinted on forms sent to external parties?

Main Body
- Is logically related information (e.g., customer name, address) grouped together?
- Is there sufficient room to record each data item?
- Is data entry consistent with the sequence the data is acquired?
- Are codes or check-offs that are used instead of written entries adequately explained?

Conclusion
- Is space provided to record the final disposition of the form?
- Is space provided for a signature(s) to indicate transaction approval?
- Is space provided to record the approval date?
- Is space provided for a dollar or numeric total?
- Is the distribution of each copy of the form clearly indicated?

---

conceptual systems design and may carry over to physical design. Most of steps 3 and 4 are done during systems design and are completed during systems implementation. Steps 5 and 6 are begun in systems design, but most of the work is done during systems implementation. Step 7 is done during systems implementation and conversion. Step 8 is part of operation and maintenance.

1. *Determine user needs.* Systems analysts consult with users and reach an agreement on user needs and software requirements.
2. *Create and document a development plan.*
3. *Write program instructions (computer code).* Program preparation time may range from a few days to a few years, depending on program complexity. Programming standards (rules for writing programs) contribute to program consistency, making them easier to read and maintain. Computer programs should be subdivided into small, well-defined modules to reduce complexity and enhance reliability and modifiability, a process called *structured programming.* Modules should interact with a control module rather than with each other. To facilitate testing and modification, each module should have only one entry and exit point.
4. *Test the program.* *Debugging* is the process of discovering and eliminating program errors. A program is tested for logic errors using test data that simulate as many real processing situations and input data combinations as possible. Large programs are often tested in three stages: individual program modules, the linkages between modules and a control module, and interfaces with other application programs.

   It is important to find errors as soon as possible during the development process. The Gartner Group estimates that bugs discovered later in the SDLC cost 80% to 1,000% more to fix than those discovered earlier. Focus 22-1 discusses the difficulty of testing software and the consequences of releasing software with undetected errors. Between 20% and 30% of software development costs should be allocated to testing, debugging, and rewriting software.

FOCUS 22-1   Software Bugs Take Their Toll

An $18.5 million rocket explodes seconds after liftoff. Because of three missing digits in several million lines of programming code, telephone networks crash, leaving 10 million customers without service. A nuclear plant releases hundreds of gallons of radioactive water near Lake Huron. A device that uses X-rays to treat cancer victims delivered a radiation overdose, killing one patient and leaving two others deeply burned and partly paralyzed. A software error prevented a Patriot missile from destroying an incoming Iraqi Scud missile that killed 28 people.

These events have one disturbing fact in common. They were caused by program errors called bugs. The term *bug* was coined during World War II when a researcher, puzzled by a computer shutdown, removed a moth stuck between two electric relays. A program containing bugs can work adequately for quite some time until, with no warning, the bug triggers something, and the computer goes haywire. One incorrect letter—even a missing period—can cause a computer to issue an incorrect command or no command at all.

Bugs exist in most software, and it is almost impossible to eliminate all of them. The sheer volume of software code in a complex program makes finding bugs difficult. There are over 2.5 million lines of code in systems that check for cracks in the engine wheel of the space shuttle and 12 million in a phone company's call-switching computer. Finding a flaw in this code is as difficult as looking for one misspelled name in the New York City phone book. It is estimated that flawed or bug-ridden software cost businesses worldwide over $175 billion last year.

Programmers go to great pains to detect and eliminate bugs, but no one has the time or money to find every bug or to simulate every situation the program will encounter in the real world. Instead, software is tested with assumptions about how it will be used and what processing volumes it must handle.

One product manager estimated that his company often found 5,000 bugs in each product. They fixed serious flaws and ignored minor flaws that were unlikely to cause a problem. If developers took the time to find and correct every flaw, they would risk not getting their product to market on a timely basis and losing market share.

Software developers also cannot predict whether computer users will work faster than the software itself. The linear accelerators that killed and maimed cancer patients were controlled by an operator who typed extremely fast. She accidentally selected the X-ray mode and then switched to the electron beam. The software was not quick enough to recognize the change, and the machine beamed radiation at full power to a tiny spot on the patients' bodies. The bug was so subtle it took programmers a year to detect and eliminate it.

---

5. *Document the program.*   Documentation explains how programs work and is used to correct errors. Program documentation includes flowcharts, data flow diagrams, E-R diagrams, data models, record layouts, and narrative descriptions. These items are stored in a documentation manual.

6. *Train program users.*   Program documentation is often used to train users.

7. *Install the system.*   All system components, including the programs and the hardware, are combined, and the company begins to use the system.

8. *Use and modify the system.*   Factors that require existing programs to be revised, referred to as **program maintenance**, include requests for new or revised reports; changes in input, file content, or values such as tax rates; error detection; and conversion to new hardware.

Procedures and Controls Design

Everyone who interacts with a system needs procedures that answer the who, what, when, where, why, and how questions related to IS activities. Procedures should cover input preparation, transaction processing, error detection and correction, controls, reconciliation of balances, database access, output preparation and distribution, and computer operator instructions. Procedures documentation and training may take the form of system manuals, user instruction classes, training materials, or online help screens. Developers, users, or teams representing both groups may write procedures.

The adage "garbage in, garbage out" emphasizes that improperly controlled input, processing, and data storage functions produce unreliable information. Controls must be built into an AIS to ensure its effectiveness, efficiency, and accuracy. They should minimize errors as well as detect and correct them when they occur. Accountants play a vital role in this area. Important control concerns are summarized in Table 22-6. Controls are discussed in detail in Chapters 7 through 11.

TABLE 22-6 Controls Design Considerations

Consideration	Concern
Validity	Are system interactions valid (e.g., all cash disbursements are made to legitimate vendors)?
Authorization	Are input, processing, storage, and output activities authorized by the appropriate managers?
Accuracy	Is input verified to ensure accuracy? Are data processed and stored accurately?
Security	Is the system protected against (a) unauthorized physical and logical access to prevent the improper use, alteration, destruction, or disclosure of information and software and (b) the theft of system resources?
Numerical control	Are documents prenumbered to prevent errors and fraud and to detect when documents are misused, missing, or stolen?
Availability	Is the system available at times set forth in service-level agreements? Can users enter, update, and retrieve data during the agreed-upon times?
Maintainability	Can the system be modified without affecting system availability, security, and integrity? Are only authorized, tested, and documented changes made? Are resources available to manage, schedule, document, and communicate the changes?
Integrity	Is data processing complete, accurate, timely, and authorized? Is data processing free from unauthorized or inadvertent system manipulation?
Audit trail	Can transactions be traced from source documents to final output?

Failing to produce good policies and procedures and failing to implement controls can be devastating. Nonexistent governance kept Kaiser Kidney Transplant Center from developing good policies and procedures. As a result, hundreds of patients did not receive life-saving transplant surgeries, and the transplant center was forced to close two years after opening. Inadequate controls at Heartland Payment Systems, a credit card processor, allowed hackers to steal sensitive information from more than 100 million credit card accounts.

A *physical systems design report* summarizes what was accomplished and serves as the basis for management's decision whether or not to proceed to the implementation phase. Table 22-8 shows a table of contents for the report prepared at Shoppers Mart.

Systems Implementation

Systems implementation is the process of installing hardware and software and getting the AIS up and running. Implementation processes are shown in Figure 22-3 and described below. Focus 22-2 describes the improvements the state of Virginia made to its AIS.

Implementation Planning and Site Preparation

An *implementation plan* consists of implementation tasks, expected completion dates, cost estimates, and who is responsible for each task. The plan specifies when the project should be complete and when the AIS is operational. The implementation team identifies factors that decrease the likelihood of successful implementation, and the plan contains a strategy for coping with each factor.

AIS changes may require adjustments to a company's existing organizational structure. New departments may be created, existing ones may be eliminated or downsized, or the IS department itself may change. Technical staff at Blue Cross and Blue Shield of Wisconsin who did not understand the company's business or vision contracted for a $200 million system that did not work properly. It sent checks to a nonexistent town, made $60 million in overpayments, and resulted in the loss of 35,000 clients. One reason the system failed was that its implementation should have included an organizational restructuring.

Site preparation is a lengthy process and should begin well in advance of the installation date. A large computer may require extensive changes, such as additional electrical outlets, data communications facilities, raised floors, humidity controls, special lighting, air conditioning, fire protection, and an emergency power supply. Space is needed for equipment, storage, and offices.

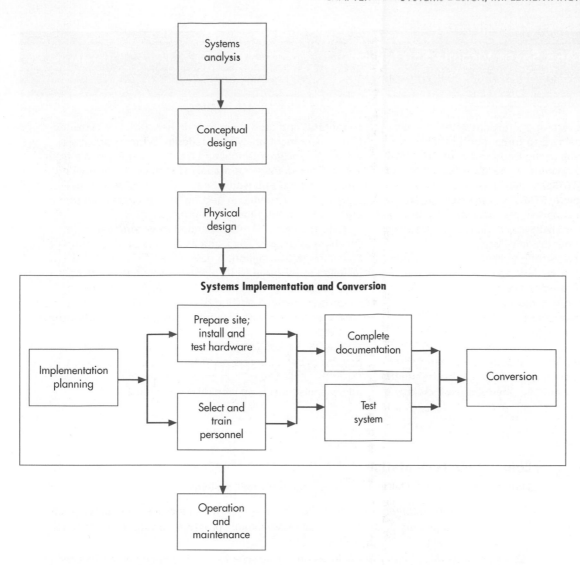

FIGURE 22-3
Systems Implementation Activities

Selecting and Training Personnel

Employees are hired from outside the company or transferred internally, which often is the less costly alternative because they already understand the firm's business and operations. Transferring employees who are displaced because of the new system could boost employee loyalty and morale.

When users are not adequately trained, the company will not achieve the expected benefits and return on its investment. Companies provide insufficient training because it is time-consuming and expensive. The hidden cost of inadequate training is that users turn for help to coworkers who have mastered the system, decreasing the productivity of coworkers and increasing company costs.

Employees must be trained on the hardware, software, and any new policies and procedures. Training should be scheduled for just before systems testing and conversion. Many training options are available, such as vendor training, self-study manuals, computer-assisted instruction, videotape presentations, role-playing, case studies, and experimenting with the system under the guidance of experienced users.

Boots the Chemists, a British pharmacy chain with over 1,000 stores, developed a novel approach to training employees nervous about a forthcoming system. They were invited to a party at a store where a new POS system had been installed. They were invited to try to harm the system by pushing the wrong buttons or fouling up a transaction. Employees quickly found they could not harm the system and that it was easy to use.

Most Virginia taxpayers receive tax refunds within a week of filing instead of the usual two to three months thanks to Jane Bailey, director of AIS at the Department of Taxation. Jane managed the development of the State Tax Accounting and Reporting System (STARS), a multisystem project that took nine years to complete. STARS was so successful that the IRS, 27 states, and a Canadian province sent teams to Richmond to see whether STARS could improve their systems development and implementation efforts.

The state's IT group had strongly recommended outside contractors for the job, saying Jane's six-person staff was far too small and unsophisticated to overhaul the state's disjointed manual and batch systems. Jane insisted on going with an inside job. She was able to convince management by stating that she would maintain the system and respond quickly to tax law changes.

Jane insisted on hiring first-rate people, and her staff eventually swelled to 45 employees. If she could not hire the experts and specialists she needed, she retained them as consultants and used them to train her staff. She recruited five management analysts to redesign business processes, write user documentation, and train users. Ten people from her staff are management analysts who work full-time on user procedures and issues. Seeing user involvement as crucial, Jane succeeded in getting six managers from user areas assigned full-time to the project.

Over the years, STARS expanded to encompass more functions and more users, and its budget climbed from $3 million to $11 million. A new piece of software was installed every three to six months. Users had to adapt, often getting 15 new screens at a time. The megaproject eventually involved putting together 1,500 programs, 40 IBM databases, and 350 online screens in 25 applications for 1,800 users.

The state asked for a Chevrolet and got a Cadillac; the payoff has been impressive. STARS users estimate that it saved the state $80 million over five years, most of it from added collections from would-be tax cheats.

Complete Documentation

Three types of documentation must be prepared for new systems:

1. *Development documentation* describes the new AIS. It includes a system description; copies of output, input, and file and database layouts; program flowcharts; test results; and user acceptance forms.
2. *Operations documentation* includes operating schedules; files and databases accessed; and equipment, security, and file-retention requirements.
3. *User documentation* teaches users how to operate the AIS. It includes a procedures manual and training materials.

Testing the System

Inadequate system testing was another reason for the Blue Cross and Blue Shield system failure. The developers underestimated system complexity and promised an unrealistic delivery time of 18 months. One shortcut they took to meet the deadline was to deliver an untested system. Documents and reports, user input, controls, operating and processing procedures, capacity limits, recovery procedures, and computer programs should all be tested in realistic circumstances. Following are three common forms of testing:

1. *Walk-throughs* are step-by-step reviews of procedures or program logic to find incorrect logic, errors, omissions, or other problems. The development team and system users attend walk-throughs early in system design. The focus is on the input, files, outputs, and data flows of the organization. Subsequent walk-throughs, attended by programmers, address logical and structural aspects of program code.
2. *Processing test data*, including all valid transactions and all possible error conditions, is performed to determine whether a program operates as designed; that is, valid transactions are handled properly and errors are detected and dealt with appropriately. To evaluate test results, the correct system response for each test transaction must be specified in advance.
3. *Acceptance tests* use copies of real transactions and files rather than hypothetical ones. Users develop the acceptance criteria and make the final decision whether to accept the AIS.

Chemical Bank did not adequately test an ATM upgrade, and customers who withdrew cash had their accounts debited twice. Over 150,000 withdrawals with a total value of $8 million were posted twice. Thousands of small accounts were overdrawn or emptied, which annoyed and angered customers. Chemical Bank lost a great deal of customer credibility because of the glitch.

Even software purchased from an outside vendor must be tested thoroughly before being installed. As soon as Kane Carpets installed an AIS custom tailored to the floor-covering industry, its inventory control system told salespeople that orders could not be filled when the product was available, and vice versa. As a result, Kane lost many of its customers.

Systems Conversion

Conversion is changing from the old to the new AIS. Many elements must be converted: hardware, software, data files, and procedures. The process is complete when the new AIS is a routine, ongoing part of the system. Four conversion approaches are used:

- *Direct conversion* terminates the old AIS when the new one is introduced. For example, Shoppers Mart could discontinue its old system on Saturday night and use its new AIS on Monday morning. Direct conversion is appropriate when a new system is so different that comparisons between the two are meaningless. The approach is inexpensive, but it provides no backup AIS. Unless a system has been carefully developed and tested, direct conversion carries a high risk of failure. Focus 22-3 discusses the problems at Sunbeam, caused in part by attempting a direct conversion.
- *Parallel conversion* operates the old and new systems simultaneously for a period. For example, Shoppers Mart could process transactions with both systems, compare the output, reconcile the differences, correct problems, and discontinue the old system after the new system proves itself. Parallel processing protects companies from errors, but it is costly and stressful to process transactions twice. Because companies often experience problems during conversion, parallel processing has gained widespread popularity.

FOCUS 22-3   Sunbeam and the Price of Direct Conversion

Sunbeam hired CEO Al Dunlap to turn the company around. While turning Scott Paper around, Al made such drastic cost cuts that he was nicknamed Chainsaw Al. At Sunbeam, Al also made drastic cost-cutting moves, many of which went too far and ended up hurting the company much more than they helped. He eliminated 87% of the company's products and half of its 6,000 employees, including outsourcing the information systems staff. Terminated computer personnel making $35,000 a year were replaced with contract workers paid significantly more than $35,000. Ironically, some of the contract workers turned out to be terminated employees.

To minimize costs during an information system modernization, Sunbeam used a direct conversion approach that did not work. Because there was no backup system, the entire system was down for months. The result was total chaos. Orders were lost, and customers did not receive their shipments, received their orders two or three times, or received the wrong order. Sunbeam had no way to respond to upset customers, because employees could not track orders or

shipments. Customers could not be billed automatically, and Sunbeam had to bill its customers manually.

Because of poor management and no AIS for a long time, Sunbeam's stock plummeted. Al Dunlap was fired, shareholder lawsuits were filed, and governmental entities investigated the company. The SEC claimed that Al perpetrated an accounting fraud, because $62 million of Sunbeam's $189 million in income in 1997 did not comply with accounting rules. Sunbeam filed for Chapter 11 bankruptcy protection, and several Sunbeam executives paid fines to settle charges of participating in a scheme to inflate the worth of the company. Al Dunlap agreed to a $500,000 fine without admitting or denying the SEC's accusations. Arthur Andersen, their auditors, paid $110 million in damages to settle a shareholder class-action suit. Phillip Harlow, the Andersen partner in charge of Sunbeam's 1997 year-end financial audit, was barred from practicing public accounting before the SEC for three years in exchange for having fraud charges against him dropped.

- *Phase-in conversion* gradually replaces elements of the old AIS with the new one. For example, Shoppers Mart could implement its inventory system, then disbursements, then sales collection, and so forth, until the whole system is functional. Gradual changes allow data processing resources to be acquired over time. The disadvantages are the cost of creating the temporary interfaces between the old and the new AIS and the time required to make the gradual changeover.
- *Pilot conversion* implements a system in one part of the organization, such as a branch location. For example, Shoppers Mart could install its new POS system at one of its stores using a direct, parallel, or phase-in approach. When problems with the system are resolved, the new system could be implemented at the remaining locations. This localizes conversion problems and allows training in a live environment. The disadvantages are the long conversion time and the need for interfaces between the old and the new systems, which coexist until all locations have been converted. Owens-Corning Fiberglass implemented its accounts payable, travel expense, and payroll systems by getting the system up and running in one plant and then moving it to all the others.

Data conversion can be time-consuming, tedious, and expensive; its difficulty and magnitude are easily underestimated. Data files may need to be modified in three ways. First, files may be moved to a different storage medium—for example, from tapes to disks. Second, data content may be changed—for example, fields and records may be added or deleted. Third, file or database format may be changed.

The first step in data conversion is to decide which data files need to be converted. Then the data are checked for completeness and errors, and inconsistencies are removed. Following data conversion, the new files are validated to ensure data were not lost during conversion. If data conversion is lengthy, the new files must be updated with the transactions that occurred during data conversion. Once the files and databases have been converted and tested for accuracy, the new system is functional. The system should be monitored for a time to make sure it runs smoothly and accurately. The final activity is to document the conversion activities.

Operation and Maintenance

The final SDLC step is to operate and maintain the new system. A *post-implementation review* is conducted to determine whether the system meets its planned objectives. Important review considerations are listed in Table 22-7. Problems uncovered during the review are brought to

TABLE 22-7 Factors to Investigate During Post-Implementation Review

Factors	Questions
Goals and objectives	Does the system help the organization meet its goals, objectives, and overall mission?
Satisfaction	Are users satisfied? What would they like changed or improved?
Benefits	How have users benefited? Were the expected benefits achieved?
Costs	Are actual costs in line with expected costs?
Reliability	Is the system reliable? Has it failed? If so, what caused its failure?
Accuracy	Does the system produce accurate and complete data?
Timeliness	Does the system produce information on a timely basis?
Compatibility	Are hardware, software, data, and procedures compatible with existing systems?
Controls and security	Is the system safeguarded against errors, fraud, and intrusion?
Errors	Do adequate error-handling procedures exist?
Training	Are systems personnel and users trained to support and use the system?
Communications	Is the communications system adequate?
Organizational changes	Are organizational changes beneficial or harmful? If harmful, how can they be resolved?
Documentation	Is system documentation complete and accurate?

TABLE 22-8 Table of Contents for Shoppers Mart Reports

Conceptual Systems Design Report	Physical Systems Design Report	Postimplementation Review Report
Table of Contents	Table of Contents	Table of Contents

I. Executive Summary of Conceptual Systems Design
II. Overview of Project Purpose and Summary of Findings to Date
III. Recommended Conceptual Design(s)
  A. Overview of Recommended Design(s)
  B. Objectives to Be Achieved by Design(s)
  C. Impact of Design(s) on Information System and Organization
  D. Expected Costs and Benefits of Design(s)
  E. Audit, Control, and Security Processes and Procedures
  F. Hardware, Software, and Other Resource Requirements
  G. Processing Flows: Relationships of Programs, Databases, Inputs, and Outputs
  H. Description of System Components (Programs, Databases, Inputs, and Outputs)
IV. Assumptions and Unresolved Problems
V. Summary
VI. Appendixes, Glossary
	I. Executive Summary of Physical Systems Design
	II. Overview of Project Purpose and Summary of Findings to Date
	III. Physical Design Recommendations
	  A. Output Design
	  B. Input Design
	  C. Database Design
	  D. Software Design
	  E. Hardware Design
	  F. Controls Design
	  G. Procedures Design
	IV. Assumptions and Unresolved Problems
	V. Summary
	VI. Appendixes, Glossary
		I. Executive Summary of Postimplementation Review
		II. Overview of Development Project
		III. Evaluation of the Development
		  A. Degree to Which System Objectives Were Met
		  B. Analysis of Actual Versus Expected Costs and Benefits
		  C. User Reactions and Satisfaction
		IV. Evaluation of Project Development Team
		V. Recommendations
		  A. Recommendations for Improving the New System
		  B. Recommendations for Improving the System Development Process
		VI. Summary

management's attention, and the necessary adjustments are made. Table 22-8 illustrates what the *post-implementation review report* should contain. User acceptance of the report is the final activity in the systems development process.

Control of the AIS is passed to the data processing department, but work on the new system is not finished. Over the life of a typical system, 30% of the work takes place during development, and 70% is spent on software modifications and updates. At Hartford Insurance Group, 70% of its personnel resources are devoted to maintaining an inventory of 34,000 program modules containing 24 million lines of code. The job is even more difficult because changes in insurance regulations and business strategies reduced the structure of the code and increased its complexity.

Summary and Case Conclusion

Ann Christy tackles the sales processing system first. She gives the project development team her systems analysis report and accompanying data. During conceptual systems design, the team visits stores with similar operations and identifies ways to meet AIS requirements. Alternative approaches are discussed with users, management, and the steering committee. They are narrowed down to Ann's original approach. Ann has considered buying software but does not find a package that accomplishes what she and the company want. The team develops conceptual design specifications for the output, input, processing, and data storage elements.

The company decides to use screen-based output and to capture data electronically using point of sale (POS) devices. Data that cannot be captured electronically will be entered using PCs. Each store will have a network that connects its PCs and POS devices to a local database. The POS cash registers will capture and feed sales data electronically to this database. Each store will be linked to the central office using a wide area network. All sales data, store orders, and other summary-level information will be uploaded to the corporate database daily. The corporate database will download the information needed to manage the store. The central office will use electronic data interchange to order goods and pay suppliers.

During physical design, the development team designs each report identified during conceptual design. Users and designers rework the reports until everyone is satisfied. The team designs all files, databases, and input screens. Then they design the software programs that collect and process data and produce the output. The team develops new procedures for handling data and operating the AIS. The accountants and the internal audit staff are especially helpful during the design of the controls needed to protect the system against errors and fraud.

Implementation planning starts early. A location for the new mainframe is identified, and site preparation begins during the design phase. The hardware and software are installed and tested and then the entire AIS is tested. The new AIS is staffed with existing employees that are trained as the system is tested. System documentation is completed before data from the old AIS are converted to the new one.

For the corporate system, the new and old systems are operated in parallel for a month, and the results compared. The bugs are ironed out, and the old AIS is discontinued. For the store systems, a pilot approach is used. The AIS is installed at three stores, and all problems are resolved before the system is implemented at the remaining stores. Conversion requires a fair amount of overtime and duplicate processing. After a few months, Ann and her staff conduct a post-implementation review and make some adjustments to enhance the high user acceptance of the new AIS.

Ann makes a final presentation to top management after the AIS is installed and operating. She is widely congratulated and even hears the president mention that she "is worth keeping an eye on" for even more responsibility in the firm. Table 22-8 is a summary of the contents of the conceptual, physical, and post-implementation reports.

Key Terms

conceptual systems
  design 641
conceptual design
  specifications 643
conceptual systems design
  report 643
physical systems design 643
scheduled report 644
special-purpose analysis
  report 644
triggered exception
  report 644

demand report 644
structured programming 646
debugging 646
program maintenance 647
physical systems design
  report 648
systems implementation 648
implementation plan 648
walk-through 650
processing test
  data 650

acceptance test 650
conversion 651
direct conversion 651
parallel conversion 651
phase-in conversion 652
pilot conversion 652
post-implementation
  review 652
post-implementation
  review report 653

AIS IN ACTION

Chapter Quiz

1. The developers of your new system have proposed two different AIS designs and have asked you to evaluate them. This evaluation process is most likely to be a part of which SDLC step?
   a. systems analysis
   b. conceptual design
   c. physical design
   d. implementation and conversion
   e. operation and maintenance

2. What is the purpose of the conceptual systems design report?
   a. to guide physical systems design activities
   b. to communicate how management and user information needs are met
   c. to help the steering committee assess system feasibility
   d. a and b
   e. a, b, and c

3. Which of the following is the correct order of the steps in physical systems design?
   a. input, file and database, output, controls, procedures, program
   b. file and database, output, input, procedures, program, controls
   c. output, input, file and database, procedures, program, controls
   d. output, file and database, input, program, procedures, controls

4. A monthly payroll register showing all hourly employees, the number of hours they worked, their deductions, and their net pay is most likely which of the following?
   a. scheduled report
   b. special-purpose analysis
   c. triggered exception report
   d. demand report

5. Which of the following is NOT a consideration in input design?
   a. Which errors are possible, and how can they be detected and corrected?
   b. How can data be entered (keyboards, OCR, or POS terminal)?
   c. Which format efficiently captures the input data with the least effort and cost?
   d. How often should the system produce reports?

6. Which of the following is most likely to help improve program development?
   a. physical model
   b. IT strategic plan
   c. walk-through
   d. record layout

7. Which of the following statements is true?
   a. The Gartner Group estimates that programming bugs not found until later in the SDLC cost 25% to 30% more to correct than if they had been found earlier in the SDLC.
   b. Direct system conversion is the least risky of the system conversion methods.
   c. Many software developers state that 5% to 10% of software development costs should be allocated to testing, debugging, and rewriting software.
   d. Over the life of a system, only 30% of information systems work takes place during development; the remaining 70% is spent maintaining the system.

8. Which of the following describes the systems testing approach that uses real transactions and files rather than hypothetical ones?
   a. walk-through
   b. processing of test transactions
   c. acceptance test
   d. parallel conversion test

9. What is the process of discontinuing an old system as soon as a new one is introduced?
   a. direct conversion
   b. parallel conversion
   c. phase-in conversion
   d. pilot conversion

10. Which of the following describes designing a program from the top down to more detailed levels?
    a. hierarchical program design
    b. top-down program design
    c. parallel program design
    d. unstructured program design

Chapter Case Hershey's Big Bang ERP

Halloween is the biggest candy season of them all, with $1.8 billion in sales. For Hershey's, Halloween 1999 was the scariest of all time. Hershey's had planned to implement a $112 million ERP system in 48 months. Instead, it was implemented in an accelerated 30-month time frame. Hershey's "flipped the switch" in July 1999, right during its busiest ordering season. Issues with inventory and ordering processes promptly gummed up the order-distribution system. By August 1999, Hershey's was 15 days behind in shipping orders. Many distributors who placed orders in September were still waiting for their shipment at Halloween. Hershey had plenty of candy in inventory; it just could not move the candy from its warehouses to its customers. The implementation problem contributed to a 19% drop in revenue. It took a full year for the company to bounce back.

The new ERP system employed over 5,000 PCs, network hubs, and servers. The ERP software was supplied by three firms and implemented by a large consulting firm. Despite the system's size and complexity, Hershey chose to implement most of it in one step called the "big bang."

Required

What could Hershey have done to properly design, implement, and operate this new ERP?

Discussion Questions

22.1. Prism Glass is converting to a new information system. To expedite and speed up implementation, the CEO asked your consulting team to postpone establishing standards and controls until after the system is fully operational. How should you respond to the CEO's request?

22.2. When a company converts from one system to another, many areas within the organization are affected. Explain how conversion to a new system will affect the following groups, both individually and collectively.
   a. Personnel
   b. Data storage
   c. Operations
   d. Policies and procedures
   e. Physical facilities

22.3. The following notice was posted in the employee cafeteria on Monday morning:

To:	All Accounting and Clerical Employees
From:	I.M. Krewel, President
Subject:	Termination of Employee Positions

Effective this Friday, all accounting and clerical employees not otherwise contacted will be terminated. Our new computer system eliminates the need for most of these jobs. We're grateful for the loyal service you've rendered as employees and wish you success. You may wish to pick up your final checks on Friday before you go.

Discuss the president's approach to human resource management. What are the possible repercussions of this episode? Assuming that job termination is the best alternative available, how should management approach the situation?

22.4. In which phase of the systems development cycle would each of the following positions be most actively involved? Justify your answers.
   a. Managerial accountant
   b. Programmer
   c. Systems analyst
   d. Financial vice president
   e. Information systems manager
   f. Internal auditor

22.5. During which of the five SDLC stages is each task, labeled (a) through (m), performed? More than one answer may apply for each activity.

—— 1. Systems analysis	a. Writing operating procedures manuals
—— 2. Conceptual (general) systems design	b. Developing program and process controls
—— 3. Physical (detailed) systems design	c. Identifying alternative systems designs
—— 4. Implementation and conversion	d. Developing a logical model of the system
—— 5. Operation and maintenance	e. Identifying external and administrative controls
	f. Testing the system
	g. Training personnel
	h. Evaluating the existing system

i. Analyzing the achievement of systems benefits

j. Modifying and altering programs

k. Analyzing total quality management (TQM) performance measures

l. Conducting a feasibility analysis

m. Aligning AIS development plans with business objectives

Problems

22.1. You were hired to manage the accounting and control functions at the Glass Jewelry Company. During your introductory meeting, the president asked you to design and implement a new AIS within six months. Company sales for the past year were $10 million, and they are expected to double in the next 18 months.

Required

a. Outline the procedures you would follow to complete the assigned project. Include a description of the following:

1. Sources of information
2. Methods of documenting information collected
3. Methods of verifying the information collected

b. The accounts payable system will contain a number of programs, including Enter Invoices and Print Payable Checks. For each program, describe its purpose, and outline application control considerations. *(SMAC Examination, adapted)*

22.2. Wang Lab's tremendous growth left the company with a serious problem. Customers would often wait months for Wang to fill orders and process invoices. Repeated attempts by Wang's understaffed IS department to solve these problems met with failure. Finally, Wang hired a consulting firm to solve its revenue tracking problems and expedite prompt receipt of payments. The 18-month project turned into a doubly long nightmare. After three years and $10 million, the consultants were dismissed from the unfinished project.

The project failed for many reasons. The systems development process was so dynamic that the failure to complete the project quickly became self-defeating as modifications took over the original design. Second, management did not have a clear vision of the new AIS and lacked a strong support staff. As a result, a number of incompatible tracking systems sprang from the company's distributed computer system. Third, the project was too large and complex for the consulting firm, who had little experience with the complex database at the heart of the new system. Finally, the project had too many applications. Interdependencies among subprograms left consultants with few completed programs. Every program was linked to several subprograms, which in turn were linked to several other programs. Programmers eventually found themselves lost in a morass of subroutines with no completed program.

The IS department finally developed a system to solve the problem, but their revenue tracking system suffered quality problems for years.

Required

Wang asked you to write a memo explaining the failure of the systems development project.

a. Why did the development project fail? What role did the consultants play in the failure?

b. Identify the organizational issues that management must address in the future.

c. Recommend steps the company could take to guarantee consulting service quality.

22.3. Tiny Toddlers, a manufacturer of children's toys and furniture, is designing and implementing a distributed system to assist its sales force. Each of the 10 sales offices in Canada and 20 in the United States maintains its own customers and is responsible for granting credit and collecting receivables. Reports used by each sales office to maintain the customer master file and to enter the daily sales orders are shown in Figures 22-4 and 22-5.

Required

Evaluate the reports shown in Figures 22-4 and 22-5 using the following format:

| Weakness | Explanation | Recommendation(s) |

(SMAC Examination, adapted)

22.4. Mickie Louderman is the new assistant controller of Pickens Publishers. She was the controller of a company in a similar industry, where she was in charge of accounting and had considerable influence over computer center operations. Pickens wants to revamp its information system, placing increased emphasis on decentralized data access and online systems. John Richards, the controller, is near retirement. He has put Mickie in charge of developing a new system that integrates the company's accounting-related functions. Her promotion to controller will depend on the success of the new AIS.

Mickie uses the same design characteristics and reporting format she used at her former company. She sends details of the new AIS to the departments that interface with accounting, including inventory control, purchasing, human resources, production control, and marketing. If they do not respond with suggestions by a prescribed date, she will continue the development process. Mickie and John have established a new schedule for many of the reports, changing the frequency from weekly to monthly. After a meeting with the director of IS, Mickie selects a programmer to help her with the details of the new reporting formats.

Most control features of the old system are maintained to decrease the installation time, with a few new ones added for unusual situations. The procedures for maintaining the controls are substantially changed. Mickie makes all the AIS control change and program-testing decisions, including screening the control features related to payroll, inventory control, accounts receivable, cash deposits, and accounts payable.

FIGURE 22-4
Customer Maintenance Form for Tiny Toddlers

CUSTOMER MAINTENANCE FORM	
New Customer?	☐
	Yes _____
	☑
	No _____ 24671 _____
Name	The Little Ones Furniture Store
New Address	5 St. Antoine Street N.
	Quebec City
Old Address	305 St. Antoine Street S.
	Quebec City
Salesperson #	02
Requested Credit Limit	50,000
Sales Office	Eastern Canada
Pricing Code	25
Estimated Sales	300,000
Credit Limit	10,000
Currency	U.S.A. ☐, Canada ☐
Bank	Canadian Credit Bank
	50 St. Antoine Street
	Quebec City
Bank Line	
Rating	Satisfactory
_____ Sales Manager	
_____ Credit Manager	

SALES ORDER FORM

Customer: 24671   Date: _____
           The Little Ones Furniture Store
           5 St. Antoine Street N.
           Quebec City

Product Code	Description	Quantity
24571	Crib	4
M0002	Mattress	102
HG730	High chair—white	32
HG223	High chair—natural wood	22
CT200	Changing table	300
D0025	Desk—modern design	2
C9925	Chair—modern design	5
BP809	Bumper pads	1200

Salesperson No.: _____

Entered by: _____

FIGURE 22-5

Sales Order Form for Tiny Toddlers

As each module is completed, Mickie has the corresponding department implement the change immediately to take advantage of the labor savings. Incomplete instructions accompany these changes, and specific implementation responsibility is not assigned to departmental personnel. Mickie believes operations people should learn as they go, reporting errors as they occur.

Accounts payable and inventory control are implemented first, and several problems arise. The semimonthly payroll runs, which had been weekly under the old system, have abundant errors, requiring numerous manual paychecks. Payroll run control totals take hours to reconcile with the computer printout. To expedite matters, Mickie authorizes the payroll clerk to prepare payroll journal entries.

The new inventory control system fails to improve the carrying level of many stock items. This causes critical stock outs of raw material that result in expensive rush orders. The new system's primary control procedure is the availability of ordering and user information. The information is available to both inventory control and purchasing personnel so that both departments can issue timely purchase orders. Because the inventory levels are updated daily, Mickie discontinues the previous weekly report.

Because of these problems, system documentation is behind schedule, and proper backup procedures have not been implemented. Mickie has requested budget approval to hire two systems analysts, an accountant, and an administrative assistant to help her implement the new system. John is disturbed by her request because her predecessor had only one part-time assistant.

Required

a. List the steps Mickie should have taken while designing the AIS to ensure that end-user needs were satisfied.

b. Identify and describe three ways Mickie violated internal control principles during the AIS implementation.

c. Identify and describe the weaknesses in Mickie's approach to implementing the new AIS. How could you improve the development process for the remaining parts of the AIS? (*CMA Examination, adapted*)

22.5. Ryon Pulsipher, manager of Columbia's property accounting division, has had difficulty responding to the following departmental requests for information about fixed assets.

1. The controller has requested individual fixed assets schedules to support the general ledger balance. Although Ryon has furnished the information, it is late. The way the records are organized makes it difficult to obtain information easily.

2. The maintenance manager wants to verify the existence of a punch press that he thinks was repaired twice. He has asked Ryon to confirm the asset number and the location of the press.
3. The insurance department wants data on the cost and book values of assets to include in its review of current insurance coverage.
4. The tax department has requested data to determine whether Columbia should switch depreciation methods for tax purposes.
5. The internal auditors have spent significant time in the property accounting division to confirm the annual depreciation expense.

Ryon's property account records, kept in an Excel spreadsheet, show the asset acquisition date, its account number, the dollar amount capitalized, and its estimated useful life for depreciation purposes. After many frustrations, Ryon realizes his records are inadequate and that he cannot supply data easily when requested. He discusses his problems with the controller, Gig Griffith.

RYON: Gig, something has to give. My people are working overtime and can't keep up. You worked in property accounting before you became controller. You know I can't tell the tax, insurance, and maintenance people everything they need to know from my records. Internal auditing is living in my area, and that slows down the work. The requests of these people are reasonable, and we should be able to answer their questions and provide the needed data. I think we need an automated property accounting system. I want to talk with the AIS people to see if they can help me.

GIG: I think that's a great idea. Just be sure you are personally involved in the design of any system so you get all the info you need. Keep me posted on the project's progress.

Required

a. Identify and justify four major objectives Columbia's automated property accounting system should possess to respond to departmental requests for information.
b. Identify the data that should be included in the database for each asset. *(CMA Examination, adapted)*

22.6. A credit union is developing a new AIS. The internal auditors suggest planning the systems development process in accordance with the SDLC concept. The following nine items are identified as major systems development activities that will have to be completed.
1. System test
2. User specifications
3. Conversion
4. Systems survey
5. Technical specifications
6. Post-implementation planning
7. Implementation planning
8. User procedures and training
9. Programming

Required

a. Arrange the nine items in the sequence in which they should logically occur.
b. One major activity is to convert data files from the old system to the new one. List three types of file conversion documentation that would be of particular interest to an auditor. *(CMA Examination, adapted)*

 22.7. MetLife, an insurance company, spent $11 billion to acquire Travelers Life and Annuity from Citicorp in one of the largest insurance company acquisitions of all time. The Metlife CIO estimated it would take three years to integrate the two systems. Because the integration project was especially critical, he figured he could accomplish the integration in 18 months if he pulled out all the stops. The MetLife CEO gave him nine months to complete the task. To pull off the integration in nine months, he had to:

- Integrate over 600 IS applications, all with their own infrastructure and business processes. The new systems had to comply with "One MetLife," a company policy that all information systems had to have a common look and feel companywide and be able to function seamlessly with other MetLife systems.
- Work with over 4,000 employees located in 88 offices scattered all over the globe.
- Supervise an oversight team and 50 integration teams in seven project management offices.
- Work with hostile, uncooperative Travelers employees for the six months it took to get regulatory approval and close the deal. The systems had to be integrated three months after the deal closed.
- Identify integration deliverables (144 in total) and manage the process to deliver them.
- Negotiate with Citicorp for hundreds of transition services that would not be immediately converted to MetLife's systems

Required

a. What tasks would MetLife have to perform to integrate the Traveler systems into MetLife's?
b. Search the Internet for articles that describe the integration process. Write a two-page summary of the problems and successes that MetLife experienced while integrating the two systems.

22.8. During final testing, just before launching a new payroll system, the project manager at Reutzel Legal Services found that the purchased payroll system was doing the following:

- Writing checks for negative amounts
- Printing checks with names and employee numbers that did not match
- Making errors; for example, $8 per hour became $800 per hour if a decimal point was not entered
- Writing checks for amounts greater than a full year's salary

Fortunately, payroll was still installed on time, and only 1.5% of the checks had to be manually reissued every payday until the problem was solved.

Other problems were that no one had made sure the new system was compatible with the existing payroll database, and there appeared to be no formal transition between the development of the project and the implementation of the project. The system was never run in parallel.

Although the programming manager lost his job, the payroll problems helped raise awareness of the company's growing dependence on IT. Lacking a major problem, there was a perception that the information system did not affect operations.

Required

a. What does "the system was never run in parallel" mean?
b. If the company had run the system in parallel, what should have occurred?
c. What other testing methodologies could have been used by the firm?
d. What other types of problems are evident from reading the case?

22.9. A new program at Jones and Carter Corporation (JCC) was supposed to track customer calls. Unfortunately, the program took 20 minutes to load on a PC, and it crashed frequently. The project did not have a traditional reporting structure, and it appeared that no one was actually in charge. The lead project manager quit halfway through the project, the in-house programmers were reassigned to other projects or let go, and two layers of management loosely supervised the systems analyst.

Management hired consultants to fix the application, but after three months and $200,000, the project was discontinued. JCC did not check the references of the consulting firm it hired to create the new system. The consultants, who were located two states away, made many programming errors. Although the systems analyst caught some of the consultant's mistakes, they grew increasingly distant and difficult to work with. They would not even furnish the source code to the project managers, most likely because they were afraid of revealing their incompetence.

Required

a. Identify potential causes for the system implementation failure.
b. What steps should JCC have taken to successfully design and implement the call tracking system?

Case 22-1 Citizen's Gas Company

Citizen's Gas Company (CGC) provides natural gas service to 200,000 customers. The customer base is divided into the following three revenue classes:

Class	Customers	Sales in Cubic Feet	Revenues
Residential	160,000	80 billion	$160 million
Commercial	38,000	15 billion	$ 25 million
Industrial	2,000	50 billion	$ 65 million
Totals		145 billion	$250 million

Residential customer gas usage is highly correlated with the weather. Commercial customer usage is partially weather dependent. Industrial customer usage is governed almost entirely by business factors.

The company buys natural gas from 10 pipeline companies in the amounts specified in contracts that run for 5 to 15 years. For some contracts, the supply is in equal monthly increments; for other contracts, the supply varies according to the heating season. Supply over the contract amounts is not available, and some contracts contain take-or-pay clauses. That is, the company must pay for the gas volume specified in the contract, regardless of the amount used.

To match customer demand with supply, gas is pumped into a storage field when supply exceeds customer demand. Gas is withdrawn when demand exceeds supply. There are no restrictions on the gas storage field except that the field must be full at the beginning of each gas year (September 1). Consequently, when the contractual supply for the remainder of the gas year is less than that required to satisfy projected demand and fill the storage field, CGC curtails service to industrial customers (except for heating quantities). The curtailments must be carefully controlled to prevent either an oversupply at year-end or a curtailing of commercial or residential customers so the storage field can be filled at year-end.

In recent years, CGC's planning efforts have not been able to control the supply during the gas year or provide the information needed to establish long-term contracts. Customer demand has been projected only as a function of the total number of customers. Commercial and industrial customers' demand for gas has been curtailed. This has resulted in lost sales and caused an excess of supply at the end of the gas year.

To correct the problems, CGC has hired a director of corporate planning. She is presented with a conceptual design for an information system that will help analyze gas supply and demand. The system will provide a monthly gas plan for the next five years, with particular emphasis on the first year. The plan will provide detailed reports that assist in the decision-making process. The system will use actual data during the year to project demand for the year. The president has indicated that she will base her decisions on the effect alternative plans have on operating income.

Required

1. Discuss the criteria to consider in specifying the structure and features of CGC's new system.
2. Identify the data that should be incorporated into CGC's new system to provide adequate planning capability. Explain why each data item is important and the level of detail needed for the data to be useful. *(CMA Examination, adapted)*

AIS IN ACTION SOLUTIONS

Quiz Key

1. The developers of your new system have proposed two different AIS designs and have asked you to evaluate them. This evaluation process is most likely to be a part of which SDLC step?
   a. systems analysis [Incorrect. During systems analysis, analysts identify user requirements and establish objectives and specifications for the design phases of the SDLC.]
   ▶ b. conceptual design [Correct. During conceptual design, users develop and evaluate appropriate design alternatives.]
   c. physical design [Incorrect. During physical design, the company translates the broad, user-oriented requirements of the conceptual design into detailed specifications that are used to develop and test computer programs.]
   d. implementation and conversion [Incorrect. During implementation and conversion, the company installs and tests hardware, software, and procedures, as well as converts from the old system to the new system.]
   e. operation and maintenance [Incorrect. During operation and maintenance, the company runs the system and performs ongoing maintenance and minor modifications.]

2. What is the purpose of the conceptual systems design report?
   a. to guide physical systems design activities [Incorrect. The conceptual design report also includes communicating how management and users' needs are met and helping the steering committee assess system feasibility.]
   b. to communicate how management and user information needs are met [Incorrect. The conceptual design report also includes guiding physical systems design activities and helping the steering committee assess system feasibility.]
   c. to help the steering committee assess system feasibility [Incorrect. The conceptual design report also includes communicating how management and users' needs are met and guiding physical systems design activities.]
   d. a and b [Incorrect. The conceptual design report also includes helping the steering committee assess system feasibility.]
   ▶ e. a, b, and c [Correct. The conceptual design report guides physical systems design activities, communicates how management and users' needs are met, and helps the steering committee assess system feasibility.]

3. Which of the following is the correct order of the steps in physical systems design?
   a. input, file and database, output, controls, procedures, program [Incorrect. See Figure 22-2.]
   b. file and database, output, input, procedures, program, controls [Incorrect. See Figure 22-2.]
   c. output, input, file and database, procedures, program, controls [Incorrect. See Figure 22-2.]
   ▶ d. output, file and database, input, program, procedures, controls [Correct. See Figure 22-2.]

4. A monthly payroll register showing all hourly employees, the number of hours they worked, their deductions, and their net pay is most likely which of the following?
   ▶ a. scheduled report [Correct. Scheduled reports have a specified content, format, and delivery time. A monthly payroll register exhibits these characteristics.]
   b. special-purpose analysis [Incorrect. A special-purpose analysis has no specified content, format, or delivery schedule.]
   c. triggered exception report [Incorrect. A triggered exception report has specified content and format, but it is generated only if a certain event occurs.]
   d. demand report [Incorrect. A demand report has specified content and format, but it is generated only on request.]

5. Which of the following is NOT a consideration in input design?
   a. Which errors are possible, and how can they be detected and corrected? [Incorrect. Error identification and correction should be considered during input design. See Table 22-4.]

b. How can data be entered (keyboards, OCR, or POS terminal)? [Incorrect. Data entry methods should be considered during input design. See Table 22-4.]

c. Which format efficiently captures the input data with the least effort and cost? [Incorrect. Data format should be considered during input design. See Table 22-4.]

▶ d. How often should the system produce reports? [Correct. Report generation frequency is not normally considered during input design. See Table 22-4.]

6. Which of the following is most likely to help improve program development?

a. physical model [Incorrect. A physical model is most commonly used to describe the physical characteristics of a database.]

b. IT strategic plan [Incorrect. An entity's strategic plan provides a roadmap for achieving long-range goals.]

▶ c. walk-through [Correct. During walk-throughs, people associated with designing the project review it step by step so any problems can be identified and corrected.]

d. record layout [Incorrect. A record layout illustrates how data items are stored in a file.]

7. Which of the following statements is true?

a. The Gartner Group estimates that programming bugs not found until later in the SDLC cost 25% to 30% more to correct than if they had been found earlier in the SDLC. [Incorrect. The correct estimate is 80% to 1,000% more.]

b. Direct system conversion is the least risky of the system conversion methods. [Incorrect. Direct conversion is the most risky rather than the least risky method for converting from an old system to a new system.]

c. Many software developers state that 5% to 10% of software development costs should be allocated to testing, debugging, and rewriting software. [Incorrect. Software developers recommend that 20% to 30% of software development costs be allocated to testing, debugging, and rewriting software.]

▶ d. Over the life of a system, only 30% of information systems work takes place during development; the remaining 70% is spent maintaining the system. [Correct.]

8. Which of the following describes the systems testing approach that uses real transactions and files rather than hypothetical ones?

a. walk-through [Incorrect. Walk-throughs are step-by-step reviews of procedures or programs so any problems can be identified and corrected.]

b. processing of test transactions [Incorrect. Processing of test transactions uses valid and erroneous data to test for the proper handling of transactions, as well as the proper detection and handling of errors.]

▶ c. acceptance test [Correct. An acceptance test uses real transaction data to test a new system.]

d. parallel conversion test [Incorrect. Parallel conversion is a system conversion method, not a testing method.]

9. What is the process of discontinuing an old system as soon as a new one is introduced?

▶ a. direct conversion [Correct. In direct conversion, the old system is discontinued as soon as the new one is activated.]

b. parallel conversion [Incorrect. A parallel conversion involves operating both the old and the new system in parallel until the users accept the new system.]

c. phase-in conversion [Incorrect. Phase-in conversion gradually replaces elements of the old system with the new one.]

d. pilot conversion [Incorrect. A pilot conversion activates and tests the new system in one or a few locations.]

10. Which of the following describes designing a program from the top down to more detailed levels?

▶ a. hierarchical program design [Correct. Hierarchical program design is the process of programming from the general level to the detailed level.]

b. top-down program design [Incorrect. This is not a program design method described in the text.]

c. parallel program design [Incorrect. This is not a program design method described in the text.]

d. unstructured program design [Incorrect. This is not a program design method described in the text.]

Chapter Case Solution

To properly design, implement, and operate this new ERP system, Hershey could have taken the following steps.

Conceptual Design

In designing its new ERP system, Hershey should have looked at all possible designs, evaluated their strengths and weaknesses, and selected the best one. Once the system was selected, Hershey needed to address the design specifications, such as what distribution output is needed to meet customer demands, how to store order and shipping data, how to input order and shipping data, and how to process the inputs and data to produce the outputs. Hershey should have prepared a detailed report to guide the physical design phase and communicate with management and the steering committee the project's progress, requirements, and feasibility.

Physical Design

Once the conceptual design was approved, physical design should have been planned. During this design phase, the following should have been created: order and shipment output documents, reports, files and databases; and the input forms and computer screens needed to capture order and shipment data. Hershey needed to choose which ERP modules to implement and to decide how to structure and modify those modules to meet its needs. Hershey also needed to decide how employees will interact with the system and to develop policies and procedures to formalize that interaction. Controls should have been designed to make sure those procedures and the system in general perform as intended and to prevent fraud and abuse. All of the physical design elements also should have been put into a report to guide Hershey in the actual implementation of the system.

Systems Implementation

Once the new ERP system had been designed and created, the actual hardware, software, procedures, and controls should have been implemented. An installation plan includes all tasks needed to prepare the physical location of the new ERP system, train managers and users to operate the ERP system, document the system, and test it. Based on the information in the case, it appears that Hershey failed to test its new ERP system adequately before converting from the old system.

System Conversion

Of the four primary system conversion approaches, Hershey chose direct conversion—the highest-risk approach. Hershey called the approach the "big bang"—and the big bang that was heard was a drop in market capitalization (stock price) and a damaged reputation due to the loss of orders and the loss of supplier confidence. In hindsight, Hershey should have used one of the other three approaches—parallel, phase-in, or pilot—with the parallel approach probably being the most effective. If Hershey had been able to convert to the new ERP system more successfully, it could have then focused on operating and maintaining the new system and making improvements to make it more effective and efficient.

Glossary

A

acceptance tests Tests of new systems using specially developed transactions and acceptance criteria. The test results are evaluated to determine whether the system is acceptable.

access control list (ACL) A set of rules that determines which packets of information transmitted over a network are allowed entry and which are dropped.

access control matrix An internally maintained table specifying which portions of the system users are permitted to access and what actions they can perform. The matrix contains a list of user codes, a list of all files and programs maintained on the system, and a list of the accesses each user is authorized to make.

accounting information system (AIS) A system that collects, records, stores, and processes data to produce information for decision makers. AIS components include: people, procedures and instructions, data, software, information technology infrastructure, and internal controls and security measures.

accounts receivable aging schedule A report listing customer account balances by length of time outstanding. The report provides useful information for evaluating current credit policies, for estimating bad debts, and for deciding whether to increase the credit limit for specific customers.

activity-based costing (ABC) A cost system designed to trace costs to the activities that create them. Once costs are traced to their specific activities, they are allocated to their corresponding products or departments.

Address Resolution Protocol (ARP) spoofing Sending fake ARP messages to an Ethernet LAN. ARP is a computer networking protocol for determining a network host's hardware address when only its IP or network address is known.

ad hoc queries Nonrepetitive requests for reports or answers to specific questions about the contents of the system's data files.

adware Spyware that (1) causes banner ads to pop up on a monitor as a user surfs the Internet; and (2) collects information about the user's Web-surfing and spending habits and forwards it to the company gathering the data, often an advertising or media organization. Adware usually comes bundled with freeware and shareware downloaded from the Internet.

agents In the REA data model, the people and organizations who participate in events and about whom information is desired.

aggression Resistance to change intended to destroy, cripple, or lessen the effectiveness of a system. It may take the form of increased error rates, disruptions, or deliberate sabotage.

analytical review The examination of the relationships between different sets of data.

application The data processing task to which a computer's processing power is applied.

application controls Controls that prevent, detect, and correct transaction errors and fraud in application programs. They are concerned with the accuracy, completeness, validity, and authorization of the data captured, entered into the system, processed, stored, transmitted to other systems, and reported. Contrast with *general controls.*

application programmer A person who uses a programming language to write an application program.

application service provider (ASP) A company that provides access to and use of application programs via the Internet. The ASP owns and hosts the software; the contracting organization accesses the software remotely via the Internet.

application software The programs that perform data or information processing tasks, such as accounts receivable and payable, inventory control, and payroll.

archive A copy of a database, master file, or software that is retained indefinitely as a historical record, usually to satisfy legal and regulatory requirements.

asymmetric encryption systems *See public key infrastructure (PKI).*

asynchronous transmission Data transmission in which each character is transmitted separately. A start bit is required before the character and a stop bit after it because the interval of time between transmission of characters can vary. Contrast with *synchronous transmission.*

attributes Characteristics of interest in a file or database; the different individual properties of an entity. Examples of attributes are employee number, pay rate, name, and address.

audit committee The committee responsible for overseeing a corporation's internal control structure, financial reporting process, and compliance with related laws and regulations. It is usually made up of outside members of the board of directors.

audit hooks A concurrent audit technique that embeds audit routines into application software to flag transactions that might indicate an error or fraud.

audit log A log of all transactions that have audit significance.

audit trail A path that allows a transaction to be traced through a data processing system from point of origin (whether paper or electronic) to final output or backwards from from final output to point of origin. It is used to check the accuracy and validity of ledger postings and to trace changes in general ledger accounts from their beginning balance to their ending balance.

auditing A systematic process of (1) objectively obtaining and evaluating evidence regarding assertions about economic actions and events to ascertain the degree of correspondence between those assertions and established criteria; and (2) communicating the results to interested parties.

authentication Verifying the identity of the person or device attempting to access the system.

authorization Granting an employee power to perform certain organizational functions, such as purchasing or selling on behalf of the company. Employees who are allowed to handle routine transactions without special approval have *general* authorization. An employee needing approval to handle a transaction receives *specific* authorization.

automated decision table programs Programs that generate a decision table representing the program's logic.

automated flowcharting program A program that interprets the source code of a program and generates a flowchart of the logic used by the program.

avoidance A way of resisting change by not using the new system.

B

back door See *trap door*.

back order A document authorizing the purchase or production of items that is created when there is insufficient inventory to meet customer orders.

background check An investigation conducted by a potential or current employer regarding a prospective or current employee. A background check often involves verifying the educational and work experience data on the person's resume, talking to references, checking for a criminal record, checking credit records, and checking other publicly available information about the individual.

backup A copy of a database, file, or software program.

balance-forward method Method of maintaining accounts receivable in which customers typically pay according to the amount shown on a monthly statement, rather than by individual invoices. Remittances are applied against the total account balance, rather than specific invoices.

balanced scorecard A management report that measures four dimensions of performance: financial, internal operations, innovation and learning, and customer perspectives of the organization.

bandwidth The difference between the highest and the lowest frequencies of a communications channel. Usually expressed in cycles per second (hertz).

bar code An identification label found on most merchandise with vertical lines of differing widths that represent binary information that is read by an optical scanner.

batch processing Accumulating transaction records into groups or batches for processing at a regular interval such as daily or weekly. The records are usually sorted into some sequence (such as numerically or alphabetically) before processing.

batch total The sum of a numerical item for a batch of documents. These totals are calculated prior to processing the batch and are compared with machine-generated totals at each subsequent processing step to verify that the data was processed correctly.

behavioral aspects of change New systems can change organizations, which may result in people changing their behavior. Organizations must be sensitive to and consider the feelings and reactions of persons affected by such changes.

belief system A corporate attitude enstilled by upper management that communicates company core values to employees and inspires them to live by these values. A belief system should draw attention to how the organization creates values and help employees understand the direction management wants the company to take.

benchmark problem A data processing task executed by different computer systems. The results are used to measure systems performance and to make comparative evaluations among systems.

bill of lading A legal contract that defines responsibility for goods while they are in transit. It identifies the carrier, source, destination, shipping instructions, and the party (customer or vendor) that must pay the carrier.

bill of materials A document that specifies the part number, description, and quantity of each component used in a product.

biometric identification Using unique physical characteristics such as fingerprints, voice patterns, retina prints, and signature dynamics to identify people.

bits Binary digits are the smallest storage location in a computer. A bit may be either "on" or "off," or "magnetized" or "nonmagnetized." A combination of bits (usually eight) is used to represent a single character of data.

bits per second (BPS) A unit of measurement describing the number of bits of data transmitted electronically in one second.

blanket purchase order or **blanket order** A commitment to purchase specified items at designated prices from a particular supplier for a set time period, often one year.

block code Blocks of numbers within a numerical sequence that are reserved for categories having meaning to the user.

border router A device that connects an organization's information system to the Internet.

boundary system An established system that helps employees act ethically by setting limits beyond which an employee must not pass. Employees can solve problems and meet customer needs as long as they operate within certain limits, such as meeting minimum standards of performance, shunning activities that are off limits, and avoiding courses of action that would damage the company's reputation.

broadband lines Communications channels capable of handling high-speed data transmissions.

budget The formal expression of goals in financial terms. Budgets are financial planning tools. Contrast with *performance report*.

buffer overflow attack When an attacker sends a program more data than it can handle. Buffer overflows may cause the system to crash or may provide a command prompt that gives the attacker full administrative privileges and control of the device.

business continuity plan (BCP) A plan that specifies how to resume all business processes in the event of a major calamity.

business cycle A group of related business processes. The major business cycles are sales and cash receipts, purchasing and cash disbursements, production and inventory control, human resources and payroll, and finance.

business process A set of related, coordinated, and structured activities and tasks that help accomplish a specific organizational goal.

business intelligence Accessing and using data for strategic decision making. There are two main business intelligence techniques: online analytical processing (OLAP) and data mining.

business process management (BPM) Managing the process of improving business processes. Software has been developed to automate business process improvement tasks.

business process management system (BPMS) System that automates and facilitates business process improvements throughout the SDLC. It can improve communication and collaboration, automate activities, and integrate with other systems and with other partners in the value chain.

business process reengineering (BPR) The thorough analysis and redesign of business processes and information systems to achieve dramatic performance improvements.

byte A group of adjacent bits (usually eight) used to represent an alphabetic, numeric, or special character, or even two numeric characters "packed" into a single eight-bit byte.

C

callback system A routing verification procedure. After the user dials in and is authenticated, the computer disconnects and calls the user back as an additional security precaution.

Caller ID spoofing Displaying an incorrect number on the recipient's caller ID display to hide the identity of the caller.

canned software Programs for sale on the open market to a broad range of users with similar needs.

capital budgeting model An estimate of funds to be appropriated for the acquisition of major capital assets and for investment in long-term projects. The estimated benefits are compared with the costs to determine if the system is cost beneficial.

cardinality A property of a database relationship indicating the number of occurrences of one entity that may be associated with a single occurrence of the other entity. Three types of cardinalities are one-to-one, one-to-many, and many-to-many.

cash flow budget A budget that shows projected cash inflows and outflows for a specified period so that an organization can anticipate the need for short-term borrowing.

centralized system or **network** A system where user terminals are linked to the centralized host computer so that users can send data to the host computer for processing and access data as needed. It provides an "economy of scale" advantage in data processing operations.

central processing unit (CPU) The hardware that contains the circuits that control the interpretation and execution of instructions and that serves as the principal data processing device. Its major components are the arithmetic-logic unit, the memory, and the control unit.

certificate authority An independent organization that issues public and private keys and records the public key in a digital certificate.

change control The process that ensures that hardware, software, or process modifications do not reduce systems reliability. Careful testing prior to implementing changes reduces the likelihood of changes that cause system downtime. Companies with a good change control process are less likely to suffer financial or reputational harm from security incidents.

change management Making sure that system changes minimize negative effects on users and do not negatively affect systems reliability, security, confidentiality, integrity, and availability.

character A letter, numeric digit, or symbol that is entered into a computer system.

chart of accounts A listing of all balance sheet and income statement account number codes.

check digit ID numbers (such as employee number) can contain a **check digit** computed from the other digits. For example, the system could assign employees a nine-digit number, calculate a tenth digit from the nine, and append it to form a ten-digit ID number.

check digit verification Recalculating a check digit to verify that an error has not been made. This calculation can be made only on a data item that has a check digit.

checkpoint The point(s) during a long processing run where a copy of all data values and status indicators of a program are captured. If a system failure occurs, the system is backed up to the most recent checkpoint and processing restarts at the checkpoint rather than at the beginning of the program.

ciphertext Plaintext that was transformed into unreadable gibberish using encryption.

client/server system A system where information requested by a user is processed as much as possible by the server and then transmitted to the user.

closed-loop verification An input validation method that uses data entered into the system to retrieve and display other related information so the accuracy of the input data can be verified.

cloud computing Purchasing software, storage, infrastructure, or platforms from a third-party (referred to as the cloud provider) on a pay-for-use or subscription basis. Cloud providers use virtualization technology to economically provide shared access simultaneously to multiple customers. The resulting economies of scale mean that organizations can often cut their total costs for IT with cloud computing and transforms IT into a utility.

coding (1) The systematic assignment of numbers or letters to items to classify and organize them. (2) Writing program instructions that direct a computer to perform specific data processing tasks.

cold site A location that provides everything necessary to quickly install computer equipment in the event of a disaster.

collusion Cooperation between two or more people in an effort to thwart internal controls.

Committee of Sponsoring Organizations (COSO) A private-sector group consisting of the American Accounting Association, the AICPA, the Institute of Internal Auditors, the Institute of Management Accountants, and the Financial Executives Institute.

compatibility check (or **test**) Determining whether a person attempting to access an information system resource is authorized to do so. The computer matches the user's authentication credentials against the access control matrix to determine whether the employee is allowed access to that resource or to perform the requested operation.

compensating controls Control procedures that compensate for the deficiency in other controls.

completeness test (or **check**) An online data entry control in which the computer determines whether all data required for a particular transaction have been entered.

compliance audit Determines compliance with applicable laws, regulations, policies, and procedures. These audits often result in recommendations to improve processes and controls that ensure compliance with regulations.

compliance objectives Objectives to help the company comply with applicable laws and regulations.

computer-assisted audit techniques (CAATS) Audit software, often referred to as generalized audit software (GAS) or computer audit software (CAS), that uses auditor-supplied specifications to generate a program that performs audit functions, thereby automating or simplifying the audit process.

computer crime Any illegal act for which knowledge of a computer is essential for the crime's perpetration, investigation, or prosecution.

computer forensics specialists Computer experts whose job entails discovering, extracting, safeguarding, and documenting computer evidence so that its authenticity, accuracy, and integrity will not succumb to legal challenges.

computer fraud See *computer crime.*

computer incident response team (CIRT) A team that is responsible for dealing with major security incidents. The CIRT should include technical specialists as well as senior operations management, because some security incident responses may have significant economic consequences.

computer-integrated manufacturing (CIM) A manufacturing approach in which much of the manufacturing process is performed and monitored by computerized equipment, in part through the use of robotics and real-time data collection of manufacturing activities.

computer operators People who operate the company's computers. They ensure that data are properly input to the computer and processed correctly, and needed output is produced.

computer programmers Persons who develop, code, and test computer programs.

computer security The policies, procedures, tools, and other means of safeguarding information systems from unauthorized access or alteration, intentional or unintentional damage, or theft.

computer security officer An employee independent of the information system function who monitors the system and disseminates information about improper system uses and their consequences.

concatenated key Two or more primary keys of other database tables that, together, become a unique identifier or primary key of another table. A multiple-attribute primary key.

conceptual design specifications System requirement specifications for systems output, data storage, input, processing procedures, and operations.

conceptual-level schema The organization-wide view of the entire database. It lists all data elements and the relationships between them. Contrast with *external-level schema* and *internal-level schema.*

conceptual systems design The systems development life cycle phase in which a general framework is created to implement user requirements and solve problems identified in the analysis phase.

conceptual systems design report A document specifying the findings and results of conceptual systems design. The report is used in physical systems design to identify the hardware, software, and procedures necessary to deliver the system.

concurrent audit techniques Software that continuously monitors an information system as it processes live data in order to collect, evaluate, and report information about system reliability.

concurrent update controls Controls that lock out users to protect individual records from errors that could occur if multiple users attempted to update the same record simultaneously.

context diagram The highest data flow diagram level. It provides a summary-level view of a system. It shows the data processing system, system input(s) and output(s), and the external entities that are the sources and destinations of the input(s) and output(s).

continuous and intermittent simulation (CIS) A concurrent audit technique that embeds an audit module into a database management system, rather than the application software.

control account A general ledger account that summarizes the total amounts recorded in a subsidiary ledger. The accounts payable control account in the general ledger represents the total amount owed to all vendors. The balances in the subsidiary accounts payable ledger indicate the amount owed to each specific vendor.

control activities Policies, procedures, and rules that provide reasonable assurance that control objectives are met and their risk responses are carried out.

control environment The organization's environment relating to controls, including management's philosophy, the audit committee, and the organizational structure.

Control OBjectives for Information and related Technology (COBIT) An information systems security and control framework that allows (1) management to benchmark the security and control practices of IT environments, (2) users of IT services to be assured that adequate security and control exist, and (3) auditors to substantiate their internal control opinions and advise on IT security and control matters.

control risk The risk that a significant control problem will not be prevented or detected by the internal control system.

control totals Batch totals used to ensure that all data are processed correctly. Examples are the number of transactions processed and the dollar amount of all updates.

conversion The process of changing from one computer format to another.

cookie A text file created by a Web site and stored on a visitor's hard drive. Cookies store information about who the user is and what the user has done on the site.

corrective controls Procedures that remedy problems that occur.

cost driver Anything that has a cause-and-effect relationship to costs. For example, the number of purchase orders processed is a purchasing department cost driver.

cracking See *hacking.*

credit limit The maximum allowable credit account balance for each customer, based on past credit history and ability to pay.

credit memo A document authorizing the billing department to credit a customer's account. Usually issued for sales returns, for allowances granted for damaged goods kept by the customer, or to write off uncollectible accounts. Approved by the credit manager.

critical path The path requiring the greatest amount of time to complete a project. If an activity on the critical path is delayed, the whole project is delayed. If possible, resources are shifted to critical path activities to reduce project completion time.

cross-footing balance test A procedure in which worksheet data are totaled both across and down. Then, the total of the horizontal totals is compared to the total of the vertical totals to ensure that the worksheet balances.

cross site scripting (XSS) Exploits Web page security vulnerabilities to bypass browser security mechanisms and create a malicious link that injects unwanted code into a Web site.

cryptography See *data encryption.*

customer relationship management (CRM) systems Software that organizes information about customers in a manner that facilitates efficient and personalized service.

custom software Software developed and written in-house to meet the unique needs of a particular company.

cyber-bullying Using computer technology to harm another person.

cycle billing Producing monthly statements for subsets of customers at different times. For example, each week monthly statements would be prepared for one-fourth of the customers.

D

data Facts that are collected, recorded, stored, and processed by an information system to produce information.

data administrator (DA) The person responsible for developing general policies and procedures governing all organizational data, not just what is stored in the database. The DA is responsible for understanding the organization's information needs and deciding what should be included in the database.

database A set of interrelated, centrally controlled data files that are stored with as little data redundancy as possible. A database consolidates records previously stored in separate files into a common pool and serves a variety of users and data processing applications.

database administrator The person responsible for coordinating, controlling, and managing the database.

database management system (DBMS) The program that manages and controls the data and the interfaces between the data and the application programs.

database query language An easy-to-use DBMS language that lets users ask questions about the data stored in a database.

database system The combination of the database, the database management system, and the application programs that access the database through the database management system.

data communications The transmission of data from a point of origin to a point of destination.

data communications network A communication system that bridges geographical distances, giving users immediate access to a company's computerized data. It allows multiple companies or computer services to be linked to information.

data control group The group charged with ensuring that source data have been properly approved, monitoring the flow of work through the computer, reconciling input and output, maintaining a record of input errors to ensure their correction and resubmission, and distributing systems output.

data definition language (DDL) A DBMS language that ties the logical and physical views of data together. It is used to build the data dictionary, initialize or create the database, describe the logical views for each individual user or programmer, and specify any limitations or constraints on security imposed on database records or fields.

data destination An entity outside the system that receives data produced by the system. A component of a data flow diagram.

data dictionary A description of each data element that is stored in the database. For example, customer numbers are stored in the database and there is a record in the data dictionary describing that data element.

data diddling Changing data before, during, or after it is entered into the system. The change can be made to add, delete, or alter system data.

data flow The data flow diagram component that represents data flowing into or out of a process.

data flow diagram (DFD) A graphical description of the flow of data within an organization. It is used to document existing systems and to plan and design new ones.

data independence Storing data such that the data and the application programs that use it are independent. This means that one may be changed without affecting the other.

data leakage The unauthorized copying of company data, often without leaving any indication that it was copied.

data loss prevention (DLP) Software which works like antivirus programs in reverse, blocking outgoing messages (e-mail, instant messages, etc.) that contain key words or phrases associated with intellectual property or other sensitive data the organization wants to protect.

data maintenance The periodic processing of transactions to update stored data. The four types of data maintenance are create, read, update, and delete (often referred to as CRUD).

data manipulation language (DML) A DBMS language used create, read, update, and delete items in the database.

data mart A smaller data warehouse for functions such as finance and human resources.

data masking A program that protects privacy by replacing customers' personal information with fake values before sending that data to the program development and testing system. For example, a real Social Security number might be replaced with a different set of numbers that have the same characteristics, such as 123-45-6789.

data mining Accessing information stored in a data warehouse through statistical analysis or artificial intelligence techniques to "discover" unhypothesized relationships in the data.

data model An abstract representation of the contents of a database.

data modeling Defining a database so that it faithfully represents all key components of an organization's environment. The objective is to explicitly capture and store data about every business activity the organization wishes to plan, control, or evaluate.

data processing center The room that houses the hardware, software, data, and people who operate a computer system.

data processing cycle The operations performed on data to generate meaningful and relevant information. It has four stages: data input, data storage, data processing, and information output.

data processing schedule A schedule of data processing tasks designed to maximize the use of scarce computer resources.

data query language (DQL) A high-level, English-like, DBMS language that retrieves, sorts, orders, and presents subsets of the database in response to user queries.

data redundancy The storage of the same data item in two or more files within an organization.

data source The entity that produces or sends the data that is entered into the system. A component of a data flow diagram.

data store The place or medium where system data is stored. A component of a data flow diagram.

data transmission controls Methods of monitoring the network to detect weak points, maintain backup components, and ensure that the system can still communicate if one of the communications paths fails.

data value The actual value stored in a field. It describes a particular attribute of an entity.

data warehouses Very large databases that contain detailed and summarized data for a number of years and that are used for analysis rather than transaction processing.

debit memo A document used to record a reduction to the balance due to a vendor.

debugging The process of checking for and correcting the errors found in a computer program.

decentralized system An information system that has an independent CPU and data processing manager at each location.

decision support system (DSS) An interactive computer system designed to help with the decision-making process by providing access to a database or decision-making model.

decryption Transforming ciphertext back into plaintext.

deduction register A report listing the miscellaneous voluntary deductions for each employee.

deep packet inspection When the firewall examines the data in the body of an IP packet rather than looking only at the information in the IP header.

default value A control that helps preserve the integrity of data processing and stored data by leaving a field blank if a standard value is to be used.

defense-in-depth Employing multiple layers of controls to avoid a single point-of-failure. Overlapping, complementary, and redundant controls buy time for the organization to detect and react to attacks. It also increases effectiveness because if one procedure fails or is circumvented, another may function as planned.

delete anomaly When deleting a row from a table results in the loss of all information about an entity. For example, if customer addresses are stored only in the sales invoice table, then deleting the row representing the only sale to a particular customer results in the loss of all information about that customer.

demand reports Reports that have a prespecified content and format but are prepared only in response to a request from a manager or other employee.

demilitarized zone (DMZ) Placing the organization's Web servers and e-mail servers in a separate network that sits outside the corporate network but is accessible from the Internet.

denial-of-service attack A computer attack in which the attacker sends so many e-mail bombs (thousands per second), often from randomly generated false addresses, that the Internet service provider's e-mail server is overloaded and shuts down. Another denial-of-service attack involves sending so many requests for Web pages that the Web server crashes.

detection risk The risk that auditors and their procedures will not detect a material misstatement.

detective controls Controls designed to discover control problems when they arise.

diagnostic control system A performance measurement system that compares actual performance to planned performance.

dictionary attack Using special software to guess company addresses and send them blank e-mail messages. Unreturned messages are usually valid e-mail addresses that can be added to spammer e-mail lists.

differential backup Copying all changes made since the last full backup. Thus, each new differential backup file contains the cumulative effects of all activity since the last full backup.

digital certificate An electronic document, created and digitally signed by a trusted third party, that certifies the identity of the owner of a particular public key. The digital certificate contains that party's public key. Thus, digital certificates provide an automated method for obtaining an organization's or an individual's public key.

digital fingerprint A hash number that identifies and validates a digital certificate.

digital signature (1) A piece of data signed on a document by a computer. A digital signature cannot be forged and is useful in tracing authorization. (2) Information encrypted with the creator's private key.

digital watermark Code embedded in documents that enables an organization to identify confidential information that has been disclosed. A digital watermark is a detective control and organizations should investigate how a compromise occurred and take appropriate corrective action.

direct access An access method that allows the computer to access a particular record without reading other records. Because each storage location on a direct access storage device has a unique address, the computer can find the record needed as long as it has the record's address.

direct access storage device (DASD) A storage device (such as a disk drive) that can directly access individual storage locations to store or retrieve data.

direct conversion An approach to converting from one system to another in which the old system is discontinued, after which the new system is started (also known as "burning the bridges" or "crash conversion").

disaster recovery plan A plan to recover data processing capacity as smoothly and quickly as possible in the event of an emergency that disables the computer system.

disbursement voucher A document that identifies the vendor, lists the outstanding invoices, and indicates the net amount to be paid after deducting any applicable discounts and allowances.

distributed data processing (DDP) A system in which computers are set up at remote locations and then linked to a centralized mainframe computer.

DNS spoofing Sniffing the ID of a Domain Name System (server that converts a Web site name to an IP address) request and replying before the real DNS server.

documentation The narratives, flowcharts, diagrams, and other written materials that explain how a system works. It covers the who, what, when, where, why, and how of data entry, processing, storage, information output, and system controls.

document flowchart Flowchart that traces a document from its cradle to its grave. They show where each document originates, its distribution, the purposes for which it is used, its ultimate disposition, and everything that happens as it flows through the system. They illustrate the flow of documents and information among areas of responsibility within an organization.

documents Records of transaction or other company data such as checks, invoices, receiving reports, and purchase requisitions.

dumpster diving See *scavenging*.

E

earnings statement A report listing the amount of gross pay, deductions, and net pay for the current period and the year-to-date totals for each category.

eavesdropping Observing data transmissions intended for someone else. One way unauthorized individuals can intercept signals is by setting up a wiretap.

e-business All uses of advances in information technology, particularly networking and communications technology, to improve the ways an organization performs its business processes.

echo check A hardware control that verifies transmitted data by having the receiving device send the message back to the sending device so that the message received can be compared with the message sent.

economic espionage The theft of information and intellectual property.

economic exchange An event in which one agent gives a resource to another agent in exchange for some other resource.

economic feasibility The dimension of feasibility concerned with whether the benefits of a proposed system will exceed the costs.

economic order quantity (EOQ) The optimal order size to minimize the sum of ordering, carrying, and stockout costs. Ordering costs are expenses associated with processing purchase transactions. Carrying costs are the costs associated with holding inventory. Stockout costs, such as lost sales or production delays, result from inventory shortages.

edit checks Accuracy checks performed by an edit program.

edit programs Computer programs that verify the validity and accuracy of input data.

electronic data interchange (EDI) The use of computerized communications and a standard coding scheme to submit business documents electronically in a format that can be automatically processed by the recipient's information system.

electronic data processing (EDP) Processing data utilizing a computer system.

electronic funds transfer (EFT) The transfer of funds between two or more organizations or individuals using computers and other automated technology. This eliminates the delay associated with the time the remittance is in the mail.

electronic lockbox A lockbox arrangement (see *lockbox*) in which the bank electronically sends the company information about the customer account number and the amount remitted as soon as it receives payments. This enables the company to begin applying remittances to customer accounts before the photocopies of the checks arrive.

electronic vaulting Electronically transmitting backup copies of data to a physically different location. Electronic vaulting permits online access to backup data when necessary.

element A specific data item in an XBRL instance document, such as a financial statement line item.

e-mail bomb A denial-of-service attack in which the receiver's e-mail server is bombarded with hundreds of e-mail messages per second.

e-mail spoofing (forgery) Making a sender address and other parts of an e-mail header appear as though the e-mail originated from a different source.

e-mail threats Threats sent to victims by e-mail. The threats usually require some follow-up action, often at great expense to the victim.

embedded audit modules Special portions of application programs that track items of interest to auditors, such as unauthorized attempts to access the data files.

embezzlement The fraudulent appropriation of business property by an employee to whom it has been entrusted. It is often accompanied by falsification of records.

encryption The process of transforming normal text, called *plaintext*, into unreadable gibberish, called *ciphertext*. Encryption is particularly important when confidential data is being transmitted from remote terminals because data transmission lines can be electronically monitored without the user's knowledge.

endpoints Collective term for the workstations, servers, printers, and other devices that comprise an organization's network. Supplementing preventive controls on the network perimeter with additional preventive controls on the endpoints enhances the security of information systems.

end-user computing (EUC) The creation, control, and implementation by end users of their own information system.

end-user system (EUS) A system developed by users, rather than information systems professionals, to meet their information needs. An EUS often draws upon the information in existing corporate databases to meet users' information needs.

enterprise resource planning (ERP) system A system that integrates all aspects of an organization's activities into one accounting information system.

Enterprise Risk Management—Integrated Framework (ERM) A COSO-developed internal framework that expands on the elements of COSO's Internal Control Integrated Framework and provides an all-encompassing focus on the broader subject of enterprise risk management.

entity The item about which information is stored in a record. Examples include an employee, an inventory item, and a customer.

entity integrity rule A design constraint in a relational database, requiring that the primary key have a non-null value. This ensures that a specific object exists in the world and can be identified by reference to its primary key value.

entity-relationship (E-R) diagram A graphical depiction of a database's contents showing the various entities being modeled and the important relationships among them. An entity is any class of objects about which data are collected, such as the resources, events, and agents that comprise the REA data model. An E-R diagram represents entities as rectangles; lines and diamonds represent relationships between entities.

error log The record of data input and data processing errors.

error message A message indicating that the computer encountered a mistake or malfunction.

error report A report summarizing errors by record type, error type, and cause.

evaluated receipt settlement (ERS) An invoiceless approach to accounts payable that replaces the three-way matching process (vendor invoice, receiving report, and purchase order) with a two-way match of the purchase order and receiving report. ERS saves time and money by reducing the number of mismatches and the time and expense of generating and tracking invoices.

event (1) In the REA data model, a business activity about which management wants to collect information for planning or control purposes. (2) An incident or occurrence from internal or external sources that affects the implementation of strategy or the achievement of objectives.

expected loss The mathematical product of the potential dollar loss that would occur should a threat become a reality (called *exposure*) and the risk or probability that the threat will occur (called *likelihood*).

expenditure cycle A recurring set of business activities and related data processing operations associated with the purchase of and payment for goods and services.

exploit The set of instructions for taking advantage of a vulnerability.

exposure The potential dollar loss should a particular threat become a reality.

extension taxonomy A set of custom XBRL tags to define elements unique to the reporting organization that are not part of the standard generally accepted taxonomies for that industry.

external label A label on the outside of a storage medium that identifies the data it contains.

external-level schema An individual user's or application program's view of a subset of the organization's database. Each of these individual user views is also referred to as a subschema. Contrast with *conceptual-level schema* and *internal-level schema*.

F

fault tolerance The capability of a system to continue performing when there is a hardware failure.

feasibility study An investigation to determine whether the development of a new application or system is practical. One of the first steps in the systems evaluation and selection process.

field The part of a data record that contains the data value for a particular attribute. For example, fields in all accounts receivable records would include customer account number, customer address, and balance due.

field check An edit check in which the characters in a field are examined to ensure they are of the correct field type (e.g., numeric data in numeric fields).

file A set of logically related records, such as the payroll records of all employees.

file maintenance The periodic processing of transaction data, which is the most common task in data processing systems. It includes creating, reading, updating, and deleting records. After file maintenance, the master file will contain all current information.

file organization The way data are stored on physical storage media. File organization may be either sequential or direct (random) access.

financial audit A review of the reliability and integrity of financial and operating information and the means used to identify, measure, classify, and report such information.

financial electronic data interchange (FEDI) The combination of EFT and EDI that enables both remittance data and funds transfer instructions to be included in one electronic package.

financial total The total of a dollar field, such as total sales, in a set of records. It is usually generated manually from source documents prior to input and compared with machine-generated totals at each subsequent processing step. A discrepancy may indicate a loss of records or errors in data transcription or processing.

financial value-added network (FVAN) An independent organization that offers specialized hardware and software to link various EDI networks with the banking system for EFT.

financing cycle The business activities and data processing operations associated with obtaining funds to operate, repay creditors, and distribute profits to investors.

firewall A combination of security algorithms and router communications protocols that prevent outsiders from tapping into corporate databases and e-mail systems.

flexible benefits plan A plan under which each employee receives some minimum coverage in medical insurance and pension contributions, plus additional benefit "credits" that can be used to acquire extra vacation time or additional health insurance. These plans are sometimes called *cafeteria-style benefit plans* because they offer a menu of options.

flexible budget A budget in which the amounts are stated in terms of formulas based upon actual level of activity.

flowchart An analytical technique used to describe some aspect of an information system in a clear, concise, and logical manner. Flowcharts use a standard set of symbols to describe pictorially transaction processing procedures and the flow of data through a system.

flowcharting symbols A set of objects that are used in flowcharts to show how and where data move. Each symbol has a special meaning that is easily conveyed by its shape.

flowcharting template A piece of hard, flexible plastic on which the shapes of flowcharting symbols have been die cut.

Foreign Corrupt Practices Act (1977) Legislation that, among other things, requires all publicly owned corporations subject to the Securities Exchange Act of 1934 to keep reasonably detailed records and maintain a system of internal accounting controls.

foreign key An attribute appearing in one table that is itself the primary key of another table. Foreign keys are used to link tables.

forensic accountants Accountants who specialize in fraud auditing and investigation. Upon qualification, forensic accountants may receive a Certified Fraud Examiner (CFE) certificate.

fraud Any and all means a person uses to gain an unfair advantage over another person.

fraud hot line A phone number employees can call to anonymously report fraud and abuse.

fraudulent financial reporting Intentional or reckless conduct, whether by act or omission, that results in materially misleading financial statements.

G

Gantt chart A bar graph used for project planning and control. Project activities are shown on the left and units of time across the top. The time period each activity is expected to take is represented with a horizontal bar on the graph.

general authorization The authorization given to regular employees to handle routine transactions without special approval.

general controls Controls designed to make sure an organization's information system and control environment is stable and well managed. Contrast with *application controls*.

generalized audit software (GAS) A software package that can be used to perform audit tests on the data files of a company.

general journal A journal used to record infrequent or nonroutine transactions, such as loan payments and end-of-period adjusting and closing entries.

general journal listing A report showing the details (account number, source reference code, description, and amount debited or credited) of each entry posted to the general ledger. This report indicates whether the total debits equal the total credits posted to the general ledger.

general ledger Ledger that contains summary-level data for every asset, liability, equity, revenue, and expense account of the organization.

general ledger and reporting system The information-processing operations involved in updating the general ledger and preparing reports that summarize organizational activities.

give-get exchange An event in which two entities exchange items, such as cash for goods or services.

goal conflict Occurs when a decision or action of a subsystem is inconsistent with another subsystem or the system as a whole.

goal congruence Achieved when a subsystem achieves its goals while contributing to the organization's overall goal.

grandfather-father-son concept Retaining the three most current copies of the master files (the son is the most recent) and transaction files. If a master file is destroyed, it can be recreated using a prior master file and the appropriate transaction file.

group codes Two or more subgroups of digits that are used to code an item. A group code is often used in conjunction with a block code.

H

hacking Unauthorized access and use of computer systems, usually by means of a personal computer and telecommunications networks.

hardening The process of turning off unnecessary program features.

hash Plaintext that has been transformed into short code.

hashing Transforming plaintext of any length into a short code called a hash.

hash total A total generated from values for a field that would not usually be totaled, such as customer account numbers. It is usually generated manually from source documents prior to input and compared with machine-generated totals at each subsequent processing step. Any discrepancy may indicate a loss of records or errors in data transcription or processing.

header label/record Type of internal label that appears at the beginning of each file and contains the file name, expiration date, and other file identification information.

help desk An in-house group of analysts and technicians who answer employees' questions with the purpose of encouraging, supporting, coordinating, and controlling end-user activity.

hijacking Gaining control of someone else's computer to carry out illicit activities, such as sending spam without the computer user's knowledge.

home page A "storefront" or site on the Internet set up by individuals and firms to provide useful and interesting information.

hot site Completely operational data processing facility configured to meet the user's requirement that can be made available to a disaster-stricken organization on short notice.

human resources management (HRM)/payroll cycle The recurring set of business activities and data processing operations associated with effectively managing the employee workforce.

I

identity theft Assuming someone's identity, usually for economic gain, by illegally obtaining confidential information such as a social security number.

impact See *exposure.*

impersonation See *masquerading.*

implementation The process of installing a computer system. It includes selecting and installing equipment, training personnel, establishing operating and control policies and procedures, testing and documenting the system, installing software, and getting the system to function properly.

implementation and conversion phase The capstone phase in the systems development life cycle where the elements and activities of the system come together.

implementation plan A written plan that outlines how the new system will be implemented. The plan includes a timetable for completion, the employee who is responsible for each activity, cost estimates, and task milestones.

imprest fund A cash account with two characteristics: (1) It is set at a fixed amount, such as $100; and (2) vouchers are required for every disbursement. At all times, the sum of cash plus vouchers should equal the preset fund balance.

incremental backup Copying data items that have changed since the last backup. This produces a set of incremental backup files, each containing the results of one day's transactions.

information Data that have been organized and processed to provide meaning to a user.

information overload The state in which additional information cannot be used efficiently and has no marginal value.

information processing The process of turning data into information. This process has four stages: data input, data processing, data storage, and information output.

information rights management (IRM) Software that offers the capability not only to limit access to specific files or documents, but also to specify the actions (read, copy, print, download, etc.) that individuals who are granted access to that resource can perform. Some IRM software even has the capability to limit access privileges to a specific period of time and to remotely erase protected files.

information system An organized way of collecting, processing, managing, and reporting information so that an organization can achieve its objectives and goals. Formal information systems have an explicit responsibility to produce information. An informal information system meets a need that is not satisfied by a formal channel and operates without formal designation of responsibility.

information system library A collection of corporate databases, files, and programs stored in a separate storage area.

information systems audit Reviews the general and application controls of an AIS to assess its compliance with internal control policies and procedures and its effectiveness in safeguarding assets.

information systems steering committee Plans and oversees the information systems function. The committee often consists of high-level management people, such as the controller and systems and user-department management. The steering committee sets policies that govern the AIS and ensures top-management participation, guidance, and control.

inherent risk The susceptibility of a set of accounts or transactions to significant control problems in the absence of internal control.

initial investigation A preliminary investigation to determine whether a proposed new system is both needed and possible.

input Data entered into the computer system either from an external storage device or from the keyboard of the computer.

input controls Controls that ensure that only accurate, valid, and authorized data are entered into the system.

input controls matrix A matrix that shows the control procedures applied to each field of an input record.

input validation routines Computer programs or routines designed to check the validity or accuracy of input data.

inquiry processing Processing user information queries by searching databases for the desired information and then organizing the information into an appropriate response.

insert anomaly A problem that arises when attributes that are not characteristics of the primary key are stored in a table. The problem arises because new information about those attributes cannot be entered in the database without violating integrity rules. For example, assume that information about vendors is stored only as part of the purchases table. Data about potential new vendors, or about alternative suppliers, could not be added until a purchase from them was made. Otherwise, the purchase order number column, the primary key of the purchases table, would have a null value, violating the entity integrity rule.

instance document An XBRL report that contains tagged data.

integrated test facility A testing technique in which a dummy company or division is introduced into the company's computer system. Test transactions may then be conducted on these fictitious records without affecting the real records. Test transactions may be processed along with real transactions, and the employees of the computer facility need not be aware that testing is being done.

integration Eliminating duplicate recording, storage, reporting, and other processing activities in an organization. For example, companies that used to have separate programs to prepare customer statements, collect cash, and maintain accounts receivable records now combine these functions into a single application.

integrity Protecting data from unauthorized tampering.

interactive control system Helps top-level managers with high-level activities that demand frequent and regular attention, such as developing company strategy, setting company objectives, understanding and assessing threats and risks, monitoring changes in competitive conditions and emerging technologies, and developing responses and action plans to proactively deal with these high-level issues.

internal auditing An independent, objective assurance and consulting activity designed to add value and improve organizational effectiveness and efficiency. Internal auditing helps an organization accomplish its objectives by using a systematic, disciplined approach to evaluate and improve the effectiveness of the risk management, control, and governance processes.

internal control flowchart A document flowchart that describes and evaluates internal controls. Often used by auditors in the planning stage of an audit.

Internal Control Integrated Framework A framework developed by COSO to define internal controls as well as to provide guidance for evaluating and enhancing internal control systems. It is widely accepted as the authority on internal controls.

internal controls Controls within a business organization that ensure information is processed correctly.

internal control system The plan of organization and the methods and measures adopted within a business to safeguard its assets, maintain records that accurately and fairly reflect company assets, check the accuracy and reliability of its accounting data, provide assurance that financial reporting is prepared in accordance with GAAP, promote operational efficiency, comply with applicable laws and regulations, and encourage adherence to prescribed managerial policies.

internal environment The tone or culture of a company that helps determine the risk consciousness of employees. It is the foundation for all other ERM components, providing discipline and structure. It is essentially the same thing as the control environment in the internal control framework.

internal labels Labels written in machine-readable form on a magnetic storage medium that identify the data contained on the storage medium. Internal labels include volume, header, and trailer labels.

internal-level schema A low-level view of the entire database describing how the data are actually stored and accessed. It includes information about record layouts, definitions, addresses, indexes, and so forth. Contrast with *external-level schemas* and *conceptual-level schemas.*

internal rate of return (IRR) The effective interest rate that equates the present value of total costs to the present value of total savings.

Internet auction fraud Using an Internet auction site to defraud another.

Internet misinformation Using the Internet to spread false or misleading information. This can be done in a number of ways, including inflammatory messages in online chats, setting up Web sites, and spreading urban legends.

Internet Protocol (IP) Protocol that specifies the structure of the TCP packets and how to route them to the proper destination.

Internet pump-and-dump fraud Using the Internet to pump up the price of a stock and then sell it.

Internet service providers (ISPs) Companies that provide connections to the Internet for individuals and other companies.

Internet terrorism Hackers using the Internet to disrupt electronic commerce and destroy company or individual communications.

intranet An internal network that can connect to the main Internet and be navigated with browser software. It is usually closed off from the general public.

intrusion detection systems (IDS) A system that creates logs of all network traffic that was permitted to pass the firewall and then analyzes those logs for signs of attempted or successful intrusions.

intrusion prevention systems (IPS) A new type of filter designed to identify and drop packets that are part of an attack.

inventory control The function of determining what, when, and how much inventory to purchase.

investigative audit Examines incidents of possible fraud, misappropriation of assets, waste and abuse, or improper governmental activities, looking for evidence of impropriety.

IP address spoofing Creating Internet Protocol packets with a forged IP address to hide the sender's identity or to impersonate another computing system.

J

job-order costing A cost system that assigns costs to specific production batches or jobs; it is used when the product or service being produced can be distinctly identified.

job-time ticket A document used to collect data about labor activity by recording the amount of time a worker spent on each specific job task.

journal voucher A form used to document one or more journal entries such as those made to update the general ledger.

journal voucher file A file that stores all journal entries used to update the general ledger.

just-in-time (JIT) inventory system A system that minimizes or virtually eliminates manufacturing inventories by scheduling inventory deliveries at the precise times and locations needed. Instead of making infrequent bulk deliveries to a central receiving and storage facility, suppliers deliver materials in small lots at frequent intervals to the specific locations that require them.

just-in-time (JIT) manufacturing Manufacturing systems with short planning horizons whose goal is to minimize or eliminate inventories of raw materials, work in process, and finished goods. JIT is often referred to as *pull manufacturing* because goods are produced in response to customer demand. Theoretically, JIT manufacturing systems produce only in response to customer orders. In practice, however, most JIT manufacturing systems develop short-run production plans.

K

key A unique identification code assigned to each data record within a system.

key escrow The process of storing a copy of an encryption key in a secure location.

key logger Spyware that records a user's keystokes, e-mails sent and received, Web sites visited, and chat session participation.

key-to-disk encoder Several keying stations linked to a computer. Data may be entered simultaneously from each of the key stations and pooled on a disk file.

key-to-tape encoder A device for keying in data and recording the data on magnetic tape.

key verification Checking the accuracy of data entry by having two people enter the same data using a key-operated device. The computer then compares the two sets of keystrokes to determine whether the data were entered correctly.

kickbacks Gifts given by vendors to purchasing agents for the purpose of influencing their choice of suppliers.

kiting A fraud scheme where the perpetrator conceals a theft of cash by creating cash through the transfer of money between banks. For example, suppose a fraud perpetrator opens checking accounts in banks A, B, and C. Then the perpetrator "creates" cash by depositing a $1,000 check from bank A into bank B and then withdraws the $1,000 from bank B. Since there are insufficient funds in bank A to cover the $1,000 check, the perpetrator deposits a $1,000 check from bank C to bank A before his check to bank B clears bank A. Since bank C also has insufficient funds, $1,000 must be deposited to bank C before the check to bank A clears. The check to bank C is written from bank B, which also has insufficient funds. The scheme continues, with checks and deposits occurring as needed to keep the checks from bouncing.

L

LAN See *local area network.*

lapping Concealing the theft of cash by means of a series of delays in posting collections to accounts. For example, a perpetrator steals customer A's accounts receivable payment. Funds received at a later date from customer B are used to pay off customer A's balance. Funds from customer C are used to pay off B's balance, and so forth.

lean manufacturing The goal of lean manufacturing is to minimize or eliminate inventories of raw materials, work in process, and finished goods. Lean manufacturing is often referred to as *pull manufacturing* because goods are produced in response to customer demand.

Lebanese looping Inserting a sleeve into an ATM that will not eject a card, pretending help for the purpose of obtaining a PIN, and then using the card and PIN to drain the account.

legal feasibility The dimension of feasibility that determines whether there will be any conflicts between the system under consideration and the organization's ability to discharge its legal obligations.

likelihood The probability that a threat to an AIS will come to pass.

limit check An edit check to ensure that a numerical amount in a record does not exceed some predetermined limit.

line count Total number of lines entered during a data processing session.

Linkbases One or more XBRL files that define the relationships among elements found in a specific instance document.

local area network (LAN) A network that links computers, printers, and other electronic equipment located within a limited geographical area, such as a single building.

lockbox A postal address to which customers send their remittances. This Post Office box is maintained by the participating bank, which picks up the checks each day and deposits them to the company's account. The bank sends the remittance advices, an electronic list of all remittances, and digital copies of all checks to the company.

log analysis The process of examining logs to monitor security.

logical access The ability to use computer equipment to access company data.

logical models Descriptions of a system that focus on the essential activities and flow of information in the system irrespective of how the flow is actually accomplished.

logical view The manner in which a user or programmer conceptually organizes, views, and understands the relationships among data items. Contrast with *physical view.*

logic errors Errors that occur when the instructions given to the computer do not accomplish the desired objective. Contrast with *syntax errors.*

logic time bomb A program that lies idle until some specified circumstance or a particular time triggers it. Once triggered, the program sabotages the system by destroying programs or data.

M

MAC address A Media Access Control address is a hardware address that uniquely identifies each node on a network.

magnetic disks Magnetic storage media consisting of one or more flat, round disks with a magnetic surface on which data can be written.

magnetic ink character recognition (MICR) The recognition of characters printed by a machine that uses special magnetic ink.

magnetic tape A secondary storage medium that is about 1/2 inch in width and that has a magnetic surface on which data can be stored. The most popular types are seven-track and nine-track tapes.

mainframe computers Large digital computers, typically with a separate stand-alone CPU.

management audit A review of how well management is utilizing company resources and how well company operations and programs follow established objectives.

management by exception A method for interpreting variances displayed on performance reports. If the performance report shows actual performance to be at or near budgeted figures, a manager can assume that the item is under control and that no action needs to be taken. Significant deviations from budgeted amounts, in *either* direction, signal the need to investigate the cause of the discrepancy and take appropriate action to correct the problem.

management information system The set of human and capital resources that are dedicated to collecting and processing data so that all levels of management have the information they need to plan and control the activities of the organization.

man-in-the-middle (MITM) attack A hacker placing himself between a client and a host to intercept network traffic; also called *session hijacking.*

manual information system Information system in which most data processing is completed by people without the use of computers.

manufacturing overhead All manufacturing costs that are not economically feasible to trace directly to specific jobs or processes.

manufacturing resource planning (MRP-II) An extension of materials resource planning that seeks to balance existing production capacity and raw materials needs to meet forecasted sales demands. Also referred to as *push manufacturing* because goods are produced in expectation of customer demand.

many-to-many (M:N) relationship A relationship between two entities where each entity can be associated with many instances of the other entity. For example, each inventory item can be sold to many different customers and each customer can order many different inventory items.

mapping programs Programs that provide information as to which portions of an application program are not executed.

masquerading Gaining access to a system by pretending to be an authorized user. This approach requires that the perpetrator know the legitimate user's identification numbers and passwords.

master file A permanent file of records that stores cumulative information about an organization's resources and the agents with whom it interacts. As transactions take place, individual records within a master file are updated to keep them current.

master plan A long-range planning document that specifies the overall information system plan of an organization. It shows what the system will consist of, how it will be developed, who will develop it, how needed resources will be acquired, and where the AIS is headed.

master production schedule (MPS) Specifies how much of each product is to be produced during the planning period and when that production should occur.

materiality The concept that an auditor should focus on detecting and reporting only those errors, deficiencies, and omissions that could possibly have a significant impact on decisions.

materials requirements planning (MRP) An approach to inventory management that seeks to reduce required inventory levels by improving the accuracy of forecasting techniques to better schedule purchases to satisfy production needs.

materials requisition Authorizes the removal of the necessary quantity of raw materials from the storeroom to the factory location where production operations are to begin.

maximum cardinality The maximum number of instances that an entity can be linked to the other entity in the relationship.

message The data transmitted over a data communication system.

message acknowledgment techniques Techniques that let the sender of an electronic message know that a message was received. They include echo checks, trailer records, and numbered batches.

minimum cardinality The minimum number of instances that an entity can be linked to the other entity in the relationship.

misappropriation of assets See *employee fraud.*

mnemonic code Letters and numbers that are interspersed to identify an item. The mnemonic code is derived from the description of the item and is usually easy to memorize. For example, Dry300W05 could represent a low end (300), white (W) dryer (Dry) made by Whirlpool (05).

modular conversion An approach for converting from an old system to a new system in which parts of the old system are gradually replaced by the new until the old system has been entirely replaced.

monthly statement A document summarizing all transactions that occurred during the past month and informing customers of their current account balance.

move tickets Documents that identify the internal transfer of parts, the location to which they are transferred, and the time of the transfer.

multifactor authentication The use of two or more authentication methods (passwords, ID badges, biometrics, etc.) in conjunction to achieve a greater level of security.

multimodal authentication The use of multiple authentication credentials of the same type to achieve a greater level of security.

mutual authentication scheme A routing verification procedure that requires both computers to exchange their passwords before communication takes place.

N

narrative description Written, step-by-step explanation of system components and how the components interact.

net present value (NPV) A value determined by discounting all estimated future cash flows back to the present, using a discount rate that reflects the time value of money.

network A group of interconnected computers and terminals; a series of locations tied together by communications channels.

network administrator One who installs, manages, and supports a network. The network administrator also controls access to the network and maintains the shared software and data.

network interface card (NIC) The device needed to connect a computer or peripheral to a data communications network.

network managers The people responsible for ensuring that all applicable devices are linked to the organization's internal and external networks and that the networks operate continuously and properly.

neural networks Computing systems that imitate the brain's learning process by using a network of interconnected processors that perform multiple operations simultaneously and interact dynamically. Neural networks recognize and understand voice, face, and word patterns much more successfully than do regular computers and humans.

nonoperational (or **throwaway**) **prototypes** Prototypes that are discarded, but the system requirements identified from the prototypes are used to develop a new system.

nonrepudiation Creating legally binding agreements that cannot be unilaterally repudiated by either party. This is done by signing documents and giving both parties copies. In today's digital world, the same level of nonrepudiation is accomplished by using hashing and asymmetric encryption to create a digital signature.

nonvoucher system A method for processing accounts payable in which each approved invoice is posted to individual vendor records in the accounts payable file and is then stored in an open invoice file. When a check is written to pay for an invoice, the invoice is removed from the open invoice file, marked paid, and stored in the paid invoice file. Contrast with *voucher system*.

normalization The process of following the guidelines for properly designing a relational database that is free from delete, insert, and update anomalies.

O

off-line devices Devices that are not connected to or controlled by a computer or network. Off-line devices are used to prepare data for entry into the computer system (e.g., key-to-tape encoder, key-punch/verification equipment). Contrast with *online devices*.

one-to-many (1:N) relationship A relationship between two entities where one entity in the relationship can be associated with many instances of the other entity in that relationship.

one-to-one (1:1) relationship A relationship between two entities where one entity in the relationship is associated with only one instance of the other entity in the relationship.

online analytical processing (OLAP) Tools that provide access to information stored in a data warehouse by using queries to investigate hypothesized relationships.

online batch processing Processing in which the computer captures data electronically and stores it so that it can be processed later.

online devices Hardware devices that are connected directly to the CPU by a cable or telephone line.

online processing Processing individual transactions as they occur and from their point of origin rather than accumulating them to be processed in batches. Online processing requires the use of online data entry devices and direct access file storage media so that each master record can be accessed directly.

online, real-time processing The computer system processes data immediately after capture and provides updated information to the user on a timely basis.

open-invoice method Method for maintaining accounts receivable in which customers typically pay according to each invoice. Usually, two copies of the invoice are mailed to the customer, who is requested to return one copy with the payment.

operating budget A report that projects an organization's revenues and expenses for a given time period, usually a month or a year.

operating system A software program that controls the overall operation of a computer system. Its functions include controlling the execution of computer programs, scheduling, debugging, assigning storage areas, managing data, and controlling input and output.

operational audit See *management audit*.

operational feasibility The dimension of feasibility concerned with whether a proposed system will be used by the people in an organization. It also is concerned with how useful the system will be within the operating environment of the organization.

operational prototypes Prototypes that are further developed into fully functional systems.

operations and maintenance The last phase of the system development life cycle where follow-up studies are conducted to detect and correct design deficiencies. Minor modifications will be made as problems arise in the new system.

operations list A document that specifies the labor and machine requirements needed to manufacture a product. It indicates how a product moves through the factory, specifying what is done at each step and how much time each operation should take.

operations objectives Objectives that deal with the effectiveness and efficiency of company operations, such as performance and profitability goals and safeguarding assets.

opportunity The condition or situation that allows a person or organization to commit and conceal a dishonest act and convert it to personal gain.

Optical Character Recognition (OCR) The use of light-sensitive hardware devices to convert characters readable by humans into computer input. Because OCR readers can read only certain items, a special machine-readable font must be used.

ordering costs All expenses associated with processing purchase transactions.

output The information produced by a system. Output is typically produced for the use of a particular individual or group of users.

output controls Controls that regulate system output.

outsourcing Hiring an outside company to handle all or part of the data processing activities.

P

packet sniffers Programs that capture data from information packets as they travel over the Internet or company networks. Captured data is sifted to find confidential or proprietary information that can be sold or otherwise used.

packing slip A document listing the quantity and description of each item included in a shipment.

parallel conversion A systems conversion approach in which the new and old systems are run simultaneously until the organization is assured that the new system is functioning correctly.

parallel simulation An approach auditors use to detect unauthorized program changes and data processing accuracy. The auditor writes his or her own version of a program and then reprocesses data. The output of the auditor's program and the client's program are compared to verify that they are the same.

parity bit An extra bit added to a byte and magnetized as needed to ensure that there is always an odd (or even) number of magnetized bits. The computer uses the odd (or even) parity scheme to check the accuracy of each item of data.

parity checking Process in which a computer, as it reads or receives a set of characters, verifies that the proper number of magnetized bits is in each character received. If not, the corresponding character may contain an error.

password A series of letters, numbers, or both that must be entered to access and use system resources. Password use helps prevent unauthorized tampering with hardware, software, and the organization's data.

password cracking Occurs when an intruder penetrates a system's defenses, steals the file containing valid passwords, decrypts them, and uses them to gain access to system resources such as programs, files, and data.

patch Code released by software developers that fixes a particular vulnerability.

patch management The process of regularly applying patches and updates to software.

payback period The number of years required for the net savings to equal the initial cost of an investment.

payroll clearing account A general ledger account used to check the accuracy and completeness of recording payroll costs and their subsequent allocation to appropriate cost centers.

payroll register A listing of payroll data for each employee for a payroll period.

payroll service bureau An organization that maintains the payroll master file for each of its clients and performs their payroll processing activities for a fee.

penetration test An authorized attempt to break into the organization's information system.

performance evaluations A project development control that requires evaluating each module or task as it is completed.

performance objectives The overall performance goals that an entity wishes to achieve.

performance report A report that compares standard, or expected, performances with actual performance and also shows the variances, or differences, between the two. Used for financial control. Contrast with *budget*.

peripherals The hardware devices (input, output, processing, and data communications) that are connected to a CPU.

personal identification number (PIN) A confidential code that allows an individual to gain access to a system and the data or resources stored in that system.

phase-in conversion See *modular conversion.*

phishing Sending an e-mail pretending to be a legitimate company, usually a financial institution, and requesting information. The recipient is asked to either respond to the e-mail request or visit a Web page and submit data. The request is bogus, and the information gathered is used to commit identity theft or to steal funds from the victim's account.

phreaker A hacker who attacks phone systems.

physical access Ability to physically use computer equipment.

physical design A phase of the system development life cycle where the broad, user-oriented requirements of the conceptual design are implemented by creating a detailed set of specifications that are used to code and test the computer programs.

physical model The description of how a system functions by describing the flow of documents, the computer processes performed and the people performing them, the equipment used, and other physical elements of the system.

physical systems design The phase of the systems development life cycle in which the designer specifies the hardware, software, and procedures for delivering the conceptual systems design.

physical systems design report A report prepared at the end of the physical design phase that describes the system and summarizes what was accomplished. Management uses this report to decide whether or not to proceed to the implementation phase.

physical view The way data are physically arranged and stored in the computer system. Contrast with *logical view.*

picking ticket A document authorizing the inventory control function to release merchandise to the shipping department. The picking ticket is often printed so that the item numbers and quantities are listed in the sequence in which they can be most efficiently retrieved from the warehouse.

piggybacking When a perpetrator latches onto a user who is logging in to a system. The legitimate user unknowingly carries the perpetrator with him into the system.

pilot conversion The implementation of a system in part of the organization, such as a branch location. This localizes conversion problems and allows training in a live environment. Disadvantages are the long conversion times and the need to interface the old system with the new system.

plaintext Normal text that has not been encrypted.

podslurping Using a small device with storage capacity (iPod, flash drive) to download unauthorized data from a computer.

point-of-sale (POS) devices Electronic devices used to record sales information at the time of the sale and to perform other data processing functions.

point scoring An objective procedure in which weighted selection criteria are used to evaluate the overall merits of vendor proposals.

policies The rules that provide a formal direction for achieving performance objectives and that enable performance.

policy and procedures manual A management tool for assigning authority and responsibility. It explains proper business practices, describes the knowledge and experience needed by key personnel, spells out management policy for handling specific transactions, and documents the systems and procedures employed to process those transactions.

post-implementation review Review made after a new system has been operating for a brief period. The purpose is to ensure that the new system is meeting its planned objectives, to identify the adequacy of system standards, and to review system controls.

post-implementation review report A report that analyzes a newly delivered system to determine if the system achieved its intended purpose and was completed within budget.

preformatting An online data entry control in which the computer displays a form on the screen and the user fills in the blanks on the form as needed.

pressure A person's incentive or motivation for committing fraud.

preventive controls Controls that deter problems before they arise. Effective preventive controls include hiring qualified accounting personnel; appropriately segregating employee duties; and effectively controlling physical access to assets, facilities, and information.

preventive maintenance A program of regularly examining the hardware components of a computer and replacing any that are found to be weak.

primary activities Activities in the value chain that are performed to create, market, and deliver products and services to customers and provide post-delivery service and support. Primary activities include production, shipping and receiving, and marketing.

primary key The attribute, or combination of attributes, that uniquely identifies a row in a database table. The primary key is used to distinguish, order, and reference records in a database.

private key system An encryption system in which both the sender and the receiver have access to the key but do not allow others access to the same key.

process A set of actions, automated or manual, that transform data into other data or information.

process costing A cost system that assigns costs to each process, or work center, in the production cycle, and then calculates the average cost for all units produced. Process costing is used when masses of similar goods or services are produced or sold.

processing controls Controls that ensure that all transactions are processed accurately and completely and that all files and records are properly updated.

processing test transactions Running hypothetical transactions through a new system to test for processing errors.

procurement card A corporate credit card that employees can use to purchase specific kinds of items.

production cycle The recurring set of business activities and related data processing operations associated with the manufacture of products.

production order A document authorizing the manufacture of a specified quantity of a particular product. It lists the operations to be performed, the quantity to be produced, and the location to which the finished product is to be delivered.

professional employer organization (PEO) An organization that processes payroll and also provides human resource management services such as employee benefit design and administration.

program A set of instructions that can be executed by a computer.

program evaluation and review technique (PERT) A commonly used technique for planning, coordinating, controlling, and scheduling complex projects such as systems implementation.

program flowchart A diagrammatical representation of the sequence of logical operations performed by a computer in executing a program. A program flowchart describes the specific logic to perform a process shown on a system flowchart.

program maintenance The revision of a computer program to meet new program instructions, satisfy system demands such as the need for a new report, correct an error, or make changes in file content.

programmer The person who takes the design provided by systems analysts and creates an information system by writing the computer programs.

programming The process of writing software programs to accomplish a specific task or set of tasks.

program tracing A technique used to obtain detailed knowledge of the logic of an application program as well as to test the program's compliance with its control specifications.

project development plan A document that shows how a project will be completed, including the modules or tasks to be performed and who will perform them, the dates they should be completed, and project costs.

project development team A group of people consisting of specialists, management, and users that develop a project's plan and direct the steps of the systems development life cycle. The team monitors costs, progress, and employees, and also gives status reports to top management and to the steering committee.

projection A way of resisting change by blaming anything and everything on the new system. The system becomes the scapegoat for all real and imagined problems and errors.

project milestones Significant points in a development effort where a formal review of progress is made.

prompting An online data entry control that uses the computer to control the data entry process. The system requests each required item of input data and then waits for an acceptable response before requesting the next required item.

proposal to conduct systems analysis A document calling for the analysis of either an existing or a proposed system. This document is prepared by a user or department and requests the information systems function to analyze the feasibility of developing a system to perform a specific function.

protocol The set of rules governing the exchange of data between two systems or components of a system.

prototype A simplified working model of an information system.

prototyping An approach to systems design in which a simplified-working model, or prototype, of an information system is developed. The users experiment with the prototype to determine what they like and do not like about the system. The developers make modifications until the users are satisfied with the system.

Public Company Accounting Oversight Board (PCAOB) A five-member board that regulates the auditing profession. The PCAOB was created as part of the Sarbanes–Oxley Act, and its members are appointed and overseen by the SEC.

public key infrastructure (PKI) An approach to encryption that uses two keys: a public key that is publicly available and a private key that is kept secret and known only by the owner of that pair of keys. With PKI, either key (the public or private) can be used to encode a message, but only the other key in that public-private pair can be used to decode that message.

purchase order A document that formally requests a vendor to sell and deliver specified products at designated prices. It is also a promise to pay and becomes a contract once the vendor accepts it.

purchase requisition A document or electronic form that identifies the requisitioner; specifies the delivery location and date needed; identifies the item numbers, descriptions, quantity, and price of each item requested; and may suggest a vendor.

Q

query A request for specific information from a computer. When the information is found, it is retrieved, displayed, or analyzed as requested. Queries are often used with a database management system to extract data from the database.

query-by-example (QBE) languages Graphical query languages for retrieving information from a relational database.

query languages Languages used to process data files and to obtain quick responses to questions about those files.

R

random access memory (RAM) A temporary storage location for computer instructions and data.

range check An edit check designed to verify that a data item falls within a certain predetermined range of acceptable values.

ransomware Software that encrypts programs and data until a ransom is paid to remove it.

rationalization The excuse that fraud perpetrators use to justify their illegal behavior.

REA data model A data model used to design AIS databases. It contains information about three fundamental objects: resources, events, and agents. Resources represent identifiable objects that have economic value to the organization. Events represent an organization's business activities. Agents represent the people or organizations about which data are collected.

real-time notification A variation of the embedded audit module in which the auditor is notified of each transaction as it occurs by means of a message printed on the auditor's terminal.

real-time system A system that is able to respond to an inquiry or provide data fast enough to make the information meaningful to the user. Real-time systems are usually designed for very fast response.

reasonable assurance The concept that an auditor cannot obtain complete assurance that information is correct, because to do so would be prohibitively expensive. Instead, the auditor accepts a reasonable degree of risk that the audit conclusion is incorrect.

reasonableness test An edit check of the logical correctness of relationships among data items. For example, a journal entry that debits inventory and credits wages payable is not reasonable.

receiving report A document that records details about each delivery, including the date received, shipper, vendor, quantity received.

record A set of logically related data items that describe specific attributes of an entity, such as all payroll data relating to a single employee.

record count A total of the number of input documents in a process or the number of records processed at a given time.

record layout A document that illustrates the arrangement of items of data in input, output, and file records.

recovery point objective (RPO) The length of time between the last backup and the time that an incident occurred. The RPO represents the period of time for which management is willing to have to reenter data about past transactions.

recovery procedures A set of procedures that is followed if the computer quits during data processing. The procedures allow the user to recover from hardware or software failures.

recovery time objective (RTO) The time by which the organization's information system must be available again following a disaster.

redundant arrays of independent drives (RAID) Writing data to multiple disk drives simultaneously so that if one disk drive fails the data can be readily accessed from another.

redundant data check An edit check that requires the inclusion of two identifiers in each input record (e.g., the customer's account number and the first five letters of the customer's name). If these input values do not match those on the record, the record will not be updated.

reengineering See *business process reengineering.*

referential integrity rule A constraint in relational database design requiring that any non-null value of a foreign key must correspond to a primary key in the referenced table. For example, if vendor number is a foreign key in the inventory table, to indicate the preferred source of that item, then any vendor number appearing in that table must appear as a primary key value in the vendor table. This constraint ensures consistency in the database. Note, however, that the foreign key can be null, if there is no existing relationship between the two tables. For example, a null value for vendor number in any row in the inventory table would indicate that there is no preferred vendor for that inventory item.

relational data model A database model in which all data elements are logically viewed as being stored in two-dimensional tables called *relations*. In these tables each row represents a unique entity or record. Each column represents a field where the record's attributes are stored. The tables serve as the building blocks from which data relationships can be created.

relational database A database management system that uses the relational data model developed by Dr. E. F. Codd in 1970.

remittance advice An enclosure included with a customer's payment that indicates the invoices, statements, or other items paid.

remittance list A document listing all checks received in the mail.

Remote Authentication Dial-In User Service (RADIUS) A standard method for verifying the identity of users attempting to connect via dial-in access. Users connect to a remote access server and submit their login credentials. The remote access server passes those credentials to the RADIUS server, which performs compatibility tests to authenticate the identity of that user.

remote batch processing Accumulating transaction records in batches at some remote location and then transmitting them electronically to a central location for processing.

reorder point The level to which the inventory balance of an item must fall before an order to replenish stock is initiated.

report System output organized in a meaningful fashion. Used by employees to control operational activities, by managers to make decisions and design strategies, and by investors and creditors to gather information about a company's business activities. Prepared for both internal and external use.

reporting objectives Objectives to help ensure the accuracy, completeness, and reliability of internal and external company reports, of both a financial and nonfinancial nature. They also improve decision making and monitor company activities and performance more efficiently.

report writers A language that simplifies report creation. Typically, users need specify only which data elements they want printed and how the report should be formatted. The report writer searches the database, extracts the specified data items, and prints them according to the user-specified format.

reprocessing An approach auditors use to detect unauthorized program changes. The auditor verifies the integrity of an application program and then saves it for future use. At subsequent intervals, and on a surprise basis, the auditor uses the previously verified version of the program to reprocess transaction data. The output of the two runs is compared and discrepancies are investigated.

request for proposal (RFP) A request by an organization or department for vendors to bid on hardware, software, or services.

request for systems development A written request for a new or improved system. The request describes the current system's problems, why the change is needed, and the proposed system's goals and objectives as well as its anticipated benefits and costs.

requirements costing A system evaluation method in which a list is made of all required features. If a proposed system does not have a desired feature, the cost of developing or purchasing that feature is added to the basic cost of the system. This method allows different systems to be compared and evaluated based on the costs of providing the required features.

residual risk The risk that remains after management implements internal controls or some other form of response to risk.

resources Those things that have economic value to an organization such as cash, inventory, supplies, factories, and land.

response time The amount of time that elapses between making a query and receiving a response.

responsibility accounting A system of reporting financial results on the basis of managerial responsibilities within an organization.

restoration The process of installing the backup copy of a database or file for use in data processing.

revenue cycle The recurring set of business activities and data processing operations associated with providing goods and services to customers and collecting cash in payment for those sales.

risk The likelihood that a threat or hazard will actually come to pass.

risk appetite The amount of risk a company is willing to accept to achieve its goals and objectives.

rollback A process whereby a log of all pre-update values is prepared for each record that is updated within a particular interval. If there is a system failure, the records can be restored to the pre-update values and the processing restarted.

round-down technique A fraud technique used in financial institutions that pay interest. The programmer instructs the computer to round down all interest calculations to two decimal places. The fraction of a cent rounded down on each calculation is put into the programmer's own account.

routers Special purpose devices that are designed to read the destination address fields in IP packet headers to decide where to send (route) the packet next.

routing verification procedures Controls to ensure that messages are not routed to the wrong system address. Examples are header labels, mutual authentication schemes, and dial-back.

run-to-run totals Comparison of the new balance of an updated general ledger account to its prior balance plus the sum of all current period debits and credits.

S

sabotage An intentional act where the intent is to destroy a system or some of its components.

salami technique A fraud technique in which tiny slices of money are stolen from many different accounts.

sales invoice A document notifying customers of the amount of a sale and where to send payment.

sales order The document created during sales order entry listing the item numbers, quantities, prices, and terms of the sale.

Sarbanes–Oxley Act (SOX) A law passed by Congress in 2002. SOX applies to publicly held companies and their auditors and is intended to prevent financial statement fraud, make financial reports more transparent, provide protection to investors, strengthen the internal controls at public companies, and punish executives who perpetrate fraud.

scanning routines Software routines that search a program for the occurrence of a particular variable name or other combinations of characters.

scareware Malicious software of no benefit that is sold using scare tactics.

scavenging Searching for corporate or personal records to gain unauthorized access to confidential information. Scavenging methods include searching garbage cans, communal trash bins, and city dumps to find documents with confidential information.

scheduled reports Reports that are generated by a system at specified time intervals.

scheduling feasibility The dimension of feasibility that determines if the system being developed can be implemented in the time allotted.

schema (1) A description of the data elements in a database, the relationships among the data elements, and the structure or overall logical model used to organize and describe the data. (2) An XBRL file that defines every element that appears in a specific instance document.

secondary key A field that can be used to identify records in a file. Unlike the primary key, it does not provide a unique identification.

security management Ensures that all aspects of the system are secure and protected from all internal and external threats.

segregation of accounting duties Separating the accounting functions of authorization, custody, and recording so as to minimize an employee's ability to comitt fraud.

segregation of duties The separation of assigned duties and responsibilities in such a way that no single employee can both perpetrate and conceal errors or irregularities.

segregation of systems duties Implementing control procedures to clearly divide authority and responsibility within the information system function to prevent employees from perpetrating and concealing fraud.

sequence check An edit check that determines if a batch of input data is in the proper numerical or alphabetical sequence.

sequence codes Documents are numbered consecutively to account for them. Gaps in the sequence code indicate missing documents that should be investigated. Examples of documents that are given sequence codes include prenumbered checks, invoices, and purchase orders.

sequential access An access method that requires data items to be accessed in the same order in which they were written.

sequential file A way of storing numeric or alphabetical records according to a key (e.g., customer numbers from 00001 to 99999). To access a sequential file record, the system starts at the beginning of the file and reads each record until the desired record is located.

sequential file processing Processing a master file sequentially from beginning to end. The master and transaction files are processed in the same predetermined order, such as alphabetically.

server High-capacity computer that contains the network software to handle communications, storage, and resource-sharing needs of other computers in the network. The server also contains the application software and data common to all users.

sexting Exchanging sexually explicit text messages and pictures with other people by means of a phone.

shoulder surfing Watching people enter telephone calling card or credit card numbers or listening as they give credit card numbers over the telephone or to a clerk.

sign check An edit check that verifies that the data in a field have the appropriate arithmetic sign.

size check An edit check that ensures the input data will fit into the assigned field.

smart cards Plastic cards containing a microprocessor, memory chips, and software that can store up to three pages of text. Used in Europe as a credit or ATM card.

SMS spoofing Using short message service (SMS) to change the name or number a text message appears to come from.

snapshot technique An audit technique that records the content of both a transaction record and a related master file record before and after each processing step.

social engineering Using deception to obtain unauthorized access to information resources. Access is usually obtained by fooling an employee.

software agents Computer programs that learn how to do often-performed, tedious, time consuming, or complex tasks.

software piracy The unauthorized copying of software.

source code (or **source program**) A computer program written in a programming language that is translated into the object (machine language) program by a translation program such as a compiler or assembler.

source code comparison program Compares the current version of a program with the source code of the program. If no changes were authorized, the two versions should be identical and any differences should be investigated. If the difference is an authorized change, auditors examine program change specifications to ensure that the changes were authorized and correctly incorporated.

source data automation (SDA) The collection of transaction data in machine-readable form at the time and place of origin. Examples of SDA devices are optical scanners and ATMs.

source documents Contain the initial record of a transaction that takes place. Examples of source documents, which are usually recorded on preprinted forms, include sales invoices, purchase orders, and employee time cards. Contrast with *operational document*.

spamming Simultaneously e-mailing the same unsolicited message to many people, often in an attempt to sell them some product.

special-purpose analysis reports Reports that have no prespecified content or format and are not prepared according to any regular schedule; rather, they are generally prepared in response to a management request to investigate a specific problem or opportunity.

specialized journals Journals where large numbers of repetitive transactions—such as credit sales, cash receipts, purchases on account, and cash disbursements—are recorded.

specific authorization Special approval an employee needs in order to be allowed to handle a transaction.

spoofing Altering something, such as an e-mail message, to make it look as if someone else sent it.

spyware Software that monitors computing habits and sends the data to someone else, often without the computer user's permission.

SQL injection (insertion) Inserting a malicious SQL query in input in such a way that it is passed to and executed by an application program.

standards The required procedures implemented to meet the policies.

stateful packet filtering A technique employed by firewalls in which a table is maintained that lists all established connections between the organization's computers and the Internet. The firewall consults this table to determine whether an incoming packet is part of an ongoing communication initiated by an internal computer.

static packet filtering A process that screens individual IP packets based solely on the contents of the source and/or destination fields in the IP packet header.

steering committee An executive-level committee to plan and oversee the information systems function. The committee typically consists of management from the systems department, the controller, and other management affected by the information systems function.

strategic master plan An organization's multiple-year plan that serves as a technological road map and lays out the projects the company must complete to achieve its long-range goals.

strategic objectives High-level goals that are aligned with and support the company's mission.

strategic planning Decisions that establish the organization's objectives and policies for accomplishing those objectives.

structured programming A modular approach to programming in which each module performs a specific function and is coordinated by a control module.

structured query language (SQL) A text-based query language provided by most relational database management systems. Powerful queries can be built using basic keywords such as: SELECT, FROM, and WHERE.

structured relationships Relationships in program design in which every event entity is linked to a resource entity and two agent entities.

structured walkthrough A formal program design review process. One or more programmers walk through another programmer's logic and code to detect weaknesses and errors in program design.

style sheet An XBRL file that provides instructions on how to display (render) an instance document on either a computer screen or printed report.

subschema (1) A subset of the schema that includes only those data items used in a particular application program or by a particular user. (2) The way the user defines the data and the data relationships.

subsidiary ledgers Ledgers used to record the detailed data for any general ledger account that has many individual subaccounts. Subsidiary ledgers are commonly used for accounts receivable, inventory, fixed assets, and accounts payable.

subsystems Smaller systems that are a part of the entire information system. Each subsystem performs a specific function that is important to and that supports the system of which it is a part.

superzapping The unauthorized use of a special system program to bypass regular system controls and perform illegal acts. The superzap utility was originally written to handle emergencies, such as restoring a system that had crashed.

supply chain An extended system that includes an organization's value chain as well as its suppliers, distributors, and customers.

support activities Activities in the value chain that enable the primary activities to be performed efficiently and effectively. Examples include administration, purchasing, and human resources.

symmetric encryption systems Encryption systems that use the same key both to encrypt and to decrypt.

synchronous transmission Data transmission in which start and stop bits are required only at the beginning and end of a block of characters. Contrast with *asynchronous transmission*.

syntax errors Errors that result from using the programming language improperly or from incorrectly typing the source program.

system (1) An entity consisting of two or more components or subsystems that interact to achieve a goal. (2) The equipment and programs that comprise a complete computer installation. (3) The programs and related procedures that perform a single task on a computer.

system control audit review file (SCARF) A concurrent audit technique that embeds audit modules into application software to continuously monitor all transaction activity and collect data on transactions having special audit significance.

system flowchart A diagrammatical representation that shows the flow of data through a series of operations in an automated data processing system. It shows how data are captured and put into the system, the processes that operate on the data, and system outputs.

system performance measurements Measurements used to evaluate and assess a system. Common measurements include throughput (output per unit of time), utilization (percentage of time the system is being productively used), and response time (how long it takes the system to respond).

system review A step in internal control evaluation in which it is determined if the necessary control procedures have been prescribed.

systems administrator Ensures that an information system operates smoothly and efficiently.

systems analysis (1) A rigorous and systematic approach to decision making, characterized by a comprehensive definition of available alternatives and an exhaustive analysis of the merits of each alternative as a basis for choosing the best alternative. (2) Examination of user information requirements in an organization to establish objectives and specifications for the design of an information system.

systems analysis report Comprehensive report prepared at the end of the systems analysis and design phase that summarizes and documents the findings of analysis activities.

systems analysts The people who help users determine their information needs and then design an information system to meet those needs.

systems design The process of preparing detailed specifications for the development of a new information system.

systems development life cycle (SDLC) Five processes a company goes through when it decides to design and implement a new system. The five steps are systems analysis, conceptual design, physical design, implementation and conversion, and operation and maintenance.

systems documentation A complete description of all aspects of each systems application, including narrative material, charts, and program listings.

systems implementation The task of delivering a completed system to an organization for use in day-to-day operations.

systems integrator A vendor who uses common standards and manages a cooperative systems development effort involving its own development personnel and those of the client and other vendors.

systems software Software that interfaces between the hardware and the application program. Systems software includes operating systems, database management systems, utility programs, language translators, and communications software.

systems survey The systematic gathering of facts relating to the existing information system. A systems analyst generally carries out this task.

systems survey report The culmination of the systems survey. It contains documentation such as memos; interview and observation notes; questionnaire data; file and record layouts and descriptions; input and output descriptions; and copies of documents, flowcharts, and data flow diagrams.

T

tagging An audit procedure in which certain records are marked with a special code before processing. During processing, all data relating to the marked records are captured and saved so that the auditors can verify them later.

taxonomy A set of XBRL files that defines elements and the relationships among them.

technical feasibility The dimension of feasibility concerned with whether a proposed system can be developed given the available technology.

terminal An input/output device for entering or receiving data directly from the computer.

test data Data that have been specially developed to test the accuracy and completeness of a computer program. The results from the test data are compared with hand-calculated results to verify that the program operates properly.

test data generator program A program that takes the specifications describing the logic characteristics of the program to be tested and automatically generates a set of test data that can be used to check the logic of the program.

test of control A test whose objective it is to determine whether control procedures are being followed correctly.

threats Any potential adverse occurrence or unwanted event that could be injurious to either the AIS or the organization. Also referred to as an *event*.

throughput (1) The total amount of useful work performed by a computer system during a given period of time. (2) A measure of production efficiency representing the number of "good" units produced in a given period of time.

time-based model of security Implementing a set of preventive, detective, and corrective controls that enable an organization to recognize that an attack is occurring and take steps to thwart it before any assets have been compromised.

time card A document that records the employee's arrival and departure times for each work shift. The time card records the total hours worked by an employee during a pay period.

time sheet A data entry screen (or paper document) used by salaried professionals to record how much time was spent performing various tasks for specific clients.

trailer label (record) Type of internal label that appears at the end of each file and serves as an indicator that the end of the file has been reached. The trailer label contains the batch totals calculated during input.

transaction An agreement between two entities to exchange goods or services. Any exchange that can be measured in economic terms by an organization.

transaction cycles A group of related business activities (e.g., sales order entry, shipping, billing, and cash receipts constitutes the revenue cycle). The four transaction cycles covered in the text are revenue, expenditure, production, and human resource management/payroll.

transaction file File that contains the individual business transactions that occur during a specific fiscal period. A transaction file is conceptually similar to a journal in a manual AIS.

transaction log A detailed record of every transaction entered in a system.

transaction processing A process that begins with capturing transaction data and ends with an informational output.

transcription error An error in which a digit of a number is written incorrectly (e.g., a 4 in the tens position transcribed as a 9, which would cause an error of 50 in the value of the number).

Transmission Control Protocol/Internet Protocol (TCP/IP) The protocol enabling communications on the Internet. It creates what is called a packet-switching network. When a message is ready to be sent over the Internet, the TCP breaks it up into small packets. Each packet is then given a header, which contains the destination address, and the packets are then sent individually over the Internet. The IP uses the information in the packet header to guide the packets so that they arrive at the proper destination. Once there, the TCP reassembles the packets into the original message.

transposition error An error that results when numbers in two adjacent columns are inadvertently exchanged (for example, 64 is written as 46).

trap door A set of computer instructions that allows a user to bypass the system's normal controls.

trial balance A report listing the balances of all general ledger accounts. It is so named because one of its purposes is to allow the accountant to verify that the total debit balances in various accounts equal the total credit balances in other accounts.

triggered exception reports Preformatted reports generated only when certain conditions exist (e.g., the amount of raw materials on hand falls below the safety stock amount). The reports bring the information about the existing conditions to the attention of a decision maker.

Trojan horse A set of unauthorized computer instructions in an authorized and otherwise properly functioning program. It performs some illegal act at a preappointed time or under a predetermined set of conditions.

tuple (rhymes with *couple*). A row in a relation. A tuple contains data about a specific occurrence in a database table. For example, each row in the inventory table contains all the pertinent data about a particular inventory item.

turnaround document Records of company data sent to an external party and then returned to the system as input. Turnaround documents are prepared in machine-readable form to facilitate their subsequent processing as input records. An example is a utility bill.

turnkey system A system that is delivered to customers ready (theoretically) to be turned on. A turnkey system supplier buys hardware, writes application software that is tailored both to that equipment and to the specific needs of its customers, and then markets the entire system.

U

uninterruptible power supply (UPS) An alternative power supply device that protects against the loss of power and fluctuations in the power level by using battery power to enable the system to operate long enough to back up critical data and safely shut down.

Universal Product Code (UPC) A machine-readable code that is read by optical scanners. The code consists of a series of bar codes and is printed on most products sold in grocery stores.

UNIX A flexible and widely used operating system for 16-bit machines.

update anomaly If attributes that are not characteristics of the primary key of a relation are stored in that table, then that data item is stored in many different rows. For example, if customer addresses are stored in the sales invoice table, then the address for a given customer is stored many times (once for each sale). Consequently, if the value of that data item is not changed in every row in which it is stored, inconsistencies in the database will result.

updating Changing stored data to reflect more recent events (e.g., changing the accounts receivable balance because of a recent sale or collection).

user ID A knowledge identifier, such as an employee number or account number, that users enter to identify themselves when signing on to a system.

user identification (ID) and authentication system A system that requires users to identify themselves by entering a unique user ID when they sign on to the system.

users People who interact with the system. Users are those who record data, manage the system, and control the system's security. Those who use information from the system are end users.

utility programs A set of prewritten programs that perform a variety of file and data-handling tasks (e.g., sorting or merging files) and other housekeeping chores.

utilization The percentage of time a system is being productively used.

V

validity check An edit test in which an identification number or transaction code is compared with a table of valid identification numbers or codes maintained in computer memory.

value-added network (VAN) A public network that adds value to the data communications process by handling the difficult task of interfacing with the multiple types of hardware and software used by different companies.

value chain The linking together of all the primary and support activities in a business. Value is added as a product passes through the chain.

value of information The benefit produced by the information minus the cost of producing it.

value system The combination of several value chains into one system. A value system includes the value chains of a company, its suppliers, its distributors, and its customers.

vendor-managed inventory (VMI) Practice in which manufacturers and distributors manage a retail customer's inventory using EDI. The supplier accesses its customer's point-of-sale system in order to monitor inventory and automatically replenish products when they fall to agreed-upon levels.

virtualization Taking advantage of the power and speed of modern computers to run multiple systems simultaneously on one physical computer. This reduces the number of servers needed and thereby reduces hardware, maintenance, and data center costs.

virtual private network (VPN) A network that controls access to an extranet using encryption and authentication technology.

virus A segment of executable code that attaches itself to an application program or some other executable system component. When the hidden program is triggered, it makes unauthorized alterations to the way a system operates.

voucher A document that summarizes the data relating to a disbursement and represents final authorization of payment.

voucher package The set of documents used to authorize payment to a vendor. It consists of a purchase order, receiving report, and vendor invoice.

voucher system A method for processing accounts payable in which a disbursement voucher is prepared instead of posting invoices directly to vendor records in the accounts payable subsidiary ledger. The disbursement voucher identifies the vendor, lists the outstanding invoices, and indicates the net amount to be paid after deducting any applicable discounts and allowances. Contrast with *nonvoucher system*.

vulnerabilities Flaws in programs that can be exploited to either crash the system or take control of it.

vulnerability scans Automated tools designed to identify whether a given system possesses any well-known vulnerabilities. The scanning tool can also identify unused and unnecessary programs that represent potential security threats. The process of identifying and turning off unnecessary programs is called *hardening*.

W

walk-throughs Meetings, attended by those associated with a project, in which a detailed review of systems procedures and/or program logic is carried out in a step-by-step manner.

war dialing Searching for an idle modem by programming a computer to dial thousands of phone lines. Finding an idle modem often enables a hacker to gain access to the network to which it is connected.

war driving The practice of looking for unprotected home or corporate wireless networks.

Web cramming Developing a free and worthless trial-version Web site and charging the phone bill of the consumer for months even if the consumer cancels.

Web-page spoofing See *phishing*.

white-collar criminals Typically, businesspeople who commit fraud. White-collar criminals usually resort to trickery or cunning, and their crimes usually involve a violation of trust or confidence.

wide area network (WAN) A telecommunications network that covers a large geographic area anywhere in size from a few cities to the whole globe. A WAN uses telephone lines, cables, microwaves, or satellites to connect a wide variety of hardware devices in many different locations.

wiretap To listen in (eavesdrop) on an unprotected communications line.

worm Similar to a virus, except that it is a program rather than a code segment hidden in a host program. A worm also copies itself automatically and actively transmits itself directly to other systems.

X

XBRL eXtensible Business Reporting Language is a variant of XML (eXtensible Markup Language) specifically designed for use in communicating the content of financial data. It does this by creating tags for each data item that look much like the tags used by HTML.

Z

zero-balance check An internal check that requires the balance of an account to be zero after all entries to it have been made.

Index